$4\sqrt{5} + 6\sqrt{16}$

ELEMENTS OF
LITERATURE
FOURTH COURSE

The Authors

Robert Anderson is a playwright, novelist, screenwriter, and teacher. His plays include *Tea and Sympathy; Silent Night, Lonely Night; You Know I Can't Hear You When the Water's Running;* and *I Never Sang for My Father.* His screenplays include *The Nun's Story* and *The Sand Pebbles.* Mr. Anderson has taught at the Writer's Workshop at the University of Iowa, the American Theatre Wing Professional Training Program, and the Salzburg Seminar in American Studies. He is a Past President of the Dramatists' Guild, Vice-President of the Authors' League of America, and a member of the Theatre Hall of Fame. He makes his home in Connecticut and New York City.

John Malcolm Brinnin, author of six volumes of poetry that have received many prizes and awards, is a member of the American Academy and Institute of Arts and Letters. He is also a critic of poetry and a biographer of poets and was for a number of years Director of New York's famous Poetry Center. His teaching career, begun at Vassar College, included long terms at the University of Connecticut and Boston University, where he succeeded Robert Lowell as Professor of Creative Writing and Contemporary Letters. Mr. Brinnin has also written *Dylan Thomas in America: An Intimate Journal* and *Sextet: T. S. Eliot & Truman Capote & Others.* He divides his time between Duxbury, Massachusetts, and Key West, Florida.

John Leggett is a novelist, biographer, and teacher who went to the Writer's Workshop at the University of Iowa in the spring of 1969, expecting to put in a single semester. In 1970 he assumed temporary charge of the program and was its Director for the next seventeen years. Mr. Leggett's novels include *Wilder Stone, The Gloucester Branch, Who Took the Gold Away, Gulliver House,* and *Making Believe.* He is also the author of the highly acclaimed biography *Ross and Tom: Two American Tragedies.* His short fiction, articles, and reviews have appeared in *Harper's, Esquire, Mademoiselle, The Ladies Home Journal,* and the *Los Angeles Times.* A native New Yorker, Mr. Leggett now lives in San Francisco. He is currently at work on a biography of William Saroyan.

Janet Burroway is a novelist and teacher who has also written children's books and a textbook on fiction writing. She has taught at the University of Sussex, England; the University of Illinois; and the Writer's Workshop at the University of Iowa. Ms. Burroway is currently FSU Foundation Professor of English at Florida State University in Tallahassee. Her novels include *Descend Again, The Dancer from the Dance, Eyes, The Buzzards* (nominated for the Pulitzer Prize), *Raw Silk* (nominated for the National Book Award), and *Opening Nights.*

Virginia Hamilton is one of America's most highly acclaimed writers of books for children and young adults. She has received many awards, including the Newbery Award for *M. C. Higgins, the Great;* the Newbery Honor Award for *In the Beginning: Creation Stories from Around the World;* the Coretta Scott King Award for *Sweet Whispers, Brother Rush;* and the Edgar Allan Poe Award for *The House of Dies Drear.* Among her collections of folktales are *The People Could Fly* and *The Dark Way: Stories from the Spirit World.* The *All Jahdu Storybook* is a collection of Hamilton's own tales about a trickster hero who was born in an oven between two loaves of bread. In 1990 Hamilton received an honorary doctorate from the Bank Street College of Education in New York City. She lives in Yellow Springs, Ohio.

David Adams Leeming is Professor of English at the University of Connecticut and the author of several books on mythology: *Mythology: The Voyage of the Hero; Flights: Readings in Magic, Mysticism, Fantasy, and Myth;* and *The World of Myth.* For several years he taught English at the Robert College in Istanbul, Turkey. He also served as secretary-assistant to the writer James Baldwin in New York and Istanbul. Dr. Leeming lives in Stonington, Connecticut.

ELEMENTS OF LITERATURE
FOURTH COURSE

Holt, Rinehart and Winston, Inc.

Harcourt Brace Jovanovich, Inc.

Austin • Orlando • San Diego • Chicago • Dallas • Toronto

Thomas Shea assisted with the planning of the lessons in critical thinking and writing. Dr. Shea was for several years Chairman of the English Department of the Middle Island Central School in New York. He received his doctorate from St. John's University, where he was particularly interested in research on learning and teaching styles.

Thomas Monsell of Greenport, New York, assisted in the annotation of *Julius Caesar.* Mr. Monsell taught English 12 at the Lindenhurst Senior High School for twenty years, where he also directed plays, including works by Shakespeare, Shaw, Molière, Barrie, Anouilh, and Coward. He majored in English and drama at Ithaca College and has acted and directed in stock and community theaters.

Nancy E. Wiseman Seminoff has served as Consultant in Reading and Questioning Strategies for the program. Dr. Seminoff is Dean of the School of Education and Professional Studies at the William Paterson College of New Jersey. She has served as a reading consultant at the secondary level and as a classroom teacher. She has published widely in national and state educational periodicals.

Cover: *Nichols Canyon* by David Hockney (1980). Acrylic on canvas, 84″ × 60″.
   © David Hockney.
Page v: *In a Village Near Paris* (detail) by Lyonel Feininger.
   The University of Iowa Museum of Art.

Acknowledgments

Grateful acknowledgment is made to the teachers who reviewed materials for the 1989 edition of ELEMENTS OF LITERATURE, in manuscript or in classroom tests.

Reviewers

Peggy Anatol
Warren High School
Downey, California

Larry W. Anders
Caroline County Schools
Denton, Maryland

Bernice Causey
Mobile County Public Schools
Mobile, Alabama

Edward Deluzain
Mosley High School
Panama City, Florida

Suzanne Mitoraj
Mark Sheehan High School
Wallingford, Connecticut

Carl Moyler
Dayton City Schools
Dayton, Ohio

Sylvia Skarstad
Cleveland High School
Portland, Oregon

Susan Stevens
South High School
Youngstown, Ohio

Joe Wilson
Corpus Christi Independent School District
Corpus Christi, Texas

Grateful acknowledgment is also made to the teachers who evaluated materials for the 1993 edition of ELEMENTS OF LITERATURE and who recommended new selections:

Kansas City School District, Kansas City, Missouri:

Dr. Ula Manzo
Coordinator of Language Arts K–12

Ann Crockett
Metro Tech High School

Michael Lyons
Southwest High School

Patricia Lyons
Southwest High School

Elizabeth M. Smith
Van Horn High School

Linda Watkins
East High School

Killeen Independent School District, Killeen, Texas:

Phyllis Wheeler
Secondary Language Arts Consultant

Paula Brock
Killeen High School

Roberta Brooks
Ellison High School

Susie De Vault
Killeen High School

Glen Martin
Killeen High School

Bunnie Montgomery
Killeen High School

Mark Noblitt
Killeen High School

Debbie Prude
Ellison High School

Debbie Siegman
Killeen High School

Barbara Teer
Ellison High School

Veda Kay Waheed
Ellison High School

Washoe County School District, Reno, Nevada:

Joanne Walen
English/Language Arts Program Coordinator K–12

Rita Hambleton
Hug High School

Phil Harriman
Sparks High School

Olivia Martin
Reno High School

Mel Shields
McQueen High School

Beverly Wooster
Reed High School

CONTENTS

UNIT ONE: THE ELEMENTS OF A SHORT STORY

Introduction: The Purpose of Storytelling by John Leggett   **2**

Plot: The Story's Framework   **4**

Tom Godwin	The Cold Equations	7
Isaac Bashevis Singer	The Fatalist	24
Guy de Maupassant	The Piece of String	30

LITERATURE AND LANGUAGE: Using the Narrative Mode   36

EXERCISES IN CRITICAL THINKING AND WRITING:
Predicting Outcomes   38

Character: The Story's Actors   **41**

Amy Tan	Two Kinds	46
Sandra Cisneros	The House on Mango Street	54
Bernard Malamud	The First Seven Years	59
Laurie Colwin	Mr. Parker	68

LITERATURE AND LANGUAGE: Using the Descriptive Mode in
Characterization   74

EXERCISES IN CRITICAL THINKING AND WRITING:
Analyzing a Character   76

Theme: The Story's Meaning and Roots   **78**

Anne Tyler	With All Flags Flying	81
Anton Chekhov	The Bet	90
Alice Munro	Boys and Girls	98

LITERATURE AND LANGUAGE: Combining Sentences   110

EXERCISES IN CRITICAL THINKING AND WRITING:
Making Generalizations and Stating a Theme   113

Point of View and Tone: The Story's Voice   **116**

Stephen Crane	The Bride Comes to Yellow Sky	120
Alice Walker	Everyday Use	129
Ray Bradbury	The Pedestrian	137

LITERATURE AND LANGUAGE: Using Pronouns Correctly   143

EXERCISES IN CRITICAL THINKING AND WRITING:
Comparing and Contrasting Stories   145

Setting: "Putting Us There"   **146**

    Louis L'Amour   Trap of Gold   149

    Leslie Marmon Silko   The Man to Send Rain Clouds   156

LITERATURE AND LANGUAGE: Using Words to Create Atmosphere   161

EXERCISES IN CRITICAL THINKING AND WRITING:
Evaluating a Short Story   163

Symbol: An Object That Suggests an Idea   **165**

    Edgar Allan Poe   The Pit and the Pendulum   168

    Katherine Mansfield   The Doll's House   180

    Gabriel García Márquez   A Very Old Man with
                        Enormous Wings   187

LITERATURE AND LANGUAGE: Using Subordinate Clauses   193

EXERCISES IN CRITICAL THINKING AND WRITING:
Recognizing Faulty Reasoning   196

Irony and Satire: The Might of the Word   **197**

    O. Henry   The Gift of the Magi   200

    Saki   The Storyteller   206

    Tim O'Brien   Where Have You Gone,
                        Charming Billy?   212

LITERATURE AND LANGUAGE: Punctuating Dialogue   219

EXERCISES IN CRITICAL THINKING AND WRITING:
Analyzing and Responding to a Story   222

UNIT TWO: THE ELEMENTS OF POETRY

Introduction: The Elements of Poetry
by John Malcolm Brinnin   **226**

Figurative Language: Language Shaped by Imagination   **227**

    Lucille Clifton   Miss Rosie   230

    Langston Hughes   Mother to Son   232

    Luis Lloréns Torres   Love Without Love   234

    Anne Sexton   Courage   237

    John Stone   Double Header   239

    Andrei Voznesensky   Foggy Street   244

LITERATURE AND LANGUAGE: Using Similes, Metaphor, and
Personification   246

Figurative Language: Symbols   **248**

    Robert Frost   Stopping by Woods on a
                        Snowy Evening   251

Robert Frost	The Road Not Taken	253
Edgar Lee Masters	George Gray	256
Elizabeth Bishop	The Fish	258
David Wagoner	Tumbleweed	261

LITERATURE AND LANGUAGE: Using Symbols   264

EXERCISES IN CRITICAL THINKING AND WRITING:
Paraphrasing and Interpreting a Poem   265

Imagery in Poetry   **267**

Ted Kooser	Abandoned Farmhouse	270
A. E. Housman	Loveliest of Trees	272
Hugh McNamar	The Elk	274
Theodore Roethke	The Meadow Mouse	276
William Wordsworth	I Wandered Lonely as a Cloud	278
Allen Ginsberg	In Back of the Real	282
Louise Erdrich	Walking in the Breakdown Lane	284
William Shakespeare	Shall I Compare Thee to a Summer's Day?	286
Bashō, Buson, Issa, Raizan	Four Haiku	289
William Carlos Williams	The Artist	290
Robert Hayden	The Whipping	292

LITERATURE AND LANGUAGE: Using Imagery   294

EXERCISES IN CRITICAL THINKING AND WRITING:
Comparing and Contrasting Poems   296

The Sounds of Poetry: Rhythm and Meter   **298**

Anonymous	Bonny Barbara Allan	305
John Updike	Ex-Basketball Player	308
Ishmael Reed	.05	311
John Masefield	Sea Fever	312
Gwendolyn Brooks	The Bean Eaters	314
Naomi Shihab Nye	The Flying Cat	317

LITERATURE AND LANGUAGE: Creating Rhythm and Meter   319

The Sounds of Poetry: Rhyme, Alliteration, and Onomatopoeia   **322**

Arthur Guiterman	Bears	324
Emily Dickinson	I Like to See It Lap the Miles	327
E. E. Cummings	in Just-	330

| David Ignatow | Simultaneously | 332 |
| John Updike | Pop Smash, Out of Echo Chamber | 334 |

LITERATURE AND LANGUAGE: Creating Sound Effects   336

EXERCISES IN CRITICAL THINKING AND WRITING:
Evaluating a Poem   339

Tone: ''Overhearing'' an Attitude   **341**

Anne Sexton	Cinderella	344
Julia Alvarez	What Could It Be?	348
Thomas Hardy	The Children and Sir Nameless	351
Percy Bysshe Shelley	Ozymandias	353
Pablo Neruda	Tonight I Can Write	356
Langston Hughes	Theme for English B	358
A. E. Housman	Oh, When I Was in Love with You	361
Patrick Worth Gray	Bread Loaf to Omaha, Twenty-eight Hours	362
Richard Moore	Willy	364
Alfred, Lord Tennyson	Flower in the Crannied Wall	367
George MacBeth	Bedtime Story	369
Richard Brautigan	All Watched Over by Machines of Loving Grace	372

LITERATURE AND LANGUAGE: Creating a Tone   374

EXERCISES IN WRITING: Writing a Poem   376

UNIT THREE: THE ELEMENTS OF NONFICTION

Introduction: The Elements of Nonfiction
by Janet Burroway   **380**

Journals and Travel Literature   **384**

John Steinbeck	The Mojave	385
Mark Twain	The Genuine Mexican Plug (Carson City, Nevada)	391
Andrea Lee	An Apartment in Moscow	397

LITERATURE AND LANGUAGE: Using Parallel Structure   406

EXERCISES IN CRITICAL THINKING AND WRITING:
Distinguishing Between Subjective and Objective Details   408

Informal Essays **410**

Janet Frame — You Are Now Entering the Human Heart — 411

Marjorie Kinnan Rawlings — My Friend Moe — 415

William Allen — A Whole Society of Loners and Dreamers — 424

Alice Walker — *from* In Search of Our Mothers' Gardens — 429

Lewis Thomas — On Warts — 434

A. M. Rosenthal — No News from Auschwitz — 439

LITERATURE AND LANGUAGE: Using Vivid Adjectives — 442

EXERCISES IN CRITICAL THINKING AND WRITING: Evaluating an Essay — 444

Autobiography: "Written Memory" **445**

Russell Baker — Make Something of Yourself — 446

Harry Crews — The Mail-Order Catalogue — 453

Susan Allen Toth — Nothing Happened — 460

LITERATURE AND LANGUAGE: Using Effective Diction — 468

EXERCISES IN CRITICAL THINKING AND WRITING: Inferring the Main Idea — 470

History: Seeking the Truth **473**

Evan S. Connell — Amundsen and Scott — 474

Hanson W. Baldwin — R.M.S. Titanic — 486

Tom Wolfe — The Limits of the Envelope — 499

LITERATURE AND LANGUAGE: Using the Expository and Persuasive Aims — 506

EXERCISES IN CRITICAL THINKING AND WRITING: Evaluating History — 510

UNIT FOUR: THE ELEMENTS OF DRAMA

Introduction: The Elements of Drama by Robert Anderson — **512**

Thornton Wilder — Our Town — 519

Robert Anderson — I Never Sang for My Father — 561

Anton Chekhov — The Brute — 601

LITERATURE AND LANGUAGE: Recognizing Sentence Fragments in Dialogue — 613

EXERCISES IN CRITICAL THINKING, SPEAKING, AND LISTENING: Debating: Developing a Logical Argument — 616

Unit Five: WILLIAM SHAKESPEARE

Introduction: William Shakespeare by Robert Anderson **620**

William Shakespeare   The Tragedy of Julius Caesar 630

Literature and Language: Famous Passages from the Play 727

Exercises in Critical Thinking and Writing:
Analyzing and Evaluating Persuasion 728

Unit Six: THE WESTERN TRADITION IN LITERATURE

Introduction: The Western Tradition
by David Adams Leeming **732**

The Literature of Classical Mythology **733**

Homer, *translated by* Richmond Lattimore   Hektor's Farewell to Andromache 736

Sophocles, *translated by* Dudley Fitts and Robert Fitzgerald   Antigone 748

Ovid, *translated by* Horace Gregory   Daedalus and Icarus 798

Literature and the Bible **803**

Tanakh: The New Jewish Publication Society Translation   Abraham and Isaac 806

King James Bible   The Book of Ruth 810

King James Bible   The Twenty-third Psalm 817

King James Bible   I Am the Rose of Sharon 819

King James Bible   To Every Thing There Is a Season 825

New English Bible   The Parable of the Prodigal Son 828

The Literature of Romance **831**

Sir Thomas Malory, *retold by* John Steinbeck   Merlin: The Coming of Arthur 835

Translated by N. J. Dawood   The Fourth Voyage of Sindbad the Sailor 842

Miguel de Cervantes, *translated by* Samuel Putnam	Tilting at Windmills	851
LITERATURE AND LANGUAGE: Recognizing Allusions		860

UNIT SEVEN: FOLKTALES FROM AROUND THE WORLD

Introduction: Folktales from Around the World
by Virginia Hamilton   **864**

The Wise and the Foolish		**868**
Chinese anecdote, *told by* Lieh Tzu	The Missing Axe	868
Chinese anecdote, *told by* Liu An	The Lost Horse	869
Chinese anecdote, *told by* Chang Shih-nan	A Clever Judge	870
Italian tale, *told by* Italo Calvino	The Happy Man's Shirt	872

Tales of Wonder		**875**
Japanese tale, *told by* Keigo Seki	Urashima Taro	875
African American tale, *told by* Virginia Hamilton	The People Could Fly	878

How-and-Why Stories		**883**
Nigerian tale, *told by* Chinua Achebe and John Iroaganachi	How the Leopard Got His Claws	883
African American tale, *told by* Zora Neale Hurston	How the Snake Got Poison	888

Trickster Tales		**891**
Zuni tale, *told by* Alfonso Ortiz and Richard Erdoes	Coyote Steals the Sun and Moon	891
Indian tale, *told by* Joseph Jacobs	The Tiger, the Brahman, and the Jackal	893
LITERATURE AND LANGUAGE: Recognizing Storytelling Motifs		896

UNIT EIGHT: THE ELEMENTS OF A NOVEL

Introduction: The Elements of a Novel by John Leggett   **898**

   John Knowles   A Separate Peace   901

EXERCISES IN CRITICAL THINKING AND WRITING:
Developing and Supporting a Thesis Statement   987

Writing About Literature   **989**

   Writing Answers to Essay Questions   989

   Writing and Revising an Essay About a Literary Work   990

   A Model Essay   991

   Documenting Sources   994

Handbook of Literary Terms   **995**

Grammar, Usage, and Mechanics: A Reference Guide   **1008**

   Parts of Speech   1008

   The Sentence   1010

   Problems of Agreement   1011

   Using Verbs Correctly   1014

   Using Pronouns Correctly   1018

   Using Modifiers Correctly   1020

   Common Usage Problems   1022

   The Rules for Capitalization   1025

   Punctuation   1028

   Spelling   1036

Glossary   **1040**

Index of Skills and Features   **1048**

   Literature and Language Skills   1048

   Language and Vocabulary Exercises   1049

   Composition Skills   1050

   Speaking and Listening Skills   1051

   Literature and Language Exercises   1052

   Critical Thinking and Writing Exercises   1052

   Index of Features   1052

Index of Authors and Titles   **1054**

THE ELEMENTS OF A SHORT STORY

In a Village Near Paris (Street in Paris, Pink Sky)
by Lyonel Feininger (1909). Oil on canvas, 39¾" × 32".

UNIT ONE   **John Leggett**

THE PURPOSE OF STORYTELLING

An introduction by **John Leggett**

Statue of the great Danish storyteller Hans Christian Andersen in Central Park, New York.

I love the pleasures of the short story. One of them is the fast payoff. Whatever happens happens quickly. The writer mounts his personal Pegasus, even if it is an absent-minded nag who never made it on the race track; an ascension occurs and the ride begins. The scenery often surprises, and so do some of the people one meets. Somewhere I've said that a short story packs a self in a few pages predicating a lifetime. The drama is tense, happens fast, and is more often than not outlandish. In a few pages a good story portrays the complexity of a life while producing the surprise and effect of knowledge—not a bad payoff.

—Bernard Malamud

Storytelling is not the quickest or the most efficient way to communicate with other people, but it is a curiously effective way, and there may be no form of communication that is more enjoyable.

Tribal societies, our own Native American societies in particular, have always depended on storytelling to hand down their collective wisdom to the young. Their stories, passed on from generation to generation, ensured that the young would understand their people's truths and that they would choose to live by them.

Storytelling was also important to the early settlers of America's frontier society. When there were no screens with moving images to watch, storytelling was one of the principal entertainments. Around the campfires and the cast-iron stoves of log cabins, American folk heroes emerged, characters like Davy Crockett, Paul Bunyan, and Johnny Appleseed. And from this tradition emerged the great American storytellers—Washington Irving, Nathaniel Hawthorne, Edgar Allan Poe, Herman Melville, Mark Twain.

What exactly accounts for the appeal of a story? At the center of any good story is the truth it reveals. An abstract truth is likely to be indigestible in its raw form, but if it is wrapped in a well-told story, the revelation of truth can be an intellectual and emotional pleasure.

Stories also provide vicarious experience. That is, they take us places and put us into situations we would never know otherwise. Such experience allows us to lead more productive lives, to make more intelligent choices, and to test our sense of values.

Nowadays, with children growing up on a video diet, there is concern that our society is losing its storytelling heritage. There is concern that we no longer take joy in language, that we are losing not only our ability to tell stories well, but also our ability to communicate ideas and images through words and sentences.

This is not just a concern in the classroom. In corporations, in research communities, in government agencies, individuals seem to have increasing difficulty in getting their ideas across to others in a clear and persuasive way. It is as though our dependence on the machines—the computer and the TV set—is eroding our own human transmitters and receivers.

Reading can help to correct this erosion of our language skills. Reading is the best insurance we can take out to protect not only our language, that great and lovely instrument, but also our access to the wonders that lie stored in the literature of our past.

The Gossips, rendered by Carmel Wilson (c. 1935). Watercolor from original object.
Index of American Design, National Gallery of Art, Washington, D.C.

> " **R**eading is the best insurance we can take out to protect not only our language, that great and lovely instrument, but also our access to the wonders that lie stored in the literature of our past.''

Plot: The Story's Framework

Stories differ from one another as widely as the people who tell them, but common to, and essential to, any story is a plot. The **plot** is the "framework" of the story; it is the arrangement of related events that makes the story hang together.

What Makes Up a Plot?

The typical plot is made up of four parts. The first is what we call the **basic situation** (sometimes called the **exposition**). The basic situation of a story usually presents a character who is placed in a situation that contains the possibility of action. Usually, this character wants something very much, or has a conflict or problem that is causing trouble:

> Nancy is worried about rumors of a thief in her English class. She wonders if it could be the girl at the next desk, who has dirty fingernails and pops her gum.

The second part of a plot must develop the basic situation. This means that **complications** develop:

> The teacher warns the class that two thefts have been reported this morning and that students should not leave money in their lockers. Nancy ignores this advice, and when she goes to her locker after math class, she finds that her blue purse and her lunch money have disappeared.

The third part of a plot is the **climax,** the most tense or exciting moment in the story, when something happens to decide the outcome of the conflict. The climax is the moment that brings about a change in the situation or in the main character or in both.

> Nancy opens her neighbor's locker, sees a blue purse, pockets it quickly—and looks up into the teacher's eyes. Nancy explains that the purse is hers, but as she displays it, she sees that it bears her neighbor's initials. Nancy is led off weeping to the principal's office.

The fourth part of a plot is the **resolution,** often described as the **denouement,** a French word for "untying the knot." At this moment, all the problems are resolved, either happily or unhappily, and the story is "closed":

> How will Nancy's story end? If the writer wants a happy ending, Nancy will persuade the principal that she was not stealing, and she will apologize to her neighbor for harboring suspicions of her. If the writer wants a different ending, Nancy might be released by the principal, who believes her story, but be ostracized by the other students, who do not.

These four parts of a plot make up the framework, or structure, of a story. They are the "bare bones" on which all the other elements of storytelling are hung.

> " **T**he basic situation of a story usually presents a character who is placed in a situation that contains the possibility of action. Usually, this character wants something very much . . ."

"Once upon a time, they lived happily ever after."

Drawing by H. Martin; © 1991
The New Yorker Magazine, Inc.

Some modern stories, often the best of them, depend so little on plot that the story's structure may be hard to find. But the plot will be there all the same, doing its work under the surface. The plot will support whichever element of storytelling the writer wants to emphasize—the portrayal of characters or the portrayal of a setting or the presentation of a strong theme.

Conflict: External and Internal

As important as it is, plot alone will not work unless it is energized—and the energy of storytelling is human emotion. In fiction, if the emotions sleep, so does the reader.

It is the conflict in a story that stirs our emotions. **Conflict** exists when a character is struggling with something—another person, a grizzly bear, or even some aspect of his or her own personality.

In the plot outline of Nancy's case, Nancy's own suspicion and anger create the conflict. These feelings cause Nancy to make a series of mistakes and even a false accusation. If there were no conflict—if Nancy had controlled her suspicion and anger—there would have been no story. If Nancy's story is told well, we will also find our own emotions stirred, for all of us have experienced these disturbing emotions or been victimized by them.

Most commonly, conflict occurs when the main character's desire is blocked in some way. It is hard to write an interesting story without a main character who *wants* something badly and is capable of struggling to get it. If you remember the story of the *Odyssey,* you know that a major conflict springs from Odysseus's desire to get home, a desire that is blocked by the raging anger of the sea god Poseidon. And so Odysseus keeps trying to get home, despite storms and whirlpools and cannibals, even despite the beautiful witches who try to keep him for themselves.

> " **I**n fiction,
> if the emotions sleep,
> so does the reader."

The Capture of Antioch (detail), illustration from the manuscript *The History of the Emperors.*

Paris, Bibliothèque Arsenale.

Conflict is likely to originate with something external blocking the character's desire: In Odysseus's case, the major external block is the rage of Poseidon. In other stories, external conflict might be supplied by a turbulent river that must be crossed, by the emptiness of the family cupboard, or by a bully in one's path. These are called **external conflicts** because they are caused by something outside the character. External conflicts are often sorted into five basic types: person against person, person against nature, person against machine, person against society, and person against supernatural beings.

All of these external conflicts become infinitely more interesting—in that they tell us more about life—when they also become internal. An **internal conflict** occurs when a character struggles against some personal quality that is causing trouble. Often the battle outside also causes a battle inside the character's head and heart. The character struggling with a bully might really be struggling between the will to win and the temptation to give up and submit to the bully's mockery. Such a struggle truly grips our attention because we sense that we ourselves carry these conflicting qualities and that they are forever at odds. (In fact, in some stories the *only* conflict is internal.) Our laziness struggles against our ambition; our courage struggles against our fear; our compassion struggles against our indifference.

Foreshadowing: Clues That Point to "What Happens Next"

We usually think of foreshadowing as a device by which a writer creates suspense, but we can also think of it as *all* the ways in which the writer tells the reader what to expect next. **Foreshadowing** refers to clues about what is going to happen as the story unfolds.

If we are told at the outset of a story that it's a gorgeous, sunny day, the events we anticipate will be very different from those we'd expect after an opening raging with thunderclaps. We expect comic things to happen to a heroine who, when we meet her, is convulsed by giggles, but we expect tragic things to happen when a story opens with the passing of a funeral procession.

If a writer mentions, however casually, that a prisoner has escaped from the local prison, we can expect that prisoner to appear at a window or door before too long. In the same way, the gun we are told is in the top desk drawer is certain to go off later in the story or to be found in the hero's car, much to his surprise.

All of these hints that foreshadow coming events, strewn with such apparent carelessness in our path, are intended to create **suspense**—to quicken our curiosity, to increase our anxiety, and to lead us forward into the story with ever sharper appetites.

The raising of our expectations in a story has a great deal to do with our sense of satisfaction at the end when we flip over the pages to see what clues we missed or how shrewd our suspicions and hunches turned out to be. The hungrier the writer has made us, the more enjoyable is the feast.

Suspense

Drawing by Victoria Roberts; © 1990
The New Yorker Magazine, Inc.

"**The** hungrier the writer has made us, the more enjoyable is the feast."

THE COLD EQUATIONS

Tom Godwin

He was not alone.

There was nothing to indicate the fact but the white hand of the tiny gauge on the board before him. The control room was empty but for himself; there was no sound other than the murmur of the drives—but the white hand had moved. It had been on zero when the little ship was launched from the *Stardust;* now, an hour later, it had crept up. There was something in the supplies closet across the room, it was saying, some kind of a body that radiated heat.

It could be but one kind of a body—a living, human body.

He leaned back in the pilot's chair and drew a deep, slow breath, considering what he would have to do. He was an EDS pilot, inured to the sight of death, long since accustomed to it and to viewing the dying of another man with an objective lack of emotion, and he had no choice in what he must do. There could be no alternative—but it required a few moments of conditioning for even an EDS pilot to prepare himself to walk across the room and coldly, deliberately, take the life of a man he had yet to meet.

He would, of course, do it. It was the law, stated very bluntly and definitely in grim Paragraph L, Section 8, of Interstellar Regulations: *"Any stowaway discovered in an EDS shall be jettisoned immediately following discovery."*

It was the law, and there could be no appeal.

It was a law not of men's choosing, but made imperative by the circumstances of the space frontier. Galactic expansion had followed the devel-opment of the hyperspace drive, and as men scattered wide across the frontier, there had come the problem of contact with the isolated first colonies and exploration parties. The huge hyperspace cruisers were the product of the combined genius and effort of Earth and were long and expensive in the building. They were not available in such numbers that small colonies could possess them. The cruisers carried the colonists to their new worlds and made periodic visits, running on tight schedules, but they could not stop and turn aside to visit colonies scheduled to be visited at another time; such a delay would destroy their schedule and produce a confusion and uncertainty that would wreck the complex interdependence between old Earth and the new worlds of the frontier.

Some method of delivering supplies or assistance when an emergency occurred on a world not scheduled for a visit had been needed, and the Emergency Dispatch Ships had been the answer. Small and collapsible, they occupied little room in the hold of the cruiser; made of light metal and plastics, they were driven by a small rocket drive that consumed relatively little fuel. Each cruiser carried four EDS's, and when a call for aid was received, the nearest cruiser would drop into normal space long enough to launch an EDS with the needed supplies or personnel, then vanish again as it continued on its course.

The cruisers, powered by nuclear converters, did not use the liquid rocket fuel, but nuclear converters were far too large and complex to permit their installation in the EDS's. The cruisers were forced by necessity to carry a limited amount of bulky rocket fuel, and the fuel was rationed with care, the cruiser's computers determining the exact amount of fuel each EDS would require for its mission. The computers considered the course coordinates, the mass of the EDS, the mass of pilot and cargo; they were very precise and accurate and omitted nothing from their calculations. They could not, however, foresee and allow for the added mass of a stowaway.

The *Stardust* had received the request from one of the exploration parties stationed on Woden, the six men of the party already being stricken with the fever carried by the green kala midges and their own supply of serum destroyed by the tornado that had torn through their camp. The *Stardust* had gone through the usual procedure, dropping into normal space to launch the EDS with the fever serum, then vanishing again in hyperspace. Now, an hour later, the gauge was saying there was something more than the small carton of serum in the supplies closet.

He let his eyes rest on the narrow white door of the closet. There, just inside, another man lived and breathed and was beginning to feel assured that discovery of his presence would now be too late for the pilot to alter the situation. It *was* too late; for the man behind the door it was far later than he thought and in a way he would find it terrible to believe.

There could be no alternative. Additional fuel would be used during the hours of deceleration to compensate for the added mass of the stowaway; infinitesimal increments of fuel that would not be missed until the ship had almost reached its destination. Then, at some distance above the ground that might be as near as a thousand feet or as far as tens of thousands feet, depending upon the mass of ship and cargo and the preceding period of deceleration, the unmissed increments of fuel would make their absence known; the EDS would expend its last drops of fuel with a sputter and go into whistling free fall. Ship and pilot and stowaway would merge together upon impact as a wreckage of metal and plastic, flesh and blood, driven deep into the soil. The stowaway had signed his own death warrant when he concealed himself on the ship; he could not be permitted to take seven others with him.

He looked again at the telltale white hand, then rose to his feet. What he must do would be unpleasant for both of them; the sooner it was over, the better. He stepped across the control room to stand by the white door.

"Come out!" His command was harsh and abrupt above the murmur of the drive.

It seemed he could hear the whisper of a furtive movement inside the closet, then nothing. He visualized the stowaway cowering closer into one corner, suddenly worried by the possible consequences of his act, his self-assurance evaporating.

"I said *out!*"

He heard the stowaway move to obey, and he waited with his eyes alert on the door and his hand near the blaster at his side.

The door opened and the stowaway stepped through it, smiling. "All right—I give up. Now what?"

It was a girl.

He stared without speaking, his hand dropping away from the blaster and acceptance of what he saw coming like a heavy and unexpected physical blow. The stowaway was not a man—she was a girl in her teens, standing before him in little white gypsy sandals, with the top of her brown, curly head hardly higher than his shoulder, with a faint, sweet scent of perfume coming from her, and her smiling face tilted up so her eyes could look unknowing and unafraid into his as she waited for his answer.

Now what? Had it been asked in the deep, defiant voice of a man he would have answered it with action, quick and efficient. He would have taken the stowaway's identification disk and ordered him into the air lock. Had the stowaway refused to obey, he would have used the blaster. It would not have taken long; within a minute the body would have been ejected into space—had the stowaway been a man.

He returned to the pilot's chair and motioned her to seat herself on the boxlike bulk of the drive-control units that were set against the wall beside him. She obeyed, his silence making the smile fade into the meek and guilty expression of a pup that has been caught in mischief and knows it must be punished.

"You still haven't told me," she said. "I'm guilty, so what happens to me now? Do I pay a fine, or what?"

"What are you doing here?" he asked. "Why did you stow away on this EDS?"

"I wanted to see my brother. He's with the government survey crew on Woden and I haven't seen him for ten years, not since he left Earth to go into government survey work."

"What was your destination on the *Stardust?*"

"Mimir. I have a position waiting for me there. My brother has been sending money home all the time to us—my father and mother and me—and he paid for a special course in linguistics I was taking. I graduated sooner than expected and I was offered this job on Mimir. I knew it would be almost a year before Gerry's job was done on Woden so he could come on to Mimir, and that's why I hid in the closet there. There was plenty of room for me and I was willing to pay the fine. There were only the two of us kids—Gerry and I—and I haven't seen him for so long, and I didn't want to wait another year when I could see him now, even though I knew I would be breaking some kind of a regulation when I did it.''

I knew I would be breaking some kind of a regulation. In a way, she could not be blamed for her ignorance of the law; she was of Earth and had not realized that the laws of the space frontier must, of necessity, be as hard and relentless as the environment that gave them birth. Yet, to protect such as her from the results of their own ignorance of the frontier, there had been a sign over the door that led to the section of the *Stardust* that housed the EDS's; sign that was plain for all to see and heed: UNAUTHORIZED PERSONNEL KEEP OUT!

"Does your brother know that you took passage on the *Stardust* for Mimir?"

"Oh, yes. I sent him a spacegram telling him about my graduation and about going to Mimir on the *Stardust* a month before I left Earth. I already knew Mimir was where he would be stationed in a little over a year. He gets a promotion then, and he'll be based on Mimir and not have to stay out a year at a time on field trips, like he does now."

There were two different survey groups on Woden, and he asked, "What is his name?"

"Cross—Gerry Cross. He's in Group Two—that was the way his address read. Do you know him?"

Group One had requested the serum: Group Two was eight thousand miles away, across the Western Sea.

"No, I've never met him," he said, then turned to the control board and cut the deceleration to a fraction of a gravity, knowing as he did so that it could not avert the ultimate end, yet doing the only thing he could do to prolong that ultimate end. The sensation was like that of the ship suddenly dropping, and the girl's involuntary movement of surprise half lifted her from the seat.

"We're going faster now, aren't we?" she asked. "Why are we doing that?"

He told her the truth. "To save fuel for a little while."

"You mean we don't have very much?"

He delayed the answer he must give her so soon to ask, "How did you manage to stow away?"

"I just sort of walked in when no one was looking my way," she said. "I was practicing my Gelanese on the native girl who does the cleaning in the Ship's Supply office when someone came in with an order for supplies for the survey crew on Woden. I slipped into the closet there after the ship was ready to go just before you came in. It was an impulse of the moment to stow away, so I could get to see Gerry—and from the way you keep looking at me so grim, I'm not sure it was a very wise impulse. But I'll be a model criminal—or do I mean prisoner?" She smiled at him again. "I intended to pay for my keep on top of paying the fine. I can cook and I can patch clothes for everyone and I know how to do all kinds of useful things, even a little bit about nursing."

There was one more question to ask:

"Did you know what the supplies were that the survey crew ordered?"

"Why, no. Equipment they needed in their work, I supposed."

Why couldn't she have been a man with some ulterior motive? A fugitive from justice hoping to lose himself on a raw new world; an opportunist seeking transportation to the new colonies where he might find golden fleece for the taking; a crackpot with a mission. Perhaps once in his lifetime an EDS pilot would find such a stowaway on his ship—warped men, mean and selfish men, brutal and dangerous men—but never before a smiling, blue-eyed girl who was willing to pay her fine and work for her keep that she might see her brother.

He turned to the board and turned the switch that would signal the *Stardust*. The call would be futile, but he could not, until he had exhausted that one vain hope, seize her and thrust her into the air lock as he would an animal—or a man. The delay, in the meantime, would not be dangerous with the EDS decelerating at fractional gravity.

A voice spoke from the communicator. "*Stardust.* Identify yourself and proceed."

"Barton, EDS 34GII. Emergency. Give me Commander Delhart."

There was a faint confusion of noises as the request went through the proper channels. The girl was watching him, no longer smiling.

"Are you going to order them to come back after me?" she asked.

The communicator clicked and there was the sound of a distant voice saying, "Commander, the EDS requests . . ."

"Are they coming back after me?" she asked again. "Won't I get to see my brother after all?"

"Barton?" The blunt, gruff voice of Commander Delhart came from the communicator. "What's this about an emergency?"

"A stowaway," he answered.

"A stowaway?" There was a slight surprise to the question. "That's rather unusual—but why the 'emergency' call? You discovered him in time, so there should be no appreciable danger, and I presume you've informed Ship's Records so his nearest relatives can be notified."

"That's why I had to call you, first. The stowaway is still aboard and the circumstances are so different—"

"Different?" the commander interrupted, impatience in his voice. "How can they be different? You know you have a limited supply of fuel; you also know the law as well as I do: 'Any stowaway discovered in an EDS shall be jettisoned immediately following discovery.'"

There was the sound of a sharply indrawn breath from the girl. *"What does he mean?"*

"The stowaway is a girl."

"What?"

"She wanted to see her brother. She's only a kid and she didn't know what she was really doing."

"I see." All the curtness was gone from the commander's voice. "So you called me in the hope I could do something?" Without waiting for an answer he went on, "I'm sorry—I can do nothing. This cruiser must maintain its schedule; the life of not one person but the lives of many depend on it. I know how you feel but I'm powerless to help you. You'll have to go through with it. I'll have you connected with Ship's Records."

The communicator faded to a faint rustle of

sound, and he turned back to the girl. She was leaning forward on the bench, almost rigid, her eyes fixed wide and frightened.

"What did he mean, to go through with it? To jettison me . . . to go through with it—what did he mean? Not the way it sounded . . . he couldn't have. What did he mean—what did he really mean?"

Her time was too short for the comfort of a lie to be more than a cruelly fleeting delusion.

"He meant it the way it sounded."

"No!" She recoiled from him as though he had struck her, one hand half upraised as though to fend him off and stark unwillingness to believe in her eyes.

"It will have to be."

"No! You're joking—you're insane! You can't mean it!"

"I'm sorry." He spoke slowly to her, gently. "I should have told you before—I should have, but I had to do what I could first; I had to call the *Stardust*. You heard what the commander said."

"But you can't—if you make me leave the ship, I'll *die*."

"I know."

She searched his face, and the unwillingness to believe left her eyes, giving way slowly to a look of dazed horror.

"You know?" She spoke the words far apart, numb and wonderingly.

"I know. It has to be like that."

"You mean it—you really mean it." She sagged back against the wall, small and limp like a little rag doll, and all the protesting and disbelief gone. "You're going to do it—you're going to make me die?"

"I'm sorry," he said again. "You'll never know how sorry I am. It has to be that way and no human in the universe can change it."

"You're going to make me die and I didn't do anything to die for—I didn't *do* anything——"

He sighed, deep and weary. "I know you didn't, child. I know you didn't."

"EDS." The communicator rapped brisk and metallic. "This is Ship's Records. Give us all information on subject's identification disk."

He got out of his chair to stand over her. She clutched the edge of the seat, her upturned face white under the brown hair and the lipstick standing out like a blood-red cupid's bow.

"*Now?*"

"I want your identification disk," he said.

She released the edge of the seat and fumbled at the chain that suspended the plastic disk from her neck with fingers that were trembling and awkward. He reached down and unfastened the clasp for her, then returned with the disk to his chair.

"Here's your data, Records: Identification Number T837——"

"One moment," Records interrupted. "This is to be filed on the gray card, of course?"

"Yes."

"And the time of execution?"

"I'll tell you later."

"Later? This is highly irregular; the time of the subject's death is required before——"

He kept the thickness out of his voice with an effort. "Then we'll do it in a highly irregular manner—you'll hear the disk read first. The subject is a girl and she's listening to everything that's said. Are you capable of understanding that?"

There was a brief, almost shocked silence, then Records said meekly, "Sorry. Go ahead."

He began to read the disk, reading it slowly to delay the inevitable for as long as possible, trying to help her by giving her what little time he could to recover from her first horror and let it resolve into the calm of acceptance and resignation.

"Number T8374 dash Y54. Name, Marilyn Lee Cross. Sex, female. Born July 7, 2160." *She was only eighteen.* "Height, five-three. Weight, a hundred and ten." *Such a slight weight, yet enough to add fatally to the mass of the shell-thin bubble that was an EDS.* "Hair, brown. Eyes, blue. Complexion, light. Blood type, O." *Irrelevant data.* "Destination, Port City, Mimir." *Invalid data.*

He finished and said, "I'll call you later," then turned once again to the girl. She was huddled back against the wall, watching him with a look of numb and wondering fascination.

"They're waiting for you to kill me, aren't they? They want me dead, don't they? You and everybody on the cruiser want me dead, don't you?" Then the numbness broke and her voice was that of a frightened and bewildered child. "Everybody wants me dead and I didn't *do* any-

thing. I didn't hurt anyone—I only wanted to see my brother."

"It's not the way you think—it isn't that way at all," he said. "Nobody wants it this way; nobody would ever let it be this way if it was humanly possible to change it."

"Then why is it? I don't understand. Why is it?"

"This ship is carrying kala fever serum to Group One on Woden. Their own supply was destroyed by a tornado. Group Two—the crew your brother is in—is eight thousand miles away across the Western Sea, and their helicopters can't cross it to help Group One. The fever is invariably fatal unless the serum can be had in time, and the six men in Group One will die unless this ship reaches them on schedule. These little ships are always given barely enough fuel to reach their destination, and if you stay aboard your added weight will cause it to use up all its fuel before it reaches the ground. It will crash then, and you and I will die and so will the six men waiting for the fever serum."

It was a full minute before she spoke, and as she considered his words, the expression of numbness left her eyes.

"Is that it?" she asked at last. "Just that the ship doesn't have enough fuel?"

"Yes."

"I can go alone or I can take seven others with me—is that the way it is?"

"That's the way it is."

"And nobody wants me to have to die?"

"Nobody."

"Then maybe—— Are you sure nothing can be done about it? Wouldn't people help me if they could?"

"Everyone would like to help you, but there is nothing anyone can do. I did the only thing I could do when I called the *Stardust*."

"And it won't come back—but there might be other cruisers, mightn't there? Isn't there any hope at all that there might be someone, somewhere, who could do something to help me?"

She was leaning forward a little in her eagerness as she waited for his answer.

"No."

The word was like the drop of a cold stone and

she again leaned back against the wall, the hope and eagerness leaving her face. "You're sure— you *know* you're sure?"

"I'm sure. There are no other cruisers within forty light-years: there is nothing and no one to change things."

She dropped her gaze to her lap and began twisting a pleat of her skirt between her fingers, saying no more as her mind began to adapt itself to the grim knowledge.

It was better so; with the going of all hope would go the fear; with the going of all hope would come resignation. She needed time and she could have so little of it. How much?

The EDS's were not equipped with hull-cooling units; their speed had to be reduced to a moderate level before entering the atmosphere. They were decelerating at .10 gravity, approaching their destination at a far higher speed than the computers had calculated on. The *Stardust* had been quite near Woden when she launched the EDS; their present velocity was putting them nearer by the second. There would be a critical point, soon to be reached, when he would have to resume deceleration. When he did so the girl's weight would be multiplied by the gravities of deceleration, would become, suddenly, a factor of paramount importance, the factor the computers had been ignorant of when they determined the amount of fuel the EDS should have. She would have to go when deceleration began; it could be no other way. When would that be—how long could he let her stay?

"How long can I stay?"

He winced involuntarily from the words that were so like an echo of his own thoughts. How long? He didn't know; he would have to ask the ship's computers. Each EDS was given a meager surplus of fuel to compensate for unfavorable conditions within the atmosphere, and relatively little fuel was being consumed for the time being. The memory banks of the computers would still contain all data pertaining to the course set for the EDS; such data would not be erased until the EDS reached its destination. He had only to give the computers the new data—the girl's weight and the exact time at which he had reduced the deceleration to .10.

"Barton." Commander Delhart's voice came abruptly from the communicator as he opened his mouth to call the *Stardust*. "A check with Records shows me you haven't completed your report. Did you reduce the deceleration?"

So the commander knew what he was trying to do.

"I'm decelerating at point ten," he answered. "I cut the deceleration at seventeen fifty and the weight is a hundred and ten. I would like to stay at point ten as long as the computers say I can. Will you give them the question?"

It was contrary to regulations for an EDS pilot to make any changes in the course or degree of deceleration the computers had set for him, but the commander made no mention of the violation. Neither did he ask the reason for it. It was not necessary for him to ask; he had not become commander of an interstellar cruiser without both intelligence and an understanding of human nature. He said only, "I'll have that given to the computers."

The communicator fell silent and he and the girl waited, neither of them speaking. They would not have to wait long; the computers would give the answer within moments of the asking. The new factors would be fed into the steel maw of the first bank, and the electrical impulses would go through the complex circuits. Here and there a relay might click, a tiny cog turn over, but it would be essentially the electrical impulses that found the answer; formless, mindless, invisible, determining with utter precision how long the pale girl beside him might live. Then five little segments of metal in the second bank would trip in rapid succession against an inked ribbon and a second steel maw would spit out the slip of paper that bore the answer.

The chronometer on the instrument board read 18:10 when the commander spoke again.

"You will resume deceleration at nineteen ten."

She looked toward the chronometer, then quickly away from it. "Is that when . . . when I go?" she asked. He nodded and she dropped her eyes to her lap again.

"I'll have the course correction given to you," the commander said. "Ordinarily I would never permit anything like this, but I understand your

position. There is nothing I can do, other than what I've just done, and you will not deviate from these new instructions. You will complete your report at nineteen ten. Now—here are the course corrections."

The voice of some unknown technician read them to him, and he wrote them down on the pad clipped to the edge of the control board. There would, he saw, be periods of deceleration when he neared the atmosphere when the deceleration would be five gravities—and at five gravities one hundred ten pounds would become five hundred fifty pounds.

The technician finished and he terminated the contact with a brief acknowledgement. Then, hesitating a moment, he reached out and shut off the communicator. It was 18:13 and he would have nothing to report until 19:10. In the meantime, it somehow seemed indecent to permit others to hear what she might say in her last hour.

He began to check the instrument readings, going over them with unnecessary slowness. She would have to accept the circumstances, and there was nothing he could do to help her into acceptance; words of sympathy would only delay it.

It was 18:20 when she stirred from her motionlessness and spoke.

"So that's the way it has to be with me?"

He swung around to face her. "You understand now, don't you? No one would ever let it be like this if it could be changed."

"I understand," she said. Some of the color had returned to her face and the lipstick no longer stood out so vividly red. "There isn't enough fuel for me to stay. When I hid on this ship I got into something I didn't know anything about and now I have to pay for it."

She had violated a man-made law that said KEEP OUT, but the penalty was not for men's making or desire and it was a penalty men could not revoke. A physical law had decreed: *h amount of fuel will power an EDS with a mass of m safely to its destination;* and a second physical law had decreed: *h amount of fuel will not power an EDS with a mass of m plus x safely to its destination.*

EDS's obeyed only physical laws, and no amount of human sympathy for her could alter the second law.

"But I'm afraid. I don't want to die—not now. I want to live, and nobody is doing anything to help me; everybody is letting me go ahead and acting just like nothing was going to happen to me. I'm going to die and nobody *cares*."

"We all do," he said. "I do and the commander does and the clerk in Ship's Records; we all care and each of us did what little he could to help you. It wasn't enough—it was almost nothing—but it was all we could do."

"Not enough fuel—I can understand that," she said, as though she had not heard his own words. "But to have to die for it. *Me* alone . . ."

How hard it must be for her to accept the fact. She had never known danger of death; had never known the environments where the lives of men could be as fragile and fleeting as sea foam tossed against a rocky shore. She belonged on gentle Earth, in that secure and peaceful society where she could be young and gay and laughing with the others of her kind; where life was precious and well guarded and there was always the assurance that tomorrow would come. She belonged in that world of soft winds and a warm sun, music and moonlight and gracious manners, and not on the hard, bleak frontier.

"How did it happen to me so terribly quickly? An hour ago I was on the *Stardust,* going to Mimir. Now the *Stardust* is going on without me and I'm going to die and I'll never see Gerry and Mama and Daddy again—I'll never see anything again."

He hesitated, wondering how he could explain it to her so she would really understand and not feel she had somehow been the victim of a reasonlessly cruel injustice. She did not know what the frontier was like; she thought in terms of safe, secure Earth. Pretty girls were not jettisoned on Earth; there was a law against it. On Earth her plight would have filled the newscasts and a fast black patrol ship would have been racing to her rescue. Everyone, everywhere, would have known of Marilyn Lee Cross, and no effort would have been spared to save her life. But this was not Earth and there were no patrol ships; only the *Stardust,* leaving them behind at many times the speed of light. There was no one to help her, there would be no Marilyn Lee Cross smiling from the newscasts tomorrow. Marilyn Lee Cross would be but a poignant memory for an EDS pilot and a name on a gray card in Ship's Records.

"It's different here; it's not like back on Earth," he said. "It isn't that no one cares; it's that no one can do anything to help. The frontier is big, and here along its rim the colonies and exploration parties are scattered so thin and far between. On Woden, for example, there are only sixteen men—sixteen men on an entire world. The exploration parties, the survey crews, the little first colonies—they're all fighting alien environments, trying to make a way for those who will follow after. The environments fight back, and those who go first usually make mistakes only once. There is no margin of safety along the rim of the frontier; there can't be until the way is made for the others who will come later, until the new worlds are tamed and settled. Until then men will have to pay the penalty for making mistakes, with no one to help them, because there is no one *to* help them."

"I was going to Mimir," she said. "I didn't know about the frontier; I was only going to Mimir and *it's* safe."

"Mimir is safe, but you left the cruiser that was taking you there."

She was silent for a little while. "It was all so wonderful at first; there was plenty of room for me on this ship and I would be seeing Gerry so soon. I didn't know about the fuel, didn't know what would happen to me . . ."

Her words trailed away, and he turned his attention to the viewscreen, not wanting to stare at her as she fought her way through the black horror of fear toward the calm gray of acceptance.

Woden was a ball, enshrouded in the blue haze of its atmosphere, swimming in space against the background of star-sprinkled dead blackness. The great mass of Manning's Continent sprawled like a gigantic hourglass in the Eastern Sea, with the western half of the Eastern Continent still visible. There was a thin line of shadow along the right-hand edge of the globe, and the Eastern Continent was disappearing into it as the planet turned on its axis. An hour before, the entire continent had been in view; now a thousand miles of it had gone into the thin edge of shadow and around to the night that lay on the other side of the world. The dark blue spot that was Lotus Lake was approaching the shadow. It was somewhere near the southern edge of the lake that Group Two had their camp. It would be night there soon, and quick behind the coming of night the rotation of Woden on its axis would put Group Two beyond the reach of the ship's radio.

He would have to tell her before it was too late for her to talk to her brother. In a way, it would be better for both of them should they not do so, but it was not for him to decide. To each of them the last words would be something to hold and cherish, something that would cut like the blade of a knife yet would be infinitely precious to remember, she for her own brief moments to live and he for the rest of his life.

He held down the button that would flash the grid lines on the viewscreen and used the known diameter of the planet to estimate the distance the southern tip of Lotus Lake had yet to go until it passed beyond radio range. It was approximately five hundred miles. Five hundred miles; thirty minutes—and the chronometer read 18:30. Allowing for error in estimating, it would not be later than 19:05 that the turning of Woden would cut off her brother's voice.

The first border of the Western continent was already in sight along the left side of the world. Four thousand miles across it lay the shore of the Western Sea and the camp of Group One. It had been in the Western Sea that the tornado had originated, to strike with such fury at the camp and destroy half their prefabricated buildings, including the one that housed the medical supplies. Two days before, the tornado had not existed; it had been no more than great gentle masses of air out over the calm Western Sea. Group One had gone about their routine survey work, unaware of the meeting of air masses out at sea, unaware of the force the union was spawning. It had struck their camp without warning—a thundering, roaring destruction that sought to annihilate all that lay before it. It had passed on, leaving the wreckage in its wake. It had destroyed the labor of months and had doomed six men to die and then, as though its task was accomplished, it once more began to resolve into gentle masses of air. But, for all its deadliness, it had destroyed with neither malice nor intent. It had been a blind and mindless force, obeying the laws of nature, and it would have followed the same course with the same fury had men never existed.

Existence required order, and there was order; the laws of nature, irrevocable and immutable. Men could learn to use them, but men could not change them. The circumference of a circle was always pi times the diameter, and no science of man would ever make it otherwise. The combination of chemical A with chemical B under condition C invariably produced reaction D. The law of gravitation was a rigid equation, and it made no distinction between the fall of a leaf and the ponderous circling of a binary star system. The nuclear conversion process powered the cruisers that carried men to the stars; the same process in the form of a nova would destroy a world with equal efficiency. The laws *were*, and the universe moved in obedience to them. Along the frontier were arrayed all the forces of nature, and sometimes they destroyed those who were fighting their way outward from Earth. The men of the frontier had long ago learned the bitter futility of cursing the forces that would destroy them, for the forces were blind and deaf; the futility of looking to the heavens for mercy, for the stars of the galaxy swung in their long, long sweep of two hundred million years, as inexorably controlled as they by the laws that knew neither hatred nor compassion. The men of the frontier knew—but how was a girl from Earth to fully understand? *H amount of fuel will not power an EDS with a mass of m plus x safely to its destination.* To himself and her brother and parents she was a sweet-faced girl in her teens; to the laws of nature she was x, the unwanted factor in a cold equation.

She stirred again on the seat. "Could I write a letter? I want to write to Mama and Daddy. And I'd like to talk to Gerry. Could you let me talk to him over your radio there?"

"I'll try to get him," he said.

He switched on the normal-space transmitter and pressed the signal button. Someone answered the buzzer almost immediately.

"Hello. How's it going with you fellows now—is the EDS on its way?"

"This isn't Group One; this is the EDS," he said. "Is Gerry Cross there?"

"Gerry? He and two others went out in the helicopter this morning and aren't back yet. It's almost sundown, though, and he ought to be back right away—in less than an hour at the most."

"Can you connect me through to the radio in his 'copter?"

"Huh-uh. It's been out of commission for two months—some printed circuits went haywire and we can't get any more until the next cruiser stops by. Is it something important—bad news for him, or something?"

"Yes—it's very important. When he comes in get him to the transmitter as soon as you possibly can."

"I'll do that; I'll have one of the boys waiting at the field with a truck. Is there anything else I can do?"

"No, I guess that's all. Get him there as soon as you can and signal me."

He turned the volume to an inaudible minimum, an act that would not affect the functioning of the signal buzzer, and unclipped the pad of paper from the control board. He tore off the sheet containing his flight instructions and handed the pad to her, together with pencil.

"I'd better write to Gerry too," she said as she took them. "He might not get back to camp in time."

She began to write, her fingers still clumsy and uncertain in the way they handled the pencil, and the top of it trembling a little as she poised it between words. He turned back to the viewscreen, to stare at it without seeing it.

She was a lonely little child trying to say her last goodbye, and she would lay out her heart to them. She would tell them how much she loved them and she would tell them to not feel bad about it, that it was only something that must happen eventually to everyone and she was not afraid. The last would be a lie and it would be there to read between the sprawling, uneven lines: a valiant little lie that would make the hurt all the greater for them.

Her brother was of the frontier and he would understand. He would not hate the EDS pilot for doing nothing to prevent her going; he would know there had been nothing the pilot could do. He would understand, though the understanding would not soften the shock and pain when he learned his sister was gone. But the others, her father and mother—they would not understand. They were of Earth and they would think in the manner of those who had never lived where the safety margin of life was a thin, thin line—and sometimes not at all. What would they think of the faceless, unknown pilot who had sent her to her death?

They would hate him with cold and terrible intensity, but it really didn't matter. He would never see them, never know them. He would have only the memories to remind him; only the nights of fear, when a blue-eyed girl in gypsy sandals would come in his dreams to die again. . . .

He scowled at the viewscreen and tried to force his thoughts into less emotional channels. There was nothing he could do to help her. She had unknowingly subjected herself to the penalty of a law that recognized neither innocence nor youth nor beauty, that was incapable of sympathy or leniency. Regret was illogical—and yet, could knowing it to be illogical ever keep it away?

She stopped occasionally, as though trying to find the right words to tell them what she wanted them to know, then the pencil would resume its whispering to the paper. It was 18:37 when she folded the letter in a square and wrote a name on it. She began writing another, twice looking up at the chronometer, as though she feared the black hand might reach its rendezvous before she had finished. It was 18:45 when she folded it as she had done the first letter and wrote a name and address on it.

She held the letters out to him. "Will you take care of these and see that they're enveloped and mailed?"

"Of course." He took them from her hand and placed them in a pocket of his gray uniform shirt.

"These can't be sent off until the next cruiser stops by, and the *Stardust* will have long since told them about me, won't it?" she asked. He nodded and she went on: "That makes the letters not important in one way, but in another way they're very important—to me, and to them."

"I know. I understand, and I'll take care of them."

She glanced at the chronometer, then back to him. "It seems to move faster all the time, doesn't it?"

He said nothing, unable to think of anything to say, and she asked, "Do you think Gerry will come back to camp in time?"

"I think so. They said he should be in right away."

She began to roll the pencil back and forth between her palms. "I hope he does. I feel sick and scared and I want to hear his voice again and maybe I won't feel so alone. I'm a coward and I can't help it."

"No," he said, "you're not a coward. You're afraid, but you're not a coward."

"Is there a difference?"

He nodded. "A lot of difference."

"I feel so alone. I never did feel like this before; like I was all by myself and there was nobody to care what happened to me. Always, before, there were Mama and Daddy there and my friends around me. I had lots of friends, and they had a going-away party for me the night before I left."

Friends and music and laughter for her to remember—and on the viewscreen Lotus Lake was going into the shadow.

"Is it the same with Gerry?" she asked. "I mean, if he should make a mistake, would he have to die for it, all alone and with no one to help him?"

"It's the same with all, along the frontier; it will always be like that so long as there is a frontier."

"Gerry didn't tell us. He said the pay was good, and he sent money home all the time because Daddy's little shop just brought in a bare living, but he didn't tell us it was like this."

"He didn't tell you his work was dangerous?"

"Well—yes. He mentioned that, but we didn't understand. I always thought danger along the frontier was something that was a lot of fun; an exciting adventure, like in the three-D shows." A wan smile touched her face for a moment. "Only

it's not, is it? It's not the same at all, because when it's real you can't go home after the show is over."

"No," he said. "No, you can't."

Her glance flicked from the chronometer to the door of the air lock, then down to the pad and pencil she still held. She shifted her position slightly to lay them on the bench beside her, moving one foot out a little. For the first time he saw that she was not wearing Vegan gypsy sandals, but only cheap imitations; the expensive Vegan leather was some kind of grained plastic, the silver buckle was gilded iron, the jewels were colored glass. *Daddy's little shop just brought in a bare living . . .* She must have left college in her second year, to take the course in linguistics that would enable her to make her own way and help her brother provide for her parents, earning what she could by part-time work after classes were over. Her personal possessions on the *Stardust* would be taken back to her parents—they would neither be of much value nor occupy much storage space on the return voyage.

"Isn't it——" She stopped, and he looked at her questioningly. "Isn't it cold in here?" she asked, almost apologetically. "Doesn't it seem cold to you?"

"Why, yes," he said. He saw by the main temperature gauge that the room was at precisely normal temperature. "Yes, it's colder than it should be."

"I wish Gerry would get back before it's too late. Do you really think he will, and you didn't just say so to make me feel better?"

"I think he will—they said he would be in pretty soon." On the viewscreen Lotus Lake had gone into the shadow but for the thin blue line of its western edge, and it was apparent he had overestimated the time she would have in which to talk to her brother. Reluctantly, he said to her, "His camp will be out of radio range in a few minutes; he's on that part of Woden that's in the shadow"—he indicated the viewscreen—"and the turning of Woden will put him beyond contact. There may not be much time left when he comes in—not much time to talk to him before he fades out. I wish I could do something about it—I would call him right now if I could."

"Not even as much time as I will have to stay?"

"I'm afraid not."

"Then——" She straightened and looked toward the air lock with pale resolution. "Then I'll go when Gerry passes beyond range. I won't wait any longer after that—I won't have anything to wait for."

Again there was nothing he could say.

"Maybe I shouldn't wait at all. Maybe I'm selfish—maybe it would be better for Gerry if you just told him about it afterward."

There was an unconscious pleading for denial in the way she spoke and he said, "He wouldn't want you to do that, to not wait for him."

"It's already coming dark where he is, isn't it? There will be all the long night before him, and Mama and Daddy don't know yet that I won't ever be coming back like I promised them I would. I've caused everyone I love to be hurt, haven't I? I didn't want to—I didn't intend to."

"It wasn't your fault," he said. "It wasn't your fault at all. They'll know that. They'll understand."

"At first I was so afraid to die that I was a coward and thought only of myself. Now I see how selfish I was. The terrible thing about dying like this is not that I'll be gone but that I'll never see them again; never be able to tell them that I didn't take them for granted; never be able to tell them I knew of the sacrifices they made to make my life happier, that I knew all the things they did for me and that I loved them so much more than I ever told them. I've never told them any of those things. You don't tell them such things when you're young and your life is all before you— you're so very afraid of sounding sentimental and silly. But it's so different when you have to die— you wish you had told them while you could and you wish you could tell them you're sorry for all the little mean things you ever did or said to them. You wish you could tell them that you didn't really mean to ever hurt their feelings and for them to only remember that you always loved them far more than you ever let them know."

"You don't have to tell them that," he said. "They will know—they've always known it."

"Are you sure?" she asked. "How can you be sure? My people are strangers to you."

"Wherever you go, human nature and human hearts are the same."

"And they will know what I want them to know—that I love them?"

"They've always known it, in a way far better than you could ever put in words for them."

"I keep remembering the things they did for me, and it's the little things they did that seem to be the most important to me, now. Like Gerry— he sent me a bracelet of fire rubies on my sixteenth birthday. It was beautiful—it must have cost him a month's pay. Yet I remember him more for what he did the night my kitten got run over in the street. I was only six years old and he held me in his arms and wiped away my tears and told me not to cry, that Flossy was gone for just a little while, for just long enough to get herself a new

fur coat, and she would be on the foot of my bed the very next morning. I believed him and quit crying and went to sleep dreaming about my kitten coming back. When I woke up the next morning, there was Flossy on the foot of my bed in a brand-new white fur coat, just like he had said she would be. It wasn't until a long time later that Mama told me Gerry had got the pet-shop owner out of bed at four in the morning and, when the man got mad about it, Gerry told him he was either going to go down and sell him the white kitten right then or he'd break his neck."

"It's always the little things you remember people by; all the little things they did because they wanted to do them for you. You've done the same for Gerry and your father and mother; all kinds of things that you've forgotten about, but that they will never forget."

"I hope I have. I would like for them to remember me like that."

"They will."

"I wish—" She swallowed. "The way I'll die— I wish they wouldn't ever think of that. I've read how people look who die in space—their insides all ruptured and exploded and their lungs out between their teeth and then, a few seconds later, they're all dry and shapeless and horribly ugly. I don't want them to ever think of me as something dead and horrible like that."

"You're their own, their child and their sister. They could never think of you other than the way you would want them to, the way you looked the last time they saw you."

"I'm still afraid," she said. "I can't help it, but I don't want Gerry to know it. If he gets back in time, I'm going to act like I'm not afraid at all and——"

The signal buzzer interrupted her, quick and imperative.

"Gerry!" She came to her feet. "It's Gerry now!"

He spun the volume control knob and asked, "Gerry Cross?"

"Yes," her brother answered, an undertone of tenseness to his reply. "The bad news—what is it?"

She answered for him, standing close behind him and leaning down a little toward the communicator, her hand resting small and cold on his shoulder.

"Hello, Gerry." There was only a faint quaver to betray the careful casualness of her voice. "I wanted to see you——"

"Marilyn!" There was sudden and terrible apprehension in the way he spoke her name. "What are you doing on that EDS?"

"I wanted to see you," she said again. "I wanted to see you, so I hid on this ship——"

"You *hid* on it?"

"I'm a stowaway . . . I didn't know what it would mean——"

"Marilyn!" It was the cry of a man who calls, hopeless and desperate, to someone already and forever gone from him. "What have you done?"

"I . . . it's not——" Then her own composure broke and the cold little hand gripped his shoulder convulsively. "Don't, Gerry—I only wanted to see you; I didn't intend to hurt you. Please, Gerry, don't feel like that——"

Something warm and wet splashed on his wrist, and he slid out of the chair, to help her into it and swing the microphone down to her level.

"Don't feel like that. Don't let me go knowing you feel like that——"

The sob she had tried to hold back choked in her throat, and her brother spoke to her. "Don't cry, Marilyn." His voice was suddenly deep and infinitely gentle, with all the pain held out of it. "Don't cry, Sis—you mustn't do that. It's all right, honey—everything is all right."

"I——" Her lower lip quivered and she bit into it. "I didn't want you to feel that way—I just wanted us to say goodbye, because I have to go in a minute."

"Sure—sure. That's the way it'll be, Sis. I didn't mean to sound the way I did." Then his voice changed to a tone of quick and urgent demand. "EDS—have you called the *Stardust*? Did you check with the computers?"

"I called the *Stardust* almost an hour ago. It can't turn back, there are no other cruisers within forty light-years, and there isn't enough fuel."

"Are you sure that the computers had the correct data—sure of everything?"

"Yes—do you think I could ever let it happen if I wasn't sure? I did everything I could do. If there was anything at all I could do now, I would do it."

"He tried to help me, Gerry." Her lower lip was no longer trembling and the short sleeves of her blouse were wet where she had dried her tears. "No one can help me and I'm not going to cry any more and everything will be all right with you and Daddy and Mama, won't it?"

"Sure—sure it will. We'll make out fine."

Her brother's words were beginning to come in more faintly, and he turned the volume control to maximum. "He's going out of range," he said to her. "He'll be gone within another minute."

"You're fading out, Gerry," she said. "You're going out of range. I wanted to tell you—but I can't now. We must say goodbye so soon—but maybe I'll see you again. Maybe I'll come to you in your dreams with my hair in braids and crying because the kitten in my arms is dead; maybe I'll be the touch of a breeze that whispers to you as it goes by; maybe I'll be one of those gold-winged larks you told me about, singing my silly head off to you; maybe, at times, I'll be nothing you can see, but you will know I'm there beside you. Think of me like that, Gerry; always like that and not—the other way."

Dimmed to a whisper by the turning of Woden, the answer came back:

"Always like that, Marilyn—always like that and never any other way."

"Our time is up, Gerry—I have to go now. Good——" Her voice broke in mid-word and her mouth tried to twist into crying. She pressed her hand hard against it and when she spoke again the words came clear and true:

"Goodbye, Gerry."

Faint and ineffably poignant and tender, the last words came from the cold metal of the communicator:

"Goodbye, little sister . . ."

She sat motionless in the hush that followed, as though listening to the shadow-echoes of the words as they died away, then she turned away from the communicator, toward the air lock, and he pulled down the black lever beside him. The inner door of the air lock slid swiftly open, to reveal the bare little cell that was waiting for her, and she walked to it.

She walked with her head up and the brown curls brushing her shoulders, with the white sandals stepping as sure and steady as the fractional gravity would permit and the gilded buckles twinkling with little lights of blue and red and crystal. He let her walk alone and made no move to help her, knowing she would not want it that way. She stepped into the air lock and turned to face him, only the pulse in her throat to betray the wild beating of her heart.

"I'm ready," she said.

He pushed the lever up and the door slid its quick barrier between them, enclosing her in black and utter darkness for her last moments of life. It clicked as it locked in place and he jerked down the red lever. There was a slight waver to the ship as the air gushed from the lock, a vibration to the wall as though something had bumped the outer door in passing, then there was nothing and the ship was dropping true and steady again. He shoved the red lever back to close the door on the empty air lock and turned away, to walk to the pilot's chair with the slow steps of a man old and weary.

Back in the pilot's chair he pressed the signal button of the normal-space transmitter. There was no response; he had expected none. Her brother would have to wait through the night until the turning of Woden permitted contact through Group One.

It was not yet time to resume deceleration, and he waited while the ship dropped endlessly downward with him and the drives purred softly. He saw that the white hand of the supplies-closet temperature gauge was on zero. A cold equation had been balanced and he was alone on the ship. Something shapeless and ugly was hurrying ahead of him, going to Woden, where her brother was waiting through the night, but the empty ship still lived for a little while with the presence of the girl who had not known about the forces that killed with neither hatred nor malice. It seemed, almost, that she still sat, small and bewildered and frightened, on the metal box beside him, her words echoing hauntingly clear in the void she had left behind her:

I didn't do anything to die for . . . I didn't do anything . . .

Responding to the Story

Analyzing the Story

Identifying Facts

1. Describe the **basic situation** of this plot. Explain why the pilot has no choice but to eject Marilyn.
2. Explain why this particular stowaway causes **complications** for Barton as he seeks to resolve his problem.
3. Describe the characters' **external conflict**—who or what is preventing them from getting what they want?
4. How would you describe the **internal conflict** that Marilyn undergoes as she gradually learns what her fate will be? Explain how Barton helps her to face that fate.
5. How would you describe Barton's internal conflict? How is it **resolved**?

Interpreting Meanings

6. What would you say is the source of this story's **suspense**—that is, what questions keep you turning the pages? Were you prepared for the way the story ended, or did you expect a different **resolution**? Explain.
7. The story contrasts life on Earth with life on the space frontiers. In what important ways are they different? Did you find the depiction of the space frontier believable? Explain.
8. Find the line toward the middle of the story that explains the **title**. What are the "cold equations" the story deals with? What other "cold equations" can you name that affect our lives?
9. The title of this story seems to imply that the more technology influences our lives, the less room there will be for human emotions. How does the story illustrate this idea? Do you think this is a general truth? Explain.
10. How did you feel about the story's **resolution**—do you think the writer should have ended it differently? How would the story's effect have been different if the ending had been changed?
11. Would you say that this story is emotionally loaded—that is, does it work by stirring up your emotions? If you think it does, try to pinpoint exactly what aspects of the story evoke all these strong feelings.

Writing About the Story

A Creative Response

1. **Changing the Resolution.** Beginning with Marilyn's words "I'm ready" on page 21, write a new resolution for the story. Try to think of a plausible way to end the conflict. Is it possible to find a happy ending?
2. **Writing About the Future.** Take some aspect of your present life—making breakfast, getting to school, acquiring information, buying clothes, taking a bath—and imagine how it will be better or worse in a hundred years. Write one paragraph explaining how technology might change the way you ordinarily carry out this activity.

A Critical Response

3. **Evaluating the Plot.** The plot of this story is carefully worked out to convince us, first, that Marilyn could actually have been able to stow away on the ship and, second, that Barton had no choice but to eject her. Write a paragraph telling whether or not you find the story believable. Are there any flaws in the plot? Cite specific details to support your evaluation.
4. **Supporting an Opinion.** On page 9, Barton says that he could have immediately carried out the regulation to eject the stowaway if the offender had been a man. His reaction is entirely different because the stowaway is a teen-age girl. (Remember that this story first appeared more than thirty years ago.) What do you think about this different treatment for women or children? Write a paragraph telling what you think of Barton's response, giving reasons to support your opinion.

Analyzing Language and Vocabulary

Context Clues

Context refers to the words that surround another word or phrase. When you read, you can often make an "educated guess" about the meaning of an unfamiliar word by looking at clues provided by its context. For example, what in the world is the *green kala midge* mentioned in this passage?

The *Stardust* had received the request from one of the exploration parties stationed on Woden, the six men of the party already being stricken with the fever carried by the *green kala midges* and their own supply of serum destroyed by the tornado that had torn through their camp.

You might not recognize a green kala midge if you saw one, but you do find out enough from this sentence to continue reading without stopping to use a dictionary. From the context clues, you can tell that a green kala midge is some kind of life form (either plant or animal) and that it causes a fever, which can be treated by a certain type of serum. For the purposes of the story, that is all you need to know about the green kala midge.

There are several kinds of context clues:

1. One type of context clue involves apposition. An **appositive** is a word or phrase that is placed next to another word to explain or define it. Appositives usually come right after the word they are explaining, sometimes right before.

    > He was an EDS pilot, *inured* to the sight of death, long since accustomed to it and to viewing the dying of another man with an objective lack of emotion. . . .

    a. What phrase in the sentence is in apposition to the word *inured*?
    b. What does *inured* mean?

2. Sometimes a context clue will give one or more **examples** of the unfamiliar word, as in the following passage. Here, the context helps us guess at the meanings of two unfamiliar words:

    > Existence required order, and there was order; the laws of nature, *irrevocable* and *immutable*. Men could learn to use them, but men could not change them. The circumference of a circle was always pi times the diameter, and no science of man would ever make it otherwise. The combination of chemical A with chemical B under condition C invariably produced reaction D. . . .

    a. The second sentence in this passage suggests that one or both of the italicized words—*irrevocable* and *immutable*—mean "unchangeable." What examples are given of the unchangeable laws of nature?
    b. Do the two words have exactly the same meaning or somewhat different meanings? Use a dictionary to find out.

3. A third kind of context clue comes from the **structure** of the word itself. Suppose that you know that the prefix *inter-* means "between" or "among" or "mutually." You could guess then what *interdependence* means in the following passage:

    > . . . such a delay would destroy their schedule and produce a confusion and uncertainty that would wreck the complex *interdependence* between old Earth and the new worlds of the frontier.

    a. What is the difference between *dependence* and *interdependence*?
    b. In this sentence, what things are interdependent?

Reading About the Writer

Tom Godwin (1915–1980) lived for many years in small towns throughout the Mojave Desert. His popular science-fiction stories began appearing in magazines during the early fifties, and his first novel, *The Survivors*, was published in 1958. Godwin's other novels are *The Space Barbarians*, which describes warfare on the planet Ragnarok, and *Beyond Another Sun*. "The Cold Equations" is one of the best known of all modern science-fiction stories.

THE FATALIST

Isaac Bashevis Singer, translated by **Joseph Singer**

"The Fatalist" is a lighthearted story, but it springs from a profound question that philosophers have been asking throughout time: Do we humans have a choice in determining our future, or are all our actions predetermined? See if you think Singer's story answers the question—or is that not his point at all? The story takes place in Poland some years ago.

Nicknames given in small towns are the homely, familiar ones: Haim Bellybutton, Yekel Cake, Sarah Gossip, Gittel Duck, and similar names. But in the Polish town where I came as a teacher in my young days, I heard of someone called Benjamin Fatalist. I promptly became curious. How did they come to the word *fatalist* in a small town? And what did that person do to earn it? The secretary of the Young Zion organization where I taught Hebrew told me about it.

The man in question wasn't a native here. He stemmed from somewhere in Courland. He had come to town in 1916 and posted notices that he was a teacher of German. It was during the Austrian occupation, and everyone wanted to learn German. German is spoken in Courland and he, Benjamin Schwartz—that was his real name—got many students of both sexes. Just as the secretary was talking, he pointed to the window and exclaimed: "There he goes now!"

I looked through the window and saw a short man, dark, in a derby and with a curled mustache that was already long out of style. He was carrying a briefcase. After the Austrians left, the secretary continued, no one wanted to study German any more and the Poles gave Benjamin Schwartz a job in the archives. If someone needed a birth certificate, they came to him. He had a fancy handwriting. He had learned Polish, and he also became a kind of hedge-lawyer.[1]

The secretary said: "He came here as if dropping from heaven. At that time, he was a bachelor of some twenty-odd. The young people had a club, and when an educated person came to our town, this was cause for a regular celebration. He was invited to our club and a box evening was arranged in his honor. Questions were placed in a box, and he was supposed to draw them out and answer them. A girl asked whether he believed in Special Providence, and, instead of replying in a few words, he spoke for a whole hour. He said that . . . all things were determined, every trifle. If one ate an onion for supper, it was because one *had* to eat an onion. It had been so preordained a billion years ago. If you walked in the street and tripped over a pebble, it was fated that you should fall. He described himself as a fatalist. It had been destined that he come to our town, though it appeared accidental.

"He spoke too long; nevertheless, a discussion followed. 'Is there no such thing as chance?' someone asked, and he replied: 'No such thing as chance.' 'If that is so,' another asked, 'what's the point of working, of studying? Why learn a trade or bring up children? Well, and why contribute to Zionism and agitate for a Jewish homeland?'

" 'The way it is written in the books of fate, that's how it has to be,' Benjamin Schwartz replied. 'If it was destined that someone open a store and go bankrupt, he has to do this.' All the efforts man made were fated, too, because free choice is nothing but an illusion. The debate lasted well into the night and from that time on, he was called the Fatalist. A new word was added to the town's vocabulary. Everyone here knows what a fatalist

---

1. **hedge-lawyer:** an unofficial lawyer.

The Wedding by Marc Chagall (1909).

Foundation E. G. Bührle Collection, Zurich.

is, even the beadle[2] of the synagogue and the poor-house attendant.

"We assumed that after that evening the crowd would get tired of these discussions and turn back to the real problems of our time. Benjamin himself said that this wasn't a thing that could be decided by logic. Either one believed in it or not. But somehow, all our youth became preoccupied with the question. We would call a meeting about certificates to Palestine or about education, but instead of sticking to these subjects, they would discuss fatalism. At that time our library acquired a copy of Lermontov's *A Hero of Our Time*, translated into Yiddish, which describes a fatalist, Petchorin. Everyone read this novel, and there were those among us who wanted to test their luck. We already knew about Russian roulette and some of us might have tried it if a revolver were available. But none of us had one.

---

2. **beadle:** a minor official, a person who keeps order.

"Now listen to this. There was a girl among us, Heyele Minz, a pretty girl, smart, active in our movement, a daughter of a wealthy man. Her father had the biggest dry-goods store in town, and all the young fellows were crazy about her. But Heyele was choosy. She found something wrong in everybody. She had a sharp tongue, what the Germans call *schlagfertig*. If you said something to her, she came right back at you with a sharp and cutting retort. When she wanted to, she could ridicule a person in a clever, half-joking way. The Fatalist fell in love with her soon after he arrived. He wasn't at all bashful. One evening he came up to her and said: 'Heyele, it's fated that you marry me, and since that is so, why delay the inevitable?'

"He said this aloud so that everyone would hear, and it created an uproar. Heyele answered: 'It's fated that I should tell you that you're an idiot and that you've got lots of nerve besides, and therefore I'm saying it. You'll have to forgive me; it was all preordained in the celestial books a billion years ago.'

"Not long afterward, Heyele became engaged to a young man from Hrubieszów, the chairman of the Paole Zion there. The wedding was postponed for a year because the fiancé had an older sister who was engaged and who had to be married first. The boys chided the Fatalist, and he said: 'If Heyele is to be mine, she will be mine,' and Heyele replied: 'I am to be Ozer Rubinstein's, not yours. That's what fate wanted.'

"One winter evening the discussion flared up again about fate, and Heyele spoke up: 'Mr. Schwartz, or Mr. Fatalist, if you really believe in what you say, and you are even ready to play Russian roulette if you had a revolver, I have a game for you that's even more dangerous.'

"I want to mention here that at that time, the railroad didn't reach to our town yet. It passed two miles away, and it never stopped there at all. It was the train from Warsaw to Lvov. Heyele proposed to the Fatalist that he lie down on the rails a few moments before the train passed over them. She argued: 'If it's fated that you live, you will live and have nothing to fear. However, if you don't believe in fatalism, then . . .'

"We all burst out laughing. Everyone was sure that the Fatalist would come up with some pretext to get out of it. Lying down on the tracks meant certain death. But the Fatalist said: 'This, like Russian roulette, is a game, and a game requires another participant who must risk something, too.' He went on: 'I'll lie down on the tracks as you propose, but you must make a sacred vow that if I should live, you'll break your engagement with Ozer Rubinstein and marry me.'

"A deadly silence fell over the hall. Heyele grew pale, and she said: 'Good, I accept your conditions.' 'Give me your sacred vow on it,' the Fatalist said, and Heyele gave him her hand and said: 'I have no mother; she died of the cholera. But I swear on her soul that if you will keep your word, I will keep mine. If not, then let my honor be stained forever.' She turned to us and went on: 'You are all witnesses. If I should break my word, you can all spit in my face.'

"I'll make it short. Everything was settled that evening. The train would pass our town around two in the afternoon. At one-thirty, our whole group would meet by the tracks, and the Fatalist would demonstrate whether he was a real fatalist or just a braggart. We all promised to keep the matter secret because if the older people had found out about it, there would have been a terrible fuss.

"I didn't sleep a wink that night, and, as far as I know, none of the others did either. Most of us were convinced that at the last minute, the Fatalist would have second thoughts and back out. Some also suggested that when the train came into sight or the rails started to hum, we should drag the Fatalist away by force. Well, but all this posed a gruesome danger. Even now as I speak of it a shudder runs through me.

"The next day we all got up early. I was so scared that I couldn't swallow any food at breakfast. The whole thing might not have happened if we hadn't read Lermontov's book. Not all of us went; there were only six boys and four girls, including Heyele Minz. It was freezing cold outside. The Fatalist, I remember, wore a light jacket and a cap. We met on the Zamosc Road, on the outskirts of town. I asked him: 'Schwartz, how did you sleep last night?' and he answered: 'Like any other night.' You actually couldn't tell what he was feeling, but Heyele was as white as if she had just gotten over the typhoid. I went up to her and said: 'Heyele, do you know that you're sending a person to his death?' And she said: 'I'm not sending him. He has plenty of time to change his mind.'

"I'll never forget that day as long as I live. None of us will ever forget it. We walked along and the snow kept falling on us the whole time. We came to the tracks. I thought that on account of the snow the train might possibly not be running, but apparently someone had cleared the rails. We had arrived a good hour too early, and, believe me, this was the longest hour I ever spent. Around fifteen minutes before the train was due to come by, Heyele said: 'Schwartz, I've thought it all over and I don't want you to lose your life because of me. Do me a favor and let's forget the whole thing.' The Fatalist looked at her and asked: 'So you've changed your mind? You want that fellow from Hrubieszów at any price, huh?' She said: 'No, it's not the fellow from Hrubieszów; it's your life. I hear that you have a mother and I don't want her to lose a son on account of me.' Heyele could barely utter these words. She spoke and she trembled. The Fatalist said: 'If you will keep your promise, I'm ready to keep mine, but under one condition: stand a little farther away. If you try to force me back at the last minute, the game is over. Then he cried out: 'Let everyone move twenty paces back!' He seemed to hypnotize us with his words, and we began to back up. He cried again: 'If someone tries to pull me away, I'll grab him by his coat and he will share my fate.' We realized how dangerous this could be. It happens more than once that when you try to save someone from drowning, you both get pushed down and drown.

"As we moved back, the rails began to vibrate and hum and we heard the whistle of the locomotive. We began to yell as one: 'Schwartz, don't do it! Schwartz, have pity!' But even as we yelled he stretched out across the tracks. There was then just one line of track. One girl fainted. We were sure that in a second we would see a person cut in half. I can't tell you what I went through in those few seconds. My blood literally began to seethe from excitement. At that moment, a loud screech was heard and a thud and the train came to a halt no more than a yard away from the Fatalist. I saw in a mist how the engineer and fireman jumped down from the locomotive. They yelled at him and dragged him away. Many passengers disembarked. Some of us ran away out of fear of being arrested. It was a real commotion. I myself stayed where I was and watched everything. Heyele ran up to me, put her arms around me, and started to cry. It was more than a cry, it was like the howling of a beast—give me a cigarette. I can't talk about it. It chokes me. Excuse me. . . ."

I gave the secretary a cigarette and watched how it shook between his fingers. He drew in the smoke and said: "That is actually the whole story."

"She married him?" I asked.

"They have four children."

"I guess the engineer managed to halt the train in time," I remarked.

"Yes, but the wheels were only one yard away from him."

"Did this convince you about fatalism?" I asked.

"No. I wouldn't make such a bet even if you offered me all the fortunes in the world."

"Is he still a fatalist?"

"He still is."

"Would he do it again?" I asked.

The secretary smiled. "Not for Heyele."

Responding to the Story

Analyzing the Story

Identifying Facts

1. Who is the Fatalist, and how did he get his nickname?
2. The **complication** in this story comes when Heyele challenges Benjamin to prove his belief in fatalism. Describe the bargain that Heyele and Benjamin strike.
3. The **climax** occurs when Benjamin comes nose to nose with the Warsaw train. Explain how the climax "proves" Benjamin's theory of fatalism.

4. Summarize how all the problems in the story are finally **resolved**.

Interpreting Meanings

5. What surprise is revealed in the story's salty last line? Did the description of Heyele in the story prepare you for Benjamin's feelings about his fate? If so, how?
6. What do you think the story's major **conflict** is? Does it involve two people in conflict (Benjamin versus the elusive Heyele) or a person in conflict

with society (Benjamin versus those doubters whom he must persuade by his risky experiment)? Keep in mind that either answer, or both, may be correct. Your answer depends on how you perceive the story—is it primarily a love story or a story about fate and free will?

7. The fate-versus-free-will argument is presented in the opening paragraphs of the story. What are Benjamin's arguments to support his belief that everything is controlled by fate? Do you think his theory can be either "proved" or "disproved"? Explain.

Writing About the Story

A Creative Response

1. **Expressing an Opinion.** Which side of the fate-versus-free-will argument are you on? Do you believe, like Benjamin in the story, that all things are determined by fate? Or do you believe that human beings can—at least in part—control what happens to them? Write a paragraph expressing your opinion. Begin with a topic sentence that clearly states your opinion, and then give at least two reasons to support that opinion.

2. **Writing a Journal Entry.** How do you imagine Heyele feels about her fate? How is she responsible for her own fate? Do you think she realizes this? Write a journal entry that Heyele might have written on the evening after the railroad episode or on the day when the narrator hears this story. Let Heyele reveal her thoughts and feelings.

A Critical Response

3. **Evaluating the Frame Story.** Singer uses a **frame story** to tell the story of Benjamin and Heyele. In the frame story, an unknown narrator is talking to the secretary of the Young Zion organization, who tells him the story of the Fatalist. Look back at the story's beginning and ending to see how the frame story works. Then suppose that there were no frame story and no unknown narrator. Suppose instead that the story of Benjamin's test at the railroad tracks were told directly to the reader by someone who witnessed the event when he or she was young. Where would that story probably begin? Where would it end? How would it work in the surprise in the final line? Write a paragraph telling what you think are the advantages or disadvantages of the frame story structure used in "The Fatalist."

Analyzing Language and Vocabulary

Suffixes

A **suffix** is a group of letters added to the end of a word to create a new word. The suffix -*ist* means "a person who makes, believes, or practices something," as in *machinist, optimist,* and *artist.*

The suffix -*ism* has several meanings, including "the doctrine or theory of," "devotion to [a cause]," and "action characteristic of," as in *capitalism, communism,* and *humanism.* What would a writer mean by referring to "the various '-isms' of our time?"

Identify the words and suffixes that have been put together to form the italicized words. What does each word mean?

1. ". . . I heard of someone called Benjamin *Fatalist.*"
2. "Well, and why contribute to *Zionism* and agitate for a Jewish homeland?"
3. ". . . but instead of sticking to these subjects, they would discuss *fatalism.*"

Using your knowledge of suffixes, write out the meaning of each word. Check your guesses in a dictionary.

pessimist	cartoonist	anarchist
archaeologist	pharmacist	terrorist
nationalism	vegetarianism	commercialism

Reading About the Writer

At eighty, **Isaac Bashevis Singer** (1904–1991) explained that he was a vegetarian not for his health "but for the health of the chickens."

Singer was born in Poland, the son of a rabbi. He was planning to become a rabbi himself, but he became captivated by stories and storytelling. When he was about twelve, he read the Sherlock Holmes stories and Dostoyevsky's *Crime and Punishment* in Yiddish. He decided right then that he would become a Yiddish writer, just as he thought Doyle and Dostoyevsky were. (It never occurred to him that the stories he read had been translated into Yiddish.) And so, over his parents' objections, Isaac Singer decided to be a writer.

With the rise of Nazism in 1935, Singer left Warsaw for New York City, where his older brother and fellow writer, I. J. Singer, had already settled. Yiddish was his only language, and at first he felt he would "never grow any roots in this country."

Then he began to teach himself English. "I bought cards and I wrote down on each card a word as if I would be the author of a dictionary, and every night before I went to sleep I repeated them. And I tried to read the Bible in English. I would say that after a year I was able to make myself understood."

Nevertheless, Singer wrote all his stories in Yiddish. In 1945, when Singer was forty-one, the *For-ward* serialized his novel *The Family Moskat,* a chronicle about the Jewish community he had known in Poland. The novel, translated into English and published as a book, became the first of his profoundly comic and moving stories and books to find favor throughout the literary world. In 1978 Singer won the Nobel Prize in literature.

Focusing on Background
Singer on Yiddish, Ghosts, and Stories for Children

STOCKHOLM, Dec. 10 (AP)—Following is the text of the address by Isaac Bashevis Singer, winner of the Nobel Prize in literature, at the banquet in City Hall tonight following the award ceremony.

"People ask me often: Why do you write in a dying language? And I want to explain it in a few words.

"Firstly, I like to write ghost stories and nothing fits a ghost better than a dying language. The deader the language, the more alive is the ghost. Ghosts love Yiddish, and as far as I know, they all speak it.

"Secondly, not only do I believe in ghosts but also in resurrection. I am sure that millions of Yiddish-speaking corpses will rise from their graves one day and their first question will be: 'Is there any new Yiddish book to read?' For them, Yiddish will not be dead.

"Thirdly, for two thousand years Hebrew was considered a dead language. Suddenly it became strangely alive. What happened to Hebrew may also happen to Yiddish one day (although I haven't the slightest idea how this miracle can take place).

"There is still a fourth minor reason for not forsaking Yiddish and this is: Yiddish may be a dying language, but it is the only language I know really well. Yiddish is my mother tongue and a mother is never really dead.

"Ladies and gentlemen, there are five hundred reasons why I began to write for children, but to save time I will mention only ten of them.

"Number one—Children read books, not reviews. They do not give a hoot about the critics.

"Number two—Children don't read to find their identity.

"Number three—They don't read to free themselves of guilt, to quench the thirst for rebellion, or to get rid of alienation.

"Number four—They have no use for psychology.

"Number five—They detest sociology.

"Number six—They don't try to understand Kafka or *Finnegans Wake.*

"Number seven—They still believe in good, the family, angels, devils, witches, goblins, logic, clarity, punctuation, and other such obsolete stuff.

"Number eight—They love interesting stories, not commentary, guides, or footnotes.

"Number nine—When a book is boring, they yawn openly, without any shame or fear of authority.

"Number ten—They don't expect their beloved writer to redeem humanity. Young as they are, they know that it is not in his power. Only the adults have such childish illusions."

—Isaac B. Singer

THE PIECE OF STRING

Guy de Maupassant, translated by **Roger Colet**

This seemingly simple story (you could almost retell it as a joke) is a classic known throughout the world. Why is it so famous? What gives it that quality of greatness?

First, Maupassant gives us an insight into a particular nineteenth-century French market town that might also be any town in the world. He shows us how the people there behave and, more importantly, what they value. The town is in Normandy and is called Goderville, but see if you think it could just as well be Jersey City or Fresno or your home town.

Second, Maupassant gives us an insight into a particular individual who might be any one of us. The main character, Hauchecorne (ōsh′kôrn),

makes some discoveries about reputation and self-respect that are relevant to all our lives.

Finally, the story gives us an insight into a great truth about life. Often our lives are changed not by a disaster (or by a major accomplishment), but by some trivial, perhaps accidental act—such as picking up a piece of string.

Before you read, spend a few minutes on this dilemma: Imagine that you've been accused of a crime you didn't commit. There isn't enough evidence to try or convict you, but everyone still believes you're guilty. How would you feel? What would you do? Would you be able to shrug your shoulders and say, "Well, I know I'm innocent, and that's all that really matters"?

O n all the roads around Goderville the peasants and their wives were making their way toward the little town, for it was market day. The men were plodding along, their bodies leaning forward with every movement of their long bandy legs—legs deformed by hard work, by the pressure of the plow which also raises the left shoulder and twists the spine, by the spreading of the knees required to obtain a firm stance for reaping, and by all the slow, laborious tasks of country life. Their blue starched smocks, shining as if they were varnished, and decorated with a little pattern in white embroidery on the collar and cuffs, bellied out around their bony frames like balloons ready to fly away, with a head, two arms and two feet sticking out of each one.

Some were leading a cow or a calf by a rope, while their wives hurried the animal on by whipping its haunches with a leafy branch. The women carried large baskets on their arms from which protruded the heads of chickens or ducks. And they walked with a shorter, brisker step than their

husbands, their gaunt, erect figures wrapped in skimpy little shawls pinned across their flat chests and their heads wrapped in tight-fitting white coifs topped with bonnets.

Then a cart went by, drawn at a trot by a small horse, with two men sitting side by side bumping up and down and a woman at the back holding on to the sides to lessen the jolts.

The square in Goderville was crowded with a confused mass of animals and human beings. The horns of the bullocks, the tall beaver hats of the well-to-do peasants, and the coifs of the peasant women stood out above the throng. And the high-pitched, shrill, yapping voices made a wild, continuous din, dominated now and then by a great deep-throated roar of laughter from a jovial countryman or the long lowing of a cow tied to the wall of a house.

Everywhere was the smell of cowsheds and milk and manure, of hay and sweat, that sharp, unpleasant odor of men and animals which is peculiar to people who work on the land.

Farmhouse in Provence, Arles by Vincent van Gogh (1888). Oil on canvas.

Maître[1] Hauchecorne of Bréauté[2] had just arrived in Goderville and was making his way toward the market square when he caught sight of a small piece of string on the ground. Maître Hauchecorne, a thrifty man like all true Normans, reflected that anything which might come in useful was worth picking up, so he bent down—though with some difficulty, for he suffered from rheumatism. He picked up the piece of thin cord and was about to roll it up carefully when he noticed Maître Malandain,[3] the saddler, standing at his door watching him. They had had a quarrel some time before over a halter and they had remained on bad terms ever since, both of them being the sort to nurse a grudge. Maître Hauchecorne felt a little shamefaced at being seen by his enemy like this, picking a bit of string up out of the muck. He hurriedly concealed his find, first under his smock, then in his trouser pocket; then he pretended to go on looking for something on the ground which he couldn't find, before continuing on his way to the square, leaning forward, bent double by his rheumatism.

He was promptly lost in the noisy slow-moving crowd, in which everyone was engaged in endless and excited bargaining. The peasants were prodding the cows, walking away and coming back in an agony of indecision, always afraid of being taken in and never daring to make up their minds, watching the vendor's eyes, and perpetually trying to spot the man's trick and the animal's defect.

---

1. **Maître** (me′tr′): a French word meaning something like ''mister'' (literally, ''master'').
2. **Bréauté** (brā′ō·tā′).
3. **Malandain** (ma′lan·dan′).

After putting their big baskets down at their feet, the women had taken out their fowls, which now lay on the ground, tied by their legs, their eyes terrified and their combs scarlet. They listened to the offers they were made and either stuck to their price, hard-faced and impassive, or else, suddenly deciding to accept the lower figure offered, shouted after the customer who was slowly walking away: "All right, Maître Anthime,[4] it's yours."

Then, little by little, the crowd in the square thinned out, and as the Angelus[5] rang for noon, those who lived too far away to go home disappeared into the various inns.

At Jourdain's[6] the main room was crowded with people eating, while the vast courtyard was full of vehicles of all sorts—carts, gigs, wagons, tilburies, and indescribable shandrydans,[7] yellow with dung, broken down and patched together, raising their shafts to heaven like a pair of arms, or else heads down and bottoms up.

Close to the people sitting at table, the bright fire blazing in the huge fireplace was scorching the backs of the row on the right. Three spits were turning, carrying chickens, pigeons, and legs of mutton; and a delicious smell of meat roasting and gravy trickling over browning flesh rose from the hearth, raising people's spirits and making their mouths water.

All the aristocracy of the plow took its meals at Maître Jourdain's. Innkeeper and horse dealer, he was a cunning rascal who had made his pile.

Dishes were brought in and emptied, as were the jugs of yellow cider. Everybody talked about the business he had done, what he had bought and sold. News and views were exchanged about the crops. The weather was good for the greens but rather damp for the wheat.

All of a sudden the roll of a drum sounded in the courtyard in front of the inn. Except for one or two who showed no interest, everybody jumped up and ran to the door or windows with his mouth still full and his napkin in his hand.

After finishing his roll on the drum, the town crier made the following pronouncement, speaking in a jerky manner and pausing in the wrong places: "Let it be known to the inhabitants of Goderville, and in general to all—persons present at the market that there was lost this morning, on the Beuzeville[8] road, between—nine and ten o'clock, a black leather wallet containing five hundred francs and some business documents. Anybody finding the same is asked to bring it immediately—to the town hall or to return it to Maître Fortuné Houlbrèque[9] of Manneville. There will be a reward of twenty francs."

Then the man went away. The dull roll of the drum and the faint voice of the town crier could be heard once again in the distance.

Everybody began talking about the incident, estimating Maître Houlbrèque's chances of recovering or not recovering his wallet.

The meal came to an end.

They were finishing their coffee when the police sergeant appeared at the door and asked: "Is Maître Hauchecorne of Bréauté here?"

Maître Hauchecorne, who was sitting at the far end of the table, replied: "Yes, here I am."

The sergeant went on: "Maître Hauchecorne, will you be good enough to come with me to the town hall? The Mayor would like to have a word with you."

The peasant, surprised and a little worried, tossed down his glass of brandy, stood up, and even more bent than in the morning, for the first few steps after a rest were especially difficult, set off after the sergeant, repeating: "Here I am, here I am."

The Mayor was waiting for him, sitting in an armchair. He was the local notary, a stout, solemn individual, with a penchant for pompous phrases.

"Maître Hauchecorne," he said, "you were seen this morning, on the Beuzeville road, picking up the wallet lost by Maître Houlbrèque of Manneville."

The peasant gazed in astonishment at the

---

4. **Anthime** (an·tēm′).
5. **Angelus** (an′jə·ləs): a church bell that rings three times a day, calling people to say a prayer beginning "The angel of the Lord . . . ."
6. **Jourdain's** (jôr·danz′).
7. **tilburies . . . shandrydans:** two-wheeled carriages and rickety vehicles.
8. **Beuzeville** (bōz·vēl′).
9. **Fortuné Houlbrèque** (fôr·tyōō·nā′ ōōl·brek′).

Mayor, already frightened by this suspicion which had fallen upon him, without understanding why.

"Me? I picked up the wallet?"

"Yes, you."

"Honest, I don't know nothing about it."

"You were seen."

"I were seen? Who seen me?"

"Monsieur Malandain, the saddler."

Then the old man remembered, understood, and flushed with anger.

"So he seen me, did he, the bastard! He seen me pick up this bit of string, Mayor—look!"

And rummaging in his pocket, he pulled out the little piece of string.

But the Mayor shook his head incredulously.

"You'll never persuade me, Maître Hauchecorne, that Monsieur[10] Malandain, who is a man who can be trusted, mistook that piece of string for a wallet."

The peasant angrily raised his hand and spat on the floor as proof of his good faith, repeating: "But it's God's truth, honest it is! Not a word of it's a lie, so help me God!"

The Mayor went on: "After picking up the object you even went on hunting about in the mud for some time to see whether some coin might not have fallen out."

The old fellow was almost speechless with fear and indignation.

"Making up . . . making up . . . lies like that to damn an honest man! Making up lies like that!"

In spite of all his protestations, the Mayor did not believe him.

He was confronted with Maître Malandain, who repeated and maintained his statement. They hurled insults at each other for an hour. Maître Hauchecorne was searched, at his own request. Nothing was found on him.

Finally the Mayor, not knowing what to think, sent him away, warning him that he was going to report the matter to the public prosecutor and ask for instructions.

The news had spread. As he left the town hall, the old man was surrounded by people who questioned him with a curiosity which was sometimes serious, sometimes ironical, but in which there was no indignation. He started telling the story of the piece of string. Nobody believed him. Everybody laughed.

As he walked along, other people stopped him, and he stopped his acquaintances, repeating his story and his protestations over and over again, and showing his pockets turned inside out to prove that he had got nothing.

Everybody said: "Get along with you, you old rascal!"

And he lost his temper, irritated, angered, and upset because nobody would believe him. Not knowing what to do, he simply went on repeating his story.

Darkness fell. It was time to go home. He set off with three of his neighbors to whom he pointed out the place where he had picked up the piece of string; and all the way home he talked of nothing else.

In the evening he took a turn round the village of Bréauté in order to tell everybody his story. He met with nothing but incredulity.

He felt ill all night as a result.

The next day, about one o'clock in the afternoon, Marius Paumelle,[11] a laborer on Maître Breton's farm at Ymauville,[12] returned the wallet and its contents to Maître Houlbrèque of Manneville.

The man claimed to have found the object on the road; but, as he could not read, he had taken it home and given it to his employer.

The news spread round the neighborhood and reached the ears of Maître Hauchecorne. He immediately went out and about repeating his story, this time with its sequel. He was triumphant.

"What really got my goat," he said, "wasn't so much the thing itself, if you see what I mean, but the lies. There's nothing worse than being blamed on account of a lie."

He talked about his adventure all day; he told the story to people he met on the road, to people drinking in the inn, to people coming out of church the following Sunday. He stopped total strangers and told it to them. His mind was at rest now, and yet something still bothered him without his know-

---

10. **Monsieur** (mə·syʉr'): French title of respect, meaning "Mister."

11. **Marius Paumelle** (ma'rē·us pō·mel').
12. **Breton . . . Ymauville** (bre·tôn'', ē·mō·vēl'').

ing exactly what it was. People seemed to be amused as they listened to him. They didn't appear to be convinced. He had the impression that remarks were being made behind his back.

The following Tuesday he went to the Goderville market, simply because he felt an urge to tell his story.

Malandain, standing at his door, burst out laughing when he saw him go by. Why?

He accosted a farmer from Criquetot,[13] who didn't let him finish his story, but gave him a dig in the ribs and shouted at him: "Go on, you old rogue!" Then he turned on his heels.

Maître Hauchecorne was taken aback and felt increasingly uneasy. Why had he been called an old rogue?

Once he had sat down at table in Jourdain's inn, he started explaining the whole business all over again.

A horse dealer from Montivilliers[14] called out to him: "Get along with you, you old rascal! I know your little game with the bit of string."

Hauchecorne stammered: "But they found the wallet!"

The other man retorted: "Give over, Grandpa! Him as brings a thing back isn't always him as finds it. But mum's the word!"

The peasant was speechless. At last he understood. He was being accused of getting an accomplice to return the wallet.

He tried to protest, but the whole table burst out laughing.

He couldn't finish his meal and went off in the midst of jeers and laughter.

He returned home ashamed and indignant, choking with anger and embarrassment, all the more upset in that he was quite capable, with his Norman cunning, of doing what he was accused of having done, and even of boasting of it as a clever trick. He dimly realized that, since his duplicity was widely known, it was impossible to prove his innocence. And the injustice of the suspicion cut him to the quick.

Then he began telling the story all over again, making it longer every day, adding fresh arguments at every telling, more energetic protestations, more solemn oaths, which he thought out and prepared in his hours of solitude, for he could think of nothing else but the incident of the piece of string. The more complicated his defense became, and the more subtle his arguments, the less people believed him.

"Them's a liar's arguments," people used to say behind his back.

Realizing what was happening, he ate his heart out, exhausting himself in futile efforts.

He started visibly wasting away.

The local wags[15] now used to get him to tell the story of the piece of string to amuse them, as people get an old soldier to talk about his battles. His mind, seriously affected, began to give way.

Towards the end of December he took to his bed.

He died early in January, and in the delirium of his death agony he kept on protesting his innocence, repeating over and over again: "A bit of string . . . a little bit of string . . . look, Mayor, here it is . . ."

---

13. **Criquetot** (krēk·tō').
14. **Montivilliers** (môn·tə·vē·yā').

---

15. **wags:** jokers.

Responding to the Story

Analyzing the Story

Identifying Facts

1. The **plot** is set in motion when Hauchecorne picks up the piece of string. Why does he pick it up and then attempt to cover up his action?

2. Hauchecorne's innocent act results in incredible **conflicts** and **complications**. What does the saddler Malandain claim he has seen Hauchecorne do?

3. After the wallet is found, Hauchecorne assumes that his problem has been **resolved**—that his good name has been cleared. What does he discover instead?

4. In the story's **resolution,** Hauchecorne finally realizes that he will never be able to prove his innocence. Why do people continue to believe he took the wallet?

Interpreting Meanings

5. What details in the story suggest that suspicion and distrust are common in Goderville? Do you think most towns are like this, or is Goderville different? Explain.

6. Do you think Malandain really believes Hauchecorne picked up the wallet? If not, why does he lie?

7. Think about the story's major **external conflict.** Would you say it's primarily a struggle between two people, or between a person and a whole society? Explain.

8. How would you describe Hauchecorne's **internal conflict?** Do you agree with what Maupassant seems to be saying about the powers of obsession and mental anguish?

9. **Irony** occurs when what happens is the opposite of what we expect to happen, or the opposite of what a character intended to happen. Explain the irony in this story. Did you find the story's ironic ending believable? Why or why not?

10. The power of this story comes from our sense of justice: We feel that a man should not be punished for a crime he didn't commit. Do you think Hauchecorne helped bring about his own punishment? Discuss your opinion.

Writing About the Story

A Creative Response

1. **Updating the Story for a Movie.** Suppose you were making a movie version of "The Piece of String" set in the United States today. You want to keep the bare bones of the plot, but you decide to change the setting, the occupation of the characters, and the specific incident that brings about the conflict. In one or two paragraphs, explain how this story could be updated to apply to life in a town or neighborhood you know well.

A Critical Response

2. **Responding to the Story.** Maupassant creates a cruel world dominated by suspicion, injustice, and obsession. Do you agree with this dark view of human nature, or do you believe that truth and justice ultimately triumph in life? Write a paragraph in which you clearly state your response to Maupassant's portrayal of human nature. Support your opinion with specific evidence from the story and from your own experience.

Reading About the Writer

Guy de Maupassant (1850–1893) was born near Dieppe, in Normandy, the French province that serves as the setting for much of his fiction. His parents separated when he was young, and Maupassant was raised by his mother. As a young man, he became a disciple of his mother's close friend, the great writer and master stylist Gustave Flaubert, who is most famous for his novel *Madame Bovary*. Lonely and aging, Flaubert took Maupaussant under his wing and for many years instructed him in the art of prose. (Some speculate that Maupassant was really Flaubert's son.)

In 1880 Maupassant became an overnight sensation with the publication of "Ball-of-Fat," a story set during the Franco-Prussian War of 1870, when he was a soldier. His success enabled him to quit his deadly civil service job and devote his full time to writing. Over the next eleven years, Maupassant published nearly three hundred short stories, six novels, three volumes of travel sketches, and dozens of newspaper articles. At the same time, he was leading a feverish, extravagant social life as an obsessive womanizer and fashionable man about town.

By the time he was forty, Maupassant had begun to suffer a physical and mental breakdown brought on by syphilis. After a suicide attempt, he was committed to an asylum, where he died at the age of forty-three.

Maupassant is one of the masters of the short-story form. Like "The Piece of String," his stories are often darkly ironic. His closely observed characters, drawn from all ranks of society, are usually the victims of their own greed, desire, vanity, or psychological obsessions.

Literature & Language

Using the Narrative Mode

Literary Model

The following passage is from the novel *True Grit*. A girl named Mattie has been tracking down her father's murderer, who is hiding out with a band of outlaws in the mountains of present-day Oklahoma. At this point in the story, Mattie has just come upon the outlaws and has shot the killer in self-defense, but the kick of the pistol has sent her reeling backward into a pit. She is wedged in a deep hole, and her arm is broken. Above her is the corner of a man's blue shirt, wedged in the rocks. Mattie is telling the story.

My legs swung free below and my jeans were bunched up so that portions of bare leg were exposed. I felt something brush against one of my legs and I thought, *Spider!* I kicked and flailed my feet, and then I stopped when my body settled downward another inch or so.

Now more squeaks, and it came to me that there were *bats* in the cavern below. *Bats* were making the noise and it had been a bat that attached himself to my leg. Yes, I had disturbed them. Their roosting place was below. This hole I now so effectively plugged was their opening to the outside.

I had no unreasonable fear of bats, knowing them for timid little creatures, yet I knew them too for carriers of the dread "hydrophobia,"[1] for which there was no specific.[2] What would the bats do, come night and their time to fly, and they found their opening to the outer world closed off? Would they bite? If I struggled and kicked against them, I would surely shake myself through the hole. But I knew I had not the will to remain motionless and let them bite.

Night! Was I to be here then till night? I must keep my head and guard against such thoughts. . . . The thing was to hold tight. Help was sure to come. At least there were no snakes. I settled on this course: I would give cries for help every five minutes or as near on that interval as I could guess it to be.

I called out at once and was again mocked by the echo of my own voice and by the wind and the dripping of the cave water and the squeaking of the bats. I told numbers to measure the time. It occupied my mind and gave me a sense of purpose and method.

I had not counted far when my body slipped down appreciably, and with panic in my breast I realized that the moss which gripped me in a tight seal was tearing loose. I looked about for something to hold to, broken arm or not, but my hand found only slick and featureless planes of rock. I was going through. . . .

Another lurch down, to the level of my right elbow. That bony knob served as a momentary check, but I could feel the moss giving way against it. A wedge! That was what I needed. Something to stuff in the hole with me to make the cork fit more snugly. Or a long stick to pass under my arm.

I cast my eyes about for something suitable. The few sticks lying about were none of them long enough or stout enough for my purpose. If only I could reach the blue shirt! It would be just the thing for packing. I broke one stick scratching and pulling at the shirttail. With the second one I managed to bring it within reach of my fingertips. Weakened as my hand was, I got a purchase on the cloth with thumb and finger and pulled it out of the dark. It was unexpectedly heavy. Something was attached to it.

Suddenly I jerked my hand away as though from a hot stove. The *something* was the corpse of a man! Or more properly, a skeleton. He was wearing the shirt. I did nothing for a minute, so frightful and astonishing was the discovery. I could see a good part of the remains, the head with patches of bright orange hair showing under a piece of rotted black hat, one shirt-sleeved arm and that portion of the trunk from about the waist upwards. . . .

I soon recovered my wits. *I am falling. I need that shirt.* These thoughts bore upon me with urgency. I had no stomach for the task ahead, but there was nothing else to be done in my desperate

---

1. **hydrophobia:** rabies.
2. **specific:** a remedy.

circumstances. My plan was to give the shirt a smart jerk in hopes of tearing it free from the skeleton. I will have that shirt!

Thus I took hold of the garment again and snatched it toward me with such sharp force as I could muster. My arm seized up with a stab of pain and I let go. After a little tingling the pain subsided and gave way to a dull and tolerable ache. I examined the result of my effort. The buttons had torn free and now the body was within reach. The shirt itself remained clothed about the shoulders and arm bones in a careless fashion. I saw too that the maneuver had exposed the poor man's rib cage.

One more pull and I would have the body close enough so that I could work the shirt free. As I made ready for the job my eyes were attracted to something—movement?—within the cavity formed by the curving gray ribs. I leaned over for a closer look. *Snakes! A ball of snakes!* I flung myself back, but of course there was no real retreat for me, imprisoned as I was in the mossy trap.

I cannot accurately guess the number of rattlesnakes in the ball, as some were big, bigger than my arm, and others small, ranging down to the size of lead pencils, but I believe there were not fewer than forty. With trembling heart I looked on as they writhed sluggishly about in the man's chest. I had disturbed their sleep in their curious winter quarters, and now, more or less conscious, they had begun to move and detach themselves from the tangle, falling this way and that.

This, thought I, is a pretty fix. . . .

—from *True Grit,*
Charles Portis

A Note on the Narrative Mode

A **narrative** tells a story or relates a series of connected events.

1. The events in a narrative are usually presented in **chronological order**—that is, the order in which they occur.
2. In some narratives, the narrator might move back and forth in time, jumping ahead to the future or **flashing back** to relate something from the past.

3. Narratives, whether fictional or actual, often try to create **suspense** by including details that arouse our curiosity about what will happen next.
4. Narratives present a series of connected events, so it is important that the writer clarify the **causes** of events and their **effects**. The **cause** of Mattie being in the pit was the kick of the pistol firing.

Examining the Writer's Techniques

Working with a partner, complete a chart like this one on the narrative techniques in the selection.

Actions in chronological order	Details that create suspense	Causes and effects
1. 2. etc.	1. 2. etc.	1. Mattie's body slips down farther. (Cause:) 2. Mattie discovers bats. (Effect:)

Using the Narrative Mode in Your Writing

Narrating a Scene. Imagine that you are alone and face a threatening situation. Perhaps you are trapped in a tunnel, a maze, or a pit (as Mattie is). Write a narrative telling "what happens."

1. Before you begin writing, list the major events that you will cover.
2. Will you narrate your events in chronological order? Or will you skip around in time, perhaps even **flash back** to describe some event in the past?
3. How will you create **suspense**?
4. Trade narratives with a partner. Identify the most interesting events of your classmate's narrative. Has the writer held your interest? Are the **causes** and **effects** of the actions clear?
5. Rewrite your own narrative, using your partner's comments as a guide. Then read your narrative to the class for other reactions.

PREDICTING OUTCOMES

Writing Assignment

Write an essay of at least four paragraphs in which you propose several possible endings for the following story, "Just Lather, That's All" by the Colombian writer Hernando Téllez. Decide which ending you think is most logical, and why. Then state which ending you like best.

Background

As we read any story, we wonder, "What will happen next? How will the story end?" We use both our reason and our imagination to **predict outcomes**—to make guesses about what will happen next.

To predict outcomes, we need to be able to judge whether an event *could* actually happen. We must judge whether something is possible, probable, impossible, or improbable.

- An event is **possible** if there is any chance at all that it will take place.
- An event is **probable** if it is likely to happen, but not absolutely certain.
- An **impossible** event can never happen, and an **improbable** one is very unlikely to occur.

1. Read each of the following statements about events that might take place *after* "The Cold Equations" (page 7) ends. Given what you know about the story and its characters, decide whether you think the event is possible, probable, improbable, or impossible. Explain why you think so.

   a. After the EDS returns to its base, Barton will be tried for murder.
   b. The people in charge of the EDS will improve security to prevent future stowaways.
   c. Barton will resign as EDS pilot and return to Earth.
   d. Marilyn's body will be recovered for burial.
   e. After being jettisoned from the EDS, Marilyn will be rescued by a passing aircraft.
   f. Marilyn's parents will sue the government for their daughter's cold-blooded murder.

2. Think about "The Fatalist" (page 24):

   a. What other outcomes could you propose for the story's plot?
   b. Which of these outcomes would have been probable, and which would have been possible but not probable?

Prewriting

Here is the beginning of the story. The responses of one reader are noted at the right.

He said nothing when he entered. I was passing the best of my razors back and forth on a strop.[1] When I recognized him, I started to tremble. But he didn't notice. Hoping to conceal my emotion, I continued sharpening the razor. I tested it on the meat of my thumb, and then held it up to the light.

At that moment he took off the bullet-studded belt that his gun holster dangled from. He hung it up on a wall hook and placed his military cap over it. Then he turned to me, loosening the knot of his tie, and said, "It's hot as hell. Give me a shave." He sat in the chair.

This guy must be a barber.

Why is he trembling? Is he afraid of this guy? Why doesn't he want him to see his emotion?

He must be a soldier. I wonder why he's taking off his gun. That could be a big mistake. I wonder if the gun will go off during the course of the story.

---

1. **strop:** a thick leather strap used for sharpening razors.

I estimated he had a four-day beard—the four days taken up by the latest expedition in search of our troops. His face seemed reddened, burned by the sun. Carefully, I began to prepare the soap. I cut off a few slices, dropped them into the cup, mixed in a bit of warm water, and began to stir with the brush. Immediately the foam began to rise. "The other boys in the group should have this much beard, too," he remarked. I continued stirring the lather.

"But we did all right, you know. We got the main ones. We brought back some dead, and we got some others still alive. But pretty soon they'll all be dead."

"How many did you catch?" I asked.

"Fourteen. We had to go pretty deep into the woods to find them. But we'll get even. Not one of them comes out of this alive, not one."

He leaned back on the chair when he saw me with the lather-covered brush in my hand. I still had to put the sheet on him. No doubt about it, I was upset. I took a sheet out of a drawer and knotted it around his neck. He wouldn't stop talking. He probably thought I was in sympathy with his party.

"The town must have learned a lesson from what we did," he said.

"Yes," I replied, securing the knot at the base of his dark, sweaty neck.

"That was a fine show, eh?"

"Very good," I answered, turning back for the brush.

The man closed his eyes with a gesture of fatigue and sat waiting for the cool caress of the soap. I had never had him so close to me. The day he ordered the whole town to file into the patio of the school to see the four rebels hanging there, I came face to face with him for an instant. But the sight of the mutilated bodies kept me from noticing the face of the man who had directed it all, the face I was now about to take into my hands.

It was not an unpleasant face, and the beard, which made him look a bit older than he was, didn't suit him badly at all. His name was Torres—Captain Torres. A man of imagination, because who else would have thought of hanging the naked rebels and then holding target practice on their bodies?

I began to apply the first layer of soap. . . .

—from "Just Lather, That's All,"
Hernando Téllez

Who are "our troops"? Is there a civil war going on? If the barber calls them "our troops," he must be an enemy of the soldier. That explains why he was trembling.

The boys in the group must be the other soldiers who went on the expedition.

They probably want them alive so they can get information out of them—probably by torturing them.

The barber must be a secret rebel. That could be dangerous to the guy getting shaved.

Why isn't he out fighting with the other rebels? Maybe he's a spy.

The barber could slit his throat with the razor.

The barber must hate this soldier.

You can't always judge a person by his face.

He's being ironic when he says "imagination." He really thinks Torres is a brutal monster.

I wonder if he'll kill him? It must be so tempting. But how would he get away with it? And if he doesn't, what will the other rebels do to him if they find out he let Torres get away?

In predicting the outcome of any story, answer these questions.

1. What **problem** needs solving in the story?
2. Does the **ending** have to conform to the ordinary laws of nature? Or could "anything happen"?
3. What details or events presented in the beginning of the story *must* be taken into consideration by the story's end? (For example, if a writer mentions a loaded gun hidden in the drawer at the start of the story, that gun should figure later in the story's plot.)
4. What is the **tone** of the story? How might that tone affect the ending of the story?
5. What are four possible **outcomes** (endings) for the story? (Are there more?)
6. Decide whether each of the outcomes is possible, probable, impossible, or improbable.
7. Which outcome do you like best?
8. Why do you prefer this ending?

Writing

Here is an introductory paragraph for an essay predicting possible outcomes for the Téllez story. You can use this introduction or write your own.

> The opening paragraphs of Hernando Téllez's story "Just Lather, That's All" present an intriguing situation. During a civil war, a vicious military leader, Captain Torres, walks into a barber shop and asks for a shave. He apparently doesn't realize that the barber secretly sides with the rebels. My guess is that the plot of the story will revolve around whether or not the barber decides to kill Torres, whose throat he could slit with his razor.

In paragraphs two and three of your essay, discuss at least three possible endings for the story. In the final paragraph, choose which ending you prefer, and explain why.

Checklist for Revision

1. Have you cited the story's title and author?
2. Have you included an introductory paragraph that identifies the characters, summarizes their basic situation, and states the problem that they want to solve?
3. Have you suggested and discussed at least four possible outcomes for the story that resolve the characters' problem?
4. For each outcome you've considered, have you determined whether it is possible, probable, impossible, or improbable?
5. Have you made predictions about all the significant details and events mentioned in the beginning of the story?
6. In your final paragraph, have you clearly stated which outcome you prefer?
7. Have you given reasons to support your choice, telling why you think this outcome works best?
8. Have you checked: Spelling? Punctuation? Capitalization? Sentence structure? Paragraph organization?

A short story is frequently the celebration of character at bursting point.

—V. S. Pritchett

Fiction can tell us more about ourselves—about how human beings behave in every conceivable situation—than any other form of art or science yet devised.

Good fiction, as opposed to stories told only for entertainment, can tell us how it feels to be a woman who has lived on the prairie all her life and has never heard the sound of a piano; how it feels to be a soldier lying wounded on a battlefield; how it feels to be a lonely girl waiting for the phone to ring. By sharing the particular feelings offered by a writer's fictional world, we come to understand some all-embracing truths about being alive—or about what being alive would be like if only we were able to find and grasp the right opportunities.

The revelation fiction offers us lies largely in the element we call **character**—that is, in the story's actors. When the characters in a story behave in convincing ways—when we are persuaded that they are like actual people—then we not only believe in them, but we also identify with them, admire them, envy them, fear them, or even love them, just as we do the real people we know. Perhaps we might also learn how to live our own lives better.

One of the pleasures of fiction is that it lets us know characters more intimately than we know most people in real life. This is because fiction can share with us a character's innermost thoughts—thoughts a person might never tell another living soul.

If a story has a memorable character—a Huck Finn, a Jane Eyre, an Oliver Twist—the plot becomes secondary. Our fascination with the story will lie in its revelation of this character. All the suspense of the unfolding narrative is carried by our desire to get to know that character better.

A story that puts its emphasis on revealing character is likely to be a story of higher quality than a simple narrative with an action-packed plot. Of course, we all enjoy these plots: we are gripped by the adventures of the rancher who faces an army of flesh-eating ants or of the spy caught as a double agent. But literature's main concern is more often with the portrayal of character than with action itself. In literature, we are usually much more interested in what a character *is* than in what a character *does*.

How a Writer Reveals Character

There are many ways for a writer to reveal what a character is. The easiest way is to use **direct characterization**—to tell us directly what the character is like. When a writer uses direct characterization, we don't have to interpret the nature of the character for ourselves. The writer does all the work for us.

Character: The Story's Actors

Mickey Rooney as Huckleberry Finn in the 1939 movie.

" **O**ne of the pleasures of fiction is that it lets us know characters more intimately than we know most people in real life. "

"Dickie, I hardly recognized you! You've changed your format."

Drawing by Koren; © 1973
The New Yorker Magazine, Inc.

Joe was a mean, lying, stealing varmint from the day he first drew breath.

But direct characterization has a number of disadvantages. For one thing, we may not believe the writer. For another, we may want to make up our minds about Joe for ourselves, just as we would when we meet any new acquaintance. So a more subtle writer will let Joe *show* us his nature—and this is where the real art of characterization begins. We call this **indirect characterization.**

Since we generally see people before we hear them speak, **appearance** is a natural place for a writer to start. Consider the assumptions we make about people because of their appearance. Even though we know we're being illogical and unfair, most of us are drawn to regular features, good posture, and clean clothes. Until that upright fellow with the strong chin, alert expression, and neatly pressed gray suit proves otherwise, we'd trust him to watch our suitcase while we use the telephone. But how would we feel about that other character—the one with the weak chin, the three-day stubble, and the shifty eyes, slouching there in his filthy brown raincoat?

A person's **speech** tells us even more about his or her character.

> "Oh goodness, Henrietta, is that a car off the road up ahead?"
>
> "You're right, George. I think it's an accident."
>
> "No, no, Henrietta, don't stop, for heaven's sake. And don't LOOK. It might be something awful."
>
> "But maybe we could help, George."
>
> "There's another car behind us. They'll help. Now please, just drive ON."

Just from George's expressions—his "Oh goodness" and "for heaven's sake"—we might guess that he's rather prim. But the content of what he says also tells us that he is fearful of unfamiliar situations and afraid to get involved, even to help someone who is in trouble. From Henrietta's lines, we know that she is agreeable and well-intentioned. Although she is driving, it is George who calls the shots.

In showing us what a character is like, the writer can also take us right into a person's mind to reveal his or her **private thoughts.**

> Luke thought Doris was pretty and flirted with her as she demonstrated how to use the power saw, but what really interested him was that moment when she turned to open the cash register. He could see that the bill compartments, even the one for tens, were full. He guessed there were a couple of hundred dollars in there.

What do you think about Luke, now that you know what's going on behind those flirty eyes? Is he deceitful? Will he be hanging around after the other customers leave?

We can also learn a lot about a character from observing his or her **effect on other characters.** Suppose we know nothing yet about an old woman but that dogs, cats, and small children love her.

Chances are we'd be disposed to think well of her—more so than if we'd been told that dogs bark, cats arch their backs, and children scurry away whenever she walks by.

As in real life, most of what we learn about characters in fiction we discover by observing their **actions.**

> The bleachers grew still as Jeb sauntered toward the plate, the crowd watching in awe as he fanned three bats and discarded two of them contemptuously. He examined his cleats and spat in the dust. Then a single, adoring voice cried out "Jebbie!" and it was picked up by the others, a regular chorus rising from the stands until he silenced it with a baleful glare. Then he smiled, tipped his cap to the crowd, and turned to face the pitcher.

Can you infer from the way Jeb acts that he is pretty impressed with his own importance? (Perhaps you even find yourself hoping that this arrogant character strikes out.) In this case, we might tend to disregard the opinion of the adoring fans and make our own judgment about Jeb's character.

We have seen, then, that writers can reveal character in these five indirect ways:

1. By appearance
2. By speech
3. By private thoughts
4. By the responses of other characters
5. By actions

With all of these methods, we interpret the character for ourselves; the writer doesn't do it for us.

The Protagonist: The "First Actor"

Most stories have a main character, called the **protagonist,** and this is the person our attention focuses on. The word *protagonist* comes from two Greek words: *protos* meaning "first," and *agonistes,* meaning "actor." Thus, the protagonist is "the first (or primary) actor" in a story. Usually, but not always, the protagonist is admirable and likable, the sort of person we tend to identify with. It is also possible to have a protagonist who is a rascal. For example, Scrooge is the protagonist in Charles Dickens's *A Christmas Carol,* and he's a mean, grasping old skinflint until he reforms at the end of the story. But the protagonist is usually neither a saint nor a villain. In a good story, the protagonist is a real, complicated human being, with just enough strengths, weaknesses, and contradictions in character to remind us of ourselves.

However interesting the other characters in a story may be, they are not as important to us as the protagonist is. As a rule, the story's action begins when this main character wants something and sets out to get it. (The **antagonist** in a story is the character or force that comes into conflict with the protagonist. And just as the protagonist is rarely all good, the antagonist is rarely all bad.)

Printed by permission of the Norman Rockwell Family Trust, copyright © 1922 the Norman Rockwell Family Trust. Cover © The Curtis Publishing Company.

> " **I**n a good story, the protagonist is a real, complicated human being, with just enough strengths, weaknesses, and contradictions in character to remind us of ourselves."

Thus, the protagonist generates the conflict that hooks our interest. We feel suspense because we *care* about the protagonist. We need to know the outcome of his or her conflict, and this outcome will usually involve some change in character.

Dynamic Characters and Static Characters

The protagonist of a story is almost always a **dynamic character**—that is, someone who changes in an important way during the course of the story. By the end of the story, a dynamic character has gained a new understanding of something or made an important decision or taken a crucial action. Dynamic characters are capable (as we hope we are) of growing and learning and changing.

In contrast, **static characters** are exactly the same at the end of the story as they were at the beginning. They haven't changed in any significant way. It is important to remember that static characters do not necessarily represent failures of the writer's art. In good fiction, static characters are supposed to be static—that is their function in the story. Too many characters undergoing important changes would be distracting, especially in a short story, where we want to focus on what is happening to the main characters.

The change that a dynamic character undergoes (he learns not to be so arrogant; she learns not to be ashamed of her father) must be **believable.** It should not be some miraculous, magic-wand transformation that neatly wraps up the plot. When that change is believable, not only does it provide the key to our understanding of the character, but it also tells us what the story is about. How the protagonist changes or what the protagonist learns is usually our best clue to the story's **meaning.**

Flat Characters and Round Characters

Critics often refer to flat or round characters. A **flat character** is like a paper doll, with only one surface. This character has only one or two key personality traits and can be described in a single sentence. A round character, on the other hand, cannot be summed up so neatly. A **round character** is fleshed out. He or she is more complex—there are more sides to this character's personality, more three-dimensionality.

As with static characters, in good fiction flat characters are not necessarily artistic flaws. The writer has included them for a reason: too many round characters, like too many dynamic characters, would be distracting. Most works of fiction, particularly short stories, require a certain number of flat characters to get the story told.

The problem with second-rate fiction is that even the main characters are flat characters. These flat characters found in inferior fiction are often also stock characters. A **stock character** is a person who fits our preconceived notions about a "type" (a

> " **D**ynamic characters are capable (as we hope we are) of growing and learning and changing.''

Drawing by Chas. Addams; © 1987
The New Yorker Magazine, Inc.

typical old man, a typical teen-ager, a typical detective, a typical nun). Stock characters have lost their individuality; there are dozens just like them on the shelf.

You know stock characters on sight (they exist on TV and in the movies too): the mad scientist; the narrow-eyed villain twirling his waxed mustache; the greedy miser who counts his cash at night; the virtuous, impoverished, but beautiful heroine; the poor little rich girl; the gullible country bumpkin with enormous hands and hay in his overalls; the stuffy, pipe-smoking Englishman with his walrus mustache and trumpeting delivery.

These and other stock characters have become so familiar to us that by now, as soon as we encounter one of their well-known traits (say, a downeast Maine twang), we can guess the rest of the formula (the character's economy with words, his diligence in mending his roof, his shrewdness and honesty, his suspicion of all strangers). It is their predictability that makes these stock characters so stale. We've met them all before in countless other stories, and we know that the writer has simply taken them off the shelf (or out of the "stock" room) and set them in motion by winding each character's key. We know that real people aren't like this—that real people are endlessly complex and never wholly predictable. What fascinates and delights us in fiction is the portrayal of characters who somehow manage to confound our expectations, yet still seem true to life.

A Character's Motivation

One of the ways a writer rounds out a character is to show us what **motivates,** or moves, that person to act as he or she does. Unless we understand *why* an otherwise dutiful daughter suddenly lashes out at her mother, her behavior will strike us as inconsistent and unbelievable. But once we recognize the need she is trying to satisfy (say, to punish someone—anyone she can get her hands on—for the way her boyfriend has neglected her), her behavior begins to make sense, and she is no longer the two-dimensional "dutiful daughter." She seems like a real person—someone who is usually kind but who is also capable (as all of us are) of cruelty.

Writers do not often state a character's motives directly. ("She screamed at her mother because Bill hadn't called in two weeks.") Instead, they imply what those motives are—maybe even scatter clues throughout the story—and trust their readers to make intelligent guesses about why their characters act the way they do.

Trying to understand the motivation of characters in literature can be as puzzling and satisfying as it is in real life. While we may know instinctively that real people surprise us with their behavior, we also know that there are reasons for what they do. In real life, we may never find out what those reasons are. In fiction, we do.

An episode from the movie *The Perils of Pauline,* showing two stock characters from melodrama, the threatened heroine and the mustachioed villain.

> "**W**hat fascinates and delights us in fiction is the portrayal of characters who somehow manage to confound our expectations, yet still seem true to life."

TWO KINDS

Amy Tan

On the surface, this story about a Chinese immigrant mother and her American-born daughter is about a conflict between two cultures. The daughter's modern notions about being herself collide with her mother's traditional Chinese values of duty and obedience.

But there's another conflict in the story, one that's common to every culture. It results from the powerful desire parents often feel to have their children surpass them in accomplishment, as if life were a relay race.

The mother in this story fervently believes that in America her daughter can accomplish anything she sets her mind to. She can even become a *prodigy*—a child of exceptional talent or genius.

Read the first paragraph of this story, and then take a few moments to discuss its main point: Do you agree with the mother's convictions about America?

The story is set in San Francisco's Chinatown during the early 1960's.

My mother believed you could be anything you wanted to be in America. You could open a restaurant. You could work for the government and get good retirement. You could buy a house with almost no money down. You could become rich. You could become instantly famous.

"Of course you can be prodigy, too," my mother told me when I was nine. "You can be best anything. What does Auntie Lindo know? Her daughter, she is only best tricky."

America was where all my mother's hopes lay. She had come here in 1949 after losing everything in China: her mother and father, her family home, her first husband, and two daughters, twin baby girls. But she never looked back with regret. There were so many ways for things to get better.

We didn't immediately pick the right kind of prodigy. At first my mother thought I could be a Chinese Shirley Temple.[1] We'd watch Shirley's old movies on TV as though they were training films. My mother would poke my arm and say,

"*Ni kan*"—You watch. And I would see Shirley tapping her feet, or singing a sailor song, or pursing her lips into a very round O while saying, "Oh my goodness."

"*Ni kan*," said my mother as Shirley's eyes flooded with tears. "You already know how. Don't need talent for crying!"

Soon after my mother got this idea about Shirley Temple, she took me to a beauty training school in the Mission district and put me in the hands of a student who could barely hold the scissors without shaking. Instead of getting big fat curls, I emerged with an uneven mass of crinkly black fuzz. My mother dragged me off to the bathroom and tried to wet down my hair.

"You look like Negro Chinese," she lamented, as if I had done this on purpose.

The instructor of the beauty training school had to lop off these soggy clumps to make my hair even again. "Peter Pan is very popular these days," the instructor assured my mother. I now had hair the length of a boy's, with straight-across bangs that hung at a slant two inches above my eyebrows. I liked the haircut and it made me actually look forward to my future fame.

In fact, in the beginning, I was just as excited as my mother, maybe even more so. I pictured this prodigy part of me as many different images,

---

1. **Shirley Temple:** child movie star who became America's darling during the thirties and forties. Mothers all across America tried to set or perm their daughters' hair to reproduce Shirley's sausage curls.

trying each one on for size. I was a dainty ballerina girl standing by the curtains, waiting to hear the right music that would send me floating on my tiptoes. I was like the Christ child lifted out of the straw manger, crying with holy indignity. I was Cinderella stepping from her pumpkin carriage with sparkly cartoon music filling the air.

In all of my imaginings, I was filled with a sense that I would soon become *perfect*. My mother and father would adore me. I would be beyond reproach. I would never feel the need to sulk for anything.

But sometimes the prodigy in me became impatient. "If you don't hurry up and get me out of here, I'm disappearing for good," it warned. "And then you'll always be nothing."

Every night after dinner, my mother and I would sit at the Formica kitchen table. She would present new tests, taking her examples from stories of amazing children she had read in *Ripley's Believe It or Not*, or *Good Housekeeping, Reader's Digest*, and a dozen other magazines she kept in a pile in our bathroom. My mother got these magazines from people whose houses she cleaned. And since she cleaned many houses each week, we had a great assortment. She would look through them all, searching for stories about remarkable children.

The first night she brought out a story about a three-year-old boy who knew the capitals of all the states and even most of the European countries. A teacher was quoted as saying the little boy could also pronounce the names of the foreign cities correctly.

"What's the capital of Finland?" my mother asked me, looking at the magazine story.

All I knew was the capital of California, because Sacramento was the name of the street we lived on in Chinatown. "Nairobi!"[2] I guessed, saying the most foreign word I could think of. She checked to see if that was possibly one way to pronounce "Helsinki" before showing me the answer.

The tests got harder—multiplying numbers in my head, finding the queen of hearts in a deck of cards, trying to stand on my head without using my hands, predicting the daily temperatures in Los Angeles, New York, and London.

One night I had to look at a page from the Bible for three minutes and then report everything I could remember. "Now Jehoshaphat had riches and honor in abundance and . . . that's all I remember, Ma," I said.

And after seeing my mother's disappointed face once again, something inside of me began to die. I hated the tests, the raised hopes and failed expectations. Before going to bed that night, I looked in the mirror above the bathroom sink and when I saw only my face staring back—and that it would always be this ordinary face—I began to cry. Such a sad, ugly girl! I made high-pitched noises like a crazed animal, trying to scratch out the face in the mirror.

And then I saw what seemed to be the prodigy side of me—because I had never seen that face before. I looked at my reflection, blinking so I could see more clearly. The girl staring back at me was angry, powerful. This girl and I were the same. I had new thoughts, willful thoughts, or rather thoughts filled with lots of won'ts. I won't let her change me, I promised myself. I won't be what I'm not.

So now on nights when my mother presented her tests, I performed listlessly, my head propped on one arm. I pretended to be bored. And I was. I got so bored I started counting the bellows of the foghorns out on the bay while my mother drilled me in other areas. The sound was comforting and reminded me of the cow jumping over the moon. And the next day, I played a game with myself, seeing if my mother would give up on me before eight bellows. After a while I usually counted only one, maybe two bellows at most. At last she was beginning to give up hope.

Two or three months had gone by without any mention of my being a prodigy again. And then one day my mother was watching *The Ed Sullivan Show* on TV. The TV was old and the sound kept shorting out. Every time my mother got halfway up from the sofa to adjust the set, the sound would go back on and Ed would be talking. As soon as she sat down, Ed would go silent again. She got

---

2. **Nairobi** (nī·rō′bē): capital of the African nation of Kenya.

up, the TV broke into loud piano music. She sat down. Silence. Up and down, back and forth, quiet and loud. It was like a stiff embraceless dance between her and the TV set. Finally she stood by the set with her hand on the sound dial.

She seemed entranced by the music, a little frenzied piano piece with this mesmerizing quality, sort of quick passages and then teasing lilting ones before it returned to the quick playful parts.

"*Ni kan,*" my mother said, calling me over with hurried hand gestures, "Look here."

I could see why my mother was fascinated by the music. It was being pounded out by a little Chinese girl, about nine years old, with a Peter Pan haircut. The girl had the sauciness of a Shirley Temple. She was proudly modest like a proper Chinese child. And she also did this fancy sweep of a curtsy, so that the fluffy skirt of her white dress cascaded slowly to the floor like the petals of a large carnation.

In spite of these warning signs, I wasn't worried. Our family had no piano and we couldn't afford to buy one, let alone reams of sheet music and piano lessons. So I could be generous in my comments when my mother bad-mouthed the little girl on TV.

"Play note right, but doesn't sound good! No singing sound," complained my mother.

"What are you picking on her for?" I said carelessly. "She's pretty good. Maybe she's not the best, but she's trying hard." I knew almost immediately I would be sorry I said that.

"Just like you," she said. "Not the best. Because you not trying." She gave a little huff as she let go of the sound dial and sat down on the sofa.

The little Chinese girl sat down also to play an encore of "Anitra's Dance" by Grieg.[3] I remember the song, because later on I had to learn how to play it.

Three days after watching *The Ed Sullivan Show,* my mother told me what my schedule would be for piano lessons and piano practice. She had talked to Mr. Chong, who lived on the first floor

of our apartment building. Mr. Chong was a retired piano teacher, and my mother had traded housecleaning services for weekly lessons and a piano for me to practice on every day, two hours a day, from four until six.

When my mother told me this, I felt as though I had been sent to hell. I whined and then kicked my foot a little when I couldn't stand it anymore.

"Why don't you like me the way I am? I'm *not* a genius! I can't play the piano. And even if I could, I wouldn't go on TV if you paid me a million dollars!" I cried.

My mother slapped me. "Who ask you be genius?" she shouted. "Only ask you be your best. For you sake. You think I want you be genius? Hnnh! What for! Who ask you!"

"So ungrateful," I heard her mutter in Chinese. "If she had as much talent as she has temper, she would be famous now."

Mr. Chong, whom I secretly nicknamed Old Chong, was very strange, always tapping his fingers to the silent music of an invisible orchestra. He looked ancient in my eyes. He had lost most of the hair on top of his head and he wore thick glasses and had eyes that always looked tired and sleepy. But he must have been younger than I thought, since he lived with his mother and was not yet married.

I met Old Lady Chong once and that was enough. She had this peculiar smell like a baby that had done something in its pants. And her fingers felt like a dead person's, like an old peach I once found in the back of the refrigerator; the skin just slid off the meat when I picked it up.

I soon found out why Old Chong had retired from teaching piano. He was deaf. "Like Beethoven!" he shouted to me. "We're both listening only in our head!" And he would start to conduct his frantic silent sonatas.

Our lessons went like this. He would open the book and point to different things, explaining their purpose: "Key! Treble! Bass! No sharps or flats! So this is C major! Listen now and play after me!"

And then he would play the C scale a few times, a simple chord, and then, as if inspired by an old, unreachable itch, he gradually added more notes and running trills and a pounding bass until the music was really something quite grand.

---

3. **Edvard Grieg** (grēg): nineteenth-century Norwegian composer. "Anitra's Dance" is from *Peer Gynt* (1876).

I would play after him, the simple scale, the simple chord, and then I just played some nonsense that sounded like a cat running up and down on top of garbage cans. Old Chong smiled and applauded and then said, "Very good! But now you must learn to keep time!"

So that's how I discovered that Old Chong's eyes were too slow to keep up with the wrong notes I was playing. He went through the motions in half-time. To help me keep rhythm, he stood behind me, pushing down on my right shoulder for every beat. He balanced pennies on top of my wrists so I would keep them still as I slowly played scales and arpeggios.[4] He had me curve my hand around an apple and keep that shape when playing chords. He marched stiffly to show me how to make each finger dance up and down, staccato[5] like an obedient little soldier.

He taught me all these things, and that was how I also learned I could be lazy and get away with mistakes, lots of mistakes. If I hit the wrong notes because I hadn't practiced enough, I never cor-

rected myself. I just kept playing in rhythm. And Old Chong kept conducting his own private reverie.

So maybe I never really gave myself a fair chance. I did pick up the basics pretty quickly, and I might have become a good pianist at that young age. But I was so determined not to try, not to be anybody different, that I learned to play only the most ear-splitting preludes, the most discordant hymns.

Over the next year, I practiced like this, dutifully in my own way. And then one day I heard my mother and her friend Lindo Jong both talking in a loud bragging tone of voice so others could hear. It was after church, and I was leaning against the brick wall wearing a dress with stiff white petticoats. Auntie Lindo's daughter, Waverly, who was about my age, was standing farther down the wall about five feet away. We had grown up together and shared all the closeness of two sisters squabbling over crayons and dolls. In other words, for the most part, we hated each other. I thought she was snotty. Waverly Jong had gained a certain amount of fame as "Chinatown's Littlest Chinese Chess Champion."

"She bring home too many trophy," lamented Auntie Lindo that Sunday. "All day she play chess. All day I have no time do nothing but dust

---

4. **arpeggios** (är·pej'ē·ōz): chords whose notes are played in quick succession, rather than simultaneously.
5. **staccato** (stə·kät'ō): a style of playing or singing music in which there is a clear-cut, distinct break between notes (the opposite of *legato*).

off her winnings." She threw a scolding look at Waverly, who pretended not to see her.

"You lucky you don't have this problem," said Auntie Lindo with a sigh to my mother.

And my mother squared her shoulders and bragged: "Our problem worser than yours. If we ask Jing-mei wash dish, she hear nothing but music. It's like you can't stop this natural talent."

And right then, I was determined to put a stop to her foolish pride.

A few weeks later, Old Chong and my mother conspired to have me play in a talent show which would be held in the church hall. By then, my parents had saved up enough to buy me a second-hand piano, a black Wurlitzer spinet with a scarred bench. It was the showpiece of our living room.

For the talent show, I was to play a piece called "Pleading Child" from Schumann's[6] *Scenes from Childhood*. It was a simple, moody piece that sounded more difficult than it was. I was supposed to memorize the whole thing, playing the repeat parts twice to make the piece sound longer. But I dawdled over it, playing a few bars and then cheating, looking up to see what notes followed. I never really listened to what I was playing. I daydreamed about being somewhere else, about being someone else.

The part I liked to practice best was the fancy curtsy: right foot out, touch the rose on the carpet with a pointed foot, sweep to the side, left leg bends, look up and smile.

My parents invited all the couples from the Joy Luck Club[7] to witness my debut. Auntie Lindo and Uncle Tin were there. Waverly and her two older brothers had also come. The first two rows were filled with children both younger and older than I was. The littlest ones got to go first. They recited simple nursery rhymes, squawked out tunes on miniature violins, twirled Hula Hoops, pranced in pink ballet tutus, and when they bowed or curtsied, the audience would sigh in unison, "Awww," and then clap enthusiastically.

When my turn came, I was very confident. I remember my childish excitement. It was as if I knew, without a doubt, that the prodigy side of me really did exist. I had no fear whatsoever, no nervousness. I remember thinking to myself, This is it! This is it! I looked out over the audience, at my mother's blank face, my father's yawn, Auntie Lindo's stiff-lipped smile, Waverly's sulky expression. I had on a white dress layered with sheets of lace, and a pink bow in my Peter Pan haircut. As I sat down I envisioned people jumping to their feet and Ed Sullivan rushing up to introduce me to everyone on TV.

And I started to play. It was so beautiful. I was so caught up in how lovely I looked that at first I didn't worry how I would sound. So it was a surprise to me when I hit the first wrong note and I realized something didn't sound quite right. And then I hit another and another followed that. A chill started at the top of my head and began to trickle down. Yet I couldn't stop playing, as though my hands were bewitched. I kept thinking my fingers would adjust themselves back, like a train switching to the right track. I played this strange jumble through two repeats, the sour notes staying with me all the way to the end.

When I stood up, I discovered my legs were shaking. Maybe I had just been nervous and the audience, like Old Chong, had seen me go through the right motions and had not heard anything wrong at all. I swept my right foot out, went down on my knee, looked up and smiled. The room was quiet, except for Old Chong, who was beaming and shouting, "Bravo! Bravo! Well done!" But then I saw my mother's face, her stricken face. The audience clapped weakly, and as I walked back to my chair, with my whole face quivering as I tried not to cry, I heard a little boy whisper loudly to his mother, "That was awful," and the mother whispered back, "Well, she certainly tried."

And now I realized how many people were in the audience, the whole world it seemed. I was aware of eyes burning into my back. I felt the shame of my mother and father as they sat stiffly throughout the rest of the show.

---

6. **Robert Schumann** (shōō'män): nineteenth-century German composer.
7. **Joy Luck Club:** a social club at which Jing-mei's mother and three other Chinese mothers get together to play mah-jongg, eat Chinese specialties, and tell stories.

We could have escaped during intermission. Pride and some strange sense of honor must have anchored my parents to their chairs. And so we watched it all: the eighteen-year-old boy with a fake mustache who did a magic show and juggled flaming hoops while riding a unicycle. The breasted girl with white makeup who sang from *Madama Butterfly*[8] and got honorable mention. And the eleven-year-old boy who won first prize playing a tricky violin song that sounded like a busy bee.

After the show, the Hsus, the Jongs, and the St. Clairs from the Joy Luck Club came up to my mother and father.

"Lots of talented kids," Auntie Lindo said vaguely, smiling broadly.

"That was somethin' else," said my father, and I wondered if he was referring to me in a humorous way, or whether he even remembered what I had done.

Waverly looked at me and shrugged her shoulders. "You aren't a genius like me," she said matter-of-factly. And if I hadn't felt so bad, I would have pulled her braids and punched her stomach.

But my mother's expression was what devastated me: a quiet, blank look that said she had lost everything. I felt the same way, and it seemed as if everybody were now coming up, like gawkers at the scene of an accident, to see what parts were actually missing. When we got on the bus to go home, my father was humming the busy-bee tune and my mother was silent. I kept thinking she wanted to wait until we got home before shouting at me. But when my father unlocked the door to our apartment, my mother walked in and then went to the back, into the bedroom. No accusations. No blame. And in a way, I felt disappointed. I had been waiting for her to start shouting, so I could shout back and cry and blame her for all my misery.

I assumed my talent-show fiasco meant I never had to play the piano again. But two days later,

after school, my mother came out of the kitchen and saw me watching TV.

"Four clock," she reminded me as if it were any other day. I was stunned, as though she were asking me to go through the talent-show torture again. I wedged myself more tightly in front of the TV.

"Turn off TV," she called from the kitchen five minutes later.

I didn't budge. And then I decided. I didn't have to do what my mother said anymore. I wasn't her slave. This wasn't China. I had listened to her before and look what happened. She was the stupid one.

She came out from the kitchen and stood in the arched entryway of the living room. "Four clock," she said once again, louder.

"I'm not going to play anymore," I said nonchalantly. "Why should I? I'm not a genius."

She walked over and stood in front of the TV. I saw her chest was heaving up and down in an angry way.

"No!" I said, and I now felt stronger, as if my true self had finally emerged. So this was what had been inside me all along.

"No! I won't!" I screamed.

She yanked me by the arm, pulled me off the floor, snapped off the TV. She was frighteningly strong, half pulling, half carrying me toward the piano as I kicked the throw rugs under my feet. She lifted me up and onto the hard bench. I was sobbing by now, looking at her bitterly. Her chest was heaving even more and her mouth was open, smiling crazily as if she were pleased I was crying.

"You want me to be someone that I'm not!" I sobbed. "I'll never be the kind of daughter you want me to be!"

"Only two kinds of daughters," she shouted in Chinese. "Those who are obedient and those who follow their own mind! Only one kind of daughter can live in this house. Obedient daughter!"

"Then I wish I wasn't your daughter. I wish you weren't my mother," I shouted. As I said these things I got scared. It felt like worms and toads and slimy things crawling out of my chest, but it also felt good, as if this awful side of me had surfaced, at last.

"Too late change this," said my mother shrilly.

---

8. *Madama Butterfly:* an opera by the Italian composer Giacomo Puccini (jä′kō·mō pōōt·chē′nē), first performed in 1904.

And I could sense her anger rising to its breaking point. I wanted to see it spill over. And that's when I remembered the babies she had lost in China, the ones we never talked about. "Then I wish I'd never been born!" I shouted. "I wish I were dead! Like them."

It was as if I had said the magic words. Alakazam!—and her face went blank, her mouth closed, her arms went slack, and she backed out of the room, stunned, as if she were blowing away like a small brown leaf, thin, brittle, lifeless.

It was not the only disappointment my mother felt in me. In the years that followed, I failed her so many times, each time asserting my own will, my right to fall short of expectations. I didn't get straight As. I didn't become class president. I didn't get into Stanford.[9] I dropped out of college.

For unlike my mother, I did not believe I could be anything I wanted to be. I could only be me.

And for all those years, we never talked about the disaster at the recital or my terrible accusations afterward at the piano bench. All that remained unchecked, like a betrayal that was now unspeakable. So I never found a way to ask her why she had hoped for something so large that failure was inevitable.

And even worse, I never asked her what frightened me the most: Why had she given up hope?

For after our struggle at the piano, she never mentioned my playing again. The lessons stopped. The lid to the piano was closed, shutting out the dust, my misery, and her dreams.

So she surprised me. A few years ago, she offered to give me the piano, for my thirtieth birthday. I had not played in all those years. I saw the offer as a sign of forgiveness, a tremendous burden removed.

"Are you sure?" I asked shyly. "I mean, won't you and Dad miss it?"

"No, this your piano," she said firmly. "Always your piano. You only one can play."

"Well, I probably can't play anymore," I said. "It's been years."

---

9. **Stanford:** a prestigious university in Palo Alto, California.

"You pick up fast," said my mother, as if she knew this was certain. "You have natural talent. You could been genius if you want to."

"No I couldn't."

"You just not trying," said my mother. And she was neither angry nor sad. She said it as if to announce a fact that could never be disproved. "Take it," she said.

But I didn't at first. It was enough that she had offered it to me. And after that, every time I saw it in my parents' living room, standing in front of the bay windows, it made me feel proud, as if it were a shiny trophy I had won back.

Last week I sent a tuner over to my parents' apartment and had the piano reconditioned, for purely sentimental reasons. My mother had died a few months before and I had been getting things in order for my father, a little bit at a time. I put the jewelry in special silk pouches. The sweaters she had knitted in yellow, pink, bright orange—all the colors I hated—I put those in moth-proof boxes. I found some old Chinese silk dresses, the kind with little slits up the sides. I rubbed the old silk against my skin, then wrapped them in tissue and decided to take them home with me.

After I had the piano tuned, I opened the lid and touched the keys. It sounded even richer than I remembered. Really, it was a very good piano. Inside the bench were the same exercise notes with handwritten scales, the same secondhand music books with their covers held together with yellow tape.

I opened up the Schumann book to the dark little piece I had played at the recital. It was on the left-hand side of the page, "Pleading Child." It looked more difficult than I remembered. I played a few bars, surprised at how easily the notes came back to me.

And for the first time, or so it seemed, I noticed the piece on the right-hand side. It was called "Perfectly Contented." I tried to play this one as well. It had a lighter melody but the same flowing rhythm and turned out to be quite easy. "Pleading Child" was shorter but slower; "Perfectly Contented" was longer, but faster. And after I played them both a few times, I realized they were two halves of the same song.

Responding to the Story

Analyzing the Story

Identifying Facts

1. The narrator says that at first she was excited about becoming a prodigy. Why does she eventually turn against the idea?
2. Explain how Jing-mei takes advantage of her piano teacher's deafness.

Interpreting Meanings

3. What do you think **motivates** the mother to push Jing-mei into being a prodigy? (What do we learn about the mother's past that might explain her high ambitions for her daughter?)
4. Find at least three details in the story that reveal something about Jing-mei's **character.** In your opinion, why is she so determined not to let her mother change her?
5. Although Jing-mei expects and almost wants her mother to blow up at her after the talent-show fiasco, the confrontation doesn't come until two days later. Why does her mother want Jing-mei to keep playing the piano, even after her disastrous performance? What kind of daughter does she *really* want Jing-mei to be?
6. At the end of the story, the narrator discovers that "Pleading Child" and "Perfectly Contented" are "two halves of the same song." How does this realization relate to the story's **title?** Is Jing-mei both of these, or only one, or neither?
7. Do you think high expectations can make someone *want* to fail? Or do you think failure results more often from low expectations? Explain your opinion.

Writing About the Story

A Critical Response

Responding to Characters. Do you agree with the narrator that her mother's pride is foolish? Do you think her mother is right to push Jing-mei so hard? Do you think Jing-mei is cruel to her mother? Write one or two paragraphs expressing your response to the characters of this mother and daughter. If you sided with one character, be sure to explain why.

Reading About the Writer

Amy Tan (1952—   ) was born in Oakland, California, two and a half years after her parents immigrated to the United States from Communist China.

Although Tan's parents had wanted her to become a surgeon, with piano as a hobby, Tan instead got a master's degree in linguistics, became a consultant to programs for disabled children, and later a freelance technical writer. She wrote her first short story at a writer's workshop in 1985. It was published in a small literary magazine and then in *Seventeen*. Eventually it caught the eye of a literary agent, who asked to see more stories. Tan wrote another, and at the agent's request, she drafted a proposal for a novel based on the stories (they later became chapters in her book). Then she left on a trip to China with her mother, who had just recovered from a serious illness.

When she returned, Tan was amazed to find that her agent had obtained a sizable advance for the novel she hadn't even written yet. She immediately devoted herself full time to writing, and in four months had completed *The Joy Luck Club*. Published in 1989 to rave reviews, it became an instant best-seller. "Two Kinds" is one of four stories in the novel narrated by Jing-mei. (Half the stories are told by mothers, the other half by their daughters.) Tan has turned "The Moon Lady," one of the mothers' stories, into a separate children's book.

Afraid of bombing after the huge success of her first novel, Tan agonized over her second novel, *The Kitchen God's Wife*. In writing that book, she says she "had to fight for every single character, every image, every word." She needn't have worried: The novel, chiefly another mother's story of her incredible life in pre-Communist China, is another blockbuster.

THE HOUSE ON MANGO STREET

Sandra Cisneros

The House on Mango Street is a book written in episodic form, consisting of a series of short short stories and sketches. What links all of the episodes is the voice of the narrator—Esperanza—who, appropriately, opens her story with a reflection on her name. You might read these sketches as if they were a series of journal entries written by a young girl who is very skillful at revealing the secrets of her own character.

My Name

In English my name means hope. In Spanish it means too many letters. It means sadness, it means waiting. It is like the number nine. A muddy color. It is the Mexican records my father plays on Sunday mornings when he is shaving, songs like sobbing.

It was my great-grandmother's name and now it is mine. She was a horse woman too, born like me in the Chinese year of the horse—which is supposed to be bad luck if you're born female— but I think this is a Chinese lie because the Chinese, like the Mexicans, don't like their women strong.

My great-grandmother. I would've liked to have known her, a wild horse of a woman, so wild she wouldn't marry until my great-grandfather threw a sack over her head and carried her off. Just like that, as if she were a fancy chandelier. That's the way he did it.

And the story goes she never forgave him. She looked out the window all her life, the way so many women sit their sadness on an elbow. I wonder if she made the best with what she got or was she sorry because she couldn't be all the things she wanted to be. Esperanza. I have inherited her name, but I don't want to inherit her place by the window.

At school they say my name funny as if the syllables were made out of tin and hurt the roof of your mouth. But in Spanish my name is made out of a softer something like silver, not quite as thick as sister's name Magdalena, which is uglier than mine. Magdalena, who at least can come home and become Nenny. But I am always Esperanza.

I would like to baptize myself under a new name, a name more like the real me, the one nobody sees. Esperanza as Lisandra or Maritza or Zeze the X. Yes. Something like Zeze the X will do.

A Rice Sandwich

The special kids, the ones who wear keys around their necks, get to eat in the canteen. The canteen! Even the name sounds important. And these kids at lunch time go there because their mothers aren't home or home is too far away to get to.

My home isn't far but it's not close either, and somehow I got it in my head one day to ask my mother to make me a sandwich and write a note to the principal so I could eat in the canteen too.

Oh no, she says pointing the butter knife at me as if I'm starting trouble, no sir. Next thing you know everybody will be wanting a bag lunch—I'll be up all night cutting bread into little triangles, this one with mayonnaise, this one with mustard,

Girl Writing by Milton
Avery (1941). Oil.

The Phillips Collection,
Washington, D.C.

no pickles on mine, but mustard on one side please. You kids just like to invent more work for me.

But Nenny says she doesn't want to eat at school—ever—because she likes to go home with her best friend Gloria who lives across the schoolyard. Gloria's mama has a big color T.V. and all they do is watch cartoons. Kiki and Carlos, on the other hand, are patrol boys. They don't want to eat at school either. They like to stand out in the cold especially if it's raining. They think suffering is good for you ever since they saw that movie *300 Spartans*.

I'm no Spartan and hold up an anemic wrist to prove it. I can't even blow up a balloon without getting dizzy. And besides, I know how to make my own lunch. If I ate at school there'd be less dishes to wash. You would see me less and less and like me better. Everyday at noon my chair would be empty. Where is my favorite daughter, you would cry, and when I came home finally at three p.m. you would appreciate me.

Okay, okay, my mother says after three days of this. And the following morning I get to go to school with my mother's letter and a rice sandwich because we don't have lunch meat.

Mondays or Fridays, it doesn't matter, mornings always go by slow and this day especially. But lunch time came finally and I got to get in line with the stay-at-school kids. Everything is fine until the nun who knows all the canteen kids by heart looks at me and says: you, who sent you here? And since I am shy, I don't say anything, just hold out my hand with the letter. This is no good, she says, till Sister Superior gives the okay. Go upstairs and see her. And so I went.

I had to wait for two kids in front of me to get hollered at, one because he did something in class, the other because he didn't. My turn came and I stood in front of the big desk with holy pictures under the glass while the Sister Superior read my letter. It went like this:

Dear Sister Superior, Please let Esperanza eat in the lunch room because she lives too far away and she gets tired. As you can see she is very skinny. I hope to God she does not faint. Thanking you, Mrs. E. Cordero.

You don't live far, she says. You live across the boulevard. That's only four blocks. Not even. Three maybe. Three long blocks away from here. I bet I can see your house from my window. Which one? Come here. Which one is your house?

And then she made me stand up on a box of books and point. That one? she said pointing to a row of ugly three-flats, the ones even the raggedy men are ashamed to go into. Yes, I nodded even though I knew that wasn't my house and started to cry. I always cry when nuns yell at me, even if they're not yelling.

Then she was sorry and said I could stay—just for today, not tomorrow or the day after—you go home. And I said yes and could I please have a Kleenex—I had to blow my nose.

In the canteen, which was nothing special, lots of boys and girls watched while I cried and ate my sandwich, the bread already greasy and the rice cold.

Chanclas[1]

It's me—Mama, Mama said. I open up and she's there with bags and big boxes, the new clothes and, yes, she's got the socks and a new slip with a little rose on it and a pink and white striped dress. What about the shoes? I forgot. Too late now. I'm tired. Whew!

Six-thirty already and my little cousin's baptism is over. All day waiting, the door locked, don't open up for nobody, and I don't 'til Mama gets back and buys everything except the shoes.

Now Uncle Nacho is coming in his car and we have to hurry to get to Precious Blood Church quick because that's where the baptism party is, in the basement rented for today for dancing and tamales and everyone's kids running all over the place.

Mama dances, laughs, dances. All of a sudden Mama is sick. I fan her hot face with a paper plate. Too many tamales, but Uncle Nacho says too many this and tilts his thumb to his lips.

Everybody is laughing except me because I'm wearing the new dress, pink and white, with stripes and new underclothes and the new socks

1. **Chanclas:** shoes.

and the old saddle shoes I wear to school, brown and white, the kind I get every September because they last long and they do. My feet are scuffed and round and the heels all crooked that look dumb with this dress, so I just sit.

Meanwhile that boy who is my cousin by first communion or something, asks me to dance and I can't. Just stuff my feet under the metal folding chair stamped Precious Blood and pick on a wad of brown gum that's stuck beneath the seat. I shake my head no. My feet grow bigger and bigger.

Then Uncle Nacho is pulling and pulling my arm and it doesn't matter how new the dress Mama bought is because my feet are ugly until my uncle who is a liar says you are the prettiest girl here, will you dance, but I believe him and, yes, we are dancing, my Uncle Nacho and me, only I don't want to at first. My feet swell big and heavy like plungers, but I drag them across the linoleum floor straight center where Uncle wants to show off the new dance we learned. And Uncle spins me and my skinny arms bend the way he taught me and my mother watches and my little cousins watch and the boy who is my cousin by first communion watches and everyone says, wow, who are those two who dance like in the movies, until I forget that I am wearing only ordinary shoes, brown and white, the kind my mother buys each year for school.

And all I hear is the clapping when the music stops. My uncle and me bow and he walks me back in my thick shoes to my mother who is proud to be my mother. All night the boy who is a man watches me dance. He watched me dance.

Mango Says Goodbye Sometimes

I like to tell stories. I tell them inside my head. I tell them after the mailman says here's your mail. Here's your mail he said.

I make a story for my life, for each step my brown shoe takes. I say, "And so she trudged up the wooden stairs, her sad brown shoes taking her to the house she never liked."

I like to tell stories. I am going to tell you a story about a girl who didn't want to belong.

We didn't always live on Mango Street. Before that we lived on Loomis on the third floor, and before that we lived on Keeler. Before Keeler it was Paulina, but what I remember most is Mango Street, sad red house, the house I belong but do not belong to.

I put it down on paper and then the ghost does not ache so much. I write it down and Mango says goodbye sometimes. She does not hold me with both arms. She sets me free.

One day I will pack my bags of books and paper. One day I will say goodbye to Mango. I am too strong for her to keep me here forever. One day I will go away.

Friends and neighbors will say, What happened to that Esperanza? Where did she go with all those books and paper? Why did she march so far away?

They will not know I have gone away to come back. For the ones I left behind. For the ones who cannot get out.

Responding to the Stories

Analyzing the Stories

Identifying Facts

1. In "My Name," what private thoughts about her name does the narrator share with the reader?
2. Explain why, in "A Rice Sandwich," Esperanza wants to eat her lunch at school. How does she convince her mother to let her?
3. In "Chanclas," what is Esperanza's **conflict**?

Interpreting Meanings

4. On page 54, what does Esperanza mean when she says she doesn't want to inherit her great-

grandmother's place by the window? Based on what you have seen of Esperanza, do you think she ever will?

5. What does the name Esperanza chooses for herself reveal about her **character**?

6. What changes does Esperanza undergo in "A Rice Sandwich" and "Chanclas"? What does she learn about the world and about herself?

7. What is the significance of the title of the last sketch? What do you think Mango Street represents for Esperanza, and why does she believe she will have to leave it someday?

8. Explain what Esperanza means when she says she has "gone away to come back" (page 57). What is her purpose in writing, according to the last two phrases of this sketch?

9. Given all that she has revealed about herself, how would you **characterize** Esperanza? Describe at least four character traits, and then identify three details from these sketches that you think are most significant in revealing what she is really like.

10. Did you find touches of humor in Esperanza's story? What passages might make a reader smile? How would you describe the way the adult writer feels about her "persona"?

Writing About the Stories

A Creative Response

Imitating the Writer's Technique. These little episodes might be called "vignettes." A **vignette** is a very short literary sketch, often one that is suggestive and poetic in style. Imitate Cisneros's first vignette here, and write one of your own about a name—your name or the name of another character. You might open with Cisneros's first line. Be sure to tell what your narrator thinks the name means, what color it feels like, and what music it sounds like. End your vignette with the name your character would prefer to be known by.

Analyzing Language and Vocabulary

Figures of Speech

These vignettes have a poetic feel to them, in part because Cisneros uses **figures of speech**—imagina-

tive phrasings in which one thing is usually compared to something much different from it. Figurative language is an economical way of expressing ourselves—explaining a figure of speech usually takes far more words than the figure of speech itself contains.

1. What does Cisneros mean in the first story when she describes women who "sit their sadness on an elbow"? What visual **image** is suggested by this figure of speech?

2. Find the figures of speech that describe Esperanza's name. What **feelings** about the sounds of Spanish and English is Cisneros expressing here?

3. What figures of speech describe Esperanza's feet at the dance? Do these suggest positive or negative feelings, and why? Suppose she had gotten the shoes she wanted. What figure of speech might she have used to describe her feet in them?

4. Find the passage that **personifies** Mango Street—that talks of Mango Street as if it had the feelings and body of a person. What is the emotional impact of this way of describing a street?

Reading About the Writer

Sandra Cisneros (1954–) spent her childhood moving back and forth between Chicago, where she was born, and Mexico City, where her parents were from. She graduated from the Writer's Workshop at the University of Iowa, has won a National Endowment for the Arts Fellowship, and is a prize-winning poet. Of her writing, Cisneros says: "There are so few of us writing about the powerless, and that world, the world of thousands of silent women, women like my mama . . . , must be recorded so that their stories can finally be heard."

The poet Gwendolyn Brooks (see page 314) has called Cisneros "one of the most brilliant of today's young writers." One critic has written that the stories in her most recent collection, *Woman Hollering Creek,* "invite us into the souls of characters as unforgettable as a first kiss." Cisneros currently lives in San Antonio, Texas.

THE FIRST SEVEN YEARS

Bernard Malamud

This story is set in New York City. Feld, a shoe-maker, is a poor Jewish immigrant who has come to America from Poland. But Feld has a daughter, born in America, whose ideas about education—and love—are different from her father's. After you read the first paragraph of this story, stop and ask yourself this question: What do you expect is going to happen to the four main characters—Feld, the shoemaker; Sobel, his assistant; Miriam, the independent daughter; and Max, the admirable college boy whom Feld believes could make a better life for his daughter?

Feld, the shoemaker, was annoyed that his helper, Sobel, was so insensitive to his reverie that he wouldn't for a minute cease his fanatic pounding at the other bench. He gave him a look, but Sobel's bald head was bent over the last[1] as he worked and he didn't notice. The shoemaker shrugged and continued to peer through the partly frosted window at the nearsighted haze of falling February snow. Neither the shifting white blur outside nor the sudden deep remembrance of the snowy Polish village where he had wasted his youth could turn his thoughts from Max the college boy (a constant visitor in the mind since early that morning when Feld saw him trudging through the snowdrifts on his way to school), whom he so much respected because of the sacrifices he had made throughout the years—in winter or direst heat—to further his education. An old wish returned to haunt the shoemaker: that he had had a son instead of a daughter, but this blew away in the snow, for Feld, if anything, was a practical man. Yet he could not help but contrast the diligence of the boy, who was a peddler's son, with Miriam's unconcern for an education. True, she was always with a book in her hand, yet when the opportunity arose for a college education, she had said no she would rather find a job. He had begged her to go, pointing out how many fathers could not afford to send their children to college, but she said she wanted to be independent. As for education, what was it, she asked, but books, which Sobel, who diligently read the classics, would as usual advise her on. Her answer greatly grieved her father.

A figure emerged from the snow and the door opened. At the counter the man withdrew from a wet paper bag a pair of battered shoes for repair. Who he was the shoemaker for a moment had no idea; then his heart trembled as he realized, before he had thoroughly discerned the face, that Max himself was standing there, embarrassedly explaining what he wanted done to his old shoes. Though Feld listened eagerly, he couldn't hear a word, for the opportunity that had burst upon him was deafening.

He couldn't exactly recall when the thought had occurred to him, because it was clear he had more than once considered suggesting to the boy that he go out with Miriam. But he had not dared speak, for if Max said no, how would he face him again? Or suppose Miriam, who harped so often on independence, blew up in anger and shouted at him for his meddling? Still, the chance was too good to let by: all it meant was an introduction. They might long ago have become friends had they

---

1. **last:** a wooden or metal model of a foot that the shoemaker uses to make or repair a shoe.

Sixth Avenue El by Peter Berent
(1938). Oil on masonite, 63″ × 35¾″.
83.5.10.

The Mitchell Wolfson, Jr., Collection.
Courtesy, The Wolfsonian Foundation,
Miami, Florida.

happened to meet somewhere; therefore was it not his duty—an obligation—to bring them together, nothing more, a harmless connivance to replace an accidental encounter in the subway, let's say, or a mutual friend's introduction in the street? Just let him once see and talk to her, and he would for sure be interested. As for Miriam, what possible harm for a working girl in an office, who met only loudmouthed salesmen and illiterate shipping clerks, to make the acquaintance of a fine scholarly boy? Maybe he would awaken in her a desire to go to college; if not—the shoemaker's mind at last came to grips with the truth—let her marry an educated man and live a better life.

When Max finished describing what he wanted done to his shoes, Feld marked them, both with enormous holes in the soles which he pretended not to notice, with large white-chalk x's, and the rubber heels, thinned to the nails, he marked with o's, though it troubled him he might have mixed up the letters. Max inquired the price, and the shoemaker cleared his throat and asked the boy, above Sobel's insistent hammering, would he please step through the side door there into the hall. Though surprised, Max did as the shoemaker requested, and Feld went in after him. For a minute they were both silent, because Sobel had stopped banging, and it seemed they understood neither was to say anything until the noise began again. When it did, loudly, the shoemaker quickly told Max why he had asked to talk to him.

"Ever since you went to high school," he said, in the dimly lit hallway, "I watched you in the morning go to the subway to school, and I said always to myself, this is a fine boy that he wants so much an education."

"Thanks," Max said, nervously alert. He was tall and grotesquely thin, with sharply cut features, particularly a beaklike nose. He was wearing a loose, long slushy overcoat that hung down to his ankles, looking like a rug draped over his bony shoulders, and a soggy, old brown hat, as battered as the shoes he had brought in.

"I am a business man," the shoemaker abruptly said to conceal his embarrassment, "so I will explain you right away why I talk to you. I have a girl, my daughter Miriam—she is nineteen—a very nice girl and also so pretty that everybody looks on her when she passes by in the street. She is smart, always with a book, and I thought to myself that a boy like you, an educated boy—I thought maybe you will be interested sometime to meet a girl like this." He laughed a bit when he had finished and was tempted to say more, but had the good sense not to.

Max stared down like a hawk. For an uncomfortable second he was silent, then he asked, "Did you say nineteen?"

"Yes."

"Would it be all right to inquire if you have a picture of her?"

"Just a minute." The shoemaker went into the store and hastily returned with a snapshot that Max held up to the light.

"She's all right," he said.

Feld waited.

"And is she sensible—not the flighty kind?"

"She is very sensible."

After another short pause, Max said it was okay with him if he met her.

"Here is my telephone," said the shoemaker, hurriedly handing him a slip of paper. "Call her up. She comes home from work six o'clock."

Max folded the paper and tucked it away into his worn leather wallet.

"About the shoes," he said. "How much did you say they will cost me?"

"Don't worry about the price."

"I just like to have an idea."

"A dollar—dollar fifty. A dollar fifty," the shoemaker said.

At once he felt bad, for he usually charged two twenty-five for this kind of job. Either he should have asked the regular price or done the work for nothing.

Later, as he entered the store, he was startled by a violent clanging and looked up to see Sobel pounding with all his might upon the naked last. It broke, the iron striking the floor and jumping with a thump against the wall, but before the enraged shoemaker could cry out, the assistant had torn his hat and coat from the hook and rushed out into the snow.

So Feld, who had looked forward to anticipating how it would go with his daughter and Max, instead had a great worry on his mind. Without his temperamental helper he was a lost man, especially since it was years now that he had carried the store alone. The shoemaker had for an age suffered from a heart condition that threatened collapse if he dared exert himself. Five years ago, after an attack, it had appeared as though he would have either to sacrifice his business upon the auction block and live on a pittance thereafter, or put himself at the mercy of some unscrupulous employee who would in the end probably ruin him. But just at the moment of his darkest despair, this Polish refugee, Sobel, appeared one night from the street and begged for work. He was a stocky man, poorly dressed, with a bald head that had once been blond, a severely plain face, and soft blue eyes prone to tears over the sad books he read, a young man but old—no one would have guessed thirty. Though he confessed he knew nothing of shoemaking, he said he was apt and would work for a very little if Feld taught him the trade. Thinking that with, after all, a landsman,[2] he would have less to fear than from a complete stranger, Feld took him on, and within six weeks the refugee rebuilt as good a shoe as he, and not long thereafter expertly ran the business for the thoroughly relieved shoemaker.

Feld could trust him with anything and did, frequently going home after an hour or two at the store, leaving all the money in the till, knowing Sobel would guard every cent of it. The amazing thing was that he demanded so little. His wants were few; in money he wasn't interested—in nothing but books, it seemed—which he one by one lent to Miriam, together with his profuse, queer written comments, manufactured during his lonely rooming-house evenings, thick pads of commentary which the shoemaker peered at and twitched his shoulders over as his daughter, from her fourteenth year, read page by sanctified page, as if the word of God were inscribed on them. To protect Sobel, Feld himself had to see that he received more than he asked for. Yet his conscience bothered him for not insisting that the assistant accept a better wage than he was getting, though Feld

2. **landsman:** a fellow countryman; someone from the same town or section of eastern Europe.

had honestly told him he could earn a handsome salary if he worked elsewhere, or maybe opened a place of his own. But the assistant answered, somewhat ungraciously, that he was not interested in going elsewhere, and though Feld frequently asked himself what keeps him here? why does he stay? he finally answered it that the man, no doubt because of his terrible experiences as a refugee, was afraid of the world.

After the incident with the broken last, angered by Sobel's behavior, the shoemaker decided to let him stew for a week in the rooming house, although his own strength was taxed dangerously and the business suffered. However, after several sharp nagging warnings from both his wife and daughter, he went finally in search of Sobel, as he had once before, quite recently, when over some fancied slight—Feld had merely asked him not to give Miriam so many books to read because her eyes were strained and red—the assistant had left the place in a huff, an incident which, as usual, came to nothing for he had returned after the shoemaker had talked to him, and taken his seat at the bench. But this time, after Feld had plodded through the snow to Sobel's house—he had thought of sending Miriam, but the idea became repugnant to him—the burly landlady at the door informed him in a nasal voice that Sobel was not at home, and though Feld knew this was a nasty lie, for where had the refugee to go? still for some reason he was not completely sure of—it may have been the cold and his fatigue—he decided not to insist on seeing him. Instead he went home and hired a new helper.

Having settled the matter, though not entirely to his satisfaction, for he had much more to do than before and so, for example, could no longer lie late in bed mornings because he had to get up to open the store for the new assistant, a speechless, dark man with an irritating rasp as he worked, whom he would not trust with the key as he had Sobel. Furthermore, this one, though able to do a fair repair job, knew nothing of grades of leather or prices, so Feld had to make his own purchases; and every night at closing time it was necessary to count the money in the till and lock up. However, he was not dissatisfied, for he lived much in his thoughts of Max and Miriam. The college boy had called her, and they had arranged a meeting for this coming Friday night. The shoemaker would personally have preferred Saturday, which he felt would make it a date of the first magnitude, but he learned Friday was Miriam's choice, so he said nothing. The day of the week did not matter. What mattered was the aftermath. Would they like each other and want to be friends? He sighed at all the time that would have to go by before he knew for sure. Often he was tempted to talk to Miriam about the boy, to ask whether she thought she would like his type—he had told her only that he considered Max a nice boy and had suggested he call her—but the one time he tried, she snapped at him—justly—how should she know?

At last Friday came. Feld was not feeling particularly well so he stayed in bed, and Mrs. Feld thought it better to remain in the bedroom with him when Max called. Miriam received the boy, and her parents could hear their voices, his throaty one, as they talked. Just before leaving, Miriam brought Max to the bedroom door and he stood there a minute, a tall, slightly hunched figure wearing a thick, droopy suit, and apparently at ease as he greeted the shoemaker and his wife, which was surely a good sign. And Miriam, although she had worked all day, looked fresh and pretty. She was a large-framed girl with a well-shaped body, and she had a fine open face and soft hair. They made, Feld thought, a first-class couple.

Miriam returned after 11:30. Her mother was already asleep, but the shoemaker got out of bed and after locating his bathrobe went into the kitchen, where Miriam, to his surprise, sat at the table, reading.

"So where did you go?" Feld asked pleasantly.

"For a walk," she said, not looking up.

"I advised him," Feld said, clearing his throat, "he shouldn't spend so much money."

"I didn't care."

The shoemaker boiled up some water for tea and sat down at the table with a cupful and a thick slice of lemon.

"So how," he sighed after a sip, "did you enjoy?"

"It was all right."

He was silent. She must have sensed his disappointment, for she added, "You can't really tell much the first time."

"You will see him again?"

Turning a page, she said that Max had asked for another date.

"For when?"

"Saturday."

"So what did you say?"

"What did I say?" she asked, delaying for a moment—"I said yes."

Afterwards she inquired about Sobel, and Feld, without exactly knowing why, said the assistant had got another job. Miriam said nothing more and began to read. The shoemaker's conscience did not trouble him; he was satisfied with the Saturday date.

During the week, by placing here and there a deft question, he managed to get from Miriam some information about Max. It surprised him to learn that the boy was not studying to be either a doctor or lawyer but was taking a business course leading to a degree in accountancy. Feld was a little disappointed because he thought of accountants as bookkeepers and would have preferred "a higher profession." However, it was not long before he had investigated the subject and discovered that Certified Public Accountants were highly respected people, so he was thoroughly content as Saturday approached. But because Saturday was a busy day, he was much in the store and therefore did not see Max when he came to call for Miriam. From his wife he learned there had been nothing especially revealing about their meeting. Max had rung the bell and Miriam had got her coat and left with him—nothing more. Feld did not probe, for his wife was not particularly observant. Instead, he waited up for Miriam with a newspaper on his lap, which he scarcely looked at, so lost was he in thinking of the future. He awoke to find her in the room with him, tiredly removing her hat. Greeting her, he was suddenly inexplicably afraid to ask anything about the evening. But since she volunteered nothing he was at last forced to inquire how she had enjoyed herself. Miriam began something noncommittal but apparently changed her mind, for she said after a minute, "I was bored."

When Feld had sufficiently recovered from his anguished disappointment to ask why, she answered without hesitation, "Because he's nothing more than a materialist."

"What means this word?"

"He has no soul. He's only interested in things."

He considered her statement for a long time but then asked, "Will you see him again?"

"He didn't ask."

"Suppose he will ask you?"

"I won't see him."

He did not argue; however, as the days went by he hoped increasingly she would change her mind. He wished the boy would telephone, because he was sure there was more to him than Miriam, with her inexperienced eye, could discern. But Max didn't call. As a matter of fact, he took a different route to school, no longer passing the shoemaker's store, and Feld was deeply hurt.

Then one afternoon Max came in and asked for his shoes. The shoemaker took them down from the shelf where he had placed them, apart from the other pairs. He had done the work himself and the soles and heels were well built and firm. The shoes had been highly polished and somehow looked better than new. Max's Adam's apple went up once when he saw them, and his eyes had little lights in them.

"How much?" he asked, without directly looking at the shoemaker.

"Like I told you before," Feld answered sadly. "One dollar fifty cents."

Max handed him two crumpled bills and received in return a newly minted silver half dollar.

He left. Miriam had not been mentioned. That night the shoemaker discovered that his new assistant had been all the while stealing from him, and he suffered a heart attack.

Though the attack was very mild, he lay in bed for three weeks. Miriam spoke of going for Sobel, but sick as he was, Feld rose in wrath against the idea. Yet in his heart he knew there was no other way, and the first weary day back in the shop thoroughly convinced him, so that night after supper he dragged himself to Sobel's rooming house.

He toiled up the stairs, though he knew it was bad for him, and at the top knocked at the door. Sobel opened it and the shoemaker entered. The room was a small, poor one, with a single window facing the street. It contained a narrow cot, a low table, and several stacks of books piled haphazardly around on the floor along the wall, which made him think how queer Sobel was, to be uneducated and read so much. He had once asked him, Sobel, why you read so much? and the assistant could not answer him. Did you ever study in a college someplace? he had asked, but Sobel shook his head. He read, he said, to know. But to know what, the shoemaker demanded, and to know, why? Sobel never explained, which proved he read so much because he was queer.

Feld sat down to recover his breath. The assistant was resting on his bed with his heavy back to the wall. His shirt and trousers were clean, and his stubby fingers, away from the shoemaker's bench, were strangely pallid. His face was thin and pale, as if he had been shut in this room since the day he had bolted from the store.

"So when you will come back to work?" Feld asked him.

To his surprise, Sobel burst out, "Never."

Jumping up, he strode over to the window that looked out upon the miserable street. "Why should I come back?" he cried.

"I will raise your wages."

"Who cares for your wages!"

The shoemaker, knowing he didn't care, was at a loss what else to say.

"What do you want for me, Sobel?"

"Nothing."

"I always treated you like you was my son."

Sobel vehemently denied it. "So why you look for strange boys in the street they should go out with Miriam? Why you don't think of me?"

The shoemaker's hands and feet turned freezing cold. His voice became so hoarse he couldn't speak. At last he cleared his throat and croaked, "So what has my daughter got to do with a shoemaker thirty-five years old who works for me?"

"Why do you think I worked so long for you?" Sobel cried out. "For the stingy wages I sacrificed five years of my life so you could have to eat and drink and where to sleep?"

"Then for what?" shouted the shoemaker.

"For Miriam," he blurted—"for her."

The shoemaker, after a time, managed to say, "I pay wages in cash, Sobel," and lapsed into silence. Though he was seething with excitement, his mind was coldly clear, and he had to admit to himself he had sensed all along that Sobel felt this way. He had never so much as thought it consciously, but he had felt it and was afraid.

"Miriam knows?" he muttered hoarsely.

"She knows."

"You told her?"

"No."

"Then how does she know?"

"How does she know?" Sobel said. "Because she knows. She knows who I am and what is in my heart."

Feld had a sudden insight. In some devious way, with his books and commentary, Sobel had given Miriam to understand that he loved her. The shoemaker felt a terrible anger at him for his deceit.

"Sobel, you are crazy," he said bitterly. "She will never marry a man so old and ugly like you."

Sobel turned black with rage. He cursed the shoemaker, but then, though he trembled to hold it in, his eyes filled with tears and he broke into deep sobs. With his back to Feld, he stood at the window, fists clenched, and his shoulders shook with his choked sobbing.

Watching him, the shoemaker's anger diminished. His teeth were on edge with pity for the man, and his eyes grew moist. How strange and sad that a refugee, a grown man, bald and old with his miseries, who had by the skin of his teeth escaped Hitler's incinerators, should fall in love, when he had got to America, with a girl less than half his age. Day after day, for five years he had sat at his bench, cutting and hammering away, waiting for the girl to become a woman, unable to ease his heart with speech, knowing no protest but desperation.

"Ugly I didn't mean," he said half aloud.

Then he realized that what he had called ugly was not Sobel but Miriam's life if she married him. He felt for his daughter a strange and gripping sorrow, as if she were already Sobel's bride, the wife, after all, of a shoemaker, and had in her life no more than her mother had had. And all his dreams for her—why he had slaved and destroyed his heart with anxiety and labor—all these dreams of a better life were dead.

The room was quiet. Sobel was standing by the window reading, and it was curious that when he read he looked young.

"She is only nineteen," Feld said brokenly. "This is too young yet to get married. Don't ask her for two years more, till she is twenty-one; then you can talk to her."

Sobel didn't answer. Feld rose and left. He went slowly down the stairs, but once outside, though it was an icy night and the crisp falling snow whitened the street, he walked with a stronger stride.

But the next morning, when the shoemaker arrived, heavy-hearted, to open the store, he saw he needn't have come, for his assistant was already seated at the last, pounding leather for his love.

Responding to the Story

Analyzing the Story

Identifying Facts

1. Which character in "The First Seven Years" is the **protagonist**? (If you think there is more than one possibility, consider which character sets the action of the plot in motion.)

2. Explain what the protagonist wants—that is, what is his or her **conflict**? Is it **internal** or **external** or both?

3. List the steps the protagonist takes to get what he or she wants. What block gets in the way of this goal?

4. Explain how the conflict is finally **resolved**.

Interpreting Meanings

5. What is Miriam's opinion of Max after she has gone out with him twice? Find evidence in the story that seems to support her assessment of his **character**.

6. How would you describe Miriam's **character**? Find passages in which the writer establishes her character **indirectly** (by her appearance, by her behavior, by other people's response to her, and by what she says). Do you think Miriam is in love with Sobel? Why or why not?

7. Sobel is certainly not the typical romantic hero. What do we learn about his background, appearance, work habits, living habits, and values? Do you agree with Feld that Miriam's life with Sobel would be "ugly"? Why or why not?

8. When did it first occur to you that Sobel was in love with Miriam? Find the **foreshadowing**—the clues that hint at Sobel's secret long before it is fully revealed.

9. How did you feel about Feld at the end of the story? Did you sympathize with him, or did you feel that he was insulting the nature of Sobel's love for Miriam by saying, "I pay wages in cash, Sobel" (page 65)? Explain your response.

10. The title of this story is an **allusion** to the Biblical account of Jacob and Rachel. (See "Focusing on Background," page 67.) What exactly are the first seven years in the Biblical account? What extra level of meaning does this allusion add to Malamud's story?

11. The conflict in this story pivots on two very different views of the purpose of education. (Some people might define this clash as the difference between education and knowledge.) What is Feld's view of education, and how is it different from Miriam's? Which view do you agree with—or do you have a completely different idea about education? Explain.

Writing About the Story

A Creative Response

1. **Writing a Resolution for the Story.** What do you think will happen to Sobel and Miriam after two years? Will Feld really let Sobel marry Miriam? Will Miriam say yes? Or might she have met somebody else in the meantime? In a paragraph or two, write a resolution for the story. Before you begin writing, you might want to read the Biblical story alluded to in Malamud's title.

A Critical Response

2. **Evaluating a Character.** Sobel's love for Miriam is strong, but he keeps it secret for five years and then agrees to endure *another* two years of waiting for her. Do you think any man could really behave this way? In a paragraph, tell whether or not you think Sobel is a believable character.

Analyzing Language and Vocabulary

Dialects

If you have ever traveled to another part of the country, you may have been surprised to discover that, like most people, you have an "accent." That is, you speak a **dialect**—a form of English that is peculiar to the region where you live or grew up. In some cases, your "accent" even might make it easy for people to place you geographically. For instance, they might guess that you are from Chicago if you flatten your *a*'s so that you pronounce *marry, merry,* and *Mary* exactly the same way. Or they might guess that you are from Boston if you broaden your *a*'s so that *park* sounds almost like *pack*. And they'll certainly spot you as a native of Brooklyn, New York, if you pronounce the section called *Greenpoint* as *Greenpernt* and *Bensonhurst* as *Bensonhoist*.

Pronunciation differences are one characteristic of a dialect. Dialects are also distinguished by differences in syntax and vocabulary. It is important to realize that everyone speaks in dialect and that no one dialect is right or wrong.

The dialect spoken by a particular ethnic group often reflects the syntax of that group's native language. For instance, a Russian person speaking English will frequently omit the definite article *the* and the indefinite article *a* because in Russian these forms are not always necessary. ("He has big house in country.")

On the other hand, a French person speaking English will often add unnecessary articles because in French articles are used more often than they are in English. A French speaker might also invert the standard English word order to reflect a direct translation of the correct French word order. ("Do you know where is the Fifth Avenue?")

Another common feature of ethnic dialects is the literal, or word-for-word, translation of their own foreign idioms into English. (An **idiom** is an expression peculiar to a certain language, which cannot be translated word for word.) For example, a Spanish speaker might say "I have twenty years" (instead of "I am twenty years old") or "I have to make my grocery shopping" (rather than "I have to do my grocery shopping").

In "The First Seven Years," Feld and Sobel speak the dialect of their ethnic group—Polish Jews whose native language is Yiddish. Malamud captures the sound of this dialect perfectly. Look back through the story, and find at least ten passages in which a Yiddish-speaking character inverts normal word order, misuses prepositions, omits words, or mixes up tenses. Then rewrite the sentences in **standard English,** the formal way of speaking and writing taught in schools.

Reading About the Writer

Bernard Malamud (1914–1986), the son of Russian immigrants, grew up in Brooklyn and was well acquainted with poverty. His mother died when he was fourteen, and his father kept a neighborhood grocery store, working at the counter from dawn until late at night. Malamud recalls that there were no books in his family's apartment, no pictures, and no music beyond that of a neighbor's piano heard occasionally through the living-room window.

Malamud drew on the immigrant experience of his parents for his first stories, and in fact, the grocer in one of his earliest novels, *The Assistant,* is modeled after his father.

Malamud's characters live precarious lives in an alien world, and they are invariably steeped in sadness. They are lovelorn, yet often redeemed by love. The author once described the essential Malamud character as "someone who fears his fate, is caught up in it, yet manages to outrun it; he's the subject and object of laughter and pity."

Malamud's most celebrated novel, *The Fixer*, won both the National Book Award and the Pulitzer Prize for fiction in 1966. His other novels include *The Natural* (which was made into a movie starring Robert Redford), *Dubin's Lives,* and *God's Grace.* "The First Seven Years" is from Malamud's first collection of stories, *The Magic Barrel*, which also won the National Book Award.

Focusing on Background
A Biblical Allusion

The title of this story is an **allusion,** or reference, to the Biblical account of Jacob, who worked twice seven years for Laban, Rachel's father, in order to win Rachel as his wife. Here is the Biblical account:

"Laban said to Jacob, 'Why should you work for me for nothing simply because you are my kinsman? Tell me what your wages ought to be.' Now Laban had two daughters: The elder was called Leah, and the younger Rachel. Leah was dull-eyed, but Rachel was graceful and beautiful. Jacob had fallen in love with Rachel and he said, 'I will work seven years for your younger daughter Rachel.' Laban replied, 'It is better that I should give her to you than to anyone else; stay with me.'

"So Jacob worked seven years for Rachel, and they seemed like a few days because he loved her. Then Jacob said to Laban, 'I have served my time. Give me my wife. . . .'

"So Laban gathered all the men of the place together and gave a feast. In the evening he took his daughter Leah and brought her to Jacob. . . . But when morning came, Jacob saw that it was Leah[1] and said to Laban, 'What have you done to me? Did I not work for Rachel? Why have you deceived me?' Laban answered, 'In our country it is not right to give the younger sister in marriage before the elder. Go through with the seven days' feast for the elder, and the younger shall be given you in return for a further seven years' work.' Jacob agreed, and completed the seven days for Leah.

"Then Laban gave Jacob his daughter Rachel as wife; and . . . Jacob . . . loved her rather than Leah, and he worked for Laban for a further seven years."

—Genesis 29:15–30,
New English Bible

---

1. Probably, the deception was possible because Leah wore a veil.

MR. PARKER

Laurie Colwin

Most readers would naturally assume that a story entitled ''Mr. Parker'' features that character as its protagonist. But this story is actually about Mr. Parker's effect on the protagonist—his young neighbor and piano student. As you read about the relationship between these two people, think about the following questions: When did an adult neighbor, relative, or teacher treat *you* like an equal for the first time? Why did it happen—was it the result of something you had accomplished? Did it happen suddenly or gradually? How did you feel as a result?

Mrs. Parker died suddenly in October. She and Mr. Parker lived in a Victorian house next to ours, and Mr. Parker was my piano teacher. He commuted to Wall Street, where he was a securities analyst, but he had studied at Juilliard[1] and gave lessons on the side—for the pleasure of it, not for money. His only students were me and the church organist, who was learning technique on a double-keyboard harpsichord Mr. Parker had built one spring.

Mrs. Parker was known for her pastry; she and my mother were friends, after a fashion. Every two months or so they spent a day together in the kitchen baking butter cookies and cream puffs, or rolling out strudel leaves. She was thin and wispy, and turned out her pastry with abstract expertness. As a girl, she had had bright red hair, which was now the color of old leaves. There was something smoky and autumnal about her: she wore rust-colored sweaters and heather-colored skirts, and kept dried weeds in ornamental jars and pressed flowers in frames. If you borrowed a book from her, there were petal marks on the back pages. She was tall, but she stooped as if she had spent a lifetime looking for something she had dropped.

The word ''tragic'' was mentioned in connection with her death. She and Mr. Parker were in the middle of their middle age, and neither of them had ever been seriously ill. It was heart failure, and unexpected. My parents went to see Mr. Parker as soon as they got the news, since they took their responsibilities as neighbors seriously, and two days later they took me to pay a formal condolence call. It was Indian summer, and the house felt closed in. They had used the fireplace during a recent cold spell, and the living room smelled faintly of ash. The only people from the community were some neighbors, the minister and his wife, and the rabbi and his wife and son. The Parkers were Episcopalian, but Mr. Parker played the organ in the synagogue on Saturday mornings and on High Holy Days. There was a large urn of tea and the last of Mrs. Parker's strudel. On the sofa were Mrs. Parker's sisters, and a man who looked like Mr. Parker ten years younger leaned against the piano, which was closed. The conversation was hushed and stilted. On the way out, the rabbi's son tried to trip me, and I kicked him in return. We were adolescent enemies of a loving sort, and since we didn't know what else to do, we expressed our love in slaps and pinches and other mild attempts at grievous bodily harm.

I loved the Parkers' house. It was the last Victorian house on the block and was shaped like a wedding cake. The living room was round, and all the walls curved. The third floor was a tower, on top of which sat a weathervane. Every five years the house was painted chocolate brown, which faded gradually to the color of weak tea. The

---

1. **Juilliard** ($j\overline{oo}'$lē·ärd): a prestigious music, dance, and drama school in New York City.

La Petite Pianiste by Henri Matisse (1924). Oil.

© Succession H. Matisse, 1993. Musée Matisse, Nice.

front-hall window was a stained-glass picture of a fat Victorian baby holding a bunch of roses. The baby's face was puffy and neuter, and its eyes were that of an old man caught in a state of surprise. Its white dress was milky when the light shone through.

On Wednesday afternoons, Mr. Parker came home on an early train, and I had my lesson. Mr. Parker's teaching method never varied. He never scolded or corrected. The first fifteen minutes were devoted to a warm-up in which I could play anything I liked. Then Mr. Parker played the lesson of the week. His playing was terrifically precise, but his eyes became dreamy and unfocused. Then I played the same lesson, and after that we worked on the difficult passages, but basically he wanted me to hear my mistakes. When we began a new piece, we played it part by part, taking turns, over and over.

After that, we sat in the solarium and discussed the next week's lesson. Mr. Parker usually played a record and talked in detail about the composer, his life and times, and the form. With the exception of Mozart and Schubert, he liked Baroque music almost exclusively. The lesson of the week was always Bach, which Mr. Parker felt taught elegance and precision. Mrs. Parker used to leave us a tray of cookies and lemonade, cold in the summer and hot in the winter, with cinnamon sticks. When the cookies were gone, the lesson was over and I left, passing the Victorian child in the hallway.

In the days after the funeral, my mother took several casseroles over to Mr. Parker and invited him to dinner a number of times. For several weeks he revolved between us, the minister, and the rabbi. Since neither of my parents cared much about music, except to hear my playing praised, the conversation at dinner was limited to the stock market and the blessings of country life.

In a few weeks, I got a note from Mr. Parker enclosed in a thank-you note to my parents. It said that piano lessons would begin the following Wednesday.

I went to the Parkers' after school. Everything was the same. I warmed up for fifteen minutes, Mr. Parker played the lesson, and I repeated it. In the solarium were the usual cookies and lemonade.

"Are they good, these cookies?" Mr. Parker asked.

I said they were.

"I made them yesterday," he said. "I've got to be my own baker now."

Mr. Parker's hair had once been blond, but was graying into the color of straw. Both he and Mrs. Parker seemed to have faded out of some bright time they once had lived in. He was very thin, as if the friction of living had burned every unnecessary particle off him, but he was calm and cheery in the way you expect plump people to be. On teaching days, he always wore a blue cardigan, buttoned, and a striped tie. Both smelled faintly of tobacco. At the end of the lesson, he gave me a robin's egg he had found. The light was flickering through the bunch of roses in the window as I left.

When I got home, I found my mother in the kitchen, waiting and angry.

"Where were you?" she said.

"At my piano lesson."

"What piano lesson?"

"You know what piano lesson. At Mr. Parker's."

"You didn't tell me you were going to a piano lesson," she said.

"I always have a lesson on Wednesday."

"I don't want you having lessons there now that Mrs. Parker's gone." She slung a roast into a pan.

I stomped off to my room and wrapped the robin's egg in a sweat sock. My throat felt shriveled and hot.

At dinner, my mother said to my father, "I don't want Jane taking piano lessons from Mr. Parker now that Mrs. Parker's gone."

"Why don't you want me to have lessons?" I said, close to shouting. "There's no reason."

"She can study with Mrs. Murchison." Mrs. Murchison had been my first teacher. She was a fat, myopic[2] woman who smelled of bacon grease and whose repertoire was confined to "Little Classics for Children." Her students were mostly under ten, and she kept an asthmatic chow who was often sick on the rug.

"I won't go to Mrs. Murchison!" I shouted. "I've outgrown her."

"Let's be sensible about this," said my father. "Calm down, Janie."

I stuck my fork into a potato to keep from crying and muttered melodramatically that I would hang myself before I'd go back to Mrs. Murchison.

The lessons continued. At night I practiced quietly, and from time to time my mother would look up and say, "That's nice, dear." Mr. Parker had given me a Three-Part Invention, and I worked on it as if it were granite. It was the most complicated piece of music I had ever played, and I learned it with a sense of loss; since I didn't know when the ax would fall, I thought it might be the last piece of music I would ever learn from Mr. Parker.

The lessons went on and nothing was said, but when I came home after them, my mother and I faced each other with division and coldness. Mr. Parker bought a kitten called Mildred to keep him company in the house. When we had our cookies and lemonade, Mildred got a saucer of milk.

At night, I was grilled by my mother as we washed the dishes. I found her sudden interest in the events of my day unnerving. She was systematic, beginning with my morning classes, ending in the afternoon. In the light of her intense focus, everything seemed wrong. Then she said, with arch sweetness, "And how is Mr. Parker, dear?"

"Fine."

"And how are the lessons going?"

"Fine."

"And how is the house now that Mrs. Parker's gone?"

"It's the same. Mr. Parker bought a kitten." As I said it, I knew it was betrayal.

---

2. **myopic** (mī·äp′ik): nearsighted.

"What kind of kitten?"

"A sort of pink one."

"What's its name?"

"It doesn't have one," I said.

One night she said, "Does Mr. Parker drink?"

"He drinks lemonade."

"I only asked because it must be so hard for him," she said in an offended voice. "He must be very sad."

"He doesn't seem all that sad to me." It was the wrong thing to say.

"I see," she said, folding the dish towel with elaborate care. "You know how I feel about this, Jane. I don't want you alone in the house with him."

"He's my *piano* teacher." I was suddenly in tears, so I ran out of the kitchen and up to my room.

She followed me up and sat on the edge of my bed while I sat at the desk, secretly crying onto the blotter.

"I only want what's best for you," she said.

"If you want what's best for me, why don't you want me to have piano lessons?"

"I *do* want you to have piano lessons, but you're growing up and it doesn't look right for you to be in a house alone with a widowed man."

"I think you're crazy."

"I don't think you understand what I'm trying to say. You're not a little girl anymore, Jane. There are privileges of childhood and privileges of adulthood, and you're in the middle. It's difficult, I know."

"You don't know. You're just trying to stop me from taking piano lessons."

She stood up. "I'm trying to protect you," she said. "What if Mr. Parker touched you? What would you do then?" She made the word "touch" sound sinister.

"You're just being mean," I said, and by this time I was crying openly. It would have fixed things to throw my arms around her, but that meant losing, and this was war.

"We'll discuss it some other time," she said, close to tears herself.

I worked on the Invention until my hands shook. When I came home, if the house was empty, I practiced in a panic, and finally, it was almost right. On Wednesday, I went to Mr. Parker's and stood at the doorway, expecting something drastic and changed, but it was all the same. There were cookies and lemonade in the solarium. Mildred took a nap on my coat. My fifteen-minute warm-up was terrible; I made mistakes in the simplest parts, in things I knew by heart. Then Mr. Parker played the lesson of the week and I tried to memorize his phrasing exactly. Before my turn came, Mr. Parker put the metronome on the floor and we watched Mildred trying to catch the arm.

I played it, and I knew it was right—I was playing music, not struggling with a lesson.

When I was finished, Mr. Parker grabbed me by the shoulders. "That's perfect! Really perfect!" he said. "A real breakthrough. These are the times that make teachers glad they teach."

We had lemonade and cookies and listened to some Palestrina motets. When I left, it was overcast, and the light was murky and green.

I walked home slowly, divided by dread and joy in equal parts. I had performed like an adult and had been congratulated by an adult, but something had been closed off. I sat under a tree and cried like a baby. He had touched me after all.

Responding to the Story

Analyzing the Story

Identifying Facts

1. Describe how Mr. Parker treats Jane. How are his piano lessons different from Mrs. Murchison's?
2. Jane's mother provides the **conflict** in this story. Explain what it is that Jane wants, and how her mother tries to block her from getting it.

Interpreting Meanings

3. Find the details in the story that suggest that Jane sees Mr. Parker, as well as the deceased Mrs. Parker, in an idealized light. For clues, look closely at the way Jane describes them, their house, and the difference between Mr. Parker and the repugnant Mrs. Murchison. Why do you think a girl like Jane so idealizes the Parkers?
4. How do you think the writer wants us to feel about Jane's mother—that is, how would you say she is **characterized**? Do you think she has an unkind, suspicious nature? Or is she really worried about what might happen to Jane? Or is she just concerned about appearances? Explain your response.
5. On page 71 Jane's mother tells her that she is "not a little girl anymore"—that she is somewhere between childhood and adulthood. What evidence in Jane's encounter with the rabbi's son suggests that she is still partly a child? Is there evidence in the story that she is also partly an adult?
6. "Mr. Parker" is a story about a girl's coming of age, about her passage into adulthood. Why does the piano lesson at the end of the story mark Jane's movement into the adult world? What do you think Jane realizes when she feels that "something has been closed off"?
7. At the end of the story, when Mr. Parker grabs Jane by the shoulders, it is merely an adult gesture of admiration, not the sinister event her mother had feared. Why do you think Jane cries about it, and why is it **ironic** that she cries like a "baby"?
8. As Jane walks home after her piano lesson, she is "divided by dread and joy." What does she dread? What brings the joy?

Writing About the Story

A Creative Response

1. **Contrasting Two Characters.** In this story, the writer establishes a sharp contrast between Mr. Parker and Mrs. Murchison. Notice how she uses contrasting but parallel images to characterize them. We are told, among other things, that Mrs. Murchison has "an asthmatic chow who was often sick on the rug"—not a terribly appealing image. Mr. Parker, on the other hand, has a kitten who naps on Jane's coat during her lesson and plays with the arm of the metronome. Of course, we all know wonderful people who have sick dogs and unpleasant people who have cute kittens. But here our emotions contradict our sense of fairness, and we get very different impressions of these characters based on the contrasting images the writer uses to describe them. Another example of contrasting imagery relates to our sense of smell; while Mr. Parker "smelled faintly of tobacco," Mrs. Murchison "smelled of bacon grease." Although readers may certainly disagree about which smell is more appealing (if either is appealing at all), nevertheless the writer clearly intends to establish a contrast between a romantic and even elegant character and a coarse, rather vulgar one. Write a paragraph in which you use contrasting but parallel images to characterize two very different people. Let your images communicate your feelings about these characters. Filling out a chart like the following one might help you develop the images.

	Character 1	Character 2
Appearance	1. 2.	1. 2.
Scent	3.	3.
Pet	4.	4.
Home	5.	5.
Clothing	6.	6.
Voice	7.	7.

A Critical Response

2. **Describing the Main Character.** Here are some adjectives that could be used to describe a person's character:

sensitive	cruel	timid
cynical	romantic	rebellious

Choose three adjectives that you think apply to Jane. Then write a brief essay in which you show how Jane displays these three traits. Support your discussion with passages from the story. Look for examples of how Jane acts, thinks, and feels, and how other characters respond to her. Open your essay with a topic sentence that uses your three adjectives.

Analyzing Language and Vocabulary

Connotations

In addition to their strict, literal meanings, most words also carry **connotations**—that is, they have strong associations, implications, and emotional overtones.

Consider this example from "Trademark," a story by the writer Jessamyn West. When a columnist for the school newspaper describes Cress Delahanty, the story's thirteen-year-old protagonist, as "the ice-blond freshman," her father gets upset about the connotations of "ice blond."

> "Ice blond! Why, Cress is nothing but a mere child."
> "A color is a color, I suppose," Mrs. Delahanty answered mildly, "regardless of age."
> "Ice blond is something more than a color," Mr. Delahanty argued, but when Mrs. Delahanty asked him to explain he could do no more than mention two or three movie stars.

The expression *ice blond* connotes someone who is glamorous, sophisticated, and cool (usually not the sort of qualities a father likes to envision in his thirteen-year-old daughter)—very different from the connotations of, say, *golden blond* or *towheaded* or *fair-haired*. When Mr. Delahanty says that "ice blond is something more than a color," he is talking about its connotations.

What feelings do the italicized words create in these passages from "Mr. Parker"? Rewrite each passage, using other descriptive words to convey completely different feelings.

1. "As a girl, [Mrs. Parker] had had *bright red hair,* which was now *the color of old leaves.* There was something *smoky and autumnal* about her: she wore *rust-colored* sweaters and *heather-colored* skirts. . . ."
2. "Every five years the house was painted *chocolate brown,* which faded gradually to the color of *weak tea.*"
3. "Its white dress was *milky* when the light shone through."
4. "Mr. Parker's hair had once been *blond,* but was graying into the color of *straw.*"
5. "When I left, it was overcast, and the light was *murky and green.*"

Reading About the Writer

Laurie Colwin (1945–1992) grew up in Chicago and Philadelphia and later lived in New York City. She is one of our most admired contemporary writers. The heroines of her stories and novels are usually sophisticated, observant young women who endure the awesome complexities of their own changing hearts. She tells their stories with an understanding, a wit, and a skill that remint the worn-out coin of the love story. Colwin's short stories have appeared in many magazines, including *The New Yorker, Redbook,* and *Mademoiselle.* "Mr. Parker" is from her first collection of stories, *Passion and Affect,* which was published in 1974. Since then she wrote two other collections: *The Lone Pilgrim* and *Another Marvelous Thing.* Colwin is the author of four novels: *Shine On, Bright and Dangerous Object; Happy All the Time; Family Happiness;* and *Goodbye Without Leaving.* Colwin also helped Isaac Bashevis Singer (see page 24) translate some of his stories from Yiddish into English.

Literature & Language

Using the Descriptive Mode in Characterization

Literary Model

In this passage from his novel *David Copperfield*, Charles Dickens describes Uriah Heep, one of the most memorable **characters** in literature. This story is narrated by its hero, David Copperfield, who at this point is still a young boy. David has arrived at Mr. Wickfield's, where he is to board while attending school. Mr. Wickfield has a law practice. The story is set in the mid-nineteenth century.

. . . I found Uriah reading a great fat book, with such demonstrative attention that his lank forefinger followed up every line as he read and made clammy tracks along the page (or so I fully believed) like a snail.

"You are working late tonight, Uriah," says I.

"Yes, Master Copperfield," says Uriah.

As I was getting on the stool opposite to talk to him more conveniently, I observed that he had not such a thing as a smile about him and that he could only widen his mouth and make two hard creases down his cheeks, one on each side, to stand for one.

"I am not doing office work, Master Copperfield," said Uriah.

"What work, then?" I asked.

"I am improving my legal knowledge, Master Copperfield," said Uriah. "I am going through Tidd's *Practice*. Oh, what a writer Mr. Tidd is, Master Copperfield!"

My stool was such a tower of observation that, as I watched him reading on again, after this rapturous exclamation, and following up the lines with his forefinger, I observed that his nostrils, which were thin and pointed, with sharp dints in them, had a singular and most uncomfortable way of expanding and contracting themselves—that they seemed to twinkle instead of his eyes, which hardly ever twinkled at all.

"I suppose you are quite a great lawyer?" I said, after looking at him for some time.

"Me, Master Copperfield?" said Uriah. "Oh, no! I'm a very umble person."

It was no fancy of mine about his hands, I observed, for he frequently ground the palms against each other as if to squeeze them dry and warm, besides often wiping them, in a stealthy way, on his pocket handkerchief.

"I am well aware that I am the umblest person going," said Uriah Heep, modestly, "let the other be where he may. My mother is likewise a very umble person. We live in an umble abode, Master Copperfield, but have much to be thankful for. My father's former calling was umble. He was a sexton."[1]

"What is he now?" I asked.

"He is a partaker of glory at present, Master Copperfield," said Uriah Heep. "But we have much to be thankful for. How much have I to be thankful for in living with Mr. Wickfield!"

I asked Uriah if he had been with Mr. Wickfield long.

"I have been with him going on four year, Master Copperfield," said Uriah, shutting up his book, after carefully marking the place where he had left off. "Since a year after my father's death. How much have I to be thankful for in that! How much have I to be thankful for in Mr. Wickfield's kind intention to give me my articles,[2] which would otherwise not lay within the umble means of mother and self!"

"Then, when your articled time is over, you'll be a regular lawyer, I suppose?" said I.

"With the blessing of Providence, Master Copperfield," returned Uriah.

"Perhaps you'll be a partner in Mr. Wickfield's business one of these days," I said, to make myself agreeable, "and it will be Wickfield and Heep, or Heep late Wickfield."

"Oh no, Master Copperfield," returned Uriah, shaking his head, "I am much too umble for that!"

—from *David Copperfield*,
Charles Dickens

---

1. **sexton:** church custodian.

2. **give me my articles:** bind me as an apprentice to learn a trade or profession.

A Note on the Descriptive Mode

Descriptive writing uses **images** to help us picture (and perhaps hear, smell, touch, and taste) a thing, a person, a place, an event, or an experience. Depending on the details chosen, descriptive writing can also create a **mood** or an **emotional effect.**

Writers use a number of descriptive techniques to create a **character.** These include the following:

1. Describing the character's **appearance** (such as Uriah's thin and pointed nostrils)
2. Describing the person's **actions** (such as Uriah's grinding his palms)
3. Describing what the character **thinks or says** (such as Uriah's repeating the fact that he is humble)
4. Describing **what others think or say** of the character (such as David's thinking that Uriah's eyes "hardly ever twinkled")
5. **Directly describing the character's qualities** as a person. (Does Dickens ever have David say directly if Uriah is admirable, repellent, devious, honest, etc.?)

Examining the Writer's Techniques

Working with a partner, use these questions to complete a chart like the one at the top of the next column.

1. How does the narrator describe Uriah's hands and fingers?
2. What **simile** describes the way the narrator imagines Uriah's fingers moving across the page?
3. How does the narrator describe Uriah's facial expression?
4. How does Uriah's enthusiasm over a thick law book make you feel about him?
5. How are Uriah's nose and nostrils described?
6. What word does Uriah repeatedly use to describe himself?
7. How does Uriah show that he, ironically, is proud of his humility?

Using the Descriptive Mode in Your Writing

1. **Using the Descriptive Mode to Create a Character.** Describe two people: one you want the reader to

Method of Characterization	Uriah Heep
Appearance	
Actions	
Thoughts and words	
Responses of others	
Direct statement of person's qualities	
Overall emotional effect of description	

trust and one you want the reader to distrust. Tell about each person's hat, eyes, and shoes. Describe how he or she orders lunch at a counter. Describe how each person behaves when asked to contribute to charity. Give each character a name that suggests his or her nature. Try to use comparisons, as Dickens does, to suggest the way you feel about each character. Before you start to write, gather your descriptive details together in a chart like the one you filled in above for the humble Uriah. Exchange your descriptions in class for evaluation.

2. **Reworking Uriah Heep.** Suppose you were Charles Dickens and you wanted the character of Uriah Heep to create a different **emotional effect.** Change Dickens's descriptive details to paint a different portrait. For example, you might change Uriah's "lank" forefinger to one that is "slender" or "elegant." Change Heep's other physical features, habits, and thoughts to make the narrator—and the reader—feel differently toward him. Exchange your description with a partner. Write down the emotional effect created by your partner's description. Is the effect achieved the one that the writer intended? Revise your own description, using your partner's response as a guide.

ANALYZING A CHARACTER

Writing Assignment

Write a four-paragraph essay in which you analyze the character of Sobel in "The First Seven Years" by Bernard Malamud (page 59). In your analysis, discuss at least two aspects of Sobel's character, and state your response to Sobel as a person.

Background

When you **analyze** anything, you look at it closely and break it up into its separate parts. To make a character analysis, you locate all the ways the writer reveals the character's nature. Then you synthesize all your material and sum up your idea of what the character is really like.

Prewriting

To gather ideas for your character analysis of Sobel, skim the story and locate every passage that refers to him. Then gather your information into a chart like the following one, which refers to Feld.

Feld in "The First Seven Years"

Summary of Character Traits
1. Practical (*too* practical; approaches Max in business-like manner; realizes when his pride must be swallowed and he must ask Sobel to return).
2. A loving father (waits up for Miriam; wants her to have a better life; wants to give her a college education).
3. Not well (two heart attacks).
4. Disappointed with his life (difficult struggle to earn a living; wanted a son; great respect for the education he doesn't have; wanted Miriam to go to college; disappointed in Miriam's refusal of Max; disappointed in Sobel as a future son-in-law).

---

5. Not perceptive (doesn't realize that Sobel and Miriam love each other; doesn't understand why Sobel reads so much, why he works for so little).

Appearance
Not mentioned.

What Character Wants
Wants to see Miriam marry a college man so that she can have a better life than he has had.

How Character Changes
Realizes that Miriam and Sobel are in love and will get married; sadly but bravely accepts his disappointment.

Key Statements About Character
1. ". . . for Feld, if anything, was a practical man." (Page 59)
2. "He had never so much as thought it consciously, but he had felt it and was afraid." (Page 65)
3. "And all his dreams for her—why he had slaved and destroyed his heart with anxiety and labor—all these dreams of a better life were dead." (Page 65)

Key Actions
1. Asks Max to go out with Miriam.
2. Asks Sobel to come back to work.

What Others Think of Character
1. Not clear in story. Miriam seems cool and remote, though she probably loves Feld.
2. Sobel has been loyal to Feld, but is angry at him.

Use the information in your chart to write a **thesis statement,** a sentence or two that sums up your idea of Sobel's character. Here is a thesis statement based on the information in the Prewriting chart:

> Malamud portrays Feld as a practical man, who mistakenly equates happiness with money and who must deal with the loss of his dream.

Writing

Now that you have your thesis statement and your chart of supporting information, you're ready to begin writing. In your first paragraph, introduce the character and include your thesis statement. Then go on to develop your thesis statement in succeeding paragraphs.

Here is a sample character analysis of Feld:

An Analysis of the Character of Feld

Feld, the shoemaker, is the central character of "The First Seven Years" by Bernard Malamud. It is Feld who sets the story's action in motion and whose thoughts we "overhear." Malamud portrays Feld as a practical man, who mistakenly equates happiness with money and who must accept the loss of his dream.

Introductory paragraph. States title and author.

Thesis statement covers three main aspects of character.

The writer states directly that Feld is practical: ". . . for Feld, if anything, was a practical man" (page 59). Although he is embarrassed in approaching Max, Feld states his case like a businessman. He is also practical when he admits that he needs Sobel—that there is "no other way" (page 64).

Topic sentence.
Cites line from story.
Supports topic sentence with three details.

Malamud clearly wants us to understand that Feld is mistaken in equating money with happiness. Because Feld has struggled all his life to earn a living, he cherishes a dream of a "better life" for Miriam. Feld is disappointed when he learns that Max is not studying to be a "professional man" but pleased when he learns that accountants make good money. Miriam rejects Max because he has no soul, because he is a materialist. We infer that she loves Sobel, who will never be rich but who definitely *has* a soul.

Topic sentence.

Supports topic sentence with specific details.

Malamud paints Feld as a disappointed man dealing with loss—the loss of his health, the loss of his dream for his daughter. I think Feld is somewhat admirable, but not entirely. He never values or understands Sobel; and though he claims to love his daughter, he does not understand her. It is *his* dream for Miriam that he must give up, and he accepts this with resignation. I think the writer wants us to see Feld as a person whose own materialistic dreams are conquered by true love.

Concluding paragraph.

Discusses response and gives reasons.

Summary of reader's response to character.

Checklist for Revision

1. Have you cited the story's title and author?
2. Have you included a thesis statement?
3. Have you discussed two aspects of the character in two separate paragraphs?
4. In your concluding paragraph, have you given your response to the character?

Theme: The Story's Meaning and Roots

When I was teaching writing, I read a student's story that was full of action—a pair of mountain climbers were about to plunge down a ravine, a skier was schussing into peril, and a killer was waiting in the valley below. Despite all this action and intrigue, I found the story both boring and infuriating to read because it was impossible to tell what the student writer meant by it. As it turned out, the student didn't know either. The story had no theme.

A story's characters and events take on significance only when we recognize what the author intended them to mean. In other words, all the elements of a good story must add up to a **theme**—some idea or insight about human life and human nature that gives meaning to the story. In fact, theme can do more than just reveal the meaning of the story. Theme can also reveal the author's whole view of life, of how the world works—or fails to work.

Suppose, for example, that a writer has a heroine work diligently at her job in the fish cannery and be rewarded by a two-dollar-an-hour raise and a trip to Vancouver. We recognize this author's world as a demanding but benign place, where human beings have some control over their destiny. But suppose another writer takes this same heroine and has her fired for her pains. As she leaves for home, she even finds that her bicycle has been stolen. We recognize in this story another kind of world—a barren world swept by cold and indifferent winds.

What Do We Mean by Theme?

The story's theme is really its roots. Theme is unseen and usually unstated, yet it is vital. It gives meaning to the story's characters and events, and at the same time it reveals the writer's own personal attitude toward the world, toward how people should behave and how they actually do behave. If we like the writer's view of the world, we may well come back for more; we may even adopt the writer's attitude as our own. But if that view of the world is one we don't accept as "true," we probably will stop reading that writer altogether.

We do not have to accept every theme. But it is important to realize that we should not simply condemn or dismiss a story because we disagree with its theme. A writer's view of the world or of human nature may be different from our own, but it may nevertheless be a worthwhile viewpoint to explore. It is always interesting to learn how other people see the world.

> " **If** we like the writer's view of the world, we may well come back for more; we may even adopt the writer's attitude as our own."

Theme is neither the story's plot (what happens) nor the story's subject (which might be boxing or prospecting for gold). Rather, theme is an *idea*; it is what the author means by everything he or she has set down. A story's theme may give us insight into some aspect of life that we have never really thought about before, or it may make us understand on an emotional level some truth that we have previously only understood on an intellectual level.

Determining a Story's Theme

Often a writer's theme cannot be stated easily or completely. (Remember that the writer has had to write the whole story to get that theme across to us.) After we have read a story, we may feel that we understand what it is about, and yet for some reason we cannot put that knowledge into words. The story has struck us as true—it has touched our emotions on some profound, wordless level—but still we cannot state the truth it has revealed to us.

The attempt to put a story's theme into words can often help us understand the story more fully—it can reveal aspects of the story that we may have ignored. It is one thing to understand *what has happened* in a story, but it is quite another thing to understand *what those events mean*. Here are some general guidelines for discovering a story's theme:

1. A theme may be stated in a single sentence, or it may require a full essay to do it justice. But we must use at least one complete sentence to state a theme. In other words, a theme must be a statement about the subject of the story, rather than a phrase such as "the rewards of old age." (Sometimes this type of phrase can be reworded to form a sentence: "Old age can be a time of great satisfaction.")

2. A theme is not the same as a moral, which is a rule of conduct. A work of serious fiction is not a sermon intended to teach us how to live better or more successful lives. One critic has said that, in getting at a story's theme, it is better to ask ourselves "What does this story *reveal*?" rather than "What does this story *teach*?" Thus, it is usually a mistake to reduce a theme (at least a serious writer's theme) to a familiar saying or cliché, such as "Crime doesn't pay" or "Waste not, want not." A theme is usually a much more complex and original revelation about life—even if it does strike us as something we have always known.

3. One of the best ways to determine a story's theme is to ask how the protagonist has changed during the course of the story. Often, what this character has learned about life is the truth the writer also wants to reveal to the reader.

4. Another good way to discover the theme of the story is to consider its title. Often (but not always), the title will hint at the meaning of the story. There may also be statements in the story itself—either dialogue spoken by one of the characters or comments made by the narrator—that point to the writer's view of the world or of human nature.

The Letter by Pierre Bonnard (c. 1906). Oil on canvas.

National Gallery of Art, Washington, D.C. Chester Dale Collection.

" **I**n getting at a story's theme, it is better to ask ourselves 'What does this story *reveal*?' rather than 'What does this story *teach*?' "

5. A theme must be expressed as a generalization about life or human nature; it should not refer to specific characters or events in the story. For example, if we were to state the theme of "The First Seven Years" (page 59), we would not begin by saying, "Feld learns that . . ." Instead, we might begin by saying, "People who have plans for their children learn that . . ."

6. This generalization about life should not be broader than is justified by the story itself. In other words, we should not claim that the writer is saying something about *all* people if the story is only revealing what is true for a certain type of person. For example, we would not want to express the theme of "Mr. Parker" (page 68) in terms of how "all parents" and "all children" behave toward one another—because the writer's insight seems to be more specifically focused.

7. A theme should explain the whole story, not just parts of it. If what we think is the theme does not apply to all the major events and characters in the story, then chances are we have not discovered its true theme.

8. There is no one correct way to state the theme of a story. If there are twenty-five students in your English class, for instance, you will have twenty-five distinct ways of putting a story's central insight into words.

> "**If** there are twenty-five students in your English class, you will have twenty-five distinct ways of putting a story's central insight into words."

The Power of Theme

In the writing class I mentioned earlier, I also read another student's story. This time it was a good story, about a girl who finds her car broken into and her stereo stolen. The girl is crazy with rage, and all she can think to do is call up an ex-boyfriend because he'll know what to do. He does. He calms her, gets the car fixed, and talks her out of her anger.

As I read, I realized that the girl is still in love with her ex-boyfriend, though he no longer is in love with her, and the story is really about *that* misfortune. In the end, the girl accepts both facts, and I realized, with all the force of sudden revelation, that the heroine has been undergoing a major growing-up experience. She has learned to accept loss. Now *that's* theme. Telling that by means of a story is about sixty times more memorable and more emotionally compelling than simply saying: "One of the lessons you must learn in growing up is how to deal with loss."

WITH ALL FLAGS FLYING

Anne Tyler

Self-Portrait Between the Clock and the Bed by Edvard Münch (1940–1942). Münch Museum, Oslo.
Oil on canvas, 58⅞″ × 47⅜″.

Weakness was what got him in the end. He had been expecting something more definite—chest pains, a stroke, arthritis—but it was only weakness that put a finish to his living alone. A numbness in his head, an airy feeling when he walked. A wateriness in his bones that made it an effort to pick up his coffee cup in the morning. He waited some days for it to go away, but it never did. And meanwhile the dust piled up in corners; the refrigerator wheezed and creaked for want of defrosting. Weeds grew around his rosebushes.

He was awake and dressed at six o'clock on a Saturday morning, with the patchwork quilt pulled up neatly over the mattress. From the kitchen cabinet he took a hunk of bread and two Fig Newtons, which he dropped into a paper bag. He was wearing a brown suit that he had bought on sale in 1944, a white T-shirt and copper-toed work boots. Those and his other set of underwear, which he put in the paper bag along with a razor, were all the clothes he took with him. Then he rolled down the top of the bag and stuck it under his arm, and stood in the middle of the kitchen, staring around him for a moment.

The house had only two rooms, but he owned it—the last scrap of the farm that he had sold off years ago. It stood in a hollow of dying trees beside a superhighway in Baltimore County. All it held was a few sticks of furniture, a change of clothes, a skillet, and a set of dishes. Also odds and ends, which disturbed him. If his inventory were complete, he would have to include six clothespins, a salt and a pepper shaker, a broken-toothed comb, a cheap ball point pen—oh, on and on, past logical numbers. Why should he be so cluttered? He was eighty-two years old. He had grown from an infant owning nothing to a family man with a wife, five children, everyday and Sun-

day china, and a thousand appurtenances, down at last to solitary old age and the bare essentials again, but not bare enough to suit him. Only what he needed surrounded him. Was it possible he needed so much?

Now he had the brown paper bag; that was all. It was the one satisfaction in a day he had been dreading for years.

He left the house without another glance, heading up the steep bank toward the superhighway. The bank was covered with small, crawling weeds planted especially by young men with scientific training in how to prevent soil erosion. Twice his knees buckled. He had to sit and rest, bracing himself against the slope of the bank. The scientific weeds, seen from close up, looked straggly and gnarled. He sifted dry earth through his fingers without thinking, concentrating only on steadying his breath and calming the twitching muscles in his legs.

Once on the superhighway, which was fairly level, he could walk for longer stretches of time. He kept his head down and his fingers clenched tight upon the paper bag, which was growing limp and damp now. Sweat rolled down the back of his neck, fell in drops from his temples. When he had been walking maybe half an hour he had to sit down again for a rest. A black motorcycle buzzed up from behind and stopped a few feet away from him. The driver was young and shabby, with hair so long that it drizzled out beneath the back of his helmet.

"Give you a lift, if you like," he said, "You going somewhere?"

"Just into Baltimore."

"Hop on."

He shifted the paper bag to the space beneath his arm, put on the white helmet he was handed, and climbed on behind the driver. For safety he took a clutch of the boy's shirt, tightly at first and then more loosely when he saw there was no danger. Except for the helmet, he was perfectly comfortable. He felt his face cooling and stiffening in the wind, his body learning to lean gracefully with the tilt of the motorcycle as it swooped from lane to lane. It was a fine way to spend his last free day.

Half an hour later they were on the outskirts of

Baltimore, stopped at the first traffic light. The boy turned his head and shouted, "Whereabouts did you plan on going?"

"I'm visiting my daughter, on Belvedere near Charles Street."

"I'll drop you off, then," the boy said. "I'm passing right by there."

The light changed, the motor roared. Now that they were in traffic, he felt more conspicuous, but not in a bad way. People in their automobiles seemed sealed in, overprotected; men in large trucks must envy the way the motorcycle looped in and out, hornetlike, stripped to the bare essentials of a motor and two wheels. By tugs at the boy's shirt and single words shouted into the wind, he directed him to his daughter's house, but he was sorry to have the ride over so quickly.

His daughter had married a salesman and lived in a plain, square stone house that the old man approved of. There were sneakers and a football in the front yard, signs of a large, happy family. A bicycle lay in the driveway. The motorcycle stopped just inches from it. "Here we are," the boy said.

"Well, I surely do thank you."

He climbed off, fearing for one second that his legs would give way beneath him and spoil everything that had gone before. But no, they held steady. He took off the helmet and handed it to the boy, who waved and roared off. It was a really magnificent roar, ear-dazzling. He turned toward the house, beaming in spite of himself, with his head feeling cool and light now that the helmet was gone. And there was his daughter on the front porch, laughing, "Daddy, what on *earth?*" she said. "Have you turned into a teeny-bopper?" Whatever that was. She came rushing down the steps to hug him—a plump, happy-looking woman in an apron. She was getting on toward fifty now. Her hands were like her mother's, swollen and veined. Gray had started dusting her hair.

"You never *told* us," she said. "Did you ride all this way on a motorcycle? Oh, why didn't you find a telephone and call? I would have come. How long can you stay for?"

"Now . . ." he said, starting toward the house. He was thinking of the best way to put it. "I came

to a decision. I won't be living alone anymore. I want to go to an old folks' home. That's what I *want*," he said, stopping on the grass so she would be sure to get it clear. "I don't want to live with you—I want an old folks' home." Then he was afraid he had worded it too strongly. "It's nice *visiting* you, of course," he said.

"Why, Daddy, you know we always asked you to come and live with us."

"I know that, but I decided on an old folks' home."

"We couldn't do that. We won't even talk about it."

"Clara, my mind is made up."

Then in the doorway a new thought hit her, and she suddenly turned around. "Are you sick?" she said. "You always said you would live alone as long as health allowed."

"I'm not up to that anymore," he said.

"What is it? Are you having some kind of pain?"

"I just decided, that's all," he said. "What I *will* rely on you for is the arrangements with the home. I know it's a trouble."

"We'll talk about that later," Clara said. And she firmed the corners of her mouth exactly the way her mother used to do when she hadn't won an argument but wasn't planning to lose it yet either.

In the kitchen he had a glass of milk, good and cold, and the hunk of bread and the two Fig Newtons from his paper bag. Clara wanted to make him a big breakfast, but there was no sense wasting what he had brought. He munched on the dry bread and washed it down with milk, meanwhile staring at the Fig Newtons, which lay on the smoothed-out bag. They were the worse for their ride—squashed and pathetic-looking, the edges worn down and crumbling. They seemed to have come from somewhere long ago and far away. "Here, now, we've got cookies I baked only yesterday," Clara said; but he said, "No, no," and ate the Fig Newtons, whose warmth on his tongue filled him with a vague, sad feeling deeper than homesickness. "In my house," he said, "I left things a little messy. I hate to ask it of you, but I didn't manage to straighten up any."

"Don't even think about it," Clara said. "I'll take out a suitcase tomorrow and clean everything up. I'll bring it all back."

"I don't want it. Take it to the poor people."

"Don't want any of it? But, Daddy——"

He didn't try explaining it to her. He finished his lunch in silence and then let her lead him upstairs to the guest room.

Clara had five boys and a girl, the oldest twenty. During the morning as they passed one by one through the house on their way to other places, they heard of his arrival and trooped up to see him. They were fine children, all of them, but it was the girl he enjoyed the most. Francie. She was only thirteen, too young yet to know how to hide what she felt. And what she felt was always about love, it seemed: whom she just loved, who she hoped loved her back. Who was just a darling. Had thirteen-year-olds been so aware of love in the old days? He didn't know and didn't care; all he had to do with Francie was sit smiling in an armchair and listen. There was a new boy in the neighborhood who walked his English sheepdog past her yard every morning, looking toward her house. Was it because of her, or did the dog just like to go that way? When he telephoned her brother Donnie, was he hoping for her to answer? And when she did answer, did he want her to talk a minute or to hand the receiver straight to Donnie? But what would she say to him, anyway? Oh, all her questions had to do with where she might find love, and everything she said made the old man wince and love her more. She left in the middle of a sentence, knocking against a doorknob as she flew from the room, an unlovable-looking tangle of blond hair and braces and scrapes and Band-Aids. After she was gone the room seemed too empty, as if she had accidentally torn part of it away in her flight.

Getting into an old folks' home was hard. Not only because of lack of good homes, high expenses, waiting lists; it was harder yet to talk his family into letting him go. His son-in-law argued with him every evening, his round, kind face anxious and questioning across the supper table. "Is it that you think you're not welcome here? You are, you know. You were one of the reasons we bought this big house." His grandchildren when they talked to him had a kind of urgency in their voices, as if they were trying to impress him with their acceptance of him. His other daughters called long distance from all across the country and begged him to come to them if he wouldn't stay with Clara. They had room, or they would make room; he had no idea what homes for the aged were like these days. To all of them he gave the same answer: "I've made my decision." He was proud of them for asking, though. All his children had turned out so well, every last one of them. They were good, strong women with happy families, and they had never given him a moment's worry. He was luckier than he had a right to be. He had felt lucky all his life, dangerously lucky, cursed by luck; it had seemed some disaster must be waiting to even things up. But the luck had held. When his wife died, it was at a late age, sparing her the pain she would have had to face, and his life had continued in its steady, reasonable pattern with no more sorrow than any other man's. His final lot was to weaken, to crumble, and to die—only a secret disaster, not the one he had been expecting.

He walked two blocks daily, fighting off the weakness. He shelled peas for Clara and mended little household articles, which gave him an excuse to sit. Nobody noticed how he arranged to climb the stairs only once a day, at bedtime. When he had empty time he chose a chair without rockers, one that would not be a symbol of age and weariness and lack of work. He rose every morning at six and stayed in his room a full hour, giving his legs enough warning to face the day ahead. Never once did he disgrace himself by falling down in front of people. He dropped nothing more important than a spoon or a fork.

Meanwhile the wheels were turning; his name was on a waiting list. Not that that meant anything, Clara said. "When it comes right down to driving you out there, I just won't let you go," she told him. "But I'm hoping you won't carry things that far. Daddy, won't you put a stop to this foolishness?"

He hardly listened. He had chosen long ago what kind of old age he would have; everyone does. Most, he thought, were weak and chose to be loved at any cost. He had seen women turn soft and sad, anxious to please, and had watched with pity and impatience their losing battles. And he had once known a school teacher, no weakling at all, who said straight out that when she grew old she would finally eat all she wanted and grow fat without worry. He admired that—a simple plan, dependent upon no one. "I'll sit in an armchair," she had said, "with a lady's magazine in my lap and a box of homemade fudge on the lampstand. I'll get as fat as I like and nobody will give a hang." The schoolteacher was thin and pale, with a kind of stooped, sloping figure that was popular at the time. He had lost track of her long ago, but he liked to think that she had kept her word. He imagined her fifty years later, cozy and fat in a puffy chair, with one hand moving constantly between her mouth and the candy plate. If she had died young or changed her mind or put off her eating till another decade, he didn't want to hear about it.

He had chosen independence. Nothing else had even occurred to him. He had lived to himself, existed on less money than his family would ever guess, raised his own vegetables, and refused all gifts but an occasional tin of coffee. And now he would sign himself into the old folks' home and enter on his own two feet, relying only on the impersonal care of nurses and cleaning women. He could have chosen to die alone of neglect, but for his daughters that would have been a burden too—a different kind of burden, much worse. He was sensible enough to see that.

Meanwhile, all he had to do was to look as busy as possible in a chair without rockers and hold fast against his family. Oh, they gave him no peace. Some of their attacks were obvious—the arguments with his son-in-law over the supper table—and some were subtle; you had to be on your guard every minute for those. Francie, for instance, asking him questions about what she called the "olden days." Inviting him to sink unnoticing into doddering reminiscence. "Did I see Granny ever? I don't remember her. Did she like me? What kind of person was she?" He stood his ground, gave monosyllabic answers. It was easier

than he had expected. For him, middle age tempted up more memories. Nowadays events had telescoped. The separate agonies and worries—the long, hard births of each of his children, the youngest daughter's chronic childhood earaches, his wife's last illness—were smoothed now into a single, summing-up sentence: He was a widowed farmer with five daughters, all married, twenty grandchildren, and three great-grandchildren. "Your grandmother was a fine woman," he told Francie; "just fine." Then he shut up.

Francie, not knowing that she had been spared, sulked and peeled a strip of sunburned skin from her nose.

Clara cried all the way to the home. She was the one who was driving; it made him nervous. One of her hands on the steering wheel held a balled-up tissue, which she had stopped using. She let tears run unchecked down her face and drove jerkily with a great deal of brake slamming and gear gnashing.

"Clara, I wish you wouldn't take on so," he told her. "There's no need to be sad over *me*."

"I'm not sad so much as mad," Clara said. "I feel like this is something you're doing *to* me, just throwing away what I give. Oh, why do you have to be so stubborn? It's still not too late to change your mind."

The old man kept silent. On his right sat Francie, chewing a thumbnail and scowling out the window, her usual self except for the unexplainable presence of her other hand in his, tight as wire. Periodically she muttered a number; she was counting red convertibles and had been for days. When she reached a hundred, the next boy she saw would be her true love.

He figured that was probably the reason she had come on this trip—a greater exposure to red convertibles.

Whatever happened to DeSotos? Didn't there used to be a car called a roadster?

They parked in the U-shaped driveway in front of the home, under the shade of a poplar tree. If he had had his way, he would have arrived by motorcycle, but he made the best of it—picked up his underwear sack from between his feet, climbed the front steps ramrod straight. They were met by

Hospital Corridor at Saint Rémy by Vincent van Gogh (1889).
Gouache and watercolor on paper, 24⅛″ × 18⅝″.

a smiling woman in blue who had to check his name on a file and ask more questions. He made sure to give all the answers himself, overriding Clara when necessary. Meanwhile Francie spun on one squeaky sneaker heel and examined the hall, a cavernous, polished square with old-fashioned parlors on either side of it. A few old people were on the plush couches, and a nurse sat idle beside a lady in a wheelchair.

They went up a creaking elevator to the second

floor and down a long, dark corridor deadened by carpeting. The lady in blue, still carrying a sheaf of files, knocked at number 213. Then she flung the door open on a narrow green room flooded with sunlight.

"Mr. Pond," she said, "this is Mr. Carpenter. I hope you'll get on well together."

Mr. Pond was one of those men who run to fat and baldness in old age. He sat in a rocking chair with a gilt-edged Bible on his knees.

"How-do," he said. "Mighty nice to meet you."

They shook hands cautiously, with the women ringing them like mothers asking their children to play nicely with each other. "Ordinarily I sleep in the bed by the window," said Mr. Pond, "but I don't hold it in much importance. You can take your pick."

"Anything will do," the old man said.

Clara was dry-eyed now. She looked frightened.

"You'd best be getting on back now," he told her. "Don't you worry about me. I'll let you know," he said, suddenly generous now that he had won, "if there is anything I need."

Clara nodded and kissed his cheek. Francie kept her face turned away, but she hugged him tightly, and then she looked up at him as she stepped back. Her eyebrows were tilted as if she were about to ask him one of her questions. Was it her the boy with the sheepdog came for? Did he care when she answered the telephone?

They left, shutting the door with a gentle click. The old man made a great business out of settling his underwear and razor in a bureau drawer, smoothing out the paper bag and folding it, placing it in the next drawer down.

"Didn't bring much," said Mr. Pond, one thumb marking his page in the Bible.

"I don't need much."

"Go on—take the bed by the window. You'll feel better after awhile."

"I *wanted* to come," the old man said.

"That there window is a front one. If you look out, you can see your folks leave."

He slid between the bed and the window and looked out. No reason not to. Clara and Francie were just climbing into the car, the sun lacquering the tops of their heads. Clara was blowing her nose with a dot of tissue.

"*Now* they cry," said Mr. Pond, although he had not risen to look out himself. "Later they'll buy themselves a milkshake to celebrate."

"I wanted to come. I made them bring me."

"And so they did. *I* didn't want to come. My son wanted to put me here—his wife was expecting. And so he did. It all works out the same in the end."

"Well, I could have stayed with one of my daughters," the old man said, "But I'm not like some I have known. Hanging around making burdens of themselves, hoping to be loved. Not me."

"If you don't care about being loved," said Mr. Pond, "how come it would bother you to be a burden?"

Then he opened the Bible again, at the place where his thumb had been all the time, and went back to reading.

The old man sat on the edge of the bed, watching the tail of Clara's car flash as sharp and hard as a jewel around the bend of the road. Then, with nobody to watch that mattered, he let his shoulders slump and eased himself out of his suit coat, which he folded over the foot of the bed. He slid his suspenders down and let them dangle at his waist. He took off his copper-toed work boots and set them on the floor neatly side by side. And although it was only noon, he lay down full-length on top of the bedspread. Whiskery lines ran across the plaster of the ceiling high above him. There was a cracking sound in the mattress when he moved; it must be covered with something waterproof.

The tiredness in his head was as vague and restless as anger; the weakness in his knees made him feel as if he had just finished some exhausting exercise. He lay watching the plaster cracks settle themselves into pictures, listening to the silent, neuter voice in his mind form the words he had grown accustomed to hearing now: Let me not give in at the end. Let me continue gracefully till the moment of my defeat. Let Lollie Simpson be alive somewhere even as I lie on my bed; let her be eating homemade fudge in an overstuffed armchair and growing fatter and fatter and fatter.

Responding to the Story

Analyzing the Story

Identifying Facts

1. As the story opens, the old man is leaving his house because he has made an important decision. What is his decision, and what are his **motives** for making it?
2. Describe how the old man makes the journey to his daughter's home. How does this incredible journey make him feel?
3. What problem, or **conflict**, is central to the story? In other words, what does the old man want, and how do his children try to block his wants? What are the children's **motives**?

Interpreting Meanings

4. How does the story's **title** relate to the old man and to what he wants? How does the motorcycle ride relate to the title?
5. At the end of the story, the old man is thinking about Lollie Simpson eating homemade fudge. What does Lollie represent to the old man? How does she relate to the title?
6. Why do you think the writer put the character of Mr. Pond in the story? What does Mr. Pond help us to understand about the **character** of the old man?
7. On page 82 we find this passage: "He had grown from an infant owning nothing to a family man with a wife, five children, everyday and Sunday china, and a thousand appurtenances, down at last to solitary old age and the bare essentials again. . . ." In summing up the old man's life this way, what point does the writer make about human existence? How would you like to have your life summed up when you are a very old person?
8. Look back over the story, and locate the passages where love is mentioned and where loving or caring actions occur. What do you think the story reveals about love and all its manifestations? State in at least one sentence the story's **theme**, as you interpret it.
9. Would you describe this story as an optimistic, "upbeat" story, or as a cynical, "downbeat" one? Explain what aspects of the story give you this impression.

Writing about the Story

A Creative Response

1. **Describing a Character.** On page 82 the writer characterizes the old man by describing his house. In a paragraph or a brief essay, characterize an old person you know by describing his or her surroundings. Be specific about naming the things the person lives with. Note how Anne Tyler names the six clothespins, a salt and a pepper shaker, a broken-toothed comb, and a cheap ball point pen.

A Critical Response

2. **Evaluating a Character's Actions.** When she drives her father to the old-age home, Clara weeps and says, "I feel like this is something you're doing *to* me, just throwing away what I give." How do you feel about the old man in this story? Do you consider him heroic for wanting to end his life "with all flags flying," or do you think he has made a serious mistake in hurting his children? In a paragraph, give your opinion about the old man's actions, and give one or two reasons *why* you feel as you do.

Analyzing Language and Vocabulary

Strong Verbs

How can you make your writing strong and vivid and inventive? One of the most influential books ever written about the art of composition gives the following advice:

> Write with nouns and verbs, not with adjectives and adverbs. The adjective hasn't been built that can pull a weak or inaccurate noun out of a tight place. This is not to disparage adjectives and adverbs; they are indispensable parts of speech. . . . In general, however, it is nouns and verbs, not their assistants, that give good writing its toughness and color.
>
> —from *The Elements of Style,*
> William Strunk, Jr., and E. B. White

In "With All Flags Flying," Anne Tyler makes particularly imaginative use of verbs. For example, in the first paragraph of the story, she says, ". . . the refrigerator wheezed and creaked for want of defrosting." Consider how diluted her description would have been if she had merely said, " . . . the refrigerator made noises for want of defrosting."

Here are some other examples of Tyler's use of tough and colorful verbs. Try rewriting each passage the way a less inventive writer might have written it. You'll have to replace the italicized verbs and perhaps add adjectives or adverbs.

1. "A black motorcycle *buzzed* up from behind and stopped a few feet away from him."
2. "The driver was young and shabby, with hair so long it *drizzled* out beneath the back of his helmet."
3. "He felt his face *cooling* and *stiffening* in the wind, his body learning to lean gracefully with the tilt of the motorcycle as it *swooped* from lane to lane."
4. "Gray had started *dusting* her hair."
5. "And she *firmed* the corners of her mouth exactly the way her mother used to do. . . ."
6. "He *munched* on the dry bread and *washed* it down with milk. . . ."
7. "Nowadays events had *telescoped*."
8. "Clara and Francie were just climbing into the car, the sun *lacquering* the tops of their heads."

Reading About the Writer

Anne Tyler (1941—   ) was born in Minneapolis, Minnesota, but grew up in Raleigh, North Carolina. She graduated from high school at the age of sixteen and from Duke University at nineteen. She then went on to Columbia University to do graduate work in Russian.

Tyler wrote her first novel at the age of twenty-two while she was looking for work in Montreal. Since then, she has written twelve novels and more than fifty stories, many of them set in Baltimore. Eudora Welty, she says, has been the strongest influence on her writing because from her she learned that "there were stories to be written about the mundane life around me."

Anne Tyler's perceptions about life and her precise, immaculate style have won her widespread praise. One critic says that she has ". . . a kind of innocence in her view of life, a sense of wonder at all the crazy things in the world, and an abiding affection for her own flaky characters."

Some of Tyler's most recent novels are *Dinner at the Homesick Restaurant; The Accidental Tourist,* which was made into a movie starring William Hurt; *Breathing Lessons,* which won the Pulitzer Prize in 1989; and *Saint Maybe.*

Focusing on Background
A Comment from the Writer

Here is an excerpt from an essay by Anne Tyler entitled "Still Just Writing," in which she examines her life as a writer:

"I think I was born with the impression that what happened in books was much more reasonable, and interesting, and *real,* in some ways, than what happened in life. I hated childhood and spent it sitting behind a book waiting for adulthood to arrive. When I ran out of books, I made up my own. At night, when I couldn't sleep, I made up stories in the dark. Most of my plots involved girls going west in covered wagons. I was truly furious that I'd been born too late to go west in a covered wagon. . . .

"I spent my adolescence planning to be an artist, not a writer. After all, books had to be about major events, and none had ever happened to me. All I knew were tobacco workers, stringing the leaves I handed them and talking up a storm. Then I found a book of Eudora Welty's short stories in the high-school library. She was writing about Edna Earle, who was so slow-witted she could sit all day just pondering how the tail of the *C* got through the loop of the *L* on the Coca-Cola sign. Why, I knew Edna Earle. You mean you could *write* about such people? I have always meant to send Eudora Welty a thank-you note, but I imagine she would find it a little strange. . . ."

—Anne Tyler

THE BET

Anton Chekhov, translated by Constance Garnett

The theme of a story reveals something about the way people act, what they value, and what they believe in. In "The Bet," the Russian writer Anton Chekhov (chek'ôf) asks us to examine our notions of freedom by taking it away from one of his main characters. There is a popular saying, "You don't know what you have until it's gone." Like love, health, or good weather, freedom is often taken for granted.

Before you read, write a few sentences in your journal about your feelings on what freedom is, and what makes life meaningful to you. As you write, remember that the theme of a story is not a moral—often, it raises more questions than it answers. How long could you survive without human companionship, or the freedom of movement? Is there such a thing as complete freedom from other people, or do individuals depend upon one another in the way that different countries do?

A biography of Anton Chekhov appears on page 612, following his play *The Brute*.

I

It was a dark autumn night. The old banker was walking up and down his study and remembering how, fifteen years before, he had given a party one autumn evening. There had been many clever men there, and there had been interesting conversations. Among other things, they had talked of capital punishment. The majority of the guests, among whom were many journalists and intellectual men, disapproved of the death penalty. They considered that form of punishment out of date, immoral, and unsuitable for Christian states.[1] In the opinion of some of them, the death penalty ought to be replaced everywhere by imprisonment for life.

"I don't agree with you," said their host, the banker. "I have not tried either the death penalty or imprisonment for life, but if one may judge *a priori*,[2] the death penalty is more moral and more humane than imprisonment for life. Capital punishment kills a man at once, but lifelong imprisonment kills him slowly. Which executioner is the more humane, he who kills you in a few minutes or he who drags the life out of you in the course of many years?"

"Both are equally immoral," observed one of the guests, "for they both have the same object—to take away life. The state is not God. It has not the right to take away what it cannot restore when it wants to."

Among the guests was a young lawyer, a young man of five-and-twenty. When he was asked his opinion, he said:

"The death sentence and the life sentence are equally immoral, but if I had to choose between the death penalty and imprisonment for life, I would certainly choose the second. To live anyhow is better than not at all."

A lively discussion arose. The banker, who was younger and more nervous in those days, was suddenly carried away by excitement; he struck the table with his fist and shouted at the young man:

"It's not true! I'll bet you two millions you wouldn't stay in solitary confinement for five years."

"If you mean that in earnest," said the young man, "I'll take the bet, but I would stay not five, but fifteen years."

---

1. **Christian states:** countries in which Christianity is the prevalent religion.
2. *a priori* (ä prē·ôr'ē): based on theory, not experience.

The House of Mystery (The Rose House)
by W. Degouve de Nuncques (1892). Oil on canvas.

Collection: State Museum Kröller-Müller,
Otterlo, The Netherlands.

"Fifteen? Done!" cried the banker. "Gentlemen, I stake two millions!"

"Agreed! You stake your millions and I stake my freedom!" said the young man.

And this wild, senseless bet was carried out! The banker, spoiled and frivolous, with millions beyond his reckoning, was delighted at the bet. At supper he made fun of the young man, and said:

"Think better of it, young man, while there is still time. To me two millions are a trifle, but you are losing three or four of the best years of your life. I say three or four, because you won't stay longer. Don't forget either, you unhappy man, that voluntary confinement is a great deal harder to bear than compulsory. The thought that you have the right to step out in liberty at any moment will poison your whole existence in prison. I am sorry for you."

And now the banker, walking to and fro, remembered all this, and asked himself: "What was the object of that bet? What is the good of that man's losing fifteen years of his life and my throwing away two millions? Can it prove that the death penalty is better or worse than imprisonment for life? No, no. It was all nonsensical and meaningless. On my part it was the caprice of a pampered man, and on his part simple greed for money. . . ."

Then he remembered what followed that evening. It was decided that the young man should spend the years of his captivity under the strictest supervision in one of the lodges in the banker's garden. It was agreed that for fifteen years he should not be free to cross the threshold of the lodge, to see human beings, to hear the human voice, or to receive letters and newspapers. He was allowed to have a musical instrument and books, and was allowed to write letters, to drink wine, and to smoke. By the terms of the agreement, the only relations he could have with the outer world were by a little window made purposely for that object. He might have anything he wanted—books, music, wine, and so on—in any quantity he desired, by writing an order, but could receive them only through the window. The agreement provided for every detail and every trifle that would make his imprisonment strictly solitary, and bound the young man to stay there *exactly* fifteen years, beginning from twelve o'clock of November 14, 1870, and ending at twelve o'clock of November 14, 1885. The slightest attempt on his part to break the conditions, if only two minutes before the end, released the banker from the obligation to pay him two millions.

For the first year of his confinement, as far as one could judge from his brief notes, the prisoner suffered severely from loneliness and depression. The sounds of the piano could be heard continually day and night from his lodge. He refused wine and tobacco. Wine, he wrote, excites the desires, and desires are the worst foes of the prisoner; and besides, nothing could be more dreary than drinking good wine and seeing no one. And tobacco spoiled the air of his room. In the first year the books he sent for were principally of a light character; novels with a complicated love plot, sensational and fantastic stories, and so on.

In the second year the piano was silent in the lodge, and the prisoner asked only for the classics. In the fifth year music was audible again, and the prisoner asked for wine. Those who watched him through the window said that all that year he spent doing nothing but eating and drinking and lying on his bed, frequently yawning and talking angrily to himself. He did not read books. Sometimes at night he would sit down to write; he would spend hours writing, and in the morning tear up all that he had written. More than once he could be heard crying.

In the second half of the sixth year the prisoner began zealously studying languages, philosophy, and history. He threw himself eagerly into these studies—so much so that the banker had enough to do to get him the books he ordered. In the course of four years, some six hundred volumes were procured at his request. It was during this period that the banker received the following letter from his prisoner:

"My dear Jailer, I write you these lines in six languages. Show them to people who know the languages. Let them read them. If they find not one mistake, I implore you to fire a shot in the garden. That shot will show me that my efforts have not been thrown away. The geniuses of all ages and of all lands speak different languages,

Portrait of Jacques-Emile Blanche
by John Singer Sargent.

Musée des Beaux Arts, Rouen.

but the same flame burns in them all. Oh, if you only knew what unearthly happiness my soul feels now from being able to understand them!" The prisoner's desire was fulfilled. The banker ordered two shots to be fired in the garden.

Then, after the tenth year, the prisoner sat immovably at the table and read nothing but the Gospel. It seemed strange to the banker that a man who in four years had mastered six hundred learned volumes should waste nearly a year over one thin book easy of comprehension. Theology and histories of religion followed the Gospels.

In the last two years of his confinement, the prisoner read an immense quantity of books quite indiscriminately. At one time he was busy with the natural sciences, then he would ask for Byron[3] or Shakespeare. There were notes in which he demanded at the same time books on chemistry, and a manual of medicine, and a novel, and some treatise on philosophy or theology. His reading suggested a man swimming in the sea among the wreckage of his ship, and trying to save his life by greedily clutching first at one spar and then at another.

II

The old banker remembered all this, and thought: "Tomorrow at twelve o'clock he will regain his freedom. By our agreement I ought to pay him two millions. If I do pay him, it is all over with me: I shall be utterly ruined."

Fifteen years before, his millions had been beyond his reckoning; now he was afraid to ask himself which were greater, his debts or his assets. Desperate gambling on the Stock Exchange, wild speculation, and the excitability which he could not get over even in advancing years, had by degrees led to the decline of his fortune, and the proud, fearless, self-confident millionaire had become a banker of middling rank, trembling at every rise and fall in his investments. "Cursed bet!" muttered the old man, clutching his head in despair. "Why didn't the man die? He is only forty now. He will take my last penny from me, he will marry, will enjoy life, will gamble on the Exchange; while I shall look at him with envy like a beggar, and hear from him every day the same sentence: 'I am indebted to you for the happiness of my life, let me help you!' No, it is too much! The one means of being saved from bankruptcy and disgrace is the death of that man!"

It struck three o'clock. The banker listened; everyone was asleep in the house, and nothing could be heard outside but the rustling of the chilled trees. Trying to make no noise, he took from a fireproof safe the key of the door which had not been opened for fifteen years, put on his overcoat, and went out of the house.

It was dark and cold in the garden. Rain was falling. A damp, cutting wind was racing about the garden, howling and giving the trees no rest. The banker strained his eyes, but could see neither the earth nor the white statues, nor the lodge, nor the trees. Going to the spot where the lodge stood, he twice called the watchman. No answer followed. Evidently the watchman had sought shelter from the weather, and was now asleep somewhere either in the kitchen or in the greenhouse.

"If I had the pluck to carry out my intention," thought the old man, "suspicion would fall first upon the watchman."

He felt in the darkness for the steps and the door, and went into the entry of the lodge. Then he groped his way into a little passage and lighted a match. There was not a soul there. There was a bedstead with no bedding on it, and in the corner there was a dark cast-iron stove. The seals on the door leading to the prisoner's rooms were intact.

When the match went out the old man, trembling with emotion, peeped through the little window. A candle was burning dimly in the prisoner's room. He was sitting at the table. Nothing could be seen but his back, the hair on his head, and his hands. Open books were lying on the table, on the two easy chairs, and on the carpet near the table.

Five minutes passed and the prisoner did not once stir. Fifteen years' imprisonment had taught him to sit still. The banker tapped at the window with his finger, and the prisoner made no movement whatever in response. Then the banker cau-

---

3. **Byron:** George Gordon, Lord Byron (1788–1824), English Romantic poet.

tiously broke the seals off the door and put the key in the keyhole. The rusty lock gave a grating sound and the door creaked. The banker expected to hear at once footsteps and a cry of astonishment, but three minutes passed and it was as quiet as ever in the room. He made up his mind to go in.

At the table a man unlike ordinary people was sitting motionless. He was a skeleton with the skin drawn tight over his bones, with long curls like a woman's, and a shaggy beard. His face was yellow with an earthy tint in it, his cheeks were hollow, his back long and narrow, and the hand on which his shaggy head was propped was so thin and delicate that it was dreadful to look at it. His hair was already streaked with silver, and seeing his emaciated, aged-looking face, no one would have believed that he was only forty. He was asleep. . . . In front of his bowed head there lay on the table a sheet of paper, on which there was something written in fine handwriting.

"Poor creature!" thought the banker, "he is asleep and most likely dreaming of the millions. And I have only to take this half-dead man, throw him on the bed, stifle him a little with the pillow, and the most conscientious expert would find no sign of a violent death. But let us first read what he has written here. . . ."

The banker took the page from the table and read as follows:

"Tomorrow at twelve o'clock I regain my freedom and the right to associate with other men, but before I leave this room and see the sunshine, I think it necessary to say a few words to you. With a clear conscience I tell you, as before God, who beholds me, that I despise freedom and life and health, and all that in your books is called the good things of the world.

"For fifteen years I have been intently studying earthly life. It is true I have not seen the earth nor men, but in your books I have drunk fragrant wine, I have sung songs, I have hunted stags and wild boars in the forests, have loved women. . . . Beauties as ethereal as clouds, created by the magic of your poets and geniuses, have visited me at night, and have whispered in my ears wonderful tales that have set my brain in a whirl. In your books I have climbed to the peaks of Elburz and Mont Blanc,[4] and from there I have seen the sun rise and have watched it at evening flood the sky, the ocean, and the mountaintops with gold and crimson. I have watched from there the lightning flashing over my head and cleaving the storm clouds. I have seen green forests, fields, rivers, lakes, towns. I have heard the singing of the sirens,[5] and the strains of the shepherds' pipes; I have touched the wings of comely devils who flew down to converse with me of God. . . . In your books I have flung myself into the bottomless pit, performed miracles, slain, burned towns, preached new religions, conquered whole kingdoms. . . .

"Your books have given me wisdom. All that the unresting thought of man has created in the ages is compressed into a small compass in my brain. I know that I am wiser than all of you.

"And I despise your books, I despise wisdom and the blessings of this world. It is all worthless, fleeting, illusory, and deceptive, like a mirage. You may be proud, wise, and fine, but death will wipe you off the face of the earth as though you were no more than mice burrowing under the floor, and your posterity, your history, your immortal geniuses will burn or freeze together with the earthly globe.

"You have lost your reason and taken the wrong path. You have taken lies for truth, and hideousness for beauty. You would marvel if, owing to strange events of some sorts, frogs and lizards suddenly grew on apple and orange trees instead of fruit, or if roses began to smell like a sweating horse; so I marvel at you who exchange heaven for earth. I don't want to understand you.

"To prove to you in action how I despise all that you live by, I renounce the two millions of which I once dreamed as of paradise and which now I despise. To deprive myself of the right to the money I shall go out from here five minutes before the time fixed, and so break the compact. . . ."

---

4. **Elburz** (el·bo͞orz′) **and Mont Blanc** (môn blän′): Elburz is a mountain range in northern Iran; Mont Blanc, in France, is the highest peak in the Alps.
5. **sirens:** in Greek mythology, sea nymphs whose beautiful voices lured sailors to their island; the sailors, enchanted, wasted away and died.

When the banker had read this he laid the page on the table, kissed the strange man on the head, and went out of the lodge, weeping. At no other time, even when he had lost heavily on the Stock Exchange, had he felt so great a contempt for himself. When he got home he lay on his bed, but his tears and emotion kept him for hours from sleeping.

Next morning the watchmen ran in with pale faces, and told him they had seen the man who lived in the lodge climb out of the window into the garden, go to the gate, and disappear. The banker went at once with the servants to the lodge and made sure of the flight of his prisoner. To avoid arousing unnecessary talk, he took from the table the writing in which the millions were renounced, and when he got home locked it up in the fireproof safe.

Responding to the Story

Analyzing the Story

Identifying Facts

1. What is the topic of the lively debate at the banker's party?
2. Why does the young lawyer agree to give up his freedom for fifteen years?
3. How does the writer's use of **flashback** at the beginning of the story add to your understanding of the **plot?**

Interpreting Meanings

4. As the banker looks back on the events that led up to the bet, he believes that he acted on "the caprice of a pampered man." What explanation does he give for the lawyer's **motivation** for accepting the bet? Do you agree with this interpretation? Why or why not?
5. There are many levels of **conflict** in "The Bet." For example, there is **external conflict** between people. (The banker's guests argue about capital punishment.) Conflicts also rage within the two main characters. Why does the banker feel self-contempt at the end of the story? What **internal conflict** do you think the lawyer experiences?
6. Chekhov lists the books the lawyer reads while he is imprisoned. Does this reading matter reveal something about the transformation the lawyer is undergoing? Discuss.
7. In your opinion, who wins the bet?
8. Think about the change that has taken place in the lawyer. How would you interpret the story's **theme**—the insight it reveals about basic human needs? Do you think it expresses a truth about life as you know it? Compare your responses with those of your classmates.
9. Do you believe there is such a thing as "internal freedom"? (This is the kind of freedom the lawyer comes to know as he rises above his circumstances, though he is imprisoned.) Think of people in the news who have been imprisoned for their beliefs. In your opinion, are they "freer" than their jailers? If so, how?
10. How do you feel about the question of life imprisonment versus capital punishment? Do you believe, as the lawyer does, that "to live anyhow is better than not at all"? Or do you agree with the banker that capital punishment is more humane?

Writing About the Story

A Creative Response

1. **Writing a Letter.** By the terms of the agreement, the young lawyer is allowed to write letters from his prison. Imagine that you are the lawyer in the first few days after the bet takes effect. It is extremely quiet in the lodge, and many thoughts, like summer lightning, keep you awake. "Is my freedom worth two millions?" you ask yourself. You remember your best friend, who still lives "on the outside." You decide to write a letter to him or her. As clearly as possible, try to describe your feelings and thoughts about your crucial decision.

A Critical Response

2. **Analyzing a Character.** Read, once again, the passages describing the lawyer's solitary confinement in the lodge. The description begins with the words, "For the first year of his confinement. . . ." Write a brief essay describing the ways in which the lawyer's character changes across time. Describe not only his changes in mood, but also the gradual change in his outlook on life. In your last paragraph, give your response to the conclusions the lawyer arrives at, as expressed in his letter.

A 1977 production of Anton Chekhov's *The Three Sisters* at the Brooklyn Academy of Music, New York.

BOYS AND GIRLS

Alice Munro

Have you ever resented the fact that somebody expected you to act a certain way simply because you were a girl or because you were a boy? Do you think there are any differences in personality or ability between the sexes? If so, do you think we are born with these differences, or are they forced upon us by society and its expectations?

Before you begin this story, think about your answers to these questions. After you have finished reading, see if this writer has reinforced, challenged, or even changed your ideas about boys and girls.

The story takes place in rural Canada.

My father was a fox farmer. That is, he raised silver foxes, in pens; and in the fall and early winter, when their fur was prime, he killed them and skinned them and sold their pelts to the Hudson's Bay Company or the Montreal Fur Traders. These companies supplied us with heroic calendars to hang, one on each side of the kitchen door. Against a background of cold blue sky and black pine forests and treacherous northern rivers, plumed adventurers planted the flags of England or of France; magnificent savages bent their backs to the portage.

For several weeks before Christmas, my father worked after supper in the cellar of our house. The cellar was whitewashed, and lit by a hundred-watt bulb over the worktable. My brother Laird and I sat on the top step and watched. My father removed the pelt inside out from the body of the fox, which looked surprisingly small, mean, and ratlike, deprived of its arrogant weight of fur. The naked, slippery bodies were collected in a sack and buried at the dump. One time the hired man, Henry Bailey, had taken a swipe at me with this sack, saying, "Christmas present!" My mother thought that was not funny. In fact she disliked the whole pelting operation—that was what the killing, skinning, and preparation of the furs was called—and wished it did not have to take place in the house. There was the smell. After the pelt had been stretched inside out on a long board, my father scraped away delicately, removing the little clotted webs of blood vessels, the bubbles of fat; the smell of blood and animal fat, with the strong primitive odor of the fox itself, penetrated all parts of the house. I found it reassuringly seasonal, like the smell of oranges and pine needles.

Henry Bailey suffered from bronchial troubles. He would cough and cough until his narrow face turned scarlet, and his light blue, derisive eyes filled up with tears; then he took the lid off the stove and, standing well back, shot out a great clot of phlegm—hsss—straight into the heart of the flames. We admired him for this performance and for his ability to make his stomach growl at will and for his laughter, which was full of high whistlings and gurglings and involved the whole faulty machinery of his chest. It was sometimes hard to tell what he was laughing at and always possible that it might be us.

After we had been sent to bed, we could still smell fox and still hear Henry's laugh, but these things, reminders of the warm, safe, brightly lit downstairs world, seemed lost and diminished, floating on the stale, cold air upstairs. We were afraid at night in the winter. We were not afraid of *outside,* though this was the time of year when snowdrifts curled around our house like sleeping whales and the wind harassed us all night, coming up from the buried fields, the frozen swamp, with its old bugbear chorus of threats and misery. We were afraid of *inside,* the room where we slept. At this time the upstairs of our house was not finished. A brick chimney went up one wall. In the middle of the floor was a square hole, with a

American Dreams by Miriam Schapiro (1977–1980).
Acrylic and fabric on canvas.

Collection of Lynn Plotkin.
Courtesy of Bernice Steinbaum Gallery, New York.

wooden railing around it; that was where the stairs came up. On the other side of the stairwell were the things that nobody had any use for anymore— a soldiery roll of linoleum, standing on end; a wicker baby carriage; a fern basket; china jugs and basins with cracks in them; a picture of the Battle of Balaclava, very sad to look at. I had told Laird, as soon as he was old enough to understand such things, that bats and skeletons lived over

there; whenever a man escaped from the county jail, twenty miles away, I imagined that he had somehow let himself in the window and was hiding behind the linoleum. But we had rules to keep us safe. When the light was on, we were safe as long as we did not step off the square of worn carpet which defined our bedroom space; when the light was off, no place was safe but the beds them- selves. I had to turn out the light kneeling on the end of my bed and stretching as far as I could to reach the cord.

In the dark we lay on our beds, our narrow life rafts, and fixed our eyes on the faint light coming up the stairwell, and sang songs. Laird sang "Jingle Bells," which he would sing anytime, whether it was Christmas or not, and I sang "Danny Boy." I loved the sound of my own voice, frail and supplicating, rising in the dark. We could make out the tall frosted shapes of the windows now, gloomy and white. When I came to the part, *When I am dead, as dead I well may be*—a fit of shivering caused not by the cold sheets but by pleasurable emotion almost silenced me. *You'll kneel and say, an Ave there for me*—What was an Ave? Every day I forgot to find out.

Laird went straight from singing to sleep. I could hear his long, satisfied, bubbly breaths. Now for the time that remained to me, the most perfectly private and perhaps the best time of the whole day, I arranged myself tightly under the covers and went on with one of the stories I was telling myself from night to night. These stories were about myself, when I had grown a little older; they took place in a world that was recognizably mine, yet one that presented opportunities for courage, boldness, and self-sacrifice, as mine never did. I rescued people from a bombed building (it discouraged me that the real war had gone on so far away from Jubilee). I shot two rabid wolves who were menacing the schoolyard (the teachers cowered terrified at my back). I rode a fine horse spiritedly down the main street of Jubilee, acknowledging the townspeople's gratitude for some yet-to-be-worked-out piece of heroism (nobody ever rode a horse there, except King Billy in the Orangemen's Day parade). There was always riding and shooting in these stories, though I had only been on a horse twice—bareback because we did not own a saddle—and the second time I had slid right around and dropped under the horse's feet; it had stepped placidly over me. I really was learning to shoot, but I could not hit anything yet, not even tin cans on fence posts.

Alive, the foxes inhabited a world my father made for them. It was surrounded by a high guard fence, like a medieval town, with a gate that was padlocked at night. Along the streets of this town were ranged large, sturdy pens. Each of them had a real door that a man could go through, a wooden ramp along the wire for the foxes to run up and down on, and a kennel—something like a clothes chest with airholes—where they slept and stayed in winter and had their young. There were feeding and watering dishes attached to the wire in such a way that they could be emptied and cleaned from the outside. The dishes were made of old tin cans, and the ramps and kennels, of odds and ends of old lumber. Everything was tidy and ingenious; my father was tirelessly inventive, and his favorite book in the world was *Robinson Crusoe*. He had fitted a tin drum on a wheelbarrow, for bringing water down to the pens. This was my job in summer, when the foxes had to have water twice a day. Between nine and ten o'clock in the morning, and again after supper, I filled the drum at the pump and trundled it down through the barnyard to the pens, where I parked it and filled my watering can and went along the streets. Laird came too, with his little cream and green gardening can, filled too full and knocking against his legs and slopping water on his canvas shoes. I had the real watering can, my father's, though I could only carry it three-quarters full.

The foxes all had names, which were printed on a tin plate and hung beside their doors. They were not named when they were born, but when they survived the first year's pelting and were added to the breeding stock. Those my father had named were called names like Prince, Bob, Wally, and Betty. Those I had named were called Star or Turk or Maureen or Diana. Laird named one Maud after a hired girl we had when he was little, one Harold after a boy at school, and one Mexico, he did not say why.

Naming them did not make pets out of them, or anything like it. Nobody but my father ever went into the pens, and he had twice had blood poisoning from bites. When I was bringing them their water, they prowled up and down on the paths they had made inside their pens, barking seldom—they saved that for nighttime, when they might get up a chorus of community frenzy—but always watching me, their eyes burning, clear gold, in their pointed, malevolent faces. They were beautiful for their delicate legs and heavy, aristocratic tails and the bright fur sprinkled on dark down their backs—which gave them their name—but especially for their faces, drawn exquisitely sharp in pure hostility, and their golden eyes.

Besides carrying water I helped my father when he cut the long grass and the lamb's quarter and flowering money-musk that grew between the pens. He cut with the scythe and I raked into piles. Then he took pitchfork and threw fresh-cut grass all over the top of the pens, to keep the foxes cooler and shade their coats, which were browned by too much sun. My father did not talk to me unless it was about the job we were doing. In this he was quite different from my mother, who if she was feeling cheerful, would tell me all sorts of things—the name of a dog she had had when she was a little girl, the names of boys she had gone out with later on when she was grown up, and what certain dresses of hers had looked like—she could not imagine now what had become of them. Whatever thoughts and stories my father had were private, and I was shy of him and would never ask him questions. Nevertheless I worked willingly under his eyes, and with a feeling of pride. One time a feed salesman came down into the pens to talk to him, and my father said, "Like to have you meet my new hired man." I turned away and raked furiously, red in the face with pleasure.

"Could of fooled me," said the salesman. "I thought it was only a girl."

After the grass was cut, it seemed suddenly much later in the year. I walked on stubble in the earlier evening, aware of the reddening skies, the entering silences, of fall. When I wheeled the tank out of the gate and put the padlock on, it was almost dark. One night at this time I saw my mother and father standing talking on the little rise of ground we called the gangway, in front of the barn. My father had just come from the meat-house; he had his stiff bloody apron on and a pile of cut-up meat in his hand.

It was an odd thing to see my mother down at the barn. She did not often come out of the house unless it was to do something—hang out the wash or dig potatoes in the garden. She looked out of place, with her bare lumpy legs not touched by the sun, her apron still on and damp across the stomach from the supper dishes. Her hair was tied up in a kerchief, wisps of it falling out. She would tie her hair up like this in the morning, saying she did not have time to do it properly, and it would stay tied up all day. It was true, too; she really did not have time. These days our back porch was piled with baskets of peaches and grapes and pears, bought in town, and onions and tomatoes and cucumbers grown at home, all waiting to be made into jelly and jam and preserves, pickles, and chili sauce. In the kitchen there was a fire in the stove all day, jars clinked in boiling water; sometimes a cheesecloth bag was strung on a pole between two chairs, straining blue-black grape pulp for jelly. I was given jobs to do, and I would sit at the table peeling peaches that had been soaked in the hot water or cutting up onions, my eyes smarting and streaming. As soon as I was done, I ran out of the house, trying to get out of earshot before my mother thought of what she wanted me to do next. I hated the hot, dark kitchen in summer, the green blinds and the fly-papers, the same old oilcloth table and wavy mirror and bumpy linoleum. My mother was too tired and preoccupied to talk to me; she had no heart to tell about the Normal School Graduation Dance; sweat trickled over her face, and she was always counting under her breath, pointing at jars, dumping cups of sugar. It seemed to me that work in the house was endless, dreary, and peculiarly depressing; work done out-of-doors, and in my father's service, was ritualistically important.

I wheeled the tank up to the barn, where it was kept, and I heard my mother saying, "Wait till Laird gets a little bigger; then you'll have a real help."

What my father said I did not hear. I was pleased by the way he stood listening, politely as he would to a salesman or a stranger, but with an air of wanting to get on with his real work. I felt my mother had no business down here and I wanted him to feel the same way. What did she mean about Laird? He was no help to anybody. Where was he now? Swinging himself sick on the swing, going around in circles, or trying to catch caterpillars. He never once stayed with me till I was finished.

"And then I can use her more in the house," I heard my mother say. She had a dead-quiet, regretful way of talking about me that always made me uneasy. "I just get my back turned and she runs off. It's not like I had a girl in the family at all."

I went and sat on a feed bag in the corner of the barn, not wanting to appear when this conversation was going on. My mother, I felt, was not to be trusted. She was kinder than my father and more easily fooled, but you could not depend on her, and the real reasons for the things she said and did were not to be known. She loved me, and she sat up late at night making a dress of the difficult style I wanted, for me to wear when school started, but she was also my enemy. She was always plotting. She was plotting now to get me to stay in the house more, although she knew I hated it (*because* she knew I hated it) and keep me from working for my father. It seemed to me she would do this simply out of perversity, and to try her power. It did not occur to me that she could be lonely or jealous. No grown-up could be; they were too fortunate. I sat and kicked my heels monotonously against a feed bag, raising dust, and did not come out till she was gone.

At any rate, I did not expect my father to pay any attention to what was said. Who could imagine Laird doing my work—Laird remembering the padlock and cleaning out the watering-dishes with a leaf on the end of a stick, or even wheeling the tank without it tumbling over? It showed how little my mother knew about the way things really were.

I have forgotten to say what the foxes were fed. My father's bloody apron reminded me. They were fed horsemeat. At this time most farmers still kept horses, and when a horse got too old to work or broke a leg or got down and would not get up, as they sometimes did, the owner would call my father, and he and Henry went out to the farm in the truck. Usually they shot and butchered the horse there, paying the farmer from five to twelve dollars. If they had already too much meat on hand, they would bring the horse back alive and keep it for a few days or weeks in our stable, until the meat was needed. After the war the farmers were buying tractors and gradually getting rid of horses altogether, so it sometimes happened that we got a good healthy horse that there was just no use for any more. If this happened in the winter, we might keep the horse in our stable till spring, for we had plenty of hay, and if there was a lot of snow—and the plow did not always get our road cleared—it was convenient to be able to go to town with a horse and cutter.

The winter I was eleven years old we had two horses in the stable. We did not know what names they had had before, so we called them Mack and Flora. Mack was an old black workhorse, sooty and indifferent. Flora was a sorrel mare, a driver. We took them both out in the cutter. Mack was slow and easy to handle. Flora was given to fits of violent alarm, veering at cars and even at other horses, but we loved her speed and high-stepping, her general air of gallantry and abandon. On Saturdays we went down to the stable and as soon as we opened the door on its cozy, animal-smelling darkness, Flora threw up her head, rolled her eyes, whinnied despairingly, and pulled herself through a crisis of nerves on the spot. It was not safe to go into her stall; she would kick.

This winter also I began to hear a great deal more on the theme my mother had sounded when she had been talking in front of the barn. I no longer felt safe. It seemed that in the minds of the people around me there was a steady undercurrent of thought, not to be deflected, on this one subject. The word *girl* had formerly seemed to me innocent and unburdened, like the word *child;* now it appeared that it was no such thing. A girl was not, as I had supposed, simply what I was; it was what I had to become. It was a definition, always touched with emphasis, with reproach and disappointment. Also it was a joke on me. Once Laird and I were fighting, and for the first time ever I had to use all my strength against him; even so, he caught and pinned my arm for a moment, really hurting me. Henry saw this and laughed, saying, "Oh, that there Laird's gonna show you, one of these days!" Laird was getting a lot bigger. But I was getting bigger too.

My grandmother came to stay with us for a few weeks and I heard other things. "Girls don't slam doors like that." "Girls keep their knees together when they sit down." And worse still, when I asked some questions, "That's none of girls' business." I continued to slam the doors and sit as awkwardly as possible, thinking that by such measures I kept myself free.

When spring came, the horses were let out in the barnyard. Mack stood against the barn wall trying to scratch his neck and haunches, but Flora trotted up and down and reared at the fences, clattering her hooves against the rails. Snowdrifts dwindled quickly, revealing the hard gray and brown earth, the familiar rise and fall of the ground, plain and bare after the fantastic landscape of winter. There was a great feeling of opening out, of release. We just wore rubbers now, over our shoes; our feet felt ridiculously light. One Saturday we went out to the stable and found all the doors open, letting in the unaccustomed sunlight and fresh air. Henry was there, just idling around looking at his collection of calendars, which were tacked up behind the stalls in a part of the stable my mother had probably never seen.

"Come to say goodbye to your old friend Mack?" Henry said. "Here, you give him a taste of oats." He poured some oats into Laird's cupped hands and Laird went to feed Mack. Mack's teeth were in bad shape. He ate very slowly, patiently shifting the oats around in his mouth, trying to find a stump of a molar to grind it on. "Poor old Mack," said Henry mournfully. "When a horse's teeth's gone, he's gone. That's about the way."

"Are you going to shoot him today?" I said. Mack and Flora had been in the stable so long I had almost forgotten they were going to be shot.

Henry didn't answer me. Instead he started to sing in a high, trembly, mocking-sorrowful voice, *Oh, there's no more work for poor Uncle Ned, he's gone where the good folks go.* Mack's thick, blackish tongue worked diligently at Laird's hand. I went out before the song was ended and sat down on the gangway.

I had never seen them shoot a horse, but I knew where it was done. Last summer Laird and I had come upon a horse's entrails before they were buried. We had thought it was a big black snake, coiled up in the sun. That was around in the field that ran up beside the barn. I thought that if we went inside the barn and found a wide crack or a knothole to look through, we would be able to see them do it. It was not something I wanted to see;

just the same, if a thing really happened, it was better to see it and know.

My father came down from the house, carrying the gun.

"What are you doing here?" he said.

"Nothing."

"Go on up and play around the house."

He sent Laird out of the stable. I said to Laird, "Do you want to see them shoot Mack?" and without waiting for an answer led him around to the front door of the barn, opened it carefully, and went in. "Be quiet or they'll hear us," I said. We could hear Henry and my father talking in the stable, then the heavy, shuffling steps of Mack being backed out of his stall.

In the loft it was cold and dark. Thin, crisscrossed beams of sunlight fell through the cracks. The hay was low. It was a rolling country, hills and hollows, slipping under our feet. About four feet up was a beam going around the walls. We piled hay up in one corner and I boosted Laird up and hoisted myself. The beam was not very wide; we crept along it with our hands flat on the barn walls. There were plenty of knotholes, and I found one that gave me the view I wanted—a corner of the barnyard, the gate, part of the field. Laird did not have a knothole and began to complain.

I showed him a widened crack between two boards. "Be quiet and wait. If they hear you, you'll get us in trouble."

My father came in sight carrying the gun. Henry was leading Mack by the halter. He dropped it and took out his cigarette papers and tobacco; he rolled cigarettes for my father and himself. While this was going on, Mack nosed around in the old, dead grass along the fence. Then my father opened the gate and they took Mack through. Henry led Mack away from the path to a patch of ground, and they talked together, not loud enough for us to hear. Mack again began searching for a mouthful of fresh grass, which was not to be found. My father walked away in a straight line and stopped short at a distance which seemed to suit him. Henry was walking away from Mack too, but sideways, still negligently holding on to the halter. My father raised the gun and Mack looked up as if he had noticed something and my father shot him.

Mack did not collapse at once but swayed,

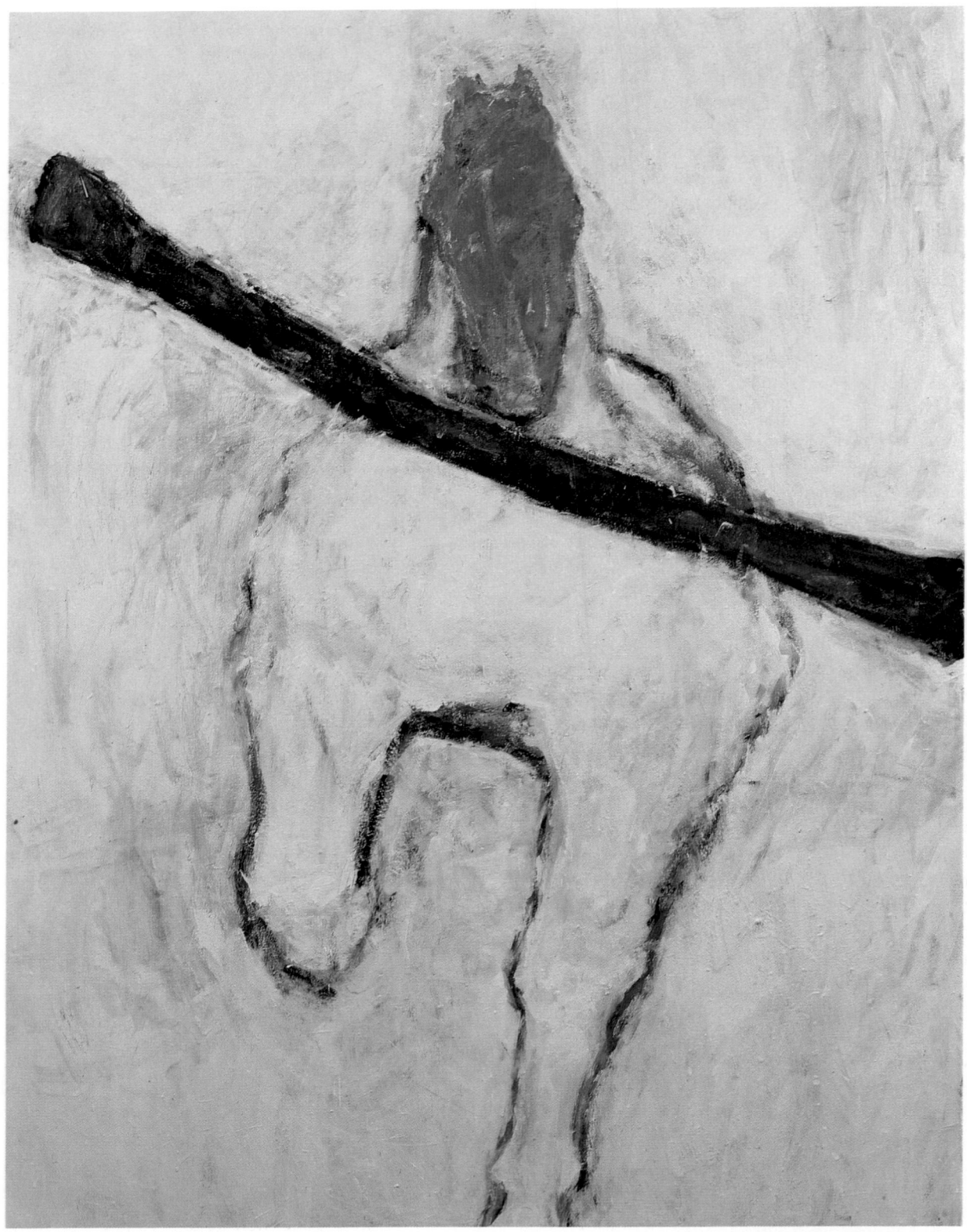

Pontiac by Susan Rothenberg (1979). Acrylic and flashe.

Collection Miani Johnson, New York.

lurched sideways and fell, first on his side; then he rolled over on his back and, amazingly, kicked his legs for a few seconds in the air. At this Henry laughed, as if Mack had done a trick for him. Laird, who had drawn a long, groaning breath of surprise when the shot was fired, said out loud, "He's not dead." And it seemed to me it might be true. But his legs stopped, he rolled on his side again, his muscles quivered and sank. The two men walked over and looked at him in a business-like way; they bent down and examined his fore-head where the bullet had gone in, and now I saw his blood on the brown grass.

"Now they just skin him and cut him up," I said. "Let's go." My legs were a little shaky, and I jumped gratefully down into the hay. "Now you've seen how they shoot a horse," I said in a congratulatory way, as if I had seen it many times before. "Let's see if any barn cat's had kittens in the hay." Laird jumped. He seemed young and obedient again. Suddenly I remembered how, when he was little, I had brought him into the barn and told him to climb the ladder to the top beam. That was in the spring, too, when the hay was low. I had done it out of a need for excitement, a desire for something to happen so that I could tell about it. He was wearing a little bulky brown and white checked coat, made down from one of mine. He went all the way up, just as I told him, and sat down on the top beam with the hay far below him on one side, and the barn floor and some old machinery on the other. Then I ran screaming to my father, "Laird's up on the top beam!" My father came, my mother came, my father went up the ladder, talking very quietly, and brought Laird down under his arm, at which my mother leaned against the ladder and began to cry. They said to me, "Why weren't you watching him?" but no-body ever knew the truth. Laird did not know enough to tell. But whenever I saw the brown and white checked coat hanging in the closet or at the bottom of the ragbag, which was where it ended up, I felt a weight in my stomach, the sadness of unexorcised guilt.

I looked at Laird, who did not even remember this, and I did not like the look on his thin, winter-pale face. His expression was not frightened or upset, but remote, concentrating. "Listen," I

said, in an unusually bright and friendly voice, "you aren't going to tell, are you?"

"No," he said absently.

"Promise."

"Promise," he said. I grabbed the hand behind his back to make sure he was not crossing his fingers. Even so, he might have a nightmare; it might come out that way. I decided I had better work hard to get all thoughts of what he had seen out of his mind—which, it seemed to me, could not hold very many things at a time. I got some money I had saved and that afternoon we went into Jubilee and saw a show, with Judy Canova, at which we both laughed a great deal. After that I thought it would be all right.

Two weeks later I knew they were going to shoot Flora. I knew from the night before, when I heard my mother ask if the hay was holding out all right, and my father said, "Well, after tomor-row there'll just be the cow, and we should be able to put her out to grass in another week." So I knew it was Flora's turn in the morning.

This time I didn't think of watching it. That was something to see just one time. I had not thought about it very often since, but sometimes when I was busy, working at school, or standing in front of the mirror combing my hair and wondering if I would be pretty when I grew up, the whole scene would flash into my mind: I would see the easy, practiced way my father raised the gun and hear Henry laughing when Mack kicked his legs in the air. I did not have any great feeling of horror and opposition, such as a city child might have had; I was too used to seeing the death of animals as a necessity by which we lived. Yet I felt a little ashamed, and there was a new wariness, a sense of holding-off, in my attitude to my father and his work.

It was a fine day, and we were going around the yard picking up tree branches that had been torn off in winter storms. This was something we had been told to do, and also we wanted to use them to make a teepee. We heard Flora whinny, and then my father's voice and Henry's shouting, and we ran down to the barnyard to see what was going on.

The stable door was open. Henry had just brought Flora out, and she had broken away from him. She was running free in the barnyard, from one end to the other. We climbed up on the fence. It was exciting to see her running, whinnying, going up on her hind legs, prancing and threatening like a horse in a Western movie, an unbroken ranch horse, though she was just an old driver, an old sorrel mare. My father and Henry ran after her and tried to grab the dangling halter. They tried to work her into a corner, and they had almost succeeded when she made a run between them, wild-eyed, and disappeared around the corner of the barn. We heard the rails clatter down as she got over the fence, and Henry yelled, "She's into the field now!"

That meant she was in the long L-shaped field that ran up by the house. If she got around the center, heading towards the lane, the gate was open; the truck had been driven into the field this morning. My father shouted to me, because I was on the other side of the fence, nearest the lane, "Go shut the gate!"

I could run very fast. I ran across the garden, past the tree where our swing was hung, and jumped across a ditch into the lane. There was the open gate. She had not got out; I could not see her up on the road; she must have run to the other end of the field. The gate was heavy. I lifted it out of the gravel and carried it across the roadway. I had it halfway across when she came in sight, galloping straight towards me. There was just time to get the chain on. Laird came scrambling through the ditch to help me.

Instead of shutting the gate, I opened it as wide as I could. I did not make any decision to do this; it was just what I did. Flora never slowed down; she galloped straight past me, and Laird jumped up and down, yelling, "Shut it, shut it!" even after it was too late. My father and Henry appeared in the field a moment too late to see what I had done. They only saw Flora heading for the township road. They would think I had not got there in time.

They did not waste any time asking about it. They went back to the barn and got the gun and the knives they used and put these in the truck; then they turned the truck around and came bouncing up the field toward us. Laird called to them, "Let me go too, let me go too!" and Henry

stopped the truck and they took him in. I shut the gate after they were all gone.

I supposed Laird would tell. I wondered what would happen to me. I had never disobeyed my father before, and I could not understand why I had done it. Flora would not really get away. They would catch up with her in the truck. Or if they did not catch her this morning, somebody would see her and telephone us this afternoon or tomorrow. There was no wild country here for her to run to, only farms. What was more, my father had paid for her, we needed the meat to feed the foxes, we needed the foxes to make our living. All I had done was make more work for my father, who worked hard enough already. And when my father found out about it, he was not going to trust me anymore; he would know that I was not entirely on his side. I was on Flora's side, and that made me no use to anybody, not even to her. Just the same, I did not regret it; when she came running at me and I held the gate open, that was the only thing I could do.

I went back to the house, and my mother said, "What's all the commotion?" I told her that Flora had kicked down the fence and got away. "Your poor father," she said, "now he'll have to go chasing over the countryside. Well, there isn't any use planning dinner before one." She put up the ironing board. I wanted to tell her, but thought better of it and went upstairs and sat on my bed.

Lately I had been trying to make my part of the room fancy, spreading the bed with old lace curtains and fixing myself a dressing table with some leftovers of cretonne for a skirt. I planned to put up some kind of barricade between my bed and Laird's, to keep my section separate from his. In the sunlight, the lace curtains were just dusty rags. We did not sing at night anymore. One night when I was singing Laird said, "You sound silly," and I went right on, but the next night I did not start. There was not so much need to, anyway; we were no longer afraid. We knew it was just old furniture over there, old jumble and confusion. We did not keep to the rules. I still stayed awake after Laird was asleep and told myself stories, but even in these stories something different was happening; mysterious alterations took place. A story might start off in the old way, with a spectacular danger, a fire or wild animals, and for a while I might rescue people; then things would change around, and instead, somebody would be rescuing me. It might be a boy from our class at school or even Mr. Campbell, our teacher, who tickled girls under the arms. And at this point the story concerned itself at great length with what I looked like—how long my hair was and what kind of dress I had on; by the time I had these details worked out, the real excitement of the story was lost.

It was later than one o'clock when the truck came back. The tarpaulin was over the back, which meant there was meat in it. My mother had to heat dinner up all over again. Henry and my father had changed from their bloody overalls into ordinary working overalls in the barn, and they washed their arms and necks and faces at the sink and splashed water on their hair and combed it. Laird lifted his arm to show off a streak of blood. "We shot old Flora," he said, "and cut her up in fifty pieces."

"Well I don't want to hear about it," my mother said. "And don't come to my table like that."

My father made him go and wash the blood off.

We sat down and my father said grace and Henry pasted his chewing gum on the end of his fork, the way he always did; when he took it off, he would have us admire the pattern. We began to pass the bowls of steaming, overcooked vegetables. Laird looked across the table at me and said proudly, distinctly, "Anyway it was her fault Flora got away."

"What?" my father said.

"She could of shut the gate and she didn't. She just open' it up and Flora run out."

"Is that right?" my father said.

Everybody at the table was looking at me. I nodded, swallowing food with great difficulty. To my shame, tears flooded my eyes.

My father made a curt sound of disgust. "What did you do that for?"

I did not answer. I put down my fork and waited to be sent from the table, still not looking up.

But this did not happen. For some time nobody said anything, then Laird said matter-of-factly, "She's crying."

"Never mind," my father said. He spoke with resignation, even good humor, the words which absolved and dismissed me for good. "She's only a girl," he said.

I didn't protest that, even in my heart. Maybe it was true.

Responding to the Story

Analyzing the Story

Identifying Facts

1. In the second paragraph of the story, what contrast do you discover between the narrator and her mother?
2. Describe how the narrator feels about helping her father with his work. How does she feel about helping her mother?
3. The **conflict** in this story arises when the narrator overhears her mother complaining about her to her father. Why is her mother frustrated and disappointed with her? Why does the narrator feel that her mother is her "enemy?"

4. How does the narrator resist the pressure put on her to act like a girl? Why does she resist?

Interpreting Meanings

5. How does the salesman's conversation with the narrator's father (page 101) **foreshadow** the change that will occur in her relationship to the world of men?
6. After the narrator watches her father shoot Mack, how does her attitude to his work begin to change? What other changes does she begin to experience as well: in the nature of her daydreams, in her relationship with Laird, in her feelings about her bedroom?

7. The two horses, Flora and Mack, are completely different from one another in temperament. What details in the story suggest that, in many respects, the narrator resembles—and even identifies with—Flora? What do you think the narrator means when she says, "I was on Flora's side. . . ." (page 106)?

8. Why do you think the narrator decides to let Flora escape, even though she knows that she is only delaying the inevitable? Do you think her action is primarily a rejection of the male world of brutality and death—or is it a statement in favor of freedom? Explain your interpretation.

9. How would you state the **theme** of this story—the major idea that all the events seem to point toward? Do you accept this theme as true, or do you have arguments with it? Explain.

10. How did you feel at the end of the story when the narrator didn't protest, even in her heart, against her father's dismissal of her as "only a girl"? Were you disappointed in her, or did you understand her feelings? Explain your response to the ending of the story.

Writing About the Story

A Creative Response

1. **Writing a Different Ending.** Write a different ending to "Boys and Girls"—one in which the narrator *does* protest against her father's rejection. If she voices this protest, what does she say to defend herself? If she protests only in her heart, what does she feel?

A Critical Response

2. **Supporting a Topic Sentence.** *Many of the images and events in "Boys and Girls" have to do with the idea of freedom—or the lack of it.* Develop this topic sentence in a paragraph in which you use specific details from the story to support your main idea. In particular, consider the following questions: How does the narrator seem to define freedom? In her limited world, who is free and who is not? What images of confinement and release does the story contain? How do you think the concept of freedom relates to the theme of the story?

3. **Expressing an Opinion.** In life as you know it, are the worlds of boys and girls (or of men and women) as distinct and cut off from one another

as they are in this story? Do you think that parents today expect their children to assume such rigid roles? Or do you think it is possible for a girl to share her father's work and for a boy to share his mother's work? Write a paragraph explaining your opinion on these questions.

Analyzing Language and Vocabulary

Connotations

On page 102 the narrator makes a startling discovery. For the first time in her life, she realizes that a familiar word has levels of meaning that she had not been aware of before.

The word *girl* had formerly seemed to me innocent and unburdened, like the word *child;* now it appeared that it was no such thing. A girl was not, as I had supposed, simply what I was; it was what I had to become. It was a definition, always touched with emphasis, with reproach and disappointment.

What the narrator discovers is that even the simplest word can come burdened with emotional overtones, or **connotations,** that go well beyond its **denotation,** or literal definition. For example, the narrator learns that to most people other than herself, the word *girl* carries with it a whole set of assumptions and standards of behavior that she would never find mentioned in the dictionary.

Some words, like *home* and *death,* have more emotional overtones than other words (and some words, like *it* and *then,* have no connotative power at all). Here are some passages from the story that use words with strong connotations. Answer the questions following each passage.

1. "My father removed the pelt inside out from the body of the fox, which looked surprisingly small, mean, and ratlike, deprived of its arrogant weight of fur."

    a. What are the connotations of "ratlike"? How would our feelings about the fox be different if it had been described as "kittenlike"?

    b. What are the connotations of "arrogant"? How would we feel if the fox had been described as having a "proud weight of fur"?

2. "My mother . . . disliked the whole pelting operation—that was what the killing, skinning, and preparation of the furs was called—and wished it did not have to take place in the house."

a. What is the difference, in emotional terms, between calling something the "pelting operation" and calling it the "killing, skinning, and preparation of the furs"?

b. Which expression do you think a fox farmer would normally use to describe the job? Why?

3. ". . . the smell of blood and animal fat, with the strong primitive odor of the fox itself, penetrated all parts of the house. I found it reassuringly seasonal, like the smell of oranges and pine needles."

a. What words reveal the narrator's feelings about the smell of the fox?

b. Would we normally associate the smell she is describing with "the smell of oranges and pine needles"?

c. How might the narrator have described this smell if she had been disgusted by it?

4. "[The foxes] were beautiful for their delicate legs and heavy, aristocratic tails and the bright fur sprinkled on dark down their backs . . . but especially for their faces, drawn exquisitely sharp in pure hostility, and their golden eyes."

a. What mixed emotions does this description make you feel about the foxes? Which words account for your different feelings?

b. Suggest a different attitude toward the foxes by finding words to replace "delicate," "aristocratic," "bright fur," "exquisitely sharp," and "golden eyes."

5. "I hated the hot, dark kitchen in summer, the green blinds and the flypapers, the same old oilcloth table and wavy mirror and bumpy linoleum. . . . It seemed to me that work in the house was endless, dreary, and peculiarly depressing."

a. What words in the narrator's description of the kitchen make it and everything associated with it seem dreary and depressing?

b. How would you describe a kitchen that was cheerful and cozy? Could such a kitchen look exactly the same as the narrator's?

Reading About the Writer

Alice Munro (1931—   ) is a Canadian writer who grew up in rural Ontario and lived for many years in British Columbia. Munro has been writing fiction since her early twenties. Her stories explore the tensions and terrors that underlie commonplace lives. Her heroines are usually sensitive girls or women who discover the uneasiness of adolescence, the tension that can exist within families or between neighbors, the despair of confronting a life of closed-off possibilities, the emptiness of material goals, or the impermanence of human relationships. Munro's stories frequently appear in *The New Yorker.* "Boys and Girls" is from her first collection of stories, *Dance of the Happy Shades,* which won Canada's highest literary prize, the Governor-General's Award for Fiction. Her second book, the much-acclaimed novel *Lives of Girls and Women,* was followed by several collections of short stories, including *The Progress of Love* and *Friend of My Youth.* Munro has been called one of the foremost contemporary short-story writers.

Focusing on Background
A Comment from the Writer

Here is what Alice Munro told a *New York Times* interviewer about why she writes short stories rather than novels:

"I never intended to be a short-story writer. I started writing them because I didn't have time to write anything else—I had three children. And then I got used to writing stories, so I saw my material that way, and now I don't think I'll ever write a novel. I don't really understand a novel. I don't understand where the excitement is supposed to come in a novel, and I do in a story. There's a kind of tension that if I'm getting a story right I can feel right away, and I don't feel that when I try to write a novel. I kind of want a moment that's explosive, and I want everything gathered into that."

—Alice Munro

Combining Sentences

Literary Model

How do writers capture and hold our attention? Sentence structure can play a large part in creating **suspense** and in making our reading experience a pleasure, rather than a struggle. Here is a short short story by a contemporary Italian writer. Notice how he opens his first sentence with a phrase that invites you into an exotic world. Read the story aloud to hear the rhythm of its sentences. Watch particularly for the way the writer alternates short sentences with longer ones. Notice also how dialogue brings the action to life.

The Walls of Anagoor

Deep inside Tibet, a native guide offered to accompany me, if by chance I wanted to see the walls of the city of Anagoor. I looked at the map, but there was no city of Anagoor. It wasn't even mentioned in the tourist guidebooks, which are usually so rich in detail. I said, "What sort of city can this be if it isn't indicated on the maps?" The native guide, whose name was Magalon, answered, "It is a great city, very wealthy and powerful, yet it is not indicated on any maps because our Ruler ignores it, or pretends to ignore it. It acts as it will and does not obey. It lives for itself alone, and not even the King's ministers can enter it. It has no commerce with any other country near or far. It is closed. It has existed for centuries within the perimeter of its solid walls. And the fact that no one has ever left it—does not this perhaps signify that whoever lives there is happy?"

"But the maps," I insisted, "do not record any city by the name of Anagoor, a fact which suggests that it may be one of the many legends of this country. The entire thing is probably the result of the mirages created by the reflections in the desert, nothing more."

"It is advisable for us to depart two hours before dawn," said Magalon, as if he hadn't heard me. "With your car, my lord, we shall arrive within sight of Anagoor near noon. I shall come to pick you up at three in the morning."

"A city like the one you describe would be recorded on the maps with a double circle, its name printed in bold letters. Yet I find no reference at all to a city by the name of Anagoor, which evidently does not exist. I shall be ready at three, Magalon."

At three in the morning, with our headlights burning, we departed and headed roughly in a southerly direction over the desert trails. While I smoked one cigarette after another, trying to warm myself, I saw the horizon on my left brighten and at once the sun appeared, already beating on the desert until everywhere it was hot and shimmering. The heat was so intense that all round one could see lakes and marshes reflecting the contours of the rocks with precision, yet in reality there was no water, not even a bucketful, only sand and incandescent stones.

But the car continued to run very efficiently, and precisely at 11:37 Magalon, who sat beside me, said, "Look, sir," and then I saw the walls of the city which stretched for many kilometers. They were a yellowish color, twenty to thirty meters high, uninterrupted, surmounted at intervals by turrets.

As I drew closer, I noted that at various points, very close to the walls, there were encampments of all kinds, ranging from poor and ordinary tents to those of rich noblemen, which were shaped like pavilions and topped with banners.

"Who are they?" I asked, and Magalon explained: "They are the people who hope to enter the city, and so they pitch their tents before the gates."

"Ah, then there are gates?"

"There is a multitude of gates, perhaps more than a hundred, large as well as small ones. But the perimeter of the city is so vast that a considerable distance stretches between each gate."

"And these gates—when do they open?"

"The gates are almost never opened. Yet it is said that a few of them will be opened. Tonight, or tomorrow, or in three months, or fifty years, one never knows: This is precisely the great secret of the city of Anagoor."

So here we are. We stopped in front of a gate which seemed made of solid iron. Many people were waiting there: emaciated Bedouins[1], beggars, veiled women, monks, warriors armed to the teeth, even a prince with his small personal court. Every so often someone with a mallet knocked on the gate, which resounded at each blow.

"They knock," said the guide, "so that the people of Anagoor, hearing the blows, will come to open the gate. In fact, the general opinion is that if one does not knock, no one will ever open the gate."

A doubt crossed my mind: "But is it certain, then, that someone lives beyond the walls? Could not the city be extinct at this point?"

Magalon smiled: "Everyone has the same thought when they first come here. At one time I myself suspected that no one lived within the walls any longer. But there is evidence to the contrary. On certain evenings, when the light is favorable, one can perceive trails of smoke rising from the city toward the sky, as from so many censers.[2] It is a sign that men live inside there, that they light fires and cook their meals. And then there is an even more persuasive fact: Some time ago one of the gates was opened."

"When?"

"To be honest, the date is uncertain. Some people say a month to a month and a half ago; others maintain, however, that the incident occurred much earlier, that it is two, three, even four years old. Someone actually assigns it to the time when the sultan Ahm-er-Ehrgun reigned."

"And when was the reign of Ahm-er-Ehrgun?"

"About three centuries ago. . . . But you are most fortunate, my lord. . . . Look: Even though it is midday and the air is burning, the smoke appears."

Notwithstanding the heat, a sudden excitement had spread through the heterogeneous[3] encampment. Everyone had left the tents and they were now pointing to the two quivering coils of gray smoke rising in the motionless air beyond the edge of the walls. I didn't understand a word of the agitated voices which merged into a confused roar. Yet the enthusiasm was obvious. It seemed as if those two scanty trails of smoke might have been the most marvelous things in creation, as if they promised the onlookers that happiness was close at hand. This reaction seemed exaggerated to me for several reasons.

First of all, the appearance of the smoke did not in fact signify any greater likelihood that a gate might be opened. Therefore, there was no sensible reason for exaltation.

Second, such a great uproar, if heard inside the walls (as was probable), would have dissuaded the inhabitants from opening the gates, rather than encouraged them—assuming, of course, that the uproar had any effect at all.

Third, the curls of smoke, in themselves, did not even demonstrate that Anagoor was inhabited. In fact, could they not be the result of an accidental fire due to the torrid sun? But there was an even more probable hypothesis: They were fires lit by plunderers who entered through some secret opening in the walls to sack the dead and uninhabited city. "It is most strange," I thought, "that apart from the smoke, no other sign of life had been noted in Anagoor: There were never any voices, or music, or the howling of dogs, or sentinels, or curious people on the edge of the walls. It is most strange."

Then I said, "Tell me, Magalon, when the gate you mentioned was opened, how many people managed to enter?"

"Only one," said Magalon.

"And what about the others? Were they driven back?"

"There were no others. The gate that opened was one of the smallest, and it was neglected by the pilgrims. That day no one was waiting there. Toward evening a traveler arrived and knocked. He did not

---

1. **Bedouins** (bedˈoo · winz): wandering Arabs of the desert.
2. **censers:** ornamental vessels used for burning incense during religious ceremonies.
3. **heterogeneous** (hetˈər · ōˊ jēˊ nē · əs): composed of diverse elements.

know what the city of Anagoor might be, nor did he have any particular expectations about what he would find when he entered. He asked only for refuge that night. He did not know anything at all; he was there by sheer chance. Perhaps for this reason alone they opened the gate for him."

As for myself, I have waited nearly twenty-four years, camped outside the walls. But the gate has not been opened. And now I am about to return to my country. The pilgrims waiting at the walls watch my preparations and shake their heads.

  "Ah, friend, how hasty you are!" they say. "What is a little patience? You expect too much from life."

—Dino Buzzati,
translated by Lawrence Venuti

A Grammar Note

One of the characteristics of immature writing is the use of many simple, subject-first sentences. Mature writers use a variety of more sophisticated sentences to show the relationships among ideas and to create a pleasing rhythm for the reader. (For examples of the different types of sentences, see *Grammar, Usage, and Mechanics: A Reference Guide,* page 1011.)

Examining the Writer's Style

Work with a partner to study the way Buzzati and his translator have combined ideas to avoid a choppy and repetitive style.

1. Reduce the following **compound-complex sentence** to as many **simple sentences** as you can:

   As I drew closer, I noted that at various points, very close to the walls, there were encampments of all kinds, ranging from poor and ordinary tents to those of rich noblemen, which were shaped like pavilions and topped with banners.

   Compare your reduction with your partner's. Did both of you come up with the same number of simple sentences? Can Buzzati's sentence be reduced even further?

2. Find two other passages from the story in which a series of related ideas have been combined into one long, sophisticated sentence. Reduce each of these sentences to a series of simple sentences. Read the simple sentences aloud. Note how they contrast in rhythm with Buzzati's sentences.

3. Find examples of simple sentences in the story, paying special attention to the next-to-last paragraph. Do the simple sentences usually come one after the other, in a long series, or are they interspersed with longer, more complicated sentences?

4. Can you revise the next-to-last paragraph, making it into one long compound-complex sentence?

5. English has such flexibility that a passage can be written in a number of ways and still be effective. Rewrite the fifth paragraph of the story (beginning "At three in the morning"), joining sentences and sentence parts in ways different from those in the original. You may want to use a short simple sentence or two for effect. Be sure to compare your versions in class.

6. What do you think are the most important sentences in this mysterious story? Are they long or short?

Combining Sentences in Your Writing

Extending the Story. Write a sequel to this story in which the narrator is admitted into the walled city. Continue writing from the point of view of the same narrator, who speaks as "I."

1. Begin by imagining what the narrator will find behind the walls of the mysterious city. Freewrite, listing words and images as they come into your mind. Will the narrator be pleased or horrified by what he discovers? Will he want to stay forever or escape as soon as possible?

2. As you write your second draft, be aware of your sentence structure. Combine ideas into the type of mature sentences characteristic of the rational and reliable narrator of "The Walls of Anagoor." Use occasional short, punchy sentences for variety and emphasis.

3. Pay particular attention to your first and final sentences. The first sentence should grab your reader's attention (notice how Buzzati at once places us "deep inside Tibet"); the last should be a satisfying "clincher" sentence.

MAKING GENERALIZATIONS AND STATING A THEME

Writing Assignment

Write a two-paragraph essay in which you first state the theme of "With All Flags Flying" by Anne Tyler (page 81) and then discuss your response to that theme.

Background

A **generalization** makes a general or broad statement about a number of specific facts, statistics, events, etc. For example, "All teen-agers are careless drivers" is an example of a generalization. In making a generalization, we leap from **specific experiences** or **observations** ("I saw three accidents involving teen-agers last month") to a **universal statement**—one that often begins with a word such as *all, every, some, many,* or *no* ("All teen-agers are careless drivers").

The trouble with generalizations, of course, is that they're not always true. Some generalizations are completely false. "Cows can fly" is clearly a **false generalization.** A **hasty generalization** is one that is based on insufficient evidence. Just because you have observed something once or twice, you can't say that it is always true. "All teen-agers are careless drivers" is a hasty generalization.

Some of the following statements are generalizations, and some are not. Identify each generalization, and then decide whether it is possible to prove that the generalization is true or false. (Propose at least one means by which it might be proved.)

1. Shakespeare wrote the world's greatest plays.
2. Most movies present a false picture of life.
3. *Home Alone* was a popular movie.
4. Most modern fiction is depressing.
5. Most high school students prefer short stories to poetry.
6. All literature is about conflict.

Theme as Generalization. The **theme** of a short story is usually expressed as a generalization—a general statement about life and human nature that the writer reveals through the action of the story. No two readers will state a story's theme in exactly the same way, so there is no single correct statement of a theme. Remember that a story's theme is *not* a summary of the plot. In stating the theme, you should not mention the specific events or characters in the story. Compare, for example, the following statements of subject, plot, and theme for "Mr. Parker," page 68.

1. **Subject.** A girl's coming of age
2. **Plot Summary.** A girl struggles with her mother, who feels it is improper for her to be alone with her piano teacher, a recent widower. The mother wants the girl to stop her lessons, but the girl resists. Sensing that her piano lessons will soon end, the girl practices her lesson more seriously than ever before and performs expertly. In congratulating her, Mr. Parker treats the girl like an adult for the first time. The girl responds by weeping.
3. **Theme.** For some young people, being treated as an adult for the first time can be both a painful and a moving experience.

In a statement of theme, don't refer to the specific characters in the story. Instead of saying "The girl is finally treated as an adult," generalize to "For some young people, being treated as an adult . . ." Also be sure to *qualify,* or limit, your generalization appropriately. Qualifying words like *some, many, may, probably, sometimes,* and *often* make a generalization more likely to be true.

Evaluating a Statement of Theme. Once you've stated the writer's theme as a generalization about life and people, you should **evaluate** it in two ways. First, think about whether your statement adequately accounts for all the major events in the story. If not, revise it until you think it does. Second, you need to think about your own response to the theme. Do you agree with the story's theme? Why or why not?

Consider the following general statements about the theme of "Boys and Girls" (page 98). Discuss which (if any) generalization best expresses what you think is the story's theme. Then tell why you think the others don't work. If you think that no generalization in this list adequately expresses the story's theme, write one of your own.

1. Boys and girls—men and women—have different life work to do, and growing up involves acceptance of our roles in life.
2. As young people grow up, they must learn to act against actions and attitudes they see as wrong.
3. Young people are often in conflict with their parents, but the real cause of this conflict is the young person's need to become independent.
4. Boys are stronger than girls physically as well as emotionally; girls are more emotional and so are the "weaker" sex.
5. Boys and girls—men and women—should not be forced into set roles. Every person is an individual who should have the freedom to choose his or her own life's work.

Prewriting

In this writing assignment, you are to discuss the theme of "With All Flags Flying" (page 81) and your response to that theme. Reread the story, and answer the following questions.

1. What is the writer's **purpose**? (Not all stories have a theme. Some are meant merely to entertain. A story has a theme if the writer is trying to reveal some serious idea about life, some truth about human beings and the way we behave.)
2. What does the action of the story reveal about life or people? What is its **central insight**?
3. Does the writer state the theme **directly** somewhere in the story? If so, where? Or is the theme **implied**?
4. Does the **title** of the story have special significance? (Some titles do not.)
5. Try writing several possible statements of the story's **theme**. (Remember that there is no one correct way of stating a theme.)
6. Do your statements of theme take into account the whole story—all its events and characters—and not just part of it?
7. Decide what your **response** is to the theme. Do you think it is a valid theme, one that expresses a truth about life as you know it? Why or why not?

Writing

Begin your first paragraph with an introductory sentence that identifies the story and writer and briefly states the story's subject. Then state what you think is the story's theme. In your second paragraph, tell how you responded to the story and to its theme. The following essay is one reader's response to Alice Munro's "Boys and Girls":

The Theme of "Boys and Girls"

The narrator of "Boys and Girls" by Alice Munro is a young girl who tells us what she thinks and feels about her parents and her brother, and their life on a fox farm. The events of this story seem to show us how some young people may not like the stereotyped sex roles that say that girls should do certain work and boys should do certain work. But in the process of growing up, they do come to accept these roles. The men and women in this story are essentially quite different—not only in their work, but also in the way they feel and think. The narrator tells us this

Mentions title, author, and subject.

Expresses story's theme in three sentences.

Exercises in Critical Thinking and Writing/*cont.*

directly: "My father did not talk to me unless it was about the job we were doing. In this he was quite different from my mother, who if she was feeling cheerful, would tell me all sorts of things—the name of a dog she had had when she was a little girl, the names of boys she had gone out with later on when she was grown up, and what certain dresses of hers had looked like . . ." (page 101).

I think this story is very interesting because it made me think. For instance, I liked it when the girl let the horse Flora go free, but in another sense it was a useless act of defiance because the horse would be caught sooner or later. I disagree with parts of the story's theme, or I think it applies only to people in certain areas. I think the idea of sexual stereotypes for boys and girls—for men and women—has changed during the last twenty years. Maybe it's not true in rural areas, but in cities and towns, anyway, women are no longer confined to the kitchen, as the mother is in this story. And girls are not usually told that the kitchen is their destiny. Many women do the same jobs as men today. Also, I'm sure that many boys today would have been disgusted at the bloody job of pelting foxes and would have let the horse go free. I think the story is controversial, but it is a true picture of how a girl grew up in the time and place that Alice Munro is writing about.

Cites quotation from the story to support preceding point.

Expresses reader's response.

Gives example (reason).

Evaluates story's theme.

Checklist for Revision

1. Have you cited the story's title and author?
2. Have you included a sentence or two citing the story's subject?
3. Have you expressed as clearly and accurately as you can what you think the story's theme is?
4. Have you included your response to the theme and given reasons why you feel this way?
5. If you have quoted directly from the story, have you checked the quotation for accuracy, used quotation marks, and cited the page on which the quotation appears?
6. Have you checked: Spelling? Punctuation? Capitalization? Sentence structure? Paragraph organization?

Point of View and Tone: The Story's Voice

Point of view—the vantage point from which a writer tells a story—has a more important effect on us than you might imagine.

The Omniscient Point of View

The traditional vantage point for storytelling, the one we are probably most familiar with, is the **omniscient point of view.** *Omniscient* means "all-knowing." The omniscient narrator is a godlike observer who knows everything that is going on in the story and who can see into each character's heart and mind. This storyteller is outside the story's action altogether.

> Once upon a time, in a mountainous country called Gulp, there lived a plump princess who wanted to be thinner. She knew that Alfred, the troubadour, would not sing beneath her window until she had lost twenty pounds. Actually, Alfred was willing to settle for ten.

The omniscient narrator can tell us as much—or as little—as the writer of the story permits. This narrator may tell us what all—or only some—of the characters are thinking, feeling, and observing. This narrator may comment on the meaning of the story or make asides about the story's characters or events.

The First-Person Point of View

At the very opposite extreme from the omniscient point of view lies the **first-person point of view.** In stories told in the first-person, an "I" tells the story. This "I" also participates in the action (though, depending on the story, in varying degrees of importance). Unlike the omniscient point of view, which can keep us at a distance from the action, the first-person point of view draws us directly into the story. When we hear the first-person narrator speak, we feel as if we are listening to a friend telling his or her own story, or as if we are reading someone's letters or diary.

> I am a princess from a small country in the Alps called Gulp. Every morning I step on my scale and get hopelessly depressed. How could I have allowed myself (Me! A princess!) to have gotten so fat? Now don't think I want to lose weight because of some *man*. That's not the case at all.

> " **W**hen we hear the first-person narrator speak, we feel as if we are listening to a friend telling his or her own story, or as if we are reading someone's letters or diary."

This first-person point of view sees only what the "I" character can see, hears only what the "I" character can hear, knows only what the "I" character can know—and tells us only what the "I" character chooses to tell. Consequently, we must always keep in mind that a first-person narrator may or may not be objective or reliable or honest—or even terribly perceptive about what's going on in the story. We must always ask ourselves how much the *writer* of the story is allowing the *narrator* to know and understand—and how much the writer agrees with the narrator's perspective on life. In fact, the whole point of a story told from the first-person point of view may lie in the contrast between what the narrator tells us and what the writer allows us to understand in spite of the narrator.

The Limited Third-Person Point of View

Between the two extremes of the omniscient and first-person points of view lies the **limited third-person point of view.** Here the story is told by an outside observer (like the godlike narrator of the omniscient point of view). But this narrator views the action only from the vantage point of a single character in the story. It is as if the narrator is standing alongside this one character and recording only his or her thoughts, perceptions, and feelings. Chances are, this narrator will tell us more than what that character would be able to tell us (or might choose to tell us) if he or she were narrating the story. (This point of view is called "third-person" because the narrator never refers to himself or herself as "I." The third-person pronouns are used to refer to all characters.)

> Helena wondered if Alfred was going to ask her to dance. Their eyes had met over the punch bowl, and his seemed to linger. But of course she had no way of knowing how he felt about her. If only she hadn't broken her diet last week, she kept chiding herself. Without realizing what she was doing, she nervously stuffed a piece of cake into her mouth.

In choosing a point of view, the writer must consider how much information to tell the reader and how much to withhold. And in reading a story, we should always ask ourselves, "How would this story have been different if it had been told by someone else?"

The Narrator's Tone

Tone is the attitude a speaker or writer takes toward a subject, audience, or character.

You've probably heard this kind of complaint before: "It's not *what* Mary Anne says that bothers me; it's the *way* she says it." In speaking and in writing, tone is revealed by the way we say something, just as much as by what we actually say.

Take a word that has a sweet sound to it: *Dear.* Whisper it: "Dear . . ." Make it impatient: "Dear!" Make it a question: "Dear?" Make it a summons: "Dee-ar!" Do you notice a change in

The False Mirror by René Magritte (1928). Oil on canvas, 21¼″ × 31⅞″.

Collection, The Museum of Modern Art, New York. Purchase.

> " **I**n reading a story, we should always ask ourselves, 'How would this story have been different if it had been told by someone else?' "

tone, in the attitude you communicate to the person you are addressing?

Use *dear* as a descriptive word. Let's say you are describing Stephanie, who has just done the breakfast dishes, mopped the kitchen floor, and arranged fresh flowers on the table. Your tone will probably be admiring, grateful, and affectionate as you say of her, "She's a dear." But if you are feeling a bit resentful that this saintly Stephanie is always making you look bad by comparison, your tone might be bitter, jealous, and maybe even insincere when you say exactly the same words.

Or suppose you use the phrase to describe Hazel, who is trying on lipsticks at the cosmetics counter and has just turned to swat the little child tugging at her skirt. If you said of Hazel, "*She's* a dear," your tone would express still a different attitude. It would be scornful, sarcastic, and ironic—because you are trying to communicate that Hazel is anything but a dear.

When we speak, we convey tone through sounds—pauses, inflections, volume, stresses, pitch. We can even use facial expressions or gestures. Writers, of course, cannot rely on sounds to convey tone; they can use only words.

Words and Attitudes: Connotations

Many words carry a tone or attitude with them (this is what we mean by the **connotations** of words). The word *skinny,* for example, suggests a critical tone, but the word *slender* suggests approval. The same applies to *red-faced* as opposed to *rosy,* or *fat* as opposed to *plump,* or *cheap* as opposed to *reasonable.*

Tone can also be conveyed through the details a writer uses. If a writer introduces a six-year-old child and describes her ragged clothes, her sweet face, and her cheery disposition, we can be certain that the writer's attitude toward this character is positive and compassionate. The writer is directing us to feel love and pity for the child. But a different writer, with a different attitude toward the child, might emphasize her ignorance, her dirty face, and her jealousy of her baby sister.

Tone is also conveyed by the way a writer manipulates the plot and characters in a story. If a writer provides a happy or satisfying ending to a conflict, we might say that the story conveys a romantic, positive, or hopeful attitude toward life. But if a story ends tragically, we might say that the story conveys an ironic tone, or maybe a cynical or fatalistic attitude toward life.

Point of view also affects tone. The story on page 68, "Mr. Parker," is told from the point of view of a girl whose mother wants her to stop taking piano lessons from a neighbor whose wife has recently died. The girl is enchanted by her piano teacher and angry and confused by her mother's suspicions of him. The tone of the story is understated—the emotions it suggests seem to lie beneath the surface, as if perhaps the narrator hadn't quite sorted out her conflicting feelings. We might describe her tone as "bittersweet." If the story had been told from the mother's point of view, her tone

> " **The** word *skinny* suggests a critical tone, but the word *slender* suggests approval. The same applies to *red-faced* as opposed to *rosy,* or *fat* as opposed to *plump,* or *cheap* as opposed to *reasonable.*"

would have been completely different. The mother might have expressed frustration at her daughter's behavior or fear for her safety or maybe even confusion about her own responsibilities as a mother—confusion that she perhaps never allows her daughter to see.

Many writers, like many other people, carry the same tone along from situation to situation and from story to story. Some will always have their characters respond to challenge and adversity in a sunny, optimistic way. Others will always have them respond in a cynical, gloomy way. In fact, we are often attracted to a particular writer because his or her tone reveals an attitude toward life that resembles our own—or because it provides a welcome contrast. And perhaps we say of another writer, "I'll never read another one of his books because his tone is just too cynical."

Like point of view, the writer's attitude is an essential element of the story's meaning. We might even view the difference between comedy and tragedy as the difference between two opposite attitudes toward life.

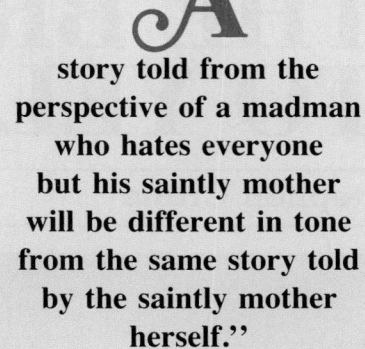

"**A** story told from the perspective of a madman who hates everyone but his saintly mother will be different in tone from the same story told by the saintly mother herself."

Determining a Story's Point of View

Whenever we read a work of fiction, we should ask ourselves five important questions about its point of view:

1. Who is telling the story?
2. How much does this narrator know?
3. How much does this narrator understand?
4. How much does this narrator want us to know?
5. In what ways would the story be different if someone else were telling it?

In any story, we must always keep in mind that the narrator is not necessarily an objective or reliable observer of what is happening. In fact, our feelings about the characters and events may be very different from the narrator's feelings—and the writer may intend for us to feel this way. Thus a story's point of view has a tremendous effect on its tone. A story told from the perspective of a madman who hates everyone but his saintly mother will be different in tone from the same story told by the saintly mother herself. It will be different still from the story told by an outside narrator who can penetrate the mysteries of both mother and son.

"Once upon a time, allegedly . . ."

Drawing by D. Reilly; © 1987
The New Yorker Magazine, Inc.

THE BRIDE COMES TO YELLOW SKY

Stephen Crane

"They were evidently very happy."

Marjorie Steele and Robert Preston in the 1952 film of Crane's story.

I.

The great Pullman was whirling onward with such dignity of motion that a glance from the window seemed simply to prove that the plains of Texas were pouring eastward. Vast flats of green grass, dull-hued spaces of mesquite and cactus, little groups of frame houses, woods of light and tender trees, all were sweeping into the east, sweeping over the horizon, a precipice.

A newly married pair had boarded this coach at San Antonio. The man's face was reddened from many days in the wind and sun, and a direct result of his new black clothes was that his brick-colored hands were constantly performing in a most conscious fashion. From time to time he looked down respectfully at his attire. He sat with a hand on each knee, like a man waiting in a barber's shop. The glances he devoted to other passengers were furtive and shy.

The bride was not pretty, nor was she very young. She wore a dress of blue cashmere, with small reservations of velvet here and there, and with steel buttons abounding. She continually twisted her head to regard her puff sleeves, very stiff, straight, and high. They embarrassed her. It was quite apparent that she had cooked, and that she expected to cook, dutifully. The blushes caused by the careless scrutiny of some passengers as she had entered the car were strange to see upon this plain, underclass countenance, which was drawn in placid, almost emotionless lines.

They were evidently very happy. "Ever been in a parlor car before?" he asked, smiling with delight.

"No," she answered; "I never was. It's fine, ain't it?"

"Great! And then after a while we'll go forward to the diner, and get a big layout. Finest meal in the world. Charge a dollar."

"Oh, do they?" cried the bride. "Charge a dollar? Why, that's too much—for us—ain't it, Jack?"

"Not this trip, anyhow," he answered bravely. "We're going to go the whole thing."

Later he explained to her about the trains. "You see, it's a thousand miles from one end of Texas to the other; and this train runs right across it and never stops but four times." He had the pride of an owner. He pointed out to her the dazzling fittings of the coach; and in truth her eyes opened wider as she contemplated the sea-green figured velvet, the shining brass, silver, and glass, the wood that gleamed as darkly brilliant as the surface of a pool of oil. At one end a bronze figure sturdily held a support for a separated chamber, and at convenient places on the ceiling were frescoes in olive and silver.

To the minds of the pair, their surroundings reflected the glory of their marriage that morning in San Antonio; this was the environment of their new estate; and the man's face in particular beamed with an elation that made him appear ridiculous to the Negro porter. This individual at times surveyed them from afar with an amused and superior grin. On other occasions he bullied them with skill in ways that did not make it exactly plain to them that they were being bullied. He subtly used all the manners of the most unconquerable kind of snobbery. He oppressed them; but of this oppression they had small knowledge, and they speedily forgot that infrequently a number of travelers covered them with stares of derisive enjoyment. Historically there was supposed to be something infinitely humorous in their situation.

"We are due in Yellow Sky at 3:42," he said, looking tenderly into her eyes.

"Oh, are we?" she said, as if she had not been aware of it. To evince surprise at her husband's statement was part of her wifely amiability. She took from a pocket a little silver watch; and as she held it before her and stared at it with a frown of attention, the new husband's face shone.

"I bought it in San Anton' from a friend of mine," he told her gleefully.

"It's seventeen minutes past twelve," she said, looking up at him with a kind of shy and clumsy coquetry. A passenger, noting this play, grew excessively sardonic and winked at himself in one of the numerous mirrors.

At last they went to the dining car. Two rows of Negro waiters, in glowing white suits, surveyed their entrance with the interest, and also the equanimity, of men who had been forewarned. The pair fell to the lot of a waiter who happened to feel pleasure in steering them through their meal. He viewed them with the manner of a fatherly pilot, his countenance radiant with benevolence. The patronage, entwined with the ordinary deference, was not plain to them. And yet, as they returned to their coach, they showed in their faces a sense of escape.

To the left, miles down a long purple slope, was a little ribbon of mist where moved the keening Rio Grande. The train was approaching it at an angle, and the apex was Yellow Sky. Presently it was apparent that as the distance from Yellow Sky grew shorter, the husband became commensurately restless. His brick-red hands were more insistent in their prominence. Occasionally he was even rather absent-minded and faraway when the bride leaned forward and addressed him.

As a matter of truth, Jack Potter was beginning to find the shadow of a deed weigh upon him like a leaden slab. He, the town marshal of Yellow Sky, a man known, liked, and feared in his corner, a prominent person, had gone to San Antonio to meet a girl he believed he loved, and there, after the usual prayers, had actually induced her to marry him, without consulting Yellow Sky for any part of the transaction. He was now bringing his bride before an innocent and unsuspecting community.

Of course people in Yellow Sky married as it pleased them, in accordance with a general cus-

tom; but such was Potter's thought of his duty to his friends, or of their idea of his duty, or of an unspoken form which does not control men in these matters, that he felt he was heinous. He had committed an extraordinary crime. Face to face with this girl in San Antonio, and spurred by his sharp impulse, he had gone headlong over all the social hedges. At San Antonio he was like a man hidden in the dark. A knife to sever any friendly duty, any form, was easy to his hand in that remote city. But the hour of Yellow Sky—the hour of daylight—was approaching.

He knew full well that his marriage was an important thing to his town. It could only be exceeded by the burning of the new hotel. His friends could not forgive him. Frequently he had reflected on the advisability of telling them by telegraph, but a new cowardice had been upon him. He feared to do it. And now the train was hurrying him toward a scene of amazement, glee, and reproach. He glanced out of the window at the line of haze swinging slowly in toward the train.

Yellow Sky had a kind of brass band, which played painfully, to the delight of the populace. He laughed without heart as he thought of it. If the citizens could dream of his prospective arrival with his bride, they would parade the band at the station and escort them, amid cheers and laughing congratulations, to his adobe home.

He resolved that he would use all the devices of speed and plains-craft in making the journey from the station to his house. Once within that safe citadel, he could issue some sort of vocal bulletin, and then not go among the citizens until they had time to wear off a little of their enthusiasm.

The bride looked anxiously at him. "What's worrying you, Jack?"

He laughed again. "I'm not worrying, girl; I'm only thinking of Yellow Sky."

She flushed in comprehension.

A sense of mutual guilt invaded their minds and developed a finer tenderness. They looked at each other with eyes softly aglow. But Potter often laughed the same nervous laugh; the flush upon the bride's face seemed quite permanent.

The traitor to the feelings of Yellow Sky narrowly watched the speeding landscape. "We're nearly there," he said.

Presently the porter came and announced the proximity of Potter's home. He held a brush in his hand, and, with all his airy superiority gone, he brushed Potter's new clothes as the latter slowly turned this way and that way. Potter fumbled out a coin and gave it to the porter, as he had seen others do. It was a heavy and muscle-bound business, as that of a man shoeing his first horse.

The porter took their bag, and as the train began to slow they moved forward to the hooded platform of the car. Presently the two engines and their long string of coaches rushed into the station of Yellow Sky.

"They have to take water here," said Potter, from a constricted throat and in mournful cadence, as one announcing death. Before the train stopped, his eye had swept the length of the platform, and he was glad and astonished to see there was none upon it but the station agent, who, with a slightly hurried and anxious air, was walking toward the water tanks. When the train had halted, the porter alighted first and placed in position a little temporary step.

"Come on, girl," said Potter, hoarsely. As he helped her down, they each laughed on a false note. He took the bag from the porter and bade his wife cling to his arm. As they slunk rapidly away, his hangdog glance perceived that they were unloading the two trunks, and also that the station agent, far ahead near the baggage car, had turned and was running toward him, making gestures. He laughed, and groaned as he laughed, when he noted the first effect of his marital bliss upon Yellow Sky. He gripped his wife's arm firmly to his side, and they fled. Behind them the porter stood, chuckling fatuously.

II.

The California express on the Southern Railway was due at Yellow Sky in twenty-one minutes. There were six men at the bar of the Weary Gentleman saloon. One was a drummer[1] who talked a

---

1. **drummer:** a traveling salesman.

great deal and rapidly; three were Texans who did not care to talk at that time; and two were Mexican sheepherders, who did not talk as a general practice in the Weary Gentleman saloon. The barkeeper's dog lay on the boardwalk that crossed in front of the door. His head was on his paws, and he glanced drowsily here and there with the constant vigilance of a dog that is kicked on occasion. Across the sandy street were some vivid green grassplots, so wonderful in appearance, amid the sands that burned near them in a blazing sun, that they caused a doubt in the mind. They exactly resembled the grass mats used to represent lawns on the stage. At the cooler end of the railway station, a man without a coat sat in a tilted chair and smoked his pipe. The fresh-cut bank of the Rio Grande circled near the town, and there could be seen beyond it a great plum-colored plain of mesquite.

Save for the busy drummer and his companions in the saloon, Yellow Sky was dozing. The newcomer leaned gracefully upon the bar and recited many tales with the confidence of a bard who has come upon a new field.

"——and at the moment that the old man fell downstairs with the bureau in his arms, the old woman was coming up with two scuttles of coal, and of course——"

The drummer's tale was interrupted by a young man who suddenly appeared in the open door. He cried: "Scratchy Wilson's drunk and has turned loose with both hands." The two Mexicans at once set down their glasses and faded out of the rear entrance of the saloon.

The drummer, innocent and jocular, answered: "All right, old man. S'pose he has? Come in and have a drink, anyhow."

But the information had made such an obvious cleft in every skull in the room that the drummer was obliged to see its importance. All had become instantly solemn. "Say," said he, mystified, "what is this?" His three companions made the introductory gesture of eloquent speech; but the young man at the door forestalled them.

"It means, my friend," he answered, as he came into the saloon, "that for the next two hours this town won't be a health resort."

The barkeeper went to the door and locked and

barred it; reaching out of the window, he pulled in heavy wooden shutters and barred them. Immediately a solemn, chapellike gloom was upon the place. The drummer was looking from one to another.

"But say," he cried, "what is this, anyhow? You don't mean there is going to be a gunfight?"

"Don't know whether there'll be a fight or not," answered one man, grimly; "but there'll be some shootin'—some good shootin'."

The young man who had warned them waved his hand. "Oh, there'll be a fight fast enough, if anyone wants it. Anybody can get a fight out there in the street. There's a fight just waiting."

The drummer seemed to be swayed between the interest of a foreigner and a perception of personal danger.

"What did you say his name was?" he asked.

"Scratchy Wilson," they answered in chorus.

"And will he kill anybody? What are you going to do? Does this happen often? Does he rampage around like this once a week or so? Can he break in that door?"

"No; he can't break down that door," replied the barkeeper. "He's tried it three times. But when he comes, you'd better lay down on the floor, stranger. He's dead sure to shoot at it, and a bullet may come through."

Thereafter the drummer kept a strict eye upon the door. The time had not yet been called for him to hug the floor, but, as a minor precaution, he sidled near to the wall. "Will he kill anybody?" he said again.

The men laughed low and scornfully at the question.

"He's out to shoot, and he's out for trouble. Don't see any good in experimentin' with him."

"But what do you do in a case like this? What do you do?"

A man responded: "Why, he and Jack Potter——"

"But," in chorus the other men interrupted, "Jack Potter's in San Anton'."

"Well, who is he? What's he got to do with it?"

"Oh, he's the town marshal. He goes out and fights Scratchy when he gets on one of these tears."

"Wow!" said the drummer, mopping his brow. "Nice job he's got."

The voices had toned away to mere whisperings. The drummer wished to ask further questions, which were born of an increasing anxiety and bewilderment; but when he attempted them, the men merely looked at him in irritation and motioned him to remain silent. A tense waiting hush was upon them. In the deep shadows of the room, their eyes shone as they listened for sounds from the street. One man made three gestures at the barkeeper; and the latter, moving like a ghost, handed him a glass and a bottle. The man poured a full glass of whiskey and set down the bottle noiselessly. He gulped the whiskey in a swallow and turned again toward the door in immovable silence. The drummer saw that the barkeeper, without a sound, had taken a Winchester from beneath the bar. Later he saw this individual beckoning to him, so he tiptoed across the room.

"You better come with me back of the bar."

"No, thanks," said the drummer, perspiring; "I'd rather be where I can make a break for the back door."

Whereupon the man of bottles made a kindly but peremptory gesture. The drummer obeyed it, and, finding himself seated on a box with his head below the level of the bar, balm was laid upon his soul at sight of various zinc and copper fittings that bore a resemblance to armor plate. The barkeeper took a seat comfortably upon an adjacent box.

"You see," he whispered, "this here Scratchy Wilson is a wonder with a gun—a perfect wonder; and when he goes on the war trail, we hunt our holes—naturally. He's about the last one of the old gang that used to hang out along the river here. He's a terror when he's drunk. When he's sober he's all right—kind of simple—wouldn't hurt a fly—nicest fellow in town. But when he's drunk—whoo!"

There were periods of stillness. "I wish Jack Potter was back from San Anton'," said the barkeeper. "He shot Wilson up once—in the leg—and he would sail in and pull out the kinks in this thing."

Presently they heard from a distance the sound of a shot, followed by three wild yowls. It instantly removed a bond from the men in the darkened saloon. There was a shuffling of feet. They looked at each other. "Here he comes," they said.

III.

A man in a maroon-colored flannel shirt, which had been purchased for purposes of decoration, and made principally by some Jewish women on the East Side of New York, rounded a corner and walked into the middle of the main street of Yellow Sky. In either hand the man held a long, heavy, blue-black revolver. Often he yelled, and these cries rang through a semblance of a deserted village, shrilly flying over the roofs in a volume that seemed to have no relation to the ordinary vocal strength of a man. It was as if the surrounding stillness formed the arch of a tomb over him. These cries of ferocious challenge rang against walls of silence. And his boots had red tops with gilded imprints, of the kind beloved in winter by little sledding boys on the hillsides of New England.

The man's face flamed in a rage begot of whiskey. His eyes, rolling, and yet keen for ambush, hunted the still doorways and windows. He walked with the creeping movement of the midnight cat. As it occurred to him, he roared menacing information. The long revolvers in his hands were as easy as straws; they were moved with an electric swiftness. The little fingers of each hand played sometimes in a musician's way. Plain from the low collar of the shirt, the cords of his neck straightened and sank, straightened and sank, as passion moved him. The only sounds were his terrible invitations. The calm adobes preserved their demeanor at the passing of this small thing in the middle of the street.

There was no offer of fight—no offer of fight. The man called to the sky. There were no attractions. He bellowed and fumed and swayed his revolvers here and everywhere.

The dog of the barkeeper of the Weary Gentleman saloon had not appreciated the advance of events. He yet lay dozing in front of his master's door. At sight of the dog, the man paused and raised his revolver humorously. At sight of the man, the dog sprang up and walked diagonally away, with a sullen head, and growling. The man yelled, and the dog broke into a gallop. As it was about to enter an alley, there was a loud noise, a whistling, and something spat the ground directly before it. The dog screamed and, wheeling in terror, galloped headlong in a new direction. Again there was a noise, a whistling, and sand was kicked viciously before it. Fear-stricken, the dog turned and flurried like an animal in a pen. The man stood laughing, his weapons at his hips.

Ultimately the man was attracted by the closed door of the Weary Gentleman saloon. He went to it and, hammering with a revolver, demanded drink.

The door remaining imperturbable, he picked a bit of paper from the walk, and nailed it to the framework with a knife. He then turned his back contemptuously upon this popular resort and, walking to the opposite side of the street and spinning there on his heel quickly and lithely, fired at the bit of paper. He missed it by a half-inch. He swore at himself and went away. Later he comfortably fusilladed the windows of his most intimate friend. The man was playing with this town; it was a toy for him.

But still there was no offer of fight. The name of Jack Potter, his ancient antagonist, entered his mind, and he concluded that it would be a glad thing if he should go to Potter's house and by bombardment induce him to come out and fight. He moved in the direction of his desire, chanting Apache scalp-music.

When he arrived at it, Potter's house presented the same still front as had the other adobes. Taking up a strategic position, the man howled a challenge. But this house regarded him as might a great stone god. It gave no sign. After a decent wait, the man howled further challenges, mingling with them wonderful epithets.

Presently there came the spectacle of a man churning himself into deepest rage over the immobility of a house. He fumed at it as the winter wind attacks a prairie cabin in the North. To the distance there should have gone the sound of a tumult like the fighting of two hundred Mexicans. As necessity bade him, he paused for breath or to reload his revolvers.

IV.

Potter and his bride walked sheepishly and with speed. Sometimes they laughed together shamefacedly and low.

"Next corner, dear," he said finally.

They put forth the efforts of a pair walking bowed against a strong wind. Potter was about to raise a finger to point the first appearance of the new home when, as they circled the corner, they came face to face with a man in a maroon-colored shirt, who was feverishly pushing cartridges into a large revolver. Upon the instant the man dropped his revolver to the ground and, like lightning, whipped another from its holster. The second weapon was aimed at the bridegroom's chest.

There was a silence. Potter's mouth seemed to be merely a grave for his tongue. He exhibited an instinct to at once loosen his arm from the woman's grip, and he dropped the bag to the sand. As for the bride, her face had gone as yellow as old cloth. She was a slave to hideous rites, gazing at the apparitional snake.

The two men faced each other at a distance of three paces. He of the revolver smiled with a new and quiet ferocity.

"Tried to sneak up on me," he said. "Tried to sneak up on me!" His eyes grew more baleful. As Potter made a slight movement, the man thrust his revolver venomously forward. "No; don't you do it, Jack Potter. Don't you move a finger toward a gun just yet. Don't you move an eyelash. The time has come for me to settle with you, and I'm goin' to do it my own way and loaf along with no interferin'. So if you don't want a gun bent on you, just mind what I tell you."

Potter looked at his enemy. "I ain't got a gun on me Scratchy," he said. "Honest, I ain't." He was stiffening and steadying, but yet somewhere at the back of his mind a vision of the Pullman floated: the sea-green figured velvet, the shining brass, silver, and glass, the wood that gleamed as darkly brilliant as the surface of a pool of oil—all the glory of the marriage, the environment of the new estate. "You know I fight when it comes to fighting, Scratchy Wilson; but I ain't got a gun on me. You'll have to do all the shootin' yourself."

His enemy's face went livid. He stepped forward and lashed his weapon to and fro before Potter's chest. "Don't you tell me you ain't got no gun on you, you whelp. Don't tell me no lie like that. There ain't a man in Texas ever seen you without no gun. Don't take me for no kid." His eyes blazed with light, and his throat worked like a pump.

"I ain't takin' you for no kid." answered Potter. His heels had not moved an inch backward. "I'm takin' you for a damn fool. I tell you I ain't got a gun, and I ain't. If you're goin' to shoot me up, you better begin now; you'll never get a chance like this again."

So much enforced reasoning had told on Wilson's rage; he was calmer. "If you ain't got a gun, why ain't you got a gun?" he sneered. "Been to Sunday School?"

"I ain't got a gun because I've just come from San Anton' with my wife. I'm married," said Potter. "And if I'd thought there was going to be any galoots like you prowling around when I brought my wife home, I'd had a gun, and don't you forget it."

"Married!" said Scratchy, not at all comprehending.

"Yes, married. I'm married," said Potter, distinctly.

"Married?" said Scratchy. Seemingly for the first time, he saw the drooping, drowning woman at the other man's side. "No!" he said. He was like a creature allowed a glimpse of another world. He moved a pace backward, and his arm, with the revolver, dropped to his side. "Is this the lady?" he asked.

"Yes; this is the lady," answered Potter.

There was another period of silence.

"Well," said Wilson at last, slowly, "I s'pose it's all off now."

"It's all off if you say so, Scratchy. You know I didn't make the trouble." Potter lifted his valise.

"Well, I 'low it's off, Jack," said Wilson. He was looking at the ground. "Married!" He was not a student of chivalry; it was merely that in the presence of this foreign condition he was a simple child of the earlier plains. He picked up his starboard revolver, and, placing both weapons in their holsters, he went away. His feet made funnel-shaped tracks in the heavy sand.

Responding to the Story

Analyzing the Story

Identifying Facts

1. Explain why Jack Potter is nervous about coming home with his new wife.
2. In the second part of the story, what do we learn about the situation awaiting the couple in Yellow Sky?
3. Most Westerns draw upon our romantic notions of frontier life. Chief among these is a belief that the hero's fast draw and sure aim will triumph over the nastiest villain. In the last part of the story, however, it is not the sheriff's gun that pacifies the terrible Scratchy Wilson. What does?

Interpreting Meanings

4. In the first part of the story, what do we learn about Jack Potter and his bride through **indirect characterization**—from their appearance, actions, words, and from the way other people on the train respond to them?
5. Explain why the sight of the new Mrs. Potter prevents Scratchy from shooting it out with Jack Potter. What does the writer mean when he says that Scratchy "was not a student of chivalry; it was merely that in the presence of this foreign condition he was a simple child of the earlier plains" (page 126)?
6. In literature, a **parody** is a humorous imitation of a serious work or of a particular style of writing. A parody pokes fun at its subject, usually through exaggeration and mockery, sometimes to make it seem ridiculous, sometimes simply to make us stop taking it so seriously. The portrait of Scratchy Wilson terrifying the town of Yellow Sky for the joy of it is surely the center of the story's mockery. What passages indicate that Scratchy is a parody of the traditional "bad guy" in a Western? (For example, what kind of clothing does he wear?) What other aspects of parody do you see in the story?
7. Is the story told from an **omniscient** or **limited third-person point of view**? Find passages in the story to support your answer. Did this point of view keep you at a distance from the characters and help you laugh at their situation, or did it take you inside the story by letting you know what everyone was thinking? Explain.
8. If you have seen the movie *High Noon,* you know that the subject of "The Bride Comes to Yellow Sky" (a newly married town marshal facing a shoot-out) can be treated quite seriously. How would you describe the **tone** in Crane's story? What passages in the story support your opinion?
9. Do you think the ending of this story is believable? That is, do you think that an angry drunkard would really refrain from shooting the enemy he has wanted to "settle with" for so long, simply because that enemy has just gotten married? Does Crane's explanation for Scratchy's remarkable change of heart convince you? Did you enjoy the twist, or did you miss the big shoot-out scene? Explain your response to the ending of the story.

Writing About the Story

A Creative Response

1. **Writing a Parody.** Think of another fictional cliché—the detective story set in the big city, the romance saga set on a mysterious moor, the spy thriller, the science-fiction epic, the soap opera. How could you parody this literary form? Which elements of the cliché would you mock—the **basic situation,** the **characters,** the **conflict,** the **resolution,** the writing **style**? Write a paragraph describing how you would parody another story type. Or better yet, write the parody.
2. **Writing a Plan for a Movie Version.** James Agee wrote the script for the movie version of "The Bride Comes to Yellow Sky," which was released in 1952. The movie has two lines of action that move the story forward simultaneously. One shows Potter and his bride on the train; the other shows the events that are taking place in Yellow Sky. Suppose you were taking the first step in adapting this story to the screen. Block out the important scenes you'd include in the movie. Describe the scenes you'd shoot on the Pullman, the scenes you'd film in the town, and the scenes you'd film when Potter and his bride arrive in Yellow Sky and the main action of the story begins.

A Critical Response

3. **Evaluating the Story.** When Crane sent this story to *McClure's Magazine* in 1897, he told his agent, "It is a daisy and don't let them talk funny about it." Crane's biographer, R. W. Stallman, calls "The Bride Comes to Yellow Sky" a masterpiece, and the English writer Ford Madox Ford once referred to it as "the greatest story ever written." Do you agree or disagree with these evaluations of Crane's story? Write a paragraph in which you state your opinion and support it with specific evidence from the story.

Analyzing Language and Vocabulary

Americanisms

In 1806 Noah Webster, the dictionary maker, made this prediction: "In each of the countries peopled by Englishmen, a distinct dialect of the language will gradually be formed; the principal of which will be that of the United States. In fifty years from this time, the *American English* will be spoken by more people than all the other dialects of the language." The passages that follow contain **Americanisms,** words and expressions that either originated in America or are peculiar to American English.

In most college dictionaries, a star or other symbol before an entry word or a definition identifies it as an Americanism. Use your dictionary to find the meanings and origins of these italicized words. Which words name things that are found in America but not in Britain? Which words were coined in America to name new inventions?

1. "The great *Pullman* was whirling onward. . . ."
2. "Vast flats of green grass, dull-hued spaces of *mesquite* and cactus, little groups of *frame* houses . . ."
3. "Ever been in a *parlor car* before?"
4. "And then after a while we'll go forward to the *diner*. . . ."
5. "He, the town *marshal* of Yellow Sky . . ."
6. " . . . they would parade the band at the station and escort them . . . to his *adobe* home."
7. "He goes out and fights Scratchy when he gets on one of these *tears*."
8. "In either hand the man held a long, heavy, blue-black *revolver*."
9. "I'm goin' to do it my own way and *loaf* along with no interferin'."
10. "And if I'd thought there was going to be any *galoots* like you prowling around . . ."

Reading About the Writer

Stephen Crane (1871–1900) was born in Newark, New Jersey, the son of a Methodist minister and the youngest of fourteen children. At the age of fifteen, Crane announced that he was going to be a professional baseball player: "But ma says it's not a serious occupation and Will [his brother] says I have to go to college first." Crane then decided to become a soldier and spent several years at a military prep school in New York. Moody and rebellious, he flunked out of both Lafayette College and Syracuse University after one semester at each, and then he moved to New York City.

Crane wrote his first story at the age of fourteen; by the time he was sixteen, his unsigned newspaper articles were appearing occasionally in the New York *Tribune*. For a short time Crane worked as a reporter for a New York newspaper, but he was fired for an article criticizing middle-class attitudes toward the poor. Broke and living in slums, Crane eked out a living as a free-lance reporter while writing his first novel about urban poverty, *Maggie: A Girl of the Streets*. At the time, the novel was considered so frank and shocking that Crane had to pay to have it printed, and even then no bookseller would handle it.

Crane's second novel was *The Red Badge of Courage*. This story of a young soldier's experiences in the Civil War was so realistic that people found it hard to believe that Crane himself had never fought in the Civil War—or in any war for that matter. The novel was immensely popular, and as a result of his celebrity, Crane became a star reporter. As a correspondent, he traveled to the West and to Mexico, covered wars in Greece and Cuba, and was shipwrecked in a tiny dinghy off the Florida coast (an experience he described in one of his most famous stories, "The Open Boat").

Worn out by his hectic pace and by efforts to pay off debts, Crane died of tuberculosis when he was only twenty-eight years old.

EVERYDAY USE

For Your Grandmama

Alice Walker

The power of this story comes from its very narrow point of view. After you have read the first two paragraphs, write down what you know about the "I" character telling the story. When you **have finished the story, think about how its impact would have changed if the writer had used one of the other characters as the narrator. The story is set in the rural South.**

I will wait for her in the yard that Maggie and I made so clean and wavy yesterday afternoon. A yard like this is more comfortable than most people know. It is not just a yard. It is like an extended living room. When the hard clay is swept clean as a floor and the fine sand around the edges lined with tiny, irregular grooves, anyone can come and sit and look up into the elm tree and wait for the breezes that never come inside the house.

Maggie will be nervous until after her sister goes: She will stand hopelessly in corners, homely and ashamed of the burn scars down her arms and legs, eyeing her sister with a mixture of envy and awe. She thinks her sister had held life always in the palm of one hand, that "no" is a word the world never learned to say to her.

You've no doubt seen those TV shows where the child who has "made it" is confronted, as a surprise, by her own mother and father, tottering in weakly from backstage. (A pleasant surprise, of course: What would they do if parent and child came on the show only to curse out and insult each other?) On TV mother and child embrace and smile into each other's faces. Sometimes the mother and father weep; the child wraps them in her arms and leans across the table to tell how she would not have made it without their help. I have seen these programs.

Sometimes I dream a dream in which Dee and I are suddenly brought together on a TV program of this sort. Out of a dark and soft-seated limousine I am ushered into a bright room filled with many people. There I meet a smiling, gray, sporty man like Johnny Carson who shakes my hand and tells me what a fine girl I have. Then we are on the stage, and Dee is embracing me with tears in her eyes. She pins on my dress a large orchid, even though she had told me once that she thinks orchids are tacky flowers.

In real life I am a large, big-boned woman with rough, man-working hands. In the winter I wear flannel nightgowns to bed and overalls during the day. I can kill and clean a hog as mercilessly as a man. My fat keeps me hot in zero weather. I can work outside all day, breaking ice to get water for washing; I can eat pork liver cooked over the open fire minutes after it comes steaming from the hog. One winter I knocked a bull calf straight in the brain between the eyes with a sledge hammer and had the meat hung up to chill before nightfall. But of course all this does not show on television. I am the way my daughter would want me to be: a hundred pounds lighter, my skin like an uncooked barley pancake. My hair glistens in the hot bright lights. Johnny Carson has much to do to keep up with my quick and witty tongue.

But that is a mistake. I know even before I wake up. Who ever knew a Johnson with a quick tongue? Who can even imagine me looking a strange white man in the eye? It seems to me I have talked to them always with one foot raised in flight, with my head turned in whichever way is farthest from them. Dee, though. She would always look anyone in the eye. Hesitation was no part of her nature.

"How do I look, Mama?" Maggie says, showing just enough of her thin body enveloped in pink skirt and red blouse for me to know she's there, almost hidden by the door.

"Come out into the yard," I say.

Have you ever seen a lame animal, perhaps a dog run over by some careless person rich enough to own a car, sidle up to someone who is ignorant enough to be kind to him? That is the way my Maggie walks. She has been like this, chin on chest, eyes on ground, feet in shuffle, ever since the fire that burned the other house to the ground.

Dee is lighter than Maggie, with nicer hair and a fuller figure. She's a woman now, though sometimes I forget. How long ago was it that the other house burned? Ten, twelve years? Sometimes I can still hear the flames and feel Maggie's arms sticking to me, her hair smoking and her dress falling off her in little black papery flakes. Her eyes seemed stretched open, blazed open by the flames reflected in them. And Dee. I see her standing off under the sweet gum tree she used to dig gum out of; a look of concentration on her face as she watched the last dingy gray board of the house fall in toward the red-hot brick chimney. Why don't you do a dance around the ashes? I'd wanted to ask her. She had hated the house that much.

I used to think she hated Maggie, too. But that was before we raised the money, the church and me, to send her to Augusta to school. She used to read to us without pity; forcing words, lies, other folks' habits, whole lives upon us two, sitting trapped and ignorant underneath her voice. She washed us in a river of make-believe, burned us with a lot of knowledge we didn't necessarily need to know. Pressed us to her with the serious ways she read, to shove us away at just the moment, like dimwits, we seemed about to understand.

Dee wanted nice things. A yellow organdy dress to wear to her graduation from high school; black pumps to match a green suit she'd made from an old suit somebody gave me. She was determined to stare down any disaster in her ef-

forts. Her eyelids would not flicker for minutes at a time. Often I fought off the temptation to shake her. At sixteen she had a style of her own: and knew what style was.

I never had an education myself. After second grade the school was closed down. Don't ask me why: In 1927 colored asked fewer questions than they do now. Sometimes Maggie reads to me. She stumbles along good-naturedly but can't see well. She knows she is not bright. Like good looks and money, quickness passed her by. She will marry John Thomas (who has mossy teeth in an earnest face) and then I'll be free to sit here and I guess just sing church songs to myself. Although I never was a good singer. Never could carry a tune. I was always better at a man's job. I used to love to milk till I was hooked in the side in '49. Cows are soothing and slow and don't bother you, unless you try to milk them the wrong way.

I have deliberately turned my back on the house. It is three rooms, just like the one that burned, except the roof is tin; they don't make shingle roofs anymore. There are no real windows, just some holes cut in the sides, like the portholes in a ship, but not round and not square, with rawhide holding the shutters up on the outside. This house is in a pasture, too, like the other one. No doubt when Dee sees it she will want to tear it down. She wrote me once that no matter where we "choose" to live, she will manage to come see us. But she will never bring her friends. Maggie and I thought about this and Maggie asked me, "Mama, when did Dee ever *have* any friends?"

She had a few. Furtive boys in pink shirts hanging about on washday after school. Nervous girls who never laughed. Impressed with her, they worshiped the well-turned phrase, the cute shape, the scalding humor that erupted like bubbles in lye. She read to them.

When she was courting Jimmy T she didn't have much time to pay to us, but turned all her faultfinding power on him. He *flew* to marry a cheap city girl from a family of ignorant, flashy people. She hardly had time to recompose herself.

When she comes, I will meet—but there they are!

Maggie attempts to make a dash for the house, in her shuffling way, but I stay her with my hand. "Come back here," I say. And she stops and tries to dig a well in the sand with her toe.

It is hard to see them clearly through the strong sun. But even the first glimpse of leg out of the car tells me it is Dee. Her feet were always neat-looking, as if God himself had shaped them with a certain style. From the other side of the car comes a short, stocky man. Hair is all over his head a foot long and hanging from his chin like a kinky mule tail. I hear Maggie suck in her breath. "Uhnnnh," is what it sounds like. Like when you see the wriggling end of a snake just in front of your foot on the road. "Uhnnnh."

Dee next. A dress down to the ground, in this hot weather. A dress so loud it hurts my eyes. There are yellows and oranges enough to throw back the light of the sun. I feel my whole face warming from the heat waves it throws out. Earrings gold, too, and hanging down to her shoulders. Bracelets dangling and making noises when she moves her arm up to shake the folds of the dress out of her armpits. The dress is loose and flows, and as she walks closer, I like it. I hear Maggie go "Uhnnnh" again. It is her sister's hair. It stands straight up like the wool on a sheep. It is black as night and around the edges are two long pigtails that rope about like small lizards disappearing behind her ears.

"Wa-su-zo-Tean-o!" she says, coming on in that gliding way the dress makes her move. The short, stocky fellow with the hair to his navel is all grinning, and he follows up with "Asalamalakim, my mother and sister!" He moves to hug Maggie but she falls back, right up against the back of my chair. I feel her trembling there, and when I look up I see the perspiration falling off her chin.

"Don't get up," says Dee. Since I am stout, it takes something of a push. You can see me trying to move a second or two before I make it. She turns, showing white heels through her sandals, and goes back to the car. Out she peeks next with a Polaroid. She stoops down quickly and lines up picture after picture of me sitting there in front of the house with Maggie cowering behind me. She never takes a shot without making sure the house is included. When a cow comes nibbling around the edge of the yard, she snaps it and me and Maggie *and* the house. Then she puts the Polaroid in the back seat of the car, and comes up and kisses me on the forehead.

Meanwhile, Asalamalakim is going through motions with Maggie's hand. Maggie's hand is as limp as a fish, and probably as cold, despite the sweat, and she keeps trying to pull it back. It looks like Asalamalakim wants to shake hands but wants to do it fancy. Or maybe he don't know how people shake hands. Anyhow, he soon gives up on Maggie.

"Well," I say. "Dee."

"No, Mama," she says. "Not 'Dee,' Wangero Leewanika Kemanjo!"

"What happened to 'Dee'?" I wanted to know.

"She's dead," Wangero said. "I couldn't bear it any longer, being named after the people who oppress me."

"You know as well as me you was named after your aunt Dicie," I said. Dicie is my sister. She named Dee. We called her "Big Dee" after Dee was born.

"But who was *she* named after?" asked Wangero.

"I guess after Grandma Dee," I said.

"And who was she named after?" asked Wangero.

"Her mother," I said, and saw Wangero was getting tired. "That's about as far back as I can trace it," I said. Though, in fact, I probably could have carried it back beyond the Civil War through the branches.

"Well," said Asalamalakim, "there you are."

"Uhnnnh," I heard Maggie say.

"There I was not," I said, "before 'Dicie' cropped up in our family, so why should I try to trace it that far back?"

He just stood there grinning, looking down on me like somebody inspecting a Model A car. Every once in a while he and Wangero sent eye signals over my head.

"How do you pronounce this name?" I asked.

"You don't have to call me by it if you don't want to," said Wangero.

"Why shouldn't I?" I asked. "If that's what you want us to call you, we'll call you."

"I know it might sound awkward at first," said Wangero.

"I'll get used to it," I said. "Ream it out again."

Well, soon we got the name out of the way. Asalamalakim had a name twice as long and three times as hard. After I tripped over it two or three times, he told me to just call him Hakim-a-barber. I wanted to ask him was he a barber, but I didn't really think he was, so I didn't ask.

"You must belong to those beef-cattle peoples down the road," I said. They said "Asalamalakim" when they met you, too, but they didn't shake hands. Always too busy: feeding the cattle, fixing the fences, putting up salt-lick shelters, throwing down hay. When the white folks poisoned some of the herd, the men stayed up all night with rifles in their hands. I walked a mile and a half just to see the sight.

Hakim-a-barber said, "I accept some of their doctrines, but farming and raising cattle is not my style." (They didn't tell me, and I didn't ask, whether Wangero—Dee—had really gone and married him.)

We sat down to eat and right away he said he didn't eat collards and pork was unclean. Wangero, though, went on through the chitlins and cornbread, the greens, and everything else. She talked a blue streak over the sweet potatoes. Everything delighted her. Even the fact that we still used the benches her daddy made for the table when we couldn't afford to buy chairs.

"Oh, Mama!" she cried. Then turned to Hakim-a-barber. "I never knew how lovely these benches are. You can feel the rump prints," she said, running her hands underneath her and along the bench. Then she gave a sigh, and her hand closed over Grandma Dee's butter dish. "That's it!" she said. "I knew there was something I wanted to ask you if I could have." She jumped up from the table and went over in the corner where the churn stood, the milk in it clabber by now. She looked at the churn and looked at it.

"This churn top is what I need," she said. "Didn't Uncle Buddy whittle it out of a tree you all used to have?"

"Yes," I said.

"Uh huh," she said happily. "And I want the dasher, too."

"Uncle Buddy whittle that, too?" asked the barber.

Dee (Wangero) looked up at me.

"Aunt Dee's first husband whittled the dash," said Maggie so low you almost couldn't hear her. "His name was Henry, but they called him Stash."

"Maggie's brain is like an elephant's," Wangero said, laughing. "I can use the churn top as a centerpiece for the alcove table," she said, sliding a plate over the churn, "and I'll think of something artistic to do with the dasher."

When she finished wrapping the dasher, the handle stuck out. I took it for a moment in my hands. You didn't even have to look close to see where hands pushing the dasher up and down to make butter had left a kind of sink in the wood. In fact, there were a lot of small sinks; you could see where thumbs and fingers had sunk into the wood. It was beautiful light yellow wood, from a tree that grew in the yard where Big Dee and Stash had lived.

After dinner Dee (Wangero) went to the trunk at the foot of my bed and started rifling through it. Maggie hung back in the kitchen over the dishpan. Out came Wangero with two quilts. They had been pieced by Grandma Dee, and then Big Dee and me had hung them on the quilt frames on the front porch and quilted them. One was in the Lone Star pattern. The other was Walk Around the Mountain. In both of them were scraps of dresses Grandma Dee had worn fifty and more years ago. Bits and pieces of Grandpa Jarrell's paisley shirts. And one teeny faded blue piece, about the size of a penny matchbox, that was from Great Grandpa Ezra's uniform that he wore in the Civil War.

"Mama," Wangero said sweet as a bird. "Can I have these old quilts?"

I heard something fall in the kitchen, and a minute later the kitchen door slammed.

"Why don't you take one or two of the others?" I asked. "These old things was just done by me and Big Dee from some tops your grandma pieced before she died."

"No," said Wangero. "I don't want those. They are stitched around the borders by machine."

"That'll make them last better," I said.

"That's not the point," said Wangero. "These

Red, white, and blue Star quilt, Ohio.
Anonymous (c. 1900). Cotton.

Collection of the Chase Manhattan Bank, N.A.

are all pieces of dresses Grandma used to wear. She did all this stitching by hand. Imagine!'' She held the quilts securely in her arms, stroking them.

"Some of the pieces, like those lavender ones, come from old clothes her mother handed down to her,'' I said, moving up to touch the quilts. Dee (Wangero) moved back just enough so that I couldn't reach the quilts. They already belonged to her.

"Imagine!'' she breathed again, clutching them closely to her bosom.

"The truth is,'' I said, "I promised to give them quilts to Maggie, for when she marries John Thomas.''

She gasped like a bee had stung her.

"Maggie can't appreciate these quilts!" she said. "She'd probably be backward enough to put them to everyday use."

"I reckon she would," I said. "God knows I been saving 'em for long enough with nobody using 'em. I hope she will!" I didn't want to bring up how I had offered Dee (Wangero) a quilt when she went away to college. Then she had told me they were old-fashioned, out of style.

"But they're *priceless*!" she was saying now, furiously; for she has a temper. "Maggie would put them on the bed and in five years they'd be in rags. Less than that!"

"She can always make some more," I said. "Maggie knows how to quilt."

Dee (Wangero) looked at me with hatred. "You just will not understand. The point is these quilts, *these* quilts!"

"Well," I said, stumped. "What would *you* do with them?"

"Hang them," she said. As if that was the only thing you *could* do with quilts.

Maggie by now was standing in the door. I could almost hear the sound her feet made as they scraped over each other.

"She can have them, Mama," she said, like somebody used to never winning anything or having anything reserved for her. "I can 'member Grandma Dee without the quilts."

I looked at her hard. She had filled her bottom lip with checkerberry snuff, and it gave her face a kind of dopey, hangdog look. It was Grandma Dee and Big Dee who taught her how to quilt

herself. She stood there with her scarred hands hidden in the folds of her skirt. She looked at her sister with something like fear, but she wasn't mad at her. This was Maggie's portion. This was the way she knew God to work.

When I looked at her like that, something hit me in the top of my head and ran down to the soles of my feet. Just like when I'm in church and the spirit of God touches me and I get happy and shout. I did something I never had done before: hugged Maggie to me, then dragged her on into the room, snatched the quilts out of Miss Wangero's hands, and dumped them into Maggie's lap. Maggie just sat there on my bed with her mouth open.

"Take one or two of the others," I said to Dee.

But she turned without a word and went out to Hakim-a-barber.

"You just don't understand," she said, as Maggie and I came out to the car.

"What don't I understand?" I wanted to know.

"Your heritage," she said. And then she turned to Maggie, kissed her, and said, "You ought to try to make something of yourself, too, Maggie. It's really a new day for us. But from the way you and Mama still live, you'd never know it."

She put on some sunglasses that hid everything above the tip of her nose and her chin.

Maggie smiled; maybe at the sunglasses. But a real smile, not scared. After we watched the car dust settle, I asked Maggie to bring me a dip of snuff. And then the two of us sat there just enjoying, until it was time to go in the house and go to bed.

Responding to the Story

Analyzing the Story

Identifying Facts

1. Find the passage in the story where the **title** is explained.
2. Describe how Maggie feels about the quilts. Why does Dee want them?

3. At the end of the story, how has Maggie changed? What has caused the change?

Interpreting Meanings

4. How would you **characterize** each of the women in this story? Find passages of the story that support each characterization.

5. Which character did you side with in the conflict over the quilts? Do you think the writer makes you feel sympathetic toward one sister and unsympathetic toward the other? Which passages do you think control your feelings?

6. At the end of the story, Dee says that her mother doesn't understand her own heritage. Do you think she is right—or is this story about a clash between two different heritages?

7. The title of a story often provides a good clue to its **theme.** What would you say is the theme of "Everyday Use," and how does it relate to the title? Do you agree with this theme, or do you feel there is something to be said for Dee's point of view? Explain your response.

8. The very first word of the story tells us that it will be narrated from the **first-person point of view.** How well do you think the narrator understands each of the other characters in the story? That is, how reliable or trustworthy or perceptive is she? How does this narrator affect the **tone** of the story and our response to it? Cite specific passages from the story to support your opinion.

9. Are you convinced that a woman like Mama would tell the story in this way? In other words, is this a realistic, plausible voice? After having read her story, do you agree with the narrator's assessment of herself: "Who ever knew a Johnson with a quick tongue"? Explain.

10. Why do you think Alice Walker dedicated this story: *"For Your Grandmama"*?

Writing About the Story

A Creative Response

1. **Using a Different Point of View.** In at least three paragraphs, let Maggie narrate the **resolution** of the story in her own voice. Why does she offer Dee the quilts? How does she feel when Mama dumps the quilts in her lap? Why does she smile at the end? What **tone** will Maggie use?

2. **Describing an Object.** Is there an heirloom in your family—some piece of art, jewelry, tableware, or furniture that is prized by family members? Or is there an object in your home that you value because it once belonged to a family member who is no longer living? Describe the object in a paragraph. Tell what you see when you look at it, what it reminds you of, and how you would put it to use in your own home.

A Critical Response

3. **Comparing a Poem to the Story.** Read the excerpt from the poem by Alice Walker in "Focusing on Background" (page 136). Then write a two-paragraph essay comparing and contrasting Dee (in the story) and Molly (in the poem). In your opinion, which sister is more sympathetically portrayed? Which work, the story or the poem, presents the clearer character portrait?

Analyzing Language and Vocabulary

Figures of Speech

Like many writers, Alice Walker uses figures of speech to make her descriptions vivid. A **figure of speech** is a comparison between two things that are basically unlike, but that have some quality in common. Here are some figures of speech from "Everyday Use." Answer the questions following each example.

1. "I am the way my daughter would want me to be: a hundred pounds lighter, my skin like an uncooked barley pancake."

   a. What color is a pancake before it is cooked?
   b. Do you think this is a pleasant comparision or an unpleasant one?

2. "Have you ever seen a lame animal, perhaps a dog run over by some careless person rich enough to own a car, sidle up to someone who is ignorant enough to be kind to him? That is the way my Maggie walks."

   a. What does this comparison tell us about the way Maggie feels about herself?
   b. In what way is Maggie like a "lame" animal?

3. "She used to read to us without pity; forcing words, lies, other folks' habits, whole lives upon us two, sitting trapped and ignorant underneath her voice."

   a. How could Dee "force words" and "whole lives" upon her mother and sister?
   b. How could her voice "trap" them?

4. "She washed us in a river of make-believe, burned us with a lot of knowledge we didn't necessarily need to know."

   a. What kinds of books do you think Dee read to her mother and sister? Which figure of speech tells you this?

b. Which figure of speech suggests that her listeners found Dee's teaching harmful or even cruel?

c. How could knowledge be harmful?

5. "Impressed with her, they worshiped the well-turned phrase, the cute shape, the scalding humor that erupted like bubbles in lye."

a. What do we usually use "scalding" in reference to?

b. If Dee's humor is compared with lye, what is it like?

Reading About the Writer

Alice Walker (1944–   ) is a novelist, short-story writer, poet, and essayist. She was born in Eatontown, a small town in rural Georgia, the youngest of eight children. Her father was a sharecropper farmer, and her mother worked as a maid. Walker says of her mother: "I grew up believing that there was nothing, literally nothing, my mother couldn't do once she set her mind to it. . . ." When the women's movement began, ". . . I was really delighted because I felt they were trying to go where my mother was and where I always assumed I would go."

When she was eight years old, Alice Walker was blinded in one eye by a shot from a BB gun. The resulting scar tissue made her painfully shy and self-conscious, and she spent her free time alone—outdoors, reading and writing stories. With the aid of a scholarship for handicapped students, she attended Spelman College, a college for African American women in Atlanta.

Her first published work, a book of poems called *Once*, was followed by many other collections of poems and short stories, and several novels. Her third novel, *The Color Purple*, won the Pulitzer Prize for fiction in 1983 and was made into a popular movie. Walker is a contributing editor of *Ms.* magazine and has been active in both the women's movement and the civil rights movement. An essay by Walker appears on page 429.

Focusing on Background
Another View of Sisters

In the following excerpt from a poem by Alice Walker, the speaker tells about her sister Molly. How are Molly in this poem and Dee in "Everyday Use" alike? How are they different?

For My Sister Molly Who in the Fifties

Once made a fairy rooster from
Mashed potatoes
Whose eyes I forget
But green onions were his tail
And his two legs were carrot sticks
A tomato slice his crown.
Who came home on vacation
When the sun was hot
and cooked
and cleaned
And minded least of all
The children's questions
A million or more
Pouring in on her
Who had been to school

And knew (and told us too) that certain
Words were no longer good
And taught me not to say us for we
No matter what "Sonny said" up the
road.

FOR MY SISTER MOLLY WHO IN THE FIFTIES
Knew Hamlet well and read into the night
And coached me in my songs of Africa
A continent I never knew
But learned to love
Because "they" she said could carry
A tune
And spoke in accents never heard
In Eatonton.
Who read from *Prose and Poetry*
And loved to read "Sam McGee from Tennessee"
On nights the fire was burning low
And Christmas wrapped in angel hair
And I for one prayed for snow. . . .

—Alice Walker

THE PEDESTRIAN

Ray Bradbury

The idea for this next story occurred to Ray Bradbury during a late-night walk in a Southern California suburb. Such behavior is so rare that police officers in a patrol car stopped Bradbury and questioned him about who he was and why he was out walking. If this innocent act could seem so dangerously suspicious in today's society, Bradbury wondered, how might it be viewed in a society of the future?

Stop when you get to the end of the third paragraph and ask yourself this: What questions has the writer planted in your mind to hook your curiosity? Before you begin reading, make sure you know two meanings of the word *pedestrian*.

To enter out into that silence that was the city at eight o'clock of a misty evening in November, to put your feet upon that buckling concrete walk, to step over grassy seams and make your way, hands in pockets, through the silences, that was what Mr. Leonard Mead most dearly loved to do. He would stand upon the corner of an intersection and peer down long moonlit avenues of sidewalk in four directions, deciding which way to go, but it really made no difference; he was alone in this world of 2053 A.D., or as good as alone, and with a final decision made, a path selected, he would stride off, sending patterns of frosty air before him like the smoke of a cigar.

Sometimes he would walk for hours and miles and return only at midnight to his house. And on his way he would see the cottages and homes with their dark windows, and it was not unequal to walking through a graveyard where only the faintest glimmers of firefly light appeared in flickers behind the windows. Sudden gray phantoms seemed to manifest upon inner room walls where a curtain was still undrawn against the night, or there were whisperings and murmurs where a window in a tomblike building was still open.

Mr. Leonard Mead would pause, cock his head, listen, look, and march on, his feet making no noise on the lumpy walk. For long ago he had wisely changed to sneakers when strolling at night, because the dogs in intermittent squads would parallel his journey with barkings if he wore hard heels, and lights might click on and faces appear and an entire street be startled by the passing of a lone figure, himself, in the early November evening.

On this particular evening he began his journey in a westerly direction, toward the hidden sea. There was a good crystal frost in the air; it cut the nose and made the lungs blaze like a Christmas tree inside; you could feel the cold light going on and off, all the branches filled with invisible snow. He listened to the faint push of his soft shoes through autumn leaves with satisfaction and whistled a cold, quiet whistle between his teeth, occasionally picking up a leaf as he passed, examining its skeletal pattern in the infrequent lamplights as he went on, smelling its rusty smell.

"Hello, in there," he whispered to every house on every side as he moved. "What's up tonight on Channel 4, Channel 7, Channel 9? Where are the cowboys rushing, and do I see the United States Cavalry over the next hill to the rescue?"

The street was silent and long and empty, with only his shadow moving like the shadow of a hawk in mid-country. If he closed his eyes and stood very still, frozen, he could imagine himself upon the center of a plain, a wintry, windless Arizona desert with no house in a thousand miles, and only dry riverbeds, the streets, for company.

"What is it now?" he asked the houses, notic-

Night Shadows by Edward Hopper (1921). Etching.

University of Iowa Museum of Art, Iowa City.
Gift of the Print and Drawing Study Club.

ing his wristwatch. "Eight-thirty P.M.? Time for a dozen assorted murders? A quiz? A revue? A comedian falling off the stage?"

Was that a murmur of laughter from within a moon-white house? He hesitated, but went on when nothing more happened. He stumbled over a particularly uneven section of sidewalk. The cement was vanishing under flowers and grass. In ten years of walking by night or day, for thousands of miles, he had never met another person walking, not one in all that time.

He came to a cloverleaf intersection, which stood silent where two main highways crossed the town. During the day it was a thunderous surge of cars, the gas stations open, a great insect rustling, and a ceaseless jockeying for position as the scarab beetles, a faint incense puttering from their exhausts, skimmed homeward to the far directions. But now these highways, too, were like streams in a dry season, all stone and bed and moon radiance.

He turned back on a side street, circling around

toward his home. He was within a block of his destination when the lone car turned a corner quite suddenly and flashed a fierce white cone of light upon him. He stood entranced, not unlike a night moth, stunned by the illumination, and then drawn toward it.

A metallic voice called to him:

"Stand still. Stay where you are! Don't move!"

He halted.

"Put up your hands!"

"But——" he said.

"Your hands up! Or we'll shoot!"

The police, of course, but what a rare, incredible thing; in a city of three million, there was only *one* police car left, wasn't that correct? Ever since a year ago, 2052, the election year, the force had been cut down from three cars to one. Crime was ebbing; there was no need now for the police, save for this one lone car wandering and wandering the empty streets.

"Your name?" said the police car in a metallic whisper. He couldn't see the men in it for the bright light in his eyes.

"Leonard Mead," he said.

"Speak up!"

"Leonard Mead!"

"Business or profession?"

"I guess you'd call me a writer."

"No profession," said the police car, as if talking to itself. The light held him fixed, like a museum specimen, needle thrust through chest.

"You might say that," said Mr. Mead. He hadn't written in years. Magazines and books didn't sell any more. Everything went on in the tomblike houses at night now, he thought, continuing his fancy. The tombs, ill-lit by television light, where the people sat like the dead, the gray or multicolored lights touching their faces, but never really touching them.

"No profession," said the phonograph voice, hissing. "What are you doing out?"

"Walking," said Leonard Mead.

"Walking!"

"Just walking," he said simply, but his face felt cold.

"Walking, just walking, walking?"

"Yes, sir."

"Walking where? For what?"

"Walking for air. Walking to *see*."

"Your address!"

"Eleven South Saint James Street."

"And there is air *in* your house, you have an air *conditioner,* Mr. Mead?"

"Yes."

"And you have a viewing screen in your house to see with?"

"No."

"No?" There was a crackling quiet that in itself was an accusation.

"Are you married, Mr. Mead?"

"No."

"Not married," said the police voice behind the fiery beam. The moon was high and clear among the stars and the houses were gray and silent.

"Nobody wanted me," said Leonard Mead with a smile.

"Don't speak unless you're spoken to!"

Leonard Mead waited in the cold night.

"Just *walking,* Mr. Mead?"

"Yes."

"But you haven't explained for what purpose."

"I explained; for air, and to see, and just to walk."

"Have you done this often?"

"Every night for years."

The police car sat in the center of the street with its radio throat faintly humming.

"Well, Mr. Mead," it said.

"Is that all?" he asked politely.

"Yes," said the voice. "Here." There was a sigh, a pop. The back door of the police car sprang wide. "Get in."

"Wait a minute, I haven't done anything!"

"Get in."

"I protest!"

"Mr. Mead."

He walked like a man suddenly drunk. As he passed the front window of the car he looked in. As he had expected, there was no one in the front seat, no one in the car at all.

"Get in."

He put his hand to the door and peered into the back seat, which was a little cell, a little black jail with bars. It smelled of riveted steel. It smelled of harsh antiseptic; it smelled too clean and hard and metallic. There was nothing soft there.

"Now, if you had a wife to give you an alibi," said the iron voice. "But——"

"Where are you taking me?"

The car hesitated, or rather gave a faint whirring click, as if information, somewhere, was dropping card by punch-slotted card under electric eyes. "To the Psychiatric Center for Research on Regressive Tendencies."

He got in. The door shut with a soft thud. The police car rolled through the night avenues, flashing its dim lights ahead.

They passed one house on one street a moment later, one house in an entire city of houses that were dark, but this one particular house had all of its electric lights brightly lit, every window a loud yellow illumination, square and warm in the cool darkness.

"That's *my* house," said Leonard Mead.

No one answered him.

The car moved down the empty riverbed streets and off away, leaving the empty streets with the empty sidewalks and no sound and no motion all the rest of the chill November night.

Responding to the Story

Analyzing the Story

Identifying Facts

1. What ominous fact about this future society is **foreshadowed** at once by the description of the "buckling concrete walk" in the first paragraph? As the story develops, what else are you told about the pedestrian's **setting**?
2. Find the sentences and phrases that at first make you think that Leonard Mead is the only person living in this setting in 2053 A.D. Find the passage that reveals that there are indeed other living people in this setting.
3. Leonard Mead is the only human character in the story. Who, or what, appears to be in charge of this future world?
4. Explain the "regressive tendencies" that Leonard Mead exhibits. Describe the police automaton's response when Mead says he is a writer.

Interpreting Meanings

5. What does the police car's response to Mead's profession suggest about freedom of expression in this future society?
6. The writer doesn't tell us directly what has happened to bring about the **basic situation** in the story. What is this situation? From the details of the story, make an educated guess about what caused it.
7. Most of "The Pedestrian" is told from a **limited third-person point of view**, with the narrator fo-

cusing on Leonard Mead's thoughts and feelings. Find at least three passages in the story where the narrator shows us that he knows what is going on in Leonard Mead's mind, but that he does *not* know what any other character is thinking or feeling.

8. Where does Bradbury use a very rare point of view—the **second person**? How does this point of view pull you directly into the story?
9. Why do you think Bradbury didn't write this story from the **first-person** point of view, using Leonard Mead's own voice? Why do you think he didn't use a completely **omniscient** narrator? Describe how the impact and **tone** of the story would have changed if a different point of view had been used.
10. How did you respond to this story? Did you find it compelling and well written, or did you find it obvious and predictable? Cite details from the story to support your opinion.

Writing About the Story

A Creative Response

1. **Continuing the Story.** Imagine what happens when Leonard Mead arrives at the Psychiatric Center for Research on Regressive Tendencies. Write the interview that Mead might have with the authorities there. Are the researchers humans or automatons? Does Mead defend his way of life? If so, how? What decision do the authorities make about Mead?

2. **Using Another Point of View.** How might this strange city appear to someone else—someone who enjoyed the silence? Rewrite paragraph 2 from the point of view of another pedestrian. What words would he or she use instead of *graveyard, gray,* and *tomblike?*

A Critical Response

3. **Responding to the Story's Theme.** What are your views on the story's theme and on the view of the future the story seems to embody? What do you think of Bradbury's attitude toward technology? Do you share his fears, or do you think he is being overly pessimistic? Write two or three paragraphs in which you answer these questions. Begin by clearly stating what you think the story's theme is.

4. **Comparing and Contrasting Stories.** In a paragraph, compare Bradbury's view of the future with the view presented in Godwin's "Cold Equations" (page 7). You might cover these aspects of the stories in your paragraph:

   a. The effect of technology on human freedom
   b. Technology and individuality
   c. Technology and emotions

Analyzing Language and Vocabulary

Connotations

As you know, certain words have emotional overtones, or **connotations,** that go beyond their literal meanings. For instance, consider the difference between the following pairs of words: *unusual* and *odd, young* and *immature, proud* and *smug, assertive* and *pushy, frugal* and *stingy.* In each pair, the first word has positive connotations, while the second has negative ones. We might describe ourselves by using the first word, but someone else using the second. In fact, the British philosopher Bertrand Russell once gave a classic example of the different connotations of words: "I am firm. You are obstinate. He is a pig-headed fool."

Here are some passages from the story that use words or phrases with powerful connotations. Answer the questions following each passage to show that you understand what emotional overtones the writer is suggesting.

1. "And on his way home he would see the cottages and homes with their dark windows, and it was not unequal to walking through a graveyard."

   a. How does the writer make you feel about his walk home by comparing it to a walk through a graveyard at night?
   b. Rephrase the comparison so that you have different feelings about his walk.

2. "Sudden gray phantoms seemed to manifest upon inner room walls . . . or there were whisperings and murmurs where a window in a tomb-like building was still open."

   a. What words suggest that this world is not alive and vigorous?
   b. Are these "whisperings and murmurs" pleasant or unpleasant sounds?

3. "During the day it [the intersection] was a thunderous surge of cars, the gas stations open, a great insect rustling, and a ceaseless jockeying for position as the scarab beetles . . . skimmed homeward to the far directions."

   a. Is a "great insect rustling" a pleasant or an unpleasant sound?
   b. How would this sound make you feel?
   c. How would you feel about this scene if the cars had been compared, not with beetles, but with butterflies?

4. "A metallic voice called to him."

   a. In some contexts, *metallic* might have positive connotations. Does it here?
   b. How would a metallic voice be different from a velvety voice? Or a musical voice?

5. "It [the inside of the car] smelled of harsh antiseptic; it smelled too clean and hard and metallic. There was nothing soft there."

   a. What things or places do you associate with the word *antiseptic?*
   b. What words in this passage suggest that the odor of this car is threatening?

Reading About the Writer

Ray Bradbury (1920–   ) calls himself "that special freak—the man with the child inside who remembers all." Bradbury was born in Waukegan, Illinois, and began writing when he was seven. He was an amateur magician and lived, he says, immersed completely in the world of fantasy and illusion—the world of the comic strip characters Buck Rogers and Flash Gordon. In high school he founded and edited a mimeographed magazine called *Futuria Fantasia.* After graduating from high school, Bradbury wrote stories that didn't sell and supported himself by selling newspapers in downtown Los Angeles. At the age of twenty-three, he became a full-time writer.

Bradbury says that his first book of stories, *Dark Carnival,* "got all my night sweats and terrors down on paper. My second, *The Martian Chronicles,* showed my concern for the future, as did my third, *The Illustrated Man."* Bradbury calls himself "a magic realist" and says that he is a disciple of Edgar Allan Poe (see page 168). Like many of his stories, "The Pedestrian" warns of what can go wrong in our future. Bradbury explains that his hatred of thought-investigation or thought-control of any kind comes from the fact that his ancestor, Mary Bradbury, was tried as a witch in Salem, Massachusetts, during the seventeenth century. According to Bradbury, "Science fiction is a wonderful hammer; I intend to use it when and if necessary to bark a few shins or knock a few heads, in order to make people leave people alone."

Focusing on Background
A Comment from the Writer

Here is an excerpt from Ray Bradbury's introduction to a collection of his short stories:

"When I was three my mother snuck me in and out of movies two or three times a week. My first film was Lon Chaney in *The Hunchback of Notre Dame.* I suffered permanent curvature of the spine *and* of my imagination that day a long time ago in 1923. From that hour on, I knew a kindred and wonderfully grotesque compatriot of the dark when I saw one. I ran off to see all the Chaney films again and again to be deliciously frightened. The Phantom of the Opera stood astride my life with his scarlet cape. And when it wasn't the Phantom it was the terrible hand that gestured from behind the bookcase in *The Cat and the Canary,* bidding me to come find more darkness hid in books.

"I was in love, then, with monsters and skeletons and circuses and carnivals and dinosaurs and, at last, the red planet, Mars.

"From these primitive bricks I have built a life and a career. By my staying in love with all of these amazing things, all of the good things in my existence have come about.

"In other words, I was *not* embarrassed at circuses. Some people are. Circuses are loud, vulgar, and smell in the sun. By the time many people are fourteen or fifteen, they have been divested of their loves, their ancient and intuitive tastes, one by one, until when they reach maturity there is no fun left, no zest, no gusto, no flavor. Others have criticized, and they have criticized themselves, into embarrassment. When the circus pulls in at five of a dark cold summer morn, and the calliope sounds, they do not rise and run, they turn in their sleep, and life passes by.

"I did rise and run. . . ."

—Ray Bradbury

Literature & Language

Using Pronouns Correctly

Literary Model

Connie is fifteen, and growing up is not easy for her. The following passage is from a short story by a well-known American writer. (The story was made into a movie starring Laura Dern.)

Her name was Connie. She was fifteen, and she had a quick, nervous, giggling habit of craning her neck to glance into mirrors or checking other people's faces to make sure her own was all right. Her mother, who noticed everything and knew everything and who hadn't much reason any longer to look at her own face, always scolded Connie about it. "Stop gawking at yourself; who are you? You think you're so pretty?" she would say. Connie would raise her eyebrows at these familiar complaints and look right through her mother, into a shadowy vision of herself as she was right at that moment: She knew she was pretty and that was everything. Her mother had been pretty once too, if you could believe those old snapshots in the album, but now her looks were gone and that was why she was always after Connie.

"Why don't you keep your room clean like your sister? How've you got your hair fixed—what stinks? Hair spray? You don't see your sister using that junk."

Her sister June was twenty-four and still lived at home. She was a secretary in the high school Connie attended, and if that wasn't bad enough—with her in the same building—she was so plain and chunky and steady that Connie had to hear her praised all the time by her mother and her mother's sisters. June did this, June did that, she saved money and helped clean the house and cooked and Connie couldn't do a thing, her mind was all filled with trashy daydreams. Their father was away at work most of the time, and when he came home he wanted supper, and he read the newspaper at supper, and after supper he went to bed. He didn't bother talking much to them, but around his bent head Connie's mother kept picking at her. . . . "She makes me want to throw up sometimes," she complained to her friends. She had a high, breathless, amused voice which made everything she said sound a little forced, whether it was sincere or not.

There was one good thing: June went places with girlfriends of hers, girls who were just as plain and steady as she, and so when Connie wanted to do that, her mother had no objections. The father of Connie's best girlfriend drove the girls the three miles to town and left them off at a shopping plaza, so that they could walk through the stores or go to a movie, and when he came to pick them up again at eleven he never bothered to ask what they had done. . . .

—from "Where Are You Going,
Where Have You Been?"
Joyce Carol Oates

A Grammar Note

There are four main characters in this excerpt: Connie; Connie's mother; Connie's sister, June; and Connie's father. The narrator uses the third-person pronouns to refer to these characters and their relationship to Connie. This use of pronouns tells us that the passage is written from either the **omniscient** or the **limited third-person point of view**.

A **pronoun** is a word that takes the place of one or more nouns. The following is a list of the personal pronouns:

Personal Pronouns			
	Singular	**Plural**	**Possessive**
1st person	I, me	we, us	my, mine, our, ours
2nd person	you	you	your, yours
3rd person	he, she, him, her, it	they, them	his, hers, its, their, theirs

Note how the italicized third-person personal pronouns in the passage below replace the names of Connie, her sister, and her father, and reduce the need to repeat the same names over and over.

> June did this, June did that, *she* saved money and helped clean the house and cooked and Connie couldn't do a thing, *her* mind was all filled with trashy daydreams. *Their* father was away at work most of the time, and when *he* came home *he* wanted supper, and *he* read the newspaper at supper, and after supper *he* went to bed.

The word a pronoun refers to (whose place it takes) is the **antecedent** of the pronoun. The antecedents of the italicized personal pronouns in the preceding passage are as follows.

Personal Pronouns	Antecedents
she	June
her	Connie's
Their	June and Connie's
he	father

In your writing, take care that all the pronouns you use have clear antecedents. In other words, be sure that the **context,** or the text surrounding each pronoun, makes it clear whom or what each pronoun is referring to. In most cases, the antecedent of a pronoun is a nearby noun.

Sometimes the antecedent of a pronoun is ambiguous—that is, it's not clear which noun the pronoun is replacing:

Confusing: My sister and her friend Doris talked to me about the job. She said I had nothing to worry about.

This passage is ambiguous because we can't tell if *she* refers to *sister* or *Doris*. In cases such as this, you should rewrite the passage:

Clear: My sister and her friend Doris talked to me about the job. Doris said I had nothing to worry about.

Often writers use the pronoun *it* in such a way that its antecedent is vague:

Vague: Connie is self-centered, and it is a serious problem.

Clearer: Connie's self-centeredness is a serious problem.

Examining the Writer's Style

The following activities will help you analyze the way Oates has used pronouns. Work with a partner.

1. Make a chart like the preceding one, listing each pronoun and its antecedent in the first and last paragraphs of the passage.
2. Rewrite the last paragraph, substituting a noun (the antecedent) for every pronoun. What is the effect of your revision?
3. The third paragraph opens with a pronoun. What is its antecedent? What are the antecedents of the pronouns *she* and *her* in the second sentence of this same paragraph?

Using Pronouns in Your Writing

Using Another Point of View. Pronouns help signal the writer's point of view. In this extract, you know at once that Oates is telling Connie's story from either the **omniscient** or the **limited third-person point of view,** because she refers to all characters with the third-person pronouns *she, her, hers, he, his, him, them,* and so on. Rewrite this extract using the **first-person point of view.** You will now have a character tell the story using the first-person pronoun *I.* (You might even try a rare point of view, and tell the story using the second-person pronoun *you.* If you attempt the second-person, you might open your story like this: "You knew her name was Connie. . . .")

COMPARING AND CONTRASTING STORIES

Writing Assignment

Write a four-paragraph essay in which you compare and contrast one of these pairs of stories: "Two Kinds" (page 46) and "Mr. Parker" (page 68); "Two Kinds" and "Boys and Girls" (page 98); "The Cold Equations" (page 7) and "The Pedestrian" (page 137).

Background

Comparing and contrasting are critical thinking skills that enable you to see similarities and differences. When you **compare** stories, you point out specific ways in which they are alike. When you **contrast** stories, you tell how they are different.

Prewriting

Review the two stories you've selected, analyzing the ways they use the short-story elements you've studied so far in this unit. A chart like the following one will help you gather information for your essay.

	Story 1	Story 2
Plot (What is the conflict, and how is it resolved?)		
Characters (What does the main character learn? Or how does he or she change?)		
Theme (What insight about life does the story reveal?)		
Point of view (Who tells the story? How does the point of view make you feel about the characters?)		
Tone (What is the writer's attitude toward the characters?)		

When you've finished the chart, make two lists summarizing the stories' similarities and differences. Here is the beginning of a list for an essay comparing "Two Kinds" and "Boys and Girls."

Similarities	Differences
1. Both stories are about strong-willed girl's struggle to be herself.	1. In Tan story she fights mother's high expectations; in Munro story she fights a limited view of girls' life.

When you've listed as many similarities and differences as you can, look over your lists and decide on a **thesis statement**. Here is a thesis statement for an essay on the Tan and Munro stories:

"Two Kinds" by Amy Tan and "Boys and Girls" by Alice Munro are both stories about a strong-willed girl who struggles to be herself.

Writing

In your first paragraph, cite the titles and authors of the stories you are comparing, and briefly state the thesis of your essay. In paragraphs 2 and 3, discuss at least two differences in the stories and two ways in which the stories are similar. End your essay with a paragraph that summarizes your findings and states your response to the stories.

Checklist for Revision
1. Have you included a thesis statement in the introductory paragraph?
2. Have you discussed at least two differences and two similarities?
3. In your last paragraph, have you summarized your points and stated your response?
4. Have you checked: Spelling? Punctuation? Capitalization? Sentence structure? Paragraph organization?

Setting: "Putting Us There"

It is undoubtedly possible for an interesting story to have no **setting** at all—that is, no indication of when or where the action is set. If the characters and their situation are strong enough, they will hold our attention in empty space, so to speak, just as a play presented on a bare stage might hold our interest.

But in life, all events occur somewhere. Often a story's place or landscape and its **atmosphere**—its feeling of harshness or mildness, of gloom or cheer, of beauty or ugliness—affect the characters and the way they lead their lives. Think of how crucial setting would be to a story about a prisoner or to a story about three castaways adrift on the Pacific or to a story about a high-school graduation in a coal town.

Setting puts us there—it gives us readers a feeling of being *in* the situation with the characters. If we are in the square of a town in Honduras, we should feel hot, sweaty, and thirsty. We should see how the sun is baking the back of the little burro tethered at the side of the church. We should smell the *zozo,* the native delicacy of fish heads and banana skins, as it sizzles over the charcoal.

Not only does setting tell us *where* we are, but it also tells us *when.* If the passing traffic is horse drawn, we can guess we have gone back in history. An inch of new-fallen snow on the porch rail tells us it's winter. If the sun is just up over the pine ridge or if the paper boy is sailing a copy of the *Clarion Ledger* onto the front steps, it is morning.

Setting can be a pit in Spain during the Inquisition, the deck of a boat crossing the Atlantic, a winter evening in a New York brownstone. Setting can be a reservation in the American Southwest or a colony on Mars or a town named Yellow Sky in Texas.

Setting, accurately portrayed, can give the story a kind of truth or believability. We call this **verisimilitude,** which means "like truth." If we are persuaded that this really is a war zone, complete with bomb bursts and the groans of the wounded, we are likely to accept the soldiers' behavior as an accurate portrayal of the way people behave in battle.

Setting and Imagination

When a writer deftly describes the setting of a story, we readers tend to fill in some details for ourselves, and we tend to store the scene in our memory alongside our own actual experiences. We are also likely to recall that setting as a particular writer's "country." When we read William Faulkner's fiction, we need not have seen the rural South in order to have a strong sense of what it is like. Similarly, Ernest Hemingway's stories give us a "memory" of Upper Michigan without our ever having been there.

It is this sense of place in fiction that gives us the opportunity for armchair travel—to visit faraway places without leaving home.

Setting and Our Emotions

A more important function of setting, however, is to contribute to a story's total **emotional effect.** We all know that some settings can make us feel gloomy and others can make us feel cheerful. An autumnal setting can add a sense of loss to a story about a doomed love. A spring setting can give a note of hope to a story of a girl's coming of age. A small-town setting can bring a sense of comfort and stability to a story about a family that endures in spite of difficulty. Setting can also be used to create ironic contrasts: that spring setting might also be used to create a poignant sense of inappropriateness in a story about loss or death.

Here are descriptions of two outdoor settings, one on a beach in New Hampshire and one in a rice paddy in Vietnam. See how one setting creates an emotional effect of pleasure, one of disgust.

> The beach shed its deadness and became a spectral gray-white, then more white than gray, and finally it was totally white and stainless, as pure as the shores of Eden.
>
> —from *A Separate Peace*,
> John Knowles, page 918

> . . . his boots sank into the thick paddy water and he smelled it all around him. He would tell his mother how it smelled: mud and algae and cattle manure and chlorophyll; decay, breeding mosquitoes and leeches as big as mice; the fecund warmth of the paddy waters rising up to his cut knee.
>
> —from "Where Have You Gone, Charming Billy?"
> Tim O'Brien, page 212

This Vietnam jungle setting is used in another part of the story to contrast with the young soldier's comforting memories of home in Iowa. The emotional effect of that contrast can be shattering.

> He was pretending he was a boy again, camping with his father in the midnight summer along the Des Moines River. In the dark, with his eyes pinched shut, he pretended. He pretended that when he opened his eyes, his father would be there by the campfire and they would talk softly about whatever came to mind and then roll into their sleeping bags. . . .
>
> —from "Where Have You Gone, Charming Billy?"
> Tim O'Brien, page 212

Setting and Characters

Setting also reveals character. We all affect our environment in one way or another, so a writer wishing to portray an untidy Alice will show us the mess in her bedroom. Look—pajamas, hangers, sneakers in a snarl on the floor of her closet, records and magazines strewn beneath the unmade bed. We'll know something about Alice the moment we see her.

Here is Jimmy's room with a set of dumbbells and heavier weights in one corner; on the bedside table a copy of the *Guinness Book of World Records;* on the wall, school pennants, photographs of the basketball team, a set of antlers; and hanging from a hook on the closet door, a pair of boxing gloves. How much do we know about Jimmy before he even opens the door?

Here are two houses: one is the home of a very old man whose life is almost over. The other is the home of a romanticized music teacher. What do their settings reveal about these characters, even before they appear?

> The house had only two rooms, but he owned it—the last scrap of the farm that he had sold off years ago. It stood in a hollow of dying trees beside a superhighway in Baltimore County. All it held was a few sticks of furniture, a change of clothes, a skillet, and a set of dishes.
>
> —from "With All Flags Flying," Anne Tyler, page 81

> I loved the Parkers' house. It was the last Victorian house on the block and was shaped like a wedding cake. The living room was round, and all the walls curved. . . . The front-hall window was a stained-glass picture of a fat Victorian baby holding a bunch of roses. . . . Its white dress was milky when the light shone through.
>
> —from "Mr. Parker," Laurie Colwin, page 68

Setting As a Character

Though you will find that in some stories setting hardly matters, in others the setting can carry all the importance of a major character. We'd find this situation in a story where setting is portrayed as the antagonist, such as a story about a polar expedition fighting against the harshness of the arctic tundra. We also find it in the story "The Cold Equations" (page 7), where the characters are in conflict with the harsh laws of the space frontier.

Let's look now at the way a famous Western writer creates a setting that carries all the importance of a character.

Cottage City Window (detail) by Ken Davies. Oil.

Private Collection. Photo courtesy Hirschl & Adler Galleries, Inc., New York.

TRAP OF GOLD

Louis L'Amour

Western stories are usually about heroic loners who save the settlement from the threats of violent gunslingers. "The Bride Comes to Yellow Sky" on page 120 is an example of a story that parodies this conventional plot. Louis L'Amour was an enormously popular writer who took the Western se-riously. Here is one of his typical heroes taking a risk that puts readers on the edge of their seats. Ask yourself this before you read: How much would you risk for ten thousand dollars? What would it take to make you risk your life?

What do you guess the title might mean?

Wetherton had been three months out of Horsehead before he found his first color.[1] At first it was a few scattered grains taken from the base of an alluvial fan[2] where millions of tons of sand and silt had washed down from a chain of rugged peaks; yet the gold was ragged under the magnifying glass.

Gold that has carried any distance becomes worn and polished by the abrasive action of the accompanying rocks and sand, so this could not have been carried far. With caution born of harsh experience, he seated himself and lighted his pipe, yet excitement was strong within him.

A contemplative man by nature, experience had taught him how a man may be deluded by hope, yet all his instincts told him the source of the gold was somewhere on the mountain above. It could have come down the wash that skirted the base of the mountain, but the ragged condition of the gold made that impossible.

The base of the fan was a half-mile across and hundreds of feet thick, built of silt and sand washed down by centuries of erosion among the higher peaks. The point of the wide V of the fan lay between two towering upthrusts of granite, but from where Wetherton sat he could see that the actual source of the fan lay much higher.

Wetherton made camp near a tiny spring west of the fan, then picketed his burros and began his climb. When he was well over two thousand feet higher, he stopped, resting again, and while resting he dry-panned some of the silt. Surprisingly, there were more than a few grains of gold even in that first pan, so he continued his climb and passed at last between the towering portals of the granite columns.

Above this natural gate were three smaller alluvial fans that joined at the gate to pour into the greater fan below. Dry-panning two of these brought no results, but the third, even by the relatively poor method of dry-panning, showed a dozen colors, all of good size.

The head of this fan lay in a gigantic crack in a granitic upthrust that resembled a fantastic ruin. Pausing to catch his breath, his gaze wandered along the base of this upthrust, and right before him the crumbling granite was slashed with a vein of quartz that was literally laced with gold!

Struggling nearer through the loose sand, his heart pounding more from excitement than from altitude and exertion, he came to an abrupt stop. The band of quartz was six feet wide, and that six feet was cobwebbed with gold.

It was unbelievable, but here it was.

Yet even in this moment of success, something about the beetling[3] cliff stopped him from going forward. His innate caution took hold, and he drew back to examine it at greater length. Wary of what he saw, he circled the batholith and then climbed to the ridge behind it from which he could

---

1. **color:** here, a trace of gold.
2. **alluvial fan:** a fan-shaped deposit of mud and sand.

3. **beetling:** projecting.

look down upon the roof. What he saw from there left him dry-mouthed and jittery.

The granitic upthrust was obviously a part of a much older range, one that had weathered and worn, suffered from shock and twisting until finally this tower of granite had been violently upthrust, leaving it standing, a shaky ruin among younger and sturdier peaks. In the process the rock had been shattered and riven by mighty forces until it had become a miner's horror. Wetherton stared, fascinated by the prospect. With enormous wealth here for the taking, every ounce must be taken at the risk of life.

One stick of powder might bring the whole crumbling mass down in a heap, and it loomed all of three hundred feet above its base in the fan. The roof of the batholith was riven with gigantic cracks, literally seamed with breaks like the wall of an ancient building that has remained standing after heavy bombing. Walking back to the base of the tower, Wetherton found he could actually break loose chunks of the quartz with his fingers.

The vein itself lay on the downhill side and at the very base. The outer wall of the upthrust was sharply tilted so that a man working at the vein would be cutting his way into the very foundations of the tower, and any single blow of the pick might bring the whole mass down upon him. Furthermore, if the rock did fall, the vein would be hopelessly buried under thousands of tons of rock and lost without the expenditure of much more capital than he could command. And at this moment Wetherton's total of money in hand amounted to slightly less than forty dollars.

Thirty yards from the face he seated himself upon the sand and filled his pipe once more. A man might take tons out of there without trouble, and yet it might collapse at the first blow. Yet he knew he had no choice. He needed money, and it lay here before him. Even if he were at first successful, there were two things he must avoid. The first was tolerance of danger that might bring carelessness; the second, that urge to go back for that "little bit more" that could kill him.

It was well into the afternoon and he had not eaten, yet he was not hungry. He circled the batholith, studying it from every angle, only to reach the conclusion that his first estimate had been correct. The only way to get at the gold was to go into the very shadow of the leaning wall and attack it at its base, digging it out by main strength. From where he stood it seemed ridiculous that a mere man with a pick could topple that mass of rock, yet he knew how delicate such a balance could be.

The tower was situated on what might be described as the military crest of the ridge, and the alluvial fan sloped steeply away from its lower side, steeper than a steep stairway. The top of the leaning wall overshadowed the top of the fan, and if it started to crumble and a man had warning, he might run to the north with a bare chance of escape. The soft sand in which he must run would be an impediment, but that could be alleviated by making a walk from flat rocks sunken into the sand.

It was dusk when he returned to his camp. Deliberately, he had not permitted himself to begin work, not by so much as a sample. He must be deliberate in all his actions, and never for a second should he forget the mass that towered above him. A split second of hesitation when the crash came—and he accepted it as inevitable—would mean burial under tons of crumbled rock.

The following morning he picketed his burros on a small meadow near the spring, cleaned the spring itself, and prepared a lunch. Then he removed his shirt, drew on a pair of gloves, and walked to the face of the cliff. Yet even then he did not begin, knowing that upon this habit of care and deliberation might depend not only his success in the venture, but life itself. He gathered flat stones and began building his walk. "When you start moving," he told himself, "you'll have to be fast."

Finally, and with infinite care, he began tapping at the quartz, enlarging cracks with the pick, removing fragments, then prying loose whole chunks. He did not swing the pick, but used it as a lever. The quartz was rotten, and a man might obtain a considerable amount by this method of picking or even pulling with the hands. When he had a sack filled with the richest quartz, he carried it over his path to a safe place beyond the shadow of the

The Mirage (detail) by Thomas Moran (1837–1926). Oil on canvas.   Stark Museum of Art, Orange, Texas.

tower. Returning, he tamped a few more flat rocks into his path and began on the second sack. He worked with greater care than was, perhaps, essential. He was not and had never been a gambling man.

In the present operation he was taking a careful calculated risk in which every eventuality had been weighed and judged. He needed the money and he intended to have it; he had a good idea of his chances of success, but he knew that his gravest danger was to become too greedy, too much engrossed in his task.

Dragging the two sacks down the hill, he found a flat block of stone and with a single jack proceeded to break up the quartz. It was a slow and a hard job, but he had no better means of extracting the gold. After breaking or crushing the quartz, much of the gold could be separated by a knife blade, for it was amazingly concentrated. With water from the spring, Wetherton panned the remainder until it was too dark to see.

Out of his blankets by daybreak, he ate breakfast and completed the extraction of the gold. At a rough estimate, his first day's work would run to four hundred dollars. He made a cache for the gold sack and took the now empty ore sacks and climbed back to the tower.

The air was clear and fresh, the sun warm after the chill of night, and he liked the feel of the pick in his hands.

Laura and Tommy awaited him back in Horsehead, and if he was killed here, there was small chance they would ever know what had become of him. But he did not intend to be killed. The gold he was extracting from this rock was for them, and not for himself.

It would mean an easier life in a larger town, a home of their own and the things to make the home a woman desires, and it meant an education for Tommy. For himself, all he needed was the thought of that home to return to, his wife and son—and the desert itself. And one was as necessary to him as the other.

The desert would be the death of him. He had been told that many times and did not need to be told, for few men knew the desert as he did. The desert was to him what an orchestra is to a fine conductor, what the human body is to a surgeon.

It was his work, his life, and the thing he knew best. He always smiled when he looked first into the desert as he started a new trip. Would this be it?

The morning drew on, and he continued to work with an even-paced swing of the pick, a careful filling of the sack. The gold showed bright and beautiful in the crystalline quartz, which was so much more beautiful than the gold itself. From time to time as the morning drew on, he paused to rest and to breathe deeply of the fresh, clear air. Deliberately, he refused to hurry.

For nineteen days he worked tirelessly, eight hours a day at first, then lessening his hours to seven, and then to six. Wetherton did not explain to himself why he did this, but he realized it was becoming increasingly difficult to stay on the job. Again and again he would walk away from the rock face on one excuse or another, and each time he would begin to feel his scalp prickle, his steps grow quicker, and each time he returned more reluctantly.

Three times, beginning on the thirteenth, again on the seventeenth and finally on the nineteenth day, he heard movement within the tower. Whether that whispering in the rock was normal he did not know. Such a natural movement might have been going on for centuries. He only knew that it happened now, and each time it happened, a cold chill went along his spine.

His work had cut a deep notch at the base of the tower, such a notch as a man might make in felling a tree, but wider and deeper. The sacks of gold, too, were increasing. They now numbered seven, and their total would, he believed, amount to more than five thousand dollars—probably nearer to six thousand. As he cut deeper into the rock, the vein was growing richer.

He worked on his knees now. The vein had slanted downward as he cut into the base of the tower and he was all of nine feet into the rock with the great mass of it above him. If that rock gave way while he was working, he would be crushed in an instant with no chance of escape. Nevertheless, he continued.

The change in the rock tower was not the only change, for he had lost weight and he no longer slept well. On the night of the twentieth day he decided he had six thousand dollars and his goal would be ten thousand. And the following day the rock was the richest ever! As if to tantalize him into working on and on, the deeper he cut, the richer the ore became. By nightfall of that day he had taken out more than a thousand dollars.

Now the lust of the gold was getting into him, taking him by the throat. He was fascinated by the danger of the tower as well as the desire for the gold. Three more days to go—could he leave it then? He looked again at the tower and felt a peculiar sense of foreboding, a feeling that here he was to die, that he would never escape. Was it his imagination, or had the outer wall leaned a little more?

On the morning of the twenty-second day he climbed the fan over a path that use had built into a series of continuous steps. He had never counted those steps, but there must have been over a thousand of them. Dropping his canteen into a shaded hollow and pick in hand, he started for the tower.

The forward tilt *did* seem somewhat more than before. Or was it the light? The crack that ran behind the outer wall seemed to have widened, and when he examined it more closely, he found a small pile of freshly run silt near the bottom of the crack. So it had moved!

Wetherton hesitated, staring at the rock with wary attention. He was a fool to go back in there again. Seven thousand dollars was more than he had ever had in his life before, yet in the next few hours he could take out at least a thousand dollars more, and in the next three days he could easily have the ten thousand he had set for his goal.

He walked to the opening, dropped to his knees, and crawled into the narrowing, flat-roofed hole. No sooner was he inside than fear climbed up into his throat. He felt trapped, stifled, but he fought down the mounting panic and began to work. His first blows were so frightened and feeble that nothing came loose. Yet when he did get started, he began to work with a feverish intensity that was wholly unlike him.

When he slowed and then stopped to fill his sack, he was gasping for breath, but despite his hurry the sack was not quite full. Reluctantly, he lifted his pick again, but before he could strike a blow, the gigantic mass above him seemed to creak like something tired and old. A deep shudder went through the colossal pile and then a deep grinding that turned him sick with horror. All his plans for instant flight were frozen, and it was not until the groaning ceased that he realized he was lying on his back, breathless with fear and expectancy. Slowly, he edged his way into the air and walked, fighting the desire to run, away from the rock.

When he stopped near his canteen he was wringing with cold sweat and trembling in every muscle. He sat down on the rock and fought for control. It was not until some twenty minutes had passed that he could trust himself to get to his feet.

Despite his experience, he knew that if he did not go back now he would never go. He had out but one sack for the day and wanted another. Circling the batholith, he examined the widening crack, endeavoring again, for the third time, to find another means of access to the vein.

The tilt of the outer wall was obvious, and it could stand no more without toppling. It was possible that by cutting into the wall of the column and striking down, he might tap the vein at a safer point. Yet this added blow at the foundation would bring the tower nearer to collapse and render his other hole untenable. Even this new attempt would not be safe, although immeasurably more secure than the hole he had left. Hesitating, he looked back at the hole.

Once more? The ore was now fabulously rich, and the few pounds he needed to complete the sack he could get in just a little while. He stared at the black and undoubtedly narrower hole, then looked up at the leaning wall. He picked up his pick and, his mouth dry, started back, drawn by a fascination that was beyond all reason.

His heart pounding, he dropped to his knees at the tunnel face. The air seemed stifling and he could feel his scalp tingling, but once he started to crawl it was better. The face where he now worked was at least sixteen feet from the tunnel mouth. Pick in hand, he began to wedge chunks from their seat. The going seemed harder now, and the chunks did not come loose so easily.

Above him the tower made no sound. The crushing weight was now something tangible. He could almost feel it growing, increasing with every move of his. The mountain seemed resting on his shoulder, crushing the air from his lungs.

Suddenly he stopped. His sack almost full, he stopped and lay very still, staring up at the bulk of the rock above him.

No.

He would go no further. Now he would quit. Not another sackful. Not another pound. He would go out now. He would go down the mountain without a backward look, and he would keep going. His wife waiting at home, little Tommy, who would run gladly to meet him—these were too much to gamble.

With the decision came peace, came certainty. He sighed deeply, and relaxed, and then it seemed to him that every muscle in his body had been knotted with strain. He turned on his side and with great deliberation gathered his lantern, his sack, his hand-pick.

He had won. He had defeated the crumbling tower, he had defeated his own greed. He backed easily, without the caution that had marked his earlier movements in the cave. His blind, trusting foot found the projecting rock, a piece of quartz that stuck out from the rough-hewn wall.

The blow was too weak, too feeble to have brought forth the reaction that followed. The rock seemed to quiver like the flesh of a beast when stabbed; a queer vibration went through that ancient rock, then a deep, gasping sigh.

He had waited too long!

Fear came swiftly in upon him, crowding him, while his body twisted, contracting into the smallest possible space. He tried to will his muscles to move beneath the growing sounds that vibrated through the passage. The whispers of the rock grew into a terrible groan, and there was a rattle of pebbles. Then silence.

The silence was more horrifying than the sound. Somehow he was crawling, even as he expected the avalanche of gold to bury him. Abruptly, his feet were in the open. He was out.

He ran without stopping, but behind him he heard a growing roar that he couldn't outrace. When he knew from the slope of the land that he must be safe from falling rock, he fell to his knees. He turned and looked back. The muted, roaring sound, like thunder beyond mountains, continued, but there was no visible change in the tower. Suddenly, as he watched, the whole rock formation seemed to shift and tip. The movement lasted only seconds, but before the tons of rock had found their new equilibrium, his tunnel and the area around it had utterly vanished from sight.

When he could finally stand, Wetherton gathered up his sack of ore and his canteen. The wind was cool upon his face as he walked away; and he did not look back again.

Responding to the Story

Analyzing the Story

Identifying Facts

1. Draw the rock formation in which Wetherton mined his gold, using the description in the opening pages. Compare your drawing with those of other readers. Do you all agree?
2. What two things does Wetherton know he must avoid? Where, later in the story, does it seem he might succumb to the two dangers?

3. Trace the way the writer builds up **suspense** by gradually "paying out" information about Wetherton's progress toward his goal.

Interpreting Meanings

4. Find the moments in the story when the writer makes you think Wetherton will fail in his quest. What passages help you share his physical responses to his ordeal?

5. Find at least three **images** that make the **setting** of the story—the tower of granite—seem like a human **antagonist**. Is the tower characterized as an evil antagonist, as a good antagonist, or as something else?

6. What do you find especially horrifying about Wetherton's situation? That is, what deep-seated fears do you think are aroused by this particular setting?

7. Did you believe from the start that Wetherton would escape his golden trap? Or did you expect another outcome? Explain.

8. What is the **point of view** in "Trap of Gold"? Suppose Wetherton himself were telling the story. How would this change in point of view affect the impact of the story—particularly the element of suspense?

9. On one level, the **title** refers to a real rock formation. What else is the "trap of gold"?

Writing About the Story

A Creative Response

1. **Writing a Different Ending.** Write a different ending to "Trap of Gold"—one in which Wetherton loses his struggle with the setting. Begin your new ending right after the sentence "He had waited too long!" on page 154.

A Critical Response

2. **Comparing and Contrasting Stories.** In "The Cold Equations" on page 7, the characters are also pitted against a hostile setting. In a two-paragraph essay, compare and contrast "Trap of Gold" with "The Cold Equations." Before you write, gather details by filling out a chart like the following one.

	L'Amour Story	Godwin Story
Setting		
Reasons characters are pitted against setting		
Power characters have over setting		
Outcome of conflict with setting		
Emotional effect of story		

Analyzing Language and Vocabulary

Specialized Vocabularies

Every job and hobby has a **specialized vocabulary:** words that refer to raw materials, tools, and procedures specific to the trade. For example, the word *color* has a specialized meaning in the first sentence of "Trap of Gold." It refers to a trace of a valuable mineral, especially gold, in rock. The specialized vocabulary in "Trap of Gold" comes from geology (the study of land formation) and mining. Use a dictionary to find the meanings of the italicized words and phrases in the following passages. Does your dictionary include *field labels* that indicate definitions for the specialized fields of *Mining* or *Geol.* (Geology)?

1. "The point of the wide V of the fan lay between two towering *upthrusts* of *granite*. . . ."
2. ". . . and while resting, he *dry-panned* some of the *silt.*"
3. ". . . and right before him the crumbling granite was slashed with a *vein of quartz* that was literally laced with gold!"
4. ". . . he circled the *batholith.* . . ."

Reading About the Writer

Louis L'Amour (1908–1988) is still a best-selling writer of Western fiction, with more than seventy novels and four hundred short stories in print. L'Amour was born in Jamestown, North Dakota. As a child, he was intrigued with stories of his pioneer ancestors and read every book he could about frontier life. He dropped out of school at fifteen and traveled throughout the West, working as a fruit picker, lumberjack, miner, and elephant handler.

During World War II L'Amour began telling Western and autobiographical tales to his fellow soldiers. Encouraged by their response, he wrote down some of his stories and published them.

The writer Louise Erdrich comments: "The best parts of Mr. L'Amour's novels are the tight spots in which we find our hero—bushwacked, surrounded, hanging over deep chasms, enslaved, defying no-good cowards who have somehow got him in their thrall." L'Amour summed up his own work by saying: "I feel like a midwife to a thousand stories that have to be told and never would be unless I told them . . . not the lives of generals and public men, but all those people buried in anonymous graves who suffered to build the country."

THE MAN TO SEND RAIN CLOUDS

Leslie Marmon Silko

This story, by a contemporary Native American writer, has one setting in which two different cultures exist side by side. One culture is that of the Laguna, a Pueblo tribe in New Mexico. The Laguna survive alongside the culture of the Euro-pean settlers who have come to their country and introduced their own way of life. Before you begin reading, write down briefly what you think the title means. Which culture do you think this man will belong to?

Earth Knower by Maynard Dixon (c. 1933). Oil.

The Oakland Museum, Oakland, California.
Bequest of Dr. Abilio Reis.

They found him under a big cottonwood tree. His Levi jacket and pants were faded light blue so that he had been easy to find. The big cottonwood tree stood apart from a small grove of winter-bare cottonwoods which grew in the wide, sandy arroyo. He had been dead for a day or more, and the sheep had wandered and scattered up and down the arroyo. Leon and his brother-in-law, Ken, gathered the sheep and left them in the pen at the sheep camp before they returned to the cottonwood tree. Leon waited under the tree while Ken drove the truck through the deep sand to the edge of the arroyo. He squinted up at the sun and unzipped his jacket—it sure was hot for this time of year. But high and northwest the blue mountains were still in snow. Ken came sliding down the low, crumbling bank about fifty yards down, and he was bringing the red blanket.

Before they wrapped the old man, Leon took a piece of string out of his pocket and tied a small gray feather in the old man's long white hair. Ken gave him the paint. Across the brown, wrinkled forehead he drew a streak of white and along the high cheekbones he drew a strip of blue paint. He paused and watched Ken throw pinches of corn-meal and pollen into the wind that fluttered the small gray feather. Then Leon painted with yellow under the old man's broad nose, and finally, when he had painted green across the chin, he smiled.

"Send us rain clouds, Grandfather." They laid the bundle in the back of the pickup and covered it with a heavy tarp before they started back to the pueblo.

They turned off the highway onto the sandy pueblo road. Not long after they passed the store and post office, they saw Father Paul's car coming toward them. When he recognized their faces, he slowed his car and waved for them to stop. The young priest rolled down the car window.

"Did you find old Teofilo?" he asked loudly.

Leon stopped the truck. "Good morning, Father. We were just out to the sheep camp. Everything is O.K. now."

"Thank God for that. Teofilo is a very old man. You really shouldn't allow him to stay at the sheep camp alone."

"No, he won't do that anymore now."

"Well, I'm glad you understand. I hope I'll be seeing you at Mass this week—we missed you last Sunday. See if you can get old Teofilo to come with you." The priest smiled and waved at them as they drove away.

Louise and Teresa were waiting. The table was set for lunch, and the coffee was boiling on the black iron stove. Leon looked at Louise and then at Teresa.

"We found him under a cottonwood tree in the big arroyo near sheep camp. I guess he sat down to rest in the shade and never got up again." Leon walked toward the old man's bed. The red plaid shawl had been shaken and spread carefully over the bed, and a new brown flannel shirt and pair of stiff new Levi's were arranged neatly beside the pillow. Louise held the screen door open while Leon and Ken carried in the red blanket. He looked small and shriveled, and after they dressed him in the new shirt and pants, he seemed more shrunken.

It was noontime now, because the church bells rang the Angelus. They ate the beans with hot bread, and nobody said anything until after Teresa poured the coffee.

Ken stood up and put on his jacket. "I'll see about the gravediggers. Only the top layer of soil is frozen. I think it can be ready before dark."

Leon nodded his head and finished his coffee. After Ken had been gone for a while, the neighbors and clanspeople came quietly to embrace Teofilo's family and to leave food on the table because the gravediggers would come to eat when they were finished.

The sky in the west was full of pale yellow light. Louise stood outside with her hands in the pockets of Leon's green army jacket that was too big for her. The funeral was over, and the old men had taken their candles and medicine bags and were gone. She waited until the body was laid into the pickup before she said anything to Leon. She touched his arm, and he noticed that her hands were still dusty from the cornmeal that she had sprinkled around the old man. When she spoke, Leon could not hear her.

"What did you say? I didn't hear you."

"I said that I had been thinking about something."

"About what?"

"About the priest sprinkling holy water for Grandpa. So he won't be thirsty."

Leon stared at the new moccasins that Teofilo had made for the ceremonial dances in the summer. They were nearly hidden by the red blanket. It was getting colder, and the wind pushed gray dust down the narrow pueblo road. The sun was approaching the long mesa, where it disappeared during the winter. Louise stood there shivering and watching his face. Then he zipped up his jacket and opened the truck door. "I'll see if he's there."

Ken stopped the pickup at the church, and Leon got out; and then Ken drove down the hill to the graveyard where people were waiting. Leon knocked at the old carved door with its symbols of the Lamb. While he waited, he looked up at the twin bells from the king of Spain with the last sunlight pouring around them in their tower.

The priest opened the door and smiled when he saw who it was. "Come in! What brings you here this evening?"

The priest walked toward the kitchen, and Leon stood with his cap in his hand, playing with the earflaps and examining the living room—the brown sofa, the green armchair, and the brass lamp that hung down from the ceiling by links of chain. The priest dragged a chair out of the kitchen and offered it to Leon.

"No thank you, Father. I only came to ask you if you would bring your holy water to the graveyard."

The priest turned away from Leon and looked out the window at the patio full of shadows and the dining-room windows of the nuns' cloister across the patio. The curtains were heavy, and the light from within faintly penetrated; it was impossible to see the nuns inside eating supper. "Why didn't you tell me he was dead? I could have brought the Last Rites anyway."

Leon smiled. "It wasn't necessary, Father."

The priest stared down at his scuffed brown loafers and the worn hem of his cassock. "For a Christian burial it was necessary."

His voice was distant, and Leon thought that his blue eyes looked tired.

"It's O.K. Father, we just want him to have plenty of water."

The priest sank down into the green chair and picked up a glossy missionary magazine. He turned the colored pages full of lepers and pagans without looking at them.

"You know I can't do that, Leon. There should have been the Last Rites and a funeral Mass at the very least."

Leon put on his green cap and pulled the flaps down over his ears. "It's getting late, Father. I've got to go."

When Leon opened the door, Father Paul stood up and said, "Wait." He left the room and came back wearing a long brown overcoat. He followed Leon out the door and across the dim churchyard to the adobe steps in front of the church. They both stooped to fit through the low adobe entrance. And when they started down the hill to the graveyard, only half of the sun was visible above the mesa.

The priest approached the grave slowly, wondering how they had managed to dig into the frozen ground; and then he remembered that this was New Mexico and saw the pile of cold loose sand beside the hole. The people stood close to each other with little clouds of steam puffing from their faces. The priest looked at them and saw a pile of jackets, gloves, and scarves in the yellow, dry tumbleweeds that grew in the graveyard. He looked at the red blanket, not sure that Teofilo was so small, wondering if it wasn't some perverse Indian trick—something they did in March to ensure a good harvest—wondering if maybe old Teofilo was actually at sheep camp corraling the sheep for the night. But there he was, facing into a cold, dry wind and squinting at the last sunlight, ready to bury a red wool blanket while the faces of his parishioners were in shadow with the last warmth of the sun on their backs.

His fingers were stiff, and it took him a long time to twist the lid off the holy water. Drops of water fell on the red blanket and soaked into dark icy spots. He sprinkled the grave and the water disappeared almost before it touched the dim, cold sand; it reminded him of something—he tried to remember what it was, because he thought if he could remember he might understand this. He sprinkled more water; he shook the container until it was empty, and the water fell through the light from sundown like August rain that fell while the sun was still shining, almost evaporating before it touched the wilted squash flowers.

The wind pulled at the priest's brown Franciscan robe and swirled away the cornmeal and pollen that had been sprinkled on the blanket. They lowered the bundle into the ground, and they didn't bother to untie the stiff pieces of new rope that were tied around the ends of the blanket. The sun was gone, and over on the highway the eastbound lane was full of headlights. The priest walked away slowly. Leon watched him climb the hill, and when he had disappeared within the tall, thick walls, Leon turned to look up at the high blue mountains in the deep snow that reflected a faint red light from the west. He felt good because it was finished, and he was happy about the sprinkling of the holy water; now the old man could send them big thunderclouds for sure.

Mogui child's blanket (Navajo).
Anonymous. Wool.

Collection of the Chase Manhattan Bank, N.A.

Responding to the Story

Analyzing the Story

Identifying Facts

1. The **setting** in this story includes two distinct cultures. What are some of the symbols and rites of the Laguna culture?
2. What symbols and rites of Father Paul's culture are mentioned in the story?
3. In Christian tradition, holy water is often used symbolically as a sign of purification. Name the two reasons Louise and Leon want the priest to sprinkle holy water on Teofilo's grave. Why does the priest say he can't?

Interpreting Meanings

4. Why do you think Leon and Ken withhold the news of Teofilo's death from Father Paul when they meet him on the way home?

5. Explain why the priest's eyes look "tired" when he says that he should have administered the Last Rites to Teofilo.
6. Why do you think the old man's family wants both kinds of burial ceremony?
7. Why do you suppose Father Paul agrees to sprinkle the holy water on Teofilo's grave? When he sprinkles the water ". . . it reminded him of something—he tried to remember what it was, because he thought if he could remember he might understand this" (pages 158–159). What do you think the falling water reminds the priest of? What exactly is he trying to understand?
8. What do you think the story's **title** means? Who *is* the man to send rainclouds—old Teofilo or Father Paul? Is there more than one possible answer? Explain.

9. By the end of the story, do you think the priest *does* come to understand his Laguna neighbors and what they want from him?

10. How does the narrator of this story seem to feel about these characters and their different cultures? Do you think the narrator is critical of any characters or cultures, or do you think she is sympathetic to everyone? What passages support your interpretation of the story's **tone**?

Writing About the Story

A Creative Response

1. **Describing a Ceremony.** Every culture has ceremonies to mark important events in human life, such as birth, coming of age, marriage, and death. There are also ceremonies for meals, for launching a boat, for inaugurating a leader, for making war and peace. There are ceremonies marking the arrival of spring, the end of the year, planting, and harvest. Choose a particular ceremony that is part of your culture, and describe it in a paragraph. Include an explanation of the significance of the actions, words, and objects used in the ceremony.

A Critical Response

2. **Responding to the Story.** In two paragraphs, explain what you think of this story and the way it is written. Did the writer make the **characters** seem real to you? Did you understand what they were feeling, or did their behavior and **motives** seem puzzling? Were you satisfied by the ending, or did you expect something different to happen? Cite passages from the story to support your response.

Analyzing Language and Vocabulary

Americanisms

Americanisms are words or meanings that either originated in America or are used only by speakers of American English. Many Americanisms came into English from Native American languages and from Spanish, which once was the predominant language of the white settlers in the American Southwest. Americanisms often were adapted into English to name objects, plants, and land formations that do not exist in other parts of the world.

In a dictionary, look up the origin of each itali-

cized word, and tell what language it comes from. (Note: An etymology may list a specific American Indian language.) Which words name things that would not have been found in England? Which name things that originated in America?

1. "His *Levi* jacket and pants were faded light blue. . . ."
2. "The big *cottonwood* tree stood apart from a small grove of winter-bare cottonwoods which grew in the wide, sandy *arroyo*."
3. "They laid the bundle in the back of the *pickup* and covered it with a heavy *tarp* before they started back to the *pueblo*."
4. "Leon stared at the new *moccasins*. . . ."
5. "The sun was approaching the long *mesa*. . . ."
6. "The priest turned away from Leon and looked out the window at the *patio*. . . ."
7. "The priest stared down at his scuffed brown *loafers* and the worn hem of his cassock."
8. "He followed Leon out the door and across the dim churchyard to the *adobe* steps. . . ."
9. ". . . a pile of jackets, gloves, and scarves in the yellow, dry *tumbleweeds* that grew in the graveyard."
10. ". . . it touched the wilted *squash* flowers."

Reading About the Author

Leslie Marmon Silko (1948–   ) was born in Albuquerque, New Mexico, and is of both Laguna Pueblo and Mexican ancestry. She was educated at the Bureau of Indian Affairs School in Old Laguna, New Mexico, and she graduated from the University of New Mexico in 1969. Although she entered law school, in 1971 she decided to make a career of writing.

As a child, Silko had listened to her great-aunts and great-grandmother tell stories about the Native American past. She soon came to believe in stories and in storytelling as central to the strong feelings she has for her Pueblo people, and as a necessary bond for any community. Her own fiction and poetry often touch on the exploitation of Native Americans and on what happens when their children must choose between contemporary, materialistic values and their own tribal tradition.

Silko is the first Native American woman to publish a full-length novel. *Ceremony,* which appeared in 1977, deals with a World War II veteran returning home after a terrifying battle experience.

Literature & Language

Using Words to Create Atmosphere

Literary Model

Here's the opening of a story by Gabriel García Márquez, a Colombian writer who sets much of his fiction in an imaginary South American town called Macondo. In Macondo the cold, wet winter arrives in May—after a long, dry summer. How does this narrator feel about her **setting**? (Another García Márquez story is on page 187.)

Winter fell one Sunday when people were coming out of church. Saturday night had been suffocating. But even on Sunday morning, nobody thought it would rain. After Mass, before we women had time to find the catches on our parasols, a thick, dark wind blew, which with one broad, round swirl swept away the dust and hard tinder of May. Someone next to me said: "It's a water wind." And I knew it even before then. From the moment we came out onto the church steps, I felt shaken by a slimy feeling in my stomach. The men ran to the nearby houses with one hand on their hats and a handkerchief in the other, protecting themselves against the wind and the dust storm. Then it rained. And the sky was a gray, jellyish substance that flapped its wings a hand away from our heads.

During the rest of the morning, my stepmother and I were sitting by the railing, happy that the rain would revive the thirsty rosemary and nard[1] in the flowerpots after seven months of intense summer and scorching dust. At noon the reverberation of the Earth stopped and a smell of turned earth, of awakened and renovated vegetation mingled with the cool and healthful odor of the rain in the rosemary. My father said at lunchtime: "When it rains in May, it's a sign that there'll be good tides." Smiling, crossed by the luminous thread of the new season, my stepmother told me: "That's what I heard in the sermon." And my father smiled. And he ate with a good appetite and even let his food digest leisurely beside the railing, silent, his eyes closed, but not sleeping, as if to think that he was dreaming while awake.

It rained all afternoon in a single tone. In the uniform and peaceful intensity you could hear the water fall, the way it is when you travel all afternoon on a train. But without our noticing it, the rain was penetrating too deeply into our senses. Early Monday morning, when we closed the door to avoid the cutting, icy draft that blew in from the courtyard, our senses had been filled with rain. And on Monday morning they had overflowed. My stepmother and I went back to look at the garden. The harsh gray earth of May had been changed overnight into a dark, sticky substance like cheap soap. A trickle of water began to run off the flowerpots. "I think they had more than enough water during the night," my stepmother said. And I noticed that she had stopped smiling and that her joy of the previous day had changed during the night into a lax and tedious seriousness. "I think you're right," I said. "It would be better to have the Indians put them on the veranda until it stops raining." And that was what they did, while the rain grew like an immense tree over the other trees. My father occupied the same spot where he had been on Sunday afternoon, but he didn't talk about the rain. He said: "I must have slept poorly last night because I woke up with a stiff back." And he stayed there, sitting by the railing with his feet on a chair and his head turned toward the empty garden. Only at dusk, after he had turned down lunch, did he say: "It looks as if it will never clear." And I remembered the months of heat. I remembered August, those long and awesome siestas in which we dropped down to die under the weight of the hour, our clothes sticking to our bodies, hearing outside the insistent and dull buzzing of the hour that never passed. I saw the washed-down walls, the joints of the beams all puffed up by the water. I saw the small garden, empty for the first time, and the jasmine bush against the wall, faithful to the

---

1. **nard:** a fragrant plant.

memory of my mother. I saw my father sitting in a rocker, his painful vertebrae resting on a pillow and his sad eyes lost in the labyrinth of the rain. I remembered the August nights in whose wondrous silence nothing could be heard except the millenary[2] sound that the Earth makes as it spins on its rusty, unoiled axis. Suddenly I felt overcome by an overwhelming sadness.

> —from "Monologue of Isabel
> Watching It Rain in Macondo,"
> Gabriel García Márquez,
> translated by Gregory Rabassa

2. **millenary:** suggesting a millennium—a thousand years.

A Note on Atmosphere

Atmosphere is the mood or feeling a work of literature evokes—an almost intangible emotional overtone that sets up the reader's expectations and attitudes.

Often a work's atmosphere is established by its **setting,** by the words, **images,** and details a writer uses to create a sense of place. For example, in the García Márquez passage, the first paragraph immediately produces an atmosphere of **foreboding.** Why? Although the rain is presumably a welcome event after the "suffocating" heat of summer, the narrator describes this rain with images that evoke fear and disgust. Isabel feels "shaken by a slimy feeling" in her stomach, and she sees the rainy sky as a repulsive, threatening bird: "a gray, jellyish substance that flapped its wings a hand away from our heads." The reader can't help feeling queasy and apprehensive.

Examining the Writer's Style

Working with a partner, analyze the way García Márquez establishes the mood of this passage.

1. What **images** in the second paragraph describe the smell, appearance, and sound of the rain during the first day of the downpour? Are these pleasant or unpleasant images?

2. On Monday morning the "peaceful intensity" of the rain turns sinister. What **words, images,** and **figures of speech** reveal the physical and emotional changes that take place?

3. Toward the end of the passage, Isabel remembers the months of heat and drought that preceded the rain. List the key words and details that describe this period.

4. One of the ways a writer establishes a particular mood is to use words with strong **connotations,** or emotional overtones. What different feelings would Isabel have conveyed if she had described the Earth as spinning on its "shiny, well-oiled axis," rather than its "rusty, unoiled axis"?

5. In the last line of the passage, Isabel is suddenly "overcome by an overwhelming sadness." What clues suggest that her feeling is more than simply a response to the monotonous intensity of the unending rain?

6. How would you summarize the **atmosphere** of this passage? List ten words whose **connotations** contribute to this **mood.**

Creating Atmosphere in Your Writing

Evoking a Mood. Write a description of weather that creates a completely different atmosphere from the one in the García Márquez passage.

1. Include at least two characters, and show how the weather affects their emotions. Use words with strong **connotations,** and include **images** and **figures of speech** that help the reader share your characters' feelings. Begin with a strong opening paragraph that sets the reader's expectations in motion.

2. Exchange descriptions with a partner. Underline all the words and details that affect your emotional response to your classmate's paper. If your partner can't identify the mood you are trying to evoke, revise your description.

EVALUATING A SHORT STORY

Writing Assignment

Write a five-paragraph essay evaluating the short story ''The Cold Equations'' by Tom Godwin (page 7). In your essay, evaluate the writer's use of the short-story elements you've studied in this unit.

Background

When you **evaluate** something, you judge how ''good'' or ''bad'' it is. An evaluation should be based on objective **criteria,** or standards, established by people who are knowledgeable in the field. In this writing assignment you are asked to judge a short story by applying criteria that have been established by short-story writers, critics, and experienced readers.

Because an evaluation is really a type of **opinion,** it can never be proved absolutely true (as a fact can be proved). But an evaluation can be judged by looking at the kind of evidence that is used to back it up. You should include good examples from the story (incidents, specific details, quotations) to support each of your evaluations.

Prewriting

Look carefully at the following criteria for evaluating short stories:

Criteria for Evaluating a Short Story

1. **Plot**
   a. Is the plot believable and consistent, or does it seem contrived? (Does it rely too much on coincidence and chance?)
   b. Given the events of the story, is its ending logical and fair (even if sad)? Or is it a forced or a cliché ending?
   c. Does the plot hold your interest?
   d. Is the conflict subtle and complex, or is it a simple struggle between an all-good hero or heroine and an all-bad villain?

2. **Characters**
   a. Are the characters realistic? (Do they behave the way real people behave?)
   b. Are their **motives** clear? Is their behavior consistent with their natures?
   c. Are the main characters **rounded** (fully developed), or are they all **flat** (one-dimensional) and shallow? Does the writer use any **stock characters**?
   d. Are the main characters **dynamic**? Do they change or develop during the course of the story, or are all of the characters **static**?

3. **Theme**
   a. Is the story told to reveal a theme, or is it told principally for entertainment?
   b. Does the theme deal with an important aspect of life? Does it present a new idea or an old cliché? Does it present an oversimplified view of life?
   c. Does the theme seem valid to you? Does it express a truth about life as you know it?

4. **Point of View**
   a. What is the point of view? Is it the best point of view for telling this particular story?
   b. Is the point of view consistent? If not, does the writer have a good reason for switching the point of view?
   c. Does the point of view help you understand the characters? Does the point of view conceal important information? Is this concealment essential to the meaning of the story?

5. **Tone**
   a. What seems to be the writer's attitude toward the characters or toward the world? Is it mocking, admiring, cynical, bemused, pitying? How does the writer convey that **tone**?
   b. Is the story sentimental—is it a ''tear-jerker''? Does the writer manipulate your emotions unfairly, or do the emotions evoked by the story seem natural and uncontrived?

6. **Setting**
   a. Does the story have a recognizable setting? Is it believable?

b. What does the setting reveal about the characters? Does the setting itself function as a character?

c. What **mood** does the setting evoke? How does the setting contribute to the **emotional effect** of the story?

7. Style (Language)

a. Is the story well written? Are the sentences clear? Are the words carefully chosen? Does the **diction** seem appropriate to the subject matter of the story?

b. Is the language original, the **imagery** fresh and evocative? Does the writer avoid clichés (except where appropriate in dialogue)?

c. Do the people talk the way real people talk, or does the dialogue seem forced? If there is **dialect,** does it sound authentic?

Read "The Cold Equations" straight through again, and give yourself some time to think about it. Then skim the story a second (and maybe even a third) time, taking notes on each of the criteria listed here. You might make a chart like the following one; give yourself plenty of space to jot down your ideas and observations for each element. Be sure to cite passages and page numbers that you can use to support your points.

Story Element	Answers to Questions (Criteria) on Pages 163–164	Examples
Plot		
Characters		
Theme		
Point of view		
Tone		
Setting		
Style		

Writing

Before you begin writing, look at your Prewriting chart, which should be full of notes. Reread your notes, and decide on the overall evaluation you'd give this story. Is it great, average, weak—or something else? Write a **thesis statement** that expresses your overall evaluation. Now, think of the rest of the essay as evidence supporting this evaluation. You might follow a plan such as the following:

1. **Paragraph 1:** Introductory paragraph, mentioning title and author. Include thesis statement.
2. **Paragraphs 2–4:** Discuss and evaluate each of the seven elements listed in the criteria. Support your evaluation with specific details from the story.
3. **Paragraph 5:** Write a concluding paragraph summarizing your main points and restating your thesis statement.

Checklist for Revision

1. Have you cited the story's title and author?
2. Have you included a thesis statement that states your overall evaluation of the story?
3. In the rest of the essay, have you discussed and evaluated each of the elements listed in the criteria for evaluating short stories (pages 163–164)?
4. Have you supported your evaluations with good, specific details from the story?
5. If you have quoted directly from the story, have you checked the quotation for accuracy, used quotation marks, and cited the page on which the quotation appears?
6. In the concluding paragraph, have you summarized your main points and/or restated your thesis statement?
7. Have you checked: Spelling? Punctuation? Capitalization? Sentence structure? Paragraph organization?

We are symbols, and inhabit symbols.

—Ralph Waldo Emerson

G ood fiction is often about the things in life that we can neither see nor touch: emotions, experiences, and ideas. Evil, for example, is a factor in real life and in stories, but it is a concept: It cannot be seen or touched. So throughout the ages, writers (and painters) have used a figure to suggest the idea of evil. Traditionally, this figure has worn a red suit (red is associated with fire), has had a forked tail, cloven hoofs, and glowing eyes. There is no mistaking this character, in whatever dark alley or sunny garden he is encountered. The snake or serpent is another figure that writers and painters have traditionally chosen to suggest the ideas of evil and cunning. These are concepts that we can't see or touch, but they are often given symbolic form in the figure of the serpent.

Symbols aren't limited to literature and art. Our everyday lives are heaped with symbols. The key in your pocket, though only a jagged piece of metal with a hole in it, may work as a symbol. When you hold it, it may symbolize for you the idea of security, for it makes you think of the door to your house and the supper and bed awaiting you there.

There are many other symbols in our culture that we know and recognize at once. We automatically make the associations suggested by a cross, a six-pointed star, a crown, a skull and crossbones, a clenched fist, the stars and stripes, the hammer and sickle, and a dove with an olive branch. These commonly accepted symbols are often called **public symbols,** and we recognize at once what they stand for.

Symbols in Literature

Writers of fiction, poetry, and drama create new, personal symbols for their work. Some literary symbols, like the great white whale in *Moby-Dick* and like that stubborn spot of blood on Lady Macbeth's hands, become so widely known that eventually they too become a part of our public stockpile of symbols.

In literature, a **symbol** is an object, a setting, an event, an animal, or even a person that functions in a story the way you'd expect it to but that, more importantly, also stands for something greater than itself, usually for something abstract. The white whale in *Moby-Dick* is a very real white whale in the novel, and Captain Ahab spends the whole book chasing it. But certain passages in that novel make clear to us that this killer whale is also associated with all the mystery of evil in the world. That is how symbols

Symbol: An Object That Suggests an Idea

Greek coin showing an owl, the symbol of Athena, goddess of wisdom (c. 440 B.C.)

" **O**ur everyday lives are heaped with symbols."

work—by natural association. We naturally associate the color green with new life and hope. We usually associate the color white with innocence and purity. We associate gardens with joy, and wastelands with futility and despair; winter with sterility, and spring with fertility; cooing doves with peace, and pecking ravens with death.

One of the most interesting aspects of the use of symbols in fiction is the enthusiastic way some readers take to them. Rather like children excited by finding Easter eggs in the strangest places, some readers begin to discover symbols under every bush.

I once was interviewed by a priest about a scene in one of my novels in which a small boy brings home a cake for a family celebration. The priest was convinced that this celebration was a symbol of the Last Supper. I had no such conscious intent. It was simply a family gathering to me, but the fact that it was more to the reader (who had good reasons for his interpretation) made us both happy.

So occasionally what the writer intends is actually less important than what the reader finds. After all, the best symbols are the unconscious ones. They emerge from some deep and secret place in the heart. Just as in the Easter egg hunt, what matters is not what somebody deliberately put out for you to find, but what you have carefully discovered and placed in your basket.

Is It a Symbol?

However, you must also be careful not to start looking for symbols in everything you read: they won't be there. Here are some guidelines to follow when you sense that a story is operating on a symbolic level:

1. Symbols are often visual.

2. When some event or object or setting is used as a symbol in a story, you will usually find that the writer has given it a great deal of emphasis. Often it reappears throughout the story.

> If you remember a story called "The Scarlet Ibis" by James Hurst, you will recall the rare bird that appears suddenly at the narrator's farm and dies because it has strayed out of its natural tropical setting. That bird, the scarlet ibis, is used in the story to symbolize the special delicacy and beauty of the narrator's younger brother. The bird is mentioned many times in the story and even is used in the title.

3. A symbol is a form of **figurative language.** Like a metaphor, a symbol is something that is identified with something else that is *very different* from it, but that shares some quality. When you are thinking about whether something is used symbolically, ask yourself: Does this item also stand for something essentially different from itself?

> Think of "The Scarlet Ibis" again. The ibis is identified with the little handicapped boy, who is very different from a bird.

> " **S**o occasionally what the writer intends is actually less important than what the reader finds. After all, the best symbols are the unconscious ones. They emerge from some deep and secret place in the heart."

The beautiful, fragile ibis functions as a real bird in the story (it actually falls into the family's yard), but it also functions as a symbol of the frail little boy and his beautiful nature.

4. A symbol usually has something to do with a story's **theme.**

When we think about the ibis, we realize that the death of the exotic bird points to the fact that the little brother also died because he could not survive in a world in which he was an outsider.

Why Do We Use Symbols?

Why do writers use symbols? Why don't they just come out and tell us directly what they want to say?

One answer is that people are born symbol-makers. It seems to be part of our nature. Even in our earliest paintings and writings, we find symbols. Think of all those mysterious markings on the walls of caves. Think of the owl used in ancient Greek art and stories to symbolize the great goddess of wisdom, Athena. Think of our language itself, which uses sounds to symbolize certain abstract and concrete things in the world.

No one knows why we are such consistent symbol-makers. But one advantage of symbols in stories is that they can express and suggest—by means of a single vivid object or event or person—a whole range of ideas and meanings.

In some sense, we never fully exhaust the significance of the great symbols. For example, critics have written whole books to explain *Moby-Dick,* yet probably no one is certain that the meaning of that white whale has been fully explored.

You may not be able to articulate fully what a symbol means. But you will find that the symbol, if it is powerful and well-chosen, will speak forcefully to your emotions and to your imagination. You may also find that you will remember and think about the symbol long after you have forgotten other details of the story's plot.

Illustration by A. Burnham Shute of Moby-Dick, the great white whale.

THE PIT AND THE PENDULUM

Edgar Allan Poe

Here is Edgar Allan Poe's famous story of confinement in an extraordinary prison cell in Toledo, Spain, during the brutal Spanish Inquisition. The purpose of the Inquisition, which began in Spain in 1478, was to discover and punish people who were suspected of not being true believers in the Christian faith.

Poe's story is powerful for many reasons, one being its point of view. It is the prisoner himself who tells this story. Given this fact, do you already know at the outset that he will survive the torture? Or could he possibly die?

The other powerful device in the story is the form of torture itself, which, as you will see, gradually takes on symbolic meaning. Before you read the story, make a list of all the feelings and images you associate with the word *pit*.

Read through to the end of the third paragraph, and discuss what the narrator has told you. What is his basic situation? What have the judges sentenced him to?

As you continue reading, ask yourself another question: Is this a simple horror story, or do you sense another level of meaning?

I was sick—sick unto death with that long agony; and when they at length unbound me, and I was permitted to sit, I felt that my senses were leaving me. The sentence—the dread sentence of death—was the last of distinct accentuation which reached my ears. After that the sound of the inquisitorial voices seemed merged in one dreamy, indeterminate hum. It conveyed to my soul the idea of *revolution*—perhaps from its association in fancy with the burr of a mill wheel. This only for a brief period, for presently I heard no more. Yet for a while I saw—but with how terrible an exaggeration! I saw the lips of the black-robed judges. They appeared to me white—whiter than the sheet upon which I trace these words—and thin even to grotesqueness; thin with the intensity of their expression of firmness—of immovable resolution—of stern contempt of human torture. I saw that the decrees of what to me was Fate were still issuing from those lips. I saw them writhe with a deadly locution. I saw them fashion the syllables of my name; and I shuddered because no sound succeeded. I saw, too, for a few moments of delirious horror, the soft and nearly imperceptible waving of the sable draperies which enwrapped the walls of the apartment. And then my vision fell upon the seven tall candles upon the table. At first they wore the aspect of charity and seemed white, slender angels who would save me; but then all at once there came a most deadly nausea over my spirit, and I felt every fiber in my frame thrill as if I had touched the wire of a galvanic battery, while the angel forms became meaningless specters, with heads of flame, and I saw that from them there would be no help. And then there stole into my fancy, like a rich musical note, the thought of what sweet rest there must be in the grave. The thought came gently and stealthily, and it seemed long before it attained full appreciation; but just as my spirit came at length properly to feel and entertain it, the figures of the judges vanished, as if magically, from before me; the tall candles sank into nothingness; their flames went out utterly; the blackness of darkness supervened; all sensations appeared swallowed up in a mad, rushing descent as of the soul into Hades. Then silence and stillness and night were the universe.

I had swooned; but still will not say that all of consciousness was lost. What of it there remained I will not attempt to define, or even to describe; yet all was not lost. In the deepest slumber—no! In delirium—no! In a swoon—no! In death—no! even in the grave all *is not lost*. Else there is no immortality for man. Arousing from the most profound of slumbers, we break the gossamer web of *some* dream. Yet in a second afterward (so frail may that web have been), we remember not that we have dreamed. In the return to life from the swoon there are two stages: first, that of the sense of mental or spiritual; secondly, that of the sense of physical existence. It seems probable that if, upon reaching the second stage, we could recall the impressions of the first, we should find these impressions eloquent in memories of the gulf beyond. And that gulf is—what? How at least shall we distinguish its shadows from those of the tomb? But if the impressions of what I have termed the first stage are not, at will, recalled, yet, after long interval, do they not come unbidden, while we marvel whence they come? He who has never swooned is not he who finds strange palaces and wildly familiar faces in coals that glow; is not he who beholds floating in midair the sad visions that the many may not view; is not he who ponders over the perfume of some novel flower—is not he whose brain grows bewildered with the meaning of some musical cadence which has never before arrested his attention.

Amid frequent and thoughtful endeavors to remember; amid earnest struggles to regather some token of the state of seeming nothingness into which my soul had lapsed, there have been moments when I have dreamed of success; there have been brief, very brief, periods when I have conjured up remembrances which the lucid reason of a later epoch assures me could have had reference only to that condition of seeming unconsciousness. These shadows of memory tell, indistinctly, of tall figures that lifted and bore me in silence down—down—still down—till a hideous dizziness oppressed me at the mere idea of the interminableness of the descent. They tell also of a vague horror at my heart, on account of that heart's unnatural stillness. Then comes a sense of sudden

motionlessness throughout all things; as if those who bore me (a ghastly train!) had outrun, in their descent, the limits of the limitless and paused from the wearisomeness of their toil. After this I call to mind flatness and dampness; and then all is *madness*—the madness of a memory which busies itself among forbidden things.

Very suddenly there came back to my soul motion and sound—the tumultuous motion of the heart and, in my ears, the sound of its beating. Then a pause in which all is blank. Then again sound and motion and touch—a tingling sensation pervading my frame. Then the mere consciousness of existence, without thought—a condition which lasted long. Then, very suddenly, *thought* and shuddering terror and earnest endeavor to comprehend my true state. Then a strong desire to lapse into insensibility. Then a rushing revival

Illustration by Arthur Rackham.

of soul and a successful effort to move. And now a full memory of the trial, of the judges, of the sable draperies, of the sentence, of the sickness, of the swoon. Then entire forgetfulness of all that followed; of all that a later day and much earnestness of endeavor have enabled me vaguely to recall.

So far I had not opened my eyes. I felt that I lay upon my back, unbound. I reached out my hand, and it fell heavily upon something damp and hard. There I suffered it to remain for many minutes, while I strove to imagine where and *what* I could be. I longed, yet dared not, to employ my vision. I dreaded the first glance at objects around me. It was not that I feared to look upon things horrible, but that I grew aghast lest there should be *nothing* to see. At length, with a wild desperation at heart, I quickly unclosed my eyes. My worst thoughts, then, were confirmed. The blackness of eternal night encompassed me. I struggled for breath. The intensity of the darkness seemed to oppress and stifle me. The atmosphere was intolerably close. I still lay quietly and made effort to exercise my reason. I brought to mind the inquisitorial proceedings and attempted from that point to deduce my real condition. The sentence had passed; and it appeared to me that a very long interval of time had since elapsed. Yet not for a moment did I suppose myself actually dead. Such a supposition, notwithstanding what we read in fiction, is altogether inconsistent with real existence—but where and in what state was I? The condemned to death, I knew, perished usually at the *auto-da-fé*,[1] and one of these had been held on the very night of the day of my trial. Had I been remanded to my dungeon, to await the next sacrifice, which would not take place for many months? This I at once saw could not be. Victims had been in immediate demand. Moreover, my dungeon, as well as all the condemned cells at Toledo, had stone floors, and light was not altogether excluded.

A fearful idea now suddenly drove the blood in torrents upon my heart, and for a brief period I once more relapsed into insensibility. Upon recovering, I at once started to my feet, trembling convulsively in every fiber. I thrust my arms wildly above and around me in all directions. I felt nothing; yet dreaded to move a step, lest I should be impeded by the walls of a *tomb*. Perspiration burst from every pore and stood in cold, big beads upon my forehead. The agony of suspense grew at length intolerable, and I cautiously moved forward, with my arms extended and my eyes straining from their sockets in the hope of catching some faint ray of light. I proceeded for many paces; but still all was blackness and vacancy. I breathed more freely. It seemed evident that mine was not, at least, the most hideous of fates.

And now, as I still continued to step cautiously onward, there came thronging upon my recollection a thousand vague rumors of the horrors of Toledo. Of the dungeons there had been strange things narrated—fables I had always deemed them—but yet strange and too ghastly to repeat, save in a whisper. Was I left to perish of starvation in this subterranean world of darkness; or what fate, perhaps even more fearful, awaited me? That the result would be death, and a death of more than customary bitterness, I knew too well the character of my judges to doubt. The mode and the hour were all that occupied or distracted me.

My outstretched hands at length encountered some solid obstruction. It was a wall, seemingly of stone masonry—very smooth, slimy, and cold. I followed it up; stepping with all the careful distrust with which certain antique narratives had inspired me. This process, however, afforded me no means of ascertaining the dimensions of my dungeon, as I might make its circuit and return to the point whence I set out without being aware of the fact, so perfectly uniform seemed the wall. I therefore sought the knife which had been in my pocket when led into the inquisitorial chamber; but it was gone; my clothes had been exchanged for a wrapper of coarse serge. I had thought of forcing the blade in some minute crevice of the masonry, so as to identify my point of departure. The difficulty, nevertheless, was but trivial; although, in the disorder of my fancy, it seemed at

---

1. *auto-da-fé* (ôt′ō·də·fā′): "act of faith." Actually, public executions of those condemned by the Inquisition, usually by burning at the stake.

first insuperable. I tore a part of the hem from the robe and placed the fragment at full length, and at right angles to the wall. In groping my way around the prison, I could not fail to encounter this rag upon completing the circuit. So at least I thought; but I had not counted upon the extent of the dungeon or upon my own weakness. The ground was moist and slippery. I staggered onward for some time, when I stumbled and fell. My excessive fatigue induced me to remain prostrate; and sleep soon overtook me as I lay.

Upon awakening, and stretching forth an arm, I found beside me a loaf and a pitcher with water. I was too much exhausted to reflect upon this circumstance, but ate and drank with avidity. Shortly afterward, I resumed my tour around the prison and with much toil, came at last upon the fragment of the serge. Up to the period when I fell, I had counted fifty-two paces, and upon resuming my walk, I had counted forty-eight more—when I arrived at the rag. There were in all, then, a hundred paces; and, admitting two paces to the yard, I presumed the dungeon to be fifty yards in circuit. I had met, however, with many angles in the wall, and thus I could form no guess at the shape of the vault, for vault I could not help supposing it to be.

I had little object—certainly no hope—in these researches; but a vague curiosity prompted me to continue them. Quitting the wall, I resolved to cross the area of the enclosure. At first I proceeded with extreme caution, for the floor, although seemingly of solid material, was treacherous with slime. At length, however, I took courage and did not hesitate to step firmly—endeavoring to cross in as direct a line as possible. I had advanced some ten or twelve paces in this manner, when the remnant of the torn hem of my robe became entangled between my legs. I stepped on it and fell violently on my face.

In the confusion attending my fall, I did not immediately apprehend a somewhat startling circumstance, which yet, in a few seconds afterward and while I still lay prostrate, arrested my attention. It was this: My chin rested upon the floor of the prison, but my lips and the upper portion of my head, although seemingly at a less elevation than the chin, touched nothing. At the same time,

my forehead seemed bathed in a clammy vapor, and the peculiar smell of decayed fungus arose to my nostrils. I put forward my arm and shuddered to find that I had fallen at the very brink of a circular pit, whose extent, of course, I had no means of ascertaining at the moment. Groping about the masonry just below the margin, I succeeded in dislodging a small fragment and let it fall into the abyss. For many seconds I hearkened to its reverberations as it dashed against the sides of the chasm in its descent; at length there was a sullen plunge into water, succeeded by loud echoes. At the same moment there came a sound resembling the quick opening and as rapid closing of a door overhead, while a faint gleam of light flashed suddenly through the gloom and as suddenly faded away.

I saw clearly the doom which had been prepared for me and congratulated myself upon the timely accident by which I had escaped. Another step before my fall and the world had seen me no more. And the death just avoided was of that very character which I had regarded as fabulous and frivolous in the tales respecting the Inquisition.

To the victims of its tyranny, there was the choice of death with its direst physical agonies or death with its most hideous moral horrors. I had been reserved for the latter. By long suffering my nerves had been unstrung, until I trembled at the sound of my own voice and had become in every respect a fitting subject for the species of torture which awaited me.

Shaking in every limb, I groped my way back to the wall—resolving there to perish rather than risk the terrors of the wells, of which my imagination now pictured many in various positions about the dungeon. In other conditions of mind, I might have had courage to end my misery at once by a plunge into one of these abysses; but now I was the veriest of cowards. Neither could I forget what I had read of these pits—that the *sudden* extinction of life formed no part of their most horrible plan.

Agitation of spirit kept me awake for many long hours, but at length I again slumbered. Upon arousing, I found by my side, as before, a loaf and a pitcher of water. A burning thirst consumed me, and I emptied the vessel at a draught. It must have been drugged—for scarcely had I drunk, before I became irresistibly drowsy. A deep sleep fell upon me—a sleep like that of death. How long it lasted, of course I know not; but when once again I unclosed my eyes, the objects around me were visible. By a wild, sulfurous luster, the origin of which I could not at first determine, I was enabled to see the extent and aspect of the prison.

In its size I had been greatly mistaken. The whole circuit of its walls did not exceed twenty-five yards. For some minutes this fact occasioned me a world of vain trouble; vain indeed—for what could be of less importance, under the terrible circumstances which environed me, than the mere dimensions of my dungeon? But my soul took a wild interest in trifles, and I busied myself in endeavors to account for the error I had committed in my measurement. The truth at length flashed upon me. In my first attempt at exploration, I had counted fifty-two paces up to the period when I fell: I must then have been within a pace or two of the fragment of serge; in fact, I had nearly performed the circuit of the vault. I then slept—and, upon awaking, I must have returned upon my steps—thus supposing the circuit nearly double what it actually was. My confusion of mind prevented me from observing that I began my tour with the wall to the left and ended it with the wall to the right.

I had been deceived, too, in respect to the shape of the enclosure. In feeling my way I had found many angles and thus deduced an idea of great irregularity; so potent is the effect of total darkness upon one arousing from lethargy or sleep! The angles were simply those of a few slight depressions, or niches, at odd intervals. The general shape of the prison was square. What I had taken for masonry seemed now to be iron, or some other metal, in huge plates, whose sutures or joints occasioned the depression. The entire surface of this metallic enclosure was rudely daubed in all the hideous and repulsive devices to which the charnel superstition of the monks has given rise. The figures of fiends in aspects of menace, with skeleton forms, and other more really fearful images overspread and disfigured the walls. I observed that the outlines of these monstrosities were sufficiently distinct, but that the colors seemed faded and blurred, as if from the effects of a damp atmosphere. I now noticed the floor, too, which was of stone. In the center yawned the circular pit from whose jaws I had escaped; but it was the only one in the dungeon.

All this I saw indistinctly and by much effort—for my personal condition had been greatly changed during slumber. I now lay upon my back, and at full length, on a species of low framework of wood. To this I was securely bound by a long strap resembling a surcingle.[2] It passed in many convolutions about my limbs and body, leaving at liberty only my head and my left arm to such extent that I could, by dint of much exertion, supply myself with food from an earthen dish which lay by my side on the floor. I saw, to my horror, that the pitcher had been removed. I say to my horror—for I was consumed with intolerable thirst. This thirst it appeared to be the design of my persecutors to stimulate—for the food in the dish was meat pungently seasoned.

---

2. **surcingle** (sər·sin′gəl): a belt that holds a saddle.

Looking upward, I surveyed the ceiling of my prison. It was some thirty or forty feet overhead and constructed much as the side walls. In one of its panels a very singular figure riveted my whole attention. It was the painted figure of Time as he is commonly represented, save that, in lieu of a scythe, he held what, at a casual glance, I supposed to be the pictured image of a huge pendulum, such as we see on antique clocks. There was something, however, in the appearance of this machine which caused me to regard it more attentively. While I gazed directly upward at it (for its position was immediately over my own) I fancied that I saw it in motion. In an instant afterward the fancy was confirmed. Its sweep was brief and, of course, slow. I watched it for some minutes somewhat in fear, but more in wonder. Wearied at length with observing its dull movement, I turned my eyes upon the other objects in the cell.

A slight noise attracted my notice, and looking to the floor, I saw several enormous rats traversing it. They had issued from the well which lay just within view to my right. Even then, while I gazed, they came up in troops, hurriedly, with ravenous eyes, allured by the scent of the meat. From this it required much effort and attention to scare them away.

It might have been half an hour, perhaps even an hour (for I could take but imperfect note of time), before I again cast my eyes upward. What I then saw confounded and amazed me. The sweep of the pendulum had increased in extent by nearly a yard. As a natural consequence its velocity was also much greater. But what mainly disturbed me was the idea that it had perceptibly *descended*. I now observed—with what horror it is needless to say—that its nether extremity was formed of a crescent of glittering steel, about a foot in length from horn to horn; the horns upward, and the under edge evidently as keen as that of a razor. Like a razor also, it seemed massy and heavy, tapering from the edge into a solid and broad structure above. It was appended to a weighty rod of brass, and the whole *hissed* as it swung through the air.

I could no longer doubt the doom prepared for me by monkish ingenuity in torture. My cognizance of the pit had become known to the inquisitorial agents—*the pit,* whose horrors had been destined for so bold a recusant[3] as myself—*the pit,* typical of hell and regarded by rumor as the Ultima Thule[4] of all their punishments. The plunge into this pit I had avoided by the merest of accidents, and I knew that surprise, or entrapment into torment, formed an important portion of all the grotesquerie of these dungeon deaths. Having failed to fall, it was no part of the demon plan to hurl me into the abyss, and thus (there being no alternative) a different and a milder destruction awaited me. Milder! I half smiled in my agony as I thought of such application of such a term.

What boots it to tell of the long, long hours of horror more than mortal during which I counted the rushing oscillations of the steel! Inch by inch—line by line—with a descent only appreciable at intervals that seemed ages—down and still down it came! Days passed—it might have been that many days passed—ere it swept so closely over me as to fan me with its acrid breath. The odor of the sharp steel forced itself into my nostrils. I prayed—I wearied heaven with my prayer for its more speedy descent. I grew frantically mad and struggled to force myself upward against the sweep of the fearful scimitar. And then I fell suddenly calm and lay smiling at the glittering death, as a child at some rare bauble.

There was another interval of utter insensibility; it was brief; for, upon again lapsing into life, there had been no perceptible descent in the pendulum. But it might have been long—for I knew there were demons who took note of my swoon, and who could have arrested the vibration at pleasure. Upon my recovery, too, I felt very—oh! inexpressibly—sick and weak, as if through long inanition.[5] Even amid the agonies of that period, the human nature craved food. With painful effort I outstretched my left arm as far as my bonds permitted and took possession of the small remnant which had been spared me by the rats. As I

---

3. **recusant** (rek′yoo·zənt): a person who refuses to obey an established authority.
4. **Ultima Thule** (ul′ti·mə thoo′ lē): in ancient geography, the northernmost region inhabited by humans; here the most extreme form.
5. **inanition** (in′ə·nish′ən): weakness from lack of food.

The Pit and the Pendulum   173

upon the sound of the crescent as it should pass across the garment—upon the peculiar thrilling sensation which the friction of cloth produces on the nerves. I pondered upon all this frivolity until my teeth were on edge.

Down—steadily down it crept. I took a frenzied pleasure in contrasting its downward with its lateral velocity. To the right—to the left—far and wide—with the shriek of a damned spirit! to my heart, with the stealthy pace of the tiger! I alternately laughed and howled, as the one or the other idea grew predominant.

Down—certainly, relentlessly down! It vibrated within three inches of my bosom! I struggled violently—furiously—to free my left arm. This was free only from the elbow to the hand. I could reach the latter from the platter beside me to my mouth with great effort, but no farther. Could I have broken the fastenings above the elbow, I would have seized and attempted to arrest the pendulum. I might as well have attempted to arrest an avalanche!

Down—still unceasingly—still inevitably down! I gasped and struggled at each vibration. I shrank convulsively at its every sweep. My eyes followed its outward or upward whirls with the eagerness of the most unmeaning despair; they closed themselves spasmodically at the descent, although death would have been a relief, oh, how unspeakable! Still I quivered in every nerve to think how slight a sinking of the machinery would precipitate that keen, glistening axe upon my bosom. It was *hope* that prompted the nerve to quiver—the frame to shrink. It was *hope*—the hope that triumphs on the rack—that whispers to the death-condemned even in the dungeons of the Inquisition.

I saw that some ten or twelve vibrations would bring the steel in actual contact with my robe—and with this observation there suddenly came over my spirit all the keen, collected calmness of despair. For the first time during many hours—or perhaps days—I *thought*. It now occurred to me that the bandage, or surcingle, which enveloped me was *unique*. I was tied by no separate cord. The first stroke of the razorlike crescent athwart any portion of the band would so detach it that it might be unwound from my person by means of

put a portion of it within my lips, there rushed to my mind a half-formed thought of joy—of hope. Yet what business had *I* with hope? It was, as I say, a half-formed thought—man has many such, which are never completed. I felt that it was of joy—of hope; but I felt also that it had perished in its formation. In vain I struggled to perfect—to regain it. Long suffering had nearly annihilated all my ordinary powers of mind. I was an imbecile—an idiot.

The vibration of the pendulum was at right angles to my length. I saw that the crescent was designed to cross the region of the heart. It would fray the serge of my robe—it would return and repeat its operations—again—and again. Notwithstanding its terrifically wide sweep (some thirty feet or more) and the hissing vigor of its descent, sufficient to sunder these very walls of iron, still the fraying of my robe would be all that, for several minutes, it would accomplish. And at this thought I paused. I dared not go further than this reflection. I dwelt upon it with a pertinacity of attention—as if, in so dwelling, I could arrest *here* the descent of the steel. I forced myself to ponder my left hand. But how fearful, in that case, the proximity of the steel! The result of the slightest struggle, how deadly! Was it likely, moreover, that the minions of the torturer had not foreseen and provided for this possibility? Was it probable that the bandage crossed my bosom in the track of the pendulum? Dreading to find my faint and, as it seemed, my last hope frustrated, I so far elevated my head as to obtain a distinct view of my breast. The surcingle enveloped my limbs and body close in all directions—*save in the path of the destroying crescent.*

Scarcely had I dropped my head back into its original position, when there flashed upon my mind what I cannot better describe than as the unformed half of that idea of deliverance to which I have previously alluded, and of which a moiety[6] only floated indeterminately through my brain when I raised food to my burning lips. The whole thought was now present—feeble, scarcely sane, scarcely definite—but still entire. I proceeded at once, with the nervous energy of despair, to attempt its execution.

For many hours the immediate vicinity of the low framework upon which I lay had been literally swarming with rats. They were wild, bold, ravenous—their red eyes glaring upon me as if they waited but for motionlessness on my part to make me their prey. "To what food," I thought, "have they been accustomed in the well?"

They had devoured, in spite of all my efforts to prevent them, all but a small remnant of the contents of the dish. I had fallen into a habitual seesaw or wave of the hand about the platter; and, at length, the unconscious uniformity of the movement deprived it of effect. In their voracity the vermin frequently fastened their sharp fangs in my fingers. With the particles of the oily and spicy viand[7] which now remained, I thoroughly rubbed the bandage wherever I could reach it; then, raising my hand from the floor, I lay breathlessly still.

At first the ravenous animals were startled and terrified at the change—at the cessation of movement. They shrank alarmedly back; many sought the well. But this was only for a moment. I had

___

6. **moiety:** part.
7. **viand:** food.

not counted in vain upon their voracity. Observing that I remained without motion, one or two of the boldest leaped upon the framework and smelt at the surcingle. This seemed the signal for a general rush. Forth from the well they hurried in fresh troops. They clung to the wood—they overran it and leaped in hundreds upon my person. The measured movement of the pendulum disturbed them not at all. Avoiding its strokes, they busied themselves with the anointed bandage. They pressed—they swarmed upon me in ever-accumulating heaps. They writhed upon my throat; their cold lips sought my own; I was half stifled by their thronging pressure; disgust for which the world has no name swelled my bosom and chilled, with a heavy clamminess, my heart. Yet one minute, and I felt that the struggle would be over. Plainly I perceived the loosening of the bandage. I knew that in more than one place it must be already severed. With a more than human resolution I lay *still.*

Nor had I erred in my calculations—nor had I endured in vain. I at length felt that I was *free.* The surcingle hung in ribbons from my body. But the stroke of the pendulum already pressed upon my bosom. It had divided the serge of the robe. It had cut through the linen beneath. Twice again it swung, and a sharp sense of pain shot through every nerve. But the moment of escape had arrived. At a wave of my hand my deliverers hurried tumultuously away. With a steady movement—cautious, sidelong, shrinking, and slow—I slid from the embrace of the bandage and beyond the reach of the scimitar. For the moment, at least, *I was free.*

Free!—and in the grasp of the Inquisition! I had scarcely stepped from my wooden bed of horror upon the stone floor of the prison when the motion of the hellish machine ceased, and I beheld it drawn up, by some invisible force, through the ceiling. This was a lesson which I took desperately to heart. My every motion was undoubtedly watched. Free!—I had but escaped death in one form of agony to be delivered unto worse than death in some other. With that thought I rolled my eyes nervously around on the barriers of iron that hemmed me in. Something unusual—some change which at first I could not appreciate distinctly—it was obvious, had taken place in the apartment. For many minutes of a dreamy and trembling abstraction, I busied myself in vain, unconnected conjecture. During this period I became aware for the first time of the origin of the sulfurous light which illumined the cell. It proceeded from a fissure about half an inch in width extending entirely around the prison at the base of the walls, which thus appeared and were completely separated from the floor. I endeavored, but of course in vain, to look through the aperture.

As I arose from the attempt, the mystery of the alteration in the chamber broke at once upon my understanding. I have observed that, although the outlines of the figures upon the walls were sufficiently distinct, yet the colors seemed blurred and indefinite. These colors had now assumed, and were momentarily assuming, a startling and most intense brilliancy that gave to the spectral and fiendish portraitures an aspect that might have thrilled even firmer nerves than my own. Demon eyes of a wild and ghastly vivacity glared upon me in a thousand directions where none had been visible before, and gleamed with the lurid luster of a fire that I could not force my imagination to regard as unreal.

Unreal!—Even while I breathed, there came to my nostrils the breath of the vapor of heated iron! A suffocating odor pervaded the prison! A deeper glow settled each moment in the eyes that glared at my agonies! A richer tint of crimson diffused itself over the pictured horrors of blood. I panted! I gasped for breath! There could be no doubt of the design of my tormentors—oh! most unrelenting! oh! most demoniac of men! I shrank from the glowing metal to the center of the cell. Amid the thought of the fiery destruction that impended, the idea of the coolness of the well came over my soul like balm. I rushed to its deadly brink. I threw my straining vision below. The glare from the enkindled roof illumined its inmost recesses. Yet for a wild moment did my spirit refuse to comprehend the meaning of what I saw. At length it forced—it wrestled its way into my soul—it burned itself in upon my shuddering reason. Oh! for a voice to speak!—oh! horror!—oh! any horror but this!

With a shriek I rushed from the margin and buried my face in my hands—weeping bitterly.

The heat rapidly increased, and once again I looked up, shuddering as with a fit of ague. There had been a second change in the cell—and now the change was obviously in the *form.* As before, it was in vain that I at first endeavored to appreciate or understand what was taking place. But not long was I left in doubt. The Inquisitorial vengeance had been hurried by my twofold escape, and there was to be no more dallying with the King of Terrors. The room had been square. I saw that two of its iron angles were now acute—two, consequently, obtuse. The fearful difference quickly increased with a low rumbling or moaning sound. In an instant the apartment had shifted its form into that of a lozenge.[8] But the alteration stopped not here—I neither hoped nor desired it to stop. I could have clasped the red walls to my bosom as a garment of eternal peace. "Death," I said, "any death but that of the pit!" Fool! might I not have known that *into the pit* it was the object of the burning iron to urge me? Could I resist its glow? or if even that, could I withstand its pressure? And now, flatter and flatter grew the lozenge, with a rapidity that left me no time for contemplation. Its center, and of course its greatest width, came just over the yawning gulf. I shrank back—but the closing walls pressed me resistlessly onward. At length, for my seared and writhing body there was no longer an inch of foothold on the firm floor of the prison. I struggled no more, but the agony of my soul found vent in one loud, long, and final scream of despair. I felt that I tottered upon the brink—I averted my eyes—

There was a discordant hum of human voices! There was a loud blast as of many trumpets! There was a harsh grating as of a thousand thunders! The fiery walls rushed back! An outstretched arm caught my own as I fell, fainting, into the abyss. It was that of General Lasalle. The French army had entered Toledo. The Inquisition was in the hands of its enemies.

---

8. **lozenge** (läz′nj): a diamond shape.

Responding to the Story

Analyzing the Story

Identifying Facts

1. As the story opens, the narrator sits in front of his judges. What colors and sounds does he describe? Find the details at the start of the story that suggest that his experience might be part of a dream or a lapse into madness.
2. When the narrator first regains consciousness, what "most hideous of fates" does he think the Inquisition has planned for him? How does he finally discover the truth?
3. After he falls into a drugged sleep, the narrator discovers that he is in a second and even worse crisis. What new torture does he face? How does he escape this crisis?
4. What third crisis does he face when he has scarcely stepped "from his bed of pain"?

Interpreting Meanings

5. We aren't told what the narrator sees in that horrified glance into the pit (page 176). If you were to draw the pit, what would you put in it?
6. Did General Lasalle's arrival seem an exceptionally lucky coincidence to you? Did it lessen the story's credibility or your enjoyment of it? If there had been no rescue, could we have had a story at all? Why or why not?
7. The scary aspect of the story comes from the details of **setting**. List as many of these details as you can. Do they emerge from a real, daytime world or from a nightmare one? What part of this story might in fact *be* a nightmare?
8. Poe's stories of terror can be read as mere horror stories, but many of them can also be interpreted **symbolically**. On one level, this is the story of a man tortured at the hands of the Inquisition. On another level, some critics read it as the story of a man who dies, almost loses his soul to Hell, and is rescued at the end by God. Let's see if the story "works" if it is read symbolically with this interpretation:

   a. The man, above all, fears falling into the pit. What could the pit symbolize?
   b. What does a pendulum suggest to you, and what does an old man with a scythe represent? What connection might there be between these symbols and the scythe on the pendulum in this story?
   c. What could the paintings on the walls of the cell suggest?
   d. Rats are conventionally used as symbols of death, decay, and the lower world. How does the prisoner's response to these rats—especially when they crawl all over him—suggest that he might see them in this way?
   e. What sounds are usually associated with Judgment Day at the end of the world? Do you hear these sounds at the story's end?

   Do you think this symbolic reading makes sense, or is it stretching the meaning of a "simple" horror story too much? Explain.

Writing About the Story

A Creative Response

1. **Updating the Story.** "The Pit and the Pendulum" is a famous psychological horror story. Do you think the story has relevance to events that could take place today? In a paragraph or two, tell how you would update the story but maintain its basic plot. Filling out the following chart might help you organize your ideas.

	Poe Story	Updated Story
Setting (When and where?)		
Protagonist (What is his or her crime?)		
Punishment		
Opponents or jailers		
Rescuer		

A Critical Response

2. **Evaluating the Story's Plot.** Here are two evaluations of "The Pit and the Pendulum":

   a. *Poe overdid this story by having three episodes in which the tortured prisoner escapes from death. I think the story would have been*

> *more effective if he had omitted the first episode.*
>
> **b.** *Poe steadily builds up suspense in this story by using three episodes, each of which is essential to the story's effect.*

Which opinion do you agree with? Use one of these statements as a topic sentence for a paragraph. Then support your opinion with evidence from the story. Be sure to identify the three episodes, and tell how each contributes to the effect of the story.

Analyzing Language and Vocabulary

Poe's Style

Language—words and the order in which they are arranged—is the primary element of fiction, and yet it is the hardest to talk about. At its simplest, language is a set of signals by which we communicate information: *I'm hungry. The Sox lost 3–2.*

Most languages are also capable of a lot more: of revealing subtle shades of meaning, of explaining intricate ideas, of evoking laughter and tears, of changing the minds and hearts of multitudes.

Many people read fiction for the joy of its language as well as for the story it tells or the ideas it contains. Such readers find pleasure in the precision of the words used and in the rhythm of the sentences that sound in our inner ear.

Like fabric, language has color: vivid and arresting, or pale and delicate. It has texture: rough, shaggy, abrasive, smooth, supple. It has pattern: clear, regular, sharp, suggestive, random, obscure. Language appeals to our organs of sense: eye, fingertip, nose, ear, and palate.

Edgar Allan Poe is a writer known for his **style**—the way he uses language. The emotional effects of "The Pit and the Pendulum" come in large part from the **images** Poe uses to describe the **setting.**

1. Read the following passages from the story and tell which senses each description appeals to:

   a. "It was a wall, seemingly of stone masonry—very smooth, slimy, and cold."

   b. ". . . my forehead seemed bathed in a clammy vapor, and the peculiar smell of decayed fungus arose to my nostrils."

   c. "The figures of fiends in aspects of menace, with skeleton forms, and other more really fearful images overspread and disfigured the walls."

   d. "They pressed—they swarmed upon me in ever-accumulating heaps. They writhed upon my throat; their cold lips sought my own; I was half stifled by their thronging pressure; disgust for which the world has no name swelled my bosom and chilled, with a heavy clamminess, my heart."

   e. "Even while I breathed, there came to my nostrils the breath of the vapor of heated iron! A suffocating odor pervaded the prison!"

2. Read aloud the sentences in item d. Where does Poe use repetition to create **rhythm**?

3. Read aloud the passage in the story that describes the descent of the pendulum, beginning on page 173 with the words "Down—steadily down it crept." How does Poe use repetition here to create **suspense** and even to suggest the steady downward movement of the knife?

4. Poe's theory of storytelling held that a story should create a single, unique emotional **effect.** Given Poe's language, what would you say is the single effect he aimed at in this story? Do you think he succeeded?

5. Poe also believed that the very first sentence of a story should contribute to this effect. If it did not, he believed the story was a failure. Do you think this story is a success or a failure? Why?

Reading About the Writer

Edgar Allan Poe (1809–1849) was born in Boston, the son of an actor and actress. His father deserted his mother, and when she died in 1811, Edgar was left an orphan of sorts before his third birthday. The little boy was taken in by the Allans, a prosperous couple in Richmond, Virginia.

The Allans were childless, and they gave Edgar the best education, with every expectation that the boy would become John Allan's business successor. However, Edgar was a moody child and sensitive about his peculiar origins. His resentment of Allan's ambitions for him became a resistance, and he pursued an interest in writing despite his guardian's impatience with it.

In his freshman year at the University of Virginia, Poe gambled his way into debt, quarreled with Allan, and left Richmond to seek his fortune elsewhere. He worked on a coal barge and did a hitch in the army. In a last attempt at reconciliation with his guardian, he enrolled at West Point. But when reconciliation still seemed impossible, Poe got himself dismissed from his cadet class for disobedience and neglect of duty, and Allan finally disowned him—this time forever.

Earlier, in 1827, Poe had published *Tamerlane and Other Poems,* a volume of poetry addressed to a sweetheart who had jilted him. Now he entered upon a full-time literary life. His writing, which was to bring him little comfort or security, would reflect the dark, nightmare quality of his imagination. It would also alter the shape of American literature.

In 1836 Poe married his thirteen-year-old cousin, Virginia Clemm, and he moved in with her and her mother. He did his best to support the household with income from his poems and stories and from his accomplished work as an editor. He was employed by a number of periodicals in Baltimore and then in New York, but his drinking—another burden to his life—often embroiled him in destructive quarreling, especially with other literary figures of his day.

Throughout these painful years of his young manhood, Poe wrote consistently. He produced two classic mystery stories, "The Murders in the Rue Morgue" and "The Gold Bug." In 1845 he published his most famous poem, "The Raven."

Poe's stories often have to do with death, even premature burial, as in his celebrated tales "The Fall of the House of Usher" and "The Cask of Amontillado." Another of his recurring subjects is wickedness and crime, as in "The Tell-Tale Heart" and "The Purloined Letter."

When Virginia died of tuberculosis in 1847, Poe's despair and drinking increased. A five-day drinking binge in Baltimore ended his life when he was only forty years old.

Focusing on Background
Where Did the Story Come From?

The American literary scholar and Poe specialist Thomas O. Mabbott has traced some of the sources that Poe seems to have drawn upon for "The Pit and the Pendulum."

1. Poe's plot idea may have come from this paragraph in *Philosophy of Religion* (1825) by Thomas Dick. Poe is known to have read this author's works.

"On the entry of the French into Toledo [in 1808], General Lasalle visited the palace of the Inquisition. The great number of instruments of torture, especially the instruments to stretch the limbs, and the drop-baths, which cause a lingering death, excited horror, even in the minds of soldiers hardened in the field of battle."

2. Poe's description of the pictures on the walls of the narrator's cell (page 171) may have had their origin in an 1820 novel by Charles Maturin, called *Melmoth the Wanderer.*

"I started up with horror . . . on perceiving myself surrounded by demons, who, clothed in fire, were breathing forth clouds of it around me. . . . What I touched was cold . . . and I comprehended that these were hideous figures scrawled in phosphorus to terrify me."

3. Poe may have gotten his idea for the pendulum from a book by Juan Antonio Llorente on the history of the Inquisition. Poe is known to have read a review of this book, which contained the following passage:

". . . the Inquisition was thrown open, in 1820, by the orders of the Cortes of Madrid. Twenty-one prisoners were found in it, not one of whom knew the name of the city in which he was: some had been confined three years, some a longer period, and not one knew perfectly the nature of the crime of which he was accused.

One of these prisoners had been condemned and was to have suffered on the following day. His punishment was to be death by the *Pendulum*. The method of thus destroying the victim is as follows: The condemned is fastened in a groove, upon a table, on his back; suspended above him is a Pendulum, the edge of which is sharp, and it is so constructed as to become longer with every movement. The wretch sees this implement of destruction swinging to and fro above him, and every moment the keen edge approaching nearer and nearer: at length it cuts the skin of his nose, and gradually cuts on, until life is extinct."

THE DOLL'S HOUSE

Katherine Mansfield

The notion of social class and of people who are considered "untouchables" is the basis for this story about snobbishness and cruelty among children. The story is set in New Zealand, but its basic situation should be familiar to all of us. Is there anyone who has not known what it is to be a Burnell—or a Kelvey? As you read the story, think about what motivates each character.

When dear old Mrs. Hay went back to town after staying with the Burnells, she sent the children a doll's house. It was so big that the carter[1] and Pat carried it into the courtyard, and there it stayed, propped up on two wooden boxes beside the feed-room door. No

harm could come of it; it was summer. And perhaps the smell of paint would have gone off by the time it had to be taken in. For, really, the smell of paint coming from that doll's house ("Sweet of old Mrs. Hay, of course; most sweet and generous!")—but the smell of paint was quite enough to make any one seriously ill, in Aunt Beryl's opinion. Even before the sacking was taken off. And when it was. . . .

There stood the doll's house, a dark, oily, spinach green, picked out with bright yellow. Its two solid little chimneys, glued onto the roof, were painted red and white, and the door, gleaming with yellow varnish, was like a little slab of toffee. Four windows, real windows, were divided into panes by a broad streak of green. There was actually a tiny porch, too, painted yellow, with big lumps of congealed paint hanging along the edge.

But perfect, perfect little house! Who could possibly mind the smell? It was part of the joy, part of the newness.

"Open it quickly, someone!"

The hook at the side was stuck fast. Pat pried it open with his penknife, and the whole house front swung back, and—there you were, gazing at one and the same moment into the drawing room and dining room, the kitchen and two bedrooms. That is the way for a house to open! Why don't all houses open like that? How much more exciting than peering through the slit of a door into a mean little hall with a hat stand and two umbrellas! That is—isn't it?—what you long to know about a house when you put your hand on the knocker.

---

1. **carter:** someone who carries things in a cart.

Perhaps it is the way God opens houses at dead of night when He is taking a quiet turn with an angel. . . .

"O-oh!" The Burnell children sounded as though they were in despair. It was too marvelous; it was too much for them. They had never seen anything like it in their lives. All the rooms were papered. There were pictures on the walls, painted on the paper, with gold frames complete. Red carpet covered all the floors except the kitchen; red plush chairs in the drawing room, green in the dining room; tables, beds with real bedclothes, a cradle, a stove, a dresser with tiny plates, and one big jug. But what Kezia liked more than anything, what she liked frightfully, was the lamp. It stood in the middle of the dining room table, an exquisite little amber lamp with a white globe. It was even filled all ready for lighting, though, of course, you couldn't light it. But there was something inside that looked like oil and that moved when you shook it.

The father and mother dolls, who sprawled very stiff, as though they had fainted in the drawing room, and their two little children asleep upstairs were really too big for the doll's house. They didn't look as though they belonged. But the lamp was perfect. It seemed to smile at Kezia, to say, "I live here." The lamp was real.

The Burnell children could hardly walk to school fast enough the next morning. They burned to tell everybody, to describe, to—well—to boast about their doll's house before the school bell rang.

"I'm to tell," said Isabel, "because I'm the eldest. And you two can join in after. But I'm to tell first."

There was nothing to answer. Isabel was bossy, but she was always right, and Lottie and Kezia knew too well the powers that went with being eldest. They brushed through the thick buttercups at the road edge and said nothing.

"And I'm to choose who's to come and see it first. Mother said I might."

For it had been arranged that while the doll's house stood in the courtyard they might ask the girls at school, two at a time, to come and look. Not to stay to tea, of course, or to come traipsing through the house. But just to stand quietly in the courtyard while Isabel pointed out the beauties, and Lottie and Kezia looked pleased. . . .

But hurry as they might, by the time they had reached the tarred palings[2] of the boys' playground the bell had begun to jangle. They only just had time to whip off their hats and fall into line before the roll was called. Never mind. Isabel tried to make up for it by looking very important and mysterious and by whispering behind her hand to the girls near her, "Got something to tell you at playtime."

Playtime came and Isabel was surrounded. The girls of her class nearly fought to put their arms round her, to walk away with her, to beam flatteringly, to be her special friend. She held quite a court under the huge pine trees at the side of the playground. Nudging, giggling together, the little girls pressed up close. And the only two who stayed outside the ring were the two who were always outside, the little Kelveys. They knew better than to come anywhere near the Burnells.

For the fact was, the school the Burnell children went to was not at all the kind of place their parents would have chosen if there had been any choice. But there was none. It was the only school for miles. And the consequence was all the children in the neighborhood, the Judge's little girls, the doctor's daughters, the storekeeper's children, the milkman's, were forced to mix together. Not to speak of there being an equal number of rude, rough little boys as well. But the line had to be drawn somewhere. It was drawn at the Kelveys. Many of the children, including the Burnells, were not allowed even to speak to them. They walked past the Kelveys with their heads in the air, and as they set the fashion in all matters of behavior, the Kelveys were shunned by everybody. Even the teacher had a special voice for them, and a special smile for the other children when Lil Kelvey came up to her desk with a bunch of dreadfully common-looking flowers.

They were the daughters of a spry, hardworking little washerwoman, who went about from house to house by the day. This was awful enough. But where was Mr. Kelvey? Nobody knew for certain. But everybody said he was in prison. So they were

---

2. **palings:** the wooden strips of a fence.

the daughters of a washerwoman and a jailbird. Very nice company for other people's children! And they looked it. Why Mrs. Kelvey made them so conspicuous was hard to understand. The truth was they were dressed in "bits" given to her by the people for whom she worked. Lil, for instance, who was a stout, plain child with big freckles, came to school in a dress made from a green art-serge tablecloth of the Burnells', with red plush sleeves from the Logans' curtains. Her hat, perched on top of her high forehead, was a grown-up woman's hat, once the property of Miss Lecky, the postmistress. It was turned up at the back and trimmed with a large scarlet quill. What a little guy[3] she looked! It was impossible not to laugh. And her little sister, our Else, wore a long white dress, rather like a nightgown, and a pair of little boy's boots. But whatever our Else wore she would have looked strange. She was a tiny wishbone of a child, with cropped hair and enormous solemn eyes—a little white owl. Nobody had ever seen her smile; she scarcely ever spoke. She went through life holding on to Lil, with a piece of Lil's skirt screwed up in her hand. Where Lil went, our Else followed. In the playground, on the road going to and from school, there was Lil marching in front and our Else holding on behind. Only when she wanted anything, or when she was out of breath, our Else gave Lil a tug, a twitch, and Lil stopped and turned round. The Kelveys never failed to understand each other.

Now they hovered at the edge; you couldn't stop them listening. When the little girls turned round and sneered, Lil, as usual, gave her silly, shamefaced smile, but our Else only looked.

And Isabel's voice, so very proud, went on telling. The carpet made a great sensation, but so did the beds with real bedclothes, and the stove with an oven door.

When she finished, Kezia broke in. "You've forgotten the lamp, Isabel."

"Oh, yes," said Isabel, "and there's a teeny little lamp, all made of yellow glass, with a white globe that stands on the dining-room table. You couldn't tell it from a real one."

"The lamp's best of all," cried Kezia. She

thought Isabel wasn't making half enough of the little lamp. But nobody paid any attention. Isabel was choosing the two who were to come back with them that afternoon and see it. She chose Emmie Cole and Lena Logan. But when the others knew they were all to have a chance, they couldn't be nice enough to Isabel. One by one they put their arms round Isabel's waist and walked her off. They had something to whisper to her, a secret. "Isabel's *my* friend."

Only the little Kelveys moved away forgotten; there was nothing more for them to hear.

Days passed, and as more children saw the doll's house, the fame of it spread. It became the one subject, the rage. The one question was, "Have you seen Burnells' doll's house? Oh, ain't it lovely!" "Haven't you seen it? Oh, I say!"

Even the dinner hour was given up to talking about it. The little girls sat under the pines, eating their thick mutton sandwiches and big slabs of johnny cake spread with butter. While always, as near as they could get, sat the Kelveys, our Else holding on to Lil, listening too, while they chewed their jam sandwiches out of a newspaper soaked with large red blobs. . . .

"Mother," said Kezia, "can't I ask the Kelveys just once?"

"Certainly not, Kezia."

"But why not?"

"Run away, Kezia; you know quite well why not."

At last everybody had seen it except them. On that day the subject rather flagged. It was the dinner hour. The children stood together under the pine trees, and suddenly, as they looked at the Kelveys eating out of their paper, always by themselves, always listening, they wanted to be horrid to them. Emmie Cole started the whisper.

"Lil Kelvey's going to be a servant when she grows up."

"O-oh, how awful!" said Isabel Burnell, and she made eyes at Emmie.

Emmie swallowed in a very meaning way and nodded to Isabel as she'd seen her mother do on those occasions.

"It's true—it's true—it's true," she said.

---

3. **guy:** in British usage, a person who has an odd appearance.

Then Lena Logan's little eyes snapped. "Shall I ask her?" she whispered.

"Bet you don't," said Jessie May.

"Pooh, I'm not frightened," said Lena. Suddenly she gave a little squeal and danced in front of the other girls. "Watch! Watch me! Watch me now!" said Lena. And sliding, gliding, dragging one foot, giggling behind her hand, Lena went over to the Kelveys.

Lil looked up from her dinner. She wrapped the rest quickly away. Our Else stopped chewing. What was coming now?

"Is is true you're going to be a servant when you grow up, Lil Kelvey?" shrilled Lena.

Dead silence. But instead of answering, Lil only gave her silly, shamefaced smile. She didn't seem to mind the question at all. What a sell for Lena! The girls began to titter.

Lena couldn't stand that. She put her hands on her hips; she shot forward. "Yah, yer father's in prison!" she hissed, spitefully.

This was such a marvelous thing to have said that the little girls rushed away in a body, deeply, deeply excited, wild with joy. Someone found a long rope, and they began skipping. And never did they skip so high, run in and out so fast, or do such daring things as on that morning.

In the afternoon Pat called for the Burnell children with the buggy and they drove home. There were visitors. Isabel and Lottie, who liked visitors, went upstairs to change their pinafores. But Kezia thieved out at the back. Nobody was about; she began to swing on the big white gates of the courtyard. Presently, looking along the road, she saw two little dots. They grew bigger; they were coming towards her. Now she could see that one was in front and one close behind. Now she could see that they were the Kelveys. Kezia stopped swinging. She slipped off the gate as if she was going to run away. Then she hesitated. The Kelveys came nearer, and beside them walked their shadows, very long, stretching right across the road with their heads in the buttercups. Kezia clambered back on the gate; she had made up her mind; she swung out.

"Hullo," she said to the passing Kelveys.

They were so astounded that they stopped. Lil gave her silly smile. Our Else stared.

"You can come and see our doll's house if you want to," said Kezia, and she dragged one toe on the ground. But at that Lil turned red and shook her head quickly.

"Why not?" asked Kezia.

Lil gasped, then she said, "Your ma told our ma you wasn't to speak to us."

"Oh, well," said Kezia. She didn't know what to reply. "It doesn't matter. You can come and see our doll's house all the same. Come on. Nobody's looking."

But Lil shook her head still harder.

"Don't you want to?" asked Kezia.

Suddenly there was a twitch, a tug at Lil's skirt. She turned round. Our Else was looking at her with big, imploring eyes; she was frowning; she wanted to go. For a moment Lil looked at our Else very doubtfully. But then our Else twitched her skirt again. She started forward. Kezia led the way. Like two little stray cats they followed across the courtyard to where the doll's house stood.

"There it is," said Kezia.

There was a pause. Lil breathed loudly, almost snorted; our Else was still as a stone.

"I'll open it for you," said Kezia kindly. She undid the hook and they looked inside.

"There's the drawing room and the dining room, and that's the—"

"Kezia!"

Oh, what a start they gave!

"Kezia!"

It was Aunt Beryl's voice. They turned round. At the back door stood Aunt Beryl, staring as if she couldn't believe what she saw.

"How dare you ask the little Kelveys into the courtyard?" said her cold, furious voice. "You know as well as I do you're not allowed to talk to them. Run away, children, run away at once. And don't come back again," said Aunt Beryl. And she stepped into the yard and shooed them out as if they were chickens.

"Off you go immediately!" she called, cold and proud.

They did not need telling twice. Burning with shame, shrinking together, Lil huddling along like her mother, our Else dazed, somehow they crossed the big courtyard and squeezed through the white gate.

"Wicked, disobedient little girl!" said Aunt Beryl bitterly to Kezia, and she slammed the doll's house to.

The afternoon had been awful. A letter had come from Willie Brent, a terrifying, threatening letter, saying if she did not meet him that evening in Pulman's Bush, he'd come to the front door and ask the reason why! But now that she had frightened those little rats of Kelveys and given Kezia a good scolding, her heart felt lighter. That ghastly pressure was gone. She went back to the house humming.

When the Kelveys were well out of sight of Burnells', they sat down to rest on a big red drainpipe by the side of the road. Lil's cheeks were still burning; she took off the hat with the quill and held it on her knee. Dreamily they looked over the hay paddocks, past the creek, to the group of wattles[4] where Logan's cows stood waiting to be milked. What were their thoughts?

Presently our Else nudged up close to her sister. But now she had forgotten the cross lady. She put out a finger and stroked her sister's quill; she smiled her rare smile.

"I seen the little lamp," she said, softly.

Then both were silent once more.

---

4. **wattles:** fences woven of twigs or branches.

Responding to the Story

Analyzing the Story

Identifying Facts

1. There are many characters in "The Doll's House," almost all of them female. Which character would you say is the **protagonist**? Why?
2. We would all probably agree that the values of these schoolgirls, which encourage them to taunt the poor Kelvey sisters, are deplorable. Find the passages that tell why the Kelveys are considered outcasts. Where do the other children, those who scorn the Kelveys, get their values? How do you know?
3. At the story's **climax,** one character takes action to get what she "wants." Who is this? What does she want, and what does she do to get it?
4. It seems safe to call the point of view in this story **omniscient.** Indeed, during the early part of the story, it is difficult to focus our attention on any one character. Find at least one passage in which we enter the minds of the following characters:

    Aunt Beryl
    The Burnell girls
    Kezia alone
    The Kelveys
    The other schoolgirls

Interpreting Meanings

5. What do you think **motivates** Aunt Beryl to act as she does?
6. Both Isabel and Kezia want to share their doll's house with other children, yet their **motives** differ. Why does Isabel invite her friends to see the doll's house? Why do you think Kezia wants to invite the two little outsiders?
7. Since it makes up the story's title, the doll's house must have some significance. In fact, it seems more important to the characters than an ordinary toy would be. Find the passage at the opening of the story where we learn what the children think of the little house. What details here suggest that the doll's house could be a **symbol** of an imaginary world that is more perfect and more ordered than the one the girls

live in? How would this add significance to Kezia's desire to share that world with the little Kelveys?

8. The little lamp within the house is also mentioned often, and it too seems to carry some **symbolic** weight. Candles, lamps, and lights of all sorts are very old images. Sometimes they symbolize these things:

    > Warmth and comfort (a light in the window that welcomes a traveler)
    > Hope (a ray of light in the darkness)
    > The presence of God (the sanctuary lights in a church or synagogue)

    Explain what you think the little lamp might symbolize in this story. What added significance does it give to Else's "rare" smile as she says at the end, "I seen the little lamp"?

9. Did you find the responses of the children in this story believable? Why do you suppose that after Lena's humiliation of the Kelveys, the other girls were "wild with joy" and more daring in their games than ever (page 183)? Can you think of other instances where people might be exhilarated for the same reasons?
10. Did you find the story's ending a satisfying one? Explain your response.

Writing About the Story

A Creative Response

1. **Updating the Story.** Could the scenes in this schoolyard take place in a contemporary schoolyard? Would the snobbishness today be based on social class, as it is in this story, or might the cruelty have some other source? In a paragraph, explain what might be altered in the story if it were to take place in a contemporary setting. Consider the toy itself, the characters, their dress, their games, their values, and the roles of the adults.

A Critical Response

2. **Evaluating the Story's Point of View.** Support or refute one of the following statements in a paragraph. Refer to specific passages from the story to support your opinion.

a. *The lack of a clear, sustained point of view in "The Doll's House" is very confusing. I am inside the thoughts of too many characters, and it is often difficult to know whose "voice" is speaking.*

b. *The range of the point of view in "The Doll's House" helps me understand the motives and feelings of all the characters in the story. Each of the switches in point of view adds to the power of the story, because I can see how the Kelveys are victimized by everyone in this nasty society.*

Analyzing Language and Vocabulary

Figures of Speech

Some writers write very straightforward prose with almost no **figures of speech.** Others, like Katherine Mansfield, use figurative language, often to create subtle emotional effects. Answer the following questions about Mansfield's use of figurative language.

1. On page 181 the doll's house is described as "dark, oily, spinach green, picked out with bright yellow."

   a. Do the colors make the house seem pleasant or unpleasant? Which words account for your feelings?

   b. How would the effect change if the house were described as "rosebud pink with watermelon-green trim" or as "mud brown with seaweed-green trim"?

2. Find the **simile** that describes the little door.

   a. Is this a pleasant association or an unpleasant one? Why?

   b. What simile might an adult have used to describe the door?

3. Else is described as a "tiny wishbone of a child" on page 182.

   a. What does this suggest about her size, weight, and strength?

   b. Can you think of other reasons why it is appropriate to compare Else to a wishbone?

4. Find the other **metaphor** that describes Else in this passage.

   a. What physical trait makes the writer describe her this way?

   b. How do these two descriptions of Else make you feel about her? Why?

5. Find three figures of speech on page 184 that identify the Kelveys with animals.

   a. Do these comparisons reveal the way the writer feels about the Kelveys or the way the people in the story feel about them?

   b. How do these descriptions of the Kelveys make you feel about them?

Reading About the Writer

Katherine Mansfield (1888–1923) was born in New Zealand. She grew up in a small town outside of Wellington, where she attended school with the milk boy and the washwoman's daughters. At fourteen she was sent to England to study at Queen's College.

Mansfield gave her early stories European backgrounds and a satiric edge. But later, with the help of her diaries, she turned to her New Zealand childhood for her material. These stories were taken by John Middleton Murry for his magazines *Rhythm* and *The Blue Review.* Mansfield eventually married Murry and became his publishing partner.

As her stories were published in periodicals and later in collections (*In a German Pension, The Garden Party and Other Stories,* and *Bliss and Other Stories*), Mansfield came to be recognized as a supremely gifted writer and an innovator of the short-story form.

Just as her contemporaries Virginia Woolf and James Joyce were changing the concept of the novel, so Katherine Mansfield was remaking the short story. Drawn from autobiographical material— often the world of childhood—her stories depend on a revelation of interior moods and on the power of poetic language. Up to this time, stories were written with straightforward plots, often with clever, trick endings. Mansfield's stories do away with attention to plot and action and instead try to illuminate moments of significance. Some people complain that in stories like Katherine Mansfield's "nothing happens." Very little happens externally, but a lot is going on inside the characters' minds.

A VERY OLD MAN WITH ENORMOUS WINGS
A TALE FOR CHILDREN

Gabriel García Márquez, translated by **Gregory Rabassa**

Like many contemporary South American writers, García Márquez writes a kind of fiction called *magic realism*. This style of writing is characterized by fantastic elements (often borrowed from mythology and religion) that are casually inserted into realistic settings. The magic realists force us to confront our fixed ideas about "reality" and "normality."

This story hangs on that stimulating hook of suppose, *what if?* What if one day an old man with huge, bug-infested wings dropped out of the sky into your backyard? How would people respond to this fantastic event?

Read to the end of the fourth paragraph, and then write down two questions you have about this very old man with enormous wings. What do you predict is going to happen to him?

On the third day of rain they had killed so many crabs inside the house that Pelayo had to cross his drenched courtyard and throw them into the sea, because the newborn child had a temperature all night and they thought it was due to the stench. The world had been sad since Tuesday. Sea and sky were a single ash-gray thing and the sands of the beach, which on March nights glimmered like powdered light, had become a stew of mud and rotten shellfish. The light was so weak at noon that when Pelayo was coming back to the house after throwing away the crabs, it was hard for him to see what it was that was moving and groaning in the rear of the courtyard. He had to go very close to see that it was an old man, a very old man, lying face down in the mud, who, in spite of his tremendous efforts, couldn't get up, impeded by his enormous wings.

Frightened by that nightmare, Pelayo ran to get Elisenda, his wife, who was putting compresses on the sick child, and he took her to the rear of the courtyard. They both looked at the fallen body with mute stupor. He was dressed like a ragpicker. There were only a few faded hairs left on his bald skull and very few teeth in his mouth, and his pitiful condition of a drenched great-grandfather had taken away any sense of grandeur he might have had. His huge buzzard wings, dirty and half-plucked, were forever entangled in the mud. They looked at him so long and so closely that Pelayo and Elisenda very soon overcame their surprise and in the end found him familiar. Then they dared speak to him, and he answered in an incomprehensible dialect with a strong sailor's voice. That was how they skipped over the inconvenience of the wings and quite intelligently concluded that he was a lonely castaway from some foreign ship wrecked by the storm. And yet, they called in a neighbor woman who knew everything about life and death to see him, and all she needed was one look to show them their mistake.

"He's an angel," she told them. "He must have been coming for the child, but the poor fellow is so old that the rain knocked him down."

On the following day everyone knew that a flesh-and-blood angel was held captive in Pelayo's house. Against the judgment of the wise neighbor woman, for whom angels in those times were the fugitive survivors of a celestial conspiracy,[1] they

---

1. **celestial conspiracy:** According to the New Testament, Satan was originally an angel who led a rebellion in heaven. He and his followers, called the fallen angels, were exiled to hell.

did not have the heart to club him to death. Pelayo watched over him all afternoon from the kitchen, armed with his bailiff's club, and before going to bed he dragged him out of the mud and locked him up with the hens in the wire chicken coop. In the middle of the night, when the rain stopped, Pelayo and Elisenda were still killing crabs. A short time afterward the child woke up without a fever and with a desire to eat. Then they felt magnanimous and decided to put the angel on a raft with fresh water and provisions for three days and leave him to his fate on the high seas. But when they went out into the courtyard with the first light of dawn, they found the whole neighborhood in front of the chicken coop having fun with the angel, without the slightest reverence, tossing him things to eat through the openings in the wire, as if he weren't a supernatural creature but a circus animal.

Father Gonzaga arrived before seven o'clock, alarmed at the strange news. By that time onlookers less frivolous than those at dawn had already arrived, and they were making all kinds of conjectures concerning the captive's future. The simplest among them thought that he should be named mayor of the world. Others of sterner mind felt that he should be promoted to the rank of five-star general in order to win all wars. Some visionaries hoped that he could be put to stud in order to implant on earth a race of winged wise men who could take charge of the universe. But Father Gonzaga, before becoming a priest, had been a robust woodcutter. Standing by the wire, he reviewed his catechism[2] in an instant and asked them to open the door so that he could take a closer look at that pitiful man who looked more like a huge decrepit hen among the fascinated chickens. He was lying in a corner drying his open wings in the sunlight among the fruit peels and breakfast leftovers that the early risers had thrown him. Alien to the impertinences of the world, he only lifted his antiquarian eyes and murmured something in his dialect when Father Gonzaga went into the chicken coop and said good morning to him in Latin. The parish priest had his first suspicion of an impostor when he saw that he did not understand the language of God or know how to greet His ministers. Then he noticed that seen close up he was much too human: He had an unbearable smell of the outdoors, the back side of his wings was strewn with parasites and his main feathers had been mistreated by terrestrial winds, and nothing about him measured up to the proud dignity of angels. Then he came out of the chicken coop and in a brief sermon warned the curious against the risks of being ingenuous.[3] He reminded them that the devil had the bad habit of making use of carnival tricks in order to confuse the unwary. He argued that if wings were not the essential element in determining the difference between a hawk and an airplane, they were even less so in the recognition of angels. Nevertheless, he promised to write a letter to his bishop so that the latter would write to his primate[4] so that the latter would write to the Supreme Pontiff[5] in order to get the final verdict from the highest courts.

His prudence fell on sterile hearts. The news of the captive angel spread with such rapidity that after a few hours the courtyard had the bustle of a marketplace, and they had to call in troops with fixed bayonets to disperse the mob that was about to knock the house down. Elisenda, her spine all twisted from sweeping up so much marketplace trash, then got the idea of fencing in the yard and charging five cents admission to see the angel.

The curious came from far away. A traveling carnival arrived with a flying acrobat who buzzed over the crowd several times, but no one paid any attention to him because his wings were not those of an angel but, rather, those of a sidereal[6] bat. The most unfortunate invalids on earth came in search of health: a poor woman who since childhood had been counting her heartbeats and had run out of numbers; a Portuguese man who couldn't sleep because the noise of the stars disturbed him; a sleepwalker who got up at night to

---

2. **catechism** (kat′ə·kiz′m): a book of religious doctrine consisting of a series of questions and answers. Children in the Roman Catholic Church, especially, are taught about their religion through a catechism.

3. **ingenuous** (in·jen′yōō·wəs): naive, too easily persuaded to believe.
4. **primate** (prī′māt): a high-ranking bishop.
5. **Supreme Pontiff:** the Pope.
6. **sidereal** (sī·dir′ē·əl): of or pertaining to the stars.

Carved and painted wood
canoe ornament.
Tlingit tribe, northwest
coast of North America.

Field Museum of Natural History, Chicago.

undo the things he had done while awake; and many others with less serious ailments. In the midst of that shipwreck disorder that made the earth tremble, Pelayo and Elisenda were happy with fatigue, for in less than a week they had crammed their rooms with money, and the line of pilgrims waiting their turn to enter still reached beyond the horizon.

The angel was the only one who took no part in his own act. He spent his time trying to get comfortable in his borrowed nest, befuddled by the hellish heat of the oil lamps and sacramental candles that had been placed along the wire. At first they tried to make him eat some mothballs, which, according to the wisdom of the wise neighbor woman, were the food prescribed for angels. But he turned them down, just as he turned down the papal[7] lunches that the penitents brought him, and they never found out whether it was because he was an angel or because he was an old man that in the end he ate nothing but eggplant mush. His only supernatural virtue seemed to be patience. Especially during the first days, when the hens pecked at him, searching for the stellar parasites that proliferated in his wings, and the cripples pulled out feathers to touch their defective parts with, and even the most merciful threw stones at him, trying to get him to rise so they could see him standing. The only time they succeeded in arousing him was when they burned his side with an iron for branding steers, for he had been motionless for so many hours that they thought he was dead. He awoke with a start, ranting in his hermetic[8] language and with tears in his eyes, and he flapped his wings a couple of times, which brought on a whirlwind of chicken dung and lunar dust and a gale of panic that did not seem to be of this world. Although many thought that his reaction had been one not of rage but of pain, from then on they were careful not to annoy him, because the majority understood that his passivity was not that of a hero taking his ease but that of a cataclysm[9] in repose.

Father Gonzaga held back the crowd's frivolity with formulas of maidservant inspiration while awaiting the arrival of a final judgment on the nature of the captive. But the mail from Rome showed no sense of urgency. They spent their time finding out if the prisoner had a navel, if his dialect had any connection with Aramaic,[10] how many times he could fit on the head of a pin, or whether he wasn't just a Norwegian with wings. Those meager letters might have come and gone until the end of time if a providential event had not put an end to the priest's tribulations.

It so happened that during those days, among so many other carnival attractions, there arrived in town the traveling show of the woman who had been changed into a spider for having disobeyed her parents. The admission to see her was not only less than the admission to see the angel, but people were permitted to ask her all manner of questions about her absurd state and to examine her up and down so that no one would ever doubt the truth of her horror. She was a frightful tarantula the size of a ram and with the head of a sad maiden. What was most heart-rending, however, was not her outlandish shape, but the sincere affliction with which she recounted the details of her misfortune. While still practically a child she had sneaked out of her parents' house to go to a dance, and while she was coming back through the woods after having danced all night without permission, a fearful thunderclap rent the sky in two, and through the crack came the lightning bolt of brimstone that changed her into a spider. Her only nourishment came from the meatballs that charitable souls chose to toss into her mouth. A spectacle like that, full of so much human truth and with such a fearful lesson, was bound to defeat without even trying that of a haughty angel who scarcely deigned to look at mortals. Besides, the few miracles attributed to the angel showed a certain mental disorder, like the blind man who didn't recover his sight but grew three new teeth, or the paralytic who didn't get to walk but almost won the lottery, and the leper whose sores sprouted sunflowers. Those consolation miracles, which were more like mocking fun, had already ruined the angel's reputation when the woman who had been changed into a spider finally crushed him completely. That was how Father Gonzaga was cured forever of his insomnia and Pelayo's courtyard went back to being as empty as during the time it had rained for three days and crabs walked through the bedrooms.

The owners of the house had no reason to lament. With the money they saved they built a two-story mansion with balconies and gardens and high netting so that crabs wouldn't get in during

---

7. **papal** (pā′pəl): of, relating to, or fit for the Pope.
8. **hermetic:** difficult or impossible to understand.
9. **cataclysm** (kat′ə·kliz′m): any great upheaval or disaster.
10. **Aramaic** (ar′ə·mā′ik): Middle Eastern language spoken by Jesus and his disciples.

the winter, and with iron bars on the windows so that angels wouldn't get in. Pelayo also set up a rabbit warren close to town and gave up his job as bailiff for good, and Elisenda bought some satin pumps with high heels and many dresses of iridescent silk, the kind worn on Sunday by the most desirable women in those times. The chicken coop was the only thing that didn't receive any attention. If they washed it down with creolin[11] and burned tears of myrrh[12] inside it every so often, it was not in homage to the angel but to drive away the dungheap stench that still hung everywhere like a ghost and was turning the new house into an old one. At first, when the child learned to walk, they were careful that he not get too close to the chicken coop. But then they began to lose their fears and got used to the smell, and before the child got his second teeth he'd gone inside the chicken coop to play, where the wires were falling apart. The angel was no less standoffish with him than with other mortals, but he tolerated the most ingenious infamies with the patience of a dog who had no illusions. They both came down with chicken pox at the same time. The doctor who took care of the child couldn't resist the temptation to listen to the angel's heart, and he found so much whistling in the heart and so many sounds in his kidneys that it seemed impossible for him to be alive. What surprised him most, however, was the logic of his wings. They seemed so natural on that completely human organism that he couldn't understand why other men didn't have them too.

When the child began school it had been some time since the sun and rain had caused the collapse of the chicken coop. The angel went dragging himself about here and there like a stray dying man. They would drive him out of the bedroom with a broom and a moment later find him in the kitchen. He seemed to be in so many places at the same time that they grew to think that he'd been duplicated, that he was reproducing himself all through the house, and the exasperated and unhinged Elisenda shouted that it was awful living in that hell full of angels. He could scarcely eat, and his antiquarian eyes had also become so foggy that he went about bumping into posts. All he had left were the bare cannulae[13] of his last feathers. Pelayo threw a blanket over him and extended him the charity of letting him sleep in the shed, and only then did they notice that he had a temperature at night, and was delirious with the tongue twisters of an old Norwegian. That was one of the few times they became alarmed, for they thought he was going to die, and not even the wise neighbor woman had been able to tell them what to do with dead angels.

And yet he not only survived his worst winter, but seemed improved with the first sunny days. He remained motionless for several days in the farthest corner of the courtyard, where no one would see him, and at the beginning of December some large, stiff feathers began to grow on his wings, the feathers of a scarecrow, which looked more like another misfortune of decrepitude. But he must have known the reason for those changes, for he was quite careful that no one should notice them, that no one should hear the sea chanteys[14] that he sometimes sang under the stars. One morning Elisenda was cutting some bunches of onions for lunch when a wind that seemed to come from the high seas blew into the kitchen. Then she went to the window and caught the angel in his first attempts at flight. They were so clumsy that his fingernails opened a furrow in the vegetable patch, and he was on the point of knocking the shed down with the ungainly flapping that slipped on the light and couldn't get a grip on the air. But he did manage to gain altitude. Elisenda let out a sigh of relief, for herself and for him, when she saw him pass over the last houses, holding himself up in some way with the risky flapping of a senile vulture. She kept watching him even when she was through cutting the onions, and she kept on watching until it was no longer possible for her to see him, because then he was no longer an annoyance in her life but an imaginary dot on the horizon of the sea.

---

11. **creolin** (krē'ə·lin'): a kind of antiseptic.
12. **myrrh** (mʉr): a fragrant, bitter-tasting gum resin used in making incense and perfume.

13. **cannulae** (kan'yōō·lē'): pl., hollow shafts; tubes.
14. **sea chanteys** (shan'tēz): songs that sailors sing while they work.

Responding to the Story

Analyzing the Story

Identifying Facts

1. The townspeople draw various conclusions about who, or rather what, the winged old man is. What do Pelayo and Elisenda think he is? Their know-it-all neighbor? Father Gonzaga?
2. How does this old man change the lives of Pelayo and Elisenda?
3. What miracles are attributed to the old man?
4. What happens when a new novelty, the spider-woman, comes to town?

Interpreting Meanings

5. If an angel did fall into a backyard on earth, what would you expect it to look like? How is the old man **ironically** unlike an angel?
6. What human shortcomings might García Márquez be poking fun at in this story? Think about

   a. how Pelayo and Elisenda treat the old man;
   b. why Father Gonzaga and his superiors decide he's not an angel;
   c. how people react to the "spectacle" of the angel and then of the spider-woman.

7. What aspects of this story are **fantastic** or **absurd?** (But what things that happen in our "real" world might seem illogical or ridiculous to someone observing us from another world?)
8. Do you think the old man is a divine figure or an evil one? Are there any other possibilities? Explain your opinion.
9. Do you think this story is merely intended to amuse and astonish us, or does it mean something? Discuss your responses to these two interpretations:

   a. The old man **symbolizes** the world of miracles we wish for but are unable to accept when they happen.
   b. The old man **symbolizes** the artist, who is mocked and misunderstood by other people and whose imagination longs to soar.

10. How do you suppose people in your community would act if an angel or a creature from outer space fell into someone's backyard?

Writing About the Story

A Creative Response

1. **Assuming a Character's Point of View.** The old winged man never says anything the townspeople can understand. What do you think is going through his mind as he patiently endures all the indignities of the chicken coop? Write a letter the old man might have left Pelayo and Elisenda—or the whole town—before flying away. He might include details about his home, the reason he fell into the yard, how "humanity" looked from his perspective, and where he is going now. Use the first-person *I.*
2. **Using Magic Realism.** Perhaps this old man is Daedalus, the Greek artisan who made wings to escape from prison. (See page 798.) Maybe the story began when García Márquez thought, "What would happen if . . . ?" Write a fantastic story of your own about another person from mythology or folklore who falls into your world. You might consider what would happen if

   Odysseus joined the U.S. Marines;
   A fairy godmother appeared to a poor girl in New York City;
   Hercules, the strongest teen-ager in the world, enrolled at a local high school;
   A dragon asked to be admitted to the zoo.

Reading About the Writer

Gabriel García Márquez (1928–   ) sets much of his work in the imaginary town of Macondo, which in many ways resembles the sleepy, decaying, backwater town of Aracataca, Colombia, where he was born. After studying law and working abroad for many years as a journalist, García Márquez achieved international acclaim during the 1970's, primarily as a result of his best-selling novel *One Hundred Years of Solitude.* This epic masterpiece tells the tragic and comic saga of seven generations of Maconda's founding family. The Chilean poet Pablo Neruda (see page 356) called the novel "the greatest revelation in the Spanish language since *Don Quixote.*" In 1982 García Márquez won the Nobel Prize in literature.

Literature & Language

Using Subordinate Clauses

Literary Model

The following story takes place in an industrial city in northern Italy.

Mushrooms in the City

The wind, coming to the city from far away, brings it unusual gifts, noticed by only a few sensitive souls, such as hay-fever victims, who sneeze at the pollen from flowers of other lands.

One day, to the narrow strip of ground flanking a city avenue came a gust of spores from God knows where; and some mushrooms germinated. Nobody noticed them except Marcovaldo, the worker who caught his tram just there every morning.

This Marcovaldo possessed an eye ill-suited to city life: Billboards, traffic lights, shop windows, neon signs, posters, no matter how carefully devised to catch the attention, never arrested his gaze, which might have been running over the desert sands. Instead, he would never miss a leaf yellowing on a branch, a feather trapped by a roof tile; there was no horsefly on a horse's back, no wormhole in a plank, or fig peel squashed on the sidewalk that Marcovaldo didn't remark and ponder over, discovering the changes of season, the yearnings of his heart, and the woes of his existence.

Thus, one morning, as he was waiting for the tram that would take him to Sbav and Co., where he was employed as an unskilled laborer, he noticed something unusual near the stop, in the sterile, encrusted strip of earth beneath the avenue's line of trees; at certain points, near the tree trunks, some bumps seemed to rise, and here and there they had opened, allowing roundish subterranean[1] bodies to peep out.

Bending to tie his shoes, he took a better look: they were mushrooms, real mushrooms, sprouting right in the heart of the city! To Marcovaldo the gray and wretched world surrounding him seemed suddenly generous with hidden riches; something could still be expected of life, beyond the hourly wage of his stipulated salary, with inflation index, family grant, and cost-of-living allowance.

On the job he was more absentminded than usual; he kept thinking that while he was there unloading cases and boxes, in the darkness of the earth the slow, silent mushrooms, known only to him, were ripening their porous flesh, were assimilating[2] underground humors;[3] breaking the crust of clods. "One night's rain would be enough," he said to himself, "then they would be ready to pick." And he couldn't wait to share his discovery with his wife and six children.

"I'm telling you!" he announced during their scant supper. "In a week's time we'll be eating mushrooms! A great fry! That's a promise!"

And to the smaller children, who did not know what mushrooms were, he explained ecstatically the beauty of the numerous species, the delicacy of their flavor, the way they should be cooked; and so he also drew into the discussion his wife, Domitilla, who until then had appeared rather incredulous and abstracted.

"Where are these mushrooms?" the children asked. "Tell us where they grow!"

At this question Marcovaldo's enthusiasm was curbed by a suspicious thought; Now, if I tell them the place, they'll go and hunt for them with the usual gang of kids, word will spread through the neighborhood, and the mushrooms will end up in somebody else's pan! And so that discovery, which had promptly filled his heart with universal love, now made him wildly possessive, surrounded him with jealous and distrusting fear.

"I know where the mushrooms are, and I'm the only one who knows," he said to his children, "and God help you if you breathe a word to anybody."

The next morning, as he approached the tram stop, Marcovaldo was filled with apprehension. He

---

1. **subterranean** (sub´tə·rā´nē·ən): underground.

2. **assimilating** (ə·sim´ə·lāt´iŋ): absorbing.
3. **humors:** fluids, moisture.

bent to look at the ground and, to his relief, saw that the mushrooms had grown a little, but not much and were still almost completely hidden by the earth.

He was bent in this position when he realized there was someone behind him. He straightened up at once and tried to act indifferent. It was the street cleaner, leaning on his broom and looking at him.

This street cleaner, whose jurisdiction included the place where the mushrooms grew, was a lanky youth with eyeglasses. His name was Amadigi, and Marcovaldo had long harbored a dislike of him, perhaps because of those eyeglasses that examined the pavement of the streets, seeking any trace of nature, to be eradicated[4] by his broom.

It was Saturday; and Marcovaldo spent his free half-day circling the bed of dirt with an absent air, keeping an eye on the street cleaner in the distance and on the mushrooms, and calculating how much time they needed to ripen.

That night it rained: Like peasants who, after months of drought, wake up and leap with joy at the sound of the first drops, so Marcovaldo, alone in all the city, sat up in bed and called to his family: "It's raining! It's raining!" and breathed in the smell of moistened dust and fresh mold that came from outside.

At dawn—it was Sunday—with the children and a borrowed basket, he ran immediately to the patch. There were the mushrooms, erect on their stems, their caps high over the still-soaked earth. "Hurrah!"—and they fell to gathering them.

"Papà! Look how many that man over there has found," Michelino said, and his father, raising his eyes, saw Amadigi standing beside them, also with a basket full of mushrooms under his arm.

"Ah, you're gathering them, too?" the street cleaner said. "Then they're edible? I picked a few, but I wasn't sure. . . . Farther down the avenue some others have sprouted, even bigger ones. . . . Well, now that I know, I'll tell my relatives; they're

down there arguing whether it's a good idea to pick them or not. . . ." And he walked off in a hurry.

Marcovaldo was speechless: Even bigger mushrooms, which he hadn't noticed, an unhoped-for harvest, being taken from him like this, before his very eyes. For a moment he was almost frozen with anger, fury, then—as sometimes happens—the collapse of individual passion led to a generous impulse. At that hour, many people were waiting for the tram, umbrellas over their arms, because the weather was still damp and uncertain. "Hey, you! Do you want to eat fried mushrooms tonight?" Marcovaldo shouted to the crowd of people at the stop. "Mushrooms are growing here by the street! Come along! There's plenty for all!" And he walked off after Amadigi, with a string of people behind him.

They all found plenty of mushrooms, and lacking baskets, they used their open umbrellas. Somebody said: "It would be nice to have a big feast, all of us together!" But, instead, each took his own share and went home.

They saw one another again soon, however; that very evening, in fact, in the same ward of the hospital, after the stomach pump had saved them all from poisoning. It was not serious, because the number of mushrooms eaten by each person was quite small.

Marcovaldo and Amadigi had adjacent beds; they glared at each other.

— Italo Calvino,
translated by William Weaver

---

4. **eradicated** (i · rad´ ə · kāt´ ed): torn up by the roots, destroyed.

A Grammar Note

A **clause** is a group of words that contains a **subject** and a **verb** and is used as part of a sentence. A clause that expresses a complete thought and could stand by itself as a sentence is called an **independent clause.** A clause that doesn't express a complete thought is called a **subordinate clause.** (For examples of various sentence structures, see *Grammar, Usage, and Mechanics: A Reference Guide,* page 1011.) Writers

Literature & Language / *cont.*

use subordinate clauses to combine ideas and show relationships among ideas. In this sentence from Calvino's story, the independent clause is in boldface and the subordinate clause is in italics:

He was bent in this position *when he realized there was someone behind him.*

Subordinate clauses function as nouns, adjectives, or adverbs, just as single words do. In the sentence above, the subordinate clause is an **adverb clause** modifying the adjective *bent* in the independent clause. In the following sentence from the story, a **noun clause** acts as the direct object of the verb *tell:*

"Tell us *where they grow*!"

In this sentence from the story, an **adjective clause** modifies the noun *worker:*

Nobody noticed them except Marcovaldo, the worker *who caught his tram just there every morning.*

Here are some rules that will help you write and punctuate subordinate clauses:

1. Use a comma after an adverb clause that comes at the beginning of a sentence. (You usually don't need a comma before an adverb clause at the end of a sentence.)

   When he got home, he told his family.

2. Use a comma before a **nonessential** adjective clause but not before an **essential** one. A clause beginning with *which* is always nonessential; one beginning with *that* is always essential.

   The mushrooms, which were growing wild, made him sick.

   The mushrooms that he ate made him sick.

3. Sometimes you can omit the **relative pronoun** (*who, whom, that,* or *which*) at the beginning of an essential adjective clause or the **conjunction** at the beginning of a noun clause.

   The mushrooms he ate made him sick.

A man [whom] we know ate wild mushrooms.
I can't believe [that] he ate them.

4. In some adverb clauses, called **elliptical clauses,** you can omit certain words:

   Marcovaldo ate more than Amadigi [did].

Examining the Writer's Style

Working with a partner, find as many subordinate clauses as you can in the Calvino story.

1. On a sheet of paper, copy the sentences containing the clauses. Then use three different colored pencils to underline the adjective, adverb, and noun clauses. (Which sentence has all three?)
2. For each clause, explain how it functions in the sentence as an adjective, adverb, or noun. For example, for the adjective clause in the first sentence of the story, you would write, "Modifies the noun *victims*."
3. State which adjective clauses are essential and which are nonessential.
4. Now turn each sentence into two or more sentences made up of only independent clauses. What changes do you notice?

Using Subordinate Clauses in Your Writing

Analyzing Symbolism. Write a brief essay analyzing the symbolism of Calvino's mushrooms. Be sure to take into account their effect on the people who encounter them, as well as the fact that they're poisonous. How are the mushrooms like the city itself?

1. Check your essay to see if you've used subordinate clauses to combine ideas and show the relationship among ideas. Pay careful attention to correct punctuation style.
2. Trade papers with a partner. Underline all the subordinate conjunctions in your classmate's essay. Act as an editor and mark any punctuation errors. If passages seem choppy or confusing, suggest ways to combine sentences and connect ideas by using subordinate clauses. Revise your essay according to your partner's comments.

RECOGNIZING FAULTY REASONING

Writing Assignment

Suppose the following review of Italo Calvino's "Mushrooms in the City" (page 193) appeared in a newspaper. Write a letter to the editor of the newspaper pointing out the faulty reasoning in the review and stating your own evaluation of the story.

Calvino's Rotten "Mushrooms"

"Mushrooms in the City" by Italo Calvino is pointless and boring. A man finds some mushrooms growing in the city. They turn out to be poisonous, and he has to get his stomach pumped. Big deal. He should have suspected they were poisonous to begin with. I can't get too worked up about the problems of some poor Italian factory worker. If he doesn't like the city, why doesn't he just move to the country? And if he's so crazy about mushrooms, why doesn't he just go to the store and buy some? This is the sort of story teachers like because it seems "deep." Normal people will just think it's dull.

Background

When you read critical reviews, you should always evaluate the reviewer's reasoning. (You should do the same, by the way, for your own writing.) Here are some common errors in reasoning:

1. **Hasty Generalizations.** This means that the writer has made a general statement about the story or play or movie without providing sufficient evidence to back it up. ("I've started to read two stories by this writer and couldn't finish either one. He is a boring writer.")

2. **Stereotypes.** This means that the writer has based a judgment on a stereotyped view of a group of people—a blind prejudice. ("No European short-story writer today has a sense of humor.")

3. **Loaded Words and Snide Comments.** This means that the writer uses emotionally charged words to win you over to a certain point of view. ("This movie is the sort of thing that would only appeal to effete, intellectual snobs.")

4. **Circular Reasoning.** This means that the writer keeps restating the main point but never gives specific reasons for it. ("This novel is gripping. I couldn't put it down, and I'll bet no one would stop in the middle without finishing it.")

Writing

1. In your opening paragraph, state the purpose of your letter.
2. Then cite one or more errors in reasoning used by the writer.
3. Quote passages from the review to support or illustrate your point.
4. In your second paragraph, state your own evaluation of the story and provide evidence to support it. (You might agree with the reviewer's main premise, but you have to support it with evidence from the story.)

Checklist for Revision

1. Have you cited the article's title and author?
2. Have you stated the purpose of your letter?
3. Have you cited at least one error in reasoning and quoted from the review to illustrate it?
4. Have you checked the quotation for accuracy and used quotation marks?
5. In your second paragraph, have you clearly stated your own evaluation of the story and given evidence to support it?
6. Have you checked: Spelling? Punctuation? Capitalization? Sentence structure? Paragraph organization?

> *We have art in order not to die of the truth.*
>
> —Friedrich Nietzsche

Irony, in its original Greek sense, means the pretense of ignorance in order to ridicule a person or to expose the truth about a situation. We see this very old kind of irony still at work today when a story or movie shows a shrewd country person pretending to be dumb in order to make fun of a city slicker. But irony has also come to have far broader meanings.

Three Types of Irony

We find three kinds of irony in stories, each of them involving some kind of contrast between expectation and reality. **Verbal irony**—the simplest kind—is when we *say* one thing but *mean* the opposite. We use verbal irony ourselves every day.

> If we say, "You sure can pick 'em" to the man whose team finished last, we are using verbal irony. A parent uses verbal irony when he or she looks up from the string of D's on Willie's report card and says, "It is certainly gratifying to find you are getting so much out of your education."

If the speaker goes on to use words in a particularly harsh and cruel way, we see the use of **sarcasm.** Sarcasm intends to wound, to bite in a hurtful way. The person looking at Willie's report card would be sarcastic if he or she went on to say, "You're so dumb it's a wonder you have the sense to get out of the rain."

Situational irony is much more important to the storyteller: It describes an occurrence that is not just surprising; it is the *opposite* of what we expected. In an ironic situation, what actually happens is so contrary to our expectations that it seems to mock human intentions and the confidence with which we plan our futures. The ironic possibility that this haughty rich man will come begging from us tomorrow or that this girl who is dreading tonight's party will meet her future husband there keeps our lives interesting. Of course, it does the same for our fiction.

> An example of situational irony would be found in a story that told how, after years of searching and after many bloody quarrels over the treasure map, the characters discover the treasure chest and find that it is full of old bottle caps.

> A classic example of situational irony is found in the myth of King Midas. This greedy king wishes for a golden touch, but when his wish is granted, something unexpected happens: Midas can no longer eat because even his food turns to gold when he touches it. The golden touch has brought him not only riches, but misery, even death, as well.

Irony and Satire: The Might of the Word

The Far Side.

Dramatic irony is the kind of irony that occurs when *we* know what is in store for a character, but the character does *not* know. This is called dramatic irony because it's so often used on stage.

> Jean arranges a surprise party for Fred's birthday, and all his friends are hiding behind the curtains waiting for him to arrive home. When Fred, looking haggard, calls into an apparently empty hall, "Hello? Jean? Anybody home? Boy, am I *tired*!" we recognize dramatic irony. Our sense that in a few seconds the exhausted Fred is going to be astonished by a happy-birthday chorus heightens our interest in Fred (we wonder how he will respond).

Dramatic irony adds to our enjoyment of a story because it mimics life, which is forever pulling surprises on us.

Irony of all kinds is somehow enormously satisfying, perhaps because we know instinctively that our carefully laid plans and ambitions and strivings often come to little, while good luck (or bad) often finds unlikely targets.

The Ironic World of Fiction

In its very largest sense, irony describes one of two broad attitudes a writer may take toward the fictional world. As their creator and the master of their destinies, a writer totally controls the characters of a story. Some storytellers arrange the characters' fates to *mock* all their plans. Suppose a storyteller tells of an old prospector who has been searching for a secret lode of gold all his life. But the storyteller decides that when the old man finds the gold and begins chipping away at the rock, he will cause an avalanche that will bury him and the gold under a ton of debris. That author is depicting a very **ironic world,** where humans, however ambitious and fortunate, have no control over an uncaring destiny.

The opposite of this ironic writer is the author who creates a world in which the characters' dreams and quests *do* come true and where they all "live happily ever after." We know then that we are enjoying a **romance,** a fictional world that is far from ironic and one that sometimes is more entertaining than truthful. (Think of the difference between the unlucky prospector described above and the protagonist in "Trap of Gold," page 149.)

One of the very oldest plots is the one that goes this way: Boy meets girl, boy almost loses girl, boy wins girl. (Today the characters' roles are often reversed: Girl meets boy, etc.) A romantic writer would stick to that plot line: The boy (or girl) would get what he is seeking, even though he has had to go through various ordeals testing the strength of his devotion. The story would end with the two young people together at last and the promise of a happy future rather securely planted in the reader's mind.

What would an ironic writer do with this plot? The ending would not necessarily be happy. The boy (or girl) might win his heart's desire, but perhaps there are hints that the girl might not be right for him (as in "The Fatalist," page 24), or that she is only marrying

> "*Irony* of all kinds is somehow enormously satisfying, perhaps because we know instinctively that our carefully laid plans and ambitions and strivings often come to little."

him because she was rejected by her true love. Or perhaps by the time she wants to marry him, it's too late—he wants someone else.

The story of Cinderella meeting her Prince on a crowded dance floor and then being rescued from a life in the ash heap is a romance. To realize how different irony is, think of all the movies today that are based on this old plot, but that give it an ironic twist. In an ironic version of the Cinderella plot, the hero and heroine would not be rewarded at the end with happiness ever after. There would probably be no fairy godmother transforming mice into footmen and pumpkins into golden coaches. The mice would remain mice, and if Cinderella said she saw a fairy god-mother, she'd probably be admitted to the hospital for psychiatric tests. (Another version of a modern, ironic Cinderella plot is on page 344.)

Satire: A Social Purpose

Satire is a close relative of irony and often uses irony to accomplish its purpose. **Satire** is any writing that uses ridicule to bring about social reform: The satirist wants to expose and eliminate human stupidity and wickedness. Greed, injustice, cruelty, and deceit are all targets of the satirist. To make people recognize these human insufficiencies, satirists will often exaggerate their characters' faults—so much so that we have to laugh at them.

Jonathan Swift's novel *Gulliver's Travels* is one of the most famous satires in the English language. The story is merciless (and hilarious) in mocking people in seventeenth-century England who thought their nation was the most civilized on earth. George Orwell's novel *Animal Farm* is another famous satire, one that uses barnyard animals to mock the way people abuse political power.

Comedians on television use satire all the time, often to make fun of themselves. The long-running television show *M*A*S*H* used satire to make us laugh (and cry) at the insanity of war.

Satire and irony are often confused. This is probably because both are often found in the same story. But irony can work without a satiric intent, and a satire can hit its target without using any of the forms of irony.

These two forms of expression—irony and satire—come out of a common inkwell, which holds plenty of acid. Ironic and satiric writing can be humorous: it can lay bare a weakness or a pretense, and it can also invite laughter at someone's expense. Irony and satire may sometimes sting; they may sometimes be cruel in purpose and in effect; but it would be a mistake to reject them.

Whenever I hear the ancient claim that "the pen is mightier than the sword," I think of irony and satire. A pen that uses irony or satire can even become a sword, and it can be taken up in a good cause. Irony and satire can hold up to us the mirror of art and reveal out own faults and foolishnesses. They can make us aware of all the ways in which we humans persuade ourselves that we are righteous and right-minded—when, in fact, we just may be dead wrong.

> " **I**n an ironic version of the Cinderella plot, the hero and heroine would not be rewarded at the end with happiness ever after . . . and if Cinderella said she saw a fairy godmother, she'd probably be admitted to the hospital for psychiatric tests."

Hawkeye (Alan Alda) and Radar (Gary Burghoff) see eye-to-eye. Scene from the television show *M*A*S*H*.

THE GIFT OF THE MAGI

O. Henry

This famous O. Henry tale carries a strong theme. Before you begin reading, see if you understand the allusion found in the title. What do the Magi have to do with gift giving? Why do we give gifts? In what ways can giving gifts be more pleasurable than receiving them?

The story takes place in New York City in the early 1900's. Though prices and salaries are much higher today, the human impulses that give the story its emotional flavor haven't changed at all. As you read the story, think about what your most cherished possession is.

One dollar and eighty-seven cents. That was all. And sixty cents of it was in pennies. Pennies saved one and two at a time by bulldozing the grocer and the vegetable man and the butcher until one's cheeks burned with the silent imputation of parsimony that such close dealing implied. Three times Della counted it. One dollar and eighty-seven cents. And the next day would be Christmas.

There was clearly nothing to do but flop down on the shabby little couch and howl. So Della did it. Which instigates the moral reflection that life is made up of sobs, sniffles, and smiles, with sniffles predominating.

While the mistress of the home is gradually subsiding from the first stage to the second, take a look at the home. A furnished flat[1] at eight dollars per week. It did not exactly beggar description, but it certainly had that word on the lookout for the mendicancy squad.[2]

In the vestibule below was a letter box into which no letter would go and an electric button from which no mortal finger could coax a ring. Also appertaining thereunto was a card bearing the name "Mr. James Dillingham Young."

The "Dillingham" had been flung to the breeze during a former period of prosperity when its possessor was being paid thirty dollars per week. Now, when the income was shrunk to twenty dol-

lars, the letters of "Dillingham" looked blurred, as though they were thinking seriously of contracting to a modest and unassuming D. But whenever Mr. James Dillingham Young came home and reached his flat above, he was called "Jim" and greatly hugged by Mrs. James Dillingham Young, already introduced to you as Della. Which is all very good.

Della finished her cry and attended to her cheeks with the powder rag. She stood by the window and looked out dully at a gray cat walking a gray fence in a gray backyard. Tomorrow would be Christmas Day, and she had only one dollar and eighty-seven cents with which to buy Jim a present. She had been saving every penny she could for months, with this result. Twenty dollars a week doesn't go far. Expenses had been greater than she had calculated. They always are. Only one dollar and eighty-seven cents to buy a present for Jim. Her Jim. Many a happy hour she had spent planning for something nice for him. Something fine and rare and sterling—something just a little bit near to being worthy of the honor of being owned by Jim.

There was a pier glass[3] between the windows of the room. Perhaps you have seen a pier glass in an eight-dollar flat. A very thin and very agile person may, by observing his reflection in a rapid sequence of longitudinal strips, obtain a fairly ac-

---

1. **flat:** an apartment.
2. **mendicancy squad:** police that pick up beggars (mendicants) and tramps.

3. **pier glass:** a tall mirror hung between two windows.

Lady Lilith by Dante Gabriel Rossetti (1867). Watercolor, 20″ × 16⅞″.

curate conception of his looks. Della, being slender, had mastered the art.

Suddenly she whirled from the window and stood before the glass. Her eyes were shining brilliantly, but her face had lost its color within twenty seconds. Rapidly she pulled down her hair and let it fall to its full length.

Now, there were two possessions of the James

Dillingham Youngs in which they both took a mighty pride. One was Jim's gold watch that had been his father's and his grandfather's. The other was Della's hair. Had the Queen of Sheba lived in the flat across the airshaft, Della would have let her hair hang out the window some day to dry just to depreciate Her Majesty's jewels and gifts. Had King Solomon been the janitor, with all his treasures piled up in the basement, Jim would have pulled out his watch every time he passed, just to see him pluck at his beard from envy.

So now Della's beautiful hair fell about her, rippling and shining like a cascade of brown waters. It reached below her knee and made itself almost a garment for her. And then she did it up again nervously and quickly. Once she faltered for a minute and stood still while a tear or two splashed on the worn red carpet.

On went her old brown jacket; on went her old brown hat. With a whirl of skirts and with the brilliant sparkle still in her eyes, she fluttered out the door and down the stairs to the street.

Where she stopped, the sign read: "Mme. Sofronie. Hair Goods of All Kinds." One flight up Della ran, and collected herself, panting. Madame, large, too white, chilly, hardly looked the "Sofronie."

"Will you buy my hair?" asked Della.

"I buy hair," said Madame. "Take yer hat off and let's have a sight at the looks of it."

Down rippled the brown cascade.

"Twenty dollars," said Madame, lifting the mass with a practiced hand.

"Give it to me quick," said Della.

Oh, and the next two hours tripped by on rosy wings. Forget the hashed metaphor. She was ransacking the stores for Jim's present.

She found it at last. It surely had been made for Jim and no one else. There was no other like it in any of the stores, and she had turned all of them inside out. It was a platinum fob chain,[4] simple and chaste in design, properly proclaiming its value by substance alone and not by meretricious[5] ornamentation—as all good things

should do. It was even worthy of The Watch. As soon as she saw it, she knew that it must be Jim's. It was like him. Quietness and value—the description applied to both. Twenty-one dollars they took from her for it, and she hurried home with the eighty-seven cents. With that chain on his watch, Jim might be properly anxious about the time in any company. Grand as the watch was, he sometimes looked at it on the sly on account of the old leather strap that he used in place of a chain.

When Della reached home, her intoxication gave way a little to prudence and reason. She got out her curling irons and lighted the gas and went to work repairing the ravages made by generosity added to love. Which is always a tremendous task, dear friends—a mammoth task.

Within forty minutes her head was covered with tiny, close-lying curls that made her look wonderfully like a truant schoolboy. She looked at her reflection in the mirror long, carefully, and critically.

"If Jim doesn't kill me," she said to herself, "before he takes a second look at me, he'll say I look like a Coney Island chorus girl. But what could I do—oh! what could I do with a dollar and eighty-seven cents?"

At seven o'clock the coffee was made and the frying pan was on the back of the stove, hot and ready to cook the chops.

Jim was never late. Della doubled the fob chain in her hand and sat on the corner of the table near the door that he always entered. Then she heard his step on the stair away down on the first flight, and she turned white for just a moment. She had a habit of saying little silent prayers about the simplest everyday things, and now she whispered: "Please God, make him think I am still pretty."

The door opened and Jim stepped in and closed it. He looked thin and very serious. Poor fellow, he was only twenty-two—and to be burdened with a family! He needed a new overcoat, and he was without gloves.

Jim stepped inside the door, as immovable as a setter at the scent of quail. His eyes were fixed upon Della, and there was an expression in them that she could not read, and it terrified her. It was not anger nor surprise nor disapproval nor horror nor any of the sentiments that she had been pre-

---

4. **fob chain:** a short chain attached to a pocket watch and hanging out of the trouser pocket.
5. **meretricious:** flashy in a cheap way.

pared for. He simply stared at her fixedly with that peculiar expression on his face.

Della wriggled off the table and went for him.

"Jim, darling," she cried, "don't look at me that way. I had my hair cut off and sold it because I couldn't have lived through Christmas without giving you a present. It'll grow out again—you won't mind, will you? I just had to do it. My hair grows awfully fast. Say 'Merry Christmas!' Jim, and let's be happy. You don't know what a nice—what a beautiful, nice gift I've got for you."

"You've cut off your hair?" asked Jim, laboriously, as if he had not arrived at that patent[6] fact yet, even after the hardest mental labor.

"Cut it off and sold it," said Della. "Don't you like me just as well, anyhow? I'm me without my hair, ain't I?"

Jim looked about the room curiously.

"You say your hair is gone?" he said, with an air almost of idiocy.

"You needn't look for it," said Della. "It's sold, I tell you—sold and gone, too. It's Christmas Eve, boy. Be good to me, for it went for you. Maybe the hairs on my head were numbered," she went on with a sudden serious sweetness, "but nobody could ever count my love for you. Shall I put the chops on, Jim?"

Out of his trance Jim seemed quickly to wake. He enfolded his Della. For ten seconds let us regard with discreet scrutiny some inconsequential object in the other direction. Eight dollars a week or a million a year—what is the difference? A mathematician or a wit would give you the wrong answer. The Magi brought valuable gifts, but that was not among them. This dark assertion will be illuminated later on.

Jim drew a package from his overcoat pocket and threw it upon the table.

"Don't make any mistake, Dell," he said, "about me. I don't think there's anything in the way of a haircut or a shave or a shampoo that could make me like my girl any less. But if you'll unwrap that package, you may see why you had me going a while at first."

White fingers and nimble tore at the string and paper. And then an ecstatic scream of joy; and

"Beautiful combs, pure tortoise shell . . ."

then, alas! a quick feminine change to hysterical tears and wails, necessitating the immediate employment of all the comforting powers of the lord of the flat.

For there lay The Combs—the set of combs, side and back, that Della had worshiped for long in a Broadway window. Beautiful combs, pure tortoise shell, with jeweled rims—just the shade to wear in the beautiful vanished hair. They were expensive combs, she knew, and her heart had simply craved and yearned over them without the least hope of possession. And now they were hers, but the tresses that should have adorned the coveted adornments were gone.

But she hugged them to her bosom, and at length she was able to look up with dim eyes and a smile and say: "My hair grows so fast, Jim!"

And then Della leaped up like a little singed cat and cried, "Oh, oh!"

Jim had not yet seen his beautiful present. She held it out to him eagerly upon her open palm. The dull precious metal seemed to flash with a reflection of her bright and ardent spirit.

---

6. **patent:** obvious.

"Isn't it a dandy, Jim? I hunted all over town to find it. You'll have to look at the time a hundred times a day now. Give me your watch. I want to see how it looks on it."

Instead of obeying, Jim tumbled down on the couch and put his hands under the back of his head and smiled.

"Dell," said he, "let's put our Christmas presents away and keep 'em a while. They're too nice to use just at present. I sold the watch to get the money to buy your combs. And now suppose you put the chops on."

The Magi, as you know, were wise men—wonderfully wise men—who brought gifts to the Babe in the manger. They invented the art of giving Christmas presents. Being wise, their gifts were no doubt wise ones, possibly bearing the privilege of exchange in case of duplication. And here I have lamely related to you the uneventful chronicle of two foolish children in a flat who most unwisely sacrificed for each other the greatest treasures of their house. But in a last word to the wise of these days, let it be said that of all who give gifts these two were the wisest. Of all who give and receive gifts, such as they are wisest. Everywhere they are wisest. They are the Magi.

Responding to the Story

Analyzing the Story

Identifying Facts
1. According to the very first paragraph of the story, what is the **conflict** going to be?
2. What action does Della take to resolve the conflict, and what surprising **complication** develops?

Interpreting Meanings
3. An **ironic situation** is one that turns out to be just the opposite of what we—or the characters in the story—expected. Describe the situational irony in this story. Were you as surprised by this twist as Della and Jim were?
4. As O. Henry explains in the final paragraph, the Magi are the Biblical "wise men of the East," who bore the first Christmas presents. In what way are the gifts in this story—Della's to Jim and Jim's to Della—at first foolish and yet finally and ironically the wisest of gifts?
5. What is the real "gift" referred to in the title? (Note that O. Henry uses the word *gift*, not *gifts*.)
6. In light of Della's and Jim's wisdom, how would you state the **theme** of "The Gift of the Magi"? Do you find this theme a true or relevant statement about life as you know it? Explain your response.
7. O. Henry's poverty-stricken young people are so sustained by love for each other that it is hard to imagine a cross word between them. How would you describe the writer's fictional territory? That is, do you think his story is set in the world of **irony** or in the world of **romance**? Explain. Suppose a writer with a different view of the world were to write this same story. How would it have to change?

Writing About the Story

A Creative Response
1. **Updating the Story.** O. Henry sets his story in the early 1900's in New York City. How would you update the details of the plot if the story were set in Dallas or Los Angeles today? How would wages, prices, rents, living quarters, and jobs have to change? Would Della have a job? Open your update of "The Gift of the Magi" with the same famous sentence, but alter the amount of money that Della would have saved but still found insufficient.

A Critical Response
2. **Responding to the Writer's Style.** When O. Henry says in the first paragraph, ". . . one's cheeks burned with the silent imputation of parsimony that such close dealing implied," he is showing off his literary skills in a way that was once considered funny. In plain English, we might say, "It was embarrassing to think that this haggling over prices suggested stinginess." Make a

list of at least five expressions from the story that strike you as pompous or overwritten or just old-fashioned. Then rephrase each expression in your own plain words. When you have finished, write a paragraph telling what you think of O. Henry's style.

Analyzing Language and Vocabulary

Allusions

In his title O. Henry **alludes** to the Biblical Magi; that is, he refers to them but does not explain who they were or what they have to do with this story. He assumes we will know. Similarly, when Della says, "Maybe the hairs on my head are numbered . . ." (page 203), she is alluding to the New Testament (see Matthew 10:30).

Here are some allusions from this story and from other stories in the unit. Two allusions are to the Bible, and two are to Greek mythology.

1. "Had the Queen of Sheba lived in the flat across the airshaft, Della would have let her hair hang out the window some day to dry just to depreciate Her Majesty's jewels and gifts." ("The Gift of the Magi," page 202)

   a. What was the Queen of Sheba famous for?
   b. How does Della surpass her?

2. "Had King Solomon been the janitor, with all his treasures piled up in the basement, Jim would have pulled out his watch every time he passed just to see him pluck at his beard from envy." (Page 202)

   a. Who was King Solomon?
   b. Why would King Solomon envy Jim?

3. ". . . an opportunist seeking transportation to the new colonies where he might find golden fleece for the taking. . . ." ("The Cold Equations," page 7)

   a. Look up the ancient Greek myth of Jason and tell what the golden fleece was.
   b. What does the golden fleece stand for in this sentence?

Reading About the Writer

O. Henry (1862–1910), whose real name was William Sidney Porter, was brought up in Greensboro, North Carolina. At the age of twenty he went to Texas, where he became a rancher, worked as a bank teller, and wrote his first stories. For a short time he also published a weekly newspaper called the *Rolling Stone.*

When he was accused of embezzling a thousand dollars from the First National Bank of Austin, where he had been a teller, Porter unwisely fled to Central America. In Honduras he traveled with the outlawed Jennings brothers and helped them spend the loot of a recent robbery. But news of his wife's illness brought him back to Austin. There he was arrested, tried, and sentenced to five years in jail. (He actually served a little more than three years in the Ohio Federal Penitentiary in Columbus.)

In jail Porter wrote more than a dozen stories and absorbed the underworld lore that he would use in stories such as "A Retrieved Reformation." He also seems to have found his pen name there: One of the prison guards was named Orrin Henry.

Porter left prison in 1901 and went to New York. He loved the city at once, and he wrote about it and its inhabitants for the rest of his life. "There are stories in everything," he once said. "I've got some of my best yarns from park benches, lamp-posts, and newspaper stands."

O. Henry wrote more than six hundred stories during his lifetime—sixty-five stories in 1904 alone. However, he also drank heavily—two quarts of whiskey a day, according to one source—and tuberculosis killed him when he was only forty-seven. His last words were, "Pull up the shades so I can see New York. I don't want to go home in the dark."

THE STORYTELLER

Saki

What do you expect from a children's story? Do you expect a happy ending? Do you expect a strong moral? Do you ever expect violence? Here is a satiric story set in England that might have been written as an antidote to the kinds of stories that were published for children many years ago. You will have to decide if the story's satiric point is still relevant today.

It was a hot afternoon, and the railway carriage was correspondingly sultry, and the next stop was at Templecombe, nearly an hour ahead. The occupants of the carriage were a small girl and a smaller girl and a small boy. An aunt belonging to the children occupied one corner seat, and the further corner seat on the opposite side was occupied by a bachelor who was a stranger to their party, but the small girls and the small boy emphatically occupied the compartment. Both the aunt and the children were conversational in a limited, persistent way, reminding one of the attentions of a housefly that refused to be discouraged. Most of the aunt's remarks seemed to begin with "Don't," and nearly all of the children's remarks began with "Why?" The bachelor said nothing out loud.

"Don't, Cyril, don't," exclaimed the aunt, as the small boy began smacking the cushions of the seat, producing a cloud of dust at each blow.

"Come and look out of the window," she added.

The child moved reluctantly to the window. "Why are those sheep being driven out of that field?" he asked.

"I expect they are being driven to another field where there is more grass," said the aunt weakly.

"But there is lots of grass in that field," protested the boy; "there's nothing else but grass there. Aunt, there's lots of grass in that field."

"Perhaps the grass in the other field is better," suggested the aunt fatuously.

"Why is it better?" came the swift, inevitable question.

"Oh, look at those cows!" exclaimed the aunt. Nearly every field along the line had contained cows or bullocks, but she spoke as though she were drawing attention to a rarity.

"Why is the grass in the other field better?" persisted Cyril.

The frown on the bachelor's face was deepening to a scowl. He was a hard, unsympathetic man, the aunt decided in her mind. She was utterly unable to come to any satisfactory decision about the grass in the other field.

The smaller girl created a diversion by beginning to recite "On the Road to Mandalay."[1] She only knew the first line, but she put her limited knowledge to the fullest possible use. She repeated the line over and over again in a dreamy but resolute and very audible voice; it seemed to the bachelor as though someone had had a bet with her that she could not repeat the line aloud two thousand times without stopping. Whoever it was who had made the wager was likely to lose his bet.

"Come over here and listen to a story," said the aunt, when the bachelor had looked twice at her and once at the communication cord.

The children moved listlessly towards the aunt's end of the carriage. Evidently her reputa-

---

1. **"On the Road to Mandalay"**: a long, energetic poem by Rudyard Kipling, in dialect. The first line is: "By the old Moulmein Pagoda, lookin' eastward to the sea."

tion as a storyteller did not rank high in their estimation.

In a low, confidential voice, interrupted at frequent intervals by loud, petulant questions from her listeners, she began an unenterprising and deplorably uninteresting story about a little girl who was good, and made friends with every one on account of her goodness, and was finally saved from a mad bull by a number of rescuers who admired her moral character.

"Wouldn't they have saved her if she hadn't been good?" demanded the bigger of the small girls. It was exactly the question that the bachelor had wanted to ask.

"Well, yes," admitted the aunt lamely, "but I don't think they would have run quite so fast to her help if they had not liked her so much."

"It's the stupidest story I've every heard," said the bigger of the small girls, with immense conviction.

"I didn't listen after the first bit, it was so stupid," said Cyril.

The smaller girl made no actual comment on the story, but she had long ago recommenced a murmured repetition of her favorite line.

"You don't seem to be a success as a storyteller," said the bachelor suddenly from his corner.

The aunt bristled in instant defense at this unexpected attack.

"It's a very difficult thing to tell stories that children can both understand and appreciate," she said stiffly.

"I don't agree with you," said the bachelor.

"Perhaps *you* would like to tell them a story," was the aunt's retort.

"Tell us a story," demanded the bigger of the small girls.

"Once upon a time," began the bachelor, "there was a little girl called Bertha, who was extraordinarily good."

The children's momentarily aroused interest began at once to flicker; all stories seemed dreadfully alike, no matter who told them.

"She did all that she was told, she was always truthful, she kept her clothes clean, ate milk puddings as though they were jam tarts, learned her lessons perfectly, and was polite in her manners."

"Was she pretty?" asked the bigger of the small girls.

"Not as pretty as any of you," said the bachelor, "but she was horribly good."

There was a wave of reaction in favor of the story; the word horrible in connection with goodness was a novelty that commended itself. It seemed to introduce a ring of truth that was absent from the aunt's tales of infant life.

"She was so good," continued the bachelor, "that she won several medals for goodness, which she always wore, pinned on to her dress. There was a medal for obedience, another medal for punctuality, and a third for good behavior. They were large metal medals, and they clicked against one another as she walked. No other child in the town where she lived had as many as three medals, so everybody knew that she must be an extra good child."

"Horribly good," quoted Cyril.

"Everybody talked about her goodness, and the Prince of the country got to hear about it, and he said that as she was so very good, she might be allowed once a week to walk in his park, which was just outside the town. It was a beautiful park, and no children were ever allowed in it, so it was a great honor for Bertha to be allowed to go there."

"Were there any sheep in the park?" demanded Cyril.

"No," said the bachelor, "there were no sheep."

"Why weren't there any sheep?" came the inevitable question arising out of that answer.

The aunt permitted herself a smile, which might almost have been described as a grin.

"There were no sheep in the park," said the bachelor, "because the Prince's mother had once had a dream that her son would either be killed by a sheep or else by a clock falling on him. For that reason the Prince never kept a sheep in his park or a clock in his palace."

The aunt suppressed a gasp of admiration.

"Was the Prince killed by a sheep or by a clock?" asked Cyril.

"He is still alive, so we can't tell whether the dream will come true," said the bachelor uncon-

Bermuda Settlers by Winslow Homer (1901). Watercolor over graphite on cream wove paper.

Worcester Art Museum, Worcester, Massachusetts.
(1911.12; Museum purchase.)

cernedly; "anyway, there were no sheep in the park, but there were lots of little pigs running all over the place."

"What color were they?"

"Black with white faces, white with black spots, black all over, gray with white patches, and some were white all over."

The storyteller paused to let a full idea of the park's treasures sink into the children's imaginations; then he resumed:

"Bertha was rather sorry to find that there were no flowers in the park. She had promised her aunts, with tears in her eyes, that she would not pick any of the kind Prince's flowers, and she had meant to keep her promise, so of course it made her feel silly to find that there were no flowers to pick."

"Why weren't there any flowers?"

"Because the pigs had eaten them all," said the bachelor promptly. "The gardeners had told the Prince that you couldn't have pigs and flowers, so he decided to have pigs and no flowers."

There was a murmur of approval at the excellence of the Prince's decision; so many people would have decided the other way.

"There were lots of other delightful things in the park. There were ponds with gold and blue and green fish in them, and trees with beautiful parrots that said clever things at a moment's notice, and humming birds that hummed all the popular tunes of the day. Bertha walked up and down and enjoyed herself immensely, and thought to herself: 'If I were not so extraordinarily good, I should not have been allowed to come into this beautiful park and enjoy all that there is to be seen in it,' and her three medals clinked against one another as she walked and helped to remind her how very good she really was. Just then an enormous wolf came prowling into the park to see if it could catch a fat little pig for its supper."

"What color was it?" asked the children, amid an immediate quickening of interest.

"Mud color all over, with a black tongue and pale grey eyes that gleamed with unspeakable ferocity. The first thing that it saw in the park was Bertha; her pinafore was so spotlessly white and clean that it could be seen from a great distance. Bertha saw the wolf and saw that it was stealing towards her, and she began to wish that she had never been allowed to come into the park. She ran as hard as she could, and the wolf came after her with huge leaps and bounds. She managed to reach a shrubbery of myrtle bushes and she hid herself in one of the thickest of the bushes. The wolf came sniffing among the branches, its black tongue lolling out of its mouth and its pale gray eyes glaring with rage. Bertha was terribly frightened and thought to herself: 'If I had not been so extraordinarily good, I should have been safe in the town at this moment.' However, the scent of the myrtle was so strong that the wolf could not sniff out where Bertha was hiding, and the bushes were so thick that he might have hunted about in them for a long time without catching sight of her, so he thought he might as well go off and catch a little pig instead. Bertha was trembling very much at having the wolf prowling and sniffing so near her, and as she trembled the medal for obedience clinked against the medals for good conduct and punctuality. The wolf was just moving away when he heard the sound of the medals clinking and stopped to listen; they clinked again in a bush quite near him. He dashed into the bush, his pale gray eyes gleaming with ferocity and triumph, and dragged Bertha out and devoured her to the last morsel. All that was left of her were her shoes, bits of clothing, and the three medals for goodness."

"Were any of the little pigs killed?"

"No, they all escaped."

"The story began badly," said the smaller of the small girls, "but it had a beautiful ending."

"It is the most beautiful story that I ever heard," said the bigger of the small girls, with immense decision.

"It is the *only* beautiful story I have ever heard," said Cyril.

A dissentient[2] opinion came from the aunt.

"A most improper story to tell to young children! You have undermined the effect of years of careful teaching."

"At any rate," said the bachelor, collecting his belongings preparatory to leaving the carriage, "I kept them quiet for ten minutes, which was more than you were able to do."

"Unhappy woman!" he observed to himself as he walked down the platform of Templecombe station; "for the next six months or so those children will assail her in public with demands for an improper story!"

---

2. **dissentient:** dissenting, disagreeing.

Responding to the Story

Analyzing the Story

Identifying Facts

1. A **frame story** is a narrative that contains another story or stories. What **basic situation** on the train provides the frame for the storytellers' two very different stories?
2. In the instructive story about infant life that the aunt tells the children, why is the little girl saved? Why do the children object to her story?

3. What is the first "ring of truth" that the children notice in the bachelor's story?

Interpreting Meanings

4. What a vastly superior storyteller the bachelor is! He understands that he must supply both logic and information as he builds his extraordinary setting for Bertha's downfall. What surprises does he fill the park with? How do they conform to peculiar but explainable laws?

5. What is comically **ironic** about Bertha's fate in the bachelor's story? What would you say is the **theme** of the bachelor's story? How about the aunt's?

6. Cyril's verdict is that the bachelor is a better storyteller than the aunt. What does the bachelor's story reveal about him as a person? Is he **romantic,** or does he have an **ironic** attitude toward life? What does the aunt's story and her theory about children reveal about her?

7. In this story, the irony is used for the purpose of **satire.** What is Saki mocking?

8. Why do you suppose Saki, a bachelor himself, made his victorious storyteller a bachelor?

9. What does the children's preference for the bachelor's story reveal about children in general? Does this point about children and their literary preferences seem true to you? Why or why not?

Writing About the Story

A Creative Response

1. **Describing an Imaginary Place.** Suppose you were telling a story about a prince, such as the one in the bachelor's story, who could equip a park with unexpected attractions. What would you put in the park? Write a paragraph describing an imaginary park setting that doesn't make much logical sense—one that is very different from the parks that we are used to.

2. **Imitating the Writer's Technique.** Take a familiar story pattern—a fairy tale, a Western, a detective story, or a romance—and make it a **parody** by giving it an **ironic** twist. Before you write, list the traditional elements of the type of story you have chosen. Think of the **plot** and how it usually ends, the **characterization,** and the "moral" of the tale. Use the bachelor's story as your model.

A Critical Response

3. **Responding to a Story.** For an exercise in responding to "The Storyteller," see page 222.

Analyzing Language and Vocabulary

Implied Meanings

Satirists often use language in subtle ways, challenging us by leaving their most important ideas unsaid. They **imply** ideas by leaving a trail of clues, and they allow us the pleasure of **inferring** their meanings by making intelligent guesses. Saki, for example, says in the first paragraph that the children "emphatically" occupied the train compartment. The word *emphatic* means "expressive, forceful, insistent." The word usually refers to a way of talking or writing: His rejection letter was emphatic.

In Saki's story, the word is used in an unusual way. By using our imaginations and by making inferences, we can guess that the children were probably jumping all over the place and talking. Their presence was clear: It was definitely something that could not be overlooked. It was "emphatic."

Saki expects us to catch his implied meanings in these passages:

1. "Both the aunt and the children were conversational in a limited, persistent way, reminding one of the attentions of a housefly that refused to be discouraged."

   a. What do a housefly's "attentions" consist of? Are they pleasant or unpleasant?

   b. Whose behavior is like that of a housefly? In what exact way?

2. "Most of the aunt's remarks seemed to begin with 'Don't,' and nearly all of the children's remarks began with 'Why?' The bachelor said nothing out loud."

   a. What can we infer about the content of the aunt's remarks? About the children's?

   b. What is implied by the fact that the bachelor said nothing out loud?

   c. What do you think he said to himself?

3. " 'Perhaps the grass in the other field is better,' suggested the aunt fatuously."

   a. What does the word *fatuously* suggest about the accuracy of the aunt's reply?

   b. What can we infer about the aunt's **tone** of voice?

   c. What does the word imply about Saki's attitude toward the aunt?

4. " 'Come over here and listen to a story,' said the aunt, when the bachelor had looked twice at her and once at the communication cord."

   a. What is a communication cord?

   b. What is implied by the fact that the bachelor was looking at it?

   c. What can we infer about the aunt's reason for telling her story?

5. " . . . the word horrible in connection with goodness was a novelty that commended itself."

   a. What might the children think is implied by "horrible goodness"?

   b. Why are the children pleased by the connection of these two qualities?

6. "There was a murmur of approval at the excellence of the Prince's decision [to have pigs and no flowers in his park]; so many people would have decided the other way."

   a. Why do you think the children prefer pigs over flowers?

   b. Why is this preference **ironic**?

   c. Is it believable? Why or why not?

Reading About the Writer

Saki is the pen name of Hector Hugh Munro (1870–1916), a Scot who was born in Burma, the son of a military officer. When their mother died before Munro was two, he and his brother and sister were sent back to England, where they were reared by their grandmother and two strict, puritanical aunts, whose mark may be seen in several stories, including "The Storyteller." (In another story, Munro has an aunt eaten by a polecat.) Hector was a sickly child, and he had little formal schooling until he was sent to boarding school at fourteen.

At twenty-three Munro returned to Burma to join his father and older brother. He took a police job arranged by his father, but he fell ill almost at once and returned to England a little more than a year later. There he began his writing career. He eventually found a wide audience for his stories, which are usually satiric and often cynical, but always tempered by a sense of humor. Some of Saki's most widely anthologized stories are "The Open Window," "The Interlopers," "Tobermory," and "Sredni Vashtar."

The now-famous pen name *Saki* comes from the Persian poem *The Rubáiyát of Omar Khayyam,* which was popular in England in Munro's day. The poem praises the pleasures of life, especially the pleasures of love and wine; Saki was the person who passed the wine cup around.

Though Munro was forty-three when World War I began, he enlisted in the British army and was killed by a German sniper in France.

Focusing on Background
A Sister's View of Saki

Here is an excerpt from a biography of Saki written by his sister, Ethel M. Munro:

"Fortunately, there were the three of us, and we lived a life of our own, in which the grown-ups had no part. . . . Our pleasures were of the very simplest—other children hardly came into our lives—once a year, at Christmas, we went to a children's party, where we were not allowed to eat any attractive, exciting-looking food, 'for fear of the consequences,' and in *case* the party might have done us harm, Granny gave us hot brandy and water on our return.

"Also, once a year, in the summer, the child of some friend visiting the neighborhood would come to play with us. 'So good a boy,' we would be told. 'He always does what he is bid.'

"From that moment a look of deep purpose settled on Hector's face, and on the day when the good Claud arrived, an entirely busy and happy time for Hector was the result.

"He saw to it that Claud did all the things we must never do, the easier to accomplish since his mother would be indoors tongue-wagging with Granny and the aunts. Poor Claud really was a good child, with no inclination to be anything else, but under Hector's ruthless tuition, . . . he put in a breathless day of bad deeds.

"And when Aunt Tom (Charlotte she was never called), after the visitors' departure, remarked, 'Claud is not the good child I imagined him to be,' Hector felt it was the end of a perfect day."

—Ethel M. Munro

WHERE HAVE YOU GONE, CHARMING BILLY?

Tim O'Brien

The platoon of twenty-six soldiers moved slowly in the dark, single file, not talking. One by one, like sheep in a dream, they passed through the hedgerow, crossed quietly over a meadow, and came down to the rice paddy. There they stopped. Their leader knelt down, motioning with his hand, and one by one the other soldiers squatted in the shadows, vanishing in the primitive stealth of warfare. For a long time they did not move. Except for the sounds of their breathing, the twenty-six men were very quiet: some of them excited by the adventure, some of them afraid, some of them exhausted from the long night march, some of them looking forward to reaching the sea, where they would be safe. At the rear of the column, Private First Class Paul Berlin lay quietly with his forehead resting on the black plastic stock of his rifle, his eyes closed. He was pretending he was not in the war, pretending he had not watched Billy Boy Watkins die of a heart attack that afternoon. He was pretending he was a boy again, camping with his father in the midnight summer along the Des Moines River. In the dark, with his eyes pinched shut, he pretended. He pretended that when he opened his eyes, his father would be there by the campfire and they would talk softly about whatever came to mind and then roll into their sleeping bags, and that later they'd wake up and it would be morning and there would not be a war, and that Billy Boy Watkins had not died of a heart attack that afternoon. He pretended he was not a soldier.

In the morning, when they reached the sea, it would be better. The hot afternoon would be over, he would bathe in the sea, and he would forget how frightened he had been on his first day at the war. The second day would not be so bad. He would learn.

There was a sound beside him, a movement, and then a breathed: "Hey!"

He opened his eyes, shivering as if emerging from a deep nightmare.

"Hey!" a shadow whispered. "We're *moving*. Get up."

"Okay."

"You sleepin', or something?"

"No." He could not make out the soldier's face. With clumsy, concrete hands he clawed for his rifle, found it, found his helmet.

The soldier shadow grunted. "You got a lot to learn, buddy. I'd shoot you if I thought you was sleepin'. Let's go."

Private First Class Paul Berlin blinked.

Ahead of him, silhouetted against the sky, he saw the string of soldiers wading into the flat paddy, the black outline of their shoulders and packs and weapons. He was comfortable. He did not want to move. But he was afraid, for it was his first night at the war, so he hurried to catch up, stumbling once, scraping his knee, groping as though blind; his boots sank into the thick paddy water, and he smelled it all around him. He would tell his mother how it smelled: mud and algae and cattle manure and chlorophyll; decay, breeding mosquitoes and leeches as big as mice; the fecund warmth of the paddy waters rising up to his cut knee. But he would not tell how frightened he had been.

Once they reached the sea, things would be better. They would have their rear guarded by three thousand miles of ocean, and they would swim and dive into the breakers and hunt crayfish and smell the salt, and they would be safe.

He followed the shadow of the man in front of him. It was a clear night. Already the Southern Cross was out. And other stars he could not yet name—soon, he thought, he would learn their names. And puffy night clouds. There was not yet a moon. Wading through the paddy, his boots made sleepy, sloshing sounds, like a lullaby, and he tried not to think. Though he was afraid, he now knew that fear came in many degrees and types and peculiar categories, and he knew that his fear now was not so bad as it had been in the hot afternoon, when poor Billy Boy Watkins got killed by a heart attack. His fear now was diffuse and unformed: ghosts in the tree line, nighttime fears of a child, a boogieman in the closet that his father would open to show empty, saying "See? Nothing there, champ. Now you can sleep." In the afternoon it had been worse, the fear had been bundled and tight and he'd been on his hands and knees, crawling like an insect, an ant escaping a giant's footsteps and thinking nothing, brain flopping like wet cement in a mixer, not thinking at all, watching while Billy Boy Watkins died.

Now as he stepped out of the paddy onto a narrow dirt path, now the fear was mostly the fear of being so terribly afraid again.

He tried not to think.

There were tricks he'd learned to keep from thinking. Counting: He counted his steps, concentrating on the numbers, pretending that the steps were dollar bills and that each step through the night made him richer and richer, so that soon he would become a wealthy man, and he kept counting and considered the ways he might spend the money after the war and what he would do. He would look his father in the eye and shrug and say, "It was pretty bad at first, but I learned a lot and I got used to it." Then he would tell his father the story of Billy Boy Watkins. But he would never let on how frightened he had been. "Not so bad," he would say instead, making his father feel proud.

Songs, another trick to stop from thinking: *Where have you gone, Billy Boy, Billy Boy, oh, where have you gone, charming Billy? I have gone to seek a wife, she's the joy of my life, but she's a young thing and cannot leave her mother,* and other songs that he sang in his thoughts as he walked toward the sea. And when he reached the sea, he would dig a deep hole in the sand and he would sleep like the high clouds and he would not be afraid anymore.

The moon came out. Pale and shrunken to the size of a dime.

The helmet was heavy on his head. In the morning he would adjust the leather binding. He would clean his rifle, too. Even though he had been frightened to shoot it during the hot afternoon, he would carefully clean the breech and the muzzle and the ammunition so that next time he would be ready and not so afraid. In the morning, when they reached the sea, he would begin to make friends with some of the other soldiers. He would learn their names and laugh at their jokes. Then when the war was over, he would have war buddies, and he would write to them once in a while and exchange memories.

Walking, sleeping in his walking, he felt better. He watched the moon come higher.

Once they skirted a sleeping village. The smells again—straw, cattle, mildew. The men were quiet. On the far side of the village, buried in the dark smells, a dog barked. The column stopped until the barking died away; then they marched fast away from the village, through a graveyard filled with conical-shaped burial mounds and tiny altars made of clay and stone. The graveyard had a perfumy smell. A nice place to spend the night, he thought. The mounds would make fine battlements, and the smell was nice and the place was quiet. But they went on, passing through a hedgerow and across another paddy and east toward the sea.

He walked carefully. He remembered what he'd been taught: Stay off the center of the path, for that was where the land mines and booby traps were planted, where stupid and lazy soldiers like to walk. Stay alert, he'd been taught. Better alert than inert. Ag-ile, mo-bile, hos-tile. He wished he'd paid better attention to the training. He could not remember what they'd said about how to stop being afraid; they hadn't given any lessons in courage—not that he could remember—and they hadn't mentioned how Billy Boy Watkins would die of a heart attack, his face turning pale and the veins popping out.

Private First Class Paul Berlin walked carefully.

Stretching ahead of him like dark beads on an invisible chain, the string of shadow soldiers whose names he did not yet know moved with the silence and slow grace of smoke. Now and again moonlight was reflected off a machine gun or a wristwatch. But mostly the soldiers were quiet and hidden and faraway-seeming in a peaceful night, strangers on a long street, and he felt quite separate from them, as if trailing behind like the caboose on a night train, pulled along by inertia, sleepwalking, an afterthought to the war.

So he walked carefully, counting his steps. When he had counted to 3,485, the column stopped.

One by one the soldiers knelt or squatted down.

The grass along the path was wet. Private First Class Paul Berlin lay back and turned his head so that he could lick at the dew with his eyes closed, another trick to forget the war. He might have slept. "I *wasn't* afraid," he was screaming or dreaming, facing his father's stern eyes. "I wasn't afraid," he was saying. When he opened his eyes, a soldier was sitting beside him, quietly chewing a stick of Doublemint gum.

"You sleepin' again?" the soldier whispered.

"No," said Private First Class Paul Berlin. "Hell, no."

The soldier grunted, chewing his gum. Then he twisted the cap off his canteen, took a swallow, and handed it through the dark.

"Take some," he whispered.

"Thanks."

"You're the new guy?"

"Yes." He did not want to admit it, being new to the war.

The soldier grunted and handed him a stick of gum. "Chew it quiet—okay? Don't blow no bubbles or nothing."

"Thanks. I won't." He could not make out the man's face in the shadows.

They sat still and Private First Class Paul Berlin chewed the gum until all the sugars were gone; then the soldier said, "Bad day today, buddy."

Private First Class Paul Berlin nodded wisely, but he did not speak.

"Don't think it's always so bad," the soldier whispered. "I don't wanna scare you. You'll get used to it soon enough. . . . They been fighting wars a long time, and you get used to it."

"Yeah."

"You will."

They were quiet awhile. And the night was quiet, no crickets or birds, and it was hard to imagine it was truly a war. He searched for the soldier's face, but could not find it. It did not matter much. Even if he saw the fellow's face, he would not know the name; and even if he knew the name, it would not matter much.

"Haven't got the time?" the soldier whispered.

"No."

"Rats. . . . Don't matter, really. Goes faster if you don't know the time, anyhow."

"Sure."

"What's your name, buddy?"

"Paul."

"Nice to meet ya," he said, and in the dark beside the path, they shook hands. "Mine's Toby. Everybody calls me Buffalo, though." The soldier's hand was strangely warm and soft. But it was a very big hand. "Sometimes they just call me Buff," he said.

And again they were quiet. They lay in the grass and waited. The moon was very high now and very bright, and they were waiting for cloud cover. The soldier suddenly snorted.

"What is it?"

"Nothin'," he said, but then he snorted again. "A bloody *heart attack!*" the soldier said. "Can't get over it—old Billy Boy croaking from a lousy heart attack. . . . A heart attack—can you believe it?"

The idea of it made Private First Class Paul Berlin smile. He couldn't help it.

"Ever hear of such a thing?"

"Not till now," said Private First Class Paul Berlin, still smiling.

"Me neither," said the soldier in the dark. "Gawd, dying of a heart attack. Didn't know him, did you."

"No."

"Tough as nails."

"Yeah."

"And what happens? A heart attack. Can you imagine it?"

"Yes," said Private First Class Paul Berlin. He wanted to laugh. "I can imagine it." And he imagined it clearly. He giggled—he couldn't help it. He imagined Billy's father opening the telegram: SORRY TO INFORM YOU THAT YOUR SON BILLY BOY WAS YESTERDAY SCARED TO DEATH IN ACTION IN THE REPUBLIC OF VIETNAM, VALIANTLY SUCCUMBING TO A HEART ATTACK SUFFERED WHILE UNDER ENORMOUS STRESS, AND IT IS WITH GREATEST SYMPATHY THAT . . . He giggled again.

He rolled onto his belly and pressed his face into his arms. His body was shaking with giggles.

The big soldier hissed at him to shut up, but he could not stop giggling and remembering the hot afternoon, and poor Billy Boy, and how they'd been drinking Coca-Cola from bright-red aluminum cans, and how they'd started on the day's march, and how a little while later poor Billy Boy stepped on the mine, and how it made a tiny little sound—*poof*—and how Billy Boy stood there with his mouth wide open, looking down at where his foot had been blown off, and how finally Billy Boy sat down very casually, not saying a word, with his foot lying behind him, most of it still in the boot.

He giggled louder—he could not stop. He bit his arm, trying to stifle it, but remembering: "War's over, Billy," the men had said in consolation, but Billy Boy got scared and started crying and said he was about to die. "Nonsense," the medic said, Doc Peret, but Billy Boy kept bawling, tightening up, his face going pale and transparent and his veins popping out. Scared stiff. Even when Doc Peret stuck him with morphine, Billy Boy kept crying.

"Shut up!" the big soldier hissed, but Private First Class Paul Berlin could not stop. Giggling and remembering, he covered his mouth. His eyes stung, remembering how it was when Billy Boy died of fright.

"Shut up!"

But he could not stop giggling, the same way Billy Boy could not stop bawling that afternoon.

Afterward Doc Peret had explained: "You see, Billy Boy really died of a heart attack. He was scared he was gonna die—so scared he had himself a heart attack—and that's what really killed him. I seen it before."

So they wrapped Billy in a plastic poncho, his eyes still wide open and scared stiff, and they carried him over the meadow to a rice paddy, and then when the Medevac helicopter arrived, they carried him through the paddy and put him aboard, and the mortar rounds were falling everywhere, and the helicopter pulled up, and Billy Boy came tumbling out, falling slowly and then faster, and the paddy water sprayed up as if Billy Boy had just executed a long and dangerous dive, as if trying to escape Graves Registration, where he would be tagged and sent home under a flag, dead of a heart attack.

"Shut up!" the soldier hissed, but Paul Berlin could not stop giggling, remembering: scared to death.

Later they waded in after him, probing for Billy Boy with their rifle butts, elegantly and delicately probing for Billy Boy in the stinking paddy, singing—some of them—*Where have you gone, Billy Boy, Billy Boy, Oh, where have you gone, charming Billy?* Then they found him. Green and covered with algae, his eyes still wide open and scared stiff, dead of a heart attack suffered while——

"Shut up!" the soldier said loudly, shaking him.

But Private First Class Paul Berlin could not stop. The giggles were caught in his throat, drowning him in his own laughter: scared to death like Billy Boy.

Giggling, lying on his back, he saw the moon move, or the clouds moving across the moon. Wounded in action, dead of fright. A fine war story. He would tell it to his father, how Billy Boy had been scared to death, never letting on . . . He could not stop.

The soldier smothered him. He tried to fight back, but he was weak from the giggles.

The moon was under the clouds and the column was moving. The soldier helped him up. "You okay now, buddy?"

"Sure."

"What was so bloody funny?"

"Nothing."

"You can get killed, laughing that way."

"I know. I know that."

"You got to stay calm, buddy." The soldier handed him his rifle. "Half the battle, just staying calm. You'll get better at it," he said. "Come on, now."

He turned away and Private First Class Paul Berlin hurried after him. He was still shivering.

He would do better once he reached the sea, he thought, still smiling a little. A funny war story that he would tell to his father, how Billy Boy Watkins was scared to death. A good joke. But even when he smelled salt and heard the sea, he could not stop being afraid.

Responding to the Story

Analyzing the Story

Identifying Facts

1. Where in the first two paragraphs is Paul Berlin's **conflict,** or problem, made clear to us?
2. As Paul marches, we overhear his thoughts, and the name "Billy Boy" keeps coming up. What questions about Billy Boy does the writer plant in your mind? Trace how the writer gradually "pays out" information about what happened to Billy Boy.
3. What is the incident that gives the story its title? What details make this incident both absurd and terrible?

Interpreting Meanings

4. On page 214 the author quotes a bit of the song that gives the story its title. (If you do not know the rest of the words to this song, find a copy.) What is **ironic** about the author's use of this particular song in a war story?
5. There is a central **irony** in most stories about modern warfare, which has to do with the fact that soldiers use explosives to kill people they do not even know. What is ironic about the way that Billy Boy dies? About the way that his body is removed?
6. What is **ironic,** or unexpected and inappropriate, about Paul's reaction to Billy Boy's death when he begins talking to the other soldier? Does his reaction strike you as believable? Tell why or why not.
7. What **theme,** or central idea, about war would you say is revealed by Paul's reactions to his first day of battle?
8. In a sense, this is a story about a hero's journey, which often takes the form of a **quest**—a search for something of great value. What is it that Paul expects to find at the sea, the endpoint of his journey? Considering what he does find, would you describe this writer's view of the world as **ironic** or **romantic**? Why?
9. Do you think this story is about an important topic, or is it trivial? What do you think of the writer's treatment of the subject? How does it compare to other war stories you have read (or war movies you have seen)?

Writing About the Story

A Creative Response

1. **Imitating the Writer's Technique.** To comfort himself in the face of death and terror, Paul summons up memories of the "safe world" of home and of camping with his father (page 213). If you were in such a situation, what ideal world would you think about? Describe a place and time and experience that would give you comfort. Use sensory details to describe sights, sounds, smells, textures, and tastes.

A Critical Response

2. **Responding to the Story's Subject.** War is a recurring subject in fiction. In the light of this story (and other stories and movies you know of that deal with war), consider why writers so often use war as a subject. In a brief essay of one or two paragraphs, explain why you think people *write* about war and why others *read* about it. Explain in your final sentence how war stories like this one affect you.

Analyzing Language and Vocabulary

Imagery

Image comes from the Latin word *imago,* which means "copy." In a sense, an **image** is a copy of a sensory experience—a sight, a sound, a smell, a taste, or a touch. Most images are visual, but many also evoke sensations of smell, taste, or touch. For example, we read that Paul pretends "that when he opened his eyes, his father would be there by the campfire and they would talk softly about whatever came to mind and then roll into their sleeping bags." We can share Paul's remembered experience here because the writer gives us images of sight (a campfire in the darkness), of sound (talking softly), and of touch (rolling into the softness of a sleeping bag on the hard ground).

Look back through the story, and write down at least five passages that use images to make vivid the sights, smells, and sounds of Paul's journey through an alien land. Identify the senses that each image appeals to.

Reading About the Writer

Tim O' Brien (1946–   ) is a novelist and journalist who has been national affairs reporter for the *Washington Post.* During the Vietnam War O'Brien was a foot soldier and was later promoted to the rank of sergeant. When he returned from Vietnam, O'Brien began writing about his experiences. Many of his stories were told from the point of view of a young soldier named Paul Berlin. These stories eventually grew into a novel called *Going After Cacciato,* which won the National Book Award in 1978. Cacciato, the novel's roguish hero, simply walks away from the war one day and heads in the direction of Paris. "Where Have You Gone, Charming Billy?" was used, with some slight changes, as Chapter 31 of the novel. One critic has called the Cacciato novel "one of the finest books to emerge from the Vietnam War." O'Brien's most recent book is *The Things They Carried.*

Focusing on Background
An Episode from Real Life

The following account is from a collection of Tim O'Brien's reports on his actual experiences as a foot soldier in Vietnam. Mad Mark was the platoon leader.

"One of the most persistent and appalling thoughts which lumbers through your mind as you walk through Vietnam at night is the fear of getting lost, of becoming detached from the others, of spending the night alone in that frightening and haunted countryside. It was dark. We walked in a single file, perhaps three yards apart. Mad Mark took us along a crazy, wavering course. We veered off the road, through clumps of trees, through tangles of bamboo and grass, zigzagging through graveyards of dead Vietnamese who lay there under conical mounds of dirt and clay. The man to the front and the man to the rear were the only holds on security and sanity. We followed the man in front like a blind man after his dog, like Dante following Virgil through the Inferno, and we prayed that the man had not lost his way, that he hadn't lost contact with the man to his front. We tensed the muscles around our eyeballs and peered straight ahead. We hurt ourselves staring at the man's back. We strained. We dared not look away for fear the man might fade and dissipate and turn into absent shadow. Sometimes, when the jungle closed in, we reached out to him, touched his shirt.

"The man to the front is civilization. He is the United States of America and every friend you have

ever known; he is Erik and blond girls and a mother and a father. He is your life, and he is your altar and God combined. And, for the man stumbling along behind you, you alone are his torch."

—from *If I Die in a Combat Zone, Box Me Up and Ship Me Home,* Tim O'Brien

Punctuating Dialogue

Literary Models

Ever since ancient times, people have written fables to **satirize** human behavior. Fable writers make our weaknesses seem especially foolish because they use animals to stand for certain human "types." (It is devastating to see ourselves cast as common barnyard animals.) Here's a fable by a twentieth-century American satirist:

© 1956 James Thurber. © 1984 Helen Thurber.
From *Further Fables for Our Time*,
published by Simon & Schuster.

What Happened to Charles

A farm horse named Charles was led to town one day by his owner, to be shod. He would have been shod and brought back home without incident if it hadn't been for Eva, a duck, who was always hanging about the kitchen door of the farmhouse, eavesdropping, and never got anything quite right. Her farm-mates said of her that she had two mouths but only one ear.

On the day that Charles was led away to the smithy, Eva went quacking about the farm, excitedly telling the other animals that Charles had been taken to town to be shot.

"They're executing an innocent horse!" cried Eva. "He's a hero! He's a martyr! He died to make us free!"

"He was the greatest horse in the world," sobbed a sentimental hen.

"He just seemed like Old Charley to me," said a realistic cow. "Let's not get into a moony mood."

"He was wonderful!" cried a gullible goose.

"What did he ever do?" asked a goat.

Eva, who was as inventive as she was inaccurate, turned on her lively imagination. "It was butchers who led him off to be shot!" she shrieked. "They would have cut our throats while we slept if it hadn't been for Charles!"

"I didn't see any butchers, and I can see a burnt-out firefly on a moonless night," said a barn owl. "I didn't hear any butchers, and I can hear a mouse walk across moss."

"We must build a memorial to Charles the Great, who saved our lives," quacked Eva. And all the birds and beasts in the barnyard except the wise owl, the skeptical goat, and the realistic cow set about building a memorial.

Just then the farmer appeared in the lane, leading Charles, whose new shoes glinted in the sunlight.

It was lucky that Charles was not alone, for the memorial builders might have set upon him with clubs and stones for replacing their hero with just plain old Charley. It was lucky, too, that they could not reach the barn owl, who quickly perched upon the weather vane of the barn, for none is so exasperating as he who is right. The sentimental hen and the gullible goose were the ones who finally called attention to the true culprit—Eva, the one-eared duck with two mouths. The others set upon her and tarred and unfeathered her, for none is more unpopular than the bearer of sad tidings that turn out to be false.

MORAL: *Get it right or let it alone. The conclusion you jump to may be your own.*

—James Thurber

The next extract from a story uses **parody,** or humorous imitation, to make us laugh at something we're all familiar with: the ridiculous characters and situations in certain TV shows.

We scan the cornfields and the wheatfields winking gold and goldbrown and yellowbrown in the midday sun, on up the grassy slope to the barn redder than red against the sky bluer than blue, across the smooth stretch of the barnyard with its pecking chickens, and then right on up to the screen door at the back of the house. The door swings open, a black hole in the sun, and Timmy emerges with his corn-silk hair, corn-fed face. He is dressed in crisp overalls, striped T-shirt, stubby blue Keds. There'd have to be a breeze—and we're not disappointed—his clean fine cup-cut hair waves and settles as he scuffs across the barnyard and out to the edge of the field. The boy stops there to gaze out over the nodding wheat, eyes unsquinted despite the sun, and blue as tinted lenses. Then he brings three fingers to his lips in a neat triangle and whistles long and low, sloping up sharp to cut off at the peak. A moment passes: he whistles again. And then we see it—way out there at the far corner of the field—the ripple, the dashing furrow, the blur of the streaking dog, white chest, flashing feet. . . .

Night: the barnyard still, a bulb burning over the screen door. Inside the family sit at dinner, the table heaped with pork chops, mashed potatoes, applesauce and peas, a pitcher of clean white milk. Home-baked bread. Mom and Dad, their faces bland, perpetually good-humored and sympathetic, poise stiff-backed, forks in midswoop, while Timmy tells his story: "So then Lassie grabbed me by the collar and golly I musta blanked out cause I don't remember anything more till I woke up on the rock——"

"Well I'll be," says Mom.

"You're lucky you've got such a good dog, son," says Dad, gazing down at the collie where she lies patiently, snout over paw, tail wapping the floor. She is combed and washed and fluffed, her lashes mascaraed and curled, her chest and paws white as dish soap. She looks up humbly. But then her ears leap, her neck jerks round—and she's up at the door, head cocked, alert. A high yipping yowl like a stuttering fire whistle shudders through the room. And then another. The dog whines.

"Darn," says Dad. "I thought we were rid of those coyotes—next thing they'll be after the chickens again." . . .

The screen door slaps behind Timmy as he bolts from the house, Lassie at his heels. Mom's head emerges on the rebound. "Timmy!" (He stops as if jerked by a rope, turns to face her.) "You be home before lunch, hear?"

"Sure, Mom," he says, already spinning off, the dog by his side. We get a close-up of Mom's face: She is smiling a benevolent boys-will-be-boys smile. Her teeth are perfect.

In the woods Timmy steps on a rattler, and the dog bites its head off. "Gosh," he says. "Good girl, Lassie." Then he stumbles and slips over an embankment, rolls down the brushy incline and over a sudden precipice, whirling out into the breathtaking blue space like a skydiver. He thumps down on a narrow ledge twenty feet below. And immediately scrambles to his feet, peering timorously down the sheer wall to the heap of bleached bone at its base. Small stones break loose, shoot out like asteroids. Dirt slides begin. But Lassie yarps reassuringly from above, sprints back to the barn for a winch and cable, hoists the boy to safety.

> — from "Heart of a Champion,"
> T. Coraghessan Boyle

A Note on Punctuating Dialogue

You're writing **dialogue** when you write the exact words used by two or more speakers having a conversation. In short stories, novels, nonfiction, and even poetry, this quoted speech usually appears in quotation marks.

When you write dialogue, you want to make sure your readers understand who is speaking. Dialogue

Literature & Language/*cont.*

that isn't carefully punctuated, capitalized, and paragraphed can be confusing. For clarity always follow these rules:

1. Begin a direct quotation with a capital letter.
2. When you identify a speaker with an expression like *she said* or *he asked,* place these phrases outside the quotation marks, separated by some form of punctuation. ("I'm tired," she whined. He said, "Go to sleep.")
3. If these "words of saying" interrupt a quoted sentence, begin the second part of the sentence with a small letter. ("Let's call," Tom suggested, "to say we'll be late.")
4. If a quotation ends with a question mark or an exclamation point, omit the comma that would otherwise separate it from the rest of the sentence. ("Watch out!" screamed Claire. "Where are we going?" demanded Ethan.)
5. Place commas and periods inside closing quotation marks. ("Let's go," he pleaded.) Colons and semicolons go outside closing quotation marks. (First Matt said, "Let's go"; then he decided he wanted to stay.)
6. Place question marks and exclamation points inside the closing quotes if they're part of the quotation itself. ("That's great news!" shouted Holly.) Place them outside if the sentence that contains the quote is the question or exclamation. (Was Kate upset when Max said, "Let's just be friends"?)
7. Start a new paragraph every time the speaker changes.

Examining the Writers' Techniques

Working with a partner, answer these questions about Thurber's and Boyle's dialogue.

1. Look back through "What Happened to Charles," and find all the "words of saying" that identify the characters' speech. How many different verbs does Thurber use? Where does he use humorous

alliteration, or the repetition of similar consonant sounds?

2. Now look at "Heart of a Champion." Does Boyle use as many different "words of saying"? (What tense are they in?)
3. How many different speakers does Thurber quote? How many does Boyle quote? How does each writer indicate that a new character has begun speaking?
4. Where does Boyle interrupt a character's speech to describe another character's response? What punctuation does he use to indicate the interruption?
5. Look back through both passages, and find examples of commas, periods, exclamation points, and question marks that are properly placed inside closing quotation marks. Are any punctuation marks placed outside the closing quotes?
6. Which writer makes his characters sound like real "people" talking? Which one writes stilted, unrealistic dialogue? What is the purpose of the stilted dialogue?

Punctuating Dialogue in Your Writing

Writing a Dialogue. Write a dialogue that takes place between two or more people who are discussing something. Before you write, brainstorm with a partner to come up with possible topics for the discussion. You might want to write your dialogue as a parody of a conversation you have heard on TV or at the mall or on the bus or in the local coffee shop.

1. Try to make your characters sound like real people talking. Use "words of saying" phrases that describe each character's tone of voice. Pay attention to punctuation, capitalization, and paragraph style.
2. Exchange papers with a partner. Revise your dialogue if your partner notices any punctuation mistakes or is confused about which characters are speaking. How will you make your dialogue clearer?

ANALYZING AND RESPONDING TO A STORY

Writing Assignment

Write an essay of at least four paragraphs in which you analyze the elements of one of the stories in this unit. In your essay, explain how you responded to the story's plot, characters, and theme.

Background

You use a critical thinking skill called **evaluating** whenever you make a judgment. If you say that something is "the best," "the worst," "the most exciting," "boring," or "disgusting"—you are making an evaluation (see page 163).

Your **response** to a story is also an evaluation. You may think that a story is true to life or upsetting or that the characters seem unreal. When you explain your response to a story, listen to your own inner voice, not to somebody else's. Never say you like a story because you think you should like it. Always say what you really feel about it, even if you think your view will be unpopular. When you state your response, be sure you give reasons explaining why you feel the way you do.

Prewriting

1. Choose a story that you had a strong response to—whether favorable or unfavorable. Start with your *feeling,* and try to state your response. ("I *loved* it!" "I *hated* it!" "I *kind of liked* it." "I liked the storm part.")
2. Then list the reasons you feel that way. ("I didn't like the ending, when the girl and boy finally get together. I think it would have been much truer to life if she'd decided to leave town.")
3. Next analyze the elements of the story, and decide how you responded to them. Give specific reasons to back up your response.

a. What is the story's **plot**? What is its **conflict,** and how is it resolved? Did the plot hook your interest; and if so, how did it do this? Or why did it fail to do so?

b. Do you find the **characters** believable, realistic people? Did any of the characters change in the course of the story; and if so, what caused the change? Did you find the change convincing? Why or why not?

c. What is the story's **theme**—the truth about life or people that the story reveals? What do you think of that theme, and *why*?

You might organize your thoughts in an outline like the following one, which is based on one reader's response to Saki's "The Storyteller" (page 206):

1. **How do I feel about the story?** It's funny and appealing and true to life. However, I think the very last part isn't necessary.
2. **Elements in the story**
   a. **Satire.** Story makes fun of children's literature. (Funniest part is satire of a fairy tale.)
   b. **Plot.** Children, aunt, and bachelor are on a train. Aunt and bachelor tell stories to children to see who is the better storyteller. There is a "frame story" (children, aunt, and bachelor on train) and an "inner story" (bachelor's story).
   c. **Conflict.** In frame story, conflict is between aunt and bachelor. In bachelor's story, conflict is between Bertha and wolf.
   d. **Climax.** In bachelor's story, climax comes when wolf finds Bertha because he hears her good-conduct medals clinking (very funny). In frame story, climax comes when Cyril pronounces bachelor's story beautiful. (Funny because bachelor's story is really gory.)
   e. **Theme.** Adults offer children two kinds of information, and children know which kind is true. Aunt tells them that girl in her story was saved *because she was good.* Bachelor tells them that her goodness does *not* save Bertha. (Good theme, and true).

Writing

Follow the rough outline that you have created by answering the Prewriting questions. You can state your response to the story either in the introductory paragraph or at the end of the essay.

The following essay is based on the preceding outline. Notice that the writer begins with one response to the story and concludes with a second response.

"The Storyteller": An Analysis and a Response

I think "The Storyteller" by Saki radiates fun and mischief. It should appeal to the rebel in all of us, and it carries a wallop of truth. Its humor derives from both satire and irony. Saki is mimicking the conventional fairy tale here, turning it and its moralizing upside down. He has the bachelor tell a familiar kind of story, so that we expect a familiar outcome. Then he makes something totally different occur. That surprise—the unexpectedness of it— is what makes the story so ironic, funny, and satisfying.

States response.

Gives reasons.

Analyzes story's satire.

Two stories are told in "The Storyteller." First there is the frame story about the children, their aunt, and the bachelor, who are all on a train together. The aunt tries to entertain the children with a typical moralistic story, which the children—of course— reject. Challenged by the aunt to do better, the bachelor tells a story about Bertha, who is so good that she has medals to prove it.

Analyzes story's structure and summarizes plot.

Both stories—the frame story and the bachelor's— have conflicts. The aunt and the bachelor are in conflict in the frame story, and in the inner story the conflict is between the virtuous Bertha and a world (or wolf) indifferent to her goodness.

Identifies conflicts in both stories.

The carefully prepared climax of the bachelor's story is that great moment when Bertha's trembling sets her good-behavior medals clinking, thus giving away her location to the wolf. The climax of the frame story occurs when the children, sitting as a jury evaluating the aunt's versus the bachelor's views of the world, bring in their verdict. Cyril gives the bachelor's story his highest praise: "It is the *only* beautiful story I have ever heard" (page 209).

Quotes from story.

The aunt first fails Cyril with her lazy falsehood about the grass. Then she fails the children more seriously on ethical grounds with the false theme of her story— that people are saved *because* they are good. Both Cyril and the bachelor catch her out on that error.

Analyzes theme of aunt's story.

The aunt's smug confidence finally collapses before the bachelor's cynicism, as surely as Bertha becomes lunch for that mud-colored wolf. The bachelor's story is about reality: His theme is that life is *not* always fair, that goodness is *not* always rewarded. The bachelor's story also reminds us that nothing is more repellent to the healthy mind than people like the narrow-minded aunt, with her instructive tales about infant life.

Analyzes theme of bachelor's story.

Saki's own theme in "The Storyteller" is that there are two kinds of information that the adult world offers children. These two types of information are represented by the aunt's story and the bachelor's. Saki believes that children have an unfailing preference for the truth, and that they instinctively recognize the truth when they hear it. Saki also knows that children dislike people who are smug about their virtue—and that children (like the rest of us) enjoy seeing such smugness defeated.

Analyzes theme of story as a whole.

I think that this story is excellent, except for one flaw—its final paragraph. It must be obvious to all but the dimmest reader that the bachelor is the victor, and that the children will be reminding their aunt of this for some time to come. And so the bachelor's last mutterings are unnecessary. They make me feel like saying, "Yes, yes, Saki, we know. No need to—(yawn)—drag in this anticlimax."

Evaluates story and expresses response.

Checklist for Revision

1. Have you cited the story's title and author?
2. Have you clearly stated your response to the story?
3. Have you included reasons to support your response?
4. Have you discussed the story's plot, characters, and theme?
5. Have you supported your ideas with specific details from the story?
6. If you have quoted directly from the story, have you checked the quotation for accuracy, used quotation marks, and cited the page on which the quotation appears?
7. Have you checked: Spelling? Punctuation? Capitalization? Sentence structure? Paragraph organization?

THE ELEMENTS OF POETRY

Flower Abstraction by Marsden Hartley (1914). Oil.

Collection of Mr. and Mrs. Meyer Potamkin.

UNIT TWO   **John Malcolm Brinnin**

THE ELEMENTS OF POETRY

An introduction by **John Malcolm Brinnin**

Metaphor, in the large sense and the small, is the main property of poetry.

—Richard Wilbur

> "**O**ur instinct for poetry may be more useful than a thousand definitions."

Long before people began to communicate through writing, they uttered combinations of words having the sound of poetry. Yet after thousands of years, no one has produced a single definition of poetry that takes into account all the ways in which poetry can make itself heard. Though you could find enough definitions to fill a book, you still wouldn't be able to put your finger on any one of them and say, "That's it."

Yet we all know poetry when we hear it—whether it's a passage from the Bible, the chorus of a song, or some striking phrase overheard on a city street. Poetry is different from the plain prose we speak and from the flat language of the committee report we read. Poetry has a beat or a roll, a melody and a texture. It's full of expressions that please us, surprise us, and make us laugh or cry. Our instincts alone tell us that when words are put together in a certain way, they are poetry. In the long run, our instinct for poetry may be more useful than a thousand definitions.

Autumn by Giuseppe Arcimboldo (1527–1593). Oil.

The Louvre, Paris.

O ne of the elements that makes poetry poetry is **figurative language**—language that is always based on some kind of comparison that is not literally true.

Figurative language is so natural to us that it is even found in our everyday conversations. For example, if you're like most people and it's time to go to bed, you'll just say, "I'm going to bed." Here you are speaking the literal, ordinary, efficient language of prose. But if you have a touch of the poet in you, you might use a common figurative expression and say, "I'm going to hit the hay."

Let's say you read this in the newspaper:

"The House Budget Committee hammered at the Treasury Secretary for three hours."

You don't ask in horror: What hospital was he taken to? You understand instantly that the writer is speaking figuratively. A **figure of speech** is language shaped by the play of the imagination, in which one thing (here, constant questioning) is compared with something that seems to be entirely different (repeated blows made by a hammer). A figure of speech is never literally true, but a good one always suggests a forceful truth to our imaginations.

In this unit we'll look at three common figures of speech: similes, metaphors, and personification.

Seeing Likenesses: Similes

A **simile** is a figure of speech that uses the words *like, as, than,* or *resembles* to compare things that seem to have little or nothing in common. In a literal comparison, we might say, "His face was

Figurative Language: Language Shaped by Imagination

"Remorse sits in my stomach like a piece of stale bread. How does that sound?"

Drawing by Booth; © 1991
The New Yorker Magazine, Inc.

Yei-bi-chei in the Desert by Rufina Begay, age 9. Watercolor with crayon. (Yei-bi-chei is the Navajo grandfather spirit.)

" 'I wandered lonely as a cloud.'
Hey, wild!"

Drawing by Donald Reilly; © 1970
The New Yorker Magazine, Inc.

> " **O**ne of the main functions of metaphor is to allow us to express ourselves in a kind of imaginative shorthand."

as red as his father's." But when we use a simile, the comparison becomes more striking and imaginative: "His face was as red as a desert sunset," or "His face was like a stoplight."

Similes are part of any poet's equipment—they are tools of the imagination. In a good simile, the connection between one thing and another must be unexpected, but entirely reasonable. William Wordsworth opens a poem with this now-famous simile:

> I wandered lonely as a cloud

The simile helps us see at once how a wanderer has no more sense of direction than does a cloud driven by the winds.

Wordsworth's simile was written in the early part of the nineteenth century, when figures of speech were often drawn from the wonders of nature. Today a poet might make different connections and come up with different similes. Twentieth-century poet Phyllis McGinley did a humorous take-off on Wordsworth's simile in a poem called "Westminster Abbey":

> I wandered lonely as a fareless cabby
> Through miles and miles of the Royal Abbey

Making Identifications: Metaphors

Like a simile, a **metaphor** is a comparison between unlike things in which some reasonable connection is instantly revealed. But a metaphor is a more forceful version of a simile because the connective *like, as, resembles,* or *than* is dropped. A metaphor says that something *is* something else: not "I wandered lonely *as* a cloud" but rather "I *was* a lonely cloud."

Metaphors, in fact, are basic even in everyday communication. One of the main functions of metaphor is to allow us to express ourselves in a kind of imaginative shorthand. In the following dialogue, compare the lengthy order given by the customer with the concise and picturesque words of the waiter:

> A man enters a diner and sits at the counter.
> "What's yours?" says the waiter.
> "I'll have two scrambled eggs on an English muffin," says the customer.
> "Two wrecks on a raft," calls out the waiter.
> ". . . and a cup of black coffee and one of those home-made doughnuts you advertise."
> "Java and a sinker," the waiter calls out.

What we use most, what we hear every day, are the kinds of metaphors found in this dialogue—suggested, or **implied,** comparisons. Other familiar examples of implied metaphors are "the long arm of the law," "the table legs," "this neck of the woods," "the foot of the mountain." These terms suggest comparisons between parts of the body and things quite different from the body. Expressions like these are so familiar that we forget they represented, once upon a time, brand new ways of seeing the world.

Even single words can contain implied metaphors. If we say that a person "barked a command," we imply a resemblance to a dog. If we say that someone "hissed a remark," we imply a resemblance to a snake. If we say that someone "squawked in protest," we imply a resemblance to a bird.

But metaphors in poetry are something more than this; they must also be fresh, even startling. Here is how the American poet Robert Lowell uses a metaphor to describe a section of twentieth-century Boston in a poem called "For the Union Dead":

> . . . Behind their cage,
> yellow dinosaur steamshovels were grunting
> as they cropped up tons of mush and grass
> to gouge their underworld garage.

Humanizing the World: Personification

When we attribute human qualities to a nonhuman thing or to an abstract idea, we are using **personification.** The figure of Uncle Sam in his top hat, long beard, and striped pants is the personification of the United States, just as stout John Bull in his brass buttons and breeches personifies Great Britain. Personification is a special kind of metaphor: In the case of Uncle Sam, a nation is compared to a person whom we recognize on sight.

When we say that a computer is "user-friendly," that "misery loves company," or that "the future beckons," we are also personifying—that is, we are giving human qualities to nonhuman things (a computer) or to abstract ideas (misery and the future).

Personification is widely used by cartoonists, especially political cartoonists. You've probably seen justice personified as a blindfolded woman carrying scales, goodness personified as a person with wings and a halo, and love personified as a chubby infant with a bow and arrow.

Poets also make use of personification, but usually in a subtler way. Here is a poem in which a mountain is personified as a grandfather, while the seasons are personified as little children playing at his knees. (An *inquest* is an investigation.)

> The Mountain sat upon the Plain
> In his tremendous Chair—
> His observation omnifold,
> His inquest, everywhere—
>
> The Seasons played around his knees
> Like Children round a sire—
> Grandfather of the Days is He
> Of Dawn, the Ancestor—
>
> —Emily Dickinson

In poetry figurative language is the most important means of imaginative expression. It is a tool that poets have used down through the centuries to translate all the various experiences of their worlds and times into very personal statements.

"**W**hen we say that a computer is 'user-friendly' or that 'the future beckons,' we are personifying."

The author of this poem is an African American woman who writes about the life she herself has experienced in the city of Baltimore. She does this truthfully and without any attempt to hide the harsh realities of what she has seen. No one could say that this portrait of a woman is very pretty. Nevertheless, beauty—and what can happen to it—is the subject of the poem. Notice how figures of speech help you see contrasting pictures—past and present—of Miss Rosie.

Miss Rosie

Lucille Clifton

When I watch you
wrapped up like garbage
sitting, surrounded by the smell
of too old potato peels
5   or
when I watch you
in your old man's shoes
with the little toe cut out
sitting, waiting for your mind
10   like next week's grocery
I say
when I watch you
you wet brown bag of a woman
who used to be the best looking gal
in Georgia
15   used to be called the Georgia Rose
I stand up
through your destruction
I stand up

Portrait of a Farmer's Wife by Robert Gwathmey (1951). Gouache.
Courtesy Terry Dintenfass Gallery, New York.

Responding to the Poem

Analyzing the Poem

Identifying Details

1. Identify the two **similes** and one **metaphor** that describe Miss Rosie.
2. What details tell you how Miss Rosie *used* to look? In what way is the term "Georgia Rose" also a **metaphor**?

Interpreting Meanings

3. Which **figure of speech** in this poem did you think was most powerful? What picture of Miss Rosie did it create for you?
4. How would you describe Miss Rosie's current state of mind?
5. The words "I stand up," repeated twice, give the most important clue as to how the writer wants us to feel about Miss Rosie. Miss Rosie, as she is presented here, is a sad figure. Why do you think the speaker is moved to "stand up" for her?
6. In a way, Miss Rosie seems to represent something more than herself, something never named. What do you think that might be?
7. What do you think might have happened to Miss Rosie?

Writing About the Poem

A Creative Response

Expressing a Different Attitude. Suppose you want to express feelings for Miss Rosie that are different from this speaker's feelings. Write at least three new lines to end the poem that would express a different attitude. Use a figure of speech to express the way the speaker feels about Miss Rosie.

Analyzing Language and Vocabulary

Idioms

An **idiom** is an expression that is peculiar to a certain language and that cannot be understood by a mere literal definition of its individual words. For example, the literal meaning of the expression "to fall in love" would be absurd. Like many idioms, this one implies a comparison. The experience of love can be so overwhelming it is like falling down to the ground. Or the idiom might suggest that being in love is like falling into a trap, although not necessarily an unpleasant one.

Idioms exist in all languages; one of the problems in translating a work from one language to another is the difficulty in translating the idioms.

1. What is the literal meaning of the phrase "to stand up for"? What is its idiomatic meaning? What comparison is implied in the idiom?
2. Identify the meanings of each of the following idioms. Check your dictionary if necessary. Which of these idioms suggest comparisons?

   a. To stand on your own two feet
   b. To stand a chance
   c. To stand by
   d. To stand to reason
   e. To stand fast
   f. To stand up to
   g. To take a stand

Reading About the Writer

Lucille Clifton (1936–   ) writes both fiction and poetry, and has published many books for children. One of Clifton's best-known works is *Generations*, a poetic memoir composed of portraits of five generations of her family. It begins with her great-great-grandmother, who was brought from Africa to New Orleans and sold into slavery. Like all of Clifton's work, *Generations* is honest but rarely bitter. As one critic observed, her purpose is perpetuation and celebration, not judgment.

This poem is a monologue, a speech spoken by one person to another person without interruption. This monologue is written in such a way as to suggest the natural speech of a woman who doesn't pay much attention to formal grammar, but who can nevertheless say what she means.

Read the poem aloud, and listen to the forceful figure of speech the speaker uses to make her point to her son. How does this metaphor show us the kind of life this woman has led? What kind of life do you think she wants her son to lead?

Mother to Son

Langston Hughes

Well, son, I'll tell you:
Life for me ain't been no crystal stair.
It's had tacks in it,
And splinters,
5   And boards torn up,
And places with no carpet on the floor—
Bare.
But all the time
I'se been a-climbin' on,
10   And reachin' landin's,
And turnin' corners,
And sometimes goin' in the dark
Where there ain't been no light.
So boy, don't you turn back.
15   Don't set you down on the steps
'Cause you finds it's kinder hard.
Don't you fall now—
For I'se still goin', honey,
I'se still climbin',
20   And life for me ain't been no crystal stair.

Responding to the Poem

Analyzing the Poem

Identifying Details

1. This poem consists of an **extended metaphor**— that is, a metaphor that is stated and then developed throughout the poem. What metaphor is the poem based on?
2. What has the mother's "stairway" been like?
3. Name four things the mother has done on this stairway.
4. Name three things she tells her son *not* to do.

Interpreting Meanings

5. What do you associate with the word *crystal*? Why do you think the poet has the mother use the image of a "crystal stair"?
6. How might you describe the mother's stairway, if it isn't crystal?
7. What kinds of human experiences do you think the mother is talking about in lines 3–7? What kind of response to these experiences is she describing in lines 8–13?
8. What do you think has motivated this mother's "speech" to her son? Has he asked for her advice, or has he done something she disapproves of, or is he just discouraged?
9. What fears do you think this mother has about her son's life? Do you think these are universal fears, or do they apply only to the mother in this poem? Explain.
10. Don't, don't, don't, says the mother in this poem. What is she really telling her son to *do*?

Writing About the Poem

A Creative Response

1. **Extending the Poem.** Write a paragraph or poem entitled "Son to Mother," and let the son respond to his mother's advice.

A Critical Response

2. **Evaluating the Metaphor.** In a paragraph, evaluate the poem's central metaphor—of life as a tenement stairway. How effective is it in communicating the poem's meaning? What feelings does it add to the poem?

Analyzing Language and Vocabulary

Dialects

A **dialect** is a way of speaking peculiar to a geographic region, a social group, or a whole community. A dialect is distinguished from the standard form of the language by its pronunciation, grammar, and vocabulary.

1. Many features of the dialect used in this poem are common throughout the United States in a variety of dialects. Lines 2 and 10 provide examples of two of those common features. What are they?
2. What is the meaning of the contraction "I'se" (lines 9, 18, and 19)?
3. How would line 9 be written in standard English? Line 15? Line 16?
4. This poem presents a moving message from a mother to her son. Do you think it would have been more or less effective if Hughes had written it in standard English? Why or why not?

Reading About the Writer

Langston Hughes (1902–1967), was born in Joplin, Missouri, but is primarily identified with Harlem, the African American community in New York City of which he became the unofficial poet laureate. A man of many talents, Hughes wrote plays and novels and worked as an administrator in groups dedicated to bringing black experiences to the theater. But his fame rests firmly on his poetry, most notably for its use of jazz rhythms and for the tender lyrics in which street talk and urban dialect are elevated into a form of art. The most prominent and widely honored black poet of his time, Hughes lived to see his influence inspire and shape the careers of many other remarkable African American poets. Other poems by Hughes appear on pages 264 and 359.

Over the centuries, poets have been particularly creative in finding new metaphors to describe the feeling of love. Like many poets of his day, Shakespeare (see page 286), drew his metaphors from the world of nature. Modern poet Ishmael Reed (see page 311) draws his metaphors from contemporary life. Watch for the unusual metaphor that describes love at the end of this poem. Before you start reading, make a guess about what you think the title means.

Love Without Love

Luis Lloréns Torres, translated by Julio Marzán

> I love you, because in my thousand and one nights of dreams,
> I never once dreamed of you.
> I looked down paths that traveled from afar,
> but it was never you I expected.
> 5   Suddenly I've felt you flying through my soul
> in quick, lofty flight,
> and how beautiful you seem way up there, far
> from my always idiot heart!
> Love me that way, flying over everything.
> 10   And, like the bird on its branches, land in my arms
> only to rest,
> then fly off again.
> Be not like the romantic ones who, in love, set me on fire.
> When you climb up my mansion,
> 15   enter so lightly, that as you enter
> the dog of my heart will not bark.

Responding to the Poem

Analyzing the Poem

Identifying Details

1. According to the first four lines, why does the speaker love this particular person?
2. Explain the **metaphor** that is implied in lines 5–6. Point out how this figure of speech is **extended** in lines 9–12.
3. What totally new **metaphor** describes the loved one in lines 14–16?

Interpreting Meanings

4. How would you describe the person this speaker is in love with?

5. How do you interpret the first two lines of the poem? Why do you think the speaker would love someone *because* he has never once dreamed of that person?
6. In the last line, why do you think the "dog" might bark? What would it be warning against?
7. What kinds of experiences with love do you think the speaker has had? Would you say this is a sad or happy love poem? Explain your answer.
8. How do you interpret the **title**—what two different meanings could the second *love* have?
9. Do you agree with the speaker's view of love, or do you think that it is impossible to have "love without love"? Explain.

Le Soleil de Paris by Marc Chagall (1975).

Amor sin amor

Te amo, porque en mis mil y una noches de
  ensueño,
jamás contigo yo soñé.
Yo miraba las sendas que venían de lejos,
pero a ti nunca te esperé.
Te he sentido de pronto volando por mi espíritu
en ardua y rápida aviación.
¡Qué bella me pareces por allá arriba, lejos
del siempre idiota corazón!
Amame así, volando por encima de todo.
Y solo para descansar,
aterriza en mis brazos, como el ave en la rama,
y vuelve otra vez a volar.
No seas de las románticas que en amor me
  encendieron.
Cuando tú escales mi mansión,
entra tan levemente, que al entrar no te ladre
el perro de mi corazón.

—Luis Lloréns Torres

Writing About the Poem

A Creative Response

1. **Imitating the Poem.** Write a short poem in which
   you describe an emotion other than love using
   at least three **figures of speech.** To show the
   contradictory nature of this emotion, model your
   title after Lloréns Torres's (for instance: "Fear
   Without Fear," "Hope Without Hope," "Anger
   Without Anger," "Loneliness Without Loneliness," or "Compassion Without Compassion").
   Write at least six lines.
2. **Translating a Poem.** If you know Spanish, make
   your own translation of the poem, using the
   Spanish text that follows. What words in the
   poem rhyme in the original Spanish? Can you
   think of any rhymes you might use in your translation?

Analyzing Language and Vocabulary

Related Words

Even if you don't know Spanish, you can find words
in the poem that are related to familiar English
words. These words are related through their common ancestor, Latin. Use a dictionary to help you
answer the following questions:

1. What Spanish word is related to the words *mirror*
   and *mirage*? What Latin word do they all come
   from?
2. What Spanish word is *amorous* related to? What
   Latin word do they both come from?
3. How are *embrace* and *brazos* related? What Latin
   word do they both come from?
4. What English words are related to *aviación*?
   What Latin word do they come from?
5. What English word is *encendieron* related to?
   What Latin word do they both come from?

Reading About the Writer

Luis Lloréns Torres (1876–1944) was born in Juana
Díaz, Puerto Rico. One of Puerto Rico's most important modern poets, Lloréns Torres edited an influential literary magazine, worked as a newspaper
columnist and lawyer, and served as a member of
the Puerto Rican legislature from 1900 to 1910.

Courage

Anne Sexton

It is in the small things we see it.
The child's first step,
as awesome as an earthquake.
The first time you rode a bike,
5   wallowing up the sidewalk.
The first spanking when your heart
went on a journey all alone.
When they called you crybaby
or poor or fatty or crazy
10   and made you into an alien,
you drank their acid
and concealed it.

Later,
if you faced the death of bombs and bullets
15   you did not do it with a banner,
you did it with only a hat to
cover your heart.
You did not fondle the weakness inside you
though it was there.
20   Your courage was a small coal
that you kept swallowing.
If your buddy saved you
and died himself in so doing,
then his courage was not courage,
25   it was love; love as simple as shaving soap.

Later,
if you have endured a great despair,
then you did it alone,
getting a transfusion from the fire,
30   picking the scabs off your heart,
then wringing it out like a sock.

Next, my kinsman, you powdered your
    sorrow,
you gave it a back rub
and then you covered it with a blanket
35   and after it had slept a while
it woke to the wings of the roses
and was transformed.

Later,
when you face old age and its natural
    conclusion
your courage will still be shown in the
40   little ways,
each spring will be a sword you'll sharpen,
those you love will live in a fever of love,
and you'll bargain with the calendar
and at the last moment
45   when death opens the back door
you'll put on your carpet slippers
and stride out.

Responding to the Poem

Analyzing the Poem

Identifying Details

1. In what "small things" does the speaker see courage at work during childhood?
2. Name the times the speaker sees courage at work later on in life.

Interpreting Meanings

3. How many **similes** and **metaphors** can you find in the first stanza alone? Which ones make the "small things" of childhood seem heroic?
4. In stanza 2, the speaker talks about courage in battle. How is going into battle "with a banner" different from going into battle "with only a hat to cover your heart"? (On what occasions would you see people covering their hearts with their hats, and what does the gesture mean?)
5. The speaker uses a **simile** when she says that the soldier's love for his buddy is "as simple as shaving soap." What is the speaker suggesting about the soldier's courage? (What other simple things might the speaker have compared to love?)
6. In stanza 3, the speaker talks about courage in the face of despair. If "scabs" have formed on the heart, what has happened? (What is the speaker comparing "scabs" to?)
7. In line 31, the speaker talks of "wringing" out the heart. What is being wrung out of it?
8. In lines 32–37, the speaker **personifies** sorrow. What does this personification tell about what we do with our sorrow? What causes sorrow's marvelous change?
9. For a person who is growing old and nearing death, why would each spring be like a "sword" to sharpen? (What enemy is the person fighting off?) When people "bargain with the calendar," what are they asking for?
10. The poet moves us through the stages of a human life. What final picture do you see, and how is this different from the way most of us think of courage? How is death **personified**?
11. What resemblances do you see between this poem and Anne Tyler's story "With All Flags Flying" (page 81)? Could the **titles** be interchanged? Explain.

Writing About the Poem

A Creative Response

1. **Imitating the Poem.** Some people have courage without knowing it. Others find that they have courage when they face situations that demand it. "It is in the small things we see it," says Anne Sexton in line 1. List at least five other "small things" in a person's life in which you see courage. Then describe each of these small things by using a dramatic **figure of speech,** such as Sexton uses in this poem.

A Critical Response

2. **Responding to Figures of Speech.** This poem is loaded with figures of speech: **similes, direct** and **implied metaphors,** and **personification.** Fill out a chart like the following one in which you identify as many figures of speech as you can. Then write a paragraph responding to Sexton's use of figurative language. Give reasons to support your response.

Similes	Direct Metaphors	Implied Metaphors	Personification
1. 2. etc.	1. 2. etc.	1. 2. etc.	1. 2. etc.

Reading About the Writer

Anne Sexton (1928–1974) was born in Massachusetts and began studying poetry at the age of 28 with the poet Robert Lowell. She soon became a central figure in a scattered group of poets who tended to write openly about the most intimate (and often painful) details of their lives. Their frankness earned them the label "confessional poets." Sexton believed that poetry "should be a shock to the senses," that "it should almost hurt." One critic has described her poems as turning "wounds into words." Another has said that her poetry "delights even as it disturbs." In 1966 Sexton received the Pulitzer Prize for poetry for her collection *Live or Die.* Another of her poems, "Cinderella," appears on page 344.

Our response to a poem often depends on the knowledge and expectations we bring to it. For example, when you read the title of this poem, what do you expect it to be about? Does this make you want to read the poem, or does the subject fail to interest you? What about the short quotation from the truck driver? Do you think the poet is referring only to truck drivers' schedules, or is he probably talking about something broader? What sort of "schedules" do you predict he has in mind? How might he be using the word metaphorically?

Double Header

John Stone

*Each and every one of us
has got a schedule to keep.*
—a truck driver being
interviewed on radio

I've made it
have been left alone in the stadium
locked here after the baseball
twilight game, having hidden
5   where I won't tell

on a bet with someone I invented
and therefore had to win.
I can hear the Security Guard
locking up, watch him making his way out,
10   turning off the lights as he goes

toward home and supper, away from
the smell of popcorn and beer.
I can see him look
with a question at my car,
15   the only one besides his

still in the lot and see him
look back once at the stadium without
knowing or even thinking I could be
looking back at him, my face barbed
20   with wire. I turn now to the stadium

that is all mine, bought
with my money, purchased with
a three dollar ticket for the top tier,
the stadium that is coming alive again
25   with the crowd that is coming back

but of course isn't coming back
to watch me play, with DiMaggio in center,
Cobb in left, Hornsby at second,
Rizzuto at short, and all the others
30   who have been tagged out more than once

themselves, and who will get me later
or sooner, trying to stretch a single
into a double, catching up with my lost breath
that I can remember now from when
35   I was eleven, with a stitch in my side

sprinting still in spite of the stitch
for the inside-the-park home run
I almost had when I was twelve
for the girl I almost got when I got
40   old enough but didn't know the rules

dusting my pants off now
to the music I never learned, for
the symphony orchestra I never conducted,
my hands rough with rosin
45   for the truck I never drove

and the fish I never caught
and wouldn't have known if I had
how to take him off the hook,
for my father who is in the crowd
50   cheering out his heart

but who of course isn't there
as I pull up lame at second
with a stand-up double
in this game that goes on for hours,
55   my hands stinging with the bat,

the All-Stars aligned against me
in this stadium I own for the night,
one great circle and inside this circle
this square that seems the only one
60   on this curving darkening ball of earth

or the only one anyway
marked by bases I must run all night
for everything I should
by now
65   be worth.

Night Baseball by Marjorie Phillips (1951). Oil.

The Phillips Collection, Washington, D.C.

Responding to the Poem

Analyzing the Poem

Identifying Details

1. At the beginning of the poem, where is the speaker, and what has he just done?
2. What line in stanza 5 tells us that the man has begun his fantasy?
3. What does the speaker do in the empty ball park?

Interpreting Meanings

4. How would you summarize what the speaker regrets about his life? (Think about what the experiences he describes in stanzas 8–10 have in common.) Why do you think the speaker imagines that his father is in the crowd, "cheering out his heart"?
5. What do you think the speaker is comparing his imaginary baseball game to? In what way is his game a "double header"?
6. When the speaker says the "All-Stars" are aligned against him, what is he comparing the stars to? When he talks of "this square" within the "one great circle," what is he talking about, literally and figuratively? What are the bases that the speaker "must run all night"? Why does he feel compelled to run them?
7. Look back at the truck driver's comment at the beginning of the poem. How is the poet using the word *schedule* **metaphorically**—in other words, what is the schedule that the speaker must keep?
8. The poem opens with the words "I've made it." In what ways has the speaker made it? In what ways *hasn't* he made it? Do you think he is more affected by his success or his failure?
9. Do you think fantasies like this are common? Explain.

Writing About the Poem

A Creative Response

1. **Extending the Poem.** Pretend you are someone who is acting out a fantasy. In a paragraph, tell what the fantasy is, where the person acts it out, and how the fantasy makes the person feel. Open with the words "I've made it."

A Critical Response

2. **Analyzing the Poem's Effect.** In two paragraphs, identify the main effect this poem had on you, and then try to account for that effect. Answer the following questions before you write. Be prepared to compare your response with those of your classmates.

   a. Did I identify with the speaker?
   b. Was I bored, intrigued, confused, moved?
   c. How did the poem's language affect me? (Was it difficult? Easy? Interesting?)
   d. What knowledge did I bring (or not bring) to the poem? How did this affect my response?
   e. What did I *expect* the poem to be about? How did this affect my response?

Analyzing Language and Vocabulary

Jargon

In one sense of the word, **jargon** is the specialized vocabulary of a group of people who share a particular occupation or interest. This poem includes several words and phrases that are baseball jargon. As you answer the following questions, refer to your dictionary as necessary. Jargon often includes both **idioms** (see page 66) and **figures of speech**.

1. Identify five examples of baseball jargon in stanza 6. What does each one mean?
2. Define the expression "trying to stretch a single into a double" (lines 32–33). Explain the metaphor in this phrase.
3. Define an "inside-the-park home run" (line 37). How might someone who knows nothing about baseball be confused by this expression?
4. Define "stand-up double" (line 53).
5. Define the title of the poem. What metaphor is implied by that phrase?

Reading About the Writer

John Stone (1936–   ) is a physician and a poet, who received his medical degree from Washington University in St. Louis. His joint interests in medicine and literature are reflected in his unique career at Emory University, Atlanta, where he is both a professor of cardiology and a lecturer in English.

Focusing on Background
A Comment from the Poet

Here is what John Stone has written about how he came to write "Double Header," and about his dual career as a doctor and poet:

"A poet is always on the lookout for metaphors. Sometimes a metaphor slips up on a poet when he or she least expects it. I've often had a poem begin to 'happen' to me while doing something entirely unpoetic: such as driving a car—or, as in this case, sitting with friends in a baseball stadium.

"Some medical students at Emory University School of Medicine (where I teach and see patients) had invited me to be their guest at an Atlanta Braves baseball game. I went along, with pleasure. We sat high in the stands above the playing field, eating popcorn and peanuts. It was August in Atlanta, and the evening was quite warm. The Braves were losing. As I sat there, I began to muse about a recurring idea I'd had: What would it be like to hide in the stadium until the crowd had all left; to be left alone there after the stadium workers had closed up and gone home; what would happen to me in that situation? I took a 3 x 5 card from my shirt pocket (I've carried such cards with me ever since I was an intern); on the card I began to make notes toward the poem that was to become 'Double Header.' It was in the writing of the poem that I discovered what it might be like to be 'left alone in the stadium.' Discovery is one of the great pleasures of writing—to find out what one may have known all along, but didn't know that one knew.

"Many physicians have been writers: The names that come immediately to mind are those of John Keats, Anton Chekhov, Somerset Maugham, Arthur Conan Doyle, and, closer to our own time, William Carlos Williams, Walker Percy, and Lewis Thomas. For me, medicine and poetry both come from the same place: the human encounter, the living of a life. After all, what each of us tells our physician when we are seen for a check-up is, in some respects, a short story. And a person's 'short stories' taken together, over time, constitute a truly wondrous and highly individualistic 'novel.' The physician-poet hopes to transmute the 'stories' that he hears into art.

"Incidentally, I like the derivation of the word *poet.* It comes from the Greek word *poiein,* which means 'to make.' The medical word *hematopoiesis,* for example, means 'the making of blood' (as in the bone marrow). A poet, then, is *one who makes.* Being both a poet and a physician assures one of an interesting life: Each vocation complements and informs the other. As a result, there's never a dull moment."

—John Stone

If you've ever experienced a foggy day, you'll recognize what this poem is about—at least on its surface. Before you read, talk about what we mean by "going through life in a fog."

This poem was written by a citizen of the Soviet Union during a period of political repression. What kind of fog could he really be describing? What is he afraid of?

Foggy Street

Andrei Voznesensky, translated by Richard Wilbur

The air is gray-white as a pigeon-feather.
       Police bob up like corks on a fishing-net.
Foggy weather.
What century is it? What era? I forget.

5   As in a nightmare, everything is crumbling;
       people have come unsoldered; nothing's intact.
I plod on, stumbling,
Or flounder in cotton wool, to be more exact.

Noses. Parking-lights. Badges flash and blur.
10   All's vague, as at a magic-lantern show.°
Your hat-check, Sir?
Mustn't walk off with the wrong head, you know.

It's as if a woman who's scarcely left your lips
       Should blur in the mind, yet trouble it with recall—
15   Bereft now, widowed by your love's eclipse—
Still yours, yet suddenly not yours at all . . .

Can that be Venus? No—an ice-cream vendor!
       I bump into curbstones, bump into passersby.
Are they friends, I wonder?
20   Home-bred Iagos,° how covert you are, how sly!

Why it's you, my darling, shivering there alone!
       Your overcoat's too big for you, my dear.
But why have you grown
That moustache? Why is there frost in your hairy ear?

25   I trip, I stagger, I persist.
       Murk, murk . . . there's nothing visible anywhere.
Whose is the cheek you brush now in the mist?
Ahoy there!
One's voice won't carry in this heavy air.

30   When the fog lifts, how brilliant it is, how rare!

10. **magic-lantern show:** an old-fashioned slide show that uses a device containing a lamp to project images.

20. **Iago** (ē·ä′gō): the false friend and villain in Shakespeare's play *Othello*.

East Germans celebrate the fall of the Berlin Wall, November 1989.

Responding to the Poem

Analyzing the Poem

Identifying Facts

1. Find three or more **similes** and **metaphors** that convey the unreal appearance of the world.
2. Find the stanza in which the speaker **personifies** his impression of the foggy street. Explain how this person appears to the speaker.
3. How does the world appear when the fog lifts?

Interpreting Meanings

4. This poem was written by a Soviet citizen during a time when the government and its secret police kept strict controls over what people were allowed to know and say. In light of this fact, what kind of "fog" might the poet really be describing? According to the poem, what effects might a repressive government have on the average person?
5. Line 20 **alludes** to Shakespeare's play *Othello*. Iago is the sly villain who lies to Othello and tells him that his wife is unfaithful. What might this speaker fear that makes him refer to strangers as "Iagos"?
6. By now you've realized there's more meaning lurking within the fog in this poem than first meets the eye. What broader meaning might line 29 have for a Soviet writer? How about line 30?

Writing About the Poem

A Creative Response

Using Figures of Speech. Write a poem or paragraph describing how you might feel during an unsettling or disorienting or otherwise strange experience. Before you write, think of some figures of speech that will convey your feelings about the experience. You might freewrite for a few minutes, finding as many ways to complete this sentence as you can: "The experience of ____ feels like ____."

Reading About the Writer

Andrei Voznesensky (vōj'nə·shen'skē) (1933–) grew up in the Soviet Union under the repressive police state run by Josef Stalin. During Stalin's dictatorship, millions of people were arrested and either sent to slave labor camps or murdered. Voznesensky has long been a vocal advocate of literary freedom. Now one of the most popular poets in Eastern Europe, he draws enormous crowds whenever he reads his work.

Literature & Language

Using Similes, Metaphors, and Personification

1. Identify the **simile** in each of the following quotations, and then tell what you imagine the two different things being compared have in common. Which simile seems the most modern?

   a. Sweet are the thoughts that savor of content,
   The quiet mind is richer than a crown.

   > —from "Sweet Are the Thoughts,"
   > Robert Greene

   b. It is a beauteous evening, calm and free;
   The holy time is quiet as a nun
   Breathless with adoration

   > —from "It Is a Beauteous Evening,"
   > William Wordsworth

   c. She walks in beauty, like the night
   Of cloudless climes and starry skies,
   And all that's best of dark and bright
   Meet in her aspect and her eyes

   > —from "She Walks in Beauty,"
   > Lord Byron

   d. I am poured out like water . . . my heart is like wax.

   > —from Psalm 22

   e. And the night shall be filled with music,
   And the cares, that infest the day,
   Shall fold their tents, like the Arabs,
   And as silently steal away.

   > —from "The Day Is Done,"
   > Henry Wadsworth Longfellow

   f. O my love's like a red, red rose,
   That's newly sprung in June:
   O my love's like the melody
   That's sweetly played in tune.

   > —from "A Red, Red Rose,"
   > Robert Burns

   g. The streets shimmered like laboratory beakers.

   > —from "Some Collisions Bring Luck,"
   > Marge Piercy

2. Here is an entire poem built around a single **simile,** which is announced in the first line:

   Spring is like a perhaps hand
   (which comes carefully
   out of Nowhere)arranging
   a window, into which people look(while
5 people stare
   arranging and changing placing
   carefully there a strange
   thing and a known thing here)and

   changing everything carefully

10 spring is like a perhaps
   Hand in a window
   (carefully to
   and fro moving New and
   Old things, while
15 people stare carefully
   moving a perhaps
   fraction of flower here placing
   an inch of air there)and

   without breaking anything.

   > —E. E. Cummings

   a. What is the speaker comparing spring to?
   b. Where does the speaker **extend** this simile into a **personification** of spring?
   c. What action do you see spring doing that only a (human) window dresser can do?
   d. What verbs tell what spring does?
   e. Is spring a gentle person, or a rough one? How do you know?
   f. By using the adverb "perhaps" as an adjective, the poet redefines the word. What would you say "perhaps" means in the poem?

3. In each of the following quotations, name the two different things the poet is bringing together in his **metaphor.** Then tell what you imagine these two things have in common.

   a. There is a garden in her face,
   Where roses and white lilies grow

   > —from "Cherry Ripe,"
   > Thomas Campion

b. This lovely flower fell to seed.
Work gently, sun and rain—
She held it as her dying creed
That she would grow again.

—"For My Grandmother,"
Countee Cullen

4. If two or more **metaphors** are used together, the images suggested by them must be consistent and logical, or a **mixed metaphor** results. For instance, when a poet writes of life as a voyage on stormy seas, we expect further images to be consistent: The voyage of life ends "in a safe harbor" or "on the shores of an unknown island." But if the poet says that life is a voyage on stormy seas that brings us to "a crash landing in the jungle," we realize that the poet has lost control of the metaphor. Since metaphors are common in speech, people tend to mix them without thinking. Explain what is inconsistent about the following metaphors:

a. That snake-in-the-grass is barking up the wrong tree.
b. The House sub-committee has a lot of bottlenecks to iron out of the budget.
c. If you rock the boat, you'll find yourself sitting on a time bomb.

5. Sometimes even a single word can suggest a **metaphor** that gives away the meaning of a whole poem.

Fear

The host, he says that all is well,
And the fire-wood glow is bright;
The food has a warm and tempting smell,—
But on the window licks the night.

Pile on the logs. . . . Give me your hands,
Friends! No,—it is not fright. . . .
But hold me . . . somewhere I heard demands. . . .
And on the window licks the night.

—Hart Crane

a. "The host" in this poem says that everything is fine, and most of the details show that he and his friends should be having a warm and pleasant evening together. But a single verb in the last line of each stanza suggests a **metaphor** that puts a different interpretation on the gathering. What is that verb? What is the night being compared to?
b. What does this verb suggest might be threatening the host and his friends?
c. What kinds of demands do you imagine he has heard? Why do they scare him?

6. In each of the following lines, tell what is being **personified,** and name the words that create the personification:

a. The little waves, with their soft white hands,
Efface the footprints in the sand

—from "The Tide Rises, the Tide Falls,"
Henry Wadsworth Longfellow

b. It is not enough that yearly, down this hill,
April
Comes like an idiot, babbling and strewing flowers.

—from "Spring,"
Edna St. Vincent Millay

c. I hear America singing, the varied carols I hear

—from "I Hear America Singing,"
Walt Whitman

Writing

Extending a Metaphor. Write four or more lines of poetry in which you start with a metaphor (or simile) and see how far you can extend it and still make sense. You might start with one of these metaphors:

Life is a dream . . .
Time is a river . . .
Joy is a bird . . .
Courage is a hot coal . . .
Doubt is like a buzzing fly . . .

Figurative Language: Symbols

All things are filled full of signs, and it is a wise man who can learn about one thing from another.

—Plotinus

A **symbol** is often an ordinary object, event, animal, or person to which we have attached extraordinary meaning and significance. We use an apple to symbolize one of the biggest cities in the world. We use two snakes wrapped around a stick to symbolize the profession of medicine. We use a skull and crossbones to symbolize poison or danger. We use a rectangle of dyed cloth to symbolize a country. We use red flowers to symbolize love.

Inherited and Invented Symbols

Symbols can be inherited, and they can be invented. The most familiar symbols have been inherited—that is, they have been handed down through history. For example, no one knows exactly who first thought of using the lion to symbolize power, courage, and domination. But once these qualities were assigned to it, images of lions began to appear on flags, banners, coats of arms, and castle walls, and the lion became a **public symbol** that has maintained its significance in art and literature to this day.

Like the lion, most symbols have been defined by history—by the collective imaginations of people who endowed certain objects with meanings far beyond their simple characters or functions. By this process, a lamb or a fish came to symbolize Christ; a curved sword came to symbolize the nations of the Muslim world; a six-pointed star came to symbolize the people of Israel; an eagle came to symbolize the United States; an image of the rising sun came to symbolize Japan; a winged horse came to symbolize poetry; and a dove came to symbolize peace.

Symbols can also be invented. Writers often take a new object, character, or event and make it the embodiment of some human concern. Some invented symbols in literature have by now also become universal. Shakespeare's monstrous character Caliban in *The Tempest* is often referred to as a symbol of the uncivilized side of human nature. Melville's great white whale Moby-Dick symbolizes the mystery of evil. Cervantes' Don Quixote symbolizes the hero whose high aspirations are defeated by a lack of realism. Peter Pan symbolizes eternal childhood.

Why do poets use symbols? Why don't they just come right out and say what they mean? Symbols, like all **figures of speech,** allow the poet to suggest layers and layers of meanings—meanings that a simple, literal statement could never convey. A symbol is like a pebble cast in the water: It sends off many, ever-widening ripples of meaning. Some symbols (like Melville's great white whale) are even so rich in meanings that their significance has never been fully understood.

In the following poem, Walt Whitman uses a symbol that is often found in literature: a ship that stands for the human soul. Notice how the poet talks of a literal ship for nine lines, describing how it veers away from the rocks that would wreck it. Then in the last two lines the poet reveals the ship's symbolic meaning.

Aboard at a Ship's Helm

Aboard at a ship's helm.
A young steersman steering with care.

Through fog on a sea coast dolefully ringing,
An ocean bell—O a warning bell, rocked by the waves.

O you give good notice indeed, you bell by the sea reefs ringing,
Ringing, ringing, to warn the ship from its wreck place.

For as on the alert O steersman, you mind the loud admonition,
The bows turn, the freighted ship tacking speeds away under her
   gray sails,
The beautiful and noble ship with all her precious wealth speeds
   away gaily and safe.

But O the ship, the immortal ship! O ship aboard the ship!
Ship of the body, ship of the soul, voyaging, voyaging, voyaging.

—Walt Whitman

A Fresh Breeze (detail) by John Callow.

York City Art Gallery, Great Britain.

Pine Forest in the Snow, Yosemite National Park
by Ansel Adams (1932).

250   The Elements of Poetry

This famous poem has been the subject of a great deal of critical analysis. Why? On a quick reading, the poem seems to be a simple, straightforward account of a man who stops briefly to watch snow falling in the woods at night. But there is much more to this poem than meets the eye. If we read it only on a literal level, we will miss its deeper, symbolic meanings.

When we read something on the literal level, we absorb the actual, the observable, the matter-of-fact. When we go deeper and read something on the symbolic level, we deal with those unseen or unspoken connections that only the imagination can make. On the literal level, this is a simple poem about a simple event. Read the poem twice. Monitor your reading the second time around by writing down your reactions to any deeper meanings or connections you sense in the text.

Stopping by Woods on a Snowy Evening

Robert Frost

Whose woods these are I think I know.
His house is in the village, though;
He will not see me stopping here
To watch his woods fill up with snow.

5   My little horse must think it queer
To stop without a farmhouse near
Between the woods and frozen lake
The darkest evening of the year.

10   He gives his harness bells a shake
To ask if there is some mistake.
The only other sound's the sweep
Of easy wind and downy flake.

The woods are lovely, dark, and deep,
But I have promises to keep,
15   And miles to go before I sleep,
And miles to go before I sleep.

Responding to the Poem

Analyzing the Poem

Identifying Details

1. On the literal level, why does the speaker decide to move on just as he's enjoying the beauty of the woods?

Interpreting Meanings

2. To understand the poem on a **symbolic** level, we have to make those connections that will convince us that the poem is about much more than our simple literal reading indicates. What might the harness bells remind the speaker of? (What other bells summon us to do things in life?)
3. In contrast to the bells, what do you think the wind "says" to the speaker? Why is it significant that the speaker hears only those two sounds? What **conflict** do they establish?
4. "The woods are lovely, dark, and deep," says the speaker, and follows this statement with "But"—as though scolding himself for being so enchanted with the beautiful scene. This indicates that he has come to his senses and realizes he has commitments—but to what, or to whom? What do you suppose his "promises" are?
5. Robert Frost was asked many times what the "miles to go" and the "sleep" in this poem symbolize, but he never answered the questions. When the speaker first says he has "miles to go" before he can "sleep," what is he probably thinking of? What **metaphorical** "sleep" do you think he might mean when he repeats the line?

6. The big question set up by the poem is what those lovely, dark, and deep woods **symbolize** to this traveler. What idea or value in life has he said "no" to in passing them by?
7. Whatever the woods stand for, what has the speaker said "yes" to in passing them by? In other words, what choice has he made?
8. Do you think this poem is about a feeling that we all might have at one time or another in our lives? Explain.

Writing About the Poem

A Creative Response

1. **Extending the Poem.** Imagine that this traveler arrives at his destination late because he stopped to look at the woods. How does he explain his lateness to whoever is waiting for him? Write out what he says when he gets home.

A Critical Response

2. **Comparing and Contrasting Poems.** Written hundreds of years apart, Frost's poem and the following poem have much the same setting (although in different seasons), and they both use English that is simple enough to be understood in any century. Their differences, however, are also apparent. In an essay, compare and contrast the two poems. In a final paragraph, tell which poem you prefer and why. Consider these topics as you prepare to write:

   a. The season the poem is set in
   b. The poem's language
   c. The speaker's feelings about the night
   d. The speaker's feelings about beauty
   e. The poem's message or meaning
   f. The symbolism in the poem (if any)
   g. Your opinion of the poem's message

Night of Spring

Slow, horses, slow,
As through the wood we go—
We would count the stars in heaven,
Hear the grasses grow:

5   Watch the cloudlets few
Dappling the deep blue,
In our open palms outspread
Catch the blessèd dew.

10   Slow, horses, slow,
As through the wood we go—
We would see fair Dian° rise
With her huntress bow:

We would hear the breeze
Ruffling the dim trees,
15   Hear its sweet love-ditty set
To endless harmonies.

Slow, horses, slow,
As through the wood we go—
All the beauty of the night
20   We would learn and know!
             —Thomas Westwood

Reading About the Writer

Robert Frost (1874–1963) was born in San Francisco—a fact often forgotten when his poetry is celebrated as the most distinctive voice to come out of New England in the twentieth century. His first book of poetry was published in England, and with its immediate success in America, Frost began a long career. Despite the influence of modernism on literature, as represented by the poetry of Ezra Pound and T. S. Eliot, Frost continued on his own way. In appearance, he looked like the kind of homespun New Englander for whom he spoke. He was actually a sophisticated man of the world whose use of native scenes and native accents sometimes disguised the fact that his vision of the world was far from simple. As the most honored and famous poet of his time, Frost made one of his last public appearances at the inauguration of President John F. Kennedy in 1961. Other poems by Frost appear on pages 253 and 337.

---

11. **Dian:** the moon, here personified as Diana, the goddess of the hunt.

Anyone who has ever had to make a decision affecting his or her life and future has wondered, "What would have happened *if* . . . ?" By putting that question in terms of a traveler who has to choose between one road and another, the poet symbolizes a common human dilemma. After you read the first stanza, stop and see if you can predict the kind of road this speaker did *not* choose.

The Road Not Taken

Robert Frost

Two roads diverged in a yellow wood,
And sorry I could not travel both
And be one traveler, long I stood
And looked down one as far as I could
5   To where it bent in the undergrowth;

Then took the other, as just as fair,
And having perhaps the better claim,
Because it was grassy and wanted wear;
Though as for that, the passing there
10 Had worn them really about the same,

And both that morning equally lay
In leaves no step had trodden black.
Oh, I kept the first for another day!
Yet knowing how way leads on to way,
15 I doubted if I should ever come back.

I shall be telling this with a sigh
Somewhere ages and ages hence:
Two roads diverged in a wood, and I—
I took the one less traveled by,
20 And that has made all the difference.

Responding to the Poem

Analyzing the Poem

Identifying Details

1. Describe the road the speaker chooses. Why doesn't he think he will ever get a chance to travel down the other road?
2. How does the speaker think he will feel about his choice in the future?

Interpreting Meanings

3. At what time of year does the speaker come upon the two roads? Name at least three feelings that are normally associated with this season. What different emotional effect would the poem have if the decision about the roads had been made in spring?
4. Instead of roads through a garden or a wide-open plain, why do you think the poet uses roads that go through woods? (Think about what the word *woods* suggests, as in the statement "We're not out of the woods yet.")
5. Even though he says the two roads are "really about the same," some factor leads the speaker to choose one over the other. What do you think that factor is? Can you see any special significance in the road he finally chooses? Explain.
6. Explain what you think the speaker means when he says that he "kept" the first road for another day. How do we know that he realizes his choice of paths is utterly final?
7. Do you think the speaker is pleased with his decision, sorry about it, or does he seem to have mixed feelings? Explain.
8. According to Frost himself (see "Focusing on Background," page 255), what is this poem about on a literal level? How might these two roads also be interpreted **symbolically**? What do you think the speaker's choice represents? Is there more than one possibility?
9. Why do you think the speaker's choice has made "all the difference"?
10. What light does the **title** shed on the speaker's feelings about his choice? Is this a common feeling about decisions we make in life?

Writing About the Poem

A Critical Response

1. **Connecting Ideas.** In a paragraph, explain how the following quotation relates to the ideas expressed in "The Road Not Taken." (If you think there is no relationship, explain why.)

> If a man does not keep pace with his companions, perhaps it is because he hears a different drummer. Let him step to the music which he hears, however measured or far away.
>
> —from *Walden,*
> Henry David Thoreau

2. **Explaining the Poet's Comment.** In "Focusing on Background," you'll read that Frost occasionally warned his readers that this was a "tricky poem." In a paragraph, explain what you think Frost meant. In a second paragraph, explain whether or not you agree with him. Before you write, discuss in class what Frost might have meant by the word *tricky.*
3. **Analyzing a Poem.** In a famous introduction to a collection of his poems, Frost made the following comment about poetry. Read his remarks, and then write a brief essay in which you show how you think they apply to either "Stopping by Woods on a Snowy Evening" or "The Road Not Taken." Before you write, restate Frost's remarks in your own words. If any details confuse you, say so in your essay.

> The figure a poem makes. It begins in delight and ends in wisdom. . . . It begins in delight, it inclines to the impulse, it assumes direction with the first line laid down, it runs a course of lucky events, and ends in a clarification of life—not necessarily a great clarification, such as sects and cults are founded on, but in a momentary stay against confusion.
>
> —from "The Figure a Poem Makes,"
> Robert Frost

Analyzing Language and Vocabulary

Words Often Confused

The word *diverged*, a key word in "The Road Not Taken," is sometimes confused with other words that have similar spellings. Match the words in the column on the left with the most appropriate sentence on the right. Then give the meaning of the word you've chosen. Consult your dictionary if you do not know the meaning of a word.

diverge
divert
diverse
divest
divulge

1. The city of San Francisco has a _____ population.
2. Agnes refused to _____ the secrets of her past.
3. The engineers were attempting to _____ the river from its course.
4. The law required them to _____ themselves of all their assets.
5. The railroad tracks began to _____ at the edge of the city.

Focusing on Background
A Tricky Poem

The following note is from a biography of Robert Frost. (Edward Thomas is a British poet who was a friend of Frost's during Frost's years in England.)

". . . [Frost] characterized himself in that poem particularly ['The Road Not Taken'] as 'fooling my way along.' He also said that it was really about his friend Edward Thomas, who when they walked together always castigated himself for not having taken another path than the one they took. When Frost sent 'The Road Not Taken' to Thomas he was disappointed that Thomas failed to understand it as a poem about himself; but Thomas in return insisted to Frost that 'I doubt if you can get anybody to see the fun of the thing without showing them and advising them which kind of laugh they are to turn on.' And though this sort of advice went exactly contrary to Frost's notion of how poetry should work, he did on occasion warn his audiences and other readers that it was a tricky poem."

—from *Frost: A Literary Life Reconsidered*,
William H. Pritchard

THE ROAD NOT TAKEN, TAKEN.

Cartoon for *Unscientific Americans* by Roy Chast.

Spoon River Anthology, from which this poem is taken, is one of the most famous books in American literature. For many years, it was one of the most widely read collections of poetry. What made *Spoon River Anthology* so appealing to millions of readers was its combination of down-to-earth realism and poetic imagination. The realism came from Masters's close observation of life in a small Illinois town. The poetic imagination came from the lawyer-poet's grasp of psychology. These gifts enabled Masters to reveal the deeper meanings of what, on the surface, looked like ordinary lives being lived by ordinary people. Underneath and behind the scenes, however, are lives full of drama and secret desires.

Each poem in *Spoon River Anthology* is spoken by a former inhabitant of Spoon River. Each speaker now "sleeps" on the hill of Spoon River Cemetery. Here, George Gray comes forward to comment on the symbol chiseled onto his tombstone. Read the poem aloud to hear the speaker's tone of voice.

George Gray

Edgar Lee Masters

I have studied many times
The marble which was chiseled for me—
A boat with a furled sail at rest in a harbor.
In truth it pictures not my destination
5   But my life.
For love was offered me and I shrank from its disillusionment;
Sorrow knocked at my door, but I was afraid;
Ambition called to me, but I dreaded the chances.
Yet all the while I hungered for meaning in my life.
10 And now I know that we must lift the sail
And catch the winds of destiny
Wherever they drive the boat.
To put meaning in one's life may end in madness,
But life without meaning is the torture
15 Of restlessness and vague desire—
It is a boat longing for the sea and yet afraid.

Responding to the Poem

Analyzing the Poem

Identifying Details

1. What does George Gray say about the **symbol** chiseled on his tombstone?
2. Explain why he rejected love.
3. What words in lines 7 and 8 **personify** two human experiences? How did George Gray respond to them, and why?
4. According to George Gray, what is the danger of putting "meaning" into one's life? What is the danger of failing to do so?

Interpreting Meanings

5. The central **symbol** in this poem is a sailboat. Why would a boat with a furled sail be an appropriate **metaphor** for death?
6. Why do you think George Gray thinks this boat is really a better **symbol** for his life?
7. In your own words, explain what it means to "lift the sail / And catch the winds of destiny." What do you think "the sea" in the last line stands for?
8. Given what you know of George Gray, explain what he might have done in his life. Describe the sort of meaning you think he wanted and never found.
9. Suppose George Gray had led a life that answered his need for "meaning." Describe the kind of **symbol** that would have been appropriate for his tombstone.

Writing About the Poem

A Creative Response

Creating Metaphors. The speaker of this poem says that "life without meaning . . . is a boat longing for the sea and yet afraid." Create four metaphors that could suggest the quality of a life *with* meaning. Model your metaphors after the one George Gray uses: "Life with meaning is . . ."

Analyzing Language and Vocabulary

What's in a Name?

Names don't always have significance in literature, but at times we do notice a connection between a name and a characteristic of the person who bears it. For example, Charles Dickens, a genius at making up names, called a cruel schoolmaster Wackford Squeers; Shakespeare named a brilliant, mercurial character Mercutio; and Emily Brontë named a brooding man of the out-of-doors Heathcliff.

1. What associations do you make with the color gray? Do you think George Gray led a gray life?
2. What name would you give a character who was just the opposite of George Gray—aggressive, confident, and fearless?
3. What name with symbolic significance would you give the mother in Langston Hughes's poem "Mother to Son" (page 232)?

Reading About the Writer

Edgar Lee Masters (1869–1950) was born in Garnett, Kansas, and brought up in Lewiston, Illinois. Like his father, Masters became a lawyer, but later gave up law for literature. Though he wrote novels and biographies as well as poetry, Masters's literary reputation is based on only one volume of poetry, *Spoon River Anthology*. In this collection of over two hundred poems, the dead people of Spoon River speak their own epitaphs, and from the grave they reveal the truth about their own lives. Masters struck a new note in American literature when he looked under the surface of small-town life. Much of what he saw and recorded was disturbing. Often it did not conform to conventional notions about the American dream, or to those traditional values that stress the harmony of rich and poor and the belief in the even hand of justice.

Ever since storytellers from ancient India began telling beast fables, people have used creatures from the natural world to illustrate all aspects of human behavior, from the wisest to the most absurd. This poem begins as a closely observed description of a creature from the sea, but it ends as something much more than that. Notice the steps by which the poet moves from a literal description of the fish to where she begins to see the fish as a symbol, or as a thing that stands for something more than itself. Read the first four lines of the poem and then stop: What do you predict the speaker is going to do with her catch from the sea?

The Fish

Elizabeth Bishop

I caught a tremendous fish
and held him beside the boat
half out of water, with my hook
fast in a corner of his mouth.
5   He didn't fight.
He hadn't fought at all.
He hung a grunting weight,
battered and venerable°
and homely. Here and there
10   his brown skin hung in strips
like ancient wallpaper,
and its pattern of darker brown
was like wallpaper:
shapes like full-blown roses
15   stained and lost through age.
He was speckled with barnacles,
fine rosettes of lime,
and infested
with tiny white sea lice,
20   and underneath two or three
rags of green weed hung down.
While his gills were breathing in
the terrible oxygen
—the frightening gills,
25   fresh and crisp with blood,
that can cut so badly—
I thought of the coarse white flesh
packed in like feathers,
the big bones and the little bones,
30   the dramatic reds and blacks

of his shiny entrails,
and the pink swim bladder
like a big peony.
I looked into his eyes
35   which were far larger than mine
but shallower, and yellowed,
the irises backed and packed
with tarnished tinfoil
seen through the lenses
40   of old scratched isinglass.°
They shifted a little, but not
to return my stare.
—It was more like the tipping
of an object toward the light.
45   I admired his sullen face,
the mechanism of his jaw,
and then I saw
that from his lower lip
—if you could call it a lip—
50   grim, wet, and weaponlike,
hung five old pieces of fish line,
or four and a wire leader
with the swivel still attached,
with all their five big hooks
55   grown firmly in his mouth.
A green line, frayed at the end
where he broke it, two heavier lines,
and a fine black thread
still crimped from the strain and snap
60   when it broke and got away.

---

8. **venerable:** worthy of respect because of age.

40. **isinglass:** mica; also a type of gelatin made from fish bladders.

Leaping Trout by Winslow Homer (1889).

Portland Museum of Art, Portland, Maine.
Charles Shipman Payson Collection.

Like medals with their ribbons
frayed and wavering,
a five-haired beard of wisdom
trailing from his aching jaw.
65 I stared and stared
and victory filled up
the little rented boat,
from the pool of bilge°

where oil had spread a rainbow
70 around the rusted engine
to the bailer rusted orange,
the sun-cracked thwarts,°
the oarlocks on the strings,
the gunnels°—until everything
75 was rainbow, rainbow, rainbow!
And I let the fish go.

---

68. **bilge:** the water that collects in the bottom of a boat.

72. **thwarts:** the seats of a boat.
74. **gunnels:** the upper sides of a boat.

Responding to the Poem

Analyzing the Poem

Identifying Details

1. As the speaker examines her catch, she uses a series of **similes** and **metaphors** to describe him. Find at least six **figures of speech** in lines 1–40 that help us see the fish.
2. Upon close observation, what does the speaker discover about the history of this fish?

Interpreting Meanings

3. Name the two figures of speech in lines 61–64 that **personify** the fish. How would you characterize the type of person these figures of speech suggest?
4. Explain what you think the speaker means when she says that "victory filled up / the little rented boat."
5. If you know the Biblical account of Noah and the flood that was sent by God to punish human wickedness, you'll recall that when the waters subsided, God arched the rainbow in the sky as a sign of His promise never to threaten the world again. Over the centuries, the rainbow has been seen as a **symbol** of victory over tragedy, of hope over despair. Why, for this speaker, does the little oily rainbow that appears late in the poem suddenly become such a symbol?
6. What clues suggest that the fish might also have **symbolic** meaning? What do you think it symbolizes? How does this explain why the speaker decides to "let the fish go"?
7. "Miss Rosie" (page 230) is much shorter than "The Fish," yet the poems share an idea and a way of expressing it. What idea do the poems have in common?
8. What do you think of the speaker's decision to let the old fish go?

Writing About the Poem

A Creative Response

1. **Writing a Poem.** Write a short poem telling this story from the point of view of the fish. You might begin with the line "I was caught," and end with the line "I was let go." Write at least six lines.

A Critical Response

2. **Analyzing "What Happened" in the Poem.** The first line of this poem is a very simple statement: "I caught a tremendous fish." So is the last line: "And I let the fish go." Between the moment when the speaker announces her catch and the moment when she returns it to the ocean, something important happens, and that is what the poem is all about. Make a list of the speaker's actions in the poem. Then arrange these actions in chronological order—the order in which they happen in the poem. Then, in a few sentences, identify the moment when "something happens" that makes the speaker give up what any other fisher would be only too happy to keep.

Analyzing Language and Vocabulary

Word Histories

Many English words have very long histories—they may have been borrowed from the French, who borrowed from the Romans, who in turn borrowed from the Greeks. In this poem, three words have histories that can be traced back to Greek or Roman gods and goddesses. Use a dictionary to answer the following questions:

1. From what Roman goddess is the word *venerable* derived? Explain the connection between the meaning of *venerable* and this goddess.
2. From what Greek goddess is the word *iris* derived? Explain the connection between one meaning of this word and the goddess.
3. The word *peony* is derived from another name for the Greek god Apollo. What is that name?

Reading About the Writer

Elizabeth Bishop (1911–1979) was born in Worcester, Massachusetts, spent part of her early life in Nova Scotia, attended Vassar College, and then lived for extended periods of time in New York, Key West, Brazil, and Boston. All these places figure importantly in her work, which is notable for simple language that conveys complex ideas and feelings. Bishop is considered one of the most distinctive poetic voices of the twentieth century.

Before you begin reading this poem, make sure you know what a tumbleweed is. (If you didn't know, how could the word itself give you a clue?) You'll find a photograph of tumbleweeds, ready to take off as soon as the wind comes up, on the next page. Tumbleweeds are a number of different types of plants that grow in the American West.

In autumn they break off near the ground and tumble over and over as the wind lifts them up. The sage and greasewood mentioned in the first two lines are other plants that grow in the dry areas of the American West.

Where do you imagine this person is standing (or sitting) as he speaks?

Tumbleweed

David Wagoner

Here comes another, bumping over the sage
Among the greasewood, wobbling diagonally
Downhill, then skimming a moment on its edge,
Tilting lopsided, bouncing end over end
5   And springing from the puffs of its own dust
To catch at the barbed wire
And hang there, shaking, like a riddled prisoner.

Half the sharp seeds have fallen from this tumbler,
Knocked out for good by head-stands and pratfalls°
10   Between here and wherever it grew up.
I carry it in the wind across the road
To the other fence. It jerks in my hands,
Butts backwards, corkscrews, lunges and swivels,
Then yaws away as soon as it's let go,
15   Hopping the scrub uphill like a kicked maverick.
The air goes hard and straight through the wires and weeds.
Here comes another, flopping among the sage.

9. **pratfalls:** falls on the rear end, usually for comic effect; blunders.

Owens Lake and Valley, Inyo Mountains, California.

Responding to the Poem

Analyzing the Poem

Identifying Details

1. If you have ever seen a tumbleweed, you know that this poet has given you a picture of how it "behaves." List at least ten verbs in the poem that tell what the tumbleweed *does*.
2. Identify two **similes** that give the tumbleweed human or animal qualities.
3. What other words **personify** the tumbleweed?

Interpreting Meanings

4. On a literal level, this poem is a detailed description of tumbleweeds, plants that break off from their roots and are carried away by the wind. On a **symbolic** level, however, the poem is about something quite different—something that concerns people. Describe the kinds of people the tumbleweed might symbolize.
5. Name some of the conditions that might make people feel like a tumbleweed—"rootless" and at the mercy of any "wind." How might such people behave?
6. Describe how the speaker seems to feel toward the tumbleweed and the people it represents. Are his feelings critical, or do you detect a tone of amusement as he watches these "mavericks"? Explain.

Writing About the Poem

A Creative Response

Writing a Poem. Pick a type of person or a group of people—artists, athletes, politicians, flirts, wallflowers, teacher's pets, wanderers, hypochondriacs, punk rockers—and see if you can find some object from nature (like a tumbleweed) that could **symbolize** them. Then write a short poem of five to ten lines that describes the actions or behavior of this natural object.

Analyzing Language and Vocabulary

Multiple Meanings

Several words in this poem have multiple meanings. Words with multiple meanings may be of two types.

In one type, the words not only have different meanings but also different origins. The fact that such words are spelled identically is an accident. In the other type, a single word has developed more than one meaning. In this latter type, the meanings of the word are usually related in some way. Use a dictionary to answer the following questions:

1. The poet uses the word *sage* (line 1) to mean a kind of plant. What is another meaning for this word? What are the origins of these two words?
2. What is the meaning of the word *riddled* in line 7? What is another meaning for this word? Do these meanings have the same origin?
3. The word *tumbler* has several meanings. What is its meaning in line 8? In what sense is the word *tumbler* related to a lock? What type of drinking glass does the word *tumbler* refer to? How are all these meanings related?
4. In line 13, the word *corkscrews* is used as a verb. What does it mean? As a noun, what does it mean? Explain the origins of the two words.
5. The word *scrub* (line 15) has many different meanings and two distinct origins. What are the two origins of *scrub*? Identify the meaning of *scrub* as it relates to:

   a. Shrubs or trees
   b. Sports
   c. Cleanliness
   d. Rockets

6. The word *flopping* (line 17) is said to be of "echoic" origin—this means that it is a word that imitates (echoes) the sound of the action it describes (as the words *buzz* and *snap* do). (See page 323.) What action is suggested by the verb *flop?* If you call someone a flop at sports, are you using a related word? Explain.

Reading About the Writer

David Wagoner (1926–   ), who was born in Massillon, Ohio, writes fiction and drama as well as poetry. One reviewer compared the depths of Wagoner's poetry to a well that "goes deeper than one can see." Wagoner has had a long career as a teacher of English; since 1954 he has been on the faculty of the University of Washington in Seattle.

Literature & Language

Using Symbols

1. Many familiar **symbols** have come down to us from the Bible. For example, in the Book of Genesis, Adam and Eve are cast out of the Garden of Eden into a wilderness where the ground is "accursed" and where thorns and thistles grow. For centuries this landscape of the "wilderness" (or wasteland or desert) has symbolized hardship, or the world of bitter experience. Its opposite is the garden, which symbolizes perfect happiness or innocence. See if you can identify what each person or thing below symbolizes. Research in a Bible will help.

   a. An apple
   b. The Ark
   c. A lamb
   d. Leviathan
   e. The Tower of Babel
   f. A mustard seed
   g. Babylon
   h. Goliath

2. In Greek mythology, Hercules took on the task of twelve labors, tasks that no ordinary human being could perform. But he accomplished the labors, and for centuries Hercules has been a symbol of superhuman strength and endurance. See if you can identify what each person or thing below **symbolizes**. Research in a good mythology collection will help.

   a. A trident (a three-pronged spear)
   b. A satyr
   c. A centaur
   d. Venus
   e. Laurel
   f. Apollo
   g. Dionysus

3. Spend an evening looking critically at TV commercials and magazine advertisements. What **public symbols** can you find?

4. Here is a very brief poem that makes its point about human life by using two **symbols**—dust and the rainbow:

   > Oh, God of dust and rainbows, help us see
   > That without dust the rainbow would not be.
   >
   > —Langston Hughes

   a. On a literal level, what is the poet saying about dust and rainbows?

   b. The poet is saying much more than what a literal interpretation would suggest. Suppose dust symbolizes hardship, ugliness, emptiness, death. What, then, does the rainbow symbolize? What is the poet saying?

5. In the following little poem, William Blake uses two **symbols**—a rose and a worm:

   > **The Sick Rose**
   >
   > O Rose, thou art sick!
   > The invisible worm,
   > That flies in the night,
   > In the howling storm,
   > Has found out thy bed
   > Of crimson joy:
   > And his dark secret love
   > Does thy life destroy.
   >
   > —William Blake

   a. On a literal level, what is this poet saying about a rose and a worm?

   b. Any reader would realize at once that there is much more to this mysterious poem than meets the eye. When we look for symbolic meanings, we might begin to understand the poem's message. The rose, for example, usually symbolizes beauty, goodness, perfection, love. Here, the rose might also symbolize innocence. What, then, does the worm that "destroys" the rose symbolize?

Writing

Using Symbols. Write a brief poem based on one of the poems you've read in this exercise.

1. Write two lines constructed like Hughes's, in which you tell how an ugly or undesirable part of creation is necessary to create beauty.

2. Write a poem that describes the destruction of beauty. Open with the line "Oh _____, you are sick!"

PARAPHRASING AND INTERPRETING A POEM

Writing Assignment

Write a five-paragraph essay in which you first paraphrase the poem "Mother to Son" (page 232) or "Tumbleweed" (page 261) and then interpret and respond to the poem's message.

Background

Understanding a poem's meaning is a two-step thinking process that involves paraphrasing and interpreting—in that order. Before you can interpret a poem, you must understand what it says.

To **paraphrase** a poem is to explain in your own words what the poem says line by line, sentence by sentence. When you paraphrase a poem, you must rephrase each **figure of speech** to be sure you understand the poet's comparisons. You must also supply missing words and rephrase **inverted** sentences so they are in normal English word order.

Yet even if you were to restate a poem completely in your own words, you might still have no idea what the poem means—what point the poet is trying to make. To **interpret** a poem is to explain what it means. When you interpret a poem, you have to *think* about all the details that you've stated in your paraphrase and try to see what they add up to. In nearly every case, you'll find that if you read carefully and listen closely, the poet will help you out. Sometimes a single line or phrase gives the meaning away. At other times, you'll have to read between the lines to catch the poet's message.

Think of a paraphrase as a listing of information leading to an interpretation. But remember that a paraphrase can never be a substitute for the poem itself, any more than the most eloquent description of a beautiful day can ever replace the actual experience of the day itself.

Prewriting

Before you begin your writing assignment, read "The Courage That My Mother Had" by Edna St. Vincent Millay and the model essay that follows.

The Courage That My Mother Had

The courage that my mother had
Went with her, and is with her still:
Rock from New England quarried;
Now granite on a granite hill.

5 The golden brooch my mother wore
She left behind for me to wear;
I have no thing I treasure more:
Yet, it is something I could spare.

Oh, if instead she'd left to me
10 The thing she took into the grave!—
That courage like a rock, which she
Has no more need of, and I have.

—Edna St. Vincent Millay

"The Courage That My Mother Had"

The subject of "The Courage That My Mother Had" by Edna St. Vincent Millay is the courage and strength of character of the speaker's mother.

In the first stanza, the speaker looks to nature to find something that will show us exactly what her mother's courage was like. In the New England countryside, she finds something solid and enduring—something that can survive heat and cold, rain and wind, time and tide.

Cites title and author.
Sums up poem's subject.

Begins paraphrase of first stanza.

Instead of describing her mother's courage literally by saying, "My mother was a woman who could face up to anything," she uses a metaphor. She tells us that her mother's courage was "Rock from New England quarried." Now, she points out, her mother and her courage are "granite on a granite hill." In other words, her mother has died; both she and her courage lie buried beneath a granite tombstone.

Rephrases a metaphor.

In the second stanza, the speaker introduces a new image: a golden brooch, a piece of jewelry that her mother wore and left behind for her daughter to wear. The speaker says she has nothing of her mother's that she treasures more than the brooch, yet it is something she "could spare." That is, it is something she could do without.

Explains a term.

In the last stanza, the speaker expresses feelings of loss and regret. She wishes that her mother could have left her courage instead of the gold pin. Her mother no longer needs the courage, but her living daughter needs it badly.

Rephrases a line.
Describes tone of stanza.

The poem reveals a contrast between material possessions and human values. Material possessions can be bought and sold, passed from one generation to another. But human values like courage cannot be traded in the marketplace or left behind in wills. The speaker made me feel her sadness in thinking about how her mother's courage is now gone forever. It is strange that parents can give us gold and jewels, but they cannot give us qualities like courage that are even more precious and important to our lives.

States interpretation of poem's meaning.

Gives response to poem.

Writing

Reread "Mother to Son" or "Tumbleweed" carefully several times. Notice the questions you ask yourself as you read. Write these questions down, and try to answer them as you go along. As you read, record your responses to the poem as well: *I liked this line. I'm not sure I agree with this idea. This reminds me of someone I know. I don't get this wording.*

Your paraphrase of the poem will deal with the poem line by line. Treat every idea in the order in which the poet presents it. Rephrase each figure of speech in your own words; be sure to explain what is being compared with what.

In your interpretation, tell what message the poem suggests to you. How do the poet's figures of speech help convey this message?

Checklist for Revision

1. Have you cited the poem's title and author?
2. Have you paraphrased *all* of the poem's details and figures of speech in the order in which they occur in the poem?
3. If you have quoted directly from the poem, have you checked the quotation for accuracy, used quotation marks, and cited line numbers?
4. In the final paragraph, have you clearly stated your interpretation of the poem's message, and your response to it?
5. Have you checked: Spelling? Punctuation? Capitalization? Sentence structure? Paragraph organization?

O for a life of sensations rather than of thoughts!

—John Keats

Imagery in Poetry

An **image** is a representation of anything we can see, hear, taste, touch, or smell. Realistic painters and sculptors make images that imitate what they see. Poets do not draw lines, make shapes, or use colors; they confine themselves to words. Poets use nouns to name people, places, and things; verbs to name actions; and adjectives and adverbs to add shades of detail and meaning. A painter or sculptor can create an image of an apple so true-to-life that we'd like to eat it or feel its weight and roundness in our hands. A poet can only use words to make us see and feel a "ruddy," "plump," or "heavy" apple.

Consequently, when we read poetry, we cannot remain passive. We must participate with the poet by seeing not only with our eyes but also with our minds. We must apply our own imaginations to the apple when the poet describes it.

What Imagery Reveals

Imagery, then, names something we can see, smell, taste, touch, or hear. Imagery is also the particular descriptive shading the poet chooses to give that sensory experience: a *ruddy* apple, a *swollen* apple, an apple *sweet* and *juicy,* an apple as *shiny as marble.*

We can even make distinctions among poets purely on the basis of the imagery they use. We can tell whether poets are identified with city life or country life, with the nineteenth century or the twentieth. We can tell whether they are more concerned with nature or with human society. We can often tell, just by examining their imagery, what kinds of personalities the poets have and from what perspectives they view their own experiences and times.

To see how images work, let's look at two poems that use the moon as their central image. The first poem introduces many variations on its main image. Notice that there's one image in this poem that could only have come from a poet writing after 1969, when humans first explored the moon.

"**W**hen we read poetry, we cannot remain passive. We must participate with the poet by seeing not only with our eyes but also with our minds."

Moons

There are moons like continents,
diminishing to a white stone
softly smoking
in a fog-bound ocean.

5   Equinoctial moons,
immense rainbarrels spilling
their yellow water.

Moons like eyes turned inward,
hard and bulging
10 on the blue cheek of eternity.

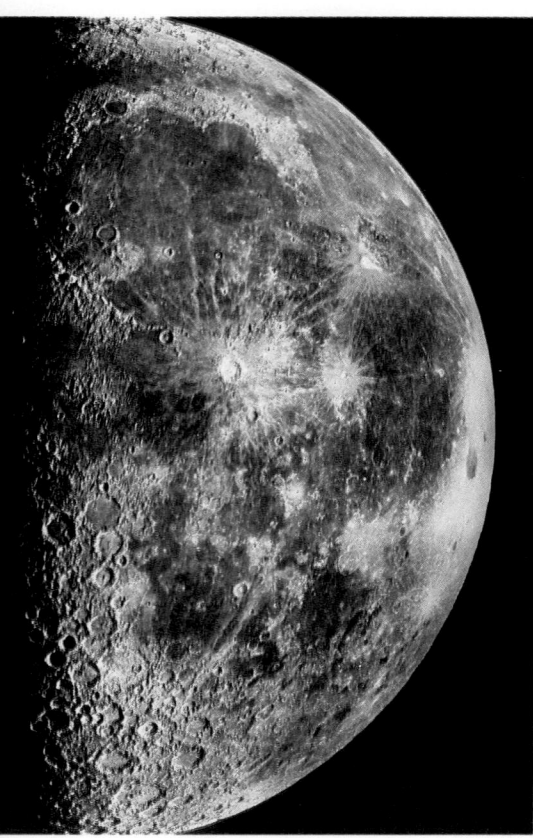

And moons half-broken,
eaten by eagle shadows . . .

But the moon of the poet
is soiled and scratched, its seas
15   are flowing with dust.

And other moons are rising,
swollen like boils—

in their bloodshot depths
the warfare of planets
20   silently drips and festers.

—John Haines

Although the moon is the central image in this poem, we see more than just one moon. As the imagination of the poet transforms this central image into many images, we see many different moons.

Stanza 1. When the moon is full and the night clear, the moon could be seen as a continent viewed from space, especially the icy-white continent of Antarctica. And when, days later, the moon begins to wane, or diminish, we might see it on a cloudy night exactly as the poet wants us to—as a "white stone" that seems to smoke in the "fog-bound ocean" of the sky.

Stanza 2. An "equinoctial" moon is one that rises during late September and March, when day and night are of equal length. (This is the type of moon that causes especially high tides.) At these times, says the poet, the golden moonlight that we see on fields or lakes or the ocean seems to be yellow water spilling from a huge rain barrel.

Stanza 3. Suddenly the moon is seen in human terms. "Turned inward" is the way the eyes of a saint or a mystic might be described. This image leads to another image based on the comparison of the sky with "the blue cheek of eternity."

Stanza 4. This poet does not have a sentimental picture of the new moon as a little boat, or as a crescent, or even as a fingernail. To him, the new moon is "half-broken," as though it had been gnawed away by an eagle (perhaps by *The Eagle* spaceship).

Stanza 5. *This* moon is the moon of our time—the only moon that has ever been visited by human beings. "The moon of the poet" is the moon of romance and mystery and love songs. This romantic and beautiful moon is now, thanks to modern technology, "soiled and scratched." Furthermore, we now know that its great craters, or "seas," are really covered with dust that clings to the boots of astronauts.

Stanzas 6 and 7. Even after all these images of the moon, the poet still has "other moons" in mind. Notice how the imagery turns particularly ugly. The poet doesn't say what he thinks these "rising" moons are, but he describes them as "swollen like boils" and "bloodshot." Perhaps the poet identifies these moons with the troubles of humanity, especially the threat of war, which for the first time in history could involve a planet other than our own and could destroy our own planet.

To see how another poet, living in a different time and place, can take the same noun—*moon*—and give it an entirely different character, look at the following poem by Emily Dickinson. This poem was written more than a hundred years before Haines's poem, long before the romantic moon of the poets had become "soiled and scratched" by scientific instruments, and long before the two great wars changed the way poets looked at the world. Dickinson's moon is personified as a beautiful woman.

> The Moon was but a Chin of Gold
> A Night or two ago—
> And now she turns Her perfect Face
> Upon the World below—
>
> 5   Her Forehead is of Amplest Blonde—
> Her Cheek—a Beryl° hewn—
> Her Eye unto the Summer Dew
> The likest I have known—
>
> Her Lips of Amber never part—
> 10 But what must be the smile
> Upon Her Friend she could confer
> Were such Her Silver Will—
>
> And what a privilege to be
> But the remotest Star—
> 15 For Certainty She takes Her Way
> Beside Your Palace Door—
>
> Her Bonnet is the Firmament°—
> The Universe—Her Shoe—
> The Stars—the Trinkets at Her Belt—
> 20 Her Dimities°—of Blue—
>
>   —Emily Dickinson

6. Beryl: a mineral that usually occurs in crystals of blue, green, pink, or yellow.

17. Firmament: the sky.

20. Dimities: dresses made of dimity, a sheer, cool, cotton material.

Imagery and Feelings

These two "moon" poems show us something else that imagery can do. The poets, through their use of imagery, tell us how they *feel* about the moon. Haines's images of the "moon of the poet" are ironic and violent. As we see this moon in our minds, we share his feelings of sadness and even rage or fear over the human capacity for destruction.

Dickinson, on the other hand, uses images that help us see another moon and share other kinds of feelings. All of her images are romantic. Images of gold, beryl, dew, amber, silver, trinkets, and dimities help us perceive feelings of wonder, admiration, and perhaps playfulness.

Thus, images are not made just for the eye; when we read poetry, we also must perceive the feelings carried by the images. We must arrive at that point where we can say to the poet not only "I see the picture you are creating" but also "I see what you are feeling," or "I see what you mean."

"Images are not made just for the eye; when we read poetry, we also must perceive the feelings carried by the images."

Think of this poem as one of those picture puzzles in which you move your pencil from number to number until a whole scene emerges. Here, let your imagination move from image to image, just as though they were numbers in a puzzle. Then describe the picture that the images create.

Abandoned Farmhouse

Ted Kooser

He was a big man, says the size of his shoes
on a pile of broken dishes by the house;
a tall man too, says the length of the bed
in an upstairs room; and a good, God-fearing man,
5   says the Bible with a broken back
on the floor below the window, dusty with sun;
but not a man for farming, say the fields
cluttered with boulders and the leaky barn.

A woman lived with him, says the bedroom wall
10   papered with lilacs and the kitchen shelves
covered with oilcloth, and they had a child
says the sandbox made from a tractor tire.
Money was scarce, say the jars of plum preserves
and canned tomatoes sealed in the cellar-hole,
15   and the winters cold, say the rags in the window frames.
It was lonely here, says the narrow gravel road.

Something went wrong, says the empty house
in the weed-choked yard. Stones in the fields
say he was not a farmer; the still-sealed jars
20   in the cellar say she left in a nervous haste.
And the child? Its toys are strewn in the yard
like branches after a storm—a rubber cow,
a rusty tractor with a broken plow,
a doll in overalls. Something went wrong, they say.

Responding to the Poem

Analyzing the Poem

Identifying Details

1. By piling **image** upon image, this poem is like a series of close-up photographs that tell a story about people by showing us their things. Cite the things and tell what each one says.

Interpreting Meanings

2. In stanzas 1 and 2, the speaker analyzes each thing and comes up with a fact or conclusion about it. In stanza 3, the speaker tries to put some of the facts together to come up with a larger picture or story. In some cases, the speaker simply looks harder at the original fact

Taylor, Arizona, 1945 by Frederick Sommer. The Center for Creative Photography, University of Arizona, Tucson.

to see if there is any further meaning to be found in it—like a detective poring over the evidence, hoping for a flash of insight. For instance, at first (line 13) the sealed jars in the cellar merely "say" that "Money was scarce." But then in lines 19–20, what new interpretation of their meaning does the speaker discover? Find another **image** that reinforces this interpretation.

3. Reread the poem. When you've finished, summarize what you know about the man, the woman, and the child. What inferences can you make to explain what happened?

4. Are there any clues in the poem indicating whether the "something" that "went wrong" came from outside or inside the farm itself? Explain.

5. What meaning or feeling would be lost from the poem if the child's sandbox had been made from plastic and wood, or if the toys had been a Barbie doll and a battery-powered racing car?

6. How do the **images** in this poem make you feel? Do you think the poem has any meaning for life as you know it today?

Writing About the Poem

A Creative Response

1. **Writing a Journal Entry.** Suppose you are one of the family members about to leave your home. Write an entry in your journal describing your last night in the house.

2. **Imitating the Writer's Technique.** In a paragraph or a poem, describe a room, a house, or a shop by presenting a series of **images** that "say" something about the person who lived or worked there. Imitate Kooser and tell directly what your images "say" about the person.

Reading About the Writer

Ted Kooser (1939–   ) graduated from Iowa State University and received his master's degree from the University of Nebraska. Although he has built a successful career in insurance, Kooser has also found time to write poetry. He has received two fellowships from the National Endowment for the Arts. Another of his poems is on page 374.

A. E. Housman spent the early years of his life near a part of western England called Shropshire. He wrote about its people, towns, and countryside in poems as clear as water from a brook. Spring comes early and suddenly to Shropshire. Its cherry trees are in bloom even by an early Easter (in parts of the United States they might not blossom until late April or the middle of May). This fact makes Housman's connection between cherry blossoms and snow quite natural, since one quickly follows the other.

What you might remember best about this poem is the image of the cherry trees laden with blooms that look like snow. But notice how, for the poet, this image sets up some very sober thoughts.

Loveliest of Trees

A. E. Housman

In a Shoreham Garden by Samuel Palmer. Watercolor.

Victoria and Albert Museum, London.

Loveliest of trees, the cherry now
Is hung with bloom along the bough,
And stands about the woodland ride°
Wearing white for Eastertide.

5 Now, of my threescore years and ten,°
Twenty will not come again,
And take from seventy springs a score,
It only leaves me fifty more.

And since to look at things in bloom
10 Fifty springs are little room,
About the woodlands I will go
To see the cherry hung with snow.

---

3. **ride:** a bridle path.
6. **threescore years and ten:** the Biblical span of life, seventy years.

Responding to the Poem

Analyzing the Poem

Identifying Details

1. What words **personify** the cherry tree?
2. What line tells you how old the speaker is?
3. How many more "springs" does the speaker have left to see the cherry trees in bloom?
4. The last stanza suggests the reason the speaker has decided to make a tour of the woodlands to see the cherry trees. What is that reason?
5. What final startling **image** helps us see the way he sees the cherry trees now?

Interpreting Meanings

6. Some readers believe that the "snow" the speaker sees is really snow. Others believe that Housman is only comparing the white blossoms to snow. What do you think, and why?
7. How is his last wintry **image** appropriate, considering what is really on the speaker's mind?
8. What does the speaker's final resolution tell us about the kind of life he wants to live?
9. What other experiences in life might make someone feel the way this speaker feels?

Writing About the Poem

A Creative Response

1. **Imitating the Poem.** Suppose you want to describe one thing you would miss when your "threescore years and ten" (probably more, nowadays) are completed. Write at least two lines of poetry (or prose if you prefer), beginning with these words:

   > I will go about the . . .
   > To see . . .

   If you prefer, write from the point of view of another person, real or fictional.

A Critical Response

2. **Comparing and Contrasting Poems.** In at least one paragraph, compare and contrast Housman's poem with Robert Frost's "Stopping by Woods on a Snowy Evening" (page 251). Before you write, fill in a chart like the following one to help you organize your thoughts.

	Housman	Frost
What happens to speaker in each poem?		
What does nature remind each speaker of?		
What is poem's main image?		
What is speaker's philosophy of life?		

Analyzing Language and Vocabulary

Connotations

In addition to their strict dictionary definitions, some words also have **connotations**—associations and emotions that usage has attached to the word. In this poem, the word *snow* has strong connotations, or emotional power.

1. List all the emotions (good and bad) that you feel when you hear the word *snow*. List all the things that you associate with *snow*.
2. Suppose the poet had compared the blossoms to one of the following white things, instead of to snow. What feeling or surprise would be lost? What would be added? Which of these images would be inappropriate in the poem?

   a. White cotton
   b. Curly white hair
   c. A swan's feathers
   d. Scoops of vanilla ice cream

Reading About the Writer

A. E. Housman (1859–1936) is one of those rare poets whose whole career is associated with one book. In his case it is *A Shropshire Lad,* a collection of poems drawing upon the customs and scenes of his own region and of Shropshire (where oddly enough, Housman never lived). But local color is merely a factor in Housman's work. His themes are universal, particularly those he dwelt upon most: the sad beauty of nature as it reminds us of our mortality, the brevity of youth, and life as a continual state of mourning for what has past. Another of Housman's poems appears on page 361.

A poacher is a trespasser—usually someone who hunts or fishes on someone else's land. A poacher invades private property and uses it as if he or she had every right to be there. See how the imagery describing their setting helps to characterize the poachers in this poem.

The Elk

Hugh McNamar

In winter poachers had used the cabin.
Their empty beer and spaghetti
cans were in one corner,
and fence posts had been burned
5 in the old pot-bellied stove. Some
were left smoldering when,
hearing the truck turn up the road,
the three of them left by the
sun porch door. There,
10 not even gutted or bled,
we found him hanging
from the rafter beam,
hard and turning on the creaking rope.
Just that morning he had probably come

15 down to where the snow was blown
from the grass around the house.

We stayed one weekend in summer
to fish the stream.
Away from the city sounds
20 at night, we could only turn
in our sleeping bags on the floor
and listen: outside insects moved
against the screen; and in such
stillness, almost heard, was
25 the turning of a rope
and something large and restless.

Responding to the Poem

Analyzing the Poem

Identifying Details

1. What did the poachers leave behind when they hurried away from the cabin?
2. How long had the elk been dead? How do you know this?

Interpreting Meanings

3. Based on the **images** of what they left behind, describe the kind of people you think the poachers are. How do the people referred to as "we" differ?
4. Explain what the speaker means when he says that the elk was "not even gutted or bled." Why do you think this fact offends him?
5. One sound **image** dominates this poem, even in the stillness of the night. Find the line that describes that sound. What mood or feeling does it create?
6. What could the last **image** of "something large and restless" be—besides (or in addition to) the body of the elk?
7. If this poem did not have a **title,** would you know what it was about? Do you think this is the best title for the poem? Explain.

Writing About the Poem

A Creative Response

Creating Sound Images. Create two or three images that suggest each of the following moods or feelings. Have your images describe particular *sounds.*

Horror	Tension	Stillness
Loneliness	Despair	Relief

Alvaro and Christina by Andrew Wyeth (1968). Watercolor.

William A. Farnsworth Library and
Art Museum, Rockland, Maine.

Analyzing Language and Vocabulary

Multiple Meanings

In this poem, McNamar uses at least four words that have more than one meaning. However, he intends only one precise meaning for each of the words. Refer to the poem or to a dictionary as needed to answer the following questions:

1. What would we mean by *poacher* if we said that "we had cooked the salmon" in one?
2. *Smoldering* can mean "burning without smoke or flame," and it can also mean "showing subdued signs of anger or hatred." Which meaning is intended in line 6? Can you think of any connection between those two meanings? If so, what do you think it is based on?
3. As a noun, the word *post* has three meanings. Which two meanings were *not* intended in this poem?
4. A *beam* can be any of a variety of long, heavy, horizontal crosspieces in a structure or a machine. It can also mean "the widest part," as in the breadth of a ship. How is the word used in this poem? What is the meaning of *beam* as it relates to light? To a person's face? What connection do you think might exist among all of these meanings?

Before you begin reading the poem, think about what the word *courtesy* means. What does it mean to say "by courtesy of the Queen," or "by courtesy of the management"?

The Meadow Mouse

Theodore Roethke

I

In a shoe box stuffed in an old nylon stocking
Sleeps the baby mouse I found in the meadow,
Where he trembled and shook beneath a stick
Till I caught him up by the tail and brought him in,
5 Cradled in my hand,
A little quaker, the whole body of him trembling,
His absurd whiskers sticking out like a cartoon-mouse,
His feet like small leaves,
Little lizard-feet,
10 Whitish and spread wide when he tried to struggle away,
Wriggling like a minuscule puppy.

Now he's eaten his three kinds of cheese and drunk from
    his bottle-cap watering-trough—
So much he just lies in one corner,
His tail curled under him, his belly big
15 As his head; his batlike ears
Twitching, tilting toward the least sound.

Do I imagine he no longer trembles
When I come close to him?
He seems no longer to tremble.

II

20 But this morning the shoe-box house on the back porch is
    empty.
Where has he gone, my meadow mouse,
My thumb of a child that nuzzled in my palm?—
To run under the hawk's wing,
Under the eye of the great owl watching from the elm
    tree,
25 To live by courtesy of the shrike,° the snake, the tomcat.

I think of the nestling fallen into the deep grass,
The turtle gasping in the dusty rubble of the highway,
The paralytic stunned in the tub, and the water rising—
All things innocent, hapless,° forsaken.

25. **shrike:** a songbird that impales its prey
on thorns.

29. **hapless:** unfortunate.

Responding to the Poem

Analyzing the Poem

Identifying Details

1. Find at least three **images** that emphasize the smallness of the meadow mouse. Name the image you think is most effective in making us realize just how tiny the mouse is.
2. Which of these images are created by **similes** and **metaphors**?
3. What **images** of other helpless creatures does the speaker present?

Interpreting Meanings

4. Why do you think the meadow mouse disappeared, even though he had "eaten his three kinds of cheese" and seemed "no longer to tremble"?
5. The speaker worries that his little mouse will survive only "by courtesy of the shrike, the snake, the tomcat." The unexpected word here is *courtesy*. Does the speaker really mean that these predators are courteous or polite to small creatures like the meadow mouse? What does he really want us to feel about the fate of the weak in the natural world?
6. At the end of the poem, the speaker's concern for his own little creature broadens to a concern for other creatures also in need of rescue and protection. Describe what would be lost from the meaning of the poem if the speaker had omitted the last four lines.
7. If you were reading this poem aloud, what tone of voice would you use to read lines 20–25?
8. Add at least two other "innocent, hapless, forsaken" creatures to the list in the last stanza.

Writing About the Poem

A Creative Response

Imitating the Poem. In a paragraph or poem, describe another tiny creature. Use at least three **images,** including at least one that describes its food and drink, to help your reader imagine how very small it is. (Roethke does that here by calling a bottle cap the little mouse's "watering trough.") At the end of your description, tell what larger creatures of nature your subject lives "by courtesy of."

Analyzing Language and Vocabulary

Context Clues

As you read a poem like "The Meadow Mouse," you will occasionally find a word that is not already in your vocabulary. When that happens, you may be able to guess at the word's meaning by studying its context. **Context clues** may be found in the words surrounding the unknown word, or they may come from the circumstances, or "context," of the entire poem or story. For example, in a phrase such as "tiny, almost infinitesimal creature," *tiny* is a clue to the meaning of *infinitesimal* (which means "too small to be measured," "infinitely small"). In an article about dentistry, the subject itself is a clue that the word *bridge* does not refer to a structure built across a body of water.

1. The words *shrike* and *hapless* are footnoted. Suppose there were no footnotes to tell you the meanings of these words; are there any context clues you could use to guess at their meanings?
2. In another context, what could *quaker* (line 6) mean? How do you know what it means here?
3. What word in line 11 is a clue to the meaning of *minuscule?* (What clue in the structure of the word itself also points to its meaning?)
4. From context clues, what do you think might be the meaning of *nestling* (line 26)? Compare your guess with the dictionary meaning.

Reading About the Writer

Theodore Roethke (1908–1963) was born in Saginaw, Michigan, to a family of German descent whose business was to supply florists from huge greenhouses on their own property. These greenhouses eventually played a great part in Roethke's poetic career. Roethke spent most of his life as a teacher in college classrooms; he became famous when his poetry evolved from its strict formal beginnings into the open forms of which he was a master. His great theme is nature, but with a difference. While many poets observe and record natural phenomena, Roethke attempts to reunite human consciousness with the powers of nature that have been obscured by civilization. He won the Pulitzer Prize in 1954.

I Wandered Lonely as a Cloud

William Wordsworth

I wandered lonely as a cloud
That floats on high o'er vales and hills,
When all at once I saw a crowd,
A host, of golden daffodils,
5   Beside the lake, beneath the trees,
Fluttering and dancing in the breeze.

Continuous as the stars that shine
And twinkle on the milky way,
They stretched in never-ending line
10   Along the margin of a bay;
Ten thousand saw I at a glance,
Tossing their heads in sprightly dance.

The waves beside them danced, but they
Outdid the sparkling waves in glee;
15   A poet could not but be gay,
In such a jocund° company;
I gazed—and gazed—but little thought
What wealth the show to me had brought:

For oft, when on my couch I lie
20   In vacant or in pensive mood,
They flash upon that inward eye
Which is the bliss of solitude;
And then my heart with pleasure fills,
And dances with the daffodils.

Cloud Study by John Constable.

16. **jocund:** merry.

Courtauld Institute Galleries, London. Witt Collection.

Responding to the Poem

Analyzing the Poem

Identifying Details

1. This famous lyric starts with a strong **simile.** What does it tell you about what the speaker is doing and what his mood is?
2. Line 3 introduces the **personification** of the daffodils. Find at least three human qualities or activities that the speaker attributes to them.
3. Name the ways in which the daffodils and their behavior contrast with the speaker's mood. How does the encounter change the speaker's mood?

Interpreting Meanings

4. Only much later does the speaker experience the true "wealth" of his encounter with the daffodils. Explain what you think a "vacant" or "pensive" mood is.
5. What do you think the speaker means by "that inward eye" (line 21)—is he referring to memory or imagination? In either case, how might the "inward eye" be the "bliss of solitude"?
6. Do you think any person would have reacted the same way to this experience—or did this speaker create the richness of the experience for himself? Explain.
7. In the nineteenth century, when this poem was written, people felt that it was important to "commune with nature." They looked for security and comfort in the beauty of natural things and in their ability to renew themselves in endless cycles. Do you think it is possible to experience nature in this way in the last part of the twentieth century? Can you remember seeing something in nature—in growing things, in animals, in weather—that remains in your own "inward eye"? Explain.

Writing About the Poem

A Creative Response

1. **Making a Poem Out of a Journal Entry.** Without changing her words, see if you can make a poem out of Dorothy Wordsworth's journal entry (see "Focusing on Background," which follows). Use just those details you think are "right," and omit the rest.

A Critical Response

2. **Comparing a Journal Entry and a Poem.** Dorothy Wordsworth's account of what she and her brother saw on an April day in 1802 is highly detailed. Her brother's poetic version of what they saw is comparatively lean and spare. Write at least one paragraph comparing the journal entry and the poem. Before you write, use the following chart to identify the similarities and differences between the two accounts.

	Journal Entry
Details not in poem	
Details that contradict poem	
Figurative language in journal similar to that in poem	
Figurative language that is different	
Lesson journal draws from experience (if any)	

Analyzing Language and Vocabulary

Poetic Words and Inverted Sentences

Many dictionaries label contractions like *e'er, 'mid,* and *'tis* (*ever, amid,* and *it is*) as **poetic,** meaning that their use today is mainly confined to poetry. The use of such **contractions,** or shortened word forms, often indicates that a poem was written before the twentieth century, during a time when poets regularly used shortened forms of words to make their lines fit a particular rhythmic beat.

Another poetic device that is still used today is the **inverted sentence.** The word order of the normal English sentence is subject–verb–complement. When one of those elements is out of order, we say that the sentence is inverted, or reversed. When Wordsworth says in another poem, "Strange fits of passion have I known," he is using inverted word order to accommodate his rhythm. (In a normal English sentence, the words would have been in this order: "I have known strange fits of passion.") Notice that another thing happens when this sentence is inverted: more emphasis is given to the important words: "strange fits of passion."

1. Find the three places where Wordsworth uses poetic contractions. What words are they shortened from? If you use the longer word in each line, what happens to the rhythm?
2. Find two inverted sentences in the poem. Rewrite each sentence in normal English word order and read it aloud in the context of the poem. What happens to the rhythm?
3. In either of these inverted sentences, do you think the poet used inversion to emphasize particular words?
4. Too many poetic contractions and inversions can make a poem sound artificial and stiff to modern readers. How did the language of this poem affect you?

Reading About the Writer

William Wordsworth (1770–1850), born in Cumberland, England, was an orphan by the time he entered his teens. A passionate supporter of the French Revolution, Wordsworth and his friend, the poet Samuel Taylor Coleridge, caused a revolution of another sort in 1798. This was the year the two poets published a collection of "revolutionary" new poems called *Lyrical Ballads,* the book that ushered in the Romantic movement in English poetry. In the famous introduction to this volume, Wordsworth and Coleridge urged poets to abandon the formal language and elaborate verse styles of the eighteenth century and to use the words and rhythms of everyday speech. Another feature of this "new" poetry was a deep emotional identification of the human mind with nature—a feature you can see in "I Wandered Lonely as a Cloud." Wordsworth was made England's Poet Laureate in 1843.

Focusing on Background
Where Did the Poem Come From?

William Wordsworth and his sister Dorothy were close companions all their lives. Much of what we know of the poet was recorded in journals that Dorothy kept for many years. Most of her journal entries are about their goings and comings in the Lake District of England, where they lived, about the friends who came to visit them, and about the customs that prevailed in a countryside inhabited by poor and simple people. But, as in this journal entry, now and then Dorothy would record an experience, usually of something in nature, that inspired her brother to write a poem.

"April 15, 1802: The wind seized our breath. The lake was rough. There was a boat by itself floating in the middle of the bay below Water Millock. We rested again in the Water Millock Lane. The hawthorns are black and green, the birches here and there greenish, but there is yet more of purple to be seen on the twigs. We got over into a field to avoid some cows—people working. A few primroses by the roadside—woodsorrel flower, the anemone, scentless violets, strawberries, and that starry, yellow flower which Mrs. C. calls pile wort. When we were in the woods beyond Gowbarrow Park, we saw a few daffodils close to the waterside. We fancied that the lake had floated the seeds ashore, and that the little colony had so sprung up. But as we went along there were more and yet more; and at last, under the boughs of the trees, we saw that there was a long belt of them along the shore, about the breadth of a country turnpike road. I never saw daffodils so beautiful. They grew along the mossy stones about and about them; some rested their heads upon these stones as on a pillow for weariness; and the rest tossed and reeled and danced, and seemed as if they verily laughed with the wind, that blew upon them over the lake, they looked so gay, ever glancing, ever changing. This wind blew directly over the lake to them. There was here and there a little knot, and a few stragglers a few yards higher up; but they were so few as not to disturb the simplicity, unity, and life of that one busy highway. We rested again and again. The bays were stormy, and we heard the waves at different distances, and in the middle of the water. Rain came on—we were wet when we reached Luff's. . . ."

—Dorothy Wordsworth

Allen Ginsberg wrote this poem more than a hundred years after William Wordsworth wrote "I Wandered Lonely as a Cloud." As you read, look for at least one simile that would have never occurred to Wordsworth. Also look for examples of imagery that the earlier poet and his readers would have considered ugly. Yet the two poems have much in common. They both begin with characters who unexpectedly "wander" into a particular scene, and they both end when these characters make statements about the meaning of what they saw. In Ginsberg's poem, the title must be read as the first line. The "Real" (rā·al') is the name of a railroad line.

In Back of the Real

Allen Ginsberg

railroad yard in San Jose
    I wandered desolate
in front of a tank factory
    and sat on a bench
5 near the switchman's shack.

A flower lay on the hay on
    the asphalt highway
—the dread hay flower
    I thought—It has a
10 brittle black stem and
    corolla° of yellowish dirty
spikes like Jesus' inchlong
    crown, and a soiled
dry center cotton tuft
15   like a used shaving brush
that's been lying under
    the garage for a year.

Yellow, yellow flower, and
    flower of industry,
20 tough spikey ugly flower,
    flower nonetheless,
with the form of the great yellow
    Rose in your brain!
This is the flower of the World.

Industry by Preston Dickinson (before 1924). Oil.

Collection of Whitney Museum of American Art, New York. Gift of Gertrude Vanderbilt Whitney. Acq. #31.173.

11. **corolla:** the outer part of the flower, or the petals.

Responding to the Poem

Analyzing the Poem

Identifying Details

1. Where does the speaker wander? Find the word that defines his mood.
2. What kind of flower does the speaker see? What **images** and **similes** does he use to describe it?

Interpreting Meanings

3. How does each of the **similes** in stanza 2 make you feel about the flower? Do the two images seem to go together, or do they seem incompatible? Explain.
4. Good poets are able to draw general truths from very particular events or objects. Why do you think the speaker in Ginsberg's poem calls this ugly but tough flower the "flower of industry" and the "flower of the World"?
5. What more beautiful flower does this ugly "flower of the World" have in its "brain"? Do you think the poet is suggesting that the world we know also reflects a more beautiful and perfect world? What do you think of this idea?
6. The Real is a railroad line, but perhaps the poet is **punning** on the word. What point do you think the poet might be making in the **title**?

Writing About the Poem

A Creative Response

1. **Describing an Object.** In a paragraph or a poem, describe another flower or natural object that you think reflects the world you know. End your paragraph with the last line of this poem. Use at least three **images** that will help your readers see, smell, taste, touch, or hear your object.

A Critical Response

2. **Comparing and Contrasting Poems.** Write at least one paragraph comparing and contrasting Ginsberg's poem and Wordsworth's "I Wandered Lonely as a Cloud." You may come to the conclusion that the connections between the poems are minor; you may feel that the two poems, written more than a century apart, express similar feelings about nature; or you may decide

that Ginsberg's poem is an **ironic** reply or rebuttal to Wordsworth's. Use a chart like the following one to collect your points of comparison and contrast.

	Wordsworth	Ginsberg
What happens in poem		
Setting of poem		
Imagery in poem		
Language of poem		
Message of poem		

Analyzing Language and Vocabulary

Connotations

In this poem, Ginsberg uses many words with strong **connotations**—emotional overtones that go beyond their literal meanings.

1. In line 2, the speaker says, "I wandered *desolate*." In Wordsworth's poem, the speaker says, "I wandered *lonely*." Explain the different connotations of these two words.
2. In stanza 3, Ginsberg uses the synonyms *dirty* and *soiled*. Are these words interchangeable?
3. The word *dread* is used to describe the hay flower in line 8. Would your image of the flower be the same if it were described as *disliked*?
4. In line 20, the flower is described as "tough." What other words could be used in place of *tough*? Do those other words call up the same associations as *tough* does?

Reading About the Writer

Allen Ginsberg (1926–   ) who grew up in Paterson, New Jersey, exploded into public notice with the publication of *Howl,* a furious, passionate attack against what he saw as the complacency of the Eisenhower years. Though many critics condemned this long, free-verse work as crude in style and content, its impact was immediate and unstoppable. *Howl* inspired a whole generation of experimental writers in the 1950's and 1960's, called the Beat Poets.

Open Road from the *Landscape of the Apocalypse* series
by Martin Hoffman (1972). Acrylic.

Virginia Museum of Fine Arts, Richmond.
Gift of Sydney and Frances Lewis.

The breakdown lane is the lane on a highway that is reserved for cars that have to pull over for some reason, usually because of mechanical trouble.

There's a line in the poem that tells you where this highway is headed—Fargo is a city in North Dakota.

Walking in the Breakdown Lane

Louise Erdrich

Wind has stripped
the young plum trees
to a thin howl.
They are planted in squares
5   to keep the loose dirt from wandering.
Everything around me is crying to be
    gone.
The fields, the crops humming to be cut
    and done with.

Walking in the breakdown lane, margin of
    gravel,
between the cut swaths and the road to
    Fargo,

10   I want to stop, to lie down
in standing wheat or standing water.

Behind me thunder mounts as trucks of
    cattle
roar over, faces pressed to slats for air.
They go on, they go on without me.
15   They pound, pound and bawl,
until the road closes over them farther on.

Responding to the Poem

Analyzing the Poem

Identifying Details

1. Where is the speaker and what is she doing?
2. What does the speaker wish she could do?
3. Exactly what **images** does she see in the break-down lane? What does she hear?
4. What details tell you what season it is?

Interpreting Meanings

5. Whose faces are pressed to the slats in the last stanza? How does this **image** make you feel?
6. How would you describe the speaker's mood?
7. What line in the poem do you think is most important in explaining her mood? Do the **images** in the poem support this mood? Explain.

Writing About the Poem

A Creative Response

1. **Using Images.** Write a poem or paragraph of your own called "Walking . . ." (name where you are walking in your title). Use images to evoke your own mood as a walker. Describe what you see and hear as you walk, both on the road and on the sides of the road.

A Critical Response

2. **Comparing and Contrasting Poems.** In a brief essay, compare and contrast this poem with Ginsberg's "In Back of the Real" (page 282). Before you start to write, collect your points of comparison and contrast by filling out a chart like the following one.

	Erdrich	Ginsberg
Speaker of poem and what he or she is doing		
Setting of poem (images)		
Mood of speaker		
Message of poem (if any)		

Analyzing Language and Vocabulary

Diction

Diction, or word choice, can make a great difference in a poem's emotional effect. That is why a poet may spend many hours searching for a fresh, original word that expresses just the right shade of meaning.

1. What kind of sound does the word *bawl* in line 15 make you hear? Would the emotional effect have been different if the verb *snort* or *moo* were used?
2. Does the verb *pound* in line 15 suggest that someone is trying to escape from something? If the poet had used the verb *knock* instead, explain how the emotional effect of the image would be different.
3. The poet could have said in line 8 that she was walking "along the highway" or "on the shoulder of the highway." In using the phrase *breakdown lane*, what emotional overtones does she add to the poem?
4. Do you think the phrase *breakdown lane* has a double meaning in the poem? Explain.

Reading About the Writer

Louise Erdrich (1954–   ), who grew up in Wahpeton, North Dakota, is of Chippewa and German ancestry. (She belongs to the Turtle Mountain Band of Chippewa.) Erdrich has written both poetry and fiction; her novel *Love Medicine* won the National Book Critics Circle Award in 1984. Most of what she writes (like this poem) is set in the part of the country she knows from childhood. Her vivid characters are usually Chippewa—many of them victimized by a raw, new world in which their old traditions no longer apply. Of all Erdrich's considerable talents, one of the most significant is her ability to evoke a sense of place. Erdrich's most recent novels are *The Beet Queen, Tracks,* and *The Crown of Columbus,* the last written in collaboration with her husband, Michael Dorris. Erdrich's most recent collection of poetry is *Baptism of Desire.*

In William Shakespeare's day, any gentleman was expected to be able to produce a sonnet in praise of someone he loved. (Very few sonnets seem to have been written by the women of those times.) To write a sonnet was a challenge, a kind of game. The writer wanted to see how well he could express his feelings while following certain rules. He also wanted to see how close to natural speech his formal poem could sound.

A *sonnet* consists of fourteen lines of poetry with a strict meter and rhyme scheme. The partic- ular form of sonnet favored (but not invented) by Shakespeare came to be known as the Shakespear- ean, or English, sonnet. Its fourteen lines are di- vided into three *quatrains* (rhyming stanzas of four lines each) and a concluding *couplet* (a pair of rhyming lines). Each quatrain usually makes a point or presents an example, and the couplet sums up the message of the sonnet.

Before you read, predict how you think the speaker of this sonnet will answer his own opening question.

Shall I Compare Thee to a Summer's Day?

William Shakespeare

Shall I compare thee to a summer's day?
Thou art more lovely and more temperate.
Rough winds do shake the darling buds of May,
And summer's lease hath all too short a date.
5 Sometime too hot the eye of heaven shines,
And often is his gold complexion dimmed;
And every fair from fair sometime declines,
By chance, or nature's changing course, untrimmed;°
But thy eternal summer shall not fade,
10 Nor lose possession of that fair thou ow'st,°
Nor shall Death brag thou wand'rest in his shade,
When in eternal lines to time thou grow'st:
So long as men can breathe or eyes can see,
So long lives this, and this gives life to thee.

8. **untrimmed:** without trimmings (decorations).

10. **ow'st:** own.

La femme à l'ombrelle tournée vers la gauche by Claude Monet (1886).   Musée d'Orsay, Paris.

Responding to the Poem

Analyzing the Poem

Identifying Details

1. In Shakespeare's day, poets often made extravagant claims about the person they loved. Often they compared the loved one's charms to the beauties of nature. In the first line of the poem, what extravagant comparison does the speaker consider?
2. In the next line, what two general reasons does he give for rejecting this comparison?
3. In lines 3–8, the speaker continues to consider the aptness of his comparison. What **image** does he use to show that summer weather is unpredictable? What is the "eye of heaven," and why is it not constant, or trustworthy?
4. According to lines 7–8, what might happen to any kind of beauty?
5. In the third quatrain (lines 9–12), the speaker makes a daring statement to his lover. What does he claim will never happen?

Interpreting Meanings

6. What does the speaker mean by "eternal lines to time" (line 12)? What is the connection between those eternal lines and the prediction he has made in lines 9–11?
7. The speaker opened the sonnet with a question about whether or not he might find an appropriate **simile** or **metaphor** to describe the person he loves. How has he answered that question? In the final couplet, what does *this* refer to?
8. Would you say that this sonnet is a love poem, or is it really about something else? Explain your opinion.
9. Do you think the poet's bold assertion in the couplet has proved true? In what ways can other kinds of art immortalize someone?

Writing About the Poem

A Creative Response

1. **Answering the Poet.** Suppose you were the person being addressed in this sonnet. Write your answer to the speaker in a prose paragraph or in verse. Do you like what the speaker says, or do you have arguments with it?

A Critical Response

2. **Comparing Two Poems.** The following sonnet is by a contemporary of Shakespeare's, the English poet Edmund Spenser. Write a brief essay comparing and contrasting this sonnet with Shakespeare's. Before you write, think about each poem's **subject, imagery,** and **message.** Which sonnet do you prefer, and why?

> One day I wrote her name upon the strand,°
> But came the waves and washèd it away;
> Again I wrote it with a second hand,
> But came the tide, and made my pains his prey.
> "Vain man," said she, "that dost in vain assay°
> A mortal thing so to immortalize!
> For I myself shall like to this decay,
> And eke° my name be wipèd out likewise."
> "Not so," quod° I, "let baser things devise
> To die in dust, but you shall live by fame:
> My verse your virtues rare shall eternize
> And in the heavens write your glorious name;
> Where, whenas death shall all the world subdue,
> Our love shall live, and later life renew."
>
> —Edmund Spenser

Analyzing Language and Vocabulary

Inverted Sentences

As you know, the word order in the normal English sentence is subject–verb–complement, with the modifier following the word it modifies. When a sentence is not in this order, we say it is **inverted,** or reversed. Poets often use inverted meters to accommodate their rhyme schemes or to emphasize a particular word.

1. What would be the normal English word order in line 5?
2. What words are reversed in line 6?
3. In line 7, where would the prepositional phrase "from fair" normally be placed?
4. What would be the normal word order in line 12?

---

1. **strand:** beach. 5. **assay:** attempt. 8. **eke:** also.
9. **quod:** said.

The form of poetry known as *haiku* (hī′kōō) developed in Japan during the 1500's and remains an important part of Japanese culture to this day. Using only three lines and usually only seventeen syllables, haiku work by means of suggestion and association. By capturing one or two images of daily life, the poet hopes to communicate the experience of a single, frozen moment. As you read these haiku, think about the pictures and associations their images conjure up in your mind.

Four Haiku

Whiter, whiter
Than the stones of Stone Mountain—
This autumn wind.
  —Matsuo Bashō,
    translated by Donald Keene

What piercing cold I feel:
 my dead wife's comb, in our bedroom,
  under my heel. . . .
  —Yosa Buson,
    translated by Donald Keene

Garden butterfly
The child crawls, it flutters,
Crawls again, it flies.
  —Kobayashi Issa,
    translated by Lewis Mackenzie

Girls planting paddy:
Only their song
Free of the mud.
  —Konishi Raizan,
    translated by Geoffrey Bownas
    and Anthony Thwaite

Responding to the Poems

Writing Haiku

It's not easy to define haiku; not even all Japanese people would agree on a definition. How many of these characteristics of the form can you find in the haiku here?

1. A haiku presents an **image** of daily life.
2. Often a word (called a *kigo*) gives a clue to the season the haiku is describing.
3. A haiku only sketches a picture; the reader must fill in the details through association.
4. A haiku conveys a moment of discovery or enlightenment (*satori*).
5. A haiku has three lines and seventeen syllables (five, seven, five). (Not all translators reproduce this syllable count.)

Before you write your own haiku, think of some important moment in your daily life that you want to capture. Then create at least one image that will crystallize this moment and how you felt about it. Include a *kigo,* or seasonal clue. You might write a seasonal cycle of haiku.

Reading About the Writers

Matsuo Bashō (1644—1694), the great haiku master, often expresses the Zen Buddhist belief that all forms of life are one. **Yosa Buson** (1715—1783), second in fame to Bashō, was a painter as well as a poet. He wrote sophisticated haiku filled with clear images and the warmth of romantic love. The life of **Kobayashi Issa** (1763—1827) was filled with poverty and personal tragedy, yet his poetry is noted for its tenderness toward small creatures and children. (His haiku here is about his own daughter.) The haiku of **Konishi Raizan** (1654—1716) have been praised for their bold colloquial language.

The conversational phrasing in this poem is borrowed more from prose than from formal poetry, and its aim is to make the movement of the poem imitate the action of what is being described. Here the "action" is both physical and mental. Before you read, describe the expectations that the word *artist* in the title sets up in your mind. See if the poet surprises you.

The Artist

William Carlos Williams

Little Fourteen-Year-Old Dancer
by Edgar Degas (c. 1880–1881).
Bronze, tulle skirt, and satin hair ribbon. H.39″

    Mr. T.
                bareheaded
                    in a soiled undershirt
        his hair standing out
5   on all sides
                        stood on his toes
        heels together
                arms gracefully
                        for the moment
10   curled above his head.
                    Then he whirled about
                        bounded
        into the air
                and with an *entrechat*°
15   perfectly achieved
        completed the figure.
                My mother
                        taken by surprise
        where she sat
20   in her invalid's chair
                            was left speechless
        Bravo! she cried at last
                    and clapped her hands.
                        The man's wife
25   came from the kitchen:
                    What goes on here? she said.
                            But the show was over.

14. *entrechat* (än′trə·shä′): a leap in ballet during which the
dancer crosses his or her feet several times.

Responding to the Poem

Analyzing the Poem

Identifying Details

1. In lines 1–5, what **images** tell us what Mr. T. looks like?

Interpreting Meanings

2. What do you think of when you hear the word *artist*? Were you surprised at what you see when Mr. T. appears? Why?
3. How does Mr. T.'s appearance contrast with what he achieves?
4. Why is it significant that one of the people who witnesses Mr. T.'s "show" cannot use her own legs? What is her response to the performance?
5. Why is it significant that Mr. T. performs his *entrechat* while his wife is out of the room?
6. An *entrechat* is something that only a highly trained ballet dancer can do—it's not the sort of feat we expect an ordinary person to accomplish. What point do you think the poem is making about the nature of art—about where and when we might expect to find it?
7. What do you think of this idea? Do you agree that our expectations are often confounded? Explain your response.

Writing About the Poem

A Creative Response

1. **Imitating the Poem.** In a few lines of poetry, describe a surprising and extraordinary action that some person accomplishes. This action could occur in a sport, in a dance, in a pool, or walking down a flight of stairs. Imitate Williams's line arrangement, and call your poem "The Artist." You might want to contrast your performer's achievement with his or her appearance.

A Critical Response

2. **Comparing and Contrasting Poems.** Write a brief essay comparing and contrasting "The Artist" and "Miss Rosie" (page 230). Before you write, list the details describing each character's appearance. Then decide how each speaker seems to feel about the character, and *why*. Be sure to state whether you feel these two poems have more similarities or more differences.

Analyzing Language and Vocabulary

Syntax

Syntax refers to the structure of a sentence, to the way the words, phrases, and clauses are arranged to show their relation to one another.

1. How many sentences are in Williams's poem?
2. Tell whether each sentence is simple, compound, or complex.
3. Poets often break their lines to indicate pauses, instead of using punctuation. Rewrite the poem in paragraph form, adding punctuation as needed to make each sentence clear.
4. How has the new form and punctuation changed the way you'd read the poem aloud?

Reading About the Writer

William Carlos Williams (1883–1963) was born in Rutherford, New Jersey, where he lived almost all of his life, and where he died. His profession was that of a pediatrician, who also attended the births of thousands of infants. His practice provided him with unusual opportunities to observe the gritty realities of life as lived by the families of the industrial workers who were his patients. As a poet, Williams was a crusader, determined to rid American poetry of British and academic influences. He wanted American poetry to speak for itself in its own native rhythms and idioms. As a result, in the early part of his career, Williams was considered radical, eccentric, and out of the mainstream of poetry. But he persisted in what he believed and lived to see the day when he was regarded as the most influential voice in American poetry.

Williams won the Pulitzer Prize in 1963, the year he died. Three of his other poems appear on pages 294, 304, and 860.

The speaker describes two experiences in this poem. One is taking place in the present; the other took place many years ago. Watch for images that help you feel that you are witnessing both experiences. (Notice the imagery that includes plants: Elephant ears are plants with large, floppy leaves; zinnias are flowering plants with colorful, sturdy petals.)

The Whipping

Robert Hayden

The old woman across the way
    is whipping the boy again
and shouting to the neighborhood
    her goodness and his wrongs.

5   Wildly he crashes through elephant ears,
    pleads in dusty zinnias,
while she in spite of crippling fat
    pursues and corners him.

She strikes and strikes the shrilly circling
10   boy till the stick breaks
in her hand. His tears are rainy weather
    to woundlike memories:

My head gripped in bony vise
    of knees, and writhing struggle
15   to wrench free, the blows, the fear
    worse than blows that hateful

Words could bring, the face that I
    no longer knew or loved . . .
Well, it is over now, it is over,
20   and the boy sobs in his room,

And the woman leans muttering against
    a tree, exhausted, purged—
avenged in part for lifelong hidings
    she has had to bear.

Gamin by Augusta Savage (c. 1930). Plaster.

The Schomberg Center for Research in Black Culture, New York Public Library.

Responding to the Poem

Analyzing the Poem

Identifying Details

1. What scene is the speaker observing? What experience does it remind him of?
2. At what point in the poem does the speaker stop describing the scene he is observing and start describing the experience he is remembering? At what point does he switch back again to the present? (What punctuation signals each change?)
3. List the **images** that help you to see and hear what is happening in each scene.
4. Find the line that gives the old woman's explanation of why she is whipping the boy. In what line does the speaker tell us what he believes her real reason is?
5. What **metaphor** does the speaker use to describe how the boy's tears affect his own memory? How would you paraphrase this metaphor—that is, express it in your own words?

Interpreting Meanings

6. As used in line 23, the word *hidings* has two possible meanings. What are they? How might each meaning apply to the old woman's life?
7. At the end of the poem, whom do you feel the most sympathy for: the boy, the old woman, or the speaker? Explain.
8. What phrase would you select as the most significant in the poem? Could this phrase have been used as the poem's **title**?
9. What message do you think this poem conveys about the causes and effects of violence? Do you agree with the poet, or do you think he is just making excuses?

Writing About the Poem

A Creative Response

1. **Questioning the Poet.** Suppose you had been able to interview this poet and ask him questions about his poem. What would you want to know about the poem and about his reasons for writing it? Write out three questions you would ask about "The Whipping."

A Critical Response

2. **Interpreting the Poem's Message.** In line 19, the speaker says, "Well, it is over now, it is over." *Yet in a sense, it isn't over at all, certainly not for the speaker and probably not for the boy.* Use this italicized statement as a topic sentence for a paragraph in which you explain how the poem suggests that the whipping each boy received will continue for a long time. Be sure to explain what "it" refers to.

Reading About the Writer

Robert Hayden's (1913–1980) deep respect for the American and British poets who influenced him led to a career that was both successful and controversial. By his mastery of traditional forms, Hayden came to be regarded as the outstanding black poet of his time. Yet in the view of many African American poets, Hayden had "sold out" by losing touch with the freer kinds of poetry being written by his younger contemporaries. Despite these controversies, Hayden was as much involved in black expression and in the promotion of African American aspirations as any of his contemporaries.

A native of Detroit, Hayden attended the University of Michigan. He later pursued a distinguished academic career that took him to Fisk University, the University of Louisville, the University of Washington, and finally back to his alma mater as Professor of English. From 1977 to 1979, Hayden was Incumbent of the Chair of Poetry at the Library of Congress, the first African American poet to hold that office.

Literature & Language

Using Imagery

1. To see how observation can lead to effective **imagery,** make a list of colors that you associate with different aspects of nature or daily life. Starting with the color *red*, see how many different shadings you can add ("blood red," "ruby red," "fire-engine red," and so on). Then do the same thing with *green* ("lime green," "grass green," "sea green," and so on). Continue your list with as many other colors as you like.

2. **Imagery** helps convey meaning by revealing a poet's attitude. In a poem about animals, for instance, the way animals are described can provide important clues to meaning. If the poem shows us images of mangy dogs, scruffy cats, listless elephants, bare-ribbed horses, and moth-eaten lions, we might feel that we are in the midst of a depressing menagerie. But if the dogs are combed and frisky, the cats sleek, the elephants trumpeting, the horses glistening, and the lions thick-maned, chances are the poem will turn out to be a happy one. Take a look around the room and pick out six objects.

   a. What adjectives would you apply to these objects on a cold, cloudy day when you are gloomy and bored?

   b. What adjectives would you apply to them on a bright day when life seems promising and everything reflects your own happiness?

3. Here are poems by three Imagists—poets who believed that **imagery** alone could carry the full emotional message of a poem:

Images

Like a gondola of green scented fruits
Drifting along the dank canals of Venice,
You, O exquisite one
Have entered into my desolate city.

—Richard Aldington

---

   a. Describe what you see happening in this poem.

   b. Do any words in the poem evoke a sensation other than sight?

   c. How do the "dank canals" contrast with the image in line 1?

   d. Who is like the gondola?

   e. Who or what is like the dank canals?

   f. What does the speaker mean by his "desolate city"? What **metaphor** is implied?

   g. What emotions do these images suggest the speaker is feeling?

Wind and Silver

Greatly shining,
The autumn moon floats in the thin sky;
And the fish-ponds shake their backs and flash their dragon scales
As she passes over them.

—Amy Lowell

---

   a. Describe what you see happening in this poem.

   b. How could the sky be "thin"?

   c. What is causing the ponds to "shake" and "flash" in line 3?

   d. What does the silver in the title refer to?

   e. How does the speaker feel about this scene?

The Red Wheelbarrow

so much depends
upon

a red wheel
barrow

glazed with rain
water

beside the white
chickens

—William Carlos Williams

---

a. Name the visual **images** you see in this poem. Are any of these images **figures of speech**?

b. Williams's famous edict about poetry, "No ideas but in things," expressed his belief in the importance of concrete **images** to stir the emotions. What do you think the speaker in this poem means when he says that "so much depends upon" the images he is describing? What idea or meaning would you say these things express?

c. Suppose you had to give new **titles** to each of the preceding poems in this review exercise, and that the titles had to be the name of an emotion or mood. What titles would you choose? Why?

4. The following cartoon is about what **imagery** and **figures of speech** reveal about a writer. What do this writer's images and figures of speech have in common? What do they reveal about him? Do any of them seem interesting to you? Which of them are old clichés?

"*The face of the pear-shaped man reminded me of the mashed turnips that Aunt Mildred used to serve alongside the Thanksgiving turkey. As he got out of the strawberry-hued car, his immense fists looked like two slabs of slightly gnawed ham. He waddled over to the counter and snarled at me under his lasagna-laden breath, 'Something, my little bonbon, is fishy in Denmark.' Slowly, I lowered my grilled cheese sandwich . . .*"

Drawing by Ziegler; © 1983 The New Yorker Magazine, Inc.

5. Suppose you were drawing another cartoon about a writer who draws his or her images from another source: perhaps from sports, TV, clothing, the seashore, the city. Rewrite this cartoon story, using the new images.

Writing

Using Imagery to Express Emotion. To learn how objects can carry a message when they are turned into imagery, write a short poem in which you express an emotion. First choose a title—"Joy," "Sorrow," "Fear," "Contentment," or any other emotion you prefer. Next decide which of the following sets of objects would be more useful to you: the set drawn from city life, or the one from country life:

1. sidewalk, skyscraper, cat, fountain, park bench, street musician, streetlamp
2. barn, road, sheep, pond, flower, schoolhouse, graveyard

Now supply these objects with appropriate adjectives (for instance, *deserted sidewalks* or *wind-ruffled pond*). Or, using similes, compare these objects to something else (*a fountain blowing like a bridal veil* or *sheep like tombstones on a hill*).

Finally, weave these images or similes together to "paint" a scene or to recall a memory that expresses the emotion you've chosen.

Should the objects you choose from these lists suggest other objects you'd like to add, use them too. But in your poem, be sure to use all seven objects from whichever list you've picked.

COMPARING AND CONTRASTING POEMS

Writing Assignment

Write a four-paragraph essay in which you first compare and contrast the following poems by Emily Dickinson and Wendell Berry and then describe your responses to the poems.

Background

Two poems that have at least one thing in common (such as subject, imagery, figures of speech, or theme) can be compared and contrasted. When you **compare** the poems, you tell the specific ways in which they are alike. When you **contrast** them, you tell the specific ways in which they differ.

Prewriting

Begin by reading each poem carefully, recording your responses and questions as you read. Notice that one reader's responses are recorded in the margin of each poem.

A Narrow Fellow in the Grass

A narrow Fellow in the Grass
Occasionally rides—
You may have met Him—did you not?
His notice sudden is—

5   The Grass divides as with a Comb—
A spotted shaft is seen—
And then it closes at your feet
And Opens further on—

He likes a Boggy Acre
10   A floor too cool for corn—
Yet when a Boy, and Barefoot—
I more than once at Noon

Have passed, I thought, a Whip lash
Unbraiding in the Sun
15   When stooping to secure it
It wrinkled, and was gone—

Several of Nature's People
I know, and they know me—
I feel for them a transport
20   Of cordiality—

But never met this Fellow
Attended, or alone
Without a tighter breathing
And zero at the bone—

—Emily Dickinson

Marginal responses:

Who is the narrow fellow? Human or animal?

This must mean "You notice him suddenly."

What's the "spotted shaft"? This is like a riddle.
What does "it" refer to? (The grass.)

"He" is the narrow fellow. He likes wet ground. Must be animal.

Who is the speaker? The poet is a woman.

"Whip lash unbraiding" must be a figure of speech. What is like a whip?

This syntax is not quite normal. It means "When I stooped to secure it."

Who are "nature's people"—people or animals?

The speaker likes other creatures.

The subject of this sentence has been omitted: "But I never met . . ."

"Zero at the bone" sounds like a metaphor. What would it feel like?

The Snake

At the end of October
I found on the floor of the woods
a small snake whose back
was patterned with the dark
5   of the dead leaves he lay on.
His body was thickened with a mouse
or small bird. He was cold,
so stuporous with his full belly
and the fall air that he hardly
10   troubled to flicker his tongue.
I held him a long time, thinking
of the perfection of the dark
marking on his back, the death
that swelled him, his living cold.
15   Now the cold of him stays
in my hand, and I think of him
lying below the frost,
big with a death to nourish him
during a long sleep.

—Wendell Berry

The subject of this poem is clear.

Who is this speaker?

Is the snake alive or dead?

What does this mean? Had he eaten the mouse or bird? What do I have to know about snakes to understand why he was "cold"?

What is the speaker's attitude toward snakes?
What is this "perfection"?

Is "living cold" a contradiction or only an apparent one?

Where is the snake now?
Seems to be thinking of death and life—the "perfection" of nature's cycle?

Go back over the poems at least once and try to answer your own questions. Once you feel you know the poems fairly well, examine each poem to see how it uses the elements of poetry you've studied so far. Focus on one element at a time, and ask yourself these questions: Are the poems alike in this respect or different—and how? Be sure to find specific details from the poems to support your points. Organize your data into two lists, using a chart like the following one.

	Similarities	Differences
Subject		
Speaker		
Figures of speech		
Imagery		
Meaning		

Writing

In your first paragraph, cite the poems' titles and authors. Include a **thesis statement** that tells whether you think the poems are basically more alike than different, or vice versa. In paragraphs 2 and 3, discuss the specific ways in which the poems are similar and different. Support your points by quoting lines or phrases from the poems. In paragraph 4, describe your response to the poems. Tell which one you prefer, and why.

Checklist for Revision
1. In the introductory paragraph, have you included a thesis statement?
2. Have you discussed at least two similarities and two differences?
3. Have you cited lines or phrases from the poems to support your points?
4. In the final paragraph, have you explained your responses to the poems?

A poem is a small . . . machine made of words. . . . Its movement is intrinsic, undulant, a physical more than a literary character.

—William Carlos Williams

The Sounds of Poetry: Rhythm and Meter

History shows us that almost all remembered poetry has something formal about it—that is, it has a distinct **form,** or structure. When a poem is remembered by an individual, it may be as simple as this:

> Mary had a little lamb,
> Its fleece was white as snow.
> And everywhere that Mary went,
> The lamb was sure to go.

What that individual remembers is not so much a statement about a child and her pet, but the *way* that statement is made: the sing-song way it sounds and the predictable way it rhymes. Let's put the same statement in an *in*formal way—that is, without that modest form apparent in the poem's regular beat and rhyme:

> There was this little kid—her name was Mary—and she had a white lamb that kept following her.

Few people would remember anything as ordinary as that.

When a poem is remembered by a nation and becomes part of its literature, the same elements of formality in rhyme and beat are usually apparent. For example, here is a verse from a famous poem that was written to commemorate the first battle in the United States's war for independence. For years this poem could be recited from memory by almost every American schoolchild.

> By the rude bridge that arched the flood,
>   Their flag to April's breeze unfurled,
> Here once the embattled farmers stood,
>   And fired the shot heard round the world. . . .

> —from "The Concord Hymn,"
> Ralph Waldo Emerson

Form, then, is one distinguishing element of poetry, and poetic form is based mainly on the organization of *sounds*.

Sound and Sense

Poets may be idealists or cynics, prophets or philosophers. But first of all they are dealers in language, and they pay a great deal of attention to sounds. Words are sounds—whether they are spoken out loud or merely "heard" by the inner ear. For sounds to make sense, to add up to something more than gibberish, they have to occur in some order or pattern. Let's examine some of the particular forms the sound patterns of poetry can take.

> **"Poets** are dealers in language, and they pay a great deal of attention to sounds."

Refrain: The Oldest Pattern

We'll begin with refrain because it is the oldest sound pattern of all. A **refrain** is a word, a phrase, a line, or even a whole stanza that is repeated exactly, or almost exactly, throughout the poem according to some regular pattern. Often a refrain occurs at the end of a stanza.

Poets have used refrains ever since language was invented. In ancient times, poets used refrains to achieve the power of an incantation—a magic spell brought about by the hypnotic repetition of certain words. Later poets have used refrains for dramatic and emotional effects, as in the following poem.

This poem was written in 1586 by an 18-year-old boy who was imprisoned in the Tower of London and about to be executed. (After he wrote the poem, he was hanged.) Young Tichborne wrote his own elegy using a refrain that sounds and resounds like a tolling bell. (An **elegy** is a poem expressing sorrow over someone who has died.) Notice how Tichborne's refrain—a line repeated at the end of each stanza—reminds us over and over again of how suddenly a life can be snuffed out.

Tichborne's Elegy

*Written with His Own Hand
in the Tower Before His Execution*

My prime of youth is but a frost of cares,
  My feast of joy is but a dish of pain,
My crop of corn is but a field of tares,°
    And all my good is but vain hope of gain;
5   The day is past, and yet I saw no sun,
      And now I live, and now my life is done.

My tale was heard and yet it was not told,
  My fruit is fallen and yet my leaves are green,
My youth is spent and yet I am not old,
10   I saw the world and yet I was not seen;
      My thread is cut and yet it is not spun,
      And now I live, and now my life is done.

I sought my death and found it in my womb,
  I looked for life and saw it was a shade,
15   I trod the earth and knew it was my tomb,
      And now I die, and now I was but made;
My glass° is full, and my glass is run,
      And now I live, and now my life is done.

—Chidiock Tichborne

3. **tares:** weeds.   17. **glass:** hourglass.

Today refrain is only a small part of written poetry, but it occurs constantly in the kind of poetry heard in ballads and popular songs. In fact, many of the songs that make it to the top of the charts are composed of very few words and a heavy refrain repeated over and over again.

> " **T**oday refrain occurs constantly in the kind of poetry heard in ballads and popular songs. In fact, many of the songs that make it to the top of the charts are composed of very few words and a heavy refrain . . ."

Rhythm: The Rise and Fall of Speech

Poetry is a musical kind of speech. Like music, it is based on **rhythm**—that is, on the alternation of stressed and unstressed sounds that make the voice rise and fall. Here's a famous little poem that many children memorize and say at bedtime. Say this out loud, and you'll feel the rise and fall of its rhythm:

> Now I lay me down to sleep.
> I pray the Lord my soul to keep.
> If I die before I wake,
> I pray the Lord my soul to take.

If you listen closely to this poem, you'll hear exactly four stressed syllables repeated in each line. The first and third lines balance these four stressed syllables against three unstressed (or weak) syllables (Now I lay me down to sleep). The second and fourth lines balance the four stressed syllables against four unstressed syllables (I pray the Lord my soul to keep). This repetition of stressed syllables balanced by unstressed syllables creates the rhythm in the poem.

What we have in this little poem is repetition—and repetition is what creates pattern in poetry. To hear the difference, let's abandon the *sound* of our child's poem and express its sense in prose, without worrying about the musical effect:

> Now I'm ready to get in bed and go to sleep. I hope the Lord keeps me well for the night. But if something unexpected happens and I die during the night, I hope my soul goes to heaven.

This is prose. There is a natural rise and fall to the language, a natural rhythm, but there is no *pattern* of stressed and unstressed sounds. Try to memorize it, and you'll find that this lack of pattern makes it more difficult to remember than the poem.

Poets have a choice in the kind of rhythm they can use. They can use **meter**—a strict rhythmic pattern of stressed and unstressed syllables in each line (as in the child's poem and in Tichborne's elegy). Or they can write in **free verse**—a loose kind of rhythm in which the sounds of long phrases are balanced against the sounds of short phrases. A poem written in free verse sounds more like natural speech than like formal poetry.

Meter: A Pattern of Stressed and Unstressed Syllables

Technically speaking, emphasis on a word or syllable is called an accent or a **stress.** In poetry, as well as in ordinary speech, stress is determined both by the meaning of what is being said and by accepted pronunciation. In **metrical poetry** (poetry that has a meter), the stressed and unstressed syllables are arranged in a regular pattern.

" **L**ike music, poetry is based on rhythm."

Here's a stanza written in meter:

He práyeth bést, who lóveth bést
All things bóth gréat and smáll;
For the déar Gód who lóveth ús,
He máde and lóveth áll.

—from *The Rime of the Ancient Mariner*, Samuel Taylor Coleridge

Manuscript of a poem by William Blake (1757–1827).

The Pierpont Morgan Library, New York.

The mark ´ indicates a stressed syllable. The mark ˘ indicates an unstressed syllable. Indicating the stresses this way is called **scanning** the poem.

You'll notice how these lines sound alike and are about the same length. The first and third lines have four stressed syllables and four unstressed syllables. The second and fourth lines have three stressed syllables and three unstressed syllables. The poet sets up his pattern in the first two lines, and then sticks to it with only one variation. Notice the third line. Read it aloud and hear how the first three syllables break the pattern of one unstressed syllable followed by a stressed syllable. Note that we *could* read that line like this:

For the déar Gód who lóveth ús.

But our good sense tells us that an unimportant word like *the* should not receive more emphasis than an important word like *dear*.

In metrical poetry, variation is important. Without any variation at all, meter can become mechanical and monotonous, like the steady tick-tock-tick-tock of a clock. An occasional change in rhythm, as in the third line of the stanza from *The Rime of the Ancient Mariner*, also allows the poet to draw attention to key words in the poem.

Here, just for fun, is a poem that shows what happens when a strict rhythmical pattern is deliberately broken up.

There was a young man from Japan
Whose verses never would scan.
    When they said this was so,
    He said, "Yes, I know,
But I always try to get as many words in the last line
    as I possibly can."

> " **W**ithout any variation at all, meter can become mechanical and monotonous, like the steady tick-tock-tick-tock of a clock."

Five "Feet"

A line of poetry written in meter is made up of metrical units called feet. A **foot** is a unit consisting of at least one stressed syllable and usually one or more unstressed syllables. There are five common types of feet used by poets writing in English. Their names come from Greek:

iamb (iambic): An unstressed syllable followed by a stressed syllable, as in forget, deceive, compare. This line by Tennyson is in iambs:

> The wrinkled sea beneath him crawls

trochee (trochaic): A stressed syllable followed by an unstressed syllable, as in listen, over, lonely. This line from Shakespeare's *Macbeth* is in trochees:

> Double, double, toil and trouble

anapest (anapestic): Two unstressed syllables followed by one stressed syllable, as in understand, seventeen, luncheonette. This line by Byron is in anapests:

> The Assyrian came down like the wolf on the fold

dactyl (dactylic): One stressed syllable followed by two unstressed syllables, as in excellent, opening, temperate. This line from a nursery rhyme uses two dactyls:

> Hickory, dickory, dock

spondee (spondaic): Two stressed syllables, as in heartbeat, airplane, football. This foot would not be used for an entire poem. If it were, it would sound like someone relentlessly hammering nails. But spondees are used several times for emphasis in these lines by Tennyson:

> Break, break, break
> On thy cold gray stones, O sea!

A Trochee (left) encountering a Spondee.

Free Verse

Early in this century, some American and English poets decided that they would rid poetry of its prettiness, sentimentality, and artificiality by concentrating on a new kind of poetry. Calling themselves **Imagists,** they declared that imagery alone could carry the full emotional message of a poem, and that imagery could do this without all the elaborate metrics and stanza patterns of the old poetry they had grown up with. These poets took on the roles of reformers. "We do not insist upon 'free verse' as the only method of writing poetry," they said. "We do believe that the individuality

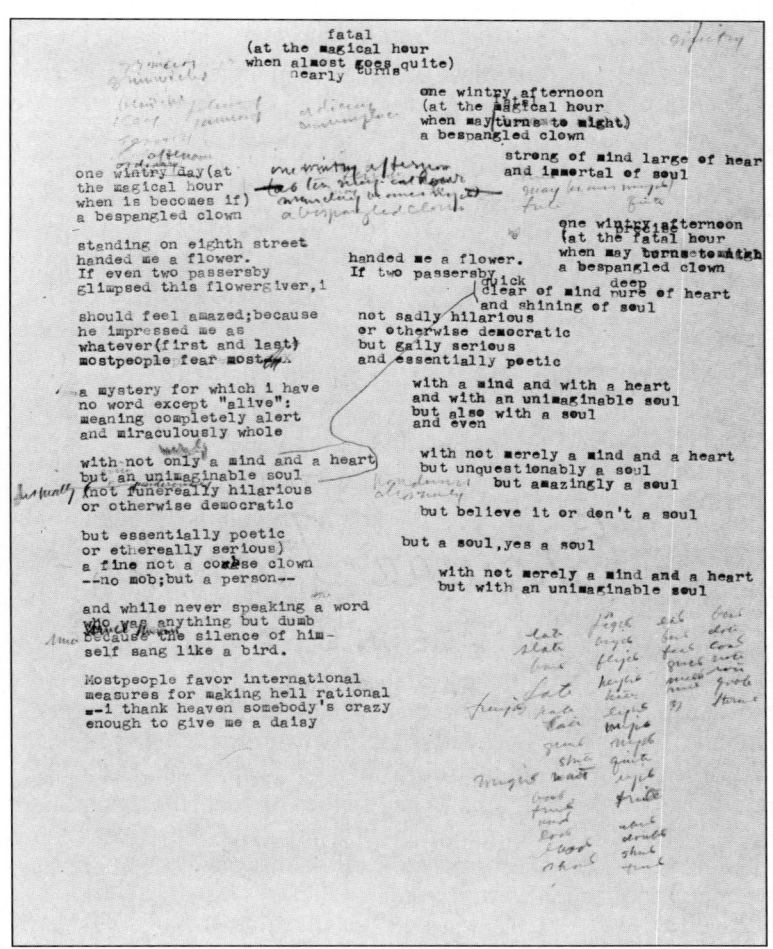

Manuscript of ''one winter afternoon''
by E. E. Cummings.

Houghton Library, Harvard University,
Cambridge.

of the poet may often be better expressed in free verse than in conventional forms.'' The term **free verse** simply means poetry that is free from the old metric rules.

To tradition-minded poets and readers, ''free verse'' seemed to represent a rejection of all poetic standards and a dismissal of every element that made a poem a poem. These people regarded free verse as a threat that would mean the end of poetry as they knew it. As the history of poetry in the following decades has shown, these people were right, but not entirely. In their fears about the decline of poetic standards they were mistaken, for they did not realize that successful free verse is at least as difficult to achieve as metered verse. And they did not realize that practitioners of free verse would develop high standards of their own.

The following poem by William Carlos Williams may serve as an example of free verse. When Williams first began to write poems like this, hardly anybody took him seriously. His lines had no meter or rhyme, no similes or metaphors. They had none of the familiar elements of poetry, except for imagery and a kind of rhythm that seemed more conversational than poetic. He did not even use punctuation. But gradually readers and poetry critics began to see that the simplest expressions of everyday life can be poetry.

> "**G**radually readers and poetry critics began to see that the simplest expressions of everyday life can be poetry.''

This Is Just to Say

I have eaten
the plums
that were in
the icebox

5 and which
you were probably
saving
for breakfast

Forgive me
10 they were delicious
so sweet
and so cold

—William Carlos Williams

Traditional poets have found the freedom from the old metric rules to be a handicap. Robert Frost, who disliked free verse, said that writing in this manner is "like playing tennis with the net down." What he meant was that the net on the tennis court is like the meter in poetry—the essential thing that the player and the poet must both respect and overcome. But in the twentieth century, more and more poets have accepted free verse as a kind of challenge. Instead of conforming to a meter, they write in cadences that follow "curves of thought" or "shapes of speech": Each line begins a new thought or variation on a thought. They trust their own sense of balance and measure to lead to poems that are as well composed as any written in meter.

Sound and Style: Reading Poetry Aloud

As in ancient days, when poetry was not written down but only spoken or sung, poetry today is still mainly addressed to the ear. You can't really say that you "know" a poem until you've heard it read aloud—preferably by the writer, in person or on a recording, or if that's not possible, by your teacher, a classmate, or you yourself. Poets at work are not apt to be silent; they test what they are writing by reading it aloud to *hear* what it sounds like. And there are times when the meaning of a poem changes in the course of searching for just that particular sequence of sounds that the poet finds satisfying. This does not indicate that meaning is unimportant; it only indicates that meaning is also expressed by the sound of a poem.

A good poet will eventually find a voice—an unmistakable combination of sound and sense that adds up to a style. When you've read enough poetry and heard the voices of a sufficient number of poets to be able to distinguish one from another, chances are you'll have a favorite. And when you do find a favorite, you'll probably find that you've selected that poet not only for what his or her poems *say*, but also for the way they *sound*.

> "**You** can't really say that you 'know' a poem until you've heard it read aloud."

Greek vase painting of the poet Sappho (c. 440 B.C.).

"Bonny Barbara Allan" is a ballad—a story-poem meant to be sung. You can easily recognize a ballad because it always contains two of the oldest elements of poetry: a strong meter and a refrain. Old ballads like this one were sung for generations before they were ever written down.

Think for a moment of popular songs today. Do they use refrains? What are their usual topics? Do any of them tell tragic stories of betrayal and death?

Bonny Barbara Allan

Anonymous

Oh, in the merry month of May,
When all things were a-blooming
Sweet William came from the Western
     states,
And courted Barbara Allan.

5   But he took sick, and very sick
And he sent for Barbara Allan,
And all she said when she got there,
"Young man, you are a-dying."

"Oh yes, I'm sick, and I'm very sick,
10 And I think that death's upon me;
But one sweet kiss from Barbara's lips
Will save me from my dying."

"But don't you remember the other day
You were down in town a-drinking?
You drank your health to the ladies all
15   around,
And slighted Barbara Allan."

"Oh yes, I remember the other day
I was down in town a-drinking;
I drank my health to the ladies all 'round,
20 But my love to Barbara Allan."

He turned his face to the wall;
She turned her back upon him;
The very last word she heard him say,
"Hard-hearted Barbara Allan."

25 As she passed on through London Town,
She heard some bells a-ringing,
And every bell, it seemed to say,
"Hard-hearted Barbara Allan."

She then passed on to the country road,
30 And heard some birds a-singing;
And every bird it seemed to say,
"Hard-hearted Barbara Allan."

She hadn't got more than a mile from
     town
When she saw his corpse a-coming;
35 "O bring him here, and ease him down,
And let me look upon him.

"Oh, take him away! Oh, take him away!
For I am sick and dying!
His death-cold features say to me,
40 'Hard-hearted Barbara Allan.'

"O father, O father, go dig my grave,
And dig it long and narrow;
Sweet William died for me today;
I'll die for him tomorrow."

They buried them both in the old grave-
45   yard,
All side and side each other.
A red, red rose grew out of his grave,
And a green briar out of hers.

They grew and grew so very high
50 That they could grow no higher;
They lapped, they tied in a true-love-
     knot—
The rose ran 'round the briar.

Lady Anne Pope by Robert Peake, the Elder (1615). Oil.

Responding to the Poem

Analyzing the Poem

Identifying Details

1. In stanza 3, what favor does William ask of Barbara Allan? According to the next stanza, why does she refuse him?
2. Describe what happens to Barbara Allan after William calls her "hard-hearted."
3. Explain how William and Barbara Allan are united in death.
4. Read this ballad aloud, and then **scan** it, marking each stressed syllable with the mark ′ and each unstressed syllable with the mark ˘. What **metrical pattern** do you find? Do any lines vary from the regular meter of the ballad?
5. What is the ballad's **refrain**?

Interpreting Meanings

6. Ballads never tell us the whole story. Do you know what caused William to sicken and die? What inference do you have to make to explain his death?
7. What evidence can you find in the ballad to suggest that Barbara Allan is, in fact, "hard-hearted"? Does anything about her behavior indicate that she is not hard-hearted? Explain.
8. A red rose is commonly regarded as a **symbol** of love. What do you think the tough-stemmed, prickly briar might symbolize in this ballad? Why is it appropriate that a rose grows out of William's grave, while a briar grows out of Barbara Allan's?
9. We'd expect the aggressive vines of a briar to grow around any nearby plant. Which plant entwines the other in this story? What do you think this suggests about which character and which emotion have triumphed? Explain.
10. If you had to set this story to music, what sort of sound and mood would you aim for? What instruments would you use?

Writing About the Poem

A Critical Response

1. **Comparing Poetry to Prose.** To see how rhythm and all the other musical devices of language affect a story, try this experiment. Rewrite this ballad, stanza by stanza, in ordinary prose. Forget about the meter and the rhymes and the repetitions. Then write a paragraph comparing the prose version with the original poem. Does the story lose its "magic" and take on a different tone? What emotional effect is lost without the refrain? Is the story as interesting once it has been stripped of its music? Is it more difficult or less difficult to understand?
2. **Explaining the Actions in the Ballad.** One of the characteristics of traditional ballads is that they omit many of the story's details. Some people think that as the poems were sung and repeated throughout the years, various details were omitted until only the high points of the plot were left. In this ballad, we learn that Barbara Allan died after her lover died, but we are not told how she died, or why. In a paragraph, give your opinion as to the cause of Barbara Allan's death. If possible, use details from the poem to support your explanation.

Analyzing Language and Vocabulary

Ballad Formulas

Traditional ballads often use certain formulas. Usually these are phrases such as "white as milk," "red, red lips," "red-roan steed," and "true, true love." The images of plants that grow on lovers' graves are also common formulas. All of these formulas would be part of the ballad singer's repertoire; whenever the singer needed to describe a woman's skin, for example, he could dip into this vast stock of descriptive phrases and find the formula. (See page 743 for a discussion of a similar technique that Homer used in his epics.)

1. The first stanza contains a phrase that is still well used today. What is it?
2. A common image in ballads is that of the red rose. How is that image used here? (In what famous Scottish poem by Robert Burns have you also heard that phrase?)
3. Beds in ballads are often described as "long and narrow." This usually indicates that the person about to lie down in the bed is going to die. What phrase here might explain the source of this formula?

Ex-Basketball Player

John Updike

Pearl Avenue runs past the high-school lot,
Bends with the trolley tracks, and stops, cut off
Before it has a chance to go two blocks,
At Colonel McComsky Plaza. Berth's Garage
5   Is on the corner facing west, and there,
Most days, you'll find Flick Webb, who helps Berth out.

Flick stands tall among the idiot pumps—
Five on a side, the old bubble-head style,
Their rubber elbows hanging loose and low.
10 One's nostrils are two S's, and his eyes
An E and O. And one is squat, without
A head at all—more of a football type.

Once Flick played for the high-school team, the Wizards.
He was good: in fact, the best. In '46
15 He bucketed three hundred ninety points,
A county record still. The ball loved Flick.
I saw him rack up thirty-eight or forty
In one home game. His hands were like wild birds.

He never learned a trade, he just sells gas,
20 Checks oil, and changes flats. Once in a while,
As a gag, he dribbles an inner tube,
But most of us remember anyway.
His hands are fine and nervous on the lug wrench.
It makes no difference to the lug wrench, though.

25 Off work, he hangs around Mae's Luncheonette,
Grease-gray and kind of coiled, he plays pinball,
Sips lemon cokes, and smokes those thin cigars;
Flick seldom speaks to Mae, just sits and nods
Beyond her face towards bright applauding tiers
30 Of Necco Wafers, Nibs, and Juju Beads.

Responding to the Poem

Analyzing the Poem

Identifying Details

1. Find details in the poem that tell us how Flick spends his time. Find details that tell us about his past and how he feels about it.
2. Read this poem aloud and listen to its beat. Then scan the poem (see page 301). Which lines are written in a regular meter? Where does the poet use **run-on lines** to make his poem sound natural and conversational?

Interpreting Meanings

3. In stanza 2, find words that **personify** the gas pumps. Considering Flick's background, explain why it is significant that they are arranged "Five on a side," with their "elbows hanging loose and low." How is Flick similar to the pumps?
4. In line 16, the speaker uses **personification** again when he says, "The ball loved Flick." Then he tells us, in line 24, that the lug wrench is indifferent to him. Explain why these details are important.

Gas by Edward Hopper (1940). Oil on canvas, 26¼ × 40¼.

Collection, The Museum of Modern Art, New York.
Mrs. Simon Guggenheim Fund.

5. In the last stanza, the candy is **personified** in the phrase "bright applauding tiers." What is the candy compared to, and who sees it this way? Explain what this personification suggests about Flick's fantasies.

6. Look back at the opening description of Pearl Avenue. Explain how this street could be seen as a **metaphor** for Flick's life.

7. Considering how Flick's life has turned out, what **irony** do you see in the **simile** in line 18 that compares his hands to "wild birds"?

8. Describe how this poem would be different if it had been entitled "Gas-station Attendant," or simply "Flick Webb."

9. How does this poem make you feel about Flick, and other people like him? Do you think there are a lot of Flick Webbs in the world?

Writing About the Poem

A Creative Response

1. **Using Another Point of View.** What would it be like to be Flick and have people feel that the best part of your life was over? What is Flick thinking? Pretend you are Flick Webb and that you are writing to an old friend you went to high school with. In one or more paragraphs, tell that friend what you are doing and how you feel about it. (Perhaps the speaker in the poem is entirely wrong about Flick.)

A Critical Response

2. **Inferring an Explanation.** "In American life," said the novelist F. Scott Fitzgerald, "there are no second acts." He was, of course, exaggerating in order to make a point. And yet Fitzgerald's experience—as well as that of many other talented people who shine like stars for a while and then fade away—tells us that there is more than a grain of truth in his statement.

If someone should ask, "What's become of Flick Webb?" this poem would be the answer. But perhaps someone who really cared about Flick might be left wondering why he has faded away. While the poem tells us *what* became of him, it doesn't tell us *why* he's known only as an "ex-basketball player." From the evidence presented in the poem, and from your own experience, make an inference, or guess, as to *why* Flick is living the way he is now. Present your explanation in a paragraph.

Analyzing Language and Vocabulary

Jargon

The specialized vocabulary that is common to a particular occupation or group is called **jargon.** In this poem, Updike uses several examples of basketball jargon—vocabulary that has a special or unique meaning in the world of basketball.

1. For someone talking about basketball, what does the word *bucketed* in line 15 mean? What comparison is the term based on? What would the word *bucketed* mean if you said, "I bucketed the car across the continent"?

2. Explain what the term *rack up* (line 17) means in basketball jargon. Does it mean the same thing in other sports? What might it mean to someone unfamiliar with basketball?

3. Explain the everyday meaning of the word *dribble* (line 21). What does it mean in basketball? What comparison is the basketball term based on?

Reading About the Writer

John Updike (1923–   ) was born in the small town of Shillington, Pennsylvania. A year after he graduated from Harvard, he got a job on the staff of *The New Yorker,* which has published much of his writing. Though Updike's fiction has won him fame and many prizes, he is also a poet of great wit. He is particularly drawn to humorous occasional poems—those based on odd or funny incidents reported in the newspapers, or observed in the suburban landscape of housing developments, service stations, and supermarkets. But Updike's comical approach should not disguise the fact that his poems, like his novels, are the products of an acute social observer and a serious moralist. One of his novels, *Rabbit, Run,* is also about an ex-basketball player whose life has gone downhill. Two of Updike's novels have won Pulitzer Prizes: *Rabbit Is Rich* in 1982 and *Rabbit at Rest* in 1991. Another of his poems appears on page 334.

Written in free verse, this poem should be read aloud so that you can hear how the rhythms of ordinary speech can be made into poetry. How would you "say" the title?

.05

Ishmael Reed

If i had a nickel
For all the women who've
Rejected me in my life
I would be the head of the
5 World Bank with a flunkie
To hold my derby as i
Prepared to fly chartered
Jet to sign a check
Giving India a new lease
10 On life

If i had a nickel for
All the women who've loved
Me in my life i would be
The World Bank's assistant
15 Janitor and wouldn't need
To wear a derby
All i'd think about would
Be going home

Responding to the Poem

Analyzing the Poem

Interpreting Meanings

1. Can you infer from the poem how many rejections the speaker has had in life? How do you know?
2. Does the lower-case *i* give you a clue as to how the speaker feels about himself?
3. What can you infer about the number of women who have loved him?
4. The last two lines could mean that the speaker has such a boring job that all he wants to do is get away from it and go home. But could the line also signify something else? Explain. Which interpretation do you agree with?
5. Do you think this speaker would rather be rich or loved? Explain.
6. This is a good example of a **free-verse** poem written to imitate the cadences of everyday speech. Identify the parts of the poem where repetition helps create rhythm. Would you have broken the lines any differently from the way the poet did? Do you think the lack of punctuation makes the poem difficult to read?

Writing About the Poem

A Creative Response

1. **Writing a Poem.** Write a two-verse poem imitating the structure of Reed's poem. Start each verse with the words, "If I had a nickel for all . . ."

A Critical Response

2. **Evaluating the Poem.** What makes this a poem? Answer this question in a brief essay, discussing the elements of poetry you've looked at so far:

   a. Figures of speech   c. Sounds
   b. Imagery   d. Feeling

Reading About the Writer

Ishmael Reed (1938–   ) is known chiefly for his satiric novels, but he has also written books of poetry and was nominated for the Pulitzer Prize for poetry in 1973. Reed was born in Chattanooga, Tennessee, and grew up in Buffalo, New York. He is one of the best-known African American writers today. Reed says he sees life "as mysterious, holy, profound, exciting, serious, and fun."

Today, even though supertankers and cruise ships are actually much taller than any ships moved by wind power, the term "tall ship" still denotes a sailing vessel with high masts.

"Sea Fever" might fall into the category of the "sea chantey." A sea chantey originally was a work-song chanted by sailors at their shipboard tasks; later it came to mean any song about life at sea in the days of sailing. Typically, sea chanteys were rousing songs meant to help keep up the spirits of sailors who were on duty much of the day on trips that sometimes seemed endless.

"The wheel's kick" in line 3 is a reference to what can happen when a sudden shift in the wind or the tide causes a ship's steering wheel to "kick over"—to spin out of control until the helmsman can grab it and put the vessel back on course.

"Trick" (line 12) was a sailing term for a voyage out and back to home. A "long trick" might involve a voyage from England to China and back that could last for more than a year.

What do you suppose the poem's title means?

Sea Fever

John Masefield

I must go down to the seas again, to the lonely sea and the sky,
And all I ask is a tall ship and a star to steer her by;
And the wheel's kick and the wind's song and the white sail's shaking,
And a gray mist on the sea's face and a gray dawn breaking.

5　I must go down to the seas again, for the call of the running tide
Is a wild call and a clear call that may not be denied;
And all I ask is a windy day with the white clouds flying,
And the flung spray and the brown spume, and the sea gulls crying.

I must go down to the seas again, to the vagrant gypsy life,
10　To the gull's way and the whale's way where the wind's like a whetted knife;
And all I ask is a merry yarn from a laughing fellow-rover,
And quiet sleep and a sweet dream when the long trick's over.

Responding to the Poem

Analyzing the Poem

Identifying Details

1. What specific **images** in the poem help you see, hear, and even "touch" the kind of life the speaker longs for?
2. **Scan** the first stanza of the poem, marking the stressed syllables ´ and the unstressed syllables ˘. How many strong beats are there in each line? Do you hear variations in the meter?

Interpreting Meanings

3. What action does the poem's **meter** suggest to you? Where does a series of strongly stressed syllables, or **spondees**, suggest the repeated slap of the waves on the bow of a ship?
4. What is the poem's **refrain**, and what does it reveal about the speaker's feelings?
5. In the final line of the poem, what **metaphor** describes life in terms of a sea voyage? What sort of afterlife does this speaker ask for?

U.S. Ship "Constellation" by James Henry Wright. Oil.

6. You are probably familiar with a variety of expressions that use "fever" **metaphorically**— "spring fever," "gold rush fever," and even "Saturday night fever." What exactly is "sea fever," and why is it a good **title** for the poem? Can you imagine other "fevers" that might grip someone the way the sea has gripped this speaker?

7. From the intensity of the speaker's feelings, what kind of life do you imagine he is leading as he speaks?

Writing About the Poem

A Creative Response

Writing a Poem. Write four lines of a poem that opens with the words "I must go" and includes the words "And all I ask." Use at least three specific **images** that describe what the speaker wants to see, hear, smell, taste, or feel.

Analyzing Language and Vocabulary

Diction

Masefield's **diction,** like his rhythm, is full of suggestive power. For example, in line 1 he might have called the sea *uninhabited* or *desolate,* rather than *lonely.* How would each of these words change the emotional tone of the poem? For each of the following words from the poem, suggest at least two possible **synonyms** that Masefield could have used instead. Then explain how the word he did choose creates a different feeling. You may consider sound as well as sense.

flung (line 8)	gypsy (line 9)
spume (line 8)	whetted (line 10)
vagrant (line 9)	yarn (line 11)

Reading About the Writer

John Masefield (1878–1967), born in Ledbury, Herefordshire, England, is best remembered for poems inspired by his years as a seaman, first on windjammers in the last days of the sailing ships and then on tramp steamers and ocean liners. No one has better evoked for the landlubber the sense of freedom and adventure, the taste of salt and spray, associated with sailing "before the mast," or the pride that marked the crews of even the rustiest and dingiest of freighters. For more than thirty years, Masefield served as Britain's Poet Laureate.

This poet says that she is not "form-conscious," that she sees herself as chiefly writing free verse, experimenting with it as much as she can, and "dotting a little rhyme here and there sometimes." Read this famous poem aloud to feel its rhythm—is it free verse or metered?

The Bean Eaters

Gwendolyn Brooks

They eat beans mostly, this old yellow pair.
Dinner is a casual affair.
Plain chipware on a plain and creaking wood,
Tin flatware.

5   Two who are Mostly Good.
Two who have lived their day,
But keep on putting on their clothes
and putting things away.

And remembering . . .
10   Remembering, with twinklings and twinges,
As they lean over the beans in their rented back room that
      is full of beads and receipts and dolls and cloths,
      tobacco crumbs, vases and fringes.

Responding to the Poem

Analyzing the Poem

Identifying Details

1. List the details in the poem that tell you that this couple does not have much money.
2. Explain the difference between "twinklings" and "twinges" in line 10.
3. Read the poem aloud several times. Would you say this poem is written in **meter** or in **free verse**?

Interpreting Meanings

4. Explain what you think the speaker means when she says that her characters are "Mostly Good."
5. Do you think the poet intends you to admire these people for their courage, or pity them for their poverty? Do you find any kind of "message" or special commentary in the poem? Explain.

6. Notice the poet's use of rhyming words (for a discussion of **rhyme,** see page 322). Do you think these rhyming sounds make the poem seem a little lighter? Do they make the poem seem more structured? Explain your response.
7. What do you think is the most important word in this poem?

Writing About the Poem

A Creative Response

1. **Filling in the Gaps.** In a paragraph, tell who this old pair might be and how they might have come to live the way they do. What inferences can you make about their past? In your paragraph, be sure to tell how you imagine the old couple feels about their lot in life.

The Apartment by Jacob Lawrence (1943).

Courtesy Terry Dintenfass Gallery, New York.

A Critical Response

2. **Evaluating the Title.** What do you think of the poem's title? Can you propose two other titles for the poem—titles that might make you feel differently about the old couple? Write a paragraph explaining your evaluation.

3. **Analyzing the Poem's Message.** In a comment made in an interview (see page 316), Brooks said that critics of the collection *The Bean Eaters* felt that her poems were "getting too social," and that she had forsaken lyricism for polemics. In a paragraph, explain what you think the critics meant (define *polemics*), explain whether you think their claim is justified, and tell how you feel about poetry with "social" messages.

Analyzing Language and Vocabulary

Connotations

The associations and emotions that come to be attached to a word through usage are called its **connotations.** Connotations are usually distinguished from **denotations,** which are the strict dictionary definitions of a word. In this poem, Brooks uses several words for their emotional effects.

1. List all the feelings and associations the word *beans* has for you. (Does everyone agree?)
2. What would be the effect if Brooks had used the word *noodles* or *sandwiches* or *rice* instead? (Can you think of other words she might have used?)

3. Put the word *regrets* in place of the word *twinges* in line 10. Does this change the impression you have of the old couple? Explain.
4. Suppose that in place of the catalogue of items in the last line, the poet had simply used the word *junk*. How would this change the emotional effect of the poem?

Reading About the Writer

Gwendolyn Brooks (1917–   ) was born in Topeka, Kansas. For nearly all of her lifetime, she has been identified with Chicago, especially with its enormous African American population, for whom she has become a kind of unofficial spokesperson. Skilled in many kinds of poetry, Brooks sometimes writes with formal elegance and at other times with an ear closely attuned to the street talk, jive talk, and bebop of South Side Chicago. Like her contemporary, the late Robert Hayden (see page 292), she uses her art to communicate the rhythms and diction of black speech in ways that give permanence to even the most casual of expressions. And like her poetic ancestor, Langston Hughes (see pages 232 and 358), she deals with the deepest concerns of African Americans in twentieth-century America without losing the voice, style, and vision of a highly individual poet. Brooks received the Pulitzer Prize for poetry in 1950.

Focusing on Background
A Comment from the Poet

In an interview in 1969, Gwendolyn Brooks was asked about her poetry, specifically about a collection called *The Bean Eaters,* which had recently been published:

". . . many people hated *The Bean Eaters;* such people as would accuse me of forsaking lyricism for polemics despised *The Bean Eaters* because they said that it was 'getting too social. Watch it, Miss Brooks!' (Laughs)"

In another interview, Brooks spoke about writing:

"Well, here are answers to questions I am often asked. 1. What is the significance of the Pulitzer Prize? I would say that it is a pleasant salute. It is a smile, usually accepted. 2. Why do you write poetry? I like the concentration, the crush; I like working with language, as others like working with paints and clay, or notes. 3. Has much of your poetry a racial element? Yes. It is organic, not imposed. It is my privilege to state 'Negroes' not as curios but as people. 4. What is your Poet's Premise? 'Vivify the contemporary fact,' said Whitman. I like to vivify the *universal* fact, when it occurs to me. But the universal wears contemporary clothing very well."

—Gwendolyn Brooks

If you've ever worried about an animal, you know how the speaker in this poem feels. Before you read, write down three metaphors or similes to describe the way you think fear feels. (Say "Fear is ____" or "Fear is like ____.")

Read the poem aloud to hear how the speaker uses the natural rhythms of free verse to convey her anxiety.

The Flying Cat

Naomi Shihab Nye

Never, in all your career of worrying, did you imagine
what worries could occur concerning the flying cat.
You are traveling to a distant city.
The cat must travel in a small box with holes.

5   Will the baggage compartment be pressurized?
       Will a soldier's footlocker fall on the cat during take-off?
       Will the cat freeze?

You ask these questions one by one, in different voices
over the phone. Sometimes you get an answer,
10 sometimes a click.
Now it's affecting everything you do.
At dinner you feel nauseous, like you're swallowing
at twenty thousand feet.
In dreams you wave fish-heads, but the cat has grown propellers,
15 the cat is spinning out of sight!

       Will he faint when the plane lands?
       Is the baggage compartment soundproofed?
       Will the cat go deaf?

"Ma'am, if the cabin weren't pressurized, your cat would explode."
20 And spoken in a droll impersonal tone, as if
the explosion of cats were another statistic!

Hugging the cat before departure, you realize again
the private language of pain. He purrs. He trusts you.
He knows little of planets or satellites,
25 black holes in space or the weightless rise of fear.

Responding to the Poem

Analyzing the Poem

Identifying Details

1. What does the speaker imagine might happen to her cat during the airplane trip?
2. Although this **free-verse** poem is written without rhyme or meter, it's designed with care. What structural element do you immediately notice as you look at the poem on the page? Find and read aloud some examples of **parallelism**—words, phrases, or sentences with a similar grammatical structure.

Interpreting Meanings

3. How do you know the speaker is a worrier?
4. Why do you think she uses "different voices" on the phone? How do the airline personnel respond to her?
5. Explain what you think the speaker means in line 23 by "the private language of pain." Why does she say she realizes that pain "again"?
6. How do the cat's feelings contrast with his owner's? Do you agree that an animal doesn't know the "rise of fear"? Why or why not?
7. This poem might seem funny to some readers. Do you think it's comical, or is it something else?

Writing About the Poem

A Creative Response

Using a Different Point of View. Imagine you're the flying cat. Write a brief **free-verse** poem (or paragraph) describing the airplane trip from your point of view. Describe how you feel about your worried owner, what happens during the trip, what you think about, and how you feel when you arrive at your destination. Before you write, reread the poem for any clues to the cat's attitude—but feel free to disagree with the poet's interpretation of those feelings.

Reading About the Writer

Naomi Shihab Nye (1952–   ) is a poet, storyteller, teacher, and songwriter who was born in St. Louis, Missouri, and now lives in San Antonio, Texas. She has helped elementary and secondary school students write poetry, taught at universities, and worked as a writer-in-residence throughout the country. Nye's writings reflect not only her private thoughts and experiences, but also her observations of the Native American and Hispanic cultures of the Southwest.

Focusing on Background
A Comment from the Poet

"Here is an example of an incident that gradually assumes epic proportions the more we worry about it.

"I speak to myself in this poem, as one often does when preoccupied. 'What do you think?' we keep asking ourselves. 'What next?' One thing I did in this case was call the airlines over and over, asking questions, till I received the reply contained within quotes.

"After that, I thought it might be better not to know.

"My cat, of course, was completely oblivious to my fears. I liked the images of outer space that came to me at the end of the poem—they seemed like gifts, and reminded me how worrying always distances us from solid ground, till we feel we're floating off in the outer limits alone."

—Naomi Shihab Nye

Literature & Language

Creating Rhythm and Meter

1. **Rhythm**—any recurrence of stressed and unstressed syllables—is, of course, not restricted to poetry. Rhythm is also found in ordinary speech and in prose. For example, what words would you stress in the following common expressions? **Scan** each phrase, marking the stressed syllables with the mark ⁄ and the unstressed syllables with the mark ⌣.

   a. Have a good day.
   b. Ham on rye.
   c. The score is tied, two to two.
   d. Take a break.
   e. Easy does it.
   f. Walk the dog.
   g. I can't believe it.
   h. Let's get going.

2. **Meter**—a regular pattern of stressed and unstressed syllables—occurs in many common jingles. Two examples are marching songs and jump-rope songs, where stress marks the moment when the marchers' or jumper's feet hit the ground. In the old military marching cadence that follows, see if you can identify the strong beats. Keep in mind that marchers always lead with the left foot. (Can you locate the refrain that the marchers shout back to the drill sergeant?)

   > Sound off, one, two
   > Sound off, three, four
   > Sound off, one, two, three, four,
   > One, two
   > Three, FOUR!
   > You had a good home and you left,
   > You're RIGHT!
   > Mary was there when you left,
   > You're RIGHT! . . .

3. The following poetic lines are written in **meter**.

Read the lines and then answer the questions that follow.

   a. Never seek to tell thy love,
      Love that never told can be
      > —from "Never Seek to Tell Thy Love,"
      > William Blake

   b. Whose woods these are I think I know,
      His house is in the village, though
      > —from "Stopping by Woods on a Snowy
      > Evening," Robert Frost

   c. My heart's in the Highlands, my heart
         is not here;
      My heart's in the Highlands a-chasing
         the deer
      > —from "My Heart's in the Highlands,"
      > Robert Burns

   d. Boot, saddle, to horse, and away!
      Rescue my castle before the hot day
      Brightens to blue from its silvery gray
      > —from "Boot and Saddle,"
      > Robert Browning

Which lines primarily use iambs (⌣⁄)?
Which lines primarily use trochees (⁄⌣)?
Which lines primarily use anapests (⌣⌣⁄)?
Which lines primarily use dactyls (⁄⌣⌣)?

4. Without words, **meter** in itself cannot convey meaning. But poets often choose certain meters to enforce their meaning, or to echo the sense of their lines. How do hard-hitting spondees (⁄⁄) suit the subjects of the following lines?

   a. Bang Bang Bang
      Said the nails in the Ark.
      > —from "The History of the Flood,"
      > John Heath-Stubbs

   b. Beat! beat! drums! blow! bugles! blow!
      > —from "Beat! Beat! Drums,"
      > Walt Whitman

How do the dactyls (∕⌣⌣) in this verse imitate its subject: the movement into battle of soldiers on horseback?

> Half a league, half a league
> Half a league onward
> All in the valley of death
> Rode the six hundred.
>
> —from "The Charge of the Light Brigade,"
> Alfred, Lord Tennyson

5. To accommodate their meter or their rhymes, poets will often **invert** the natural order of words in their sentences. How would the following lines be rewritten to conform to normal English word order? What happens to the rhythm or the rhyme when you reorder them?

   a. Then felt I like some watcher of the skies
      When a new planet swims into his ken.

      —from "On First Looking into
      Chapman's Homer," John Keats

   b. A slumber did my spirit seal;
      I had no human fears:
      She seemed a thing that could not feel
      The touch of earthly years.

      —from "A Slumber Did My Spirit Seal,"
      William Wordsworth

   c. The day returns, but nevermore
      Returns the traveler to the shore.

      —from "The Tide Rises, the Tide Falls,"
      Henry Wadsworth Longfellow

   d. A narrow Fellow in the grass
      Occasionally rides—
      You may have met Him—did you not?
      His notice sudden is—

      —from "A Narrow Fellow in the Grass,"
      Emily Dickinson

6. If a poet stuck rigidly to a particular **meter** in every line of a poem, the result would be a kind of singsong verse. Most poems depart from their meter occasionally, and then get back into the basic beat. You'll recognize the variations if you simply read the lines aloud and notice which words you would stress naturally. For example, in English we would rarely stress the articles *the*, *an*, or *a*, or the prepositions *with*, *on*, or *to*. Here is a famous poem that has the underpinnings of a strong meter—but the poet slips out of it at times:

On the Grasshopper and Cricket

The poetry of earth is never dead:
  When all the birds are faint with the hot
    sun,
  And hide in cooling trees, a voice will run
From hedge to hedge about the new-mown
    mead;
5 That is the Grasshopper's—he takes the lead
  In summer luxury—he has never done
  With his delights; for when tired out with
    fun
He rests at ease beneath some pleasant
    weed.
The poetry of earth is ceasing never:
10 On a lone winter evening, when the frost
    Has wrought a silence, from the stove
      there shrills
The Cricket's song, in warmth increasing
    ever,
  And seems to one in drowsiness half lost,
    The Grasshopper's among some grassy
      hills.

—John Keats

---

   a. **Scan** the poem to show how it consists of five **iambs** a line.

   b. Line 5 could be scanned like this:

      ⌣ ∕ ⌣ ∕ ⌣ ∕ ⌣ ⌣ ∕ ⌣ ∕ ⌣
      That is the Grasshopper's—he takes the
      ∕
      lead.

   But this is not the way you'd naturally place the stresses in this line. Reading the line in this mechanical way distorts its meaning. How should this line be scanned?

c. Find at least five other lines in whch the basic **iambic** pattern is broken.

d. Which lines in the poem are **end-stopped**—that is, which lines use punctuation marks to signal you to pause at the end?

e. Which lines are **run-on**—that is, which lines run on to the next line in order to complete their sense?

f. Read the poem aloud to hear how run-on lines and variations in meter prevent the poem from sounding mechanical and singsong.

7. Poets who write in **free verse** do not follow any metrical "rules." Instead they try to imitate the natural rhythms of spoken language. They pay careful attention to balancing the sounds of long and short phrases, and often they aim for rhythms that echo the sense of the poem. Here is a poem in free verse:

The High School Band

On warm days in September the high school band
Is up with the birds and marches along our street,
Boom boom,
To a field where it goes boom boom until eight forty-five
When it marches, as in the old rhyme, back,
5   boom boom,
To its study halls, leaving our street
Empty except for the leaves that descend, to no drum,
And lie still.
In September
A great many high school bands beat a
10 great many drums,
And the silences after their partings are very deep.

—Reed Whittemore

---

a. Lines in free verse often conform to "curves of thought." A new line begins a new thought or variation on a thought. Usually the poet expects you to pause briefly at the end of each line of free verse, even though there may be no punctuation mark. Lines ending with punctuation marks call for more pronounced pauses. Do the lines in this poem follow "curves of thought"?

b. Where would you pause in reading this poem?

c. What **refrain** beats out a kind of rhythm and echoes the subject of the poem?

d. How does the rhythm of the poem change when the band leaves "our street"?

e. How does the speaker feel about the silence that follows?

Writing

Writing a Free-Verse Poem. Take the basic idea and the major **images** of Keats's "On the Grasshopper and Cricket," and write a free-verse poem. Arrange your phrases so that they conform to "curves of thought." Do not use any inverted sentences.

> *A poet is a nightingale, who sits in darkness and sings to cheer its own solitude with sweet sounds. . . .*
>
> —Percy Bysshe Shelley

Rhyme works along with rhythm to create the special music of a poem. **Rhyme** is the repetition of the accented vowel sound and all subsequent sounds in a word (*time/dime, history/mystery, lobster/mobster*). Rhyme sets up our expectations that the pattern of chiming sounds we first hear in the opening lines will continue throughout the poem. Chiming sounds that punctuate the rhythm of a poem also make it easy to remember.

Rhyme is the most familiar aspect of sound in poetry, and not long ago it was part of every poet's craft. Today rhyme has fallen out of favor with some serious poets, though many poets still continue to explore its possibilities.

In poetry, rhymes may occur at the ends of lines—**end rhyme**—or within a line—**internal rhyme.** End rhymes are used much more frequently than internal rhymes. A perfect rhyme like *cat/mat* or *verging/merging* is called an **exact rhyme.** When the repetition of sound is similar but not exact, as in *fellow/follow* or *mystery/mastery,* it is called **approximate rhyme.** Approximate rhymes are also called "half rhymes" or "slant rhymes" or, by readers who don't like them, "imperfect rhymes." The following lines contain examples of exact rhyme:

> "You are old, Father William," the young man said,
>   "And your hair has become very white;
> And yet you incessantly stand on your head—
>   Do you think, at your age, it is right?"
>
> —from "Father William,"
> Lewis Carroll

In these lines the rhymes are approximate (*washes/rushes, bales/orioles*) and exact (*sea/mystery*):

> This is the land the Sunset washes—
> These are the banks of the Yellow Sea—
> Where it rose—or whither it rushes—
> These are the Western Mystery!
>
> Night after night her purple traffic
> Strews the landing with Opal Bales—
> Merchantmen poise upon horizons—
> Dip—and vanish like Orioles!
>
> —Emily Dickinson

This is the original wording of Dickinson's poem. Editors who prepared the poem for publication after her death changed one of the approximate rhymes to an exact rhyme: They changed the words "like orioles" to "with fairy sails."

Drawing by Chas. Addams; © 1983
The New Yorker Magazine, Inc.

Alliteration: Repeated Consonant Sounds

The tongue twister "Peter Piper picked a peck of pickled peppers" uses alliteration, and so does "She sells seashells by the seashore." **Alliteration** is the repetition of consonant sounds in words that appear close together; strictly speaking, alliteration occurs at the beginning of words or on accented syllables. Tongue twisters make exaggerated use of alliteration just for the fun of it. But alliteration used with restraint can result in lines as memorable as this one from Percy Bysshe Shelley's "Ode to the West Wind":

> O wild west wind, thou breath of autumn's being

Or this one from John Masefield's "Sea Fever" (page 312):

> To the gull's way and the whale's way where the wind's
>   like a whetted knife

Or this one from Robert Frost's "Acquainted with the Night":

> I have stood still and stopped the sound of feet

Onomatopoeia: The Making of Words

Beyond rhythm, the most important aspect of sound in poetry is onomatopoeia. **Onomatopoeia** (än′ə·mat′ə·pē′ə) is the use of words that sound like what they mean (*snap, crackle, pop*). This forbidding sounding word itself came into the English language from the Greek. Literally, it means "the making of words," but it has come to mean the making of words by imitating or suggesting sounds.

In its most basic form, onomatopoeia is a single word (such as *gurgle, bang, rattle, boom, hiss, buzz, sputter, honk, thud, sizzle, fizzle, twitter, clunk,* or *whine*) that echoes a natural or mechanical sound. For the poet, onomatopoeia is a way of conveying meaning while providing musical accompaniment—like background music in the movies.

In the next two lines from Isabella Gardner's poem "Summer Remembered," alliteration creates onomatopoeia—the sounds of *p*'s, *k*'s, and *t*'s imitate the sound of ice in a glass:

> The pizzicato plinkle of ice in an auburn
> uncle's amber glass

Here the sounds of *s*'s and *p*'s imitate the sound of waves breaking against the side of a sloop, or wooden boat:

> The slap and slop of waves on little sloops

The use of onomatopoeia can be so obvious that it seems deliberately or accidentally comic. But, as in this famous example from Tennyson's *The Princess,* onomatopoeia can be used with such exactitude that the sounds of the poem voice a particular feeling that the words alone could otherwise only approximate:

> The moan of doves in immemorial elms
> And murmuring of innumerable bees

> "**O**nomatopoeia is a way of conveying meaning while providing musical accompaniment—like background music in the movies."

Satire is a kind of writing that makes fun of human weakness or vice, usually in an attempt to make people change their ways. On the surface, this poem is about bears—and it might remind you of one of those children's books that have animal characters. But it shouldn't take you long to see that, like a fable, the poem is not really about animals at all. Read the first few stanzas of the poem aloud. From the way the poem sounds, do you predict it's going to be funny or serious?

Bears

Arthur Guiterman

High up among the mountains, through a lovely grove of cedars
    They came on ferny forest ways and trails that lift and wind,
The bears of many ranges under celebrated leaders
    Assembling in a congress for the weal° of all their kind.

5   Black bears, brown bears,
        Sober bears and clown bears,
Chubby bears and tubby bears and bears austerely planned,
        Bears of mild benignity,°
        Bears of simple dignity,
10 Coming to the Council of the Bruins of the Land.

A most tremendous Grizzly was Exalted Cockalorum;°
    He didn't need a gavel for his paw was hard and square.
The meeting was conducted with unparalleled decorum,
    For no one ever questioned the decisions of the Chair.

15   Fat bears, lean bears,
        Muddy bears and clean bears,
Tawny bears and brawny bears and bears in heavy coats,
        Bears of perspicacity,°
        Bears of much loquacity,°
20 Rumbling ghostly noises in their tummies and their throats.

They argued that their greatest need was more and better honey,
    That berries ought to propagate° in every vacant space;
They voted that the Teddy Bear was anything but funny,
    Demanding his suppression as a Libel on the Race.

25   Dark bears, light bears,
        Stupid bears and bright bears,
Gabby bears and flabby bears and bears of force and will,
        Bears of deep humility,
        Bears of marked ability,
30 Dealing with Conditions with extraordinary skill.

---

4. **weal:** general good. 8. **benignity:** kindliness. 11. **Cockalorum:** a self-important little man.
18. **perspicacity:** understanding. 19. **loquacity:** talkativeness. 22. **propagate:** grow, multiply.

Their orators orated on the laxity° of morals
    Contrasted with the beauty of the early forest den;
They favored arbitration for the settlement of quarrels
    And instant abolition of the armaments of men.

35 Weak bears, strong bears,
        Proper bears and wrong bears,
    Eager bears and meager bears and bears morose and glum,
        Locally admired bears,
        Splendidly inspired bears,
40 Working for the Future and the Bear that Is to Come.

    They settled mighty matters with miraculous discernment,
        They voted a Committee on the Stinginess of Bees,
    They voted for a banquet and immediate adjournment
        And rolled away like shadows through the vistas of the trees.

45   Red bears, gray bears,
        Gloomy bears and gay bears,
    Ambling off in bevies° down the boulder-bordered run,
        Bears in sweet amenity,°
        Bears in calm serenity,
50 Sure that what is voted for is just as good as done.

---

31. **laxity:** looseness.   47. **bevies:** groups.   48. **amenity:** agreeableness.

Group of Bears by Paul H. Manship
(1939). Bronze.

Collection, Minnesota Museum of Art, St. Paul.
Bequest of the Estate of Paul Howard Manship.

Responding to the Poem

Analyzing the Poem

Identifying Details

1. What issues do the bears discuss? What conclusions do they arrive at?
2. The sounds of this poem—its bouncy **rhythms** and comic **rhymes**—reveal the poet's sense of humor. List all the comic or clever examples of **internal rhyme** you can find.
3. The **end rhymes** in the poem vary. Sometimes every other line rhymes. Sometimes the lines rhyme consecutively in clever **couplets**. List all the examples of couplets you can find.

Interpreting Meanings

4. While it's meant to be funny in the way that political cartoons are funny, the poem is about something very serious. List the ways the actions and decisions of the bears mock the ways our politicians behave. Explain the "human" weaknesses revealed by the bears as they settle the "mighty matters" of honey, berries, armaments, and stingy bees.
5. Like groups of humans who give their leader a fancy title, the bears call their leader "Exalted Cockalorum." Of all the kinds of bears they might have picked for this position, why do you think they chose a grizzly bear? What does the bears' choice show about the kinds of people who sometimes gain power in human politics?
6. Why would the bears consider the teddy bear "a libel on the race" of bears? Explain where we might see this attitude in human behavior.
7. What does it mean that orators orated on the "laxity of morals" as contrasted with the "beauty of the early forest den" (lines 31–32)? Do you find people complaining about the same thing today? Do you think the "early forest den" really was a better place? Explain.
8. In the last line, the poet touches on a failing that could be ascribed to humans as well as to these bears. What is that failing? Do you think the poet's criticism is justified?
9. Take a close look at the **rhymes** in this poem. See if you can come up with a theory or definition about what makes a rhyme seem clever or comic or inventive.

Writing About the Poem

A Creative Response

Writing a Fable. Write a fable that **satirizes** human politics, but use animals other than bears to make your satiric points. (You might consider mice, cockroaches, or dogs.) How will you describe the various sizes, colors, and abilities of the creatures? What will they decide is their greatest need? What will their orators orate on, and what committee will they set up? Write up to three paragraphs, and then conclude with a brief moral about your creatures and their congress.

Analyzing Language and Vocabulary

Pronunciation and Oral Reading

To enjoy this poem fully, you must read it aloud. Before you read, be certain you can pronounce all of the unusual words the poet uses in his rhymes.

1. Practice sounding out these rhymed pairs:

   a. mild benignity / simple dignity
   b. Exalted Cockalorum / unparalleled decorum
   c. Bears of perspicacity / Bears of much loquacity
   d. Locally admired bears / Splendidly inspired bears
   e. Bears in sweet amenity / Bears in calm serenity

   Write out each phrase and indicate where the stresses fall. Use the mark ′ to indicate each stress point. Use a dictionary if you need help with pronunciations.

2. Now prepare the poem for a choral reading. Decide which lines will be read by a single person and which will be read by the chorus.

Reading About the Writer

Arthur Guiterman's (1871–1943) clever rhymes and wry humor were common features in magazines such as *Life,* the *Saturday Evening Post, Harper's,* and the *New York Times.* He disapproved of "modern" poetry, and his several thousand published poems all use traditional rhyme and meter.

Before the coming of the railroad, people depended on horses to take them where they wanted to go. Railroads were still relatively new when Emily Dickinson was a young woman, and so it was entirely natural that while watching a train traveling through her part of Massachusetts, she would compare its movements to those of a horse. Notice that the word *horse* appears nowhere in the poem. Dickinson's metaphor is implied: We know only that we are watching the movement of something referred to as "it" that seems to be an animal. Only when we get to the last line do we know for certain what that animal is.

This poem is a famous example of onomatopoeia: All the train's movements are described in words that *sound* like a train. As you read the poem, you will notice something else—its structure and rhythm make the poem *move* like a train.

From what the speaker says in the first two lines of the poem, what would you think "it" is?

I Like to See It Lap the Miles

Emily Dickinson

I like to see it lap the Miles—
And lick the Valleys up—
And stop to feed itself at Tanks—
And then—prodigious° step

5   Around a Pile of Mountains—
And supercilious° peer
In Shanties—by the sides of Roads—
And then a Quarry pare

To fit its sides
10   And crawl between
Complaining all the while
In horrid—hooting stanza—
Then chase itself down Hill—

And neigh like Boanerges°—
15   Then—prompter than a Star
Stop—docile and omnipotent
At its own stable door—

Manchester Valley by Joseph Pickett (1914–18?).
Oil with sand on canvas, 45½" × 60⅝".

Collection, The Museum of Modern Art, New York.
Gift of Abby Aldrich Rockefeller.

---

4. **prodigious:** enormous.
6. **supercilious:** haughty, stuck-up.
14. **Boanerges** (bō′ə·nŭr′jēz): a Biblical name meaning "sons of thunder." In Dickinson's time, it had come to mean a preacher who gave thunderous sermons.

Responding to the Poem

Analyzing the Poem

Identifying Details

1. At what point would a reader be certain of what the poem is really about?
2. List the verbs in the poem that tell what the train does.
3. Dickinson explored the possibilities of using **approximate**, or **half, rhyme,** for which she was widely criticized at one time. (People didn't think such rhyme was "poetic.") If you listen carefully, you'll hear a fairly regular scheme of approximate rhymes. Where do they occur?
4. Where does Dickinson use **inverted** word order? What would the normal word order be?

Interpreting Meanings

5. This train does many different things very quickly. But if we accepted everything it does as logical, we might find ourselves in the position of the farmer from Iowa who saw a giraffe for the first time in his life. When the man looked at the strange beast, he took note of its neck as high as a tree; its thin, gawky legs; its ears as small as a kitten's; and its skin spotted like camouflage. Then, turning to the man next to him, he said: "There just ain't no such animal." As Dickinson leads us along, she continuously compares a mechanical thing (a train) to an animate thing (a horse). But not every comparison seems to fit. Cite the actions that suggest a horse. Which actions do not? What kind of creature might they suggest?
6. The train's movements are described in words that match sound to sense. List the **alliterated** sounds that evoke the clackety-clack sounds made by a train. Find two **onomatopoetic** words in the poem that echo a train's (or a horse's) sounds.
7. Notice that the first two stanzas end with lines that don't stop, but instead hurry right into the next stanza. In fact, the whole poem is one sentence. How is the pacing and structure of the poem appropriate to its subject?
8. *Docile* and *omnipotent* (line 16) have contrasting meanings. Explain how a train could be both docile and omnipotent at the same time.

9. Describe how you think Dickinson felt about this train. Before you answer, list all the adjectives she uses to describe it, and then try to summarize their total emotional effect.
10. Look again at the adjectives that describe the train. Would we be likely to describe a train this way today? Is there any kind of machine or technological invention that we *might* apply these adjectives to?

Writing About the Poem

A Creative Response

1. **Creating an Extended Metaphor.** Choose a mechanical object (car, vacuum cleaner, lawn mower, blow-dryer, electric shaver, helicopter), and write a brief poem comparing it to something living. Try to keep the mechanical object unnamed, as Dickinson does. Then hint at the identity of your mystery item by using suggestive or imitative sound effects.

A Critical Response

2. **Evaluating Poetic Diction.** For most of Dickinson's poems, several versions exist. Some changes were made in her poems by editors after she had died; some changes were made during her lifetime by editors of the few poems Dickinson herself had published. This poem sometimes appears with the verb *hear* used in line 1, instead of the verb *see:*

   I like to *hear* it lap the miles.

   In a brief essay, tell which word you prefer, and why. Before you write, you might want to read "Focusing on Background" on page 329.

Analyzing Language and Vocabulary

Synonyms

One word may have several **synonyms,** but synonyms are not always interchangeable. For example, synonyms for *supercilious* (line 6) include *contemptuous, haughty, proud, condescending, superior,* and *dictatorial.* How would the sense of line 6 be changed if Dickinson had used one of these synonyms instead of *supercilious*?

1. Use a dictionary of synonyms or a thesaurus to find three synonyms for each of the following words from the poem:

   a. prodigious
   b. pile
   c. pare
   d. prompter
   e. docile
   f. omnipotent

2. Use each synonym in a sentence that illustrates its particular meaning.
3. Do you think any of these synonyms could be used in the poem without a significant change in the poem's sound or sense? Explain.
4. Another version of this poem has "To fit its *ribs*" instead of "To fit its *sides*" in line 9. Are the two words synonymous here? (If not, explain how they differ.) Which word do you prefer, and why?
5. In that same version of the poem, "*punctual as* a star" replaces "*Prompter than* a star" in line 15. Which wording do you prefer, and why? Consider the sounds of the words as well as their sense.

Reading About the Writer

Emily Dickinson (1830—1886) rarely left her birthplace: Amherst, Massachusetts. There she lived unknown as a poet, except to her family and a few friends, and there she produced in obscurity the hundreds of exquisite short poems that would eventually be regarded as one of the great expressions of American genius. Shy and retiring, she dressed in nun-like white clothes, never married, and devoted her life to her close relatives and to the concerns of her small New England town. Yet her wide reading acquainted her with the social and political developments of her time, at home and abroad, and she knew the English poetry of her generation perhaps better than did her famous contemporaries, Walt Whitman and Ralph Waldo Emerson. Of her own poetry, she wrote, "This is my letter to the world / That never wrote to me. . . ." Only a handful of her poems were published (anonymously) in her lifetime and Dickinson died oblivious to the fact that the day would come when she would be honored as one of the greatest American poets. Four other of her poems are on pages 229, 269, 296, and 322.

Focusing on Background
Emily Dickinson and the Train

In his biography of Emily Dickinson, Richard Sewell talks about the day the train first came to Amherst, Massachusetts. Edward Dickinson was Emily's father, and Austin was her brother.

"On June 9, 1853, a trainload of celebrants came from New London, Connecticut, to honor the completion of the Amherst & Belchertown Rail Road. It was Edward Dickinson's big day, with appropriate pomp and circumstance. Emily describes it—and her own part in the proceedings.

'The New London Day passed off grandly—so all the people said—it was pretty hot and dusty, but nobody cared for that. Father was as usual, Chief Marshal of the day, and went marching around the town with New London at his heels like some old Roman General, upon a Triumph Day. Mrs Howe got a capital dinner, and was very much praised. Carriages flew like sparks, hither, and thither and yon, and they all said t'was fine. I spose it was—I sat in Prof Tyler's woods and saw the train move off, and then ran home again for fear somebody would see me, or ask me how I did.'

"But what seems to have thrilled her most about the new railroad was its *sound*. On May 16, 1853, she had written to Austin: 'While I write, the whistle is playing, and the cars just coming in. It gives us all new life, every time it plays. How you will love to hear it, when you come home again!' And later (November 10, 1853): 'You asked me about the railroad—Everybody seems pleased at the change in arrangement. It sounds so pleasantly to hear them come in twice. I hope there will be a bell soon.' "

—from *The Life of Emily Dickinson,* Richard Sewell

This poem is simpler than it looks. Some words are jammed together, and others are given unusual spacing on the page. But once you get the hang of it and realize that you have to supply your own punctuation, you'll find that it reads like any other poem. Think of it as a painting—a street scene full of movement and color dominated by a big bunch of bobbing balloons.

in Just-

E. E. Cummings

       in Just-
       spring   when the world is mud-
       luscious the little
       lame balloonman

5   whistles   far   and wee

       and eddieandbill come
       running from marbles and
       piracies and it's
       spring

10   when the world is puddle-wonderful

       the queer
       old balloonman whistles
       far   and   wee
       and bettyandisbel come dancing

15   from hop-scotch and jump-rope and

       it's
       spring
       and
                  the

20   goat-footed

       balloon Man   whistles
       far
       and
       wee

Responding to the Poem

Analyzing the Poem

Identifying Details

1. When does the poem take place?
2. List the actions you see taking place in the poem.
3. The central figure in this poem is a man who sells balloons and who lets the children know he's around by blowing on a whistle. How does the description of the balloonman change each time he's mentioned in the poem?

Interpreting Meanings

4. What **images** do the hyphenated words "Just-spring," "mud-luscious," and "puddle-wonder-ful" bring to your mind? What sort of person do you think would be most likely to view mud as luscious and puddles as wonderful?
5. In Greek mythology, a "goat-footed" man was a *satyr*—a creature who was half-human and half-animal, and who represented the life of the senses. The god Pan was also "goat-footed." Pan is often pictured blowing on a set of musical pipes, and he was the special god of shepherds. Why would it be appropriate to consider this balloonman a kind of shepherd? In what way might he also represent the life of the senses?
6. Do you think the balloonman is sinister or kind? Explain your response.
7. The sound the balloonman makes is repeated three times in the poem, but each time the words are spaced a little differently on the page. Can you see any reason for this? What difference would it make if the sound just went "far and wide" instead of "far and wee"?
8. This poem is filled with sound effects. List all the examples of **alliteration** and **onomatopoeia** you can find. What sounds are echoed in "eddieandbill" and "bettyandisbel"? (What is the effect of running the names together?)
9. When you read the poem, sometimes you have to hop from word to word because they're spread out; sometimes you have to read words quickly because they're squashed together; and sometimes you have to jump from line to line. Describe how these devices suggest the actions of the children in the poem.

Writing About the Poem

A Creative Response

Imitating the Poem. Imitate this poem by writing five lines of your own about the beginning of a different season and a sound that you might hear then. Open with the words "in Just-," and invent two hyphenated words. Use at least one **onomatopoetic** word.

Analyzing Language and Vocabulary

Reading Aloud

Cummings's poems are always arranged in unusual ways on the page. Words are spaced out or jammed together; sentences rush into one another as if they have run out of control. But there is a purpose behind all the strange-looking typography; it tells you how to read the poem aloud.

Prepare this famous poem for several different oral readings. Pay attention to the sense of the poem and to these questions:

1. How will you read the lines that have big spaces between words or words that are squashed together?
2. How will you read the words that move diagonally down the page? How will you read the other one-word lines?
3. Will your voice be an adult's or a child's?

Reading About the Writer

E. E. Cummings (1894–1963) was born in Cambridge, Massachusetts, the son of a minister. After graduating from Harvard, he joined an American volunteer ambulance corps serving in France during World War I. Arrested by mistake as a spy, Cummings was held for three months in a concentration camp—an experience that he wrote about in a book called *The Enormous Room*. After the war, he lived in Paris for a while, then settled permanently in New York. Cummings's poetry is distinctive for its use of lower-case letters, for its unusual distribution of words across the page, and for its eccentric punctuation. But these are merely typographical oddities. Cummings's themes are familiar: the wonder of life and the miracle of individual identity. Another of his poems is on page 338.

A good approach to this poem would be to think of it as a cartoon like the kind you find on the editorial page of a newspaper. A cartoon makes a point, and it tries to make it simply. In this case, the picture we get is simple, but its meaning is open to at least two interpretations.

Simultaneously

David Ignatow

Simultaneously, five thousand miles apart,
two telephone poles, shaking and roaring
and hissing gas, rose from their emplacements
straight up, leveled off and headed
5   for each other's land, alerted radar
and ground defense, passed each other
in midair, escorted by worried planes,
and plunged into each other's place,
steaming and silent and standing straight,
10   sprouting leaves.

Responding to the Poem

Analyzing the Poem

Identifying Details

1. What happens to the two telephone poles?

Interpreting Meanings

2. What did you *expect* to happen?
3. What details in the poem suggest that these telephone poles might be something else instead? What do you think they are? Why do you think the poet chose to describe them as telephone poles?
4. Is there any significance in the fact that these "telephone poles" are located "five thousand miles apart"? Explain.
5. Although the visual picture we get in this poem is simple, its meaning is open to at least two interpretations. Explain how the poem can be interpreted as a vision of destruction followed by the emergence of new life. Then explain how it can be interpreted as a vision of a miracle.

6. Which interpretation of the poem do you find more convincing or exciting? Why?
7. This carefully phrased poem should be read line-by-line, rather than as a paragraph of prose. The sound and sense of the poem are held together by an interweaving of *s* sounds, from the first word to the last. Read the poem aloud to hear its sounds. How many *s* sounds can you locate? What does this **alliteration** suggest to you?
8. What wishes or hopes do you think this poem is expressing?
9. What significance do you see in the poem's **title**? Why is it important that these strange events take place *simultaneously*?

Writing About the Poem

A Creative Response

Expressing a Wish. In free verse, describe another potentially nightmarish event that turns miraculously into a wish come true.

Analyzing Language and Vocabulary

Syntax

Syntax refers to the way words are arranged and interrelated in a sentence. Notice that "Simultaneously" consists of only one sentence, and that the sentence is longer than any sentence most prose writers would use. See if you can identify the syntactic parts of Ignatow's sentence.

1. Identify the sentence's subject(s).
2. Identify its verb(s).
3. Identify the adjectives that modify the subject(s) of the poem.
4. What words and phrases function as adverbs?

Can you rearrange the parts of this sentence so that the poem opens with either the subject(s) or the verb(s)?

Reading About the Writer

David Ignatow (1914–   ) was born in Brooklyn and has lived in New York most of his life. He entered the business world at the insistence of his family, and he even became president of a bindery company. But business did not satisfy him. Eventually, Ignatow became a poet-in-residence at the City University of New York. "Simultaneously" is from his collection *Figures of the Human*.

No one has ever figured out why some records make it to the top of the charts and why others that sound much like them just disappear. In this poem, John Updike hints humorously that success or failure in the world of pop music may depend on a completely unexpected turn of events. In this case, an attempted murder leads to fame and fortune for both the would-be murderer and his intended victim. Before you begin reading, write down what you *think* the title means.

Pop Smash, Out of Echo Chamber

John Updike

O truly, Lily was a lulu,
   Doll, and dilly of a belle;
No one's smile was more enameled,
No one's style was more untrammeled,°
5   Yet her records failed to sell
       Well.

Her agent, Daley, duly worried,
   Fretted, fidgeted, complained,
Daily grew so somber clever
10   Wits at parties said whenever
     Lily waxed, poor Daley waned.
       Strained

Beyond endurance, feeling either
   He or Lily must be drowned,
15   Daley, dulled to Lily's luster,
Deeply down a well did thrust her.
     Lily yelled; he dug the sound,
       Found

A phone, contacted Victor,°
20   Cut four sides; they sold, and how!
Daley disclaims credit; still, he
Likes the lucre.° As for Lily,
     She is dry and famous now.
       Wow.

---

4. **untrammeled:** unrestrained.
19. **Victor:** RCA Victor.
22. **lucre** (lōō′kər): money.

The singer Patti Page.

Responding to the Poem

Analyzing the Poem

Identifying Details

1. In your own words, summarize the story this poem tells.

Interpreting Meanings

2. Lily is described as a "lulu," "doll," and "dilly." What do these slang terms mean?
3. Before Lily's singing career takes off, we learn that whenever "Lily waxed, poor Daley waned." Look up the words *waxed* and *waned* in the dictionary. What natural phenomenon is associated with these terms? What do they mean?
4. Clearly, the sounds in this poem create a lot of its humor. How does the poet use **alliteration** to create tongue-twisters? (What consonant sounds predominate?)
5. Describe the poem's **rhyme scheme.** Where does the poet make clever rhymes by coupling a two-syllable word with two one-syllable words?
6. The last line of each stanza is a one-syllable word that **rhymes** with the preceding word. Which of these short lines run over into the next stanza? What **rhythmic** effect do these lines produce, and how does it contribute to the humor of the poem?
7. Explain the **title** of the poem. How is the poem itself like an echo chamber?
8. How would you describe the poet's attitude toward the making of pop smashes?

Writing About the Poem

A Critical Response

Analyzing the Poem's Humor. A **farce** is a type of exaggerated comedy based on improbable situations, ridiculous characters, slapstick antics, and crude wit. (Laurel and Hardy and Abbott and Costello made farces; Peter Sellers's *Pink Panther* movies are also farces.) In a paragraph, explain how this poem is farcical. Then show how the poem's language and sound effects seem to imitate the buffoonery of farce.

Analyzing Language and Vocabulary

Puns

John Updike writes fiction as well as poetry. In all his writing we find many puns hidden away for our intellectual pleasure. A **pun** is a play on words that sound alike but have different meanings. Puns are usually, but not always, humorous.

There are at least two puns in this poem:

1. What word puns on the name *Daley* in stanza 2?
2. What slang meaning does the word *waxed* have that creates another pun in line 11? (If you're not sure, look it up in the dictionary again.)

Some people (those who do not like puns) insist that the only way to respond to a pun is to groan. What do you think of that point of view? Can you contribute any puns to the discussion?

Literature & Language

Creating Sound Effects

1. In this stanza, the poet has used the sounds of the words to echo their sense:

> All movement slows and stops, machines
> Have long since reeled and sputtered
> Into stillness, abandoned in snowy
> Cliffs and reefs on empty, snow-
> Filled streets, and now
> The airy spaces—silence between
> Flake and flake—
> Elegant, uninhabited and
> Cold, persist,
> And then,
> Accumulate.
>
> —from "Snowstorm,"
> Lynne Alvarez

a. Anyone who has stood in falling snow knows how snow tends to muffle sounds so that the landscape or cityscape seems to be saying "Hush." Where does this poet use **alliteration** to suggest the muffled sound of snow falling? What consonant sound is repeated?

b. Is this particular sound harsh, or is it pleasing to the ear? Do you think a series of words beginning with the letter *k* or *t* would have the same effect?

c. How do the poem's **rhythm** and line arrangement also reinforce its meaning?

2. Here is a verse from another poem in which sounds contribute to a completely different effect. This scene is not an empty, snowy, silent street, but the bustling street called Avenue C in the Lower East Side of New York City:

> pcheek pcheek pcheek pcheek pcheek
> They cry. The motherbirds thieve the air
> To appease them. A tug on the East River
> Blasts the bass-note of its passage, lifted
> 5 From the infra-bass of the sea. A broom
> Swishes over the sidewalk like feet through
>   leaves.
> Valerio's pushcart Ice Coal Kerosene
> Moves clack
>   clack
>   clack
> On a broken wheelrim. Ringing in its
>   chains
> The New Star Laundry horse comes down
> 10 the street
> Like a roofleak whucking in a pail.
> At the redlight, where a horn blares,
> The Golden Harvest Bakery brakes on its
>   gears,
> Squeaks, and seethes in place. A propane-
> gassed bus makes its way with big, airy
> 15 sighs.
>
> Across the street a woman throws open
> Her window.
> She sets, terribly softly,
> Two potted plants on the windowledge
> 20   tic   tic
> And bangs shut her window.
>
> —from "The Avenue Bearing the Initial
> of Christ into the New World,"
> Galway Kinnell

a. List the words and phrases from the poem that use **onomatopoeia** to echo these sounds:

The birds' cries	The horn
The tugboat's horn	The bakery truck's
The broom's sound	sound
The pushcart's	The bus's sounds
movement	The sounds made by
The chains of the	the woman setting
laundry wagon	out flower pots
Water leaking into	The window being
a pail	shut

b. How would you describe the effect of these onomatopoetic words and phrases? Are these city sounds pleasing and peaceful to the ear, or are they harsh and discordant? What particular vowels and consonant sounds create this effect?

3. Rewrite the following lines without the **rhymes.** Do they lose their force? Is some of the pleasure and wit gone?

The Span of Life

The old dog barks backward without getting up,
I can remember when he was a pup.

—Robert Frost

4. The basic building block of poetry for many centuries has been the **quatrain**—four lines of verse, usually united by rhyme. Read the two quatrains at the top of the next column. The first is rhymed in **couplets;** if we used a letter of the alphabet for each new rhyming sound, the **rhyme scheme** of this quatrain would look like this: *aabb.* (A *fen* is a swamp.)

I May, I Might, I Must

If you will tell me why the fen	a
appears impassable, I then	a
Will tell you why I think that I	b
can get across it if I try.	b

—Marianne Moore

A Choice of Weapons

Sticks and stones are hard on bones.
Aimed with angry art,
Words can sting like anything.
But silence breaks the heart.

—Phyllis McGinley

a. Cite the **rhyme scheme** of McGinley's poem, using a new letter for each rhyming sound.
b. List the **internal rhymes** used in each poem.
c. **Scan** each poem to show its **meter.**
d. Which poet uses **run-on lines** to make her verse sound conversational?

5. Here is a **sonnet** by Shakespeare. The speaker is addressing the person he loves.

Sonnet 29

When, in disgrace with fortune and men's eyes,
I all alone beweep my outcast state,
And trouble deaf heaven with my bootless° cries,
And look upon myself and curse my fate,

5 Wishing me like to one more rich in hope,
Featured like him, like him with friends possessed,
Desiring this man's art, and that man's scope,°
With what I most enjoy contented least;
Yet in these thoughts myself almost despising,

10 Haply° I think on thee, and then my state,
Like to the lark at break of day arising
From sullen earth, sings hymns at heaven's gate;
   For thy sweet love remembered such wealth brings,
   That then I scorn to change my state with kings.

—William Shakespeare

3. **bootless:** useless.

7. **scope:** scope of mind.

10. **haply:** luckily.

Literature & Language/cont.

a. Indicate the **rhyme scheme** of this sonnet.

b. Where does Shakespeare use an **approximate rhyme**?

c. In which lines does Shakespeare use **internal rhyme**?

d. Which lines are **end-stopped** and which are **run-on**?

e. As a rule, Shakespeare shaped his "message" to conform to the sonnet form; that is, each **quatrain** would express one idea, and the concluding couplet would sum up the point of the sonnet. Explain the idea of each quatrain in Sonnet 29, and how the couplet sums up the poem.

6. Today, nearly four hundred years after Shakespeare and his contemporaries composed their sonnets, poets still take on the challenge of expressing their thoughts and feelings within fourteen lines. Here is a twentieth-century sonnet. (A hurdy-gurdy is a kind of hand-organ that is played by turning a crank. Street musicians used to crank out tunes on hurdy-gurdys.)

> when my love comes to see me it's
> just a little like music,a
> little more like curving color(say
> orange)
> against silence,or darkness. . . .
>
> 5 the coming of my love emits
> a wonderful smell in my mind,
>
> you should see when i turn to find
> her how my least heart-beat becomes less.
> And then all her beauty is a vise
>
> 10 whose stilling lips murder suddenly me,
>
> but of my corpse the tool her smile makes
>   something
> suddenly luminous and precise
>
> —and then we are I and She. . . .
>
> what is that the hurdy-gurdy's playing
>
>   —E. E. Cummings

a. What does the subject of Cummings's sonnet have in common with the subject of Shakespeare's sonnet?

b. Both poets use **similes** to express the intensity of their feelings. Identify the similes, and explain whether you think they have anything in common.

c. Explain how each poet says that his intense feelings of love have "transformed" him.

d. At first glance, Cummings's poem looks more like free verse than like a sonnet. But if you look at it carefully, you'll see that it consists of fourteen rhymed lines. Describe the sonnet's **rhyme scheme**. Are all the rhymes **exact**? Or are there some **approximate rhymes**? Where does the poet use **internal rhymes**?

e. Does Cummings use a regular **meter**?

f. Where does Cummings use **alliteration** to help create the music of the poem?

g. Other than the **Shakespearean sonnet** (see page 286), the major type of sonnet is called the **Petrarchan**, or **Italian, sonnet**. (The form was made popular by the fourteenth-century Italian poet Francesco Petrarch.) The Petrarchan sonnet is divided into an **octave** (eight lines) that establishes a position or problem and a **sestet** (six lines) that offers the resolution. Describe how the **rhymes** in Cummings's sonnet hold together the two distinct parts of the poem—the octave and the sestet. What statement is the poet making in each group of lines? Does the sestet present the "answer" to the octave?

Writing

Describing Sights and Sounds. Take the weather, a street scene, or some other subject that includes sounds as well as sights (a buzzing fly, a waterfall, a dripping faucet, a cat licking up food), and write four lines describing what you see. Use a few words that also suggest what you are hearing. Try to find words that will create a particular effect—harsh, discordant, peaceful, noisy, irritating, droning, monotonous, grating, and so on.

EVALUATING A POEM

Writing Assignment

Write a five-paragraph essay in which you evaluate the poem "Leisure" by W. H. Davies.

Background

Emily Dickinson once wrote: "If I feel physically as if the top of my head were taken off, I know that is poetry. . . . Is there any other way?"

There is, of course, a more objective way. A poem that takes the top off one person's head may leave another person cold (with head intact). When you **evaluate** a poem (or anything else, for that matter), you need **criteria,** or standards, to serve as a basis for your evaluation. If a poem meets these criteria, then you can judge it "good" or "effective." If it doesn't, you can give reasons to explain why the poem is "poor" or "ineffective." The following criteria for evaluating a poem are based on the elements you've been studying in this unit.

1. **Subject.** Is the poem's subject an important one? Does it say something about a universal human experience or feeling? Or is it so personal that it doesn't speak to many people?
2. **Meaning.** Does the poem contain no wasted words? Does each word contribute to the poem's meaning? Does the poet ever use words simply to fill out the meter?
3. **Images and Figures of Speech.** Are the images and figures of speech fresh and original, or are they old clichés?
4. **Sound Effects.** Do the poem's sound effects support, rather than detract from, the poem's meaning? Do these sound effects seem forced or contrived?
5. **Sincerity Versus Sentimentality.** Does the poem elicit "fake" emotions, or stock responses? Is it a "tear-jerker"? Do you feel that the poem manipulates your feelings?

Prewriting

Read the following poem several times, both silently and aloud, applying the preceding criteria. A good way to evaluate a poem is to compare it to another poem of similar content. You might use "Stopping by Woods on a Snowy Evening" by Robert Frost, page 251, as a basis for comparison.

Leisure

What is this life if, full of care,
We have no time to stand and stare?

No time to stand beneath the boughs
And stare as long as sheep or cows.

5 No time to see, when woods we pass,
Where squirrels hide their nuts in grass.

No time to see, in broad daylight,
Streams full of stars, like skies at night.

No time to turn at beauty's glance,
10 And watch her feet, how she can dance.

No time to wait till her mouth can
Enrich that smile her eyes began.

A poor life this if, full of care,
We have no time to stand and stare.

—W. H. Davies

A chart like the following one will help you plan your essay. You might rank each of the numbered criteria on a scale of 1 to 10, with 10 being the highest score and 1 the lowest. Give examples or explanations to support your rating.

Criteria	Rating	Examples
Subject		
Meaning		
Images and figures of speech		
Sound effects		
Emotional response		
OVERALL EVALUATION		

Writing

Use your Prewriting notes to organize your essay. Begin with your overall evaluation of the poem—your honest and informed opinion of the poem's merit. Think of the rest of your essay (paragraphs 2–5) as specific evidence to support this evaluation. Try to cover all of the criteria listed in your Prewriting checklist. Then discuss your personal response to the poem in the last paragraph.

You have a lot to cover in your essay by concentrating on "Leisure" alone. But contrasting "Leisure" with some of the other poems you've read in this unit may help you clarify your thinking and evaluation. Feel free to refer to specific aspects of other poems. Just be sure to mention the title, author, and page number on which each poem appears.

Checklist for Revision

1. Have you cited the poem's title and author?
2. In the introductory paragraph, have you included a thesis statement that summarizes your evaluation of the poem?
3. Have you discussed each of the criteria listed on page 339?
4. Have you cited lines or phrases from the poem to support your points? Have you checked the quotations for accuracy, used quotation marks, and cited line numbers?
5. In the final paragraph, have you described and explained your response to the poem?
6. Have you checked: Spelling? Punctuation? Capitalization? Sentence structure? Paragraph organization?

"It's a remarkable write, but not an irresistible read."

Drawing by James Stevenson; © 1987 The New Yorker Magazine, Inc.

Hearing poems read, like reading them, is different from other encounters with language. Nothing else we read prepares us for poetry.

—Mark Strand

Tone: "Overhearing" an Attitude

Tone in poetry is a quality that is not so much stated as overheard. **Tone** is the attitude of the writer or the speaker toward the subject of the poem or toward the audience.

When we speak, the inflections of our voice provide clues to our tone. By varying our volume, pitch, emphasis, and timing, we can use our voice to show feelings that range from anger to joy, from humor to anxiety. Tone can usually be identified by an adjective:

awed	contemptuous	playful	regretful
amused	cynical	mocking	satiric
angry	humorous	moralistic	sarcastic
affectionate	ironic	nostalgic	sorrowful

To see how vocal inflections can affect tone and meaning, think of at least two ways you would say each of the following expressions to reveal the tones cited in parentheses. No end punctuation is used here because you have to decide if the expressions are statements, questions, or exclamations.

Scott loves Kate (disbelieving; joyful)
Yes (uncertain; emphatic)
Maybe (playful; puzzled)
Cabbage for dinner (disgusted; delighted)
The dog's in the daffodils (humorous; angry)

In the following sentence, how would you use your voice to express the unspoken thoughts in parentheses?

"Are you going to cook dinner tonight?"	(That would be wonderful!)
"Are YOU going to cook dinner tonight?"	(Or am I going to have to do it, as usual?)
"Are you going to cook dinner TONIGHT?"	(Oh. I thought we were going to eat out for a change.)

Detecting a Poem's Tone

In poetry, we sense tone not from vocal inflection but from the poet's language—from words, from figures of speech, from rhythm, and from sound effects.

> "**I**n poetry, we sense tone not from vocal inflection but from the poet's language."

> ## "Even a single word can reveal a poet's tone."

The following poem is an example of how even a single word can reveal a poet's tone. This poem was written before legislation was passed prohibiting child labor. In those times, it was common to find very young children working in the textile mills for twelve or fourteen hours a day.

The Golf Links

The golf links lie so near the mill
That almost every day
The laboring children can look out
And see the men at play.

—Sarah N. Cleghorn

It is the word *play* in the last line that establishes the speaker's tone. We think of "play" as something that children do and "laboring" as something that adults do. But here it is the *men* who are "at play," with their game of golf, and it is the children who are "laboring" in the mill. We'd call this poet's tone **ironic** because she obviously feels that this situation is just the opposite of what should be in a well-run, just world. (If you doubt the power of a single word to convey an attitude, try this: Imagine how different the poem's effect would have been if it had ended with the words "teeing off" or "driving over the fairways.")

Notice that this poet never once says directly what she thinks of the men who play while children labor, or of a society that permits such a situation to exist; we must "hear" her tone and interpret it for ourselves. Could any other tone be heard in this poem? Is there any justification for interpreting its tone as humorous, rather than ironic? Why or why not?

Parody: The Mocking Tone

Here are the first two verses of a famous nineteenth-century poem by an American poet. Following these verses are two more written some years later by a famous British poet. The two poems could not be more different in tone. In fact, one is a **parody,** or humorous imitation, of the other. (*Excelsior* is a motto that means "Higher! Ever upward!'')

© 1940 James Thurber. © 1968 Helen Thurber. From *Fables for Our Time and Famous Poems Illustrated,* published by Harper & Row.

The shades of night were falling fast,
As through an Alpine village passed
A youth, who bore, 'mid snow and ice,
A banner with the strange device—
    Excelsior!

"Try not the pass," the old man said;
"Dark lowers the tempest overhead;
The roaring torrent is deep and wide!"
And loud that clarion voice replied,
    Excelsior!

—from "Excelsior,"
Henry Wadsworth Longfellow

The shades of night were falling fast,
　And the rain was falling faster,
When through an Alpine village passed
　An Alpine village pastor:
A youth who bore mid snow and ice
　A bird that wouldn't chirrup,
And a banner with the strange device—
　"Mrs. Winslow's soothing syrup."

"Beware the pass," the old man said,
　"My bold, and desperate fellah;
Dark lowers the tempest overhead,
　And you'll want your umberella;
And the roaring torrent is deep and wide—
　You may hear how loud it washes."
But still that clarion voice replied:
　"I've got my old goloshes." . . .

　　　　—from "The Shades of Night . . . ,"
　　　　A. E. Housman

If you like "Excelsior," you might feel that all Housman has done is ruin a beautiful poem. It is clear that Housman is making fun of Longfellow's ardently serious speaker and his moralistic tone. Our first clue to Housman's own tone comes from his silly rhymes. Another clue comes from the device carried by Housman's youth. Instead of bearing a banner with the stirring word "Excelsior," he is carrying an advertisement for cough syrup. We might describe Longfellow's tone as serious and solemn. We might describe Housman's tone as humorous and mocking.

Mixed Tones

Sometimes we can hear an echo of sadness in a poem that is otherwise joyful, or a tone of humor in a poem that is otherwise sad. Here are two lines from Shakespeare's play *Cymbeline:*

　　　Golden lads and girls all must,
　　　As chimney sweepers, come to dust.

Shakespeare is pointing out a sad fact—that even the young and beautiful must someday die and turn to dust. Yet he uses a comparison that gives his lines an almost light tone: We see the golden lads and girls just for a moment, not as beautiful young people, but as little sooty-faced figures holding heavy brooms.

No one can give you exact directions on how to "read" a poem's tone. Perhaps the best way to start is to listen to the poem read aloud and try to "hear" the speaker's voice. Then trust your instincts, and look for specific words and phrasings that you think convey a particular attitude.

Remember that tone is an important element of poetry. All of the other elements of a poem work together to create that particular shade of meaning that we can only overhear.

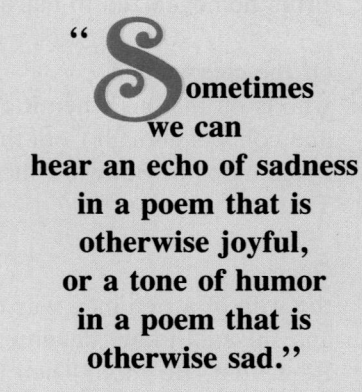

"**Sometimes we can hear an echo of sadness in a poem that is otherwise joyful, or a tone of humor in a poem that is otherwise sad.**"

What do you think of "happy-ever-after" fairy tales? Did you enjoy them as a child? Do you think they make people expect all of life's problems to be easily solved? While it's based on a famous old fairy tale, this poem offers a modern version that comes to an entirely different conclusion. Perhaps the first thing that distinguishes the story told in this poem from earlier versions of the fairy tale is its tone. What clue to the poet's attitude do you detect in the first stanza?

Cinderella

Anne Sexton

You always read about it:
the plumber with twelve children
who wins the Irish Sweepstakes.
From toilets to riches.
5   That story.

Or the nursemaid,
some luscious sweet from Denmark
who captures the oldest son's heart.
From diapers to Dior.°
10 That story.

Or a milkman who serves the wealthy,
eggs, cream, butter, yogurt, milk,
the white truck like an ambulance
who goes into real estate
15 and makes a pile.
From homogenized to martinis at lunch.

Or the charwoman
who is on the bus when it cracks up
and collects enough from the insurance.
20 From mops to Bonwit Teller°
That story.

Once
the wife of a rich man was on her deathbed
and she said to her daughter Cinderella:
25 Be devout. Be good. Then I will smile
down from heaven in the seam of a cloud.
The man took another wife who had

two daughters, pretty enough
but with hearts like blackjacks.
30 Cinderella was their maid
She slept on the sooty hearth each night
and walked around looking like Al Jolson.°
Her father brought presents home from
    town,
jewels and gowns for the other women
35 but the twig of a tree for Cinderella.
She planted that twig on her mother's grave
and it grew to a tree where a white dove sat.
Whenever she wished for anything the dove
would drop it like an egg upon the ground.
The bird is important, my dears, so heed
40   him.

Next came the ball, as you all know.
It was a marriage market.
The prince was looking for a wife.
All but Cinderella were preparing
45 and gussying up for the big event.
Cinderella begged to go too.
Her stepmother threw a dish of lentils
into the cinders and said: Pick them
up in an hour and you shall go.
50 The white dove brought all his friends;
all the warm wings of the fatherland came,
and picked up the lentils in a jiffy.
No, Cinderella, said the stepmother,
you have no clothes and cannot dance.
55 That's the way with stepmothers.

---

9. **from diapers to Dior:** an allusion to a true story: A Danish maid married one of the rich Rockefeller sons. (She went from washing diapers to wearing Christian Dior dresses.)
20. **Bonwit Teller:** an expensive department store.

32. **Al Jolson:** American jazz singer who often performed in black face.

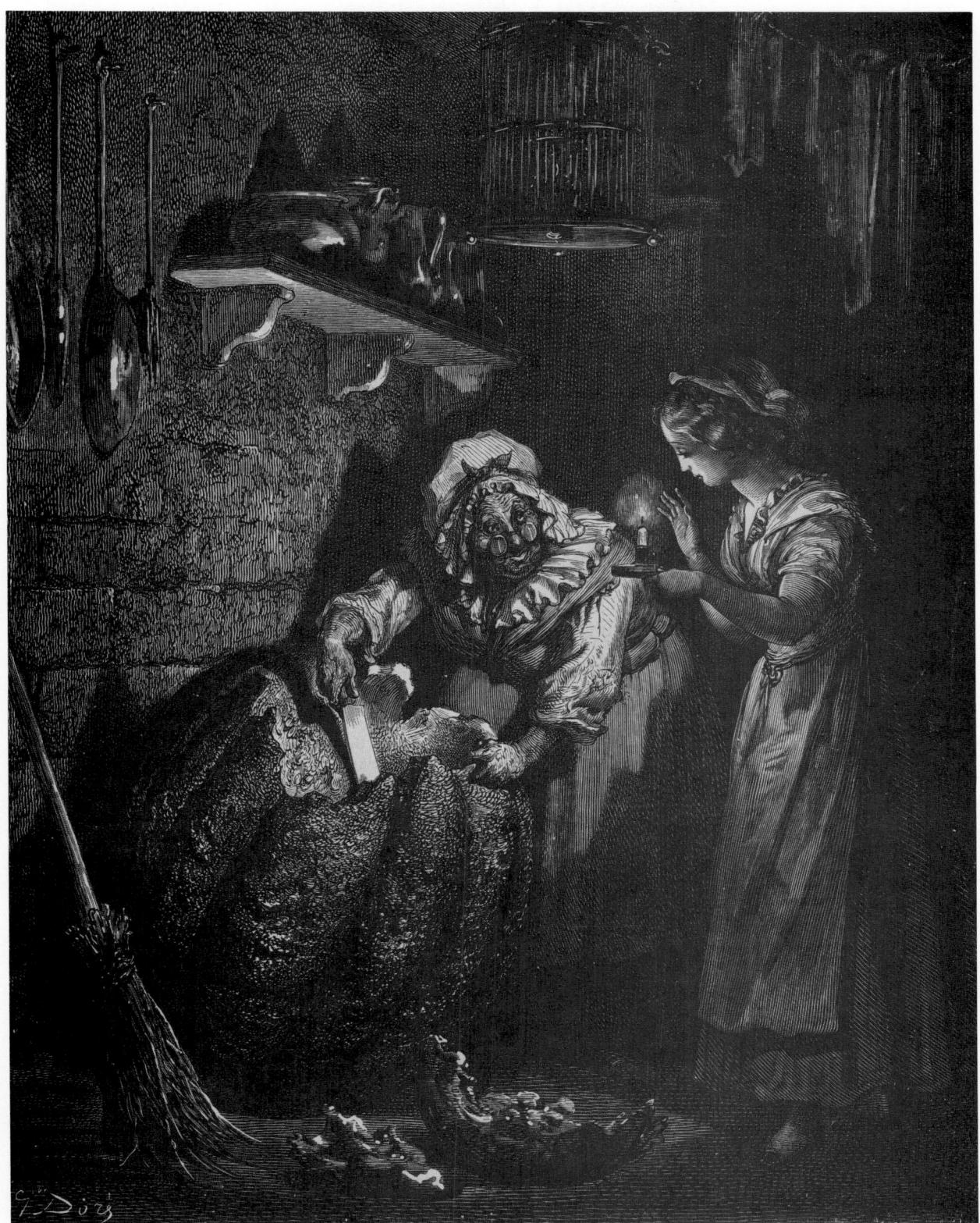

Cinderella and Her Fairy Godmother by Gustave Doré. Engraving.

Cinderella went to the tree at the grave
and cried forth like a gospel singer:
Mama! Mama! My turtledove,
send me to the prince's ball!
60 The bird dropped down a golden dress
and delicate little gold slippers.
Rather a large package for a simple bird.
So she went. Which is no surprise.
Her stepmother and sisters didn't
65 recognize her without her cinder face
and the prince took her hand on the spot
and danced with no other the whole day.

As nightfall came she thought she'd better
get home. The prince walked her home
70 and she disappeared into the pigeon house
and although the prince took an axe and
       broke
it open she was gone. Back to her cinders.
These events repeated themselves for three
       days.
However on the third day the prince
75 covered the palace steps with cobbler's wax
and Cinderella's gold shoe stuck upon it.

Now he would find whom the shoe fit
and find his strange dancing girl for keeps.
He went to their house and the two sisters
80 were delighted because they had lovely feet.
The eldest went into a room to try the slip-
       per on
but her big toe got in the way so she
       simply
sliced it off and put on the slipper.

The prince rode away with her until the
       white dove
85 told him to look at the blood pouring forth.
That is the way with amputations.
They don't just heal up like a wish.
The other sister cut off her heel
but the blood told as blood will.
90 The prince was getting tired.
He began to feel like a shoe salesman.
But he gave it one last try.
This time Cinderella fit into the shoe
like a love letter into its envelope.

95 At the wedding ceremony
the two sisters came to curry favor°
and the white dove pecked their eyes out.
Two hollow spots were left
like soup spoons.

100 Cinderella and the prince
lived, they say, happily ever after,
like two dolls in a museum case
never bothered by diapers or dust,
never arguing over the timing of an egg,
105 never telling the same story twice,
never getting a middle-aged spread,
their darling smiles pasted on for eternity.
Regular Bobbsey Twins.°
That story.

---

96. **curry favor:** win approval by flattering someone.
108. **Bobbsey Twins:** characters from a popular series of children's books about two sets of twins who were always good and always happy. (Nan and Bert and Flossie and Freddie are the Bobbsey Twins.)

Responding to the Poem

Analyzing the Poem

Identifying Details

1. At the beginning of the poem, the speaker gives four examples of the kind of story she claims "you always read about." Explain what these four stories have in common.

2. The old label for such stories is "from rags to riches." How does the poet update this old label for each story? What **refrain** does she use after three of these examples?

3. Identify at least six **similes** the speaker uses in telling her updated version of the Cinderella story.

Interpreting Meanings

4. To understand this new version of an old fairy tale, we have to catch the poet's **tone**, or her attitude toward the Cinderella story. A clue to this tone can be found in her use of slang and references to modern life. List as many examples as you can find of each. Why are they **ironic**—that is, how does this use of language confound our expectations?

5. Locate the moments where the speaker addresses the readers or comments on the story's plot in a way that is uncharacteristic of fairy tales. How does this running commentary affect you? What kind of a **tone** does it suggest?

6. How would you read the last stanza aloud? (What tone of voice would you use and what unspoken meaning would you try to communicate?)

7. We all like happy endings. Traditional storytellers usually supplied them by saying, "And they lived happily ever after." In this version of the Cinderella story, however, the poet refuses to use that convention. In the last stanza, she shows us that "happily ever after" might *not* apply to real life. What do you think this poet is saying actually does happen after even the most romantic storybook wedding, no matter what "they" say?

8. Describe how this poet feels about fairy tales. (Do you think that she is just trying to be funny, or do you think she has a serious objection to such stories?) Do you agree with her, or would you argue for another point of view?

9. If the Cinderella story and other fairy tales can be so easily mocked, why do you think they have been so popular for so long? Explain what such stories might reveal about our deepest desires.

Writing About the Poem

A Creative Response

1. **Writing a New Version of an Old Story.** Choose another old fairy tale and retell it in a new way— "The Three Little Pigs," for instance. Include all of the story's important events; change or add only certain details. (Perhaps the wolf is a bill collector.) As in "Cinderella," all sorts of changes are possible even though the narrative remains more or less the same. As you plan your story, think about your attitude toward the original fairy tale. Try to convey that attitude through the language you use in your version.

A Critical Response

2. **Responding to the Poem's Message.** In a brief essay, explain your response to this poem's message. You might use one of these passages as your topic statement:

   a. *I totally agree with this poet. I think stories like "Cinderella" have made girls expect life to turn out happily because they always expect Prince Charming to come along and rescue them.*

   b. *I disagree with this poet. I think the old fairy stories have a valuable function. They show us cruelty and horror, yet they speak to the hope in all of us that goodness will win out.*

Analyzing Language and Vocabulary

Allusions

Like many writers, Anne Sexton often **alludes,** or refers, to contemporary events, culture, and politics in her poems. Unless you catch her allusions, you will miss much of her meaning.

In a recent issue of a national news magazine, a teacher presented the results of a "general knowledge test" that he had given his students. He had asked them to identify some names and terms that writers (and teachers) frequently allude to today. Here are some of their answers. How many of these allusions would *you* have recognized?

Ralph Nader is a baseball player. Charles Darwin invented gravity. J. Edgar Hoover was a nineteenth-century president. Neil Simon wrote *One Flew Over the Cuckoo's Nest; The Great Gatsby* was a magician in the 1930's. Franz Joseph Haydn was a songwriter during the same decade. Sid Caesar was an early Roman emperor. Mark Twain invented the cotton gin. Heinrich Himmler invented the Heimlich maneuver. Jefferson Davis was a guitar player for The Jefferson Airplane. Benito Mussolini was a Russian leader of the eighteenth century; Dwight D. Eisenhower came earlier, serving as a president during the seventeenth century. William Faulkner made his name as a seventeenth-century scientist. All of these people must have appreciated the work of Pablo Picasso, who painted masterpieces in the twelfth century.

—Jaime M. O'Neill

Anyone who has ever cooked will recognize the scene in this poem—but you may not have realized that such a common experience could be made into poetry. Think for a minute of all the names of foods that are stored in an ordinary kitchen. Make a list of the first ten that come to your mind. Say them aloud. Can you hear a kind of music in these names? Watch how this writer uses the names of spices to make a poem. The scene takes place in the Dominican Republic.

What Could It Be?

Julia Alvarez

Around the kettle of chicken and rice,
the aunts were debating what flavor was missing.
Aunt Carmen guessed garlic.
Aunt Rosa, some coarsely ground pepper.
5   Aunt Fofi, so tidy she wore the apron,
shook her head, plain salt what was needed.
Aunt Ana, afraid to be wrong, echoed salt.
Just a pinch, she apologized, and reached for the shaker.
Aunt Gladys said parsley never hurt anything.
10   Aunt Victoria frowned and pronounced,
Tarragon. No one disagreed.

The tarragon dotted the rice in the cauldron.
And now, as if signaled, the spice jars popped open,
unladened their far eastern wonders:
15   cumin, turmeric, saffron, and endives.
The aunts each put in a shake of their favorites.
The steam unwrinkled the frowns from their faces.
They cackled like witches, sampled, and nodded.

Around the table the uncles were grunting,
20   wolfing their food down, gnawing their chicken bones.
And yet the aunts stopped in the middle of swallows,
heads cocked at each other as if they had heard
in some far off room their own baby crying.
It needed a pinch more of . . . saffron? Paprika?
25   What could it be they had missed putting in?
The uncles ate seconds and rose in a chorus
of chair scrapes and belches,
falling to slumber on living room couches,
empty plates glowed like the eyes of the spellbound.

Responding to the Poem

Analyzing the Poem

Identifying Details

1. The poem presents **images** of a busy kitchen scene. What are the cooks searching for?
2. By the time they are finished, what have the aunts added to their kettle?

Interpreting Meanings

3. Find three details in the poem that make you think of the aunts as storybook witches or sorcerers. What do you think the uncles are compared to?
4. Given this, we might expect that the speaker is mocking her aunts and uncles. But is she? How does she seem to feel about this lively, fragrant scene and the people in it? What would you say the poem's **tone** is: fond, humorous, critical, ironic? Defend your answer.
5. Do you think this poem is really about cooking? Or is its real subject something else? Explain.

Writing About the Poem

A Creative Response

Imitating the Poem. Write a brief poem or a paragraph describing a kitchen scene, using the names of at least ten specific foods. Be sure to name the dish that is being prepared.

Analyzing Language and Vocabulary

Food as Metaphor

If you say someone is "the salt of the earth," you mean that the person is as "basic" and "good" as salt, that substance that brings out the taste in food and that we all need to stay alive.

1. What does it mean to say that language is "salty"?
2. If you "salt away" money, what have you done with it?
3. How is the word *salary* related to the word *salt*?
4. What does it mean to say that someone is "worth his or her salt"?

Reading About the Writer

Julia Alvarez (1950–   ) spent the early years of her childhood in the Dominican Republic. She drew upon those experiences for *Homecoming,* the poetry collection in which "What Could It Be?" appears. The poet Linda Pastan (see page 378) says that in *Homecoming* Alvarez is "searching for the secret meanings of what has been known as 'women's work.'" Alvarez's most recent work is a collection of related stories called *How the García Girls Lost Their Accents,* about a Dominican family living in the Bronx. Alvarez teaches at Middlebury College in Vermont, her alma mater.

In this poem, the sculpture that Sir Nameless orders is actually a stone slab with his figure carved in relief. You see this type of tombstone in very old churches. They are laid right into the church wall or floor, with the bodies buried behind or under them. The people who are buried there are frequently knights or nobles.

What do you think of statues and paintings that are made to immortalize some powerful person? In your opinion, what is the best way for a person to make sure that his or her memory is honored?

The Children and Sir Nameless

Thomas Hardy

Sir Nameless, once of Athelhall, declared:
"These wretched children romping in my park
Trample the herbage° till the soil is bared,
And yap and yell from early morn till dark!
5 Go keep them harnessed to their set routines:
Thank God I've none to hasten my decay;
For green remembrance there are better means
Than offspring, who but wish their sires° away."

Sir Nameless of that mansion said anon:
10 "To be perpetuate° for my mightiness
Sculpture must image me when I am gone."
—He forthwith summoned carvers there express
To shape a figure stretching seven-odd feet
(For he was tall) in alabaster stone,
15 With shield, and crest, and casque,° and sword complete:
When done a statelier work was never known.

Three hundred years hied;° Church-restorers came,
And, no one of his lineage being traced,
They thought an effigy so large in frame
20 Best fitted for the floor. There it was placed,
Under the seats for schoolchildren. And they
Kicked out his name, and hobnailed off his nose;
And, as they yawn through sermon-time, they say
"Who was this old stone man between our toes?"

3. **herbage:** grass.

8. **sires:** fathers.

10. **perpetuate:** immortalized (perpetuated).

15. **casque:** helmet.

17. **hied:** went quickly.

Responding to the Poem

Analyzing the Poem

Identifying Details

1. Sir Nameless, we learn, is annoyed by noisy children who spoil the grass surrounding his estate. But he also has another attitude toward children. Find the lines that reveal how he feels about them.
2. What means of immortalizing himself does Sir Nameless devise?
3. Revenge is the act of "getting even" for some real or imagined insult or injury. What does Sir Nameless say should be done with the "romping" children? Three hundred years later, how do the children "get even" with Sir Nameless?

Interpreting Meanings

4. What is **ironic** about what happens to Sir Nameless's sculpture? In other words, what did he expect it to do for him, and what actually happens to it?
5. Why do the church restorers decide to put Sir Nameless's sculpture on the church floor? Why is this **ironic,** considering how Sir Nameless felt about having children to carry on his memory?
6. Why is it **ironic** that the poet calls his character "Sir Nameless"?
7. How would you state the lesson, **moral,** of this poem? Do you agree with it? Why or why not? Can you come up with any arguments to refute it?
8. How does this poet feel about Sir Nameless? Do you share his feelings, or do you feel some pity toward him? Explain your response.
9. Do you think that Sir Nameless's attitude toward children is common today? Explain.

Writing About the Poem

A Creative Response

Updating the Poem. This poem is about a man who lived over three hundred years ago in England. In a paragraph, describe a modern "Mr. Nameless" who lives in the United States and who might try to perpetuate his name in some contemporary way. What happens to this memorial in the next three centuries?

Analyzing Language and Vocabulary

Paraphrasing

To **paraphrase** means to restate something in your own words. Here is how the first four lines of "Sir Nameless" might be paraphrased:

> Sir Nameless, who once lived on an estate called Athelhall, said, "Those lousy kids who play on my property ruin the grass by tramping it down so that the earth shows through, and they scream from dawn to dusk."

Paraphrase the following lines, paying particular attention to the italicized words and phrases:

1. " 'For *green remembrance* there are better means
   Than offspring, who but *wish their sires away.*' "
2. " 'To be *perpetuate* for my mightiness
   Sculpture must image me when I am gone.' "
3.   "And they
   Kicked out his name, and *hobnailed off* his nose;
   And, as they yawn through sermon-time, they say,
   'Who was this old stone man *between our toes?*' "

Reading About the Writer

Thomas Hardy (1840–1928) was born near Dorchester, in that gentle and rolling part of England bordering the English Channel. While most readers know him as the author of such novels as *Jude the Obscure, The Return of the Native,* and *Tess of the d'Urbervilles,* Hardy was a prolific poet whose work assumes greater and greater importance with the passing years. Like Robert Frost, A. E. Housman, and other poets identified with a particular place, Hardy's poetic sources are found in the country life and scenes of Dorsetshire, which, for fictional purposes, he called Wessex. By prevailing critical standards, Hardy's poems are old-fashioned. Yet they convey a vision broad enough to include the most intimate personal concerns as well as a philosopher's concerns for the meanings of history and our place within it. While he was basically a lyricist (many of his poems have the feeling of songs), Hardy also used his gifts as a novelist to tell stories in his poems.

The "antique land" in this poem is Egypt, where over three thousand years ago, the Pharaoh "Ozymandias" (also known as Rameses II) built huge palaces, temples, and monuments commemorating his own greatness. The remains of some of these can be seen today in places like Karnak and Thebes, where they are popular tourist attractions.

In Shelley's time, any traveler in Egypt was apt to encounter these ruins wherever they had fallen, untended and half-buried by drifting sand.

Perhaps you have seen photographs of colossal ancient ruins—in Egypt (see page 355), Mexico, Guatemala, Greece, or Italy. When you see such ruins, what do you think of?

Ozymandias

Percy Bysshe Shelley

I met a traveler from an antique land
Who said: Two vast and trunkless legs of stone
Stand in the desert . . . Near them, on the sand,
Half sunk, a shattered visage° lies, whose frown,
5 And wrinkled lip, and sneer of cold command,
Tell that its sculptor well those passions read
Which yet survive, stamped on these lifeless things,
The hand that mocked them, and the heart that fed:
And on the pedestal these words appear:
10 "My name is Ozymandias, king of kings:
Look on my works, ye Mighty, and despair!"
Nothing beside remains. Round the decay
Of that colossal wreck, boundless and bare
The lone and level sands stretch far away.

4. **visage**: face.

Responding to the Poem

Analyzing the Poem

Identifying Details

1. How many voices do you hear speaking in this poem? Identify them.
2. Describe what the traveler has seen.
3. Describe the expression the traveler reads on the face of the broken statue.
4. The "hand" and the "heart" in line 8 are objects of the verb "survive" in line 7. Whose hand mocked the passions? Whose heart fed them?

Interpreting Meanings

5. Considering the condition of the statue, explain what is **ironic** about the words inscribed on its pedestal.
6. Apparently, the vast "works" of this tyrant once stood near the statue. What might they have been? How do the **images** in the last three lines provide an **ironic** comment on the king's "works" and how long they endured?
7. Explain why Ozymandias said, "Look on my

works, ye Mighty, and despair!'' **Ironically,** why might readers of this poem ''despair'' when they realize what has become of the king's great works?

8. Explain what Ozymandias intended his statue to **symbolize. Ironically,** what has the statue come to symbolize instead?

9. How would you describe the **tone** of the poem—that is, how do you think the poet feels about Ozymandias?

10. Do you think this poem's message is still important? Do any ''Ozymandiases'' exist today? Do you see any connections between this poem and W. H. Auden's ''Epitaph on a Tyrant'' (page 375)? Explain.

Writing About the Poem

A Critical Response

Comparing and Contrasting Poems. Write a brief essay comparing and contrasting Shelley's poem with Hardy's ''The Children and Sir Nameless'' (page 351). Use the following chart as a guide for gathering details and planning your essay. Write one or two paragraphs.

	Hardy	Shelley
Characteristics of main character in poem		
Role of sculptor in poem		
How face in poem has been ''shattered''		
Moral of poem		
Use of irony in poem		
Emotional effect of poem		

Analyzing Language and Vocabulary

Root Words

One of the key words in this poem is the noun *visage,* which means ''face.'' *Visage* comes from the Latin verb *videre,* meaning ''to see.'' Often the word *visage* is used with an adjective to suggest a kind of temperament: a stern visage, a kind visage, a tortured visage. In this poem, we read of a ''shattered visage,'' an image that helps us imagine the broken pieces of the face of Ozymandias's huge

statue. Find the lines in the poem that tell you which of these adjectives could be used to describe Ozymandias's visage:

A stern visage   A kind visage
A cold visage   A noble visage

Many English words such as *vision* are formed from the Latin verb *videre.* Some of the italicized words in the following sentences may seem at first glance to have little to do with ''seeing.'' Look these words up in a dictionary to answer these questions:

1. What does the word *review* have to do with the idea of ''seeing''?

2. Why can *revision* be thought of as ''re-seeing''?

3. How is the word *interview* related to *videre?*

4. What does the word *survey* have to do with ''seeing''?

5. A *visa* is an endorsement on a passport that enables a traveler to travel through a particular country. What does a *visa* have to do with ''seeing''?

6. Which of these words derive from *videre: video, viscous, visit, vista, vital?*

Reading About the Writer

Percy Bysshe Shelley (1792–1822) was born in Horsham, Sussex, England. His independent reading in history and literature, first at Eton and later at Oxford, led him to take intellectual positions so much at odds with authority that he was expelled from the university. This was merely the first of many stormy episodes in a brief life that was marked by a struggle against tyranny of all forms—including the tyranny of social conventions. Shelley married two remarkable women, Harriet Westbrook and Mary Wollstonecraft Godwin, who wrote the famous novel *Frankenstein.* His relations with literary critics were touchy, and his unconventional life and his ideas on love, marriage, and politics scandalized his fellow Englishmen. Shelley traveled restlessly from place to place in Europe. He was barely thirty years old when, one summer day, his boat was caught in a storm in the Bay of Lerici, off the west coast of Italy, and Shelley and his companion were drowned. Identified with the Romantic movement of the early nineteenth century, Shelley is often regarded as the purest and most lyrical of the English Romantic poets. He is especially known for a body of comparatively short poems that include ''Ode to the West Wind'' and ''To a Skylark.''

When you're feeling strong emotions—sadness, joy, anger—have you ever attempted to write down your thoughts? Here a famous Chilean poet tries to find words to express his feelings after he has lost a woman he loved—and perhaps still loves. Before you read the poem, write a few sentences in your journal describing how the world feels when you've won somebody you love. Then write how the world feels when you've lost that person.

Tonight I Can Write

Pablo Neruda, translated by W. S. Merwin

Tonight I can write the saddest lines.

Write, for example, "The night is starry
and the stars are blue and shiver in the distance."

The night wind revolves in the sky and sings.

5   Tonight I can write the saddest lines.
I loved her, and sometimes she loved me too.

Through nights like this one I held her in my arms.
I kissed her again and again under the endless sky.

She loved me, sometimes I loved her too.
10   How could one not have loved her great still eyes.

Tonight I can write the saddest lines.
To think that I do not have her. To feel that I have
    lost her.

To hear the immense night, still more immense
    without her.
And the verse falls to the soul like dew to the pasture.

15   What does it matter that my love could not keep her.
The night is starry and she is not with me.

This is all. In the distance someone is singing. In
    the distance.
My soul is not satisfied that it has lost her.

My sight tries to find her as though to bring her
    closer.
20   My heart looks for her, and she is not with me.

Woman Meditating by Giovanni Costetti.

Gallery of Modern Art, Florence.

The same night whitening the same trees.
We, of that time, are no longer the same.

I no longer love her, that's certain, but how I loved her.
My voice tried to find the wind to touch her hearing.

25   Another's. She will be another's. As she was before my kisses.
Her voice, her bright body. Her infinite eyes.

I no longer love her, that's certain, but maybe I love her.
Love is so short, forgetting is so long.

Because through nights like this one I held her in my arms
30   my soul is not satisfied that it has lost her.

Though this be the last pain that she makes me suffer
and these the last verses that I write for her.

Untitled (Trees at Night) by
Thomas B. Meteyard.

Berry-Hill Galleries, New York.

Responding to the Poem

Analyzing the Poem

Identifying Details

1. How does the speaker now feel about the woman he has lost? What **conflict** does he express in line 27?

Interpreting Meanings

2. The speaker keeps contrasting this night with previous ones. How were those other nights different? How might the speaker have described the night, the stars, and the sound of someone sighing on those other nights?
3. Describe the speaker's **tone**. What images help establish this tone?
4. Find examples of **repetition** in the poem—lines and phrases that echo previous lines. How do these echoes intensify the **emotional effect**?
5. How do you think the speaker felt last night— why was he unable to write even the saddest lines then?
6. Look at the **simile** in line 14. What is Neruda suggesting about what poetry does for us?
7. Reread line 28. Are you convinced this *will* be the last time the speaker feels pain about the woman, and the last poem he writes for her? Explain.

Writing About the Poem

A Creative Response

Telling a Story. Fill in the outlines of the love story hinted at in this poem. Describe what might have happened between the speaker and the woman. Why did their romance end? What is the woman doing now? How does *she* feel?

Reading About the Writer

Pablo Neruda (1904–1973) is the pen name of Neftalí Recardo Reyes Basualto of Chile. One of Latin America's best-known poets, Neruda was also a politician, diplomat, and social activist, as well as an important translator of English poetry into Spanish. After his involvement in an aborted revolution in Chile, Neruda wrote, ''. . . politics became part of my poetry and my life. In my poems I could not shut the door to the street, just as I could not shut the door to love, life, joy, or sadness in my young poet's heart.''

In 1971 Neruda won the Nobel Prize in literature. He died two years later during the week of the 1973 military coup that overthrew his friend President Salvadore Allende. Some people believe that both Neruda and Allende were murdered.

The speaker in the following poem has been directed by his teacher to write a paper and to "let that page come out of" him. What do you think this instruction means? How do you feel when you are faced with such assignments? Do you agree with the speaker that they aren't "that simple"?

Theme for English B

Langston Hughes

The instructor said,

Go home and write
a page tonight.
And let that page come out of you—
5 →*then, it will be true.*

6 I wonder if it's that simple?
7 I am twenty-two, colored, born in Winston-Salem.
8 I went to school there, then Durham, then here
9 to this college on the hill° above Harlem.
10 I am the only colored student in my class.
   The steps from the hill lead down into Harlem,
   through a park, then I cross St. Nicholas,
   Eighth Avenue, Seventh, and I come to the Y,
   the Harlem Branch Y, where I take the elevator
15 up to my room, sit down, and write this page:

   It's not easy to know what is true for you or me
   at twenty-two, my age. But I guess I'm what
   I feel and see and hear, Harlem, I hear you:
   hear you, hear me—we two—you, me, talk on this page.
20 (I hear New York, too.) Me—who?

   Well, I like to eat, sleep, drink, and be in love.
   I like to work, read, learn, and understand life.
   I like a pipe for a Christmas present,
   or records—Bessie,° bop, or Bach.

25 I guess being colored doesn't make me *not* like
   the same things other folks like who are other races.
   So will my page be colored that I write?
   Being me, it will not be white.
   But it will be
30 a part of you, instructor.
   You are white—
   yet a part of me, as I am a part of you.
   That's American.
   Sometimes perhaps you don't want to be a part of me.
35 Nor do I often want to be a part of you.
   But we are, that's true!
   As I learn from you,
   I guess you learn from me—
   although you're older—and white—
40 and somewhat more free.

   This is my page for English B.

9. **college on the hill:** Columbia University.

24. **Bessie:** Bessie Smith, the great jazz and blues singer.

Responding to the Poem

Analyzing the Poem

Identifying Details

1. In line 6, explain what the speaker isn't sure is "that simple" to do.
2. List the autobiographical information that the speaker provides about who he is, where he comes from, and the things he likes in life.

Interpreting Meanings

3. After presenting his autobiography, the speaker then tries to make some sense out of it—he tries to determine if it conveys the essential truth about himself. In lines 27–35, what does he struggle to understand?
4. What realization does he come to at the end of the poem? Do you think the speaker intends line 40 to be an **understatement,** a statement that means far more than it seems to say? Explain.
5. How would you describe the **tone** of this "essay"? Is the speaker bitter about his life, sad, angry, positive, hopeful, amused, or some combination of these feelings?

Writing About the Poem

A Creative Response

1. **Imitating the Poem.** Imagine that your own teacher has given you the same writing assignment that this speaker's instructor gave him. Then write a poem that in the first ten or fifteen lines tells your age and gives details about where you come from, where you live, and where you go to school. Then, in as many lines as you need, talk about your likes and dislikes, and name those particular things about yourself that would have to be included in any description of your personality. If you would prefer not to write about yourself, write as if you were another person, perhaps a friend or even a famous person whose character you think you understand. Use the first-person pronoun *I,* and if you like, address your teacher directly as *you.*
2. **Responding to the Poem.** Suppose you are the instructor of English B. Write a response to this student's essay. You might write a free-verse poem or a paragraph. Will your **tone** be understanding, confused, angry, or something else?

Focusing on Background
The Autobiography of a Poet

Here is an excerpt from the first volume of Langston Hughes's autobiography, *The Big Sea,* in which he describes meeting the poet Vachel Lindsay while working as a busboy in a hotel in Washington, D.C.:

". . . Diplomats and cabinet members in the dining room did not excite me much, but I was thrilled the day Vachel Lindsay came. I knew him because I'd seen his picture in the papers that morning. He was to give a reading of his poems in the little theater of the hotel that night. I wanted very much to hear him read his poems, but I knew they did not admit colored people to the auditorium.

"That afternoon I wrote out three of my poems, "Jazzonia," "Negro Dancers," and "The Weary Blues," on some pieces of paper and put them in the pocket of my white busboy's coat. In the evening when Mr. Lindsay came down to dinner, quickly I laid them beside his plate and went away, afraid to say anything to so famous a poet, except to tell him I liked his poems and that these were poems of mine. I looked back once and saw Mr. Lindsay reading the poems as I picked up a tray of dirty dishes from a side table and started for the dumbwaiter.

"The next morning on the way to work, as usual I bought a paper—and there I read that Vachel Lindsay had discovered a Negro busboy poet! At the hotel the reporters were already waiting for me. . . ."

—Langston Hughes

The speaker in this little lyric is the "Shropshire lad," the central figure in Housman's major collection of poems (see also page 272). As the young man talks of the time he was in love, think about this question: How does the *poet* feel about this experience?

Oh, When I Was in Love with You

A. E. Housman

Oh, when I was in love with you,
    Then I was clean and brave,
And miles around the wonder grew
    How well did I behave.

And now the fancy passes by,
    And nothing will remain,
And miles around they'll say that I
    Am quite myself again.

Responding to the Poem

Analyzing the Poem

Identifying Details

1. What does the speaker tell us he was like when he was in love?
2. What happened when the "fancy" passed by?

Interpreting Meanings

3. How does the speaker feel about his experience of being in love? How do you think the poet feels about it? (Do you think the poet's **tone** is serious and sympathetic, or light and slightly cynical?)
4. Do you think the speaker's own **tone** changes in the second stanza? Explain your answer.
5. To whom is the speaker talking? How does this affect the **tone** of his poem?
6. Some readers interpret the speaker's tone in the last two lines as **ironic.** Do you think the speaker agrees with the opinion of his neighbors, or does he perhaps feel that he was actually his true self when he was "clean and brave" and in love? How might the word "fancy" in line 5 also have **ironic** overtones? Explain your response.
7. Do you think this boy's experience with love is a common one? Is the fact that his transformation was temporary also common? Explain.
8. Could these lines have been spoken by a woman?

Writing About the Poem

A Creative Response

Changing the Speaker in the Poem. The same subject might be treated quite differently by two different writers or speakers. To show how a shift in attitude can affect a poem, select a character from another poem in this unit and have that character be the speaker of a new poem that begins: "Oh, when I was in love with you . . ." Try to capture a **tone** that you think fits this character. For the most interesting results, choose a character whose attitudes would obviously be different from those in Housman's poem. You might have Sir Nameless (page 351) talk about his childhood sweetheart. Or you might have the speaker in ".05" (page 311) tell about his experiences with love. If you think Miss Rosie (page 230) has a story to tell, you might let her be your speaker.

This poem is about a writer who is driving home to Omaha, Nebraska, from a writers' conference in Bread Loaf, Vermont. To get the full flavor of this poem, you have to catch the speaker's references to contemporary American life. What effect do they create as you read the poem?

Bread Loaf to Omaha, Twenty-eight Hours

Patrick Worth Gray

Doing 70 on Interstate 94
In the hot August dusk
My little blue Opel straining
Toward the stink of Hammond visible
On the horizon, I was whistling
5   "Hernando's
Hideaway" (you can sing "Stopping
By Woods on a Snowy Evening"
To it) and thinking what a really
Neat poet (and good-looking)
10   I am when a tractor-trailer
Loaded with new Cadillacs
Its tattooed driver chewing
A Dutch Master right
Beside me pulled left
15   I jerked left

Another truck, the gap
Narrowed, smoke appeared
From my new Sears Radials
Then I was on the shoulder
20   And the two truckers were shouting
Speed-trap bulletins across
Lanes, blasting into
The sunset, and I kneeled, losing
Anchovy pizza, Michelob,
25   Illusions. I was just another
Old man lost in Michigan,
Trying to reach my wife
And daughter, to write another
Lousy poem, just
30   Another old man, lost
In America, trying to get home.

Responding to the Poem

Analyzing the Poem

Identifying Details

1. What happens to the speaker on his way from Bread Loaf to Omaha?

Interpreting Meanings

2. Explain what the "twenty-eight hours" in the title signifies.
3. The speaker uses a **figure of speech** in line 4. Explain how the "stink of Hammond" (a steel-making city in Indiana) could be *visible* on the horizon.
4. At the beginning of the poem, the speaker's **tone** is positive. He's "full of himself," or pleased to be who he is. As the poem ends, however, the tone changes. Describe how the speaker suddenly feels about himself, and explain why his feelings have changed.
5. When the speaker says that he is "lost in America," clearly he isn't talking about being *physically* lost. Explain what you think he means and what has led him to this troubling conclusion.
6. What meanings can you propose for the word *home* in the last line?
7. Do you think this feeling of being "lost" is a common one? What events can bring the feeling on, and what experiences can make it go away?

Writing About the Poem

A Critical Response

Analyzing the Poem. Clearly, the **diction,** or word choice, in this poem indicates that it was written in the United States in the latter part of the twentieth century. In a paragraph, explain whether the **theme** of the poem is also limited to contemporary American life, or if the speaker's experience could have taken place anywhere, at any time in history.

Analyzing Language and Vocabulary

Proper Nouns and Brand Names

The reader of this poem knows exactly what road the speaker is driving on (Interstate 94), what kind of car he is driving (Opel), what song he is whistling ("Hernando's Hideaway"), what he had for lunch (anchovy pizza and Michelob), and a host of other details about the America he drives through on his way home.

1. The use of these specific names tells us something about the speaker. How would the effect have been different if he had been driving a "big, black Cadillac" or a "beat-up Ford station wagon"?
2. What impression would you have gotten if the speaker had been humming a refrain from Beethoven's Fifth Symphony, rather than a musical-comedy song?
3. How would your feelings about the speaker have been different if he had eaten poached salmon and Perrier, or a broccoli omelette and Diet Pepsi, for lunch?
4. What is the disadvantage of using these specific words? Do you know what an Opel looks like? Can *you* hum the tune of "Hernando's Hideaway"? Will readers understand this poem in a hundred years?

Rewrite the following sentences, substituting brand names or proper nouns for the italicized words. Then exchange your sentences in class. Have any of you used the same names? Do different names reveal anything distinct about the character or event mentioned in the sentence?

1. Al checked his *watch* and went into the *hotel*.
2. Julia sang a *song* as she ran down the *street*.
3. The children demanded a *soft drink* at the *fast-food restaurant*.
4. Louise drove her *car* to *town*.
5. Emily is in the *city* with a *singer*.
6. Jonathan drove down the *highway* to the *convenience store* to buy a *soda*.

Reading About the Writer

Patrick Worth Gray (1937–   ) graduated from Phillips University and received a master's degree from the University of Iowa. In 1973 he became an instructor in the Omaha Writer's Workshop at the University of Nebraska. His poetry has been published in several journals, including *Cimarron Review, Poetry Now,* and *The Saturday Review.*

In "Willy" we have a good example of *apostrophe* —a figure of speech that is closely related to personification. In apostrophe, someone who is absent (or dead) or something nonhuman is addressed as if it were alive, present, and capable of responding to the speaker.

Have you ever watched a caged animal in a zoo and wondered what it is feeling and thinking?

Reading this poem aloud will help you feel as if you are overhearing this speaker's thoughts as he stands in front of the grizzly's cage.

As you read the poem a second time, write down questions you have about the text. Note passages that puzzle you, or words that you have to look up in a dictionary. On this second reading, are any parts of the poem still unclear to you?

Willy

Richard Moore

Willy, enormous Saskatchewan° grizzly—your blood partly polar,
tranquil your temper—with only your furred face visible in there
propped up over your puddle and pool-rim, scanning the crowd for
peanuts: we're all safe on humanity's side of your cage-bars.
5 One of your elbows sits on your concrete floor, with its huge paw
coyly supporting your chin, while your eyelids droop and your mouth hangs
cavernous, wide as a hillside, opening—heavens!—you're yawning.
Seeming so spiritless—so like a man—are you mocking us, Willy?

Nuts drop near you, and sometimes your free paw, big as a tree-stump,
10 mossy with hair and with stick-sized claws on it, browned and decaying,
darts, and adroitly° you sweep one into you, Willy—you're much too
civilized, playing obsequious° tricks for these pestering people:
you who have driven whole ox-herds before you through forests and ice fields.
Do you remember your long lone nights on the stardark tundra,
15 now that you're shut in from life and this wearying crowd and its clamors?
Bored, Willy? Who can awaken you? ("Up, Willy!" someone is calling.)
Peanuts may not be enough. Do you long for some tastier tribute?
That, Willy, needs a more godlike behavior and ("Up, Willy, up, up!")
dignity, Willy; more dignity's needed to . . . Willy? What's moving?

20 Nothing is moving; yet all of you—face, paws, elbows—is rising.
Mountains of hair there are heaving up under you, streaming with waters,
up, up, up out of splashing cascades; dark shadowy body
up from the black earth's bubbling depths—and the women are shrieking.
How did they dare to confine you, those vermin alive on your shadow?
25 What is it makes you endure them, O swaying and perilous tower,
touching our day with a second of terror, our nights with a nasty
Freudian dream?° How?—deftly you've caught it—that carton of—ice cream!

---

1. **Saskatchewan:** a Canadian province.   11. **adroitly:** skillfully.   12. **obsequious:** overly servile, submissive, fawning.   27. **Freudian dream:** a dream that reveals hidden fears or desires.

Responding to the Poem

Analyzing the Poem

Identifying Details

1. When we first meet Willy, what is he doing?
2. Describe how the crowd treats Willy. What do they want him to do?
3. How does the speaker want Willy to behave?
4. Identify at least five examples of **alliteration** and **internal rhyme** in the poem.

Interpreting Meanings

5. The speaker tells Willy that he is too civilized, playing "obsequious tricks" for the crowd. Does he really mean that the bear is civilized, or is he making an **ironic** comment on the supposedly civilized crowd that is pestering the bear? Explain.
6. Beginning in line 19, Willy rises up out of the pool. What **images** and **figures of speech** make Willy's movements now seem terrifying and godlike? Who are the "vermin alive on" his shadow in line 24?
7. What outrage does the bear's new-found dignity inspire in the speaker? Describe how his **tone** changes as he addresses Willy in line 24.
8. Do you think the "second of terror" and the "nasty Freudian dream" are exactly what the crowd wanted out of Willy in the first place? Where else might we find this psychology of pleasantly manageable fear put to use?
9. The last line of the poem is deliberately anti-climactic—that is, it leads us to expect something big and then lets us down. What did you *think* the speaker was building up to? What does this last **image** of Willy tell us about what happens to nature when it is caged or tamed?
10. Do you think the poem suggests that something also happens to human beings when they treat animals this way? Explain.

Writing About the Poem

A Creative Response

1. **Using Another Point of View.** Write at least six lines of poetry that reveal Willy's thoughts. What images would he use to describe the crowd? What does *he* think of *them*?

A Critical Response

2. **Answering the Poet.** In this poem, the speaker seems to feel that Willy would be much better off if he were left in the wild. There are people, however, who would counter with the argument that zoo animals are protected and humanely cared for, and that they help people understand animal life better. What do you think? Write one or two paragraphs in response to the poet.
3. **Comparing and Contrasting Poems.** Arthur Guiterman's poem on page 324 is also about bears. In a brief essay, compare and contrast that poem with "Willy." Consider each poem's purpose, sound effects, and tone.

Analyzing Language and Vocabulary

Monitoring Your Reading

What questions did you have as you read this poem? Refer to your notes, and discuss your questions in class. In case you haven't covered these aspects of the poem, answer the following questions as well:

1. Is the word *Willy* the subject of the first sentence? If not, what word is the subject?
2. What would be the standard way of saying "tranquil your temper" in line 2?
3. What verb goes with the subject "paw" in line 9?
4. What does the pronoun "one" refer to in line 11?
5. To what or whom does the apostrophe "O swaying and perilous tower" in line 25 refer?

Reading About the Writer

Richard Moore (1927–   ) was born in Greenwich, Connecticut, and has taught college English for many years. He has published several volumes of poetry, including a long epic poem entitled *The Autobiography of a Mouse*. Moore's poems frequently appear in such magazines as *The New Yorker, The Atlantic, Harper's, Mademoiselle,* and *The Nation*. Of his work, Moore says, "I try for poems that are passionate, clear, classic in form, and darkly humorous."

This little lyric is one of the most famous poems of the nineteenth century. During that century, nature was both the main subject of poetry and the main object of scientific investigation. To the poets, nature was mysterious and romantic. To the scientists, nature had laws of its own that could be discovered by observation, secrets that could be revealed and analyzed with the help of the telescope and microscope.

Reading this poem today, you might think about why a poem so brief and so simple could have once made such an impact that anyone with even the slightest education was likely to know it by heart.

Flower in the Crannied Wall

Alfred, Lord Tennyson

Flower in the crannied° wall,
I pluck you out of the crannies,
I hold you here, root and all, in my hand,
Little flower—but *if* I could understand
What you are, root and all, and all in all,
I should know what God and man is.

1. **cranny:** a small crevice in a wall or rock face.

The Four Leaf Clover by Winslow Homer (1873). Oil.

© 1987 The Detroit Institute of Arts. Bequest of Robert H. Tannahill.

Responding to the Poem

Analyzing the Poem

Identifying Details

1. What does the speaker think an understanding of the flower would teach him?

Interpreting Meanings

2. What mystery or secret is the speaker talking about in this poem?
3. "Root and all," a handful that the speaker can study, is clear enough. But what do you think he means by "all in all"?
4. How would you describe the speaker's **tone,** or his attitude, toward the flower? Is he cynical, troubled, sarcastic, awed, or amused?
5. List at least two questions a scientist might ask about a flower he or she is given to study. How do you think the scientist would phrase the speaker's question?
6. In what ways is the speaker, in his investigation of the flower, also acting like a scientist? Do you think the subject of the speaker's investigation is still meaningful today, or have scientific advances made such questions obsolete? Explain.

Writing About the Poem

A Creative Response

1. **Extending the Poem.** The speaker in this poem imagines that he might understand "what God and man is" if he could penetrate the secret of a flower. In a paragraph, describe three other "things" that could hold the answers to questions about the mysteries of life. The "things" could be human, animal, vegetable, or mineral, or even things manufactured or created by human beings.

A Critical Response

2. **Comparing and Contrasting Poems.** In a brief essay, compare and contrast Tennyson's response to the flower in this poem to Wordsworth's response to the daffodils (page 278) and Ginsberg's response to the hay flower (page 282). Before you write, think about the following aspects of each poem:

   a. What the speaker is searching for when he encounters the flower or flowers
   b. What the speaker discovers (or what lesson he learns)
   c. The speaker's tone
   d. The speaker's feelings about nature

Reading About the Writer

Alfred, Lord Tennyson (1809–1892) was one of the great figures of the Victorian Age in England. His life span approximated that of Queen Victoria herself, in whose reign he became Poet Laureate.

Tennyson had grave doubts about what was happening to his country as industry began to replace agriculture and as scientific theories began to undermine religious beliefs, and much of his poetry addresses this issue. Yet many critics feel that his poems tend to echo the sentimentality that pervaded the popular art of his time. Today Tennyson is best known for a few of his lyrics; for his poem *In Memoriam,* a long series of elegies honoring a dead friend of his youth; and for *Idylls of the King*, a twelve-volume book of narrative poems that retell the legendary tales of King Arthur and his Knights of the Round Table. Enormously popular, *Idylls of the King* helped the English people sense their connection with a more heroic and chivalrous past.

A typical bedtime story begins with "once upon a time . . ." and ends with "and so they lived happily ever after." It is meant to comfort children and to send them off to sleep with the feeling that all's well with the world. At what moment in this poem do you realize that this "bedtime story" is *not* a comforting one?

Since a bedtime story is told aloud, read this poem orally. Notice where the poet uses run-on lines to avoid a monotonous, singsong rhythm.

Bedtime Story

George MacBeth

Long long ago when the world was a wild place
Planted with bushes and peopled by apes, our
Mission Brigade was at work in the jungle.
    Hard by the Congo

5   Once, when a foraging detail was active
Scouting for green-fly, it came on a gray man, the
Last living man, in the branch of a baobab°
    Stalking a monkey.

Earlier men had disposed of, for pleasure,
10   Creatures whose names we scarcely remember—
Zebra, rhinoceros, elephants, wart-hog,
    Lion, rats, deer. But

After the wars had extinguished the cities
Only the wild ones were left, half-naked
15   Near the Equator: and here was the last one,
    Starved for a monkey.

But then the Mission Brigade had encountered
Hundreds of such men: and their procedure,
History tells us, was only to feed them:
20   Find them and feed them;

Those were the orders. And this was the last one.
Nobody knew that he was, but he was. Mud
Caked on his flat gray flanks. He was crouched, half-
    Armed with a shaved spear,

25   Glinting beneath broad leaves. When their jaws cut
Swathes through the bark and he saw fine teeth shine,
Round eyes roll round and forked arms waver
    Huge as the rough trunks

---

7. **baobab:** an African tree.

Over his head, he was frightened. Our workers
30 Marched through the Congo before he was born, but
This was the first time perhaps that he'd seen one.
    Staring in hot still

Silence, he crouched there: then jumped. With a long swing
Down from his branch, he had angled his spear too
35 Quickly, before they could hold him, and hurled it
    Hard at the soldier

Leading the detail. How could he know Queen's
Orders were only to help him? The soldier
Winced when the tipped spear pricked him. Unsheathing his
40 Sting was a reflex.

Later the Queen was informed. There were no more
Men. An impetuous soldier had killed off,
Purely by chance, the penultimate° primate.
    When she was certain,

45 Squadrons of workers were fanned through the Congo
Detailed to bring back the man's picked bones to be
Sealed in the archives in amber. I'm quite sure
    Nobody found them

After the most industrious search, though.
50 Where had the bones gone? Over the earth, dear,
Ground by the teeth of the termites, blown by the
    Wind, like the dodo's.

---

43. **penultimate:** next-to-last. The apes and monkeys were the last primates.

Responding to the Poem

Analyzing the Poem

Identifying Details

1. The narrative of "Bedtime Story" is easy to follow: A detail of soldiers from a "Mission Brigade" encounters a man and accidentally kills him. But there is much more to the story. First of all, is the speaker a human being? How do you know?

2. What *is* the "bedtime story"? List its main events.

3. What has happened to human civilization by the time this "bedtime story" takes place?

4. What facts about the speaker's species are provided in stanzas 7 and 10?

5. According to stanzas 10–12, who governs this species?

Interpreting Meanings

6. Putting together the clues provided in the poem, identify the speaker of "Bedtime Story." Who is listening?

7. Does the speaker's species resemble any creatures you are familiar with? Explain.

8. Using your imagination and clues provided in the poem, what would you say caused the downfall of human civilization? Can you suggest why the speaker's species might have developed as it did?

9. What details in the poem suggest that the speaker and his species are superior to humans? What do you think of the way the poet depicts people in the poem?

10. How would you describe the **tone** of the "bedtime story"? How would you describe the *poet's* attitude toward contemporary civilization?

11. Explain why "Bedtime Story" is both an accurate and an **ironic** title for this poem.

12. Do you think this poem contains a warning to the human race? What do you think of its message? Why?

Writing About the Poem

A Creative Response

1. **Extending the Poem.** Write an account that explains how the speaker and his species came to dominate Earth. Tell what happened, when it happened, and why it happened.

2. **Using Another Point of View.** Write a brief poem or paragraph in which the gray man tells what he thought and felt when he was surprised by the Mission Brigade. What kind of **tone** will you use to describe his response to the soldiers?

3. **Choosing Visual Images.** If you had to illustrate this poem, what scene or image would you concentrate on? Cite the lines that contain this scene or image, and describe how you would depict it.

A Critical Response

4. **Analyzing the Poet's Attitude.** The dodo was a bird that disappeared from the earth because it could not fly and consequently could not protect itself. A comical and awkward creature, the dodo has come to stand for stupidity. When the poet says that the bones of the last man have disappeared "like the dodo's," he is making a comment on the human race. What other details in the poem reveal the poet's attitude toward the human race? In one or two paragraphs, discuss this attitude, supporting your statements with details from the poem.

Analyzing Language and Vocabulary

Related Forms of Words

A key word in "Bedtime Story" is *penultimate* (line 43), which means "next-to-last." The word comes from two Latin words: *paene*, meaning "almost," and *ultimus*, meaning "last, final, or farthest." Other English words are related to *penultimate* because they are also built on either *paene* or *ultimus*.

1. If a terrorist issues an *ultimatum*, what might happen?

2. What is an *ultimate* goal?

3. The partly lighted area around the shadow cast by a solar eclipse is called the *penumbra*. You know that *pen* means "almost." What do you think *umbra* means?

4. What do we mean when we say someone is investigating the *ultimate* nature of life?

5. What do we mean when we call a car the *ultimate* in luxury?

6. What would be the *penult* syllable in the word *penultimate*?

Reading About the Writer

George MacBeth (1932–   ) was born in Shotts, a mining village in Scotland. After graduating from Oxford, he became a producer for the British Broadcasting Corporation. Since 1976 he has divided his time between England and the United States.

All Watched Over by Machines of Loving Grace

Richard Brautigan

I like to think (and
the sooner the better!)
of a cybernetic° meadow
where mammals and computers
5   live together in mutually
programming harmony
like pure water
touching clear sky.

I like to think
10   (right now, please!)
of a cybernetic forest
filled with pines and electronics

where deer stroll peacefully
past computers
15   as if they were flowers
with spinning blossoms.

I like to think
(it has to be!)
of a cybernetic ecology
20   where we are free of our labors
and joined back to nature,
returned to our mammal
brothers and sisters,
and all watched over
25   by machines of loving grace.

---

3. **cybernetic:** having to do with computers.

Responding to the Poem

Analyzing the Poem

Identifying Details

1. Every time the poet repeats "I like to think," he follows with a remark in parentheses. List these remarks. What is he impatiently hoping for?
2. The **imagery** in this poem is striking because it mixes two categories of things that we normally think of as having nothing in common. What are these two categories? (Look at lines 4, 12, 13, and 14.)

Interpreting Meanings

3. Are machines usually regarded as the enemies of nature or as the guardians of nature? How are they regarded by this poet?
4. Why is the phrase "machines of loving grace" unusual and surprising?
5. This poem is a vision of the future, but in what sense might it be said that we already live under the guardianship of machines? Do you think of them as machines of "loving grace"? Explain why or why not.

6. Do you think any part of this poet's vision can come true? Would you *want* his vision of the future to come true—or do you find it unappealing? Explain.

7. Would you call this poem optimistic or pessimistic in **tone**? Why?

Writing About the Poem

A Creative Response

Imitating the Poem. Write a **free-verse** poem of your own in which you express your own vision of an ideal future. Open with Brautigan's words: "I like to think . . . ," and repeat these words every time you present a new **image** or set of images. You may want to present images of nature, images of tech-

nology, or other images or combinations of images. Choose your words carefully to express your **tone,** or attitude: Will you be sincere, ironic, awed, sarcastic, playful, optimistic, pessimistic, or something else? Write at least six lines.

Reading About the Writer

Richard Brautigan (1935–1984), who was born in Tacoma, Washington, spent most of his adult life in San Francisco, and was part of a group called the "San Francisco poets." Although Brautigan began his writing career as a poet, his first public recognition was for his loosely constructed comic novels. In 1967 he became a cult hero with the publication of *Trout Fishing in America.*

Literature & Language

Creating a Tone

1. In each of the two poems that follow, a speaker is addressing someone he loves:

Pocket Poem

If this comes creased and creased again
    and soiled
as if I'd opened it a thousand times
to see if what I'd written here was right
it's all because I looked for you too long
to put it in your pocket. Midnight says
the little gifts of loneliness come wrapped
by nervous fingers. What I wanted this
to say was that I want to be so close
that when you find it, it is warm from me.

                    —Ted Kooser

Lines Supposed to Have Been Written to Fanny Brawne

This living hand, now warm and capable
Of earnest grasping, would, if it were cold
And in the icy silence of the tomb,
So haunt thy days and chill thy dreaming
    nights
That thou wouldst wish thine own heart dry
    of blood
So in my veins red life might stream again,
And thou be conscience-calmed—see here
    it is—
I hold it towards you.

                    —John Keats

---

a. In the first poem, why is the speaker writing?

b. What does "midnight" have to do with loneliness?

c. What specific details tell you the speaker's tone is sincerely affectionate? What detail shows that he yearns for love and closeness?

d. In the second poem, what does the speaker say his hand will do if he dies?

e. Is there a hint in the poem that Keats thinks Fanny feels guilty about something? Explain.

f. What important word is common to Kooser's and Keats's poem? Does it mean something different in each poem? Explain.

g. The **tone** of Keats's poem cannot be expressed simply—it reveals a mixture of attitudes. Keats was in love with Fanny Brawne, but when he learned that he had contracted tuberculosis, he realized that he would never live to marry her. Which of the following sets of adjectives would you select to describe the tone of Keats's poem: Loving and desperate? Cynical and bitter? Mocking and angry?

2. This next poem is also written to someone the speaker loves, but its **tone** is different from both Kooser's and Keats's poems:

The Taxi

When I go away from you
The world beats dead
Like a slackened drum.
I call out for you against the jutted stars
And shout into the ridges of the wind.
Streets coming fast,
One after the other,
Wedge you away from me,
And the lamps of the city prick my eyes
So that I can no longer see your face.
Why should I leave you,
To wound myself upon the sharp edges of the
    night?

                    —Amy Lowell

---

a. List the **images** you find in the poem.

b. What general feeling do these images give you? (How does each image suggest something dead, or sharp, or painful?)

c. Is there a single image that suggests contentment, pleasure, or fulfillment?

d. Which of these words best describes how the speaker feels about her experience: Amused? Angry? Hurt? Regretful? Mocking?

Literature & Language/*cont.*

3. When a speaker or writer gives words a meaning different from what they seem to express, an **ironic tone** results. This ironic tone might be created by a particular word choice or by a combination of details. The next poem is an epitaph, which means the poet imagines that it is inscribed on a tomb or gravestone:

Epitaph on a Tyrant

Perfection, of a kind, was what he was after,
And the poetry he invented was easy to understand;
He knew human folly like the back of his hand,
And was greatly interested in armies and fleets;
When he laughed, respectable senators burst with laughter,
And when he cried the little children died in the streets.

—W. H. Auden

---

a. What associations does the word *tyrant* suggest? How would the poem be different if the title were simply "Epitaph on a Ruler"?
b. What does the fact that the tyrant invented poetry that was "easy to understand" suggest about him?
c. Which of the following statements would you say is implied by the last line of the poem?

   (1) The tyrant wept for the little children.
   (2) Innocent children died because the tyrant was upset about something.
   (3) Children died because they wanted the tyrant to stop crying.

d. Which of these words would you use to describe Auden's **tone,** or attitude, toward the tyrant: Critical? Regretful? Admiring?

4. **Parody** is often used by poets to mock certain sentiments they don't agree with, or styles of poetry they don't like. Here are two poems that open with the same expression. "To burn your candle at both ends" means to play or to live so hard that you exhaust yourself.

First Fig

My candle burns at both ends;
   It will not last the night;
But ah, my foes, and oh, my friends—
   It gives a lovely light!

—Edna St. Vincent Millay

I Burned My Candle at Both Ends

I burned my candle at both ends,
And now have neither foes nor friends;
For all the lovely light begotten,
I'm paying now in feeling rotten.

—Samuel Hoffenstein

---

a. How does Millay's speaker feel about burning her candle at both ends?
b. How does Hoffenstein's speaker feel?
c. How does Hoffenstein use slang to mock Millay's poem?
d. How does he destroy Millay's "message"?

Writing

1. Changing a Poem's Tone. Rewrite Amy Lowell's poem "The Taxi" so that the poem is now about a person riding in a taxi to meet someone he or she loves. Use **images** that will suggest a tone of joy and anticipation. Your imagery should also involve stars, wind, the lamps (lights) of the city, and night, but you should describe all these things in words that reveal a joyful tone.

2. Imitating a Poem. Write a poem called "Epitaph on a Ruler" (or King, Prime Minister, President, etc.). Select someone you admire, and make your epitaph reflect your admiration. You could follow the general organization of Auden's poem:

_____ was what he (or she) was after.
The poetry he invented was _____.
He knew _____.
He was greatly interested in _____.
When he laughed _____.
When he cried _____.

WRITING A POEM

To write a poem is to turn an impulse into an idea, to give inner feelings outward expression. The process begins with finding the first word, the first mark among many marks on a page, that will somehow work the magic that translates what you feel into what you say.

Like the subjects available to painters and photographers, the materials for poetry are everywhere. But these materials do not come to life until they have been selected by your feelings and combined by your thoughts. The heart makes the choice, but the mind makes the poem.

Prewriting

1. **Choosing a Subject.** When you are assigned a poem to write, your first reaction is likely to be, "What am I going to write about?" Here's a technique for finding a subject: Imagine that you've just been given a new camera and three rolls of film. The weather is beautiful and you have nothing to do all day but wander wherever you'd like and snap anything you see. At first you'll probably take shots of any object in range just because it's there. But as your supply of film gets lower and lower, you'll be more apt to snap things that have particular meaning for you. Make a list of **images** you might take pictures of. Here is a sample list:

   a. A corner of the schoolyard where you used to play when you were in the fourth grade
   b. The magnolia tree in front of the library
   c. The "For Sale" sign on your house
   d. Your Aunt Hilda, the traffic officer
   e. Rooftops silhouetted against the sky
   f. Your dog Gus chasing a squirrel
   g. Your father's chair

   Once you stop taking pictures of everything in sight, you'll begin to choose your subjects, and your choice in every case will be something that reminds you of something else—an event, a person, a place—or that evokes a particular feeling you'd like to express.

2. **Finding Details.** Once you've chosen your subject, the big question is: "How can I make this thing and what I feel about it come alive for someone besides myself?" The answer is: *describe, describe, describe.* What you feel will be made apparent by the details you emphasize. Therefore, as your next step, make another list:

   a. Write down the details you want to emphasize.
   b. Write down the colors, shapes, textures, and weights of what you see.
   c. Are there any sounds, tastes, or smells you notice?
   d. Be aware of the **connotations,** or suggestive powers, of the words and figures of speech you choose. Is that motorcycle leaning against the wall shining like a new toy, or does it look like a sinister war machine? Does the rain on that window look like tears or like a spill of diamonds? Does the wind in the trees sound like a moan or like a song?

   At this point, jot down whatever comes into your mind. Later, you can select the details you will use. As you look over your list, you will also decide on your focus. Think of yourself again as a photographer: Will your picture be wide and panoramic, or will it be a tight close-up?

Writing

1. **Finding a Form.** If you want to be informal or conversational about your chosen subject and about the feelings it arouses, write your poem in **free verse.** (See page 303.) If you want to try to be more structured, write your poem with **meter** and **rhyme.** (See pages 300 and 322.)

2. **Using Free Verse**

   a. If you choose free verse, be concise about visual particulars, and be as economical with words, phrases, and sentences as possible. Don't "string out" what you mean in the casual language of a letter writer, or in the outpourings of the school gossip. Pack your meaning into the smallest parcel that will contain it.

b. Free verse can be willowy and languorous; and it can be as clipped and terse as something measured off with a ruler. In either case, free verse is free only to this extent: It allows natural conversational rhythms to do the work of **meter,** and it allows hard, precise **images** to carry the emotional weight of the poem. Find the proper images and your poem will almost write itself. These images open a poem that describes Barstow, a town in south-central California. (Belsen was the site of a Nazi concentration camp.)

> Nervy with neons, the main drag
> was all there was. A placeless place.
> A faint flavor of Mexico in the tacos
> tasting of gasoline. Trucks refueled
> before taking off through space. Someone lived
> in the houses with their houseyards wired
> like tiny Belsens.
>
> —from ''At Barstow,''
> Charles Tomlinson

Offering a completely different tone, these images open a poem that describes a small town in New England:

> I must be mad, or very tired,
> When the curve of a blue bay beyond a railroad
>   track
> Is shrill and sweet to me like the sudden spring-
>   ing of a tune,
> And the sight of a white church above thin trees
>   in a city square
> Amazes my eyes as though it were the Parthenon.
>
> —from ''Meeting-House Hill,''
> Amy Lowell

c. Pay special attention to where you end your lines. In writing free verse, poets may break

a line to indicate a pause for breath, or to show a natural break in thought.

d. Try to open with a line that captures your reader's attention. Here is an example by Carl Sandburg from a poem called ''Soup'':

> I saw a famous man eating soup.

Here is the opening line of a poem by Mark Strand called ''Eating Poetry'':

> Ink runs from the corners of my mouth.

e. Though free verse does not usually use **end rhymes,** it does often include **alliteration, onomatopoeia,** and **internal rhyme.**

3. Using Meter and Rhyme

a. If you are writing in a metric form, you will have to experiment until you find a pattern that suits your purpose. (A list of the common metric forms is on page 302.) Two meters are easiest for beginners: Try writing lines of three or four **iambs**—an unstressed syllable alternating with a stressed syllable: *daDAH daDAH daDAH daDAH.*

b. Try to maintain your beat exactly for the most part, but allow for some variation so that your verse doesn't sound mechanical and forced. If you use a three-foot line, for example, you might occasionally vary the meter by using a **trochee:** *DAHda daDAH daDAH.*

c. A simple form of rhyme is the **couplet:** two successive lines that rhyme:

> The time you won your town the race
> We chaired you through the market-place
> —from ''To an Athlete Dying Young,''
> A. E. Housman

d. Another popular form of rhyme is the **quatrain**—four successive lines of verse that have a certain rhyme pattern. Here is a comical quatrain by John Updike. It uses **end rhyme** in the second and fourth lines, plus a **half rhyme** in the first and third lines and within the second line. (Notice that the poet got the idea for his poem from a headline in a newspaper.)

ROGER BOBO GIVES RECITAL ON TUBA

—*Headline in the* Times

Eskimos in Manitoba,
Barracuda off Aruba,
Cock an ear when Roger Bobo
Starts to solo on the tuba

—from ''Recital,''
John Updike

''*Write about dogs!*''

Drawing by Booth; © 1976 The New Yorker Magazine, Inc.

4. **Finding Your Own Style.** If you choose to write your poem in **meter** and **rhyme,** you won't have to struggle for conciseness and economy because the demands of the form will take care of that. But a poem in meter and rhyme will amount to little unless you can overcome the mechanical sound of the metrical form and allow your own voice to be heard. Think of meter and rhyme as a dress or suit hanging on a rack. Nobody can change its basic shape or cut; but anyone who tries it on will find a way to wear it just a little differently from everyone else. That difference is called *style*. When you work on your poem, try out sounds and phrasings that sound like *you*. Read your poem aloud to yourself: Does it sound like your own individual voice? Once you've found your voice, the resulting style will be all yours, and so will the poem.

Linda Pastan describes the poet's dilemma and raw materials in the poem that follows. (The *yahrzeit glass* holds the candle that, in Jewish tradition, is lighted on the anniversary of a loved one's death.)

Poet

At his right hand
silence;
at his left hand
silence;
ahead of him
the yahrzeit glass;
behind him
silence;
and above his head
all the letters of the alphabet
to choose from.

—Linda Pastan

THE ELEMENTS OF NONFICTION

Still Life, Taj Hotel, Bombay, 1977 by David Hockney (1977). Crayon on paper.

UNIT THREE   **Janet Burroway**

THE ELEMENTS OF NONFICTION

An introduction by **Janet Burroway**

The Cotton Bureau at New Orleans (detail) by Edgar Degas (c. 1872). Oil.

Musée des Beaux Arts, Pau, France.

> *Those of us who are trying to write well about the world we live in, or to teach students to write well about the world* **they** *live in, are caught in a time warp, where literature by definition consists of forms that were certified as "literary" in the nineteenth century: novels and short stories and poems. But in fact these have become quite rarefied form in American life. The great preponderance of what writers now write and sell, what book and magazine publishers publish, and what readers demand is nonfiction.*
>
> —William Zinsser

A fiction writer creates an alternate world into which we may escape. A writer of nonfiction finds story enough, and strangeness enough, in the actual world as it lies before us. Nonfiction writers are curious and careful watchers, focusing on an amazing range of subjects, examining what they know and feel about stars or warts or sports. They may be watching coyotes or cotton fields or daily life in Soviet Russia. They may be thinking about love in Iowa or death in the North Atlantic.

No one is fascinated by real life all the time. Nonfiction writers want to capture those moments when life seems especially fascinating, luminous, or tragic; they want to direct our attention to the wonder of the ordinary world. Such writers begin with facts, respond to them, interpret them, and explain them. All nonfiction writers provide us with information, but the best of them present us with some even deeper truth as well.

Sometimes we think of nonfiction as the "workhorse" of literature—useful, but lacking the power and vision of poetry, drama, and fiction. It is true that if all the world's nonfiction were to disappear, a massive amount of information would vanish with it. All written records of history would be lost, and all the accounts of famous lives. All the science books would disappear, the medical books, cookbooks, travel guides, jogging manuals, and how-to series. The encyclopedias would go, and so would newspapers. We would lose all the practical information that the watchers and explainers of the world have set down for us. But if nonfiction were to disappear one day, not only information but a great deal of humor, wisdom, beauty, and humanity would perish, too.

Although nonfiction may be the most practical of the literary arts, it is also the most versatile and adaptable. It ranges from

> "**I**f nonfiction were to disappear one day, not only information but a great deal of humor, wisdom, beauty, and humanity would perish, too."

Naranjas (Oranges) by Carmen Lomas Garza (1988). Gouache on paper. (This artist records real events that have taken place within her family or in her neighborhood.)

Courtesy of the artist.

historical investigation to psychological insight to down-home humor. Nonfiction writers philosophize on the nature of cowardice and reminisce about mail-order catalogues; they can mock our money-grubbing or celebrate our survival against odds. Nonfiction writers can take the most complex issue and render it comprehensible. They can take the simplest object and reveal its mysteries.

Nonfiction and Fact

Nonfiction is usually defined as the form of literature that is based on fact. The term may be used to describe many varied kinds of writing—newspaper reports, autobiographies, biographies, essays, magazine articles, journals, diaries, book and play reviews, editorials. The list is long, and you can probably always find another

" **W**e
expect nonfiction
to tell the truth,
the whole truth,
and nothing but the
truth. But this is
impossible.''

sort of writing to add to it, provided the writing is based on fact. We expect nonfiction to be accurate and thorough, and to include nothing that can't be somehow verified. We also expect nonfiction to tell the truth, the whole truth, and nothing but the truth.

But this is impossible. Words themselves are an approximation of experience. The moment we try to put experience into words we have changed it, because "saying it" alters the experience. We can never tell "the whole truth" because experience is too complex to capture completely and because words have multiple shades of meaning. The word *love* in the statement *I love my new puppy* means something rather different from the word *love* in *I love Linda Sanchez.* It's just as impossible to tell "nothing but the truth" because many words have **connotations,** associations that color their meaning. The way we choose and arrange such words almost invariably implies an attitude as well as a fact. *Linda Sanchez has brown eyes* may be a fact, but is it a fact that *Linda Sanchez has hot-chocolate eyes?* Experience is rich and complex, words are rich and complex, and the one can never perfectly fit the other.

What a writer can do is choose and arrange words so that they come as near as possible to representing factual accuracy and honesty of judgment. If the writer can do that, and if he or she can also make people, places, and things so vivid that they seem "alive" in our minds, then the writing is "true."

Objective Versus Subjective Writing

At the moment, you are reading this book, and that's a fact. The book is called *Elements of Literature,* and that's a fact. You are sitting somewhere—on a chair, at a desk, on the grass, in a car? You are wearing something—jeans, a skirt, sneakers, a T-shirt, a letter sweater, a locket? It is some hour of the day, some day of the week, some month of the year—and so far, all the facts are **objective,** which means they can be proved to be true by the senses or by the calendar or the clock.

But you also might feel interested or bored, eager to get an A in English, or infuriated that you can't be on the basketball court. Any of these details may also be true, but they are **subjective**— they are verifiable only by reference to your own state of mind, and nobody knows the truth of that state but you.

Furthermore, if you were asked, would you describe your text-book as "well-thumbed" or "worn out"? Would you describe your T-shirt as "shabby" or "comfortable," the sun as "bright" or "glaring"? Can any of these details be objectively verified, or do they express subjective attitudes?

Consider the following two paragraphs. Which of these paragraphs is "true"?

> It's a Monday morning in May, and I am cross-legged on the fresh tickling grass in front of the library. I roll my shoulders in my favorite old T-shirt and open the well-thumbed pages of my textbook.

Monday again—the glare of the sun makes me squint, and the grass in front of the library prickles and itches. My T-shirt's a little the worse for wear, and so is this crumby textbook.

Here, two writers start with the same objective facts, but their choice of words gives their experiences opposite effects. The writers are reporting their experiences subjectively. By their choice of words and details, we understand that one writer is relaxed and comfortable, while the other is irritable and grumpy.

The Writer's Purpose: Four Types of Writing

There are many ways of classifying types of nonfiction, and one of the most common and useful is to identify the effect the author wants to produce. What is the writer's purpose? Given the facts, what is the primary sort of truth that the writer wants to communicate about them? What effect does the writer try to produce by his or her choice and arrangement of words?

In **exposition,** the writer's major purpose is to inform. This is likely to be the most objective kind of nonfiction, in which facts are employed as neutrally as possible. Exposition might explain how something works. It might report on a historical or scientific event, define a term, or clarify an idea—all without the author's opinion intruding. It would be possible, for example, for you to detest computers and to believe that high tech will destroy civilization—and yet to write a computer software manual so that the reader would never guess you held such an opinion.

In **persuasion,** on the other hand, the writer's major purpose is to convince the reader to think, to feel, or to act in a certain way. Persuasive writers will select and arrange facts in a way that will get readers to share their opinions. A newspaper editorial, a political speech, and a letter home asking for money will use persuasion. They are likely to succeed if the reader believes that the facts support the writer's opinion or the request.

Between these two extremes of purpose are description and narration. A writer of **description** intends to recreate for the reader a person, a place, or an event, largely through language that appeals to the senses. Description tells us how something looks, smells, tastes, sounds, and feels to the touch. A traveler's journal or an autobiographical reminiscence of a home town would probably use a great deal of description.

In writing **narration,** the author's purpose is to relate a series of events, usually in chronological order. A narrative has the form of a story (it even has characters and dialogue), but in nonfiction we demand that the events be factual and accurately recorded. A historical essay or an account of a soccer game would use narrative writing.

It is most important to remember that no piece of nonfiction can pursue one of these purposes to the absolute exclusion of the others. It would be impossible, for instance, to evoke the atmos-

Leonard Sidney Woolf by Vanessa Bell (1940). Oil on canvas.

By courtesy of the National Portrait Gallery, London.

> **Y**ou'll be better able to judge the effectiveness of a piece if you can identify its purpose.''

phere of your home town (description) without giving some information about it (exposition) and without trying to convince us to have a certain feeling about it (persuasion). Few sports writers will narrate a basketball game (narration) without describing the sights and sounds of the game and even of its spectators (description).

But each nonfiction piece will, if it is written well and clearly, reveal one of these as its major purpose. You'll be better able to judge the effectiveness of a piece if you can identify its purpose. Is this piece of writing telling me what something is and how it works? Then it's exposition. Is it trying to get me to believe something or to do something? Then it's persuasion. Is it showing me how something looks, tastes, feels, sounds, smells? Then it's description. Is it telling me what happened, and what happened next? Then it's narration.

All of the selections that follow are based on fact. They illustrate the range, the variety, and the power of nonfiction. They demonstrate as well the perception of their writers' minds, which are lively and curious, and of their eyes, which know not only the trick of watching but of watching well.

Journals and Travel Literature

The journals that follow record journeys—journeys in the great world, which often are also journeys within the self. For centuries, people have kept journals, records of their personal experiences and emotions. Some journals have become famous: Samuel Pepys's gossipy diary of life in eighteenth-century London allows us to travel, as if in a time machine, back to that lost time. The journals kept by Meriwether Lewis and William Clark as they marched across the Northwest Territory chronicle one of the great adventures in American history. *The Diary of Anne Frank* gives us both a moving record of a girl growing up and a terrifying day-by-day account of a Jewish family's ordeal in Nazi-occupied Amsterdam.

Those who keep journals are fortunate because they can savor their experiences and give them form. A journal may comment on events in the outside world or explore the writer's own feelings or do both. Journal writers live significant experiences twice— once as things happen and again as the experiences are re-created.

Other people—those who stay at home—have always been fascinated by the journals of travelers to strange and distant lands. Sometimes these travel accounts are primarily educational; sometimes they are filled with wondrous and exotic tales that are nonetheless true; and sometimes they are funny.

The selections in this section give you a small sampling of the variety available in journal and travel literature. The places visited range from the Mojave Desert in southern California to the Soviet Union, and the moods range from meditative to humorous to somber. Each selection shows a writer looking at the world with a keen eye and from a unique personal perspective.

Something of the restlessness of the traveler always remained with John Steinbeck (1902–1968), whose father had traveled to California from Florida, and whose mother was the daughter of an Irish immigrant. Steinbeck worked at an enormous variety of jobs, from hod carrier to war correspondent. He sought fame, but when it came to him, he tended to flee into anonymity—on the road or in Mexico. Steinbeck's complexity was reflected in his work. Critic W. M. Frohock has said that there are "nearly two Steinbecks, . . . an angry man whose anger puts real tension in his work" and another who is "warmhearted and amused, . . . increasingly soft and often downright mushy."

Critics began to pay attention to Steinbeck when he published *Tortilla Flat*, a novel that treats a group of California *paisanos* as twentieth-century Knights of the Round Table. But it was his novel *Of Mice and Men* that brought him fame (Steinbeck also wrote a play version). The high point of his career came in 1939 when he won both the National Book Award and the Pulitzer Prize for *The Grapes of Wrath*. The "heroes" of this novel are migrant laborers, farmers displaced by the Great Depression, who set off across the country for the Promised Land of California.

After World War II, Steinbeck found it frustrating to write about the problems of an increasingly complex world. In 1960, plagued by ill health and troubled by what he saw as the decline of his power as a writer, he took his aged poodle, Charley, and set out across America in a home-made camper he called Rocinante (named after Don Quixote's run-down horse). West to the Pacific, south to Texas, east to New Orleans, and then north again—Steinbeck traveled 10,000 miles in search of America, avoiding the cities and racing through the suburbs.

In 1962 Steinbeck was awarded the Nobel Prize, the highest achievement possible for a writer. Asked by a *Life* reporter if he deserved it, Steinbeck said he was always afraid of the award because people never seemed to write anymore after they received it. "I wouldn't have accepted it," he said, "if I hadn't thought I could beat the rap." He didn't "beat the rap." He died eight years later and had published nothing more.

The selection that follows is from *Travels with Charley*. The theme of that whole book is evident in this excerpt—what Joseph Fontenrose has described as the theme of *all* of Steinbeck's work: ". . . the superiority of simple human virtues and pleasures to the accumulation of riches and property, of kindness and justice to meanness and greed, of life-asserting action to life-denying. In several ways he has asserted that all life is holy, every creature valuable." Note the key passages in this report that reveal Steinbeck's chief concerns. Read the first two sentences carefully: Like a map, they provide information on this setting.

THE MOJAVE

John Steinbeck

I bucketed Rocinante out of California by the shortest possible route—one I knew well from the old days of the 1930's. From Salinas to Los Banos, through Fresno and Bakersfield, then over the pass and into the Mojave Desert, a burned and burning desert even this late in the year, its hills like piles of black cinders in the distance, and the rutted floor sucked dry by the hungry sun. It's easy enough now, on the high-speed road in a dependable and comfortable car, with stopping places for shade and every service station vaunting its refrigeration. But I can remember when we came to it with prayer, listening for trouble in our laboring old motors, drawing a plume of steam from our boiling radiators. Then the broken-down wreck by the side of the road was in real trouble unless someone stopped to offer help. And I have never crossed it without sharing something with those early families foot-dragging through this terrestrial hell, leaving the white skeletons of horses and cattle which still mark the way.

The Mojave is a big desert and a frightening one. It's as though nature tested a man for endurance and constancy to prove whether he was good enough to get to California. The shimmering dry heat made visions of water on the flat plain. And even when you drive at high speed, the hills that mark the boundaries recede before you. Charley, always a dog for water, panted asthmatically, jarring his whole body with the effort, and a good eight inches of his tongue hung out flat as a leaf and dripping. I pulled off the road into a small gulley to give him water from my thirty-gallon

tank. But before I let him drink, I poured water all over him and on my hair and shoulders and shirt. The air is so dry that evaporation makes you feel suddenly cold.

I opened a can of beer from my refrigerator and sat well inside the shade of Rocinante, looking out at the sun-pounded plain, dotted here and there with clumps of sagebrush.

About fifty yards away two coyotes stood watching me, their tawny coats blending with sand and sun. I knew that with any quick or suspicious movement of mine they could drift into invisibility. With the most casual slowness I reached down my new rifle from its sling over my bed—the .222 with its bitter little high-speed, long-range stings. Very slowly I brought the rifle up. Perhaps in the shade of my house I was half hidden by the blinding light outside. The little rifle has a beautiful telescope sight with a wide field. The coyotes had not moved.

I got both of them in the field of my telescope, and the glass brought them very close. Their tongues lolled out so that they seemed to smile mockingly. They were favored animals, not starved, but well furred, the golden hair tempered with black guard hairs. Their little lemon-yellow eyes were plainly visible in the glass. I moved the cross hairs to the breast of the right-hand animal and pushed the safety. My elbows on the table steadied the gun. The cross hairs lay unmoving on the brisket. And then the coyote sat down like a dog and its right paw came up to scratch the right shoulder.

My finger was reluctant to touch the trigger. I must be getting very old and my ancient conditioning worn thin. Coyotes are vermin. They steal chickens. They thin the ranks of quail and all other game birds. They must be killed. They are the enemy. My first shot would drop the sitting beast, and the other would whirl to fade away. I might very well pull him down with a running shot because I am a good rifleman.

And I did not fire. My training said, "Shoot!" and my age replied, "There isn't a chicken within thirty miles, and if there are any they aren't my chickens. And this waterless place is not quail country. No, these boys are keeping their figures

with kangaroo rats and jack rabbits, and that's vermin eat vermin. Why should I interfere?"

"Kill them," my training said. "Everyone kills them. It's a public service." My finger moved to the trigger. The cross was steady on the breast just below the panting tongue. I could imagine the splash and jar of angry steel, the leap and struggle until the torn heart failed, and then, not too long later, the shadow of a buzzard, and another. By that time I would be long gone—out of the desert and across the Colorado River. And beside the sagebrush there would be a naked, eyeless skull, a few picked bones, a spot of black dried blood, and a few rags of golden fur.

I guess I'm too old and too lazy to be a good citizen. The second coyote stood sidewise to my rifle. I moved the cross hairs to his shoulder and held steady. There was no question of missing with that rifle at that range. I owned both animals. Their lives were mine. I put the safety on and laid the rifle on the table. Without the telescope they were not so intimately close. The hot blast of light tousled the air to shimmering.

Then I remembered something I heard long ago that I hope is true. It was unwritten law in China, so my informant told me, that when one man saved another's life he became responsible for that life to the end of its existence. For, having interfered with a course of events, the savior could not escape his responsibility. And that has always made good sense to me.

Now I had a token responsibility for two live and healthy coyotes. In the delicate world of relationships, we are tied together for all time. I opened two cans of dog food and left them as a votive.[1]

I have driven through the Southwest many times, and even more often have flown over it—a great and mysterious wasteland, a sun-punished place. It is a mystery, something concealed and waiting. It seems deserted, free of parasitic man, but this is not entirely so. Follow the double line of wheel tracks through sand and rock and you will find a habitation somewhere huddled in a protected place, with a few trees pointing their roots

---

1. **votive:** something given in fulfillment of a vow or pledge.

at under-earth water, a patch of starveling corn and squash, and strips of jerky[2] hanging on a string. There is a breed of desert men, not hiding exactly but gone to sanctuary from the sins of confusion.

At night in this waterless air, the stars come down just out of reach of your fingers. In such a place lived the hermits of the early church, piercing to infinity with unlittered minds. The great concepts of oneness and of majestic order seem always to be born in the desert. The quiet counting of the stars, and observation of their movements, came first from desert places. I have known desert men who chose their places with quiet and slow passion, rejecting the nervousness of a watered world. These men have not changed with the exploding times except to die and be replaced by others like them.

And always there are mysteries in the desert, stories told and retold of secret places in the desert mountains where surviving clans from an older era wait to re-emerge. Usually these groups guard treasures hidden from the waves of conquest, the golden artifacts of an archaic Montezuma,[3] or a mine so rich that its discovery would change the world. If a stranger discovers their existence, he is killed or so absorbed that he is never seen again. These stories have an inevitable pattern untroubled by the question, If none return, how is it known what is there? Oh, it's there all right, but if you find it, you will never be found.

And there is another monolithic[4] tale which never changes. Two prospectors in partnership discover a mine of preternatural[5] richness—of gold or diamonds or rubies. They load themselves with samples, as much as they can carry, and they mark the place in their minds by landmarks all around. Then, on the way out to the other world, one dies of thirst and exhaustion, but the other crawls on, discarding most of the treasure he has grown too weak to carry. He comes at last to a settlement, or perhaps is found by other prospecting men. They examine his samples with great excitement. Sometimes in the story the survivor dies after leaving directions with his rescuers, or again he is nursed back to strength. Then a well-equipped party sets out to find the treasure, and it can never be found again. That is the invariable end of the story—it is never found again. I have heard this story many times, and it never changes. There is nourishment in the desert for myth, but myth must somewhere have its roots in reality.

2. **jerky:** meat cut into strips and dried in the sun.
3. **Montezuma** (1479–1520): Aztec emperor of Mexico.

4. **monolithic:** like a monolith, an enormous block of stone.
5. **preternatural:** beyond what is normal or natural.

Responding to the Journal

Analyzing the Journal

Identifying Facts

1. Name at least four specific **details** in the opening paragraphs that make you see the Mojave as harsh and unwelcoming. What details about Charley in the second paragraph help illustrate this point?
2. Summarize the arguments (the pros and cons) that Steinbeck has with himself about shooting the coyotes. Why does he decide to save them?

Interpreting Meanings

3. Find the **images** in the description of the coyotes that suggest that Charley may have had something to do with Steinbeck's change of heart.
4. Explain in your own words what Steinbeck means when he says on page 387 that his "ancient conditioning" is "worn thin." (Tell what he was conditioned to do, and who or what "conditioned" him.)
5. Steinbeck says on page 387, "I guess I'm too old and too lazy to be a good citizen." Read this

comment in its context, and explain why it is **ironic**. (What is his real meaning?)

6. Explain what Steinbeck means by saying, "I owned both animals. Their lives were mine." How could this idea of responsibility for a life you saved be extended to other situations?

7. Explain in your own words what Steinbeck means by the following key statements about the desert and the people who are drawn to it. Explain what the statements reveal about Steinbeck's attitude toward nature and "progress."

   a. "There is a breed of desert men, not hiding exactly but gone to sanctuary from the sins of confusion." (Page 388)

   b. "In such a place lived the hermits of the early church, piercing to infinity with unlittered minds." (Page 388)

   c. "I have known desert men who chose their places with quiet and slow passion, rejecting the nervousness of a watered world." (Page 388)

Writing About the Journal

A Creative Response

1. **Imitating the Writer's Style.** In a paragraph, describe a place in a way that will reveal how you feel about it. Before you write, list five descriptive words or comparisons that suggest your feelings. Imitate Steinbeck's first paragraph.

A Critical Response

2. **Analyzing the Writer's Attitude.** Write a brief essay in which you analyze Steinbeck's attitude toward the desert and toward so-called "civilization." Support your analysis with passages from the selection. Before you write, organize your data in a chart like this.

	Author's Attitude	Supporting Details
What he finds frightening about desert		
What he finds attractive		
How he feels about urban life		

In your final paragraph, explain your response to Steinbeck's views on the merits of the wilderness over those of the city.

Analyzing Language and Vocabulary

Context Clues and Related Words

Steinbeck uses the word *vermin* several times:

1. "Coyotes are *vermin*. They steal chickens. They thin the ranks of quail and all other game birds. They must be killed. They are the enemy."

2. "No, these boys are keeping their figures with kangaroo rats and jack rabbits, and that's *vermin* eat *vermin*. Why should I interfere?' "

From the **context clues** provided, write your own definition of *vermin*. Then check a dictionary. What meanings were not apparent from the context?

1. What Latin word is *vermin* derived from?
2. What is a *vermicide*?
3. What do you suppose is the shape of the human appendix, called the *vermiform appendix*?
4. If a clay pot is decorated with *vermicular* lines, what do the decorations look like?

One of the many legends about Mark Twain (1835–1910) is that he was born on the day that Halley's comet appeared and died seventy-five years later, on the day of its next return. Twain (who said that both he and the comet were "two unaccountable frauds") shifted from job to job when he was young, making and squandering fortunes later. He was a great humorist with a prickly disposition, a natural actor who lived a series of poses and disguises and believed in all of them—believed, along with his Connecticut Yankee Hank Morgan, that "you can't throw too much style into a miracle."

"Mark Twain" was born Samuel Clemens in Florida, Missouri. He moved with his family to Hannibal on the banks of the Mississippi when he was four years old. (He later began signing newspaper reports using the boatman's call "Mark Twain," which means "Mark two fathoms [12 feet]," a safe depth for boats.) Twain seemed to have inherited the wit and vivacity of his beautiful mother and the extravagant temperament of his father. When the boy was eleven, his father died on the edge of bankruptcy. During his youth three of his six brothers and sisters died in infancy, and a fourth, Henry, was killed in a steamboat accident at the age of twenty.

After his father's death, Twain left school to become a printer's apprentice, the first of a dozen jobs that failed to satisfy him over the next fifteen years. He tried soldiering, reporting, piloting a steamboat, prospecting, lecturing, and publishing. Through his various professions and life styles, however, two began to emerge as constants: that of a writer and that of a family man.

In 1869 Twain bought an interest in a Boston newspaper, believing journalism would be his career. But almost immediately, his fictionalized account of his European adventures, *Innocents Abroad,* was published and became a best seller.

In 1870 he married the elegant and delicate Olivia Langdon of Elmira, New York, who would eventually inherit a quarter of a million dollars from her father. Twain sold his interest in the newspaper (at a loss) and moved to Hartford, Connecticut, where his first daughter, Susy, was born. The publication of *Roughing It* confirmed Twain's success as a writer, and he and his be-

loved "Livy" built a house that was a monument to domesticity. (This elaborate three-story turreted mansion is still a Hartford landmark.) Two more daughters, Clara and Jean, were born. The Clemenses lived in an atmosphere of intense familiarity, scarcely leaving one another's company except when Twain had to go on whirlwind lecture tours to pay for the cost of his extravagant establishment. The girls were educated at home, and when Susy went to college at Bryn Mawr, she was so homesick that she withdrew in the first year. When Clara went to Europe to study music, the whole family followed to set up housekeeping near her.

In the meantime, Twain wrote both *The Adventures of Tom Sawyer* and *The Adventures of Huckleberry Finn. Huckleberry Finn* is generally considered the masterpiece of American fiction, yet in Twain's own lifetime he was thought of as a mere humorist and popular writer, seldom taken seriously by critics.

In an echo of his father's extravagance, Twain invested and lost over $200,000 in an impractical typesetting machine. He was saved from bankruptcy by a Standard Oil executive, whom he insisted on paying back, mainly through lecture tours that strained his health and robbed him of time to write.

Twain's last years were marked by a series of embittering misfortunes. Between 1902 and 1909 his wife and two of his treasured daughters died: Susy died of spinal meningitis, and Jean died during an epileptic seizure. Twain himself contracted heart disease, and his energy declined as he struggled to complete unfinished novels and stories. There is no way he could have realized that within half a century he would stand as a literary giant, the one writer above all others who captured the American voice—vernacular, exuberant, ironic, and strong.

The selection that follows is from *Roughing It,* Twain's humorous account of his five-and-a-half years of "roughing it" in the American West (1861–1866). Twain describes himself as the typical "greenhorn"—gullible, inexperienced, and eager to please. How far do you have to read before you discover the joke that's been pulled on this narrator?

THE GENUINE MEXICAN PLUG
(Carson City, Nevada)

Mark Twain

Turn Him Loose, Bill! by Frederic Remington (1892). Oil.

Courtesy of the Anschutz Collection, Denver.

I resolved to have a horse to ride. I had never seen such wild, free, magnificent horsemanship outside of a circus as these picturesquely clad Mexicans, Californians, and Mexicanized Americans displayed in Carson streets every day. How they rode! Leaning just gently forward out of the perpendicular, easy and nonchalant, with broad slouch-hat brim blown square up in front, and long riata[1] swinging above the head, they swept through the town like the wind! The next minute they were only a sailing puff of dust on the far desert. If they trotted, they sat up gallantly and gracefully, and seemed part of the horse; did not go jiggering up and down after the silly Miss Nancy fashion of the riding schools. I had quickly learned to tell a horse from a cow and was full of anxiety to learn more. I was resolved to buy a horse.

While the thought was rankling in my mind, the auctioneer came scurrying through the plaza on a black beast that had as many humps and corners on him as a dromedary,[2] and was necessarily uncomely; but he was "going, going, at twenty-two!—horse, saddle and bridle at twenty-two dollars, gentlemen!" and I could hardly resist.

A man whom I did not know (he turned out to be the auctioneer's brother) noticed the wistful look in my eye and observed that that was a very remarkable horse to be going at such a price; and added that the saddle alone was worth the money. It was a Spanish saddle with ponderous *tapaderos*,[3] and furnished with the ungainly sole-leather covering with the unspellable name. I said I had half a notion to bid. Then this keen-eyed person appeared to me to be "taking my measure"; but I dismissed the suspicion when he spoke, for his manner was full of guileless candor and truthfulness. Said he:

"I know that horse—know him well. You are a stranger, I take it, and so you might think he was an American horse, maybe, but I assure you he is nothing of the kind; but—excuse my speaking in a low voice, other people being

near—he is, without the shadow of a doubt, a Genuine Mexican Plug!"

I did not know what a Genuine Mexican Plug was, but there was something about this man's way of saying it that made me swear inwardly that I would own a Genuine Mexican Plug or die.

"Has he any other—er—advantages?" I inquired, suppressing what eagerness I could.

He hooked his forefinger in the pocket of my army shirt, led me to one side, and breathed in my ear impressively these words:

"He can outbuck anything in America!"

"Going, going, going—at *twenty*-four dollars and a half, gen—"

"Twenty-seven!" I shouted, in a frenzy.

"And sold!" said the auctioneer and passed over the Genuine Mexican Plug to me.

I could scarcely contain my exultation. I paid the money, and put the animal in a neighboring livery stable to dine and rest himself.

In the afternoon I brought the creature into the plaza, and certain citizens held him by the head and others by the tail, while I mounted him. As soon as they let go, he placed all his feet in a bunch together, lowered his back, and then suddenly arched it upward and shot me straight into the air a matter of three or four feet! I came as straight down again, lit in the saddle, went instantly up again, came down almost on the high pommel, shot up again, and came down on the horse's neck—all in the space of three or four seconds. Then he rose and stood almost straight up on his hind feet, and I, clasping his lean neck desperately, slid back into the saddle and held on. He came down and immediately hoisted his heels into the air, delivering a vicious kick at the sky, and stood on his forefeet. And then down he came once more and began the original exercise of shooting me straight up again. The third time I went up I heard a stranger say:

"Oh, *don't* he buck, though!"

While I was up, somebody struck the horse a sounding thwack with a leathern strap, and when I arrived again, the Genuine Mexican Plug was not there. A Californian youth chased him up and caught him, and asked if he might have a ride. I granted him that luxury. He mounted the Genuine,

---

1. **riata** (rē·ät′ə): a lariat or lasso, used for tying animals.
2. **dromedary** (dräm′ə·der′ē): a camel.
3. *tapaderos* (täp·ə·der′ōs): leather covers for the stirrups of a Mexican saddle horse.

got lifted into the air once, but sent his spurs home as he descended, and the horse darted away like a telegram. He soared over three fences like a bird and disappeared down the road toward the Washoe Valley.

I sat down on a stone, with a sigh, and by a natural impulse one of my hands sought my forehead, and the other the base of my stomach. I believe I never appreciated, till then, the poverty of the human machinery—for I still needed a hand or two to place elsewhere. Pen cannot describe how I was jolted up. Imagination cannot conceive how disjointed I was—how internally, externally, and universally I was unsettled, mixed up, and ruptured. There was a sympathetic crowd around me, though.

One elderly-looking comforter said:

"Stranger, you've been taken in. Everybody in this camp knows that horse. Any child could have told you that he'd buck; he is the worst devil to buck on the continent of America. You hear *me*. I'm Curry. *Old* Curry. Old *Abe* Curry. And moreover, he is a simon-pure, out-and-out, genuine d—d Mexican plug, and an uncommon mean one at that, too. Why, you turnip, if you had laid low and kept dark, there's chances to buy an *American* horse for mighty little more than you paid for that bloody old foreign relic."

I gave no sign; but I made up my mind that if the auctioneer's brother's funeral took place while I was in the Territory, I would postpone all other recreations and attend it.

After a gallop of sixteen miles, the Californian youth and the Genuine Mexican Plug came tearing into town again, shedding foam flakes like the spume spray that drives before a typhoon, and, with one final skip over a wheelbarrow and a Chinaman, cast anchor in front of the "ranch."

Such panting and blowing! Such spreading and contracting of the red equine[4] nostrils and glaring of the wild equine eye! But was the imperial beast subjugated? Indeed he was not. His lordship the Speaker of the House thought he was and mounted him to go down to the capitol; but the first dash the creature made was over a pile of telegraph poles half as high as a church; and his time to the capitol—one mile and three quarters—remains unbeaten to this day. But then he took an advantage—he left out the mile and only did the three quarters. That is to say, he made a straight cut across lots, preferring fences and ditches to a crooked road; and when the Speaker got to the capitol, he said he had been in the air so much he felt as if he had made the trip on a comet.

In the evening the Speaker came home afoot for exercise and got the Genuine towed back behind a quartz wagon. The next day I loaned the animal to the clerk of the House to go down to the Dana silver mine, six miles, and *he* walked back for exercise and got the horse towed. Everybody I loaned him to always walked back; they never could get enough exercise any other way. Still, I continued to loan him to anybody who was willing to borrow him, my idea being to get him crippled and throw him on the borrower's hands, or killed and make the borrower pay for him. But somehow nothing ever happened to him. He took chances that no other horse ever took and survived, but he always came out safe. It was his daily habit to try experiments that had always before been considered impossible, but he always got through. Sometimes he miscalculated a little and did not get his rider through intact, but *he* always got through himself. Of course I had tried to sell him; but that was a stretch of simplicity which met with little sympathy. The auctioneer stormed up and down the streets on him for four days, dispersing the populace, interrupting business, and destroying children, and never got a bid—at least never any but the eighteen-dollar one he hired a notoriously substanceless bummer to make. The people only smiled pleasantly and restrained their desire to buy, if they had any. Then the auctioneer brought in his bill, and I withdrew the horse from the market. We tried to trade him off at private vendue[5] next, offering him at a sacrifice for secondhand tombstones, old iron, temperance tracts—any kind of property. But holders were stiff, and we retired from the market again. I never tried to ride the horse anymore. Walking

---

4. **equine** (ē′kwīn): horselike.

5. **vendue** (ven·dōō′): public auction.

was good enough exercise for a man like me, that had nothing the matter with him except ruptures, internal injuries, and such things. Finally I tried to *give* him away. But it was a failure. Parties said earthquakes were handy enough on the Pacific coast—they did not wish to own one. As a last resort I offered him to the governor for the use of the brigade.[6] His face lit up eagerly at first, but toned down again, and he said the thing would be too palpable.

Just then the livery-stable man brought in his bill for six weeks' keeping—stall room for the horse, fifteen dollars; hay for the horse, two hundred and fifty! The Genuine Mexican Plug had eaten a ton of the article, and the man said he would have eaten a hundred if he had let him.

I will remark here, in all seriousness, that the regular price of hay during that year and a part of the next was really two hundred and fifty dollars

---

6. **brigade:** a unit of soldiers in the army.

a ton. During a part of the previous year it had sold at five hundred a ton, in gold, and during the winter before that there was such scarcity of the article that in several instances small quantities had brought eight hundred dollars a ton in coin! The consequence might be guessed without my telling it: People turned their stock loose to starve, and before the spring arrived, Carson and Eagle valleys were almost literally carpeted with their carcasses! Any old settler there will verify these statements.

I managed to pay the livery bill, and that same day I gave the Genuine Mexican Plug to a passing Arkansas emigrant whom fortune delivered into my hand. If this ever meets his eye, he will doubtless remember the donation.

Now whoever has had the luck to ride a real Mexican plug will recognize the animal depicted in this chapter and hardly consider him exaggerated—but the uninitiated will feel justified in regarding his portrait as a fancy sketch, perhaps.

Responding to the Journal

Analyzing the Journal

Identifying Facts

1. Who encourages Twain to purchase the horse? Find the statement that gives *us* a clue to this man's motive.
2. Describe what happens the first time Twain tries to ride the horse. What experiences have other riders had with the plug?
3. Describe the ways in which Twain tries to get rid of the horse. What success does he have?
4. Summarize the "last straw" for Twain—the incident that makes getting rid of the Mexican plug absolutely necessary. What does fortune deliver "into his hand"?

Interpreting Meanings

5. Why would no one who knows better buy a horse described as a "plug"? What is comically **ironic** about the term "genuine plug"? (How is it like saying a "genuine fake"?)

6. What concrete **descriptive details** does Twain use to *show* us and therefore convince us that the horsemen of Carson City are magnificent riders?

7. After painting a romantic picture of the local horsemen, Twain says about himself: "I had quickly learned to tell a horse from a cow and was full of anxiety to learn more." What does this tell us about Twain's knowledge of horses? How does the comment **foreshadow** what will happen in the rest of the essay?

8. At what point in this story did you know it was going to be comical? Twain's humor is delivered in part by his use of **irony**—the contrast between what he states and what we know to be true. Read each of these passages in its context, and explain the irony in the use of each italicized word or group of words:

   a. "A Californian youth chased him up and caught him, and asked if he might have a ride. I granted him that *luxury*." (Page 392)

   b. ". . . I made up my mind that if the auctioneer's brother's funeral took place while I was in the Territory, I would postpone all other *recreations* and attend it." (Page 393)

   c. "In the evening the Speaker came home afoot *for exercise*. . . ." (Page 393)

   d. "Everybody I loaned him to always walked back; *they never could get enough exercise any other way*." (Page 393)

9. What incidents here show that Twain is presenting himself as a victim, or "greenhorn," preyed on by tricky con men? How does he turn the tables on the townspeople and become a trickster himself?

10. Have you seen these two character types—victim and trickster—portrayed in other comic stories or in movies or TV shows? Why do you think people enjoy watching this "victim" character get tricked?

Writing About the Journal

A Creative Response

1. **Narrating an Experience.** When Twain buys the Genuine Mexican Plug, he thinks he will become a dashing horseman. Instead he is dashed—bruised both in body and ego. He is, in short, quickly disillusioned. Disillusionment—sometimes comical, sometimes tragic—is a common motif in literature, perhaps because it is such a universal human experience. Write a short narrative about such an experience. Describe what you expected, what you got, and how you felt

The illustrations on pages 394 and 395 are from the 1872 edition of *Roughing It*.

about what happened. Before you write, decide if you will use comedy, as Twain does, or if you will make your narrative serious. (If you don't want to write about yourself, write about someone else.)

A Critical Response

2. **Analyzing the Humor.** E. B. White, a humorist himself, said that "Humorists fatten on trouble. They have always made trouble pay." In other words, humorists turn trouble and disruption into a cause for laughter. And they do this by means of language. Examine Twain's report carefully. Write a brief essay in which you cite all the major *bad* things that happen in the course of the story. Then describe the techniques Twain uses to make these troublesome events seem funny. Before you write, gather your details in a chart like the following one.

Humorous Devices	Examples from Twain
Describing situations in a comical way	
Describing characters in a comical way	
Use of exaggeration	
Use of comic irony	

Analyzing Language and Vocabulary

Overstatement

Overstatement means "exaggeration." When writers use overstatement, they exaggerate actions, emotions, or other qualities such as size and speed. Writers have used overstatement for humor for centuries; Twain is one of its masters.

1. Twain says of the auctioneer (page 393) that he "stormed up and down the streets on him for four days, dispersing the populace, interrupting business, and destroying children. . . ." What detail in this sentence is an overstatement?

2. Describe the comical pictures that Twain's statements about the auctioneer put in your mind.

3. List at least three other examples of obvious overstatement in Twain's narrative.

4. At what points near the end of the story does Twain protest that he is being completely truthful and not exaggerating? What is the effect of his protestations of honesty?

5. Exaggeration is sometimes called **hyperbole** (hī·pur′bə·lē), a word built on two Greek roots meaning "an excess" (literally, "to throw beyond"). Explain how *hyperactive* and *hypercritical* are related to *hyperbole*.

6. Is the word *hype* related to *hyperbole,* or is it derived from an altogether different word?

Focusing on Background
A Comment from the Writer

In his *Autobiography,* Mark Twain relates how he and his brother Orion set out for the Nevada Territory in 1861:

"Orion and I cleared for that country in the overland stagecoach, I paying the fares, which were pretty heavy, and carrying with me what money I had been able to save—this was eight hundred dollars, I should say—and it was all in silver coin and a good deal of a nuisance because of its weight. And we had another nuisance, which was an Unabridged Dictionary. It weighed about a thousand pounds and was a ruinous expense, because the stagecoach company charged for extra baggage by the ounce. We could have kept a family for a time on what that dictionary cost in the way of extra freight—and it wasn't a good dictionary, anyway—didn't have any modern words in it—only had obsolete ones that they used to use when Noah Webster was a child. . . .

"There were many practical jokers in the new Territory. I do not take pleasure in exposing this fact, for I liked those people; but what I am saying is true. I wish I could say a kindlier thing about them instead. If I could say they were burglars or hat-rack thieves or something like that, that wouldn't be utterly uncomplimentary. I would prefer it, but I can't say those things. They would not be true. These people were practical jokers, and I will not try to disguise it. In other respects they were plenty good enough people; honest people; reputable and likable. They played practical jokes upon each other with success and got the admiration and applause and also the envy of the rest of the community."

—Mark Twain

Essayist, novelist, and short-story writer, Andrea Lee (1953–   ) grew up in Yeadon, Pennsylvania, near Philadelphia. Yeadon was, she says, "the kind of town few people believe exists: a black upper-middle-class suburb full of colonial-style houses and Volkswagen Rabbits, . . . tree houses and two-car garages and fathers who commuted into the city." Lee spent her childhood protected from racial prejudice in an "idyll of shady streets and bicycles and ice cream from a drugstore called Doc's."

But in the 1960's and 1970's the teen-agers of Yeadon began to realize that they had been especially protected from the realities of black America. In high school and in college, Lee and her friends became more socially aware and, to some extent, radicalized. They came home from Ivy League colleges wearing African clothes and speaking of their "urban brothers and sisters," much to the chagrin of their middle-class parents. The writer recalls mothers who would say, "Yes, she used to look so *sweet,* and now she's gone and gotten one of those . . . Afros." Now, Andrea Lee says, she thinks affectionately of Yeadon as a place with "a lively mixture of materialism, idealism, and ironic humor that prevents the minds of its children from stagnating."

In 1979 Andrea Lee and her husband, Tom, graduated from Harvard College and traveled to Moscow, where Tom was to do research on Russian history. Andrea produced a journal of her Russian experiences that was serialized in *The New Yorker* magazine (where she is now a staff writer) and later published as a book.

Both Andrea and Tom Lee spoke fluent Russian, which often startled the Muscovites and which gained them access to experiences usually denied to American tourists. Andrea Lee found much to admire in Moscow: the dramatic vegetable vendors of the great market, the opulence and camaraderie of the public baths, the spirit and freshness of the Russian students. But she also encountered the tedious and terrifying realities of living in a totalitarian state. The journal excerpt that follows details one such encounter. (Lee changed the names of all the Russians.)

This selection is provocative—it should make you think and respond. As you read, write down questions that come to you about the text. Note any passages that confuse you or that you want to reread. Note your other responses: "I like this part. I disagree. I think this is biased. This would not be true today . . ." Use your questions to discuss the journal later in class.

AN APARTMENT IN MOSCOW

Andrea Lee

September 24

I should write this down while it is still fresh. We have just come back home, tired. It's not weariness brought on by physical exertion; it's the gutless exhaustion that follows shock. Early this morning—a beautiful, hazy autumn morning—we set off for the apartment of our friend Seryozha. We three planned to visit the monastery at Zagorsk, a town about forty-five miles outside Moscow, and make a day of it; Tom was carrying a bottle of cognac and six *pirozhki* (meat dumplings), still warm in their paper wrapping. Now, barely two hours later, we're back, and we don't know when we can see Seryozha again. When we left his apartment, he told us that after everything was over he would send us a letter giving only a date and a time for a meeting. The place we would already know; it would be a Metro station where we had met before. After Seryozha said this, he told us to run, not walk, away from his apartment, avoiding anyone we might see. The danger, of course, was to him, not to us, but I still felt panicky. We dashed down the stairs and out of the place, the bag of food banging absurdly against Tom's legs, and then walked rapidly until we reached a bus stop around a corner. There we stood, catching our breath. Both of us felt a little sick.

We had known very little about Seryozha's troubles at first. American friends had introduced us. He is a thin young man with the mobile face and the expressive body of an actor or a mime. He has curly blond hair, which he wears long, and hazel eyes, which reveal a lively and ironic wit. Seryozha works as a chemical researcher, but, like so many Russians, he is in a profession that has little to do with his real interests: art, literature, music, and anything concerning the West. (Strange that so many scientists we've met here are passionately devoted to the arts. In the past month, I've met three or four young poets and novelists whose nominal[1] calling is chemistry or physics.)

The first time we visited Seryozha, he met us at a Metro stop near Arbat Street, and we took a trolley to his apartment. He was with his friend, Anya, an attractive, dark-haired young art student. Tom and I were both struck by their stylish Western clothes: Seryozha wore jeans and an English tweed cap, Anya, a subtly striped sweater dress and heavy silver bracelets. In Moscow, such clothing is a mark of high status, of black-market connections, or of a devotion to taste and quality extreme enough to sustain days and weeks of combing the barren stores. In any case, it is a statement of nonconformity. I was also impressed by Seryozha's apartment. It was closer than anything else I have seen in the Soviet Union to the apartment of a student or a young professional in the United States. Most of the apartments I've visited here combine sheer bleakness with depressingly gaudy attempts at modishness; this one was not only spacious and comfortable but tastefully, even imaginatively, furnished. The kitchen, where we spent most of our time, was a snug place

---

1. **nominal:** in name only.

decorated with English and American photographs and posters; there were plants, an old brass lamp, and an elegant china tea set. The bathroom, in true student fashion, was lined with metal signs stolen from construction sites. In Seryozha's bedroom, a wall of books faced a wall covered with photographs of poets and other writers.

That night, we drank tea and then vodka with lemon peel steeped in it. The four of us talked in Russian and English about mutual friends and American railroads and the Rolling Stones. Seryozha loves the Stones, and his face grew wistful as we spoke about their recent album, "Some Girls." He played a tape of "Let It Bleed" over and over, until we could translate some difficult phrases for him; after that, he came out with the phrases at intervals during the evening, in a pretty decent imitation of Jagger's Cockney snarl. He was an adroit and oddly formal host, inconspicuously filling our teacups and politely urging us to eat bread and cheese and chocolate. While he talked to us, he teased Anya, calling her "Piglet," and she shook back her bangs and glowered at him. It was clear that theirs was a fiery relationship. After a while, we talked about ourselves. Anya told us about painting and printmaking, and about how hard it was to buy supplies in Moscow. There had been something angry in her dark face since the beginning of the evening; I thought at first that it meant she didn't like Americans, but now I realized that it was constant, barely suppressed rage at her own situation. Imagine being a painter, she said, and having only four colors of acrylics to choose from and being unable to buy canvas. A little later, I mentioned the Louvre. Anya gave a sardonic smile. "Oh, *Paris*!" she said, and her voice was full of bitter humor.

She left the room for a moment, and Seryozha told us that her deepest desire was to travel. "She's ready to do anything," he said. "But it's no good—she won't be allowed." He explained that Anya's father, a Pole living in Moscow, had been sent to a labor camp[2] in the late fifties. The sentence had left a mark on the entire family, and

it was unlikely that Anya would ever get to Paris.

"And what about you?" Tom asked.

Seryozha said, "I have some problems of my own." He put his slim hands on the table, looked down, and then hesitated. "I'll tell you about them later," he said. "Not now—the next time."

He took us into his bedroom to see his collection of photographs: heads of Pasternak and Mandelstam; Akhmatova[3] leaning backward in black draperies. Among these was a small sepia portrait of several children in identical sailor suits sitting under a tree.

We asked who they were.

"This is my grandmother, sitting with her brothers and sisters," said Seryozha, pointing to a girl with a long blond braid. "And this is their village," he added, pointing to another old picture. From his intonation and from the look of the children, it was clear that this was not a village that they inhabited, but one that they owned. Seryozha explained to us that his family had for generations been noble landowners in the Volga region. He told us his mother's maiden name, and we recognized it. The family has a long tradition of literary and artistic achievement. One ancestor of Seryozha's was a distinguished minor poet of the eighteen-twenties, and his maternal grandmother is well known as a woman of letters, a friend of Pasternak and other writers. Seryozha showed us two daguerreotypes[4]—one a portrait of a beautiful young woman in a riding habit and the other a formal shot of an officer with sharply pointed mustaches. "Two of my great-grandparents," he said. The family, he told us, was listed in the General Armorial of Noble Families of the Russian Empire, Imperial Russia's oldest and most distinguished book of heraldry.

Seryozha had given us all this information in a flat, half-mocking voice. Now he flashed his wrist at us and gave the same sardonic smile Anya had given. "We say in Russian, 'blue, blue blood,' " he said.

"But how in the world did your family manage to survive the Revolution?" I asked.

---

2. **labor camp:** an isolated prison, often in Siberia, where inmates do forced labor.

3. Boris **Pasternak,** Osip **Mandelstam,** and Anna **Akhmatova** are twentieth-century Soviet poets.
4. **daguerreotype** (da·ger′ə·tīp): an early type of photograph made on a plate of chemically treated metal or glass.

Seryozha shrugged. "They managed." A little later, he explained that his grandparents on both sides had quietly decided to go along with the new regime. His father joined the Party in the early thirties and has remained active in it ever since. This membership eventually placed the once-noble family in a position of privilege under Soviet rule. But Seryozha hates the Party and feels that his father's devotion to Communism springs from willful blindness. "My grandfather—my father's own father—was shot down in the street during the purges,"[5] he said. "And my father pretends that it was an accident—that his dear Party could not have deliberately killed an innocent man. The rest of my family think differently." Seryozha's refusal to be active in the Komsomol[6] has become a focal point of tension between father and son, in much the same way that draft resistance did in American families ten years ago. In fact, listening to Seryozha talk about his father made me think of endless conversations I'd heard in the late sixties. "We can go for a drive together and not agree on one single thing," he said. "My father hates the Rolling Stones, my books, my foreign friends, my long hair." Seryozha prefers his grandparents, who carry on the genteel family tradition of literary and artistic involvement. Often, he talks to his grandmothers for hours about their life before the Revolution. It's interesting to me that one way in which the minor sixties-type rebellion taking place in Russia manifests itself is in a devotion to all things pre-Revolutionary. Many of my student friends pointedly call Leningrad St. Petersburg[7] or "Piter."

Seryozha doesn't entirely condemn his father, however. "In the thirties, the family had no money, and my grandmother was sick," he said. The entire family was starving in the big old town house they'd been allowed to retain. (The place,

Virginia Museum of Fine Arts, Richmond.
Bequest from the Estate of Lillian Thomas Pratt, 1947.

torn down in the early sixties, was a crumbling wooden mansion like many that still cluster in the formerly aristocratic neighborhood around Arbat Street. Seryozha was born in the house. He remembers it as a series of big, dark rooms full of old people and enormous stoves.) Seryozha showed us a picture of his father, a dour-faced man in his late fifties. He glanced at the picture himself and began to whistle through his teeth; the tune was the Stones's "Ruby Tuesday." He was leaning against the bookcase, looking very slim in his jeans and sweater. "My father had to do it, I know," he said. "But he started to believe in it, and that was his great mistake."

On the Metro going home, I said to Tom, "I think it shows."

"What shows?" said Tom.

"The blue, blue blood."

Tom laughed and said that I was in love with anything that had to do with fallen fortunes. "If you hadn't heard that story, you would think he was an ordinary Russian," he said.

I disagreed. I thought I recognized in Seryozha

---

5. During the 1930's and then after World War II, the dictator Joseph Stalin conducted bloody purges in which thousands of Communist Party leaders and army chiefs were forced to confess to being traitors and were then executed.
6. **Komsomol:** the young people's Communist organization in the Soviet Union.
7. **St. Petersburg:** the former capital of Russia in the days of the Tsars. After the Russian Revolution in 1917, the city was renamed Leningrad (after Lenin), and the capital was moved to Moscow. In 1991 the city became known as St. Petersburg again.

a courtesy so ingrained that it operated by reflex, an instinctive delicacy of wit. There was something else, too—a peculiar frailty. I think that most Russians are tougher, physically and spiritually, than anything we can imagine. . . . But Seryozha was not tough. I thought of this as the train crossed the Moskva River and we looked out at Moscow. The huge city was well lit in the cold fall night; with the gigantic Stalin Gothic towers poking up at intervals, it looked a little like a sinister Oz. In this context, the apartment we had just left seemed like a refuge, a shelter for a very fragile way of life. I wished suddenly and intensely that Seryozha lived in any other city in the world.

The following Sunday, we visited Seryozha again, arriving half an hour later than we had agreed. (The end of a visit with Russian friends is always occupied with elaborate arrangements for the next meeting—time, place. No one likes to use the phone in Moscow.) After we knocked, we heard quiet footsteps coming toward the door. They stopped, and there was a long pause. We knocked again. There was another pause, and finally two heavy bolts were shot back. Seryozha's face appeared through a crack in the door. "Come in, come in," he said rapidly. Once we were inside, he berated us for being late. "You see, when you come to visit me, you have to be on time," he said. "Exactly. I will unlock my door for you and only you."

This was our first glimpse of what we took to be Seryozha's paranoia. We learned that there was a reason for it after he made us tea and sandwiches. He put on a Rod Stewart tape, and then sat down and looked at us gravely. There was a pause, which I could not help thinking was a little stagy; like many of my Russian friends, Seryozha has an exaggerated sense of the moment, the grand gesture. "I'll tell you my story now," he said, in his stilted English. Then he laughed. "I sound like a novel. But it's a very dirty story."

It was a very dirty story, and one that unfortunately seems not at all out of the ordinary in this country. Here it is, briefly: Seryozha is married, and he and his wife are separated. Like many of our friends here, he married very young; Masha, the wife he chose, was a young Siberian woman. She didn't share his high education or his

cultural interests; her parents, Party members in Irkutsk, were conservative and thought their aristocratic son-in-law a bad bargain, with his interest in literature and Western music, and his disdain for the Party. After a few years, Seryozha and Masha separated amicably, leading independent lives in a way that seems common in this country. (Many young Russians we know seem to have a shadowy spouse, even a child, off somewhere—perhaps in another province, perhaps across town.) All fine. But Masha's family, as families will, intervened, pressing their daughter to get a divorce until she finally agreed. They also wanted to make trouble for Seryozha; the most effective method of accomplishing this was to denounce him to the K.G.B.[8] (Strange, incidentally, to hear these letters whispered against rock music in a kitchen. The power of their mere sound to awaken nervousness in Russians is incredible. Tom once casually mentioned the K.G.B. as he sat with a Russian friend in a remote corner of a park. She shivered and stopped him from saying the name again. "It makes me very nervous to hear that," she said.) Seryozha's small desk, which he kept locked, was broken into and searched—he described this to us with a peculiar wincing delicacy, as if he were talking about the loss of a limb. Inside were copies of *The Gulag Archipelago* and Mikhail Bulgakov's *The Master and Margarita*, a modern classic novel banned by the government. There was also a picture of Tsar Nicholas II. ("I used to light candles to it," Seryozha said ironically.) These possessions, along with his aristocratic background, a reputation for associating with foreigners, and his dislike of the Party, were enough to compromise him thoroughly.

What was behind this ugly action was the most commonplace of Russian personal motives. From far away in Siberia, Seryozha's parents-in-law had long had their eye on Seryozha's gem of an apartment—and on the alluring possibility of life in the capital. A Moscow *propiska,* or residence permit, is extremely difficult to obtain; one major requirement, as they well knew, is the existence of an available apartment. The denunciation of their son-in-law might mean that he must forfeit the

---

8. **K.G.B.:** the Russian secret police.

apartment to Masha in a divorce settlement. Seryozha sighed as he told us this, and I thought of the nightmarish housing shortage in Moscow. The loss of a good apartment is a very serious thing. But the other consequences of the denunciation are more serious. One of them was that Seryozha would certainly forfeit any chance of fulfilling his dream of travel outside the Soviet Union. Moreover, his father might be demoted from his rather high position in the Party. This was what Seryozha feared most of all. Anonymous letters concerning Seryozha had already been sent to his father's superiors. "Russian families have strong ties," he told us, "but this would create a rift nothing could bridge."

For the next month, Tom and I visited Seryozha twice a week. It was a period of limbo for him. The divorce hearing was set for the indefinite future; the outcome of the denunciation was uncertain. Although we thought that meeting with foreigners at this time might compromise him further, he insisted on inviting us over. He acted with a strange mixture of recklessness and paranoia. We spent one amazing afternoon with him and Anya at the sixteenth-century Novo-Devichy Convent. Seryozha showed us how to slip through a wooden reconstruction barricade and climb to the forbidden top of the ramparts. He laughed as hard as any of us as he led us running around the top of the convent walls, ducking to avoid being seen by guards or tourists. In a taxi going home, however, he forbade us to speak any English—too dangerous for him, he said. At home, he would often lecture us on our naiveté about the Soviet Union. "You are not critical enough," he said. He told us about hidden cameras and listening devices. Often, as he spoke, he would get up and turn the tape player up louder. He told us about a friend of his who had been reading a forbidden book while riding on the Metro and had been spotted by a K.G.B. agent. The agent hustled his friend off the train and threatened to turn him in. But Seryozha's friend had the presence of mind to offer a bribe of forty rubles, and the agent went away after only issuing a warning. "The danger always exists," Seryozha said, drumming his fingers on the table. "But it is not often the kind of danger you envision. For most of us, it is an ugly,

petty danger. The long arm ends in greedy little men."

When we saw Seryozha in the middle of last week, he was uneasy. He had heard rumors that his wife's parents were now in Moscow; this meant they were planning some decisive move. But he promised to visit the monastery at Zagorsk with us on Sunday morning—today. When we knocked on the door this morning, we heard the usual footsteps, then silence, then the rattling of the locks. Seryozha finally opened the door and pulled us inside. The apartment was unlit. Seryozha wore jeans and a shrunken black sweater that made his slim body look theatrically thin. He was very pale, and his mouth wore a trembling smile. He hurried us into the kitchen, putting a finger to his lips until he had shut the kitchen door. He said, "I'll explain to you very quickly, and then you have to go."

He told us that his wife's family had pulled some strings to advance the date of the hearing, that it was set for noon on Monday, and that until then he was being watched constantly—by his wife's family, by his own family, and by the K.G.B. His lawyer had told him that the denunciation was uncontestable; it was almost certain that he would lose his apartment and that his father would suffer as well. Our presence there was dangerous to him: If he should be seen with Americans right now, it would make his case far worse. As he told us this, there was a loud knock at the front door. We froze. The knock was repeated. We heard a slight commotion of voices in the hall, and the sound of someone trying the lock. Seryozha crept out of the kitchen to listen through the door, and then returned to us. "They're all there," he said. "My wife's family—the vultures! But they can't come in. I've changed the locks. They'll leave for a while, and when they do, you must go quickly. Run down the stairs, don't walk." He said this last in English; then he added, still in English. "It's a very dirty thing. Very dirty."

The knocking and rattling went on for a few minutes while the three of us sat in the dim little kitchen. The knocking disturbed me very much. It was not loud, but it seemed to be breaking through something inside me, a membrane of privacy I hadn't known existed. I saw Seryozha wincing, and I thought of the purges, of Anya's father—times past when a knock on the door meant the breaking apart of lives.

The knocking stopped, and there was silence. The three of us took several deep breaths. Seryozha grabbed our arms and hurried us out of the kitchen. He set his ear against the door. Then he thrust our coats at us. "All right, go, go!" he said. Then: "Wait. I'll see you sometime when this is over." And he made the arrangements for getting in touch with us which I have described. As he shook our hands and said goodbye, I took a good look at him. I thought that in the States he would have been a student friend of mine: well-mannered, idle, artistic, mildly radical—in short, someone to frequent a coffeehouse in Harvard Square, not to head a list of political victims. Then I thought of the family who had just left his door. He had got entangled in this shabby web of denunciation not through the operation of some gigantic, all-seeing machine but through the greed and petty vindictiveness of those near to him. Seryozha's life was not shattered—it had only been disrupted in a particularly degrading way. I remembered his story of his friend's encounter with the K.G.B. agent on the Metro. This, it seemed to me, showed the same theme, which is one I've run into constantly since I've been in the Soviet Union: that the evil of the system is aided less by a desire to uphold that system than by some of the nastier personal motives that drive human nature. The greedy little men are everywhere.

All this went through my mind in a rush, confused by fear. For a few seconds, Tom and I stood in the hall, looking at Seryozha across the barrier that misfortune erects around a friend. There was nothing to say except "Good luck" and "We will think of you." He opened the door and gave us a slight push. "Go, go!" he whispered, with his trembling smile. I gave him a kiss, and then we bolted down the stairs.

Responding to the Journal

Analyzing the Journal

Identifying Facts

1. At what point do we learn why Andrea and Tom have run away from their friend's apartment?
2. Seryozha's clothing, his apartment, and his taste in music would be ordinary enough in any American city. Find at least three details describing these aspects of Seryozha's life that suggest he is making a "statement of nonconformity" (page 398). What does *nonconformity* mean?
3. Explain why Anya is angry and bitter (page 400). Why does Seryozha tell the story of his ancestry in a "flat, half-mocking voice"?
4. Seryozha's father and grandparents have different attitudes toward the Russian Revolution and the Communist Party. Find the passages of this account where these attitudes are revealed. How are they different from Seryozha's views?

5. Define *denunciation,* and explain the in-laws' motive in denouncing Seryozha. Name the two consequences of the denunciation that would cause serious trouble for Seryozha.

Interpreting Meanings

6. The apartment is of central importance to Seryozha's trouble with the K.G.B. Explain how the problem with the apartment illustrates Andrea Lee's **main idea:** ". . . the evil of the system is aided less by a desire to uphold that system than by some of the nastier personal motives that drive human nature. The greedy little men are everywhere" (page 404).
7. Do you think Lee is presenting a prejudiced or distorted view of Soviet life? How could you determine whether or not her account is fair or biased?
8. Do you agree that the "greedy little men" might exist anywhere? Explain.

9. What would you say is the writer's main **purpose** in recording this excerpt in her journal? Is she describing events and people, or does she want to persuade you to feel and think a certain way? Do you think she accomplishes her purpose? Explain.

Writing About the Journal

A Creative Response

1. Describing the United States from an Outsider's Point of View. You have seen what Seryozha's country looks like to Andrea Lee. Imagine that Seryozha could visit the United States. What do you think this country would seem like to him? If he visited the area where you live, what might he find strange, confusing, disturbing, pleasing, or intriguing? Write a paragraph.

A Critical Response

2. Analyzing Character. Andrea Lee uses the same methods of creating character that fiction writers use. In a paragraph, explain what you learned about Seryozha from (a) his appearance, (b) his actions, (c) what he says, (d) the response of other characters, (e) the writer's direct comments about his character. Cite details from the journal to illustrate what you say.

3. Responding to the Journal. In at least one paragraph, state your general response to Andrea Lee's journal, and cite passages to support what you say. Remember, nonfiction can be evaluated in terms of the following elements:

   a. The use of facts
   b. The vividness of language
   c. Objectivity or subjectivity in reporting
   d. The writer's purpose
   e. The writer's insights into human experience

Analyzing Language and Vocabulary

Metaphors and Similes

Metaphors and similes are comparisons between things that are basically dissimilar. A **metaphor** identifies two things, either directly ("The clouds are white wool in the sky") or indirectly ("White woolly clouds graze in the sky"). A **simile** uses terms such as *like* or *as* to make the comparison explicit ("The clouds in the sky are *like* white, woolly sheep").

Virginia Museum of Fine Arts, Richmond. Bequest from the Estate of Lillian Thomas Pratt, 1947.

1. " 'The long arm ends in greedy little men.' "
   a. The whole phrase Seryozha is referring to is "the long arm of the law." What is the law being compared to?
   b. Why would its arm be "long"?
   c. At which end of the arm are the greedy little men?

2. " 'My wife's family—the vultures!' "
   a. In what sense could people be like vultures?
   b. How is this comparison supposed to make you feel about the family?

3. "He had got entangled in this shabby web of denunciation. . . ."
   a. What are Seryozha's problems being compared to? What word suggests the comparison?
   b. In what sense is he "entangled"?
   c. What is the effect of the word *shabby*?

Literature & Language

Using Parallel Structure

Literary Model

N. Scott Momaday is a Kiowa writer who often writes about Native American life. The Kiowa are one of several Southwestern tribes known collectively as the Pueblos because they live in terraced, adobe villages called *pueblos.* Here Momaday is describing his boyhood in the Jemez (hā´māz) Pueblo in New Mexico, the "land of light."

The landscape was full of mystery and of life. The autumn was in full bloom. The sun cast a golden light upon the adobe walls and the cornfields; it set fire to the leaves of willows and cottonwoods along the river; and a fresh cold wind ran down from the canyons and carried the good scents of pine and cedar smoke, of bread baking in the beehive ovens, and of rain in the mountains. There were horses in the plain and angles of geese in the sky.

Gradually and without effort, I entered into the motion of life there. In the winter dusk, I heard coyotes barking by the river, the sound of drums in the kiva,[1] and the voice of the village crier, ringing at the rooftops. . . .

Above Jemez Pueblo, San Diego Canyon ascends from the plain to the mountains. On Saturdays and Sundays, when the good people of Albuquerque and Corrales and Bernalillo drive up to take the mountain air, the women of Jemez Pueblo sell fresh bread at the side of the road at Cañon. The bread is baked in outdoor ovens, or *hornos,* and it is heavy and sweet and delicious, especially good for dipping into the very hot chili that is served in the pueblo on feast days. . . .

Jemez Springs is named for the hot waters that rise out of the earth in this vicinity and which are said to be as rich in their mineral content as any springs in the country. In the center of the village is a bathhouse where an attendant will wrap you up after your bath and you can melt yourself down through your pores. . . .

—from "Discovering the Land of Light," N. Scott Momaday

A Note on Parallel Structure

One of the ways a writer can create a smooth, pleasing rhythm and a feeling of order and clarity is by using **parallel structure,** or **parallelism.** Parallel structure exists when sentence elements of equal importance are expressed in the same grammatical form. Parallelism is a common device in poetry, sermons, and speeches (see page 826), but it's also a feature of all good writing.

What does it mean to express parallel ideas in the same grammatical form? It means you're consistent in your use of **articles** and **prepositions.** It means you don't mix a **noun** into a series of **adjectives,** or a **clause** into a list of **phrases.** It means you don't use a **passive construction** with a series of **active verbs,** or pair an **infinitive** (*to see*) with a **gerund** (*believing*).

Sometimes the lack of parallel structure in a sentence creates a true grammatical error (*Seeing is to believe*). But there are other times when a grammatically acceptable sentence would simply be stronger or clearer if its elements were parallel.

| **Unparallel:** | Sonya is not only an actress, but she also plays the violin. |
| **Parallel:** | Sonya is not only an actress but also a violinist. |

Notice that Momaday uses two parallel **prepositional phrases** in the first paragraph of this passage:

There were horses *in the plain* and angles of geese *in the sky.*

If Momaday had written, "There were horses in the plain and angles of geese *flying in the sky*," his construction would have been grammatically

---

1. **kiva:** a large underground room in a pueblo dwelling, used for religious and other purposes.

acceptable but not parallel. He would have been pairing a prepositional phrase with a gerund phrase.

Later in the passage, Momaday presents another parallel construction: a series of adjectives connected by the **coordinating conjunction** *and:*

> . . . [the bread] is *heavy* and *sweet* and *delicious* . . . .

If Momaday had said the bread was "heavy and sweet and *it tasted delicious,*" his sentence would not have been parallel, because he would have been combining two adjectives with a clause.

See if you can make the following sentences parallel. (There is more than one correct answer in each case.) Can you also explain *why* each construction is unparallel?

1. Tom wanted to shop for an outfielder's glove, a pair of sneakers and hat.
2. My father likes baking bread and to make fresh pasta.
3. We rode our bicycles to the card shop, the cafe, and to the museum.
4. Allison is more interested in going to South America than she is to visit Europe.
5. On our vacation we traveled by airplane, train, and we took a boat trip.

Examining the Writer's Style

1. Working with a partner, see how many examples of parallel structure you can find in the Momaday passage. Pick three of these constructions, and rewrite them so that they're no longer parallel. (Has everyone rewritten them the same way?)
2. Working in small groups, prepare the passage for oral reading. Try to emphasize Momaday's use of parallel structure, and pay close attention to the pauses signaled by commas and semicolons. Which words in the passage do you think require greatest emphasis? (Does everyone agree?) How does parallelism contribute to the **rhythm** Momaday establishes? What adjective would you use to describe that rhythm?

Using Parallel Structure in Your Writing

1. **Describing an Ideal Place.** If you could create the perfect place to live, what would it be like? Write a description of your utopia. Give specific details about how the place would look, sound, smell, feel, and perhaps taste. What foods would you eat there?
   a. Before you write, list details about your place under headings for the five senses. You might want to make drawings or collect images that illustrate your idea of perfection.
   b. As you write, be aware of the **rhythm** of your words and sentences. Try to use parallel structure to emphasize the balanced, serene order of your ideal place. Write your description so that it has a pleasing cadence when read aloud.
2. **Rewriting the Passage as a Poem.** On page 826 you'll find a description of how parallelism is used in poetry, particularly in the ancient Hebrew religious poems known as Psalms. Rewrite Momaday's tribute to the Land of Light as a poem in the style of the Biblical Psalms. You'll have to break the passage into lines, and you'll have to be sure that some of your lines contain parallel structure. Read your new "Discovering the Land of Light" aloud to hear its cadences. Does the parallelism help create the effect of a kind of hymn or chant?

DISTINGUISHING BETWEEN SUBJECTIVE AND OBJECTIVE DETAILS

Writing Assignment

Write a three-paragraph essay in which you discuss the subjective and objective details in "An Apartment in Moscow" by Andrea Lee (page 397). In your essay, state your response to the excerpt.

Background

In **subjective reporting,** the writer makes judgments about people, actions, and events. A **journal** is by definition subjective because the writer's intention is to record personal experiences, feelings, and thoughts. Part of the pleasure of reading a journal comes from being able to "eavesdrop" on the writer's private thoughts so that we get a sense of the writer's "real self."

In **objective reporting,** the writer presents only facts—no opinions or personal comments or responses. The writer is completely invisible. Encyclopedia articles are almost always objective writing. Some newspaper articles are also, but it is very difficult for a reporter to be totally objective. Even the *selection* of facts to report is a subjective decision.

Good **travel writing** is a mixture of objective and subjective reporting. Writers try to describe accurately—objectively—sights, sounds, smells, and tastes to make us feel as if we are at their elbow. But they also give us subjective responses and comment on what they observe. Here is a traveler's description of a marketplace in Marrakesh during the month-long holiday of Ramadan, when Moslems fast from sunrise to sundown. One reader's responses are noted in the side notes.

By four or five, the square is beginning a second run of life. Young girls, still unveiled because unmarried, come out in their best clothes for a promenade. The streets roar with the sound of mopeds, bearing, sometimes, whole families, including baby on the handlebars. . . .	Seems to be providing a fact about when Moslem women wear veils.
	Gives a mixture of objective and subjective details. She assumes these are families.
As the sun's rays slant across the square, outdoor kitchens are carried out. A fire is set in the middle, burning a kind of charcoal that sends up a pungent, sweet-smelling smoke and increasing the scenic haze. Around the fire are placed benches that are soon filled by ravenous-looking men—no women, of course. During the fast of Ramadan they wait tensely for the sun to drop altogether and the siren to announce the time to eat. The poorer clients eat a thick chicken-based soup of vegetables and beans, served in painted earthenware bowls. To my amazement, hungry men sit for quite half an hour with their soup in front of them, wooden spoon in hand, even bread dipped in soup, waiting for the proper moment. The power of the Moslem faith could not be illustrated more vividly.	Gives objective details about sights and smells.
	Uses descriptive words that are pleasant: "pungent," "sweet-smelling," "scenic." They are all subjective.
	"Ravenous-looking" is subjective. How does she know?
	"Tensely" seems subjective. Maybe they are not tense at all, but only alert.
	Gives objective details.
	States own emotion—subjective detail.
	States conclusion—subjective.

—from "A Day in the Life of the Jemaa el Fna," Rachel Billington

Prewriting

Reread Lee's journal entry and make notes monitoring your reading. What are your responses? What questions do you have? Where is she subjective? Where is she strictly objective? Then fill out a chart like the following.

	Examples and Responses
Give three examples of objective details, and tell what sense (sight, sound, smell, etc.) each detail appeals to.	
Give three examples of subjective reporting.	
Which part of the journal entry did you enjoy most? Did you dislike any part? Give at least two reasons for your answer.	
What is your overall response to this journal entry? Do you think it is well written? Tell why or why not.	

Writing

Use the information in your chart to plan your essay. You might organize it this way:

1. **Paragraph 1:** Discuss the objective reporting— how much, effect of, response to.
2. **Paragraph 2:** Discuss the subjective reporting— how much, effect of, response to.
3. **Paragraph 3:** Give your response to excerpt as a whole.

Make sure your introductory paragraph contains a **thesis statement** that expresses your general analysis of the amount of subjective versus objective reporting in the excerpt. You might use one of the following thesis statements, or one of your own:

> Andrea Lee in "An Apartment in Moscow" presents a carefully balanced, chiefly objective and factual account of an incident that occurred while she and her husband were in Moscow.

> "An Apartment in Moscow" by Andrea Lee is a subtly subjective report of an incident that reveals the writer's feelings about the Soviet political system in the early 1980's.

Checklist for Revision

1. Have you cited the journal excerpt's title and author?
2. Have you included a thesis statement in the first paragraph?
3. Have you given at least two examples each of subjective and objective reporting?
4. Have you stated your response to the excerpt as a whole and given reasons to explain your response?
5. If you have quoted directly from the excerpt, have you checked the quotation for accuracy, used quotation marks, and cited the page on which the quotation appears?
6. Have you checked: Spelling? Punctuation? Capitalization? Sentence structure? Paragraph organization?

The essay is an old literary form. As the name of a particular kind of writing, the term *essay* was first used in France more than four hundred years ago by Michel de Montaigne, a retired lawyer. For his own amusement, Montaigne wrote short prose pieces about various topics that interested him. He called these pieces *essais,* which means "attempts" or "tries." English writers quickly adopted Montaigne's form, and it has flourished ever since.

Basically, the **essay** is a brief discussion of a single subject. But this definition does not begin to hint at the great variety the essay takes today. In fact, the essay has assumed so many forms and purposes that it is like the "shape-shifter" of folklore, the creature that so constantly changes its appearance that it is difficult to say what its true form is.

Formal and Informal Essays

Critics often classify essays according to their tone and style as either formal or informal. A **formal essay** is serious in tone and uses formal language (full sentences, no slang, no colloquial expressions). Today we tend to associate formal essays with the master writers of the past. America's great formal essayist is the nineteenth-century writer Ralph Waldo Emerson, who addressed himself to such topics as "The Poet," "Self-Reliance," "Fate," and "Illusions." (Some people call these **traditional essays**.)

Most modern essays are **informal essays**—essays that manage to sound as if the writer were speaking directly to us, in informal conversation. (Sometimes they are called **personal essays**.) These essays can range from very serious to very comic.

Essays and Their Purposes

Essays combine information with entertainment in a proportion that varies greatly according to the writer's purpose. The intent of a **narrative** essay is to tell a true story, and so it will use such fictional devices as plot, dialogue, suspense, and characterization. The intent of a **descriptive** essay is to create a mood or an atmosphere or to help us experience a particular place or person, so it will use sensory and concrete details. The intent of an **expository** essay is to explain or give information, so it will contain facts and examples that will help us understand something complicated or unfamiliar or unusual. The intent of a **persuasive** essay is to persuade us to think or act in a certain way, so it will use language in a way that will appeal to our emotions.

The modern essay includes editorials, magazine articles, personal reflections, historical reports, critical reviews, biographical accounts, and humorous pieces. Almost any subject is—and has been—treated by the essayist, from the mysteries of the cosmos to how the clothes dryer seems to steal socks and eat them.

essay
d so many
purposes that
the 'shape-
shifter' of folklore."

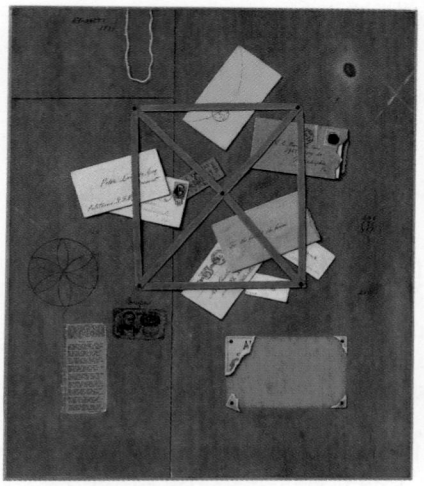

The Artist's Letter Rack by William Michael Harnett (1879). Oil on canvas.

The Metropolitan Museum of Art, New York. Morris K. Jesup Fund, 1966.

"Almost any subject is—and has been—treated by the essayist, from the mysteries of the cosmos to how the clothes dryer seems to steal socks and eat them."

Janet Frame (1924–   ) was raised in the little town of Oamaru, New Zealand, and as a young woman she trained for a career as a teacher. Her life story, told in three volumes—*To the Is-land*, *An Angel at My Table*, and *The Envoy from Mirror City*—reads like a horror story. (Her autobiography was made into a movie in 1991.) Pathologically shy as a child, Frame lived for a time with her aunt and her dying uncle in a cottage where there was not enough space, food, or heat. Her two beloved sisters died in drowning accidents. Though she "delighted in the children at school and in teaching," Frame was so shy that she could not face the inspection needed to earn her teaching certificate.

When she sought help for her timidity, Frame became the victim of a devastating mistaken diagnosis. She was labeled "schizophrenic" and whisked off to a psychiatric ward. For the next eight years she was in and out of mental institutions. Eight years of her life were needlessly lost.

Through all the horror of those years, she never forgot her childhood dream to be recognized "as a true poet." When a New Zealand writer offered her an army hut in which to live and write, she accepted and began her first novel. Eventually, tests made doctors conclude that Frame was not mentally ill; what's more, she never had been.

Though she still lives in New Zealand, Frame has traveled in America and worked at two famous writers' retreats, the Yaddo Foundation and the MacDowell Colony. "You Are Now Entering the Human Heart," an essay about an experience she had in Philadelphia, first appeared in *The New Yorker* magazine. Before you begin reading Frame's essay, discuss the various meanings the title might have.

YOU ARE NOW ENTERING THE HUMAN HEART

Janet Frame

I looked at the notice. I wondered if I had time before my train left Philadelphia for Baltimore in one hour. The heart, ceiling high, occupied one corner of the large exhibition hall, and from wherever you stood in the hall, you could hear it beating, *thum-thump-thum-thump*. It was a popular exhibit, and sometimes, when there were too many children about, the entrance had to be roped off, as the children loved to race up and down the blood vessels and match their cries to the heart's beating. I could see that the heart had already been punished for the day—the floor of the blood vessel was worn and dusty, the chamber walls were covered with marks, and the notice "You Are Now Taking the Path of a Blood Cell Through the Human Heart" hung askew. I wanted to see more of the Franklin Institute and the Natural Science Museum across the street, but a journey through the human heart would be fascinating. Did I have time?

Later. First, I would go across the street to the Hall of North America, among the bear and the bison, and catch up on American flora and fauna.

I made my way to the Hall. More children, sitting in rows on canvas chairs. An elementary class from a city school, under the control of an elderly teacher. A museum attendant holding a basket, and all eyes gazing at the basket.

"Oh," I said. "Is this a private lesson? Is it all right for me to be here?"

The attendant was brisk. "Surely. We're having a lesson in snake handling," he said. "It's something new. Get the children young and teach them that every snake they meet is not to be killed. People seem to think that every snake has to be knocked on the head. So we're getting them young and teaching them."

"May I watch?" I said.

"Surely. This is a common grass snake. No harm, no harm at all. Teach the children to learn the feel of them, to lose their fear."

He turned to the teacher. "Now, Miss—Mrs.——" he said.

"Miss Aitcheson."

He lowered his voice. "The best way to get through to the children is to start with teacher," he said to Miss Aitcheson. "If they see you're not afraid, then they won't be."

She must be near retiring age, I thought. A city woman. Never handled a snake in her life. Her face was pale. She just managed to drag the fear from her eyes to some place in their depths, where it lurked like a dark stain. Surely the attendant and the children noticed?

"It's harmless," the attendant said. He'd worked with snakes for years.

Miss Aitcheson, I thought again. A city woman born and bred. All snakes were creatures to kill, to be protected from, alike the rattler, the copperhead, king snake, grass snake—venom and victims. Were there not places in the South where you couldn't go into the streets for fear of the rattlesnakes?

Her eyes faced the lighted exit. I saw her fear. The exit light blinked, hooded. The children, none of whom had ever touched a live snake, were sitting hushed, waiting for the drama to begin; one or two looked afraid as the attendant withdrew a green snake about three feet long from the basket and with a swift movement, before the teacher could protest, draped it around her neck and stepped back, admiring and satisfied.

"There," he said to the class. "Your teacher has a snake around her neck and she's not afraid."

Miss Aitcheson stood rigid; she seemed to be holding her breath.

"Teacher's not afraid, are you?" the attendant persisted. He leaned forward, pronouncing judgment on her, while she suddenly jerked her head and lifted her hands in panic to get rid of the snake. Then, seeing the children watching her, she whispered, "No, I'm not afraid. Of course not." She looked around her.

"Of course not," she repeated sharply.

I could see her defeat and helplessness. The attendant seemed unaware, as if his perception had grown a reptilian covering. What did she care for the campaign for the preservation and welfare of copperheads and rattlers and common grass snakes? What did she care about someday walking through the woods or the desert and deciding between killing a snake and setting it free, as if there would be time to decide, when her journey to and from school in downtown Philadelphia held enough danger to occupy her? In two years or so, she'd retire and be in that apartment by herself and no doorman, and everyone knew what happened then, and how she'd be afraid to answer the door and to walk after dark and carry her pocketbook in the street. There was enough to think about without learning to handle and love the snakes, harmless and otherwise, by having them draped around her neck for everyone, including the children—most of all the children—to witness the outbreak of her fear.

"See, Miss Aitcheson's touching the snake. She's not afraid of it at all."

As everyone watched, she touched the snake. Her fingers recoiled. She touched it again.

"See, she's not afraid. Miss Aitcheson can stand there with a beautiful snake around her neck and touch it and stroke it and not be afraid."

The faces of the children were full of admiration for the teacher's bravery, and yet there was a cruelly persistent tension; they were waiting, waiting.

"We have to learn to love snakes," the attendant said. "Would someone like to come out and stroke teacher's snake?"

Silence.

One shamefaced boy came forward. He stood petrified in front of the teacher.

"Touch it," the attendant urged. "It's a friendly snake. Teacher's wearing it around her neck and she's not afraid."

The boy darted his hand forward, rested it

lightly on the snake, and immediately withdrew his hand. Then he ran to his seat. The children shrieked with glee.

"He's afraid," someone said, "He's afraid of the snake."

The attendant soothed. "We have to get used to them, you know. Grown-ups are not afraid of them, but we can understand that when you're small you might be afraid, and that's why we want you to learn to love them. Isn't that right, Miss Aitcheson? Isn't that right? Now who else is going to be brave enough to touch teacher's snake?"

Two girls came out. They stood hand in hand side by side and stared at the snake and then at Miss Aitcheson.

I wondered when the torture would end. The two little girls did not touch the snake, but they smiled at it and spoke to it, and Miss Aitcheson smiled at them and whispered how brave they were.

"Just a minute," the attendant said. "There's really no need to be brave. It's not a question of bravery. The snake is absolutely *harmless*. Where's the bravery when the snake is harmless?"

Suddenly the snake moved around to face Miss Aitcheson and thrust its flat head toward her cheek. She gave a scream, flung up her hands, and tore the snake from her throat and threw it on the floor, and rushing across the room, she collapsed into a chair beside the Bear Cabinet.

I didn't feel I should watch any longer. Some of the children began to laugh, some to cry. The attendant picked up the snake and nursed it. Miss Aitcheson, recovering, sat helplessly exposed by the small piece of useless torture. It was not her fault she was city-bred, her eyes tried to tell us. She looked at the children, trying in some way to force their admiration and respect; they were shut against her. She was evicted from them and from herself and even from her own fear-infested tomorrow, because she could not promise to love and preserve what she feared. She had nowhere, at that moment, but the small canvas chair by the Bear Cabinet of the Natural Science Museum.

I looked at my watch. If I hurried, I would catch the train from Thirtieth Street. There would be no time to make the journey through the human heart. I hurried out of the museum. It was freezing cold. The icebreakers would be at work on the Delaware and the Susquehanna; the mist would have risen by the time I arrived home. Yes, I would just catch the train from Thirtieth Street. The journey through the human heart would have to wait until some other time.

Responding to the Essay

Analyzing the Essay

Identifying Facts

1. Explain the purpose of the museum attendant's demonstration. Why does he pick Miss Aitcheson to aid him?
2. Describe Miss Aitcheson's attitude toward the snake. List four **objective details** that tell you how Miss Aitcheson looks, moves, and speaks.
3. How do the children feel about the snake? What is their attitude toward Miss Aitcheson after she shows her fear?
4. On page 412 the writer says that the children "were sitting hushed, waiting for the drama to begin. . . ." List the specific events that occur during this "drama." What is the high point, or **climax,** of the narrative?

Interpreting Meanings

5. Frame doesn't directly express her judgment about the museum attendant, yet her feelings are clear, as are her feelings about Miss Aitcheson. How would you describe her attitude toward the principal actors in this drama? Find examples of **subjective details**—words, phrases, and sentences that reveal the writer's feelings.

6. Where does the writer also give us completely imagined details about Miss Aitcheson's life and about her thoughts and feelings? Since she cannot really know what is in Miss Aitcheson's mind, how would you justify the inclusion of these details? (What "truth" is she seeking to show?)

7. Frame mentions both cruelty and torture in this essay. Precisely what kind of torture is Miss Aitcheson put through?

8. The final line of the essay says: "The journey through the human heart would have to wait until some other time." In what sense had the narrator already journeyed through the human heart?

9. In your own words, explain what you think Frame means in these statements. Which of the **figures of speech** here suggest snakes?

   a. "The exit light blinked, hooded." (Page 412)

   b. "She just managed to drag the fear from her eyes to some place in their depths, where it lurked like a dark stain." (Page 412)

   c. "The attendant seemed unaware, as if his perception had grown a reptilian covering." (Page 412)

10. Explain how you felt about Miss Aitcheson and about the museum attendant as you read this essay. How do you think you would have reacted if you had been, like Frame, a witness to what happened in the museum?

Writing About the Essay

A Creative Response

1. **Describing a Fear.** Fear is a universal experience; everyone is afraid of something. Some people fear flying in airplanes; others fear heights or the dark. Even people whom we think of as brave are sometimes fearful. The girl who can break in a wild colt may be terrified of speaking in front of a group. In at least two paragraphs, describe a person in the grip of a specific fear. (Write about yourself or someone you know or an imagined character.) In one paragraph, use specific details to show how the person looks, talks, and moves in the presence of the feared object or situation. In the second paragraph, tell what the person is thinking and feeling.

2. **Writing a Persuasive Essay.** The museum attendant is not very convincing in his attempt to teach the students to like and respect snakes. Write an essay in which you do a better job. Give facts and reasons to persuade your reader that not all snakes should be feared or killed and that a snake is worthy of awe and even admiration. Use an encyclopedia or a book about snakes to gather information for your essay.

A Critical Response

3. **Analyzing the Essay's Purpose.** In one paragraph, explain what you see as the writer's main purpose in writing this essay. In a second paragraph, describe your response to the essay and tell whether or not you think Frame accomplished her purpose.

Analyzing Language and Vocabulary

Strong Verbs

A good writer uses strong, specific verbs to make an action vivid for the reader. In the passage that follows, each set of parentheses contains two verb choices. One of these is the verb Frame used; the other is a different choice. Decide which is the more effective verb in each pair, and tell why.

Suddenly the snake moved around to face Miss Aitcheson and (*put, thrust*) its flat head toward her cheek. She gave a scream, (*raised, flung up*) her hands, and (*tore, removed*) the snake from her throat and (*put, threw*) it on the floor, and (*moving, rushing*) across the room, she (*collapsed into, sat down on*) a chair beside the Bear Cabinet.

Rewrite the following sentences, replacing each italicized verb with a stronger, more specific verb.

1. Jason *got up* from the couch and *went* inside.
2. Grace *walked* against the wind.
3. The cat *sat* on the windowsill, and her tail *moved*.
4. Ida *closed* the door and *left* the house.
5. Helen is *doing* her nails.

Marjorie Kinnan Rawlings (1896–1953) was the daughter of a Washington, D.C., patent attorney. Her own inventions took a literary turn from the earliest years of her life: at the age of eleven she won a two-dollar prize for a short story published in the *Washington Post*.

For nine years after her graduation from the University of Wisconsin, Rawlings worked as a reporter for newspapers in Louisville, Kentucky, and Rochester, New York. She once said that her newspaper experience was "a rough school, but I wouldn't have missed it. . . . You learn a lot when you must put down what people said and how they acted in great crises of their lives. And it teaches you objectivity."

Nevertheless, it was always her ambition to write fiction, and as the years went by and she had not sold a single short story, she became increasingly frustrated. Impulsively, she quit her newspaper job, bought an orange grove in Cross Creek in Central Florida, "at the jungle edge between two lakes," and settled down to write full-time. The Florida countryside and her neighbors proved to be her natural subjects: when she began to write about Florida, her stories sold "like a shot" to *Scribners* magazine.

Her editor at *Scribners* was the powerful Maxwell Perkins, friend and mentor to Thomas Wolfe, Ernest Hemingway, and F. Scott Fitzgerald—all of whom Rawlings came to know. Having found Florida as her subject and Perkins as her editor, Rawlings entered a rich and productive life, and her books followed each other in quick succession. Of all her books, the most famous is *The Yearling*, a novel set in Florida about a boy and a fawn. The book won the Pulitzer Prize, was translated into thirteen languages, and was made into a successful movie.

Rawlings was a small, dark, intense woman, who impressed people with the firmness of her chin, her gray-blue eyes, and her quick wit. She was generous to a fault, but she also had a tendency to melancholy and a love of solitude. Writing was never easy for her—sometimes it was even agony. "I stay at my typewriter for eight hours every day. . . . I aim to do six pages a day, but I'm satisfied with three. Often there are only a few lines to show. . . ."

Rawlings's last novel, *The Sojourner,* was set in Michigan and represented a deliberate attempt to deal with a setting other than the South. But it is for her portrait of the South that Rawlings is mainly celebrated today. Her vision of rural poverty presents not its violence and decadence, as so many other writings have done, but its decency, courage, comedy, and beauty.

The essay that follows is from *Cross Creek,* a collection of essays about her neighbors and her experiences in this tiny Florida town. (Years after its publication, *Cross Creek* was made into a critically acclaimed movie.)

After you read the first two paragraphs, stop and discuss in class what Rawlings says about friendship. Does everyone agree?

MY FRIEND MOE

Marjorie Kinnan Rawlings

Sometimes there are friendships that have no apparent reason for existence, between people set apart by every circumstance of life, yet so firm in their foundations that they survive conditions that would separate friends of more apparent suitability. My friendship with Moe was one of these. Moe said and believed that we were friends because we needed each other.

In the village he said once, "Me and her is buddies, see? If her gate falls down, I go and fix it. If I git in a tight for money, she helps me if she's got it, and if she ain't got it, she gits it for me. We stick together. You got to stick to the bridge that carries you across."

If he had never fixed a gate for me, waving aside any offer of pay, leaving a profitable carpenter's job to do it—for I certainly could not be bothered with the neighbors' stock coming in, could I?—if I had never scratched up a dollar for him, Moe and I would have been friends. Beyond our admiration of something in each other that might pass for courage, beyond our mutual helpfulness, there was a warm tenderness that made us like just to sit down together on the back steps and talk about the world as we saw it, while three or four of his boys squatted patiently on their heels waiting for us to be finished.

Sometimes he would wave his arm at them and boom in his deep voice, "You scapers go on and eat oranges now. Me and her ain't half done talkin'."

He introduced himself on my first Christmas Day at the Creek. He came out with a man named Whitey and it was a formal Christmas call. I was bustling about cooking Christmas dinner, some of the family was there, and Moe and Whitey sat on the back steps and visited with the men. It was long past the country noon dinner hour and I grew uneasy as the turkey browned and the squash and potatoes were done and the hard sauce finished for the plum pudding. I took my outdoor shower and dressed. I delayed, pushing the gravy to the back of the wood range. Moe and Whitey sat on. The turkey was beginning to dry out and the sauce had stood too long on the oyster cocktails in the icebox.

In desperation, I said, "Dinner is ready. Won't you men join us?"

According to my bringing up, that was the signal for uninvited guests to be on their way. I found that in rural Florida to refuse an invitation to a meal, if one is there at the time it is ready or nearly so, is to insult hospitality so grievously that the damage can seldom be repaired. Moe and Whitey had of course had their dinner, but to my horror Moe said, "Thank you, Ma'am," led Whitey to the pump stand to wash up, and came in. The family dinner was ruined for me. The intruders were as unhappy as I, but applied themselves with lowered heads and high-lifted elbows to their plates. Whitey was plainly only a follower and I stole a look at Moe. He was a great burly man with long arms and thick shoulders, slightly hunched from years of labor. His head was mas-

sive, and beyond a full fine forehead, the receding hair was shaggy and leonine. There was the look there of a man who might have been a statesman. He had one of the most beautiful speaking voices that I have ever heard. It had the deep resonance of a bass fiddle.

He plowed his way through the many-coursed dinner without comment. When I served the plum pudding that had taken so long to make and decorate he looked briefly at the blanched almonds and sugared fruits on the top and scraped them to one side, as I should scrape unexpected insects. The dinner had been one of my best, and it seemed to me from the rough worn clothes and the backwoods speech that it must surely have been a little out of the ordinary for these men. My vanity about my cooking is known and pandered to, and it seemed incredible to me that uninvited guests like these should not only pay me no compliments, but should have put down the choice dishes like so much hay.

I said, "You men have just eaten a typical Yankee Christmas dinner. Now tell me, what is the usual Cracker Christmas dinner?"

Moe lifted his big head and looked at me gravely.

"Whatever we can git, Ma'am," he said. "Whatever we can git."

I should have given the dinner and all my work over it, not to have asked that question.

I heard later that in the village Moe described the meal dish by dish. He spoke even of the edible decorations on the plum pudding that he rejected.

"A meal like that," I was told he said, "a feller don't know what's cold-out rations and what's fancy fixin's. When I seed her face, I knowed I'd ought to of run the risk and et everything."

I do not remember when we became friends. The occasion is bound to have been one when he did me some kindness. It seems to me that it was the hot Sunday morning when he passed by with his boys from a night's frog-hunting and found me in hell. I shall always associate my conception of hell with hot Sunday summer mornings at the Creek. And why Sunday morning? Because that is when the drinking portion of the help fails to arrive.

The Sunday morning that Moe stopped by was

one of these. I was without household help at the time and I slept late without hearing a sound on the place to disturb me. The lowing of the cow finally penetrated my sleep and I awoke in a humid heat with an uneasy sense that all was not well. I dressed and went out to the stillness of a desert island. I do not remember which of the procession of men was the culprit, but whoever he was, he was not there.

The cow was old Laura, weather-beaten, gray, and gaunt, and the only cow I have known with a more evil nature than hers, is her daughter Dora. Laura was busily and angrily engaged in tearing down the pasture fence. An early daughter, then a calf, little Atrocia, a repulsive creature whom I later traded for a week's hoeing, was jumping back and forth through the hole in the fence that Laura had begun. The young bull had broken through the fence by the road and at sight of me began bellowing and pawing the earth. The chickens, unfed and protesting, got under my feet and tripped me as I made my way through the sandspurs to the pasture gate. It had been fastened with an intricate African arrangement of chains, and by the time I had them loosened and the gate swung wide, Laura had knocked down two more fence posts and was making her way loftily to the barn.

She then decided to be coy and, food being what I supposed she wanted, refused to go into the pen where it waited. She gamboled like a heifer through the grove, her bony hips heaving, little Atrocia at her heels in delight at the sudden friskiness of her aged parent. I was obliged to give up getting her into the pen. I lugged the feed trough out into the open by the barn and brought a bucket of water, for the lake was low beside the pasture and the stock must be watered by hand. I went into the barn for feed. A new sack had to be opened and I bruised my fingers working at the chain-stitched binding. I took a bucket of the feed and emptied it into the trough. Laura was in front of the house eating blue plumbago blossoms and asparagus fern. I climbed up the rickety ladder to the hayloft to pitch down hay, for the bull must have some of this too. A chicken snake and two rats ran across my feet as I lifted a forkful. A leather-winged bat, disturbed from its slumbers in the rafters, swooped out of the loft, brushing my hair. A setting hen under the hay flew into my face and floated to earth, squawking and shrilling. I pitched down the hay and descended the ladder. The next to the last rung broke under me and I slid to the ground and walked limping to the feed trough. Laura had come, eaten all the feed, and was now over by the tenant house. Being full, she had no intention of standing for milking. She had a greedy nature and I lured her back to the trough with another bucket of feed. The calf was only two months old, though weaned, and Laura's bag in mid-morning was full and tight. I had never milked in my life. I had never expected to milk in my life. I should not have tried it now, but I was certain Laura would burst if she were not somehow relieved.

I knelt down beside her, put the milk bucket under her, and tightened my fingers around two of the teats. Nothing happened. With her mouth dripping feed, Laura turned her head over her shoulder and looked at me, as though to say, "What on earth are you doing?" In annoyance, she moved a foot to the side. I moved too. I began again. I constricted desperately, trying to recall the motion I had seen the milkers use. The knack suddenly came to me, and I saw the first thin streams of milk drop into the bucket as though I had brought up pearls from the sea. By this time the second bucket of feed was gone; Laura walked off, and I was obliged to go for a third bucket and lure her back again. She was indifferent, but she had become also a little lethargic, and I got her back to the trough. This time, because she ate so slowly, I got a quart of milk. A sense of proud competence filled me. I was dripping with perspiration and the flies hummed around us. When they stung me, I went frantically on with my milking. When they stung Laura, she switched her long tail across my face. Now she stood immobile, ruminating placidly. With no provocation at all, because the stinging flies were on me, she lifted a hind foot and kicked the bucket of milk into my lap. I looked at her bag. It seemed as full as ever. I went back to the milking. Humanitarian motives had left me, but I did not want a good milch cow to swell up and die. I got another pint, and Laura lifted a hind leg and kicked me square in the mid-

dle. There was only one thing left to do. I kicked her in the middle, said to her, "You may burst for all of me," and she stalked off into the coffee-weed. I tottered to the pen to close the gate. It was at this moment that Moe and his boys drew up by the fence and hailed me.

His big voice boomed out, "What you doin' with a milk bucket?"

I leaned weakly on the fence to answer him.

"My man didn't show up and I tried to milk the cow."

"Where is she?"

He was already putting his long legs out of the old car. His boys tumbled out behind him.

"Over there in the coffee-weed. I hope she pops wide open."

I must have begun then to know him as a friend, for he did not laugh. He gave directions to the boys and they scattered to the points of the compass. Two of them drove back the cow. Two made a noose of a rope from the barn. All together they held her tied tight to an orange tree while Moe rested on his heels and milked and stripped her.

"What else you got around here ain't done?"

The chickens had not been fed and water for all the animals had not been pumped. They did that.

Moe said, "Now if that man don't show up by evenin', you leave me know. I'll go find him and take a whip to him, leavin' you like this."

He was always indignant when he found me doing work that he considered too difficult and too heavy, and called his boys in a swarm to take over. They were silent, unsmiling youngsters, undersized and pale. They went to school passively, and since they showed no interest in education, Moe was trying to train them in his own profession of carpentering and was teaching them frog hunting on the side.

"Them scapers is the best frog hunters in the county," he said. "No fear o' them or their mammy starvin' when I'm done for, long as they can haul in a hundred pounds o' frogs of a night."

The boys smiled then, wanly. The irresponsible night hunting was to their taste. I am sure the carpentering was not, though they did accurate enough work under Moe's critical eye. Moe's true love was an orange grove, and he would have liked

to raise oranges for a living. His father, and his grandfather before him, had been superintendent for the Fairbanks grove, one of the oldest Florida groves, of which my choice seven acres in Big Hammock is a part. Moe had lived on the grove as a boy. One day I heard his voice giving orders at the gate. The boys were bringing in a bedstead. It was handmade, spool turned, of pine, put together with wooden pegs. It had the grace of all good handmade things.

"This mought seem like pure trash to you," Moe said, and the boys set the bed down in front of me. "But if you want it, it's yours. It was made for Major Fairbanks, and before he died he give it to my daddy. It's been out in the barn for fifty years. You want it?"

The bed had real value as Floridiana. There are almost no native Florida antiques. Major Fairbanks was not only a famous early grove owner, but the founder and first president of the Florida Historical Society and the author of *Fairbanks' History of Florida* and the *History and Antiquities of St. Augustine,* both now collectors' items.

I said, "It's beautiful, Moe, but it's valuable. You should keep it."

"We got no use fer it," he said contemptuously, not of the bed, but of his household's way of life, which grieved him. "The way I got to figgerin', a thing belongs to be used and used right, and you livin' nice, and havin' a piece o' the Major's old grove, why, you're the one to have it. Been layin' up all these years waitin' for the right person."

The bed is now my own, and it is promised when I am done with it to the Historical Society.

I did not understand it at the time but as I look back on our friendship, I believe that Moe lived vicariously in my grove and in my "livin' nice." He was intrigued with every detail of my housekeeping. He put in a new kitchen floor for me, saying of the old one through which 'Geechee[1] had scrubbed a hole, "Why, Ma'am, they was places you could of throwed a dog through it." As he worked, he noticed a row of glass jars of huckleberries that I had canned. His grave face brightened.

"Now that's the way to live," he said. "All the

---

1. 'Geechee: Rawlings's housekeeper and cook.

good things we got here in Florida, blueberries and blackberries and beans and cowpeas, all them things had ought to be canned and put up on a clean cupboard shelf with white paper on it. That's the way my Ma did. She lived fine, not the way you live, but just as good when it come to cannin' things and keepin' things clean." His face darkened. "I've tried and I've done tried to get my wife to do that-a-way, but it just ain't no use. One time I bought two dozen glass jars and I went out by myself and I picked about a bushel o' blackberries and I went to the store and bought a twenty-five pound sack o' sugar and I takened it home and I said, 'Wife, here's a bait o' blackberries to put up for us for jam and jelly for the winter.' " He hesitated, his loyalty pricking him.

"She probably didn't have time to do it," I suggested.

"She had time. She let the blackberries spoil and the antses got in the sugar and I found the jars throwed out in the back yard."

I had light on the matter when I met his mother, who came to visit in the village. Moe brought her out and left her with me for the day. She was of the admirable Florida pioneer type, plump, immaculate, wise, and kindly. We talked of her life on the Fairbanks grove and we talked of Moe.

"It like to killed me when he married," she said. "Moe did love bein' to home and havin' things nice. I said to him, 'Son, don't you marry that girl. She ain't your kind and she'll not make you the home you want.' He looked kind o' sorrowful, and he said, real slow, 'I know, Ma. But I love the little old thing.' "

Moe followed the fortunes of my grove as closely as if it had been his own. When I planted ten acres of Valencias[2] across the road where the dingy pecan trees had been cut down and the vacant space had stared at me, he rejoiced with me. We were sure that the new ten acres would make the needed difference between profit and loss. I had put my last hundreds of dollars in the planting and was obliged to watch my simple grocery supplies in consequence. I went to the Everglades in the winter on a hunting trip with Dessie and the Chanceys. The weather in late November

was warm when we left Tampa. Cold weather set in the second day at camp. Even so far south, we were obliged to have a roaring campfire night and morning, and the pond water in which we bathed struck us with icy power. We wore sweaters under our hunting clothes and were hard put to it, as we stood motionless on our deer and turkey stands, not to stamp our feet and clap our hands to keep our circulation moving against the cold. The hunt and the companions were so delightful that I did not think to associate the cold with any menace to my new young grove.

When I returned to the Creek, I found that a disastrous freeze had come in to north and central Florida. Old groves showed much damage, fruit was nipped, and many young groves had been frozen to the ground. I looked across the road to my small, frail Valencia trees. A miracle had happened. They had been mounded with earth almost to their tops and below the frozen tips they were safe. No one could have done this but Moe. That evening I drove in to his house to see him.

"Bet you was surprised," he chuckled. "The cold begun comin' in that afternoon and it got wuss and wusser. I drove out to the Creek to tell you somethin' had ought to be done. You wasn't there and Martha said you was off huntin' in the south and likely didn't know it was freezin' up here. Dogged if I aimed to let them trees freeze behind your back. I got my boys together and Ivey Sykes and Whitey and a couple more, and I borried all the spades and shovels in Island Grove, and we went out and we worked all night 'til sunrise. The wust cold come in about day and by that time we had the job done."

Such things that Moe did for me could never be paid for.

He tried me out a little later. He came out one evening with the boys and sat stiffly on the veranda.

He burst out, "I got to have forty dollars. How about it?" He looked me in the eye with something like belligerence.

I said, "As long as I've got it, it's yours."

The loan caught me very short. I wrote out the check and as I handed it to the man, I sensed in him a feeling of triumph. He returned the money a week later. I happened to know that he had not

---

2. **Valencias:** a type of orange.

worked that week. He was only making certain that he could count on me. After that, he borrowed only when he was in dire straits. Sometimes I myself had to borrow the money when half of his immense family was sick, but my credit was better than his. If he could not pay me back in cash, he paid in work worth twice what he owed me.

One summer I decided to make a hurried trip to New York to consult with my editor. I put my car in storage and bought my ticket for New York. My grove man would drive me in the truck to the train at the village stop. The morning that I was to leave, Moe drove out to see me. His face was gray.

He said, "I'm in trouble. Mary's dyin'. Seems like I'm turned to stone. I cain't think. I cain't figger out what to do."

Mary was one of the youngest of his brood of twelve, a shy child with a certain brightness of face the others did not possess.

I said, "I'll come," and drove the farm truck behind him to his house.

The child lay like a crumpled rag doll on her small bed, her blue eyelids closed, her breathing hoarse and labored. The mother sat nearby in a slovenly incompetence. Moe had taken Mary to the doctor two days before, and while there was a chance, he had said, that her illness might pass into pneumonia, there was an equal chance, with proper nursing, of no danger at all. The pneumonia had developed rapidly, and literally nothing had been done. Moe had been ill and unable to work, and his funds were exhausted. His wife thought the illness was unimportant. The child was plainly in a critical condition.

A heavy downpour of rain had set in, the roof of the farm truck leaked like a sieve, I was dressed for my trip and had only two hours before train time. But my own plans were trivial before Moe's trouble. I drove to Ocala in the rain, arranged for a doctor and a nurse, drew money out of the bank for Moe, and went back to tell him that help was on the way. The doctor and nurse had arrived ahead of me and were working over the sick child. Moe looked at my soaked clothes. He dropped down on the porch of his house and tears ran down the deep furrows of his face.

He said, "I hadn't ought to of let you do this. I reckon you can't figger why I'd take on so over one young un, and me with a whole houseful of 'em."

He wiped away his tears unashamed with the back of his big hand.

"Mary's different," he said. "All them other young uns, and their Ma, they don't pay me a bit o' mind. When I come home, times they don't even pass the time o' day with me, lessen to ask maybe did I bring home meat for supper. They don't none of 'em care do I come or go. But Mary sets by the road and waits for me. She comes runnin' and I carry her in on my shoulder. She called me 'Bubber.' "

The tears ran like rain.

"I don't know how I'll live if she dies," he said. "I just couldn't make out without Mary."

I took my train for New York, but I had almost forgotten why I was going. I could not get Moe out of my mind. All day, far up into Georgia, the rain fell, and they were Moe's tears, falling for Mary, the only one who cared whether he came or went. All night, the wheels of the train repeated, "Moe and Mary! Moe and Mary!" It seemed to me that I should be obliged to get off the train and go back to them.

I had a brief interview with my editor and hurried home. Mary was safe. She smiled shyly when Moe took me to her bed. The nurse had the sickroom in order and Moe was in his best bib and tucker. His face was luminous.

"I shore went to pieces," he apologized. "When I think o' you comin', all dressed in your best clothes and soppin' wet from helpin' me, I'm ashamed. But them things gits made up somehow. I'll git a chance to do somethin' for you sometime. Tell you what I'll do. I'll take you alligator huntin'. You ain't never been and I'll bet you could write a fine story about it if you saw it yourself."

Moe continued to keep an eye on my grove and on tottering fences, leaking roofs, and broken plumbing. He tried to keep his own garden, single-handed, and he brought me always the first of his crop; lettuce, squash, watermelons. He brought up the matter of the 'gator hunt every time he came, but somehow we never got together on it.

"How about that 'gator hunt tonight?" he

would say and I would have some engagement that prevented it.

He could not have been much past fifty in age, but he began to break like a man much older. There were increasing periods when he could not do his carpentering and when he could not go frog hunting with his boys. The last summer of his life he was very ill. He asked if the boys might help with my summer grove pruning. I was glad of the extra labor. At the time Moe owed me twenty-five dollars and since I knew it fretted him, I asked if he wanted the boys' pay applied on the debt. He hesitated.

"No, jest pay 'em right out," he said. "That other's somethin' between you and me."

There was no hope for him. Years of improper food and overwork, of anxiety over the future of his family, above all, I think, despair at not living

as he longed to have them live, had eaten at his big burly frame and great gentle mind. He knew that he was going. He sent the boys out for me one day. He sat propped in a chair, his face gaunt, his hair tousled above the broad forehead.

"I ain't goin' to make it," he said and his voice was deep and rich as ever. "I ain't never taken you on that 'gator hunt like I promised, and I hate that."

A few days later I stopped by his place, drawn by an uneasy instinct. Moe was still propped in his chair. As I stood in the doorway, his breath made a strangling sound in his throat and the big head dropped forward on his chest and did not lift again. The family stood stonily. Only Mary huddled behind his chair with a desperate small face. Only she and I have missed him, finding the world less generous for his going.

Responding to the Essay

Analyzing the Essay

Identifying Facts

1. When Moe and his friend come to call on Christmas Day, how does their Cross Creek behavior surprise the author? Explain why she says (on page 416) that she would have "given the dinner and all my work over it, not to have asked that question."
2. List at least ten specific **details** Rawlings uses to describe Moe. Which of them are **factually** true? Which of them are **subjective**—revealing how Rawlings feels about her friend?
3. Describe Moe's home life. Why is he particularly attached to Mary?
4. In the first paragraph, Rawlings says that Moe believes they are friends because they need each other. How did these two different people need each other? Despite their differences, how were they alike?

Interpreting Meanings

5. This essay begins with a generalization about friendship. Do you think the rest of the essay

bears out the generalization? Do you agree with it? Explain.
6. Rawlings reveals Moe's character indirectly in a series of brief stories, or **anecdotes.** Explain what each of the following anecdotes reveals about Moe's character:

   a. The cow-milking scene (pages 417–419)
   b. The gift of a bedstead (page 419)
   c. The freeze that threatens the young orange trees (page 420)
   d. Mary's illness (page 421)

7. Find the passages where Rawlings reports her own generosity. This is an extremely dangerous thing for a writer to do because it can so easily seem like bragging. In your opinion, does Rawlings survive the risk? Explain.
8. Rawlings's essay is about herself and a neighbor in a tiny town in central Florida more than fifty years ago. What does the essay reveal about people and life in general, and at all times?
9. How did you respond to the **characters** of Rawlings and Moe? Which incidents in this essay affected your feelings most strongly?

Writing About the Essay

A Creative Response

1. **Imitating the Writer's Technique.** Rawlings uses anecdotes to *show* us Moe's **character.** Write a brief character sketch of someone you know and like—a friend, a store owner, a relative, a town character. Tell at least one anecdote that will reveal something important about the person's character. Use your subject's name in the title.

A Critical Response

2. **Analyzing the Essay's Beginning.** Many writers believe that the most important paragraph in an essay is the first one, because it must make the reader want to read on. Write a paragraph in which you analyze Rawlings's opening paragraph and evaluate its effectiveness. Before you write, organize your material in a chart like the following one.

	Opening of the Essay
What is the first sentence?	
Does it hook my interest?	
What are the supporting details?	
How far do I have to read before I know the essay's topic?	

Analyzing Language and Vocabulary

Dialect

Like novelists, poets, and playwrights, nonfiction writers sometimes use dialect to help us ''hear'' the actual words a character says. A **dialect** is the variety of spoken language peculiar to a region or community, or to a social or occupational group. Rawlings's depiction of Moe's character depends, in part, on letting us hear exactly how he speaks. Use the following chart to identify the Cross Creek dialect used in these passages. How would you say the same thing if you were talking to a friend?

1. '' 'If I get in a tight for money, she helps me if she's got it, and if she ain't got it, she gits it for me.' ''

2. '' 'Me and her ain't half done talkin'.' ''
3. '' 'Them scapers is the best frog hunters in the county. . . .' ''
4. '' 'This mought seem like pure trash to you. . . .' ''
5. '' 'Wife, here's a bait o' blackberries to put up for us for jam and jelly for the winter.' ''
6. '' 'The cold begun comin' in that afternoon and it got wuss and wusser.' ''
7. '' 'When I come home, times they don't even pass the time o' day with me, lessen to ask maybe did I bring home meat for supper.' ''

Dialect	
Specialized vocabulary	1. 2. etc.
Characteristic ways of pronouncing words	1. 2. etc.
Unorthodox syntax (arrangement of words) and grammar	1. 2. etc.

William Allen (1940–   ), born in Dallas, Texas, teaches nonfiction writing at Ohio State University. He has also written articles for *The Antioch Review*, the *New York Times*, and *The Saturday Review*, which is where this essay first appeared. In 1976 he published *Starkweather: The Story of a Mass Murderer*, a nonfiction book about a notorious murder spree that took place in Nebraska in 1959.

Allen, who has been writing since he was twelve years old, is interested especially in American history, his regional Texas background, and humor. When asked about his theory of fiction, he once said, "Every good story should have at least one chicken in it."

As you might expect from this last comment, the article that follows is humorous. But, like most humor, it makes a serious point. The title hints at Allen's message about writing and writers: What do you think it means? Read the first five paragraphs and discuss this question with your classmates: Would you be influenced by this kind of advertising, as the narrator was? What desires do the ads appeal to?

A WHOLE SOCIETY OF LONERS AND DREAMERS

William Allen

On Sunday afternoons here, if you're tired of taking walks in the country and fighting off the green-bellied hogflies, your next best choice is thumbing magazines at the downtown drugstore. One Sunday not long ago, when I ran out of anything else to thumb, I started looking through one of those magazines geared toward helping new writers achieve success. I used to pore over them a lot when I was a teenager, and the first thing I noticed now was that the ads haven't changed much over the past fifteen years:

"IMAGINE MAKING $5,000 A YEAR WRITING IN YOUR SPARE TIME! Fantastic? Not at all. . . . Hundreds of People Make That Much or More Every Year—and Have Fun Doing It!"

"TO PEOPLE WHO WANT TO WRITE FOR PROFIT BUT CAN'T GET STARTED. Have You Natural Writing Ability? Now a Chance to Test Yourself—FREE!"

"I FIRE WRITERS . . . with enthusiasm for developing God-given talent. You'll 'get fired' too with my 48-lesson home study course. Over-the-shoulder coaching . . . personalized critiques! Amazing sales opportunity the first week. Write for my FREE STARTER KIT."

The ad that struck me the most showed a picture of a handsome and darkly serious young man sitting on a hill, picking his teeth with a weed, and gazing out over the countryside. The caption read: DO YOU HAVE THE "FAULTS" THAT COULD MEAN YOU WERE MEANT TO BE A WRITER? The ad went on to list the outstanding characteristics of writers. They are dreamers, loners, bookworms. They are too impractical, too intense, too idealistic.

When I was fourteen and had just started trying to write, I saw an ad much like this and was overwhelmed by it. That fellow on the hill was just like me, I thought. It was a tremendous feeling

The Plaid Sweater by Grant Wood (1931).
Oil, 29½″ × 24⅛″.

The University of Iowa Museum of Art, Iowa City.
Partial gift of Melvin R. and Carole Blumberg.

to discover that I might not be alone—that there was a whole society of loners and dreamers, that they were called writers, and that by sending off for a free writing IQ test I could find out by return mail if I qualified to climb the hill and chew straw with them.

I took the test and blew the top off it. The writing school said I demonstrated a rare creative potential unlike anything they had seen in years. They did wonder, though, if I had what it took to stick with them through long months of arduous training to develop my raw talent. If I really did have that kind of fortitude, the next step would be to send in some actual samples of my writing.

Spurred, I sent off everything I had ever written—two stories of about two hundred words each. One was about some unidentified creatures who lived in dread of an unidentified monster who came around every week or so to slaughter as many of them as he could. Some of the persecuted creatures had the option of running, hopping, scurrying, or crawling to safety, but the others, for some unexplained reason, couldn't move and had just to stand there and take it. There was a description of the monster's roaring approach. Then the last line hit the reader like a left hook: "The lawn mower ran swiftly over. . . ."

The other story I have preserved these many years:

THE RACE

Two gleaming hot rods stand side by side, poised and tensed—eager to scream down the hot asphalt track, each secretly confident that he will be the supreme victor. The time is drawing close now; in just a few minutes the race will be on.

There is a last-minute check of both cars . . . everything is ready. A yell rings out for everyone to clear the track. The flagman raises the starting flag above his head, pauses for a second, and with a downward thrust of the flag, he sends the cars leaping forward with frightening speed.

They fly down the track, side by side, neither able to take the lead. They are gaining speed with every second. Faster and faster they go, approaching the halfway mark with incredible momentum. . . .

Wait! Something is wrong—one of the cars is going out of control and skidding toward the other car! The rending sound of ripping metal and sliding tires cuts through the air as the two autos collide and spin crazily off the track.

For a moment the tragic panorama is hidden by a self-made curtain of dust, but it isn't a second before the curtain is pulled away by the wind, revealing the horrible sight. There are the two hot rods, one turned over, both broken and smashed. All is quiet. . . .

Two small children, a boy and a girl, get up from the curb where they have been sitting. They eye each other accusingly as they walk slowly across the street where the two broken toy cars lay silent. . . . "Woman driver," grumbles the little boy.

THE END

The correspondence school's copy desk quickly replied that the writing samples confirmed my aptitude test results and that they looked forward to working with me to the point of publication and beyond. I couldn't imagine what could be beyond publication but finally figured out they meant to handle my work later as agent-representative. They praised my choice of subject matter, sense of drama, and powerful surprise endings—all of which they said indicated I could sell to the sci-fi market. This made sense, because science fiction was all I had ever read voluntarily except for *Comic Classics* and, as a child, *Uncle Wiggily*. The school was particularly impressed by my style, which they said was practically poetry, in places. They made reference to my use of alliteration ("rending sound of ripping metal") and of metaphor ("self-made curtain of dust . . . pulled away by the wind").

They were quick to make clear, however, that what I had here were only germs of stories. They needed to be expanded to publishable lengths and had to have better character development—particularly the one about the bugs and grass being slaughtered by the lawn mower. They said a good writer could give even an insect an interesting personality.

The next step was to send them $10 for each of the two stories—the standard fee for detailed, over-the-shoulder copy-desk criticism. Then after these stories had been redone and rushed off for publication, I should enroll in their thirty-six-lesson course, in which I would be taught the ins and outs of plotting, characterization, point of view, theme, tone, and setting. The fee was $10 a lesson, and after my successful completion of the course, they would then handle my literary properties, protect my legal rights, etc., for the regular ten percent.

At this point I began to wonder if I might be going in over my head. I was getting only a dollar a week from my folks and didn't understand half of what the writing school was talking about. In English class I had heard of such terms as "alliteration," "tone," and "point of view" but had no clear idea what they meant. Also I felt like an impostor. I had given my age as twenty-one. Of course, I was strutting because at fourteen I was doing better than anybody they had worked with in years, but I wondered if I could keep it up. "Rending sound of ripping metal" was genius, but could I crank out lines like that on a daily basis? I decided to try.

First I wrote them that I was a little short of cash this month and asked if just to get started, it would be all right to work on one story for $10 instead of two for $20. They replied that that would be fine—just send in the ten bucks so they could get rolling.

Meanwhile I hadn't been able to get even that much money together. I approached my family and was turned down flat because my father thought there was something unhealthy about people who wanted to write. He was bothered by the school's remark that my writing was like poetry. "If you were a girl, it might be different," he said, and showed me a copy of *Men's Adventure*.

"Look here, why don't you get one of these two ninety-eight worm ranches? Or one of these small-game boomerangs?"

After a few days of trying to drum up work around the neighborhood, I realized I wasn't going to be able to pull it off and decided just not to write back. But in a week I got a curt note saying they wanted to help me, were trying to be patient, but I was going to have to be more responsible. They said that writing was one percent inspiration and ninety-nine percent perspiration and wondered if in my case the figures might be reversed.

This both goaded and scared me. I wrote back that on account of unexpected medical expenses I could afford to give them only $5 at first. Could they possibly let me have a cut rate? They replied that it was strictly against their policy, but in view of my undeniably vast potential the copy-desk team had voted to go along with me just this once—send the $5.

By mowing lawns and selling bottles, I had by this time scraped together $3, but there my earning potential dropped sharply. Another week went by, and I made only 48 cents more. Then a letter arrived stamped in red, front and back: URGENT! IMPORTANT! DO NOT DISCARD! It said I had violated an agreement based on mutual trust and had exactly twenty-four hours to send in the $5. Without exactly spelling it out, they gave the impression that legal action might be taken. The letter ended: "Frankly, Mr. Allen, we're about at our wits' end with you."

I was hurt as well as shaken. I felt that I just didn't have what it takes. If there ever had been a chance of my climbing that hill and sitting with that elite group of loners and dreamers, it was gone now. I had my mother write them that I had suddenly been struck down with polio and was unable even to write my name, much less take their course. I hung onto the little money I had in case I had to give it to them to avoid a lawsuit, but I didn't hear from them after that. In a few weeks I relaxed and mailed off for the $2.98 worm ranch.

Responding to the Essay

Analyzing the Essay

Identifying Facts

1. Look back at the essay's beginning. How does the author lead in to the **flashback** about his experiences as an aspiring writer?
2. Why is Allen attracted to the writing school's offer?
3. Describe what happens when Allen takes the correspondence school's free test. List the specific steps—each involving a fee—that the school suggests will improve Allen's writing.
4. Explain how Allen finally gets out of his problem with the correspondence school.

Interpreting Meanings

5. We are shown directly that Allen is lying in his letters to the writing school—about being short of cash, about medical expenses, about having polio—but the school's dishonesty is more subtly signaled. Find several passages from which we can **infer** what Allen did not realize at the time: that the school is conning him.
6. Why does his father show Allen a copy of *Men's Adventures*? Why do you think some people regard poetry the way the father does?
7. Do you think everyone in some way is a ''loner'' and a ''dreamer''? Explain.
8. In a **satire** a writer makes the faults of something or someone seem ridiculous. Would you consider this essay a satire? Explain why or why not. If it is a satire, who or what is its target?

Writing About the Essay

A Critical Response

1. **Analyzing Advertisements.** Advertisements appeal to our strongest emotions and deepest desires by promising all sorts of things—wealth, health, physical attractiveness, pleasure, ease, popularity. For example, the magazine ads cited on page 424 appeal to the reader's desire to have money and need to feel talented and ''superior.'' Choose two specific advertisements from television, newspaper, radio, or billboards. In two paragraphs, analyze each ad; base your analysis on the items in the chart that follows. Be sure to consider all aspects of the advertisement: images, sounds, and words.

Analysis of an Advertisement	
What it is selling	
What it promises	
What emotions or desires or fears it appeals to	
Elements of the ad that work on your feelings or desires	

2. **Evaluating a Story.** Reread Allen's childhood story on page 426, and decide whether you agree or disagree with the correspondence school's evaluation of it. Write a brief essay giving what you think is a fair evaluation of his story.

Analyzing Language and Vocabulary

Language That Persuades

Language is a powerful tool, and the correspondence school uses it craftily. Remember that the school's goal is to persuade Allen to send them money—as much as they can get. Examine the methods they use to get what they want.

1. After his free test, the writing school tells Allen that he has ''rare creative potential.'' List at least three other flattering phrases used to persuade Allen that he has talent.
2. Next the school needs to persuade Allen that it is qualified to help him improve his writing. List three literary terms it uses to impress its impressionable client. Where does the school use the specialized vocabulary of publishing to imply that it can get his stories published?
3. Finally the school must persuade Allen to put the money in the mail. At first it flatters him, but then it scolds and warns him. List the words or phrases that are intended to make Allen feel guilty and frighten him into sending the money.

You'll find a brief biography of Alice Walker on page 136, along with her short story "Everyday Use."

The selection that follows is the second part of a long essay about the intense creative spirit of black women. In this section of the essay, Walker is attempting to answer, on a personal level, some questions she has raised earlier:

"What did it mean for a black woman to be an artist in our grandmothers' time? In our great-grandmothers' day? It is a question with an answer cruel enough to stop the blood. . . .

"How was the creativity of the black woman kept alive, year after year and century after century, when for most of the years black people have been in America, it was a punishable crime for a black person to read or write? And the free-dom to paint, to sculpt, to expand the mind with action did not exist."

Walker explores these questions by examining her own mother's life. She writes: "I found, while thinking about the far-reaching world of the creative black woman, that often the truest answer to a question that really matters can be found very close."

Before you begin reading about Walker's un-usual "search," write down a sentence or two de-scribing what you think the word *creative* means. Who is the most creative person you know? What does he or she create? Is this person famous, or likely to become famous someday? Now think about this question: Do you know anyone who might have become a great artist or writer or mu-sician if the circumstances of his or her life had been different?

IN SEARCH OF OUR MOTHERS' GARDENS

Alice Walker

In the late 1920's, my mother ran away from home to marry my father. Marriage, if not running away, was expected of seventeen-year-old girls. By the time she was twenty, she had two children and was pregnant with a third. Five children later, I was born. And this is how I came to know my mother: She seemed a large, soft, loving-eyed woman who was rarely impatient in our home. Her quick, violent temper was on view only a few times a year, when she battled with the white landlord who had the misfortune to suggest to her that her children did not need to go to school.

She made all the clothes we wore, even my brothers' overalls. She made all the towels and sheets we used. She spent the summers canning vegetables and fruits. She spent the winter eve-nings making quilts enough to cover all our beds.

During the "working" day, she labored be-side—not behind—my father in the fields. Her day began before sunup, and did not end until late at night. There was never a moment for her to sit down, undisturbed, to unravel her own private thoughts; never a time free from interruption—by work or the noisy inquiries of her many children. And yet, it is to my mother—and all our mothers who were not famous—that I went in search of the secret of what has fed that muzzled and often mutilated, but vibrant, creative spirit that the black woman has inherited, and that pops out in wild and unlikely places to this day.

But when, you will ask, did my overworked mother have time to know or care about feeding the creative spirit?

The answer is so simple that many of us have spent years discovering it. We have constantly

Maudell Sleet by
Romare Bearden (1980). Watercolor.

Collection C. E. Boulware, New York. Reprinted courtesy of
the Estate of Romare Bearden. Photograph, Dawoud Bey.

looked high, when we should have looked high—and low.

For example: In the Smithsonian Institution in Washington, D. C., there hangs a quilt unlike any other in the world. In fanciful, inspired, and yet simple and identifiable figures, it portrays the story of the Crucifixion. It is considered rare, beyond price. Though it follows no known pattern of quilt-making, and though it is made of bits and pieces of worthless rags, it is obviously the work of a person of powerful imagination and deep spiritual feeling. Below this quilt I saw a note that says it was made by "an anonymous Black woman in Alabama, a hundred years ago."

If we could locate this "anonymous" black woman from Alabama, she would turn out to be one of our grandmothers—an artist who left her mark in the only materials she could afford, and in the only medium her position in society allowed her to use.

As Virginia Woolf[1] wrote further, in *A Room of One's Own*:

> Yet genius of a sort must have existed among women as it must have existed among the working class. [Change this to "slaves" and "the wives and daughters of share-croppers."] Now and again an Emily Brontë[2] or a Robert Burns[3] [change this to "a Zora Hurston[4] or a Richard Wright"[5]] blazes out and proves its presence. But certainly it never got itself onto paper. When, however, one reads of a witch being ducked, of a woman possessed by devils [or "Sainthood"[6]], of a wise woman selling herbs [our root workers], or even a very

remarkable man who had a mother, then I think we are on the track of a lost novelist, a suppressed poet, of some mute and inglorious Jane Austen.[7] . . . Indeed, I would venture to guess that Anon, who wrote so many poems without signing them, was often a woman. . . .

And so our mothers and grandmothers have, more often than not anonymously, handed on the creative spark, the seed of the flower they themselves never hoped to see: or like a sealed letter they could not plainly read.

And so it is, certainly, with my own mother. Unlike "Ma" Rainey's songs, which retained their creator's name even while blasting forth from Bessie Smith's[8] mouth, no song or poem will bear my mother's name. Yet so many of the stories that I write, that we all write, are my mother's stories. Only recently did I fully realize this: that through years of listening to my mother's stories of her life, I have absorbed not only the stories themselves, but something of the manner in which she spoke, something of the urgency that involves the knowledge that her stories—like her life—must be recorded. It is probably for this reason that so much of what I have written is about characters whose counterparts in real life are so much older than I am.

But the telling of these stories, which came from my mother's lips as naturally as breathing, was not the only way my mother showed herself as an artist. For stories, too, were subject to being distracted, to dying without conclusion. Dinners must be started, and cotton must be gathered before the big rains. The artist that was and is my mother showed itself to me only after many years. This is what I finally noticed:

Like Mem, a character in *The Third Life of Grange Copeland*,[9] my mother adorned with flowers whatever shabby house we were forced to live in. And not just your typical straggly country stand of zinnias, either. She planted ambitious gar-

---

1. **Virginia Woolf** (1882–1941): In *A Room of One's Own* (1929), Woolf says that in order to write, a woman must have privacy (a room of her own) and money to support herself. (Walker says "further" because she quoted from Woolf earlier.)
2. **Emily Brontë** (1819–1848): English novelist and poet, best known for her novel *Wuthering Heights*.
3. **Robert Burns** (1759–1796): Scottish poet whose father was a farmer and who was largely self-educated.
4. **Zora [Neale] Hurston** (1891–1960): African American novelist and folklorist. Walker edited an anthology of her writings.
5. **Richard Wright** (1908–1960): African American writer, best known for his novel *Native Son*.
6. Earlier in the essay, Walker talks about certain "crazy, loony, pitiful" black women in the South called Saints. Intensely spiritual, these women were driven to madness by their creativity, for which there was no release.

7. **Jane Austen** (1775–1817): English novelist, best known for *Pride and Prejudice*.
8. **Bessie Smith** (1898?–1937): called the "Empress of the Blues." The great blues singer and songwriter "Ma" Rainey (1886–1939) took her under her wing when Smith was a teenager.
9. This is Alice Walker's first novel, published in 1970.

dens—and still does—with over fifty different varieties of plants that bloom profusely from early March until late November. Before she left home for the fields, she watered her flowers, chopped up the grass, and laid out new beds. When she returned from the fields she might divide clumps of bulbs, dig a cold pit,[10] uproot and replant roses, or prune branches from her taller bushes or trees—until night came and it was too dark to see.

Whatever she planted grew as if by magic, and her fame as a grower of flowers spread over three counties. Because of her creativity with her flowers, even my memories of poverty are seen through a screen of blooms—sunflowers, petunias, roses, dahlias, forsythia, spirea, delphiniums, verbena . . . and on and on.

And I remember people coming to my mother's yard to be given cuttings from her flowers; I hear again the praise showered on her because whatever rocky soil she landed on, she turned into a garden. A garden so brilliant with colors, so original in its design, so magnificent with life and creativity, that to this day people drive by our house in Georgia—perfect strangers and imperfect strangers—and ask to stand or walk among my mother's art.

I notice that it is only when my mother is working in her flowers that she is radiant, almost to the point of being invisible—except as Creator: hand and eye. She is involved in work her soul must have. Ordering the universe in the image of her personal conception of Beauty.

Her face, as she prepares the Art that is her gift, is a legacy of respect she leaves to me, for all that illuminates and cherishes life. She has handed down respect for the possibilities—and the will to grasp them.

For her, so hindered and intruded upon in so many ways, being an artist has still been a daily part of her life. This ability to hold on, even in very simple ways, is work black women have done for a very long time.

This poem is not enough, but it is something, for the woman who literally covered the holes in our walls with sunflowers:

They were women then
My mama's generation
Husky of voice—Stout of
Step
With fists as well as
Hands
How they battered down
Doors
And ironed
Starched white
Shirts
How they led
Armies
Headragged Generals
Across mined
Fields
Booby-trapped
Kitchens
To discover books
Desks
A place for us
How they knew what we
Must know
Without knowing a page
Of it
Themselves.

Guided by my heritage of a love of beauty and a respect for strength—in search of my mother's garden, I found my own.

And perhaps in Africa over two hundred years ago, there was just such a mother; perhaps she painted vivid and daring decorations in oranges and yellows and greens on the walls of her hut; perhaps she sang—in a voice like Roberta Flack's—*sweetly* over the compounds of her village; perhaps she wove the most stunning mats or told the most ingenious stories of all the village storytellers. Perhaps she was herself a poet—though only her daughter's name is signed to the poems that we know.

Perhaps Phillis Wheatley's[11] mother was also an artist.

Perhaps in more than Phillis Wheatley's biological life is her mother's signature made clear.

---

10. **cold pit:** shallow pit dug into the soil and usually covered with an old window, used to shelter young plants in spring.

11. **Phillis Wheatley** (1753?–1784): the first published African poet in America. She was born in Africa and purchased as a slave by a Boston merchant.

Responding to the Essay

Analyzing the Essay

Identifying Facts

1. Describe the kind of life Alice Walker's mother led while Walker was growing up.
2. In what two ways did Walker's mother express her creativity and show herself to be an artist?
3. What secret does Walker hope to discover from examining her mother's life—and the lives of other women like her mother?

Interpreting Meanings

4. How does Walker's discussion about the quilt relate to the **theme** of her essay? That is, what does this quilt show about the creative spirit of black women?
5. On page 431, Walker uses a **metaphor** and a **simile** to describe how black women have handed down their creative spark through the generations. What do these **figures of speech** have in common? How do they relate to Virginia Woolf's ideas about the mothers of "very remarkable" men?
6. As a writer, how does Walker feel she has been enriched by her mother's storytelling? How do you think Walker feels about the fact that "no song or poem will bear" her mother's name?
7. Walker sets up a connection between her own mother and the anonymous black woman who made the quilt hanging in the Smithsonian. Explain how each woman "left her mark in the only materials she could afford, and in the only medium her position in society allowed her to use." How did Walker's mother use her creativity to improve the quality of her family's life? (Do you imagine the same might be true of the anonymous quilter? Explain.)
8. What do you think Walker means when she says her mother "has handed down respect for the possibilities—and the will to grasp them"? What do you think Walker the writer has learned from her mother the gardener?
9. In the poem at the end of the essay, Walker states a **paradox,** or apparent contradiction, when she writes that the women of her mother's generation

. . . knew what we
Must know
Without knowing a page
Of it
Themselves.

What kinds of things do you think these women knew their children had to know?

10. In your own words, explain what Walker means when she says, "in search of my mother's garden, I found my own."

Writing About the Essay

A Creative Response

1. **Writing a Character Sketch.** Write an essay about someone you admire, but who is not at all famous and who might even be regarded by some people as a failure. In your essay, be sure to indicate exactly what you admire about this person. Try to include a description of what the person looks like and what he or she does all day long. You might also consider these suggestions:

   a. Use the word *search* in your title.
   b. Write a poem of at least four lines in tribute to this person, and include it in your essay.

A Critical Response

2. **Comparing an Essay and a Short Story.** What thematic connections do you see between Walker's essay and her story "Everyday Use" (page 129)? Before you write, use the following chart to organize your ideas. Then write two or three paragraphs comparing the essay and the story.

	Story	Essay
What selection says about importance of family legacy		
What it says about place of art in our lives		
How it relates to statement "We have constantly looked high, when we should have looked high—and low."		

A native New Yorker, Lewis Thomas (1913–   ) graduated from Princeton University and Harvard Medical School. He specializes in research pathology and over the years has been associated with such institutions as the Rockefeller Institute, Tulane University, the University of Minnesota, and the Yale University School of Medicine. In 1973 he became president of the Sloan-Kettering Cancer Center in New York, and in 1980 he was made its chancellor.

Thomas's first book of essays, *The Lives of a Cell*, won the National Book Award in 1974. Of his second collection, *The Medusa and the Snail*, one reviewer said: "If it doesn't activate your sense of wonder, I can only suggest that you go to bed for a day or two."

Thomas sees the twentieth century as a time of "cultural sadness" in spite of—and also because of—our progress in the sciences. In the eighteenth century, he points out, people believed they could explain everything with pure reason. Now, he says, "We have come a long way indeed, but just enough to become conscious of our ignorance. . . . We are bewildered by the mystery of ourselves and confused by the strangeness of our uncomfortable connection to all the rest of life. . . ."

But Thomas thinks we have discovered how to ask important questions. "We need science," he says, "more and better science, not for its technology, not for leisure, not even for health and longevity, but for the hope of wisdom which our kind of culture must acquire for survival."

In *The Medusa and the Snail*, Thomas presents his own ("partial and piecemeal," he would say) wisdom on such subjects as ponds, cloning a human being, the hazards of science, worry, punctuation, magic, mistakes, and thinking about thinking. The book takes its title from a tiny jellyfish, the medusa, and the sea slug it lives on as a parasite in the Bay of Naples. At various times in the life cycle of the medusa and the sea slug, the two reverse roles and the slug becomes a parasite of the medusa, rather than the other way around. "The thought of these creatures gives me an odd feeling," Thomas writes. "They do not remind me of anything, really. They are bizarre, that's it, unique. And at the same time, like a vaguely remembered dream, they remind me of the whole earth at once."

In the following essay from *The Medusa and the Snail*, Thomas celebrates "the whole earth" as it operates through warts and their relation to the human mind. As you read, notice when the essayist lets you know that warts are not his real subject. Thomas uses scientific terminology—refer to a dictionary to look up the meanings of unfamiliar terms, or try to guess their meanings from clues provided by the context. Take notes as you read this essay, and be prepared to discuss in class any questions it raises.

ON WARTS

Lewis Thomas

Warts are wonderful structures. They can appear overnight on any part of the skin, like mushrooms on a damp lawn, full grown and splendid in the complexity of their architecture. Viewed in stained sections under a microscope, they are the most specialized of cellular arrangements, constructed as though for a purpose. They sit there like turreted mounds of dense, impenetrable horn, impregnable, designed for defense against the world outside.

In a certain sense, warts are both useful and essential, but not for us. As it turns out, the exuberant cells of a wart are the elaborate reproductive apparatus of a virus.

You might have thought from the looks of it that the cells infected by the wart virus were using

Barber Shop by Adriaen Brouwer (17th century). Engraving.

this response as a ponderous way of defending themselves against the virus, maybe even a way of becoming more distasteful, but it is not so. The wart is what the virus truly wants; it can flourish only in cells undergoing precisely this kind of overgrowth. It is not a defense at all; it is an overwhelming welcome, an enthusiastic accommodation meeting the needs of more and more virus.

The strangest thing about warts is that they tend to go away. Fully grown, nothing in the body has so much the look of toughness and permanence as a wart, and yet, inexplicably and often very abruptly, they come to the end of their lives and vanish without a trace.

And they can be made to go away by something that can only be called thinking, or something like thinking. This is a special property of warts which

is absolutely astonishing, more of a surprise than cloning or recombinant DNA[1] or endorphin[2] or acupuncture or anything else currently attracting attention in the press. It is one of the great mystifications of science: Warts can be ordered off by the skin by hypnotic suggestion.

Not everyone believes this, but the evidence goes back a long way and is persuasive. Generations of internists and dermatologists,[3] and their grandmothers for that matter, have been convinced of the phenomenon. I was once told by a

---

1. **recombinant DNA:** DNA regulates hereditary characteristics in all living cells. *Recombinant DNA* is the manipulation of genetic material that results in offspring with combinations of genes not present in either parent.
2. **endorphin:** substances secreted in the brain that have a pain-relieving effect.
3. **internists and dermatologists:** doctors who specialize in internal medicine and skin diseases.

distinguished old professor of medicine, one of Sir William Osler's original bright young men, that it was his practice to paint gentian violet[4] over a wart and then assure the patient firmly that it would be gone in a week, and he never saw it fail. There have been several meticulous studies by good clinical investigators, with proper controls. In one of these, fourteen patients with seemingly intractable generalized warts on both sides of the body were hypnotized, and the suggestion was made that all the warts on one side of the body would begin to go away. Within several weeks the results were indisputably positive; in nine patients, all or nearly all of the warts on the suggested side had vanished, while the control side had just as many as ever.

It is interesting that most of the warts vanished precisely as they were instructed, but it is even more fascinating that mistakes were made. Just as you might expect in other affairs requiring a clear understanding of which is the right and which the left side, one of the subjects got mixed up and destroyed the warts on the wrong side. In a later study by a group at the Massachusetts General Hospital, the warts on both sides were rejected even though the instructions were to pay attention to just one side.

I have been trying to figure out the nature of the instructions issued by the unconscious mind,[5] whatever that is, under hypnosis. It seems to me hardly enough for the mind to say, simply, get off, eliminate yourselves, without providing something in the way of specifications as to how to go about it.

I used to believe, thinking about this experiment when it was just published, that the instructions might be quite simple. Perhaps nothing more detailed than a command to shut down the flow through all the precapillary arterioles[6] in and around the warts to the point of strangulation. Exactly how the mind would accomplish this with precision, cutting off the blood supply to one wart while leaving others intact, I couldn't figure out, but I was satisfied to leave it there anyhow. And I was glad to think that my unconscious mind would have to take responsibility for this, for if I had been one of the subjects I would never have been able to do it myself.

But now the problem seems much more complicated by the information concerning the viral etiology[7] of warts, and even more so by the currently plausible notion that immunologic[8] mechanisms are very likely implicated in the rejection of warts.

If my unconscious can figure out how to manipulate the mechanisms needed for getting around that virus, and for deploying all the various cells in the correct order for tissue rejection, then all I have to say is that my unconscious is a lot further along than I am. I wish I had a wart right now, just to see if I am that talented.

There ought to be a better word than "Unconscious," even capitalized, for what I have, so to speak, in mind. I was brought up to regard this aspect of thinking as a sort of private sanitarium, walled off somewhere in a suburb of my brain, capable only of producing such garbled information as to keep my mind, my proper Mind, always a little off balance.

But any mental apparatus that can reject a wart is something else again. This is not the sort of confused, disordered process you'd expect at the hands of the kind of Unconscious you read about in books, out at the edge of things making up dreams or getting mixed up on words or having hysterics. Whatever, or whoever, is responsible for this has the accuracy and precision of a surgeon. There almost has to be a Person in charge, running matters of meticulous detail beyond anyone's comprehension, a skilled engineer and manager, a chief executive officer, the head of the whole place. I never thought before that I pos-

---

4. **gentian** (jen′shən) **violet:** a violet dye used to fight infections.
5. **unconscious mind:** the sum of all thoughts, memories, impulses, desires, feelings, etc., of which the individual is not conscious. The unconscious is thought to include repressed material that influences the emotions and behavior.
6. **precapillary arterioles** (är·tir′ē·ōlz′): any of the blood vessels that lead from the larger arteries to the smaller capillaries.

7. **viral etiology** (ēt′ē·äl′ə·jē): the study of the causes or origins of viral diseases.
8. **immunologic** (im′yoo·nə·läj′ik): dealing with the power to resist infection from a specific disease.

sessed such a tenant. Or perhaps more accurately, such a landlord, since I would be, if this is in fact the situation, nothing more than a lodger.

Among other accomplishments, he must be a cell biologist of world class, capable of sorting through the various classes of one's lymphocytes,[9] all with quite different functions which I do not understand, in order to mobilize the right ones and exclude the wrong ones for the task of tissue rejection. If it were left to me, and I were somehow empowered to call up lymphocytes and direct them to the vicinity of my wart (assuming that I could learn to do such a thing), mine would come tumbling in all unsorted, B cells and T cells,[10] suppressor cells and killer cells, and no doubt other cells whose names I have not learned, incapable of getting anything useful done.

Even if immunology is not involved, and all that needs doing is to shut off the blood supply locally, I haven't the faintest notion how to set that up. I assume that the selective turning off of arterioles can be done by one or another chemical mediator, and I know the names of some of them, but I wouldn't dare let things like these loose even if I knew how to do it.

---

9. **lymphocytes** (lim′fə·sīts′): special cells formed in the lymph tissue that help fight disease or infection.
10. **B cells and T cells:** blood cells that fight infection. T cells, called ''killer cells,'' are manufactured in the bone marrow.

Well, then, who does supervise this kind of operation? Someone's got to, you know. You can't sit there under hypnosis, taking suggestions in and having them acted on with such accuracy and precision, without assuming the existence of something very like a controller. It wouldn't do to fob off the whole intricate business on lower centers without sending along a quite detailed set of specifications, way over my head.

Some intelligence or other knows how to get rid of warts, and this is a disquieting thought.

It is also a wonderful problem, in need of solving. Just think what we would know, if we had anything like a clear understanding of what goes on when a wart is hypnotized away. We would know the identity of the cellular and chemical participants in tissue rejection, conceivably with some added information about the ways that viruses create foreignness in cells. We would know how the traffic of these reactants is directed, and perhaps then be able to understand the nature of certain diseases in which the traffic is being conducted in wrong directions, aimed at the wrong cells. Best of all, we would be finding out a kind of superintelligence that exists in each of us, infinitely smarter and possessed of technical knowhow far beyond our present understanding. It would be worth a War on Warts, a Conquest of Warts, a National Institute of Warts and All.

Responding to the Essay

Analyzing the Essay

Identifying Facts

1. Thomas begins with the surprising judgment that ''warts are wonderful structures,'' and in the second paragraph he calls them ''both useful and essential, but not for us.'' In what sense, and to whom or what, are warts wonderful, useful, and essential?
2. Warts can be made to go away ''by something that can only be called thinking, or something like thinking.'' Explain what Thomas means by ''something like thinking.''

3. Briefly describe the experiments that prove that warts are affected by the mind. What odd mix-ups by the subjects of the experiments made the results of the experiment seem even stranger?
4. Thomas speculates on how the unconscious mind might get rid of warts. Summarize the ''simple explanation'' he thinks of first. What more complicated explanation—involving a ''Person'' in charge—does he suggest?
5. In the last paragraph, what does Thomas say we would understand if we discovered how warts can be hypnotized away?

Interpreting Meanings

6. Part of the effect of the essay depends on a **paradox,** an apparent contradiction that is nevertheless true. The paradox is that Thomas is not nearly as clever as his unconscious, which is part of his own mind. Find the phrases and sentences in which Thomas characterizes himself as "dumb" and his unconscious as very clever. Do you think this is possible?—that our unconscious is smarter than we are?

7. Summarize in your own words Thomas's main points in the order that he makes them. How would you state his overall purpose in writing this essay?

8. The language of this essay is made vivid by the frequent use of **figurative language.** Identify the similes in the first paragraph. What metaphor in the paragraph beginning, "There ought to be a better word," describes the unconscious? Did Thomas's use of figurative language make his ideas easier to understand? Explain.

9. Why does Thomas reject the **metaphor** of "tenant" and prefer the metaphor "landlord," in the paragraph beginning "But any mental apparatus . . ." (page 436)?

10. What do you think of Thomas's theories about the mind and its powers? Are there any other things the mind can do that seem as mysterious as its ability to remove warts? Explain.

Writing About the Essay

A Creative Response

1. **Writing an Essay.** Thomas concentrates on warts, but he mentions in passing some other topics of current scientific interest. Choose one of these topics, and use library resources to find out more about it. Read at least two recent magazine or newspaper articles about your topic. Then write a brief essay of your own in which you define or explain the term and tell about some recent findings. In your opening paragraph, try to catch the reader's interest, as Thomas does, with a statement that surprises.

   a. cloning
   b. recombinant DNA
   c. endorphins
   d. acupuncture
   e. tissue rejection
   f. "killer" T cells
   g. hypnosis
   h. white blood cells

A Critical Response

2. **Analyzing the Writer's Techniques.** Thomas is a scientist writing for nonscientists about a phenomenon that science does not yet fully understand. Write a brief essay describing the techniques used in the essay that show the writer's scientific training. Consider each of the following aspects of the essay:

   a. Use of specialized language and vocabulary
   b. Logical statement of a problem
   c. Evidence to support his statements
   d. Curiosity and sense of wonder

   Use examples from the essay to support your statements.

Analyzing Language and Vocabulary

Word Analysis

Like literature and music and any other field of study, science has a specialized vocabulary. To nonscientists, this terminology can be difficult. But fortunately many scientific terms are based on familiar roots, prefixes, and suffixes which can give you clues to their meaning.

1. Sometimes the roots of words give us an idea of the word's meaning. You may never have heard of a *suppressor cell* before, but what does the word *suppress* mean? What do you think a suppressor cell might do to an invading cell?

2. You know what *puncture* means. If you know that *acu-* comes from the Latin word for needle, what technique does *acupuncture* use for treating medical conditions?

3. What root word can you find in *recombinant*? If the prefix *re-* means "again," what would you guess that *recombinant DNA* is?

4. The combining form *-ology* signifies a branch of science or of some special knowledge. What can you guess about the meanings of *immunology* and *dermatology* (knowing that *derma-* means "skin")?

5. The *lymph system* in the human body is a network of vessels that carry *lymph,* a clear fluid used to fight infections. If *-cyte* means "cell," what is a *lymphocyte*?

6. How is the word *lymph* related to the name the Greeks gave to sea goddesses—*nymphs*?

Abraham Michael Rosenthal (1922–   ) was born in Ontario, Canada, but moved with his family to New York City when he was four. For many years he served with distinction as the executive editor of the *New York Times*. When he "retired," he began a column for the *Times* called "On My Mind."

In 1958, when Rosenthal was the *New York Times* correspondent in Warsaw, Poland, he visited the concentration camp at Auschwitz. At that time, fourteen years after the camps were liberated toward the end of World War II, mention of the atrocities of the concentration camps had virtually disappeared from American newspapers. There was "no news" to report from those sites, and Americans seemed all too willing to put the ugly memories behind them. Rosenthal's piece for the *New York Times*, "No News from Auschwitz," served as a powerful reminder of the dangers of forgetting what had happened in the death camps. It has been reprinted many times.

In November 1959 the Polish government expelled Rosenthal for his "probing reporting," for which he won a Pulitzer Prize in May 1960.

Rosenthal is also the author of *38 Witnesses*, an account of a murder in a quiet residential New York neighborhood. The title refers to the thirty-eight people who witnessed a young woman's murder but did nothing to stop it.

As you read, identify the emotional tone of the essay. What feelings does it arouse in you? What do you think the title means?

NO NEWS FROM AUSCHWITZ

A. M. Rosenthal

BRZEZINKA, POLAND—The most terrible thing of all, somehow, was that at Brzezinka the sun was bright and warm, the rows of graceful poplars were lovely to look upon, and on the grass near the gates children played.

It all seemed frighteningly wrong, as in a nightmare, that at Brzezinka the sun should ever shine or that there should be light and greenness and the sound of young laughter. It would be fitting if at Brzezinka the sun never shone and the grass withered, because this is a place of unutterable terror.

And yet every day, from all over the world, people come to Brzezinka, quite possibly the most grisly tourist center on earth. They come for a variety of reasons—to see if it could really have been true, to remind themselves not to forget, to pay homage to the dead by the simple act of looking upon their place of suffering.

Brzezinka is a couple of miles from the better-known southern Polish town of Oswiecim.[1] Oswiecim has about 12,000 inhabitants, is situated about 171 miles from Warsaw, and lies in a damp, marshy area at the eastern end of the pass called the Moravian Gate. Brzezinka and Oswiecim together formed part of that minutely organized factory of torture and death that the Nazis called Konzentrationslager Auschwitz.

By now, fourteen years after the last batch of prisoners was herded naked into the gas chambers by dogs and guards, the story of Auschwitz has been told a great many times. Some of the inmates have written of those memories of which sane men cannot conceive. Rudolf Franz Ferdinand Hoess, the superintendent of the camp, before he was executed wrote his detailed memoirs of mass exterminations and the experiments on living bodies. Four million people died here, the Poles say.

---

1. **Oswiecim** (ôsh·vyan′tsim).

And so there is no news to report about Auschwitz. There is merely the compulsion to write something about it, a compulsion that grows out of a restless feeling that to have visited Auschwitz and then turned away without having said or written anything would somehow be a most grievous act of discourtesy to those who died here.

Brzezinka and Oswiecim are very quiet places now; the screams can no longer be heard. The tourist walks silently, quickly at first to get it over with and then, as his mind peoples the barracks and the chambers and the dungeons and flogging posts, he walks draggingly. The guide does not say much either, because there is nothing much for him to say after he has pointed.

For every visitor there is one particular bit of horror that he knows he will never forget. For some it is seeing the rebuilt gas chamber at Oswiecim and being told that this is the "small one."

For others it is the fact that at Brzezinka, in the ruins of the gas chambers and the crematoria[2] the Germans blew up when they retreated, there are daisies growing.

There are visitors who gaze blankly at the gas chambers and the furnaces because their minds simply cannot encompass them, but stand shivering before the great mounds of human hair behind the plate-glass window or the piles of babies' shoes or the brick cells where men sentenced to death by suffocation were walled up.

One visitor opened his mouth in a silent scream

simply at the sight of boxes—great stretches of three-tiered wooden boxes in the women's barracks. They were about six feet wide, about three feet high, and into them from five to ten prisoners were shoved for the night. The guide walks quickly through the barracks. Nothing more to see here.

A brick building where sterilization experiments were carried out on women prisoners. The guide tries the door—it's locked. The visitor is grateful that he does not have to go in, and then flushes with shame.

A long corridor where rows of faces stare from the walls. Thousands of pictures, the photographs of prisoners. They are all dead now, the men and women who stood before the cameras, and they all knew they were to die.

They all stare blank-faced, but one picture, in the middle of a row, seizes the eye and wrenches the mind. A girl, twenty-two years old, plumply pretty, blond. She is smiling gently, as at a sweet, treasured thought. What was the thought that passed through her young mind and is now her memorial on the wall of the dead at Auschwitz?

Into the suffocation dungeons the visitor is taken for a moment and feels himself strangling. Another visitor goes in, stumbles out, and crosses herself. There is no place to pray in Auschwitz.

The visitors look pleadingly at each other and say to the guide, "Enough."

There is nothing new to report about Auschwitz. It was a sunny day and the trees were green and at the gates the children played.

---

2. **crematoria:** furnaces for cremating, or burning, the dead.

Responding to the Essay

Analyzing the Essay

Identifying Facts
1. Rosenthal begins his essay by stating "the most terrible thing of all" about Brzezinka. What is it? Why is it so terrible?
2. List the **images** that Rosenthal uses to show us

that Auschwitz was normal and pleasant in 1958. What images does he use to help us imagine the horror of the war years?
3. Most of the essay deals with what visitors *see* when they tour Auschwitz today. Find some words, phrases, and sentences that also indicate what these visitors *feel*.

Interpreting Meanings

4. "No News from Auschwitz" is an **ironic** title because the author obviously feels there *is* important information at Auschwitz. What is the "news" that Rosenthal wants his American readers to know? How would you explain his **purpose** in writing this essay?

5. Rosenthal also uses **irony** to create emotional effects. What is ironic about the opening paragraph? About the daisies growing at Auschwitz? Find at least one other example of irony in the essay.

6. What do you think Rosenthal means when he says it would be "a most grievous act of discourtesy" not to write something about Auschwitz? Why do you think he chose to use the specific word *discourtesy* here?

7. Explain how Rosenthal uses the technique of **contrast** in this essay. What exactly is he contrasting, and what effect does he create?

8. Describe the feelings you experienced as you read this essay. If you had a chance to visit Auschwitz, would you go? Explain why or why not.

Writing About the Essay

A Creative Response

1. **Creating a Character from a Photograph.** Among the photographs of the concentration camp victims, Rosenthal remembers one of a young smiling woman and wonders who she was and what she was thinking. Study the photograph on page 236, and then write a paragraph about the young girl in it. Describe who she might be, where she might live, what her family might be like, what her hopes and fears might be. Tell what you imagine she was thinking when this photograph was taken.

A Critical Response

2. **Analyzing the Essay.** In **objective reporting,** a writer presents facts and observations and tries not to reveal personal judgments, emotions, or biases. In **subjective reporting,** on the other hand, the writer's judgments and feelings are evident. In writing about his experiences at Auschwitz, Rosenthal carefully maintains the stance of an objective reporter: He never uses the word *I* but instead speaks impersonally of "the tourist" and "the visitor." But do we know what his feelings are? Does he make judgments? Or does he stick closely to reporting facts and his own observations? In a brief essay, tell whether you think "No News from Auschwitz" is an example of objective reporting or subjective reporting—or some combination of both. Cite specific words, phrases, and sentences from the essay to support your view.

Analyzing Language and Vocabulary

Oral Reading

Words in this essay are arranged to produce that rhythmic rising and falling of the voice known as **cadence.** Cadence is usually most pronounced in poetry and in public orations, such as sermons or important speeches. The Gettysburg Address, for example, is a good example of a speech written in a strong cadence that makes it hypnotic to listen to and easy to memorize.

Cadence is produced by the repetition of words, phrases, and sentence structures; by dramatic pauses; and by the alternation of long and short utterances.

Read "No News from Auschwitz" aloud. Notice how it takes on the sound of a sermon. (Why is this appropriate?)

1. Look at paragraphs 1 and 2. What words and phrases are repeated?

2. What parallel structures are repeated in paragraph 3?

3. In the paragraph beginning "By now, fourteen years after . . . ," which is the shortest sentence? Why do you think the writer made it so brief? How would you read it aloud?

4. In the paragraph beginning "There are visitors . . . ," what litany of horrors is repeated?

5. Look at the sentences in the paragraph beginning "One visitor . . ." What is the emotional effect of the terse final sentence? Find two other places in the essay where this same idea is repeated.

Literature & Language

Using Vivid Adjectives

Literary Model

Here is an excerpt from an essay that uses vivid, even startling adjectives to catch our attention.

Science takes away with one hand what it gives with the other. No sooner do Russian scientists claim that they have revived two lizards that had been frozen in the Siberian tundra for five thousand years than American scientists announce that there is no life whatever on Venus. In a way, we're relieved, for there's so much life in France, Cuba, and the subway these days that it's a comfort to know there are still a few underdeveloped areas in the universe. But in a way we're sorry, for the tendrilous, polyoptical Venutian was, along with the wispy, transparent Lunite and the green-skinned, snaggle-toothed, canal-building Martian, a childhood friend. How vivid the populations of other planets once seemed—far more imaginable than the residents of Cambodia or Chicago! The people on Jupiter were terribly squat and slow, because of the intense gravity; when they moved, it was like lava pouring, and when they talked, it was like furnaces grumbling. The inhabitants of Saturn always wore wide-brimmed hats and hoopskirts, whereas the folks on Neptune swam everywhere they went, carrying tridents. Pluto, so remote, cold, and small, seemed the planetary poor relation, and we pitied the cosmic hillbillies who had to live there, clad in rags, drinking cheap sulphates, and trying to warm their shivering limbs in the rays of a sun no bigger than a star. At the opposite end of the system, but somewhat kindredly under-privileged, were the almost Caribbean individuals sweltering out their lazy days on Mercury, which always kept the same side toward the sun, and where everything this side of silicon melted, making machinery impossible and architecture unstable.

Now they tell us this is all fancy. Venus, far from being a tropical paradise beneath its mantle of perpetual clouds, is a baking limbo of eight hundred degrees Fahrenheit. Though there is still hope that a bit of moss enlivens Mars, the planets have, in effect, been given a clean slate. They are innocent of life, and the Earth, which is so guilty of it, can feel a little safer, and a little lonelier.

— from "Spatial Remarks,"
John Updike

A Note on Adjectives

An **adjective** is a word that modifies a noun or pronoun. Adjectives describe people, places, or things by answering the questions *What kind?* (a purple flower), *Which one?* (that house), *How much?* (ten dollars), or *How many?* (several students).

Some writers use short, simple, everyday adjectives:

Her arms are *pale* and *thick,* her face *wrinkled* and *white,* her mouth too *red.*
— from "In California,"
Brett Lott

Other writers use more elaborate, unusual adjectives that may send you to the dictionary:

I had expected that Mr. Gatsby would be a *florid* and *corpulent* person in his middle years.
— from *The Great Gatsby,*
F. Scott Fitzgerald

Some writers even invent their own adjectives:

The day was terrifically *hot,* a *real slap-in-the-face, dog-under-the-house sort of* day. . . .
— from *East Is East,*
T. Coraghessan Boyle

All the Christmases roll down toward the *two-tongued* sea . . . ; and they stop at the rim of the *ice-edged, fish-freezing* waves. . . .
— from "A Child's Christmas in Wales,"
Dylan Thomas

As you can see, an adjective can be a single word or a **compound** word *(ice-edged).* It can be the only adjective modifying a word, or part of a team of modifiers. This adjective, in turn, can be modified by an adverb *(terrifically hot).*

Literature & Language/*cont.*

Here are some additional points to keep in mind about adjectives:

1. An adjective can come either before or after the noun or pronoun it modifies.

    Cold weather makes me *miserable.*

2. Nouns and verbs can function grammatically as adjectives within a sentence. A verb used as an adjective is called a **participle.** There are two kinds of participles—**present participles** end in *-ing;* **past participles** usually end in *-ed* or *-d.*

    a *music* critic (noun)
    a *sleeping* dog (verb, present participle)
    a *wasted* morning (verb, past participle)

3. Whole **phrases** and **clauses** can also function as adjectives.

    the man *in the blue car* (adjective phrase)
    the woman *who was on TV* (adjective clause)
    a hat *like a muffin* (adjective phrase)

4. In general, hyphenate a **compound adjective** when it precedes the noun it modifies, unless one of the words in the compound is an adverb ending in *-ly.* Don't use a hyphen if the compound adjective follows the noun.

    She's a *well-informed* reporter.
    That reporter is *well informed.*
    She's a *highly knowledgeable* reporter.

Note that some compound adjectives have become permanent compounds—that is, they're always hyphenated or written as one word, regardless of their position in the sentence.

    It was *backbreaking* work.
    He became *tongue-tied.*

5. Use a comma to separate two or more adjectives preceding a noun, unless the final adjective is thought of as part of the noun. (If you can say *and* instead of a comma, the comma is correct.)

    a long, winding corridor
    a famous literary critic

Examining the Writer's Style

Work with a partner to analyze the way Updike uses adjectives in this passage.

1. First list all the adjectives you can find. (Skip those pertaining to number or amount.) Then organize these adjectives according to the planetary life they describe. Use ten headings, including one for adjectives describing the other planets considered collectively. In some cases, you may want to include the noun being modified.

2. What **compound adjectives** does Updike use? Does he use any nouns or verbs as adjectives? Where does he use more than one adjective to modify a noun? Which adjectives are separated by commas, and which are not?

3. How would you describe the kinds of adjectives Updike uses? Are they plain and simple? Elaborate and unusual? Inventive and quirky? How might a different writer have described someone who is "tendrilous" and "polyoptical"?

4. What do you think of Updike's adjective style? (Were you surprised to see this kind of writing in a piece of nonfiction?)

Using Vivid Adjectives in Your Writing

Reacting to a Scientific Discovery. Look through a newspaper or magazine, and find a piece of scientific or medical news that surprises you in some way. Then write a brief essay explaining what you think of this latest discovery or theory.

1. In your essay, use fresh, vivid, and precise adjectives to describe both the news itself and your response to it. Be sure to include your *visual* response to the news, as Updike does. Don't overload your writing with fancy adjectives—just pay careful attention to the ones you use. Short, simple adjectives are okay—lazy, lifeless ones are not.

2. Exchange essays with a partner. Circle any adjectives in your classmate's paper that you feel are trite or vague or boring. Revise your own essay as you wish, using your partner's response as a guide.

EVALUATING AN ESSAY

Writing Assignment

Write a four-paragraph essay in which you evaluate one of the essays you have read in this section.

Background

Essays vary more than most literary forms. They can be about any subject; they can be long or short, formal or informal, personal or impersonal, humorous or serious. How can you judge whether an essay is good or bad, effective or ineffective, or something in between? You can **evaluate** any essay by applying certain **criteria,** or standards.

Prewriting

Look carefully at the following guidelines for evaluating an essay. After you finish rereading the essay you have chosen to write about, answer each of the questions in the outline. Whenever possible, refer to actual passages in the essay.

Criteria for Evaluating an Essay

1. Audience and Purpose
   a. As far as I can tell, who is the intended audience of the essay?
   b. What is the writer's purpose (to recreate a scene or character, to amuse, to inform, to persuade, to give a message)? How well has the writer achieved that purpose?

2. Content and Language
   a. Is the **subject** important or trivial? Does it interest me?
   b. Is the writer's **diction** precise? Are the descriptions vivid and original?
   c. Are the facts accurate—as far as I can tell? Are opinions supported with sufficient and convincing evidence?

3. Organization
   a. Is every part of the essay necessary, either for meaning or effect?
   b. Are the writer's ideas presented in the best possible order? Are they logical?

4. Response
   a. Did I enjoy reading the essay? Would I like to read more essays by this writer?
   b. If the essay presents an opinion, do I agree or disagree with it? Why?

Writing

Organize your essay into four paragraphs that correspond to the four main sections of your outline. Here is the first paragraph of an evaluation of one essay in this unit:

> It is not easy to read A. M. Rosenthal's "No News from Auschwitz," and I don't mean that the essay is difficult to understand. The essay is aiming at a general American newspaper readership. The writer wants those people—most of whom have never seen Auschwitz—to see and hear and feel what this concentration camp is like today, and what it was like in the 1940's. It's my opinion that he's succeeded in communicating his own horror about Auschwitz, and his respect for the memory of the dead. The essay made me, for one, feel like crying.

Checklist for Revision
1. Have you cited the essay's title and author?
2. In your first paragraph, have you made a general statement about who the intended audience is and how well the writer has achieved his or her purpose?
3. In paragraphs 2 and 3, have you evaluated the essay's content and organization?
4. Have you summed up your evaluation and stated your response to the essay?

The linguist S. I. Hayakawa once wrote, "It is not true that we have only one life to live; if we can read, we can live as many more lives and as many kinds as we wish." When we read an **autobiography**—the story of the writer's own life—we learn of events, times, places, and people that we would otherwise not have known. But, if the story is told well, we may also experience "the shock of recognition" as we find something of ourselves in a stranger's life story. Even though we have never shared the same experiences, we may still identify with the terror of the soldier, the fear of the child who is in some way "different," the frustration of the artist.

The most interesting autobiographies are honest. These writers don't seek to glorify or glamorize or justify themselves; nor do they flinch from reporting that they are less than perfect. They try to tell the truth about themselves and about their experiences.

Honesty is difficult. Some writers would never attempt any kind of autobiography. "It does no good to write autobiographical fiction," warns fiction writer Toni Cade Bambara, "cause the minute this book hits the stand here comes your mama screamin how could you. . . ."

In the following excerpt from Russell Baker's autobiography, you will notice that Baker does *not* say that his childhood days were a wonderful time in a wonderful era and that his mother was a wonderful woman with whom he always got along wonderfully. Although he writes with humor and warmth, Baker's portrait of himself, his family, and the life they lived is frank. The writer shows human frailty and a prickliness of spirit that make his characters seem real. Anyone who has been forced by a parent to take a hated job can identify with Baker's misadventures as a reluctant young magazine salesman. Everyone who has banged heads with an iron-willed parent can recognize Baker's mother.

All three of the writers in this section try to examine their early years with honesty. All three discover truths in their own childhoods that might help us see parts of our own lives and parts of the wider world in sharper focus.

"Facts" and "Truth" in Autobiography

One of these three writers, Harry Crews, has said: "What has been most significant in my life had all taken place by the time I was six years old." He is stating his strong personal sense of something that most scientists acknowledge as a fact: The preschool years are the "formative" years, and most traits of our character are in place before we reach the age of five or six.

What an autobiographer remembers about those years is likely to be faulty from the standpoint of absolute fact. What most of us remember most accurately is the significance things had for us, which is something that only *we* can know and judge. Memory has this in common with autobiography (which is, after all, simply written memory): that the facts may be distorted or misremembered, but the significance of these facts is what we make of them.

Autobiography: "Written Memory"

"I started to write my autobiography but I can't fill up more than half a page!"

© Buresch/Rothco

> " **I**t does no good to write autobiographical fiction, cause the minute this book hits the stand here comes your mama screamin how could you . . ."
> —Toni Cade Bambara

Russell Baker (1925–   ) spent his earliest years in a small Virginia town. When his father died during the Depression, Russell, his mother, and one of his sisters were forced to live with an uncle in New Jersey whose salary of only thirty dollars a week was the only steady income in the family.

A dreamer whose favorite reading was Dick Tracy and whose "lack of gumption" was his mother's despair, Baker grew up to be a respected Washington correspondent, columnist for the *New York Times,* and twice winner of the Pulitzer Prize. "I've had an unhappy life, thank God," Baker once told an interviewer. At least one reviewer has suggested that Baker can take "raw, potentially wrenching material" and turn it into stories "so warm, so likeable, and so disarmingly funny."

By 1961 Baker felt he "had done enough reporting. . . . It came to seem to me that this wasn't a worthy way for a grown man to spend his life . . . always on the sidelines . . . not making anything." The next year the *Times* offered Baker a thrice-weekly column of his own, and he launched into twenty years of the "Observer," with his particular brand of plain talk and dry humor on every subject from dish washing to government bureaucrats.

Baker, who has been married since 1950, has a daughter and two sons. He is a lean six-foot-two, with an unruly thatch of sandy gray hair and, he says, the look of "a decaying boy." He describes the columnist's life as a "Chinese water torture . . . FridaySundayTuesday, FridaySundayTuesday . . ." He has varied the routine by writing a novel fantasizing a disastrous Presidential election, a play that never opened, and a children's book about a mad scientist in a people-making factory. Four collections of his columns have been published, and in 1979 he won the Pulitzer Prize for distinguished commentary. His second Pulitzer came in 1983 for the autobiography *Growing Up.* (Baker has continued telling his life story in *The Good Times,* which chronicles his early years in journalism.)

In the following chapter from *Growing Up,* watch for the passages that reveal Baker's tone. Do you think his purpose in writing about himself is entirely serious?

MAKE SOMETHING OF YOURSELF

Russell Baker

I began working in journalism when I was eight years old. It was my mother's idea. She wanted me to "make something" of myself and, after a levelheaded appraisal of my strengths, decided I had better start young if I was to have any chance of keeping up with the competition.

The flaw in my character which she had already spotted was lack of "gumption." My idea of a perfect afternoon was lying in front of the radio rereading my favorite Big Little Book, *Dick Tracy Meets Stooge Viller.* My mother despised inactivity. Seeing me having a good time in repose, she was powerless to hide her disgust. "You've got no more gumption than a bump on a log," she said. "Get out in the kitchen and help Doris do those dirty dishes."

My sister Doris, though two years younger than I, had enough gumption for a dozen people. She positively enjoyed washing dishes, making beds, and cleaning the house. When she was only seven, she could carry a piece of short-weighted[1] cheese back to the A&P, threaten the manager with legal

---

1. **short-weighted:** weighing less than claimed or promised.

By permission of Russell Baker.

action, and come back triumphantly with the full quarter pound we'd paid for and a few ounces extra thrown in for forgiveness. Doris could have made something of herself if she hadn't been a girl. Because of this defect, however, the best she could hope for was a career as a nurse or school-teacher, the only work that capable females were considered up to in those days.

This must have saddened my mother, this twist of fate that had allocated all the gumption to the daughter and left her with a son who was content with Dick Tracy and Stooge Viller. If disappointed, though, she wasted no energy on self-pity. She would make me make something of myself whether I wanted to or not. "The Lord helps those who help themselves," she said. That was the way her mind worked.

She was realistic about the difficulty. Having sized up the material the Lord had given her to mold, she didn't overestimate what she could do with it. She didn't insist that I grow up to be President of the United States.

Fifty years ago parents still asked boys if they wanted to grow up to be President, and asked it not jokingly, but seriously. Many parents who were hardly more than paupers still believed their sons could do it. Abraham Lincoln had done it. We were only sixty-five years from Lincoln. Many a grandfather who walked among us could remember Lincoln's time. Men of grandfatherly age were the worst for asking if you wanted to grow up to be President. A surprising number of little boys said yes and meant it.

I was asked many times myself. No, I would say, I didn't want to grow up to be President. My mother was present during one of these interrogations. An elderly uncle, having posed the usual question and exposed my lack of interest in the Presidency, asked, "Well, what *do* you want to be when you grow up?"

I loved to pick through trash piles and collect empty bottles, tin cans with pretty labels, and discarded magazines. The most desirable job on earth sprang instantly to mind. "I want to be a garbage man," I said.

My uncle smiled, but my mother had seen the first distressing evidence of a bump budding on a log. "Have a little gumption, Russell," she said. Her calling me Russell was a signal of unhappiness. When she approved of me, I was always "Buddy."

When I turned eight years old, she decided that the job of starting me on the road toward making something of myself could no longer be safely delayed. "Buddy," she said one day, "I want you to come home right after school this afternoon.

Somebody's coming and I want you to meet him.''

When I burst in that afternoon she was in conference in the parlor with an executive of the Curtis Publishing Company. She introduced me. He bent low from the waist and shook my hand. Was it true as my mother had told him, he asked, that I longed for the opportunity to conquer the world of business?

My mother replied that I was blessed with a rare determination to make something of myself.

"That's right," I whispered.

"But have you got the grit, the character, the never-say-quit spirit it takes to succeed in business?"

My mother said I certainly did.

"That's right," I said.

He eyed me silently for a long pause, as though weighing whether I could be trusted to keep his confidence, then spoke man-to-man. Before taking a crucial step, he said, he wanted to advise me that working for the Curtis Publishing Company placed enormous responsibility on a young man. It was one of the great companies of America. Perhaps the greatest publishing house in the world. I had heard, no doubt, of the *Saturday Evening Post?*

Heard of it? My mother said that everyone in our house had heard of the *Saturday Evening Post* and that I, in fact, read it with religious devotion.

Then doubtless, he said, we were also familiar with those two monthly pillars of the magazine world, the *Ladies Home Journal* and the *Country Gentleman.*

Indeed we were familiar with them, said my mother.

Representing the *Saturday Evening Post* was one of the weightiest honors that could be bestowed in the world of business, he said. He was personally proud of being a part of that great corporation.

My mother said he had every right to be.

Again he studied me as though debating whether I was worthy of a knighthood. Finally: "Are you trustworthy?"

My mother said I was the soul of honesty.

"That's right," I said.

The caller smiled for the first time. He told me

I was a lucky young man. He admired my spunk. Too many young men thought life was all play. Those young men would not go far in this world. Only a young man willing to work and save and keep his face washed and his hair neatly combed could hope to come out on top in a world such as ours. Did I truly and sincerely believe that I was such a young man?

"He certainly does," said my mother.

"That's right," I said.

He said he had been so impressed by what he had seen of me that he was going to make me a representative of the Curtis Publishing Company. On the following Tuesday, he said, thirty freshly printed copies of the *Saturday Evening Post* would be delivered at our door. I would place these magazines, still damp with the ink of the presses, in a handsome canvas bag, sling it over my shoulder, and set forth through the streets to bring the best in journalism, fiction, and cartoons to the American public.

He had brought the canvas bag with him. He presented it with reverence fit for a chasuble.[2] He showed me how to drape the sling over my left shoulder and across the chest so that the pouch lay easily accessible to my right hand, allowing the best in journalism, fiction, and cartoons to be swiftly extracted and sold to a citizenry whose happiness and security depended upon us soldiers of the free press.

The following Tuesday I raced home from school, put the canvas bag over my shoulder, dumped the magazines in, and, tilting to the left to balance their weight on my right hip, embarked on the highway of journalism.

We lived in Belleville, New Jersey, a commuter town at the northern fringe of Newark. It was 1932, the bleakest year of the Depression. My father had died two years before, leaving us with a few pieces of Sears, Roebuck furniture and not much else, and my mother had taken Doris and me to live with one of her younger brothers. This was my Uncle Allen. Uncle Allen had made something of himself by 1932. As salesman for a soft-

---

2. **chasuble** (chaz'yoo·b'l): a vestment worn by priests at Mass.

drink bottler in Newark, he had an income of $30 a week; wore pearl-gray spats, detachable collars, and a three-piece suit; was happily married; and took in threadbare relatives.

With my load of magazines I headed toward Belleville Avenue. That's where the people were. There were two filling stations at the intersection with Union Avenue, as well as an A&P, a fruit stand, a bakery, a barber shop, Zuccarelli's drugstore, and a diner shaped like a railroad car. For several hours I made myself highly visible, shifting position now and then from corner to corner, from shop window to shop window, to make sure everyone could see the heavy black lettering on the canvas bag that said THE SATURDAY EVENING POST. When the angle of the light indicated it was suppertime, I walked back to the house.

"How many did you sell, Buddy?" my mother asked.

"None."

"Where did you go?"

"The corner of Belleville and Union Avenues."

"What did you do?"

"Stood on the corner waiting for somebody to buy a *Saturday Evening Post*."

"You just stood there?"

"Didn't sell a single one."

"For God's sake, Russell!"

Uncle Allen intervened. "I've been thinking about it for some time," he said, "and I've about decided to take the *Post* regularly. Put me down as a regular customer." I handed him a magazine and he paid me a nickel. It was the first nickel I earned.

Afterward my mother instructed me in salesmanship. I would have to ring doorbells, address adults with charming self-confidence, and break down resistance with a sales talk pointing out that no one, no matter how poor, could afford to be without the *Saturday Evening Post* in the home.

I told my mother I'd changed my mind about wanting to succeed in the magazine business.

"If you think I'm going to raise a good-for-nothing," she replied, "you've got another think coming." She told me to hit the streets with the canvas bag and start ringing doorbells the instant school was out next day. When I objected that I

didn't feel any aptitude for salesmanship, she asked how I'd like to lend her my leather belt so she could whack some sense into me. I bowed to superior will and entered journalism with a heavy heart.

My mother and I had fought this battle almost as long as I could remember. It probably started even before memory began, when I was a country child in northern Virginia and my mother, dissatisfied with my father's plain workman's life, determined that I would not grow up like him and his people, with calluses on their hands, overalls on their backs, and fourth-grade educations in their heads. She had fancier ideas of life's possibilities. Introducing me to the *Saturday Evening Post,* she was trying to wean me as early as possible from my father's world where men left with their lunch pails at sunup, worked with their hands until the grime ate into the pores, and died with a few sticks of mail-order furniture as their legacy. In my mother's vision of the better life, there were desks and white collars, well-pressed suits, evenings of reading and lively talk, and perhaps—if a man were very, very lucky and hit the jackpot, really made something important of himself—perhaps there might be a fantastic salary of $5,000 a year to support a big house and a Buick with a rumble seat and a vacation in Atlantic City.

And so I set forth with my sack of magazines. I was afraid of the dogs that snarled behind the doors of potential buyers. I was timid about ringing the doorbells of strangers, relieved when no one came to the door, and scared when someone did. Despite my mother's instructions, I could not deliver an engaging sales pitch. When a door opened I simply asked, "Want to buy a *Saturday Evening Post*?" In Belleville few persons did. It was a town of 30,000 people, and most weeks I rang a fair majority of its doorbells. But I rarely sold my thirty copies. Some weeks I canvassed the entire town for six days and still had four or five unsold magazines on Monday evening; then I dreaded the coming of Tuesday morning, when a batch of thirty fresh *Saturday Evening Post*s was due at the front door.

"Better get out there and sell the rest of those magazines tonight," my mother would say.

I usually posted myself then at a busy intersection where a traffic light controlled commuter flow from Newark. When the light turned red, I stood on the curb and shouted my sales pitch at the motorists.

"Want to buy a *Saturday Evening Post*?"

One rainy night when car windows were sealed against me I came back soaked and with not a single sale to report. My mother beckoned to Doris.

"Go back down there with Buddy and show him how to sell these magazines," she said.

Brimming with zest, Doris, who was then seven years old, returned with me to the corner. She took a magazine from the bag, and when the light turned red, she strode to the nearest car and banged her small fist against the closed window. The driver, probably startled at what he took to be a midget assaulting his car, lowered the window to stare, and Doris thrust a *Saturday Evening Post* at him.

"You need this magazine," she piped, "and it only costs a nickel."

Her salesmanship was irresistible. Before the light changed half a dozen times she disposed of the entire batch. I didn't feel humiliated. To the contrary. I was so happy I decided to give her a treat. Leading her to the vegetable store on Belleville Avenue, I bought three apples, which cost a nickel, and gave her one.

"You shouldn't waste money," she said.

"Eat your apple." I bit into mine.

"You shouldn't eat before supper," she said. "It'll spoil your appetite."

Back at the house that evening, she dutifully reported me for wasting a nickel. Instead of a scolding, I was rewarded with a pat on the back for having the good sense to buy fruit instead of candy. My mother reached into her bottomless supply of maxims and told Doris, "An apple a day keeps the doctor away."

By the time I was ten, I had learned all my mother's maxims by heart. Asking to stay up past normal bedtime, I knew that a refusal would be explained with, "Early to bed and early to rise, makes a man healthy, wealthy, and wise." If I whimpered about having to get up early in the morning, I could depend on her to say, "The early bird gets the worm."

The one I most despised was, "If at first you don't succeed, try, try again." This was the battle cry with which she constantly sent me back into the hopeless struggle whenever I moaned that I had rung every doorbell in town and knew there wasn't a single potential buyer left in Belleville that week. After listening to my explanation, she handed me the canvas bag and said, "If at first you don't succeed . . ."

Three years in that job, which I would gladly have quit after the first day except for her insistence, produced at least one valuable result. My mother finally concluded that I would never make something of myself by pursuing a life in business and started considering careers that demanded less competitive zeal.

One evening when I was eleven, I brought home a short "composition" on my summer vacation which the teacher had graded with an A. Reading it with her own schoolteacher's eye, my mother agreed that it was top-drawer seventh-grade prose and complimented me. Nothing more was said about it immediately, but a new idea had taken life in her mind. Halfway through supper she suddenly interrupted the conversation.

"Buddy," she said, "maybe you could be a writer."

I clasped the idea to my heart. I had never met a writer, had shown no previous urge to write, and hadn't a notion how to become a writer, but I loved stories and thought that making up stories must surely be almost as much fun as reading them. Best of all, though, and what really gladdened my heart, was the ease of the writer's life. Writers did not have to trudge through the town peddling from canvas bags, defending themselves against angry dogs, being rejected by surly strangers. Writers did not have to ring doorbells. So far as I could make out, what writers did couldn't even be classified as work.

I was enchanted. Writers didn't have to have any gumption at all. I did not dare tell anybody for fear of being laughed at in the schoolyard, but secretly I decided that what I'd like to be when I grew up was a writer.

Responding to the Autobiography

Analyzing the Autobiography

Identifying Facts

1. Describe what Russell's mother does to start Russell on the road toward "making something of himself." How do Doris's sales techniques contrast with Russell's?
2. What gives his mother the idea that Russell should be a writer?

Interpreting Meanings

3. How would you **characterize** Doris? On page 447, Baker says "Doris could have made something of herself if she hadn't been a girl." Is he being **ironic** here or serious? Explain.
4. Underlying this selection is an **irony** that is introduced in the first sentence: "I began working in journalism . . ." Hawking magazines on a street corner is hardly "journalism," but throughout this chapter, Baker's mother and the Curtis executive overstate the grandeur of his new profession. Find at least five examples of their humorous **overstatements.** How would you describe the mother's role in this interview that is supposed to be between Russell and the executive?
5. Baker's concluding **irony** is his childish vision of "the ease of the writer's life." He describes the horrors of newspaper peddling and concludes that "what writers did couldn't even be classified as work." From your own experience, explain how the difficulties a writer faces might be as bad as angry dogs, surly strangers, and doorbell ringing.
6. How would you describe Baker's **tone** toward his mother and his childhood?
7. The childhood experiences Baker describes took place many years ago. Are any aspects of these experiences still common today? Or are some of them hopelessly dated? Explain your opinions.
8. Do you think Russell had the "faults" that meant he should be a writer? (See "A Whole Society of Loners and Dreamers," page 424.)

Writing About the Autobiography

A Creative Response

1. **Writing an Autobiographical Essay.** What were you like as a child? Did you share Russell's qualities? Or were you more like Doris? Or were you different altogether from either one? In a brief essay, describe what you think you were like when you were around eight years old. What was your idea of a perfect afternoon? Did you have any brothers and sisters? Were they like or unlike you? What did the adults want you to be when you grew up? What were your own ideas?

A Critical Response

2. **Analyzing a Character.** In a brief essay, write a character analysis of Russell's mother. Think of a **generalization** about his mother's character, and use that as your topic statement. Cite at least three passages where Baker characterizes his mother directly. Cite at least three incidents or actions that support his direct characterization and make it vivid. In a second paragraph, tell what you think of Baker's mother.

Analyzing Language and Vocabulary

Clichés

Clichés are expressions that were once fresh and original but that have been used so often they have now lost their punch (a statement that is itself a cliché). Baker deliberately uses a few clichés in this account of his career in journalism; the effect he is aiming for is humor. Explain the meaning of each cliché below. What comparison is each one based on?

1. " 'You've got no more gumption than a bump on a log,' she said."
2. ". . . my mother agreed that it was top-drawer seventh-grade prose. . . ."
3. "Brimming with zest, Doris, who was then seven years old, returned with me to the corner."
4. "I clasped the idea to my heart."

Harry Crews (1935–   ), the son of tobacco share-croppers, was born in rural Georgia in a split-pine house that his father had built by hand at a total cost of fifty dollars. This was the height of the Great Depression, but, as Crews says, the Depression "had been living in Bacon County for years." Tobacco is a fickle crop, heavily dependent on the weather, and the life was as hard as the land in a place where digging out an oak stump "might cost a man a week of his life" and where the crop would sell for three cents a pound and the mule to work it would cost two hundred dollars.

Crews was the second living son—one had died at birth. When he was not quite two years old, his father, overworked and always in danger from his "hissing, skipping heart," died in his sleep from a heart attack so sudden and massive that it did not even wake his mother.

After that, the family was, as Crews remembers, so "driven from pillar to post [that] there is nowhere I can think of as the home place. Bacon County is my home place, and I've had to make do with it." At seventeen, Crews left Bacon County, never to live there again, and entered the Marine Corps. He later enrolled at the University of Florida to take his degree on the G. I. Bill, to write, and eventually to teach writing there.

Despite what happened to him later, Crews says that "what has been most significant in my life had all taken place by the time I was six years old." Wherever he might go in the world, Bacon County—"all its people and its customs and all its loveliness and ugliness"—would go with him.

Crews has written for many major American magazines and has produced half a dozen novels, including the acclaimed *Car, The Hawk Is Dying, Feast of Snakes, Body,* and *Scar Lover.* But he is perhaps best known for the autobiography *A Childhood: The Biography of a Place.*

In the excerpt from *A Childhood* that follows, Sam is the little white dog that follows him like a shadow. The man Crews refers to as "daddy" is his stepfather, though the boy, who never knew his own father and is not quite five years old, does not yet realize this.

Unless you live in a part of the country like Crews's rural Georgia, you might never have had the specific experiences he describes here. But as you read, try to decide if any feelings expressed in this little story are common to children every-where—whether they grew up in rural Georgia or in metropolitan New York. Do you think the habit of storytelling is common to all children?

THE MAIL-ORDER CATALOGUE

Harry Crews

I opened the safe,[1] took a biscuit off a plate, and punched a hole in it with my finger. Then with a jar of cane syrup, I poured the hole full, waited for it to soak in good, and then poured again. When the biscuit had all the syrup it would take, I got two pieces of fried pork off another plate and went out and sat on the back steps, where Sam was already lying in the warm sun, his ears struck forward on his head. I ate the bread and pork slowly, chewing for a long time and shar-ing it all with Sam.

When we had finished, I went back into the house, took off my gown, and put on a cotton undershirt, my overalls with twin galluses[2] that buckled on my chest, and my straw hat, which was rimmed on the edges with a border of green cloth and had a piece of green cellophane sewn into the brim to act as an eyeshade. I was bare-

---

1. **safe:** pie safe, a cupboard with screened doors.

2. **galluses:** suspenders.

foot, but I wished very much I had a pair of brogans[3] because brogans were what men wore and I very much wanted to be a man. In fact, I was pretty sure I already was a man, but the only one who seemed to know it was my daddy. Everybody else treated me like I was still a baby.

I went out the side door, and Sam fell into step behind me as we walked out beyond the mule barn where four mules stood in the lot and on past the cotton house and then down the dim road past a little leaning shack where our tenant farmers lived, a black family in which there was a boy just a year older than I was. His name was Willalee Bookatee. I went on past their house because I knew they would be in the field, too, so there was no use to stop.

I went through a sapling thicket and over a shallow ditch and finally climbed a wire fence into the field, being very careful of my overalls on the barbed wire. I could see them all, my family and the black tenant family, far off there in the shimmering heat of the tobacco field. They were pulling cutworms off the tobacco. I wished I could have been out there with them pulling worms because when you found one, you had to break it in half, which seemed great good fun to me. But you could also carry an empty Prince Albert tobacco can in your back pocket and fill it up with worms to play with later.

Mama wouldn't let me pull worms because she said I was too little and might damage the plants. If I was alone in the field with daddy, though, he would let me hunt all the worms I wanted to. He let me do pretty much anything I wanted to, which included sitting in his lap to guide his old pickup truck down dirt roads all over the county.

I went down to the end of the row and sat under a persimmon tree in the shade with Sam and watched as daddy and mama and brother and Willalee Bookatee, who was—I could see even from this distance—putting worms in Prince Albert cans, and his mama, whose name was Katie, and his daddy, whose name was Will, I watched them all as they came toward me, turning the leaves and searching for worms as they came.

The moment I sat down in the shade, I was already wondering how long it would be before they quit to go to the house for dinner because I was already beginning to wish I'd taken two biscuits instead of one and maybe another piece of meat, or else that I hadn't shared with Sam.

Bored, I looked down at Sam and said: "Sam, if you don't quit eatin my biscuit and meat, I'm gone have to cut you like a shoat hog."

A black cloud of gnats swarmed around his heavy muzzle, but I clearly heard him say that he didn't think I was man enough to do it. Sam and I talked a lot together, had long involved conversations, mostly about which one of us had done the other one wrong and, if not about that, about which one of us was the better man. It would be a good long time before I started thinking of Sam as a dog instead of a person. But I always came out on top when we talked because Sam could only say what I said he said, think what I thought he thought.

"If you was any kind of man atall, you wouldn't snap at them gnats and eat them flies the way you do," I said.

"It ain't a thing in the world the matter with eatin gnats and flies," he said.

"It's how come people treat you like a dog," I said. "You could probably come on in the house like other folks if it weren't for eatin flies and gnats like you do."

That's the way the talk went until daddy and the rest of them finally came down to where Sam and I were sitting in the shade. They stopped beside us to wipe their faces and necks with sweat rags. Mama asked if I had got something to eat when I woke up. I told her I had.

"You all gone stop for dinner now?"

"I reckon we'll work awhile longer," daddy said.

I said: "Well, then, can Willalee and me go up to his house and play till dinnertime?"

Daddy looked at the sun to see what time it was. He could come within five or ten minutes by the position of the sun. Most of the farmers I knew could.

Daddy was standing almost dead center in his own shadow. "I reckon so," he said.

Then the whole thing had to be done over again. Willalee asked his daddy the same question. Be-

---

3. **brogans:** high, heavy work shoes.

cause my daddy had said it was all right didn't mean Willalee's daddy would agree. He usually did, but not always. So it was necessary to ask.

We climbed the fence and went across the ditch and back through the sapling thicket to the three-track road that led up to the shack, and while we walked, Willalee showed me the two Prince Albert tobacco cans he had in his back pockets. They were both filled with cutworms. The worms had lots of legs and two little things on their heads that looked like horns. They were about an inch long, sometimes as long as two inches, and round and fat and made wonderful things to play with. There was no fence around the yard where Willalee lived and the whole house leaned toward the north at about a ten-degree tilt. Before we even got up the steps, we could smell the food already cooking on the wood stove at the back of the house where his grandma was banging metal pots around over the cast-iron stove. Her name was Annie, but everybody called her Auntie. She was too old to work in the field anymore, but she was handy about the house with ironing and cooking and scrubbing floors and canning vegetables out of the field and berries out of the woods.

She also was full of stories, which, when she had the time—and she usually did—she told to me and Willalee and his little sister, whose name was Lottie Mae. Willalee and my brother and I called her Snottie Mae, but she didn't seem to mind. She came out of the front door when she heard us coming up on the porch and right away wanted to know if she could play in the book with us. She was the same age as I and sometimes we let her play with us, but most of the time we did not.

"Naw," Willalee said, "git on back in there and help Auntie. We ain't studying you."

"Bring us the book," I said.

"I git it for you," she said, "if you give me five of them worms."

"I ain't studying you," said Willalee.

She had already seen the two Prince Albert cans full of green worms because Willalee was sitting on the floor now, the lids of the cans open and the worms crawling out. He was lining two of them up for a race from one crack in the floor to the next crack, and he was arranging the rest of the worms in little designs of diamonds and tri-angles in some game he had not yet discovered the rules for.

"You bring the book," I said, "and you can have two of them worms."

Willalee almost never argued with what I decided to do, up to and including giving away the worms he had spent all morning collecting in the fierce summer heat, which is probably why I liked him so much. Lottie Mae went back into the house and got the Sears, Roebuck catalogue and brought it out onto the porch. He handed her the two worms and told her to go on back in the house, told her it weren't fitting for her to be out here playing with worms while Auntie was back in the kitchen working.

"Ain't nothing left for me to do but put them plates on the table," she said.

"See to them plates then," Willalee said. As young as she was, Lottie Mae had things to do about the place. Whatever she could manage. We all did.

Willalee and I stayed there on the floor with the Sears, Roebuck catalogue and the open Prince Albert cans, out of which deliciously fat worms crawled. Then we opened the catalogue at random as we always did, to see what magic was waiting for us there.

In the minds of most people, the Sears, Roebuck catalogue is a kind of low joke associated with outhouses. God knows the catalogue sometimes ended up in the outhouse, but more often it did not.

The Sears, Roebuck catalogue was much better used as a Wish Book, which it was called by the people out in the country, who would never be able to order anything out of it, but could at their leisure spend hours dreaming over.

Willalee Bookatee and I used it for another reason. We made up stories out of it, used it to spin a web of fantasy about us. Without that catalogue our childhood would have been radically different. The federal government ought to strike a medal for the Sears, Roebuck company for sending all those catalogues to farming families, for bringing all that color and all that mystery and all that beauty into the lives of country people.

I first became fascinated with the Sears catalogue because all the people in its pages were

perfect. Nearly everybody I knew had something missing, a finger cut off, a toe split, an ear half-chewed away, an eye clouded with blindness from a glancing fence staple. And if they didn't have something missing, they were carrying scars from barbed wire or knives or fishhooks. But the people in the catalogue had no such hurts. They were not only whole, had all their arms and legs and toes and eyes on their unscarred bodies, but they were also beautiful. Their legs were straight and their heads were never bald and on their faces were looks of happiness, even joy, looks that I never saw much of in the faces of the people around me.

Young as I was, though, I had known for a long time that it was all a lie. I knew that under those fancy clothes there had to be scars, there had to be swellings and boils of one kind or another because there was no other way to live in the world. And more than that, at some previous, unremembered moment, I had decided that all the people in the catalogue were related, not necessarily blood kin, but knew one another, and because they knew one another there had to be hard feelings, trouble between them off and on, violence, and hate between them as well as love. And it was out of this knowledge that I first began to

make up stories about the people I found in the book.

Once I began to make up stories about them, Willalee and Lottie Mae began to make up stories, too. The stories they made up were every bit as good as mine. Sometimes better. More than once we had spent whole rainy afternoons when it was too wet to go to the field turning the pages of the catalogue, forcing the beautiful people to give up the secrets of their lives: how they felt about one another, what kind of sicknesses they may have had, what kind of scars they carried in their flesh under all those bright and fancy clothes.

Willalee had his pocketknife out and was about to operate on one of the green cutworms because he liked to pretend he was a doctor. It was I who first put the notion in his head that he might in fact be a doctor, and since we almost never saw a doctor and because they were mysterious and always drove cars or else fine buggies behind high-stepping mares, quickly healing people with their secret medicines, the notion stuck in Willalee's head, and he became very good at taking cutworms and other things apart with his pocket-knife.

The Sears catalogue that we had opened at random found a man in his middle years but still strong and healthy with a head full of hair and clear, direct eyes looking out at us, dressed in a red hunting jacket and wading boots, with a rack of shotguns behind him. We used our fingers to mark the spot and turned the Wish Book again, and this time it opened to ladies standing in their underwear, lovely as none we had ever seen, all perfect in their unstained clothes. Every last one of them had the same direct and steady eyes of the man in the red hunting jacket.

I said: "What do you think, Willalee?"

Without hesitation, Willalee said: "This lady here in her step-ins[4] is his chile."

We kept the spot marked with the lady in the step-ins and the man in the hunting jacket and turned the book again, and there was a young man in a suit, the creases sharp enough to shave with, posed with his foot casually propped on a box, every strand of his beautiful hair in place.

"See, what it is," I said. "This boy right here is seeing that girl back there, the one in her step-ins, and she is the youngun of him back there, and them shotguns behind'm belong to him, and he ain't happy."

"Why he ain't happy?"

"Cause this feller standing here in this suit looking so nice, he ain't nice at all. He's mean, but he don't look mean. That gal is the only youngun the feller in the jacket's got, and he loves her cause she is a sweet child. He don't want her fooling with that sorry man in that suit. He's so sorry he done got hisself in trouble with the law. The high sheriff is looking for him right now. Him in the suit will fool around on you."

"How it is he fool around?"

"He'll steal anything he can put his hand to," I said. "He'll steal your hog, or he'll steal your cow out of your field. He's so sorry he'll take that cow if it's the only cow you got. It's just the kind of feller he is."

Willalee said: "Then how come it is she mess around with him?"

"That suit," I said, "done turned that young girl's head. Daddy always says if you give a man

a white shirt and a tie and a suit of clothes, you can find out real quick how sorry he is. Daddy says it's the quickest way to find out."

"Do her daddy know she's messing around with him?"

"Shore he knows. A man allus knows what his youngun is doing. Special if she's a girl." I flipped back to the man in the red hunting jacket and the wading boots. "You see them shotguns behind him there on the wall? Them his guns. That second one right there, see that one, the double barrel? That gun is loaded with double-ought buckshot. You know how come it loaded?"

"He gone stop that fooling around," said Willalee.

And so we sat there on the porch with the pots and pans banging back in the house over the iron stove and Lottie Mae there in the door where she had come to stand and listen to us as we talked even though we would not let her help with the story. And before it was over, we had discovered all the connections possible between the girl in the step-ins and the young man in the knife-creased suit and the older man in the red hunting jacket with the shotguns on the wall behind him. And more than that we also discovered that the man's kin people, when they had found out about the trouble he was having with his daughter and the young man, had plans of their own to fix it so the high sheriff wouldn't even have to know about it. They were going to set up and wait on him to take a shoat hog out of another field, and when he did, they'd be waiting with their own guns and knives (which we stumbled upon in another part of the catalogue) and they was gonna throw down on him and see if they couldn't make two pieces out of him instead of one. We had in the story what they thought and what they said and what they felt and why they didn't think that the young man, as good as he looked and as well as he stood in his fancy clothes, would ever straighten out and become the man the daddy wanted for his only daughter.

Before it was over, we even had the girl in the step-ins fixing it so that the boy in the suit could be shot. And by the time my family and Willalee's family came walking down the road from the to-

---

4. **step-ins:** underpants.

bacco field toward the house, the entire Wish Book was filled with feuds of every kind and violence, maimings, and all the other vicious happenings of the world.

Since where we lived and how we lived was almost hermetically sealed[5] from everything and everybody else, fabrication became a way of life. Making up stories, it seems to me now, was not only a way for us to understand the way we lived but also a defense against it. It was no doubt the first step in a life devoted primarily to men and women and children who never lived anywhere but in my imagination. I have found in them infinitely more order and beauty and satisfaction than I ever have in the people who move about me in the real world. And Willalee Bookatee and his family were always there with me in those first tentative steps. God knows what it would have been like if it had not been for Willalee and his people, with whom I spent nearly as much time as I did with my own family.

---

5. **hermetically sealed:** completely sealed; airtight.

Responding to the Autobiography

Analyzing the Autobiography

Identifying Facts

1. In the first two paragraphs, Crews gives us a dozen or so details about the boy's morning, and not all of these necessarily suggest either a poor or a rural life: A breakfast of biscuits, syrup, and bacon might be welcome in any middle-class urban household. But which details *do* reveal the boy's poverty, his "time period," and his setting?
2. Even as a not-quite-five-year-old, this little boy seems to have unusual powers of imagination. How does his relationship with Sam **foreshadow** the game with the Sears, Roebuck catalogue?
3. Why is the catalogue called a "Wish Book"?

Interpreting Meanings

4. Throughout this excerpt, Crews writes from the **point of view** of the child; he expresses attitudes and values that are not necessarily shared by the adult writer. Rarely does Crews the author comment on these attitudes and values—this would distance us from the mind of the child. What, for example, are we to think is wonderful about worms? Locate other passages that help us share the child's view.

5. How is the catalogue's value to the boys different from its value to most people? What does the boys' story tell about life in Bacon County?
6. Explain what Crews means by stating that he has found in imaginary people "infinitely more order and beauty and satisfaction than I ever have in the people who move about me in the real world." Do you agree or disagree? Why?
7. What does Crews mean when he says: "Making up stories . . . was not only a way for us to understand the way we lived but also a defense against it"? Do you think that other arts (painting and music, for example) also can both help us understand the world and defend us against it? Explain.
8. Even as a boy, Crews understood that there were hard feelings, trouble, violence, and hate among people: ". . . it was out of this knowledge that I first began to make up stories about the people I found in the book." When he says this, he is expressing a truth not only about life but also, more importantly, about literature. Think about the best stories you know. Do many of them involve trouble of some kind—danger, death, lost love, cruelty, or hurt? Why do you think writers write about worlds and lives that are less than perfect? How do you feel about this kind of writing?

Writing About the Autobiography

A Creative Response

1. **Imitating the Writer's Technique.** Write a brief narrative about an incident that you remember vividly from your early childhood. Imitate Crews's method and try to tell your story from the point of view of a child. Let the child respond to a **setting** and **characters.**
2. **Telling an Imaginary Story.** If you don't have access to a catalogue, find advertisements in a newspaper or magazine that feature at least three people. Then tell a story about these people that features a **basic situation,** a **conflict,** and a **resolution.** First you'll have to imagine relationships or connections among your characters.

A Critical Response

3. **Analyzing Relationships.** Although the narrator and Willalee are familiar with conflict, are they in conflict with their own parents? What details reveal the relationship between the narrator and his father? What details reveal Willalee's relationship with his father? What does the children's view of the father in the story (about the man and the shotgun) reveal about them? Write a brief essay discussing these families.

Analyzing Language and Vocabulary

Dialect and Oral Reading

A **dialect,** the special way of speaking characteristic of a group or a region, involves all aspects of spoken language: special pronunciation, special vocabulary, characteristic syntax (way of arranging words in sentences), and characteristic grammar.

1. Find three examples of pronunciations that differ from those in standard English.
2. What does the narrator call the meal his family eats at noon? (What do you call it?)
3. What is his word for *suspenders*? (What is yours?)
4. What does Willalee mean when he tells his sister "We ain't studying you"?
5. How is the syntax in these sentences unusual: "Why he ain't happy?" "How it is he fool around?"
6. Find at least three other examples of nonstandard grammar in the story.

Like Mark Twain's writings, Harry Crews's story cries out for oral reading. Select a passage that you think is especially vivid or comical and prepare it for oral presentation. Someone else in class must help you read the conversation with Sam.

Focusing on Background
A Comment from the Writer

"I guess I really learned, seriously learned, how to write just after I got out of college when I pretty much literally ate Graham Greene's *The End of the Affair.* My wife and I were living in a little trailer about the size of this porch in Jacksonville, Fla., where I was teaching seventh grade. Our little baby was with us—when he was four we lost him. He drowned. But I wrote a novel that year, and here's how I did it. I took *The End of the Affair,* and I pretty much reduced the thing to numbers. I found out how many characters were in it, how much time was in it—and that's hard to do as there is not only present time in a book but past time as well. I found out how many cities were in the book, how many rooms, where the climaxes were and how long it took Greene to get to them. And there were a lot of other things I reduced to numbers. I read that book until it was dogeared and was coming apart in my hands. And then I said, 'I'm going to write me a novel and do everything he did.' I knew I was going to waste—but it wasn't a waste—a year of my time. And I knew that the end result was going to be a mechanical, unreadable novel. But I was trying to find out how you do it. So I wrote the novel, and it had to have this many rooms, this many transitions, etc. It was the bad novel I knew it would be. But by doing it I learned more about writing fiction and writing a novel and about the importance of time and place—Greene is a freak about time and place—than I had from any class or anything I'd done before. I really, literally, ate that book. And that's how I learned to write."

—Harry Crews

Unlike Harry Crews, who knew brutal poverty in his childhood, Susan Allen Toth (1940–) was raised in the sheltered middle class town of Ames, Iowa, during the affluent 1950's. Curiously, Toth shares with Crews a childhood memory of the Sears, Roebuck catalogue as presenting remote images of the American ideal. "The kind of woman we thought we would become," she says, ". . . shimmered in our minds, familiar but removed as the glossy cover. . . ." Also like Crews, who took Bacon County with him, Toth records that when she left Ames to "head into a new and wonderful life, . . . it never occurred to me that I would be taking my old self, and Ames, with me."

Toth first left Ames to attend Smith College. She also studied at the University of California at Berkeley and at the University of Minnesota. In 1969 she joined the English staff of Macalester College in St. Paul.

When her daughter Jennifer was four years old and questioned her about the "old days," Toth began to think about writing her autobiography, which was eventually published under the title *Blooming*. (A second volume, called *Ivy Days,* continues the story through her college and graduate school years.) " 'Did you wear long dresses?' Jennifer asked. 'Did you ever ride in a covered wagon?' As I struggled with her questions, I realized that to her the 'old days' encompassed a cloudy past when I was young, as well as when her grandmother was young, and whatever dim days extended beyond Gramma's childhood."

Toth admits that the writing of the book resulted not in any satisfying answers but in further questions: "Does any girl today have the chance to grow up as gradually and as quietly as we did? . . . Was such innocence constricting, or did it give me shelter and space to grow? What do I see in the past that I can still value? What did I get for the price I paid? What was the price, anyway?" In exploring such questions, Toth vividly recaptures a past only recently gone, but in some places gone forever. As you read this excerpt from *Blooming,* decide if any parts of the narrator's description of her life seem "dated." What aspects might remain the same for a teenager today?

NOTHING HAPPENED

Susan Allen Toth

We huddled together in the cool spring night, whispering in hoarse voices, thrumming with the excitement that vibrated through the crowd gathering in the parking lot outside the Ames train station. All the way home from Des Moines we had hugged each other, laughed, cried, and hugged each other again. When we passed through the small farming towns between Des Moines and Ames, we rolled down the windows of the Harbingers' station wagon and shouted down the quiet streets, "We beat Marshalltown in seven overtimes! We beat Marshalltown in seven overtimes!" It had a rhythmic beat, a chant we repeated to each other in unbelieving ecstasy. We beat Marshalltown in seven overtimes! For the first time in ten years, Ames High School had won the state basketball championship. Most of us sophomores felt nothing so important could ever happen to us again.

As a string of cars began threading off the highway, filling up the lot, someone turned the lights along Main Street on full. It was close to midnight, but families were pouring down the street toward the station as though it held a George Washington's Birthday sale. We were all waiting for the team. The mayor had ordered out the two fire engines, which were waiting too, bright red and gleaming under the lights. When the bus finally came around the corner, a cheering erupted from the crowd that didn't stop until the boys had walked down the steps, grinning a little sheepishly, and climbed onto the engines. The coach rode on

one, the mayor on another. Following our cheer-leaders, voices gone but valiantly shrieking, who were leading the way in their whirling orange pleated skirts and black sweaters, we snake-danced down Main Street behind blowing sirens and paraded to the high-school auditorium. There we listened to speeches from the mayor, the principal, the coach, and the team captain. We would have no school tomorrow, the principal told us (we cheered again), just a pep assembly, then dismissal. Then Mr. J. J. Girton, who owned all three movie theaters in Ames, came to the mike and said that in honor of the occasion he would show a free movie at the New Ames tomorrow at two P.M. We cheered, but this time not as loudly. We knew whenever Mr. Girton showed free movies, he always picked the oldest Looney Tunes and a dull Western. The coach thanked everyone and sat down quickly; he looked tired. But when he introduced the team captain, who made his teammates rise, we jumped to our feet and clapped and stomped.

I was filled with love and admiration for all of them, for stocky little Tom Fisher, who had made a critical free throw; for tall, gangly Charlie Stokowski, who had racked up thirty points; for George Davis, who usually stood most of the game in front of the bench with his mouth hanging open, but who tonight in the midst of the team looked like a hero. Next to me Patsy Jones, George's girlfriend, looked smug and proud. We knew she was planning to meet him backstage for a few moments after the assembly. When our new celebrities filed off the stage, our parents, who had been sitting together in the last rows, took us home. Next morning at breakfast we could read all about ourselves, with headlines and pictures, in the Des Moines *Register*. Though we knew other stories would topple ours after a few days, it didn't matter.

Perhaps I remember that night so vividly because it stands out like a high hill in the flat, uneventful landscape that was both the physical and emotional setting for our town. Our lives were not dull, oh, no; but our adolescence bubbled and fermented in a kind of vacuum. In Ames, in the 1950's, as far as we were concerned, nothing happened.

Ames had once had a murder. It had happened a few years before we were in junior high, to someone we didn't know, a man who hadn't lived in Ames long. He had somehow accumulated gambling debts, probably on his travels out West, and one night he was found shot to death at the Round-up Motel. No one ever found a weapon or the murderers. After a few blurred photographs in the Ames *Daily Tribune* and interviews with the cleaning woman who'd found him, the motel owner, the county sheriff, and local police, even the newspaper abandoned the story. But for many years afterward, when we drove with strangers past the Round-up, we would point it out in reverential tones. It might look just like a tidy modern bungalow, stretched out into longer wings than usual, but we knew it was a bloody place.

Other than our murder, we had little experience with violence. Sometimes there were accidents. One of my girlfriends had a brother who had lost an eye when another boy had aimed badly with a bow and arrow. We stared surreptitiously at his glass eye, which was bigger and shinier than it ought to be. Someone else's sister, much younger, had toddled in front of a truck on the highway and been killed. Her picture, done in careful pastels by an artist from Des Moines, hung over the sofa in her parents' living room. When they spoke of her, I tried not to look at the picture, which made me feel uncomfortable.

When death came to Ames, it seldom took anyone we knew. We were all shocked when one morning we saw our high-school teachers whispering together in the halls, a few of them weeping openly, over the history teacher's four-year-old daughter, who had been rushed the previous night to the hospital and who had died almost immediately of heart failure. Visitation was to be that night at the Jefferson Funeral Parlor. Those of us who felt close to Mr. Sansome wanted to go to "pay our respects," a phrase someone had heard from another teacher. We discussed solemnly what to wear, what to do, what to say. When two girlfriends came to pick me up, I was nervous, with a sinking feeling in my stomach because I did not know what to expect. I had never seen a dead person before.

We didn't stay at the funeral parlor long. The

room was crowded with friends of the Sansomes. Mrs. Sansome wasn't there—home, in bed, someone said sympathetically—and Mr. Sansome stood with a glazed expression on his face, shaking hands, muttering politeness to everyone who came up to him. We shook his hand and moved on to the coffin. Mary Sansome looked just as she always did, dressed perhaps more neatly in a Sunday dress with bright pink bows tied onto her long pigtails. As we leaned closer, I thought her skin looked rubbery and waxen, like a doll I had once had. Her eyes were shut, but she looked as though she might wake up any minute, disturbed by the murmured talk around her. I looked over at Mr. Sansome, usually a gesturing, dramatic man, standing woodenly a few feet away, staring straight ahead of him. The feeling in my stomach got worse. I wanted to cry, but I couldn't. Soon my friends and I went silently home.

One reason I was so blind to common attitudes toward blacks was that Ames didn't have any. Or rather, like everything else, Ames had only one. For most of the years I was growing up, there was a single family in town who were black, or, to be precise, an unassuming shade of brown. The Elliotts, quiet and hardworking, lived far from the college campus in an unfashionable section where small businesses, warehouses, and rundown older houses crowded together. It wasn't exactly a slum, but it wasn't a place where anyone I knew lived either. Alexander Elliott was in my class, his younger sister two classes behind me. They too were hardworking and quiet, always neatly dressed, pleasant expressions on their faces, ready to respond politely. What went on behind those carefully composed smiles no one then ever wondered.

We thought the Elliott kids were nice enough, we exchanged casual greetings with them, but Alexander was never invited to any parties. He did not belong to any social groups. I do not remember seeing him anywhere, except in a crowd cheering at a football game or sitting a little apart in school assembly. Once or twice I think I remember Alexander's bringing a date, also black—though "Negro" was what we called them, enunciating the word carefully—to the Junior-Senior

Prom. Wherever she was from, it wasn't Ames. They danced by themselves all evening. Yet none of us thought we were prejudiced about Alex, and almost every year we elected him to some class office. The year Alex became student-body president, our principal pointed to Ames High proudly as an example of the way democracy really worked.

If I was unaware that Ames was prejudiced toward blacks, I could not miss the town's feelings about Catholics. I myself was fascinated by the glamour that beckoned at the door of St. Cecilia's, the imposing brick church defiantly planted right on the main road through town. Every Christmas St. Cecilia's erected a life-size nativity scene on its lawn, floodlit, Mary in blue velvet, glowing halos, real straw in the wooden manger. None of the Methodists, Lutherans, Baptists, or Presbyterians did anything quite so showy. I always begged Mother to slow down as we drove by so I could admire it. Sometimes I could see one of the nuns from the small convent behind the church billowing in her black robes down the street. If I was with my friend Peggy O'Reilly, who was Catholic, she would stop and greet the nun respectfully. She knew each one by name, though they all looked alike to me.

Peggy told me bits and pieces about Catholic doctrine, which was so different from the vague advice I was gathering haphazardly in my own Presbyterian Sunday School that I didn't know what to make of it. Catholics had exotic secrets. One of the saints—was it Bernadette?—had been given the exact date of the end of the world, Peggy said, and she on her death had bequeathed it to the Pope. Every Pope kept this secret locked in a special case, and when he was about to die, he opened it, read the date, and expired—probably, I thought, out of shock. Why didn't the Popes share this wonderful knowledge with the world, so we could all get ready for the end? I asked Peggy. Peggy couldn't say.

Even if we hadn't known from friends like Peggy that Catholics were different, our parents would have told us. One of the few rigid rules enforced on many of us was the impossibility of "getting serious" about a Catholic boy. For a Protestant to marry a Catholic in Ames produced

a major social upheaval, involving parental conferences, conversions, and general disapproval on both sides. Even our liberal minister, who encouraged his Presbyterian parishioners to call him "Doctor Bob" because he didn't want to appear uppish about his advanced degree, came to our high-school fellowship group one night to lecture on Catholicism. He probably knew that one of his deacons' daughters was going very steadily with a Catholic boy. Warning us about the autocratic nature of the Catholic Church, its iron hand, its idolatry, and most of all the way it could snatch our very children from us and bring them up in the manacles of a strange faith, Doctor Bob heated with the warmth of his topic until his cheeks glowed as he clenched and unclenched his fists.

Since I never fell in love with one of the few Catholic boys in our class, I never faced such direct fire. But my friend Peggy did. Much to her parents' disapproval, she began going steadily with Alvin Barnes, a Methodist boy who had never dated at all before he discovered Peggy. He was a quiet, withdrawn boy who seldom talked about anything, let alone his feelings, but we could all tell by the way he looked at Peggy that he loved her with a single-minded devotion. Her parents tolerated the romance for a year, though we knew they often had long talks with Peggy about it. But during their senior year, when Peggy and Alvin were still holding hands in daylight, Peggy's family decided that enough was enough. They gave Peggy an ultimatum, which she repeated to us, sobbing, one night when we girls had gathered together at someone's house for popcorn and gossip. She was distraught, but she had no thought of disobeying them; she was going to tell Alvin they must break it off. We were indignant, sympathetic, but helpless; the price Peggy's parents were willing to pay was a year away at college, and no one thought Peggy could give that up instead.

A few days later Alvin was absent from school, and the whispers were alarming. After hearing Peggy's news, he had come to her house to try to argue with her parents. They had refused to let him in, had told him to go home and not to bother their daughter again. When he called their house, they wouldn't let Peggy come to the phone. So later that night, he had returned. There in the sloping driveway he had lain down behind the rear wheels of the O'Reilly family car. All night he lay there, waiting for the still-dark morning when Mr. O'Reilly would come out, start the engine, and back the car down the driveway on his way to work.

Of course, when morning finally came, Mr. O'Reilly saw Alvin at once. Horrified, he called Alvin's parents. They came and took Alvin away, and he did not come back to school until close to the end of the semester. Then he kept aloof, refusing to talk about what had happened, and hovered silently at the edges of our games and parties. Soon we all graduated, Alvin left town, and we lost track of him entirely. But I felt as though he had somehow been sacrificed, offered up to the fierce religious hatred I had seen gleaming in Doctor Bob's eyes. For several years, until even more bitter images etched over this one, I thought of the effects of prejudice as embodied in Alvin's quiet figure, lying patiently and hopelessly in the chilly darkness behind the wheels of the O'Reilly car.

As I grew older, I began to realize that this quiet was not going to last. Time was speeding up; at some sharply definable point I would grow up and leave Ames. At odd moments in those last years I would be surprised by sadness, a strange feeling that perhaps I had missed something, that maybe life was going to pass me by. At the same time I nestled securely in the familiar landscape of streets whose every bump and jog I knew, of people who smiled and greeted me by name wherever I went, of friends who appeared at every movie, store, or swimming pool.

Nowhere did I feel this conflicting sense of security and impending loss as sharply as I did at the train station. Ames lay on some important transcontinental routes, and trains passed through daily on their way from Chicago to Portland, San Francisco, Los Angeles. I had ridden on trains for short trips, but I had never been on one overnight and I was too young to remember clearly what the country was like west of Ames when the prairies stopped and the mountains began. From a long auto trip when I was eight, I only remembered endless spaces punctuated by the Grand Canyon. So for me the crack passenger trains, the *City of San Francisco,* the *City of Denver,* the *City of Los Angeles,* had titles that rang in my imagination like the purest romance. Big cities, the golden West, life beckoned to me from every flashing train window.

On slow spring or summer nights I would often ask my friend Charlie to take me down to the station to watch the trains come in. The *City of San Francisco* was due to pass through at ten o'clock, the *City of Denver* at eleven. Down at the deserted station we sat on an abandoned luggage cart near the tracks, staring into the darkness, listening for the first telltale hoot of a faraway whistle. The night was so quiet we whispered, hearing above our voices the grasshoppers, a squeal of brakes three blocks away at the beer parlor, the loud click of the station clock. The trains were always late, but we were in no hurry.

Eventually we'd hear a rumble on the tracks and then see a searching eye of light bearing down on us. Quickly we'd leap to our feet and get as close to the tracks as we dared, plugging our ears as the train ground to a stop in front of us, its metallic clamor deafening, its cars looming in the night like visitors from another world. As we stood there, we could see people moving back and forth inside the lighted windows. If we were outside a Pullman car, we might catch a glimpse of someone seated next to the window, staring wordlessly back at us. I wondered why everyone wasn't asleep. A frowsy-haired woman with a brown felt hat pinned to her graying curls looked like someone I might know, but didn't. Two young boys, jumping on their seats and pounding silently on the glass, could have been the Evans kids down the street, but weren't. They were strangers, separated from us not only by thick glass but by chance, being whisked away from their old lives to new ones. I felt the pull of the future, of adventure waiting for them and someday for me.

After a few moments, an exchange of luggage flung by the stationmaster, who had suddenly emerged from inside the darkened hut, a few shouts, the train began to grind again. As we winced with the jarring sound of metal against metal, it picked up speed. I tried to watch the car with the frowsy-haired woman and the two jumping boys, but it was soon lost in a blur of streaming silver metal. A last long low shriek, and the train was gone, off to Denver or San Francisco.

I always felt let down when Charlie and I walked back to his car. I comforted myself with thinking that someday I too would be traveling on one of those trains, leaving Ames for college someplace far away, maybe even Denver or San Francisco. When I got on that train, I would head into a new and wonderful life. It never occurred to me that I would be taking my old self, and Ames, with me.

Responding to the Autobiography

Analyzing the Autobiography

Identifying Facts

1. Find the passage that explains the **title** of this excerpt.
2. List the events that Toth says *did* happen.

Interpreting Meanings

3. What do you think the writer means when she says on page 462 that their "adolescence bubbled and fermented in a kind of vacuum"?
4. On page 463 Toth begins a paragraph with the sentence, "One reason I was so blind to common attitudes toward blacks was that Ames didn't have any." She then proceeds to let us know by implication the attitudes that Ames did exhibit. How would you describe these attitudes? What details make them clear?
5. What details convey the sense of glamour and exoticness in her girlhood view of the Catholic Church? How would you account for the religious prejudices she describes?
6. Summarize the story of Peggy and Alvin. What significance does Toth see in the incident? How did you feel about the story and the people involved in it?

7. Why is it so important to the girl to watch the trains come into the Ames station? This whole passage about train watching may be said to be **symbolic**—details suggest that the train represents more than a mere mode of transportation. What *does* it represent?
8. In "The Mail-Order Catalogue," Harry Crews tells how as a young boy he ate breakfast, walked down to the tobacco field, came back with a friend, and made up some stories. On pages 462–463 of "Nothing Happened," Susan Toth recounts a murder, a bow-and-arrow accident to a boy's eye, the death of a toddler by a highway truck, the heart failure of a four-year-old, and a funeral. Yet which child is better acquainted with death and violence—the boy in Bacon County or the girl in Ames? How do the writers make this clear to us? What do the attitudes of the two children tell us about the **atmosphere** of life in each setting?
9. What do you think Toth means when she says in her concluding sentence, "It never occurred to me that I would be taking my old self, and Ames, with me"? Do you think most people carry their childhoods with them wherever they go? What do you think this line means?

Writing About the Autobiography

A Creative Response

1. **Narrating an Event.** One reason that sports events produce such strong emotions in people is that they come to represent—for a school, a community, or a nation—the aspirations of a whole group of people. Even those who say they "don't care" about sports are often likely to be vehemently emotional about not caring and to feel strongly that sports are boring, brutal, or a waste of time. Write about a sports event (a triumph or a disaster) in which you have been either a participant or a spectator. Let us know your exact feelings: Did you share the emotions of the team and fans? Or did you feel alienated from the general reaction?

A Critical Response

2. **Comparing and Contrasting Autobiographies.** In an essay, compare and contrast Toth's story with Crews's. Tell what they have in common and how they differ. Before you begin writing, gather your details in a chart like the following one.

	Crews Story	Toth Story
How old is the narrator when the story takes place?		
Where does the story take place (time, place, type of community)?		
What is the writer's main idea?		
Does the writer express any criticism of his or her childhood?		
Does the writer regret anything?		
Does the writer seem to be honest?		
Does the writer show any humor?		
Do death and violence play a part in the narrative?		
What is the writer's tone?		

Analyzing Language and Vocabulary

Point of View and Irony

Like Harry Crews, Susan Toth presents her story primarily through the eyes of her young self. But we can feel, in the tone and texture of her writing, the presence of an adult narrator who no longer shares all of the child's views. This awareness of an adult perspective can produce a strong sense of **irony** in the reader: We sense that the child's view, though stated, is not at all what the adult now feels.

Can you explain the irony in each of the following statements? Read the passages in context first.

1. "Most of us sophomores felt nothing so important could ever happen to us again."

   a. What was this "important" thing?
   b. Do you think the adult narrator agrees with the sophomores?
   c. Could this event really be the most important thing that ever happened to someone?

2. "The year Alex became student-body president, our principal pointed to Ames High proudly as an example of the way democracy really worked."

   a. Is there any implication as to *why* Alex was really elected?
   b. Did democracy have anything to do with it?

3. "We were indignant, sympathetic, but helpless; the price Peggy's parents were willing to pay was a year away at college, and no one thought Peggy could give that up instead."

   a. Why is it ironic that no one expected Peggy to give up the year away at college?
   b. What does this say about Peggy's values?
   c. Do you think she did the right thing?

Literature & Language

Using Effective Diction

Literary Model

Here novelist and short-story writer Eudora Welty presents her recollection of Mrs. Calloway, the librarian in the town of Jackson, Mississippi, when Welty was nine years old.

I never knew anyone who'd grown up in Jackson without being afraid of Mrs. Calloway, our librarian. She ran the Library absolutely by herself, from the desk where she sat with her back to the books and facing the stairs, her dragon eye on the front door, where who knew what kind of person might come in from the public? SILENCE in big black letters was on signs tacked up everywhere. She herself spoke in her normally commanding voice; every word could be heard all over the Library above a steady seething sound coming from her electric fan; it was the only fan in the Library and stood on her desk, turned directly onto her streaming face.

As you came in from the bright outside, if you were a girl, she sent her strong eyes down the stairway to test you; if she could see through your skirt, she sent you straight back home: You could just put on another petticoat if you wanted a book that badly from the public library. I was willing; I would do anything to read.

My mother was not afraid of Mrs. Calloway. She wished me to have my own library card to check out books for myself. She took me in to introduce me, and I saw I had met a witch. "Eudora is nine years old and has my permission to read any book she wants from the shelves, children or adult," Mother said. "With the exception of *Elsie Dinsmore*," she added. Later she explained to me that she'd made this rule because Elsie, the heroine, being made by her father to practice too long and hard at the piano, fainted and fell off the piano stool. "You're too impressionable, dear," she told me. "You'd read that and the very first thing you'd do, you'd fall off the piano stool." "Impressionable" was a new word. I never hear it yet without the image that comes with it of falling straight off the piano stool.

Mrs. Calloway made her own rules about books. You could not take back a book to the Library on the same day you'd taken it out; it made no difference to her that you'd read every word in it and needed another to start. You could take out two books at a time and two only; this applied as long as you were a child and also for the rest of your life, to my mother as severely as to me.

—from *One Writer's Beginnings*, Eudora Welty

A Note on Diction

Diction is a writer's or speaker's choice of words. People use different words depending on their subject, purpose, and audience. For instance, a report in a medical journal read by doctors would contain much more technical language than an article on the same subject in a newspaper. And the kind of colloquial or even slang words you'd use in a conversation with a friend would be different from the more formal language you'd write in a book report.

Diction is an important element of a writer's **style.** A writer's diction can be simple or fancy *(do/implement)*, modern or old-fashioned *(boyfriend/beau)*, general or specific *(flower/daffodil)*, vague or precise *(said/whispered)*, straightforward or euphemistic *(died/passed away)*. Can you think of any other adjectives that might be used to describe the kinds of words a writer uses?

Careful writers choose exactly the right words to express their precise meanings and communicate their feelings. They pay particular attention not only to the literal meanings of words (their **denotations**), but also to their **connotations**—all the associations and emotions those words suggest. For example, in the first paragraph of this passage, Eudora Welty describes Mrs. Calloway as having a "dragon eye." Her choice of the word *dragon* immediately conjures up an image of a fierce, frightening woman intent on guarding her treasured library. We'd get a completely different feeling about Mrs. Calloway if Welty had described her as having an "eagle eye" or an "observant eye."

As you can see, Welty's diction plays an important role in conveying her **tone,** or attitude toward her subject. Though the writer never comes out and directly states her feelings about Mrs. Calloway, her choice of words reveals her attitude. How would you describe Welty's tone?

Examining the Writer's Style

Working with a partner, study the effects of Welty's diction.

1. List all the adjectives, nouns, and adverbs Welty uses to describe Mrs. Calloway, her possessions, and her rules. How do these words make you feel about her? Do you and your partner agree?
2. Which of these descriptive words represent **objective** details—factual information that any observer can verify? Which are **subjective** details—unverifiable judgments, feelings, and thoughts?
3. Working independently, replace each of the words you've selected with a word or phrase that has a similar meaning but different **connotations.** Do these new words convey a different attitude toward Mrs. Calloway? Are they more **objective** than Welty's original words? Explain.
4. Now substitute words or phrases that represent a different type of **diction**—one that's more technical, colloquial, or flowery, or perhaps more

tactful than Welty's. Then compare your new word choices with your partner's. How do your changes affect the **tone** of the description?
4. What word does Welty's mother use to describe Eudora? What **connotations** does this word continue to have for the adult writer? (Would you like to be described this way?)

Using Effective Diction in Your Writing

Describing a Person. Write a paragraph describing someone you know or frequently encounter who has made a strong impression on you—a friend, relative, neighbor, mail carrier, police officer, or shopkeeper.

1. Describe this person's appearance, actions, voice, and **setting** (for example, the restaurant where you always see a certain waitress). Without coming out and directly stating your feelings about your subject, use precise, vivid words that reveal your attitude.
2. Exchange your description with a partner. Underline all the words you feel contribute to the **tone** of your classmate's description. Circle any words that strike you as vague or weak or clichéd, and suggest more vivid replacements. Then write a sentence summarizing your partner's attitude toward his or her subject. If your partner hasn't identified the tone you intended to convey, revise your description to express your feelings more precisely and vividly.

INFERRING THE MAIN IDEA

Writing Assignment

Write a two-paragraph essay in which you state the main idea of the following extract from *Hunger of Memory* by Richard Rodriguez.

Background

Writers can't, won't, and don't tell you everything. They don't define every word for you or explain every figure of speech. As you read, you have to make **inferences**—intelligent guesses based on the information you already know. Don't confuse the words *imply* and *infer*. A writer or speaker *implies* something by hinting at it but leaving it unsaid. Then a reader or listener *infers* the unstated information from the details that are given.

Prewriting

The following selection was written by a grown man looking back at his childhood. Richard Rodriguez was born in Mexico and moved to Sacramento, California, when he was a very young boy. These recollections date back to the 1950's, when he was a student in a Catholic school.

Notice that in order to understand this selection, you will have to make many inferences about words or customs that might be unfamiliar to you. To do this, you will have to use **context clues**, footnotes, and sometimes just hunches to guess at meanings.

The Church rocked through time—a cradle, an ark—to rhythms of sorrow and joy, marking the passage of man.

The Catholic calendar in my bedroom was printed by W. F. Gormley and Sons, morticians. Every month there was a different Bible picture in beautiful colors. Every day was something. The calendar noted ferial and ember days,[1] fish days and the feast days of saints. (My birthday honored St. Ignatius Loyola.) There was another, a "regular," calendar in the kitchen (Capitol Savings and Loan). It noted full moons and crescents and the official change of the seasons. My mother used the regular calendar to write down our doctors' appointments (shots; teeth).

It was the religious calendar that governed my school year. In early September there was a nine o'clock Mass on the Friday of the first week of school to pray for academic success. (Students were grouped according to class; behind my class would be my new teacher's face, a face I still wasn't used to.) In June there was a Mass of graduation for the eighth-graders. Between those events, school often stopped or flowered as routine bowed to the sacred. In the middle of a geography or an arithmetic lesson, the nuns would lead us out of our classrooms and we would walk—four hundred students in double lines—down a block to

Does this suggest something positive or negative? What do the cradle and ark suggest?

How are the calendars different? Does he seem to prefer one to the other?

---

1. **ferial and ember days:** Ferial days are days not designated for any particular festival or commemoration; ember days are days of special fasting and prayer.

church, stopping traffic (We were Catholics!) to attend a First Friday Mass or a rosary to Mary. We returned to the classroom, came back to the same paragraph in a still-opened book. Routine resumed. Sacred dramas of Church thus fitted into a day, never became the routine; rather they redeemed the routine. . . .

What does *redeemed* mean? How did he feel about the sacred "dramas"?

On Halloween night, all over Sacramento children dressed up as ghosts or Frankensteins or dime-store skeletons with phosphorescent bones. But only Catholic school kids went to Mass the next morning to honor the white-robed saints on the Feast of All Hallows. It was one of the "holy days of obligation"—a day on which I was obliged to go to morning Mass, but for the rest of the day I was free—no school. I could ride my bicycle around Sacramento; watch public school kids walking to school. And people downtown were passing just another day. (They seemed not to know.)

Did he mind being different?

In the secular[2] calendar there was no day like Ash Wednesday. All day I would see on the heedless foreheads of classmates the Hindu-like smudge of dark ash, the reminder of death. (. . . Unto dust thou shalt return.) One year a girl at school was killed in a car crash shortly after Ash Wednesday. I took the lesson.

Why does he say "Hindu-like"?

What does the saying in parentheses refer to? Is it from the Bible?
What lesson?

On those few occasions when secular Sacramento took up the sacred calendar they got it all wrong. Christmas downtown began in early November. Merchants would string tiny white lights up over K Street, where they shone through the night as pretty as heaven. But their Christmas ended in late afternoon on Christmas Eve—I saw department store clerks working against time to replace a holiday window display with deathly white piles of towels and sheets. In church, in early November there was Advent, the time for penance. On a table in front of the altar was a wreath with four candles stuck in, one of which was lit each week to mark the coming—the slow, slow coming—of Christ. In church Christmas began at midnight Mass, Christmas Eve. And the holy season continued until the Feast of Epiphany, the sixth of January, when carols were sung for the very last time and fir trees on the altar no longer cast their dark scent of damp earth.

What does "they got it all wrong" mean?

I wonder why he says "deathly white."

The secular calendar whirled like a carnival wheel and offered carnival prizes—a fat Santa instead of the infant God; colored eggs and chocolate bunnies instead of the death and resurrection of Christ. During Holy Week all pictures and statues in church were shrouded by purple silk drapes. On Holy Thursday to commemorate the Last Supper of Christ there was a "white" Mass

Which does he favor: the secular Christmas or the sacred one?

What are the connotations of "a carnival wheel"?

---

2. **secular:** nonreligious.

at sunset (when stained-glass windows burned briefly before the light failed). After that Mass the sacrament was removed to a side altar and the red sanctuary lamp was extinguished, so that the next day, Good Friday, when women in scarves and men in work clothes came to church for "the three hours," they found an altar stripped bare and the tabernacle gaping.

Do these images suggest that he found the rituals moving?

In our house on Good Friday we behaved as if a member of our family had died. There was no radio or television. But I noticed that the Standard gas station right across from church stayed open for business as usual and I saw people at the Laundromat watching their clothes tumble behind a round window—as if nothing in the world had happened. . . .

Why does he mention this observation?

The wheels turned. Two wheels of time. . . .

—from *Hunger of Memory*,
Richard Rodriguez

1. Before you write your essay, think about the answers to the marginal questions. If your teacher directs, you might discuss them in class or in small groups.
2. Next write down your own questions about the selection. What did you want to know as you read about the writer's responses to his early years? Were there any passages that you did not understand? Again, a discussion in class might help resolve some of your questions.
3. Find at least two key statements in the selection—general statements that Rodriguez makes about life or about his experiences. Write these statements down.
4. Look at the answers to your questions, and at the key statements you have written down, and make several **inferences** about the writer's **main idea.** Write your inferences down. At this point you might want to discuss your various inferences in class.
5. Select the **inference** that best covers the entire selection, not just part of it. Do the key statements you have written down relate to your **main idea?**

Writing

Organize your essay into two paragraphs. In your first paragraph, cite the title and author of the selection. Then state the main idea as you infer it, and use this as your **thesis statement.** In your second paragraph, cite at least two incidents or passages from the story (descriptions, images, or comments) that seem to support this **main idea.**

Checklist for Revision

1. Have you cited the selection's title and author?
2. Have you summed up the main idea and stated it as your thesis statement?
3. Have you cited episodes and quoted passages to support the main idea? Have you checked the quotations for accuracy, used quotations marks, and cited the pages on which the quotations appear?
4. Have you checked: Spelling? Punctuation? Capitalization? Sentence structure? Paragraph structure?

W riting history is a little like looking for the truth in a wilderness of conflicting facts and opinions. The first thing the writer finds when seeking facts is that generally there are either too few or too many. The poet William Shakespeare, for example, left behind the world's greatest poetry and drama— and amazingly few facts about his life. These facts are so few that some people have decided Shakespeare didn't even write the works attributed to him. How could he have, they reason, when he left so little evidence of himself for the biographer and historian?

The opposite problem—too many facts—sometimes obscures the subject, confuses the researcher, and makes evaluation difficult. Was General George Armstrong Custer a hero or a fool when he rode into the Battle of the Little Big Horn? Was his action one of misguided genius or pure incompetence? Mountains of facts and conflicting testimony cause historians difficulty when they try to answer questions such as these.

All along the line, historians must try to distinguish **facts** from **opinions.** A fact is something that can be proved true; an opinion cannot. It is a fact that the *Titanic* struck an iceberg and sank on the night of April 14—15, 1912; it is an opinion that the tragedy was avoidable.

Once writers have collected and evaluated their information, they face the equally difficult job of selecting and presenting their material. For example, in "R.M.S. Titanic," which you will read in this section, Hanson W. Baldwin chronicles the events of the night the *Titanic* sank. More than a thousand people were involved in the great sea disaster. Baldwin had to choose which stories to tell, which details to include, and which incidents to recount to give the reader a complete and realistic picture.

The historical accounts of the real people and real events that follow are the results of hundreds of hours of research—of interviewing, reading, sorting, discarding, arranging, and commenting. These are examples of historical writing at its best—when it can capture our imaginations and, like all literature, help us understand our complex world.

History: Seeking the Truth

(Left) A jubilant Harry S Truman displays a newspaper headline mistakenly announcing his expected defeat in the 1948 presidential election. (Below) The Apollo 12 Moonwalk, 1969.

AMUNDSEN AND SCOTT

Evan S. Connell

Novelist and essayist Evan Connell (1924–   ) was born in Kansas City, attended Dartmouth and the University of Kansas, and did graduate work at Columbia and Stanford. He is the author of several novels, including *Mr. Bridge* and *Mrs. Bridge*, which were made into a movie starring Paul Newman and Joanne Woodward.

Connell is also well known for his two collections of historical essays: *A Long Desire* and *The White Lantern*. Connell says that he is fascinated by the "age-old unappeasable desire" of human beings to seek out the unknown. His essays recount the "irrational, marvelous passion of history's adventurers" as they search for prehistoric humans, black holes, Linear B (an ancient Greek script), buried civilizations, and the South Pole.

In his essay "The White Lantern" (Chapter Five of the book of the same title), Connell traces the struggles of explorers to reach the South Pole in Antarctica. He tells about the adventures of the young Oxford graduate Apsley Cherry-Garrard, who went out one morning and returned five weeks later with frostbite, snow blindness, and three penguin eggs. He tells of the Australian physicist and geologist Sir Douglas Mawson, who survived his eighteen dogs and both of his companions while on a map-making expedition. Mawson—dangling at the end of a rope over a bottomless gorge, his clothing weighted with snow, dizzy, half starved, poisoned with overdoses of Vitamin A from eating dogs' livers—remarked to his rescuers that it was rather chilly. Connell also describes Sir Ernest Shackleton's failed attempt in 1908–1909 to reach the South Pole. Shackleton's fifty-year-old companion, Professor Edgeworth David, was so gentlemanly that when he slipped down a deep crack in a glacier, he apologized, "I am so sorry to disturb you, . . . but . . . I really don't think I can hold on much longer."

In the following excerpt from "The White Lantern," Connell describes the final conquest of the South Pole by two men of sharply contrasting temperaments. Read through to Connell's comment in paragraph 6 ("There we have it . . ."). Then stop and decide what you think his tone is going to be as he traces the journeys of the Norwegian explorer Roald Amundsen and the British explorer Robert Scott. The year is 1911.

The grand prize . . . was the mystic southern core, the symbolic end of the earth, the Geographic Pole. Shackleton almost made it but stopped ninety-seven miles short. Ninety-seven miles from immortality.

"We have shot our bolt," he writes in his journal. "We hoisted Her Majesty's flag, and the other Union Jack[1] afterward, and took possession of the plateau. . . . While the Union Jack blew out stiffly in the icy gale that cut us to the bone, we looked south with our powerful glasses, but could see nothing but the dead-white snow plain. There was no break in the plateau as it extended toward the Pole. . . ."

Amundsen and Scott are the illustrious names. They got to the Pole within five weeks of each other, which suggests nothing more than good luck and bad luck; but there was such a difference in what happened subsequently that luck cannot explain it. The explanation must be found in the characters of the two men, just as Mawson's trip can be explained only by his outrageous determination.

Roald Amundsen's opinion of luck is terse and revealing:

"Victory awaits those who have everything in order. People call this luck. Defeat awaits those who fail to take the necessary precautions. This is known as bad luck."

There we have it. To be lucky you must know what you are doing.

At the age of fifteen, after reading about Sir John Franklin's disastrous attempt to find a northwest passage, Amundsen began to get ready. He trained his body to endure hardship. He detested football, but forced himself to play it. He went skiing in the mountains whenever possible. He slept with his bedroom windows open all winter. He looked forward to the obligatory term of military service "both because I wanted to be a good citizen and because I felt that military training would be of great benefit to me as further preparation for my life."

When he was twenty-two, he persuaded a friend to go with him on a miniature polar passage. West of Oslo is a mile-high plateau extending nearly to the coast. In summer it is used by Lapp herdsmen pasturing reindeer, but when winter arrives, the Lapps descend to the valley and the plateau is deserted. There is no record of anyone ever having crossed it during winter. Amundsen resolved to cross it.

In the middle of their third night on the plateau he woke up because of a temperature change. Instead of sleeping on top of the snow he had burrowed into it, hoping to escape the wind, and while he lay snugly in the hole he had been pleased with himself for such a clever idea. He woke up lying on his back, feeling cramped. Without opening his eyes he tried to roll over but was unable to move. The damp snow of early evening had filled the entrance to his burrow, sifted over his sleeping bag, and then had frozen into a solid block of ice. He began struggling and shouting, but he was helpless—absolutely unable to move— and his voice probably was inaudible at the surface. He very soon quit shouting, he says, because it was hard to breathe, and he realized that if he did not keep quiet he would suffocate. Presumably his friend also had burrowed into the snow, which meant he must be trapped in the same way. Unless there should be a quick thaw they both would die in these ice coffins.

Amundsen does not know whether he fell asleep or fainted, but the next time he became conscious he heard the sound of digging. His friend had slept on the surface, too exhausted to do anything else, and was astonished when he woke up to find himself alone. The only trace of Amundsen was a tuft of hair at one corner of his sleeping bag. Another snow flurry would have hidden him until the Lapps returned.

They got back in such poor shape that people who had seen them eight days earlier did not recognize them.

Commenting on this experience years later, Amundsen remarks that an "adventure" is merely an interruption of an explorer's serious work and indicates bad planning.

This trip across the Norwegian plateau seems to have been rigorously educational. What he

---

1. **Union Jack:** the flag of the United Kingdom (Great Britain and Northern Ireland).

learned from it, beyond the danger of burrowing, cannot even be estimated; but it is obvious that, like most extraordinary people, he knew how to distinguish the shape of the world from a grain of sand. Again and again he talks about preparation. Planning. Attention to detail.

He chose the site of his South Polar base only after studying every existing description of the Ross Ice Shelf from the day it was discovered in 1841. Each member of his expedition was judiciously selected. Every bit of equipment, right down to the tent pegs and buttons, was inspected for weakness or inadequacy. He ordered the boots ripped apart and rebuilt according to his own ideas of comfort and safety. He insisted that a new dog whip be designed.

Aboard the *Fram,* in addition to nineteen men, were almost one hundred huskies. Amundsen was convinced that dogs were essential to success and he had a false deck constructed on the ship to protect them from the tropic sun. He watched their health as closely as he watched the health of his men. He had calculated the day-by-day weight of the sledges that must be hauled to the Pole, and he knew how much weight each animal could pull. As the journey progressed, the sledges would become lighter, which meant that fewer dogs would be required. Logistics demanded, therefore, that at a certain point a certain number of dogs be slaughtered. Yet even in death they must contribute. He had calculated that the average dog carried fifty pounds of edible meat. He worked out the precise day on which he intended to kill each dog, and he adhered to this schedule almost exactly.

Amundsen says nothing about the liver,[2] but Arctic Eskimos had known for a long time that you should not eat a husky's liver, and he probably was aware of this. He would not have known just why the liver was dangerous, but it would be characteristic of him to credit the Eskimos with some valid reason for their belief.

On the central plateau twenty-four huskies were killed.

"We had agreed to shrink from nothing," he wrote. "The pemmican[3] was cooked remarkably quickly that evening and I was unusually industrious in stirring it. I am not a nervous man, but at the sound of the first shot I found myself trembling. Shot now followed shot in quick succession, echoing uncannily over the great white plain. Each time a trusty servant lost his life."

The Norwegians afterward referred to this campground as the Butcher's Shop.

At first they were reluctant to devour their trusty servants, but the cook Wisting knew his trade. He selected a young animal named Rex.

"I could not take my eyes off his work," says Amundsen.

The delicate little cutlets had an absolutely hypnotizing effect as they were spread out one by one over the snow. They recalled memories of old days, when no doubt a dog cutlet would have been less tempting than now—memories of dishes on which the cutlets were elegantly arranged side by side, with paper frills on the bones, and a neat pile of petits pois[4] in the middle. Ah, my thoughts wandered still farther afield—but that does not concern us now, nor has it anything to do with the South Pole. . . . The meat was excellent, quite excellent, and one cutlet after another disappeared with lightninglike rapidity. I must admit that they would have lost nothing by being a little more tender, but one must not expect too much of a dog. At this first meal I finished five cutlets myself and looked in vain in the pot for more. Wisting appeared not to have reckoned on such a brisk demand.

About three o'clock on the afternoon of December 14, 1911, Amundsen's men calculated that they had reached the end of the trail.

There were no cheers, no orations. All together the five men grasped a Norwegian flag and thrust it into the snow: Amundsen, Sverre Hassel, Oskar Wisting, Helmer Hansen, Olav Bjaaland.

---

2. Dogs' livers contain high doses of Vitamin A, which makes them poisonous.

3. **pemmican:** dried lean meat, pounded into a paste with fat.
4. **petits pois** (pə·tē pwá′): (French) small green peas.

"Thus we plant thee, beloved flag, at the South Pole, and give to the plain on which it lies the name of King Haakon VII's plateau."

That brief speech was the only concession to ritual. One gets out of the way of protracted ceremonies in these regions, says Amundsen. The shorter they are, the better.

The Norwegians were in no hurry to leave. The trip had not been difficult, the weather was mild, and they had more than enough food. They stayed several days, taking measurements, circling the area on skis to be sure they truly had encompassed the Pole, and otherwise enjoyed themselves.

They were camped in the middle of a continent almost as large as Australia and Europe combined. The Ross Ice Shelf, over which they had traveled at the beginning, appears to be only a deep indentation on the map of Antarctica, although it is about the size of France. Ice has buried the entire continent—all of its mountains, plains, and valleys, with very few exceptions—in some places to a depth of two miles. Astronauts say that it is the earth's most noticeable feature and that it radiates light from the bottom of the world like a great white lantern.

Once upon a time Antarctica was different. There were pine forests, swamps, and fern jungles. Shackleton's party found a seam of coal eight feet thick near the top of Beardmore Glacier. Scott, following the same route, came across fossilized twigs and leaves:

"The best leaf impressions and the most obvious were in the rotten clumps of weathered coal which split up easily to sheath knife and hammer. Every layer of these gave abundant vegetable remains. Most of the bigger leaves were like beech leaves in shape and venation,[5] in size a little smaller than British beech."

On the Palmer Peninsula are traces of fig leaves, sequoia, and an evergreen called araucaria that reached a height of 150 feet and still grows in South America. At Mount Weaver, close to the Pole, is a petrified log eighteen inches in diameter; it dates from the Jurassic period, the age of dinosaurs. What reptiles, animals, and birds lived in prehistoric Antarctica is not known—except for

some ancestral families of the penguin, one of which grew as tall as a man.

Nor does anybody know what changed the climate. There are theories, but not much agreement.

At present more than a million people live within a radius of two thousand miles of the North Pole, yet within that radius of the South Pole—excluding the men at weather stations—there is no human life. There are no land animals or birds, only the indestructible aquatic penguin. There is not a single living tree. There are lichens clinging to exposed rocks, a little moss, some coarse grass, a few spiders and flies. The spiders do not spin webs because of the wind and the flies have no wings. These tiny creatures, as obstinate as Sir Douglas Mawson, spend most of their lives frozen stiff, but thaw out several days a year and hurriedly go about their business in order to maintain the species. Such is life today in Antarctica, which may explain why King Haakon's real estate has never been developed.

Before starting the return journey Amundsen lashed a small Norwegian flag to a tent pole. Inside the tent he left a bag containing a letter to the king, just in case they should not make it back to their ship. He discarded some items: reindeerskin foot bags, mitts, a sextant, a hypsometer case—which is an instrument for measuring heights above sea level. And he addressed a letter to Scott.

"He will be here sooner or later," Amundsen told a member of the party. "I hope for his sake it will be sooner."

What Amundsen meant was that the weather could only get worse.

Their trip home sounds idyllic. They had marked the route, and the wind and sun were at their backs. They planned to travel eighteen miles a day, which they did without effort in less than five hours. There was so much food that sometimes they threw away biscuits and pemmican, and fed chocolate to the dogs. The dogs had such an easy time pulling the sledges that they began to get fat.

"We were in high spirits and bowled along at a cracking pace. . . ."

They reached their base on January 25, the date

---

5. **venation** (vē·nā′shən): the arrangement or system of veins.

Amundsen had selected two years earlier in Norway. A week later the *Fram* sailed with all aboard in perfect health.

Scott at this time was hundreds of miles away, writing in his diary: "February 2. Three out of five of us injured. We shall be lucky if we get through. . . ."

On March 18 he wrote: "Ill fortune presses. . . ."

March 19: "The weather doesn't give us a chance. . . ."

Earlier he had told a Melbourne journalist: "We may get through, we may not. We may lose our lives. We may be wiped out. It is all a matter of providence and luck."

Shortly after that while en route to the Antarctic: ". . . fortune has determined to put every difficulty in our path."

Again, the following week: "I begin to wonder if fortune will ever turn her wheel."

At the start of the final journey: "The future is in the lap of the gods. . . ."

While struggling up Beardmore Glacier, unaware that Amundsen had just reached the Pole: "Our luck is very bad."

Eight days later: "I trust this may prove the turning point in our fortunes. . . ."

Near the end of March as he lay dying he wrote to the mother of one of his dead companions: "The ways of Providence are inscrutable. . . ."

And in his *Message to the Public,* found beside his body, he begins: "The causes of the disaster are not due to faulty organization, but to misfortune. . . ."

Perhaps. Perhaps he was right. Maybe all things rest in the lap of the gods. Maybe "faulty organization" was not the cause, though it is hard to forget something he had said ten years before:

"To my mind no journey ever made with dogs can approach the height of the fine conception which is realized when a party of men go forth to face hardships, dangers, and difficulties with their own unaided efforts, and by days and weeks of hard physical labor succeed in solving some problem of the great unknown. Surely in this case the conquest is more nobly and splendidly won."

It's arguable, of course, whether one should extract particular phrases from a man's life to

offer as proof of anything. On the subject of luck, for example, Amundsen himself occasionally referred to it without disdain, in a rather idle fashion, as something to be hoped for.

Still, there's a difference. And the difference becomes more significant when you learn what others thought about Scott. As a child he was so lethargic[6] and preoccupied that he was called "Old Moony." He seems to have been the storybook sissy: emotional, horrified at the sight of blood, physically weak, pampered by his mother and an older sister. A doctor who examined him before he joined the navy advised him to choose a different career.

Scott himself recognized his languid disposition and tried to do something about it; and considering how rapidly he was promoted in the navy, he must have changed. Yet in every photograph he looks bemused, tentative, almost doubtful. His stance, his expression—he lives far away from the frigid, brutal world of Roald Amundsen. Biographer Peter Brent speaks of a brooding, melancholy air. "His mouth, with its full, rounded lips, suggests a leaning toward sensuality and pleasure. . . ."

Scott's resemblance to his romantic kinsman, Sir Walter Scott, is startling; they look like brothers. And his written "impressions" of the Antarctic are what you might expect from a mystic poet, not an explorer:

The small green tent and the great white road.

The drift snow like finest flour penetrating every hole and corner—flickering up beneath one's head covering, pricking sharply as a sand blast.

The sun with blurred image peeping shyly through the wreathing drift giving pale shadowless light.

The eternal silence of the great white desert. Cloudy columns of snow drift advancing from the south, pale yellow wraiths, heralding the coming storm, blotting out one by one the sharp-cut lines of the land.

Given such a temperament, why was he chosen to lead an expedition? The answer seems to be

---

6. **lethargic** (li·thär'jik): abnormally drowsy or dull.

Captain Robert Falcon Scott (standing, center) and his party at the South Pole.

that as a midshipman he won a whaleboat race. This sounds like a petty triumph, but among the excited spectators was Sir Clements Markham, president of the Royal Geographical Society. He invited Scott to supper and later commented: "I was much struck with his intelligence, information, and the charm of his manner."

Because of Markham's patronage, when a British exploratory party sailed for the Antarctic in 1901, its commander was Scott. Even then he admits he is out of place: "I may as well confess that I have no predilection for polar exploration. . . ."

Subsequently he married an actress, Kathleen Bruce, and began to associate with actors, authors, painters, and musicians—a doubtful lot. How much these people unsettled him can only

be imagined. Once he wrote to Kathleen: "I seem to hold in reserve something that makes for success and yet to see no worthy field for it, and so there is this consciousness of a truly deep unrest."

Now listen to Roald Amundsen on the same subject: "Success is a woman who has to be won, not courted. You've got to seize her and carry her off, not stand under her window with a mandolin."

In 1910 when the South Polar expedition departed Scott once more was put in charge. And it is a little strange—or perhaps not—that the London *Evening Standard* should remark: "We may never see them again."

Scott's wife also had premonitions, confiding to her diary:

"I had rather a horrid day today. I woke up having a bad dream about you, and then Peter came very close to me and said emphatically, 'Daddy won't come back,' as though in answer to my silly thoughts.''

"I was very taken up with you all evening. I wonder if anything special is happening to you. Something odd happened to the clocks and watches between nine and ten p.m.''

"I was still rather taken up by you and a wee bit depressed. As you ought about now to be returning to ship I see no reason for depression. I wonder.''

Ernest Shackleton wrote to a New Zealand friend: "I suppose that we shall soon hear of Scott. I am inclined to think that we will hear from Amundsen first.''

Today, from this distance, as one reads about the expedition, a feeling of doom soars overhead like an albatross.[7] Aboard ship—even before they reach Antarctica—things do not go well. Icebergs appear father north than expected. Then a storm threatens the *Terra Nova,* and ten precious bags of coal which had not been lashed down must be jettisoned. At four in the morning the pumps become choked, water rises in the engine room, the men start bailing with buckets. A dog drowns. Two ponies die.

Upon reaching Antarctica they were unable to establish winter quarters on Cape Crozier as they had planned. Three motor sledges were brought along for heavy work, but one sledge broke through the ice and sank, so that in order to get the ponies' fodder ashore, the men harnessed themselves to bales of hay. And the expedition's photographer, standing quite literally on thin ice, was almost knocked into the water by a scheming killer whale.

About this time they got news of Amundsen, who had set up camp on an indentation sixty miles nearer the Pole. Scott wrote in his diary: "I never thought he could have got so many dogs safely to the ice. His plan for running them seems excellent. . . .''

Three more ponies died while the first depot was being stocked. Two more drowned when the ice disintegrated beneath them. And Scott writes: "I could not rid myself of the fear that misfortune was in the air. . . .''

Despite every problem he scrupulously kept his journal.

January 15: "We left our depot today with nine days' provisions, so that it ought to be a certain thing now, and the only appalling possibility the sight of the Norwegian flag forestalling ours.''

January 16: "The worst has happened. . . . Bowers's sharp eyes detected what he thought was a cairn;[8] he was uneasy about it, but argued that it might be sastrugus.[9] Half an hour later he detected a black speck ahead. Soon we knew that this could not be a natural snow feature. We marched on, found that it was a black flag tied to a sledge bearer; nearby the remains of a camp; sledge tracks and ski tracks coming and going and the clear trace of dogs' paws—many dogs.''

Next day Scott reached the Pole: "Great God! this is an awful place. . . .''

Inside the tent was Amundsen's message.

Poleheim
15 December 1911

Dear Captain Scott:

As you are probably the first to reach this area after us, I will ask you kindly to forward this letter to King Haakon VII. If you can use any of the articles left in this tent, please do not hesitate to do so. The sledge left outside may be of use to you. With best regards, I wish you a safe return.

Roald Amundsen

The British party stayed just long enough to verify the location. By their measurements, Amundsen's tent was only a few hundred yards from the geographical center.

It is hard to understand why they loitered on the way back. They did not have much food, the weather was savage, and they had nine hundred miles to go. But here is Scott's journal entry on February 8: "I decided to camp and spend the rest of the day geologizing. It has been extremely in-

---

7. **albatross:** a very large sea bird. In *The Rime of the Ancient Mariner* by Samuel Taylor Coleridge, the albatross is used as a symbol of guilt.

8. **cairn** (kern): a cone-shaped heap of stones built as a monument or landmark.
9. **sastrugus** (sas′trōō·gəs): a long, wavelike ridge of hard snow.

teresting. We found ourselves under perpendicular cliffs of Beacon sandstone, weathering rapidly and carrying veritable coal seams. From the last, Wilson, with his sharp eyes, has picked several plant impressions, the last a piece of coal with beautifully traced leaves in layers, also some excellently preserved impressions of thick stems, showing cellular structure. In one place we saw the cast of small waves in the sand.''

Why did they do this? Two explanations have been proposed. If they could bring back some scientific information that the Norwegians had overlooked, their defeat would not be total. Certainly they knew that. The other explanation, which seeps through Scott's journal like a stain, is that they sensed they could never make it. By now they were crippled and suffering from the cold. Wilson had pulled a tendon in his leg. Evans' hands were so badly frozen that his fingernails had begun to drop off. Oates's feet were turning black. Scott had injured his shoulder. Bowers seems to be the only one in good shape.

Yet the next day they again stopped to collect geological specimens. Scott remarks on "the delight of setting foot on rock after fourteen weeks of snow and ice.''

A few days later Evans died.

Temperatures dropped so low that in the mornings it took them an hour to put on their footgear. The cooking oil was almost gone. Food rations were cut. Scott meditates: "I wonder what is in store for us. . . .''

On the fifteenth of March while they waited in the tent for a blizzard to let up, Oates said, "I am just going outside and may be some time.'' His feet had become so painful that he could hardly walk, and he did not want to delay the other men.

The bodies of Scott, Bowers, and Wilson were discovered eleven miles from a food depot. Their tent was almost buried by snow. The men lay in their sleeping bags, Wilson with his hands folded on his chest. Bowers also appeared to have died without anguish. Between them lay Scott, the flaps of his sleeping bag open. His diaries were in a green wallet underneath the bag, the last letters on a groundsheet beside him. His left arm was extended, his hand resting on Wilson's shoulder. The interior of the tent had been kept neat. There

was an improvised lamp, a bag of tea, a bag of tobacco, and their scientific notes.

Outside stood the sledge. Along with the necessities, it carried thirty-five pounds of rock.

Scott's wife was aboard ship en route to New Zealand to meet him when she learned of his death—five days after the captain got the news by radio. The captain had been so distressed that he could not approach her. She reports in her diary that his hands trembled when he finally showed her the message. After reading it she said to him: "Oh, well, never mind! I expected that. Thanks very much. I will go and think about it.''

Then, as she usually did each morning on the ship, she took a Spanish lesson. Then she ate lunch and discussed American politics and in the afternoon spent a while reading about the *Titanic*, determined to avoid thinking of her husband's death until she was sure she could control herself.

She mentions that because it was too hot to go to her cabin, she stayed on deck the whole day. Immediately after this commonplace statement, and without a pause, as though it were the most natural sequence in the world, she writes the following passage: "My god is godly. I need not touch him to know that. Let me maintain a high, adoring exaltation, and not let the sorrow of contamination touch me. Within I shall be exultant. My god is glorious and could never become less so. Loneliness is a fear that I have never known. Had he died before I had known his gloriousness or before he had been the father of my son, I might have felt a loss. Now I have felt none for myself. Won't anybody understand that?—probably nobody. So I must go on and on with the tedious business of discretion. Must even the greatest visions of the heart be blurred by discretions?''

That last line, once you have memorized it, cannot ever be forgotten, although when analyzed it doesn't make much sense. It suggests some deep communication with her husband, nothing more. But that's all right; many of Shakespeare's indelible lines don't make sense.

What is curious and moving about this passage is the radiance emanating from Scott through the adoration of his wife. To arouse such transcendent feelings in a woman he must have been extraordinary. And that such a man should have been misplaced seems all the more pathetic.

Just as curious—perhaps more so—is the fact that Amundsen, the victor, is not as renowned as the loser. Quite a few people think Scott was the first man to reach the South Pole. There is no logical explanation for this belief, though his dramatic death may account for it, together with the fact that he and his companions are still there—frozen like insects or splinters on the side of the great white lantern. However, they won't stay there indefinitely. Calculations by scientists at McMurdo Sound indicate that the bodies now lie fifty feet beneath the surface and fifteen miles closer to the edge of the ice shelf. What this means is that sometime in the future Scott and his companions will be carried out to sea on an iceberg.

As for Roald Amundsen, who knows what became of him? Almost no one. He died on a gallant but useless errand, searching for General Umberto Nobile, whose dirigible crash-landed in the Arctic. Amundsen's plane may have developed engine trouble; pieces of it were found off the Norwegian coast. The plane had been lent by the French government, which had at that time two modern seaplanes: one with a water-cooled engine, the other with an air-cooled engine. The French, exhibiting that singular wisdom we have come to associate with all federal government, provided Amundsen with the water-cooled engine for his long flight through subzero temperatures.

A Swedish pilot later rescued the Italian general.

Scott is now remembered and honored throughout the English-speaking world, while Amundsen is not. One might say this is folly, because Amundsen has more to teach us. But in the end, of course, they are equally instructive.

Responding to the Account

Analyzing the Account

Identifying Facts

1. Cite the passage that explains the meaning of the essay's **title**, "The White Lantern."
2. Connell says that the explanation for the very different fates of Amundsen and Scott in the Antarctic "must be found in the characters of the two men," and throughout the excerpt he contrasts those two characters. Summarize the **characteristics** of each explorer.
3. Find the passages that present Amundsen's attitudes toward the ideas of "luck," "adventure," and "success." Find the passages that reveal, in contrast, Scott's attitudes.
4. How do dogs account for one man's success and the other's failure?

Interpreting Meanings

5. What does Connell imply is the reason (or reasons) that Scott failed and Amundsen succeeded? Cite the passages that support your answer. Do you agree with Connell?
6. When the news of Scott's death reaches his wife, both her behavior and the words she writes are unexpected. She seems to know this, for she writes, "Won't anybody understand that?—probably nobody." Do you understand? She ends a paragraph, "Must even the greatest visions of the heart be blurred by discretions?" and Connell remarks that this unforgettable line, "when analyzed, doesn't make much sense." What sense do you make of it?
7. Explain the **irony** of the following statement about the cause of Amundsen's death: "The French, exhibiting that singular wisdom we have come to associate with all federal government, provided Amundsen with the water-cooled engine for his long flight through subzero temperatures."
8. Why do you suppose that Scott is the more renowned and honored of the two explorers? Why does Connell say that, although Amundsen has more to teach us, "in the end, of course, they are equally instructive"?
9. Connell learned about his subject matter through research rather than personal experience, but he is not strictly an objective re-

porter. From time to time we hear his voice as author, interpreting, pointing out an **irony,** or intruding a sudden informal or humorous element. For example, on page 476:

> There we have it. To be lucky you must know what you are doing.

Find at least three other passages where you are aware of the author's **tone.** What did you think of the writer's intrusions?

10. What do you suppose motivates people to go to inaccessible places like the South Pole? How would you respond if you had a chance to join such an expedition?

Writing About the Account

A Creative Response

1. **Imagining a Character's Reaction.** On page 482 Connell quotes in its entirety the letter that Amundsen left at the South Pole for Captain Scott. Imagine that you are Scott. You have lost your equipment, dogs, and ponies; your companions are injured; and you sense impending doom. Then you discover that "The worst has happened, . . ." that Amundsen has beaten you to the Pole. How would Amundsen's letter affect you? How would you feel about Amundsen himself? Write a paragraph describing Scott's response. Use the first-person pronoun *I*.

2. **Writing a Letter.** What sort of letter do you think Scott might have written to Amundsen if *he* had been the first to reach the Pole? Write the imagined text of Scott's victory letter.

A Critical Response

3. **Analyzing Characters.** In a three-paragraph essay, analyze the characters of Amundsen and Scott, based on what Connell tells you here. In your first paragraph, summarize how Connell feels about each explorer. Cite passages from the account to support your statements. In your second paragraph, tell whether or not you think the writings of the two men support the impression Connell gives you. In your third paragraph, describe your own feelings for the two men—did one appeal to you more than the other? Why?

4. **Responding to an Attitude.** On page 481 Amundsen is quoted as saying: "Success is a woman who has to be won, not courted. You've got to seize her and carry her off, not stand under her window with a mandolin." In a paragraph, respond to this **metaphor.** What might it reveal about Amundsen's attitude toward women?

Analyzing Language and Vocabulary

"Loaded" Words

This account of the two explorers could have been written as an **objective** historical report, but it was not. Connell clearly has feelings about the two men, and he chooses his words to convey these feelings to his readers. For example, on page 480 Connell describes Scott when he was young:

> As a child he was so lethargic and preoccupied that he was called "Old Moony."

Another historian might have had different feelings about Scott and written the following:

> As a child he was so thoughtful that he was called "Old Moony."

The adjectives in Connell's description carry strong **connotations.** The word *lethargic* suggests a dull, sluggish state, a kind of apathy or lack of interest in anything. *Preoccupied* suggests that the person is not connected with things going on around him, but instead is engrossed only in his or her own thoughts. Both words are **loaded** with judgments.

Here are some other passages that use loaded words. Explain what impression each italicized word or phrase creates. Then rewrite the passage to convey different impressions.

1. "He seems to have been the storybook *sissy: emotional, horrified* at the sight of blood, *physically weak, pampered* by his mother and an older sister."

2. "Scott himself recognized his *languid* disposition. . . ."

3. "Yet in every photograph he looks *bemused, tentative,* almost *doubtful.*"

4. ". . . he lives far away from the *frigid, brutal* world of Roald Amundsen."

5. " 'His mouth, with its *full, rounded* lips, suggests a leaning toward *sensuality* and *pleasure.* . . .' "

6. "The other explanation, which *seeps through Scott's journal like a stain,* is that they sensed they could never make it."

7. ". . . he and his companions are still there— frozen *like insects or splinters on the side of the great white lantern.*"

Hanson Weightman Baldwin (1903–   ), born in Baltimore, Maryland, graduated with an ensign's commission from the U. S. Naval Academy at Annapolis. After three years of service aboard battleships, Baldwin resigned from the Navy and launched a new career as a military correspondent and editor. His longest association was with the *New York Times.*

During World War II Baldwin covered battles in North Africa and the Normandy invasion. He wrote a series of articles on the war in the South Pacific that won him a Pulitzer Prize in 1942. After the war, he reported on the second atom-bomb test at Bikini Island, on guided-missile and rocket-firing installations, and on the organization of American military forces in the nuclear age.

Relatively early in his writing career (1934), Baldwin wrote an article for *Harper's* magazine about the sinking of the ship *Titanic* some twenty-two years earlier. He researched thoroughly, piecing together information from logs, interviews, and written accounts of the events of the catastrophic night when the "unsinkable" ship went down.

The sinking of the *Titanic* will remind you of other disaster stories. Reporters can present such catastrophes in several ways. The worst writers aim for sensational effects; they pander to the public's appetite for thrills and shocks to a point where their accounts become not only mawkish and sentimental, but also inaccurate. Other writers strive for a dramatic, attention-riveting presentation of the facts. Still others fictionalize the event, making up details they could not possibly know about. What tone does Baldwin strike immediately, with his first paragraph?

R.M.S. TITANIC

Hanson W. Baldwin

I

The White Star liner *Titanic,* largest ship the world had ever known, sailed from Southampton on her maiden voyage to New York on April 10, 1912. The paint on her strakes was fair and bright; she was fresh from Harland and Wolff's Belfast yards, strong in the strength of her forty-six thousand tons of steel, bent, hammered, shaped, and riveted through the three years of her slow birth.

There was little fuss and fanfare at her sailing; her sister ship, the *Olympic*—slightly smaller than the *Titanic*—had been in service for some months and to her had gone the thunder of the cheers.

But the *Titanic* needed no whistling steamers or shouting crowds to call attention to her superlative qualities. Her bulk dwarfed the ships near her as longshoremen singled up her mooring lines and cast off the turns of heavy rope from the dock bollards. She was not only the largest ship afloat, but was believed to be the safest. Carlisle, her builder, had given her double bottoms and had divided her hull into sixteen watertight compartments, which made her, men thought, unsinkable. She had been built to be and had been described as a gigantic lifeboat. Her designers' dreams of a triple-screw giant, a luxurious, floating hotel, which could speed to New York at twenty-three knots, had been carefully translated from blueprints and mold loft lines at the Belfast yards into a living reality.

The *Titanic's* sailing from Southampton, though quiet, was not wholly uneventful. As the liner moved slowly toward the end of her dock that April day, the surge of her passing sucked away from the quay the steamer *New York,* moored just to seaward of the *Titanic's* berth. There were sharp cracks as the manila mooring lines of the *New York* parted under the strain. The frayed

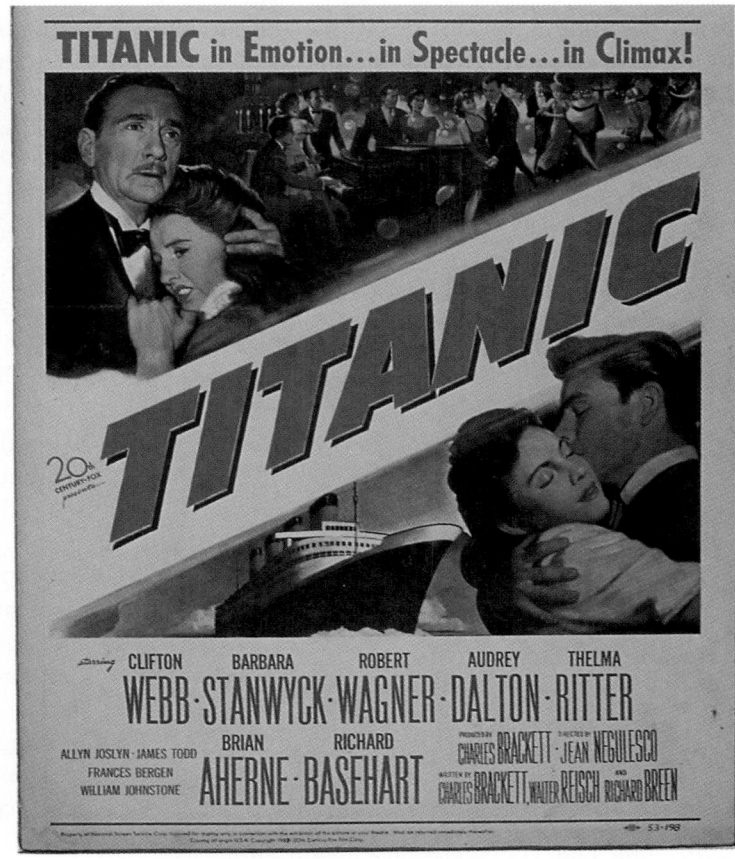

Poster for the 1953 movie *Titanic*. Survivors of the 1912 disaster were invited to the film's preview showing.

ropes writhed and whistled through the air and snapped down among the waving crowd on the pier; the *New York* swung toward the *Titanic*'s bow, was checked and dragged back to the dock barely in time to avert a collision. Seamen muttered, thought it an ominous start.

Past Spithead and the Isle of Wight the *Titanic* steamed. She called at Cherbourg at dusk and then laid her course for Queenstown.[1] At 1:30 P.M. on Thursday, April 11, she stood out of Queenstown harbor, screaming gulls soaring in her wake, with 2,201 persons—men, women, and children—aboard.

Occupying the Empire bedrooms and Georgian suites of the first-class accommodations were many well-known men and women—Colonel John Jacob Astor and his young bride; Major Archibald Butt, military aide to President Taft, and his friend Frank D. Millet, the painter; John B. Thayer, vice-president of the Pennsylvania Railroad, and Charles M. Hays, president of the Grand Trunk Railway of Canada; W. T. Stead, the English journalist; Jacques Futrelle, French novelist; H. B. Harris, theatrical manager, and Mrs. Harris; Mr. and Mrs. Isidor Straus; and J. Bruce Ismay, chairman and managing director of the White Star Line.

Down in the plain wooden cabins of the steerage class were 706 immigrants to the land of promise, and trimly stowed in the great holds was a cargo valued at $420,000: oak beams, sponges, wine, calabashes, and an odd miscellany of the common and the rare.

The *Titanic* took her departure on Fastnet Light and, heading into the night, laid her course for New York. She was due at Quarantine the following Wednesday morning.

---

1. **Queenstown:** the name the British gave to Cork City, Ireland.

Sunday dawned fair and clear. The *Titanic* steamed smoothly toward the west, faint streamers of brownish smoke trailing from her funnels. The purser held services in the saloon in the morning; on the steerage deck aft the immigrants were playing games and a Scotsman was puffing "The Campbells are Coming" on his bagpipes in the midst of the uproar.

At 9:00 A.M. a message from the steamer *Caronia* sputtered into the wireless shack:

> Captain, *Titanic*—Westbound steamers report bergs growlers and field ice in 42 degrees N. from 49 degrees to 51 degrees W. 12th April.
>
> Compliments—
Barr.

It was cold in the afternoon; the sun was brilliant, but the *Titanic,* her screws turning over at seventy-five revolutions per minute, was approaching the Banks.

In the Marconi cabin[2] Second Operator Harold Bride, earphones clamped on his head, was figuring accounts; he did not stop to answer when he heard *MWL,* Continental Morse for the nearby Leyland liner, *Californian,* calling the *Titanic.* The *Californian* had some message about three icebergs; he didn't bother then to take it down. About 1:42 P.M. the rasping spark of those days spoke again across the water. It was the *Baltic,* calling the *Titanic,* warning her of ice on the steamer track. Bride took the message down and sent it up to the bridge. The officer-of-the-deck glanced at it; sent it to the bearded master of the *Titanic,* Captain E. C. Smith, a veteran of the White Star service. It was lunchtime then; the Captain, walking along the promenade deck, saw Mr. Ismay, stopped, and handed him the message without comment. Ismay read it, stuffed it in his pocket, told two ladies about the icebergs, and resumed his walk. Later, about 7:15 P.M., the Captain requested the return of the message in order to post it in the chart room for the information of officers.

Dinner that night in the Jacobean dining room was gay. It was bitter on deck, but the night was calm and fine; the sky was moonless but studded with stars twinkling coldly in the clear air.

After dinner some of the second-class passengers gathered in the saloon, where the Reverend Mr. Carter conducted a "hymn sing-song." It was almost ten o'clock and the stewards were waiting with biscuits and coffee as the group sang:

> "O, hear us when we cry to Thee
> For those in peril on the sea."

On the bridge Second Officer Lightoller—short, stocky, efficient—was relieved at ten o'clock by First Officer Murdoch. Lightoller had talked with other officers about the proximity of ice; at least five wireless ice warnings had reached the ship; lookouts had been cautioned to be alert; captains and officers expected to reach the field at any time after 9:30 P.M. At twenty-two knots, its speed unslackened, the *Titanic* plowed on through the night.

Lightoller left the darkened bridge to his relief and turned in. Captain Smith went to his cabin. The steerage was long since quiet; in the first and second cabins lights were going out; voices were growing still, people were asleep. Murdoch paced back and forth on the bridge, peering out over the dark water, glancing now and then at the compass in front of Quartermaster Hichens at the wheel.

In the crow's-nest, Lookout Frederick Fleet and his partner, Leigh, gazed down at the water, still and unruffled in the dim, starlit darkness. Behind and below them the ship, a white shadow with here and there a last winking light; ahead of them a dark and silent and cold ocean.

There was a sudden clang. "Dong-dong. Dong-dong. Dong-dong. Dong!" The metal clapper of the great ship's bell struck out 11:30. Mindful of the warnings, Fleet strained his eyes, searching the darkness for the dreaded ice. But there were only the stars and the sea.

In the wireless room, where Phillips, first operator, had relieved Bride, the buzz of the *Californian's* set again crackled into the earphones:

Californian: "Say, old man, we are stuck here, surrounded by ice."

Titanic: "Shut up, shut up; keep out. I am talking to Cape Race; you are jamming my signals."

Then, a few minutes later—about 11:40 . . .

---

2. **Marconi cabin:** the room where messages were received and sent on the wireless telegraph.

II

Out of the dark she came, a vast, dim, white, monstrous shape, directly in the *Titanic*'s path. For a moment Fleet doubted his eyes. But she was a deadly reality, this ghastly *thing*. Frantically, Fleet struck three bells—*something dead ahead*. He snatched the telephone and called the bridge:

"Iceberg! Right ahead!"

The First Officer heard but did not stop to acknowledge the message.

"Hard-a-starboard!"

Hichens strained at the wheel; the bow swung slowly to port. The monster was almost upon them now.

Murdoch leaped to the engine-room telegraph. Bells clanged. Far below in the engine room those bells struck the first warning. Danger! The indicators on the dial faces swung round to "Stop!" Then "Full speed astern!" Frantically the engineers turned great valve wheels; answered the bridge bells. . . .

There was a slight shock, a brief scraping, a small list to port. Shell ice—slabs and chunks of it—fell on the foredeck. Slowly the *Titanic* stopped.

Captain Smith hurried out of his cabin.

"What has the ship struck?"

Murdoch answered, "An iceberg, sir. I hard-a-starboarded and reversed the engines, and I was going to hard-a-port around it, but she was too close. I could not do any more. I have closed the watertight doors."

Fourth Officer Boxhall, other officers, the carpenter, came to the bridge. The Captain sent Boxhall and the carpenter below to ascertain the damage.

A few lights switched on in the first and second cabins; sleepy passengers peered through porthole glass; some casually asked the stewards:

"Why have we stopped?"

"I don't know, sir, but I don't suppose it is anything much."

In the smoking room a quorum³ of gamblers and their prey were still sitting round a poker table; the usual crowd of kibitzers looked on. They had felt the slight jar of the collision and had seen an eighty-foot ice mountain glide by the smoking-room windows, but the night was calm and clear, the *Titanic* was "unsinkable"; they hadn't bothered to go on deck.

But far below, in the warren⁴ of passages on the starboard side forward, in the forward holds and boiler rooms, men could see that the *Titanic*'s hurt was mortal. In No. 6 boiler room, where the red glow from the furnaces lighted up the naked, sweaty chests of coal-blackened firemen, water was pouring through a great gash about two feet above the floor plates. This was no slow leak; the ship was open to the sea; in ten minutes there were eight feet of water in No. 6. Long before then the stokers had raked the flaming fires out of the furnaces and had scrambled through the watertight doors into No. 5 or had climbed up the long steel ladders to safety. When Boxhall looked at the mailroom in No. 3 hold, twenty-four feet above the keel, the mailbags were already floating about in the slushing water. In No. 5 boiler room a stream of water spurted into an empty bunker. All six compartments forward of No. 4 were open to the sea; in ten seconds the iceberg's jagged claw had ripped a three-hundred-foot slash in the bottom of the great *Titanic*.

Reports came to the bridge; Ismay in dressing gown ran out on deck in the cold, still, starlit night, climbed up the bridge ladder.

"What has happened?"

Captain Smith: "We have struck ice."

"Do you think she is seriously damaged?"

Captain Smith: "I'm afraid she is."

Ismay went below and passed Chief Engineer William Bell, fresh from an inspection of the damaged compartments. Bell corroborated the Captain's statement; hurried back down the glistening steel ladders to his duty. Man after man followed him—Thomas Andrews, one of the ship's designers, Archie Frost, the builder's chief engineer, and his twenty assistants—men who had no posts of duty in the engine room, but whose traditions called them there.

---

3. **quorum:** the number required to play a particular game.

4. **warren:** a crowded area, like a rabbit warren.

On deck, in corridor and stateroom, life flowed again. Men, women, and children awoke and questioned; orders were given to uncover the lifeboats; water rose into the firemen's quarters; halfdressed stokers streamed up on deck. But the passengers—most of them—did not know that the *Titanic* was sinking. The shock of the collision had been so slight that some were not awakened by it; the *Titanic* was so huge that she must be unsinkable; the night was too calm, too beautiful, to think of death at sea.

Captain Smith half ran to the door of the radio shack. Bride, partly dressed, eyes dulled with sleep, was standing behind Phillips, waiting.

"Send the call for assistance."

The blue spark danced: "CQD—CQD—CQD—CQ—"

Miles away Marconi men heard. Cape Race heard it, and the steamships *La Provence* and *Mt. Temple*.

The sea was surging into the *Titanic*'s hold. At 12:20 the water burst into the seamen's quarters through a collapsed fore-and-aft wooden bulkhead. Pumps strained in the engine rooms—men and machinery making a futile fight against the sea. Steadily the water rose.

The boats were swung out—slowly; for the deckhands were late in reaching their stations; there had been no boat drill, and many of the crew did not know to what boats they were assigned. Orders were shouted; the safety valves had lifted, and steam was blowing off in a great rushing roar. In the chart house Fourth Officer Boxhall bent above a chart, working rapidly with pencil and dividers.

12:25 A.M. Boxhall's position is sent out to a fleet of vessels: "Come at once; we have struck a berg."

To the Cunarder *Carpathia* (Arthur Henry Rostron, Master, New York to Liverpool, fifty-eight miles away): "It's a CQD, old man. Position 41–46 N.; 50–14 W."

The blue spark dancing: "Sinking; cannot hear for noise of steam."

12:30 A.M. The word is passed: "Women and children in the boats." Stewards finish waking their passengers below; life preservers are tied on;

some men smile at the precaution. "The *Titanic* is unsinkable." The *Mt. Temple* starts for the *Titanic;* the *Carpathia,* with a double watch in her stokeholds, radios, "Coming hard." The CQD changes the course of many ships—but not of one; the operator of the *Californian,* nearby, has just put down his earphones and turned in.

The CQD flashes over land and sea from Cape Race to New York; newspaper city rooms leap to life and presses whir.

On the *Titanic,* water creeps over the bulkhead between Nos. 5 and 6 firerooms. She is going down by the head; the engineers—fighting a losing battle—are forced back foot by foot by the rising water. Down the promenade deck, Happy Jock Hume, the bandsman, runs with his instrument.

12:45 A.M. Murdoch, in charge on the starboard side, eyes tragic, but calm and cool, orders boat No. 7 lowered. The women hang back; they want no boat ride on an ice-strewn sea; the *Titanic* is unsinkable. The men encourage them, explain that this is just a precautionary measure: "We'll see you again at breakfast." There is little confusion; passengers stream slowly to the boat deck. In the steerage the immigrants chatter excitedly.

A sudden sharp hiss—a streaked flare against the night; Boxhall sends a rocket toward the sky. It explodes, and a parachute of white stars lights up the icy sea. "God! Rockets!" The band plays ragtime.

No. 8 is lowered, and No. 5. Ismay, still in dressing gown, calls for women and children, handles lines, stumbles in the way of an officer, is told to "get the hell out of here." Third Officer Pitman takes charge of No. 5; as he swings into the boat, Murdoch grasps his hand. "Goodbye and good luck, old man."

No. 6 goes over the side. There are only twenty-eight people in a lifeboat with a capacity of sixty-five.

A light stabs from the bridge; Boxhall is calling in Morse flashes, again and again, to a strange ship stopped in the ice jam five to ten miles away. Another rocket drops its shower of sparks above the ice-strewn sea and the dying ship.

1:00 A.M. Slowly the water creeps higher; the fore ports of the *Titanic* are dipping into the sea. Rope squeaks through blocks; lifeboats drop jerk-

ily seaward. Through the shouting on the decks comes the sound of the band playing ragtime.

The "Millionaires' Special" leaves the ship—boat No. 1, with a capacity of forty people, carries only Sir Cosmo and Lady Duff Gordon and ten others. Aft, the frightened immigrants mill and jostle and rush for a boat. An officer's fist flies out; three shots are fired in the air, and the panic is quelled. . . . Four Chinese sneak unseen into a boat and hide in the bottom.

1:20 A.M. Water is coming into No. 4 boiler room. Stokers slice and shovel as water laps about their ankles—steam for the dynamos, steam for the dancing spark! As the water rises, great ash hoes rake the flaming coals from the furnaces. Safety valves pop; the stokers retreat aft, and the watertight doors clang shut behind them.

The rockets fling their splendor toward the stars. The boats are more heavily loaded now, for the passengers know the *Titanic* is sinking. Women cling and sob. The great screws aft are rising clear of the sea. Half-filled boats are ordered to come alongside the cargo ports and take on more passengers, but the ports are never opened—and the boats are never filled. Others pull for the steamer's light miles away, but never reach it; the lights disappear; the unknown ship steams off.

The water rises and the band plays ragtime.

1:30 A.M. Lightoller is getting the port boats off; Murdoch, the starboard. As one boat is lowered into the sea, a boat officer fires his gun along the ship's side to stop a rush from the lower decks. A woman tries to take her Great Dane into a boat with her; she is refused and steps out of the boat to die with her dog. Millet's "little smile which played on his lips all through the voyage" plays no more; his lips are grim, but he waves goodbye and brings wraps for the women.

Benjamin Guggenheim, in evening clothes, smiles and says, "We've dressed up in our best and are prepared to go down like gentlemen."

1:40 A.M. Boat 14 is clear, and then 13, 16, 15, and C. The lights still shine, but the *Baltic* hears the blue spark say, "Engine room getting flooded."

The *Olympia* signals, "Am lighting up all possible boilers as fast as can."

Major Butt helps women into the last boats and waves goodbye to them. Mrs. Straus puts her foot on the gunwale of a lifeboat; then she draws back and goes to her husband: "We have been together many years; where you go, I will go." Colonel John Jacob Astor puts his young wife in a lifeboat, steps back, taps cigarette on fingernail: "Goodbye, dearie; I'll join you later."

1:45 A.M. The foredeck is under water; the fo'c'sle head almost awash; the great stern is lifted high toward the bright stars; and still the band plays. Mr. and Mrs. Harris approach a lifeboat arm in arm.

Officer: "Ladies, first, please."

Harris bows, smiles, steps back: "Of course, certainly; ladies first."

Boxhall fires the last rocket, then leaves in charge of boat No. 2.

2:00 A.M. She is dying now; her bow goes deeper, her stern higher. But there must be steam. Below in the stokeholds the sweaty firemen keep steam up for the flaring lights and the dancing spark. The glowing coals slide and tumble over the slanted grate bars; the sea pounds behind that yielding bulkhead. But the spark dances on.

The *Asian* hears Phillips try the new signal—SOS.

Boat No. 4 has left now; boat D leaves ten minutes later. Jacques Futrelle clasps his wife: "For God's sake, go! It's your last chance; go!" Madame Futrelle is half forced into the boat. It clears the side.

There are about 660 people in the boats, and 1,500 still on the sinking *Titanic*.

On top of the officers' quarters, men work frantically to get the two collapsibles stowed there over the side. Water is over the forward part of A deck now; it surges up the companionways toward the boat deck. In the radio shack, Bride has slipped a coat and life jacket about Phillips as the first operator sits hunched over his key, sending—still sending—"41–46 N.; 50–14 W. CQD—CQD—SOS—SOS—"

The captain's tired white face appears at the radio-room door: "Men, you have done your full duty. You can do no more. Now, it's every man for himself." The captain disappears—back to his sinking bridge, where Painter, his personal steward, stands quietly waiting for orders. The spark dances on. Bride turns his back and goes into the inner cabin. As he does so, a stoker, grimed with coal, mad with fear, steals into the shack and reaches for the life jacket on Phillips' back. Bride wheels about and brains him with a wrench.

2:10 A.M. Below decks the steam is still holding, though the pressure is falling—rapidly. In the gymnasium on the boat deck, the athletic instructor watches quietly as two gentlemen ride the bicycles and another swings casually at the punching bag. Mail clerks stagger up the boat-deck stairways, dragging soaked mail sacks. The spark still dances. The band still plays—but not ragtime:

> "Nearer my God to Thee,
> Nearer to Thee . . ."

A few men take up the refrain; others kneel on the slanting decks to pray. Many run and scramble aft, where hundreds are clinging above the silent screws on the great uptilted stern. The spark still dances and the lights still flare; the engineers are on the job. The hymn comes to its close. Bandmaster Hartley, Yorkshireman violinist, taps his bow against a bulkhead, calls for "Autumn" as the water curls about his feet, and the eight musicians brace themselves against the ship's slant. People are leaping from the decks into the nearby water—the icy water. A woman cries, "Oh, save me, save me!" A man answers, "Good lady, save yourself. Only God can save you now." The band plays "Autumn":

> "God of Mercy and Compassion!
> Look with pity on my pain . . ."

The water creeps over the bridge where the *Titanic*'s master stands; heavily he steps out to meet it.

2:17 A.M. "CQ—" The *Virginian* hears a ragged, blurred CQ, then an abrupt stop. The blue spark dances no more. The lights flicker out; the engineers have lost their battle.

2:18 A.M. Men run about blackened decks; leap into the night; are swept into the sea by the curling wave which licks up the *Titanic*'s length. Lightoller does not leave the ship; the ship leaves him; there are hundreds like him, but only a few who live to tell of it. The funnels still swim above the water, but the ship is climbing to the perpendicular; the bridge is under and most of the foremast; the great stern rises like a squat leviathan.[5] Men swim away from the sinking ship; others drop from the stern.

The band plays in the darkness, the water lapping upwards:

> "Hold me up in mighty waters,
> Keep my eyes on things above,
> Righteousness, divine atonement,
> Peace and everlas . . ."

The forward funnel snaps and crashes into the sea; its steel tons hammer out of existence swimmers struggling in the freezing water. Streams of sparks, of smoke and steam, burst from the after funnels. The ship upends to 50—to 60 degrees.

Down in the black abyss of the stokeholds, of the engine rooms, where the dynamos have whirred at long last to a stop, the stokers and the engineers are reeling against the hot metal, the rising water clutching at their knees. The boilers, the engine cylinders, rip from their bed plates; crash through bulkheads; rumble—steel against steel.

The *Titanic* stands on end, poised briefly for the plunge. Slowly she slides to her grave—slowly at first, and then more quickly—quickly—quickly.

2:20 A.M. The greatest ship in the world has sunk. From the calm, dark waters, where the floating lifeboats move, there goes up, in the white wake of her passing, "one long continuous moan."

III

The boats that the *Titanic* had launched pulled safely away from the slight suction of the sinking ship, pulled away from the screams that came from the lips of the freezing men and women in the water. The boats were poorly manned and badly equipped, and they had been unevenly loaded. Some carried so few seamen that women bent to the oars. Mrs. Astor tugged at an oar handle; the Countess of Rothes took a tiller. Shivering stokers in sweaty, coal-blackened singlets and light trousers steered in some boats; stewards in white coats rowed in others. Ismay was in the last boat that left the ship from the starboard side; with Mr. Carter of Philadelphia and two seamen he tugged at the oars. In one of the lifeboats an Italian with a broken wrist—disguised in a woman's shawl and hat—huddled on the floorboards, ashamed now that fear had left him. In another rode the only baggage saved from the *Titanic*—the carryall of Samuel L. Goldenberg, one of the rescued passengers.

There were only a few boats that were heavily loaded; most of those that were half empty made but perfunctory efforts to pick up the moaning swimmers, their officers and crew fearing they would endanger the living if they pulled back into the midst of the dying. Some boats beat off the freezing victims; fear-crazed men and women struck with oars at the heads of swimmers. One woman drove her fist into the face of a half-dead man as he tried feebly to climb over the gunwale. Two other women helped him in and stanched the flow of blood from the ring cuts on his face.

One of the collapsible boats, which had floated off the top of the officers' quarters when the *Titanic* sank, was an icy haven for thirty or forty men. The boat had capsized as the ship sank; men swam to it, clung to it, climbed upon its slippery bottom, stood knee-deep in water in the freezing air. Chunks of ice swirled about their legs; their soaked clothing clutched their bodies in icy folds. Colonel Archibald Gracie was cast up there, Gracie who had leaped from the stern as the *Titanic* sank; young Thayer who had seen his father die; Lightoller who had twice been sucked down with the ship and twice blown to the surface by a belch of air; Bride, the second operator, and Phillips, the first. There were many stokers, half naked; it was a shivering company. They stood there in the icy sea, under the far stars, and sang and prayed—the Lord's Prayer. After a while a lifeboat came and picked them off, but Phillips was dead then or died soon afterward in the boat.

Only a few of the boats had lights; only one—No. 2—had a light that was of any use to the *Carpathia,* twisting through the ice field to the rescue. Other ships were "coming hard" too; one, the *Californian,* was still dead to opportunity.

---

5. **leviathan:** a Biblical sea monster, perhaps a whale.

The blue sparks still danced, but not the *Titanic*'s. *La Provence* to *Celtic*: "Nobody has heard the *Titanic* for about two hours."

It was 2:40 when the *Carpathia* first sighted the green light from No. 2 boat; it was 4:10 when she picked up the first boat and learned that the *Titanic* had foundered. The last of the moaning cries had just died away then.

Captain Rostron took the survivors aboard, boatload by boatload. He was ready for them, but only a small minority of them required much medical attention. Bride's feet were twisted and frozen; others were suffering from exposure; one died, and seven were dead when taken from the boats, and were buried at sea.

It was then that the fleet of racing ships learned they were too late; the *Parisian* heard the weak signals of *MPA,* the *Carpathia,* report the death of the *Titanic.* It was then—or soon afterward, when her radio operator put on his earphones— that the *Californian,* the ship that had been within sight as the *Titanic* was sinking, first learned of the disaster.

And it was then, in all its white-green majesty, that the *Titanic*'s survivors saw the iceberg, tinted with the sunrise, floating idly, pack ice jammed about its base, other bergs heaving slowly nearby on the blue breast of the sea.

IV

But it was not until later that the world knew, for wireless then was not what wireless is today, and garbled messages had nourished a hope that all of the *Titanic*'s company were safe. Not until Monday evening, when P.A.S. Franklin, vice-president of the International Mercantile Marine Company, received relayed messages in New York that left little hope, did the full extent of the disaster begin to be known. Partial and garbled lists of the survivors; rumors of heroism and cowardice; stories spun out of newspaper imagination, based on a few bare facts and many false reports, misled the world, terrified and frightened it. It was not until Thursday night, when the *Carpathia* steamed into the North River, that the full truth was pieced together.

New York Times, April 16, 1912.

Flashlights flared on the black river when the *Carpathia* stood up to her dock. Tugs nosed about her; shunted her toward Pier 54. Thirty thousand people jammed the streets; ambulances and stretchers stood on the pier; coroners and physicians waited.

In midstream the Cunarder dropped over the *Titanic*'s lifeboats; then she headed toward the dock. Beneath the customs letters on the pier stood relatives of the 711 survivors, relatives of the missing—hoping against hope. The *Carpathia* cast her lines ashore; stevedores looped them over bollards. The dense throngs stood quiet as the first survivor stepped down the gangway. The woman half staggered—led by customs guards—beneath her letter. A "low wailing" moan came from the crowd; fell, grew in volume, and dropped again.

Thus ended the maiden voyage of the *Titanic.* The lifeboats brought to New York by the *Carpathia,* a few deck chairs and gratings awash in the ice field off the Grand Bank eight hundred miles from shore, were all that was left of the world's greatest ship.

V

The aftermath of weeping and regret, of recriminations and investigations, dragged on for weeks. Charges and countercharges were hurled about; the White Star Line was bitterly criticized; Ismay was denounced on the floor of the Senate as a coward, but was defended by those who had been with him on the sinking *Titanic* and by the Board of Trade investigation in England.

It was not until weeks later, when the hastily convened Senate investigation in the United States and the Board of Trade report in England had been completed, that the whole story was told. The Senate investigating committee, under the chairmanship of Senator Smith, who was attacked in both the American and British press as a "backwoods politician," brought out numerous pertinent facts, though its proceedings verged at times on the farcical. Senator Smith was ridiculed for his lack of knowledge of the sea when he asked witnesses, "Of what is an iceberg composed?" and "Did any of the passengers take refuge in the watertight compartments?" The Senator seemed particularly interested in the marital status of Fleet, the lookout, who was saved. Fleet, puzzled, growled aside, "Wot questions they're arskin' me!"

The report of Lord Mersey, Wreck Commissioner in the British Board of Trade's investigation, was tersely damning.

The *Titanic* had carried boats enough for 1,178 persons, only one third of her capacity. Her sixteen boats and four collapsibles had saved but 711 persons; 400 people had needlessly lost their lives. The boats had been but partly loaded; officers in charge of launching them had been afraid the falls would break or the boats buckle under their rated loads; boat crews had been slow in reaching their stations; launching arrangements were confused because no boat drill had been held; passengers were loaded into the boats haphazardly because no boat assignments had been made.

But that was not all. Lord Mersey found that sufficient warnings of ice on the steamer track had reached the *Titanic,* that her speed of twenty-two knots was "excessive under the circumstances," that "in view of the high speed at which the vessel was running it is not considered that the lookout was sufficient," and that her master made "a very grievous mistake"—but should not be blamed for negligence. Captain Rostron of the *Carpathia* was highly praised. "He did the very best that could be done." The *Californian* was damned. The testimony of her master, officers, and crew showed that she was not, at the most, more than nineteen miles away from the sinking *Titanic* and probably no more than five to ten miles distant. She had seen the *Titanic*'s lights; she had seen the rockets; she had not received the CQD calls because her radio operator was asleep. She had attempted to get in communication with the ship she had sighted by flashing a light, but vainly.

"The night was clear," reported Lord Mersey, "and the sea was smooth. When she first saw the rockets, the *Californian* could have pushed through the ice to the open water without any serious risk and so have come to the assistance of the *Titanic*. Had she done so she might have saved many if not all of the lives that were lost.

"She made no attempt."

Responding to the Account

Analyzing the Account

Identifying Facts

1. Why was the *Titanic* thought to be "unsinkable"? Cite the passages in which Baldwin reminds us that the ship was "unsinkable."

2. Essentially, Baldwin's recounting of the sinking of the *Titanic* is the ancient story of human integrity against brute nature; in this case, nature wins easily. In what passages, however, does Baldwin suggest that human failure was responsible for the disaster?

3. Baldwin reports that among the garbled messages received by wireless in New York, there were "rumors of heroism and cowardice." Cite at least two examples of heroism and two of cowardice.

Interpreting Meanings

4. What devices does Baldwin use—as a fiction writer would—to build up your **suspense**? Since you know that the *Titanic* will sink, what hooks your interest to keep you reading?

5. Why do you think Baldwin switches from the past to the present tense in Part II?

6. Baldwin returns, as if in a refrain, to the band and its music. Why is it significant that they begin by playing ragtime music? What **mood** is suggested by the music they play later?

7. Baldwin makes great use of **irony** in his essay—much of it comes from our foreknowledge that the *Titanic* will sink. Find at least three ironic situations in Baldwin's story. Which irony in the story do you think creates the strongest emotional effect?

8. How did you feel as you read this story of an event that occurred more than seventy-five years ago? Do any aspects of the disaster—including human responses to it—remind you of other catastrophes? Explain.

9. Do you think Baldwin had a **purpose** in writing about this disaster other than to record the factual events? Explain.

10. How does Baldwin's report compare in **tone** with Connell's account of the explorers in Antarctica (page 474)? Do you think anyone would dare use Connell's tone in writing about the *Titanic*? Explain.

Writing About the Account

A Creative Response

1. **Writing an Eyewitness Report.** Choose one of the passengers or crew members (either a person that Baldwin names and describes or one that you imagine), and write an account of the night's events from this person's point of view. Use the first-person pronoun *I*.

2. **Writing a Narrative in the Form of a Log.** Retell an actual event in the form of a log. Begin each entry with the exact time of the incident you are recording. If your subject is serious or suspenseful (a disaster or the last minutes of an exciting game), use the passage of time to create suspense. If your subject is trivial (putting on eye makeup, eating an ice-cream cone), make the passage of time contribute to the comedy.

A Critical Response

3. **Writing a Factual Summary.** Baldwin gives a detailed account of the maiden voyage and the sinking of the *Titanic*. Using the facts in his account, write in your own words a one- to two-page summary of the same events. Report the most significant information and the most important conclusions about the disaster.

Analyzing Language and Vocabulary

Specialized Vocabulary

Every type of work or hobby has its own **jargon**, or **specialized vocabulary**, that describes its tools, equipment, and procedures. People who work with computers, for instance, talk about *hackers, floppies, NLQ modes,* and *software*. Ships and seagoing people have generated a huge specialized vocabulary. *R.M.S.* in the title is such a term: It stands for "Royal Mail Steamship."

Use a dictionary to help you answer the following questions about Baldwin's vocabulary:

1. A ship that is *moored* is tied up to a wharf with its engines off. Can a ship be moored at a *quay*? What can you guess *bollards* are, if you know that they are on a dock and the heavy *mooring ropes* are wound around them?

2. When you are on board a ship and facing its front, the side to your left is called the *port* side, and the side to your right is the *starboard*. What does the captain's order *"Hard-a-starboard"* mean? What would the captain say in order to turn the ship quickly to the left?

3. The front end of the ship is its *bow,* and the back end is its *stern*. Objects toward the bow are said to be *fore;* where are the *foredeck, foremast,* and *forecastle (fo'c'sle)* located? (Use a dictionary to find out what each of these is.) Anything at or near the stern of a ship is said to be *aft*. Where would you expect to find the ship's *afterdeck*?

4. A captain stands on the *bridge*. Who stands in the *crow's-nest,* and what does this person do?

5. A *stoker* tends a furnace, *stoking* it by shoveling in coal. Where is the *stokehold* aboard a ship, and what does it have to do with a *stoker*?

Tom Wolfe (1931–   ) had two passions during his childhood and youth: books and baseball. For a long time, it was uncertain which he would pursue as his career.

Wolfe grew up in Richmond, Virginia, where he read avidly—Arthurian legends, biographies, and the novels of Thomas Wolfe (no relation) and William Faulkner. He became co-editor of his school newspaper and pitcher for his school team. He went on to pitch for Washington and Lee University in Lexington, Virginia, to become sports editor of the paper there, and to found the literary quarterly *Shenandoah.*

When he was twenty-one, Wolfe tried out as pitcher for the New York Giants, but when he failed the tryouts, he gave up his pro-ball ambitions and entered graduate school in American Studies at Yale University. There he earned his Ph.D. in 1956 and turned to journalism. "To tell the truth," he says, "I immediately found it glamorous. Nobody else did at that late date, but I looked at it like the original 1922 Chicago Cub reporter."

In 1963 the New York newspapers were paralyzed for four months by a strike. While the *Tribune* was idle, Wolfe accepted an assignment from *Esquire* magazine to write an article on customized cars—the souped-up, lowered-chassis, fins-and-chrome "streamlined babies" of the rich young California car buffs. Wolfe researched for months but failed to write the article—"I couldn't pull the thing together"—and that failure was ironically responsible for his breakthrough in style. Since *Esquire* had already locked space and artwork for the article into the magazine, they ran Wolfe's notes just as they were—breathless, hip, full of wild metaphors, nonsense words, slap-dash punctuation, and passages of stream-of-con-sciousness. The piece was an instant—if controversial—success that freed Wolfe from the traditional who-what-when-where style of reporting and enabled him to move closer to what is now called New Journalism.

"I believe," Wolfe has said, "that it is possible to achieve a nonfiction form that combines the emotional impact usually found only in novels and short stories, the analytical insights of the best essays and scholarly writing, and the deep factual foundation of 'hard reporting.' "

Wolfe's articles are collected in *The Kandy-Kolored Tangerine-Flake Streamline Baby, The Pump House Gang,* and *Radical Chic and Mau-Mauing the Flak-Catchers.* Perhaps his most acclaimed book is *The Right Stuff,* which was made into a film. Wolfe's bestselling novel, *The Bonfire of the Vanities,* was also made into a movie.

The Right Stuff traces the lives of the early astronauts, from their beginnings as test pilots in the California desert to their national role as public heroes, "the fame and celebrity no one had trained them for." What they trained for and lived for was the tough code of Air Force professionalism that provided Wolfe with his title.

In the passage that follows, Wolfe describes one episode late in the flying life of Chuck Yeager. Yeager was a crack test pilot who had broken the sound barrier twelve years before. His laid-back Appalachian drawl and his calm in the face of fatal danger had been copied by a whole generation of Air Force and commercial pilots. Yeager had been passed over by NASA when the astronauts were chosen (he lacked a college education), and at the age of thirty-nine he returned to Edwards Air Force Base in California as commandant of the Aerospace Research Pilot School. The Air Force had plans for a manned space program of its own and hoped that ARPS would turn out astronauts both for the civilian NASA and for its own liftoff into space. If anyone could do it, it would be Chuck Yeager who would turn out the men with "the right stuff."

"As to what this ineffable quality was, . . . well, it obviously involved bravery. But it was not bravery in the simple sense of being willing to risk your life. The idea seemed to be that any fool could do that, if that was all that was required, just as any fool could throw away his life in the process." In this extract from *The Right Stuff,* Yeager displays "the right stuff" as he takes the NF–104, a sophisticated plane with a rocket engine mounted over the tailpipe, on its first test into the weightless atmosphere more than 100,000 feet above the earth.

One critic has called Wolfe's writing "a language experience" (it's what Walt Whitman called his own collection of poems). To catch Wolfe's tone and the excitement of his narrative, you should read parts of this adventure aloud.

THE LIMITS OF
THE ENVELOPE

Tom Wolfe

Yeager had taken the NF–104 up for three checkout flights, edging it up gradually toward 100,000 feet, where the limits of the envelope, whatever they were, would begin to reveal themselves. And now he was out on the flight line for the second of two major preliminary flights. Tomorrow he would let it all out and go for the record. It was another of those absolutely clear brilliant afternoons on the dome of the world. In the morning flight everything had gone exactly according to plan. He had taken the ship up to 108,000 feet after cutting in the rocket engine at 60,000. The rocket had propelled the ship up at a 50-degree angle of attack. One of the disagreeable sides of the ship was her dislike of extreme angles. At any angle greater than 30 degrees, her nose would pitch up, which was the move she made just before going into spins. But at 108,000 feet it was no problem. The air was so thin at that altitude, so close to being pure ''space,'' that the reaction controls, the hydrogen-peroxide thrusters, worked beautifully. Yeager had only to nudge the sidearm hand controller by his lap and a thruster on top of the nose of the plane pushed the nose right down again, and he was in perfect position to reenter the dense atmosphere below. Now he was going up for one final exploration of that same region before going for broke tomorrow.

At 40,000 feet Yeager began his speed run. He cut in the afterburner and it slammed him back in his seat, and he was now riding an engine with nearly 16,000 pounds of thrust. As soon as the Machmeter[1] hit 2.2, he pulled back on the stick and started the climb. The afterburner would carry him to 60,000 feet before exhausting its fuel. At precisely that moment he threw the switch for the rocket engine . . . terrific jolt . . . He's slammed back in his seat again. The nose pitches up to 70 degrees. The g-forces[2] start rising. The desert sky starts falling away. He's going straight up into the indigo. At 78,000 feet a light on the console . . . as usual . . . the main engine overheating from the tremendous exertion of the climb. He throws the switch and shuts it down, but the rocket is still accelerating. Who doesn't know this feeling if he doesn't! . . . One hundred thousand feet . . . He shuts down the rocket engine. He's still climbing. The g-forces slide off . . . makes you feel like you're pitching forward . . . He's weightless, coming over the top of the arc[3] . . . 104,000 feet . . . It's absolutely silent . . . Twenty miles up . . . The sky is almost black. He's looking straight up into it, because the nose of the ship is pitched up. His angle of attack is still about 50 degrees. He's over the top of the arc and coming down. He pushes the sidearm control to bring down the nose of the ship. Nothing happens . . . He can hear the thruster working, but the nose isn't budging. It's still pitched up. He hits the thruster again . . . She won't go down! . . . Now he can see it, the whole diagram . . . This morning at 108,000 feet the air was so thin it offered no resistance and you could easily push the nose down with the thrusters. At 104,000 feet the air remains just thick enough to exert aerodynamic pressure. The thrusters aren't strong enough to overcome it . . . He keeps hitting the reaction controls . . . The hydrogen peroxide squirts out of the jet on the nose of the ship and doesn't do a damned thing . . . He's dropping and the nose is still pitched up . . . the outside of the envelope! . . . well, here it is . . . It doesn't want to stretch . . . and here we go! . . . The ship snaps into a flat spin. It's spinning right over its center of gravity, like a pinwheel on a stick. Yeager's head is on the outer edge of the circle, spinning around. He pushes the sidearm control again. The hydrogen peroxide is finished. He has 600 pounds of fuel left in the main engine but there's no way to start it up. To relight the engine you have to put the ship nose down into a dive and force air through the intake duct and start the engine windmilling to build up the rpms. Without rpms there's no hydraulic pressure and without hydraulic pressure you can't move the stabilizer wings on the tail and without the stabilizer wings you can't control the plane at the lower altitudes . . . He's in a

---

1. **Machmeter:** a device that measures the ratio of airspeed to the speed of sound.
2. **g-forces:** units used to measure the force on a body undergoing acceleration. A g-force is a unit of acceleration equal to the acceleration of gravity.

3. **the top of the arc:** the peak of a test flight, which can be seen as making an arc.

steady-state flat spin and dropping . . . He's whirling around at a terrific rate . . . He makes himself keep his eyes pinned on the instruments . . . A little sightseeing at this point and it's vertigo[4] and you're finished . . . He's down to 80,000 feet and the rpms are at dead zero . . . He's falling 150 feet a second . . . 9,000 feet a minute . . . *And what do I do next?* . . . here in the jaws of the Gulp . . . *I've tried A!—I've tried B!*—The beast isn't making a sound . . . just spinning around like a length of pipe in the sky . . . He has one last shot . . . the speed brakes, a parachute rig in the tail for slowing the ship down after a high-speed landing . . . The altimeter keeps winding down . . . Twenty-five thousand feet . . . but the altimeter is based on sea level . . . He's only 21,000 feet above the high desert . . . The slack's running out . . . He pops the speed brake . . . *Bango!*—the chute catches with a jolt . . . It pulls the tail up . . . He pitches down . . . The spin stops. The nose is pointed down. Now he only has to jettison the chute and let her dive and pick up the rpms. He jettisons the chute . . . and the beast heaves up again! The nose goes back up in the air! . . . It's the rear stabilizer wing . . . The leading edge is locked, frozen into the position of the climb to altitude. With no rpms and no hydraulic controls he can't move the tail . . . The nose is pitched way above 30 degrees . . . Here she goes again . . . She's back into the spin . . . He's spinning out on the rim again . . . He has no rpms, no power, no more speed chute, and only 180 knots airspeed . . . He's down to 12,000 feet . . . 8,000 feet above the farm[5] . . . There's not a damned thing left in the manual or the bag of tricks or the righteousness of twenty years of military flying . . . Chosen or damned! . . . It blows at any seam! Yeager hasn't bailed out of an airplane since the day he was shot down over Germany when he was twenty . . . I've tried A!—I've tried B!—I've tried C! . . . 11,000 feet, 7,000 from the farm . . . He hunches himself into a ball, just as it says in the manual, and reaches under the seat for the cinch ring and pulls . . . He's exploded out of the cockpit with such force it's like a concussion . . . He can't

see . . . *Wham* . . . a jolt in the back . . . It's the seat separating from him and the parachute rig . . . His head begins to clear . . . He's in midair, in his pressure suit, looking out through the visor of his helmet . . . Every second seems enormously elongated . . . infinite . . . such slow motion . . . He's suspended in midair . . . weightless . . . The ship had been falling at about 100 miles an hour and the ejection rocket had propelled him up at 90 miles an hour. For one thick adrenal moment he's weightless in midair, 7,000 feet above the desert . . . The seat floats nearby, as if the two of them are parked in the atmosphere . . . The butt of the seat, the underside, is facing him . . . a red hole . . . the socket where the ejection mechanism had been attached . . . It's dribbling a charcoal red . . . lava . . . the remains of the rocket propellant . . . It's glowing . . . it's oozing out of the socket . . . In the next moment they're both falling, him and the seat . . . His parachute rig has a quarter bag over it and on the bag is a drogue chute[6] that pulls the bag off so the parachute will stream out gradually and not break the chute or the pilot's back when the canopy pops open during a high-speed ejection. It's designed for an ejection at 400 or 500 miles an hour, but he's only going about 175. In this infinitely expanded few seconds the lines stream out and Yeager and the rocket seat and the glowing red socket sail through the air together . . . and now the seat is drifting above him . . . into the chute lines! . . . The seat is nestled in the chute lines . . . dribbling lava out of the socket . . . eating through the lines . . . An infinite second . . . He's jerked up by the shoulders . . . it's the chute opening and the canopy filling . . . in that very instant *the lava*—it smashes into the visor of his helmet . . . Something slices through his left eye . . . He's knocked silly . . . He can't see a damned thing . . . The burning snaps him to . . . His left eye is gushing blood . . . It's pouring down inside the lid and down his face and his face is on fire . . . the seat rig . . . The jerk of the parachute had suddenly slowed his speed, but the seat kept falling . . . It had fallen out of the chute lines and the butt end crashed

---

4. **vertigo:** sickening dizziness.
5. **the farm:** death.

6. **drogue chute:** a type of parachute attached to the body, used to slow down a descent.

into his visor . . . 180 pounds of metal . . . a double visor . . . the damned thing has smashed through both layers . . . He's burning! . . . There's rocket lava inside the helmet . . . The seat has fallen away . . . He can't see . . . blood pouring out of his left eye and there's smoke inside the helmet . . . Rubber! . . . It's the seal between the helmet and the pressure suit . . . It's burning up . . . The propellant won't quit . . . A tremendous *whoosh* . . . He can feel the rush . . . He can even hear it . . . The whole left side of the helmet is full of flames . . . A sheet of flame goes up his neck and the side of his face . . . The oxygen! . . . The propellant has burned through the rubber seal, setting off the pressure suit's automatic oxygen system . . . The integrity of the circuit has been violated and it rushes oxygen to the helmet, to the pilot's face . . . A hundred percent oxygen! . . . It turns the lava into an inferno . . . Everything that can burn is on fire . . . everything else is melting . . . Even with the hole smashed in the visor the helmet is full of smoke . . . He's choking . . . blinded . . . The left side of his head is on fire . . . He's suffocating . . . He brings up his left hand . . . He has on pressure-suit gloves locked and taped to the sleeve . . . He jams his hand in through the hole in the visor and tries to create an air scoop with it to bring air to his mouth . . . The flames . . . They're all over it . . . They go to work on the glove where it touches his face . . . They devour it . . . His index finger is burning up . . . His damned finger is burning! . . . But he doesn't move it . . . Get some air! . . . Nothing else matters . . . He's gulping smoke . . . He has to get the visor open . . . It's twisted . . . He's encased in a little broken globe dying in a cloud of his own fried flesh . . . The stench of it! . . . rubber and a human hide . . . He has to get the visor open . . . It's that or nothing, no two ways about it . . . It's smashed all to hell . . . He jams both hands underneath . . . It's a tremendous effort . . . It lifts . . . Salvation! . . . Like a sea the air carries it all away, the smoke, the flames . . . The fire is out. He can breathe. He can see out of his right eye. The desert, the mesquite, the motherless Joshua trees are rising slowly toward him . . . He can't open his left eye . . . Now he can feel the pain . . . Half his head is broiled . . .

That isn't the worst of it . . . The damned finger! . . . He can make out the terrain, he's been over it a million times . . . Over there's the highway, 466, and there's Route 6 crossing it . . . His left glove is practically burned off . . . The glove and his left index finger . . . he can't tell them apart . . . they look as if they exploded in an oven . . . He's not far from base . . . Whatever it is with the finger, it's very bad . . . Nearly down . . . He gets ready . . . Right out of the manual . . . A terrific wallop . . . He's down on the mesquite, looking across the desert, one-eyed . . . He stands up . . . He's in one piece! . . . He can hardly use his left hand. The finger is killing him. The whole side of his head . . . He starts taking off the parachute harness . . . It's all in the manual! Regulation issue! . . . He starts rolling up the parachute, just like it says . . . Some of the cords are almost melted through, from the lava . . . His head feels like it's still on fire . . . The pain comes from way down deep . . . But he's got to get the helmet off . . . It's a hell of an operation . . . He doesn't dare touch his head . . . It feels enormous . . . Somebody's running toward him . . . It's a kid, a guy in his twenties . . . He's come from the highway . . . He comes up close and his mouth falls open and he gives Yeager a look of stone horror . . .

"Are you all right!"

The look on the kid's face! . . .

"I was in my car! I saw you coming down!"

"Listen," says Yeager. The pain in his finger is terrific. "Listen . . . you got a knife?"

The kid digs into his pocket and pulls out a penknife. Yeager starts cutting the glove off his left hand. He can't bear it any more. The kid stands there hypnotized and horrified. From the look on the kid's face, Yeager can begin to see himself. His neck, the whole left side of his head, his ear, his cheek, his eye must be burned up. His eye socket is slashed, swollen, caked shut, and covered with a crust of burned blood, and half his hair is burned away. The whole mess and the rest of his face and his nostrils and his lips are smeared with the sludge of the burning rubber. And he's standing there in the middle of the desert in a pressure suit with his head cocked, squinting out of one eye, working on his left glove with a pen-

The photographs that illustrate this selection are from the 1983 movie *The Right Stuff*, starring Sam Shepard as Chuck Yeager.

knife . . . The knife cuts through the glove and it cuts through the meat of his finger . . . You can't tell any longer . . . It's all run together . . . The finger looks like it's melted . . . He's got to get the glove off. That's all there is to it. It hurts too much. He pulls off the glove and a big hunk of melted meat from the finger comes off with it . . . It's like fried suet . . .

"Arrggghhh . . ." It's the kid. He's retching. It's too much for him. He looks up at Yeager. His eyes open and his mouth opens. All the glue has come undone. He can't hold it together any longer.

"God," he says, "you . . . look *awful!*" The Good Samaritan, A.A.D.! Also a Doctor! And he just gave his diagnosis! That's all a man needs

. . . to be forty years old and to fall one hundred thousand feet in a flat spin and punch out and make a million-dollar hole in the ground and get half his head and his hand burned up and have his eye practically ripped out of his skull . . . and have the Good Samaritan, A.A.D., arrive as if sent by the spirit of Pancho Barnes herself to render a midnight verdict among the motherless Joshua trees while the screen doors bang and the pictures of a hundred dead pilots rattle in their frames:[7]

"My God! . . . you look awful."

A few minutes later the rescue helicopter ar-

---

7. Pancho Barnes ran a bar called the Fly Inn near the base. On its walls were photographs of dead test pilots.

rived. The medics found Yeager standing out in the mesquite, him and some kid who had been passing by. Yeager was standing erect with his parachute rolled up and his helmet in the crook of his arm, right out of the manual, and staring at them quite levelly out of what was left of his face, as if they had had an appointment and he was on time.

At the hospital they discovered one stroke of good luck. The blood over Yeager's left eye had been baked into a crustlike shield. Otherwise he might have lost it. He had suffered third- and second-degree burns on his head and neck. The burns required a month of treatment in the hospital, but he was able to heal without disfigurement. He even regained full use of his left index finger.

It so happened that on the day of Yeager's flight, at just about the time he headed down the runway on takeoff, the Secretary of Defense, Rob-

ert McNamara, announced that the X–20 program had been canceled. Although the Manned Orbiting Laboratory scheme remained alive officially, it was pretty obvious that there would be no American military space voyagers. The boys in Houston[8] had the only ticket; the top of the pyramid was theirs to extend to the stars, if they were able.

Yeager was returned to flight status and resumed his duties at ARPS. In time he would go on to fly more than a hundred missions in Southeast Asia in B–57 tactical bombers.

No one ever broke the Russian mark with the NF–104 or even tried to. Up above 100,000 feet the plane's envelope was full of holes. And Yeager never again sought to set a record in the sky over the high desert.

---

8. That is, NASA.

Responding to the Account

Analyzing the Account

Identifying Facts

1. Describe the problem that develops with the NF–104 at 104,000 feet.
2. List the steps that Yeager takes to try to correct the problem before he bails out.
3. Describe what happens when Yeager ejects himself from the plane. What causes each of his injuries?
4. The last five paragraphs provide a **resolution** to Yeager's problem and answer some of the questions we are left with after his landing. Summarize the facts presented in this last part of the account.

Interpreting Meanings

5. This excerpt tells the story of a failure. On a flight that is not even an attempt to break a record but is only a preliminary to that attempt, the plane, the ejector seat, and the pressure suit all malfunction in a way that no one has fore-

seen. The plane does not even reach the height of an earlier preliminary flight. The pilot is badly injured, and in the meantime he has to abandon the ship, which makes a "million-dollar hole in the ground." Nevertheless, do you think this is the story of a triumph? Why? What sort?

6. Find three instances in the recounting of Yeager's ordeal where Wolfe repeats the phrase "right out of the manual." What does the phrase mean? What does Wolfe emphasize by its repetition?

7. On page 500, just as Yeager throws the switch for the rocket engine, Wolfe switches from the past tense to the present. The narrative remains in the present tense until the last line of page 503. Ordinarily a writer is (wisely) advised to stick to a single tense. What does this switch to the present tense accomplish for Wolfe's narrative? What is the effect of the unusual punctuation in this section?

8. Throughout *The Right Stuff,* Wolfe talks about stretching "the limits of the envelope." Based on this excerpt, what do you think the phrase means?

9. The "kid who had been passing by" is so revolted by the sight of Yeager's injuries that he retches. Wolfe hopes you will be somewhat revolted, too, by his description. Were you? Is revulsion a legitimate emotion for a writer to produce? In your opinion, are there things so ugly or painful that they should not be described? Explain.

Writing About the Account

A Creative Response

1. **Using a Different Point of View.** As Wolfe describes Yeager's battle with the malfunctioning plane, he moves in and out of the pilot's mind. Sometimes he narrates in the third person as an objective reporter. Sometimes he "overhears" Yeager's thoughts, and sometimes he writes in the third person but with the immediacy and vocabulary of a first-person narrator. Try casting a short section of Wolfe's account all in the first person; then rewrite it using the point of view of an objective reporter. What is lost?

A Critical Response

2. **Responding to the Account.** In a brief essay, describe your response to Wolfe's account of Yeager's test flight. Before you write, gather data by filling out a chart like the following one.

	Responses
What emotions did the account evoke in me?	
Does the writing tell me something about people in general?	
What do I think of the unusual way the writer has used language?	
Is the account well written?	
Is it about something important?	
Is there a lesson to be learned from the account?	

3. **Comparing and Contrasting Characters.** In a three-paragraph essay, compare and contrast the character of Yeager with the characters of Scott and Amundsen (page 474). Which of these characters do you think had "the right stuff"? Before you write, decide how *you* would define "the right stuff."

Analyzing Language and Vocabulary

The Characteristics of a Style: Jargon, Slang, and Punctuation

One of the characteristics of Wolfe's style is the use of **jargon** and **slang**. The effect of this device is to take the reader more intimately into the scene. The assumption that we know their special language makes us identify with the people who use it. The danger of this technique, of course, is that we won't know what the writer is talking about—but Wolfe is skilled at explaining words by their **context**.

1. In the first paragraph, for example, he uses the technical terms "pitch up," "hydrogen-peroxide thrusters," and "sidearm hand controller."

   a. What do you think each term means? (Look back at the passage in context, page 500.)

   b. Do context clues help you define the word or phrase? How?

2. Tell what you think the italicized words or phrases in each of these sentences means. It might help if you go back and read the passages in their context.

   a. "Now he [Yeager] was going up for one final exploration of that same region before *going for broke* tomorrow," (Page 500)

   b. "His eyes open and his mouth opens. All *the glue has come undone.* He can't *hold it together* any longer." (Page 503)

3. Jargon and slang must always be used in appropriate situations. (Wolfe's style wouldn't be appropriate for another kind of essay.) What do you think of his style? Did you feel that the jargon and slang contributed to the total effect? Or did you find the jargon and slang distracting and difficult?

4. Another characteristic of Wolfe's style is his unorthodox use of punctuation. (He once said, "I came along and saw all those punctuation marks lying dormant and decided to use them— exclamation points, dots, dashes, multiple parentheses, and multiple colons.") Find a passage that uses many different punctuation marks, and rewrite it in standard English. Then read the two passages aloud: Can you hear how punctuation contributes to Wolfe's voice?

Using the Expository and Persuasive Aims

Literary Model

In April 1963 Dr. Martin Luther King, Jr., and his civil rights organization, the Southern Christian Leadership Conference (SCLC), began a protest campaign aimed at ending segregation in Birmingham, Alabama. John F. Kennedy was President of the United States at the time; his brother Robert was Attorney General. In the following passage, Pulitzer Prize winning historian David J. Garrow explains the significance of this campaign.

[The] next city would be Birmingham, Alabama, where King's longtime SCLC colleague, Rev. Fred Shuttlesworth, had headed up an aggressive local civil rights organization, the Alabama Christian Movement for Human Rights (ACMHR), ever since state authorities had forced the NAACP[1] out of business in Alabama in 1956. Shuttlesworth was eager for King and the SCLC to help him mount a full-scale protest campaign against Birmingham's infamous Public Safety Commissioner Eugene "Bull" Connor. Although some Birmingham merchants, much like Albany's businessmen,[2] had told Shuttlesworth they would rather desegregate than pay the economic price that would result from mass demonstrations, they refused to act in the face of Connor's forceful championing of total segregation. King and the SCLC weighed a number of factors including the ACMHR's commitment, the economic vulnerability of the white merchants, Connor's quick-tempered penchant for violent responses to black activism, and the 1961–1962 lesson that the Kennedys would respond to violent civil rights repression with direct federal intervention while largely ignoring Pritchett-style repression.[3] They decided that Connor and Birmingham might well be just the tonic that the southern movement needed after the disappointments and frustrations of Albany.

The SCLC and the ACMHR launched their Birmingham demonstrations in April 1963. After a slow start, King intentionally chose to submit to arrest, hoping his incarceration might spark the campaign into greater action and win it more national—and federal—attention. When Connor's jailers placed King in solitary confinement, King's friends and aides became deeply concerned and persuaded his wife, Coretta Scott King, to phone the Kennedy White House to seek federal reassurance of her husband's safety. Both Attorney General Robert Kennedy and President John Kennedy responded with personal calls to Mrs. King, and King's jailing did help spark an intensification of the movement's Birmingham protests. "Bull" Connor employed both snarling police attack dogs and high-powered fire hoses to drive back black demonstrators who sought to march into downtown Birmingham. National and international outrage resulted as graphic photos and television footage of the police violence were printed and shown across the country and around the world. The Kennedy administration sprang into action and successfully lobbied Birmingham's economic leadership into reaching a desegregation accord with King and Shuttlesworth before the police violence and resulting black anger got totally out of hand.

Coverage of the Birmingham protests made Americans more profoundly aware of the obstacles and opposition facing the southern black freedom struggle than any events from preceding years. Several weeks later, as smaller demonstrations

---

1. **NAACP:** National Association for the Advancement of Colored People.
2. In late 1961 through August 1962, civil rights leaders attempted to desegregate the bus and train stations of Albany, Alabama. The Albany Movement ended in failure.

3. Albany police chief Laurie Pritchett carried out a policy of mass arrests but avoided using violence against protesters. His policy led to widespread media praise rather than criticism, and to the defeat of the Albany Movement.

spread across the South and Alabama governor George C. Wallace sought unsuccessfully to block the court-ordered integration of the University of Alabama, President Kennedy went on television to declare, in words far stronger than he or any previous president had ever used, that racial discrimination and injustice was a serious and profound moral evil that American society had to confront and strive to eliminate. For the first time in his presidency, Kennedy committed himself to aggressively championing federal legislation that would mandate public desegregation and racial nondiscrimination in many facets of American life.

— from *The Eyes on the Prize Civil Rights Reader,* David J. Garrow

A Note on the Expository Aim

Writers of history often have an **expository aim**—that is, their purpose is to inform, explain, or clarify what happened in the past, and why.

To do so, historians investigate historical events and then present evidence—**facts, statistics,** and **examples**—to support their **main ideas.** But historians may also inform, explain, or clarify by **narrating** a series of events or by vividly **describing** people, places, and experiences—as you can see from the three historical accounts in this unit.

In general, historical writing with an expository aim is formal, factual, and unemotional in **tone.** (But this isn't always the case, as Tom Wolfe demonstrates in "The Limits of the Envelope.") Yet even a historian who tries to be **objective** usually presents **opinions,** draws **conclusions,** and makes **judgments** about the past. Most readers would feel that a writer who had not done so had not truly explained or clarified history.

For this reason, a historian whose primary purpose is expository may also have another aim: to **persuade** readers to agree with a particular interpretation of history and the lessons it teaches us. What interpretations of history do you think Connell, Baldwin, and Wolfe are trying to persuade their readers to accept in the accounts you've just read?

Examining the Writer's Techniques

Working with a partner, answer the following questions about Garrow's historical account:

1. In the first paragraph, Garrow is explaining why King and his colleagues chose Birmingham as the site of their next protest campaign. Identify the **main idea** Garrow is explaining in each of the other two paragraphs.
2. For each paragraph, identify at least three **facts, examples, reasons,** or **narrative details** that Garrow presents to support or clarify his main idea. You might organize your information in the form of an outline, using Roman numerals for each main idea.
3. Does Garrow present any **opinions, judgments,** or **conclusions** about the events he's discussing? How would you describe his **tone?**
4. Is Garrow's main purpose to inform (tell what happened), explain (analyze why it happened), or persuade (convince readers to accept his view of what happened)? Justify your choice.

Literary Model

Martin Luther King, Jr., was arrested and jailed during the April 1963 Birmingham protests. While he was in prison, eight white Birmingham clergymen who considered themselves liberals wrote an open letter to the local newspaper, criticizing the demonstrations. Here are some excerpts from King's famous reply:

My Dear Fellow Clergymen,

While confined here in the Birmingham City Jail, I came across your recent statement calling our present activities "unwise and untimely." Seldom, if ever, do I pause to answer criticism of my work and ideas. . . . But since I feel that you are men of genuine good will and your criticisms are sincerely set forth, I would like to answer your statement in what I hope will be patient and reasonable terms. . . .

You may well ask, "Why direct action? Why sit-ins, marches, etc.? Isn't negotiation a better path?" You are exactly right in your call for negotiation.

Indeed, this is the purpose of direct action. Nonviolent direct action seeks to create such a crisis and establish such creative tension that a community that has constantly refused to negotiate is forced to confront the issue.

My friends, I must say to you that we have not made a single gain in civil rights without determined legal and nonviolent pressure. History is the long and tragic story of the fact that privileged groups seldom give up their privileges voluntarily. Individuals may see the moral light and give up their unjust posture; but as Reinhold Niebuhr[1] has reminded us, groups are more immoral than individuals.

We know through painful experience that freedom is never voluntarily given by the oppressor; it must be demanded by the oppressed. Frankly, I have never yet engaged in a direct action movement that was "well timed," according to the timetable of those who have not suffered unduly from the disease of segregation. For years now I have heard the word "Wait!" It rings in the ear of every Negro with a piercing familiarity. This "wait" has almost always meant "never." It has been a tranquilizing Thalidomide,[2] relieving the emotional stress for a moment, only to give birth to an ill-formed infant of frustration. We must come to see with the distinguished jurist of yesterday that "justice too long delayed is justice denied."[3] We have waited for more than 340 years for our constitutional and God-given rights. The nations of Asia and Africa are moving with jetlike speed toward the goal of political independence, and we still creep at horse and buggy pace toward the gaining of a cup of coffee at a lunch counter.

I guess it is easy for those who have never felt the stinging darts of segregation to say wait. But when you have seen vicious mobs lynch your mothers and fathers at will and drown your sisters and brothers at whim; when you have seen hate-filled policemen curse, kick, brutalize, and even kill your black brothers and sisters with impunity; when you see the vast majority of your 20 million Negro brothers smothering in an airtight cage of poverty in the midst of an affluent society; when you suddenly find your tongue twisted and your speech stammering as you seek to explain to your six-year-old daughter why she can't go to the public amusement park that has just been advertised on television, and see the tears welling up in her little eyes when she is told that Funtown is closed to colored children, and see the depressing clouds of inferiority begin to form in her little mental sky, and see her begin to distort her little personality by unconsciously developing a bitterness toward white people; when you have to concoct an answer for a five-year-old son who is asking in agonizing pathos: "Daddy, why do white people treat colored people so mean?"; when you take a cross country drive and find it necessary to sleep night after night in the uncomfortable corners of your automobile because no motel will accept you; when you are humiliated day in and day out by nagging signs reading "white" men and "colored"; when your first name becomes "nigger" and your middle name becomes "boy" (however old you are) and your last name becomes "John," and when your wife and mother are never given the respected title of "Mrs."; when you are harried by day and haunted by night by the fact that you are a Negro, living constantly at tip-toe stance, never quite knowing what to expect next, and plagued with inner fears and outer resentments; when you are forever fighting a degenerating sense of "nobodiness"—then you will understand why we find it difficult to wait. There comes a time when the cup of endurance runs over, and men are no longer willing to be plunged into an abyss of injustice where they experience the bleakness of corroding despair. . . .

— from "Letter from Birmingham City Jail," Martin Luther King, Jr.

---

1. **Reinhold Niebuhr** (rĭn´hold nē´boor) (1892–1971): American religious thinker, political philosopher, and social activist.
2. **Thalidomide:** drug widely prescribed to prevent morning sickness during pregnancy. It was found to cause severe birth defects.
3. King is probably thinking of a statement attributed to William E. Gladstone (1809–1898), British statesman and prime minister: "Justice delayed is justice denied."

A Note on the Persuasive Aim

Writers with a **persuasive aim** are trying to convince you to think or act in a certain way—to accept their beliefs, buy their products, vote for their candidates, join their political movements, even fight their wars.

Some persuasion is manipulative and deceptive; it is based primarily on **faulty reasoning** and **emotional appeals**. (See page 196.) But persuasive writing can also use well-reasoned, logical **arguments** based on **informed opinions**—opinions the writer can back up with facts. Keep in mind, however, that even a responsible, well-intentioned writer who's trying to persuade rarely presents all the facts about a subject or completely avoids appealing to the heart, rather than the brain.

Persuasive writers can use a variety of approaches to get their messages across. For example, someone trying to persuade people to contribute money to a charity might use **narration** to tell a story that tugs at the heartstrings (and makes readers open their checkbooks). That same writer might also use vivid **description** to evoke the misery of a hungry child or homeless family.

Some persuasive writing, such as advertising, has no purpose other than to persuade. But just as the expository writer may also have a persuasive aim, the persuasive writer may also have an **expository aim**—to inform readers about an issue, explain the validity of a point of view, or clarify the reasons for an action.

Examining the Writer's Techniques

Working with a partner, answer the following questions about King's letter:

1. King begins by laying out his **expository aim.** What is he trying to explain?
2. Considering his audience, what would you say is King's **persuasive aim**? (Is he trying to influence opinions or actions or both?)
3. Where does King support his position by using a logical, well-reasoned **argument** based on **informed opinions**? (Keep in mind that an informed opinion may be backed up by first-hand, personal experience, as well as by the kinds of facts found in books.)
4. How would you summarize King's **argument**? How does he establish his authority to pass judgment on the issue he's discussing?
5. Where does King use **emotional appeals**? What specific feelings is he trying to arouse in his readers? Were you moved by his letter?
6. Where does King use **narration** or **description** to convey his message? Where does he use **figurative language** and **parallelism**, the repetition of words, phrases, or sentences with a similar grammatical structure?

Using the Expository and Persuasive Aims

1. **Writing About an Historical Event.** Working with a partner, choose an important event in recent history, such as the Gulf War, the collapse of Communism in Eastern Europe and the Soviet Union, the 1989 San Francisco earthquake, the Exxon *Valdez* oil spill, or the sexual harassment controversy during the Senate confirmation hearings for Supreme Court Justice Clarence Thomas. Then, working independently, write a straight expository account of the event, based on library research and, if possible, eye-witness reports. (For example, you might interview a Gulf War veteran.) The primary purpose of your account is to explain what happened and why. Compare papers with your partner. Then collaborate on a single account based on your two different versions.

2. **Writing an Opinion Column.** Write an opinion column about the same historical event. Here your purpose is to persuade people to agree with your interpretation of that event (and maybe even take action). Your column should include well-reasoned arguments based on evidence drawn from your expository account. You probably will want to include an emotional appeal. Trade papers with a partner, and revise your column as you wish, based on your classmate's comments.

EVALUATING HISTORY

Writing Assignment

Write a four-paragraph essay in which you evaluate either the passage from David Garrow's *The Eyes on the Prize* or the selection from Dr. Martin Luther King, Jr.'s, letter (pages 506–508). In your essay, comment on the writer's use of facts and opinions and on his use of language to appeal to your emotions. (After you finish writing, compare your evaluations in class. Does everyone agree?)

Background

Whenever you read history, you should be able to tell whether a writer is stating a fact or an opinion.

- A **fact** is information that can be proved true.
- An **opinion** is a judgment (an evaluation) that cannot be proved either right or wrong. An opinion, however, can be persuasive when it is supported by facts, examples, quotations, and other kinds of evidence.

Nonfiction writers, historians included, often appeal to the emotions by using **loaded words** (words that are loaded with emotional overtones or associations called **connotations**). Loaded words are used to convey the writer's own attitudes and to influence the readers' feelings about the subject.

Another way of appealing to the readers' emotions is through the use of **sarcasm,** or ridicule. Sarcasm, which can be used very effectively to undercut the authority of someone, would be avoided by most serious historians (though it might be used quite effectively in a personal essay).

As you read either Garrow's or King's account, take notes and ask yourself questions. If you have answered the questions on page 507, you have already done a great deal of critical thinking about the first selection.

Prewriting

Before you write, gather your data in a chart like the following one.

	Quotations
Facts that can be proved	
Opinions that are totally unsupported	
Opinions backed up by evidence	
Language with positive connotations	
Language with negative connotations	
Sarcasm (if any)	
Your feelings about the account	

Writing

You might organize your own essay like this:

1. **Paragraph 1:** In your introductory paragraph, include a **thesis statement** that describes the **tone** of the passage in general.
2. **Paragraph 2:** Sum up the writer's attitude toward one character, with an evaluation of his supporting evidence.
3. **Paragraph 3:** Sum up the writer's attitude toward the other character, with an evaluation of his supporting evidence.
4. **Paragraph 4:** Present your conclusion, including your feelings about the excerpt.

Checklist for Revision

1. Have you cited the account's title and author?
2. Have you summarized what you think is the writer's attitude toward his subjects?
3. Have you analyzed the evidence the writer gives to support his opinions?
4. Have you mentioned at least one example in which the writer uses loaded words?
5. If you have quoted from the excerpt, have you used quotation marks, checked the quotation for accuracy, and cited the page on which the quotation appears?
6. Have you checked: Spelling? Punctuation? Capitalization? Sentence structure? Paragraph organization?

THE ELEMENTS OF DRAMA

Interior of Booth's Theater
by Charles W. Witham. Watercolor.

UNIT FOUR   Robert Anderson

THE ELEMENTS OF DRAMA

An introduction by **Robert Anderson**

> *Drama began as the act of a whole community. Ideally, there would be no spectators. In practice, every member of the audience should feel like an understudy.*
>
> —W. H. Auden

Apache Gan Dancers by Pablita Velarde. Watercolor.

The Amerind Foundation, Inc., Dragoon, Arizona.

D rama is perhaps the oldest form of storytelling, and it is likely that the original dramatists, in order to get and hold the attention of their audiences, used the same principles that later great playwrights were to follow.

Imagine a Stone Age tribesman coming in from the hunt with his companions. He is eager to tell the people in his village what happened, and he starts his story: "We came upon this bear and we followed him and then he turned on us and we killed him." As he gets to the exciting part, one of the other hunters might jump

San Geronimo Fiesta by
Leon Gaspard (1929–1953).
Oil on canvas.

Courtesy of The Anschutz Collection.
Denver, Colorado.

up and act the bear. Then another might join in to show what part
he played in the hunt by jabbing at the bear with his spear.

A week later someone might say, "Tell us again how you killed
that bear." And in repeating the performance, the tribesmen are
no longer reporting; they are acting out a drama.

The "Bare Bones" of Drama

The first time they reported the kill, the tribesmen might simply
have told what happened: They went out hunting, found the bear,
and killed it. But the second time they act out the story, they want
to make the hunt more exciting, so they include a **foreshadowing,**
or hint, of danger. Perhaps they create **suspense** by indicating that
there had been rumors of a marauding bear in the vicinity.

Now the hunter-actor-playwrights have created the story of a
desperate situation: The people in the "drama" must do something
to save themselves from the bear, who might return and destroy
the village. A great deal is at stake. After some discussion they
decide to take action: They will hunt the bear.

Since plays and stories are usually not about groups, let's imagine that the story now becomes personalized and focused as the
chief tells his young son that he must come along. Suppose further
that the playwrights decide to make it the young son's first hunt,
and he is afraid. Now we have two matters at stake: the safety of
the village and the testing of the son. We also have two different
types of **conflict:** the **external** threat posed by the bear and the
son's **internal** struggle to overcome his fear.

Greek tragedy mask (c. 86 B.C.).

National Museum, Athens.

In reenacting their drama, the hunter-actors now meet the bear and throw their spears, but they either miss or only wound the bear. Now what? The action mounts to a new crisis: Enraged, the bear charges and kills the chief. Seeing his father dead, the youth overcomes his fear, recovers one of the spears, rushes wildly at the bear, and kills it. And the play is over.

In this story of the bear hunt, we have most of the basic elements of drama. That is, we have the **bare bones,** or the framework, on which any drama is built.

1. Characters the audience cares about are placed in a more or less desperate situation with a great deal at stake.

2. The characters have a **conflict,** or problem, that engages them in a struggle—they want something (to save themselves), and they take action against a formidable opponent (the bear) to get it.

3. The story mounts in tension because **suspense** is created. Questions come to the audience's mind. (Will the hunters kill the bear? Will the boy measure up?)

4. The story progresses to its **climax,** or the moment of greatest emotional intensity, just before the outcome of the conflict is revealed. (The boy takes up his father's spear in fury.)

5. The main character undergoes a **change** (from fear to courage) under the pressure of the action. (He kills the bear.)

The Importance of Conflict and Action

Because conflict is central to any story, almost all plays involve action. But most plays do not involve physical action like hunting bears. (The movies can do this kind of thing better, though of course in some of Shakespeare's plays, there are duels and street fights and battles.) Plays are usually concerned with more subtle conflicts between characters, which must be worked out not in physical action but rather through speech.

Speech is itself a kind of action. When we open our mouths to speak, we do so with some kind of intention: We want to convey some information, to argue, to communicate with someone. In fact, we can fight and struggle and wound and try to achieve our "wants" and overcome obstacles with words. In a courtroom, two lawyers can use words to argue, to develop evidence, to drag out admissions from unwilling witnesses, and even to destroy a witness on the stand. A person trying to persuade a friend not to give up hope is engaged in an action as serious and as tense as a police officer chasing a thief through the streets of San Francisco. A man, desperately in love, trying to convince a skeptical woman that he is in love with her, is struggling in an action as important as two people dueling. He, too, is dueling—but with words.

In each of these cases, the conflict is not the result of opposing physical forces but of opposing attitudes and wants. The actions taken to work out the conflicts are not physical; they are expressions of ideas and attitudes—that is, they are *words*.

> " **M**ost plays do not involve physical action like hunting bears. . . . Plays are usually concerned with more subtle conflicts between characters, which must be worked out not in physical action but rather through speech."

From the 1957 film *Witness for the Prosecution* starring Marlene Dietrich, Tyrone Power, and Charles Laughton.

Involving the Audience

The important thing in any conflict is the meaning of the struggle to the man or woman involved: At stake might be life, self-respect, belief, security, happiness. No conflict in and of itself is very interesting for long unless the dramatist makes us care about the person, unless we become involved with the psychological complexity arising from the situation, and unless we know how desperately important the outcome is to the character.

The same is true of life itself. If we suddenly come upon a baseball game being played by teams we know nothing about, we may take a mild interest in the skill of both sides. But obviously mere skill is not what makes fans jump up and down and scream. They *care* fervently about one side or the other. They know the various problems of the team and the players. Will the rookie pitcher be demoted to the bullpen because of his fight last night with the manager? Will he be able to pitch, knowing his son is in the hospital?

The merely skillful use of the "bare bones" of playwriting does not make plays "good." What makes plays "good" is the mind and the sensitivity of the playwrights, their depth of feeling, their powers of observation and imagination, as well as their understanding of the complexities of human nature.

The "Bare Bones" of Drama in a Modern Classic

To illustrate how the principles we have been talking about operate in a modern classic, let's look at Arthur Miller's *Death of a Salesman*. Willy Loman, a traveling salesman, is old, tired, and broken in spirit. He no longer has the strength to go on the road for the company he has served for many years. But he has a problem: He still needs to earn money for his family. Here is a character whom we care about, whom we can identify with. Willy is the underdog (the "low" man); we all know people like him, in our families or among our friends. And his situation is desperate. (Indeed, a good description of the situation of almost all dramatic characters might be "desperate.") Willy makes a decision to ask his employer for a position in the main office. He knows he will be up against a "tough customer," not the kind, considerate man his employer's father was. But Willy takes action to solve his problem. He goes to his employer to make his request. The employer says he does not need him in the main office, but he also agrees that Willy should no longer work on the road. Willy pleads to be allowed to work in the office. He will take a cut in pay—anything. They argue. Finally, instead of getting the office job, Willy is fired. At the play's climax, Willy, faced with his failure to get money, chooses an action that he believes will solve his problems. Ironically, the action he takes is as futile as the life he has lived: The insurance money he hopes his family will collect after his death is not paid because he has committed suicide.

Dustin Hoffman as Willy Loman in a 1984 production of *Death of a Salesman* by Arthur Miller.

Innovators in Drama

There are, of course, plays that to a greater or lesser extent do without these "bare bones" of characters, conflict, action, suspense, climax, and change. *Our Town,* which we will be reading, is one of them. One of the pleasures and duties of artists is to challenge the form in which they work. Each time artists start to work, they are faced with the challenge of their material and the challenge of the forms and conventions of their art. We are all familiar with the break from tradition in much modern painting and sculpture. But the artists who have broken with tradition and departed from established principles are still aware of them. They know the risks they are taking in trying to find new principles or new ways of extending the old ones. Innovators are usually well versed in the traditions of their art before they try to change them.

Show, Don't Tell!

One of the pleasures of the theater is watching the *process* through which things happen. A novelist telling the story of *Our Town,* for example, might tell you, "Emily and George sat at the soda fountain and soon knew they were in love." In the theater that is not enough. In fact, it is not *anything,* because we want to see *how* it happened. *What* did they say to each other? Show us! Let us live through the experience. Play it! Sometimes a playwright may write an outline of a scene between two people but then on trying to write the scene itself, finds "it won't play." In other words, the outline might say, "Emily and George drink sodas and fall in love." But when the playwright comes to write the scene, for some reason Emily and George just won't say anything.

When I have written movies based on novels, I have frequently been faced with the difference between the *telling* done by the novelist and the *showing* demanded of the dramatic writer. Let us say that at the end of a chapter, the novelist has a boy fall down a well. At the opening of the next chapter, the novelist might say, "After his friends had helped him out of the well, the boy went home." If I had to rewrite this as a drama, where the audience delights in *seeing* and demands to see *process,* I would have to invent the whole scene of getting the boy out of the well.

Thus drama is a medium in which *process* is important—we care about "how" a scene develops, not just "what" a scene accomplishes. This is why we can go back so many times to see plays and movies when we already know the outcome. We want to see again that funny scene where . . . or that sad scene when . . .

The Playwright's Collaborators

A novel or a short story exists in its final form on the page. Readers, in a sense, "perform" the story in their own minds. But a play is meant to be presented on a stage, so the actors, directors, stage designers, lighting designers, costumers, and even musicians become the playwright's collaborators.

> " We care about 'how' a scene develops, not just 'what' a scene accomplishes. This is why we can go back so many times to see plays and movies when we already know the outcome."

It is this collaboration that can make playwriting the most rewarding kind of writing—and the most difficult. In addition to having a story to tell and the ability to conceive it in a basically dramatic form, playwrights must know *how* to write for the theater. They must know how to evoke a response from an audience, not by using words alone but by creating a "theater poetry"—by using all the talents of their collaborators, all the elements of the theater available to them.

For example, suppose a beautiful actress, who creates by her personal magnetism a kind of magic, slowly moves across a dimly lit stage to a man sitting despondently in a chair. She hesitates, then touches his shoulder. He turns, surprised, pleased. She lowers her head toward his. The lights dim slowly, finally leaving the man and woman in a faintly glowing spot of light. Then the spot fades away. Do we still see them, or don't we see them? And the curtain is finally down.

The stage direction for a scene like this might look very ordinary on the page. "She crosses slowly to him and touches his shoulder. He looks up, surprised. She lowers her head toward him and they kiss." This stage direction was not written to be read as literature. It was written with the knowledge of what a fine actress, working with a skilled director and an expert lighting designer, could do to help communicate this wordless moment. If it is done well, the audience will remember the moment forever. In the theater, we tend to remember what we *see* even more than what we *hear*.

That scene between the man and the woman is no less the playwright's scene because there is no dialogue. It is the playwright who devised the situation, created the characters, and organized the story so that this wordless scene is possible.

The Playwright and the Audience

The playwright's final collaborator is the audience. The play exists somewhere between the stage and the spectator. In a sense, we get out of a play only what we bring to it. Out of some deep feeling of joy or sadness or excitement, a playwright writes a story, sounds a note, hoping to evoke a responsive chord from the audience. This response is what might be called the "Oh, yes!" reaction. Playwrights write about particular experiences or observations. Enhancing these particulars with their imagination, they hope to reach something universal, something in everyone's experience. If they succeed, then members of the audience might ask, "How did you know what my family is like?" The playwright, of course, did not know about the audience's families, but he knew his own, and in some ways all families are the same.

One of the special qualities of the theater is that when we respond, we respond as a group. This mass response of laughter or tears or excitement gives us a reassuring feeling that we are not alone, that we are one with the people sitting around us, with everyone in the theater, and in a sense, with our community and the world.

> " **I**n the theater, we tend to remember what we *see* even more than what we *hear*."

Our Town
by Thornton Wilder

*O*ur Town, originally presented in 1938, is probably the American play most widely produced throughout the world. Although Thornton Wilder wrote that it "is not offered as a picture of life in a New Hampshire village" (see page 558), people in all countries have accepted it as just that. Americans, too—even those who have been brought up in New York City or Texas—look upon the life portrayed in Our Town as part of their own heritage. It was not too long ago that America was largely a country of villages, and Grover's Corners stands in our memory (or in our fantasy) for all those villages and for the simpler, truer life that we imagine was lived there.

After saying what Our Town is not meant to be, Wilder went on to say what it is: "It is an attempt to find a value above all price for the smallest events in our daily life." This is a clue to the **theme,** or central idea, of the play. We sit and watch with the "shock of recognition" all the small and large rituals of our own lives. We hear our mothers calling to us that we will be late for school; we relive our first hesitant contact with love; we feel the anxieties of weddings and the grieving for a loved one gone.

Someone once said, "The trouble with life is that it's so daily." Wilder wants to make us appreciate and even wonder at this "dailiness." Those of us who have been very sick for a long time, or who have been unable to use our hands or our legs for months because of an accident, have experienced sudden appreciation when we have again been able to walk, to run, to throw a ball. Unfortunately, once we are "whole" again, we take all these wonders for granted. Wilder wants us to see the world with the eyes of someone who has not yet lost this sense of wonder.

The Staging of *Our Town*

When Our Town opened its tryout tour in Boston, it was not well received. Wilder's play was different and it was strange. Many people felt particularly cheated by the absence of sets; most of them were accustomed to plays in five acts with each act having a different setting. Even after the production went on to New York and became a success, many critics continued to regard it as little more than a "stunt."

If you have never seen the play staged, you will probably visualize a small New England village as you are reading. If you have never been to such a village, you will probably build an image from pictures you have seen on Christmas cards or calendars.

The interesting thing is that when you see the play performed, you do not see a picture of the village in your mind's eye at all. What has remained in my mind over the many years since I first saw the play is the actual bare stage with the wooden chairs and the black umbrellas. Strangely, that is the proper setting for the play—the stark simplicity of a bare stage, not the stark simplicity of a New England village. I do not see a cemetery in my mind when I see the play, but when I go to an old churchyard cemetery in New England, I see Wilder's characters sitting in chairs, talking.

> "**S**omeone once said, 'The trouble with life is that it's so daily.' Wilder wants to make us appreciate and even wonder at this 'dailiness.'"

> "**W**hen I go to an old churchyard cemetery in New England, I see Wilder's characters sitting in chairs, talking."

OUR TOWN

Thornton Wilder

From a 1975 production at the American Shakespeare Theatre in Stratford, Connecticut.

Characters

(in order of appearance)

Stage Manager	Mr. Webb
Dr. Gibbs	Woman in the Balcony
Joe Crowell	Man in the Auditorium
Howie Newsome	Lady in the Box
Mrs. Gibbs	Simon Stimson
Mrs. Webb	Mrs. Soames
George Gibbs	Constable Warren
Rebecca Gibbs	Si Crowell
Wally Webb	Three Baseball Players
Emily Webb	Sam Craig
Professor Willard	Joe Stoddard

The entire play takes place in Grover's Corners, New Hampshire.

The first performance of this play took place at the McCarter Theatre, Princeton, New Jersey, on January 22, 1938. The first New York performance was at the Henry Miller Theater on February 4, 1938.

Act One

No curtain.

No scenery.

The audience, arriving, sees an empty stage in half-light.

Presently the STAGE MANAGER, *hat on and pipe in mouth, enters and begins placing a table and three chairs downstage left, and a table and three chairs downstage right. He also places a low bench at the corner of what will be the Webb house, left.*

"Left" and "right" are from the point of view of the actor facing the audience. "Up" is toward the back wall.

As the house lights go down he has finished setting the stage and, leaning against the right proscenium[1] pillar, watches the late arrivals in the audience.

When the auditorium is in complete darkness, he speaks:

Stage Manager. This play is called "Our Town." It was written by Thornton Wilder; produced and directed by A. . . . (or: produced by A. . . .; directed by B. . . .). In it you will see Miss C. . . .; Miss D. . . .; Miss E. . . .; and Mr. F. . . .; Mr. G. . . .; Mr. H. . . .; and many others. The name of the town is Grover's Corners, New Hampshire—just across the Massachusetts line: latitude 42 degrees 40 minutes; longitude 70 degrees 37 minutes. The First Act shows a day in our town. The day is May 7, 1901. The time is just before dawn. *(A rooster crows.)*

The sky is beginning to show some streaks of light over in the East there, behind our mount'in.

The morning star always gets wonderful bright the minute before it has to go, doesn't it? *(He stares at it for a moment, then goes upstage.)*

Well, I'd better show you how our town lies. Up here—*(that is: parallel with the back wall)* is Main Street. Way back there is the railway station; tracks go that way. Polish Town's across the tracks, and some Canuck[2] families. *(Toward the left)*

Over there is the Congregational Church; across the street's the Presbyterian.

Methodist and Unitarian are over there.

Baptist is down in the holla' by the river.

Catholic Church is over beyond the tracks.

Here's the Town Hall and Post Office combined; jail's in the basement.

Bryan[3] once made a speech from these very steps here.

Along here's a row of stores. Hitching posts and horse blocks in front of them. First automobile's going to come along in about five years— belonged to Banker Cartwright, our richest citizen . . . lives in the big white house up on the hill.

Here's the grocery store and here's Mr. Morgan's drugstore. Most everybody in town manages to look into those two stores once a day.

---

1. **proscenium** (prō·sē′nē·əm): a small area of the stage in front of the curtain line.

2. **Canuck** (ka·nuk′): slang for a person who is French-Canadian (from a Hawaiian word).

3. **Bryan:** William Jennings Bryan (1860–1925), a famous American statesman and orator.

"Nice town, y'know what I mean?"

From a 1959 production directed by José Quintero
at the Circle in the Square in New York.

Public School's over yonder. High School's still farther over. Quarter of nine mornings, noontimes, and three o'clock afternoons, the hull town can hear the yelling and screaming from those schoolyards. *(He approaches the table and chairs downstage right.)*

This is our doctor's house—Doc Gibbs'. This is the back door. *(Two arched trellises, covered with vines and flowers, are pushed out, one by each proscenium pillar.)* There's some scenery for those who think they have to have scenery.

This is Mrs. Gibbs's garden. Corn . . . peas . . . beans . . . hollyhocks . . . heliotrope . . . and a lot of burdock. *(Crosses the stage.)*

In those days our newspaper come out twice a week—the Grover's Corners *Sentinel*—and this is Editor Webb's house.

And this is Mrs. Webb's garden.

Just like Mrs. Gibbs's, only it's got a lot of sunflowers, too. *(He looks upward, center stage.)*

Right here . . .'s a big butternut tree. *(He returns to his place by the right proscenium pillar and looks at the audience for a minute.)*

Nice town, y'know what I mean?

Nobody very remarkable ever come out of it, s'far as we know.

The earliest tombstones in the cemetery up there on the mountain say 1670–1680—they're Grovers and Cartwrights and Gibbses and Herseys—same names as are around here now.

Well, as I said: It's about dawn.

The only lights on in town are in a cottage over by the tracks where a Polish mother's just had twins. And in the Joe Crowell house, where Joe Junior's getting up so as to deliver the paper. And in the depot, where Shorty Hawkins is gettin' ready to flag the 5:45 for Boston. *(A train whistle is heard. The* STAGE MANAGER *takes out his watch and nods.)*

Naturally, out in the country—all around—

there've been lights on for some time, what with milkin's and so on. But town people sleep late.

So—another day's begun.

There's Doc Gibbs comin' down Main Street now, comin' back from that baby case. And here's his wife comin' downstairs to get breakfast. (MRS. GIBBS, *a plump, pleasant woman in the middle thirties, comes ''downstairs'' right. She pulls up an imaginary window shade in her kitchen and starts to make a fire in her stove.*)

Doc Gibbs died in 1930. The new hospital's named after him.

Mrs. Gibbs died first—long time ago, in fact. She went out to visit her daughter, Rebecca, who married an insurance man in Canton, Ohio, and died there—pneumonia—but her body was brought back here. She's up in the cemetery there now—in with a whole mess of Gibbses and Herseys—she was Julia Hersey 'fore she married Doc Gibbs in the Congregational Church over there.

In our town we like to know the facts about everybody.

There's Mrs. Webb, coming downstairs to get her breakfast, too.

—That's Doc Gibbs. Got that call at half past one this morning.

And there comes Joe Crowell, Jr., delivering Mr. Webb's *Sentinel*.

[DR. GIBBS *has been coming along Main Street from the left. At the point where he would turn to approach his house, he stops, sets down his— imaginary—black bag, takes off his hat, and rubs his face with fatigue, using an enormous handkerchief.*

MRS. WEBB, *a thin, serious, crisp woman, has entered her kitchen, left, tying on an apron. She goes through the motions of putting wood into a stove, lighting it, and preparing breakfast.*

Suddenly, JOE CROWELL, JR., *eleven, starts down Main Street from the right, hurling imaginary newspapers into doorways.*]

Joe Crowell, Jr. Morning, Doc Gibbs.
Dr. Gibbs. Morning, Joe.
Joe Crowell, Jr. Somebody been sick, Doc?
Dr. Gibbs. No. Just some twins born over in Polish Town.

Joe Crowell, Jr. Do you want your paper now?
Dr. Gibbs. Yes, I'll take it.—Anything serious goin' on in the world since Wednesday?
Joe Crowell, Jr. Yessir. My schoolteacher, Miss Foster, 's getting married to a fella over in Concord.
Dr. Gibbs. I declare.—How do you boys feel about that?
Joe Crowell, Jr. Well, of course, it's none of my business—but I think if a person starts out to be a teacher, she ought to stay one.
Dr. Gibbs. How's your knee, Joe?
Joe Crowell, Jr. Fine, Doc, I never think about it at all. Only like you said, it always tells me when it's going to rain.
Dr. Gibbs. What's it telling you today? Goin' to rain?
Joe Crowell, Jr. No, sir.
Dr. Gibbs. Sure?
Joe Crowell, Jr. Yessir.
Dr. Gibbs. Knee ever make a mistake?
Joe Crowell, Jr. No, sir.

[JOE *goes off.* DR. GIBBS *stands reading his paper.*]

Stage Manager. Want to tell you something about that boy Joe Crowell there. Joe was awful bright—graduated from high school here, head of his class. So he got a scholarship to Massachusetts Tech. Graduated head of his class there, too. It was all wrote up in the Boston paper at the time. Goin' to be a great engineer, Joe was. But the war broke out and he died in France.—All that education for nothing.
Howie Newsome (*offstage left*). Giddap, Bessie! What's the matter with you today?
Stage Manager. Here comes Howie Newsome, deliverin' the milk.

[HOWIE NEWSOME, *about thirty, in overalls, comes along Main Street from the left, walking beside an invisible horse and wagon and carrying an imaginary rack with milk bottles. The sound of clinking milk bottles is heard. He leaves some bottles at* MRS. WEBB'S *trellis; then, crossing the stage to* MRS. GIBBS', *he stops center to talk to* DR. GIBBS.]

Howie Newsome. Morning, Doc.

Dr. Gibbs. Morning, Howie.

Howie Newsome. Somebody sick?

Dr. Gibbs. Pair of twins over to Mrs. Goruslawski's.

Howie Newsome. Twins, eh? This town's gettin' bigger every year.

Dr. Gibbs. Goin' to rain, Howie?

Howie Newsome. No, no. Fine day—that'll burn through. Come on, Bessie.

Dr. Gibbs. Hello Bessie. (*He strokes the horse, which has remained up center.*) How old is she, Howie?

Howie Newsome. Going on seventeen. Bessie's all mixed up about the route ever since the Lockharts stopped takin' their quart of milk every day. She wants to leave 'em a quart just the same—keeps scolding me the hull trip.

[*He reaches* MRS. GIBBS' *back door. She is waiting for him.*]

Mrs. Gibbs. Good morning, Howie.

Howie Newsome. Morning, Mrs. Gibbs. Doc's just comin' down the street.

Mrs. Gibbs. Is he? Seems like you're late today.

Howie Newsome. Yes. Somep'n went wrong with the separator.[4] Don't know what 'twas. (*He passes* DR. GIBBS *up center.*) Doc!

Dr. Gibbs. Howie!

Mrs. Gibbs (*calling upstairs*). Children! Children! Time to get up.

Howie Newsome. Come on, Bessie! (*He goes off right.*)

Mrs. Gibbs. George! Rebecca!

[DR. GIBBS *arrives at his back door and passes through the trellis into his house.*]

Mrs. Gibbs. Everything all right, Frank?

Dr. Gibbs. Yes. I declare—easy as kittens.

Mrs. Gibbs. Bacon'll be ready in a minute. Set down and drink your coffee. You can catch a couple hours' sleep this morning, can't you?

Dr. Gibbs. Hm! . . . Mrs. Wentworth's coming at eleven. Guess I know what it's about, too. Her stummick ain't what it ought to be.

---

4. **separator:** a dairy machine for separating cream from milk.

Mrs. Gibbs. All told, you won't get more'n three hours' sleep. Frank Gibbs, I don't know what's goin' to become of you. I do wish I could get you to go away someplace and take a rest. I think it would do you good.

Mrs. Webb. Emileeee! Time to get up! Wally! Seven o'clock!

Mrs. Gibbs. I declare, you got to speak to George. Seems like something's come over him lately. He's no help to me at all. I can't even get him to cut me some wood.

Dr. Gibbs (*washing and drying his hands at the sink.* MRS. GIBBS *is busy at the stove*). Is he sassy to you?

Mrs. Gibbs. No. He just whines! All he thinks about is that baseball—George! Rebecca! You'll be late for school.

Dr. Gibbs. M-m-m . . .

Mrs. Gibbs. George!

Dr. Gibbs. George, look sharp!

George's Voice. Yes, Pa!

Dr. Gibbs (*as he goes off the stage*). Don't you hear your mother calling you? I guess I'll go upstairs and get forty winks.

Mrs. Webb. Wallee! Emileee! You'll be late for school! Walleee! You wash yourself good or I'll come up and do it myself.

Rebecca Gibbs's Voice. Ma! What dress shall I wear?

Mrs. Gibbs. Don't make a noise. Your father's been out all night and needs his sleep. I washed and ironed the blue gingham for you special.

Rebecca. Ma, I hate that dress.

Mrs. Gibbs. Oh, hush-up-with-you.

Rebecca. Every day I go to school dressed like a sick turkey.

Mrs. Gibbs. Now, Rebecca, you always look *very* nice.

Rebecca. Mama, George's throwing soap at me.

Mrs. Gibbs. I'll come and slap the both of you—that's what I'll do.

[*A factory whistle sounds. The* CHILDREN *dash in and take their places at the tables. Right,* GEORGE, *about sixteen, and* REBECCA, *eleven. Left,* EMILY *and* WALLY, *same ages. They carry strapped schoolbooks.*]

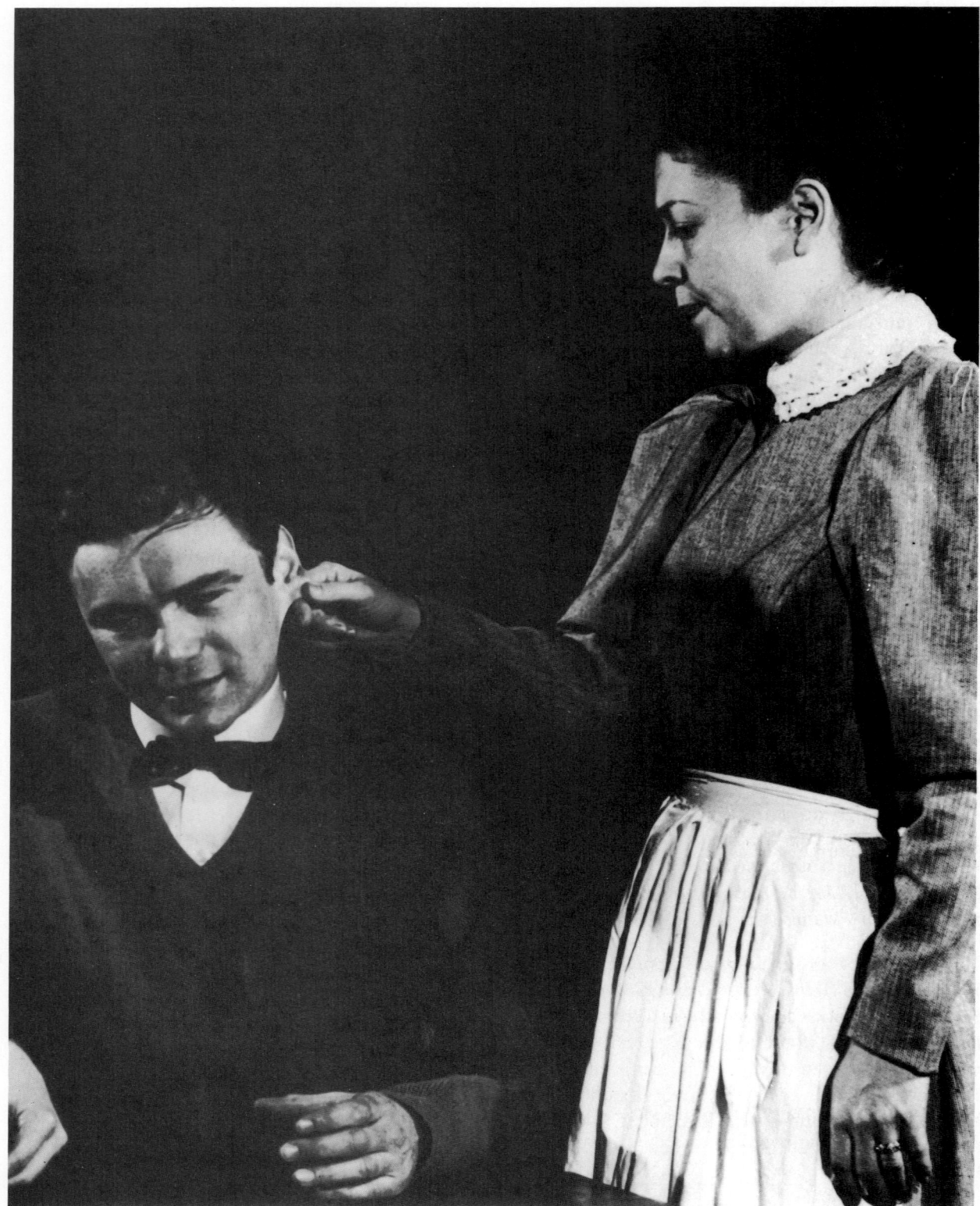

"*. . . I won't have you gobbling like wolves.*"   From the 1959 Circle in the Square production.

Stage Manager. We've got a factory in our town too—hear it? Makes blankets. Cartwrights own it and it brung 'em a fortune.

Mrs. Webb. Children! Now I won't have it. Breakfast is just as good as any other meal and I won't have you gobbling like wolves. It'll stunt your growth—that's a fact. Put away your book, Wally.

Wally. Aw, Ma! By ten o'clock I got to know all about Canada.

Mrs. Webb. You know the rule's well as I do—no books at table. As for me, I'd rather have my children healthy than bright.

Emily. I'm both, Mama: You know I am. I'm the brightest girl in school for my age. I have a wonderful memory.

Mrs. Webb. Eat your breakfast.

Wally. I'm bright, too, when I'm looking at my stamp collection.

Mrs. Gibbs. I'll speak to your father about it when he's rested. Seems to me twenty-five cents a week's enough for a boy your age. I declare I don't know how you spend it all.

George. Aw, Ma—I gotta lotta things to buy.

Mrs. Gibbs. Strawberry phosphates[5]—that's what you spend it on.

George. I don't see how Rebecca comes to have so much money. She has more'n a dollar.

Rebecca (spoon in mouth, dreamily). I've been saving it up gradual.

Mrs. Gibbs. Well, dear, I think it's a good thing to spend some every now and then.

Rebecca. Mama, do you know what I love most in the world—do you?—Money.

Mrs. Gibbs. Eat your breakfast.

The Children. Mama, there's first bell.—I gotta hurry.—I don't want any more.—I gotta hurry.

[*The* CHILDREN *rise, seize their books and dash out through the trellises. They meet, down center, and chattering, walk to Main Street, then turn left. The* STAGE MANAGER *goes off, unobtrusively, right.*]

Mrs. Webb. Walk fast, but you don't have to run. Wally, pull up your pants at the knee. Stand up straight, Emily.

---

5. **phosphates:** soft drinks (flavored syrups and soda water).

Mrs. Gibbs. Tell Miss Foster I send her my best congratulations—can you remember that?

Rebecca. Yes, Ma.

Mrs. Gibbs. You look real nice, Rebecca. Pick up your feet.

All. Goodbye.

[MRS. GIBBS *fills her apron with food for the chickens and comes down to the footlights.*]

Mrs. Gibbs. Here, chick, chick, chick.

No, go away, you. Go away.

Here, chick, chick, chick.

What's the matter with *you*? Fight, fight, fight—that's all you do.

Hm . . . *you* don't belong to me. Where'd you come from? (*She shakes her apron.*)

Oh, don't be so scared. Nobody's going to hurt you. (MRS. WEBB *is sitting on the bench by her trellis, stringing beans.*)

Good morning, Myrtle. How's your cold?

Mrs. Webb. Well, I still get that tickling feeling in my throat. I told Charles I didn't know as I'd go to choir practice tonight. Wouldn't be any use.

Mrs. Gibbs. Have you tried singing over your voice?

Mrs. Webb. Yes, but somehow I can't do that and stay on the key. While I'm resting myself I thought I'd string some of these beans.

Mrs. Gibbs (*rolling up her sleeves as she crosses the stage for a chat*). Let me help you. Beans have been good this year.

Mrs. Webb. I've decided to put up forty quarts if it kills me. The children say they hate 'em, but I notice they're able to get 'em down all winter.

[*Pause. Brief sound of chickens cackling.*]

Mrs. Gibbs. Now, Myrtle. I've got to tell you something, because if I don't tell somebody I'll burst.

Mrs. Webb. Why, Julia Gibbs!

Mrs. Gibbs. Here, give me some more of those beans. Myrtle, did one of those secondhand-furniture men from Boston come to see you last Friday?

Mrs. Webb. No-o.

Mrs. Gibbs. Well, he called on me. First I thought

he was a patient wantin' to see Dr. Gibbs. 'N he wormed his way into my parlor, and, Myrtle Webb, he offered me three hundred and fifty dollars for Grandmother Wentworth's highboy, as I'm sitting here!

Mrs. Webb. Why, Julia Gibbs!

Mrs. Gibbs. He did! That old thing! Why, it was so big I didn't know where to put it and I almost give it to Cousin Hester Wilcox.

Mrs. Webb. Well, you're going to take it, aren't you?

Mrs. Gibbs. I don't know.

Mrs. Webb. You don't know—three hundred and fifty dollars! What's come over you?

Mrs. Gibbs. Well, if I could get the Doctor to take the money and go away someplace on a real trip, I'd sell it like that.—Y'know, Myrtle, it's been the dream of my life to see Paris, France.—Oh, I don't know. It sounds crazy, I suppose, but for years I've been promising myself that if we ever had the chance——

Mrs. Webb. How does the Doctor feel about it?

Mrs. Gibbs. Well, I did beat about the bush a little and said that if I got a legacy—that's the way I put it—I'd make him take me somewhere.

Mrs. Webb. M-m-m . . . What did he say?

Mrs. Gibbs. You know how he is. I haven't heard a serious word out of him since I've known him. No, he said, it might make him discontented with Grover's Corners to go traipsin' about Europe; better let well enough alone, he says. Every two years he makes a trip to the battlefields of the Civil War and that's enough treat for anybody, he says.

Mrs. Webb. Well, Mr. Webb just *admires* the way Dr. Gibbs knows everything about the Civil War. Mr. Webb's a good mind to give up Napoleon and move over to the Civil War, only Dr. Gibbs being one of the greatest experts in the country just makes him despair.

Mrs. Gibbs. It's a fact! Dr. Gibbs is never so happy as when he's at Antietam or Gettysburg. The times I've walked over those hills, Myrtle, stopping at every bush and pacing it all out, like we were going to buy it.

Mrs. Webb. Well, if that secondhand man's really serious about buyin' it, Julia, you sell it. And then you'll get to see Paris, all right. Just keep droppin' hints from time to time—that's how I got to see the Atlantic Ocean, y'know.

Mrs. Gibbs. Oh, I'm sorry I mentioned it. Only it seems to me that once in your life before you die you ought to see a country where they don't talk in English and don't even want to.

[*The* STAGE MANAGER *enters briskly from the right. He tips his hat to the ladies, who nod their heads.*]

Stage Manager. Thank you, ladies. Thank you very much. (MRS. GIBBS *and* MRS. WEBB *gather up their things, return into their homes and disappear.*) Now we're going to skip a few hours. But first we want a little more information about the town, kind of a scientific account, you might say. So I've asked Professor Willard of our State University to sketch in a few details of our past history here. Is Professor Willard here? (PROFESSOR WILLARD, *a rural savant,*[6] *pince-nez*[7] *on a wide satin ribbon, enters from the right with some notes in his hand.*) May I introduce Professor Willard of our State University. A few brief notes, thank you, Professor—unfortunately our time is limited.

Professor Willard. Grover's Corners . . . let me see . . . Grover's Corners lies on the old Pleistocene granite of the Appalachian range. I may say it's some of the oldest land in the world. We're very proud of that. A shelf of Devonian basalt crosses it with vestiges of Mesozoic[8] shale, and some sandstone outcroppings; but that's all more recent: two hundred, three hundred million years old. Some highly interesting fossils have been found . . . I may say: unique fossils . . . two miles out of town, in Silas Peckham's cow pasture. They can be seen at the museum in our University at any time—that is, at any reasonable time. Shall I read some of Professor Gruber's notes on the meteorological situation—mean precipitation, et cetera?

---

6. **savant** (sə·vänt'): (French) a learned or experienced person; a scholar.
7. **pince-nez** (pans'nā'): eyeglasses that clip onto the bridge of the nose (from French "pinch the nose").
8. **Pleistocene** (plīs'ta·sēn') . . . **Mesozoic** (mes'ə·zō'ik): periods in geological history. Devonian means from Devon, England. (America and Europe were once parts of a single land mass.)

Stage Manager. Afraid we won't have time for that, Professor. We might have a few words on the history of man here.

Professor Willard. Yes . . . anthropological data: Early Amerindian[9] stock. Cotahatchee tribes . . . no evidence before the tenth century of this era . . . hm . . . now entirely disappeared . . . possible traces in three families. Migration toward the end of the seventeenth century of English brachycephalic[10] blue-eyed stock . . . for the most part. Since then some Slav and Mediterranean——

Stage Manager. And the population, Professor Willard?

Professor Willard. Within the town limits: 2,640.

Stage Manager. Just a moment, Professor. (*He whispers into the professor's ear.*)

Professor Willard. Oh, yes, indeed?—The population, *at the moment,* is 2,642. The Postal District brings in 507 more, making a total of 3,149.—Mortality and birth rates: constant.—By MacPherson's gauge: 6.032.

Stage Manager. Thank you very much, Professor. We're all very much obliged to you, I'm sure.

Professor Willard. Not at all, sir; not at all.

Stage Manager. This way, Professor, and thank you again. (*Exit* PROFESSOR WILLARD)

Now the political and social report: Editor Webb.—Oh, Mr. Webb?

[MRS. WEBB *appears at her back door.*]

Mrs. Webb. He'll be here in a minute. . . . He just cut his hand while he was eatin' an apple.

Stage Manager. Thank you, Mrs. Webb.

Mrs. Webb. Charles! Everybody's waitin'. (*Exit* MRS. WEBB.)

Stage Manager. Mr. Webb is Publisher and Editor of the Grover's Corners *Sentinel.* That's our local paper, y'know.

[MR. WEBB *enters from his house, pulling on his coat. His finger is bound in a handkerchief.*]

Mr. Webb. Well . . . I don't have to tell you that we're run here by a Board of Selectmen.[11]—All males vote at the age of twenty-one. Women vote indirect. We're lower middle class: sprinkling of professional men . . . ten percent illiterate laborers. Politically, we're eighty-six percent Republicans; six percent Democrats; four percent Socialists; rest, indifferent.

Religiously, we're eighty-five percent Protestants; twelve percent Catholics; rest, indifferent.

Stage Manager. Have you any comments, Mr. Webb?

Mr. Webb. Very ordinary town, if you ask me. Little better behaved than most. Probably a lot duller.

But our young people here seem to like it well enough. Ninety percent of 'em graduating from high school settle down right here to live—even when they've been away to college.

Stage Manager. Now, is there anyone in the audience who would like to ask Editor Webb anything about the town?

Woman in the Balcony. Is there much drinking in Grover's Corners?

Mr. Webb. Well, ma'am, I wouldn't know what you'd call *much.* Satiddy nights the farmhands meet down in Ellery Greenough's stable and holler some. We've got one or two town drunks, but they're always having remorses every time an evangelist comes to town. No, ma'am, I'd say likker ain't a regular thing in the home here, except in the medicine chest. Right good for snake bite, y'know—always was.

Belligerent Man at Back of Auditorium. Is there no one in town aware of——

Stage Manager. Come forward, will you, where we can all hear you.—What were you saying?

Belligerent Man. Is there no one in town aware of social injustice and industrial inequality?

Mr. Webb. Oh, yes, everybody is—somethin' terrible. Seems like they spend most of their time talking about who's rich and who's poor.

Belligerent Man. Then why don't they do something about it? (*He withdraws without waiting for an answer.*)

Mr. Webb. Well, I dunno. . . . I guess we're all hunting like everybody else for a way the diligent and sensible can rise to the top and the lazy and quarrelsome can sink to the bottom. But it ain't easy to find. Meanwhile, we do all we can to help

---

9. **Amerindian:** American Indian.
10. **brachycephalic** (brak′i·sə·fal′ik): broad-headed.
11. **Board of Selectmen:** town officers, still elected each year in many New England towns.

those that can't help themselves and those that can we leave alone.—Are there any other questions?

Lady in a Box. Oh, Mr. Webb? Mr. Webb, is there any culture or love of beauty in Grover's Corners?

Mr. Webb. Well, ma'am, there ain't much—not in the sense you mean. Come to think of it, there's some girls that play the piano at High School Commencement; but they ain't happy about it. No, ma'am, there isn't much culture; but maybe this is the place to tell you that we've got a lot of pleasures of a kind here: We like the sun comin' up over the mountain in the morning, and we all notice a good deal about the birds. We pay a lot of attention to them. And we watch the change of the seasons; yes, everybody knows about them. But those other things—you're right, ma'am—there ain't much.—*Robinson Crusoe* and the Bible; and Handel's ''Largo,'' we all know that; and Whistler's *Mother*—those are just about as far as we go.

Lady in a Box. So I thought. Thank you, Mr. Webb.

Stage Manager. Thank you, Mr. Webb. (MR. WEBB *retires.*) Now, we'll go back to the town. It's early afternoon. All 2,642 have had their dinners and all the dishes have been washed. (MR. WEBB, *having removed his coat, returns and starts pushing a lawn mower to and fro beside his house.*) There's an early-afternoon calm in our town: a buzzin' and a hummin' from the school buildings; only a few buggies on Main Street—the horses dozing at the hitching posts; you all remember what it's like. Doc Gibbs is in his office, tapping people and making them say ''ah.'' Mr. Webb's cuttin' his lawn over there; one man in ten thinks it's a privilege to push his own lawn mower.

No, sir. It's later than I thought. There are the children coming home from school already.

[*Shrill girls' voices are heard, off left.* EMILY *comes along Main Street, carrying some books. There are some signs that she is imagining herself to be a lady of startling elegance.*]

Emily. I *can't*, Lois. I've got to go home and help my mother. I *promised.*

Mr. Webb. Emily, walk simply. Who do you think you are today?

Emily. Papa, you're terrible. One minute you tell me to stand up straight and the next minute you call me names. I just don't listen to you. (*She gives him an abrupt kiss.*)

Mr. Webb. Golly, I never got a kiss from such a great lady before.

[*He goes out of sight.* EMILY *leans over and picks some flowers by the gate of her house.*
GEORGE GIBBS *comes careening down Main Street. He is throwing a ball up to dizzying heights and waiting to catch it again. This sometimes requires his taking six steps backward. He bumps into an* OLD LADY *invisible to us.*]

George. Excuse me, Mrs. Forrest.

Stage Manager (*as Mrs. Forrest*). Go out and play in the fields, young man. You got no business playing baseball on Main Street.

George. Awfully sorry, Mrs. Forrest.—Hello, Emily.

Emily. H'lo.

George. You made a fine speech in class.

Emily. Well, . . . I was really ready to make a speech about the Monroe Doctrine, but at the last minute Miss Corcoran made me talk about the Louisiana Purchase instead. I worked an awful long time on both of them.

George. Gee, it's funny, Emily. From my window up there I can just see your head nights when you're doing your homework over in your room.

Emily. Why, can you?

George. You certainly do stick to it, Emily. I don't see how you can sit still that long. I guess you like school.

Emily. Well, I always feel it's something you have to go through.

George. Yeah.

Emily. I don't mind it really. It passes the time.

George. Yeah.—Emily, what do you think? We might work out a kinda telegraph from your window to mine; and once in a while you could give me a kinda hint or two about one of those algebra problems. I don't mean the answers, Emily, of course not . . . just some little hint . . .

"Oh, I think hints are allowed."

From the 1975 American Shakespeare Theatre production.

Emily. Oh, I think *hints* are allowed.—So—ah—if you get stuck, George, you whistle to me; and I'll give you some hints.

George. Emily, you're just naturally bright, I guess.

Emily. I figure that it's just the way a person's born.

George. Yeah. But, you see, I want to be a farmer, and my Uncle Luke says whenever I'm ready I can come over and work on his farm and if I'm any good I can just gradually have it.

Emily. You mean the house and everything?

[*Enter* MRS. WEBB *with a large bowl and sits on the bench by her trellis.*]

George. Yeah. Well, thanks . . . I better be getting out to the baseball field. Thanks for the talk, Emily.—Good afternoon, Mrs. Webb.

Mrs. Webb. Good afternoon, George.

George. So long, Emily.

Emily. So long, George.

Mrs. Webb. Emily, come and help me string these beans for the winter. George Gibbs let himself have a real conversation, didn't he? Why, he's growing up. How old would George be?

Emily. I don't know.

Mrs. Webb. Let's see. He must be almost sixteen.

Emily. Mama, I made a speech in class today and I was very good.

Mrs. Webb. You must recite it to your father at supper. What was it about?

Emily. The Louisiana Purchase. It was like silk off a spool. I'm going to make speeches all my life—Mama, are these big enough?

Mrs. Webb. Try and get them a little bigger if you can.

Emily. Mama, will you answer me a question, serious?

Mrs. Webb. Seriously, dear—not serious.

Emily. Seriously—will you?

Mrs. Webb. Of course, I will.

Emily. Mama, am I good-looking?

Mrs. Webb. Yes, of course you are. All my children have got good features; I'd be ashamed if they hadn't.

Emily. Oh, Mama, that's not what I mean. What I mean is: Am I *pretty*?

Mrs. Webb. I've already told you, yes. Now that's enough of that. You have a nice young pretty face. I never heard of such foolishness.

Emily. Oh, Mama, you never tell us the truth about anything.

Mrs. Webb. I *am* telling you the truth.

Emily. Mama, were *you* pretty?

Mrs. Webb. Yes, I was, if I do say it. I was the prettiest girl in town next to Mamie Cartwright.

Emily. But, Mama, you've got to say *some*thing about me. Am I pretty enough . . . to get anybody . . . to get people interested in me?

Mrs. Webb. Emily, you make me tired. Now stop it. You're pretty enough for all normal purposes— Come along now and bring that bowl with you.

Emily. Oh, Mama, you're no help at all.

Stage Manager. Thank you. Thank you! That'll do. We'll have to interrupt again here. Thank you, Mrs. Webb; thank you, Emily. (MRS. WEBB *and* EMILY *withdraw.*)

There are some more things we want to explore about this town. (*He comes to the center of the stage. During the following speech the lights gradually dim to darkness, leaving only a spot on him.*)

I think this is a good time to tell you that the Cartwright interests have just begun building a new bank in Grover's Corners—had to go to Vermont for the marble, sorry to say. And they've asked a friend of mine what they should put in the cornerstone for people to dig up . . . a thousand years from now. . . . Of course, they've put in a copy of the *New York Times* and a copy of Mr. Webb's *Sentinel*. . . . We're kind of interested in this because some scientific fellas have found a way of painting all that reading matter with a glue—a silicate glue—that'll make it keep a thousand—two thousand years.

We're putting in a Bible . . . and the Constitution of the United States—and a copy of William Shakespeare's plays. What do you say, folks? What do you think? Y'know—Babylon once had two million people in it, and all we know about 'em is the names of the kings and some copies of wheat contracts . . . and contracts for the sale of slaves. Yet every night all those families sat down to supper and the father came home from his work and the smoke went up the chimney, same as here. And even in Greece and Rome, all we know about the *real* life of the people is what we can piece together out of the joking poems and the comedies they wrote for the theater back then.

So I'm going to have a copy of this play put in the cornerstone, and the people a thousand years from now'll know a few simple facts about us— more than the Treaty of Versailles[12] and the Lindbergh flight. See what I mean?

So—people a thousand years from now—this is the way we were in the provinces north of New York at the beginning of the twentieth century.— This is the way we were: in our growing up and in our marrying and in our living and in our dying.

[*A choir partially concealed in the orchestra pit has begun singing "Blessed Be the Tie That Binds."* SIMON STIMSON *stands directing them. Two ladders have been pushed onto the stage; they serve as indication of the second story in the Gibbs and Webb houses.* GEORGE *and* EMILY *mount them, and apply themselves to their schoolwork.* DR. GIBBS *has entered and is seated in his kitchen reading.*]

Well!—good deal of time's gone by. It's evening.

You can hear choir practice going on in the Congregational Church.

The children are at home doing their schoolwork.

The day's running down like a tired clock.

Simon Stimson. Now look here, everybody. Music come into the world to give pleasure.—Softer! Softer! Get it out of your heads that music's only good when it's loud. You leave loudness to the Methodists. You couldn't beat 'em, even if you wanted to. Now again. Tenors!

George. Hsst! Emily!

Emily. Hello.

George. Hello!

---

12. **Treaty of Versailles:** the treaty that ended World War I (in 1919).

Emily. I can't work at all. The moonlight's so *terrible*.

George. Emily, did you get the third problem?

Emily. Which?

George. The *third*?

Emily. Why, yes, George—that's the easiest of them all.

George. I don't see it. Emily, can you give me a hint?

Emily. I'll tell you one thing: The answer's in yards.

George. ! ! ! In yards? How do you mean?

Emily. In *square* yards.

George. Oh . . . in square yards.

Emily. Yes, George, don't you see?

George. Yeah.

Emily. In square yards of *wallpaper*.

George. Wallpaper—oh, I see. Thanks a lot, Emily.

Emily. You're welcome. My, isn't the moonlight *terrible*? And choir practice going on.—I think if you hold your breath you can hear the train all the way to Contoocook. Hear it?

George. M-m-m—What do you know!

Emily. Well, I guess I better go back and try to work.

George. Good night, Emily. And thanks.

Emily. Good night, George.

Simon Stimson. Before I forget it: How many of you will be able to come in Tuesday afternoon and sing at Fred Hersey's wedding?—Show your hands. That'll be fine; that'll be right nice. We'll do the same music we did for Jane Trowbridge's last month.

Now we'll do: "Art Thou Weary; Art Thou Languid?" It's a question, ladies and gentlemen, make it talk. Ready.

Dr. Gibbs. Oh, George, can you come down a minute?

George. Yes, Pa. *(He descends the ladder.)*

Dr. Gibbs. Make yourself comfortable, George; I'll only keep you a minute. George, how old are you?

George. I? I'm sixteen, almost seventeen.

Dr. Gibbs. What do you want to do after school's over?

George. Why, you know, Pa. I want to be a farmer on Uncle Luke's farm.

Dr. Gibbs. You'll be willing, will you, to get up early and milk and feed the stock . . . and you'll be able to hoe and hay all day?

George. Sure, I will. What are you . . . what do you mean, Pa?

Dr. Gibbs. Well, George, while I was in my office today I heard a funny sound . . . and what do you think it was? It was your mother chopping wood. There you see your mother—getting up early; cooking meals all day long; washing and ironing—and still she has to go out in the back yard and chop wood. I suppose she just got tired of asking you. She just gave up and decided it was easier to do it herself. And you eat her meals and put on the clothes she keeps nice for you, and you run off and play baseball—like she's some hired girl we keep around the house, but that we don't like very much. Well, I knew all I had to do was call your attention to it. Here's a handkerchief, son. George, I've decided to raise your spending money twenty-five cents a week. Not, of course, for chopping wood for your mother, because that's a present you give her, but because you're getting older—and I imagine there are lots of things you must find to do with it.

George. Thanks, Pa.

Dr. Gibbs. Let's see—tomorrow's your payday. You can count on it.—Hmm. Probably Rebecca'll feel she ought to have some more too. Wonder what could have happened to your mother. Choir practice never was as late as this before.

George. It's only half past eight, Pa.

Dr. Gibbs. I don't know why she's in that old choir. She hasn't any more voice than an old crow. . . . Traipsin' around the streets at this hour of the night . . . Just about time you retired, don't you think?

George. Yes, Pa.

[GEORGE *mounts to his place on the ladder. Laughter and good nights can be heard on stage left and presently* MRS. GIBBS, MRS. SOAMES, *and* MRS. WEBB *come down Main Street. When they arrive at the corner of the stage they stop.*]

Mrs. Soames. Good night, Martha. Good night, Mr. Foster.

Mrs. Webb. I'll tell Mr. Webb; I *know* he'll want to put it in the paper.

Mrs. Gibbs. My, it's late!

Mrs. Soames. Good night, Irma.

Mrs. Gibbs. Real nice choir practice, wa'n't it! Myrtle Webb! Look at that moon, will you! Tsk-tsk-tsk. Potato weather, for sure.

[*They are silent a moment, gazing up at the moon.*]

Mrs. Soames. Naturally I didn't want to say a word about it in front of those others, but now we're alone—really, it's the worst scandal that ever was in this town!

Mrs. Gibbs. What?

Mrs. Soames. Simon Stimson!

Mrs. Gibbs. Now, Louella!

Mrs. Soames. But, Julia! To have the organist of a church *drink* and *drunk* year after year. You know he was drunk tonight.

Mrs. Gibbs. Now, Louella! We all know about Mr. Stimson, and we all know about the troubles he's been through, and Dr. Ferguson knows too, and if Dr. Ferguson keeps him on there in his job, the only thing the rest of us can do is just not to notice it.

Mrs. Soames. *Not to notice it!* But it's getting worse.

Mrs. Webb. No, it isn't, Louella. It's getting better. I've been in that choir twice as long as you have. It doesn't happen anywhere near so often. . . . My, I hate to go to bed on a night like this.—I better hurry. Those children'll be sitting up till all hours. Good night, Louella.

[*They all exchange good nights. She hurries downstage, enters her house, and disappears.*]

Mrs. Gibbs. Can you get home safe, Louella?

Mrs. Soames. It's as bright as day. I can see Mr. Soames scowling at the window now. You'd think we'd been to a dance the way the menfolk carry on.

[*More good nights.* MRS. GIBBS *arrives at her home and passes through the trellis into the kitchen.*]

Mrs. Gibbs. Well, we had a real good time.

Dr. Gibbs. You're late enough.

Mrs. Gibbs. Why, Frank, it ain't any later'n usual.

Dr. Gibbs. And you stopping at the corner to gossip with a lot of hens.

Mrs. Gibbs. Now, Frank, don't be grouchy. Come out and smell the heliotrope in the moonlight. (*They stroll out arm in arm along the footlights.*) Isn't that wonderful? What did you do all the time I was away?

Dr. Gibbs. Oh, I read—as usual. What were the girls gossiping about tonight?

Mrs. Gibbs. Well, believe me, Frank—there is something to gossip about.

Dr. Gibbs. Hmm! Simon Stimson far gone, was he?

Mrs. Gibbs. Worst I've ever seen him. How'll that end, Frank? Dr. Ferguson can't forgive him forever.

Dr. Gibbs. I guess I know more about Simon Stimson's affairs than anybody in this town. Some people ain't made for small-town life. I don't know how that'll end; but there's nothing we can do but just leave it alone. Come, get in.

Mrs. Gibbs. No, not yet. . . . Frank, I'm worried about you.

Dr. Gibbs. What are you worried about?

Mrs. Gibbs. I think it's my duty to make plans for you to get a real rest and change. And if I get that legacy, well, I'm going to insist on it.

Dr. Gibbs. Now, Julia, there's no sense in going over that again.

Mrs. Gibbs. Frank, you're just *unreasonable*!

Dr. Gibbs (*starting into the house*). Come on, Julia, it's getting late. First thing you know you'll catch cold. I gave George a piece of my mind tonight. I reckon you'll have your wood chopped for a while anyway. No, no, start getting upstairs.

Mrs. Gibbs. Oh, dear. There's always so many things to pick up, seems like. You know, Frank, Mrs. Fairchild always locks her front door every night. All those people up that part of town do.

Dr. Gibbs (*blowing out the lamp*). They're all getting citified, that's the trouble with them. They haven't got nothing fit to burgle and everybody knows it.

[*They disappear.*
REBECCA *climbs up the ladder beside* GEORGE.]

George. Get out, Rebecca. There's only room for

one at this window. You're always spoiling everything.

Rebecca. Well, let me look just a minute.

George. Use your own window.

Rebecca. I did, but there's no moon there. . . .
George, do you know what I think, do you? I
think maybe the moon's getting nearer and nearer
and there'll be a big 'splosion.

George. Rebecca, you don't know anything. If the
moon were getting nearer, the guys that sit up all
night with telescopes would see it first and they'd
tell about it and it'd be in all the newspapers.

Rebecca. George, is the moon shining on South
America, Canada, and half the whole world?

George. Well—prob'ly is.

[*The* STAGE MANAGER *strolls on.*
Pause. The sound of crickets is heard.]

Stage Manager. Nine-thirty. Most of the lights are
out. No, there's Constable Warren trying a few
doors on Main Street. And here comes Editor
Webb, after putting his newspaper to bed.

[MR. WARREN, *an elderly policeman, comes along*
Main Street from the right, MR. WEBB *from the*
left.]

Mr. Webb. Good evening, Bill.

Constable Warren. Evenin', Mr. Webb.

Mr. Webb. Quite a moon!

Constable Warren. Yep.

Mr. Webb. All quiet tonight?

Constable Warren. Simon Stimson is rollin'
around a little. Just saw his wife movin' out to
hunt for him so I looked the other way—there he
is now.

[SIMON STIMSON *comes down Main Street from*
the left, only a trace of unsteadiness in his walk.]

Mr. Webb. Good evening, Simon. . . . Town
seems to have settled down for the night pretty
well. . . . (SIMON STIMSON *comes up to him and*
pauses a moment and stares at him, swaying
slightly.) Good evening. . . . Yes, most of the
town's settled down for the night, Simon. . . . I
guess we better do the same. Can I walk along a
ways with you? (SIMON STIMSON *continues on his*
way without a word and disappears at the right.)
Good night.

Constable Warren. I don't know how that's goin'
to end, Mr. Webb.

Mr. Webb. Well, he's seen a peck of trouble, one
thing after another. . . . Oh, Bill, . . . if you see
my boy smoking cigarettes, just give him a word,
will you? He thinks a lot of you, Bill.

Constable Warren. I don't think he smokes no
cigarettes, Mr. Webb. Leastways, not more'n two
or three a year.

Mr. Webb. Hm. . . . I hope not.—Well, good
night, Bill.

Constable Warren. Good night, Mr. Webb. (*Exit.*)

Mr. Webb. Who's that up there? Is that you,
Myrtle?

Emily. No, it's me, Papa.

Mr. Webb. Why aren't you in bed?

Emily. I don't know. I just can't sleep yet, Papa.
The moonlight's so *won*-derful. And the smell of
Mrs. Gibbs' heliotrope. Can you smell it?

Mr. Webb. Hm . . . Yes. Haven't any troubles on
your mind, have you, Emily?

Emily. *Troubles,* Papa? *No.*

Mr. Webb. Well, enjoy yourself, but don't let your
mother catch you. Good night, Emily.

Emily. Good night, Papa.

[MR. WEBB *crosses into the house, whistling*
"Blessed Be the Tie That Binds," and disappears.]

Rebecca. I never told you about that letter Jane
Crofut got from her minister when she was sick.
He wrote Jane a letter and on the envelope the
address was like this: It said: Jane Crofut; The
Crofut Farm; Grover's Corners; Sutton County;
New Hampshire; United States of America.

George. What's funny about that?

Rebecca. But listen, it's not finished: the United
States of America; Continent of North America;
Western Hemisphere; the Earth; the Solar System; the Universe; the Mind of God—that's what
it said on the envelope.

George. What do you know!

Rebecca. And the postman brought it just the
same.

George. What do you know!

Stage Manager. That's the end of the First Act,
friends. You can go and smoke now, those that
smoke.

Responding to the Play

Analyzing Act One

Identifying Facts

1. Wilder is having fun here with the usual techniques of playwriting. For example, traditional plays open with a scene of **exposition,** in which some action is presented that tells us where we are, when the action takes place, who the characters are, and what the characters want. Summarize the information the Stage Manager provides in his "exposition" to the audience. Describe how the Stage Manager also manipulates or controls the action of Act One.

2. Act One is framed by two recurring natural phenomena—the fading of the morning star and the rising of the moon. List the other natural patterns or cycles mentioned in Act One. What predictable human routines or patterns are dramatized in this act?

3. Name the **characters** from Grover's Corners who are presented to the audience. What facts do you learn about their lives at this moment in time?

4. The Stage Manager lets members of the audience (they are really actors and actresses planted in the audience) rise and ask Mr. Webb questions. What do they want to know about Grover's Corners? How does Mr. Webb answer their questions?

Interpreting Meanings

5. Find the speeches that help you to see "our town" and its people as links in an enormous cosmic chain of life that stretches back to prehistory. What details in Jane Crofut's letter contribute to this wide view of human life?

6. **Dramatic irony** is a powerful device: It occurs when the playwright lets the audience know something that the characters on stage do not know. Dramatic irony gives us a kind of godlike advantage over the characters. We watch them go about their daily lives, and we *know* what the future holds for them. At what points in this act does the Stage Manager make us feel this sense of dramatic irony—where does he share with us his own omniscience (his ability to know past, present, and future)?

Henry Fonda as the Stage Manager in a 1969 production at the ANTA Theater in New York.

7. Are there any indications in this act that "our town" has its share of good and bad qualities? Explain your opinion.

8. What does Grover's Corners decide to put in the cornerstone of the new bank? If these objects are found and analyzed one or two thousand years later, what do you think they will reveal about the values of Grover's Corners and the country it was part of? Why does the Stage Manager want to include a copy of *Our Town*?

9. Emily Webb and George Gibbs will be key characters in the play. What details **foreshadow** the fact that they might "get together" in the next act?

10. Since we see very few townspeople in this act, those that we do see must be important. Why do you think the town drunk is part of the act? What reasons are given for his drinking? Do you think there is any significance to the fact that he is also "artistic"?

11. Did you have a "double image" in reading Act One—that is, did you see here any moments of your own life or of the lives of people in your own town? Explain.

Act Two

The tables and chairs of the two kitchens are still on the stage.

The ladders and the small bench have been withdrawn.

The STAGE MANAGER has been at his accustomed place watching the audience return to its seats.

Stage Manager. Three years have gone by.

Yes, the sun's come up over a thousand times.

Summers and winters have cracked the mountains a little bit more, and the rains have brought down some of the dirt.

Some babies that weren't even born before have begun talking regular sentences already; and a number of people who thought they were right young and spry have noticed that they can't bound up a flight of stairs like they used to, without their heart fluttering a little.

All that can happen in a thousand days.

Nature's been pushing and contriving in other ways too: A number of young people fell in love and got married.

Yes, the mountain got bit away a few fractions of an inch; millions of gallons of water went by the mill; and here and there a new home was set up under a roof.

Almost everybody in the world gets married—you know what I mean? In our town there aren't hardly any exceptions. Most everybody in the world climbs into their graves married.

The First Act was called the Daily Life. This act is called Love and Marriage. There's another act coming after this: I reckon you can guess what that's about.

So:

It's three years later. It's 1904.

It's July seventh, just after High School Commencement.

That's the time most of our young people jump up and get married.

Soon as they've passed their last examinations in solid geometry and Cicero's[1] Orations, looks like they suddenly feel themselves fit to be married.

It's early morning. Only this time it's been raining.

It's been pouring and thundering.

Mrs. Gibbs' garden, and Mrs. Webb's here: drenched.

All those bean poles and pea vines: drenched.

All yesterday over there on Main Street, the rain looked like curtains being blown along.

Hm . . . it may begin again any minute.

There! You can hear the 5:45 for Boston. (MRS. GIBBS *and* MRS. WEBB *enter their kitchen and start the day as in the First Act.*) And there's Mrs. Gibbs and Mrs. Webb come down to make breakfast, just as though it were an ordinary day. I don't have to point out to the women in my audience that those ladies they see before them, both of those ladies cooked three meals a day—one of 'em for twenty years, the other for forty—and no summer vacation. They brought up two children apiece, washed, cleaned the house—and *never a nervous breakdown*.

It's like what one of those Middle West poets said: You've got to love life to have life, and you've got to have life to love life[2]. . . . It's what they call a vicious circle.

Howie Newsome (*offstage left*). Giddap, Bessie!

Stage Manager. Here comes Howie Newsome delivering the milk. And there's Si Crowell delivering the papers like his brother before him.

[SI CROWELL *has entered hurling imaginary newspapers into doorways;* HOWIE NEWSOME *has come along Main Street with Bessie.*]

Si Crowell. Morning, Howie.

Howie Newsome. Morning, Si.—Anything in the papers I ought to know?

Si Crowell. Nothing much, except we're losing about the best baseball pitcher Grover's Corners ever had—George Gibbs.

Howie Newsome. Reckon he is.

Si Crowell. He could hit and run bases, too.

Howie Newsome. Yep. Mighty fine ball player.—

---

1. **Cicero:** Roman statesman (106–43 B.C.) whose speeches are studied in Latin classes.

2. **You've . . . life:** a paraphrase of a line from the poem ''Lucinda Matlock'' in Edgar Lee Masters's *Spoon River Anthology* (1915). The line actually says: ''It takes life to love life.''

Whoa! Bessie! I guess I can stop and talk if I've a mind to!

Si Crowell. I don't see how he could give up a thing like that just to get married. Would you, Howie?

Howie Newsome. Can't tell, Si. Never had no talent that way. (CONSTABLE WARREN *enters. They exchange good mornings.*) You're up early, Bill.

Constable Warren. Seein' if there's anything I can do to prevent a flood. River's been risin' all night.

Howie Newsome. Si Crowell's all worked up here about George Gibbs's retiring from baseball.

Constable Warren. Yes, sir; that's the way it goes. Back in '84 we had a player, Si—even George Gibbs couldn't touch him. Name of Hank Todd. Went down to Maine and become a parson. Wonderful ballplayer.—Howie, how does the weather look to you?

Howie Newsome. Oh, 'tain't bad. Think maybe it'll clear up for good.

[CONSTABLE WARREN *and* SI CROWELL *continue on their way.*

HOWIE NEWSOME *brings the milk first to* MRS. GIBBS' *house. She meets him by the trellis.*]

Mrs. Gibbs. Good morning, Howie. Do you think it's going to rain again?

Howie Newsome. Morning, Mrs. Gibbs. It rained so heavy, I think maybe it'll clear up.

Mrs. Gibbs. Certainly hope it will.

Howie Newsome. How much did you want today?

Mrs. Gibbs. I'm going to have a houseful of relations, Howie. Looks to me like I'll need three-a-milk and two-a-cream.

Howie Newsome. My wife says to tell you we both hope they'll be very happy, Mrs. Gibbs. Know they *will*.

Mrs. Gibbs. Thanks a lot, Howie. Tell your wife I hope she gits there to the wedding.

Howie Newsome. Yes, she'll be there; she'll be there if she kin. (HOWIE NEWSOME *crosses to* MRS. WEBB'S *house.*) Morning, Mrs. Webb.

Mrs. Webb. Oh, good morning, Mr. Newsome. I told you four quarts of milk, but I hope you can spare me another.

Howie Newsome. Yes'm . . . and the two of cream.

Mrs. Webb. Will it start raining again, Mr. Newsome?

Howie Newsome. Well. Just sayin' to Mrs. Gibbs as how it may lighten up. Mrs. Newsome told me to tell you as how we hope they'll both be very happy, Mrs. Webb. Know they *will*.

Mrs. Webb. Thank you, and thank Mrs. Newsome and we're counting on seeing you at the wedding.

Howie Newsome. Yes, Mrs. Webb. We hope to git there. Couldn't miss that. Come on, Bessie.

[*Exit* HOWIE NEWSOME.
DR. GIBBS *descends in shirt sleeves, and sits down at his breakfast table.*]

Dr. Gibbs. Well, Ma, the day has come. You're losin' one of your chicks.

Mrs. Gibbs. Frank Gibbs, don't you say another word. I feel like crying every minute. Sit down and drink your coffee.

Dr. Gibbs. The groom's up shaving himself—only there ain't an awful lot to shave. Whistling and singing, like he's glad to leave us.—Every now and then he says "I do" to the mirror, but it don't sound convincing to me.

Mrs. Gibbs. I declare, Frank, I don't know how he'll get along. I've arranged his clothes and seen to it he's put warm things on.—Frank! they're too *young*. Emily won't think of such things. He'll catch his death of cold within a week.

Dr. Gibbs. I was remembering my wedding morning, Julia.

Mrs. Gibbs. Now don't start that, Frank Gibbs.

Dr. Gibbs. I was the scaredest young fella in the State of New Hampshire. I thought I'd make a mistake for sure. And when I saw you comin' down that aisle, I thought you were the prettiest girl I'd ever seen, but the only trouble was that I'd never seen you before. There I was in the Congregational Church marryin' a total stranger.

Mrs. Gibbs. And how do you think I felt!—Frank, weddings are perfectly awful things. Farces—that's what they are! (*She puts a plate before him.*) Here, I've made something for you.

Dr. Gibbs. Why, Julia Hersey—French toast!

Mrs. Gibbs. 'Tain't hard to make and I had to do *some*thing.

[*Pause.* DR. GIBBS *pours on the syrup.*]

Dr. Gibbs. How'd you sleep last night, Julia?

Mrs. Gibbs. Well, I heard a lot of the hours struck off.

Dr. Gibbs. Ye-e-s! I get a shock every time I think of George setting out to be a family man—that great gangling thing!—I tell you Julia, there's nothing so terrifying in the world as a *son*. The relation of father and son is the darndest, awkwardest——

Mrs. Gibbs. Well, mother and daughter's no picnic, let me tell you.

Dr. Gibbs. They'll have a lot of troubles, I suppose, but that's none of our business. Everybody has a right to their own troubles.

Mrs. Gibbs (*at the table, drinking her coffee, meditatively*). Yes . . . people are meant to go through life two by two. 'Tain't natural to be lonesome.

[*Pause.* DR. GIBBS *starts laughing.*]

Dr. Gibbs. Julia, do you know one of the things I was scared of when I married you?

Mrs. Gibbs. Oh, go along with you!

Dr. Gibbs. I was afraid we wouldn't have material for conversation more'n'd last us a few weeks. (*Both laugh.*) I was afraid we'd run out and eat our meals in silence, that's a fact.—Well, you and I been conversing for twenty years now without any noticeable barren spells.

Mrs. Gibbs. Well—good weather, bad weather—'tain't very choice, but I always find something to say. (*She goes to the foot of the stairs.*) Did you hear Rebecca stirring around upstairs?

Dr. Gibbs. No. Only day of the year Rebecca hasn't been managing everybody's business up there. She's hiding in her room.—I got the impression she's crying.

Mrs. Gibbs. Lord's sakes!—This has got to stop.—Rebecca! Rebecca! Come and get your breakfast.

[GEORGE *comes rattling down the stairs, very brisk.*]

George. Good morning, everybody. Only five more hours to live. (*Makes the gesture of cutting his throat, and a loud "k-k-k," and starts through the trellis*).

Mrs. Gibbs. George Gibbs, where are you going?

George. Just stepping across the grass to see my girl.

Mrs. Gibbs. Now, George! You put on your overshoes. It's raining torrents. You don't go out of this house without you're prepared for it.

George. Aw, Ma. It's just a *step*!

Mrs. Gibbs. George! You'll catch your death of cold and cough all through the service.

Dr. Gibbs. George, do as your mother tells you!

[DR. GIBBS *goes upstairs.*
GEORGE *returns reluctantly to the kitchen and pantomimes putting on overshoes.*]

Mrs. Gibbs. From tomorrow on you can kill yourself in all weathers, but while you're in my house you'll live wisely, thank you.—Maybe Mrs. Webb isn't used to callers at seven in the morning.—Here, take a cup of coffee first.

George. Be back in a minute. (*He crosses the stage, leaping over the puddles.*) Good morning, Mother Webb.

Mrs. Webb. Goodness! You frightened me!—Now, George, you can come in a minute out of the wet, but you know I can't ask you in.

George. Why not—?

Mrs. Webb. George, you know's well as I do: The groom can't see his bride on his wedding day, not until he sees her in church.

George. Aw!—that's just a superstition.—Good morning, Mr. Webb. (*Enter* MR. WEBB.)

Mr. Webb. Good morning, George.

George. Mr. Webb, you don't believe in that superstition, do you?

Mr. Webb. There's a lot of common sense in some superstitions, George. (*He sits at the table, facing right.*)

Mrs. Webb. Millions have folla'd it, George, and you don't want to be the first to fly in the face of custom.

George. How is Emily?

Mrs. Webb. She hasn't waked up yet. I haven't heard a sound out of her.

George. Emily's *asleep*!!!

Mrs. Webb. No wonder! We were up 'till all hours, sewing and packing. Now I'll tell you what I'll do; you set down here a minute with Mr. Webb and drink this cup of coffee; and I'll go upstairs and see she doesn't come down and surprise you. There's some bacon, too; but don't be long about it.

[*Exit* MRS. WEBB.
Embarrassed silence.
MR. WEBB *dunks doughnuts in his coffee.*
More silence.]

Mr. Webb (*suddenly and loudly*). Well, George, how are you?

George (*startled, choking over his coffee*). Oh, fine, I'm fine. (*Pause*) Mr. Webb, what sense could there be in a superstition like that?

Mr. Webb. Well, you see—on her wedding morning a girl's head's apt to be full of . . . clothes and one thing and another. Don't you think that's probably it?

George. Ye-e-s. I never thought of that.

Mr. Webb. A girl's apt to be a mite nervous on her wedding day.

[*Pause*]

George. I wish a fellow could get married without all that marching up and down.

Mr. Webb. Every man that's ever lived has felt that way about it, George; but it hasn't been any use. It's the womenfolk who've built up weddings, my boy. For a while now the women have it all their own. A man looks pretty small at a wedding, George. All those good women standing shoulder to shoulder making sure that the knot's tied in a mighty public way.

George. But . . . you *believe* in it, don't you, Mr. Webb?

Mr. Webb (*with alacrity*). Oh, yes: *oh, yes.* Don't you misunderstand me, my boy. Marriage is a wonderful thing—wonderful thing. And don't you forget that, George.

George. No, sir.—Mr. Webb, how old were you when you got married?

Mr. Webb. Well, you see: I'd been to college and I'd taken a little time to get settled. But Mrs. Webb—she wasn't much older than what Emily is. Oh, age hasn't much to do with it, George—not compared with . . . uh . . . other things.

George. What were you going to say, Mr. Webb?

Mr. Webb. Oh, I don't know.—Was I going to say something? (*Pause*) George, I was thinking the other night of some advice my father gave me when I got married. Charles, he said, Charles, start out early showing who's boss, he said. Best thing to do is to give an order, even if it don't

make sense; just so she'll learn to obey. And he said: If anything about your wife irritates you— her conversation, or anything—just get up and leave the house. That'll make it clear to her, he said. And, oh, yes! He said never, *never* let your wife know how much money you have, never.

George. Well, Mr. Webb, . . . I don't think I could . . .

Mr. Webb. So I took the opposite of my father's advice and I've been happy ever since. And let that be a lesson to you, George, never to ask advice on personal matters.—George, are you going to raise chickens on your farm?

George. What?

Mr. Webb. Are you going to raise chickens on your farm?

George. Uncle Luke's never been much interested, but I thought——

Mr. Webb. A book came into my office the other day, George, on the Philo System of raising chickens. I want you to read it. I'm thinking of beginning in a small way in the back yard, and I'm going to put an incubator in the cellar——

[*Enter* MRS. WEBB.]

Mrs. Webb. Charles, are you talking about that old incubator again? I thought you two'd be talking about things worthwhile.

Mr. Webb (*bitingly*). Well, Myrtle, if you want to give the boy some good advice, I'll go upstairs and leave you alone with him.

Mrs. Webb (*pulling* GEORGE *up*). George, Emily's got to come downstairs and eat her breakfast. She sends you her love, but she doesn't want to lay eyes on you. Goodbye.

George. Goodbye. (GEORGE *crosses the stage to his own home, bewildered and crestfallen. He slowly dodges a puddle and disappears into his house.*)

Mr. Webb. Myrtle, I guess you don't know about that older superstition.

Mrs. Webb. What do you mean, Charles?

Mr. Webb. Since the cave men: No bridegroom should see his father-in-law on the day of the wedding, or near it. Now remember that.

[*Both leave the stage.*]

Stage Manager. Thank you very much, Mr. and

Mrs. Webb.—Now I have to interrupt again here. You see, we want to know how all this began—this wedding, this plan to spend a lifetime together. I'm awfully interested in how big things like that begin.

You know how it is: You're twenty-one or twenty-two and you make some decisions; then whisssh! you're seventy: you've been a lawyer for fifty years, and that white-haired lady at your side has eaten over fifty thousand meals with you.

How do such things begin?

George and Emily are going to show you now the conversation they had when they first knew that . . . that . . . as the saying goes . . . they were meant for one another.

But before they do it, I want you to try and remember what it was like to have been very young.

And particularly the days when you were first in love; when you were like a person sleepwalking, and you didn't quite see the street you were in and didn't quite hear everything that was said to you. You're just a little bit crazy. Will you remember that, please?

Now they'll be coming out of high school at three o'clock. George has just been elected president of the Junior Class, and as it's June, that means he'll be president of the Senior Class all next year. And Emily's just been elected secretary and treasurer.

I don't have to tell you how important that is. *(He places a board across the backs of two chairs, which he takes from those at the Gibbs family's table. He brings two high stools from the wings and places them behind the board. Persons sitting on the stools will be facing the audience. This is the counter of Mr. Morgan's drugstore. The sounds of young people's voices are heard off left.)*

Yep—there they are coming down Main Street now.

[EMILY, *carrying an armful of—imaginary—schoolbooks, comes along Main Street from the left.*]

Emily. I can't, Louise. I've got to go home. Goodbye. Oh, Ernestine! Ernestine! Can you come over tonight and do Latin? Isn't that Cicero the worst thing!—Tell your mother you *have* to. G'by. G'by, Helen. G'by, Fred.

[GEORGE, *also carrying books, catches up with her.*]

George. Can I carry your books home for you, Emily?
Emily *(coolly).* Why . . . uh . . . Thank you. It isn't far. *(She gives them to him.)*
George. Excuse me a minute, Emily.—Say, Bob, if I'm a little late, start practice anyway. And give Herb some long high ones.
Emily. Goodbye, Lizzy.
George. Goodbye, Lizzy.—I'm awfully glad you were elected, too, Emily.
Emily. Thank you.

[*They have been standing on Main Street, almost against the back wall. They take the first steps toward the audience when* GEORGE *stops and says:*]

George. Emily, why are you mad at me?
Emily. I'm not mad at you.
George. You've been treating me so funny lately.
Emily. Well, since you ask me, I might as well say it right out, George—— *(She catches sight of a teacher passing.)* Goodbye, Miss Corcoran.
George. Goodbye, Miss Corcoran.—Wha—what is it?
Emily *(not scoldingly; finding it difficult to say).* I don't like the whole change that's come over you in the last year. I'm sorry if that hurts your feelings, but I've got to—tell the truth and shame the devil.
George. A *change?*—Wha—what do you mean?
Emily. Well, up to a year ago I used to like you a lot. And I used to watch you as you did everything . . . because we'd been friends so long . . . and then you began spending all your time at *baseball* . . . and you never stopped to speak to anybody anymore. Not even to your own family you didn't . . . and, George, it's a fact, you've got awful conceited and stuck-up, and all the girls say so. They may not say so to your face, but that's what they say about you behind your back, and it hurts me to hear them say it, but I've got to agree with them a little. I'm sorry if it hurts your feelings . . . but I can't be sorry I said it.

George. I . . . I'm glad you said it, Emily. I never thought that such a thing was happening to me. I guess it's hard for a fella not to have faults creep into his character.

[*They take a step or two in silence, then stand still in misery.*]

Emily. I always expect a man to be perfect, and I think he should be.
George. Oh . . . I don't think it's possible to be perfect, Emily.
Emily. Well, my *father* is, and as far as I can see *your* father is. There's no reason on earth why you shouldn't be, too.
George. Well, I feel it's the other way round. That men aren't naturally good; but girls are.
Emily. Well, you might as well know right now that I'm not perfect. It's not as easy for a girl to be perfect as a man, because we girls are more—more—nervous.—Now I'm sorry I said all that about you. I don't know what made me say it.
George. Emily——
Emily. Now I can see it's not the truth at all. And I suddenly feel that it isn't important, anyway.
George. Emily, . . . would you like an ice-cream soda, or something, before you go home?
Emily. Well, thank you. . . . I would.

[*They advance toward the audience and make an abrupt right turn, opening the door of Morgan's drugstore. Under strong emotion,* EMILY *keeps her face down.* GEORGE *speaks to some passers-by.*]

George. Hello, Stew—how are you?—Good afternoon, Mrs. Slocum.

[*The* STAGE MANAGER, *wearing spectacles and assuming the role of* MR. MORGAN, *enters abruptly from the right and stands between the audience and the counter of his soda fountain.*]

Stage Manager. Hello, George. Hello, Emily.—What'll you have?—Why, Emily Webb—what you been crying about?
George (*He gropes for an explanation*). She . . . she just got an awful scare, Mr. Morgan. She almost got run over by that hardware-store wagon.

Everybody says that Tom Huckins drives like a crazy man.
Stage Manager (*drawing a drink of water*). Well, now! You take a drink of water, Emily. You look all shook up. I tell you, you've got to look both ways before you cross Main Street these days. Gets worse every year.—What'll you have?
Emily. I'll have a strawberry phosphate, thank you, Mr. Morgan.
George. No, no, Emily. Have an ice-cream soda with me. Two strawberry ice-cream sodas, Mr. Morgan.
Stage Manager (*working the faucets*). Two strawberry ice-cream sodas, yes sir. Yes, sir. There are a hundred and twenty-five horses in Grover's Corners this minute I'm talking to you. State Inspector was in here yesterday. And now they're bringing in these auto-mo-biles, the best thing to do is to just stay home. Why, I can remember when a dog could go to sleep all day in the middle of Main Street and nothing come along to disturb him. (*He sets the imaginary glasses before them.*) There they are. Enjoy 'em. (*He sees a customer, right.*) Yes, Mrs. Ellis. What can I do for you? (*He goes out right.*)
Emily. They're so expensive.
George. No, no—don't you think of that. We're celebrating our election. And then do you know what else I'm celebrating?
Emily. N-no.
George. I'm celebrating because I've got a friend who tells me all the things that ought to be told me.
Emily. George, *please* don't think of that. I don't know why I said it. It's not true. You're——
George. No, Emily, you stick to it. I'm glad you spoke to me like you did. But you'll *see:* I'm going to change so quick—you bet I'm going to change. And, Emily, I want to ask you a favor.
Emily. What?
George. Emily, if I go away to State Agriculture College next year, will you write me a letter once in a while?
Emily. I certainly will. I certainly will, George. . . . (*Pause. They start sipping the sodas through the straws.*) It certainly seems like being away three years you'd get out of touch with things. Maybe letters from Grover's Corners wouldn't be

"Emily, if I do improve and make a big change . . .
would you be . . . I mean: could you be . . ."

From a 1946 U.S.O. camp show production.

so interesting after a while. Grover's Corners isn't a very important place when you think of all— New Hampshire; but I think it's a very nice town.

George. The day wouldn't come when I wouldn't want to know everything that's happening here. I know *that's* true, Emily.

Emily. Well, I'll try to make my letters interesting.

[*Pause*]

George. Y'know. Emily, whenever I meet a farmer, I ask him if he thinks it's important to go to Agriculture School to be a good farmer.

Emily. Why, George——

George. Yeah, and some of them say that it's even a waste of time. You can get all those things, anyway, out of the pamphlets the government sends out. And Uncle Luke's getting old—he's about ready for me to start in taking over his farm tomorrow, if I could.

Emily. My!

George. And, like you say, being gone all that time

. . . in other places and meeting other people . . . Gosh, if anything like that can happen, I don't want to go away. I guess new people aren't any better than old ones. I'll bet they almost never are. Emily, . . . I feel that you're as good a friend as I've got. I don't need to go and meet the people in other towns.

Emily. But, George, maybe it's very important for you to go and learn all that about—cattle judging and soils and those things. . . . Of course, I don't know.

George (*after a pause, very seriously*). Emily, I'm going to make up my mind right now. I won't go. I'll tell Pa about it tonight.

Emily. Why, George, I don't see why you have to decide right now. It's a whole year away.

George. Emily, I'm glad you spoke to me about that . . . that fault in my character. What you said was right; but there was *one* thing wrong in it, and that was when you said that for a year I wasn't noticing people, and . . . you, for instance. Why, you say you were watching me when I did everything. . . . I was doing the same about you all the time. Why, sure—I always thought about you as one of the chief people I thought about. I always made sure where you were sitting on the bleachers, and who you were with, and for three days now I've been trying to walk home with you; but something's always got in the way. Yesterday I was standing over against the wall waiting for you, and you walked home with *Miss Corcoran*.

Emily. George! . . . Life's awful funny! How could I have known that? Why, I thought——

George. Listen, Emily, I'm going to tell you why I'm not going to Agriculture School. I think that once you've found a person that you're very fond of . . . I mean a person who's fond of you, too, and likes you enough to be interested in your character . . . Well, I think that's just as important as college is, and even more so. That's what I think.

Emily. I think it's awfully important, too.

George. Emily.

Emily. Y-yes, George.

George. Emily, if I *do* improve and make a big change . . . would you be . . . I mean: *could* you be . . .

Emily. I . . . I am now; I always have been.

George (*pause*). So I guess this is an important talk we've been having.

Emily. Yes . . . yes.

George (*takes a deep breath and straightens his back*). Wait just a minute and I'll walk you home. (*With mounting alarm he digs into his pockets for the money. The* STAGE MANAGER *enters, right.* GEORGE, *deeply embarrassed, but direct, says to him:*) Mr. Morgan, I'll have to go home and get the money to pay you for this. It'll only take me a minute.

Stage Manager (*pretending to be affronted*). What's that? George Gibbs, do you mean to tell me—!

George. Yes, but I had reasons, Mr. Morgan.— Look, here's my gold watch to keep until I come back with the money.

Stage Manager. That's all right. Keep your watch. I'll trust you.

George. I'll be back in five minutes.

Stage Manager. I'll trust you ten years, George— not a day over.—Got all over your shock, Emily?

Emily. Yes, thank you, Mr. Morgan. It was nothing.

George (*taking up the books from the counter*). I'm ready.

[*They walk in grave silence across the stage and pass through the trellis at the Webbs' back door and disappear. The* STAGE MANAGER *watches them go out, then turns to the audience, removing his spectacles.*]

Stage Manager. Well—— (*He claps his hands as a signal.*) Now we're ready to get on with the wedding. (*He stands waiting while the set is prepared for the next scene.* STAGEHANDS *remove the chairs, tables, and trellises from the Gibbs and Webb houses. They arrange the pews for the church in the center of the stage. The congregation will sit facing the back wall. The aisle of the church starts at the center of the back wall and comes toward the audience. A small platform is placed against the back wall on which the* STAGE MANAGER *will stand later, playing the minister. The image of a stained-glass window is cast from a lantern slide upon the back wall. When all is ready the* STAGE MANAGER *strolls to the center of the stage, down front, and, musingly, addresses the audience.*)

There are a lot of things to be said about a wedding; there are a lot of thoughts that go on during a wedding.

We can't get them all into one wedding, naturally, and especially not into a wedding at Grover's Corners, where they're awfully plain and short.

In this wedding I play the minister. That gives me the right to say a few more things about it.

For a while now, the play gets pretty serious.

Y'see, some churches say that marriage is a sacrament. I don't quite know what that means, but I can guess. Like Mrs. Gibbs said a few minutes ago: People were made to live two-by-two.

This is a good wedding, but people are so put together that even at a good wedding there's a lot of confusion way down deep in people's minds, and we thought that that ought to be in our play, too.

The real hero of this scene isn't on the stage at all, and you know who that is. It's like what one of those European fellas said: Every child born into the world is nature's attempt to make a perfect human being. Well, we've seen nature pushing and contriving for some time now. We all know that nature's interested in quantity; but I think she's interested in quality, too—that's why I'm in the ministry.

And don't forget all the other witnesses at this wedding—the ancestors. Millions of them. Most of them set out to live two-by-two, also. Millions of them.

Well, that's all my sermon. 'Twan't very long, anyway.

[*The organ starts playing Handel's ''Largo.''*
The congregation streams into the church and sits in silence.
Church bells are heard.
MRS. GIBBS *sits in the front row, the first seat on the aisle, the right section; next to her are* REBECCA *and* DR. GIBBS. *Across the aisle* MRS. WEBB, WALLY, *and* MR. WEBB. *A small choir takes its place, facing the audience under the stained-glass window.*
MRS. WEBB, *on the way to her place, turns back and speaks to the audience.*]

Mrs. Webb. I don't know why on earth I should be crying. I suppose there's nothing to cry about. It came over me at breakfast this morning; there was Emily eating her breakfast as she's done for seventeen years and now she's going off to eat it in someone else's house. I suppose that's it.

And Emily! She suddenly said: I can't eat another mouthful, and she put her head down on the table and *she* cried. (*She starts toward her seat in the church, but turns back and adds:*) Oh, I've got to say it: You know, there's something downright cruel about sending our girls out into marriage this way.

I hope some of her girlfriends have told her a thing or two. It's cruel, I know, but I couldn't bring myself to say anything. I went into it blind as a bat myself. (*In half-amused exasperation*)

The whole world's wrong, that's what's the matter. There they come.

[*She hurries to her place in the pew.*
GEORGE *starts to come down the right aisle of the theater, through the audience.*
Suddenly, THREE MEMBERS *of his baseball team*

appear by the right proscenium pillar and start whistling and catcalling to him. They are dressed for the ball field.]

The Baseball Players. Eh, George, George! Hast—yaow! Look at him, fellas—he looks scared to death. Yaow! George, don't look so innocent, you old geezer. We know what you're thinking. Don't disgrace the team, big boy. Whoo-oo-oo.

Stage Manager. All right! All right! That'll do. That's enough of that. (*Smiling, he pushes them off the stage. They lean back to shout a few more catcalls.*) There used to be an awful lot of that kind of thing at weddings in the old days—Rome, and later. We're more civilized now—so they say.

[*The choir starts singing ''Love Divine, All Love Excelling.''* GEORGE *has reached the stage. He stares at the congregation a moment, then takes a few steps of withdrawal, toward the right proscenium pillar. His mother, from the front row, seems to have felt his confusion. She leaves her seat and comes down the aisle quickly to him.*]

Mrs. Gibbs. George! George! What's the matter?
George. Ma, I don't want to grow old. Why's everybody pushing me so?
Mrs. Gibbs. Why, George, . . . you wanted it.
George. No, Ma, listen to me——
Mrs. Gibbs. No, no, George—you're a man now.
George. Listen, Ma—for the last time I ask you . . . All I want to do is to be a fella——
Mrs. Gibbs. George! If anyone should hear you! Now stop. Why, I'm ashamed of you!
George (*He comes to himself and looks over the scene*). What? Where's Emily?
Mrs. Gibbs (*relieved*). George! You gave me such a turn.
George. Cheer up, Ma. I'm getting married.
Mrs. Gibbs. Let me catch my breath a minute.
George (*comforting her*). Now, Ma, you save Thursday nights. Emily and I are coming over to dinner every Thursday night . . . you'll see. Ma, what are you crying for? Come on; we've got to get ready for this.

[MRS. GIBBS, *mastering her emotion, fixes his tie and whispers to him.*
In the meantime, EMILY, *in white and wearing her wedding veil, has come through the audience and*

mounted onto the stage. She too draws back, frightened, when she sees the congregation in the church. The choir begins: "Blessed Be the Tie That Binds."]

Emily. I never felt so alone in my whole life. And George over there, looking so . . . ! I *hate* him. I wish I were dead. Papa! Papa!

Mr. Webb (*leaves his seat in the pews and comes toward her anxiously*). Emily! Emily! Now don't get upset. . . .

Emily. But Papa—I don't want to get married. . . .

Mr. Webb. Sh—sh—Emily. Everything's all right.

Emily. Why can't I stay for a while just as I am? Let's go away——

Mr. Webb. No, no, Emily. Now stop and think a minute.

Emily. Don't you remember that you used to say—all the time you used to say—all the time: that I was *your* girl! There must be lots of places we can go to. I'll work for you. I could keep house.

Mr. Webb. Sh . . . You mustn't think of such things. You're just nervous, Emily. (*He turns and calls:*) George! George! Will you come here a minute? (*He leads her toward George.*) Why you're marrying the best young fellow in the world. George is a fine fellow.

Emily. But Papa——

[MRS. GIBBS *returns unobtrusively to her seat.*
MR. WEBB *has one arm around his daughter.*
He places his hand on GEORGE'S *shoulder.*]

Mr. Webb. I'm giving away my daughter, George. Do you think you can take care of her?

George. Mr. Webb, I want to . . . I want to try. Emily, I'm going to do my best. I love you, Emily. I need you.

Emily. Well, if you love me, help me. All I want is someone to love me.

George. I will, Emily. Emily, I'll try.

Emily. And I mean for*ever*. Do you hear? Forever and ever.

[*They fall into each other's arms.*
The March from Lohengrin *is heard.*
The STAGE MANAGER, *as* CLERGYMAN, *stands on the box, up center.*]

Mr. Webb. Come, they're waiting for us. Now you know it'll be all right. Come, quick.

[GEORGE *slips away and takes his place beside the* STAGE MANAGER-CLERGYMAN.
EMILY *proceeds up the aisle on her father's arm.*]

Stage Manager. Do you, George, take this woman, Emily, to be your wedded wife, to have . . .

[MRS. SOAMES *has been sitting in the last row of the congregation.*
She now turns to her neighbors and speaks in a shrill voice. Her chatter drowns out the rest of the clergyman's words.]

Mrs. Soames. Perfectly lovely wedding! Loveliest wedding I ever saw. Oh, I do love a good wedding, don't you? Doesn't she make a lovely bride?

George. I do.

Stage Manager. Do you, Emily, take this man, George, to be your wedded husband——

[*Again his further words are covered by those of* MRS. SOAMES.]

Mrs. Soames. Don't know *when* I've seen such a lovely wedding. But I always cry. Don't know why it is, but I always cry. I just like to see young people happy, don't you? Oh, I think it's lovely.

[*The ring.*
The kiss.
The stage is suddenly arrested into silent tableau.
The STAGE MANAGER, *his eyes on the distance, as though to himself:*]

Stage Manager. I've married over two hundred couples in my day.

Do I believe in it?

I don't know.

M. . . . marries N. . . . millions of them.

The cottage, the go-cart, the Sunday afternoon drives in the Ford, the first rheumatism, the grandchildren, the second rheumatism, the deathbed, the reading of the will—— (*He now looks at the audience for the first time, with a warm smile that removes any sense of cynicism from the next line.*)

Once in a thousand times it's interesting.

—Well, let's have Mendelssohn's "Wedding March"!

"Once in a thousand times it's interesting."

From the 1975 American Shakespeare Theatre production.

[*The organ picks up the march.*
The BRIDE *and* GROOM *come down the aisle, radiant, but trying to be very dignified.*]

Mrs. Soames. Aren't they a lovely couple? Oh, I've never been to such a nice wedding. I'm sure they'll be happy. I always say: *Happiness,* that's the great thing! The important thing is to be happy.

[*The* BRIDE *and* GROOM *reach the steps leading into the audience. A bright light is thrown upon them. They descend into the auditorium and run up the aisle joyously.*]

Stage Manager. That's all the Second Act, folks. Ten minutes' intermission.

Responding to the Play

Analyzing Act Two

Identifying Facts

1. When the audience files in for Act Two, the Stage Manager sums up the action thus far and gives us hints about what's to come. Explain what Act One told us about "the Daily Life." What is Act Two going to be about?

2. The Stage Manager says that we can guess what Act Three will be about. List the details that have prepared us for the idea that death will be the subject of the last act.

3. Explain how the Stage Manager reminds us again, in his opening speech, of the eternal cycles of life. How does he also remind us that life is about change?

4. One ritual of life that the Stage Manager doesn't show us is the father-son scene of advice on the eve of the wedding. But he has substituted for it an equally touching and amusing scene of advice. What is that scene, and what is the advice given to George?

5. In his opening speech, the Stage Manager tells us that nature has been "pushing and contriving" to make changes in the world. What kind of "change" is dramatized in the scene in the drugstore?

6. "People are so put together," says the Stage Manager, "that even at a good wedding there's a lot of confusion way down deep in people's minds." Describe the confused thoughts that the various people involved in this particular wedding have. How has the Stage Manager shown, in the dialogue between Mr. and Mrs. Gibbs earlier, that these fears are universal?

Interpreting Meanings

7. According to the Stage Manager's "sermon" before the wedding, what is the ultimate purpose of all of nature's "pushing and contriving"? Do you think Wilder is saying that perfection is the real purpose of human existence? What do you think of this idea?

8. The real hero of the wedding scene isn't on stage at all, says the Stage Manager rather mysteriously. Would you say that nature itself is the real hero of this scene? Or would you say it is the new human being that might be born to George and Emily? Explain.

9. "Once in a thousand times it's interesting," says the Stage Manager. What do you think he means? What does he say in this speech at the wedding to make us feel **suspense**—even dread—as we look forward to the last act?

Caricature by Al Hirshfeld of the 1969 ANTA Theater production.

Appeared in the *New York Times* on November 23, 1969.

Act Three

During the intermission the audience has seen the STAGEHANDS *arranging the stage. On the right-hand side, a little right of the center, ten or twelve ordinary chairs have been placed in three openly spaced rows facing the audience. These are graves in the cemetery.*

Toward the end of the intermission the ACTORS *enter and take their places. The front row contains: toward the center of the stage, an empty chair; then* MRS. GIBBS; SIMON STIMSON.

The second row contains, among others, MRS. SOAMES.

The third row has WALLY WEBB.

The dead do not turn their heads or their eyes to right or left, but they sit quietly without stiffness. When they speak, their tone is matter-of-fact, without sentimentality and, above all, without lugubriousness.

The STAGE MANAGER *takes his accustomed place and waits for the house lights to go down.*

Stage Manager. This time nine years have gone by, friends—summer, 1913.

Gradual changes in Grover's Corners. Horses are getting rarer.

Farmers coming into town in Fords.

Everybody locks their house doors now at night.

Ain't been any burglars in town yet, but everybody's heard about 'em.

You'd be surprised, though—on the whole, things don't change much around here.

This is certainly an important part of Grover's Corners. It's on a hilltop—lots of sky, lots of clouds—often lots of sun and moon and stars.

You come up here on a fine afternoon and you can see range on range of hills—awful blue they are—up there by Lake Sunapee and Lake Winnipesaukee . . . and way up, if you've got a glass, you can see the White Mountains and Mt. Washington—where North Conway and Conway is. And, of course, our favorite mountain, Mt. Monadnock, 's right here—and all these towns that lie around it: Jaffrey, 'n East Jaffrey, 'n Peterborough, 'n Dublin; and *(then pointing down in the audience)* there, quite a ways down, is Grover's Corners.

Yes, beautiful spot up here. Mountain laurel and li-lacks. I often wonder why people like to be buried in Woodlawn and Brooklyn when they might pass the same time up here in New Hampshire. Over there—*(pointing to stage left)* are the old stones—1670, 1680. Strong-minded people that come a long way to be independent. Summer people walk around there laughing at the funny words on the tombstones . . . it don't do any harm. And genealogists come up from Boston—get paid by city people for looking up their ancestors. They want to make sure they're Daughters of the American Revolution and of the *Mayflower*. . . . Well, I guess that don't do any harm, either. Wherever you come near the human race, there's layers and layers of nonsense. . . .

Over there are some Civil War veterans. Iron flags on their graves . . . New Hampshire boys . . . had a notion that the Union ought to be kept together, though they'd never seen more than fifty miles of it themselves. All they knew was the name, friends—the United States of America. The United States of America. And they went and died about it.

This here is the new part of the cemetery. Here's your friend Mrs. Gibbs. 'N let me see—— Here's Mr. Stimson, organist at the Congregational Church. And Mrs. Soames who enjoyed the wedding so—you remember? Oh, and a lot of others. And Editor Webb's boy, Wallace, whose appendix burst while he was on a Boy Scout trip to Crawford Notch.

Yes, an awful lot of sorrow has sort of quieted down up here. People just wild with grief have brought their relatives up to this hill. We all know how it is . . . and then time . . . and sunny days . . . and rainy days . . . 'n snow . . . We're all glad they're in a beautiful place, and we're coming up here ourselves when our fit's over.

Now there are some things we all know, but we don't take'm out and look at'm very often. We all know that *something* is eternal. And it ain't houses, and it ain't names, and it ain't earth, and it ain't even the stars . . . everybody knows in their bones that *something* is eternal, and that something has to do with human beings. All the greatest people ever lived have been telling us that for five thousand years, and yet you'd be surprised how people are always losing hold of it. There's something way down deep that's eternal about every human being. *(Pause)*

You know as well as I do that the dead don't stay interested in us living people for very long. Gradually, gradually, they lose hold of the earth . . . and the ambitions they had . . . and the pleasures they had . . . and the things they suffered . . . and the people they loved.

They get weaned away from earth—that's the way I put it—weaned away.

And they stay here while the earth part of 'em burns away, burns out; and all that time they slowly get indifferent to what's goin' on in Grover's Corners. They're waitin'. They're waitin' for something that they feel is comin'. Something important, and great. Aren't they waitin' for the eternal part in them to come out clear?

Some of the things they're going to say maybe'll hurt your feelings—but that's the way it is: mother'n daughter . . . husband 'n wife . . . enemy 'n enemy . . . money 'n miser . . . all those terribly important things kind of grow pale around here. And what's left when memory's gone and your identity, Mrs. Smith? *(He looks at the audience a minute, then turns to the stage.)*

Well! There are some *living* people. There's Joe Stoddard, our undertaker, supervising a new-made grave. And here comes a Grover's Corners boy that left town to go out West.

[JOE STODDARD *has hovered about in the background.* SAM CRAIG *enters left, wiping his forehead from the exertion. He carries an umbrella and strolls front.*]

Sam Craig. Good afternoon, Joe Stoddard.

Joe Stoddard. Good afternoon, good afternoon. Let me see now: Do I know you?

Sam Craig. I'm Sam Craig.

Joe Stoddard. Gracious sakes' alive! Of all people! I should'a knowed you'd be back for the funeral. You've been away a long time, Sam.

Sam Craig. Yes, I've been away over twelve years. I'm in business out in Buffalo now, Joe. But I was in the East when I got news of my cousin's death, so I thought I'd combine things a

little and come and see the old home. You look well.

Joe Stoddard. Yes, yes, can't complain. Very sad, our journey today, Samuel.

Sam Craig. Yes.

Joe Stoddard. Yes, yes. I always say I hate to supervise when a young person is taken. They'll be here in a few minutes now. I had to come here early today—my son's supervisin' at the home.

Sam Craig *(reading stones).* Old Farmer McCarty, I used to do chores for him—after school. He had the lumbago.

Joe Stoddard. Yes, we brought Farmer McCarty here a number of years ago now.

Sam Craig *(staring at* MRS. GIBBS'S *knees).* Why, this is my Aunt Julia. . . . I'd forgotten that she'd . . . of course, of course.

Joe Stoddard. Yes, Doc Gibbs lost his wife two-three years ago . . . about this time. And today's another pretty bad blow for him, too.

Mrs. Gibbs *(to* SIMON STIMSON: *in an even voice).* That's my sister Carey's boy, Sam . . . Sam Craig.

Simon Stimson. I'm always uncomfortable when *they're* around.

Mrs. Gibbs. Simon.

Sam Craig. Do they choose their own verses much, Joe?

Joe Stoddard. No . . . not usual. Mostly the bereaved pick a verse.

Sam Craig. Doesn't sound like Aunt Julia. There aren't many of those Hersey sisters left now. Let me see: Where are . . . I wanted to look at my father's and mother's . . .

Joe Stoddard. Over there with the Craigs . . . Avenue F.

Sam Craig *(reading* SIMON STIMSON'*s epitaph).* He was organist at church, wasn't he?—Hm, drank a lot, we used to say.

Joe Stoddard. Nobody was supposed to know about it. He'd seen a peck of trouble. *(Behind his hand)* Took his own life, y'know?

Sam Craig. Oh, did he?

Joe Stoddard. Hung himself in the attic. They tried to hush it up, but of course it got around. He chose his own epy-taph. You can see it there. It ain't a verse exactly.

Sam Craig. Why, it's just some notes of music— what is it?

Joe Stoddard. Oh, I wouldn't know. It was wrote up in the Boston papers at the time.

Sam Craig. Joe, what did she die of?

Joe Stoddard. Who?

Sam Craig. My cousin.

Joe Stoddard. Oh, didn't you know? Had some trouble bringing a baby into the world. 'Twas her second, though. There's a little boy 'bout four years old.

Sam Craig (opening his umbrella). The grave's going to be over there?

Joe Stoddard. Yes, there ain't much more room over here among the Gibbses, so they're opening up a whole new Gibbs section over by Avenue B. You'll excuse me now. I see they're comin'.

[From left to center, at the back of the stage, comes a procession. FOUR MEN carry a casket, invisible to us. All the rest are under umbrellas. One can vaguely see: DR. GIBBS, GEORGE, the WEBBS, etc. They gather about a grave in the back center of the stage, a little to the left of center.]

Mrs. Soames. Who is it, Julia?

Mrs. Gibbs (without raising her eyes). My daughter-in-law, Emily Webb.

Mrs. Soames (a little surprised, but no emotion). Well, I declare! The road up here must have been awful muddy. What did she die of, Julia?

Mrs. Gibbs. In childbirth.

Mrs. Soames. Childbirth. (Almost with a laugh) I'd forgotten all about that. My, wasn't life awful—(with a sigh) and wonderful.

Simon Stimson (with a sideways glance). Wonderful, was it?

Mrs. Gibbs. Simon! Now, remember!

Mrs. Soames. I remember Emily's wedding. Wasn't it a lovely wedding! And I remember her reading the class poem at Graduation Exercises. Emily was one of the brightest girls ever graduated from high school. I've heard Principal Wilkins say so time after time. I called on them at their new farm, just before I died. Perfectly beautiful farm.

A Woman from Among the Dead. It's on the same road we lived on.

A Man Among the Dead. Yep, right smart farm.

[They subside. The group by the grave starts singing "Blessed Be the Tie That Binds."]

A Woman Among the Dead. I always liked that hymn. I was hopin' they'd sing a hymn.

[Pause. Suddenly EMILY appears from among the umbrellas. She is wearing a white dress. Her hair is down her back and tied by a white ribbon like a little girl. She comes slowly, gazing wonderingly at the dead, a little dazed.

She stops halfway and smiles faintly. After looking at the mourners for a moment, she walks slowly to a vacant chair beside MRS. GIBBS and sits down.]

Emily (to them all, quietly, smiling). Hello.

Mrs. Soames. Hello, Emily.

A Man Among the Dead. Hello, M's Gibbs.

Emily (warmly). Hello, Mother Gibbs.

Mrs. Gibbs. Emily.

Emily. Hello. (With surprise) It's raining. (Her eyes drift back to the funeral company.)

Mrs. Gibbs. Yes . . . They'll be gone soon, dear. Just rest yourself.

Emily. It seems thousands and thousands of years since I . . . Papa remembered that that was my favorite hymn.

Oh, I wish I'd been here a long time. I don't like being new here.—How do you do, Mr. Stimson?

Simon Stimson. How do you do, Emily.

[EMILY continues to look about her with a wondering smile; as though to shut out from her mind the thought of the funeral company she starts speaking to MRS. GIBBS with a touch of nervousness.]

Emily. Mother Gibbs, George and I have made that farm into just the best place you ever saw. We thought of you all the time. We wanted to show you the new barn and a great long ce-ment drinking fountain for the stock. We bought that out of the money you left us.

Mrs. Gibbs. I did?

Emily. Don't you remember, Mother Gibbs—the legacy you left us? Why, it was over three hundred and fifty dollars.

Mrs. Gibbs. Yes, yes, Emily.

Emily. Well, there's a patent device on the drinking fountain so that it never overflows, Mother Gibbs, and it never sinks below a certain mark they have there. It's fine. *(Her voice trails off and her eyes return to the funeral group.)*

It won't be the same to George without me, but it's a lovely farm. *(Suddenly she looks directly at* MRS. GIBBS.*)*

Live people don't understand, do they?

Mrs. Gibbs. No, dear—not very much.

Emily. They're sort of shut up in little boxes, aren't they? I feel as though I knew them last a thousand years ago. . . . My boy is spending the day at Mrs. Carter's. *(She sees* MR. CARTER *among the dead.)* Oh, Mr. Carter, my little boy is spending the day at your house.

Mr. Carter. Is he!

Emily. Yes, he loves it there.—Mother Gibbs, we have a Ford, too. Never gives any trouble. I don't drive, though. Mother Gibbs, when does this feeling go away?—Of being . . . one of *them*? How long does it . . . ?

Mrs. Gibbs. Sh, dear! Just wait and be patient.

Emily *(with a sigh).* I know.—Look, they're finished. They're going.

Mrs. Gibbs. Sh—.

[The umbrellas leave the stage. DR. GIBBS *has come over to his wife's grave and stands before it a moment.* EMILY *looks up at his face.* MRS. GIBBS *does not raise her eyes.]*

Emily. Look! Father Gibbs is bringing some of my flowers to you. He looks just like George, doesn't he? Oh, Mother Gibbs, I never realized before how troubled and how . . . how in the dark live persons are. Look at him. I love him so. From morning till night, that's all they are—troubled.

*[*DR. GIBBS *goes off.]*

The Dead. Little cooler than it was.—Yes, that rain's cooled it off a little. Those northeast winds always do the same thing, don't they? If it isn't a rain, it's a three-day blow.

[A patient calm falls on the stage. The STAGE MANAGER *appears at his proscenium pillar, smoking.* EMILY *sits up abruptly with an idea.]*

Emily. But, Mother Gibbs, one can go back; one can go back there again . . . into living. I feel it. I know it. Why just then for a moment I was thinking about . . . about the farm . . . and for a minute I *was* there, and my baby was on my lap as plain as day.

Mrs. Gibbs. Yes, of course you can.

Emily. I can go back there and live all those days over again . . . why not?

Mrs. Gibbs. All I can say is, Emily, don't.

Emily *(She appeals urgently to the* STAGE MANAGER*).* But it's true, isn't it? I can go and live . . . back there . . . again.

Stage Manager. Yes, some have tried—but they soon come back here.

Mrs. Gibbs. Don't do it, Emily.

Mrs. Soames. Emily, don't. It's not what you think it'd be.

Emily. But I won't live over a sad day. I'll choose a happy one.—I'll choose the day I first knew that I loved George. Why should that be painful?

[They are silent. Her question turns to the STAGE MANAGER.*]*

Stage Manager. You not only live it; but you watch yourself living it.

Emily. Yes?

Stage Manager. And as you watch it, you see the thing that they—down there—never know. You see the future. You know what's going to happen afterwards.

Emily. But is that—painful? Why?

Mrs. Gibbs. That's not the only reason why you shouldn't do it, Emily. When you've been here longer you'll see that our life here is to forget all that, and think only of what's ahead, and be ready for what's ahead. When you've been here longer you'll understand.

Emily *(softly).* But Mother Gibbs, how can I *ever* forget that life? It's all I know. It's all I had.

Mrs. Soames. Oh, Emily. It isn't wise. Really, it isn't.

Emily. But it's a thing I must know for myself. I'll choose a happy day, anyway.

Mrs. Gibbs. *No!*—At least, choose an unimportant day. Choose the least important day in your life. It will be important enough.

Emily *(to herself).* Then it can't be since I was married; or since the baby was born. *(To the* STAGE MANAGER, *eagerly)* I can choose a birthday at least, can't I?—I choose my twelfth birthday.

Stage Manager. All right. February 11th, 1899. A

"But Mother Gibbs, how can I ever forget that life? It's all I know."

From the original 1938 production at the McCarter Theatre in Princeton, New Jersey.

Tuesday.—Do you want any special time of day?

Emily. Oh, I want the whole day.

Stage Manager. We'll begin at dawn. You remember it had been snowing for several days; but it had stopped the night before, and they had begun clearing the roads. The sun's coming up.

Emily *(with a cry; rising).* There's Main Street . . . why, that's Mr. Morgan's drugstore before he changed it! . . . And there's the livery stable.

[*The stage at no time in this act has been very dark; but now the left half of the stage gradually becomes very bright—the brightness of a crisp winter morning.*

EMILY *walks toward Main Street.*]

Stage Manager. Yes, it's 1899. This is fourteen years ago.

Emily. Oh, that's the town I knew as a little girl. And, *look,* there's the old white fence that used to be around our house. Oh, I'd forgotten that! Oh, I love it so! Are they inside?

Stage Manager. Yes, your mother'll be coming downstairs in a minute to make breakfast.

Emily *(softly).* Will she?

Stage Manager. And you remember: Your father had been away for several days; he came back on the early-morning train.

Emily. No . . . ?

Stage Manager. He'd been back to his college to make a speech—in western New York, at Clinton.

Emily. Look! There's Howie Newsome. There's our policeman. But he's *dead; he died.*

[*The voices of* HOWIE NEWSOME, CONSTABLE WARREN, *and* JOE CROWELL, JR., *are heard at the left of the stage.* EMILY *listens in delight.*]

Howie Newsome. Whoa, Bessie!—Bessie! 'Morning, Bill.

Constable Warren. Morning, Howie.

Howie Newsome. You're up early.

Constable Warren. Been rescuin' a party; darn near froze to death, down by Polish Town thar. Got drunk and lay out in the snowdrifts. Thought he was in bed when I shook'm.

Emily. Why, there's Joe Crowell. . . .

Joe Crowell. Good morning, Mr. Warren. 'Morning, Howie.

[MRS. WEBB *has appeared in her kitchen, but* EMILY *does not see her until she calls.*]

Mrs. Webb. Chil-*dren!* Wally! Emily! . . . Time to get up.

Emily. Mama, I'm here! Oh! how young Mama looks! I didn't know Mama was ever that young.

Mrs. Webb. You can come and dress by the kitchen fire, if you like; but hurry. (HOWIE NEW-SOME *has entered along Main Street and brings the milk to* MRS. WEBB's *door.*) Good morning, Mr. Newsome. Whhhh—it's cold.

Howie Newsome. Ten below by my barn, Mrs. Webb.

Mrs. Webb. Think of it! Keep yourself wrapped up. (*She takes her bottles in, shuddering.*)

Emily (*with an effort*). Mama, I can't find my blue hair ribbon anywhere.

Mrs. Webb. Just open your eyes, dear, that's all. I laid it out for you special—on the dresser, there. If it were a snake it would bite you.

Emily. Yes, yes . . .

[*She puts her hand on her heart.* MR. WEBB *comes along Main Street, where he meets* CONSTABLE WARREN. *Their movements and voices are increasingly lively in the sharp air.*]

Mr. Webb. Good morning, Bill.

Constable Warren. Good morning, Mr. Webb. You're up early.

Mr. Webb. Yes, just been back to my old college in New York State. Been any trouble here?

Constable Warren. Well, I was called up this mornin' to rescue a Polish fella—darn near froze to death he was.

Mr. Webb. We must get it in the paper.

Constable Warren. 'Twan't much.

Emily (*whispers*). Papa.

[MR. WEBB *shakes the snow off his feet and enters his house.*

CONSTABLE WARREN *goes off, right.*]

Mr. Webb. Good morning, Mother.

Mrs. Webb. How did it go, Charles?

Mr. Webb. Oh, fine, I guess. I told'm a few things.—Everything all right here?

Mrs. Webb. Yes—can't think of anything that's happened special. Been right cold. Howie Newsome says it's ten below over to his barn.

Mr. Webb. Yes, well, it's colder than that at Hamilton College. Students' ears are falling off. It ain't Christian.—Paper have any mistakes in it?

Mrs. Webb. None that I noticed. Coffee's ready when you want it. (*He starts upstairs.*) Charles! Don't forget; it's Emily's birthday. Did you remember to get her something?

Mr. Webb (*patting his pocket*). Yes, I've got something here. (*Calling up the stairs*) Where's my girl? Where's my birthday girl? (*He goes off left.*)

Mrs. Webb. Don't interrupt her now, Charles. You can see her at breakfast. She's slow enough as it is. Hurry up, children! It's seven o'clock. Now, I don't want to call you again.

Emily (*softly, more in wonder than in grief*). I can't bear it. They're so young and beautiful. Why did they ever have to get old? Mama, I'm here. I'm grown up. I love you all, everything.—I can't look at everything hard enough. (*She looks questioningly at the* STAGE MANAGER, *saying or suggesting: "Can I go in?" He nods briefly. She crosses to the inner door to the kitchen, left of her mother, and as though entering the room, says, suggesting the voice of a girl of twelve:*) Good morning, Mama.

Mrs. Webb (*crossing to embrace and kiss her; in her characteristic matter-of-fact manner*). Well, now, dear, a very happy birthday to my girl and many happy returns. There are some surprises waiting for you on the kitchen table.

Emily. Oh, Mama, you *shouldn't* have. (*She throws an anguished glance at the* STAGE MANAGER.) I can't—I can't.

Mrs. Webb (*facing the audience, over her stove*). But birthday or no birthday, I want you to eat your breakfast good and slow. I want you to grow up and be a good, strong girl.

That in the blue paper is from your Aunt Carrie; and I reckon you can guess who brought the postcard album. I found it on the doorstep when I brought in the milk—George Gibbs . . . must have come over in the cold pretty early . . . right nice of him.

Emily *(to herself).* Oh, George! I'd forgotten that. . . .

Mrs. Webb. Chew that bacon good and slow. It'll help keep you warm on a cold day.

Emily *(with mounting urgency).* Oh, Mama, just look at me one minute as though you really saw me. Mama, fourteen years have gone by. I'm dead. You're a grandmother, Mama. I married George Gibbs, Mama. Wally's dead, too. Mama, his appendix burst on a camping trip to North Conway. We felt just terrible about it—don't you remember? But, just for a moment now we're all together. Mama, just for a moment we're happy. *Let's look at one another.*

Mrs. Webb. That in the yellow paper is something I found in the attic among your grandmother's things. You're old enough to wear it now, and I thought you'd like it.

Emily. And this is from you. Why, Mama, it's just lovely and it's just what I wanted. It's beautiful!

[*She flings her arms around her mother's neck. Her* MOTHER *goes on with her cooking, but is pleased.*]

Mrs. Webb. Well, I hoped you'd like it. Hunted all over. Your Aunt Norah couldn't find one in Concord, so I had to send all the way to Boston. *(Laughing)* Wally has something for you, too. He made it at manual-training class and he's very proud of it. Be sure you make a big fuss about it.—Your father has a surprise for you, too; don't know what it is myself. Sh—here he comes.

Mr. Webb *(offstage).* Where's my girl? Where's my birthday girl?

Emily *(in a loud voice to the* STAGE MANAGER*).* I can't. I can't go on. It goes so fast. We don't have time to look at one another. *(She breaks down sobbing. The lights dim on the left half of the stage.* MRS. WEBB *disappears.)* I didn't realize. So all that was going on and we never noticed. Take

me back—up the hill—to my grave. But first: Wait! One more look.

Goodbye, Goodbye, world. Goodbye, Grover's Corners . . . Mama and Papa. Goodbye to clocks ticking . . . and Mama's sunflowers. And food and coffee. And new-ironed dresses and hot baths . . . and sleeping and waking up. Oh, earth, you're too wonderful for anybody to realize you. *(She looks toward the* STAGE MANAGER *and asks abruptly, through her tears:)*

Do any human beings ever realize life while they live it?—every, every minute?

Stage Manager. No. *(Pause)* The saints and poets, maybe—they do some.

Emily. I'm ready to go back. *(She returns to her chair beside* MRS. GIBBS. *Pause)*

Mrs. Gibbs. Were you happy?

Emily. No . . . I should have listened to you. That's all human beings are! Just blind people.

Mrs. Gibbs. Look, it's clearing up. The stars are coming out.

Emily. Oh, Mr. Stimson, I should have listened to them.

Simon Stimson *(with mounting violence; bitingly).* Yes, now you know. Now you know! That's what it was to be alive. To move about in a cloud of ignorance; to go up and down trampling on the feelings of those . . . of those about you. To spend and waste time as though you had a million years. To be always at the mercy of one self-centered passion or another. Now you know—that's the happy existence you wanted to go back to. Ignorance and blindness.

Mrs. Gibbs *(spiritedly).* Simon Stimson, that ain't the whole truth and you know it. Emily, look at that star. I forget its name.

A Man Among the Dead. My boy Joel was a sailor—knew 'em all. He'd set on the porch evenings and tell 'em all by name. Yes, sir, wonderful!

Another Man Among the Dead. A star's mighty good company.

A Woman Among the Dead. Yes, Yes, 'tis.

Simon Stimson. Here's one of *them* coming.

The Dead. That's funny. 'Tain't no time for one of them to be here.—Goodness sakes.

Emily. Mother Gibbs, it's George.

Mrs. Gibbs. Sh, dear. Just rest yourself.

Emily. It's George.

[GEORGE *enters from the left, and slowly comes toward them.*]

A Man from Among the Dead. And my boy, Joel, who knew the stars—he used to say it took millions of years for that speck o' light to git to the earth. Don't seem like a body could believe it, but that's what he used to say—millions of years.

[GEORGE *sinks to his knees then falls full length at Emily's feet.*]

A Woman Among the Dead. Goodness! That ain't no way to behave!

Mrs. Soames. He ought to be home.

Emily. Mother Gibbs?

Mrs. Gibbs. Yes, Emily?

Emily. They don't understand, do they?

Mrs. Gibbs. No, dear. They don't understand.

[*The* STAGE MANAGER *appears at the right, one hand on a dark curtain which he slowly draws across the scene.*

In the distance a clock is heard striking the hour very faintly.]

Stage Manager. Most everybody's asleep in Grover's Corners. There are a few lights on: Shorty Hawkins, down at the depot, has just watched the Albany train go by. And at the livery stable somebody's setting up late and talking.—Yes, it's clearing up. There are the stars—doing their old, old crisscross journeys in the sky. Scholars haven't settled the matter yet, but they seem to think there are no living beings up there. Just chalk . . . or fire. Only this one is straining away, straining away all the time to make something of itself. The strain's so bad that every sixteen hours everybody lies down and gets a rest. (*He winds his watch.*) Hm. . . . Eleven o'clock in Grover's Corners.—You get a good rest, too. Good night.

The End

A Critical Comment

Our Town has sometimes been called sentimental. One dictionary defines **sentimental** as "having excessive feeling or emotion," or "giving rise to emotion that is based too much on nostalgia," or a longing for the past. *Sentimental* has become a popular word in criticism. Sometimes it is used accurately, but some people see any emotion as "excessive." It is, perhaps, up to each of us to determine for ourselves what is "excessive feeling" and what is not.

A more reliable definition of *sentimental* might be that it describes a work that limits its view so that our feelings are manipulated and we cannot see the whole truth. Now, all writers select the part of the story they want to show. That is necessary and legitimate to a point. But we have a right to object, or to call a work "sentimental," when something in us says: "Now wait a minute. That's only part of the story." We have a "gut feeling" that our emotions are being unfairly manipulated.

Our Town, of course, presents only part of the story, but Wilder has in fact laced this idealized picture of village life and love with wit and humor. The "sweetness" is cut by the tart New England "put-down" manner of the Stage Manager as he comments on the characters and their lives. For example, at the end of the wedding he comments, "Once in a thousand years it's interesting." That is hardly sentimental.

When we come to discuss the dramatic technique and structure of *Our Town,* we can only sit in wonder. Like Anton Chekhov (see page 612), who in his longer plays gave us what seemed to be just a series of scenes from life, Wilder rejects almost every principle of playwriting. There *is* a story: A boy and a girl recognize their love for each other and marry; she dies and returns to life on earth for a brief, unendurable visit. But there is no conflict, no protagonist driving the story against obstacles toward a goal. Nor is there suspense, except the question of who is going to occupy that empty chair in the cemetery in the last act. The scenes do not grow out of each other *because* of each other. They simply *follow* each other.

The play defies analysis, but it all works brilliantly. Hundreds of playwrights have tried to imitate Wilder's technique and have failed. (One who has succeeded is Tad Mosel with his play *All the Way Home,* an adaptation of James Agee's novel *A Death in the Family.*)

In *Our Town,* the movement and progression are the movement and progression of life and living. We are led through some of the stations of our brief lives by a benign, humorous Stage Manager, who serves us sodas, marries us, and, in a sense, buries us. The Stage Manager observes, "This is the way we were: in our growing up and in our marrying and in our living and in our dying." He puts the experience in perspective with his references to millions and millions of years. He makes the sadness of living bearable. We are but a speck, the subject of a small story to be put in a cornerstone to be opened a million years hence, if human life survives. Babylon didn't.

Our Town is one of the plays in which we play our own story as we watch the story of Grover's Corners unfolding on stage. We respond to this play in different ways at different times in our lives. When we are young, we ask, "Is that what life is like?" And when we are older, we nod, "Yes. That's what it is like." We return to Wilder's play as we return to music—we wait for our favorite passages, and we discover new meanings as our own experience broadens.

Responding to the Play

Analyzing Act Three

Identifying Facts

1. When the audience returns from intermission, they see the stage set has been rearranged. Describe what you see on stage as this act opens. What is unusual about the ways the actors and actresses look? When do you find out exactly *where* you are now?

2. How does the Stage Manager, in his opening speech, again remind us that earthly life is made up of recurring cycles and of eternal change?

3. According to the Stage Manager, what happens to the dead, and how do they feel about earthly life?

4. The conversation between Sam Craig and Joe Stoddard gradually reveals the purpose of the empty chair. Explain why it is there. How do we finally find out who has died?

5. What does the dialogue between Sam Craig and Joe Stoddard reveal about what has happened in Grover's Corners in the past nine years?

6. Emily at first is still very involved in the daily affairs of the living—the earthly part of her is still not burned out. Explain how she shows this when she first enters the stage.

7. Emily wants to go back and live in Grover's Corners again. According to Mrs. Gibbs, why wouldn't this be wise? Explain what Emily discovers when she relives her twelfth birthday and sees daily life from the perspective of eternity.

Interpreting Meanings

8. On page 547, the Stage Manager says that we all know that *something* is eternal and that that *something* has to do with human beings. What do you think he means? Do you agree?

9. We've heard the hymn "Blessed Be the Tie That Binds" earlier in the play. When? What *is* the tie that binds, and what do you think the song has to do with the playwright's **themes**?

10. When Emily realizes (on page 550) that it is the living who are shut up in little boxes, we feel some **irony**—a sense that this is just the opposite of what we would have thought was true. Why is this statement ironic? How is it also true?

11. Mrs. Soames was the woman who gushed about the wedding at the end of Act Two. What does she say about life (on page 549) when she finds out how Emily has died? What do you think of her remark?

From a 1971 production at the National Arts Center in Ottawa, Canada.

12. Simon Stimson has another opinion about earthly life (see page 553). How does he view life on earth, and why would he feel this way? Why do you think Mrs. Gibbs immediately calls Emily's attention to the stars?

13. The play ends when George Gibbs falls onto Emily's new grave. How does George's action refute Simon Stimson's view of life? What is it, however, that George doesn't yet understand?

14. Tell how the play opens and closes by making us think of the stars. Why do you think the playwright chose to begin and end his story from this perspective? How does this reminder of the stars make you feel?

15. If you had to select one key speech from this play, which would you choose? If you had to select one key scene from the play, which one would it be? Be ready to defend your choices.

Writing About the Play

A Creative Response

1. **Writing a Fourth Act.** Write a brief Act Four for *Our Town*. Give your act a title, and tell when it takes place (perhaps the year 2000). Describe your cast of characters. In an opening speech, have your Stage Manager describe what Grover's Corners now looks like.

2. **Writing a New Stage Manager's Speech.** Imagine that you are going to write a play about the life of one or two families in your own town or neighborhood. What would you say about your town or setting to introduce it to your audience? What characters would you create to represent life in your setting? Write an opening speech that a Stage Manager might give to introduce your own setting and characters to the audience. Use Wilder's Stage Manager's opening speech as your model.

3. **Writing a Dialogue.** What would be the equivalent of the soda-fountain scene today (page 540)? Write a dialogue between a girl and boy who are just discovering that they like each other very much. What will they say to get the action moving so that they can reveal their true feelings? (In Wilder's scene, the problem that moves the action is George's insistence that Emily tell him why she's been treating him "so funny lately.")

A Critical Response

4. **Explaining a Theme.** In the introduction to *Our Town*, we said that a clue to the theme of the play lay in Wilder's intention "to find a value above all price for the simplest events in our daily life." In a brief essay, give your own statement of the play's theme, and indicate the incidents and characters that help to reveal it. Quote at least three passages from the play that support your statement of theme.

5. **Responding to a Critic.** Not every critic has been kind to *Our Town*. Here is one who had something negative to say about Wilder's characters:

Wilder's homespun characters in Grover's Corners, N.H., are caricatures of a homespun, innocent American type that never existed. "There's an early-afternoon calm in our town: a buzzin' and hummin' from the school building; only a few buggies on Main Street—the horses dozing at the hitching posts; you all remember what it's like." The trouble is, no one does.

—James Atlas

In a paragraph, give your response to this criticism of the characters in *Our Town*. Whether you agree with this critic or disagree with him, try to give at least two convincing reasons to explain why you feel the way you do.

6. **Responding to the Play.** In a brief essay, explain your response to *Our Town*. You might want to cover several of the elements of the play in your response, or perhaps you'll want to focus on one: the characters, the theme, the setting, or the dialogue. Here are some sample responses, if you need something to spark your own:

a. I see myself as the director of a production of *Our Town*. I disagree with Thornton Wilder's Preface to the play—with how he wants to see *Our Town* staged. (See page 558.) Here's why . . .

b. The people of Grover's Corners seem to be leaving some important items out of their new bank's cornerstone. Here are some items that will be vital to future people's understanding of our "*real*" life" . . . And each of these items is vital because . . .

c. By the end of *Our Town,* I feel cheated. The playwright has not given me his *real* opinion about whether life is a comedy or a tragedy.

d. I'm neither a saint nor an artist, but I "realize" the life I live.

e. The people of *Our Town* seem to have no politics and no awareness of life outside their own town. That's no way to create a perfect human society.

f. If you want people to leave the theater more aware of their own lives, then you shouldn't keep reminding them that "this is play," and you should keep all your scenes in the *real* world.

g. I like the characters in this play. I see my own town's characters realistically reflected in the people of Grover's Corners.

Analyzing Language and Vocabulary

Related Words and Exact Meanings

The following quotations are from the stage directions to *Our Town*. Each stage direction contains at least one italicized word. The questions that follow relate to the italicized words. A dictionary will help you answer the questions.

1. ". . . [the Stage Manager], leaning against the right *proscenium* pillar, watches the late arrivals in the audience." (Page 520)

a. A *proscenium* is sometimes called the "apron" of the stage: It is the part of the stage separating the acting area from the audience. The word comes from Greek words meaning "before the tent," and it was used to refer to the stage of the ancient Greek and Roman theaters. From this information, what might you infer about these ancient theaters?

b. How do the words *scene, scenic,* and *scenario* relate in meaning to the word *proscenium*?

2. "When the *auditorium* is in complete darkness, he speaks." (Page 520)

a. *Auditorium* comes from a Latin word meaning a "place where people gather to listen to concerts, plays, speeches, etc." How are the words *audit* and *auditory* related to the word *auditorium*?

b. Is the word *audition* related too?

3. "George returns reluctantly to the kitchen and *pantomimes* putting on overshoes." (Page 537)

a. What kind of action is George involved in here?

b. How is the word *mimic* related to the word *pantomime*?

4. "The stage is suddenly arrested into silent *tableau*." (Page 544)

a. A *tableau* is a striking scene or picture. In the theater, it usually refers to a group of actors standing silently, without moving, in a scene of suddenly halted movement. How are the common words *tablet* and *table* related to the word *tableau*?

b. A *tableau* almost always suggests a mood, which is often achieved by lighting. Look back at this *tableau*, and describe the mood it creates.

Reading About the Writer

Thornton Wilder (1897–1975) was born in Madison, Wisconsin, but spent part of his youth in China, where his father was consul general. Wilder later attended schools in America, spending two years at Oberlin and taking his degree at Yale.

His second novel was a best seller. *The Bridge of San Luis Rey* (1927) is an ironic study of five travelers who happened to be crossing a rope bridge in Peru when it collapsed and plunged them all to their deaths in the gorge below. The novel won the Pulitzer Prize for fiction and made Wilder famous.

Wilder won the Pulitzer Prize twice again—this time for drama, for *Our Town* (1938) and for *The Skin of Our Teeth* (1943). In 1955 he wrote a play called *The Matchmaker*, which became the basis for the enormously successful musical comedy *Hello, Dolly!*

Though Wilder was that rare creature—both a playwright and a novelist—and though he became one of the most distinguished literary figures of his time (he was often mentioned as a candidate for the Nobel Prize), he always liked to think of himself as a teacher. Indeed, he did spend a good deal of his life as a convivial teacher and lecturer of French, classical literature, and creative writing.

Unlike most playwrights, Wilder liked to act; he frequently played the Stage Manager in regional or summer-theater productions of *Our Town*.

Though anyone familiar with his life realizes that he was aware of "the dark side of the moon," he was, to the despair of some of his critics, essentially an optimist. Wilder emphasized the positive aspects of life: In *Our Town* it is the miracle of even the most ordinary day; in *The Skin of Our Teeth* it is the human capacity through the ages to survive every conceivable calamity. Wilder once wrote to a friend, "The positive still lives about us in sufficient fragments to live by."

Focusing on Background
From the Preface to Our Town

". . . Those nineteenth-century audiences . . . loaded the stage with specific objects, because every concrete object on the stage fixes and narrows the action to one moment in time and place. (Have you ever noticed that in the plays of Shakespeare no one—except occasionally a ruler—ever sits down? There were not even chairs on the English or Spanish stages in the time of Elizabeth I.) So it was by a jugglery with time that the middle classes devitalized the theater. When you emphasize *place* in the theater, you drag down and limit and harness time to it. You thrust the action back into past time, whereas it is precisely the glory of the stage that it is always 'now' there. Under such production methods the characters are all dead before the action starts. You don't have to pay deeply from your heart's participation. No great age in the theater ever attempted to capture the audiences' belief through this kind of specification and localization. I became dissatisfied with the theater because I was unable to lend credence to such childish attempts to be 'real.' . . .

"*Our Town* is not offered as a picture of life in a New Hampshire village; or as a speculation about the conditions of life after death. It is an attempt to find a value above all price for the smallest events in our daily life. I have made the claim as preposterous as possible, for I have set the village against the largest dimensions of time and place. The recurrent words in this play (few have noticed it) are *hundreds, thousands,* and *millions.* Emily's joys and griefs, her algebra lessons, and her birthday presents—what are they when we consider all the billions of girls who have lived, who are living, and who will live? Each individual's assertion to an absolute reality can only be inner, very inner. And here the method of staging finds its justification—in the first two acts there are at least a few chairs and tables; but when she revisits the earth and the kitchen to which she descended on her twelfth birthday, the very chairs and table are gone. Our claim, our hope, our despair are in the mind—not in things, not in 'scenery.' Molière said that for the theater all he needed was a platform and a passion or two. The climax of this play needs only five square feet of boarding and the passion to know what life means to us."

—Thornton Wilder

I Never Sang for My Father was originally written as a movie, and when I was unable to get the movie produced, I turned the story into a play. After the story was produced as a play, we made it into a movie. Such are the strange workings of the theater and of the movies.

I wrote this story first as a movie because screenwriting is a freer (though not easier) form, and I knew that to tell the story I would need many locations—a railroad station, the family's home, a restaurant, a hospital room. Up to this time, each of my plays had used only one set. Sometimes the set would include several rooms in a house, but it was still one set involving no change of scenery. Like many playwrights, I liked the challenge of bringing all the action together in one setting. A single set gives a play a sense of unity and seems to be of the essence of the theater. Although movies handle movement and physical action better than the theater does, the theater seems to me best for concentrated scenes of a small group of people digging for psychological truths.

The original play script for *I Never Sang for My Father* noted on the first page, "There are no sets." After the play opened, the producer jokingly said, "Never give me another play that says, 'There are no sets.' " While I had first visualized the play on a bare stage, somewhat in the manner of a production of *Our Town,* I had then called for restaurant tables, a hospital bed, a television set, and much more. It finally took a turntable set on either side of the stage to move in the various "no sets."

The Narrator's Function in the Play

The form of this play derived from its earlier life as a movie script. Many people had admired the material, and so I was anxious to keep as much of it as possible. I used the leading character as a narrator between the scenes to bridge the many small scenes from the movie version that I wanted to keep.

Oddly, when we turned the play into a movie, we kept the son as the narrator at the opening and closing of the story. Though some of his narrations were written in the play to bridge the scenes, it turned out that the last narration had become an integral part of the story. We kept a short narration at the opening of the movie to establish the convention of a narrator because we didn't want the audience to think the narrator was something strange popping up unexpectedly at the end.

Narrators have not been used much in the theater because of the principle of "Show, don't tell." The theater audience wants to know the characters by what they *do* and *say*; the audience doesn't want to be told by a narrator *how* to feel about the characters. You will notice in Act Two of *I Never Sang for My Father* that when the major dramatic action gets under way, the narrator drops out almost entirely until the end. But the device of using a narrator has served some modern plays very well. There's a narrator in Tennessee Williams's *The Glass Menagerie;* in Arthur Miller's *After the Fall;* and, as we have seen, in Thornton Wilder's *Our Town.*

I Never Sang for My Father
by Robert Anderson

From the 1970 film of *I Never Sang for My Father* starring Gene Hackman, Dorothy Stickney, and Melvyn Douglas.

> " 'If I told you it was all made up, you'd feel cheated, and if I told you it was all real, you'd be embarrassed.' "

GILBERT CATES
in association with Doris Vidor
presents

HAL HOLBROOK   **ALAN WEBB**
TERESA WRIGHT   **LILLIAN GISH**
in

ROBERT ANDERSON'S

*I never sang
for my father*

A NEW PLAY

Setting and Lighting by   Costumes by
JO MIELZINER   THEONI V. ALDREDGE

Directed by
ALAN SCHNEIDER

LONGACRE THEATRE 220 W. 48th Street
MATINEES Wed. & Sat.

"*I* went home that night and sat at my desk and said to my father (long dead), 'All right, Dad, let's have the scene we never had.'"

Experience and Imagination: "Is It True?"

Like many other plays, *I Never Sang for My Father* has been called "autobiographical." Most authors are uncomfortable when their work is called "autobiographical." While they know there is some truth in their stories, writers also know how much they have invented, changed, and heightened during the creative process. Playwrights in particular know how often they have recollected an actual situation and then let themselves think, "What would have happened if . . . ?" The great artist Pablo Picasso said, "Art is a lie that makes us realize the truth." A biography should tell the facts, but a play is a work of art that *uses* the facts, builds on them, and takes them beyond where they really went in actual life.

Two examples from *I Never Sang for My Father* show that much of the play is imagination. First: I do not have a sister, and Alice in the play is not like my brother. Alice is an imagined character. She is, in a sense, Gene's *alter ego*, his "other self," so that the arguments Gene has with Alice are really arguments with himself.

Second: When we went into rehearsal, the play did not end the way it does now. Gene still left his father, but under different circumstances, which in fact were fairly close to the actual facts in life. The director and the producer kept urging me to invent different circumstances and end the play another way, but in the theater the playwright has the right to say no. Finally, at a run-through just before we were starting our pre-Broadway tour, I saw what the producer and director meant. I went home that night and sat at my desk and said to my father (long dead), "All right, Dad, let's have the scene we never had." And I wrote the scene that saved the play. I changed the plot, but not the story. The son still leaves the father, but the event that makes him leave is different.

This anecdote raises two important points. One, I went beyond the real experiences to find the "truth." And two, a story is not always right "because it happened that way."

Even though the facts in a play or novel may not be strictly autobiographical, what we call "the voice" often is. In fact, the works of many contemporary playwrights are very personal expressions. Tennessee Williams, who wrote *The Glass Menagerie,* said that he wrote about what "bugged" him. *I Never Sang for My Father* is obviously written about what Gene describes in the play's opening scene as ". . . a relationship, which struggles on in the survivor's mind toward some resolution, some clear meaning, which it perhaps never finds."

But when I am asked the "autobiographical" question, I say, "If I told you it was all made up, you'd feel cheated, and if I told you it was all real, you'd be embarrassed."

I NEVER SANG FOR MY FATHER

Robert Anderson

The photographs illustrating this play are from the original 1968 Broadway production.

I Never Sang for My Father was first presented on January 25, 1968, by Gilbert Cates in association with Doris Vidor at the Longacre Theatre, New York, with the following cast:

Characters

(in order of appearance)

Gene Garrison	Hal Holbrook
Porter	Earl Sydnor
Tom Garrison	Alan Webb
Margaret Garrison	Lillian Gish
Mary	Sloane Shelton
Nurse	Laurinda Barrett
Reverend Pell	Allan Frank
Marvin Scott	Matt Crowley
Waiter	James A. Spearman
Dr. Mayberry	Daniel Keyes
Alice	Teresa Wright

Directed by: Alan Schneider
Scenery and Lighting by: Jo Mielziner
Costumes by: Theoni V. Aldredge

Synopsis of Scenes: The time is the present and the past. The places are New York City and a town in Westchester County.

Act One

There are no sets. Lighting is the chief means for setting the stage.

A man comes from the shadows in the rear. He is GENE GARRISON, *age forty. He checks his watch. A* PORTER *passes through with a baggage cart.*

Gene. I wonder if you could help me. (*The* PORTER *stops.*) My father and mother are coming in on the Seaboard Express from Florida. I'd like a wheelchair for my mother if I could get one.
Porter. You have the car number?
Gene. Yes. (*He checks a slip of paper.*) One-oh-seven.
Porter. Due in at three ten. I'll meet you on the platform.

Gene. Thank you. (*The* PORTER *moves away and off.* GENE *comes down and addresses the audience.*) Death ends a life, but it does not end a relationship, which struggles on in the survivor's mind toward some final resolution, some clear meaning, which it perhaps never finds. (*He changes the mood.*) Pennsylvania Station, New York, a few years ago. My mother and father were returning from Florida. They were both bored in Florida, but they had been going each winter for a number of years. If they didn't go, my father came down with pneumonia and my mother's joints stiffened cruelly with arthritis. My mother read a great deal, liked to play bridge and chatter and laugh gaily with "the girls," . . . make her eyes sparkle in a way she had, and pretend that she had not had two operations for cancer, three heart attacks, and painful arthritis. . . . She used to say, "Old age takes courage." She had it. My father, though he had never been in the service, had the air of a retired brigadier general. He read the newspapers, all editions, presumably to help him make decisions about his investments. He watched Westerns on television and told anyone who would listen the story of his life. I loved my mother. . . . I wanted to love my father. . . .

[*The lights come up on another area of the stage, where the* PORTER *is already standing with the wheelchair and baggage cart.* TOM GARRISON *is standing amid the suitcases which have been piled up on the platform. He is a handsome man, almost eighty, erect in his bearing, neat in his dress. He speaks distinctly, and when he is irritated, his voice takes on a hard, harsh edge. At the moment he is irritated, slightly bewildered, on the brink of exasperation.*]

Tom. We had four bags. I don't see any of them. We had one in the compartment with us. That can't have been lost.

[*He fumes for a moment. As* GENE *watches his father for a moment, we can see in his face something of his feelings of tension. On the surface he shows great kindness and consideration for the old man. Underneath there is usually considerable strain.*]

Gene. Hello, Dad.

"Pennsylvania Station, New York, a few years ago."

Tom (*beaming*). Well, Gene, as I live and breathe. This *is* a surprise.

Gene. I wrote you I'd be here.

Tom. Did you? Well, my mind is like a sieve. (*They have shaken hands and kissed each other on the cheek.*) Am I glad to see you! They've lost all our bags.

Gene. I'm sure they're somewhere, Dad.

Tom (*firmly*). No. I've looked. It's damnable!

Gene. Well, let's just take it easy. I'll handle it. (*He looks around at the luggage piled on the platform.*)

Tom. I'm confident we had four bags.

Gene (*quietly showing the redcap*). There's one. . . . They'll show up. Where's mother?

Tom. What? . . . Oh, she's still on the train. Wait a minute. Are you sure that's ours? (*He looks around for bags, fussing and fuming. He shakes his head in exasperation with the world.*)

Gene. Yes, Dad. You just relax now.

[TOM *is seized with a fit of coughing.*]

Tom (*is exasperated at the cough*). Damnable cough. You know the wind never stops blowing down there.

Gene. Don't worry about anything now, Dad. We've got a porter, and everything's under control. (TOM *snorts at this idea. The redcap proceeds in a quiet, efficient, and amused way to work the luggage.*) I brought a wheelchair for Mother.

Tom. Oh. That's very considerate of you.

Gene. I'll go get her.

Tom. I didn't hear you.

Gene (*raising his voice*). I said I'll go get Mother.

Tom. Yes, you do that. I've got to get these bags straightened out. (*His rage and confusion are rising.*)

Gene (*to the* PORTER). There's one. The gray one.

Tom. That's not ours.

Gene (*patient but irritated*). Yes, it is, Dad.

Tom. No. Now wait. We don't want to get the wrong bags. Mine is brown.

Gene. The old one was brown, Dad. I got you a new one this year for the trip.

Tom (*smiling reasonably*). Now. Gene. I've had the bag in Florida all winter. I should know.

Gene. Dad. Please . . . Please let me handle this.

Tom (*barks out an order to his son without looking at him*). You go get your mother. I'll take care of the bags.

[GENE'S *mouth thins to a line of annoyance. He points out another bag to the* PORTER, *who is amused.* GENE *moves with the wheelchair to another area of the stage, where his mother,* MARGARET GARRISON, *is sitting.* MARGARET *is waiting patiently. She is seventy-eight, still a pretty woman. She has great spirit and a smile that lights up her whole face. She is a good sport about her problems. When she is put out, she says "darn." She is devoted to her son, but she is not the possessive and smothering mother. She is wearing a white orchid on her mink stole.*]

Gene. Hello, Mother.

Margaret. (*Her face lights up*). Well, Gene. (*She opens her arms, but remains seated. They embrace.*) Oh, my, it's good to see you. (*This with real feeling as she holds her son close to her.*)

Gene (*when he draws away*). You look wonderful.

Margaret. What?

Gene (*Raises his voice slightly. His mother wears a hearing aid*). You look wonderful.

Margaret (*little-girl coy*). Oh . . . a little rouge. . . . This is your Easter orchid. I had them keep it in the icebox in the hotel. This is the fourth time I've worn it.

Gene. You sure get mileage out of those things.

Margaret (*raising her voice slightly*). I say it's the fourth time I've worn it. . . . Some of the other ladies had orchids for Easter, but mine was the only white one. (*She knows she is being snobbishly proud and smiles as she pokes at the bow.*) I was hoping it would last so you could see it.

Gene. How do you feel?

Margaret (*serious, pouting*). I'm all right, but your father . . . did you see him out there?

Gene. Yes.

Margaret. He's sick and he won't do anything about it.

Gene. I heard his cough.

Margaret. It makes me so darned mad. I couldn't get him to see a doctor.

Gene. Why not?

Margaret. Oh, he's afraid they'd send him a big bill. He says he'll see Mayberry tomorrow. . . . But I can't tell you what it's been like. You tell him. Tell him he's got to see a doctor. He's got me sick with worry. (*She starts to cry.*)

Gene (*comforts her*). I'll get him to a doctor, Mother. Don't you worry.

Margaret. He makes me so mad. He coughs all night and keeps us both awake. Poor man, he's skin and bone. . . . And he's getting so forgetful. This morning he woke up here on the train and he asked me where we were going.

Gene. Well, Mother, he's almost eighty.

Margaret. Oh, I know. And he's a remarkable man. Stands so straight. Everyone down there always comments on how handsome your father is. . . . But I've given up. You get him to a doctor.

Gene. I've got a wheelchair for you, Mother. Save you the long walk up the ramp.

Margaret. Oh, my precious. What would we ever do without you?

Gene (*He is always embarrassed by these expressions of love and gratitude*). Oh, you manage pretty well.

[*He helps her up from the chair, and she gives him a big hug as she stands . . . and looks at him.*]

Margaret. Oh, you're a sight for sore eyes.

Gene (*embarrassed by the intensity*). It's good to see you.

Margaret (*She sits in the wheelchair*). You know, much as we appreciate your coming to meet us . . . I say, much as we appreciate your coming

like this, the last thing in the world I'd want to do is take you away from your work.
Gene. You're not, Mother.

[*Father coughs his hacking cough.*]

Margaret. Do you hear that? I'm so worried and so darned mad.

[*They arrive at the platform area.*]

Tom. Oh, Gene, this is damnable. They've lost a suitcase. We had four suitcases.
Gene. Let's see, Dad. There are four there.
Tom. Where?
Gene. Under the others. See?
Tom. That's not ours.
Gene. Yes. Your new one.
Tom. Well, I'm certainly glad you're here. My mind's like a sieve. (*Low, to* GENE) It's the confusion and worrying about your mother.
Gene. Well, everything's under control now. Dad, so let's go. We'll take a cab to my apartment, where I've got the car parked, and then I'll drive you out home.
Tom. Your mother can't climb the stairs to your apartment.
Gene. She won't have to. We'll just change from the cab to my car.
Tom. But she might have to use the facilities.
Margaret. No. No. I'm all right.
Tom (*with a twinkle in his eye . . . the operator*). You know, if you handle it right, you can get away with parking right out there in front of the station. When I used to come to meet the Senator . . .
Gene. I know, but I'd prefer to do it this way. I'm not very good at that sort of thing.
Tom. Well, all right. You're the boss. It's just that you can get right on the West Side Drive.
Gene. It's easier for me to go up the Major Deegan.
Tom. Rather than the Cross County?
Gene. Yes.
Tom. I don't like to question you, old man, but I'm sure if you clocked it, you'd find it shorter to go up the West Side Drive and——
Margaret (*annoyed with him*). Father, now come on. Gene is handling this.
Tom. All right. All right. Just a suggestion.

Gene. Come on, Dad.
Tom. You go along with your mother. I'll keep an eye on this luggage.
Gene (*trying to be patient*). It will be all right.
Tom (*clenching his teeth and jutting out his jaw, sarcastic*). You don't mind if I want to keep an eye on my luggage, do you? I've traveled a good deal more than you have in my day, old man, and I know what these guys will do if you let them out of your sight. (GENE *is embarrassed. The* PORTER *smiles and starts moving off.*) Hey, not so fast there.

[*And he strides after the* PORTER *and the bags.* GENE *moves to the front of the stage again, as the lights dim on the retreating wheelchair and luggage, and on* TOM *and* MARGARET.]

Gene. My father's house was in a suburb of New York City, up in Westchester County. It had been a quiet town with elms and chestnut trees, lawns and old sprawling houses with a certain nondescript elegance. My father had been mayor of this town a long time ago. . . . Most of the elms and chestnut trees had gone, and the only elegance left was in the pretentious names of the developments and ugly apartment houses . . . Parkview Meadows Estates . . . only there was no meadow, and no park, and no view except of the neon signs of the chain stores. Some old houses remained, like slightly frowzy dowagers. The lawns were not well kept, and the houses were not painted as often as they should have been, but they remained. My father's house was one of these.

[TOM *and* MARGARET *have now started coming in from the back.*]

Tom. Just look at this town.
Margaret. What, dear?
Tom (*raises his voice in irritation*). Do you have that thing turned on?
Margaret. Yes.
Tom. I said just look at this town.
Margaret. I know, dear, but time marches on.
Tom. Junky, ugly mess. When we came here . . .
Margaret. Don't get started on that. You can't play the show over again.
Tom. I can make a comment, can't I?

Margaret. But you always dwell on the gloomy side. Look at the good things.

Tom. Like what? . . . I'll bet you Murphy didn't bring the battery back for the Buick. I wrote him we'd be home today. *(He heads for the garage.)*

Margaret *(to* GENE*).* I don't know what we're going to do about that car. Your father shouldn't be driving any more. But they just keep renewing his license by mail. *(She moves stiffly, looking at her garden and trees and lawn.)* I must say, there's no place like home. *Mmmmm.* Just smell the grass.

Gene *(taking his mother's arm).* You all right?

Margaret. It's just my mean old joints getting adjusted. I want to look at my garden. I think I see some crocuses. *(And she moves into the shadows to see her garden.)*

Tom *(coming back).* Well, he did bring it back.

Gene. Good.

Tom. Can't count on anyone these days. Where's your mother?

Gene. She's walking around her garden.

Tom. What?

Gene. She's walking around her garden.

Tom. You know, Gene, I don't mean to criticize, but I notice you're mumbling a great deal. It's getting very difficult to understand you.

Gene *(friendly, his hand on his father's shoulder).* I think you need a hearing aid, Dad.

Tom. I can hear perfectly well if people would only enunciate. "Mr. Garrison, if you would only *E-NUN-CI-ATE.*" Professor Aurelio, night school. Didn't you ever have to take any public speaking?

Gene. No, Dad.

Tom. All your education. Well. . . . Where did you say your mother was?

Gene. Walking around her garden.

Tom *(Intense. He has been waiting for someone to say this to).* I tell you, the strain has been awful.

Gene. She looks well.

Tom. I know. But you never know when she might get another of those damnable seizures. *(He looks at the ground and shakes his head at the problem of it all.)*

Gene *(pats his father's shoulder).* It's rough. I know.

Tom. Well, we'll manage. She's a good soldier. But you know, she eats too fast. The doctor said she must slow down. But not your mother. Incidentally, don't forget she has a birthday coming up.

Gene *(who knows his mother's birthday and hates being reminded of it each year).* Yes, I know.

Tom. Before you go, I want to give you some money. Go get something nice for me to give her. Handkerchiefs. You know what she likes.

Gene *(who has done this every Christmas and birthday for years . . . smiles).* All right. (TOM *coughs, deep and thick.)* We're going to have to get that cough looked into.

Tom. I fully intend to, now I'm home. But I wasn't going to let them get their hands on me down there. If you're a tourist, they just soak you.

Gene. With the problems you've had with pneumonia . . .

Tom. I can take care of myself. Don't worry about me.

Gene. Let's go see if Dr. Mayberry can see you.

Tom. First thing tomorrow.

Gene. Why not make the appointment today?

Tom *(irked).* Now, look, I'm perfectly able to take care of myself.

Gene. Mother would feel better if——

Tom *(that smile again).* Now, Gene, don't you think I have the sense to take care of myself?

Gene *(smiling, but a little angry).* Sometimes, no.

Tom *(considers this, but is mollified by the smile).* Well, I appreciate your solicitude, old man. Why don't you stay for supper?

Gene. I was planning to take you to Schrafft's.

Tom. Hooray for our side! (GENE *starts out toward the garden.)* Oh, Gene. I want to talk to you a minute. We received your four letters from California . . .

Gene. I'm sorry I didn't write more often.

Tom. Well, we *do* look forward to your letters. But this girl, this woman you mentioned several times . . .

Gene. Yes?

Tom. You seemed to see a lot of her.

Gene. Yes. I did.

Tom. Carol's been dead now, what is it? . . .

Gene. About a year.

Tom. And there's no reason why you shouldn't go out with other women. (GENE *just waits.)* I was in California with the Senator, and before that.

It's a perfectly beautiful place. I can understand your enthusiasm for it. Gorgeous place.

Gene. Yes. I like it a lot.

Tom. But listen, Gene . . . *(He bites his upper lip, and his voice is heavy with emotion.)* If you were to go out there, I mean, to live, it would kill your mother. *(He looks at his son with piercing eyes, tears starting. This has been in the nature of a plea and an order.* GENE *says nothing. He is angry at this order, that his father would say such a thing.)* You know you're her whole life. *(*GENE *is further embarrassed and troubled by this statement of what he knows to be the truth from his father.)* Yes, you are! Oh, she likes your sister. But you . . . are . . . her . . . life!

Gene. Dad, we've always been fond of each other, but——

Tom. Just remember what I said.

[MARGARET *can now be heard reciting to herself, very emotionally.*]

Margaret. "Loveliest of trees, the cherry now / Is hung with bloom along the bough, / And stands about the woodland ride, / Wearing white for Eastertide."[1] *(She opens her eyes.)* Oh, Gene, I've just been looking at your garden. Give me a real hug. You haven't given me a real hug yet. *(*GENE *hugs her, uncomfortable, but loving and dutiful. It is, after all, a small thing.* MARGARET *looks at him, then kisses him on the lips.)* Mmmmmmm. *(She smiles, making a playful thing of it.)* Oh, you're a sight for sore eyes.

[TOM *has watched this, and looks significantly at* GENE.]

Tom *(moving off).* Gene is staying for dinner. We're going to Schrafft's.

Margaret. Oh. Can you give us all that time?

Tom. He said he would. Now come along. You shouldn't be standing so long. You've had a long trip. *(He exits.)*

Margaret. He worries so about me. I suppose it is a strain, but he makes me nervous reminding me I should be sitting or lying down . . . Oh, well

---

1. **"Loveliest . . . Eastertide"**: lines from the poem "Loveliest of Trees" by A. E. Housman. (See page 272.)

. . . *(She takes* GENE'S *arm.)* How are you, my precious?

Gene. Fine.

Margaret. We haven't talked about your trip to California.

Gene. No.

Margaret *(raising her voice).* I say, we haven't talked about your trip.

Gene. We will.

Margaret *(low).* Did you speak to your father about seeing a doctor?

Gene. He promised me tomorrow.

Margaret. I'll believe it when I see it. He's so darned stubborn. Alice takes after him.

Gene. Oh, I got a piece of it too.

Margaret *(her tinkling laugh).* You? You don't have a stubborn bone in your body.

[*We fade, as they move up and into the shadows. Immediately the lights come up on another part of the stage—Schrafft's.*]

Mary *(A pretty Irish waitress, she is just finishing setting up her table as* TOM *enters).* Well, good evening, Mr. Garrison. Welcome back.

Tom *(the charmer).* Greetings and salutations.

Mary. We've missed you.

Tom. It's mutual. Is this your table?

Mary. Yes.

Tom. Is there a draft here? I like to keep Mrs. Garrison out of drafts.

[*He looks around for windows.* MARGARET *and* GENE *come into the area. He is helping her, as she moves slowly and deliberately.*]

Mary. Good evening, Mrs. Garrison. Nice to have you back.

Tom. You remember Mary?

Margaret *(polite but reserved).* Yes. Good evening, Mary.

Mary. You're looking well, Mrs. Garrison.

Margaret *(as* TOM *holds the chair for her).* But look at him. *(She nods at* TOM.*)*

Mary. We'll fatten him up.

Tom *(smiling, flirtatiously).* Will you do that now? Oh, we've missed you. We've had a girl down there in Florida, no sense of humor. Couldn't get a smile out of her.

Mary. Well, we'll have some jokes. Dry martini?

"Now, this is my dinner, understand?"

Tom (*a roguish twinkle*). You twist my arm. Six to one. (*He says this as though he were being quite a man to drink his martini so dry.* GENE *finds all this byplay harmless, but uncomfortable.*) You remember my son, Gene.

Mary (*smiles*). Yes.

[GENE *smiles back.*]

Tom. What's your pleasure, Gene . . . Dubonnet?

Gene. I'll have a martini too, please.

Tom. But not six to one.

Gene. Yes. The same.

Tom. Well!

Gene. Mother?

Margaret. No, nothing. My joints would be stiff as a board.

Tom (*with a twinkle in his eye*). You said you'd be stiff?

Margaret. What?

Tom (*raising his voice*). You said you'd be stiff?

Margaret. My joints. My joints.

Tom. Oh, wouldn't want you stiff. (*He thinks he's being very funny, and tries to share his laugh with*

GENE, *who smiles reluctantly.* MARY *exits. To* GENE) Have I ever shown you this ring?

Margaret. Oh, Tom, you've shown it to him a hundred times.

Tom (*ignoring her reminder*). I never thought I'd wear a diamond ring, but when the Senator died, I wanted something of his. Last time I had it appraised, they told me it was worth four thousand.

Margaret. It's his favorite occupation, getting that ring appraised.

Tom (*again ignoring her*). Don't let anyone ever tell you it's a yellow diamond. It's a golden diamond. Of course, when I go to see a doctor, I turn it around.

[*He gives a sly smile. The others look embarrassed.*]

Margaret (*looking at the menu*). What are you going to have?

Tom (*taking out his glasses*). Now, this is my dinner, understand?

Gene. No. I invited you.

Tom. Uh-uh. You had all the expenses of coming to get us.

Gene. No, it's mine. And order what you want. Don't go reading down the prices first.

Tom (*smiles at the idea, though he knows he does it*). What do you mean?

Gene. Whenever I take you out to dinner, you always read down the prices first.

Margaret. Oh, he does that anyway.

Tom. I do not. But I think it's ridiculous to pay, look, three seventy-five for curried shrimp.

Gene. You like shrimp. Take the shrimp.

Tom. If you'll let me pay for it.

Gene (*getting annoyed*). No! Now, come on.

Tom. Look, I appreciate it, Gene, but on what you make . . .

Gene. I can afford it. Now let's not argue.

Margaret. Tell me, lovey, do you get paid your full salary on your sabbatical?[2]

Gene. No. Fifty percent.

Tom. Well, then, look . . .

Margaret. Now, Father, he wants to pay. Let him pay. (*They consult their menus.*) Incidentally, Tom, you should go over and say hello to Bert Edwards. Gene and I stopped on our way in.

Tom. Why?

Margaret. While we were gone, he lost his wife.

Tom. Where'd he lose her?

Margaret. Tom!

Tom. Just trying to get a rise.

Margaret. And Mrs. Bernard. She looks terrible.

Tom. Always did.

Margaret. She lost her husband six months ago. She told me, just before we left for Florida, "I hope I go soon."

Tom. Why are you so morbid tonight?

Margaret. I'm not morbid. They're just there. We really should see them, have them in.

Tom. Phooey! Who needs them?

Margaret. Oh, Tom! I can't have anyone in. Your father won't play bridge or do anything. He just wants to watch Westerns or tell the story of his life.

Tom. Now, wait a minute.

Margaret. I can't invite people to come over to

watch Westerns or to listen to you go on and on. You embarrass me so. You insist on going into the most gruesome details of your life.

Tom. People seem to be interested.

Margaret. What?

Tom. Have you got that turned up?

Margaret. Yes. (*She adjusts the volume.*)

Tom. I said they seem to be interested. (*He tries to take* GENE *in on an exasperated shaking of the head, but* GENE *looks the other way.*)

Margaret. I admit it's a remarkable story, your life. But there are other things to talk about. People want to talk about art or music or books.

Tom. Well, let them.

Margaret. He keeps going over and over the old times. Other people have had miserable childhoods, and they don't keep going over and over them. . . . That story of your mother's funeral. And you say I'm morbid.

Gene. What was that? I don't remember that.

Margaret. Oh, don't get him started.

Tom. Your mother wants me to play cards with a lot of women who just want to gossip and chatter about styles. That's why I won't play.

Margaret. You won't play because you can't follow the play of the cards anymore.

Tom. I beg to disagree.

Gene. Please! Don't fight . . . don't fight. (*He's said this in a mock-serious singsong.*)

Margaret. He kept telling everyone how he wouldn't allow his father to come to his mother's funeral.

Tom (*defensively angry*). Are you implying that I should have let him?

Margaret. I'm not saying——

Tom. He'd run out on us when we were kids, and I told him——

Margaret. I'm not saying you were wrong. You're so defensive about it. I'm saying you're wrong to keep bringing it up.

Tom. You brought it up this time.

Margaret. Well, I'm sorry. Imagine going around telling everyone he shoved his father off the funeral coach. (*She is consulting the menu.*)

Tom. And I'd do it again. I was only ten, but I'd do it again. We hadn't seen him in over a year, living, the four of us, in a miserable two-room tenement, and suddenly he shows up weeping and

---

2. **sabbatical:** a leave of absence.

begging, and drunk, as usual. And I shoved him off! (He almost relives it.) I never saw him again till some years later when he was dying in Bellevue . . . of drink. (The hatred and anger are held in, but barely.)
Margaret (She has been studying the menu). What looks good to you?
Tom (a hard, sharp edge to his voice). I have not finished! I went down to see him, to ask him if he wanted anything. He said he wanted an orange. I sent him in a half-dozen oranges. I would have sent more, except I knew he was dying, and there was no point in just giving a lot of oranges to the nurses. The next morning he died.

[There is a silence for a moment, while GENE and MARGARET look at the menu, and TOM grips and ungrips his hand in memory of his hatred for his father.]

Margaret (gently). Look at your menu now, Father. What are you going to eat?
Tom. I don't feel like anything. I have no appetite. (He lights a cigarette.)
Margaret (to GENE). This is the way it's been.
Gene. He'll see a doctor tomorrow. Don't get upset.

[MARY arrives with the martinis.]

Tom. Ah, here we are.
Mary. Six to one. (She puts the martini in front of him.)
Tom. Oh . . . ! (He shakes his head in exasperation and fishes out the lemon peel.)
Mary. But you always ask for lemon peel.
Tom (demonstrating). Twisted over it, not dumped in it. It's all right. It's all right. (With an Irish accent) Well, to your smilin' Irish eyes.
Mary. He hasn't changed, has he?
Tom. What county are you from, did you say?
Mary. Armagh.
Tom. I knew there was something I liked about you. That's where my people came from. To County Armagh. (He drinks.) Do you have any burnt ice cream tonight?
Mary. Ah, you.

Tom (smiling). No, I mean it. (To GENE) They have burnt ice cream here.
Mary. I'll be back.

[And she exits. MARGARET sits embarrassed and piqued by this kind of flirtation, which has gone on all their lives.]

Tom (the sport, to GENE). I like to get a rise out of them. If they kid with me, I give them a good tip. If they don't, a straight ten percent. (He draws a line on the tablecloth to emphasize this. He looks at MARGARET.) What's the matter?
Margaret. If you want to make a fool of yourself, go right ahead.

[TOM is angry, hurt, and exasperated. He looks at her, and then tries to include GENE, to make him share his anger. But GENE looks away and to the menu. TOM stares at his glass, and his jaw muscles start to work. The scene dims in the Schrafft's area, and GENE moves from the table to another side of the stage.]

Gene. We hurried through the last part of our dinner. My father ate only his dessert, burnt almond ice cream. We hurried through to rush home to one of my father's rituals, the television Western. He would sit in front of them hour after hour, falling asleep in one and waking up in the middle of the next one, never knowing the difference. When my father fell in love with a program, it was forever. All during my childhood we ate our dinner to the accompaniment of Lowell Thomas and Amos and Andy.[3] If anyone dared to talk, father would storm away from the table and have his dinner served at the radio. . . . I say, we rushed away from Schrafft's. Actually, my father rushed. We just lived down the street. I walked my mother home very slowly, stopping every fifty yards or so.

[MARGARET has joined GENE and taken his arm.]

---

3. **Lowell Thomas and Amos and Andy:** a reporter (Thomas) and a comedy team (Amos and Andy) popular on radio in the 1930's and 1940's.

Margaret. I don't know how he can sit through hour after hour of those Westerns.

Gene. I think he always wished he'd been a cowboy. "Take 'em out and shoot 'em!"

Margaret. He won't listen to the things I want to hear. Down in Florida there's only one TV in the lounge, and he rode herd on it. And then he'd fall asleep in three minutes. . . . Still, he's a remarkable man.

Gene. Good old Mom.

Margaret. Well, he is. Not many boys have fathers they could be as proud of.

Gene. I know that, Mom. I'm very . . . proud of him.

Margaret *(She catches his tone).* Everything he's done, he's done for his family. (GENE *just looks at her, smiling.*) So he didn't dance with me at parties. *(She smiles at* GENE.) You took care of that.

Gene. You were just a great dancer, Mother.

Margaret. I was a terrible dancer. You just couldn't stand seeing me sitting alone at a table at the club while your father was . . . *(She stops, realizing she's about to make* GENE's *point.)*

Gene. . . . off dancing with various other people, table-hopping, or playing poker with the boys in the locker room.

Margaret. What a shame that children can't see their parents when they're young and courting, and in love. All they see them being is tolerant, sympathetic, forbearing, and devoted. All the qualities that are so unimportant to passionate young people.

[TOM *appears.*]

Tom. Gene . . . Gene . . . Come watch this one. This is a real shoot-'em-up.

Gene. In a minute, Dad.

Margaret. Gene, I want to talk to you.

Gene. You should be in bed. You've had a big day.

[*They move to another part of the stage.*]

Margaret. I took another nitro.[4] And I've had something on my mind for a long time now. You remember you gave me that heart-shaped pillow when I was in the hospital once, when you were a boy? *(She sits on the chaise longue.)*

Gene. Yes.

Margaret. Fidget used to curl up here. *(She indicates the crook in her leg.)* And you'd sit over there, and we'd listen to the Metropolitan Opera broadcasts.

[GENE *is made uncomfortable by this attempt to evoke another time, another kind of relationship, but he doesn't show it.*]

Gene. Yes. I remember.

Margaret. You'd dress up in costumes and act in front of that mirror. I remember you were marvelous as d'Artagnan in *The Three Musketeers.* *(For the fun of it, a forty-year-old man, he assumes the dueling stance, and thrusts at his image in an imaginary mirror.* GENE *sits on a footstool and watches her adjust herself in her chaise. After a moment)* Tell me about California.

Gene *(A little taken by surprise. Here is the subject).* I loved it.

Margaret. And the girl, the woman with the children? The doctor? (GENE *doesn't say anything. He frowns, wondering what to say.)* You love her too, don't you?

Gene. I think so.

Margaret. I know when Carol died, you said you'd never marry again. But I hoped you would. I know it's hard, but I think Carol would have wanted you to.

Gene. I don't know.

Margaret. Gene, your sabbatical is over soon, isn't it?

Gene. A few more months.

Margaret. I think you want to move to California and get a job teaching there and marry this woman.

Gene *(after a moment).* Yes. I think I do. I wasn't sure while I was there. I suddenly felt I should get away and think. But when I walked into my old apartment, with all Carol's things there . . .

Margaret. I think it would be the best thing in the world for you to get away, to marry this girl.

Gene *(touched . . . very simply).* Thanks.

---

4. **nitro:** nitroglycerin, a medicine taken to relieve the chest pain of angina.

Margaret. A new place, a new wife, a new life. I would feel just terrible if you didn't go because of me. There are still planes, trains, and telephones and Alice comes from Chicago once or twice a year and brings the children.

Gene. Thanks, Mother. You've always made things very easy. I think you'll like Peggy.

Margaret. I'm sure I will. You have good taste in women. And they have good taste when they like you.

Gene. I'm not so sure. I never really knew if I made Carol happy. . . . If I did make her happy, I wish she'd let me know it.

Margaret. I guess a lot of us forget to say thank you until it's too late. *(She takes his hand and smiles at him.)* Thank you. . . . You have such nice hands. I've always loved your hands. . . . You've been so good to me, Gene, so considerate. Perhaps I've let you be too considerate. But it was your nature, and your father just withdrew behind his paper and his investments and his golf. And our interests seem to go together. You liked to sing, and I played the piano, oh, miserably, but I played. *(She strokes his hand.)* I tried not to be one of those possessive mothers, Gene. If I did things wrong, I just did the best I knew how.

Gene. You did everything just fine. *(He pats his mother's hand before he draws his own away.)*

Margaret. And your father has done the best he knew how.

Gene *(with no conviction).* Yes. *(This is her old song. She knows that* GENE *knows it's probably true, but he gets no satisfaction from the knowledge.)*

Margaret. Of course you know your father will object to your going away.

Gene. He already has. He said it would kill you.

Margaret. How sad. Why can't he say it would kill him? He doesn't think it would hold you or mean anything to you. *(She shakes her head.)* He dotes on your letters down there. Reads them and rereads them. Tells everyone what a fine relationship he has with you. "My door is always open. . . . Anything he wants, he can have. . . . We have always had each others' confidence. . . ." *(*GENE *smiles at this and sadly shakes his head.)* Well, you go to California. Your father and I can take care of each other. I'll remember where he

put his checkbook, and he'll make the beds, which is the only thing I'm really not supposed to do. And, for your information, I have my old-lady's home all picked out. That's what I want, so I won't be a burden to any of you.

Gene. You a burden!

Margaret *(wisely).* Oh, yes! Now don't mention this business to your father tonight. He's not well, and it's been such a nice day. In the next few days I'll talk to him, tell him it's important for you to——

Gene. No, I'll do it. *(He kisses her on the cheek.)*

Margaret. Good night, my precious.

Gene. Where would you like to celebrate your birthday?

Margaret. Oh, lovey, you've already given me so much time. Just call me on the phone.

Gene. No. . . . We can at least have dinner. . . . I'll make some plans.

Margaret. Gene, if your father gives you money to buy his present for me, please, no more handkerchiefs.

Gene. He always says handkerchiefs.

Margaret. I know, but I've got dozens and dozens from my past birthdays and Christmases.

Gene. What would you like?

Margaret. Get me some perfume. You choose the kind, except I don't like lily of the valley or gardenia.

Gene. You're a hard woman to please. . . . Good night. . . . You look great.

Margaret. Oh, a little rouge and lipstick. Thanks for coming to meet us. Tell your father I've gone to bed, and don't let him keep you there to all hours watching television. *(Calling after him)* I don't like carnation either.

[GENE *waves back affectionately and moves away, as the lights dim on* MARGARET's *area.* GENE *moves, then stands and looks at the back of his father's chair as the TV sounds come up, and lights come on in that area.* GENE *moves to his father's chair and gently touches his arm while turning the knob of the TV volume.*]

Tom *(stirring).* What? . . . What? *(He comes to slowly, shakes his head, and looks at* GENE, *bewildered.)*

Gene (*gently*). I'm going now, Dad.

Tom. Oh, so soon?

Gene (*Controls his irritation. This has always been his father's response, no matter how long he has been with him*). Yes. I have to go.

Tom. Where's your mother?

Gene. She's upstairs. She's fine. (TOM *starts to cough.*) You see about that in the morning, Dad.

Tom (*getting up, steadying himself*). I fully intend to. I would have done it down there, but I wasn't going to be charged outrageous prices. (*He glances at the TV screen.*) Oh, this is a good one. Why don't you just stay for this show?

Gene (*the anger building*). No, Dad. I've got to run along.

Tom. Well, all right. We see so little of you.

Gene. I'm up at least once a week, Dad.

Tom. Oh, I'm not complaining. (*But he is.*) There just doesn't seem to be any time. And when you are here, your mother's doing all the talking. The way she interrupts. She just doesn't listen. And I say, "Margaret, please." . . . But she goes right on. . . . Well, "all's lost, all's spent, when we our desires get without content . . . 'tis better to be that which we destroy, than by destruction dwell with doubtful joy."[5]

Gene (*He is always puzzled by his father's frequent use of this quotation. It never is immediately appropriate, but it indicates such unhappiness that it is sad and touching to him*). We'll get a chance to talk, Dad. (*He moves toward the porch.*)

Tom. I can't tell you what a comfort it is knowing you are just down in the city. Don't know what we'd do without you. No hat or coat?

Gene. No.

Tom. It's still chilly. You should be careful.

Gene (*kissing his father on the cheek*). Good night, Dad. I'll call you tomorrow to see if you've gone to the doctor's.

Tom. Well, I may and I may not. I've looked after myself pretty well for almost eighty years. I guess I can judge if I need to see the doctor or not.

Gene (*angry*). Look, Dad . . .

Tom. Seventy years ago when I was a snot-nosed

kid up in Harlem, a doctor looked at me and said if I were careful, I'd live to be twenty. That's what I think about doctors. Ten dollars to look at your tongue. Phooey! Out! Who needs them?

Gene. Look, Dad, you're worrying Mother to death with that cough.

Tom. All right, all right. I'll go. I'll be a good soldier. . . . You're coming up for your mother's birthday, aren't you?

Gene. Yes.

Tom. And don't forget, Mother's Day is coming up.

Gene. Well . . .

Tom. Why don't we make reservations at that restaurant in Connecticut where you took us last Mother's Day?

Gene. We'll see.

Tom. It will be my party. And, Gene, remember what I said about California!

Gene (*straining to get away from all the encirclements*). Good night, Dad. (*He moves off.*)

Tom. Drive carefully. I noticed you were inclined to push it up there a little. (GENE *burns.*) Make a full stop going out the driveway, then turn right.

Gene (*angry, moves further down*). Yes, Dad.

Tom (*calling after him*). Traffic is terrible out there now. Used to be a quiet little street. Take your first left, and your second right.

Gene (*He has driven this route for many years*). Yes.

Tom. Then left under the bridge. It's a little tricky down there. (*When he gets no response, he calls.*) Gene?

Gene (*in a sudden outburst*). I've driven this road for twenty years! (*He is immediately sorry, and turns away from his father's direction.*)

Tom. Just trying to be helpful.

[*The lights fade on* TOM *as he goes back into the house.* GENE *is now downstage.*]

Gene. Take your first left and your second right. Then turn left under the bridge. But do not go as far as California, because it would kill your mother. . . . I hated him for that, for sending up warning flares that if I left, it would not be with his blessing, but with a curse . . . as he had ban-

---

5. **"all's lost . . . doubtful joy"**: lines of regret spoken by Lady Macbeth in Shakespeare's *Macbeth*, Act III, Scene 2.

ished my sister Alice years ago for marrying some- one he didn't approve of . . . and the scene so terrified me at fourteen, I was sick. . . . He knew his man . . . that part of me at least . . . a gentle- man who gave way at intersections. . . . And yet, when I looked at those two old people, almost totally dependent on me for their happiness . . . This is the way the world ends, all right. . . .[6]

[*A phone rings. A light picks out* TOM *holding the phone.*]

Tom. I was downstairs in the kitchen, and sud- denly I heard your mother scream. . . . "Tom! Tom" . . . I ran up the stairs . . . (*He is seized with a fit of coughing.*) I ran up the stairs, and there she was stretched out on the floor of the bedroom, . . . "Nitro". . . "nitro.". . . That's all she could say. You know we have nitroglycerin all over the house.

[*A* NURSE *comes to* TOM *as the lights come up; she leads him into a hospital waiting-room area.* GENE *joins them.*]

Gene. Dad. (*He shakes his hand and kisses him on the cheek.*)
Tom. Am I glad to see you! Have you seen your mother?
Gene. Yes. She's sleeping. (TOM *starts to cough.*) That doesn't sound any better.
Tom. Well, I've had a shot. After your mother got settled over here, the doctor took me to his office and gave me a shot. I *would* have gone down there in Florida, you know, but . . . well . . . (*shakes his head*) I just don't know. I was in the kitchen getting breakfast. . . . You know I've been getting the breakfasts, when suddenly I heard her scream, "Tom. Tom." I went running up the stairs, and there she was stretched out on the floor. She'd had an attack. "Nitro," she whispered. We've got it all over the house, you know. She'd had attacks before, but I knew at once that this was something more. I gave her the pills and called the doctor, . . . "This is an emergency. Come quick." . . . The doctor came, gave her a shot . . . and called

the ambulance . . . and here we are. (*He shakes his head, partly in sorrow, but also partly in ex- asperation that such a thing could happen.*) She had a good time in Florida. I don't understand it. She ate too fast, you know. And the doctor had said she should do everything more slowly.
Gene. There's no explaining these things, Dad.
Tom. I suppose I could have seen more of her down there. But she just wanted to play bridge, and I didn't play, because the ladies just chattered all the time about styles and shops. . . . And I met some very interesting people. Oh, some of them were bores and just wanted to tell you the story of their life. But there were others. You know, I met a man from Waterbury, Connecticut, used to know Helen Moffett. . . . I've told you about Helen Moffett, haven't I? When I was a kid, when the clouds were low and dark, my grandfather'd take me up there sometimes on Sundays . . . a city slum kid in that lovely country . . . And Helen and I . . . oh . . . it never amounted to much. We'd go to church, and then we'd take a walk and sit in a hammock or under an apple tree. I think she liked that. But I didn't have any money, and I couldn't go up there often. Her mother didn't like me . . . "That young man will end up the same way as his father." . . . And that scared her off. . . . This man in Florida, I've got his name somewhere. . . . (*He fishes out a notebook and starts to go through it.*) He said Helen had never married. . . . Said she'd been in love as a kid . . . and had never married. (*Tears come to his eyes.*) Well, I can't find it. No matter. (GENE *doesn't know what to say. He is touched by this naked and unconscious revelation of an early and deeply meaningful love. But it seems so incongruous un- der the circumstances.*) Some day we might drive out there and look him up. . . . Helen's dead now, but it's nice country. I was a kid with nothing . . . living with my grandfather. . . . Maybe if she hadn't been so far away. . . . Well, that's water over the dam.
Gene (*After a long pause, he touches his father*). Yes.
Tom (*just sits for a few moments, then seems to come back to the present, and takes out his watch*). You know, I'd like to make a suggestion.
Gene. What, Dad?

6. An allusion to T. S. Eliot's poem "The Hollow Men," which ends with the lines: "This is the way the world ends / Not with a bang but a whimper."

Tom. If we move right along, we might be able to make the Rotary Club for dinner. (GENE *frowns in bewilderment.*) I've been away for three months. They don't like that very much if you're absent too often. They drop you or fine you. How about it? (*He asks this with a cocked head and a twinkle in his eye.*)

Gene. I thought we might eat something around here in the hospital.

Tom. I had lunch in the coffee shop downstairs, and it's terrible. It will only take a little longer. We won't stay for the speeches, though sometimes they're very good, very funny. We'll just say hello to the fellows and get back. . . . Your mother's sleeping now. That's what they want her to do.

Gene (*bewildered by this, but doesn't want to get into an argument*). Let's drop by and see Mother first.

Tom. They want her to rest. We'd only disturb her.

Gene. All right.

Tom (*As they turn to go, he puts his arm around* GENE's *shoulder*). I don't know what I'd do without you, old man.

[*As the lights shift, and* TOM *and* GENE *head away, we move to the Rotary gathering, held in the grill room of one of the local country clubs. A piano is heard offstage, playing old-fashioned singing-type songs (badly). A tinkle of glasses . . . a hum of men talking and laughing. This area is presumably an anteroom with two comfortable leather chairs. A man enters, wearing a large name button and carrying a glass. This is the minister,* REVEREND PELL, *a straightforward, middle-aged man.*]

Reverend Pell. Hello, Tom, good to see you back.

Tom (*His face lights up in a special "greeting the fellows" type grin*). Hello, Sam.

Reverend Pell. Did you have a good trip?

Tom. All except for the damned wind down there. *Oooops.* Excuse my French, Sam. . . . You know my son, Gene. Reverend Pell.

Reverend Pell. Yes, of course. Hello, Gene. (*They shake hands.*)

Tom. Gene was a Marine. (GENE *frowns.*) You were a Marine, weren't you, Sam?

Reverend Pell. No. Navy.

Tom. Well, same thing.

Reverend Pell. Don't say that to a Marine.

[GENE *and* REVEREND PELL *smile.*]

Tom. Gene saw the flag go up on Iwo.[7]

Gene (*embarrassed by all this inappropriate line*). Let's order a drink, Dad.

Tom. Sam, I've been wanting to talk to you. Now is not the appropriate time, but some bozo has been crowding into our pew at church. You know Margaret and I sit up close because she doesn't hear very well. Well, this guy has been there in our pew. I've given him a pretty sharp look several times, but it doesn't seem to faze him. Now, I don't want to seem unreasonable, but there is a whole church for him to sit in.

Reverend Pell. Well, we'll see what we can do, Tom.

Tom (*calling to a bartender*). A martini, George. Six to one. (*To* GENE) Dubonnet?

Gene. A martini.

Tom. Six to one?

Gene. Yes. Only make mine vodka.

Tom. Vodka? Out! Phooey!

Reverend Pell. What have you got against vodka, Tom?

Tom. It's Russian, isn't it? However, I don't want to influence you. Make his vodka. Six to one, now! These fellows like to charge you extra for a six to one, and then they don't give you all the gin you've got coming to you.

Reverend Pell. I hope you don't drink many of those, Tom, six to one.

Tom. My grandmother used to give me, every morning before I went to school, when I was knee-high to a grasshopper . . . she used to give me a jigger of gin with a piece of garlic in it, to keep away colds. I wonder what the teacher thought. Phew. I must have stunk to high heaven. . . . She used to put a camphor ball in my necktie too. That was for colds, too, I think. . . . But they were good people. They just didn't know any better. That's my grandfather and my grandmother. I lived with them for a while when I was a little

---

7. **Iwo:** Iwo Jima, a South Pacific island, the site of fierce battles in World War II.

shaver, because my father . . . well, that's another story . . . but my grandfather——

Reverend Pell (*He puts his hand on* TOM's *arm*). I don't mean to run out on you, Tom, but I was on my way to the little-boy's room. I'll catch up with you later.

Tom. Go ahead. We don't want an accident.

Reverend Pell (*as he is going, to* GENE). You got a great dad there. (*And he disappears.*)

Tom. I don't really know these fellows any more. (*Indicating people offstage*) All new faces. Most of them are bores. All they want to do is tell you the story of their lives. But sometimes you hear some good jokes. . . . Now, here's someone I know. Hello, Marvin.

[MARVIN SCOTT, *a man about sixty-five, enters.*]

Marvin Scott. Hello, Tom. Good to see you back.

Tom. You remember my son, Gene.

Marvin Scott. Yes. Hello.

Gene. Hello, Mr. Scott.

Marvin Scott (*to* TOM). Well, young feller, you're looking great!

Tom. Am I? Well, thank you.

Marvin Scott. How's Margaret?

[TOM *goes very dramatic, pauses for a moment, and bites his lip.* MARVIN *looks at* GENE.]

Gene. Mother's . . .

Tom. Margaret's in an oxygen tent in the hospital.

Marvin Scott (*Surprised that* TOM *is here, he looks at* GENE, *then at* TOM). I'm terribly sorry to hear that, Tom.

Tom. Heart. (*He shakes his head and starts to get emotional.*)

Gene (*embarrassed*). We're just going to grab a bite and get back. Mother's sleeping, and if we were there, she'd want to talk.

Marvin Scott. I'm sorry to hear that, Tom. When did it happen?

Tom (*Striving for control. His emotion is as much anger that it could happen, and self-pity, as anything else*). This morning . . . I was in the kitchen, getting something for Margaret, when suddenly I heard her scream, . . . "Tom . . . Tom . . ." and I ran upstairs . . . and there she was stretched out

on the bedroom floor. . . . "Nitro . . . nitro," . . . she said. . . . We have nitroglycerin all over the house, you know . . . since her last two attacks. . . . So, I get her the nitro and call the doctor . . . and now she's in an oxygen tent in the hospital . . .

[*The bell starts to ring to call them to dinner.*]

Marvin Scott. Well, I hope everything's all right, Tom.

Gene. Thank you.

Tom. What happened to those martinis? We've got to go into dinner and we haven't gotten them yet.

Gene. We can take them to the table with us.

Tom. I have to drink mine before I eat anything. It brings up the gas. Where are they? (*And he heads off.*)

Marvin Scott (*to* GENE). He's quite a fella.

[*And they move off as Rotarians start singing to the tune of "Auld Lang Syne," "We're awfully glad you're here," etc.*
As the lights fade on this group they come up on the hospital bed and MARGARET. *The* NURSE *is sitting there, reading a movie magazine. The oxygen tent has been moved away.*
TOM *and* GENE *enter quietly, cautiously. The* NURSE *gets up.* GENE *approaches the bed.*]

Gene (*whispers to the* NURSE). Anything?

Nurse. The doctor was just here. He said things looked much better.

Tom (*too loud*). Hooray for our side.

Margaret (*stirs*). Hm . . . What? (*She looks around.*)

Gene. Hello, Mother.

Margaret. Oh, Gene. (*She reaches as though to touch him.*) Look where I ended up.

Gene. The doctor says you're better tonight.

Margaret (*her eyes flashing*). You know how this happened, don't you? Why it happened? (*She nods her head in the direction of* TOM, *who is at the foot of the bed chatting with the* NURSE.)

Gene (*quieting*). Now, Mother. Take it easy. He's seen the doctor. He's had his shot.

Margaret. Well!

Gene. You should be sleeping.

Margaret. That's all I've been doing. *(She takes his hand.)* It makes me so mad. I was feeling so well. All the ladies down in Florida said I've never looked so well.

Gene. You've had these before, Mother. Easy does it.

Margaret. He's seen the doctor for himself?

Gene. Yes. Just a bad cold. He's had a shot.

Margaret. Why wouldn't he have that down there?

Gene. Mother, we'll have to go if you talk like this, because you should be resting.

Tom *(leaving the NURSE, cheerful)*. Well, how goes it?

Margaret. How do I know?

Tom *(takes her hand and smiles)*. You look better.

Margaret. You know I came without anything. I've still got my stockings on.

Tom *(kidding, very gentle)*. Well, it all happened pretty quick, my darling.

Margaret. I'll need some things.

Tom. Your wish is our command.

Gene. I'll write it down. But don't talk too much.

Margaret. Toothbrush . . . some night clothes. I'm still in my slip . . . a hairbrush.

Tom. We'll collect some things.

Margaret *(joshing)*. Oh, you. You wouldn't know what to bring. Gene, you look around.

Gene. Yes. Now, take it easy.

Margaret. I hate being seen this way.

Tom. We think you look beautiful.

Gene. Mother, we're just going to sit here now, because you're talking too much. You're being a bad girl. *(MARGARET makes a childlike face at him, puckering her lips and wrinkling her nose. She reaches out for his hand.)* Those are lovely flowers Alice sent. She knows your favorites. I called her. I'll keep in touch with her. She said she'd come on, but I said I didn't think she had to.

Margaret. Did you have any dinner?

Tom. We went to Rotary. Everyone asked for you.

Margaret. That's nice.

[DR. MAYBERRY *comes into the room, in the shadows of the entrance.* GENE *spots him and goes to him.*]

Dr. Mayberry. Hello, Gene. How are you?

Gene *(trying to catch him before he enters the room entirely)*. I'd like to——

Dr. Mayberry *(pleasant and hearty)*. We can talk right here. She seems to be coming along very well.

Gene. Good.

Tom. That's wonderful news.

Dr. Mayberry *(kidding her)*. She's tough. (MARGARET *smiles and makes a face at him.*) We won't know the extent of it until we're able to take a cardiogram tomorrow. It was nothing to toss off lightly, but it looks good now.

Gene. Well . . . thank you. (TOM *coughs.*) What about that?

Dr. Mayberry. He'll be all right. Just a deep cough. He'll get another shot tomorrow.

Gene *(low)*. You don't think we should . . . stay around?

Dr. Mayberry. I wouldn't say so. And she should rest.

Gene. Thanks, Doctor. *(They shake hands.)*

Dr. Mayberry. Do I have your number in New York? I'll keep in touch with you. Your dad's a little vague about things. (GENE *jots the number on a slip of paper.*) Good night, Mrs. Garrison. I'm going to kick your family out now so that you can get some rest.

Margaret *(smiles and makes a small wave of the fingers)*. Take care of Tom.

Dr. Mayberry. He's going to be fine. *(To* TOM*)* Drop into the office for another shot tomorrow.

Tom *(kidding)*. Will you ask that girl of yours to be a little more considerate next time?

Dr. Mayberry. Oh, you can take it.

Tom. Oh, I'm a good soldier. But, wow! *(He indicates a sore rump.)*

Dr. Mayberry. Good night. *(He waves his hand and disappears.)*

Gene. We'll run along now, Mother. *(She reaches her hand out.)*

Margaret. My precious.

Gene *(leans down and kisses her hand)*. Good night. Sleep well.

Tom. Well, my dearest, remember what we used to say to the children. "When you wake up, may your cheeks be as red as roses and your eyes as bright as diamonds."

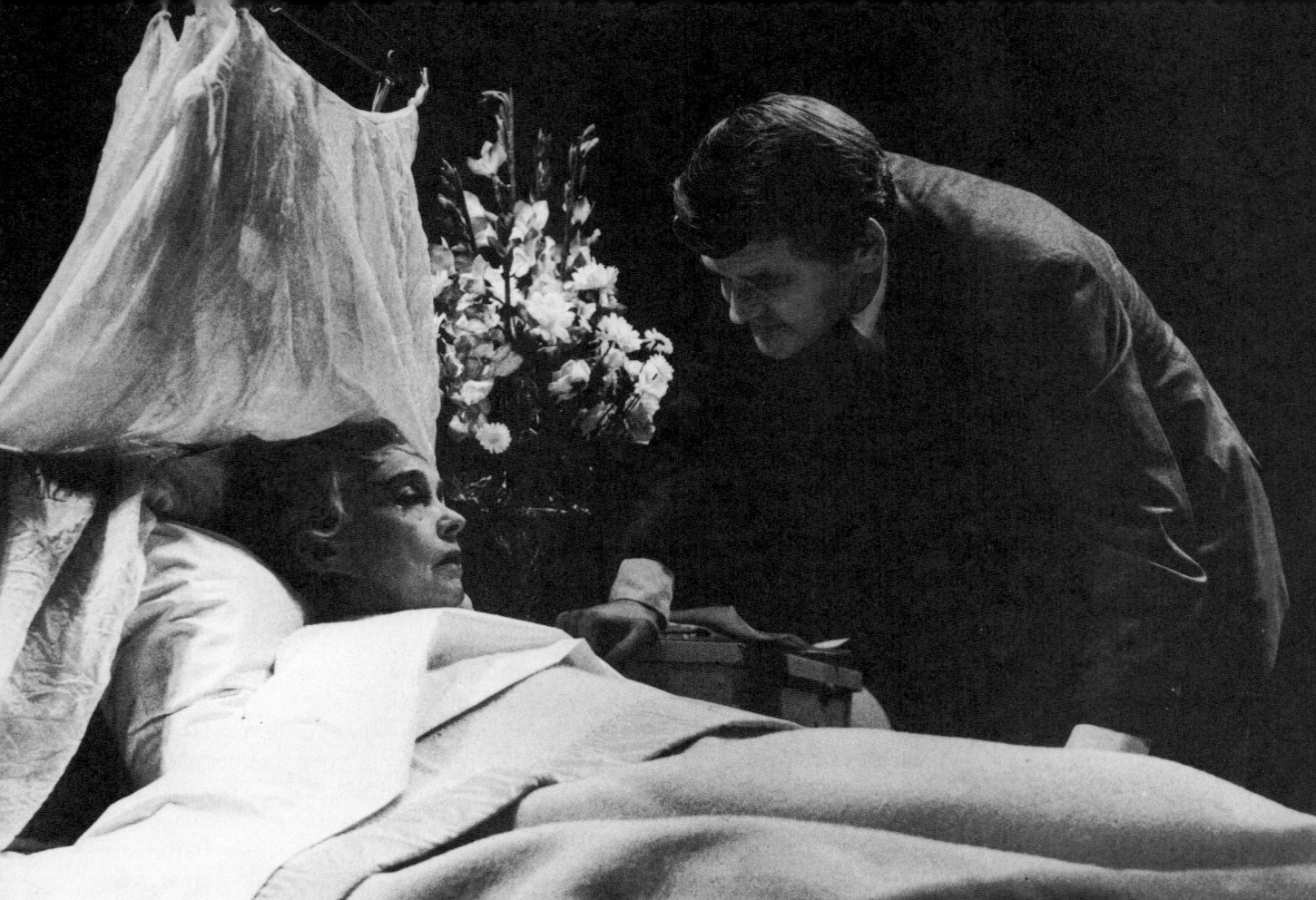

"Don't bother to come tomorrow."

Margaret (*pouts, half kidding*). Just you take care of yourself. And get the laundry ready for Annie tomorrow.

Tom (*with a flourish*). Your wish is my command.

Margaret. I put your dirty shirts from Florida in the hamper in the guest bathroom, and my things are——

Gene (*trying to stop her talking*). We'll find them.

Margaret (*to* GENE). Thanks for coming. Don't bother to come tomorrow. Father will keep in touch with you.

Gene. We'll see. Good night.

[*He stops at the door for a little wave. She wiggles her fingers in a small motion. The lights dim on the hospital scene as* TOM *and* GENE *move away.*]

Tom. Well, that's good news.

Gene. Yes.

Tom. She looks a lot better than when they brought her in here this morning, I can tell you that.

Gene. She looked pretty good.

Tom. She's a good soldier. Do you remember what she asked us to bring her? My mind is like a sieve.

Gene. I'll come along and get the bag ready and round up the laundry.

Tom. We should get the laundry ready tonight because Annie arrives at eight sharp, and she starts getting paid the minute she enters the door. But we could leave the bag till morning.

Gene (*uneasy*). I've got an early appointment at college tomorrow, Dad. I'll have to run along after we have a nightcap.

Tom. Oh, I thought you might spend the night.

Gene. I . . . uh . . . I've got an early appointment at college tomorrow.

Tom. I thought you were on your sabbatical.

Gene. I am. . . . But I arranged a meeting with someone there, Dad.

Tom. You could stay and still make it.

Gene. It's very early, Dad.

Tom. We've got an alarm. Alarm clocks all over the house.

Gene. I want to change before the appointment. . . . Shirt . . .

Tom. I've got plenty of shirts . . . underwear . . . socks . . .

Gene (*more uncomfortable*). I don't wear your sizes, Dad.

Tom. I could get you up earlier, then. I don't sleep beyond five these days.

Gene (*tense*). No, Dad . . . I just . . . No. I'll come by and——

Tom. There may be something good on television . . . Wednesday night. I think there is . . .

Gene. . . . We'll watch a little television, Dad . . . and have some drinks. . . . But then I'll have to go.

Tom (*after a moment*). All right, old man.

[GENE *instinctively reaches out to touch his father's arm, to soften the rejection. They look at each other a moment; then* TOM *drifts off into the dark, as* GENE *moves directly downstage.*]

Gene. I sat with my father much longer than I meant to . . . Because I knew I should stay the night. But . . . I couldn't. . . . We watched television. He slept on and off . . . and I went home. . . . The next morning, around nine-thirty, my mother died . . . (GENE *turns and walks upstage, as the lights dim.*)

Curtain

Responding to the Play

Analyzing Act One

Identifying Facts

1. Gene steps out of the action five times in this act to talk directly to the audience. Find the line in Gene's first speech of **exposition** that states his major problem with his father. Find details in Gene's other speeches that give important revelations about his father's **character.**

2. To prepare for the crucial **conflict** in the play, this act moves through a series of scenes. It begins at the railroad station, then goes to Tom and Margaret's home, to Schrafft's Restaurant, back home, to the hospital, and to the Rotary Club. Explain what happens in each scene to dramatize Gene's conflict with his father. Describe the conflicts between Tom and Margaret.

3. Act One introduces a fourth **character,** Alice, Gene's sister. What do you learn about her here, and how do you learn it?

Interpreting Meanings

4. Explain what each of the three characters we meet in this act wants.

5. Gene and his mother are very close. Is Gene entirely happy with this closeness? What incidents give you the answer? What do you think of the **character** of Margaret Garrison—do you find her sympathetic, unsympathetic, or both?

6. What hints are you given in this act about Tom's early life? How do these facts help explain Tom's complex **character**? How do you feel about Tom so far? What situations make you feel this way?

7. Act One is more or less static; that is, the major problem in the play does not arise until Margaret dies at the end of the act. As a result of this **crisis,** what problems will Gene and Tom face in Act Two? Explain why these problems will be especially difficult to resolve.

8. List at least three possible solutions to Gene's difficulties.

9. One of the pleasures of seeing or reading a play is feeling the "shock of recognition," the "Oh, yes!" reaction. Did you feel a shock of recognition anywhere in the play so far? Explain.

Act Two

GENE *and* DR. MAYBERRY *enter from the rear.* GENE *is carrying a small overnight case containing his mother's things.*

Gene. Thank you for all you've done for her over the years. It's been a great comfort to her, to us all.

Dr. Mayberry. I was very fond of her.

Gene. She was terribly worried about my father's health. Yesterday she said to me, "You know what put me here."

Dr. Mayberry. Well, Gene, I think that's a little too harsh. She's been living on borrowed time for quite a while, you know.

Gene. Yes. . . . Where's Dad?

Dr. Mayberry. He's gone along to the undertaker's. He wanted to wait for you, but since we couldn't reach you this morning, he went along. We sent your mother's nurse to be with him till you arrived.

Gene. Thank you.

Dr. Mayberry. He's all right. You know, Gene, old people live with death. He's been prepared for this for years. It may in some way be a relief. He's taken wonderful care of her.

Gene. Yes, he has.

Dr. Mayberry. Alice will be coming on, I suppose.

Gene. I've called her.

Dr. Mayberry. He shouldn't be staying in that house alone. (GENE *nods.*) Now, you have the suitcase and the envelope with your mother's things.

Gene. Yes. I think she should have her wedding ring.

Dr. Mayberry. Maybe you ought to check with your father . . .

Gene. No. . . . Will you? . . .

[*He hands the ring to* DR. MAYBERRY *and moves away. The lights come up on the undertaker's office.* TOM *and the* NURSE *are there.*]

Tom. I find the constant wind down there very annoying. Every year I think it's going to be different, but it isn't. You get a little overheated in the sun, and when you walk out from behind some shelter, it knifes into you.

Gene (*He has stood looking at his father for a moment. He now comes to him with tenderness, to share the experience*). Dad.

Tom (*looks up in the middle of his story*). Oh, Gene.

[*He gets up shakily. They embrace.* GENE *pats him on the back.* TOM *steps away and shakes his head. His mouth contorts, showing emotion and anger that this should have happened. He looks at the floor in moments like this.*]

Nurse. We've given him a little sedative.

Tom (*looks up*). What?

Nurse. I said we'd given you a little sedative.

Tom (*at once the charmer*). Oh, yes. This lovely lady has taken wonderful care of me.

Gene (*to the* NURSE). Thank you.

Tom. It turns out she's been to Florida, very near to where we go.

Gene (*a little surprised at this casual conversation, but playing along*). Oh, really?

Tom. I was telling her it was too bad we didn't have the pleasure of meeting her down there. But she goes in the summer. Isn't it terribly hot down there in the summer?

Nurse. The trade winds are always blowing.

Tom. Oh, yes those damnable winds. We wanted this young man to come join us there, but he went to California instead. (*To* GENE) You'll have to come down to Florida sometime. See what lovely girls you'd meet there!

Gene (*baffled and annoyed by this chatter, but passes it off*). I will.

Tom. What was your name again? My mind's like a sieve.

Nurse. Halsey.

Tom (*courtly*). Miss Halsey . . . My son, Gene.

Gene. How do you do?

Tom. Miss Halsey and I are on rather intimate terms. She . . . uh . . . gave me my shot.

Gene. Good.

Tom (*to the* NURSE). I had this terrible cough down there. The winds. But I'll be all right. Don't worry about me. If I can get some regular exercise, get over to the club.

[*For a moment they all just sit there. Obviously there is to be no sharing of the experience of the mother's death.*]

Gene. I called Alice.

Tom. Oh. Thank you. *(To the* NURSE*)* Alice was my daughter. She . . . uh . . . lives in Chicago.

Nurse *(shaking his hand, kindly)*. Goodbye, Mr. Garrison.

Tom. Oh, are you going?

Nurse. Yes. Take good care of yourself.

Tom. Oh, well. Thank you very much, my dear. You've been very kind.

Gene. Thank you.

[*The* NURSE *exits.*]

Marvin Scott *(entering with some forms and papers)*. Now, Tom, all we have to do is—*(He looks up from papers and sees* GENE.*)* Oh, hello, Gene.

Gene. Mr. Scott.

Marvin Scott. I'm terribly sorry.

Gene. Thank you.

Marvin Scott. Now, the burial is to be where, Tom? *(Throughout he is simple, considerate, and decent.)*

Tom. The upper burial ground. I've got the deed at home in my file cabinet, if I can ever find it. For years I've meant to clean out that file cabinet. But I'll find it.

Marvin Scott *(to* GENE*)*. Will you see that I get it? At least the number of the plot?

Gene. It's 542.

Marvin Scott. You're sure of that?

Gene. My wife was buried there last year.

Tom *(suddenly remembering)*. That's right.

[*He reaches out and puts his hand on* GENE*'s arm, implying that they have something to share.* GENE *doesn't really want to share his father's kind of emotionalism.*]

Marvin Scott *(He has been making notes)*. We'll need some clothes . . . uh . . .

Gene *(quickly)*. Yes, all right. I'll take care of that.

Marvin Scott. Do you want the casket open or closed while she's resting here?

[*There is a pause.*]

Gene. Dad?

Tom. What was that?

Gene. Do you want the casket open or closed?

Tom. Oh . . . open, I think.

[GENE *would have preferred it closed.*]

Marvin Scott. Now, an obituary. Perhaps you would like to prepare something, Tom.

Tom. Yes. Well, . . . Gene? Gene was very close to his mother.

[MARVIN SCOTT *looks at* GENE.]

Gene. Yes, I'll work something up.

Marvin Scott. If you could come by this afternoon, so that it would catch the——

Tom. She was my inspiration. When I met her the clouds hung low and dark. I was going to night school, studying shorthand and typing and *elocution*[1] . . . and working in a lumberyard in the daytime . . . wearing a cutaway coat, if you please, someone at the church had given me. . . . I was making a home for my brother and sister. . . . My mother had died, and my father had deserted us. . . . *(He has gone hard on his father . . . and stops a moment.)* "He did not know the meaning of the word 'quit.' " They said that some years ago when The Schoolboys of Old Harlem gave me an award. You were there, Gene.

Gene. Yes.

Tom. "Obstructions, yes. But go through them or over them, but never around them." Teddy Roosevelt said that. I took it down in shorthand for practice . . . Early in life I developed a will of iron. . . . *(You can feel the iron in the way he says it.)* Any young man in this country who has a sound mind and a sound body, who will set himself an objective, can achieve anything he wants, within reason. *(He has said all this firmly, as though lecturing or giving a speech. He now looks at his cigarette.)* Ugh. . . . Filthy habit. Twenty years ago a doctor told me to give these things up, and I did. But when things pile up . . . Well, . . . All's lost, all's spent, when we our desires get without content . . . *(He looks around. There is a pause.)*

Gene. I'll write something.

Tom. About what?

Gene. Mother. For an obituary.

Tom. Oh, yes, you do that. He's the lit'ry member of the family. You'll use the church, won't you?

---

1. **elocution:** the art of public speaking.

Not the chapel. I imagine there'll be hundreds of people there . . . Garden Club . . . Woman's Club . . . Mother's Club.

Marvin Scott. I'm sure that Reverend Pell will use whichever you want. (*He shuffles some papers.*) Now, Tom, the only thing that's left is the most difficult. We have to choose a coffin.

Tom. Do we have to do that now?

Marvin Scott. It's easier now, Tom. To get it over with.

Tom (*firm*). I want the best. That's one thing. I want the best!

Marvin Scott (*moves across the stage with* TOM *and* GENE). There are many kinds.

Tom (*As he takes a few steps, he takes* GENE'S *arm*). I don't know what I'd do without this young fellow. (*This kind of word bribery disturbs* GENE. *In the coffin area, overhead lights suddenly come on. Shafts of light in the darkness indicate the coffins.* TOM *claps his hand to his forehead.*) Do I have to look at all these?

Marvin Scott (*gently*). It's the only way, Tom. The best way is to just let you wander around alone and look at them. The prices are all marked on the cards inside the caskets. (*He lifts an imaginary card.*)

Tom (*puts on his glasses to look*). Nine hundred? For the casket?

Marvin Scott. That includes everything, Tom. All our services, and one car for the mourners. Other cars are extra.

Tom (*to* GENE, *who is standing back*). Well, we'll have your car, so we shouldn't need another. Anybody else wants to come, let them drive their own car. (*Looks back at the caskets*) Oh, dear . . . Gene! (GENE *comes alongside. He is tender and considerate to the part of his father that is going through a difficult time, though irritated by the part that has always angered him. They walk silently among the caskets for a few moments.* TOM *lifts a price tag and looks at it.*) Two thousand! (*He taps an imaginary casket.*) What are these made of?

Marvin Scott (*coming forward*). They vary, Tom. . . . Steel, bronze . . . wood.

Tom. What accounts for the variation in prices?

Marvin Scott. Material . . . workmanship . . . the finish inside. You see, this is all silk.

Tom. I suppose the metal stands up best.

Marvin Scott. Well, yes. (TOM *shakes his head, confused.*) Of course the casket does not go directly into the ground. We first sink a concrete outer vault.

Tom. Oh?

Marvin Scott. That prevents seepage, et cetera.

Tom. That's included in the price?

Marvin Scott. Yes.

[TOM *walks on.* GENE *stays in the shadows.*]

Tom. How long do any of these stand up?

[GENE *closes his eyes.*]

Marvin Scott. It's hard to say, Tom. It depends on the location. Trees, roots, and so on.

Tom. I suppose these metal ones are all welded at the seams?

Marvin Scott. Oh, yes.

Tom. Our plot up there is on a small slope. I suppose that's not so good for wear. I didn't think of that when I bought it. . . . And the trees looked so lovely. . . . I never thought.

Marvin Scott (*gently*). I don't think it makes that much difference, Tom.

Tom (*moves along, stops*). For a child?

Marvin Scott. Yes.

Tom (*shakes his head, moved*). My mother would have fit in that. She was a little bit of a thing. . . . Died when I was ten. (*Tears come to his eyes.*) I don't remember much about her funeral except my father. . . . He'd run out on us, but he came back when she died . . . and I wouldn't let him come to the cemetery. (*He gets angry all over again . . . then:*) Oh, well, . . . water over the dam. But this made me think of her . . . a little bit of a thing. (GENE *is touched by his father's memory of his own mother, but still upset at this supermarket type of shopping.*) Five hundred. What do you think of this one, Gene? (GENE *comes up.*) I like the color of the silk. Did you say that was silk or satin?

Marvin Scott. Silk.

Gene. I don't think it makes much difference, Dad. Whatever you think.

Tom. I mean, they all go into this concrete business. (*He senses some disapproval on* GENE'S *part and moves on, then adjusts his glasses.*) This one is eight hundred. I don't see the difference. Marvin, what's the difference?

Marvin Scott. It's mostly finish and workmanship. They're both steel.

Tom. I don't like the browns or blacks. Gray seems less somber. Don't you agree, Gene?

Gene. Yes, I do.

Tom. Eight hundred. Is there a tax, Marvin?

[GENE *turns away.*]

Marvin Scott. That includes the tax, Tom.

Tom. All right. Let's settle for that, then, and get out of here. (*He shivers.*)

Marvin Scott. Fine. (*to* GENE) And you'll send some clothes over?

Gene. Yes. (GENE *bobs his head up and down, annoyed with the details, though* MARVIN *has been considerate and discreet.*)

Marvin Scott. I'd estimate that Mrs. Garrison should be . . . that is, if people want to come to pay their respects, about noon tomorrow.

Gene. All right.

Marvin Scott. Would you like to see where Mrs. Garrison will be resting?

Gene (*definite*). No, thank you. I think we'll be moving along.

Marvin Scott. I assume your sister Alice will be coming on?

Gene. She arrives this evening. (*He looks around for his father and sees him standing in front of the child's coffin, staring at it. He goes over to his father and takes him gently by the arm.*) Shall we go, Dad?

Tom (*nods his head, far away*). She was just a little bit of a thing.

[*And they start moving out of the room, as the lights dim out.*

As the lights come up again on another part of the stage, ALICE, GENE's *older sister, is coming on. She is in her early forties, attractive, brisk, realistic, unsentimental.*]

Alice. Shouldn't we be getting home to Dad?

Gene (*Carrying two highballs. He is blowing off steam*). I suppose so, but I'm not ready to go home yet. . . . Let's sit over here, where we can get away from the noise at the bar.

Alice. You've had quite a day.

Gene. I'm sorry for blowing off, but damn it, Alice, our mother died this morning, and I've wanted to talk about her, but she hasn't been mentioned except as "my inspiration," which is his cue to start the story of his life.

Alice. I'm sorry you've had to take it all alone.

Gene. Well, I'm glad you're here, and I'm glad of the chance to get out of the house to come to meet you. . . . I'm so tired of hearing about "when the clouds hung low and dark." . . . I'm so tired of people coming up to me and saying, "Your dad's a remarkable man." Nobody talks about Mother. Just, "He's a remarkable man." You'd think he died! . . . I want to say to them, "My mother was a remarkable woman. . . . You don't know my father. You only know the man in the newspapers. He's a selfish man who's lived on the edge of exasperation all his life. You don't know the bite of his sarcasm. The night he banished my sister for marrying someone he didn't approve of did not get into the papers."

Alice. *Shhh* . . .

Gene. What a night that was! Mother running from the room sobbing. You shouting at him and storming out, and the two of us, father and son, left to finish dinner, in silence. Afterward I threw up.

Alice. I shouted and you threw up. That was pretty much the pattern.

Gene. I know I'm being unfair. But I'm in the mood to be unfair. I've wanted to turn to him all day and say, "Will you for once shut up about your miserable childhood and say something about Mother?" (*A little ashamed of his outburst*) But I can't say that. He's an old man and my father, and his wife has died, and he may be experiencing something, somewhere, I know nothing about. (*He shakes his head for going on like this.*) I'm sorry.

Alice. It's all right.

Gene. No. (*He touches her arm, smiles.*) Mother loved your flowers.

Alice. I've felt guilty about Mother all the way coming here. I should have seen her more, invited her more often, brought the kids more often. Instead I sent flowers.

Gene. I guess that's an inevitable feeling when a person dies. I feel the same way.

Alice. But you were so good to her. You made her life.

Gene (*He has always hated that phrase. Slowly, quietly*). A son is not supposed to make his mother's life . . . Oh, I loved Mother. You know that. But to be depended on to make her life . . . Dad says, he boasts, he never knew the meaning of the word "quit." Well, he quit on her all right. And I . . . I was just there. (ALICE *looks at this sudden revelation of his feelings, his resentment that he was left to save his mother from loneliness and unhappiness.*) Still, wait till you see him. There's something that comes through . . . the old Tiger. Something that reaches you and makes you want to cry. . . . He'll probably be asleep when we get home, in front of the television. And you'll see. The Old Man . . . the Father. But then he wakes up and becomes Tom Garrison, and I'm in trouble. . . . Last night he asked me to stay with him, and I didn't. . . . I couldn't. I'm ashamed of that now.

Alice (*Touched by the complexity of* GENE's *feelings, she looks at him a long moment, then*). Have you called California?

Gene (*Frowns. A problem*). No. (*He takes a drink, wanting to avoid the subject.*)

Alice. I suppose we have enough problems for the next few days, but . . .

Gene. After?

Alice. Yes. We'll have to start thinking about Dad, about what we're going to do.

Gene (*nods his head*). I don't know. (*They look at each other a moment, then*) Well, let's go home. (*He rises.*) Thanks for listening to all this, Alice. You had to pay good money to get someone to listen to you. I appreciate it. (*He smiles.*) I thought I wanted to talk to you about Mother, but all I've done is talk about him, just like the others.

Alice. We'll talk. There'll be time.

[*And they leave. The lights dim out on the bar area and come up on the home area.* TOM *is asleep, his head forward, his glasses on, some legal papers in his lap. Quiet like this, he is a touching picture of old age. The strong face . . . the good but gnarled hands. He is the symbol of* FATHER. *The television is on. As* GENE *and* ALICE *come in, they pause and look. They are impressed by the sad dignity. Finally* GENE *approaches and*

gently puts his hand on his father's arm, then turns down the television.]

Gene. Dad?

Tom (*barely stirs*). Hm?

Gene. Dad?

Tom. Mm? Margaret? (*Coming to a little more and looking up at* GENE) . . . Oh, Gene . . . I must have dozed off.

Gene. Alice is here.

Tom. Alice? . . . What for? (*He is genuinely confused.*)

Alice (*comes from the shadows*). Hello, Dad.

Tom (*Looks around, a bit panicky, confused. Then he remembers*). Oh . . . Oh, yes.

[*He bites his upper lip and with his gnarled hands grips theirs for a moment of affection and family strength.* ALICE *kisses him on the cheek. They help him from the chair and start putting on his coat. As the lights dim on the home area, they come up on a graveyard area.* TOM, GENE *and* ALICE, *and all the people we have met are gathering as* REVEREND PELL *starts his eulogy.*]

Reverend Pell. Margaret Garrison was a loving wife and a kind and generous mother, and a public-spirited member of the community. The many people who were touched by her goodness can attest to the pleasure and joy she brought them through her love of life and her power to communicate this love to others. The many children, now grown . . .

Gene (*turns from the family group*). Only a dozen or so people were at my mother's funeral. Most of her friends were dead or had moved to other cities or just couldn't make it. Fifteen years earlier the church would have been filled. There were a few men sent from Rotary, a few women from the Garden Club, the Mother's Club, the Woman's Club, and a few of the members of her bridge club were there. . . . The hundreds of children who had listened to her tell stories year after year on Christmas Eve were all gone, or had forgotten. . . . Perhaps some of them who were still in the neighborhood looked up from their evening papers to say, "I see Mrs. Garrison died. She was nice. . . . Well, she was an old lady." (*He turns to rejoin the family group.*)

"Only a dozen or so people were at my mother's funeral."

Reverend Pell. Earth to earth . . . ashes to ashes . . . dust to dust. . . . The Lord giveth and the Lord taketh away. . . . Blessed be the name of the Lord. . . . Amen.

[TOM *comes to shake hands with* REVEREND PELL. *The others drift about, exchanging nods, and gradually leave during the following.*]

Tom. Well, it's a nice place up here.
Gene (*who has wandered over to look at another grave*). Yes.
Tom. Your mother and I bought it soon after we were married. She thought it a strange thing to do, but we bought it. (*He looks at the grave* GENE *is looking at.*) Now, let's see, that's . . .
Gene. Carol.
Tom. Who?
Gene. Carol. My wife.

Tom. Oh, yes. (*He reaches out a sympathetic hand toward* GENE, *then moves away.*) There's room for three more burials up here, as I remember. There . . . there . . . and there. I'm to go there, when the time comes. (*He looks around for a moment.*) This plot is in terrible shape. . . . I paid three hundred dollars some years ago for perpetual care, and now look at it. Just disgraceful . . . I'm going to talk to that superintendent.

[*And he strides off. The lights change.* ALICE *and* GENE *move into another area, what might be a garden with a bench. For a moment neither says anything.* GENE *lights a cigarette and sits on the grass.*]

Alice. I don't know how you feel, but I'd like to figure out some kind of memorial for Mother. . . . Use some of the money she left.
Gene. Yes, definitely.

Alice. Maybe some shelves of books for the children's library. Christmas books with the stories she liked to tell.

Gene. That's a good idea.

[*There is a long and awkward pause.*]

Alice. Well, Gene, what are we going to do?

Gene (*frowns*). Mother always said to put her in an old-people's home. She had one all picked out.

Alice. Sidney's mother and father saw it coming and arranged to be in one of those cottage colonies for old people.

Gene. Mother and Dad didn't.

Alice. I think you should go ahead and get married and move to California. . . . But . . . I might as well get this off my chest, it would be murder if he came to live with us. In the first place, he wouldn't do it, feeling as he does about Sid, and the kids can't stand how he tells them how to do everything.

Gene. I think you're right. That would never work. (*There is a pause.* GENE *looks out at the garden.*) I can't tell you what it does to me as a man . . . to see someone like that . . . a man who was distinguished, remarkable . . . just become a nuisance.

Alice (*She is disturbed at what her brother may be thinking*). I know I sound hard, but he's had his life . . . and as long as we can be assured that he's taken care of . . . Oh, I'll feel some guilt, and you, maybe more. But my responsibility is to my husband and my children.

Gene. Yes. That's *your* responsibility.

Alice. And your responsibility is to yourself . . . to get married again, to get away from memories of Carol and her whole world. Have you called California?

Gene (*frowns*). No.

Alice. If I were the girl you were planning to marry, and you didn't call me to tell me your mother had died . . .

Gene (*gets up, disturbed*). I just haven't wanted to go into it all with her.

Alice (*understanding, but worried*). Gene, my friend . . . my brother . . . Get out of here!

Gene. Look, Alice, your situation is quite different. Mine is very complex. You fortunately see things very clearly, but it's not so easy for me.

(ALICE *looks at* GENE, *troubled by what his thinking seems to be leading to. After a moment . . . reflective*) We always remember the terrible things about Dad. I've been trying to remember some of the others . . . How much he *did* do for us.

Alice. I'm doing a lot for my kids. I don't expect them to pay me back at the other end. (GENE *wanders around, thinking, scuffing the grass.*) I'm sure we could find a full-time housekeeper. He can afford it.

Gene. He'd never agree.

Alice. It's that or finding a home. (GENE *frowns.*) Sidney's folks like where they are. Also, we might as well face it, his mind's going. Sooner or later, we'll have to think about powers of attorney, perhaps committing him to an institution.

Gene. It's all so ugly.

Alice (*smiling*). Yes, my gentle Gene, a lot of life is.

Gene. Now, look, don't go trying to make me out some softhearted . . . (*He can't find the word.*) I know life is ugly.

Alice. Yes, I think you know it. You've lived through a great deal of ugliness. But you work like a Trojan to deny it, to make it not so. (*After a moment, not arguing*) He kicked me out. He said he never wanted to see me again. He broke Mother's heart over that for years. He was mean, unloving. He beat you when you were a kid. . . . You've hated and feared him all your adult life. . . .

Gene (*cutting in*). Still he's my father, and a man. And what's happening to him appalls me as a man.

Alice. We have a practical problem here.

Gene. It's not as simple as all that.

Alice. To me it is. I don't understand this mystical haze you're casting over it. I'm going to talk to him tomorrow, after the session with the lawyer, about a housekeeper. (GENE *reacts, but says nothing.*) Just let me handle it. He can visit us, and we can take turns coming to visit him. Now, I'll do the dirty work. Only when he turns to you, don't give in.

Gene. I can't tell you how ashamed I feel . . . not to say with open arms, "Poppa, come live with me . . . I love you, Poppa, and I want to take care of you." . . . I need to love him. I've always wanted to love him.

[*He drops his arms and wanders off.* ALICE *watches her brother drift off into the garden as the lights go down in that area. The lights come up in the living room area.* TOM *is seated in his chair, writing.* ALICE *comes into the room. Small packing boxes are grouped around.*]

Alice. How are you coming?
Tom. Oh, Alice, I've written out receipts for you to sign for the jewelry your mother left you. And if you'll sign for the things she left the children.
Alice. All right.

[*Signs.* GENE *comes into the room carrying a box full of his mother's things. He exchanges a look with* ALICE, *knowing the time has come for the discussion.*]

Tom. It may not be necessary, but as executor, I'll be held responsible for these things.
Alice. Dad, I'd like to talk a little . . . with you . . . about——
Tom. Yes, all right. But first I'd like to read you this letter I've written to Harry Hall. . . . He and I used to play golf out in New Jersey. . . . He wrote a very nice letter to me about your mother . . . and I've written him as follows, . . . it will only take a minute, . . . if I can read my own shorthand . . . (*He adjusts his glasses.*) "Dear Harry, . . . How thoughtful of you to write me on the occasion of Margaret's death. It was quite a blow. As you know, she was my inspiration, and had been ever since that day fifty-five years ago when I met her, . . . when the clouds hung low and dark for me. At that time I was supporting my younger brother and my sister and my aged grandfather in a two-room flat . . . going to work every day in a lumber mill. Providence, which has always guided me, prompted me to take a night course in shorthand and typing, and also prompted me to go to the Underwood Typewriting Company seeking a position as stenographer. They sent me, God be praised, to the office of T. J. Parks . . . and a job that started at five dollars a week ended in 1929 when I retired at fifty thousand a year. . . ." That's as far as I've gotten at the moment. (*He looks up for approval.*)
Gene. Dad, I don't think financial matters are par-

ticularly appropriate in answering a letter of condolence.
Tom. Oh? (*He looks at the letter.*) But it's true. You see, it follows. I'm saying she was my inspiration . . . and it seems entirely appropriate to explain that.
Gene. Well, it's your letter, Dad.
Tom (*looks it over*). Well . . .
Alice. Dad, I'm leaving tomorrow . . . and . . .
Tom (*looking up*). What?
Alice. I'm going home tomorrow.
Tom (*formal*). Well, Alice, I'm grateful you came. I know it was difficult for you, leaving home. Your mother would have appreciated it. She was very fond of you, Alice.
Alice. I think we ought to talk over, maybe, what your plans are.
Tom. My plans? I have many letters to answer, and a whole mess in my files and accounts. If the income tax people ever asked me to produce my books . . .
Gene. They're not likely to, Dad. Your income is no longer of that size.
Tom (*with a twinkle in his eye*). Don't be too sure.
Alice. I didn't mean exactly that kind of plans. I meant . . . Well, you haven't been well.
Tom (*belligerent*). Who said so?
Alice. Mother was worried to death about——(*She stops.*)
Tom. I was under a strain. Your mother's health . . . never knowing when it might happen. Trying to get her to take care of herself, to take it easy. You know, the doctor said if she didn't eat more slowly, this might happen.
Alice. You plan to keep the house?
Tom. Oh, yes. All my things are here. . . . It's a . . . It's a . . . I'll be back on my feet, and my . . . (*points to his head*) . . . will clear up. Now this strain is over, I'm confident I'll be in shape any day now.
Alice. I worry, leaving you in this house . . . alone, Dad.
Tom (*looks around, very alert, defensively*). I'm perfectly all right. Now don't worry about me . . . either of you. Why, for the last year, since your mother's first attack, I've been getting the breakfast, making the beds, using a dust rag. . . . (*He makes quite a performance of this. It is a gallant*

struggle.) And the laundress comes in once a week and cleans up for me. . . . And Gene here . . . if Gene will keep an eye on me, drop in once or twice a week . . .

Alice. That's the point.

Gene *(low).* Alice!

Alice. We think you should have a full-time housekeeper, Dad. To live here.

Tom *(trying to kid it off, but angry).* Alone here with me? That wouldn't be very proper, would it?

Alice *(smiling).* Nevertheless . . .

Tom. No. Now that's final!

Alice. Dad, Gene and I would feel a lot better about it if——

Tom. Look, you don't have to worry about me.

Alice. Dad, you're forgetting things more and more.

Tom. Who says so?

Alice. Mother wrote me, and——

Tom. I was under a strain. I just finished telling you. Look, Alice, you can go, leave with a clear mind. I'm all right. *(GENE is touched and moved by his father's effort, his desperate effort to maintain his dignity, his standing as a functioning man.)* Of course, I will appreciate Gene's dropping in. But I'm all right.

Alice. We still would like to get a full-time housekeeper.

Tom *(bristling).* What do you mean, you would get? I've hired and fired thousands of people in my day. I don't need anyone *getting* someone for me.

Alice. Will you do it yourself, then?

Tom. No, I told you. No! *(He gets very angry. His voice sharpens and hardens.)* Since I was eight years old I've taken care of myself. What do you two know about it? You were given everything on a platter. At an age when you two were swinging on that tree out there, breaking the branches, I was selling newspapers five hours a day, and at night dancing a jig in saloons for pennies. . . . And you're trying to tell me I can't take care of myself. . . . If I want a housekeeper, and I don't, I'll hire one. . . . I've hired and fired thousands of people in my time. When I was vice-president of Colonial Brass at fifty thousand a year . . . two thousand people. And you tell me I'm incompetent . . . to hire a housekeeper. And how many people have you hired? *(To GENE)* You teach. . . . Well, all right. That's your business, if that's what you want to do. But don't talk to me about hiring and firing.

[*The children are saddened and perhaps a little cowed by this naked outburst, the defense of a man who knows that he is slipping, and an angry outburst of hatred and jealousy for his own children. Everyone is quiet for a moment . . . then:*]

Alice. Dad, you might fall down.

Tom. Why fall down? There's nothing wrong with my balance.

[*GENE is sick at this gradual attempt to bring to a man's consciousness the awareness that he is finished.*]

Alice. Sometimes, when you get up, you're dizzy.

Tom. Nonsense. *(He gets up abruptly. He makes great effort and stands for a moment, then one foot moves slightly to steady his balance . . . and the children both look away.)* Now, I appreciate your concern. . . . *(Very fatherly)* But I'm perfectly able to carry on by myself. As I said, with Gene's help from time to time. I imagine we could have dinner every once in a while, couldn't we, Gene . . . once a week or so? Take you up to Rotary. Some of the speakers are quite amusing.

[ALICE *looks at* GENE *to see if he is going to speak up.*]

Gene. Sure, Dad.

Tom. Give us some time together at last. Get to know each other.

Alice *(quietly but firmly).* Gene wants to get married.

Gene. Alice!

Tom. What?

Alice. Gene wants to move to California and get married.

Gene. Alice, shut up.

Alice *(almost in tears).* I can't help it. You've never faced up to him. You'd let him ruin your life.

Gene *(angry).* I can take care of my own life.

Alice. You can't!

Tom *(loud).* Children! . . . Children! *(They stop arguing and turn to their father at his command.* TOM *speaks with a note of sarcasm.)* I have no desire to interfere with either of your lives. I took care of myself at eight. I can take care of myself at eighty. I have never wanted to be a burden to my children.

Gene. I'm going to hang around, Dad.

Tom. There's no need to.

Gene. I'll move in here at least till you're feeling better.

[ALICE *turns away, angry and despairing.*]

Tom (*sarcastically*). I don't want to ruin your life.

Gene (*angry now at his father*). I didn't say that.

Tom. I have long gotten the impression that my only function in this family is to supply the money to——

Gene (*anguished*). Dad!

Tom. ——to supply the funds for your education, for your——

Gene. Dad, stop it!

[TOM *staggers a little, dizzy.* GENE *goes to his side to steady him.* TOM *breathes heavily in and out in rage. The rage of this man is a terrible thing to see, old as he is. He finally gets some control of himself.*]

Tom. As far as I am concerned, this conversation is ended. Alice, we've gotten along very well for some years now without your attention.

Gene (*protesting, but hating the fight*). Dad!

Alice. You sent me away. Don't forget that.

Tom. You chose to lead your own life. Well, we won't keep you now.

Gene. Dad . . .

Tom (*rage again*). I was competent to go into the city year after year to earn money for your clothes, your food, the roof over your head. Am I now incompetent? Is that what you're trying to tell me? (*He looks at* ALICE *with a terrible look. He breathes heavily for a moment or two; then, shaking his head, he turns away from both of them and leaves, disappearing into the shadows.*)

Gene (*angry, troubled*). Alice!

Alice. I'm only trying to get a practical matter accomplished.

Gene. You don't have to destroy him in the process.

Alice. I wasn't discussing his competence. Although that will be a matter for discussion soon.

Gene. Look, Alice, just leave it now, the way it is. Don't say any more.

Alice. With you staying on.

Gene. Yes. You can go with a clear conscience.

Alice. My conscience is clear.

Gene. I am doing this because I want to.

Alice. You're doing it because you can't help yourself.

Gene. Look, when I want to be analyzed, I'll pay for it.

Alice (*pleading*). But I saw you. Didn't you see yourself there, when he started to rage? Didn't you feel yourself pull in? You shrank.

Gene. I shrank at the ugliness of what was happening.

Alice. You're staying because you can't stand his wrath the day you say, "Dad, I'm leaving." You've never been able to stand up to his anger. He's cowed you.

Gene. Look, Alice . . .

Alice. He'll call you ungrateful, and you'll believe him. He'll lash out at you with his sarcasm, and that will kill this lovely, necessary image you have of yourself as the good son. Can't you see that?

Gene (*lashing out*). What do you want us to do? Shall we get out a white paper? Let it be known that we, Alice and Gene, have done all that we can to make this old man happy in his old age, without inconveniencing ourselves, of course. And he has refused our help. So, if he falls and hits his head and lies there until he rots, it is not our fault. Is that it?

Alice. You insist on——

Gene (*running on*). Haven't you learned on the couch[2] that people do *not* always do what you want them to do? It is sometimes *we* who have to make the adjustments?

Alice. The difference between us is that I accept the inevitable sadness of this world without an acute sense of personal guilt. You don't. I don't think anyone expects either of us to ruin our lives for an unreasonable old man.

Gene. It's not going to ruin my life.

Alice. It is.

Gene. A few weeks, a month.

---

2. **on the couch:** a reference to the couch often provided for patients in a psychiatrist's office.

"... *the 'old man' in me ... wants to extend some kind of mercy to that old man."*

Alice. Forever!

Gene. Alice, let's not go on discussing it. I know what I am going to do. Maybe I can't explain my reasons to you. I just know I can't do anything else. Maybe there isn't the same thing between a mother and a daughter, but the "old man" in me feels something very deep, wants to extend some kind of mercy to that old man. I never had a father. I ran away from him. He ran away from me. Maybe he's right. Maybe it is time we found each other.

Alice. Excuse me for saying so, but I find that sentimental slop! I think this is all rationalization to make tolerable a compulsion you have to stay here. You hate the compulsion, so you've dressed it up to look nice.

Gene. How do you know what you're saying isn't a rationalization to cover up a callousness, a self-ishness, a coldness in yourself? To make *it* smell nice?

Alice. What do you think you'll find?

Gene. I don't know.

Alice. You hope to find love. Couldn't you tell from what he just said what you're going to find? Don't you understand he's got to hate you? He may not think it in his head or feel it in his heart, but you are his enemy! From the moment you were born a boy, you were a threat to this man and his enemy.

Gene. That sounds like the textbooks, Alice.

Alice. He wants your guts . . . and he's had them! (GENE *stands, starts to leave the room.*) I'm sorry. I want to shock you. When has he ever regarded you as a man, an equal, a male? When you were a marine. And that you did for him. Because even back there you were looking for his love. You didn't want to be a marine. "Now, Poppa, will you love me?" And he did. No, not love. But he was proud and grateful because you gave him an extension of himself he could boast about, with his phony set of values. When was he ever proud about the things *you* do? The things *you* value?

When did he ever mention your teaching or your books, except in scorn?

Gene. You don't seem to have felt the absence of a father. But I feel incomplete, deprived. I just do not want to let my father die a stranger to me.

Alice. You're looking for something that isn't there, Gene. You're looking for a mother's love in a father. Mothers are soft and yielding. Fathers are hard and rough, to teach us the way of the world, which is rough, which is mean, which is selfish and prejudiced.

Gene. All right. That's your definition. And because of what he did to you, you're entitled to it.

Alice. I've always been grateful to him for what he did. He taught me a marvelous lesson and has made me able to face a lot. And there has been a lot to face, and I'm grateful to him. Because if I couldn't get the understanding and compassion from a father, who could I expect it from in the world? Who in the world, if not from a father? So I learned and didn't expect it, and I've found very little, and so I'm grateful to him. I'm grateful to him. (*The growing intensity ends in tears, and she turns her head.*)

Gene (*Looks in pity at the involuntary revelation of her true feeling. He moves to her and touches her*). I'll stay, Alice . . . for a while, at least . . . for whatever reasons. Let's not argue anymore.

Alice. And Peggy?

Gene. She'll be coming in a week or two, we'll see.

Alice. Don't lose her, Gene. Maybe I'm still fouled up on myself, but I think I've spoken near the truth about you.

Gene. I keep wondering why I haven't called her, or wanted to call her. Why I seem so much closer to Carol at the moment.

Alice (*gently, tentatively*). The image . . . of the eternally bereaved husband . . . forgive me . . . the dutiful son . . . they're very appealing and seductive. . . . But they're not living. (GENE *just stands, looking at her, thinking about what she has said.* ALICE *kisses him on the cheek.*) Good night, Gene.

Gene (*his hands on her shoulders*). Good night.

Alice (*She suddenly puts her head tight against his shoulder and holds him*). Suddenly I miss Mother so.

[*She sobs. He just holds her and strokes her back.*]

Gene. Yes. (*And he holds her, comforting her, as the lights dim.*)

[*After a few moments of darkness the lights come up on* TOM *in his bedroom in pajamas and bathrobe, kneeling by his bed, praying. On his bed is a small top drawer of a bureau, filled with mementos.* GENE *comes in. He stands in the shadows and watches his father at his prayers.* GENE *does not pray anymore, and he has always been touched by the sight of his father praying.* TOM *gets up and starts to untie his bathrobe.*]

Gene. You ready to be tucked in?

Tom (*smiling*). Yes. (*Loosening his robe*) Look at the weight I've lost.

Gene (*Troubled at the emaciated body, which is pathetic. The face is ruddy and strong, the body that of an old man*). Since when?

Tom. Oh, I don't know.

Gene (*tapping his father's stomach*). Well, you had quite a little pot there, Dad.

Tom (*smiling*). Did I?

Gene. Yes.

Tom. But look, all through here, through my chest.

Gene. Well, we'll put some back on you. You've been eating pretty well this last week.

Tom (*looking at his own chest*). You know, I never had hair on my chest. I don't understand it. You have hair on your chest. I just didn't have any. Well, I'm confident if I could get some exercise, . . . Do you remember when I used to get you up in the morning, and we'd go down and do calisthenics to the radio?

Gene (*smiling*). Yes.

Tom (*stands very straight, swings his arms*). One-two-three-four . . . One-two-three-four . . .

Gene. Hey, take it easy.

Tom. I used to swing the Indian clubs every day at lunchtime. I gave you a set once, didn't I?

Gene. I think so.

Tom. We'll have to dig them out. (*Starts bending exercises*) One-two-three-four . . . one-two-three-four.

Gene. Why don't you wait till morning for that?

Tom. Remember when we used to put on the gloves and spar down on the side porch? . . . I don't think you ever liked it very much. *(He crouches in boxing position.)* The manly art of self-defense . . . Gentleman Jim Corbett . . . Now it's something else again. . . . Oh, well, things to worry about. But I intend to get over to the club, play some golf, sit around and swap stories with the boys. Too bad you never took up golf. Alice could have played a good game of golf. But she had a temper. Inherited it from your mother's father. *(He fishes in the bureau drawer on the bed.)* I was looking through my bureau drawer . . . I don't know, just going over things . . . Did you ever see this? *(He takes out a small revolver.)*

Gene. Yes.

Tom. Never had occasion to use it. Oh, I took it out West one winter when we went to Arizona instead of Florida. Shot at rattlesnakes in a rock pile. *(Takes pot shots)* I don't have a permit for this anymore. *(Starts putting it back in its box)* I suppose they wouldn't give me one. I don't know anyone up there anymore. When I was Mayor, cops on every corner would wave, . . . "Hello, Mr. Garrison, . . . 'Morning, Mr. Garrison." Now, one of the young whippersnappers gave me a ticket, just before we left for Florida. Said I'd passed a full-stop sign. That's what *he* said. First ticket I had in forty or more years of driving, so keep this quiet. *(He takes out a packet of photographs wrapped in tissue paper.)* Pictures . . . I think you've seen most of them. . . . The family.

Gene *(very tentatively).* You know, Dad, I've never seen a picture of your father. *(*TOM *looks at him a long time. Then finally, with his hatred showing on his face, he unwraps another tissue and hands over a small picture.* GENE *looks at it a long moment.)* He's just a boy.

Tom. That was taken about the time he was married.

Gene. I'd always thought of him as . . . the way you talked about him . . . as . . . *(*GENE *is obviously touched by the picture.)*

Tom. Oh, he was a fine-looking man before he started to drink. Big, square, high color. But he became my mortal enemy. . . . Did I ever show you that? *(He takes out a small piece of paper.)*

Careful. . . . When I set up a home for my brother and sister, one day we were all out, and he came around and ripped up all my sister's clothes and shoes. Drunk, of course. A few days later he came around to apologize and ask for some money, and I threw him out. . . . The next day he left this note, . . . "You are welcome to your burden."

Gene. And you kept it?

Tom. Yes. I never saw him again until many years later he was dying, in Bellevue, and someone got word to me, and I went down and asked him if he wanted anything. He said he'd like some fruit. So I sent him a few oranges. He died the next day.

Gene. There must have been something there to love, to understand.

Tom. In my father? *(Shakes his head "no." Then he shows* GENE *another card.)* Do you remember this? *(He reads.)* "To the best dad in the world on Father's Day." That was in . . . *(Turns over and reads the notation)* 1946. . . . Yes. *(Emotional)* I appreciate that, Gene. That's a lovely tribute. I think I have all your Father's Day cards here. You know, your mother used to talk of you children as her jewels. Maybe because my interests were different, I've always said you were my dividends. . . . You know, I didn't want children, coming from the background I did . . . and we didn't have Alice for a long time. But your mother finally persuaded me. She said they would be a comfort in our old age. And you are, Gene.

Gene *(touched, but embarrassed and uncomfortable).* Well. . . .

Tom *(fishes in the drawer and brings out a sheet of paper).* A program of yours from college . . . some glee club concert . . . I've got everything but the kitchen stove in here. *(Looks over the program)* Do you still sing?

Gene *(smiling).* Not in years.

Tom. That's too bad. You had a good voice. But we can't do everything. . . . I remember your mother would sit at the piano, hour after hour, and I'd be up here at my desk and I'd hear you singing.

Gene. You always asked me to sing "When I Grow Too Old to Dream."

Tom. Did I? . . . I don't remember your ever singing that. . . . You always seemed to be just finishing when I came into the room. . . . (*Looks at* GENE) Did you used to sing that for me?

Gene (*not a joke anymore*). No. . . . But you always asked me to sing it for you.

Tom. Oh . . . (*puts the program away*). Well, I enjoyed sitting up here and listening. (*He pokes around in his box and takes something out . . . in tissue paper. He unwraps a picture carefully.*) And that's my mother.

Gene (*gently*). Yes. I've seen that, Dad. It's lovely.

Tom. She was twenty-five when that was taken. She died the next year. . . . I carried it in my wallet for years. . . . And then I felt I was wearing it out. So I put it away. . . . Just a little bit of a thing . . . (*He starts to cry, and the deep, deep sobs finally come, and his emaciated body is wracked by them. It is a terrible, almost soundless sobbing.* GENE *comes to his father and puts his arms around him and holds him. After moments*) I didn't think it would be this way. . . . I always thought I'd go first. (*He sobs again, gasping for air.* GENE *continues to hold him, inevitably moved and touched by this genuine suffering. Finally,* TOM *gets a stern grip on himself.*) I'm sorry. . . . (*Tries to shake it off*) It just comes over me. . . . It'll pass. . . . I'll get a hold of myself.

Gene. Don't try, Dad. . . . Believe me, it's best.

Tom (*angry with himself*). No. . . . It's just that . . . I'll be all right. (*He turns and blows his nose.*)

Gene. It's rough, Dad. . . . It's bound to be rough.

Tom (*shakes his head to snap out of it*). It'll pass . . . it'll pass. . . . (*Starts to wrap up the picture of his mother*)

Gene. Can I help you put these things away, Dad?

Tom. No . . . No . . . I can . . . (*He seems to be looking for something he can't find.*) Well, if you would. (GENE *helps him wrap the pictures.*) I don't know what we'd do without you. . . .

[*And together they put the things back in the box. As they do so,* GENE *is deeply moved with feelings of tenderness for his father. After a few moments he starts, with great consideration.*]

Gene. Dad?

Tom. Yes?

Gene (*carefully*). You remember . . . I wrote you about California . . . and Peggy?

Tom. What?

Gene. The girl . . . in California.

Tom (*on guard*). Oh, yes.

Gene (*putting it carefully, and slowly*). I'm thinking very seriously, Dad . . . of going out there . . . to marry . . . and to live. (TOM *straightens up a little.*) Now, I know this is your home, where you're used to . . . but I'd like you to come out there with me, Dad. . . . It's lovely out there, as you said, and we could find an apartment for you, near us. (*This is the most loving gesture* GENE *has made to his father in his life.*)

Tom (*thinks for a moment, then looks at* GENE *with a smile*). You know, I'd like to make a suggestion. . . . Why don't you all come live here?

Gene (*explaining calmly*). Peggy has a practice out there.

Tom. A what?

Gene. She's a doctor. I told you. And children with schools and friends.

Tom. We have a big house here. You always liked this house. It's wonderful for children. You used to play baseball out back, and there's that basketball thing.

Gene. Dad, I'd like to get away from this part of the country for a while. It's been rough here ever since Carol died. It would be good for you too, getting away.

Tom. Your mother would be very happy to have the house full of children again. I won't be around long, and then it would be all yours.

Gene. That's very kind of you, Dad. But I don't think that would work. Besides her work and the children, all Peggy's family is out there.

Tom. Your family is here.

Gene. Yes, I know.

Tom. Just me, of course.

Gene. You see, the children's father is out there, and they're very fond of him and see him a lot.

Tom. Divorced?

Gene. Yes.

Tom. You know, Gene, I'm only saying this for your own good, but you went out there very soon after Carol's death, and you were exhausted from her long illness, and well, naturally, very susceptible. . . . I was wondering if you've really waited long enough to know your own mind.

Gene. I know my own mind.

Tom. I mean, taking on another man's children. You know, children are far from the blessing they're supposed to be. . . . And then there's the whole matter of discipline, of keeping them in line. You may rule them with a rod of iron, but if this father——

Gene *(cutting in).* I happen to love Peggy.

Tom *(looks at* GENE *a long moment).* Did you mention this business of California to your mother?

Gene *(gets the point, but keeps level).* She mentioned it to me and told me to go ahead, with her blessings.

Tom. She would say that, of course. . . . But I warned you.

Gene *(turns away).* For God's sake——

Tom *(giving up, angry).* All right, go ahead. I can manage. . . . *(His sarcasm)* Send me a Christmas card, . . . if you remember.

Gene *(enraged).* Dad!

Tom. What?

Gene. I've asked you to come with me!

Tom. And I've told you I'm not going.

Gene. I understand that, but not this "send me a Christmas card, if you remember."

Tom. I'm very sorry if I offended you. Your mother always said I mustn't raise my voice to you. *(Suddenly hard and vicious)* Did you want me to make it easy for you the way your mother did? Well, I won't. If you want to go, go!

Gene. Dad!

Tom *(running on).* I've always known it would come to this when your mother was gone. I was tolerated around this house because I paid the bills and——

Gene. Shut up!

Tom *(coming at him).* Don't you——

Gene *(shouting).* Shut up! I asked you to come with me. What do you want? For God's sake, what do you want? If I lived here the rest of my life, it wouldn't be enough for you. I've tried, I've tried to be the dutiful son, to maintain the image of the good son. . . . Commanded into your presence on every conceivable occasion . . . Easter, Christmas, birthdays, Thanksgiving . . . Even that Thanksgiving when Carol was dying, and I was staying with her in the hospital. "We miss you so.

Our day is nothing without you. Couldn't you come up for an hour or two after you leave Carol?" You had no regard for what was really going on. . . . My wife was dying!

Tom. Is it so terrible to want to see your own son?

Gene. It is terrible to want to possess him . . . entirely and completely!

Tom *(coldly . . . after a moment).* There will be some papers to sign for your mother's estate. Be sure you leave an address with my lawyer . . .

Gene *(cutting in).* Dad!

Tom *(cutting, with no self-pity).* From tonight on, you can consider me dead. *(Turns on him in a rage of resentment)* I gave you everything. Since I was a snot-nosed kid I've worked my fingers to the bone. You've had everything and I had nothing. I put a roof over your head, clothes on your back——

Gene. Food on the table.

Tom. ——things I never had.

Gene. I know!

Tom. You ungrateful! . . .

Gene *(seizes him, almost as though he would hit him).* What do you want for gratitude? Nothing, nothing would be enough. You have resented everything you ever gave me. The orphan boy in you has resented everything. I'm sorry about your miserable childhood. When I was a kid, and you told me those stories, I used to go up to my room at night and cry. But there is nothing I can do about it . . . and it does not excuse everything. . . . I *am* grateful to you. I also admire you and respect you and stand in awe of what you have done with your life. I will never be able to touch it. *(TOM looks at him with contempt.)* But it does not make me love you. And I wanted to love you. *(TOM snorts his disbelief.)* You hated your father. I saw what it did to you. I did not want to hate you.

Tom. I don't care what you feel about me.

Gene. I do! *(He moves away from his father.)* I came so close to loving you tonight. . . . I'd never felt so open to you. You don't know what it cost me to ask you to come with me . . . when I have never been able to sit in a room alone with you. . . . Did you really think your door was always open to me?

Tom. It was not my fault if you never came in.

Gene (*starts to move out*). Goodbye, Dad. I'll arrange for someone to come in.

Tom (*shouting*). I don't want anyone to come in! I can take care of myself! I have always had to take care of myself. Who needs you? Get out!

[*This last, wildly at* GENE. *The lights dim out quickly, except for a lingering light on* GENE.]

Gene (*after a few moments*). That night I left my father's house forever. . . . I took the first right and the second left . . . and this time I went as far as California. . . . Peggy and I visited him once or twice . . . and then he came to California to visit us and had a fever and swollen ankles, and we put him in a hospital, and he never left. . . . The reason we gave, and which he could accept, for not leaving, . . . the swollen ankles. But the real reason . . . the arteries were hardening, and he gradually over several years slipped into complete and speechless senility . . . with all his life centered in his burning eyes. (*A* NURSE *wheels in* TOM, *dressed in a heavy, warm bathrobe and wearing a white linen golf cap to protect his head from drafts. The* NURSE *withdraws into the shadows.*) When I would visit him, and we would sit and look at each other, his eyes would mist over and his nostrils would pinch with emotion. . . . But I never could learn what the emotion was . . . anger . . . or love . . . or regret. . . . One day, sitting in his wheelchair and staring without comprehension at television . . . he died . . . alone . . . without even an orange in his hand. (*The light fades on* TOM.) Death ends a life, . . . but it does not end a relationship, which struggles on in the survivor's mind . . . toward some resolution, which it never finds. Alice said I would not accept the sadness of the world. . . . What did it matter if I never loved him, or if he never loved me? . . . Perhaps she was right. . . . But, still, when I hear the word "father" . . . (*He cannot express it . . . there is still the longing, the emotion. He looks around . . . out . . . as though he would finally be able to express it, but he can only say . . .*) It matters. (*He turns and walks slowly away, into the shadows . . . as the lights dim.*)

Curtain

A Critical Comment

"On this gray afternoon, the line at the box office for *I Never Sang for My Father* was predominantly of older women, in pairs or single, although once inside a crowded house you saw a sprinkling of men and some young girls with flowing hair.

"Word had clearly got around since the movie opened that this was a film about people over thirty, dominated by that splendid and durable actor, Melvyn Douglas; and the words *sentiment, heartwarming,* and *touching* doubtless drew many adults who had ceased being regular moviegoers because what they saw at their local cinemas had either bludgeoned or bewildered them into absence. And not just little old ladies shocked by sex . . . or middle-aged squares yearning for the traditional American values. These, I suspect, are only a part of the adult population looking for some identification with the people they see on the screen, some recognitive stirring of the heart or mind.

"Instead they are confronted with films, some of them brilliant, in which the word has no meaning, emotion no stature, and the mind no place. They see the nonhero, the bum, the drifter, even the killer, as the central focus, sex as a standard exercise, violence as an obligatory 'comment,' and obscenity as 'truth.' They see superb photography, beautiful bodies, and breathtaking juxtapositions. They hear a pounding or plaintive score. They are told that 'this is reality, this is now, this is where it's at,' and if they don't dig it, they're dead. They listen to young audiences cackling at private jokes and signs, at sexual fumbles and small crudities, and they leave the theater feeling not only disoriented but in a very real sense disenfranchised.

"At *I Never Sang for My Father*, they are at home. Not everybody, fortunately, has a father like Tom Garrison, nor, unfortunately, a mother like Margaret Garrison. But they know them to be true, as the Garrison son and daughter are true. Playwright Robert Anderson and producer Gilbert Cates have created a real family in a real house filled with real agonies in a film that is solely concerned with the human condition. Not headlines, not slogans, not movements, not cinematic or psychedelic tricks. Just people, individuals, breathing, choking, loving, hating, trying to love, dying.

"Certainly the picture is about older people, middle-aged or verging on senescence. If what they think and feel and suffer is irrelevant, then half the population of this country is irrelevant.

"But they are not. Old Garrison, so magnificently played by Melvyn Douglas, is far more relevant to our present condition than even an appreciative audience (and unappreciative critics) might think. For he is the precursor and embodiment of almost everything wrong with this country and its people today.

"Here is the American folk hero who came up the hard way and made it. Child of a hated drunken father and a mother who died when he was ten, Tom Garrison spent the rest of his life making money and taking power. Business leader, president of the Board of Education, and finally mayor of his town, he is now in his eighties, living in his past, his mighty ego subsisting on Rotarian pats on the back, smiles from a waitress, and the love of a frail wife who endures his endless recitals and pomposities with heroic sweetness. She loves him for the way he was, and for the way he walks. . . .

"Old Tom also feeds on his forty-year-old son, Gene (played by Gene Hackman), who has tried, but has never been able to love him. Gene has seen Tom crush the life out of his wife, banish his daughter, . . . and load Gene himself with a terrible guilt that turns the natural filial instinct into fury and frustration.

"Old Tom is, in fact, the prototype of the suc-cessful American man whose obsessive need for material security has stripped him of the capacity for love and pity—except for himself. Charming as he can be (the old gallant, the old quipster), he weeps only for himself. Women are dependents, children are possessions, and possessions are life.

". . . No power on earth could make his son want to be like him or think as he did. It took Gene a long time to spring his trap, but he finally did. What's more, he married a free woman (Elizabeth Hubbard), a doctor, whose love and need for him is no less real than the demands of her profession.

"The fact that he chooses to move across a continent to where her practice is may be a hopeful indication of a new breed of men who find such accommodations neither demeaning nor unnatural. For that matter, the women in *I Never Sang for My Father* share a distinction absent in the majority of films, however 'now.' They are three-dimensional human beings. The mother, superbly evoked by Dorothy Stickney, reveals capacities of mind and heart far beyond the 'little woman' image imposed by her marriage. . . . And Gene's sister Alice (Estelle Parsons) is a wife and mother compact with integrity and intelligence, a sturdy soul.

"Young people who choose to expose themselves to this film might find their compassion engaged by one more oppressed minority. When they see, as Gene does, the doom of the rejected and discarded old of this society, rotting in institutions and fearful exile, they might discover, as he does, that the parental bond transcends time, discord, even hate. Whether we like them or not, fathers and mothers are part of us and with us forever. And therefore relevant."

—from "Her Heart Belongs to 'Father' "
Marya Mannes

Responding to the Play

Analyzing Act Two

Identifying Facts

1. Up to a point, Tom seems to experience his wife's death through the death of his own mother. Where does Tom reveal that this is what he is doing? At what point does Tom finally make the shift and feel his wife's death? Describe how Gene responds to his father's behavior in this scene.

2. Alice is a key figure in Act Two. Describe the **conflicts** that are forced into the open in her scenes with Gene and in her scene with Gene and her father.

3. As you know, one of the **bare bones** of drama is a main character who wants something desperately and who initiates action to get it. Find the speech where Gene tells us what he wants. Name the steps he takes to get it.

4. The **climax** of a play is that intensely emotional moment when the major characters meet "to have it out." What big scene is the climax of this play?

5. A play is **resolved,** or closed, when the loose ends are tied up, when we know finally what has become of the characters. What is the resolution of this play?

Interpreting Meanings

6. How did you feel about the way Gene's **conflict** is **resolved**—or **unresolved**? Does the ending seem believable to you—that is, do you feel that a real person would behave this way? Explain your response.

7. The story of Tom Garrison's early life is mentioned in Act One, and more details are revealed in Act Two. Does Tom's childhood help you feel compassion for him? Explain how Tom's relationship with his father was like Gene's relationship with Tom. In what ways, though, is each man different from his father?

8. Toward the end of the play, Tom says to Gene, "It was not my fault if you never came in." When Hal Holbrook, the actor playing Gene, got this line during rehearsals, he was upset. He asked, "Do I hear that line? If I did, I wouldn't leave." The director told him, "It's the kind of line you hear ten years after it is spoken." (Do you know what he meant?) Why do *you* think Gene did not go through his father's "open door"?

9. We've said that change is a key element in drama. Remember that the most interesting change is **internal.** An internal change can be a change of heart, the reversal of a conviction, or a new awareness. Do any characters change under the pressure of the action in this play? Which character does *not* seem to change, and how do you feel about this character as the play ends?

10. Explain what Gene means when he says his father died "without even an orange in his hand."

11. Explain the significance of the play's **title.** Which of the play's titles do you prefer, its first title, *The Tiger,* (see "Focusing on Background") or its final one? Why?

12. Shortly after this play opened in New York, a good friend of the playwright's father wrote a note with a single line: "You *have* sung for your father." What do you think the friend meant? Do you agree or disagree with her?

13. Do you think this play could have been written about a mother rather than a father? What significant changes would have to be made?

Writing About the Play

A Creative Response

1. **Writing an Original Scene.** Peggy, the woman that Gene wants to marry, never appears in the play. In fact, it seems that Gene does not even want to tell her how his mother's death and his father's actions have affected him. Why doesn't he want to tell her? How do his feelings toward his father affect his relationship with Peggy? Write a scene in which Peggy finally confronts Gene and demands that he tell her about it. Be sure that under the pressure, both reveal feelings they would never have revealed otherwise. Write stage directions telling when and where the action takes place, and how the characters talk.

A Critical Response

2. **Analyzing a Character.** Although Gene controls the play and is the only character allowed to speak to the audience directly, the character who often dominates the action is Tom. In an essay, analyze the character of Tom Garrison. Before you write, gather your data in a chart like the following one. In your concluding paragraph, explain your own response to Tom's character.

	Answers	Supporting passages
What do I learn from Tom's actions?		
What do I learn from his words?		
What do I learn from his past?		
What do I learn from his affect on other people?		
How do I feel about this character?		

3. **Stating the Theme.** In a brief essay, explain the theme of this play. Remember that theme is the central idea about human life that is revealed through the play's action. A theme is usually expressed in more than one sentence—some themes are so complex it would take a book to explain them. Do not express the theme in terms of this play only. Do not say, "Gene learns in this play that . . ." Instead say, "This play reveals that . . ." Find at least two quotations from the play to support your statement of the theme.

4. **Explaining an Opinion.** In the old days, families stayed close together, often in the same village or on the same farm. Grandmothers and grandfathers took care of grandchildren, while their own children were taking care of *them.* With a more mobile population, problems have arisen. In a brief essay, present some of your thoughts on the ways this mobile and transient population has affected family life. Before you write, list the advantages of being part of a "mobile population." Then list the disadvantages, in terms of lost family closeness, friends, security, and the feeling of having set down "roots" in a particular community or landscape.

Analyzing Language and Vocabulary

Stage Directions

Note the stage directions in the passages that follow. First define the key word in each direction as fully as you can. Then explain what each word tells you about the character's feelings and intentions. Are different interpretations possible?

1. **Tom** (*considers this, but is mollified by the smile*). Well, I appreciate your solicitude, old man. Why don't you stay for supper?
2. **Gene** (*straining to get away from all the encir- clements*). Good night, Dad.
3. **Alice.** I didn't mean exactly that kind of plans. I meant . . . Well, you haven't been well.
   Tom (*belligerent*). Who said so?
4. **Alice.** I worry, leaving you in this house. . . . alone, Dad.
   Tom (*looks around, very alert, defensively*). I'm perfectly all right. Now don't worry about me . . . either of you. Why, for the last year, since your mother's first attack, I've been getting the breakfast, making the beds, using a dust rag. . . .

5. **Tom.** I have long gotten the impression that my only function in this family is to supply the money to——
   Gene (*anguished*). Dad!

Reading About the Writer

Three months after I was born in 1917 in New York City, my family moved to a suburb, New Rochelle, where I lived until I went away to school, first to Phillips Exeter Academy and then to Harvard. I stayed on at Harvard studying for graduate degrees with the idea that I would teach and write on the side.

While I was with the Pacific Fleet in World War II, I wrote a play that was judged the best play written by a serviceman overseas. This play contest changed my life.

Shortly after my return from the war, while I was living on a Rockefeller Playwriting Grant, I was fortunate to get work writing for the radio. This began my routine of writing stage plays in the morning, radio (and later television) plays in the afternoon, and teaching playwriting four nights a week. In 1953 the production of my first Broadway play, *Tea and Sympathy,* ended this routine, though I have continued writing occasionally for movies and television because, as I have often said, "You can make a killing in the theater but not a living."

With the production of *Tea and Sympathy,* I became a member of The Playwrights Producing Company (with dramatists Robert Sherwood, Maxwell Anderson, and Elmer Rice). My later plays include *I Never Sang for My Father; Silent Night, Lonely Night;* and *You Know I Can't Hear You When the Water's Running.*

In spite of the desperate situation that faces playwrights today, I intend to keep on writing till "The End." On his death bed, my good friend Marc Connelly (he wrote the classic *The Green Pastures*) came out of a coma briefly to say, "They've raised the money. We go into rehearsal tomorrow." May those also be my final words.

—Robert Anderson

Focusing on Background
Getting a Play Produced

"In the mid-sixties, discouraged by the usual battle to get a play produced (it ordinarily took me three years to get a play into production), I decided to write an original movie. Up to that time, with the exception of *Tea and Sympathy,* my movies had been based on other people's novels.

"I wrote a screenplay and called it *The Tiger,* because I had always thought of my father as a tiger. I showed the script to Fred Zinnemann, who had directed the movie *The Nun's Story,* for which I had written the screenplay. He read the script of *The Tiger* and said he wanted it to be his next picture. He would get Spencer Tracy to play the father.

"It turned out that Spencer Tracy did not want to play the father, and Fred lost interest.

"I sent the play to Elia Kazan, the extraordinary director who directed my first Broadway play, *Tea and Sympathy*. He was making a movie in Europe. He wrote me that he had been unable to sleep one night and had read my screenplay. He asked if I would consider turning it into a play for Lincoln Center, a new performing group that was just shaping up. Kazan and Robert Whitehead were to be the group's directors. I said I would be pleased to try. He said not to do anything until they found out who they would have for actors in their company. Some months later, he told me they had nobody in the company who could act the father, and they were going to open their theater with Arthur Miller's *After the Fall.*

"I then sent the screenplay to John Frankenheimer, a distinguished movie director, and one day I had an excited call from him from the desert location where he was filming *Seven Days in May*. He said he wanted *The Tiger* to be his next picture and that Fredric March, who was in the film he was directing, would play the father. Of course, no contracts were drawn.

"Some months later, I received a letter from John's secretary telling me that he had left for Europe for an extended stay, and that he would be in touch with me on his return. I wrote to John asking where we stood, and he wrote back saying that he was deeply involved with two or three other pictures and would have to drop *The Tiger.*

"Over the next months there were other 'flirtations.' Then finally I decided to turn this screenplay into a play on my own. When my agent sent it around to producers, many of them praised it, but they felt it was too 'shattering.' I took this as a compliment, since people go to the theater to be 'shattered' in one way or another—with emotion or laughter or excitement.

"I became discouraged and sat down and wrote four one-act comedies with the title *You Know I Can't Hear You When the Water's Running.* It turned out that nobody wanted to do these plays either. Who wanted to see one-act plays on Broadway? Then my agent asked me if I minded sending the plays to two young producers who had never produced anything in their lives. I said, 'What do I have to lose?'

"Those two young men, Gilbert Cates and Jack Farren, produced *You Know I Can't Hear You When the Water's Running.* It was a great success and played all over the world. Then Cates decided he would like to produce the play I had made from *The Tiger,* which I now called *I Never Sang for My Father*. We were moving ahead with production plans when a friend from Hollywood, Martin Manulis, a noted producer of movies and of the famous television show *Playhouse 90*, said that Columbia Broadcasting System had asked him to return to television and produce a very special 'Special.' He had decided he would like to do *The Tiger.*

"I told him that *The Tiger* was now a play and that we were moving ahead with production plans. He said, 'But wait a minute. Let me tell you the cast, and they have all agreed to do it. Spencer Tracy will play the father, Katherine Hepburn will play the mother, and Richard Widmark will play the son.' He assumed that my wife, Teresa Wright, would want to play the daughter.

"I conferred with Cates, and he said that with a cast like that, I should let Manulis do it. I called him to give him my approval. Two weeks later he called me to say that CBS had turned it down because it was too shattering.

"And that is how there finally happened to be a play on Broadway called *I Never Sang for My Father.*

"I like to tell this story to young writers who tell me that 'established' writers have things easy."

—Robert Anderson

The Brute
by Anton Chekhov

The Brute, subtitled "A Joke in One Act," is a short, simple **linear comedy,** which means that it has a beginning, a middle, and an end, in that order. *The Brute* is almost a comic opera in style: Two larger-than-life characters, ridiculously extreme in their attitudes, go at each other in grand fashion.

"The Battling Lovers"

In essence, we have here a nineteenth-century Russian play based on a situation also used in thousands of Hollywood romantic stories: Two characters who are originally wildly antagonistic to each other eventually fall into each other's arms, often at the final fade-out. Think of Rhett Butler and Scarlett O'Hara in *Gone with the Wind* or Sam and Diane in early episodes of the TV show *Cheers.* The tradition can even be traced back to sixteenth-century England, where we have Petruchio and Katherina (Kate) battling it out in William Shakespeare's *The Taming of the Shrew.*

People seem to be fascinated by this **paradox,** or apparent contradiction, of attraction and antagonism. The combination, of course, also gives the actors something to do for two hours, for the antagonisms must be met and overcome. Drama, as we have seen, involves characters who want something desperately (most lovers by definition are desperate), who meet an obstacle and take steps to overcome it, and who, in the end, either win or lose their struggle.

This conflict between the "battling lovers" has proved to be a very convenient framework over the years: The two characters have different beliefs or attitudes, which must be expressed, debated, and possibly reconciled before they can be together (or apart) at the end of the play. The antagonism between the man and woman may be based on real differences—differences in background, in social class, in attitudes. Many American plays and movies of the 1930's and 1940's used their antagonistic lovers to dramatize social and political problems. *He* was an arch conservative; *she* was a radical. *He* was the son of an oil tycoon; *she* was a chauffeur's daughter.

The Brute also illustrates what used to be a Hollywood requirement: that these attracted antagonists should "meet-cute." A state trooper, for example, meets his millionaire love-to-be after chasing her speeding Mercedes and snarling, "Where's the fire, lady?" as he hands her a ticket. Or two lawyers meet in court, where *her* client is suing *his* client.

In plays like *The Brute,* we are never concerned with what happens after this loving-warring couple finally gets married. We seem to be satisfied that some primitive rite of courtship has been performed. Besides, it makes a good story. "Tranquillity is of no poetic use," said the English poet Robert Graves; it might also be said that tranquillity is of no dramatic use. Obstacles, problems, strong desires, antagonisms—these are the stuff of drama. And of course, fortunately or unfortunately, they are also the stuff of life.

THE BRUTE
A Joke in One Act

Anton Chekhov

From a 1948 production starring and directed by José Ferrer at City Center in New York.

Translated by **Eric Bentley**

Characters

Mrs. Popov, widow and landowner, small, with dimpled cheeks.
Mr. Grigory S. Smirnov, gentleman farmer, middle-aged.
Luka, Mrs. Popov's footman, an old man.
Gardener
Coachman
Hired Men

The drawing room of a country house. MRS. POPOV, *in deep mourning, is staring hard at a photograph.* LUKA *is with her.*

Luka. It's not right, ma'am, you're killing yourself. The cook has gone off with the maid to pick berries. The cat's having a high old time in the yard catching birds. Every living thing is happy. But you stay moping here in the house like it was a convent, taking no pleasure in nothing. I mean it, ma'am! It must be a full year since you set foot out of doors.

Mrs. Popov. I must never set foot out of doors again, Luka. Never! I have nothing to set foot out of doors *for*. My life is done. *He* is in his grave. I have buried myself alive in this house. We are *both* in our graves.

Luka. You're off again, ma'am. I just won't listen to you no more. Mr. Popov is dead, but what can we do about that? It's God's doing. God's will be done. You've cried over him, you've done your share of mourning, haven't you? There's a limit to everything. You can't go on weeping and wailing forever. My old lady died, for that matter, and I wept and wailed over her a whole month long. Well, that was it. I couldn't weep and wail all my life, she just wasn't worth it. *(He sighs.)* As for the neighbors, you've forgotten all about them, ma'am. You don't visit them and you don't let them visit you. You and I are like a pair of spiders—excuse the expression, ma'am—here we are in this house like a pair of spiders, we never see the light of day. And it isn't like there was no nice people around either. The whole county's swarm-

ing with 'em. There's a regiment quartered at Riblov, and the officers are so good-looking! The girls can't take their eyes off them.—There's a ball at the camp every Friday.—The military band plays most every day of the week.—What do you say, ma'am? You're young, you're pretty, you could enjoy yourself! Ten years from now you may want to strut and show your feathers to the officers, and it'll be too late.

Mrs. Popov *(firmly).* You must never bring this subject up again, Luka. Since Popov died, life has been an empty dream to me, you know that. *You* may think I am alive. Poor ignorant Luka! You are wrong. I am dead. I'm in my grave. Never more shall I see the light of day, never strip from my body this . . . raiment of death! Are you listening, Luka? Let his ghost learn how I love him! Yes, *I* know, and *you* know, he was often unfair to me, he was cruel to me, and he was unfaithful to me. What of it? *I* shall be faithful to *him*, that's all. I will show him how *I* can love. Hereafter, in a better world than this, he will welcome me back, the same loyal girl I always was——

Luka. Instead of carrying on this way, ma'am, you should go out in the garden and take a bit of a walk, ma'am. Or why not harness Toby and take a drive? Call on a couple of the neighbors, ma'am?

Mrs. Popov *(breaking down).* Oh, Luka!

Luka. Yes, ma'am? What have I said, ma'am? Oh dear!

Mrs. Popov. Toby! You said Toby! He adored that horse. When he drove me out to the Korchagins and the Vlasovs, it was always with Toby! He was a wonderful driver, do you remember, Luka? So graceful! So strong! I can see him now, pulling at those reins with all his might and main! Toby! Luka, tell them to give Toby an extra portion of oats today.

Luka. Yes, ma'am.

[A bell rings.]

Mrs. Popov. Who is that? Tell them I'm not at home.

Luka. Very good, ma'am. *(Exit.)*

Mrs. Popov *(gazing again at the photograph).* You shall see, my Popov, how a wife can love and forgive. Till death do us part. Longer than that. Till death reunite us forever! *(Suddenly a titter* *breaks through her tears.)* Aren't you ashamed of yourself, Popov? Here's your little wife, being good, being faithful, so faithful she's locked up here waiting for her own funeral, while you—— doesn't it make you ashamed, you naughty boy? You were terrible, you know. You were unfaithful, and you made those awful scenes about it, you stormed out and left me alone for weeks——

[*Enter* LUKA.]

Luka *(upset)*. There's someone asking for you, ma'am. Says he must——

Mrs. Popov. I suppose you told him that since my husband's death I see no one?

Luka. Yes, ma'am. I did, ma'am. But he wouldn't listen, ma'am. He says it's urgent.

Mrs. Popov *(shrilly)*. I see no one!!

Luka. He won't take no for an answer, ma'am. He just curses and swears and comes in anyway. He's a perfect monster, ma'am. He's in the dining room right now.

Mrs. Popov. In the dining room, is he? I'll give him his come uppance. Bring him in here this minute. *(Exit* LUKA. *Suddenly sad again)* Why do they do this to me? Why? Insulting my grief, intruding on my solitude? *(She sighs.)* I'm afraid I'll have to enter a convent. I will, I *must* enter a convent!

[*Enter* MR. SMIRNOV *and* LUKA.]

Smirnov *(to* LUKA*)*. Dolt! Idiot! You talk too much! *(Seeing* MRS. POPOV. *With dignity)* May I have the honor of introducing myself, madam? Grigory S. Smirnov, landowner and lieutenant of artillery, retired. Forgive me, madam, if I disturb your peace and quiet, but my business is both urgent and weighty.

Mrs. Popov *(declining to offer him her hand)*. What is it you wish, sir?

Smirnov. At the time of his death, your late husband—with whom I had the honor to be acquainted, ma'am—was in my debt to the tune of twelve hundred rubles. I have two notes to prove it. Tomorrow, ma'am, I must pay the interest on a bank loan. I have therefore no alternative, ma'am, but to ask you to pay me the money today.

Mrs. Popov. Twelve hundred rubles? But what did my husband owe it to you for?

Smirnov. He used to buy his oats from me, madam.

Mrs. Popov *(to* LUKA, *with a sigh)*. Remember what I said, Luka: Tell them to give Toby an extra portion of oats today! *(Exit* LUKA.*)* My dear Mr.— what was the name again?

Smirnov. Smirnov, ma'am.

Mrs. Popov. My dear Mr. Smirnov, if Mr. Popov owed you money, you shall be paid—to the last ruble, to the last kopeck. But today—you must excuse me, Mr.—what was it?

Smirnov. Smirnov, ma'am.

Mrs. Popov. Today, Mr. Smirnov, I have no ready cash in the house. *(SMIRNOV* starts to speak.*)* Tomorrow, Mr. Smirnov, no, the day after tomorrow, all will be well. My steward will be back from town. I shall see that he pays what is owing. Today, no. In any case, today is exactly seven months from Mr. Popov's death. On such a day you will understand that I am in no mood to think of money.

Smirnov. Madam, if you don't pay up now, you can carry me out feet foremost. They'll seize my estate.

Mrs. Popov. You can have your money. *(He starts to thank her.)* Tomorrow. *(He again starts to speak.)* That is: the day after tomorrow.

Smirnov. I don't need the money the day after tomorrow. I need it today.

Mrs. Popov. I'm sorry, Mr.——

Smirnov *(shouting)*. Smirnov!

Mrs. Popov *(sweetly)*. Yes, of course. But you can't have it today.

Smirnov. But I can't wait for it any longer!

Mrs. Popov. Be sensible, Mr. Smirnov. How can I pay you if I don't have it?

Smirnov. You don't have it?

Mrs. Popov. I don't have it.

Smirnov. Sure?

Mrs. Popov. Positive.

Smirnov. Very well. I'll make a note to that effect. *(Shrugging)* And then they want me to keep cool. I meet the tax commissioner on the street, and he says "Why are you always in such a bad humor, Smirnov?" Bad humor! How can I help it, in God's name? I need money, I need it desperately. Take yesterday: I leave home at the crack of dawn; I call on all my debtors. Not a one of them

"Water! Water! No, make it vodka."

From a 1938 Russian film of the play.

pays up. Footsore and weary, I creep at midnight into some little dive and try to snatch a few winks of sleep on the floor by the vodka barrel. Then today, I come here, fifty miles from home, saying to myself, "At last, at last, I can be sure of something," and you're not in the mood! You give me a mood! How the devil can I help getting all worked up?

Mrs. Popov. I thought I'd made it clear, Mr. Smirnov, that you'll get your money the minute my steward is back from town?

Smirnov. What the hell do I care about your steward? Pardon the expression, ma'am. But it was you I came to see.

Mrs. Popov. What language! What a tone to take to a lady! I refuse to hear another word. *(Quickly, exit.)*

Smirnov. Not in the mood, huh? "Exactly seven months since Popov's death," huh? How about me? *(Shouting after her)* Is there this interest to pay, or isn't there? I'm asking you a question: Is there this interest to pay, or isn't there? So your husband died, and you're not in the mood, and your steward's gone off some place, and so forth and so on, but what can *I* do about all that, huh? What do *you* think I should do? Take a running jump and shove my head through the wall? Take off in a balloon? You don't know my *other* debtors. I call on Gruzdeff. Not at home. I look for Yaroshevitch. He's hiding out. I find Kooritsin. He kicks up a row, and I have to throw him through the window. I work my way right down the list. Not a kopeck. Then I come to you, and damn it, if you'll pardon the expression, you're not in the mood! *(Quietly, as he realizes he's talking to air)* I've spoiled them all, that's what; I've let them play me for a sucker. Well, I'll show them. I'll show this one. I'll stay right here till she pays up. Ugh! *(He shudders with rage.)* I'm in a rage! I'm in a positively towering rage! Every nerve in my body is trembling at forty to the dozen! I can't breathe, I feel ill, I think I'm going to faint, hey, you there!

[*Enter* LUKA.]

Luka. Yes, sir? Is there anything you wish, sir?
Smirnov. Water! Water! ! No, make it vodka. *(Exit* LUKA.)* Consider the logic of it. A fellow creature

is desperately in need of cash, so desperately in need of cash that he has to seriously contemplate hanging himself, and this woman, this mere chit of a girl, won't pay up, and why not? Because, forsooth, she isn't in the mood! Oh, the logic of women! Come to that, I never have liked them, I could do without the whole sex. Talk to a woman? I'd rather sit on a barrel of dynamite, the very thought gives me gooseflesh. Women! Creatures of poetry and romance! Just to see one in the distance gets me mad. My legs start twitching with rage. I feel like yelling for help.

[*Enter* LUKA, *handing* SMIRNOV *a glass of water.*]

Luka. Mrs. Popov is indisposed, sir. She is seeing no one.
Smirnov. Get out. (*Exit* LUKA.) Indisposed, is she? Seeing no one, huh? Well, she can see me or not, but I'll be here, I'll be right here till she pays up. If you're sick for a week, I'll be here for a week. If you're sick for a year, I'll be here for a year. You won't get around *me* with your widow's weeds and your school-girl dimples. I know all about dimples. (*Shouting through the window*) Semyon, let the horses out of those shafts, we're not leaving, we're staying, and tell them to give the horses some oats, yes, oats, you fool, what do you think? (*Walking away from the window*) What a mess, what an unholy mess! I didn't sleep last night, the heat is terrific today, not a one of 'em has paid up, and here's this—this skirt in mourning that's not in the mood! My head aches, where's that—— (*He drinks from the glass.*) Water, ugh! You there!

[*Enter* LUKA.]

Luka. Yes, sir. You wish for something, sir?
Smirnov. Where's that confounded vodka I asked for? (*Exit* LUKA. SMIRNOV *sits and looks himself over.*) Oof! A fine figure of a man *I* am! Unwashed, uncombed, unshaven, straw on my vest, dust all over me. The little woman must've taken me for a highwayman. (*Yawns*) I suppose it wouldn't be considered polite to barge into a drawing room in this state, but who cares? I'm not a visitor, I'm a creditor—most unwelcome of guests, second only to Death.

[*Enter* LUKA.]

Luka (*handing him the vodka*). If I may say so, sir, you take too many liberties, sir.
Smirnov. What?!
Luka. Oh, nothing, sir, nothing.
Smirnov. Who do you think you're talking to? Shut your mouth!
Luka (*aside*). There's an evil spirit abroad. The Devil must have sent him. Oh! (*Exit* LUKA.)
Smirnov. What a rage I'm in! I'll grind the whole world to powder. Oh, I feel ill again. You there!

[*Enter* MRS. POPOV.]

Mrs. Popov (*looking at the floor*). In the solitude of my rural retreat, Mr. Smirnov, I've long since grown unaccustomed to the sound of the human voice. Above all, I cannot bear shouting. I must beg you not to break the silence.
Smirnov. Very well. Pay me my money and I'll go.
Mrs. Popov. I told you before, and I tell you again, Mr. Smirnov: I have no cash; you'll have to wait till the day after tomorrow. Can I express myself more plainly?
Smirnov. And *I* told *you* before, and *I* tell *you* again, that I need the money today, that the day after tomorrow is too late, and that if you don't pay, and pay now, I'll have to hang myself in the morning!
Mrs. Popov. But I have no cash. This is quite a puzzle.
Smirnov. You won't pay, huh?
Mrs. Popov. I *can't* pay, Mr. Smirnov.
Smirnov. In that case, I'm going to sit here and wait. (*Sits down*) You'll pay up the day after tomorrow? Very good. Till the day after tomorrow, here I sit. (*Pause. He jumps up.*) Now look, do I have to pay that interest tomorrow, or don't I? Or do you think I'm joking?
Mrs. Popov. I must ask you not to raise your voice, Mr. Smirnov. This is not a stable.
Smirnov. Who said it was? Do I have to pay the interest tomorrow or not?
Mrs. Popov. Mr. Smirnov, do you know how to behave in the presence of a lady?
Smirnov. No, madam, I do not know how to behave in the presence of a lady.

Mrs. Popov. Just what I thought. I look at you, and I say: ugh! I hear you talk, and I say to myself: "That man doesn't know how to talk to a lady."

Smirnov. You'd like me to come simpering to you in French, I suppose. *"Enchanté, madame! Merci beaucoup* for not paying zee money, *madame! Pardonnez-moi* if I 'ave disturbed you, *madame!* How *charmante* you look in mourning, *madame!"*

Mrs. Popov. Now you're being silly, Mr. Smirnov.

Smirnov *(mimicking).* "Now you're being silly, Mr. Smirnov." "You don't know how to talk to a lady, Mr. Smirnov." Look here, Mrs. Popov, I've known more women than you've known kitty cats. I've fought three duels on their account. I've jilted twelve and been jilted by nine others. Oh, yes, Mrs. Popov, I've played the fool in my time, whispered sweet nothings, bowed and scraped and endeavored to please. Don't tell me I don't know what it is to love, to pine away with longing, to have the blues, to melt like butter, to be weak as water. I was full of tender emotion. I was carried away with passion. I squandered half my fortune on the sex. I chattered about women's emancipation. But there's an end to everything, dear madam. Burning eyes, dark eyelashes, ripe, red lips, dimpled cheeks, heaving bosoms, soft whisperings, the moon above, the lake below—I don't give a rap for that sort of nonsense any more, Mrs. Popov. I've found out about women. Present company excepted, they're liars. Their behavior is mere play acting; their conversation is sheer gossip. Yes, dear lady, women, young or old, are false, petty, vain, cruel, malicious, unreasonable. As for intelligence, any sparrow could give them points. Appearances, I admit, can be deceptive. In appearance, a woman may be all poetry and romance, goddess and angel, muslin and fluff. To look at her exterior is to be transported to heaven. But I have looked at her interior, Mrs. Popov, and what did I find there—in her very soul? A crocodile. *(He has gripped the back of the chair so firmly that it snaps.)* And, what is more revolting, a crocodile with an illusion, a crocodile that imagines tender sentiments are its own special province, a crocodile that thinks itself queen of the realm of love! Whereas, in sober fact, dear madam, if a woman can love anything except a lap dog you can hang me by the feet on that nail.

For a man, love is suffering, love is sacrifice. A woman just swishes her train[1] around and tightens her grip on your nose. Now, you're a woman, aren't you, Mrs. Popov? You must be an expert on some of this. Tell me, quite frankly, did you ever know a woman to be—faithful, for instance? Or even sincere? Only old hags, huh? Though some women are old hags from birth. But as for the others? You're right: A faithful woman is a freak of nature—like a cat with horns.

Mrs. Popov. Who *is* faithful, then? Who *have* you cast for the faithful lover? Not man?

Smirnov. Right first time, Mrs. Popov: man.

Mrs. Popov *(going off into a peal of bitter laughter).* Man! Man is faithful! That's a new one! *(Fiercely)* What right do you have to say this, Mr. Smirnov? Men faithful? Let me tell you something. Of all the men I have ever known, my late husband Popov was the best. I loved him, and there are women who know how to love, Mr. Smirnov. I gave him my youth, my happiness, my life, my fortune. I worshiped the ground he trod on—and what happened? The best of men was unfaithful to me, Mr. Smirnov. Not once in a while. All the time. After he died, I found his desk drawer full of love letters. While he was alive, he was always going away for the weekend. He squandered my money. He flirted with other women before my very eyes. But, in spite of all, Mr. Smirnov, *I* was faithful. Unto death. And beyond. I am *still* faithful, Mr. Smirnov! Buried alive in this house, I shall wear mourning till the day I, too, am called to my eternal rest.

Smirnov *(laughing scornfully).* Expect me to believe that? As if I couldn't see through all this hocus-pocus. Buried alive! Till you're called to your eternal rest! Till when? Till some little poet— or some little subaltern[2] with his first moustache— comes riding by and asks: "Can that be the house of the mysterious Tamara, who for love of her late husband has buried herself alive, vowing to see no man?" Ha!

Mrs. Popov *(flaring up).* How dare you? How dare you insinuate—?

---

1. **train:** a reference to the part of a skirt that trails on the floor. In Mrs. Popov's day most women's dresses had trains.
2. **subaltern:** a person of low rank, a subordinate.

Smirnov. You may have buried yourself alive, Mrs. Popov, but you haven't forgotten to powder your nose.

Mrs. Popov *(incoherent).* How dare you? How—?

Smirnov. Who's raising his voice now? Just because I call a spade a spade. Because I shoot straight from the shoulder. Well, don't shout at me, I'm not your steward.

Mrs. Popov. I'm not shouting, you're shouting! Oh, leave me alone!

Smirnov. Pay me the money, and I will.

Mrs. Popov. You'll get no money out of me!

Smirnov. Oh, so that's it!

Mrs. Popov. Not a ruble, not a kopeck. Get out! Leave me alone!

Smirnov. Not being your husband, I must ask you not to make scenes with me. *(He sits.)* I don't like scenes.

Mrs. Popov *(choking with rage).* You're sitting down?

Smirnov. Correct, I'm sitting down.

Mrs. Popov. I asked you to leave!

Smirnov. Then give me the money. *(Aside)* Oh, what a rage I'm in, what a rage!

Mrs. Popov. The impudence of the man! I won't talk to you a moment longer. Get out. *(Pause)* Are you going?

Smirnov. No.

Mrs. Popov. No?!

Smirnov. No.

Mrs. Popov. On your head be it. Luka! *(Enter* LUKA*)* Show the gentleman out, Luka.

Luka *(approaching).* I'm afraid, sir, I'll have to ask you, um, to leave, sir, now, um——

Smirnov *(jumping up).* Shut your mouth, you old idiot! Who do you think you're talking to? I'll make mincemeat of you.

Luka *(clutching his heart).* Mercy on us! Holy saints above! *(He falls into an armchair.)* I'm taken sick! I can't breathe!!

Mrs. Popov. Then where's Dasha? Dasha! Dasha! Come here at once! *(She rings.)*

Luka. They gone picking berries, ma'am, I'm alone here—Water, water, I'm taken sick!

Mrs. Popov *(to* SMIRNOV*).* Get out, you!

Smirnov. Can't you even be polite with me, Mrs. Popov?

Mrs. Popov *(clenching her fists and stamping her feet).* With you? You're a wild animal, you were never housebroken!

Smirnov. What? What did you say?

Mrs. Popov. I said you were a wild animal, you were never housebroken.

Smirnov *(advancing upon her).* And what right do you have to talk to me like that?

Mrs. Popov. Like what?

Smirnov. You have insulted me, madam.

Mrs. Popov. What of it? Do you think I'm scared of you?

Smirnov. So you think you can get away with it because you're a woman. A creature of poetry and romance, huh? Well, it doesn't go down with me. I hereby challenge you to a duel.

Luka. Mercy on us! Holy saints alive! Water!

Smirnov. I propose we shoot it out.

Mrs. Popov. Trying to scare me again? Just because you have big fists and a voice like a bull? You're a brute.

Smirnov. No one insults Grigory S. Smirnov with impunity! And I don't care if you *are* a female.

Mrs. Popov *(trying to outshout him).* Brute, brute, brute!

Smirnov. The sexes are equal, are they? Fine: Then it's just prejudice to expect men alone to pay for insults. I hereby challenge——

Mrs. Popov *(screaming).* All right! You want to shoot it out? All right! Let's shoot it out!

Smirnov. And let it be here and now!

Mrs. Popov. Here and now! All right! I'll have Popov's pistols here in one minute! *(Walks away, then turns)* Putting one of Popov's bullets through your silly head will be a pleasure! *Au revoir. (Exit.)*

Smirnov. I'll bring her down like a duck, a sitting duck. I'm not one of your little poets, I'm no little subaltern with his first moustache. No, sir, there's no weaker sex where I'm concerned!

Luka. Sir! Master! *(He goes down on his knees.)* Take pity on a poor old man, and do me a favor: Go away. It was bad enough before, you nearly scared me to death. But a duel—!

Smirnov *(ignoring him).* A duel! That's equality of the sexes for you! That's women's emancipation! Just as a matter of principle I'll bring her down like a duck. But what a woman! "Putting one of Popov's bullets through your silly head . . ." Her cheeks were flushed, her eyes were

"You hold it this way. (Aside) *My Lord, what eyes she has!"*

From the 1938 Russian film.

gleaming! And, by Heaven, she's accepted the challenge! I never knew a woman like this before!

Luka. Sir! Master! Please go away! I'll always pray for you!

Smirnov *(again ignoring him).* What a woman! Phew!! *She's* no sourpuss; *she's* no crybaby. She's fire and brimstone. She's a human cannonball. What a shame I have to kill her!

Luka *(weeping).* Please, kind sir, please, go away!

Smirnov *(as before).* I like her, isn't that funny? With those dimples and all? I like her. I'm even prepared to consider letting her off that debt. And where's my rage? It's gone. I never knew a woman like this before.

[*Enter* MRS. POPOV *with pistols.*]

Mrs. Popov *(boldly).* Pistols, Mr. Smirnov! *(Matter of fact)* But before we start, you'd better show me how it's done, I'm not too familiar with these things. In fact I never gave a pistol a second look.

Luka. Lord, have mercy on us, I must go hunt up the gardener and the coachman. Why has this catastrophe fallen upon us, O Lord? *(Exit.)*

Smirnov *(examining the pistols).* Well, it's like this. There are several makes: One is the Mortimer, with capsules, especially constructed for dueling. What you have here are Smith and Wesson triple-action revolvers, with extractor, first-rate job, worth ninety rubles at the very least. You hold it this way. *(Aside)* My Lord, what eyes she has! They're setting me on fire.

Mrs. Popov. This way?

Smirnov. Yes, that's right. You cock the trigger, take aim like this, head up, arm out like this. Then you just press with this finger here, and it's all over. The main thing is, keep cool, take slow aim, and don't let your arm jump.

Mrs. Popov. I see. And if it's inconvenient to do the job here, we can go out in the garden.

Smirnov. Very good. Of course, I should warn you: I'll be firing in the air.

Mrs. Popov. What? This is the end. Why?

Smirnov. Oh, well—because—for private reasons.

Mrs. Popov. Scared, huh? *(She laughs heartily.)*

Now don't you try to get out of it, Mr. Smirnov. My blood is up. I won't be happy till I've drilled a hole through that skull of yours. Follow me. What's the matter? Scared?

Smirnov. That's right. I'm scared.

Mrs. Popov. Oh, come on, what's the matter with you?

Smirnov. Well, um, Mrs. Popov, I, um, I like you.

Mrs. Popov (*laughing bitterly*). Good Lord! He likes me, does he? The gall of the man. (*Showing him the door*) You may leave, Mr. Smirnov.

Smirnov (*Quietly puts the gun down, takes his hat, and walks to the door. Then he stops, and the pair look at each other without a word. Then, approaching gingerly*). Listen, Mrs. Popov. Are you still mad at me? I'm in the devil of a temper myself, of course. But then, you see—what I mean is—it's this way—the fact is—(*roaring*) Well, is it my fault if I like you? (*Clutches the back of a chair. It breaks.*) What fragile furniture you have here! I like you. Know what I mean? I could fall in love with you.

Mrs. Popov. I hate you. Get out!

Smirnov. What a woman! I never saw anything like it. Oh, I'm lost, I'm done for, I'm a mouse in a trap.

Mrs. Popov. Leave this house, or I shoot!

Smirnov. Shoot away! What bliss to die of a shot that was fired by that little velvet hand! To die gazing into those enchanting eyes. I'm out of my mind. I know: You must decide at once. Think for one second, then decide. Because if I leave now, I'll never be back. Decide! I'm a pretty decent chap. Landed gentleman, I should say. Ten thousand a year. Good stable. Throw a kopeck up in the air, and I'll put a bullet through it. Will you marry me?

Mrs. Popov (*indignant, brandishing the gun*). We'll shoot it out! Get going! Take your pistol!

Smirnov. I'm out of my mind. I don't understand anything any more. (*Shouting*) You there! That vodka!

Mrs. Popov. No excuses! No delays! We'll shoot it out!

Smirnov. I'm out of my mind. I'm falling in love. I *have* fallen in love. (*He takes her hand vigorously; she squeals.*) I love you. (*He goes down on his knees.*) I love you as I've never loved before.

I jilted twelve and was jilted by nine others. But I didn't love a one of them as I love you. I'm full of tender emotion. I'm melting like butter. I'm weak as water. I'm on my knees like a fool, and I offer you my hand. It's a shame; it's a disgrace. I haven't been in love in five years. I took a vow against it. And now, all of a sudden, to be swept off my feet, it's a scandal. I offer you my hand, dear lady. Will you or won't you? You won't? Then don't! (*He rises and walks toward the door.*)

Mrs. Popov. I didn't say anything.

Smirnov (*stopping*). What?

Mrs. Popov. Oh, nothing, you can go. Well, no, just a minute. No, you can go. Go! I detest you! But, just a moment. Oh, if you knew how furious I feel! (*Throws the gun on the table*) My fingers have gone to sleep holding that horrid thing. (*She is tearing her handkerchief to shreds.*) And what are you standing around for? Get out of here!

Smirnov. Goodbye.

Mrs. Popov. Go, go, go! (*Shouting*) Where are you going? Wait a minute! No, no, it's all right, just go. I'm fighting mad. Don't come near me, don't come near me!

Smirnov (*who is coming near her*). I'm pretty disgusted with myself—falling in love like a kid, going down on my knees like some moon-gazing whippersnapper, the very thought gives me gooseflesh. (*Rudely*) I love you. But it doesn't make sense. Tomorrow, I have to pay that interest, and we've already started mowing. (*He puts his arm about her waist.*) I shall never forgive myself for this.

Mrs. Popov. Take your hands off me, I hate you! Let's shoot it out!

[*A long kiss. Enter* LUKA *with an axe, the* GARDENER *with a rake, the* COACHMAN *with a pitchfork,* HIRED MEN *with sticks.*]

Luka (*seeing the kiss*). Mercy on us! Holy saints above!

Mrs. Popov (*dropping her eyes*). Luka, tell them in the stable that Toby is *not* to have any oats today.

Curtain

A Critical Comment

Chekhov, who in his longer, mature plays very slowly leads us into subtle conflicts, here presents us right off with a flamboyant woman, Mrs. Popov, in an absurd situation. She has vowed to prove to an unfaithful husband, now dead, that *she* can be faithful. This situation, of course, could have been presented differently; if Chekhov had been in another mood, he might have presented a serious, pathetic study of a young widow. But in this play, Chekhov's heroine "protests too much," and her excess lets us know immediately that we can be amused by her. Her excess also tells a knowledgeable audience that she will be toppled from her "never, never" position. When a character in a play says in the first scene "I'll *never* love again," you may rest assured that she (or he) will fall in love before the end of the play.

We *hear* the heroine's antagonist, Grigory Smirnov, before we meet him. We know he is a certified "brute" before he makes his entrance, because the footman has told us that he is "a perfect monster." With a rude and abrupt entry line, suddenly Mrs. Popov's antagonist is there!

Their verbal duel begins at once. Although Smirnov comes in with his primary "want," the repayment of a loan, we know that these two must soon get around to love because why else would Chekhov have brought them together? He has prepared us with a woman grieving excessively and ridiculously for a lost husband. He must now **pay off** by presenting us with someone who will challenge her strongly held position. We soon find that Smirnov, too, has a strongly held position about love and marriage, so we sit back and watch with delight the process of one lover wearing the other down. Whether the characters themselves know it or not, we in the audience now know they are "made for each other." (Hollywood calls it "chemistry.")

Responding to the Play

Analyzing the Play

Identifying Facts

1. At first we think Mrs. Popov is grieving because she has lost a husband who was absolutely perfect. What is the truth? Explain why she has vowed to be faithful.
2. What does Mrs. Popov vow never to do again?
3. What other vow does Mrs. Popov make as the "perfect monster" enters?
4. Describe how Smirnov presents himself at once as a "brute."
5. Explain what exactly Smirnov wants and what obstacle is in his way.
6. Describe the action Smirnov takes to get what he wants, despite the formidable obstacle.
7. Describe Smirnov's views on women and love. What are his views on men and love?
8. What answer does Mrs. Popov make to Smirnov's proclamations about love and women?
9. Explain what leads up to Smirnov's challenge to a duel.
10. Why does Smirnov begin to change his mind about Mrs. Popov? At what **climactic** moment do we know that she has changed her mind too?

Interpreting Meanings

11. Explain the significance of Mrs. Popov's last remark about Toby and the oats.
12. **Repetition** is frequently used in comedies—for some reason, people seem to find something funny in repeated patterns of speech or behavior. (However, most audiences find that things repeated more than three times are for some reason no longer funny.) Find two examples of comic repetition in this play. Did you find the repetition funny? Why or why not?
13. Name the precise moment in the play that *you* knew that Smirnov had begun to change.

coachman

laborers

gardener

Watercolor costume sketch by Ted Boerner for a 1985 production at the American Players Theatre in Spring Green, Wisconsin.

14. Though these two characters profess to have entirely different views about love, in what ways were their experiences with love and with the opposite sex exactly the same?

15. Are Chekhov's battling lovers believable to you? If the play were to be set in a setting you know well, would any details have to be changed? Explain.

Writing About the Play

A Creative Response

1. **Writing the Next Act.** A comedy often ends with a marriage or with the promise of one, but comedies almost never follow the couple beyond their marriage. What do you think will happen to Smirnov and Mrs. Popov after they are married? Imagine a day in their lives ten years later, and write a dialogue for this next act. To get your dialogue going, have your two characters face a decision—how to spend some money; what to do about Luka, who still dislikes Smirnov; what to do about the photos of Mrs. Popov's husband, which are still all over the house.

A Critical Response

2. **Analyzing the Play as a Farce.** A **farce** is a kind of comedy that most of us are familiar with, since farces are standard fare in movies and on television. Here are some of the characteristics of a farce:

   a. A farce is a knockabout comedy that is not interested in developing complex characters.

   b. A farce intends to make us laugh, and it does this with a lot of physical action—people bumping into closet doors, falling on banana peels, disguising themselves in the clothing of the opposite sex, and so on.

   c. Nothing truly tragic ever happens in a farce, though situations often teeter on the brink of disaster.

   d. The characters in a farce make a lot of noise; the stage is busy with actors running on and off.

   Write a brief essay in which you explain how *The Brute* can or cannot be seen as a farce. Cite specific situations from the play that support your point of view.

3. **Comparing Plays.** Another play that uses the device of the warring lovers is George Bernard Shaw's *Pygmalion.* (The American musical comedy *My Fair Lady* was derived from Shaw's play.) Here the battling lovers consist of a crusty old upper-class bachelor named Professor Higgins, who is a professor of speech, and a pretty, charming, lower-class Cockney flower vendor named Eliza Doolittle. The plot takes off when Higgins pompously decides he can change Eliza's life merely by teaching her to speak properly. From your reading or viewing of plays, movies, and television, think of some other shows that use the "meet-cute" device, or the "attracted antagonist" situation (sometimes called the "love-hate" relationship). Write a brief essay in which you cite these other shows, and explain how they are like the Popov-Smirnov story. Concentrate on these elements of the work: (a) **plot,** (b) **characters,** and (c) **tone.** If you know the shows well enough, you can also tell whether or not the stories end with the couple falling into each other's arms.

José Ferrer in the 1948 production.

Reading About the Writer

Anton Chekhov (1860–1904) is one of the two playwrights who have most influenced modern drama. The other is the Norwegian writer Henrik Ibsen, whose best-known plays often deal with contemporary social problems and are constructed and formed into what has become known as "the well-made play." Chekhov's major plays, on the other hand, are often called "slices of life"; they meander rather than march. They are more concerned with psychological insights than they are with a well-crafted plot. Most modern American playwrights have followed Ibsen's model, not Chekhov's. Those who have tried to write slice-of-life plays have generally failed because by and large, American audiences do not seem to be attuned to plays that chart the slow ebb and flow of moods and of subtly shifting relationships.

Chekhov was born in a small seaport in southern Russia, the grandson of a serf and the son of an unsuccessful shopkeeper. As a young man, he supported his mother, father, four brothers, and sister by writing short stories and sketches for humor magazines. At the same time, he was studying medicine at the University of Moscow.

Chekhov received his medical degree, but he did not practice medicine for long. Instead he fell back on his literary work to earn a living, and over the course of his short life he produced more than a thousand short stories (one, "The Bet," appears on page 90) and four major plays. *The Brute* is one of several one-act comedies ("jokes") that he wrote early in his career. Though these little comedies do not match the achievement of his later great plays—and Chekhov himself considered them unimportant "vaudevilles"—the public loved them.

In the last years of his life, while suffering from tuberculosis, Chekhov wrote five full-length serious plays, four of which are considered masterpieces: *The Sea Gull, Uncle Vanya, The Three Sisters,* and *The Cherry Orchard.* These new plays were different from the kind of theater audiences were used to, and the first production of *The Sea Gull* was a complete failure. The audience hissed, and Chekhov left the theater after the second act, vowing never again to write a play. Fortunately, he did not keep his vow. *The Sea Gull* was restaged two years later in Moscow and was a smashing success. Each new play was a greater triumph than the last.

Chekhov died of tuberculosis when he was only forty-four years old.

Recognizing Sentence Fragments in Dialogue

Literary Model

Here's a climactic scene from the second act of Neil Simon's comedy *Barefoot in the Park*. As this scene opens, a young couple—Corie and Paul—have just returned from a late evening with Corie's widowed mother and their flamboyant next-door-neighbor. This neighbor is a gourmet, and he has taken Paul, Corie, and her mother to an Albanian restaurant on Staten Island, in New York City. Now he is gallantly accompanying Corie's mother home to New Jersey. Corie has had a perfectly wonderful evening; Paul has not had a good time at all.

Corie. What are you so angry about, Paul?

Paul (*crossing to the closet*). I just told you. I felt terrible for your mother. (*He gets the wallet out of his jacket pocket.*)

Corie (*following after him to the front of the couch*). Why? Where is she at this very minute? Alone with probably the most attractive man she's ever met. Don't tell me *that* doesn't beat . . . hair curlers and the "Late Late Show."

Paul (*crossing onto bedroom landing*). Oh, I can just hear it now. What sparkling conversation. He's probably telling her about a chicken cacciatore he once cooked for the High Lama of Tibet, and she's sitting there shoving pink pills in her mouth.

Corie (*taking her coat from the couch and putting it on the armchair at right*). You can never tell what people talk about when they're alone.

Paul. I don't understand how you can be so unconcerned about this. (*He goes into the bedroom.*)

Corie (*moving to the stairs*). Unconcerned . . . I'm plenty concerned. Do you think I'm going to get one wink of sleep until that phone rings tomorrow? I'm scared to death for my mother. But I'm grateful there's finally the opportunity for something to be scared about . . . (*She moves right, then turns back.*) What I'm really concerned about is you!

Paul (*bursts out of the bedroom, nearly slamming through the door*). Me? Me?

Corie. I'm beginning to wonder if you're capable of *having* a good time.

Paul. Why? Because I like to wear my gloves in the winter?

Corie. No. Because there isn't the least bit of adventure in you. Do you know what you are? You're a Watcher. There are Watchers in this world and there are Do-ers. And the Watchers sit around watching the Do-ers do. Well, tonight you watched and I did.

Paul (*moves down the stairs to* CORIE). Yeah . . . Well, it was harder to watch what you did than it was for you to *do* what I was watching. (*He goes back up the stairs to the landing.*)

Corie. You won't let your hair down for a minute? You couldn't even relax for one night. Boy, Paul, sometimes you act like a . . . a . . . . (*She gets her shoes from under the couch.*)

Paul (*stopping on the landing*). What . . . ? A stuffed shirt?

Corie (*drops the shoes on the couch*). I didn't say that.

Paul. That's what you're implying.

Corie (*moves to the right armchair and begins to take off her jewelry*). That's what you're anticipating. I didn't say you're a stuffed shirt. But you are extremely proper and dignified.

Paul. I'm proper and dignified? (*He moves to* CORIE.) When . . . ? When was I proper and dignified? . . .

Corie. Always. You're always dressed right, you always look right, you always say the right things. You're very close to being perfect.

Paul (*hurt to the quick*). That's . . . that's a *rotten* thing to say.

Corie (*moves to* PAUL). I have never seen you without a jacket. I always feel like such a slob compared to you. Before we were married, I was sure you slept with a tie.

Paul. No, no. Just for very *formal* sleeps.

Corie. You can't even walk into a candy store and ask the lady for a Tootsie Roll. (*Playing the scene out, she moves down to right side of the couch.*)

You've got to walk up to the counter and point at it and say, "I'll have that thing in the brown and white wrapper."

Paul (*moving to the bedroom door*). That's ridiculous.

Corie. And you're not. That's just the trouble. (*She crosses to the foot of the stairs.*) Like Thursday night. You wouldn't walk barefoot with me in Washington Square Park. Why not?

Paul (*moving to the head of the stairs*). Very simple answer. It was seventeen degrees.

Corie (*moves back to the chair and continues taking down her hair*). Exactly. That's very sensible and logical. Except it isn't any fun.

Paul (*moves down the stairs to the couch*). You know, maybe I *am* too proper and dignified for you. Maybe you would have been happier with someone a little more colorful and flamboyant . . . like the Geek! (*He starts back to the bedroom.*)

Corie. Well, he'd be a lot more laughs than a stuffed shirt.

Paul (*turns back on the landing*). Oh, oh . . . I thought you said I wasn't.

Corie. Well, you are now.

Paul (*reflectively*). I'm not going to listen to this . . . I'm not going to listen . . . (*He starts for the bedroom.*) I've got a case in court in the morning.

Corie (*moves left*). Where are you going?

Paul. To sleep.

Corie. *Now?* How can you sleep now?

Paul (*steps up on the bed and turns back, leaning on the door jamb*). I'm going to close my eyes and count knichis.[1] Good night!

Corie. You can't go to sleep now. We're having a fight.

Paul. *You* have the fight. When you're through, turn off the lights. (*He turns back into the bedroom.*)

Corie. Ooh, that gets me insane. You can even control your emotions.

Paul (*storms out to the head of the stairs*). Look, I'm just as upset as you are. . . . (*He controls

himself.*) But when I get hungry, I eat. And when I get tired, I sleep. You eat and sleep, too. Don't deny it, I've seen you . . .

Corie (*moves right with a grand gesture*). Not in the middle of a crisis.

Paul. What crisis? We're just yelling a little.

Corie. You don't consider this a crisis? Our whole marriage hangs in the balance.

Paul (*sits on the steps*). It does? When did that happen?

Corie. Just now. It's suddenly very clear that you and I have absolutely *nothing* in common.

Paul. Why? Because I won't walk barefoot in the park in winter? . . .

Corie (*seething*). Don't oversimplify this. I'm angry. Can't you see that?

Paul (*brings his hands to his eyes, peers at her through imaginary binoculars, and then looks at his watch*). Corie, it's two-fifteen. If I can fall asleep in about half an hour, I can get about five hours' sleep. I'll call you from court tomorrow, and we can fight over the phone. (*He gets up and moves to the bedroom.*)

Corie. You will *not* go to sleep. You will stay here and fight to save our marriage.

Paul (*in the doorway*). If our marriage hinges on breathing fish balls and poofla-poo pie, it's not worth saving. . . . I am now going to crawl into our tiny little single bed. If you care to join me, we will be sleeping from left to right tonight. (*He goes into the bedroom and slams the door.*)

Corie. You won't discuss it . . . You're *afraid* to discuss it . . . I married a coward!! . . . (*She takes a shoe from the couch and throws it at the bedroom door.*)

Paul (*opens the door*). Corie, would you bring in a pail? The closet's dripping.

Corie. Ohh, I hate you! I really, really hate you!

Paul (*storms to the head of the stairs*). Corie, there is one thing I learned in court. Be careful when you're tired and angry. You might say something you will soon regret. I-am-now-tired-and-angry.

Corie. And a coward.

Paul (*comes down the stairs to her at right of the

---

1. **knichis:** dough stuffed with meat, potatoes, or cheese (also spelled *knishes*).

Literature & Language /*cont.*

couch). And I will now say something I will soon regret . . . Okay, Corie, maybe you're right. Maybe we have nothing in common. Maybe we rushed into this marriage a little too fast. Maybe Love isn't enough. Maybe two people should have to take more than a blood test. Maybe they should be checked for common sense, understanding, and emotional maturity.

Corie *(that hurt).* All right . . . Why don't you get it passed in the Supreme Court? Only those couples bearing a letter from their psychiatrists proving they're well adjusted will be permitted to be married.

Paul. You're impossible.

Corie. You're unbearable.

Paul. You belong in a nursery school.

Corie. It's a lot more fun than the Home for the Fuddy Duddies.

Paul *(reaches out his hand to her).* All right, Corie, let's not get . . .

Corie. Don't you touch me . . . Don't you touch me . . .

—from *Barefoot in the Park,*
Neil Simon

From Act Two, Scene 2 of *Barefoot in the Park* by Neil Simon. © 1964 by Ellen Enterprises, Inc. Reprinted by permission of Paramount Pictures Corporation.

A Grammar Note

A **sentence fragment** is a group of words that does not express a complete thought. A fragment might be missing a **subject** or **verb** or even both. Although you should avoid using sentence fragments in formal writing, they are acceptable in colloquial speech and in any kind of writing that attempts to capture the feel of spoken language. In fact, in drama and fiction, and even in nonfiction, dialogue that contained no sentence fragments would probably sound stilted and unnatural. That's why Neil Simon uses so many sentence fragments in this passage. He wants to make his dialogue sound as though Corie and Paul are talking the way people really talk.

Corie. Before we were married, I was sure you slept with a tie.

Paul. No, no. Just for very *formal* sleeps.

Paul's response is a fragment because it's missing a subject and a verb. If Paul had used a grammatically complete sentence, he would have said, "I sleep with a tie just for very *formal* sleeps." But even proper, dignified, perfect Paul doesn't talk that way.

Examining the Writer's Style

Find all the sentence fragments Simon uses in this passage. For each fragment, identify which part or parts of speech are missing. Then rewrite each fragment as a complete sentence, underlining the parts you added. Here's how you would analyze the first fragment in the passage:

> **Fragment:** Alone with probably the most attractive man she's ever met.
> **Missing Parts:** subject and verb
> **Rewrite:** *She is* alone with probably the most attractive man she's ever met.

Using Sentence Fragments in Your Writing

Writing Realistic Dialogue. Write a short passage of dialogue that captures the sound of real speech. Use sentence fragments whenever they seem natural.

1. Before you write, pick two characters for a conversation, and then choose a subject for them to discuss. (Some sort of **conflict** will generate a lively conversation or even a heated argument.) Read the first draft of your dialogue aloud to make sure it sounds natural.

2. Trade papers with a partner, and read his or her dialogue aloud to see how it flows. Underline any passages that seem awkward or confusing. Revise your own dialogue as you wish, based on your partner's suggestions.

3. Share your dialogue in a class drama session, with you and your partner playing the two roles. (You can either read from the script or act it out from memory.)

DEBATING: DEVELOPING A LOGICAL ARGUMENT

Assignment

A **debate** is a formal speaking contest with two teams arguing opposing sides of a question. Your assignment is to prepare and conduct a debate on the following **proposition,** or statement:

> *Resolved:* Tom Garrison, the father in *I Never Sang for My Father,* is an admirable character and the central character of the play.

Notice that this proposition has two parts:

1. Tom Garrison is an admirable character.
2. Tom Garrison is the central character.

The **affirmative** team will try to prove that both parts of the proposition are true. The **negative** team will try to prove that both parts are *not* true.

Background

In a real debate, each team must be able to debate both sides of the question. So we're going to assign you a side arbitrarily. If your birthday is in January through June, you're on the affirmative side. The rest of you are on the negative side. Find a classmate who's on the same side as you: The two of you will work together as a team.

In order to win a debate, you need to assemble a great deal of **evidence.** Your evidence—arranged in the order you are going to present it—is called your **argument.** Here are some kinds of evidence you can use in a debate about any literary work:

1. **The work itself.** You can use your own **analysis** and **interpretation** of the work as evidence. You can quote lines from the work or refer to specific actions, scenes, and situations.

2. **Quotations by authorities.** An **authority** is an expert. You can look for comments on the work by critics or by the writer.

   a. **Card catalogue.** Look for books *about* the writer and *by* the writer. Sometimes an introduction or preface will comment on the work. Also, the writer's letters, essays, or autobiography may mention the work. Check the indexes of the books.

   b. **The *Readers' Guide to Periodical Literature.*** For contemporary works, look for reviews from the year the work was published. Also check for recent articles by or about the writer.

Preparing for the Debate

You and your partner will work together in getting ready for the debate:

1. **Gather your evidence.** Write each piece of evidence (each example or quotation) on a separate 3 × 5 inch index card. You need to gather sufficient evidence to convince your audience that your opinion is correct. You will need to **analyze** and **evaluate** the material that you read. Judge whether a quotation or action or scene *directly* supports the point you are making or **refutes** (disproves) your opponents' viewpoint. If so, it's **relevant;** add it to your collection. Avoid **irrelevant** material—anything unrelated or only vaguely related to your points.

Here is an excerpt from a drama critic's review of the opening night performance of *I Never Sang for My Father.* In this excerpt, Walter Kerr discusses the character of Tom Garrison. Read the review carefully to find his conclusions. Will a quotation from this review be good evidence for your argument? (Lillian Gish played the part of Margaret.)

> The patriarch [Tom Garrison] is self-made. He will repeat, at the drop of nothing at all, the whole sterling saga of his rise; he will even write it out all over again in answering a simple note of con-

dolence on the death of his own wife. At his own wife's funeral, he never speaks of his wife; his attention is centered on himself and on the mother he buried so long ago ("She was a little bit of a thing").

He is affable. Accept his invitation to dinner at a restaurant in town and you will hear jokes. The jokes are the same jokes, clapped out with fresh confidence. If the family can't laugh this time, father has a ready retreat. "Just trying to get a rise," he beams, face flushed with triumph. He is seriously obtuse and pleasantly obtuse. After wife Lillian Gish has died, he won't have a housekeeper on the premises. Not *alone* with him, he confides in all goatish innocence. He is tough. The son will by God live with him, freshly remarried or no. And when he is tucked in for the night, he is a wrinkled scarecrow in pajamas. No surprise that Lillian Gish died before he did, though. He'd been calling attention to her failing powers—not quite gloating over them, mind you—for years. He'd been barking, "Can't you turn that thing up?" at her and her hearing aid all along, unaware that she could hear him when she chose, if she chose.

He is a prickly bastion, a fortress flying a deceptive flag of friendliness, fending off in his contrary variety all efforts at penetration—astringent in the writing, superbly armored in the playing. You believe in the firmness with which Mr. Webb puts his arms halfway about Mr. Holbrook's shoulders, and also in the decisive withdrawal that says halfway is quite enough.

—Walter Kerr

2. **Select the evidence you will use.** Choose the strongest evidence you've found to support your argument. Make sure you have sufficient evidence: Three pieces of evidence are more convincing than two; one piece of evidence is usually not enough.
3. **Organize the evidence.** Once you've chosen your best evidence, write a rough outline of your argument. Decide on the most effective order. If you have three pieces of evidence to prove a point, save the strongest piece for last. It will be the idea that your listeners will remember.
4. **Anticipate your opponents' arguments.** In a debate, three things are happening all at once:

   a. You try to convince your audience that your opinion is right.
   b. You listen critically to your opponents' arguments and then try to prove that their opinions are wrong.
   c. You defend your own arguments after your opponents have attacked them.

A debate is something like a boxing match. You're not only attacking your opponent but also defending yourself at all times. Prepare your own argument carefully, but spend almost as much time preparing to refute what you expect your opponents to say. Gather evidence to attack the arguments you think they will make.

Conducting the Debate
The format and rules of debate have been simplified for this assignment.

Rules for Conducting a Debate
1. Each speaker presents his or her case without interruption.
2. Speakers are courteous to each other.
3. Speakers may refer to notes or may read a written paper.
4. Speakers must stay within the time limits.

Each team has two speakers: 1AFF and 2AFF (the affirmative team); 1NEG and 2NEG (the negative team). The first affirmative speaker (1AFF) has four minutes to present evidence proving that Tom Garrison is an admirable character. Then the first negative speaker (1NEG) must refute 1AFF's argument and also present evidence to convince the listeners that Tom Garrison is *not* an admirable character. The next two speakers (2AFF and 2NEG) follow the same format, but they debate the second part of the proposition (Tom is the central figure in the play). Each speaker should take some time to refute the preceding speaker's argument. Finally, at the end of the debate, the first affirmative (1AFF) and first negative speaker (1NEG) return to summarize their arguments.

This sounds a lot more complicated than it is. The following chart summarizes the information above.

Order	Speaker	Time	Subject
1	1AFF	4 min.	Prove: Tom is an admirable character.
2	1NEG	5 min.	Refute 1AFF argument.
			Prove: Tom is *not* an admirable character.
3	2AFF	5 min.	Refute 1NEG argument.
			Prove: Tom is the play's central character.
4	2NEG	5 min.	Refute 2AFF argument.
			Prove: Tom is *not* the play's central character.
5	1AFF	3 min.	Refute 2NEG argument.
			Summarize main points of affirmative team's arguments.
6	1NEG	2 min.	Summarize main points of negative team's arguments.

Evaluating the Debate

Listen critically to all four speakers to decide which team is more convincing. You may find it helpful to take notes outlining each speaker's main points. Keep these criteria in mind as you listen to the debate:

Criteria for Evaluating a Debate

1. Are the speakers' arguments clear and well organized?
2. Do the speakers present relevant evidence to prove their points?
3. Do the speakers present sufficient evidence?
4. Do the speakers speak clearly? Can they be understood easily?
5. Do the speakers convincingly refute their opponents' arguments?
6. Do the speakers convincingly defend their arguments from their opponents' attacks?

WILLIAM SHAKESPEARE

Shakespeare by Heather Cooper (1982). Oil.

UNIT FIVE

Robert Anderson

WILLIAM SHAKESPEARE

An introduction by **Robert Anderson**

William Shakespeare's Life

> " **B**y now, more material has been written about Shakespeare and his works than about any other writer in the world."

Stratford-on-Avon.

We know very little of William Shakespeare's life. In the early years of the 1600's, nobody realized that this actor and writer would one day become known as the world's greatest playwright. In the 1600's there were no talk shows on which Shakespeare might appear, no Sunday supplements to feature all the intimate details of his life. This neglect, however, has been corrected in the past few hundred years. By now, more material has been written about Shakespeare and his works than about any other writer in the world.

What we do know about Shakespeare comes mainly from public records. We know that he was baptized on April 26, 1564, in Stratford-on-Avon, a market town about one hundred miles northwest of London. It is assumed he was born a few days before his baptism, and his birthday is celebrated on April 23, possibly only because he died on that date in 1616. He was one of eight children.

His father, John Shakespeare, was a shopkeeper and a man of some importance in Stratford, serving at various times as alderman and "high bailiff"—the equivalent of a mayor today.

William probably went to the local grammar school, which was considerably different from grammar schools today. In those days it was rare for students to move on to a university; the Stratford grammar school provided Shakespeare with all his formal education. The curriculum included a great deal of Latin grammar and literature, including such writers as Ovid and Virgil.

In 1582 Shakespeare married Anne Hathaway, who was eight years older than he, and in 1583 their first child, Susanna, was born. In 1585 Anne gave birth to twins, Hamnet and Judith. Then, from 1585 until 1592, the history on Shakespeare goes blank.

Many people believe that the year after the twins were born, Shakespeare went to London to seek his fortune. We know for certain that by 1592 he had become an actor and a playwright, because that year a rival playwright, Robert Greene, scathingly warned other playwrights against the actor who had the nerve to become a writer:

> There is an upstart crow, beautified with our feathers, . . . that supposes he is well able to bombast out a blank verse as the best of you. . . .

Greene is referring to a fable in which a crow struts about in another bird's feathers—just as an actor can only recite the words of others. Greene was being nasty about the upstart newcomer, a mere actor, not even a university man, who dared to *write*.

As you can tell from Greene's contempt for Shakespeare, actors were held in disrepute at the time. In fact, they were often lumped together with other unsavory groups: "rogues, vagabonds, sturdy beggars, and common players." Local officials were always trying to close the theaters because they felt clerks and apprentices wasted time there (performances were in the daytime). They also felt that disease was too easily spread among the audience. In fact, the London theaters were closed for long periods during the plague years of 1592–1594.

Thus actors sought the protection and support of noblemen with the power to speak for their rights against critical town authorities. In 1594 it appears that Shakespeare became a charter member of a theatrical group called the Lord Chamberlain's Men, which became the King's Men in 1603. (The patron of the group was none other than King James himself.) Shakespeare acted and wrote for this company until he retired to Stratford in 1612. By that time, he had written thirty-seven plays—comedies, histories, tragedies, and romances—including his masterpieces: *Hamlet, Othello, King Lear,* and *Macbeth.*

The White Hart Inn, London.
Engraving.

From the Collection of The Folger
Shakespeare Library, Washington, D.C.

Detail from Cornelius Visscher's 1616 view of London, showing the Globe Theater on the south bank of the River Thames.

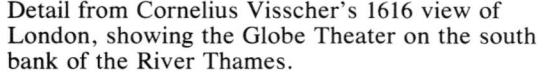

Poster showing Raul Julia in *Macbeth*.
© 1989 Paul Davis. Courtesy of the artist.

Al Pacino as Mark Antony in a New York Public Theater performance of *Julius Caesar* in 1988.

It is sometimes difficult to fix the dates of Shakespeare's works because plays were not routinely published after production as they generally are now. In Shakespeare's day plays became the property of the theaters, and the theaters were not eager to have copies made available for rival theaters to use. Some of Shakespeare's plays were published during his lifetime, but often in versions of dubious authenticity. It was not until 1623 that two men who had been with Shakespeare in the King's Men brought out what they called "True Originall Copies" of all the plays. This volume is called the First Folio.

It is believed that *Julius Caesar* was written in 1599, because a Swiss traveler who was in England in September 1599 wrote:

> After dinner on the twenty-first of September, at about two o'clock, I went with my companions over the water, and in the strewn-roof house [the playhouse with a thatched roof] saw the tragedy of the first Emperor Julius with at least fifteen characters very well acted. At the end of the comedy they danced according to their custom with extreme elegance. Two men in men's clothes and two in women's gave this performance, in wonderful combination with each other.

Shakespeare died on April 23, 1616, at the age of fifty-two. He was buried in the church at Stratford, where his grave can still be seen today. A bequest he made in his will has attracted almost as much interest and curiosity as anything in his plays—he left his wife his "second best bed."

The Elizabethan stage would have seemed very strange to American theatergoers of fifty or sixty years ago, who were accustomed to elaborate and realistic settings placed behind a proscenium (see page 557) and separated from the audience by a huge velvet curtain. Though this proscenium stage is still more or less standard today, the newer arena stages, thrust stages, and open stages have made us much more at home with Shakespeare's theater. The use of these simpler stages perhaps goes back to the saying that all you need for a theater is "a platform and a passion or two."

As with Shakespeare's life, we have only sketchy information about the early English theaters. It appears that the wandering acting companies in England had originally set up their stages—mere platforms—wherever they could find space, often in the courtyards of inns. The audience stood around three sides of the stage, or if they paid more, they sat in chairs on the balconies surrounding the inn yard.

When James Burbage (the father of Richard Burbage, the actor who was to perform most of Shakespeare's great tragic parts) decided in 1576 to build the first permanent theater just outside the city of London, it was natural that he should duplicate the courtyard theaters in which his company had been performing. Burbage called his new playhouse simply "The Theatre."

The Globe—The "Wooden O"

In 1599 the owner of the land on which Burbage had built his theater apparently decided to raise the rent. Because the theater was somewhat behind in its rent payments, the landlord threatened to take it over. On the night of January 20, 1599, James Burbage's son Cuthbert and others in the company stealthily took their theater apart timber by timber and rowed the pieces across the river, where they later reconstructed the theater and called it the Globe. This was the theater where Shakespeare's greatest plays were performed.

In *Henry V* Shakespeare calls this theater "a wooden O." It consisted of an open space, perhaps sixty-five feet in diameter, surrounded by a more or less circular building thirty feet high and consisting of three tiers of seats for spectators. As in the inn courtyards, the stage, which was forty by thirty feet and five feet off the ground, projected into the open space.

The interesting part of the stage was at the rear, where there was a small curtained inner stage, flanked by two entrances, with an upper stage above it. Stout pillars held up a narrow roof over the rear part of the stage. This was called "the Heavens." The front part of the stage was equipped with a trap door, which could be used for burial scenes, surprise entrances, and mysterious exits.

The Sets

We have seen (page 558) that Thornton Wilder asked the audience to use its imagination in viewing *Our Town*. Wilder referred to the

The Elizabethan Stage

The Swan Theater, London
by Johannes DeWitt (c. 1595). Drawing.

" **I**n *Henry V* Shakespeare calls this theater 'a wooden O.' "

Poster showing Tracy Ulmann and Lou Gossett, Jr., in *The Taming of the Shrew.*

© 1990 Paul Davis. Courtesy of the artist.

Chinese theater, where a character straddling a stick conveys to us he is on horseback. More than three hundred years earlier, Shakespeare had written these lines for the Prologue to *Henry V:*

> . . . let us . . .
> On your imaginary forces work . . .
> Think, when we talk of horses, that you see them
> Printing their proud hoofs i' th' receiving earth;
> For 'tis your thoughts that now must deck our kings.

In spite of this appeal to the audience to use its imagination, it appears that the kings were indeed royally decked out. Though the stage was bare, allowing for almost cinematic fluidity of action, scenes often called for flags and banners and musicians. Characters were also lowered from the Heavens by cranes, and there were sound effects as well. In fact, these effects caused the destruction of the Globe. In 1613, during the battle scene of *Henry VIII,* a stage hand was lighting the fuse of a cannon. A spark flew up and started a fire in the thatched roof of the Heavens, and the theater burned down.

As for lighting, because the plays were performed during the daytime in the open air, there was no need for stage illumination. In fact, Shakespeare had to convey the idea of night by having his characters carry torches. (Nowadays, when movie directors shoot a night scene in the daytime, they use filters on their cameras to darken the scene.)

The Actors

In Shakespeare's time, all actors were male. (It wasn't until 1660, when the exiled King Charles II was restored to the English throne and the repressive Puritan dominance ended, that women played in professional theaters.) Boys who had been recruited from the choir schools and professionally trained played the female roles. It was not too difficult to create the illusion that these boys were women. Shakespeare's plays were performed in contemporary Elizabethan costumes, and women's clothing of the day was very elaborate and concealing, with long, full skirts jutting out from the waist. Women of the day also wore elaborate wigs and powdered their faces heavily. So, all in all, the transformation of boys into women characters was not that unbelievable.

Hooking the Audience's Attention

The Elizabethan theater was a convivial place, where people arrived early, visited with friends, made new acquaintances, moved around freely, and ate and drank before and during the performance. (The occasion might have had something of the feeling of a Saturday matinee at a local shopping-mall movie theater.) Playwrights had to write scenes that would catch the attention of this audience, and many actors held their attention by vigorous and flamboyant acting. By comparison, today's movie cameras are so sensitive that sometimes all an actor has to do is think the right thoughts, and that is enough. Elizabethan actors had to do more than that, since they were trying to hold the interest of three thousand restless people who were also busy eating, drinking, and talking. We get the impression that, like actors working on modern thrust or arena stages, the Elizabethan players had to keep on the move so that spectators on all three sides could catch their expressions and hear their voices.

Shakespeare's Poetry: Blank Verse

As with all of Shakespeare's plays, *Julius Caesar* is written in blank verse. **Blank verse** is unrhymed **iambic pentameter,** which means that each line of poetry in the play contains five iambs. A line of formal verse is usually divided into what are called poetic "feet." A **foot** contains at least one stressed syllable and, usually, one or more unstressed syllables. An **iamb** is a foot that consists of an unstressed syllable followed by a stressed syllable, as in the word prepáre. **Pentameter** simply means that there are five of these iambs in a line. The following two lines are written in blank verse—five feet of unrhymed iambic meter:

> The evil that men do lives after them,
> The good is oft interred with their bones.

A whole play written in this unvarying pattern would become singsong. To break the monotony and alter the emphasis, Shakespeare sometimes reverses the stressed and unstressed syllables:

> This was the noblest Roman of them all.
> All the conspirators save only he
> Did what they did in envy of great Caesar.

Notice that each of these lines *could* be read in strict iambic pentameter (except for the extra final syllable in *Caesar*). However, other variations in reading are possible. For example:

> Did what they did in envy of great Caesar.

End-stopped and Run-on Lines

To follow the meaning of the lines, it is important to take note of the punctuation marks and to resist the temptation to stop at the end of each line. Thus in the passage above, we would make a full stop at the end of the first line but not at the end of the second line. There is no punctuation mark at the end of the second line, and sense requires that we move on. Lines that conclude with a punctuation mark are called **end-stopped** lines. Lines that do not end with a punctuation mark are called **run-on** lines. (To complete their meaning, you must "run on" to the next line.)

Reading Elizabethan English

Statue of Julius Caesar.

Campidoglio, Rome.

S hakespeare wrote his plays in an early form of Modern English. Though you'll find some words and phrasings difficult to understand, remember that Shakespeare did use the same English language we use today. Our difficulties in reading Shakespeare come from these factors:

1. Some words in Shakespeare's play are **archaic** (är·kā′ik), meaning that they are old-fashioned and are no longer used.

2. Some words have simply changed in meaning over the past four hundred years.

3. English grammar has changed slightly over the past four hundred years.

Archaic Words

One character in *Julius Caesar* is called a *soothsayer*. In Shakespeare's day the word *sooth* meant "truth"; today that word has gone out of common use. Now we'd call a "soothsayer" a fortune teller, a prophet, or an astrologer, depending on how the person arrived at the "truth." Here are some archaic words used in *Julius Caesar,* with their definitions:

> **ague:** fever.
> **alarum:** a call to arms, such as a trumpet sound.
> **an:** if.
> **betimes:** from time to time.
> **fleering:** flattering.
> **hence, whence, thence:** here, where, there.
> **hie:** hurry.
> **knave:** servant, or person of humble birth.
> **Marry!:** a mild oath, shortened from "By the Virgin Mary!"
> **moe:** more. *Moe* was used to refer to number and amounts; *more* to size.
> **prithee:** pray thee (beg thee).
> **smatch:** a small amount.

Archaic Pronouns: Forms of "You"

Most readers today are familiar with stories set long ago in which characters use forms of *you* that are now archaic: *thee, thou, thine,* and *thy.* It is interesting to know a little about these pronouns, which are always singular. In Shakespeare's day they could be used in two ways:

1. They could be used to address someone very familiar or intimate with the speaker, such as a wife, husband, or close friend. Thus when Brutus talks to his wife at one point, he says:

> All my engagements I will construe to thee.
> —Act II, Scene 1, line 307

2. They could also be used to address a subordinate or inferior, or a servant. Thus when Flavius orders the commoners to move on, he refers to them collectively as *you* but says to one of them:

> . . . Speak, what trade art thou?
>   —Act I, Scene 1, line 5

If *thou, thy, thine,* or *thee* are used incorrectly, they can be insulting. You'll see that just before Caesar is stabbed, Brutus deliberately uses the familiar pronoun (an insult because Caesar is Brutus's superior):

> I kiss thy hand, but not in flattery, Caesar.
>   —Act III, Scene 1, line 52

Words with Different Meanings

The words in Shakespeare that often cause the most trouble are those that are still in use today but have different meanings. For example, when Flavius calls the cobbler "Thou naughty knave" (Act I, Scene 1, line 15), we might think he is mildly rebuking the man by calling him "mischievous." But *naughty* here means "worthless," not "mischievous," and so the sense of Flavius's line is very different from what a hasty reading would suggest. At the right, you'll find a box of some other familiar words in *Julius Caesar* that had different meanings in Shakespeare's day.

Changes in Grammar

Today words are classified as nouns, verbs, adjectives, adverbs, etc., and when someone mixes up the parts of speech, an uproar might result among purists. (This happened when people began to use the noun "input" as a verb.) But Shakespeare freely used words as different parts of speech. Here he makes a verb out of the noun *conceit*:

> You have right well conceited. . . .
>   —Act I, Scene 3, line 162

Here he uses an adjective (*vulgar*) as a noun (we'd say *vulgar people*):

> . . . drive away the vulgar from the streets
>   —Act I, Scene 1, line 70

Some passages seem puzzling because a word or more has been omitted:

> . . . So Caesar may;
> Then lest he may, prevent. . . .
>   —Act II, Scene 1, lines 27–28

What's understood here is ". . . prevent him from doing it."

" **The** words in Shakespeare that often cause the most trouble are those that are still in use today but have different meanings."

Familiar Words/Different Meanings

closet: a small room, often a private study.

exhalations: meteors.

gentle: noble. A "gentleman" was once a man with a title.

ghastly: ghostly.

humor: temper or disposition.

indifferently: impartially.

just: true.

merely: wholly, entirely.

repair: go.

sad: serious.

saucy: presumptuous.

soft: slowly, or "wait a minute."

wit: intelligence.

When Shakespeare made a sentence negative or when he asked a question, he didn't have to use the auxiliary verb *do* as we must today. Where we'd say, "What do you mean?" Shakespeare could say, ". . . what mean you?" (Act II, Scene 1, line 234). Where we'd say, "Don't let him die," Shakespeare could say, ". . . let him not die" (Act II, Scene 1, line 190).

The side notes in the play will help you with vocabulary and grammar that might present a problem. Use context clues to make educated guesses about any other words that might puzzle you. And be sure to read the lines aloud—you'll often find that *hearing* Shakespeare is easier than *reading* him.

The Play

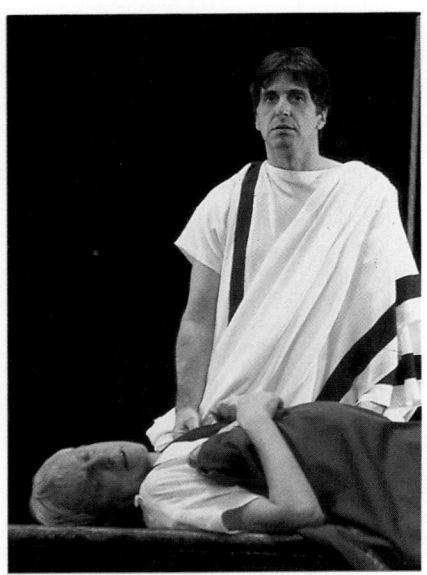

A scene from a 1988 production of *Julius Caesar,* starring Al Pacino.

Julius Caesar is about the assassination of the Roman military commander and dictator who lived from 102 to 44 B.C. Shakespeare drew his material from Sir Thomas North's translation of Plutarch's *Lives of the Noble Grecians and Romans,* which first appeared in England in 1579. Greek and Roman history and culture had a great appeal for the English of the Elizabethan Age.

The Historical Background: Rome in Caesar's Day

We get the impression that the Roman world in Caesar's time was continually at war. Powerful generals like Caesar moved with their plundering armies over the entire Mediterranean world, from Spain and France through Greece and Asia Minor and around to Egypt and Africa. These "private armies" would subdue weaker states and countries, which then would become allies or provinces ruled by Roman governors who exacted cruel taxes.

Sometimes the Roman Senate called on one general or another to help stabilize the government. In such cases, the general often took over the government, sometimes giving way to a newly elected government, sometimes not.

And sometimes the generals turned on each other, not necessarily because of differing ideologies, but simply because they were strong men battling for power. This is what happened when the generals Caesar and Pompey clashed in the civil war that began in 49 B.C.

Caesar and Pompey had been friends. Pompey had married Caesar's daughter by his first wife, and in 60 B.C. the generals together had helped bring order to a weakening government. Pompey and Caesar had then set themselves up, along with Crassus, as the First Triumvirate (three-man governing body).

Eager for still more power, and realizing that the only way to achieve it was with conquests and money, Caesar departed for what has been called the Gallic Wars. For eight years he roamed over Europe, subjugating France, Belgium, and parts of Holland, Germany, and Switzerland. In the process he amassed huge sums of money, which he sent back to Rome to gain favor with the people.

Caesar's daughter died in 54 B.C., and in 49 B.C. Pompey, jealous of Caesar's growing power and favor with the people, threw his weight with the aristocratic Senate, which was also becoming wary of Caesar's growing ambitions.

Caesar considered himself a defender of the *populares,* but critics claimed that he gained the people's support with bribes and handouts—"bread and circuses." According to his enemies, Caesar deprived the Romans of their liberty and self-respect.

Caesar refused the Senate's order to give up his command and return to Rome as a private citizen. Instead he marched his army on Rome, took control, and pursued Pompey all the way to Egypt. There, Pompey was murdered before Caesar could capture him. Caesar lingered in Egypt for nine months, bewitched by the twenty-two-year-old Cleopatra. Establishing her on the throne of Egypt under his protection, Caesar proceeded to Spain, where he defeated an army led by Pompey's sons.

When he returned to Rome this time, Caesar was invincible. He was declared dictator for ten years and saw to it that his supporters, including Brutus, became senators. As his desire for power grew obsessive, he had a statue of himself erected in the Temple with the inscription, "To the Unconquerable God." The common people loved him; eventually Caesar was declared dictator for life.

But for many Romans, Caesar's ambitions were deplorable. The Romans had overthrown their last king 450 years before and had set up a republican government. The idea of another king ruling the "free Romans" was unthinkable. As Caesar's arrogance and power became unbearable to certain senators, they made plans to assassinate him on March 15, 44 B.C. Shakespeare's play opens a month before the murder.

Marble bust of Julius Caesar (44 B.C., shortly after his assassination).

Museo Nazionale, Naples.

The Themes of the Play

In all of Shakespeare's plays, the characters (no matter what historical period they live in) all occupy a world that is run by a benevolent God who rewards good and punishes evil. In Shakespeare's day people believed that the universe was essentially good and orderly. All order stemmed from the authority of God, the supreme ruler. The monarch's right to rule came from God too, and so opposition to the anointed ruler was really opposition to God. When the chain of authority was snapped, the heavens would be offended, and a whole society might be plunged into disorder.

As you read *Julius Caesar* think about this view of the universe, and decide how these themes are parts of Shakespeare's concern:

1. Chaos results when the prescribed social order is broken.

2. The best intentions of good, noble men can lead to tragedy.

3. Language is a powerful weapon, and in the hands of a skilled person, it can be used to manipulate others.

4. Violence and bloodshed can never have morally good results.

5. Orderliness and a stable rule, even though dictatorial, are preferable to social chaos.

> " **W**hen the chain of authority was snapped, the heavens would be offended, and a whole society might be plunged into disorder."

THE TRAGEDY OF JULIUS CAESAR

William Shakespeare

Something deathless and dangerous in the world sweeps past you. . . . It is something fearful and ominous, something turbulent and to be dreaded, which distends the drama to include the life of nations as well as of men. It is an ageless warning. . . . It unrolls in your mind's eye a map of the world, which is increasingly splotched with sickening colors.

—from a review of *Julius Caesar*,
John Mason Brown

Characters

Julius Caesar
Octavius Caesar
Marcus Antonius } triumvirs after the death
M. Aemilius Lepidus } of Julius Caesar
Cicero
Publius } senators
Popilius Lena
Marcus Brutus
Cassius
Casca
Trebonius } conspirators against Julius
Ligarius } Caesar
Decius Brutus
Metellus Cimber
Cinna
Flavius } tribunes
Marullus
Artemidorus of Cnidos, a teacher of rhetoric
A Soothsayer
Cinna, a poet
Another Poet
Lucilius
Titinius
Messala } friends to Brutus and Cassius
Young Cato
Volumnius

Varro
Clitus
Claudius
Strato } servants to Brutus
Lucius
Dardanius
Pindarus, servant to Cassius
Calphurnia, wife to Caesar
Portia, wife to Brutus
Senators, Citizens, Guards
Attendants, etc.

Scene: During most of the play, at Rome; afterward, near Sardis, and near Philippi.

Note: The text of this play is taken in entirety from the Signet Classic Shakespeare. The editors of the Signet Classic Shakespeare have refrained from making abundant changes in the text, but they have added line numbers and act and scene divisions, as well as indications of locale at the beginning of scenes.

Act I

Scene 1. *Rome. A street.*

Enter FLAVIUS, MARULLUS, *and certain* COMMONERS *over the stage.*

Flavius.
Hence! Home, you idle creatures, get you home!
Is this a holiday? What, know you not,
Being mechanical,° you ought not walk
Upon a laboring day without the sign

5   Of your profession?° Speak, what trade art thou?

Carpenter. Why, sir, a carpenter.

Marullus.
Where is thy leather apron and thy rule?
What dost thou with thy best apparel on?
You, sir, what trade are you?

10 **Cobbler.** Truly, sir, in respect of a fine workman,° I am
      but, as you would say, a cobbler.°

Marullus.
But what trade art thou? Answer me directly.

Cobbler. A trade, sir, that, I hope, I may use with a safe
conscience, which is indeed, sir, a mender of bad soles.

Flavius.

15   What trade, thou knave? Thou naughty knave, what
          trade?

Cobbler. Nay, I beseech you, sir, be not out with me: yet,
if you be out, sir, I can mend you.

Marullus.
What mean'st thou by that? Mend me, thou saucy fellow?

Cobbler. Why, sir, cobble you.

Flavius.

20   Thou art a cobbler, art thou?

Cobbler. Truly, sir, all that I live by is with the awl:° I
meddle with no tradesman's matters, nor women's
matters; but withal,° I am indeed, sir, a surgeon to old
shoes: when they are in great danger, I recover them.

25   As proper men as ever trod upon neat's leather° have
gone upon my handiwork.

Flavius.
But wherefore art not in thy shop today?
Why dost thou lead these men about the streets?

Cobbler. Truly, sir, to wear out their shoes, to get myself

30   into more work. But indeed, sir, we make holiday to
see Caesar and to rejoice in his triumph.

Marullus.
Wherefore rejoice? What conquest brings he home?
What tributaries° follow him to Rome,

Stage direction. *We are on a crowded street in Rome. It is lined with statues near what is today known as the Palatine Hill (which is where the palaces, or* palatia, *were). A joyous, peaceful crowd is milling about. Two tribunes—military men—enter with the noisy mob of commoners. What tone does Flavius's first speech bring immediately to the play?*

3. mechanical: common, working-class men.

5. sign/of your profession: your working clothes and tools.

10. In other words, in comparison with a skilled laborer.

11. cobbler: In Shakespeare's day the word meant both "shoemaker" and "bungler."

15. *It is important in this play to watch the moods of the mob. Do you think these commoners are afraid of the military men, or are they acting comically and boldly?*

21. awl: a sharp, pointed tool for making holes in wood or leather.

23. withal: nevertheless.

25. neat's leather: cattle's hide.

32. *This speech signals a change in tone. How should Marullus say this line? How should the crowd respond?*
33. tributaries: captives (captive enemies who have to pay "tribute" to Rome).

To grace in captive bonds his chariot wheels?
35 You blocks, you stones, you worse than senseless
        things!
    O you hard hearts, you cruel men of Rome,
    Knew you not Pompey?° Many a time and oft
    Have you climbed up to walls and battlements,
    To tow'rs and windows, yea, to chimney tops,
40 Your infants in your arms, and there have sat
    The livelong day, with patient expectation,
    To see great Pompey pass the streets of Rome.
    And when you saw his chariot but appear,
    Have you not made an universal shout,
45 That Tiber trembled underneath her banks
    To hear the replication° of your sounds
    Made in her concave shores?°
    And do you now put on your best attire?
    And do you now cull out a holiday?
50 And do you now strew flowers in his way
    That comes in triumph over Pompey's blood?
    Be gone!
    Run to your houses, fall upon your knees,
    Pray to the gods to intermit° the plague
55 That needs must light on this ingratitude.
    Flavius.
        Go, go, good countrymen, and, for this fault,
        Assemble all the poor men of your sort;
        Draw them to Tiber banks and weep your tears
        Into the channel, till the lowest stream
60   Do kiss the most exalted shores of all.

                        [*Exeunt all the* COMMONERS.]

        See, whe'r their basest mettle° be not moved;
        They vanish tongue-tied in their guiltiness.
        Go you down that way towards the Capitol;
        This way will I. Disrobe the images,°
65   If you do find them decked with ceremonies.
    Marullus.
        May we do so?
        You know it is the feast of Lupercal.°
    Flavius.
        It is no matter; let no images
        Be hung with Caesar's trophies. I'll about
70   And drive away the vulgar° from the streets;
        So do you too, where you perceive them thick.
        These growing feathers plucked from Caesar's wing
        Will make him fly an ordinary pitch,°
        Who else would soar above the view of men
75   And keep us all in servile fearfulness.   [*Exeunt.*]

35. *What actions might Marullus be engaged in here?*

37. Pompey: the Roman politician and general who was defeated by Caesar in 48 B.C. and later murdered.

46. replication: echo, copy.

47. concave shores: carved-out banks of the river.

52. *How should this short line be spoken?*

54. intermit: hold back.

55. *What is the key word in the last line of this speech? Why is Marullus angry at the mob?*

Stage direction. *Pay attention to the movements of the mob. What mood has taken over these commoners as they leave the stage? Would you have them leave in a defiant mood, or are they ashamed?*
61. basest mettle: basic substance, their "stuff."
64. images: statues.

67. Lupercal: an old Roman fertility festival celebrated on February 15. In the ceremony young men wearing only girdles raced around the Palatine Hill (at the base of which is the Lupercal cave) and whipped bystanders with strips of goat skin. Those who were whipped were assured of fertility. The Lupercal cave is believed to be where the twins Romulus and Remus, the founders of Rome, were suckled by a wolf.
70. vulgar: common people.
73. an ordinary pitch: at an ordinary height.
75. *What does Flavius fear about Caesar?*

Scene 2. *A public place.*

Enter CAESAR, ANTONY *(dressed for the race),* CALPHUR-
NIA, PORTIA, DECIUS, CICERO, BRUTUS, CASSIUS,
CASCA, *a* SOOTHSAYER; *after them,* MARULLUS *and*
FLAVIUS.

Caesar.
    Calphurnia!
Casca.   Peace, ho! Caesar speaks.
Caesar.   Calphurnia!
Calphurnia. Here, my lord.
Caesar.
    Stand you directly in Antonius' way
    When he doth run his course. Antonius!
5 **Antony.** Caesar, my lord?
Caesar.
    Forget not in your speed, Antonius,
    To touch Calphurnia; for our elders say
    The barren, touchèd in this holy chase,
    Shake off their sterile curse.
Antony.   I shall remember:
10   When Caesar says "Do this," it is performed.
Caesar.
    Set on, and leave no ceremony out.
Soothsayer. Caesar!
Caesar. Ha! Who calls?
Casca.
    Bid every noise be still; peace yet again!
Caesar.
15   Who is it in the press° that calls on me?
    I hear a tongue, shriller than all the music,
    Cry "Caesar." Speak; Caesar is turned to hear.
Soothsayer.
    Beware the ides of March.
Caesar.   What man is that?
Brutus.
    A soothsayer bids you beware the ides of March.
Caesar.
20   Set him before me; let me see his face.
Cassius.
    Fellow, come from the throng; look upon Caesar.
Caesar.
    What say'st thou to me now? Speak once again.
Soothsayer.
    Beware the ides of March.
Caesar.
    He is a dreamer, let us leave him. Pass.

Stage direction. *Before the individual actors enter, we again are aware of the
mob—at this moment they are chanting
"Hail, Caesar!" As Caesar and his retinue
enter, the crowd makes way for them. Antony is dressed for the race held on the
Feast of Lupercal which this year also celebrates Caesar's latest victory. Caesar is
richly dressed—perhaps too much so. What
mood would Marullus and Flavius be in?*

10. *This speech suggests something important about Antony. What is it?*

13. *A lot of ceremonial music and ritual
have opened this scene, so our attention
has been focused on Caesar and his followers. But now the soothsayer is suddenly visible. This is a dramatic moment, for it
foreshadows what will happen later. Where
would you place the soothsayer? How
should Caesar react to his call?*
15. press: crowd.
17. *This line could suggest a physical
disability. What is it?*

18. *The ides of March are March 15. In
some productions this warning is heard
as an ominous and disembodied cry. In what
different ways could the line be spoken?*

"Who is it in the press that calls on me?"

The photographs illustrating this play are from a 1987 production
by the Royal Shakespeare Company in Stratford-on-Avon, England.

[*Sennet.° Exeunt all except Brutus and Cassius.*]

25 **Cassius.**
    Will you go see the order of the course?
Brutus. Not I.
Cassius. I pray you do.
Brutus.
    I am not gamesome: I do lack some part
    Of that quick spirit that is in Antony.
30   Let me not hinder, Cassius, your desires;
    I'll leave you.
Cassius.
    Brutus, I do observe you now of late;
    I have not from your eyes that gentleness

Sennet: a flourish, or fanfare of trumpets
announcing a ceremonial entrance or exit.

? **Stage direction.** *The stage is empty a
few moments as Brutus and Cassius
stand looking at the departing Caesar. The
action line of the play—the assassination—
begins now with Cassius's rather casual
question. How should Brutus answer?*

And show of love as I was wont to have;

35   You bear too stubborn and too strange a hand°
    Over your friend that loves you.

Brutus.   Cassius,
    Be not deceived: if I have veiled my look,
    I turn the trouble of my countenance
    Merely° upon myself. Vexèd I am

40   Of late with passions of some difference,°
    Conceptions only proper to myself,
    Which give some soil,° perhaps, to my behaviors;
    But let not therefore my good friends be grieved
    (Among which number, Cassius, be you one)

45   Nor construe° any further my neglect
    Than that poor Brutus, with himself at war,
    Forgets the shows of love to other men.

Cassius.
    Then, Brutus, I have much mistook your passion,°
    By means whereof this breast of mine hath buried

50   Thoughts of great value, worthy cogitations.°
    Tell me, good Brutus, can you see your face?

Brutus.
    No, Cassius; for the eye sees not itself
    But by reflection, by some other things.

Cassius.
    'Tis just:°

55   And it is very much lamented, Brutus,
    That you have no such mirrors as will turn
    Your hidden worthiness into your eye,
    That you might see your shadow.° I have heard
    Where many of the best respect° in Rome

60   (Except immortal Caesar), speaking of Brutus,
    And groaning underneath this age's yoke,
    Have wished that noble Brutus had his eyes.

Brutus.
    Into what dangers would you lead me, Cassius,
    That you would have me seek into myself

65   For that which is not in me?

Cassius.
    Therefore, good Brutus, be prepared to hear;
    And since you know you cannot see yourself
    So well as by reflection, I, your glass°
    Will modestly discover to yourself

70   That of yourself which you yet know not of.
    And be not jealous on° me, gentle Brutus:
    Were I a common laughter,° or did use
    To stale with ordinary oaths my love
    To every new protester,° if you know

75   That I do fawn on men and hug them hard,

---

35. Cassius is comparing Brutus's treatment of him with the way a trainer treats a horse.

39. Merely: wholly.

40. passions of some difference: conflicting feelings or emotions.

42. give some soil: stain or mar.

45. construe: interpret.

47. *How does Brutus explain his behavior?*

48. passion: feeling.

50. worthy cogitations: reflections of great value.

54. just: true.

58. shadow: reflection (of what others think of him).
59. respect: reputation.
60. *How would Cassius say the parenthetical remark?*

68. glass: mirror.

71. jealous on: suspicious of.

72. common laughter: butt of a joke, object of mockery.

74. In other words, if he swore to love everyone who came along.

And after scandal° them; or if you know
That I profess myself in banqueting
To all the rout,° then hold me dangerous.

[*Flourish*° *and shout.*]

Brutus.
    What means this shouting? I do fear the people
    Choose Caesar for their king.

80   **Cassius.**   Ay, do you fear it?
    Then must I think you would not have it so.

Brutus.
    I would not, Cassius, yet I love him well.
    But wherefore do you hold me here so long?
    What is it that you would impart to me?

85   If it be aught toward the general good,
    Set honor in one eye and death i' th' other,
    And I will look on both indifferently;°
    For let the gods so speed me, as I love
    The name of honor more than I fear death.

Cassius.

90   I know that virtue to be in you, Brutus,
    As well as I do know your outward favor.°
    Well, honor is the subject of my story.
    I cannot tell what you and other men
    Think of this life, but for my single self,

95   I had as lief° not be, as live to be
    In awe of such a thing as I myself.
    I was born free as Caesar; so were you:
    We both have fed as well, and we can both
    Endure the winter's cold as well as he:

100   For once, upon a raw and gusty day,
    The troubled Tiber chafing with° her shores,
    Caesar said to me "Dar'st thou, Cassius, now
    Leap in with me into this angry flood,
    And swim to yonder point?" Upon the word,

105   Accout'red as I was, I plungèd in
    And bade him follow: so indeed he did.
    The torrent roared, and we did buffet it
    With lusty sinews, throwing it aside
    And stemming it with hearts of controversy.°

110   But ere we could arrive the point proposed,
    Caesar cried "Help me, Cassius, or I sink!"
    I, as Aeneas,° our great ancestor,
    Did from the flames of Troy upon his shoulder
    The old Anchises bear, so from the waves of Tiber

115   Did I the tired Caesar. And this man
    Is now become a god, and Cassius is
    A wretched creature, and must bend his body

---

76. scandal: ruin them by gossip.

78. rout: common people, the mob.

78. *What, in sum, is Cassius telling Brutus here?*

Flourish: flourish of trumpets.

Stage direction. *The trumpet sounds offstage, and the crowd's roar is heard again. How would Cassius and Brutus react?*

81. *This is what Cassius has wanted to hear. How should he deliver this speech?*

87. indifferently: impartially, fairly.

89. *Brutus could sound noble here, or he could be played as foolishly idealistic, even priggish. How would you deliver this speech?*

91. outward favor: appearance.

95. as lief: just as soon.

97. *This is a long and important speech. What is Cassius's chief complaint about Caesar?*

101. chafing with: raging against (the river was rough with waves and currents).

109. hearts of controversy: hearts full of aggressive feelings, or fighting spirit.

112. Aeneas (i·nē′əs): legendary forefather of the Roman people who, in Virgil's *Aeneid,* fled from the burning city of Troy carrying his old father on his back. (In many accounts of the legend, Romulus and Remus were descendants of Aeneas. See note, line 67, page 633.)

If Caesar carelessly but nod on him.
He had a fever when he was in Spain,
120   And when the fit was on him, I did mark
How he did shake; 'tis true, this god did shake.
His coward lips did from their color fly,
And that same eye whose bend doth awe the world
Did lose his luster; I did hear him groan;
125   Ay, and that tongue of his, that bade the Romans
Mark him and write his speeches in their books,
Alas, it cried, "Give me some drink, Titinius,"
As a sick girl. Ye gods! It doth amaze me,
A man of such a feeble temper should
130   So get the start of the majestic world,
And bear the palm° alone.

[Shout. Flourish.]

Brutus.

Another general shout?
I do believe that these applauses are
For some new honors that are heaped on Caesar.

Cassius.

135   Why, man, he doth bestride the narrow world
Like a Colossus,° and we petty men
Walk under his huge legs and peep about
To find ourselves dishonorable graves.
Men at some time are masters of their fates:
140   The fault, dear Brutus, is not in our stars,°
But in ourselves, that we are underlings.
Brutus and Caesar: what should be in that "Caesar"?
Why should that name be sounded more than yours?
Write them together, yours is as fair a name;
145   Sound them, it doth become the mouth as well;
Weigh them, it is as heavy; conjure with 'em,
"Brutus" will start a spirit as soon as "Caesar."
Now, in the names of all the gods at once,
Upon what meat doth this our Caesar feed,
150   That he is grown so great? Age, thou art shamed!
Rome, thou hast lost the breed of noble bloods!
When went there by an age, since the great flood,°
But it was famed with more than with one man?
When could they say (till now) that talked of Rome,
155   That her wide walks encompassed but one man?
Now is it Rome indeed, and room° enough,
When there is in it but one only man.
O, you and I have heard our fathers say,
There was a Brutus once that would have brooked°
160   Th' eternal devil to keep his state in Rome
As easily as a king.°

118. *How should Cassius say this last sentence?*

121. *What word should be stressed here?*

131. **bear the palm:** hold the palm branch, an award given to a victorious general.
131. *Why has Cassius told these anecdotes about Caesar? What is his point?*

136. **Colossus:** a huge statue of Apollo (as large as the Statue of Liberty) that was said to straddle the entrance to the harbor at Rhodes, an island in the Aegean Sea. The statue, so huge that ships passed under its legs, was one of the Seven Wonders of the Ancient World. It was destroyed by an earthquake in 224 B.C.
140. **stars:** Elizabethans, like modern astrologers, believed that one's life was governed by the stars or constellation one was born under.
142. *There is often a pause here, after the famous Colossus metaphor. How would Cassius say the names "Brutus" and "Caesar"?*

152. **the great flood:** the flood sent by Zeus to drown all the wicked people on Earth. Only the faithful couple Deucalion and Pyrrha were saved.
156. **Rome . . . room:** a pun; both words were pronounced *rōōm* in Shakespeare's day.
159. **brooked:** put up with.
161. This refers to an ancestor of Brutus who, in the sixth century B.C., helped to expel the last king from Rome and set up the Republic.
161. *Why does Cassius mention Brutus's famous ancestor?*

Brutus.
    That you do love me, I am nothing jealous;
    What you would work me to, I have some aim;°
    How I have thought of this, and of these times,
165   I shall recount hereafter. For this present,
    I would not so (with love I might entreat you)
    Be any further moved. What you have said
    I will consider; what you have to say
    I will with patience hear, and find a time
170   Both meet° to hear and answer such high things.
    Till then, my noble friend, chew upon this:
    Brutus had rather be a villager
    Than to repute himself a son of Rome
    Under these hard conditions as this time
    Is like to lay upon us.
175 **Cassius.**   I am glad
    That my weak words have struck but thus much show
    Of fire from Brutus.

    [*Enter* CAESAR *and his* TRAIN.]

Brutus.
    The games are done, and Caesar is returning.
Cassius.
    As they pass by, pluck Casca by the sleeve,
180   And he will (after his sour fashion) tell you
    What hath proceeded worthy note today.
Brutus.
    I will do so. But look you, Cassius,
    The angry spot doth glow on Caesar's brow,
    And all the rest look like a chidden° train:
185   Calphurnia's cheek is pale, and Cicero
    Looks with such ferret° and such fiery eyes
    As we have seen him in the Capitol,
    Being crossed in conference by some senators.
Cassius.
    Casca will tell us what the matter is.
190 **Caesar.** Antonius.
Antony. Caesar?
Caesar.
    Let me have men about me that are fat,
    Sleek-headed men, and such as sleep a-nights.
    Yond Cassius has a lean and hungry look;
195   He thinks too much: such men are dangerous.
Antony.
    Fear him not, Caesar, he's not dangerous;
    He is a noble Roman, and well given.°
Caesar.
    Would he were fatter! But I fear him not.

163. aim: idea.

170. meet: appropriate.

177. *According to Cassius's speech, how has Brutus delivered his previous line? Has Cassius gotten what he wants?*
Stage direction. *Cassius and Brutus move downstage left to allow the procession to pass across the width of the backstage area to an entrance down right. In this way, the audience sees two acting areas at one time—one for the conspirators and their growing intimacy, and one for the pompous world of public ceremony. Would the two actors next speak openly, or are they already acting secretive?*

184. chidden: rebuked, corrected.

186. ferret: a weasel-like animal, usually considered crafty.

188. *Cicero at this time is sixty-two years old, famous as a great advocate of the Republic. (Though he had supported Pompey and opposed Caesar, Cicero liked Caesar personally and had nothing to do with the assassination. What does Brutus think of Cicero?*
190. *Cassius and Brutus move away and we focus on Caesar, who casts a suspicious look at Cassius, who is now downstage left. What does Caesar's next speech tell you about Cassius's physical appearance?*

197. well given: well disposed to support Caesar.

Yet if my name were liable to fear,
200   I do not know the man I should avoid
So soon as that spare Cassius. He reads much,
He is a great observer, and he looks
Quite through the deeds of men.° He loves no plays,
As thou dost, Antony; he hears no music;
205   Seldom he smiles, and smiles in such a sort°
As if he mocked himself, and scorned his spirit
That could be moved to smile at anything.
Such men as he be never at heart's ease
Whiles they behold a greater than themselves,
210   And therefore are they very dangerous.
I rather tell thee what is to be feared
Than what I fear; for always I am Caesar.
Come on my right hand, for this ear is deaf,
And tell me truly what thou think'st of him.

[*Sennet. Exeunt* CAESAR *and his* TRAIN.]

215   **Casca.**
You pulled me by the cloak; would you speak with me?
Brutus.
Ay, Casca; tell us what hath chanced today,
That Caesar looks so sad.°
Casca.
Why, you were with him, were you not?
Brutus.
I should not then ask Casca what had chanced.
220   **Casca.** Why, there was a crown offered him; and being
offered him, he put it by° with the back of his hand,
thus; and then the people fell a-shouting.
Brutus. What was the second noise for?
Casca. Why, for that too.
Cassius.
225   They shouted thrice; what was the last cry for?
Casca. Why, for that too.
Brutus. Was the crown offered him thrice?
Casca. Ay, marry,° was't, and he put it by thrice, every
time gentler than other; and at every putting-by mine
230   honest neighbors shouted.
Cassius.
Who offered him the crown?
Casca. Why, Antony.
Brutus.
Tell us the manner of it, gentle Casca.
Casca. I can as well be hanged as tell the manner of it:
235   it was mere foolery; I did not mark it. I saw Mark
Antony offer him a crown—yet 'twas not a crown
neither, 'twas one of these coronets°—and, as I told

203. In other words, he looks through
what men *do* to search out their hidden
feelings and motives.
205. sort: manner.

213. *Caesar's analysis of Cassius is
very accurate. Why does he fear Cassius? What does the speech tell us about
Caesar himself?*
Stage direction. *As the procession
leaves through an upstage portal at left,
Brutus pulls on the toga of Casca as he
passes. Casca is rough and sarcastic. How
is his sarcasm suggested in the following
lines?*

217. sad: serious.

221. put it by: pushed it aside.

228. marry: a mild oath meaning "By the
Virgin Mary."

233. *How would Brutus respond to this
news about the crown?*

237. coronets: small crowns.

you, he put it by once; but for all that, to my thinking,
he would fain° have had it. Then he offered it to him
again; then he put it by again; but to my thinking, he
was very loath to lay his fingers off it. And then he
offered it the third time. He put it the third time by;
and still as he refused it, the rabblement hooted, and
clapped their chopt° hands, and threw up their sweaty
nightcaps,° and uttered such a deal of stinking breath
because Caesar refused the crown, that it had, almost,
choked Caesar; for he swounded° and fell down at it.
And for mine own part, I durst not laugh, for fear of
opening my lips and receiving the bad air.

Cassius.
But, soft,° I pray you; what, did Caesar swound?

Casca. He fell down in the market place, and foamed at
mouth, and was speechless.

Brutus.
'Tis very like he hath the falling-sickness.°

Cassius.
No, Caesar hath it not; but you, and I,
And honest Casca, we have the falling-sickness.

Casca. I know not what you mean by that, but I am sure
Caesar fell down. If the tag-rag people° did not clap
him and hiss him, according as he pleased and dis-
pleased them, as they use to do the players in the
theater, I am no true man.

Brutus.
What said he when he came unto himself?

Casca. Marry, before he fell down, when he perceived
the common herd was glad he refused the crown, he
plucked me ope° his doublet° and offered them his
throat to cut. An I had been a man of any occupation,°
if I would not have taken him at a word, I would I
might go to hell among the rogues. And so he fell.
When he came to himself again, he said, if he had done
or said anything amiss, he desired their worships to
think it was his infirmity. Three or four wenches,°
where I stood, cried "Alas, good soul!" and forgave
him with all their hearts; but there's no heed to be
taken of them; if Caesar had stabbed their mothers,
they would have done no less.

Brutus.
And after that, he came thus sad away?

Casca. Ay.

Cassius.
Did Cicero say anything?

Casca. Ay, he spoke Greek.

Cassius. To what effect?

240

245

250

255

260

265

270

275

239. fain: happily.

244. chopt: chapped (raw and rough from hard work and the weather).
245. nightcaps: Casca is mockingly refer-ring to the hats of the workingmen.
247. swounded: swooned or fainted (in an epileptic seizure).

? 249. *How does Casca feel about the Ro-man mob?*

250. soft: wait a minute.

253. falling-sickness: an old term for the disease we now call epilepsy.

? 255. *What do you think Cassius means here?*

257. tag-rag: a contemptuous reference to the commoners in the mob, the riff-raff.

264. plucked me ope: plucked open. (*Plucked me* was a colloquialism for *plucked*.) **doublet:** a close-fitting jacket (actually an Elizabethan form of dress).
265. man of any occupation: a working-man.

270. wenches: girls.

? 274. *Casca gets very sarcastic here. What does he think of Caesar?*

280 **Casca.** Nay, an° I tell you that, I'll ne'er look you i' th' face again. But those that understood him smiled at one another and shook their heads; but for mine own part, it was Greek to me. I could tell you more news too: Marullus and Flavius, for pulling scarfs off Cae-

285 sar's images, are put to silence.° Fare you well. There was more foolery yet, if I could remember it.

Cassius. Will you sup with me tonight, Casca?

Casca. No, I am promised forth.°

Cassius. Will you dine with me tomorrow?

290 **Casca.** Ay, if I be alive, and your mind hold, and your dinner worth the eating.

Cassius. Good; I will expect you.

Casca. Do so. Farewell, both.   [*Exit.*]

Brutus.

What a blunt fellow is this grown to be!

295 He was quick mettle° when he went to school.

Cassius.

So is he now in execution
Of any bold or noble enterprise,
However he puts on this tardy form.°
This rudeness° is a sauce to his good wit,°

300 Which gives men stomach to disgest° his words
With better appetite.

Brutus.

And so it is. For this time I will leave you.
Tomorrow, if you please to speak with me,
I will come home to you; or if you will,

305 Come home to me, and I will wait for you.

Cassius.

I will do so. Till then, think of the world.°

             [*Exit* BRUTUS.]

Well, Brutus, thou art noble; yet I see
Thy honorable mettle may be wrought
From that it is disposed;° therefore it is meet

310 That noble minds keep ever with their likes;
For who so firm that cannot be seduced?
Caesar doth bear me hard,° but he loves Brutus.
If I were Brutus now and he were Cassius,
He should not humor° me. I will this night,

315 In several hands,° in at his windows throw,
As if they came from several citizens,
Writings, all tending to the great opinion
That Rome holds of his name; wherein obscurely
Caesar's ambition shall be glancèd at.°

320 And after this, let Caesar seat him sure;°
For we will shake him, or worse days endure. [*Exit.*]

280. an: if.

285. put to silence: silenced, perhaps by losing their positions as tribunes or by being exiled.
286. *Why are Marullus and Flavius silenced? What does this tell you about Caesar?*
288. forth: previously (he has other plans).

295. quick mettle: lively of disposition.

298. tardy form: sluggish appearance.
299. rudeness: rough manner. **wit:** intelligence.
300. disgest: digest.

306. the world: the state of affairs in Rome.

307. *Why do you think Cassius uses the respectful* you *when talking to Brutus but then switches to the familiar* thou *here?*
309. In other words, he may be persuaded against his better nature to join the conspirators.

312. bear me hard: has a grudge (hard feelings) against me.

314. humor: influence by flattery.

315. hands: forms of handwriting.

319. glancèd at: touched on.
320. seat him sure: make his position secure.
321. *What is Cassius going to write in the letters to Brutus? What does he hope these letters will accomplish?*

Scene 3. *A street.*

Thunder and lightning. Enter from opposite sides
CASCA *and* CICERO.

Cicero.
    Good even, Casca; brought you Caesar home?
    Why are you breathless? And why stare you so?

Casca.
    Are not you moved, when all the sway of earth°
    Shakes like a thing unfirm? O Cicero,
5   I have seen tempests,° when the scolding winds
    Have rived° the knotty oaks, and I have seen
    Th' ambitious ocean swell and rage and foam,
    To be exalted with° the threat'ning clouds;
    But never till tonight, never till now,
10   Did I go through a tempest dropping fire.
    Either there is a civil strife in heaven,
    Or else the world, too saucy° with the gods,
    Incenses them to send destruction.

Cicero.
    Why, saw you anything more wonderful?

Casca.
15   A common slave—you know him well by sight—
    Held up his left hand, which did flame and burn
    Like twenty torches joined, and yet his hand,
    Not sensible of° fire, remained unscorched.
    Besides—I ha' not since put up my sword—
20   Against° the Capitol I met a lion,
    Who glazed° upon me and went surly by
    Without annoying me. And there were drawn
    Upon a heap a hundred ghastly° women,
    Transformèd with their fear, who swore they saw
25   Men, all in fire, walk up and down the streets.
    And yesterday the bird of night° did sit
    Even at noonday upon the market place,
    Hooting and shrieking. When these prodigies°
    Do so conjointly meet, let not men say,
30   "These are their reasons, they are natural,"
    For I believe they are portentous° things
    Unto the climate° that they point upon.

Cicero.
    Indeed, it is a strange-disposèd time:
    But men may construe things after their fashion,
35   Clean from the purpose° of the things themselves.
    Comes Caesar to the Capitol tomorrow?

Casca.
    He doth; for he did bid Antonius
    Send word to you he would be there tomorrow.

? **Stage direction.** *In Shakespeare's day, other than a drum roll or "thunder sheet," there was no way to reproduce the drama of nature onstage. How might the actors themselves suggest the threatening weather?*

3. all the sway of earth: all the principles that govern the earth.

5. tempests: storms.

6. rived: split.

8. exalted with: elevated to.

12. saucy: disrespectful, presumptuous.

? **13.** *How is Casca different here from the way he was depicted earlier?*

18. not sensible of: not sensitive to.

20. Against: opposite or near.

21. glazed: stared.

23. ghastly: ghostly, pale.

26. bird of night: the owl (believed to be a bad omen).

28. prodigies: wonders.

31. portentous: ominous.

32. climate: region or place.

? **32.** *Shakespeare often uses disorder in nature to suggest a nation's disorder. What does Casca think?*

35. clean from the purpose: contrary to what they really do mean.

? **35.** *How does the aged Cicero respond to Casca's report?*

Cicero.
    Good night then, Casca; this disturbèd sky
    Is not to walk in.
40 **Casca.**   Farewell, Cicero.   [*Exit* CICERO.]

[*Enter* CASSIUS.]

Cassius.
    Who's there?
Casca.   A Roman.
Cassius.   Casca, by your voice.
Casca.
    Your ear is good. Cassius, what night is this?
Cassius.
    A very pleasing night to honest men.
Casca.
    Who ever knew the heavens menace so?
Cassius.
45   Those that have known the earth so full of faults.
    For my part, I have walked about the streets,
    Submitting me unto the perilous night,
    And thus unbracèd,° Casca, as you see,
    Have bared my bosom to the thunder-stone,
50   And when the cross° blue lightning seemed to open
    The breast of heaven, I did present myself
    Even in the aim and very flash of it.
Casca.
    But wherefore did you so much tempt the heavens?
    It is the part° of men to fear and tremble
55   When the most mighty gods by tokens° send
    Such dreadful heralds to astonish us.
Cassius.
    You are dull, Casca, and those sparks of life
    That should be in a Roman you do want,°
    Or else you use not. You look pale, and gaze,
60   And put on fear, and cast yourself in wonder,
    To see the strange impatience of the heavens;
    But if you would consider the true cause
    Why all these fires, why all these gliding ghosts,
    Why birds and beasts from quality and kind,°
65   Why old men, fools, and children calculate,°
    Why all these things change from their ordinance,°
    Their natures and preformèd faculties,°
    To monstrous quality,° why, you shall find
    That heaven hath infused them with these spirits°
70   To make them instruments of fear and warning
    Unto some monstrous state.
    Now could I, Casca, name to thee a man
    Most like this dreadful night,

43. *Can you explain Cassius's response to the disordered night?*

48. unbracèd: with his jacket unfastened.

50. cross: jagged.

54. part: role.
55. tokens: signs.

58. want: lack.

64. from quality and kind: act against their natures.
65. calculate: prophesy or try to predict the future.
66. ordinance: natural behavior.
67. preformèd faculties: natural or normal qualities.
68. monstrous quality: unnatural condition.
69. spirits: supernatural powers.

72. *How might Cassius's tone of voice change here?*

75

That thunders, lightens, opens graves, and roars
As doth the lion in the Capitol;
A man no mightier than thyself, or me,
In personal action, yet prodigious° grown
And fearful, as these strange eruptions are.

Casca.
'Tis Caesar that you mean, is it not, Cassius?

Cassius.

80

Let it be who it is; for Romans now
Have thews° and limbs like to their ancestors;
But, woe the while!° Our fathers' minds are dead,
And we are governed with our mothers' spirits;
Our yoke and sufferance° show us womanish.

Casca.

85

Indeed, they say the senators tomorrow
Mean to establish Caesar as a king;
And he shall wear his crown by sea and land,
In every place save here in Italy.

Cassius.

90

I know where I will wear this dagger then;
Cassius from bondage will deliver Cassius.
Therein,° ye gods, you make the weak most strong;
Therein, ye gods, you tyrants do defeat.
Nor stony tower, nor walls of beaten brass,
Nor airless dungeon, nor strong links of iron,

95

Can be retentive to° the strength of spirit;
But life, being weary of these worldly bars,
Never lacks power to dismiss itself.
If I know this, know all the world besides,
That part of tyranny that I do bear
I can shake off at pleasure.   [*Thunder still.*°]

100

Casca.   So can I;
So every bondman in his own hand bears
The power to cancel his captivity.

Cassius.
And why should Caesar be a tyrant then?
Poor man, I know he would not be a wolf

105

But that he sees the Romans are but sheep;
He were no lion, were not Romans hinds.°
Those that with haste will make a mighty fire
Begin it with weak straws. What trash is Rome,
What rubbish and what offal,° when it serves

110

For the base matter to illuminate
So vile a thing as Caesar! But, O grief,
Where hast thou led me? I, perhaps, speak this
Before a willing bondman; then I know
My answer must be made.° But I am armed,

115

And dangers are to me indifferent.

77. **prodigious:** monstrous.

81. **thews:** sinews or muscles.
82. **woe the while!:** too bad for our times!

84. **Our yoke and sufferance:** our burden and our timid acceptance of it.

? 89. *Cassius's response to this news is usually one of anger. What is he probably holding in his hand?*
91. **Therein:** in other words, in the act of suicide.

95. **be retentive to:** restrain.

100. **still:** continues.
? 100. *What is Cassius threatening to do?*

106. **hinds:** female deer. (The word also means peasants and servants.)

109. **offal:** garbage, especially the parts of a butchered animal that are considered inedible or rotten.

114. **My answer must be made:** I must later answer for my words.
? 115. *Does Cassius seriously mean that Casca is a willing slave of Caesar's? What reaction is he looking for?*

Casca.

You speak to Casca, and to such a man
That is no fleering° tell-tale. Hold, my hand.
Be factious° for redress of all these griefs,
And I will set this foot of mine as far
As who goes farthest.   [*They clasp hands.*]

120 **Cassius.**   There's a bargain made.
Now know you, Casca, I have moved already
Some certain of the noblest-minded Romans
To undergo with me an enterprise
Of honorable dangerous consequence;

125 And I do know, by this° they stay for me
In Pompey's porch,° for now, this fearful night,
There is no stir or walking in the streets,
And the complexion of the element°
In favor's like° the work we have in hand,

130 Most bloody, fiery, and most terrible.

[*Enter* CINNA.]

Casca.

Stand close° awhile, for here comes one in haste.
Cassius.
'Tis Cinna; I do know him by his gait;
He is a friend. Cinna, where haste you so?
Cinna.
To find out you. Who's that? Metellus Cimber?
Cassius.

135 No, it is Casca, one incorporate
To° our attempts. Am I not stayed for,° Cinna?
Cinna.
I am glad on't. What a fearful night is this!
There's two or three of us have seen strange sights.
Cassius.
Am I not stayed for? Tell me.
Cinna.   Yes, you are.

140 O Cassius, if you could
But win the noble Brutus to our party—
Cassius.
Be you content. Good Cinna, take this paper,
And look you lay it in the praetor's chair,°
Where Brutus may but find it; and throw this

145 In at his window; set this up with wax
Upon old Brutus' statue.° All this done,
Repair° to Pompey's porch, where you shall find us.
Is Decius° Brutus and Trebonius there?
Cinna.
All but Metellus Cimber, and he's gone

---

117. fleering: flattering.
118. Be factious: Go ahead and organize a faction opposed to Caesar.

125. by this: by this time.
126. Pompey's porch: the entrance to a theater built by Pompey.
128. complexion of the element: appearance of the sky.
129. in favor's like: in appearance is like.
130. *Cassius has begun his conversation with Casca by showing him his dagger and threatening suicide as a way to free himself from bondage. At what point does the conversation shift to an altogether different method of freeing himself?*

131. close: hidden.

136. incorporate to: bound up with.
stayed for: waited for.

139. *What is Cassius's mood?*

143. praetor's chair: chief magistrate's chair; Brutus's chair.

146. old Brutus' statue: the statue of Brutus's heroic ancestor.
147. Repair: go.
148. Decius: Decimus, a relative of Brutus.
148. *What is Cassius asking Cinna to do?*

150 To seek you at your house. Well, I will hie,°
And so bestow these papers as you bade me.
Cassius.
    That done, repair to Pompey's Theater. [*Exit* CINNA.]
    Come, Casca, you and I will yet ere day
    See Brutus at his house; three parts of him
155 Is ours already, and the man entire
    Upon the next encounter yields him ours.
Casca.
    O, he sits high in all the people's hearts;
    And that which would appear offense in us,
    His countenance,° like richest alchemy,°
160 Will change to virtue and to worthiness.
Cassius.
    Him, and his worth, and our great need of him,
    You have right well conceited.° Let us go,
    For it is after midnight, and ere day
    We will awake him and be sure of him.   [*Exeunt.*]

150. hie: hurry.

159. countenance: support; demeanor. **alchemy:** the science that was supposed to change ordinary metals into gold.

162. conceited: Cassius is punning here. The word means both "understood" and "described in an elaborate figure of speech" (called a *conceit*).

Responding to the Play

Analyzing Act I

Identifying Facts

1. Explain why the workingmen are celebrating in the first scene. Why does Marullus reproach them?
2. What is the **setting** of Scene 2? What warning does the soothsayer give Caesar, and what is Caesar's response?
3. Explain what Cassius wants to convince Brutus of in Scene 2.
4. Why does Caesar, in Scene 2, think Cassius is dangerous? What qualities disturb him?
5. Describe what happens when Caesar is offered the crown, according to Casca in Scene 2.
6. Caesar stands astride the world as a powerful ruler, yet he suffers many personal weaknesses. Various characters tell us what these are, and they say that a man who is as human as anyone else should not act like a god and rule the world. What exactly are Caesar's infirmities and weaknesses?

7. At the end of Scene 2, how does Cassius say he will pursue his plan to involve Brutus in the conspiracy against Caesar?

Interpreting Meanings

8. Believing that nature mirrors the disorders in human lives, Shakespeare heightens the atmosphere of terror as the conspirators gather to discuss their plans. What details in Scene 3 do you think evoke this sense of danger and terror?
9. Who is the moving force, the **protagonist** who drives the action, in Act I? By the act's end, what steps has he taken to achieve his goal?
10. How would you describe the play's **conflict** as it is established in Act I?
11. Shakespeare uses even minor characters in this act to set up the basic situation of the play and to **foreshadow** future conflicts and events. Explain what you learn from this act about the moods and loyalties of the Roman mob. Do you think it is like any other large group of people?

Costume sketch of the soothsayer by Tanya Moiseiwitsch for a 1955 production by the Stratford Shakespearean Festival in Ontario.

The Stratford Shakespearean Festival Foundation of Canada.

12. A healthy republic requires a reasonably intelligent and responsive citizenry. Throughout this play, the people of Rome are described as "trash" or worse. Point out passages in Act I where various nobles express their contempt for the common people. How does this make you feel about these **characters**? Do the people seem to deserve a republic?

13. Cassius tells Brutus several anecdotes about Caesar in Scene 2. What is Cassius implying through these stories? What do you think of the techniques Cassius uses to persuade Brutus to turn against Caesar? Do you see any serious flaws in his reasoning?

14. Do you have conflicting feelings about Caesar during this act? Describe your impressions of his **character,** based on what you observe of his speeches and actions and on what other characters say about him.

15. Do any events or characters in this act remind you of people involved in politics today? Is Caesar's attitude (as interpreted by Cassius) displayed by any contemporary rulers? Do you know of any contemporary Cassiuses?

Analyzing Language and Vocabulary

Puns

Although some people groan when they hear puns and complain that puns are a "low" form of humor, Shakespeare's audiences thoroughly enjoyed them. A **pun** is a word or phrase that is used to mean two different things at the same time (as in the joke "What is black and white and red all over? Answer: A newspaper").

In the very first scene of *Julius Caesar*, the sparring between the commoners and the tribunes is lively because the cobbler won't be stifled from making puns. When he says he is a "cobbler," he plays on two different meanings of the same word. In Shakespeare's day the word could mean both "shoemaker" and "bungler" or "incompetent." When Marullus questions him further, the jokester puns on the meaning of "soles." "Soles" could refer to parts of a shoe; but the word also sounds exactly the same as "souls."

As the examples show, some puns depend for their effect on the contrast between two quite different meanings of a single word (cobbler/cobbler). Other puns involve **homophones**, or words that sound exactly alike but are spelled differently and have different meanings (sole/soul).

By their very nature, puns always carry a measure of **verbal irony**, since they depend on unexpected contrasts. Many of Shakespeare's puns are humorous and lightly ironic, but some of his characters, especially Cassius in *Julius Caesar,* use puns with darker ironic effect.

Using the side notes in the play and a good dictionary, discuss in class the puns, or plays on words, in the following phrases from Act I. Read the phrase in context first. The key word or words in the pun are italicized.

1. ". . . *all* that I live by is with the *awl.* . . ." (Scene 1, line 21)
2. ". . . when they [old shoes] are in great danger, I *recover* them." (Scene 1, line 24)
3. "See, whe'r their *basest mettle* be not moved . . . " (Scene 1, line 61)
4. "His coward lips did *from their color fly.* . . ." (Scene 2, line 122)
5. "No, Caesar hath it not; but you, and I, / And honest Casca, we have the *falling-sickness*." (Scene 2, lines 255-256)
6. "He [Caesar] were no lion, were not Romans *hinds*." (Scene 3, line 106)

Act II Scene 1. *Rome.*

Enter BRUTUS *in his orchard.*

Brutus.

    What, Lucius, ho!

    I cannot, by the progress of the stars,

    Give guess how near to day. Lucius, I say!

    I would it were my fault to sleep so soundly.

5   When, Lucius, When? Awake, I say! What, Lucius!

[*Enter* LUCIUS.]

Lucius. Called you, my lord?

Brutus.

    Get me a taper° in my study, Lucius.

    When it is lighted, come and call me here.

Lucius. I will, my lord.   [*Exit.*]

Brutus.

10   It must be by his death; and for my part,

    I know no personal cause to spurn at° him,

    But for the general.° He would be crowned.

    How that might change his nature, there's the question.

    It is the bright day that brings forth the adder,

15   And that craves° wary walking. Crown him that,

    And then I grant we put a sting in him

    That at his will he may do danger with.

    Th' abuse of greatness is when it disjoins

    Remorse° from power; and, to speak truth of Caesar,

20   I have not known when his affections swayed°

    More than his reason. But 'tis a common proof°

    That lowliness° is young ambition's ladder,

    Whereto the climber upward turns his face;

    But when he once attains the upmost round,

25   He then unto the ladder turns his back,

    Looks in the clouds, scorning the base degrees°

    By which he did ascend. So Caesar may;

    Then lest he may, prevent.° And, since the quarrel°

    Will bear no color° for the thing he is,

30   Fashion it thus:° that what he is, augmented,

    Would run to these and these extremities;

    And therefore think him as a serpent's egg

    Which hatched, would as his kind grow mischievous,

    And kill him in the shell.

[*Enter* LUCIUS.]

Lucius.

35   The taper burneth in your closet,° sir.

    Searching the window for a flint, I found

Stage direction. *Brutus's garden often has a set of steps in the back, set in a half-circle. Below the steps is a stone bench. On the right and left are the doorways of an impressive residence. The door to the left is the servants' entrance, where Brutus directs his call to Lucius.* Why is Brutus so anxious about the time?

7. **taper:** candle.

10. *Whom is Brutus talking about in this soliloquy?*
11. **spurn at:** rebel against.
12. **the general:** the general good.

15. **craves:** demands.

19. **remorse:** compassion.
20. **affections swayed:** emotions ruled.
21. **common proof:** matter of common experience.
22. **lowliness:** humility.

26. **base degrees:** low rungs of the ladder. Also, the lower offices he once held, and the lower classes of people.
28. **prevent:** we must prevent it. **quarrel:** argument.
29. **bear no color:** bear no weight.
30. **Fashion it thus:** state the case this way.

34. *According to Brutus, who is like a serpent's egg, and why?*

35. **closet:** a small private room; a study.

This paper thus sealed up, and I am sure
It did not lie there when I went to bed.

[*Gives him the letter.*]

Brutus.

Get you to bed again; it is not day.

40 Is not tomorrow, boy, the ides of March?

Lucius. I know not, sir.

Brutus.

Look in the calendar and bring me word.

Lucius. I will, sir.   [*Exit.*]

Brutus.

The exhalations° whizzing in the air

45 Give so much light that I may read by them.

[*Opens the letter and reads.*]

"Brutus, thou sleep'st; awake, and see thyself.
Shall Rome, &c. Speak, strike, redress.°
Brutus, thou sleep'st; awake."
Such instigations have been often dropped

50 Where I have took them up.
"Shall Rome, &c." Thus must I piece it out:
Shall Rome stand under one man's awe? What, Rome?
My ancestors did from the streets of Rome
The Tarquin° drive, when he was called a king.

55 "Speak, strike, redress." Am I entreated
To speak and strike? O Rome, I make thee promise,
If the redress will follow, thou receivest
Thy full petition at the hand of Brutus!

[*Enter* LUCIUS.]

Lucius.

Sir, March is wasted fifteen days.

[*Knock within.*]

Brutus.

60 'Tis good. Go to the gate; somebody knocks.

[*Exit* LUCIUS.]

Since Cassius first did whet me against Caesar,
I have not slept.
Between the acting of a dreadful thing
And the first motion, all the interim is

65 Like a phantasma,° or a hideous dream.
The genius and the mortal instruments°
Are then in council, and the state of a man,
Like to a little kingdom, suffers then
The nature of an insurrection.

[*Enter* LUCIUS.]

Stage direction. *Whose letter is this?*

40. *Does Brutus know of the soothsayer's warning?*

44. **exhalations:** meteors.

47. **redress:** correct a wrong.

54. **Tarquin:** the last king of Rome, Tarquinius Superbus. See note, line 161, page 638.

58. *What actions might Brutus engage in as he reads this message? What is his tone of voice at the end?*

65. **phantasma:** apparition, hallucination.

66. **the genius and the mortal instruments:** the mind (genius) and the emotions and physical powers of the body.

Lucius.

70   Sir, 'tis your brother° Cassius at the door,
        Who doth desire to see you.

Brutus.   Is he alone?

Lucius.

        No, sir, there are moe° with him.

Brutus.   Do you know them?

Lucius.

        No, sir; their hats are plucked about their ears,
        And half their faces buried in their cloaks,

75   That by no means I may discover them
        By any mark of favor.°

Brutus.   Let 'em enter.   [*Exit* LUCIUS.]
        They are the faction. O conspiracy,
        Sham'st thou to show thy dang'rous brow by night,
        When evils are most free? O, then by day

80   Where wilt thou find a cavern dark enough
        To mask thy monstrous visage? Seek none, conspir-
            acy;
        Hide it in smiles and affability:
        For if thou path, thy native semblance on,°
        Not Erebus° itself were dim enough

85   To hide thee from prevention.

        [*Enter the conspirators,* CASSIUS, CASCA, DECIUS,
        CINNA, METELLUS CIMBER, *and* TREBONIUS.]

Cassius.

        I think we are too bold upon° your rest.
        Good morrow, Brutus; do we trouble you?

Brutus.

        I have been up this hour, awake all night.
        Know I these men that come along with you?

Cassius.

90   Yes, every man of them; and no man here
        But honors you; and every one doth wish
        You had but that opinion of yourself
        Which every noble Roman bears of you.
        This is Trebonius.

Brutus.   He is welcome hither.

Cassius.

        This, Decius Brutus.

95 **Brutus.**   He is welcome too.

Cassius.

        This, Casca; this, Cinna; and this, Metellus Cimber.

Brutus.

        They are all welcome.
        What watchful cares° do interpose themselves
        Betwixt your eyes and night?

---

70. brother: brother-in-law; Cassius is married to Brutus's sister.

72. moe: more.

76. favor: appearance.

83. In other words, if you walk (path) in your true way.
84. Erebus: a region between Earth and Hades, the Underworld.

? **Stage direction.** *Describe what the stage looks like right now. From what is said of them above, how would you imagine the conspirators are dressed?*

86. too bold upon: too bold in intruding on.

98. watchful cares: cares that keep you awake.

"Give me your hands all over, one by one."

100   **Cassius.** Shall I entreat a word?

       [*They whisper.*]

       Decius.

          Here lies the east; doth not the day break here?

       Casca. No.

       Cinna.

          O, pardon, sir, it doth; and yon gray lines

          That fret° the clouds are messengers of day.

       Casca.

105   You shall confess that you are both deceived.

          Here, as I point my sword, the sun arises,

          Which is a great way growing on° the south,

          Weighing the youthful season of the year.

          Some two month hence, up higher toward the north

110   He first presents his fire; and the high east

          Stands as the Capitol, directly here.

       Brutus.

          Give me your hands all over, one by one.

100. *How would you have the actors placed on stage as Brutus and Cassius huddle and the others talk?*

104. fret: interlace.

107. growing on: tending toward.

Cassius.

    And let us swear our resolution.

Brutus.

    No, not an oath. If not the face of men,°

115   The sufferance° of our souls, the time's abuse°

    If these be motives weak, break off betimes,°

    And every man hence to his idle bed.

    So let high-sighted tyranny range on

    Till each man drop by lottery. But if these

120   (As I am sure they do) bear fire enough

    To kindle cowards and to steel with valor

    The melting spirits of women, then, countrymen,

    What need we any spur but our own cause

    To prick° us to redress? What other bond

125   Than secret Romans that have spoke the word,

    And will not palter?° And what other oath

    Than honesty to honesty engaged

    That this shall be, or we will fall for it?

    Swear priests and cowards and men cautelous,°

130   Old feeble carrions° and such suffering souls

    That welcome wrongs; unto bad causes swear

    Such creatures as men doubt; but do not stain

    The even virtue of our enterprise,

    Nor th' insuppressive mettle of our spirits,

135   To think that or our cause or our performance

    Did need an oath; when every drop of blood

    That every Roman bears, and nobly bears,

    Is guilty of a several bastardy°

    If he do break the smallest particle

140   Of any promise that hath passed from him.

Cassius.

    But what of Cicero? Shall we sound him?

    I think he will stand very strong with us.

Casca.

    Let us not leave him out.

Cinna.   No, by no means.

Metellus.

    O, let us have him, for his silver hairs

145   Will purchase us a good opinion,

    And buy men's voices to commend our deeds.

    It shall be said his judgment ruled our hands;

    Our youths and wildness shall no whit appear,

    But all be buried in his gravity.°

Brutus.

150   O, name him not! Let us not break with him,°

    For he will never follow anything

    That other men begin.

Cassius.   Then leave him out.

---

114. If not the face of men: Our honest faces should be enough.

115. sufferance: endurance. **time's abuse:** abuses of the times.

116. betimes: at once.

124. prick: urge.

126. palter: play fast and loose.

129. cautelous: deceitful.

130. carrions: people so old or sick they're almost dead and rotting.

138. of a several bastardy: of several acts that are not truly "Roman."

149. gravity: soberness and stability.

150. break with him: break our news to him, divulge our plan.

152. *Why do they decide not to ask Cicero to join them?*

Casca.

Indeed, he is not fit.

Decius.

Shall no man else be touched but only Caesar?

Cassius.

155   Decius, well urged. I think it is not meet
Mark Antony, so well beloved of Caesar,
Should outlive Caesar; we shall find of° him
A shrewd contriver;° and you know, his means;
If he improve° them, may well stretch so far

160   As to annoy° us all; which to prevent,
Let Antony and Caesar fall together.

Brutus.

Our course will seem too bloody, Caius Cassius,
To cut the head off and then hack the limbs,
Like wrath in death and envy° afterwards;

165   For Antony is but a limb of Caesar.
Let's be sacrificers, but not butchers, Caius.
We all stand up against the spirit of Caesar,
And in the spirit of men there is no blood.
O, that we then could come by Caesar's spirit,

170   And not dismember Caesar! But, alas,
Caesar must bleed for it. And, gentle friends,
Let's kill him boldly, but not wrathfully;
Let's carve him as a dish fit for the gods,
Not hew him as a carcass fit for hounds.

175   And let our hearts, as subtle masters do,
Stir up their servants° to an act of rage,
And after seem to chide 'em. This shall make
Our purpose necessary, and not envious;
Which so appearing to the common eyes,

180   We shall be called purgers,° not murderers.
And for Mark Antony, think not of him;
For he can do no more than Caesar's arm
When Caesar's head is off.

Cassius.   Yet I fear him;
For in the ingrafted° love he bears to Caesar——

Brutus.

185   Alas, good Cassius, do not think of him.
If he love Caesar, all that he can do
Is to himself—take thought° and die for Caesar.
And that were much he should,° for he is given
To sports, to wildness, and much company.

Trebonius.

190   There is no fear in him;° let him not die,
For he will live and laugh at this hereafter.

[*Clock strikes.*]

153. *What kind of person does Casca seem to be?*

157. **of:** in.
158. **shrewd contriver:** a cunning and dangerous schemer.
159. **improve:** make good use of.
160. **annoy:** harm.

164. **envy:** malice.

170. *How should Brutus act when he speaks this sentence?*

176. **servants:** the hands or the emotions.

180. **purgers:** healers.
180. *What does Brutus want the public, or history, to think of him?*

184. **ingrafted:** firmly rooted.

187. **take thought:** take to thinking too much and become depressed.
188. In other words, that is too much to expect of him.

190. **no fear in him:** nothing to fear in him.
191. *What do Brutus, Cassius, and Trebonius think of Antony?*

Brutus.
Peace! Count the clock.

Cassius. The clock hath stricken three.

Trebonius.
'Tis time to part.

Cassius. But it is doubtful yet
Whether Caesar will come forth today or no;
195   For he is superstitious grown of late,
Quite from the main° opinion he held once
Of fantasy, of dreams, and ceremonies.°
It may be these apparent prodigies,°
The unaccustomed terror of this night,
200   And the persuasion of his augurers°
May hold him from the Capitol today.

Decius.
Never fear that. If he be so resolved,
I can o'ersway him; for he loves to hear
That unicorns may be betrayed with trees,
205   And bears with glasses, elephants with holes,
Lions with toils, and men with flatterers;
But when I tell him he hates flatterers,
He says he does, being then most flatterèd.
Let me work;
210   For I can give his humor° the true bent,
And I will bring him to the Capitol.

Cassius.
Nay, we will all of us be there to fetch him.

Brutus.
By the eighth hour; is that the uttermost?°

Cinna.
Be that the uttermost, and fail not then.

Metellus.
215   Caius Ligarius doth bear Caesar hard,
Who rated° him for speaking well of Pompey.
I wonder none of you have thought of him.

Brutus.
Now, good Metellus, go along by him.°
He loves me well, and I have given him reasons;
220   Send him but hither, and I'll fashion him.

Cassius.
The morning comes upon 's; we'll leave you, Brutus.
And, friends, disperse yourselves; but all remember
What you have said, and show yourselves true Romans.

Brutus.
Good gentlemen, look fresh and merrily.
225   Let not our looks put on° our purposes,
But bear it as our Roman actors do,

196. main: strong.
197. ceremonies: ceremonial rituals undertaken to determine the future, usually from examining signs in the entrails of slaughtered animals.
198. prodigies: disasters.
200. augurers: those who foretell the future.

210. humor: mood.

211. *According to Decius, what sort of man is Caesar? (What do you think of people like Decius?)*

213. uttermost: latest.

216. rated: berated, rebuked.

218. him: his house.

221. *How would you use lighting here to suggest the time?*

225. put on: display.

With untired spirits and formal constancy.°
And so good morrow to you every one.

[*Exeunt all except* BRUTUS.]

Boy! Lucius! Fast asleep? It is no matter;
230   Enjoy the honey-heavy dew of slumber.
Thou hast no figures nor no fantasies°
Which busy care draws in the brains of men;
Therefore thou sleep'st so sound.

[*Enter* PORTIA.]

Portia.   Brutus, my lord.
Brutus.
Portia, what mean you? Wherefore rise you now?
235   It is not for your health thus to commit
Your weak condition to the raw cold morning.
Portia.
Nor for yours neither. Y'have ungently, Brutus,
Stole from my bed; and yesternight at supper
You suddenly arose and walked about,
240   Musing and sighing, with your arms across,°
And when I asked you what the matter was,
You stared upon me with ungentle looks.
I urged you further; then you scratched your head,
And too impatiently stamped with your foot.
245   Yet I insisted, yet you answered not,
But with an angry wafter° of your hand
Gave sign for me to leave you. So I did,
Fearing to strengthen that impatience
Which seemed too much enkindled, and withal°
250   Hoping it was but an effect of humor,°
Which sometime hath his hour with every man.
It will not let you eat, nor talk, nor sleep,
And could it work so much upon your shape
As it hath much prevailed on your condition,
255   I should not know you Brutus. Dear my lord,
Make me acquainted with your cause of grief.
Brutus.
I am not well in health, and that is all.
Portia.
Brutus is wise and, were he not in health,
He would embrace the means to come by it.
Brutus.
260   Why, so I do. Good Portia, go to bed.
Portia.
Is Brutus sick, and is it physical°
To walk unbracèd° and suck up the humors°
Of the dank morning? What, is Brutus sick,

---

227. **formal constancy:** consistent good conduct.

231. **figures . . . fantasies:** figments of the imagination.

240. **arms across:** crossed arms, a sign of melancholy or depression in Shakespeare's day.

246. **wafter:** wave.

249. **withal:** also
250. **humor:** moodiness.

? 256. *Where would Portia be standing?*

? 260. *Some directors have Portia come too close to Brutus, physically and emotionally, and have him break away here. What would Portia's actions be?*
261. **physical:** healthy.
262. **unbracèd:** with his jacket opened.
humors: Here the word means dampness (of the air).

And will he steal out of his wholesome bed,
265 To dare the vile contagion of the night,
     And tempt the rheumy and unpurgèd air°
     To add unto his sickness? No, my Brutus;
     You have some sick offense within your mind,
     Which by the right and virtue of my place
270 I ought to know of; and upon my knees
     I charm° you, by my once commended beauty,
     By all your vows of love, and that great vow
     Which did incorporate and make us one,
     That you unfold to me, your self, your half,
275 Why you are heavy,° and what men tonight
     Have had resort to you; for here have been
     Some six or seven, who did hide their faces
     Even from darkness.

Brutus.   Kneel not, gentle Portia.
Portia.
     I should not need, if you were gentle Brutus.
280 Within the bond of marriage, tell me, Brutus,
     Is it exceptèd° I should know no secrets
     That appertain to you? Am I your self
     But, as it were, in sort or limitation,

266. The night was supposed to be unhealthy, since the air was not purified (purged) by the sun.

270. *What clue tells us what Portia does here? Is she becoming calmer or more agitated?*
271. charm: beg.

275. heavy: depressed (heavy-hearted).

278. *What is Brutus doing here?*

281. exceptèd: made an exception that.

"You have some sick offense within your mind."

285
To keep with you at meals, comfort your bed,
And talk to you sometimes? Dwell I but in the suburbs
Of your good pleasure? If it be no more,
Portia is Brutus' harlot, not his wife.

Brutus.
You are my true and honorable wife,
As dear to me as are the ruddy drops
290
That visit my sad heart.

Portia.
If this were true, then should I know this secret.
I grant I am a woman; but withal
A woman that Lord Brutus took to wife.
I grant I am a woman; but withal
295
A woman well reputed, Cato's daughter.°
Think you I am no stronger than my sex,
Being so fathered and so husbanded?
Tell me your counsels, I will not disclose 'em.
I have made strong proof of my constancy,
300
Giving myself a voluntary wound
Here in the thigh; can I bear that with patience,
And not my husband's secrets?

Brutus.   O ye gods,
Render me worthy of this noble wife!

[*Knock.*]

Hark, hark! One knocks. Portia, go in a while,
305
And by and by thy bosom shall partake
The secrets of my heart.
All my engagements I will construe to thee,
All the charactery of my sad brows.°
Leave me with haste.   [*Exit* PORTIA.]

[*Enter* LUCIUS *and* CAIUS LIGARIUS.]

            Lucius, who's that knocks?
Lucius.
310
Here is a sick man that would speak with you.
Brutus.
Caius Ligarius, that Metellus spake of.
Boy, stand aside. Caius Ligarius! How?
Ligarius.
Vouchsafe° good morrow from a feeble tongue.
Brutus.
O, what time have you chose out, brave Caius,
315
To wear a kerchief!° Would you were not sick!
Ligarius.
I am not sick, if Brutus have in hand
Any exploit worthy the name of honor.

295. Cato joined Pompey against Caesar and killed himself at the end to avoid living under the rule of a tyrant. He was a most respected man, famous for his integrity.

[?] 301. *What does Portia suddenly do to prove her patience and faithfulness? How should Brutus respond?*

308. In other words, the meaning of all the lines written in his forehead (from worry).

313. Vouchsafe: please accept.

315. kerchief: scarf (it shows he is sick).

Brutus.

    Such an exploit have I in hand, Ligarius,
    Had you a healthful ear to hear of it.

Ligarius.

320   By all the gods that Romans bow before,
    I here discard my sickness! Soul of Rome,
    Brave son, derived from honorable loins,
    Thou, like an exorcist, hast conjured up
    My mortifièd° spirit. Now bid me run,
325   And I will strive with things impossible,
    Yea, get the better of them. What's to do?

Brutus.

    A piece of work that will make sick men whole.

Ligarius.

    But are not some whole that we must make sick?

Brutus.

    That must we also. What it is, my Caius,
330   I shall unfold to thee, as we are going
    To whom° it must be done.

Ligarius.   Set on° your foot,
    And with a heart new-fired I follow you,
    To do I know not what; but it sufficeth
    That Brutus leads me on.   *[Thunder.]*

Brutus.   Follow me, then. *[Exeunt.]*

321. *What action might he make with this line?*

324. mortifièd: deadened.

331. To whom: to the house of whom.
Set on: set off on.

Stage direction. *Thunder is a kind of actor in Shakespeare's plays. What mood does it invoke? Would you have this thunder sound alone, or would you have it serve as background noise for these speeches?*

Scene 2. *Caesar's house.*

Thunder and lightning. Enter JULIUS CAESAR *in his nightgown.*

Caesar.

    Nor heaven nor earth have been at peace tonight:
    Thrice hath Calphurnia in her sleep cried out,
    "Help, ho! They murder Caesar!" Who's within?

[Enter a SERVANT.*]*

Servant. My lord?

Caesar.

5   Go bid the priests do present° sacrifice,
    And bring me their opinions of success.°

Servant. I will, my lord.   *[Exit.]*

[Enter CALPHURNIA.*]*

5. present (pre′zənt): immediate.

6. opinions of success: opinions about the future course of events.

Calphurnia.
What mean you, Caesar? Think you to walk forth?
You shall not stir out of your house today.

Caesar.
10 Caesar shall forth. The things that threatened me
Ne'er looked but on my back; when they shall see
The face of Caesar, they are vanishèd.

Calphurnia.
Caesar, I never stood on ceremonies,°
Yet now they fright me. There is one within,
15 Besides the things that we have heard and seen,
Recounts most horrid sights seen by the watch.°
A lioness hath whelpèd° in the streets,
And graves have yawned, and yielded up their dead;
Fierce fiery warriors fought upon the clouds
20 In ranks and squadrons and right form of war,
Which drizzled blood upon the Capitol;
The noise of battle hurtled in the air,
Horses did neigh and dying men did groan,
And ghosts did shriek and squeal about the streets.
25 O Caesar, these things are beyond all use,°
And I do fear them.

Caesar.   What can be avoided
Whose end is purposed by the mighty gods?
Yet Caesar shall go forth; for these predictions
Are to° the world in general as to Caesar.

Calphurnia.
30 When beggars die, there are no comets seen;
The heavens themselves blaze forth the death of princes.

Caesar.
Cowards die many times before their deaths;
The valiant never taste of death but once.
Of all the wonders that I yet have heard,
35 It seems to me most strange that men should fear,
Seeing that death, a necessary end,
Will come when it will come.

[*Enter a* SERVANT.]

                              What say the augurers?

Servant.
They would not have you to stir forth today.
Plucking the entrails of an offering forth,
40 They could not find a heart within the beast.

Caesar.
The gods do this in shame of cowardice:
Caesar should be a beast without a heart

---

13. ceremonies: again, a reference to the ritual ceremonies of priests that were supposed to reveal omens of the future.

16. watch: watchman.
17. whelpèd: given birth.

25. beyond all use: beyond all we are used to in our normal experience.
26. *Calphurnia can be played here as hysterical and overly emotional, or as truly frightened for her husband. Which way would you play the part?*

29. Are to: apply to.

31. *What does Calphurnia mean?*

37. *How does Caesar feel about death? How does his tone change when he addresses the servant?*

37. *The augurers were very important in ancient Rome. Their duty was to tell from certain signs whether or not some action was favored by the gods. Signs were read in the flights of birds, in thunder, in the way sacred chickens ate their food, and in the conditions of the organs of a sacrificial animal. What is Caesar's mood as he hears of the augury this morning?*

If he should stay at home today for fear.
No, Caesar shall not; Danger knows full well
45 That Caesar is more dangerous than he.
We are two lions littered in one day,
And I the elder and more terrible,
And Caesar shall go forth.

Calphurnia.   Alas, my lord,
Your Wisdom is consumed in confidence.
50 Do not go forth today. Call it my fear
That keeps you in the house and not your own.
We'll send Mark Antony to the Senate House,
And he shall say you are not well today.
Let me, upon my knee, prevail in this.

Caesar.
55 Mark Antony shall say I am not well,
And for thy humor,° I will stay at home.

[*Enter* DECIUS.]

Here's Decius Brutus, he shall tell them so.
Decius.
Caesar, all hail! Good morrow, worthy Caesar;
I come to fetch you to the Senate House.
Caesar.
60 And you are come in very happy time°
To bear my greeting to the senators,
And tell them that I will not come today.
Cannot, is false; and that I dare not, falser:
I will not come today. Tell them so, Decius.
Calphurnia.
Say he is sick.
65 **Caesar.**   Shall Caesar send a lie?
Have I in conquest stretched mine arm so far
To be afeard to tell graybeards the truth?
Decius, go tell them Caesar will not come.
Decius.
Most mighty Caesar, let me know some cause,
70 Lest I be laughed at when I tell them so.
Caesar.
The cause is in my will: I will not come.
That is enough to satisfy the Senate.
But for your private satisfaction,
Because I love you, I will let you know.
75 Calphurnia here, my wife, stays° me at home.
She dreamt tonight she saw my statue,
Which, like a fountain with an hundred spouts,
Did run pure blood, and many lusty Romans
Came smiling and did bathe their hands in it.

662   William Shakespeare

48. *Caesar could end this speech with pomposity, dignity, or even humor. How do you interpret his tone?*

54. *What is Calphurnia doing?*

56. humor: mood.
56. *Here is a sudden change. Would a kiss between lines 54 and 55 explain it?*

60. happy time: lucky time.

65. *Is Caesar angry or gentle?*

75. stays: keeps.

80   And these does she apply for° warnings and portents
      And evils imminent, and on her knee
      Hath begged that I will stay at home today.
Decius.
      This dream is all amiss interpreted;
      It was a vision fair and fortunate:
85   Your statue spouting blood in many pipes,
      In which so many smiling Romans bathed,
      Signifies that from you great Rome shall suck
      Reviving blood, and that great men shall press
      For tinctures, stains, relics, and cognizance.°
90   This by Calphurnia's dream is signified.
Caesar.
      And this way have you well expounded it.
Decius.
      I have, when you have heard what I can say;
      And know it now, the Senate have concluded
      To give this day a crown to mighty Caesar.
95   If you shall send them word you will not come,
      Their minds may change. Besides, it were a mock
      Apt to be rendered, for someone to say
      "Break up the Senate till another time,
      When Caesar's wife shall meet with better dreams."
100   If Caesar hide himself, shall they not whisper
      "Lo, Caesar is afraid"?
      Pardon me, Caesar, for my dear dear love
      To your proceeding° bids me tell you this,
      And reason to my love is liable.°
Caesar.
105   How foolish do your fears seem now, Calphurnia!
      I am ashamèd I did yield to them.
      Give me my robe, for I will go.

      [*Enter* BRUTUS, LIGARIUS, METELLUS CIMBER, CASCA,
      TREBONIUS, CINNA, *and* PUBLIUS.]

      And look where Publius is come to fetch me.
Publius.
      Good morrow, Caesar.
Caesar.   Welcome, Publius.
110   What, Brutus, are you stirred so early too?
      Good morrow, Casca. Caius Ligarius,
      Caesar was ne'er so much your enemy°
      As that same ague° which hath made you lean.
      What is't o'clock?
Brutus.   Caesar, 'tis strucken eight.
Caesar.
115   I thank you for your pains and courtesy.

80. apply for: explain as.

83. *Remember what Decius is here for. We should sense his hungry absorption of Caesar's dream. How should he explain the dream—is he confident, fawning, awed, nervous?*

89. cognizance: identifying emblems worn by a nobleman's followers.

91. *There should be a pause here. Caesar's fate is about to be sealed. Does he seem relieved or amused?*

101. *What reaction from Caesar is Decius seeking when he refers to "Caesar's wife"? How is Decius playing on Caesar's fears?*
103. proceeding: advancement.
104. liable: subordinate.

107. *Suddenly Caesar changes his mind. Decius has succeeded. How would Calphurnia react now? Do you think Caesar concedes because he foolishly believes Decius, or because he heroically accepts his fate?*
Stage direction. *What mood would the conspirators be in as they approach their victim?*

112. enemy: Ligarius had supported Pompey in the Civil War and had recently been pardoned.
113. ague: fever.
113. *Where else has Caesar mentioned that a character is lean?*

[*Enter* ANTONY.]

See! Antony, that revels long a-nights,
Is notwithstanding up. Good morrow, Antony.

Antony.

So to most noble Caesar.

Caesar.   Bid them prepare within.

I am to blame to be thus waited for.
120 Now, Cinna; now, Metellus; what, Trebonius,
I have an hour's talk in store for you;
Remember that you call on me today;
Be near me, that I may remember you.

Trebonius.

Caesar, I will (*aside*) and so near will I be,
125 That your best friends shall wish I had been further.

Caesar.

Good friends, go in and taste some wine with me,
And we (like friends) will straightway go together.

Brutus.

(*Aside*) That every like is not the same,° O Caesar,
The heart of Brutus earns° to think upon.   [*Exeunt.*]

? **117.** *How can the actors playing Antony and Caesar establish the fact that a deep friendship exists between them?*

? **124.** *Asides are addressed to the audience, out of hearing of the other actors. How would this aside be spoken?*

? **127.** *What irony do you feel here? (What do* we *know that Caesar is ignorant of?)*

128. In other words, that those who appear to be friends are not really friends at all.
129. **earns:** grieves.

Scene 3. *A street near the Capitol, close to* BRUTUS'S *house.*

Enter ARTEMIDORUS *reading a paper.*

Artemidorus. "Caesar, beware of Brutus; take heed of
Cassius; come not near Casca; have an eye to Cinna;
trust not Trebonius; mark well Metellus Cimber; Decius Brutus loves thee not; thou hast wronged Caius
5 Ligarius. There is but one mind in all these men, and
it is bent against Caesar. If thou beest not immortal,
look about you: security gives way to conspiracy.° The
mighty gods defend thee!

                              Thy lover,° Artemidorus."

10 Here will I stand till Caesar pass along,
And as a suitor° will I give him this.
My heart laments that virtue cannot live
Out of the teeth of emulation.°
If thou read this, O Caesar, thou mayest live;
15 If not, the Fates with traitors do contrive.°   [*Exit.*]

7. In other words, a feeling of security gives the conspirators their opportunity.

9. **lover:** friend (one who loves you).

11. **suitor:** one who seeks a favor.

13. **out of the teeth of emulation:** beyond the reach of envy.

15. **contrive:** plot or scheme.

Scene 4. *Another part of the street.*

Enter PORTIA *and* LUCIUS.

Portia.
    I prithee, boy, run to the Senate House;
    Stay not to answer me, but get thee gone.
    Why dost thou stay?
Lucius.   To know my errand, madam.
Portia.
    I would have had thee there and here again
5   Ere I can tell thee what thou shouldst do there.
    O constancy,° be strong upon my side;
    Set a huge mountain 'tween my heart and tongue!
    I have a man's mind, but a woman's might.
    How hard it is for women to keep counsel!°
    Art thou here yet?
10 **Lucius.**   Madam, what should I do?
    Run to the Capitol, and nothing else?
    And so return to you, and nothing else?
Portia.
    Yes, bring me word, boy, if thy lord look well,
    For he went sickly forth; and take good note
15   What Caesar doth, what suitors press to him.
    Hark, boy, what noise is that?
Lucius.
    I hear none, madam.
Portia.   Prithee, listen well.
    I hear a bustling rumor like a fray,°
    And the wind brings it from the Capitol.
Lucius.
20   Sooth,° madam, I hear nothing.

[*Enter the* SOOTHSAYER.]

Portia.
    Come hither, fellow. Which way has thou been?
Soothsayer.
    At mine own house, good lady.
Portia.
    What is't o'clock?
Soothsayer.   About the ninth hour, lady.
Portia.
    Is Caesar yet gone to the Capitol?
Soothsayer.
25   Madam, not yet; I go to take my stand,
    To see him pass on to the Capitol.
Portia.
    Thou hast some suit to Caesar, hast thou not?

6. **constancy:** resolution.

9. **counsel:** a secret.
9. *Is there a clue in this speech that Brutus has told Portia of the conspiracy to murder Caesar? According to "stage time," did he ever have an opportunity to tell her after their conversation in Scene 1?*

18. **fray:** fight.

20. **Sooth:** in truth.

Soothsayer.

That I have, lady; if it will please Caesar
To be so good to Caesar as to hear me,

30   I shall beseech him to befriend himself.

Portia.

Why, know'st thou any harm's intended towards him?

Soothsayer.

None that I know will be, much that I fear may chance.
Good morrow to you. Here the street is narrow;
The throng that follows Caesar at the heels,

35   Of senators, of praetors, common suitors,
Will crowd a feeble man almost to death.
I'll get me to a place more void,° and there
Speak to great Caesar as he comes along.   [*Exit.*]

Portia.

I must go in. Ay me, how weak a thing

40   The heart of woman is! O Brutus,
The heavens speed thee in thine enterprise!
Sure, the boy heard me—Brutus hath a suit
That Caesar will not grant—O, I grow faint.
Run, Lucius, and commend me to my lord;

45   Say I am merry; come to me again,
And bring me word what he doth say to thee.

                          [*Exeunt severally.*]

37. void: empty.

46. *What is Portia's state of mind? Does she deliver line 45 after a pause?*

Responding to the Play

Analyzing Act II

Identifying Facts

1. Look back at his **soliloquy** at the beginning of this act and list the reasons Brutus gives for killing Caesar.
2. Who proposes the murder of Antony? Why does Brutus oppose it?
3. What does Portia demand of her husband in Scene 1?
4. In Scene 2, what ominous events have taken place that night, according to Calphurnia? What is Caesar's response to her terror?
5. What does Calphurnia try to persuade her husband to do in Scene 2?

6. Describe Calphurnia's dream. Explain why Decius's interpretation of the dream persuades Caesar to go to the Senate.
7. According to Scene 3, what chance still exists that the assassination plan won't work?

Interpreting Meanings

8. At the opening of Act II, Brutus has made up his mind to kill Caesar. Critic Mark Van Doren has said that this soliloquy is "riddled with rank fallacy. The fine man is a coarse thinker. . . ." What fallacies in thinking can you spot? In your view, are Brutus's reasons valid or invalid? How else might Brutus have responded to the problem posed by Caesar?

9. Explain Brutus's opposition to swearing an oath in Scene 1, lines 114–140. Describe the **character** traits that you think emerge in this speech.
10. Caesar's scene with Calphurnia and later with Decius (Scene 2) is a perfect play-within-a-play. Describe the **conflict,** the **decision** made, and the new **complication** that changes that decision.
11. Describe the complexities of Caesar's **character** that you've observed in this act. How does Shakespeare make you feel about Caesar— does he seem to be a monstrous tyrant, as the conspirators feel he is, or does he seem sympathetic? Explain your answer.
12. Compare and contrast the relationships of Brutus and Caesar with their wives, as depicted in this act. Do you think that these relationships are portrayed in relatively modern husband-wife terms? Or do they seem old-fashioned? Explain your opinions.
13. When we have to make difficult moral choices, we look for absolutes of right and wrong behavior to guide us. Discuss the moral choices that have been made so far by Cassius and Brutus. What do you think of the absolutes that have guided them?
14. Shakespeare uses thunder and other sounds indicating storms and tempests in order to suggest wholesale cosmic disorders and conflicts. Locate the moments when thunder is called for in this act, and describe the emotional effects it has at each point. What cosmic disorders is the thunder signifying?
15. Describe how Shakespeare creates and builds **suspense** during Scenes 3 and 4. What questions are you left with as the act ends?

Analyzing Language and Vocabulary

Elizabethan English

Although the language of the Elizabethans is essentially the same as ours, we may occasionally have some difficulty understanding it. The side notes might help you answer the following questions on Elizabethan usage in Act II. You might also want to review the material on pages 626–628, "Reading Elizabethan English."

1. In Scene 1, line 3, Brutus says he cannot "Give guess how near to day." How would we expand this phrase to make sense today?

2. What word does Brutus omit after the word *general* at the end of the first sentence of his soliloquy (Scene 1, line 12)?
3. What do you think Lucius means in Scene 1, line 73, when he says of the conspirators who come to Brutus's house that "their hats are plucked about their ears"?
4. What noun in Scene 1, line 83, does Shakespeare use as a verb?
5. What unfamiliar meaning does the word *prevention* have in Scene 1, line 85?
6. From the structure of the word itself, and from context clues, what would you guess *insuppressive* means in Scene 1, line 134?
7. What does Brutus's expression "several bastardy" in Scene 1, line 138, seem to mean?
8. What does Portia mean when she uses the expression "yesternight at supper" in Scene 1, line 238?
9. In Scene 2, line 13, Calphurnia tells Caesar that she "never stood on ceremonies." How is this expression similar to, but also a bit different from, an idiomatic expression in contemporary English?

Costume sketch of Caesar by Tanya Moiseiwitsch for the 1955 Stratford Shakespearean Festival production.

The Stratford Shakespearean Festival Foundation of Canada.

Act III

Scene 1. *Rome. Before the Capitol.*

Flourish. Enter CAESAR, BRUTUS, CASSIUS, CASCA, DECIUS, METELLUS CIMBER, TREBONIUS, CINNA, ANTONY, LEPIDUS, ARTEMIDORUS, PUBLIUS, POPI-LIUS, *and the* SOOTHSAYER.

Caesar.
> The ides of March are come.

Soothsayer.
> Ay, Caesar, but not gone.

Artemidorus.
> Hail, Caesar! Read this schedule.°

Decius.
> Trebonius doth desire you to o'er-read,
5 At your best leisure, this his humble suit.

Artemidorus.
> O Caesar, read mine first; for mine's a suit
> That touches° Caesar nearer. Read it, great Caesar.

Caesar.
> What touches us ourself shall be last served.

Artemidorus.
> Delay not, Caesar; read it instantly.

Caesar.
> What, is the fellow mad?

10 **Publius.**   Sirrah,° give place.

Cassius.
> What, urge you your petitions in the street?
> Come to the Capitol.

*[*CAESAR *goes to the Capitol, the rest following.]*

Popilius.
> I wish your enterprise today may thrive.

Cassius.
> What enterprise, Popilius?

Popilius.   Fare you well.

[Advances to CAESAR.*]*

Brutus.
15 What said Popilius Lena?

Cassius.
> He wished today our enterprise might thrive.
> I fear our purpose is discoverèd.

Brutus.
> Look how he makes to° Caesar; mark him.

Cassius.
> Casca, be sudden, for we fear prevention.°
20 Brutus, what shall be done? If this be known,

Stage direction. *This scene takes place on the Capitol Hill, where the Temple of Jupiter is located. A half-circle of steps is seen at the back of the stage, with a throne on top. A statue of Pompey is seen to the side—the enemy Caesar defeated in the recent civil wars. Caesar walks to center stage and the others flank him. How should Caesar regard the soothsayer and Artemidorus? Should he address his first remark to the soothsayer or to the crowd in general?*

3. schedule: scroll of paper.

7. touches: concerns.

8. *Is this sincerity or false humility?*

10. Sirrah: like "sir," but in Shakespeare's day used to address an inferior, often intending disrespect or anger.

10. *Publius speaks to Artemidorus, and the conspirators rush the petitioner away from Caesar. Whom is Cassius addressing in the next speech?*

13. *Popilius speaks to Cassius. Do you think he knows about the conspiracy?*

18. makes to: makes his way toward.

19. prevention: being prevented from carrying out their deed.

Cassius or Caesar never shall turn back,°
For I will slay myself.

Brutus.   Cassius, be constant.°
Popilius Lena speaks not of our purposes;
For look, he smiles, and Caesar doth not change.

Cassius.
25 Trebonius knows his time; for look you, Brutus,
He draws Mark Antony out of the way.

[*Exeunt* ANTONY *and* TREBONIUS.]

Decius.
Where is Metellus Cimber? Let him go
And presently prefer his suit to Caesar.

Brutus.
He is addressed.° Press near and second him.

Cinna.
30 Casca, you are the first that rears your hand.

Caesar.
Are we all ready? What is now amiss
That Caesar and his Senate must redress?

Metellus.
Most high, most mighty, and most puissant° Caesar,
Metellus Cimber throws before thy seat
An humble heart.   [*Kneeling.*]

35 **Caesar.**   I must prevent thee, Cimber.
These couchings° and these lowly courtesies
Might fire the blood of ordinary men,
And turn preordinance and first decree°
Into the law of children. Be not fond°
40 To think that Caesar bears such rebel blood
That will be thawed from the true quality°
With that which melteth fools—I mean sweet words,
Low-crooked curtsies, and base spaniel fawning.
Thy brother by decree is banishèd.
45 If thou dost bend and pray and fawn for him,
I spurn thee like a cur out of my way.
Know, Caesar doth not wrong, nor without cause
Will he be satisfied.

Metellus.
Is there no voice more worthy than my own,
50 To sound more sweetly in great Caesar's ear
For the repealing of my banished brother?

Brutus.
I kiss thy hand, but not in flattery, Caesar,
Desiring thee that Publius Cimber may
Have an immediate freedom of repeal.°

Caesar.
What, Brutus?

---

21. **turn back:** come out alive.

22. **constant:** calm.

26. *Why is Trebonius getting Antony out of the way?*

29. **addressed:** ready.
29. *What is happening near Caesar now?*

33. **puissant** (pwē′sənt): powerful.

36. **couchings:** very low bows.

38. These are very old Roman laws. Caesar warns that the laws might be changed at whim if they are not vigilant (just as the laws of children can be changed).
39. **fond:** so foolish as.
41. **true quality:** that is, firmness.

48. *What is Caesar doing during this speech? What is Metellus doing in response to Caesar's words?*

51. *Whom is Metellus addressing here?*

52. *Brutus steps forward; notice that he uses the pronoun* thy *in an insulting way, since Caesar is neither his social inferior nor an intimate. How might Caesar react to Brutus's surprising words?*
54. **freedom of repeal:** permission to return from exile.

Cassius.   Pardon, Caesar; Caesar, pardon!
55   As low as to thy foot doth Cassius fall
          To beg enfranchisement° for Publius Cimber.
     Caesar.
          I could be well moved, if I were as you;
          If I could pray to move,° prayers would move me;
60   But I am constant as the Northern Star,
          Of whose true-fixed and resting° quality
          There is no fellow° in the firmament.
          The skies are painted with unnumb'red sparks,
          They are all fire and every one doth shine;
65   But there's but one in all doth hold his place.
          So in the world; 'tis furnished well with men,
          And men are flesh and blood, and apprehensive;
          Yet in the number I do know but one
          That unassailable holds on his rank,°
70   Unshaked of motion; and that I am he,
          Let me a little show it, even in this—
          That I was constant° Cimber should be banished,
          And constant do remain to keep him so.
     Cinna.
          O Caesar——
     Caesar.   Hence! Wilt thou lift up Olympus?°
     Decius.
          Great Caesar——
75   **Caesar.**   Doth not Brutus bootless° kneel?
     Casca.
          Speak hands for me!

     [*They stab* CAESAR.]

     Caesar.
          Et tu, Brutè?° Then fall Caesar.   [*Dies.*]
     Cinna.
          Liberty! Freedom! Tyranny is dead!
          Run hence, proclaim, cry it about the streets.
     Cassius.
80   Some to the common pulpits, and cry out
          ''Liberty, freedom, and enfranchisement!''
     Brutus.
          People, and senators, be not affrighted.
          Fly not; stand still; ambition's debt is paid.
     Casca.
          Go to the pulpit, Brutus.
     Decius.   And Cassius too.
     Brutus.
85   Where's Publius?°
     Cinna.
          Here, quite confounded with this mutiny.

57. enfranchisement: restoration of the rights of citizenship.

59. pray to move: pray to others to change their minds.

61. resting: changeless.
62. fellow: equal.

69. rank: position.

70. *At what point in this speech would Caesar rise from his throne? The senators now rush in around Caesar and, in most productions, kneel before him. Casca has worked his way in back of Caesar.*
72. constant: firmly determined.

74. Olympus: in Greek mythology, the mountain where the gods lived.

75. bootless: in vain.
75. *This line is often spoken to show Caesar's great fondness for Brutus. How else might it be spoken?*
76. *What does this line mean? What is Casca doing?*

77. *Et tu, Brutè?*: (Latin) And you also, Brutus?
77. *The murder of Caesar has been staged in many ways. Low-budget productions have to worry about laundry bills for stained togas, but most productions show blood. In some productions, each dagger has attached to it a plastic capsule, which the actors break with their fingernails. In other productions, Caesar has a ''blood'' bag concealed under his toga. To stage the murder, directors often have the conspirators standing at different places on stage—all points to which Caesar runs in his attempt to escape. The last spot is Brutus's place. What does Caesar see as he utters his last words? Why does he say ''Then fall Caesar''?*

85. *Publius is a very old senator, too old to flee.*

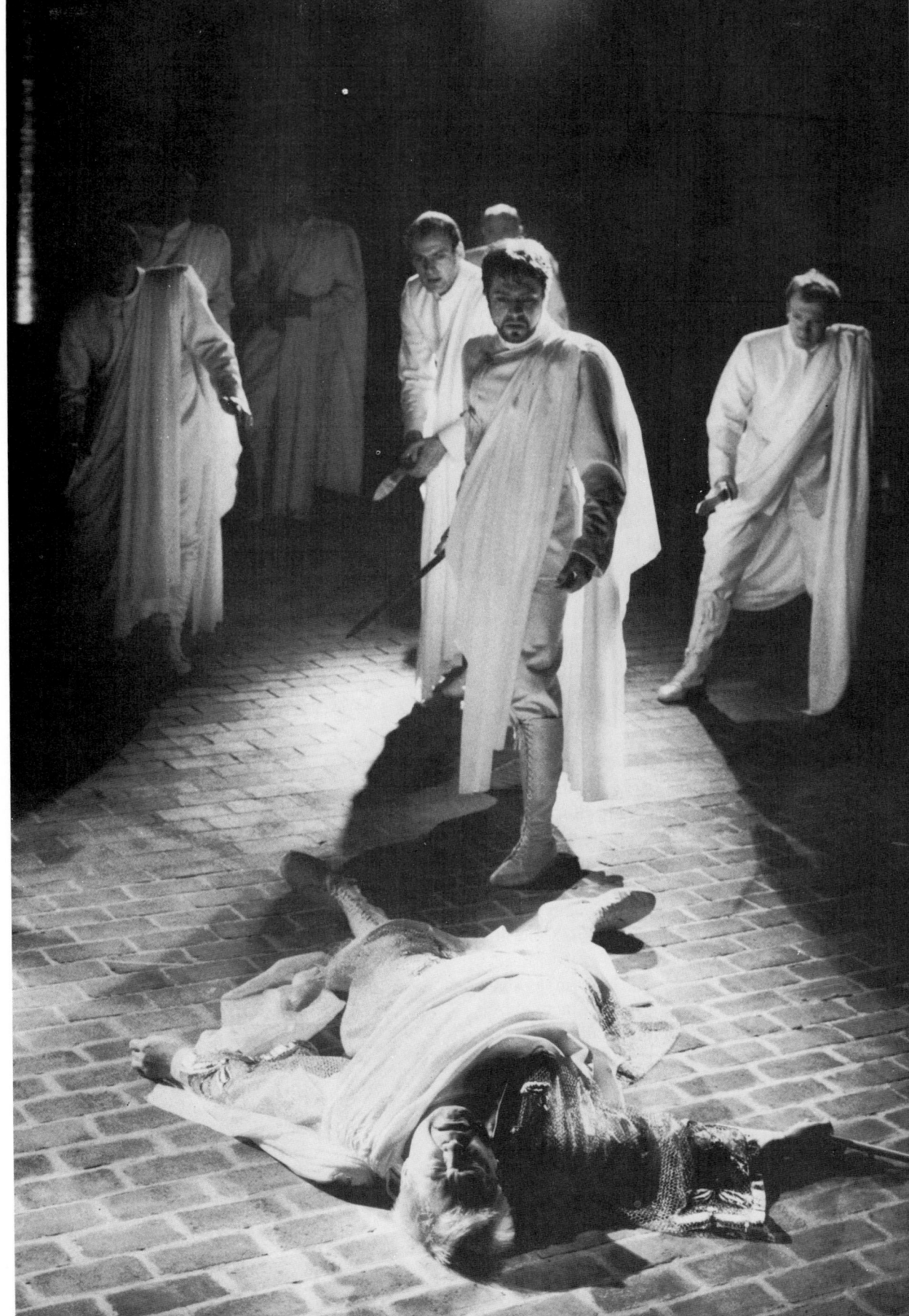

Metellus.

    Stand fast together, lest some friend of Caesar's
    Should chance——

Brutus.

    Talk not of standing. Publius, good cheer;
90   There is no harm intended to your person,
    Nor to no Roman else. So tell them, Publius.

Cassius.

    And leave us, Publius, lest that the people
    Rushing on us should do your age some mischief.

Brutus.

    Do so; and let no man abide° this deed
95   But we the doers.

94. abide: take the consequences of.

[*Enter* TREBONIUS.]

Cassius.

    Where is Antony?

Trebonius.   Fled to his house amazed.
    Men, wives, and children stare, cry out and run,
    As it were doomsday.

Brutus.   Fates, we will know your pleasures.
    That we shall die, we know; 'tis but the time
100   And drawing days out, that men stand upon.°

100. stand upon: wait for.

Casca.

    Why, he that cuts off twenty years of life
    Cuts off so many years of fearing death.

Brutus.

    Grant that, and then is death a benefit.
    So are we Caesar's friends, that have abridged
105   His time of fearing death. Stoop, Romans, stoop,
    And let us bathe our hands in Caesar's blood
    Up to the elbows, and besmear our swords.
    Then walk we forth, even to the market place,°
    And waving our red weapons o'er our heads,
110   Let's all cry "Peace, freedom, and liberty!"

105. *What are the conspirators doing now?*

108. market place: the Roman Forum, center of public and commercial life.

Cassius.

    Stoop then, and wash. How many ages hence
    Shall this our lofty scene be acted over
    In states unborn and accents yet unknown!

Brutus.

    How many times shall Caesar bleed in sport,
115   That now on Pompey's basis° lies along°
    No worthier than the dust!

Cassius.   So oft as that shall be,
    So often shall the knot of us be called
    The men that gave their country liberty.

115. basis: base (of Pompey's statue). **lies along:** stretches out.

118. *These speeches can be delivered in various ways. Would you emphasize the idealism of the conspirators, or their self-deception and short-sightedness?*

Decius.

What, shall we forth?

Cassius.   Ay, every man away.

120   Brutus shall lead, and we will grace his heels

With the most boldest and best hearts of Rome.

[*Enter a* SERVANT.]

Brutus.

Soft, who comes here? A friend of Antony's.

Servant.

Thus, Brutus, did my master bid me kneel;

Thus did Mark Antony bid me fall down;

125   And, being prostrate, thus he bade me say:

Brutus is noble, wise, valiant, and honest;

Caesar was mighty, bold, royal, and loving.

Say I love Brutus and I honor him;

Say I feared Caesar, honored him, and loved him.

130   If Brutus will vouchsafe that Antony

May safely come to him and be resolved

How Caesar hath deserved to lie in death,

Mark Antony shall not love Caesar dead

So well as Brutus living; but will follow

135   The fortunes and affairs of noble Brutus

Thorough° the hazards of this untrod state

With all true faith. So says my master Antony.

Brutus.

Thy master is a wise and valiant Roman;

I never thought him worse.

140   Tell him, so please him come unto this place,

He shall be satisfied and, by my honor,

Depart untouched.

Servant.   I'll fetch him presently.°

[*Exit* SERVANT.]

Brutus.

I know that we shall have him well to friend.

Cassius.

I wish we may. But yet have I a mind

145   That fears him much; and my misgiving still

Falls shrewdly to the purpose.°

[*Enter* ANTONY.]

Brutus.

But here comes Antony. Welcome, Mark Antony.

Antony.

O mighty Caesar! Dost thou lie so low?

Are all thy conquests, glories, triumphs, spoils,

136. Thorough: through.

137. *What does Antony ask of Brutus?*

142. presently: immediately.

146. My misgivings or doubts are usually justified.

146. *How does Cassius say this line? Notice that at this moment the play takes a turn, and that the hunters now become the hunted.*

150   Shrunk to this little measure? Fare thee well.
I know not, gentlemen, what you intend,
Who else must be let blood,° who else is rank.°
If I myself, there is no hour so fit
As Caesar's death's hour, nor no instrument
155   Of half that worth as those your swords, made rich
With the most noble blood of all this world.
I do beseech ye, if you bear me hard,°
Now, whilst your purpled hands do reek and smoke,
Fulfill your pleasure. Live a thousand years,
160   I shall not find myself so apt to die;
No place will please me so, no mean of death,
As here by Caesar, and by you cut off,
The choice and master spirits of this age.

Brutus.
     O Antony, beg not your death of us!
165   Though now we must appear bloody and cruel,
As by our hands and this our present act
You see we do, yet see you but our hands
And this the bleeding business they have done.
Our hearts you see not; they are pitiful;°
170   And pity to the general wrong of Rome—
As fire drives out fire, so pity pity—
Hath done this deed on Caesar. For your part,
To you our swords have leaden° points, Mark Antony:
Our arms in strength of malice, and our hearts
175   Of brothers' temper, do receive you in
With all kind love, good thoughts, and reverence.

Cassius.
     Your voice shall be as strong as any man's
In the disposing of new dignities.°

Brutus.
     Only be patient till we have appeased
180   The multitude, beside themselves with fear,
And then we will deliver you the cause
Why I, that did love Caesar when I struck him,
Have thus proceeded.

Antony.   I doubt not of your wisdom.
Let each man render me his bloody hand.
185   First, Marcus Brutus, will I shake with you;
Next, Caius Cassius, do I take your hand;
Now, Decius Brutus, yours; now yours, Metellus;
Yours, Cinna; and, my valiant Casca, yours;
Though last, not least in love, yours, good Trebonius.
190   Gentlemen all—alas, what shall I say?
My credit° now stands on such slippery ground
That one of two bad ways you must conceit° me,
Either a coward or a flatterer.

151. *Where should Antony position himself? In this speech, where would you have the actor playing Antony pause? What movements or gestures would he make?*
152. Antony is punning here: ''let blood'' can mean to bleed a sick person in order to cure the illness, or it can mean to shed blood (kill). **rank:** another pun—swollen with disease (and thus in need of bleeding), or swollen with power.
157. bear me hard: bear a grudge against me.

169. pitiful: full of pity.

173. leaden: blunt (not made of steel).

178. dignities: titles.
178. *What differences in character do Brutus and Cassius reveal here in replying to Antony?*

185. *This is a rather bold step on Antony's part. What is he doing? What is his motive?*

191. credit: reputation.
192. conceit: judge.

That I did love thee, Caesar, O, 'tis true!

195 If then thy spirit look upon us now,
Shall it not grieve thee dearer than thy death
To see thy Antony making his peace,
Shaking the bloody fingers of thy foes,
Most noble, in the presence of thy corse?°

200 Had I as many eyes as thou hast wounds,
Weeping as fast as they stream forth thy blood,
It would become me better than to close
In terms of friendship with thine enemies.
Pardon me, Julius! Here wast thou bayed, brave hart;°

205 Here didst thou fall, and here thy hunters stand,
Signed in thy spoil and crimsoned in thy lethe.°
O world, thou wast the forest to this hart;
And this indeed, O world, the heart of thee.
How like a deer, stroken by many princes,

210 Dost thou here lie!

Cassius.
Mark Antony——

Antony.   Pardon me, Caius Cassius.
The enemies of Caesar shall say this;
Then, in a friend, it is cold modesty.°

Cassius.
I blame you not for praising Caesar so;

215 But what compact mean you to have with us?
Will you be pricked in number of° our friends,
Or shall we on, and not depend on you?

Antony.
Therefore I took your hands, but was indeed
Swayed from the point by looking down on Caesar.

220 Friends am I with you all, and love you all,
Upon this hope, that you shall give me reasons
Why, and wherein, Caesar was dangerous.

Brutus.
Or else were this a savage spectacle.
Our reasons are so full of good regard

225 That were you, Antony, the son of Caesar,
You should be satisfied.

Antony.   That's all I seek;
And am moreover suitor that I may
Produce° his body to the market place,
And in the pulpit, as becomes a friend,

230 Speak in the order of his funeral.

Brutus.
You shall, Mark Antony.

Cassius.   Brutus, a word with you.
(*Aside to* BRUTUS) You know not what you do; do not
    consent

194. *What is Antony's position on stage now—is he standing or kneeling? Is he near the corpse or far away from it?*

199. corse: corpse.

204. Antony compares Caesar to a deer (hart) hunted down by baying (barking) hounds. "Brave hart" is also a pun on "brave heart."
206. In other words, marked with the wounds of your slaughter and reddened by your blood (compared with the river Lethe in the Underworld).

210. *Why is the imagery of the hunted deer (hart) so appropriate here? How does it make you feel about Caesar?*

213. modesty: moderation.

216. pricked in number of: counted with. In counting off a list of people, the Roman would prick a hole in a wax-covered tablet. The modern expression would be "ticked off."

228. produce: bring forth.

"Our reasons were so full of good regard . . ."

That Antony speak in his funeral.
Know you how much the people may be moved
By that which he will utter?

235 **Brutus.**   By your pardon:
I will myself into the pulpit first,
And show the reason of our Caesar's death.
What Antony shall speak, I will protest
He speaks by leave and by permission,
240 And that we are contented Caesar shall
Have all true rites and lawful ceremonies.
It shall advantage more than do us wrong.

Cassius.
I know not what may fall,° I like it not.   **243. fall:** befall, happen.

Brutus.
Mark Antony, here, take you Caesar's body.
245 You shall not in your funeral speech blame us,
But speak all good you can devise of Caesar,
And say you do't by our permission;
Else shall you not have any hand at all
About his funeral. And you shall speak
250 In the same pulpit whereto I am going,
After my speech is ended.

Antony.   Be it so;
    I do desire no more.
Brutus.
    Prepare the body then, and follow us.

            [*Exeunt all except* ANTONY.]

Antony.
    O pardon me, thou bleeding piece of earth,
255   That I am meek and gentle with these butchers!
    Thou art the ruins of the noblest man
    That ever livèd in the tide of times.
    Woe to the hand that shed this costly blood!
    Over thy wounds now do I prophesy
260   (Which like dumb mouths do ope their ruby lips
    To beg the voice and utterance of my tongue),
    A curse shall light upon the limbs of men;
    Domestic fury and fierce civil strife
    Shall cumber° all the parts of Italy;
265   Blood and destruction shall be so in use,
    And dreadful objects so familiar,
    That mothers shall but smile when they behold
    Their infants quartered° with the hands of war,
    All pity choked with custom of fell deeds,°
270   And Caesar's spirit, ranging for revenge,
    With Atè° by his side come hot from hell,
    Shall in these confines with a monarch's voice
    Cry ''Havoc,''° and let slip the dogs of war,
    That this foul deed shall smell above the earth
275   With carrion° men, groaning for burial.

    [*Enter Octavius's* SERVANT.]

    You serve Octavius Caesar, do you not?
Servant.
    I do, Mark Antony.
Antony.
    Caesar did write for him to come to Rome.
Servant.
    He did receive his letters and is coming,
280   And bid me say to you by word of mouth—
    (*Seeing the body*) O Caesar!
Antony.
    Thy heart is big;° get thee apart and weep.
    Passion, I see, is catching, for mine eyes,
    Seeing those beads of sorrow stand in thine,
285   Began to water. Is thy master coming?
Servant.
    He lies tonight within seven leagues° of Rome.

254. *How should Antony immediately change his tone? Whom is he talking to?*

263. *During this speech, some directors often let us hear the offstage noise of the crowd. At what moments in this speech would the offstage cries of the mob and even other street noises be appropriate?*
264. cumber: burden.

268. quartered: butchered (cut in four parts).
269. fell deeds: evil deeds.

271. Atè: Greek goddess of revenge.

273. Cry ''Havoc'': give the signal for the devastation and disorder to begin.

275. carrion: dead and rotting.

282. big: full of grief.

284. *What might Antony do to the servant to make us feel his compassion?*

286. Seven leagues: about twenty-one miles.

Antony.

Post° back with speed, and tell him what hath chanced.
Here is a mourning Rome, a dangerous Rome,
No Rome of safety for Octavius yet.
290   Hie° hence and tell him so. Yet stay awhile;
Thou shalt not back till I have borne this corse
Into the market place; there shall I try°
In my oration how the people take
The cruel issue° of these bloody men;
295   According to the which, thou shalt discourse
To young Octavius of the state of things.
Lend me your hand.   [*Exeunt.*]

287. Post: ride on horseback (in relays of horses).

290. Hie: hurry.

292. try: test.

294. cruel issue: cruel deed; also, the outcome or result of cruelty.

297. *Would you end this scene with Antony raising the body in his arms, or would you have him stand over it? Would you hear the noise of the crowd offstage?*

Scene 2. *The Forum.*

Enter BRUTUS *and goes into the pulpit, and* CASSIUS, *with the* PLEBEIANS.°

Plebeians.

We will be satisfied! Let us be satisfied!

Brutus.

Then follow me, and give me audience, friends.
Cassius, go you into the other street
And part the numbers.
5   Those that will hear me speak, let 'em stay here;
Those that will follow Cassius, go with him;
And public reasons shall be renderèd
Of Caesar's death.

First Plebeian.   I will hear Brutus speak.

Second Plebeian.

I will hear Cassius, and compare their reasons,
10   When severally we hear them renderèd.

[*Exit* CASSIUS, *with some of the* PLEBEIANS.]

Third Plebeian.

The noble Brutus is ascended. Silence!

Brutus. Be patient till the last.

Romans, countrymen, and lovers, hear me for my
cause, and be silent, that you may hear. Believe me
15   for mine honor, and have respect to mine honor, that

plebeians: the common people.

Stage direction. *Today the Roman Forum is a heap of ruins (see the photograph on page 630), but in Caesar's day it was a busy, crowded, open area. At one end of the Forum was the Rostrum, a "pulpit" from which Rome's great public figures would speak. In stage sets, the pulpit is usually set on a semicircular platform with steps leading up to it. This scene is tumultuous. What is Brutus's mood as he fights free of the mob and goes up to the pulpit?*

---

you may believe. Censure° me in your wisdom, and awake your senses,° that you may the better judge. If there be any in this assembly, any dear friend of Caesar's, to him I say that Brutus' love to Caesar
20 was no less than his. If then that friend demand why Brutus rose against Caesar, this is my answer: Not that I loved Caesar less, but that I loved Rome more. Had you rather Caesar were living, and die all slaves, than that Caesar were dead, to live all free men? As
25 Caesar loved me, I weep for him; as he was fortunate, I rejoice at it; as he was valiant, I honor him; but, as he was ambitious, I slew him. There is tears, for his love; joy, for his fortune; honor, for his valor; and death, for his ambition. Who is here so base that
30 would be a bondman?° If any, speak; for him have I offended. Who is here so rude° that would not be a Roman? If any, speak; for him have I offended. Who is here so vile that will not love his country? If any, speak; for him have I offended. I pause for a reply.
35 **All.** None, Brutus, none!
Brutus. Then none have I offended. I have done no more to Caesar than you shall do to Brutus. The question of his death is enrolled° in the Capitol; his glory not extenuated,° wherein he was worthy, nor his offenses
40 enforced,° for which he suffered death.

[*Enter* MARK ANTONY, *with* CAESAR'S *body.*]

Here comes his body, mourned by Mark Antony, who, though he had no hand in his death, shall receive the benefit of his dying, a place in the commonwealth, as which of you shall not? With this I depart, that, as I
45 slew my best lover for the good of Rome, I have the same dagger for myself, when it shall please my country to need my death.
All. Live, Brutus! Live, live!
First Plebeian.
Bring him with triumph home unto his house.
Second Plebeian.
50 Give him a statue with his ancestors.
Third Plebeian.
Let him be Caesar.
Fourth Plebeian.   Caesar's better parts°
Shall be crowned in Brutus.
First Plebeian.
We'll bring him to his house with shouts and clamors.
Brutus. My countrymen——
Second Plebeian.   Peace! Silence! Brutus speaks.

16. **Censure:** judge.
17. **senses:** reasoning powers.

30. **bondman:** slave.
31. **rude:** rough and uncivilized.

? **34.** *Notice that Brutus's reasoned speech is in prose, not poetry. What value does Brutus presume the people cherish—as he cherishes it?*

38. In other words, there's a record of the reasons he was killed.
39. **extenuated:** lessened.
40. **enforced:** exaggerated.

? **Stage direction.** *In some productions, Caesar's body is now formally prepared for funeral rites. In others, it is still bloody and torn, just as we saw it in the assassination scene. In your opinion, which use of the body would be more effective?*

51. **better parts:** better qualities.
? **51.** *Why is this cry from the mob ironic? Has the crowd understood Brutus's motives at all?*
? **53.** *What would you have Antony doing while the mob is talking? (Remember, he has brought Caesar's body to the Forum.)*

55   **First Plebeian.** Peace, ho!

Brutus.

    Good countrymen, let me depart alone,

    And, for my sake, stay here with Antony.

    Do grace to Caesar's corpse, and grace his speech°

    Tending to Caesar's glories, which Mark Antony

60   By our permission, is allowed to make.

    I do entreat you, not a man depart,

    Save I alone, till Antony have spoke.   [*Exit.*]

First Plebeian.

    Stay, ho! And let us hear Mark Antony.

Third Plebeian.

    Let him go up into the public chair;°

65   We'll hear him. Noble Antony, go up.

Antony.

    For Brutus' sake, I am beholding to you.

Fourth Plebeian.

    What does he say of Brutus?

Third Plebeian.   He says, for Brutus' sake,

    He finds himself beholding to us all.

Fourth Plebeian.

    'Twere best he speak no harm of Brutus here!

First Plebeian.

    This Caesar was a tyrant.

70   **Third Plebeian.**   Nay, that's certain.

    We are blest that Rome is rid of him.

Second Plebeian.

    Peace! Let us hear what Antony can say.

Antony.

    You gentle Romans——

All.   Peace, ho! Let us hear him.

Antony.

    Friends, Romans, countrymen, lend me your ears;

75   I come to bury Caesar, not to praise him.

    The evil that men do lives after them,

    The good is oft interrèd with their bones;

    So let it be with Caesar. The noble Brutus

    Hath told you Caesar was ambitious.

80   If it were so, it was a grievous fault,

    And grievously hath Caesar answered° it.

    Here, under leave of Brutus and the rest

    (For Brutus is an honorable man,

    So are they all, all honorable men),

85   Come I to speak in Caesar's funeral.

    He was my friend, faithful and just to me;

    But Brutus says he was ambitious,

    And Brutus is an honorable man.

    He hath brought many captives home to Rome,

---

58. grace his speech: listen respectfully to Antony's funeral oration.

64. public chair: pulpit or rostum.

? **74.** *An important question: Where would you place Caesar's body so that Antony can use it most effectively?*

81. answered: paid the penalty for.

90   Whose ransoms did the general coffers° fill;
      Did this in Caesar seem ambitious?
      When that the poor have cried, Caesar hath wept;
      Ambition should be made of sterner stuff.
      Yet Brutus says he was ambitous;
95   And Brutus is an honorable man.
      You all did see that on the Lupercal
      I thrice presented him a kingly crown,
      Which he did thrice refuse. Was this ambition?
      Yet Brutus says he was ambitious;
100   And sure he is an honorable man.
      I speak not to disprove what Brutus spoke,
      But here I am to speak what I do know.
      You all did love him once, not without cause;
      What cause withholds you then to mourn for him?
105   O judgment, thou art fled to brutish beasts,
      And men have lost their reason! Bear with me;
      My heart is in the coffin there with Caesar,
      And I must pause till it come back to me.
      First Plebeian.
      Methinks there is much reason in his sayings.
      Second Plebeian.
110   If thou consider rightly of the matter,
      Caesar has had great wrong.
      Third Plebeian.   Has he, masters?
      I fear there will a worse come in his place.
      Fourth Plebeian.
      Marked ye his words? He would not take the crown,
      Therefore 'tis certain he was not ambitious.
      First Plebeian.
115   If it be found so, some will dear abide it.°
      Second Plebeian.
      Poor soul, his eyes are red as fire with weeping.
      Third Plebeian.
      There's not a nobler man in Rome than Antony.
      Fourth Plebeian.
      Now mark him, he begins again to speak.
      Antony.
      But yesterday the word of Caesar might
120   Have stood against the world; now lies he there,
      And none so poor to° do him reverence.
      O masters! If I were disposed to stir
      Your hearts and minds to mutiny and rage,
      I should do Brutus wrong and Cassius wrong,
125   Who, you all know, are honorable men.
      I will not do them wrong; I rather choose
      To wrong the dead, to wrong myself and you,
      Than I will wrong such honorable men.

90. **general coffers:** public treasury.

? 99. *Remember that the crowd is pressing in on Antony. What movements or sounds would they make as Antony says things that are meant to sway their feelings?*

? 108. *What do lines 107–108 mean? What could Antony be doing at this point, as our attention is drawn again to the mob?*

115. **dear abide it:** pay dearly for it.

121. **so poor to:** so low in rank as to.

But here's a parchment with the seal of Caesar;
130 I found it in his closet; 'tis his will.
Let but the commons hear this testament,
Which, pardon me, I do not mean to read,
And they would go and kiss dead Caesar's wounds,
And dip their napkins° in his sacred blood;
135 Yea, beg a hair of him for memory,
And dying, mention it within their wills,
Bequeathing it as a rich legacy
Unto their issue.°

Fourth Plebeian.
We'll hear the will; read it, Mark Antony.

All.
140 The will, the will! We will hear Caesar's will!

Antony.
Have patience, gentle friends, I must not read it.
It is not meet you know how Caesar loved you.
You are not wood, you are not stones, but men;
And being men, hearing the will of Caesar,
145 It will inflame you, it will make you mad.
'Tis good you know not that you are his heirs;
For if you should, O, what would come of it?

Fourth Plebeian.
Read the will! We'll hear it, Antony!
You shall read us the will, Caesar's will!

Antony.
150 Will you be patient? Will you stay awhile?
I have o'ershot myself° to tell you of it.
I fear I wrong the honorable men
Whose daggers have stabbed Caesar; I do fear it.

Fourth Plebeian.
155 They were traitors. Honorable men!

All.
The will! The testament!

Second Plebeian. They were villains, murderers! The
will! Read the will!

Antony.
You will compel me then to read the will?
Then make a ring about the corpse of Caesar,
160 And let me show you him that made the will.
Shall I descend? And will you give me leave?

All. Come down.

Second Plebeian. Descend.

[ANTONY *comes down.*]

Third Plebeian. You shall have leave.
165 **Fourth Plebeian.** A ring! Stand round.

134. napkins: handkerchiefs.

138. issue: children, heirs.
138. *Antony says he is not going to read the will. But what has he already implied about its contents?*

147. *Again, how has Antony scored his point indirectly? How could an actor play Antony in this scene to make him seem manipulative?*

151. o'ershot myself: gone further than I intended.

153. *The irony here is so obvious that an actor playing Antony must make a choice about how to say these lines: Will he continue his pretense of honoring Caesar's assassins, or will he finally drop this pose and speak with obviously scathing sarcasm?*

"You all do know this mantle. . . ."

First Plebeian.

    Stand from the hearse, stand from the body!

Second Plebeian.

    Room for Antony, most noble Antony!

Antony.

    Nay, press not so upon me; stand far off.

All. Stand back! Room! Bear back.

Antony.

170   If you have tears, prepare to shed them now.
    You all do know this mantle; I remember
    The first time ever Caesar put it on:
    'Twas on a summer's evening, in his tent,
    That day he overcame the Nervii.°

175   Look, in this place ran Cassius' dagger through;
    See what a rent the envious° Casca made;
    Through this the well-belovèd Brutus stabbed,
    And as he plucked his cursèd steel away,
    Mark how the blood of Caesar followed it,

180   As rushing out of doors, to be resolved
    If Brutus so unkindly knocked, or no;
    For Brutus, as you know, was Caesar's angel.
    Judge, O you gods, how dearly Caesar loved him!
    This was the most unkindest cut of all;

185   For when the noble Caesar saw him stab,
    Ingratitude, more strong than traitors' arms,
    Quite vanquished him. Then burst his mighty heart;
    And, in his mantle muffling up his face,
    Even at the base of Pompey's statue

190   (Which all the while ran blood) great Caesar fell.
    O, what a fall was there, my countrymen!
    Then I, and you, and all of us fell down,
    Whilst bloody treason flourished over us.
    O, now you weep, and I perceive you feel

195   The dint° of pity; these are gracious drops.
    Kind souls, what weep you when you but behold
    Our Caesar's vesture° wounded? Look you here,
    Here is himself, marred as you see with traitors.

First Plebeian. O piteous spectacle!

200 **Second Plebeian.** O noble Caesar!

Third Plebeian. O woeful day!

Fourth Plebeian. O traitors, villains!

First Plebeian. O most bloody sight!

Second Plebeian. We will be revenged.

205 **All.** Revenge! About! Seek! Burn! Fire! Kill! Slay! Let
    not a traitor live!

Antony. Stay, countrymen.

First Plebeian. Peace there! Hear the noble Antony.

169. *How do you visualize the placement of the actors at this point? Where is Caesar's body?*

172. *Watch for clues that tell what Antony is doing for effect as he delivers this speech. What is he holding in line 171?*
174. Nervii: one of the tribes conquered by Caesar, in 57 B.C.

176. envious: spiteful.

194. *What is the crowd doing as Antony speaks?*
195. dint: stroke.

197. vesture: clothing.
198. *What has Antony done with the body now?*

Second Plebeian. We'll hear him, we'll follow him, we'll
210   die with him!
       Antony.
       Good friends, sweet friends, let me not stir you up
       To such a sudden flood of mutiny.
       They that have done this deed are honorable.
       What private griefs° they have, alas, I know not,
215   That made them do it. They are wise and honorable,
       And will, no doubt, with reasons answer you.
       I come not, friends, to steal away your hearts;
       I am no orator, as Brutus is;
       But (as you know me all) a plain blunt man
220   That love my friend, and that they know full well
       That gave me public leave to speak of him.
       For I have neither writ, nor words, nor worth,
       Action, nor utterance, nor the power of speech
       To stir men's blood; I only speak right on.
225   I tell you that which you yourselves do know,
       Show you sweet Caesar's wounds, poor poor dumb
           mouths,
       And bid them speak for me. But were I Brutus,
       And Brutus Antony, there were an Antony
       Would ruffle up your spirits, and put a tongue
230   In every wound of Caesar that would move
       The stones of Rome to rise and mutiny.
       All.
       We'll mutiny.
       First Plebeian.   We'll burn the house of Brutus.
       Third Plebeian.
       Away, then! Come, seek the conspirators.
       Antony.
       Yet hear me, countrymen. Yet hear me speak.
       All.
235   Peace, ho! Hear Antony, most noble Antony!
       Antony.
       Why, friends, you go to do you know not what:
       Wherein hath Caesar thus deserved your loves?
       Alas, you know not; I must tell you then:
       You have forgot the will I told you of.
       All.
240   Most true, the will! Let's stay and hear the will.
       Antony.
       Here is the will, and under Caesar's seal.
       To every Roman citizen he gives,
       To every several° man, seventy-five drachmas.°
       Second Plebeian.
       Most noble Caesar! We'll revenge his death!

214. griefs: grievances.

216. *Notice that Antony implies that reasons have not already been given. Have they?*

224. *How does Antony characterize himself, as compared to Brutus? What is his motive?*

231. *Again, the irony is obvious here. What is the key word in this speech?*

239. *Notice how many times the mob goes to run off and how Antony pulls it back again. How do you think Antony feels about this herd of people he has so cleverly manipulated?*

243. several: individual.   **drachmas:** silver coins (Greek currency).

Third Plebeian. O royal Caesar!

Antony. Hear me with patience.

All. Peace, ho!

Antony.

> Moreover, he hath left you all his walks,
> His private arbors, and new-planted orchards,
> On this side Tiber; he hath left them you,
> And to your heirs forever: common pleasures,°
> To walk abroad and recreate yourselves.
> Here was a Caesar! When comes such another?

First Plebeian.

> Never, never! Come, away, away!
> We'll burn his body in the holy place,
> And with the brands fire the traitors' houses.
> Take up the body.

Second Plebeian. Go fetch fire.

Third Plebeian. Pluck down benches.

Fourth Plebeian. Pluck down forms, windows,° anything!

[*Exeunt* PLEBEIANS *with the body.*]

Antony.

> Now let it work: Mischief, thou art afoot,
> Take thou what course thou wilt.

[*Enter* SERVANT.]

> How now, fellow?

Servant.

> Sir, Octavius is already come to Rome.

Antony. Where is he?

Servant.

> He and Lepidus are at Caesar's house.

Antony.

> And thither will I straight to visit him;
> He comes upon a wish. Fortune is merry,
> And in this mood will give us anything.

Servant.

> I heard him say, Brutus and Cassius
> Are rid° like madmen through the gates of Rome.

Antony.

> Belike° they had some notice of the people,
> How I had moved them. Bring me to Octavius.

[*Exeunt.*]

245

250

255

260

265

270

---

251. **common pleasures:** public recreation areas.

260. **forms, windows:** long benches and shutters.

? 262. *Antony is alone onstage. The noise of the mob dies off in the distance. We might in some productions see the reflection of flames, and hear the sounds of rioting. How should Antony speak these lines?*

270. **Are rid:** have ridden.

? 270. *What have Brutus and Cassius done?*

271. **Belike:** probably.

Scene 3. *A street.*

Enter CINNA *the Poet, and after him the* PLEBEIANS.

Cinna.

    I dreamt tonight that I did feast with Caesar,
    And things unluckily charge my fantasy.°
    I have no will to wander forth of doors,
    Yet something leads me forth.

5   **First Plebeian.** What is your name?

    Second Plebeian. Whither are you going?

    Third Plebeian. Where do you dwell?

    Fourth Plebeian. Are you a married man or a bachelor?

    Second Plebeian. Answer every man directly.

10 **First Plebeian.** Ay, and briefly.

    Fourth Plebeian. Ay, and wisely.

    Third Plebeian. Ay, and truly, you were best.

    Cinna. What is my name? Whither am I going? Where
    do I dwell? Am I a married man or a bachelor? Then,

15 to answer every man directly and briefly, wisely and
    truly: wisely I say, I am a bachelor.

    Second Plebeian. That's as much as to say they are fools
    that marry; you'll bear me a bang° for that, I fear.
    Proceed directly.

20 **Cinna.** Directly, I am going to Caesar's funeral.

    First Plebeian. As a friend or an enemy?

    Cinna. As a friend.

    Second Plebeian. That matter is answered directly.

    Fourth Plebeian. For your dwelling, briefly.

25 **Cinna.** Briefly, I dwell by the Capitol.

    Third Plebeian. Your name, sir, truly.

    Cinna. Truly, my name is Cinna.

    First Plebeian. Tear him to pieces! He's a conspirator.

    Cinna. I am Cinna the poet! I am Cinna the poet!

30 **Fourth Plebeian.** Tear him for his bad verses! Tear him
    for his bad verses!

    Cinna. I am not Cinna the conspirator.

    Fourth Plebeian. It is no matter, his name's Cinna; pluck
    but his name out of his heart, and turn him going.°

35 **Third Plebeian.** Tear him, tear him!

[They attack him.]

    Come, brands, ho! Firebrands! To Brutus',to Cassius'!
    Burn all! Some to Decius' house, and some to Casca's;
    some to Ligarius'! Away, go!
                     [Exeunt all the PLEBEIANS *with* CINNA.]

2. That is, events unluckily fill his imagination (with ominous ideas).

18. bear me a bang: get a blow from me.

34. turn him going: send him packing.

38. *What has the mob done to the innocent poet Cinna?*

Responding to the Play

Analyzing Act III

Identifying Facts

1. In Scene 1, there is still a chance that the conspiracy might be foiled. Explain why Artemidorus fails to get Caesar to read his warning.
2. What petition serves as an excuse for the conspirators to gather around Caesar immediately before the assassination?
3. In Scene 1, why does Cassius argue against allowing Antony to speak at Caesar's funeral? What reasons does Brutus give for overruling him?
4. For a moment after the assassination, the action seems to stop. The **protagonists** (Brutus, Cassius, and the other conspirators) have achieved their goal. An audience might say, "Well, that's that." But soon the protagonist who is to drive the rest of the play appears. Who is this protagonist, and what does he want? Explain how we have been prepared for his appearance as the avenger of Caesar.
5. What does Antony disclose to the crowd concerning Caesar's will in Scene 2? Describe the crowd's reaction.

Interpreting Meanings

6. In Scene 1, reread carefully Brutus's speech in lines 105–110 and Antony's speech in lines 184–189. These lines share a vivid **image**— that of the blood of Caesar. Yet the implications of the passages are quite different. What does the first passage suggest about Brutus's attitude toward the assassination? How does Antony's **tone** in the second passage differ from Brutus's, and what do you think are the implications of Antony's tone?
7. How does Antony's speech at the end of Scene 1 (lines 254–275) indicate his true intentions regarding the assassins? What could this speech **foreshadow** about events in the second half of the play?
8. Antony's funeral oration in Scene 2 is one of the most famous pieces of rhetoric in literature. In this oration, Antony abides by his agreement with Brutus and Cassius. Explain how he does this and yet still manages to destroy the conspirators' reputations. How does he shrewdly manipulate the Roman mob?
9. Listen to Brutus's speech and Antony's speech read aloud. Which speech would more effectively move a crowd to action today? Why?
10. Up until Act III, Antony has barely figured in the play. How have others **characterized** him? Keeping in mind what occurs in Act III, do you agree with the way he has been described? Why or why not?
11. In earlier scenes, Shakespeare has *told* us about lions wandering in the streets and people running mad through the city. Now in Scene 3, with the attack on Cinna the poet, he *shows* us something. What does this action reveal about the mob? Does this sad scene have any contemporary parallels? Explain.
12. In lines 111–118 of Scene 1, a famous passage seems to refer to Shakespeare's intuition that this play will still be staged "many ages

Costume sketch of Cassius by Tanya Moiseiwitsch for the 1955 Stratford Shakespearean Festival production.

The Stratford Shakespearean Festival Foundation of Canada.

hence." Reread these lines in context. What other interpretations do you think are possible for this passage? Defend your answer.

13. The third act of Shakespeare's tragedies usually contains the **turning point**, that moment when something happens that turns all the subsequent actions of the play downward, toward the tragic ending. This event does not necessarily *cause* the tragic ending; it simply marks the point at which the protagonist's fortunes begin to go downhill. Which of the following events marks the turning point? Why?

    a. The assassination of Caesar
    b. Brutus's decision to allow Antony to address the crowd

    What do you think will happen to the conspirators now that Antony has control of the Roman populace?

14. How do you feel about Brutus in this act? Do you think he is admirable? Naive? Idealistic and unrealistic? Dishonest about his real motives? How do you feel, on the other hand, about Antony? Do you see people like Antony in political or military life today? Do you see people like Brutus? Explain your responses.

Analyzing Language and Vocabulary

Paraphrasing

When you **paraphrase** a passage, you rephrase it by expressing all its essential ideas in your own words. As you have seen, Elizabethan English differs somewhat from contemporary English in vocabulary, grammar, and syntax. Some contemporary versions of Shakespeare's plays have removed these differences and paraphrased complex passages. (These "rewritten" Shakespearean plays are very controversial. One of the latest examples of a modernized Shakespeare is the series by the distinguished British Shakespeare scholar, A. L. Rowse.)

However we feel about modernizing Shakespeare, paraphrasing provides valuable exercises in close reading. Read the following passages in their contexts, and then paraphrase each one. Feel free to alter the vocabulary, grammar, and syntax of the passages so that they sound as if they are being spoken by twentieth-century Americans. If you find a word you do not know, use context clues or the side notes to help you figure out its meaning. The first passage is done for you.

1. **Caesar.** Thy brother by decree is banishèd.
   If thou dost bend and pray and fawn for him,
   I spurn thee like a cur out of my way.
   —Act III, Scene 1, lines 44—46
   Your brother is banished by law. If you lower yourself to grovel and beg for him, I'll treat you like a dog and kick you out of my way.

2. **Decius.** Where is Metellus Cimber? Let him go
   And presently prefer his suit to Caesar.
   —Act III, Scene 1, lines 27—28

3. **Caesar** (to the Senators). If I could pray to move, prayers would move me;
   But I am constant as the Northern Star,
   Of whose true-fixed and resting quality
   There is no fellow in the firmament.
   —Act III, Scene 1, lines 59—62

4. **Brutus** (to the servant, about Antony). Thy master is a wise and valiant Roman;
   I never thought him worse.
   Tell him, so please him come unto this place,
   He shall be satisfied and, by my honor,
   Depart untouched.
   —Act III, Scene 1, lines 138—142

5. **Antony.** That I did love thee, Caesar, O, 'tis true!
   If then thy spirit look upon us now,
   Shall it not grieve thee dearer than thy death
   To see thy Antony making his peace,
   Shaking the bloody fingers of thy foes,
   Most noble, in the presence of thy corse?
   —Act III, Scene 1, lines 194—199

6. **Antony.** Friends, Romans, countrymen, lend me your ears;
   I come to bury Caesar, not to praise him.
   The evil that men do lives after them,
   The good is oft interrèd with their bones.
   —Act III, Scene 2, lines 74—77

7. **Antony.** I tell you that which you yourselves do know,
   Show you sweet Caesar's wounds, poor dumb mouths,
   And bid them speak for me. But were I Brutus,
   And Brutus Antony, there were an Antony
   Would ruffle up your spirits, and put a tongue
   In every wound of Caesar that would move
   The stones of Rome to rise and mutiny.
   —Act III, Scene 2, lines 225—231

Act IV

Scene 1. *A house in Rome.*

Enter ANTONY, OCTAVIUS, *and* LEPIDUS.

Antony.
    These many then shall die; their names are pricked.
Octavius.
    Your brother too must die; consent you, Lepidus?
Lepidus.
    I do consent——
Octavius.   Prick him down, Antony.
Lepidus.
    Upon condition Publius shall not live,
5   Who is your sister's son, Mark Antony.
Antony.
    He shall not live; look, with a spot I damn him.
    But, Lepidus, go you to Caesar's house;
    Fetch the will hither, and we shall determine
    How to cut off some charge° in legacies.
Lepidus.
10 What, shall I find you here?
Octavius.
    Or here or at the Capitol.   [*Exit* LEPIDUS.]
Antony.
    This is a slight unmeritable man,
    Meet to be sent on errands; is it fit,
    The threefold world° divided, he should stand
15 One of the three to share it?°
Octavius.   So you thought him,
    And took his voice° who should be pricked to die
    In our black sentence and proscription.°
Antony.
    Octavius, I have seen more days than you;
    And though we lay these honors on this man,
20 To ease ourselves of divers sland'rous loads,°
    He shall but bear them as the ass bears gold,
    To groan and sweat under the business,
    Either led or driven, as we point the way;
    And having brought our treasure where we will,
25 Then take we down his load, and turn him off,
    (Like to the empty ass) to shake his ears
    And graze in commons.°
Octavius.   You may do your will;
    But he's a tried and valiant soldier.
Antony.
    So is my horse, Octavius, and for that
30 I do appoint him store of provender.°
    It is a creature that I teach to fight,

9. In other words, cut down on some of the expenses by changing the legacies.

14. **threefold world:** three parts of the Roman Empire: Europe, Asia, and Africa.
15. Antony, Octavius, and Lepidus now govern the Roman Empire as a triumvirate, or three-member ruling body.
16. **voice:** vote.
17. **proscription:** a death sentence. In Roman law, a person under proscription could be killed by anyone, and the killer had no fear of murder charges being brought against him.
? 17. *What details suggest that this triumvirate is showing signs of strain? How has Antony changed from the person we saw in Act III?*
20. **divers sland'rous loads:** blame that will be laid against them.

27. **in commons:** on commonly held pasture land.
? 27. *Who is compared to the ass?*

30. **appoint . . . provender:** allot him a supply of food.

To wind, to stop, to run directly on,
His corporal motion governed by my spirit.
And, in some taste,° is Lepidus but so.
35 He must be taught, and trained, and bid go forth.
A barren-spirited fellow; one that feeds
On objects, arts, and imitations,
Which, out of use and staled by other men,
Begin his fashion.° Do not talk of him
40 But as a property.° And now, Octavius,
Listen great things. Brutus and Cassius
Are levying powers;° we must straight make head.°
Therefore let our alliance be combined,
Our best friends made, our means stretched;
45 And let us presently go sit in council
How covert matters may be best disclosed,
And open perils surest answerèd.

Octavius.
Let us do so; for we are at the stake,
And bayed about with many enemies;°
50 And some that smile have in their hearts, I fear,
Millions of mischiefs.   [*Exeunt.*]

Scene 2. *Camp near Sardis.*

Drum. Enter BRUTUS, LUCILIUS, LUCIUS, *and the* ARMY. TITINIUS *and* PINDARUS *meet them.*

Brutus. Stand ho!
Lucilius. Give the word, ho! and stand.
Brutus.
What now, Lucilius, is Cassius near?
Lucilius.
He is at hand, and Pindarus is come
5 To do you salutation from his master.
Brutus.
He greets me well.° Your master, Pindarus,
In his own change, or by ill officers,°
Hath given me some worthy cause to wish
Things done undone; but if he be at hand,
10 I shall be satisfied.°
Pindarus.   I do not doubt
But that my noble master will appear
Such as he is, full of regard and honor.

Brutus.

    He is not doubted. A word, Lucilius,

    How he received you; let me be resolved.°

Lucilius.

15   With courtesy and with respect enough,

    But not with such familiar instances,°

    Nor with such free and friendly conference

    As he hath used of old.

Brutus.   Thou hast described

    A hot friend cooling. Ever note, Lucilius,

20   When love begins to sicken and decay

    It useth an enforcèd ceremony.

    There are no tricks in plain and simple faith;

    But hollow men, like horses hot at hand,°

    Make gallant show and promise of their mettle;

[*Low march within.*]

25   But when they should endure the bloody spur,

    They fall their crests, and like deceitful jades°

    Sink in the trial. Comes his army on?

Lucilius.

    They mean this night in Sardis to be quartered;

    The greater part, the horse in general,°

    Are come with Cassius.

[*Enter* CASSIUS *and his* POWERS.]

30   **Brutus.**   Hark! He is arrived.

    March gently on to meet him.

Cassius. Stand, ho!

Brutus. Stand, ho! Speak the word along.

First Soldier. Stand!

35   **Second Soldier.** Stand!

Third Soldier. Stand!

Cassius.

    Most noble brother, you have done me wrong.

Brutus.

    Judge me, you gods! Wrong I mine enemies?

    And if not so, how should I wrong a brother.

Cassius.

40   Brutus, this sober form of yours hides wrongs;

    And when you do them——

Brutus.   Cassius, be content.°

    Speak your griefs softly; I do know you well.

    Before the eyes of both our armies here

    (Which should perceive nothing but love from us)

45   Let us not wrangle. Bid them move away;

    Then in my tent, Cassius, enlarge° your griefs,

    And I will give you audience.

14. resolved: informed.

16. familiar instances: friendly behavior.

18. *What details show that a split might be taking place in the conspirators' ranks?*

23. hot at hand: overspirited at the start of the race.

26. jades: nags.

29. the horse in general: all the cavalry.

36. *What do you picture happening on-stage here?*

41. content: calm.

46. enlarge: express.

"Judge me, you gods! Wrong I mine enemies?"

Cassius.   Pindarus,
   Bid our commanders lead their charges off
   A little from this ground.
Brutus.
50   Lucilius, do you the like, and let no man
   Come to our tent till we have done our conference.
   Let Lucius and Titinius guard our door.
            [*Exeunt all except* BRUTUS *and* CASSIUS.]

Scene 3. *Brutus's tent.*

Cassius.
   That you have wronged me doth appear in this:
   You have condemned and noted° Lucius Pella   2. **noted:** publicly disgraced.
   For taking bribes here of the Sardians;
   Wherein my letters, praying on his side,
5   Because I knew the man, was slighted off.

Brutus.
    You wronged yourself to write in such a case.

Cassius.
    In such a time as this it is not meet
    That every nice offense should bear his comment.°

Brutus.
    Let me tell you, Cassius, you yourself

10   Are much condemned to have an itching palm,
    To sell and mart° your offices for gold
    To undeservers.

Cassius.   I an itching palm?
    You know that you are Brutus that speaks this,
    Or, by the gods, this speech were else your last.

Brutus.

15   The name of Cassius honors° this corruption,
    And chastisement doth therefore hide his head.

Cassius. Chastisement!

Brutus.
    Remember March, the ides of March remember.
    Did not great Julius bleed for justice' sake?

20   What villain touched his body, that did stab,
    And not for justice? What, shall one of us,
    That struck the foremost man of all this world
    But for supporting robbers,° shall we now
    Contaminate our fingers with base bribes,

25   And sell the mighty space of our large honors°
    For so much trash as may be graspèd thus?
    I had rather be a dog, and bay the moon,
    Than such a Roman.

Cassius.   Brutus, bait not me;
    I'll not endure it. You forget yourself

30   To hedge me in. I am a soldier, I,
    Older in practice, abler than yourself
    To make conditions.

Brutus.   Go to! You are not, Cassius.

Cassius. I am.

Brutus. I say you are not.

Cassius.

35   Urge° me no more, I shall forget myself;
    Have mind upon your health, tempt me no farther.

Brutus. Away, slight man!

Cassius.
    Is't possible?

Brutus.   Hear me, for I will speak.
    Must I give way and room to your rash choler?°

40   Shall I be frighted when a madman stares?

Cassius.
    O ye gods, ye gods! Must I endure all this?

---

8. That every trivial offense should be criticized.

11. **mart:** trade, traffic in.

? 12. *What has Brutus accused Cassius of?*

15. **honors:** gives an air of respectability to.

23. **supporting robbers:** supporting or protecting dishonest public officials.

25. **our large honors:** capacity to be honorable and generous.

35. **Urge:** goad, bully.

? 36. *What threat is Cassius making to Brutus?*

39. **choler:** anger.

Brutus.

All this? Ay, more: fret till your proud heart break.
Go show your slaves how choleric you are,
And make your bondmen tremble. Must I budge?°
45   Must I observe° you? Must I stand and crouch
Under your testy humor? By the gods,
You shall digest the venom of your spleen,°
Though it do split you; for, from this day forth,
I'll use you for my mirth, yea, for my laughter,
When you are waspish.

50 **Cassius.**   Is it come to this?

Brutus.

You say you are a better soldier:
Let it appear so; make your vaunting° true,
And it shall please me well. For mine own part,
I shall be glad to learn of noble men.

Cassius.

55   You wrong me every way; you wrong me, Brutus;
I said, an elder soldier, not a better.
Did I say, better?

Brutus.   If you did, I care not.

Cassius.

When Caesar lived, he durst not thus have moved°
    me.

Brutus.

Peace, peace, you durst not so have tempted him.

Cassius. I durst not?

60 **Brutus.** No.

Cassius.

What? Durst not tempt him?

Brutus.   For your life you durst not.

Cassius.

Do not presume too much upon my love;
I may do that I shall be sorry for.

Brutus.

65   You have done that you should be sorry for.
There is no terror, Cassius, in your threats;
For I am armed so strong in honesty
That they pass by me as the idle wind,
Which I respect not. I did send to you
70   For certain sums of gold, which you denied me;
For I can raise no money by vile means.
By heaven, I had rather coin my heart
And drop my blood for drachmas than to wring
From the hard hands of peasants their vile trash
75   By any indirection.° I did send
To you for gold to pay my legions,
Which you denied me. Was that done like Cassius?

44. budge: defer.

45. observe: wait on.

47. spleen: fiery temper. (The spleen was believed to be the seat of the emotions.)

52. vaunting: boasting.

? 57. *What did Cassius say?*

58. moved: exasperated.

75. indirection: illegal methods.

? 75. *What do you think of Brutus's moral position here? Does it seem honorable or hypocritical?*

Should I have answered Caius Cassius so?
When Marcus Brutus grows so covetous

80   To lock such rascal counters° from his friends,
Be ready, gods, with all your thunderbolts,
Dash him to pieces!

Cassius.   I denied you not.

Brutus.
You did.

Cassius.   I did not. He was but a fool
That brought my answer back. Brutus hath rived° my
    heart.

85   A friend should bear his friend's infirmities;
But Brutus makes mine greater than they are.

Brutus.
I do not, till you practice them on me.

Cassius.
You love me not.

Brutus.   I do not like your faults.

Cassius.
A friendly eye could never see such faults.

Brutus.

90   A flatterer's would not, though they do appear
As huge as high Olympus.

Cassius.
Come, Antony, and young Octavius, come,
Revenge yourselves alone on Cassius,
For Cassius is aweary of the world:

95   Hated by one he loves; braved° by his brother;
Checked like a bondman; all his faults observed,
Set in a notebook, learned and conned by rote°
To cast into my teeth. O, I could weep
My spirit from mine eyes! There is my dagger,

100   And here my naked breast; within, a heart
Dearer than Pluto's mine,° richer than gold;
If that thou be'st a Roman, take it forth.
I, that denied thee gold,° will give my heart.
Strike as thou didst at Caesar; for I know,
When thou didst hate him worst, thou lovedst him

105   better
Than ever thou lovedst Cassius.

Brutus.   Sheathe your dagger.
Be angry when you will, it shall have scope.
Do what you will, dishonor shall be humor.°
O Cassius, you are yokèd with a lamb

110   That carries anger as the flint bears fire,
Who, much enforcèd, shows a hasty spark,
And straight is cold again.

Cassius.   Hath Cassius lived

80. counters: coins.

84. rived: broken.

95. braved: defied.

97. conned by rote: learned by heart.

99. *What is Cassius doing, and why?*

101. Pluto's mine: the riches under the earth. Pluto was the Roman god of the Underworld (akin to the Greek god Hades); Shakespeare confuses him with Plutus, god of riches.

102. *Notice that Cassius switches from* you *to* thou *here. Why?*

103. That *you say* denied you gold.

108. In other words, dishonor or insults will be seen merely as the result of temperamental idiosyncrasies.

111. *Have Brutus's feelings changed? Why or why not?*

To be but mirth and laughter to his Brutus
When grief and blood ill-tempered vexeth him?

Brutus.

115   When I spoke that, I was ill-tempered too.

Cassius.

Do you confess so much? Give me your hand.

Brutus.

And my heart too.

Cassius.   O Brutus!

Brutus.   What's the matter?

Cassius.

Have not you love enough to bear with me
When that rash humor which my mother gave me
Makes me forgetful?

120   **Brutus.**   Yes, Cassius, and from henceforth,
When you are over-earnest with your Brutus,
He'll think your mother chides, and leave you so.

[*Enter a Poet, followed by* LUCILIUS, TITINIUS, *and* LU-
CIUS.]

Poet.

Let me go in to see the generals;
There is some grudge between 'em; 'tis not meet
They be alone.

125   **Lucilius.**   You shall not come to them.

Poet. Nothing but death shall stay me.

Cassius. How now. What's the matter?

Poet.

For shame, you generals! What do you mean?
Love, and be friends, as two such men should be;

130   For I have seen more years, I'm sure, than ye.

Cassius.

Ha, ha! How vilely doth this cynic° rhyme!

Brutus.

Get you hence, sirrah! Saucy fellow, hence!

Cassius.

Bear with him, Brutus, 'tis his fashion.

Brutus.

I'll know his humor when he knows his time.°

135   What should the wars do with these jigging° fools?
Companion,° hence!

Cassius.   Away, away, be gone!

[*Exit* POET.]

Brutus.

Lucilius and Titinius, bid the commanders
Prepare to lodge their companies tonight.

117. *What actions could mark the change in feelings now?*

122. *How could a humorous note be sounded here?*

131. cynic: rude person.

134. his time: the right time to speak.
135. jigging: rhyming.
136. companion: lower-class fellow.
136. *Remember that Shakespeare himself was a "jigging fool." What is the point of this scene with the poet?*

Cassius.

And come yourselves, and bring Messala with you
Immediately to us. [*Exeunt* LUCILIUS *and* TITINIUS.]

140 **Brutus.**   Lucius, a bowl of wine.

[*Exit* LUCIUS.]

Cassius.

I did not think you could have been so angry.

Brutus.

O Cassius, I am sick of many griefs.

Cassius.

Of your philosophy you make no use,
If you give place to accidental evils.

Brutus.

145   No man bears sorrow better. Portia is dead.

Cassius. Ha? Portia?

Brutus. She is dead.

Cassius.

How scaped I killing when I crossed you so?
O insupportable and touching loss!
Upon what sickness?

150 **Brutus.**   Impatient of my absence,
And grief that young Octavius with Mark Antony
Have made themselves so strong—for with her death
That tidings came—with this she fell distract,°
And (her attendants absent) swallowed fire.°

Cassius.

And died so?

Brutus.   Even so.

155 **Cassius.**   O ye immortal gods!

[*Enter* LUCIUS, *with wine and tapers.*]

Brutus.

Speak no more of her. Give me a bowl of wine.
In this I bury all unkindness, Cassius.

[*Drinks.*]

Cassius.

My heart is thirsty for that noble pledge.
Fill, Lucius, till the wine o'erswell the cup;
160   I cannot drink too much of Brutus' love.

[*Drinks. Exit* LUCIUS.]

[*Enter* TITINIUS *and* MESSALA.]

144. *This reference is to Brutus's philosophy of Stoicism, which taught that we should master our emotions, lead lives dictated by reason and duty, and submit to fate. How should Brutus deliver the next shocking line?*

153. fell distract: became distraught.

154. According to Plutarch, Portia killed herself by putting hot coals in her mouth.

155. *Who is probably more emotional in this scene—Brutus or Cassius? (Many fine actors—Anthony Quayle among them—have been unemotional as they played Brutus in this scene.)*

Brutus.
    Come in, Titinius! Welcome, good Messala.
    Now sit we close about this taper here,
    And call in question° our necessities.
Cassius.
    Portia, art thou gone?
Brutus.   No more, I pray you.
165   Messala, I have here receivèd letters
    That young Octavius and Mark Antony
    Come down upon us with a mighty power,
    Bending their expedition toward Philippi.°
Messala.
    Myself have letters of the selfsame tenure.°
Brutus.
170   With what addition?
Messala.
    That by proscription and bills of outlawry°
    Octavius, Antony, and Lepidus
    Have put to death an hundred senators.
Brutus.
    Therein our letters do not well agree.
175   Mine speak of seventy senators that died
    By their proscriptions, Cicero being one.
Cassius.
    Cicero one?
Messala.   Cicero is dead,
    And by that order of proscription.
    Had you your letters from your wife, my lord?
180 **Brutus.** No, Messala.
Messala.
    Nor nothing in your letters writ of her?
Brutus.
    Nothing, Messala.
Messala.   That methinks is strange.
Brutus.
    Why ask you? Hear you aught of her in yours?
Messala. No, my lord.
Brutus.
185   Now as you are a Roman, tell me true.
Messala.
    Then like a Roman bear the truth I tell,
    For certain she is dead, and by strange manner.
Brutus.
    Why, farewell, Portia. We must die, Messala.
    With meditating that she must die once,°
190   I have the patience to endure it now.
Messala.
    Even so great men great losses should endure.

163. **call in question:** consider.

168. **Philippi:** an ancient city in northern Greece.

169. **tenure:** tenor, meaning.

171. **bills of outlawry:** lists of proscribed people.

? 183. *A peculiar scene now takes place, in which Brutus seems to hear again for the first time the news of his wife's death. Some scholars believe that the original account of Portia's death was told in lines 179–193, and that Shakespeare later rewrote the scene, which is now lines 141–156. A production might not use both scenes. Which would you use, and why? (If a director did decide to use both scenes, how should Brutus act in the second one?)*

189. **once:** at some time.
? 190. *The actor playing Brutus must be careful not to make him seem cold and unfeeling. How could this scene be played to suggest Brutus's humanity, as well as his Stoicism?*

Cassius.
I have as much of this in art° as you,
But yet my nature could not bear it so.
Brutus.
Well, to our work alive. What do you think
195   Of marching to Philippi presently?
Cassius.
I do not think it good.
Brutus.   Your reason?
Cassius.   This it is:
'Tis better that the enemy seek us;
So shall he waste his means, weary his soldiers,
Doing himself offense, whilst we, lying still,
200   Are full of rest, defense, and nimbleness.
Brutus.
Good reasons must of force° give place to better.
The people 'twixt Philippi and this ground
Do stand but in a forced affection,°
For they have grudged us contribution.
205   The enemy, marching along by them,
By them shall make a fuller number up,
Come on refreshed, new-added and encouraged;
From which advantage shall we cut him off
If at Philippi we do face him there,
210   These people at our back.
Cassius.   Hear me, good brother.
Brutus.
Under your pardon. You must note beside
That we have tried the utmost of our friends,
Our legions are brimful, our cause is ripe.
The enemy increaseth every day;
215   We, at the height, are ready to decline.
There is a tide in the affairs of men
Which, taken at the flood, leads on to fortune;
Omitted,° all the voyage of their life
Is bound in shallows and in miseries.
220   On such a full sea are we now afloat,
And we must take the current when it serves,
Or lose our ventures.
Cassius.   Then, with your will,° go on;
We'll along ourselves and meet them at Philippi.
Brutus.
The deep of night is crept upon our talk,
225   And nature must obey necessity,
Which we will niggard with a little rest.°
There is no more to say?
Cassius.   No more. Good night.
Early tomorrow will we rise and hence.

192. in art: the art of being a Stoic.

? 200. *What plan does Cassius propose regarding Antony's forces at Philippi?*

201. of force: of necessity.

203. That is, they support us only grudgingly.

218. Omitted: neglected.

? 222. *Where does Brutus want to fight Antony, and why?*
222. with your will: as you wish.
? 223. *Which man seems to dominate the action now?*

226. niggard with a little rest: cheat with a short period of sleep.

"There is no more to say?"

[*Enter* LUCIUS.]

Brutus.
    Lucius, my gown.   [*Exit* LUCIUS.]
              Farewell, good Messala.
230   Good night, Titinius. Noble, noble Cassius,
    Good night, and good repose.
Cassius.   O my dear brother,
    This was an ill beginning of the night.
    Never come such division 'tween our souls!
    Let it not, Brutus.

[*Enter* LUCIUS, *with the gown.*]

231. *In the production photographed here, at this point in the scene Brutus takes a letter out of his pocket and burns it. What letter are we to assume he is destroying, and what does his action demonstrate?*

Brutus.   Everything is well.

Cassius.

Good night, my lord.

235 **Brutus.**   Good night, good brother.

Titinius, Messala.

Good night, Lord Brutus.

Brutus.   Farewell, every one.

[Exeunt.]

Give me the gown. Where is thy instrument?°

Lucius.

Here in the tent.

Brutus.   What, thou speak'st drowsily?

Poor knave, I blame thee not; thou art o'erwatched.°

240 Call Claudius and some other of my men;

I'll have them sleep on cushions in my tent.

Lucius. Varro and Claudius!

[Enter VARRO *and* CLAUDIUS.]

Varro. Calls my lord?

Brutus.

I pray you, sirs, lie in my tent and sleep.

245 It may be I shall raise you by and by

On business to my brother Cassius.

Varro.

So please you, we will stand and watch your pleas-

ure.°

Brutus.

I will not have it so; lie down, good sirs;

It may be I shall otherwise bethink me.

*[*VARRO *and* CLAUDIUS *lie down.*]

250 Look, Lucius, here's the book I sought for so;

I put it in the pocket of my gown.

Lucius.

I was sure your lordship did not give it me.

Brutus.

Bear with me, good boy, I am much forgetful.

Canst thou hold up thy heavy eyes awhile,

255 And touch thy instrument a strain or two?

Lucius.

Ay, my lord, an't please you.

Brutus.   It does, my boy.

I trouble thee too much, but thou art willing.

Lucius. It is my duty, sir.

Brutus.

I should not urge thy duty past thy might;

260 I know young bloods look for a time of rest.

237. **instrument:** probably a lute.

239. **o'erwatched:** exhausted.

247. **watch your pleasure:** wait for your orders.

Lucius. I have slept, my lord, already.

Brutus.

It was well done, and thou shalt sleep again;
I will not hold thee long. If I do live,
I will be good to thee.

[*Music and a song.*]

265   This is a sleepy tune. O murd'rous° slumber!
Layest thou thy leaden mace° upon my boy,
That plays thee music? Gentle knave, good night;
I will not do thee so much wrong to wake thee.
If thou dost nod, thou break'st thy instrument;

270   I'll take it from thee; and, good boy, good night.
Let me see, let me see; is not the leaf turned down
Where I left reading? Here it is, I think.

[*Enter the* GHOST *of* CAESAR.]

     How ill this taper burns. Ha! Who comes here?
I think it is the weakness of mine eyes

275   That shapes this monstrous apparition.
It comes upon° me. Art thou anything?
Art thou some god, some angel, or some devil,
That mak'st my blood cold, and my hair to stare?°
Speak to me what thou art.

Ghost.

     Thy evil spirit, Brutus.

280 **Brutus.**   Why com'st thou?

Ghost.

     To tell thee thou shalt see me at Philippi.

Brutus. Well; then I shall see thee again?

Ghost. Ay, at Philippi.

Brutus.

     Why, I will see thee at Philippi then.   [*Exit* GHOST.]

285   Now I have taken heart thou vanishest.
Ill spirit, I would hold more talk with thee.
Boy! Lucius! Varro! Claudius! Sirs, awake!
Claudius!

Lucius. The strings my lord, are false.°

Brutus.

290   He thinks he still is at his instrument.
Lucius awake!

Lucius. My lord?

Brutus.

     Didst thou dream, Lucius, that thou so criedst out?

Lucius.

     My lord, I do not know that I did cry.

Stage direction. *How could lighting be used to suggest an intimate, drowsy, and nonmilitaristic scene?*

265. murd'rous: deathlike.

266. mace: a staff carried by public officials.

276. upon: toward.

278. stare: stand on end.

279. *How would you "stage" the Ghost? Would you have him in military dress? In his bloodied toga? Or would you not show the Ghost at all, but merely project his voice onstage?*

289. Lucius sleepily supposes that his instrument is out of tune.

293. *In one production, the ghost scene was staged so that the Ghost's words seemed to come from the mouth of the sleeping Lucius. How would this explain Brutus's question to Lucius about "crying out"?*

Brutus.

295   Yes, that thou didst. Didst thou see anything?

Lucius. Nothing, my lord.

Brutus.

Sleep again, Lucius. Sirrah Claudius!

(*To* VARRO) Fellow thou, awake!

Varro. My lord?

300   **Claudius.** My lord?

Brutus.

Why did you so cry out, sirs, in your sleep?

Both.

Did we, my lord?

Brutus.   Ay. Saw you anything?

Varro.

No, my lord, I saw nothing.

Claudius.   Nor I, my lord.

Brutus.

Go and commend me to my brother Cassius;

305   Bid him set on his pow'rs betimes before,°

And we will follow.

Both.   It shall be done, my lord.

[*Exeunt.*]

305. That is, lead his forces out early in the morning, ahead of Brutus and his troops.

Responding to the Play

Analyzing Act IV

Identifying Facts

1. Describe the military situation as it is presented in Act IV. What is going on between the conspirators and the triumvirate?
2. As Scene 1 opens, what are Antony, Octavius, and Lepidus doing? What breach has opened in the triumvirate?
3. What is Brutus uneasy about at the beginning of Scene 2?
4. Describe the issues that cause Brutus and Cassius to quarrel in Scene 3.
5. According to Brutus, what were the reasons for Portia's death? How does he respond to her death?

6. Brutus and Cassius disagree over military strategy. Who finally gives in?
7. What does the Ghost report will happen in the future?

Interpreting Meanings

8. How is Antony **characterized** by his actions and words in Scene 1? In your opinion, is the portrait of Antony in this scene consistent with the play's earlier characterization of him?
9. It is in the nature of drama that, under pressure, relationships burst open and certain truths are revealed. Usually this happens toward the end of the play. After the exposure, the relationship is either renewed and strengthened, or it is ended. Brutus and Cassius have

been friends throughout the play, with Cassius clearly the subordinate. In Scene 3, they quarrel with each other. How is their **conflict** resolved? What has become of their relationship by the end of the scene?

10. How do you interpret each character's behavior in this quarrel? Do you think their conflict stems from misunderstandings or from deeper causes? (Fear of the future? Guilt about the past? Other insecurities?) Explain your answer.

11. In what ways does the meeting of the conspirators in Scene 3 seem to parallel the meeting of the triumvirate in Scene 1? In what ways are the scenes different?

12. What reason does Brutus give for summoning Varro and Claudius to his tent in Scene 3? What other dramatic purpose does their presence serve in this scene?

13. In the scene with Cassius, we have seen a harsh and overbearing Brutus. What kind of Brutus does Shakespeare show us with the boy Lucius and the guards? How does the quality of this scene contrast with the battle scenes we know are to come?

14. Comment on the significance of the Ghost's appearance. What emotional **tone** do you think this use of the supernatural gives to this scene?

15. Has your opinion of any of the major **characters** changed as the final act approaches?

Analyzing Language and Vocabulary

Anachronisms

An **anachronism** (from *ana-,* "against," and *chronos,* "time") is an event or detail in a literary work that is displaced chronologically—that is, it could not logically be placed at the time when it is portrayed. For example, if a character in a story about the Civil War were to go out and drive a car, the author would be presenting an anachronism, since cars were not invented until a generation later. Anachronisms can also be phrases or sayings. If a character in a play set in the 1920's called someone a "nerd," we'd be hearing an anachronism. *Nerd* didn't develop as slang until much later in the twentieth century.

We often miss the anachronisms in Shakespeare, since we are so far removed in time from Elizabethan England and from the dramatic settings of his plays. And it is doubtful whether Shakespeare's audiences noticed the anachronisms much either. For Shakespeare's spectators, anachronisms would

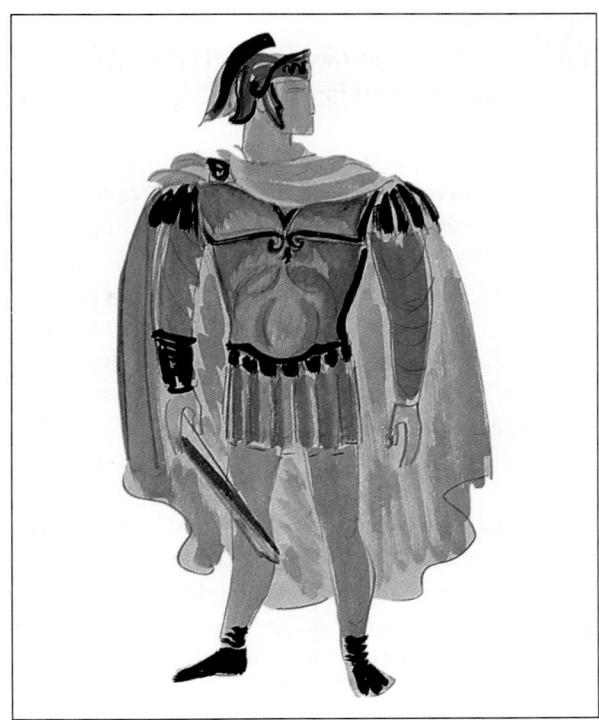

Costume sketch of Octavius by Tanya Moiseiwitsch for the 1955 Stratford Shakespearean Festival production.

The Stratford Shakespearean Festival Foundation of Canada.

have seemed minor, compared to the exciting action of his plots and the brilliance of his language. Remember that *Julius Caesar* is set in 44–43 B.C., in ancient Rome. See if you can identify the anachronism in each of the following passages:

1. Ay, marry, was't, and he put it by thrice, every time gentler than other. . . .
   —Act I, Scene 2, lines 228–229

2. . . . he plucked me ope his doublet and offered them his throat to cut.
   —Act I, Scene 2, lines 263–265

3. Peace! Count the clock.
             The clock hath stricken three.
   —Act II, Scene 1, line 192

4. O, what time have you chose out, brave Caius, To wear a kerchief! . . .
   —Act II, Scene 1, lines 314–315

5. Look, Lucius, here's the book I sought for so. I put it in the pocket of my gown.
   —Act IV, Scene 3, lines 250–251

Act V

Scene 1. *The plains of Philippi.*

Enter OCTAVIUS, ANTONY, *and their* ARMY.

Octavius.
Now, Antony, our hopes are answerèd;
You said the enemy would not come down,
But keep the hills and upper regions.
It proves not so; their battles° are at hand;

5 They mean to warn us at Philippi here,
Answering before we do demand of them.

Antony.
Tut, I am in their bosoms,° and I know
Wherefore they do it. They could be content
To visit other places, and come down

10 With fearful bravery, thinking by this face
To fasten in our thoughts that they have courage;
But 'tis not so.

[Enter a MESSENGER.*]*

Messenger.   Prepare you, generals,
The enemy comes on in gallant show;
Their bloody sign° of battle is hung out,

15 And something to be done immediately.

Antony.
Octavius, lead your battle softly on
Upon the left hand of the even° field.

Octavius.
Upon the right hand I; keep thou the left.

Antony.
Why do you cross me in this exigent?°

Octavius.

20 I do not cross you; but I will do so.

[March. Drum. Enter BRUTUS, CASSIUS, *and their* ARMY;
LUCILIUS, TITINIUS, MESSALA, *and others*.*]*

Brutus.
They stand, and would have parley.

Cassius.
Stand fast, Titinius, we must out and talk.

Octavius.
Mark Antony, shall we give sign of battle?

Antony.
No, Caesar, we will answer on their charge.

25 Make forth, the generals would have some words.

Octavius.
Stir not until the signal.

Stage direction. *This act is crammed with action and could be confusing to follow. Be alert to the movements of the armies. What props might be used to indicate that we are now on the plains of Philippi with Antony's and Octavius's armies?*

4. **battles:** armies.

7. **in their bosoms:** know their secret thoughts.

14. **sign:** flag.

17. **even:** level.

19. **exigent:** critical moment.

Stage direction. *The armies should be placed at opposite sides of the stage, with a kind of no-man's-land between them. In the next lines, notice which man in which army speaks. They are taunting one another across the short distance that separates them.*

Brutus.

    Words before blows; is it so, countrymen?

Octavius.

    Not that we love words better, as you do.

Brutus.

    Good words are better than bad strokes, Octavius.

Antony.

30   In your bad strokes, Brutus, you give good words;

    Witness the hole you made in Caesar's heart,

    Crying "Long live! Hail, Caesar!"

Cassius.   Antony,

    The posture of your blows are yet unknown;

    But for your words, they rob the Hybla° bees,

    And leave them honeyless.

35 **Antony.**   Not stingless too.

Brutus.

    O, yes, and soundless too;

    For you have stol'n their buzzing, Antony,

    And very wisely threat before you sting.

Antony.

    Villains! You did not so, when your vile daggers

40   Hacked one another in the sides of Caesar.

    You showed your teeth like apes, and fawned like
        hounds,

    And bowed like bondmen, kissing Caesar's feet;

    Whilst damnèd Casca, like a cur, behind

    Struck Caesar on the neck. O you flatterers!

Cassius.

45   Flatterers! Now, Brutus, thank yourself;

    This tongue had not offended so today,

    If Cassius might have ruled.°

Octavius.

    Come, come, the cause. If arguing make us sweat,

    The proof of it will turn to redder drops.

50   Look,

    I draw a sword against conspirators.

    When think you that the sword goes up again?

    Never, till Caesar's three and thirty wounds

    Be well avenged; or till another Caesar°

55   Have added slaughter to the sword of traitors.

Brutus.

    Caesar, thou canst not die by traitors' hands,

    Unless thou bring'st them with thee.

Octavius.   So I hope.

    I was not born to die on Brutus' sword.

Brutus.

    O, if thou wert the noblest of thy strain,

60   Young man, thou couldst not die more honorable.

34. Hybla: town in Sicily famous for its honey.

47. ruled: gotten his way.

47. *What is Cassius referring to?*

54. another Caesar: meaning Octavius himself.

Cassius.

A peevish schoolboy, worthless° of such honor,
Joined with a masker and a reveler.

Antony.

Old Cassius still!

Octavius.   Come, Antony; away!
Defiance, traitors, hurl we in your teeth.
65   If you dare fight today, come to the field;
If not, when you have stomachs.

[*Exit* OCTAVIUS, ANTONY, *and* ARMY.]

Cassius.

Why, now blow wind, swell billow, and swim bark!
The storm is up, and all is on the hazard.°

Brutus.

Ho, Lucilius, hark, a word with you.

[LUCILIUS *and* MESSALA *stand forth*.]

Lucilius.   My lord?

[BRUTUS *and* LUCILIUS *converse apart*.]

Cassius.

Messala.

Messala.   What says my general?

70   **Cassius.**   Messala,
This is my birthday; as this very day
Was Cassius born. Give me thy hand, Messala:
Be thou my witness that against my will
(As Pompey was) am I compelled to set
75   Upon one battle all our liberties.
You know that I held Epicurus strong,°
And his opinion; now I change my mind,
And partly credit things that do presage.°
Coming from Sardis, on our former ensign°
80   Two mighty eagles fell, and there they perched,
Gorging and feeding from our soldiers' hands,
Who to Philippi here consorted° us.
This morning are they fled away and gone,
And in their steads do ravens, crows, and kites
85   Fly o'er our heads and downward look on us
As we were sickly prey; their shadows seem
A canopy most fatal, under which
Our army lies, ready to give up the ghost.

Messala.

Believe not so.

Cassius.   I but believe it partly,

61. **worthless:** unworthy.

? 62. *Whom is Cassius taunting here? What does he think of this "new Caesar"?*

68. **on the hazard:** at risk.

76. **held Epicurus strong:** believed in the philosophy of Epicurus, a philosopher of the third century B.C. who believed that omens were worthless.
78. **presage:** foretell.
79. **former ensign:** foremost flag.

82. **consorted:** accompanied.

? 88. *What images in this speech suggest death and decay?*

". . . I am fresh of spirit and resolved
To meet all perils very constantly."

<table>
<tr><td>90</td><td>For I am fresh of spirit and resolved
To meet all perils very constantly.</td></tr>
</table>

90   For I am fresh of spirit and resolved
        To meet all perils very constantly.

Brutus.
        Even so, Lucilius.

Cassius.   Now, most noble Brutus,
        The gods today stand friendly, that we may,
        Lovers in peace, lead on our days to age!

95   But since the affairs of men rests still incertain,
        Let's reason with the worst that may befall.
        If we do lose this battle, then is this
        The very last time we shall speak together.
        What are you then determinèd to do?

Brutus.
100   Even by the rule of that philosophy
        By which I did blame Cato for the death

92. *Remember that the two pairs of men have been talking separately. What action should now take place onstage?*

Which he did give himself; I know not how,
But I do find it cowardly and vile,
For fear of what might fall, so to prevent
105 The time° of life, arming myself with patience
To stay the providence of some high powers
That govern us below.

Cassius.   Then, if we lose this battle,
You are contented to be led in triumph°
Thorough the streets of Rome?

Brutus.
110 No, Cassius, no; think not, thou noble Roman,
That ever Brutus will go bound to Rome;
He bears too great a mind. But this same day
Must end that work the ides of March begun;
And whether we shall meet again I know not.
115 Therefore our everlasting farewell take.
Forever, and forever, farewell, Cassius!
If we do meet again, why, we shall smile;
If not, why then this parting was well made.

Cassius.
Forever, and forever, farewell, Brutus!
120 If we do meet again, we'll smile indeed;
If not, 'tis true this parting was well made.

Brutus.
Why then, lead on. O, that a man might know
The end of this day's business ere it come!
But it sufficeth that the day will end,
125 And then the end is known. Come, ho! Away!

[*Exeunt.*]

105. **time:** term, or natural span.

[?] 107. *Brutus refers again to his Stoic philosophy, which taught that he should be ruled by reason, not by emotion. What is Brutus saying about suicide?*
108. **triumph:** the victorious procession of a conquering Roman general.
[?] 109. *According to this speech, what will happen to the losing armies?*

Scene 2. *The field of battle.*

Alarum.° Enter BRUTUS *and* MESSALA.

Brutus.
Ride, ride, Messala, ride, and give these bills°
Unto the legions on the other side.

[*Loud alarum.*]

Let them set on at once; for I perceive
But cold demeanor° in Octavius' wing,
5 And sudden push° gives them the overthrow.
Ride, ride, Messala! Let them all come down.

[*Exeunt.*]

Alarum: call to arms by drum or trumpet.

1. **bills:** orders.

4. **cold demeanor:** lack of fighting spirit.
5. **push:** attack.
[?] 6. *What orders has Brutus given his army?*

William Shakespeare

Scene 3. *The field of battle.*

Alarums. Enter CASSIUS *and* TITINIUS.

Cassius.
    O, look, Titinius, look, the villains fly!
    Myself have to mine own turned enemy.
    This ensign° here of mine was turning back;
    I slew the coward, and did take it° from him.
Titinius.
5   O Cassius, Brutus gave the word too early,
    Who, having some advantage on Octavius,
    Took it too eagerly; his soldiers fell to spoil,°
    Whilst we by Antony are all enclosed.

[*Enter* PINDARUS.]

Pindarus.
    Fly further off, my lord, fly further off!
10   Mark Antony is in your tents, my lord.
    Fly, therefore, noble Cassius, fly far off!
Cassius.
    This hill is far enough. Look, look, Titinius!
    Are those my tents where I perceive the fire?
Titinius.
    They are, my lord.
Cassius.   Titinius, if thou lovest me,
15   Mount thou my horse and hide thy spurs in him°
    Till he have brought thee up to yonder troops
    And here again, that I may rest assured
    Whether yond troops are friend or enemy.
Titinius.
    I will be here again even with a thought.°   [*Exit.*]
Cassius.
20   Go, Pindarus, get higher on that hill;
    My sight was ever thick. Regard Titinius,
    And tell me what thou not'st about the field.

[*Exit* PINDARUS.]

    This day I breathèd first. Time is come round,
    And where I did begin, there shall I end.
25   My life is run his compass.° Sirrah, what news?
Pindarus (*above*). O my lord!
Cassius. What news?
Pindarus.
    (*Above*) Titinius is enclosèd round about
    With horsemen that make to him on the spur,°

---

3. ensign: standard-bearer.

4. it: the flag (standard).

7. spoil: loot.

? 8. *What have Brutus's and Cassius's armies done?*

15. In other words, dig your spurs into him to make him go at top speed.

19. even with a thought: immediately.

? 24. *What is Cassius referring to here?*

25. run his compass: completed its appointed span.

? 26. *Pindarus stands on the upper stage, suggesting that he is on the hilltop, looking over the field of battle. What does he report to Cassius, who stands below?*

29. on the spur: at top speed.

30   Yet he spurs on. Now they are almost on him.
     Now, Titinius! Now some light. O, he lights too!
     He's ta'en! (*Shout*) And, hark! They shout for joy.

Cassius.
     Come down; behold no more.
     O, coward that I am, to live so long,
35   To see my best friend ta'en before my face!

[*Enter* PINDARUS.]

     Come hither, sirrah.
     In Parthia° did I take thee prisoner;
     And then I swore thee, saving of° thy life,
     That whatsoever I did bid thee do,
40   Thou shouldst attempt it. Come now, keep thine oath.
     Now be a freeman, and with this good sword,
     That run through Caesar's bowels, search this bosom.
     Stand not to answer. Here, take thou the hilts,
     And when my face is covered, as 'tis now,
45   Guide thou the sword—Caesar, thou art revenged,
     Even with the sword that killed thee.   [*Dies.*]

Pindarus.
     So, I am free; yet would not so have been,
     Durst I have done my will. O Cassius!
     Far from this country Pindarus shall run,
50   Where never Roman shall take note of him.   [*Exit.*]

[*Enter* TITINIUS *and* MESSALA.]

Messala.
     It is but change,° Titinius; for Octavius
     Is overthrown by noble Brutus' power,
     As Cassius' legions are by Antony.

Titinius.
     These tidings will well comfort Cassius.

Messala.
     Where did you leave him?

55   **Titinius.**   All disconsolate,
     With Pindarus his bondman, on this hill.

Messala.
     Is not that he that lies upon the ground?

Titinius.
     He lies not like the living. O my heart!

Messala.
     Is not that he?

     Titinius.   No, this was he, Messala,
60   But Cassius is no more. O setting sun,
     As in thy red rays thou dost sink to night,
     So in his red blood Cassius' day is set.
     The sun of Rome is set. Our day is gone;

37. Parthia: an ancient country (corresponding to part of modern Iran) that was the site of many Roman military campaigns.
38. saving of: sparing.

46. *What does Cassius have Pindarus do for him? What does he believe has happened?*

51. change: exchange of fortune.

53. *Titinius and Messala enter from the wings and do not see Cassius's body at first. What irony do we in the audience feel when they enter?*

Clouds, dews, and dangers come; our deeds are done!

65 Mistrust of° my success hath done this deed.

Messala.

Mistrust of good success hath done this deed.
O hateful Error, Melancholy's child,
Why dost thou show to the apt° thoughts of men
The things that are not? O Error, soon conceived,

70 Thou never com'st unto a happy birth,
But kill'st the mother° that engend'red thee!

Titinius.

What, Pindarus! Where art thou, Pindarus?

Messala.

Seek him, Titinius, whilst I go to meet
The noble Brutus, thrusting this report

75 Into his ears. I may say "thrusting" it;
For piercing steel and darts envenomèd
Shall be as welcome to the ears of Brutus
As tidings of this sight.

Titinius.   Hie you, Messala,
And I will seek for Pindarus the while.

[*Exit* MESSALA.]

80 Why didst thou send me forth, brave Cassius?
Did I not meet thy friends, and did not they
Put on my brows this wreath of victory,
And bid me give it thee? Didst thou not hear their
   shouts?
Alas, thou hast misconstrued everything!

85 But hold thee, take this garland on thy brow;
Thy Brutus bid me give it thee, and I
Will do his bidding. Brutus, come apace,°
And see how I regarded Caius Cassius.
By your leave, gods.° This is a Roman's part.

90 Come, Cassius' sword, and find Titinius' heart.

[*Dies.*]

[*Alarum. Enter* BRUTUS, MESSALA, YOUNG CATO,
STRATO, VOLUMNIUS, *and* LUCILIUS.]

Brutus.

Where, where, Messala, doth his body lie?

Messala.

Lo, yonder, and Titinius mourning it.

Brutus.

Titinius' face is upward.

Cato.   He is slain.

Brutus.

O Julius Caesar, thou art mighty yet!

65. **mistrust of:** disbelief in.

65. *What does Titinius think caused Cassius to kill himself?*

68. **apt:** credulous, easily impressed.

71. **the mother:** that is to say, Cassius, who conceived the error.

87. **apace:** quickly.

89. He asks the gods' permission to end his life before the time they have allotted to him.

95 Thy spirit walks abroad, and turns our swords
    In our own proper entrails.   [*Low alarums.*]
    Cato.   Brave Titinius!
    Look, whe'r° he have not crowned dead Cassius.
    Brutus.
    Are yet two Romans living such as these?
    The last of all the Romans, fare thee well!
100 It is impossible that ever Rome
    Should breed thy fellow.° Friends, I owe moe tears
    To this dead man than you shall see me pay.
    I shall find time, Cassius; I shall find time.
    Come, therefore, and to Thasos° send his body;
105 His funerals shall not be in our camp,
    Lest it discomfort us.° Lucilius, come,
    And come, young Cato; let us to the field.
    Labeo and Flavius set our battles on.
    'Tis three o'clock; and, Romans, yet ere night
110 We shall try fortune in a second fight.   [*Exeunt.*]

96. *Why does Brutus invoke Caesar's name?*

97. whe'r: whether.

101. fellow: equal.

104. Thasos: an island in the Aegean Sea, near Philippi.

106. discomfort us: dishearten us.

Scene 4. *The field of battle.*

Alarum. Enter BRUTUS, MESSALA, YOUNG CATO, LUCILIUS, *and* FLAVIUS.

Brutus.
    Yet, countrymen, O, yet hold up your heads!
                                [*Exit, with followers.*]
Cato.
    What bastard° doth not? Who will go with me?
    I will proclaim my name about the field.
    I am the son of Marcus Cato,° ho!
5   A foe to tyrants, and my country's friend.
    I am the son of Marcus Cato, ho!

[*Enter* SOLDIERS *and fight.*]

Lucilius.
    And I am Brutus, Marcus Brutus, I;
    Brutus, my country's friend, know me for Brutus!

[YOUNG CATO *falls.*]

    O young and noble Cato, art thou down?
10 Why, now thou diest as bravely as Titinius,
    And mayst be honored, being Cato's son.
First Soldier.
    Yield, or thou diest.

2. bastard: low fellow.

4. Thus he is Portia's brother. (See note, line 295, page 659.)

7. *Lucilius is impersonating Brutus. What are these young men doing, and why?*

Lucilius.   Only I yield to die.
    There is so much that thou wilt kill me straight,°
    Kill Brutus, and be honored in his death.
First Soldier.
15   We must not. A noble prisoner!

[*Enter* ANTONY.]

Second Soldier.
    Room, ho! Tell Antony, Brutus is ta'en.
First Soldier.
    I'll tell the news. Here comes the general.
    Brutus is ta'en, Brutus is ta'en, my lord.
Antony.
    Where is he?
Lucilius.
20   Safe, Antony; Brutus is safe enough.
    I dare assure thee that no enemy
    Shall ever take alive the noble Brutus.
    The gods defend him from so great a shame!
    When you do find him, or alive or dead,
25   He will be found like Brutus, like himself.°
Antony.
    This is not Brutus, friend, but, I assure you,
    A prize no less in worth. Keep this man safe;
    Give him all kindness. I had rather have
    Such men my friends than enemies. Go on,
30   And see whe'r Brutus be alive or dead,
    And bring us word unto Octavius' tent
    How everything is chanced.°   [*Exeunt.*]

13. That is, there is so much inducement to kill me that you will surely do so right away. (Some editors have interpreted this line to mean that Lucilius is offering his captors money to kill him rather than take him prisoner.)

25. **like himself:** true to his own noble nature.

32. **chanced:** turned out.
32. *Not long ago, Antony was compiling a list of the enemies he was to have murdered. How does he seem to have changed?*

Scene 5. *The field of battle.*

Enter BRUTUS, DARDANIUS, CLITUS, STRATO, *and* VOLUMNIUS.

Brutus.
    Come, poor remains of friends, rest on this rock.
Clitus.
    Statilius showed the torchlight, but, my lord,
    He came not back; he is or ta'en or slain.°
Brutus.
    Sit thee down, Clitus. Slaying is the word;
5   It is a deed in fashion. Hark thee, Clitus.

[*Whispers.*]

3. According to Plutarch, Statilius volunteered to see what was happening at Cassius's camp. If all was well, he was to signal with his torchlight. He did signal, but then was killed while returning to Brutus's camp.
5. *What is Brutus's mood?*

Clitus.

What, I, my lord? No, not for all the world!

Brutus.

Peace then, no words.

Clitus.   I'll rather kill myself.

Brutus.

Hark thee, Dardanius.   [*Whispers.*]

Dardanius.   Shall I do such a deed?

Clitus. O Dardanius!

10   **Dardanius.** O Clitus!

Clitus.

What ill request did Brutus make to thee?

Dardanius.

To kill him, Clitus. Look, he meditates.

Clitus.

Now is that noble vessel° full of grief,

That it runs over even at his eyes.

Brutus.

15   Come hither, good Volumnius; list° a word.

Volumnius.

What says my lord?

Brutus.   Why, this, Volumnius:

The ghost of Caesar hath appeared to me

Two several° times by night; at Sardis once,

And this last night here in Philippi fields.

I know my hour is come.

20   **Volumnius.**   Not so, my lord.

Brutus.

Nay, I am sure it is, Volumnius.

Thou seest the world, Volumnius, how it goes;

Our enemies have beat us to the pit.°

[*Low alarums.*]

It is more worthy to leap in ourselves

25   Than tarry till they push us. Good Volumnius,

Thou know'st that we two went to school together;

Even for that our love of old, I prithee

Hold thou my sword-hilts whilst I run on it.

Volumnius.

That's not an office for a friend, my lord.

[*Alarum still.*]

30   **Clitus.**

Fly, fly, my lord, there is no tarrying here.

Brutus.

Farewell to you; and you; and you, Volumnius.

Strato, thou hast been all this while asleep;

Farewell to thee too, Strato. Countrymen,

13. **vessel:** a figure of speech meaning a human being.

15. **list:** listen to.

18. **several:** separate.

23. **pit:** a trap for capturing wild animals; also, a grave.

My heart doth joy that yet in all my life
35 I found no man but he was true to me.
I shall have glory by this losing day
More than Octavius and Mark Antony
By this vile conquest shall attain unto.
So fare you well at once, for Brutus' tongue
40 Hath almost ended his life's history.
Night hangs upon mine eyes; my bones would rest,
That have but labored to attain this hour.

[*Alarum. Cry within,* "Fly, fly, fly!"]

Clitus.
Fly, my lord, fly!
Brutus.   Hence! I will follow.

[*Exeunt* CLITUS, DARDANIUS, *and* VOLUMNIUS.]

I prithee, Strato, stay thou by thy lord,
45 Thou art a fellow of a good respect.°
Thy life hath had some smatch° of honor in it;
Hold then my sword, and turn away thy face,
While I do run upon it. Wilt thou, Strato?
Strato.
Give me your hand first. Fare you well, my lord.
Brutus.
50 Farewell, good Strato—Caesar, now be still;
I killed not thee with half so good a will.   [*Dies.*]

[*Alarum. Retreat. Enter* ANTONY, OCTAVIUS, MESSALA,
LUCILIUS, *and the* ARMY.]

Octavius. What man is that?
Messala.
My master's man. Strato, where is thy master?
Strato.
Free from the bondage you are in, Messala;
55 The conquerors can but make a fire of him.
For Brutus only overcame himself,
And no man else hath honor by his death.
Lucilius.
So Brutus should be found. I thank thee, Brutus,
That thou hast proved Lucilius' saying true.
Octavius.
60 All that served Brutus, I will entertain them.
Fellow, wilt thou bestow° thy time with me?
Strato.
Ay, if Messala will prefer° me to you.
Octavius. Do so, good Messala.

41. *What does he mean that "night hangs upon" his eyes?*

45. respect: reputation.
46. smatch: trace, taste.

51. *How many bodies now lie upon the stage? It's important for a director of a Shakespearean tragedy to remember how many bodies are onstage. Getting rid of them is often a challenge.*

61. bestow: spend.
61. *How does Octavius indicate by his words to his former enemies that the strife is finally over?*
62. prefer: recommend.

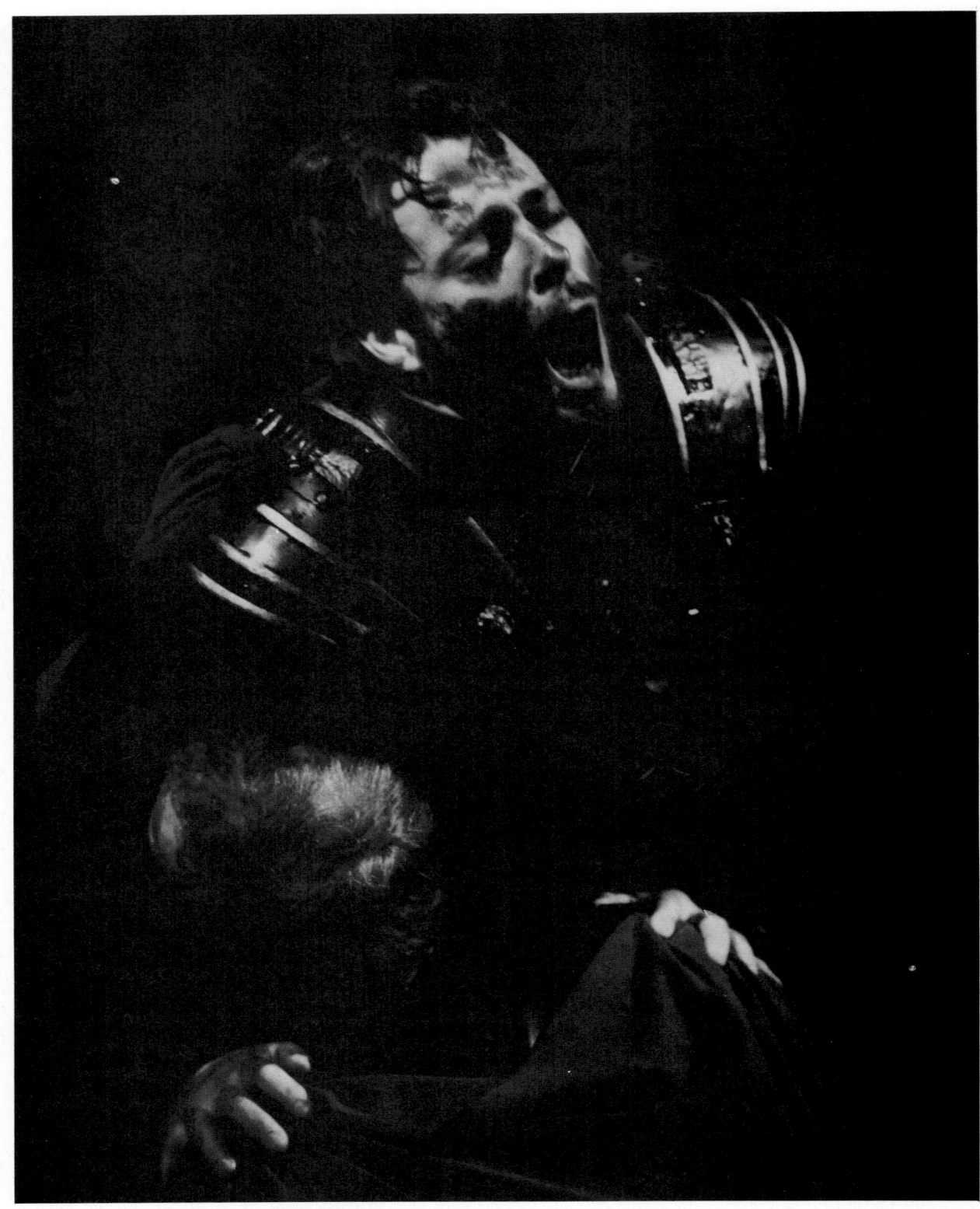

"*. . . Caesar, now be still:*
I killed not thee with half so good a will."

720   William Shakespeare

Messala. How died my master, Strato?

Strato.
65 I held the sword, and he did run on it.

Messala.
Octavius, then take him to follow thee,
That did the latest service to my master.

Antony.
This was the noblest Roman of them all.
All the conspirators save only he
70 Did that they did in envy of great Caesar;
He, only in a general honest thought
And common good to all, made one of them.°
His life was gentle, and the elements
So mixed in him that Nature might stand up
75 And say to all the world, "This was a man!"

Octavius.
According to his virtue, let us use° him
With all respect and rites of burial.
Within my tent his bones tonight shall lie,
Most like a soldier ordered honorably.
80 So call the field to rest, and let's away
To part° the glories of this happy day.

[*Exeunt omnes.*]

72. **made one of them:** joined their group.

76. **use:** treat.

81. **part:** divide.
81. *Order has been restored; healing will begin. Which actor would you have exit last?*

Two Interpretations of the Play

Julius Caesar is capable of at least two interpretations. The question is: Was Brutus heroic in helping to assassinate Caesar? Or were the wars and social chaos that resulted worse than Caesar's despotic rule? Since the dead Caesar triumphs through Antony and Octavius at the end of the play, it may be assumed that Shakespeare's contemporaries saw the play as supporting the rule of a strong monarch—their own Queen Elizabeth I. This interpretation is especially persuasive when we recall that the play was written near the end of Elizabeth's long reign. Since she (like Caesar) was childless and had named no successor, the English dreaded the outbreak of war if succession to the throne were disputed. The words of the Roman historian Plutarch, commenting on the life of Caesar, could have been used for Elizabethan England: ". . . the state of Rome (in my opinion) could not more abide to be governed by many lords, but required one only absolute governor."

But times change. Almost three hundred and fifty years after the first production of *Julius Caesar*, in an age that saw dictators such as Hitler and Mussolini rising to power, American director Orson Welles staged a modern-dress production of Shakespeare's play. In this production, Brutus, striking down the ambitious tyrant, was overwhelmingly viewed as the hero. (A portion of one critic's review of this production appears on page 724.)

Responding to the Play

Analyzing Act V

Identifying Facts

1. Name the four characters who finally confront each other in the first scene of Act V.
2. Explain what Brutus wishes for at the end of Scene 1.
3. As the battle is waged, both sides achieve mixed results. Explain who triumphs over whom?
4. What events and mistaken assumptions lead to Cassius's suicide?
5. Explain why Lucilius behaves as he does in Scene 4. Describe Antony's reaction when Lucilius is captured.
6. Summarize the reasons Brutus gives for his suicide.
7. Describe how Antony and Octavius react to Brutus's death.

Interpreting Meanings

8. Shakespeare knew from his study of Plutarch that the young Octavius, Julius Caesar's great-nephew and adopted son, would eventually eliminate his rival, Antony, and consolidate his rule of the Roman Empire under the title Augustus Caesar. In Scene 1 of this act, there are several hints that Octavius is beginning to assert himself. What are these hints? What significance do you find in the fact that Octavius delivers the final speech of the play?
9. Identify two of the ancient philosophies that are referred to in Scene 1 of this act. What do you think of them? Do you find similar codes of behavior today? Explain.
10. Numerous **ironies** attend the death of Cassius in Scene 3. Identify at least three examples of irony in this scene. How did these ironies affect your feelings about the action at this point?
11. Compare and contrast the dying words of Cassius and Brutus, in Scenes 3 and 5 respectively. In your opinion, how does each man's final speech shed light on both his attitude toward Caesar's murder and on his **character** in general?
12. Taking everything into consideration, describe your view of Brutus at the end. Did he misread the evidence that Caesar might become a dictator? Should he have betrayed a friend for the public good? Knowing that the citizens of Rome were such a fickle, irresponsible mob, was he wrong in doing away with the only strong man who could bring order out of chaos? Give evidence from the play to support your answer.
13. Could the events of the final act ever take place on a modern battlefield? Explain why or why not.

The Play as a Whole

1. Brutus makes two fatal mistakes in *Julius Caesar,* each stemming from his idealized vision of the assassination and from the image of himself as an "honorable man." One error occurs in Act II, and one in Act III. Discuss these errors, and trace the events they set in motion that bring about Brutus's downfall.
2. Many critics have argued (not least from the play's title) that Julius Caesar dominates the play as a whole, just as Cassius says in Act 1 that he "bestrides the world like a Colossus." How would you defend this view that the play is basically Caesar's? What evidence can you cite from the second half of the play that Caesar is still very much "present" in the action?
3. In his essay on tragedy entitled *The Poetics* (written in the fourth century B.C.), the Greek philosopher Aristotle described the **tragic hero** as a person who is more noble than evil, but who experiences a change from good fortune to bad owing to some error or frailty. (See page 796.) Does the Brutus of Shakespeare's play fit this description, in your opinion? Or is the tragic hero someone else, perhaps Caesar himself? Or does the play lack a tragic hero, at least in the Aristotelian sense? Defend your answer. (Remember that it is highly unlikely that Shakespeare would have read Aristotle's essay.)
4. The play makes clear that during the Roman Republic, few words inspired such anxiety in the Romans as the word *king.* Even though the last king had been driven out of Rome nearly five centuries before the time of Julius Caesar, the Romans long remembered the evils that their

ancestors had experienced under such rule.

a. Looking back at the portrayal of Julius Caesar in the play, do you think that the anxieties of Brutus and others about Caesar's potential "kingship" were justified?

b. How do you think Shakespeare's Elizabethan audience, living under a benevolent but absolute monarchy at the time the play was presented, might have regarded this choice between the evils of dictatorship and the evils of anarchy and social chaos?

c. How would people today feel about this problem of "two evils"? Which "evil" would people today fear more?

5. Certain references in Plutarch suggest that the relationship between Brutus and Caesar was so special because Brutus may, in fact, have been Caesar's illegitimate son. It is interesting to note that Caesar's famous last words, *"Et tu, Brutè,"* are reported by Plutarch in Greek as *"kai su, teknon."* In Greek, the last word may mean either "young person" or "child." Look back through the play for passages that focus on the relationship between Brutus and Caesar. Analyzing these passages, can you find any hints of a family tie? Or can you suggest another reason for Caesar to call Brutus "child"?

Writing About the Play

A Creative Response

1. **Updating the Characters.** If Cassius, Brutus, Antony, and Caesar were living today, how would you describe their beliefs, hobbies, values, and career ambitions in the modern world? Write a short personality profile of each of these characters, putting each one in a specific contemporary setting.

2. **Extending the Story.** Several contemporary writers have taken portions of older plays (or novels) and expanded on small episodes to make entirely new works of literature. Take one of the undeveloped episodes in this play and in a brief essay, explain how it might be expanded into a play or novel of its own. You might consider these scenes:

a. Portia's suicide
b. Caesar's last evening alive
c. The discovery of Cinna's body
d. Calphurnia's response to Caesar's murder

3. **Writing Persuasive Essays.** Instead of losing their lives at the conclusion of the play, let us pretend that Brutus, Cassius, and the other conspirators are captured. They are charged with treason and put on trial. Choose one of these situations:

a. You are the attorney who is prosecuting the conspirators. Write an essay that presents your closing argument for conviction to the jury. Choose those facts and details (including quotations) from the play which you feel the jury must consider to return a verdict of guilty. Use words that might have an emotional appeal to your audience. Arrange your facts and details so that your essay will be most persuasive. (For help in writing persuasion, see Exercises in Critical Thinking and Writing, page 728.)

b. You are the attorney who is defending the conspirators. Write an essay presenting your closing argument for acquittal to the jury.

c. You are sitting on the jury for the conspirators' trial. You have listened as both sides presented their cases. But the jury has not been able to come to a unanimous decision regarding the guilt or innocence of the conspirators. As a result, the judge has asked that each jury member write the reasons for voting the way he or she did. Using facts and details (including quotations) from the play explain why you voted the conspirators either guilty or not guilty.

4. **Describing a Modern-Dress Production.** On November 11, 1937, at a time when Hitler and Mussolini were extending Fascist dominance over Europe, director Orson Welles staged a modern-dress *Julius Caesar* at the Mercury Theater in New York City. John Mason Brown, reviewing the play for the *New York Post,* called it a play about "mob mischief and demagoguery," which he and the rest of the audience heard with "today's headlines screaming in our eyes." In Welles's production, Caesar wears a military uniform and boots like those worn by Hitler and Mussolini, and the conspirators wear overcoats and felt hats. The setting is a modern city; the conspirators meet in an alley. They murder Caesar with gangster daggers and Caesar lies in a modern casket in the funeral scene. Here are some extracts from Brown's review. After you read them, write a brief essay of your own in which you propose a new modern-dress version

of *Julius Caesar.* You might consider how you would present these elements of the play:

a. Settings
b. Lights
c. Props
d. Music
e. Background noise
f. Costumes
g. Murder scene
h. Funeral scene
i. Battle scenes
j. Women's roles

The astonishing, all-impressive virtue of Mr. Welles's *Julius Caesar* is that, magnificent as it is as theater, it is far larger than its medium. Something deathless and dangerous in the world sweeps past you down the darkened aisles at the Mercury and takes possession of the proud, gaunt stage. It is something fearful and ominous, something turbulent and to be dreaded, which distends the drama to include the life of nations as well as of men. It is an ageless warning, made in such arresting terms that it not only gives a new vitality to an ancient story but unrolls in your mind's eye a map of the world which is increasingly splotched with sickening colors.

. . . After this surly modern Caesar, dressed in a green uniform and scowling behind the mask-like face of a contemporary dictator, has fallen at the Mercury and new mischief is afoot, we cannot but shudder before the prophet's wisdom of those lines which read:

How many ages hence
Shall this our lofty scene be acted over
In states unborn and accents yet unknown!

He places it [the play] upon a bare stage, the brick walls of which are crimson and naked. A few steps and a platform and an abyss beyond are the setting. A few steps—and the miracle of enveloping shadows, knife-like rays, and superbly changing lights. That is all. And it is all that is needed. In its streamlined simplicity, this setting achieves the glorious, unimpeded freedom of an Elizabethan stage.

. . . Mr. Welles keeps drumming the meaning of his play into our minds by the scuffling of his mobs when they prowl in the shadows, or the herd-like thunder of their feet when they run as one threatening body. It is a memorable device. Like the setting in which it is used, it is pure theater; vibrant, unashamed, and enormously effective.

—John Mason Brown

A Critical Response

5. **Analyzing a Character.** In a brief essay, write a character analysis of Brutus. Use one of the following critical comments as your thesis statement. Be sure to use details from the play to support what the critic says about Brutus.

. . . Brutus is humorlessly good. If his duty is to know himself, his performance fails. Nobility has numbed him until he cannot see himself for his principles. When his principles are expressing themselves, they are beautiful in their clarity. . . . But when he speaks to himself he knows not who is there; he addresses a strange audience, and fumbles. . . . He is not mad or haunted or inspired or perplexed in the extreme. He is simply confused.

—Mark Van Doren

Brutus is an intellectual who can do things, who is not . . . hampered by doubts. He can do things—but he always does them wrong: His advice is invariably fatal, from the moment of the murder down to the battle of Philippi. He cannot realize that men seek their own interests, for he has never sought his own, he has lived nobly among noble thoughts, wedded to a noble wife. He is kind to his servant. Everything he does is touched with fineness. Yet Brutus is not frigid. He just avoids being a prig. We are able to take him to our hearts.

—E. M. Forster

If you do not agree with either of these assessments of Brutus, write an essay in which you provide specific details from the play to refute Van Doren's or Forster's points.

6. **Comparing and Contrasting Characters.** In a brief essay, compare and contrast the characters of Brutus and Cassius; of Cassius and Antony; or of Brutus and Antony. Name at least one way in which the two Romans are alike and at least one way in which they differ. In your final paragraph, describe your responses to each of the men.

7. **Comparing the Play with Its Source.** On page 725 you'll find an extract from Plutarch's *Life of Caesar.* In a brief essay, compare details in Plutarch with details in the pertinent scenes from Shakespeare's play. Before you write, you should organize your data in a chart or outline.

Focusing on Background
Shakespeare's Source: Plutarch

Here is an excerpt from Plutarch's *Life of Caesar,* the essay that Shakespeare used as the basis of his play. Plutarch was a moral historian. Note the lessons he draws from Caesar's tragedy.

"A soothsayer warned Caesar to be on his guard against a great danger on the day of the month of March which the Romans call the Ides; and when this day had come, Caesar, on his way to the senate house, met the soothsayer and greeted him jestingly with the words: 'Well, the Ides of March have come,' to which the soothsayer replied in a soft voice: 'Yes, but they have not yet gone.' And on the previous day Marcus Lepidus was entertaining Caesar at supper, and Caesar, according to his usual practice, happened to be signing letters as he reclined at table. Meanwhile the conversation turned to the question of what sort of death was the best, and, before anyone else could express a view on the subject, Caesar cried out: 'The kind that comes unexpectedly.' After this, when he was sleeping as usual by the side of his wife, all the doors and windows of the bedroom flew open at once; Caesar, startled by the noise and by the light of the moon shining down on him, noticed that Calphurnia was fast asleep, but she was saying something in her sleep which he could not make out and was groaning in an inarticulate way. In fact she was dreaming at that time that she was holding his murdered body in her arms and was weeping over it. Though some say that it was a different dream which she had. They say that she dreamed that she saw the gable ornament of the house torn down and for this reason fancied that she was weeping and lamenting. In any case, when it was day, she implored Caesar, if it was possible, not to go out and begged him to postpone the meeting of the senate; or if, she said, he had no confidence in her dreams, then he ought to inquire about the future by sacrifices and other methods of divination. Caesar himself, it seems, was affected and by no means easy in his mind; for he had never before noticed any superstition in Calphurnia and now he could see that she was in very great distress. And when the prophets, after making many sacrifices, told him that the omens were unfavorable, he decided to send for Antony and to dismiss the senate.

"At this point Decimus Brutus, surnamed Albinus, intervened. Caesar had such confidence in him that he had made him the second heir in his will, yet he was in the conspiracy with the other Brutus and Cassius. Now, fearing that if Caesar escaped this day the whole plot would come to light, he spoke derisively of the prophets and told Caesar that he ought not to give the senate such a good opportunity for thinking that they were being treated discourteously; they had met, he said, on Caesar's instructions, and they were ready to vote unanimously that Caesar should be declared King of all the provinces outside Italy with the right of wearing a diadem in any other place except Italy, whether on sea or land; but if, when they were already in session, someone were to come and tell them that they must go away for the time being and come back again when Calphurnia had better dreams, it would be easy to imagine what Caesar's enemies would have to say themselves and what sort of a reception they would give to Caesar's friends when they tried to prove that Caesar was not a slave master or a tyrant. If, however, he had really made up his mind to treat this day as inauspicious, then, Decimus Brutus said, it would be better for him to go himself to the senate, speak personally to the senators, and adjourn the meeting.

"While he was speaking, Brutus took Caesar by the hand and began to lead him toward the door. And before he had gone far from the door, a slave belonging to someone else tried to approach him, but being unable to get near him because of the crowds who pressed round him, forced his way into the house and put himself into the hands of Calphurnia, asking her to keep him safe until Caesar came back, since he had some very important information to give him.

"Then there was Artemidorus, a Cnidian by birth, and a teacher of Greek philosophy, who for that reason, had become acquainted with Brutus and his friends. He had thus acquired a very full knowledge of the conspiracy, and he came to Caesar with a small document in which he had written down the information which he intended to reveal to him. But when he saw that Caesar took each document that was given to him and then handed it to one of his attendants, he came close up to him and said: 'Read this one, Caesar, and read it quickly and by yourself. I assure you that it is important and that it concerns you personally.' Caesar then took the document and was several times on the point of reading it, but was prevented from doing so by the numbers of people who came to speak to him. It was the only document which he did keep with him and he was still holding it in his hand when he went on into the senate.

"It may be said that all these things could have happened as it were by chance. But the place where the senate was meeting that day and which was to be the scene of the final struggle and of the assassination made it perfectly clear that some heavenly power was at work, guiding the action and directing that it should take place just here. For here stood a statue of Pompey, and the building had been erected and dedicated by Pompey as one of the extra amenities attached to his theater. Indeed it is said that just before the attack was made on him, Caesar turned his eyes toward the statue of Pompey and silently prayed for its good will. This was in spite of the fact that Caesar was a follower of the doctrines of Epicurus; yet the moment of crisis, so it would seem, and the very imminence of the dreadful deed made him forget his former rationalistic views and filled him with an emotion that was intuitive or divinely inspired.

"Now Antony, who was a true friend of Caesar's and also a strong man physically, was detained outside the senate house by Brutus Albinus, who deliberately engaged him in a long conversation. Caesar himself went in, and the senate rose in his honor. Some of Brutus's party took their places behind his chair and others went to meet him as though they wished to support the petition being made by Tillius Cimber on behalf of his brother, who was in exile. So, all joining in with him in his entreaties, they accompanied Caesar to his chair. Caesar took his seat and continued to reject their request; as they pressed him more and more ur-

gently, he began to grow angry with them. Tillius then took hold of his toga with both hands and pulled it down from his neck. This was the signal for the attack. The first blow was struck by Casca, who wounded Caesar in the neck with his dagger. The wound was not mortal and not even a deep one, coming as it did from a man who was no doubt much disturbed in mind at the beginning of such a daring venture. Caesar, therefore, was able to turn round and grasp the knife and hold on to it. At almost the same moment the striker of the blow and he who was struck cried out together—Caesar, in Latin, 'Casca, you villain, what are you doing?' while Casca called to his brother in Greek: 'Help, brother.'

"So it began, and those who were not in the conspiracy were so horror struck and amazed at what was being done that they were afraid to run away and afraid to come to Caesar's help; they were too afraid even to utter a word. But those who had come prepared for the murder all bared their daggers and hemmed Caesar in on every side. Whichever way he turned he met the blows of daggers and saw the cold steel aimed at his face and at his eyes. So he was driven this way and that, and like a wild beast in the toils, had to suffer from the hands of each one of them; for it had been agreed that they must all take part in this sacrifice and all flesh themselves with his blood. Because of this compact, Brutus also gave him one wound in the groin. Some say that Caesar fought back against all the rest, darting this way and that to avoid the blows and crying out for help, but when he saw that Brutus had drawn his dagger, he covered his head with his toga and sank down to the ground. Either by chance or because he was pushed there by his murderers, he fell down against the pedestal on which the statue of Pompey stood, and the pedestal was drenched with his blood, so that one might have thought that Pompey himself was presiding over this act of vengeance against his enemy, who lay there at his feet struggling convulsively under so many wounds."

—from *The Life of Caesar,*
Plutarch,
translated by Rex Warner

Literature & Language

Famous Passages from the Play

Here are some famous passages of the play. Read each passage carefully (in its context, if you wish), and answer the questions that follow.

1. Why, man, he doth bestride the narrow world
   Like a Colossus, and we petty men
   Walk under his huge legs and peep about
   To find ourselves dishonorable graves.
   Men at some time are masters of their fates:
   The fault, dear Brutus, is not in our stars,
   But in ourselves, that we are underlings.
   —Act I, Scene 2, lines 135–141

   a. What **simile** is central to this passage?
   b. Describe the **image** it puts in your mind.
   c. Write a **paraphrase** of the last two lines.

2. Let's be sacrificers, but not butchers, Caius.
   —Act II, Scene 1, line 166

   a. What is a "sacrificer"?
   b. What is a "butcher"?
   c. Why does the speaker not wish to be a "butcher"?

3. Cowards die many times before their deaths;
   The valiant never taste of death but once.
   Of all the wonders that I yet have heard,
   It seems to me most strange that men should fear,
   Seeing that death, a necessary end,
   Will come when it will come.
   —Act II, Scene 2, lines 32–37

   a. **Figuratively,** what does "die" mean in line 32?
   b. What is death compared with in line 33?
   c. How would you **paraphrase** lines 32–33?

4. For Brutus, as you know, was Caesar's angel.
   Judge, O you gods, how dearly Caesar loved him!
   This was the most unkindest cut of all;
   For when the noble Caesar saw him stab,

Ingratitude, more strong than traitors' arms,
Quite vanquished him. . . .
   —Act III, Scene 2, lines 182–187

   a. Find two grammatical constructions in this speech that would be considered erroneous today.
   b. What comparison is implied with the use of the word *cut*?
   c. What **personification** can you find?
   d. How would you **paraphrase** the first line, substituting other words for the word *angel*?

5. The evil that men do lives after them,
   The good is oft interrèd with their bones.
   —Act III, Scene 2, lines 76–77

   a. **Paraphrase** these two lines.
   b. Do you agree with this statement? Explain.

6. There is a tide in the affairs of men
   Which, taken at the flood, leads on to fortune;
   Omitted, all the voyage of their life
   Is bound in shallows and in miseries.
   On such a full sea are we now afloat,
   And we must take the current when it serves,
   Or lose our ventures.
   —Act IV, Scene 3, lines 216–222

   a. Identify the two terms of the central **metaphor** in this passage.
   b. List all the words that **extend** the metaphor.
   c. What words are omitted in the third line?
   d. What other words would you substitute for *ventures*?

Writing

1. **Relating a Passage to Contemporary Life.** Select three of these passages and in a brief essay, explain how each passage could relate to some event or situation or person in contemporary life.
2. **Comparing the Passage with a Poem.** Refer back to the poem "George Gray" by Edgar Lee Masters on page 256, and in a brief essay compare it with the passage in item 6.

ANALYZING AND EVALUATING PERSUASION

Writing Assignment

Write a six-paragraph essay analyzing Antony's funeral speech (pages 682–688). Identify the persuasive devices that Antony uses, and evaluate their effectiveness.

Background

Persuasion is the use of language to influence people to think or behave in a certain way. Mark Antony's funeral speech in Act III is an example of persuasive writing at its most effective. Here are some of the persuasive devices Antony uses:

1. **Specific Evidence.** Specific, detailed evidence—and lots of it—is necessary to back up any opinion. What specific evidence (facts, statistics, incidents) does Antony give to convince his audience that Caesar's murder was *not* justified?
2. **Verbal Irony.** Antony says that Brutus is honorable, but he means the exact opposite. How can we tell? Try saying the ironic lines aloud. How can you make it clear that you mean the opposite of what you're saying?
3. **Loaded Words.** Some words are loaded with powerful **connotations,** or emotional overtones and associations. The associations may be either positive or negative. What are the connotations of the words *honorable, bloody, loved, sacred?* Find other loaded words in the speech.
4. **Repetition.** Advertisers know that people tend to remember and eventually believe messages that are repeated. What message does Antony repeat? Does he really mean what he repeats?
5. **Appeals to Self-interest and Other Emotions.** People can be made to care most about themselves, and everyone longs for a happier, "better" life. How does Antony feed his listeners' self-interests?

6. **Props.** Antony does a "show-and-tell" routine. What powerful props does he use?
7. **Suspense.** How does Antony keep his listeners curious? Why does he pause? What important information does he delay giving them?

Prewriting

After you reread the funeral speech, gather data for your essay by filling out a chart like the following one. Be sure to cite line and page numbers.

Audience and Purpose	Answers/Examples
What does Antony think of his audience?	
What is Antony's purpose? How well does he accomplish his purpose?	
Persuasive Devices	
Specific evidence	
Verbal irony	
Loaded words	
Others	
Which of these devices do you think Antony uses most effectively? Explain why. (You can choose more than one device.)	

Writing

You might organize your essay as follows:
1. **Paragraph 1:** Introductory paragraph including thesis statement. The **thesis statement** should state your **evaluation** of Antony's funeral speech. Paragraphs 2–6 will offer **evidence** to support your evaluation.
2. **Paragraph 2–6:** Discussion of five persuasive devices used in the speech. Discuss a single device in each paragraph, and cite as examples passages and evidence from text.
3. **Paragraph 7:** Concluding paragraph. Summarize your main points, or restate the **main idea.** If you wish, give your own response to the speech.

The following sample essay analyzes and evaluates
Brutus's funeral speech (pages 680–681):

Brutus's Funeral Speech

When Brutus speaks to the Romans, he has two purposes. His first (and surely more important) purpose is to convince his listeners that Caesar's murder was justified. His second purpose is to introduce Mark Antony. He accomplishes this second purpose better than the first. He implies that he's a "good guy" for letting Caesar's best friend speak, but he's naive when he decides not to stay to listen to Antony. Brutus gets a "D−" grade on his speech, while Antony walks away with an "A+." Brutus's speech is practically a failure.

Brutus makes his first mistake when he disperses half of his audience. "Those that will hear me speak, let 'em stay here; / Those that will follow Cassius, go with him . . . (Act III, Scene 2, lines 5–6). Brutus does not have the authority of a powerful leader. By showing that Cassius is equal in power and authority, Brutus makes himself less important.

The most serious flaw in Brutus's speech is that he is not specific or detailed; he is too vague. This is the essence of Brutus's argument: You know that I am an honorable man. (What does he mean by honorable? Is it honorable to assassinate a leader for the reasons Brutus offers?) I loved Caesar as much as you did, but Caesar was a threat to Rome because he was ambitious. Brutus is vague about Caesar's "crimes"; he never tells exactly how Caesar was ambitious or why his ambition was bad. In fact, the word ambitious is a poor choice because it has favorable connotations as well as negative ones. For example, we admire someone for being ambitious and striving to achieve a high goal. But Brutus assumes that ambition is all bad. Brutus's speech is weak because it is too short. He doesn't give any convincing evidence to prove that Caesar deserved to die.

Brutus's logic is faulty also. As part of his justification of Caesar's murder, he says, "Had you rather Caesar were living, and die all slaves, than that Caesar were dead, to live all free men?" (Act III, Scene 2, lines 23–24). This is an example of the either-or fallacy, one kind of faulty reasoning. Brutus says that only two positions are possible: Either Caesar remains alive and all Rome is in slavery, or Caesar is dead and all Rome is free. In fact, there

---

Introductory paragraph. Identifies two purposes.

Evaluates how well he accomplished second purpose.

Thesis statement.

Topic sentence: Gives up his "authority."

Quotes passage and gives act, scene, and line numbers.

Topic sentence: Worst flaw is lack of evidence.

Analyzes (summarizes) main points of argument.
Cites specific instance of vagueness.

Restates paragraph's main idea.

Topic sentence: faulty logic.
Cites specific instance of faulty logic.

Identifies fallacy and explains why it *is* a fallacy.

are many other possible alternatives between these two extremes. And why should we believe Brutus anyway? He doesn't substantiate either of the claims he makes: Why does Caesar alive mean slavery? Why does Caesar dead mean freedom for Rome?

Again, cites lack of evidence.

Brutus uses a powerful emotional appeal when he appeals to his listeners' patriotism, but it's not enough to justify Caesar's murder. He says, "Who is here so rude that would not be a Roman? . . . Who is here so vile that will not love his country?" (Act III, Scene 2, lines 31–33). He pauses for effect, knowing full well that no one will publicly admit to being unpatriotic. Patriotic, of course, is a loaded word; and it's "vile" to be unpatriotic.

Topic sentence: emotional appeal.

Gives example of loaded word.

If we had only Brutus's speech in this act, we'd probably think it wasn't bad. He is very sincere. But Brutus is far less passionate and thus far less convincing to the mob than Antony is. Brutus doesn't use any of the persuasive devices that Antony uses. And he ignores Rule 1 of Persuasive Speaking: Nobody believes anybody without proof. Brutus is vague and illogical, and his rational appeal to patriotism isn't enough to save his speech. Brutus may or may not be an honorable man, but he is certainly a terrible orator.

Cites some good points about speech. Compares Brutus's speech to Antony's.

Summarizes main points of essay.

Clincher sentence.

Checklist for Revision

1. In your introductory paragraph, have you included a thesis statement that states your evaluation of Antony's speech?
2. Have you supported your evaluation with specific evidence from the speech? Have you included *enough* evidence?
3. In Paragraphs 2–6, have you discussed five persuasive devices used in the speech and given specific examples?
4. Have you summarized your main points in a concluding paragraph?
5. Have you cited lines from the play to support your points? Have you checked the quotations for accuracy; used quotation marks; and cited act, scene, and line numbers?
6. Have you checked: Spelling? Punctuation? Capitalization? Sentence structure? Paragraph organization?

THE WESTERN TRADITION IN LITERATURE

The School of Athens (detail) by Raphael (c. 1510). Fresco.   Vatican Palace, Rome.

UNIT SIX   **David Adams Leeming**

THE WESTERN TRADITION

An introduction by **David Adams Leeming**

> " **W**hen the voices of Sophocles, Ovid, and the unknown writer of the Book of Ruth can penetrate the noise and static caused by distance, time, cultural differences, and translation, we are participating in an extraordinary act of communication.''

Agrigentum (detail) by Pierre Henri Valenciennes. (Agrigentum, a city in Sicily, is the site of many ancient Greek and Roman ruins.)

The Louvre, Paris.

The latest incarnation of Oedipus, the continued romance of Beauty and the Beast, stand this afternoon on the corner of Forty-second Street and Fifth Avenue, waiting for the traffic light to change.

—Joseph Campbell

The works of literature chosen for this unit are only a handful of those writings that are seminal to the Western imaginative tradition. Classical mythology and the Bible have influenced writers, painters, and musicians from the times of Moses and Homer down to the present day. The three romances presented here still provide plots, characters, and images for contemporary stories, movies, and even cartoons.

When we read these works of literature, we are experiencing a kind of miracle. When the voices of Sophocles, Ovid, and the unknown writer of the Book of Ruth can penetrate the noise and static caused by distance, time, cultural differences, and translation, we are participating in an extraordinary act of communication.

The selections you'll read in this unit, then, are ones that any educated person in the Western world should be familiar with. But in the long run, these works are basic not only to the Western imagination but to the collective mind of the whole human race as well.

You have probably heard the ancient Greek story about how Hades abducted Persephone, the daughter of the goddess Demeter, and took her to his dismal underworld palace to reign there as his queen. We are told that Demeter, who was in charge of keeping the Earth fertile, mourned for her lost daughter and refused to care for the world. No plants grew and the Earth became barren until Zeus arranged a compromise: Persephone would live with Hades in the underworld for half the year and with her mother on Earth for the other half.

Most of you also probably know the story of Narcissus, who was so self-centered that he fell in love with his reflection in a forest pool and drowned while trying to embrace his own image. Later Narcissus was transformed into a familiar spring flower, as was another unfortunate youth named Hyacinthus.

Myths: The Earliest Form of Literature

Myths are our earliest form of literature. The strange stories about Persephone, Narcissus, and Hyacinthus are probably religious in origin. It seems clear that their purpose was to "explain" the mysterious ways of gods, humans, and nature, and that they orig-

The Literature of Classical Mythology

Greek plate (detail) showing Hercules battling the sea-god Triton.

Tarquinia Museum, Tarquinia, Italy.

Detail of an amphora showing
the warriors Achilles and Ajax playing dice.

Etruscan Museum, Vatican City.

Greek water jar showing Triptolemus, who traveled throughout the world teaching people the skills of farming.

Vatican Museum, Rome.

inated with religious rituals. For example, the story of Persephone's death and revival explains the seasonal cycles. In spring and summer, when Persephone is with her mother, the Earth blooms and flourishes; but when she disappears into the underworld, Demeter's grieving brings on the barren times of autumn and winter. The stories about Narcissus and Hyacinthus suggest early rituals of sacrifice and fertility.

But to modern readers many centuries removed from the ancient rites, these myths are first and foremost entertaining stories that tell us—as all great literature does—what we fear, what we desire, and what we are capable of as human beings.

Classical Greek and Roman Myths

In the Western world, the most important myths have been those of ancient Greece and Rome. Until recently, all serious students began their study of literature with the Greco-Roman classics. In fact, it was impossible to be an educated person without knowing Homer, Sophocles, Ovid, and Virgil.

The Greco-Roman classics are based on myths that had been passed down by word of mouth for generations. Homer, through the *Iliad* and the *Odyssey*, is our main source of Greek myths. Like the great Greek playwrights who came after him—Aeschylus, Sophocles, and Euripides—Homer was a master at developing larger, more sustained works of literature out of fragmentary myths. Bits of myths about the Trojan War were probably known to the people of Homer's time, but in the *Iliad* and the *Odyssey*, Homer breathed new life into them. He turned flat characters into rounded ones and purely symbolic situations into deeply moving, human ones. In the same way, the Greek playwright Sophocles gave flesh and blood to the strange myths of Oedipus and Antigone, while the Roman poet Ovid filled out stories like the one about Daedalus and Icarus and made them leap off the page into life.

The fundamental themes of the old myths are still explored in fiction, poetry, and drama today. Here are a few of the themes found in the myths in this unit. You might recognize them from stories and plays you've read before—and you might even hear their echoes in movies and television today.

1. The idea that a true hero must be willing to sacrifice personal desires and even his family's well-being in order to save his country

2. The idea that the causes of war may not justify the enormous suffering that it produces

3. The idea that individual conscience and divine law are superior to the dictates of civil law

4. The idea that anger, stubbornness, and pride can lead to tragedy

5. The idea that youth is rash and deaf to all warnings to be moderate

6. The idea that in attempting to be "more" than human, human beings can bring disaster upon themselves

Greek water jar showing Hercules with Cerberus, the fierce three-headed watchdog of Hades.

The Louvre, Paris.

It is not known where or when—or even whether—the poet called Homer was born. The ancient Greeks believed that he was blind and that he was the author of both the *Iliad* and the *Odyssey*. Most modern scholars will only go so far as to say that Homer was probably a Greek poet from the area called Ionia who lived in the eighth or ninth century B.C. Whether he composed the two great epic poems attributed to him either alone or with others is open to question.

The War Epic

The *Iliad* is an epic poem composed in the eighth or ninth century B.C., probably by Homer, and written down by others long after that. The *Iliad* was an oral work, meant to be performed rather than read.

The story of the *Iliad* concerns an episode that takes place during the long Trojan War. The war began when a Trojan prince named Paris visited Greece and ran off with Helen, the beautiful wife of King Menelaus (men′ə·lā′əs) of Sparta. In order to punish Paris and retrieve Helen, an alliance of Greek cities attacked the walled city of Troy in Asia Minor (present-day Turkey). These forces were led by Menelaus's brother, King Agamemnon of Mycenae (mī′sə·nē).

When the *Iliad* begins, the war between the Greeks and the Trojans has been at a stalemate for some ten years. The following excerpt is from Book 6, when the tide is beginning to turn in favor of the invading Greeks. The greatest of the Greek warriors is Achilleus, a man of violent temper, whose rage at Agamemnon sets the plot of the *Iliad* in motion. The Trojan super-hero is Hektor, the son of King Priam of Troy and the brother of Paris. In this excerpt, Hektor is about to fight Achilleus and the other Greeks on the dusty plains outside the high walls of Troy. On his way to battle, Hektor rushes home to see his wife, Andromache (an·dräm′ə·kē), who senses disaster and begs him not to fight.

A Note About Greek Names

The Greek names that you are probably familiar with are based on their Latin spellings. However, many modern translators have chosen to use English spellings that are closer to the original Greek. For instance, here is how Richmond Lattimore has spelled certain names in the translation used here. (The first spelling is the traditional Latin-based spelling; the second is the Lattimore spelling.)

Hector—Hektor	Hecuba—Hekabe (hek′ə·bē)
Athena—Athene	Iliam—Ilion (another name for Troy)
Achilles—Achilleus	Achaeans—Achaians (ə·kē′ənz)

It is also important to note that Homer never refers to the Greeks as Greeks; he calls them by their old tribal or city names, such as the Achaians and the Argives.

The Iliad
by Homer

Greek drinking cup (detail) showing Helen of Troy and Priam.

Tarquinia Museum, Tarquinia, Italy.

" **The** *Iliad* was an oral work, meant to be performed rather than read."

Hektor's Farewell to Andromache

Homer, translated by **Richmond Lattimore**

. . . Hektor of the shining helm° departed and in speed
made his way to his own well-established dwelling,
but failed to find in the house Andromache of the white
    arms;
for she, with the child, and followed by one fair-robed
    attendant,
5 had taken her place on the tower in lamentation, and
    tearful.
When he saw no sign of his perfect wife within the house,
    Hektor
stopped in his way on the threshold and spoke among
    the handmaidens:
"Come then, tell me truthfully as you may, handmaidens:
where has Andromache of the white arms gone? Is she
with any of the sisters of her lord or the wives of his
10 brothers?
Or has she gone to the house of Athene where all the
    other
lovely-haired women of Troy propitiate° the grim god-
    dess?"

Then in turn the hard-working housekeeper gave him an
    answer:
"Hektor, since you have urged me to tell you the truth,
    she is not
with any of the sisters of her lord or the wives of his
15 brothers,
nor has she gone to the house of Athene, where all the
    other
lovely-haired women of Troy propitiate the grim goddess,
but she has gone to the great bastion of Ilion, because
    she heard that
the Trojans were losing, and great grew the strength of
    the Achaians.
20 Therefore she has gone in speed to the wall, like a woman
gone mad, and a nurse attending her carries the baby."

So the housekeeper spoke, and Hektor hastened from his
    home
backward by the way he had come through the well-laid
    streets. So
as he had come to the gates on his way through the great
    city,

1. **helm:** helmet.

12. **propitiate** (prə·pish′ē·āt′): appease, pac-
ify.

Hektor and Andromache. Illustration from the
oldest surviving manuscript of the *Iliad*.

Scansani-Biblioteca Ambroisiana, Milan.

the Skaian gates,° whereby he would issue into the plain, there

25

at last his own generous wife came running to meet him,
Andromache, the daughter of high-hearted Eëtion;°
Eëtion, who had dwelt underneath wooded Plakos,°
in Thebe below Plakos, lord over the Kilikian° people.
It was his daughter who was given to Hektor of the bronze helm.°

30

She came to him there, and beside her went an attendant carrying
the boy in the fold of her bosom, a little child, only a baby,
Hektor's son, the admired, beautiful as a star shining,
whom Hektor called Skamandrios, but all of the others
Astyanax—lord of the city;° since Hektor alone saved Ilion.

35

Hektor smiled in silence as he looked on his son, but she,
Andromache, stood close beside him, letting her tears fall,
and clung to his hand and called him by name and spoke to him: "Dearest,
your own great strength will be your death, and you have no pity
on your little son, nor on me, ill-starred, who soon must be your widow;

40

for presently the Achaians, gathering together,
will set upon you and kill you; and for me it would be far better
to sink into the earth when I have lost you, for there is no other
consolation for me after you have gone to your destiny—
only grief; since I have no father, no honored mother.

45

It was brilliant Achilleus who slew my father, Eëtion,
when he stormed the strong-founded citadel of the Kilikians,
Thebe of the towering gates. He killed Eëtion
but did not strip his armor, for his heart respected the dead man,

50

but burned the body in all its elaborate war-gear
and piled a grave mound over it, and the nymphs of the mountains,
daughters of Zeus of the aegis,° planted elm trees about it.
And they who were my seven brothers in the great house all went
upon a single day down into the house of the death god,

---

25. **Skaian** (sē′ən) **gates:** the northwest gates of the walled city of Troy.

27. **Eëtion** (ē·ē′tē·on): Andromache's father, king of Thebe (thē·bē), a city near Troy that Achilleus sacked during the ninth year of the Trojan War. Thebe was allied with Troy. (Thebe is not the same city as the legendary Thebes in Greece.)
28. **Plakos:** a mountain in Thebe.
29. **Kilikian** (ki·lik′ē·ən): the province in Asia Minor where Thebe was located.

35. **Astyanax . . . city:** The name *Astyanax* means "lord of the city."

52. **aegis** (ē·jis): Zeus's shield, made from the hide of the goat that had suckled him.

for swift-footed brilliant Achilleus slaughtered all of
55   them°
as they were tending their white sheep and their lumber-
      ing oxen;
and when he had led my mother, who was queen under
      wooded Plakos,
here, along with all his other possessions, Achilleus
released her again, accepting ransom beyond count, but
      Artemis°
of the showering arrows struck her down in the halls of
60   her father.
Hektor, thus you are father to me, and my honored
      mother,
you are my brother, and you it is who are my young
      husband.
Please take pity upon me then, stay here on the rampart,
that you may not leave your child an orphan, your wife
      a widow,
but draw your people up by the fig tree, there where the
65   city
is openest to attack, and where the wall may be mounted.
Three times their bravest came that way, and fought there
      to storm it
about the two Aiantes and renowned Idomeneus,
about the two Atreidai and the fighting son of Tydeus.°
Either some man well skilled in prophetic arts had spo-
70   ken,
or the very spirit within themselves had stirred them to
      the onslaught.''

Then tall Hektor of the shining helm answered her: ''All
      these
things are in my mind also, lady; yet I would feel deep
      shame
before the Trojans, and the Trojan women with trailing
      garments,
75   if like a coward I were to shrink aside from the fighting;
and the spirit will not let me, since I have learned to be
      valiant
and to fight always among the foremost ranks of the
      Trojans,
winning for my own self great glory, and for my father.
For I know this thing well in my heart, and my mind
      knows it:
80   there will come a day when sacred Ilion shall perish,
and Priam, and the people of Priam of the strong ash
      spear.

55. **slaughtered all of them:** When Achilleus sacked Thebe, he killed King Eëtion and his seven sons. Achilleus showed his respect for the king by burying him in full armor. Later, mountain nymphs planted a grove around Eëtion's grave.

59. **Artemis** (är′tə·mis): Apollo's twin sister, the chaste goddess of the hunt and of the moon. When a woman died suddenly and painlessly, she was said to have been struck down by Artemis's arrow.

69. **Aiantes** (ī·än′tēz) . . . **Tydeus** (tī·dē′əs): various Greek warriors.

Greek helmet (c. 460 B.C.). Bronze.

But it is not so much the pain to come of the Trojans
that troubles me, not even of Priam the king nor Hekabe,°
not the thought of my brothers who in their numbers and
    valor
shall drop in the dust under the hands of men who hate
85   them,
as troubles me the thought of you, when some bronze-
    armored
Achaian leads you off, taking away your day of liberty,
in tears;° and in Argos you must work at the loom of
    another,
and carry water from the spring Messeis or Hypereia,°
90   all unwilling, but strong will be the necessity upon you;
and some day seeing you shedding tears a man will say
    of you:
'This is the wife of Hektor, who was ever the bravest
    fighter
of the Trojans, breakers of horses, in the days when they
    fought about Ilion.'
So will one speak of you; and for you it will be yet a
    fresh grief,
to be widowed of such a man who could fight off the day
95   of your slavery.
But may I be dead and the piled earth hide me under
    before I
hear you crying and know by this that they drag you
    captive.''

So speaking glorious Hektor held out his arms to his
    baby,
who shrank back to his fair-girdled nurse's bosom
100   screaming, and frightened at the aspect of his own father,
terrified as he saw the bronze and the crest with its horse-
    hair,
nodding dreadfully, as he thought, from the peak of the
    helmet.
Then his beloved father laughed out, and his honored
    mother,
and at once glorious Hektor lifted from his head the
    helmet
105   and laid it in all its shining upon the ground. Then taking
up his dear son he tossed him about in his arms, and
    kissed him,
and lifted his voice in prayer to Zeus and the other im-
    mortals:
"Zeus, and you other immortals, grant that this boy, who
    is my son,
may be as I am, preeminent among the Trojans,

83. **Hekabe** (Hecuba): Priam's wife and Hektor's mother.

88. **taking . . . tears:** It was customary for the victors to take captured enemy citizens home as slaves.
89. **Messeis** (mes·ē′is) **or Hypereia** (hī′pə·rī′ə): wellsprings in Greece.

Bronze sword hilt found in Myce-naean tomb (15th century B.C.).

National Museum, Athens.

110   great in strength, as am I, and rule strongly over Ilion;
        and some day let them say of him: 'He is better by far
           than his father,'
        as he comes in from the fighting; and let him kill his
           enemy
        and bring home the blooded spoils, and delight the heart
           of his mother.''

        So speaking he set his child again in the arms of his
           beloved
115   wife, who took him back again to her fragrant bosom
        smiling in her tears; and her husband saw, and took pity
           upon her,
        and stroked her with his hand, and called her by name
           and spoke to her:
        "Poor Andromache! Why does your heart sorrow so
           much for me?
        No man is going to hurl me to Hades,° unless it is fated,
120   but as for fate, I think that no man yet has escaped it
        once it has taken its first form, neither brave man nor
           coward.
        Go therefore back to our house, and take up your own
           work,
        the loom and the distaff,° and see to it that your hand-
           maidens
        ply their work also; but the men must see to the fighting,
125   all men who are the people of Ilion, but I beyond others.''

        So glorious Hektor spoke and again took up the helmet
        with its crest of horse-hair, while his beloved wife went
           homeward,
        turning to look back on the way, letting the live tears fall.
        And as she came in speed into the well-settled household
        of Hektor the slayer of men, she found numbers of hand-
130   maidens
        within, and her coming stirred all of them into lamenta-
           tion.
        So they mourned in his house over Hektor while he was
           living
        still, for they thought he would never again come back
           from the fighting
        alive, escaping the Achaian hands and their violence.

119. **Hades** (hā′dēz): the Underworld, home of the dead. The Greeks believed that all dead souls dwelt in the Underworld, which was not primarily a place of punishment.

123. **distaff:** a staff on which flax or wool is wound for use in spinning.

Responding to the Poem

Analyzing the Poem

Identifying Details

1. What does Andromache ask of Hektor? What reasons does she give for her request?
2. How does Hektor reply to her request? What reasons does he give for his decision?
3. How does the infant Astyanax react to his father? Why?
4. What does Hektor ask of Zeus and the other gods?

Interpreting Meanings

5. Hektor begins his reply to Andromache's plea by saying, "All these things are in my mind also, lady." How would you describe Hektor's inner **conflict**? What do you think about the way he resolves it?
6. Andromache doesn't say a word in response to her husband's speech. Do you think Hektor has convinced her that his course of action is necessary? Explain.
7. In ancient days, young Greek men studied the *Iliad* to learn their culture's values. What values do you think this excerpt teaches? What does it reveal about the roles of men and women in Trojan society?
8. At the end of his speech, Hektor tries to console Andromache by discussing fate. If all that remained of Greek literature were these few lines, what could you conclude about the Greek concept of fate?
9. Remember that Hektor is an enemy of the Greeks and that the *Iliad* is a Greek epic composed for a Greek audience, many of whom claimed to trace their ancestry back to the Greek heroes of the Trojan war. Describe how Hektor is **characterized** by his words and actions in this part of the story. How is this characterization unlike what we might expect to learn about the enemy?
10. What do you think Homer is trying to say about war by including in his poem a scene of farewell between an enemy warrior and his family? Emotionally, how is this whole scene like the incident in which Hektor removes his helmet?

Writing About the Poem

A Creative Response

1. **Updating the Farewell Scene.** How would you update this scene to include a "modern Hektor" and a "modern Andromache"? Write a brief synopsis of a modern parallel, paying attention to the following elements:

   a. Setting
   b. Basic situation
   c. Nature of the conflict
   d. Characterization of Hektor and Andromache
   e. Resolution of the conflict

   If you like, include a few lines of modern dialogue between the husband and wife.

A Critical Response

2. **Responding to a Critic's Comment.** In his introduction to his translation of the *Iliad*, Richmond Lattimore makes the following comment about Hektor:

   > Hektor's tragedy is that of Troy. He, like it, is destroyed fighting a quarrel unworthy of him. He does not believe in Paris's quarrel, and he does not like to fight. . . . Not bloodthirsty enough to be a natural warrior, he fights finely from a sense of duty and a respect for the opinions of others. . . . Some hidden weakness, not cowardice but perhaps the fear of being called a coward, prevents him from liquidating a war which he knows perfectly well is unjust. . . .
   >
   > —Richmond Lattimore

   Write a brief essay stating your response to this analysis of Hektor's **character** and **motives**. Cite specific details from the excerpt to support your opinions. At the end of your essay, tell whether or not Lattimore's comment could also apply to a soldier today.

3. **Comparing and Contrasting Translations.** In this farewell scene, Andromache's first words to her husband, as translated by Richmond Lattimore, are these:

"Dearest, your own great strength will be your death. . . ."

Here are five other translations of the same lines:

1. "O noblest in desire,
   Thy mind, inflamed with other's good, will set thy self on fire."

   —George Chapman, 1598

2. "Too daring Prince! . . .
   For sure such courage length of life denies,
   And thou must fall, thy virtue's sacrifice."

   —Alexander Pope, 1715

3. "Ah, my husband, this prowess of thine will be thy doom. . . ."

   —A. T. Murray (prose), 1924

4. "Ah, Hector, possessed by a demon, your might as a fighter
   Will be the death of you yet."

   —Ennis Rees, 1963

5. "Oh, my wild one, your bravery will be your own undoing!"

   —Robert Fitzgerald, 1974

Write a brief essay of one or two paragraphs comparing and contrasting these translations. Which translation do you like best? Which do you like least? Do they all contain the same basic ideas, or are there significant differences in content?

Analyzing Language and Vocabulary

Epithets

When we call Wilt Chamberlain "Wilt the Stilt," we are using one of the **conventions,** or devices, of Homer's epics—the epithet. An **epithet** is a word or phrase that names some characteristic or object associated with a person or thing. Throughout the *Odyssey*, for example, Homer uses such epithets as *the wine-dark sea* and *the rosy-fingered dawn.*

Classical scholars believe that epithets originated in the oral tradition. Hundreds of years before Homer composed the *Iliad*, traveling storytellers recited from memory long poems about the Trojan War. Each major character, as well as many objects and places, had several epithets—stock phrases of description—that the storyteller could use to fill out the meter of a line. For example, if an epithet was needed to make the meter work in a particular line, Hektor could be called "glorious Hektor" or "Hektor of the bronze helm," depending on the number of syllables required.

Identify the epithets in each of the following excerpts from the *Iliad:*

1. ". . . where has Andromache of the white arms gone?"
2. ". . . where all the other / lovely-haired women of Troy propitiate the grim goddess . . ."
3. ". . . at last his own generous wife came running to meet him, / Andromache, the daughter of high-hearted Eëtion; . . ."
4. ". . . for swift-footed brilliant Achilleus slaughtered all of them. . . ."
5. ". . . but Artemis / of the showering arrows struck her down in the halls of her father."
6. "Then tall Hektor of the shining helm answered her. . . ."
7. ". . . there will come a day when sacred Ilion shall perish, / and Priam, and the people of Priam of the strong ash spear."
8. "And as she came in speed into the well-settled household / of Hektor the slayer of men, she found numbers of handmaidens / within. . . ."

Take five famous figures from today's news and create epithets for them.

Detail from a Parthenon frieze (c. 438–432 B.C.). Marble.

British Museum, London.

Antigone
by Sophocles

"**All** the actors were men, and the choruses were well-trained boys. By switching masks, each actor could play several roles."

Greek Dionysian mask (early 1st century A.D.). Bronze, silver inlay, and traces of copper. H.12″.

The Metropolitan Museum of Art, New York. Gift of Gérard van der Kemp, 1958.

Greek drama grew out of ancient religious rituals honoring Dionysos (dī′ə·nī′səs), the god of wine and fertility. During these celebrations, worshipers danced around the altar of the god, singing hymns to the wild, passionate accompaniment of the flute.

At some point during the sixth century B.C., these Dionysian celebrations became an annual festival held in Athens at a large outdoor amphitheater. Eventually, the dancing choruses of worshipers began competing for prizes (a bull or a goat). Tradition has it that a man named Thespis transformed these hymns into songs that still honored Dionysos but also told the story of a famous hero, or even another god. Then Thespis added another innovation: One of the chorus members would step away from the others to play the part of that hero or god. This individual actor wore a mask and entered into a dialogue with the chorus. Drama was born when the playwright Aeschylus (es′kə·ləs) added a second individual actor to the performance, thereby creating the possibility of conflict.

By the end of the fifth century B.C., this annual festival, called the Dionysia, had become a four-day extravaganza. Public business was suspended; prisoners were released on bail. As many as fourteen thousand spectators gathered in the open-air Theater of Dionysos to watch as playwrights chosen by the city magistrates competed for prizes in tragedy and comedy. After an opening day of traditional choral hymns, three dramatists in each category presented their plays over the next three days. Each morning, one of the playwrights presented three tragedies and a satyr play, and that afternoon, another playwright presented a comedy. The tragedies were serious treatments of religious and mythic questions. The **satyr plays** (named for the lecherous wood demons, or *satyrs*, who formed the chorus) were comic and even raucous treatments of the same themes.

The Greek Theater

The Theater of Dionysos looked like a semicircular football stadium. The seats were carved out of stone on a hillside; at the bottom was a performance area divided into two parts. In the front was a rounded orchestra, a fairly large space where the chorus sang and danced around the remnant of an altar. Behind the orchestra was a platform where the actors spoke their lines from behind huge masks. These masks had exaggerated mouthpieces that amplified the actors' voices. Many were stylized into familiar character types that were easily recognized by the audience. All the actors were men, and the choruses were well-trained boys. By switching masks, each actor could play several roles.

A few days before the festival of Dionysos began, that year's competing playwrights, choruses, and actors would march in a procession through the city of Athens. A herald would announce the titles of the competing plays, and masked revelers would dance through the streets, carrying a statue of Dionysos from the god's temple to his theater.

Sophocles

Sophocles (496?—406 B.C.) is generally considered the greatest of the ancient Greek playwrights. Few writers from any period have had a greater impact on drama, and few have been better loved in their own lifetimes.

A prominent citizen of Athens, Sophocles was known for his musical, poetic, and dramatic talents. He also took an active role in public life, serving as general, political leader, and priest. He is said to have been extremely handsome and graceful. At the age of seventeen, he was the *choragos*, or chorus leader, in a dramatic celebration of Greece's victory over Persia. When he was twenty-eight, he caused a sensation by winning first prize for tragedy at the festival of Dionysos, defeating Aeschylus, the leading playwright of the day. Over the next sixty-two years, Sophocles went on to win twenty-four first prizes and seven second prizes in thirty-one competitions—the best record of any Greek playwright.

Sophocles made good use of a remarkably long life, writing more than one hundred and twenty tragedies, of which only seven survive today. A religious conservative, he was deeply concerned with the individual's need to find a place in the existing moral and cosmic order. His plays always contain a moral lesson—usually a caution against pride and religious indifference. Sophocles was also a great technical innovator: He added a third actor to Aeschylus's original two, introduced painted sets, and expanded the size of the chorus to fifteen.

Few plays are more universally admired than Sophocles' three "Theban" plays—three tragedies about King Oedipus (e'də·pəs) of Thebes and his family. Sophocles wrote these plays over a forty-year period, and actually began with the third part of the story, *Antigone*, first performed in 442 B.C. Twelve years later, Sophocles backtracked and wrote the first part of the story, *Oedipus the King*. It wasn't until the last year of his life that Sophocles wrote the middle segment, *Oedipus at Colonus*.

Perhaps the ninety-year-old playwright hoped that people would soon say of him what one of his characters says after Oedipus dies and is mysteriously carried off by the gods:

> . . . he was taken without lamentation,
> Illness or suffering; indeed his end
> Was wonderful if mortal's ever was.
>
> —from *Oedipus at Colonus*

The Background of *Antigone*

The basic plot of *Antigone* was part of a long mythic story that was as familiar to Athenian audiences as stories about George Washington or Abraham Lincoln are to us. For Greek audiences watching *Antigone*, suspense came not from their anxiety about what would happen next, but rather from their knowledge of things the characters on stage did not know. As these characters spoke in their

Greek vase (late 6th century B.C.) showing Dionysos standing between a maenad and a satyr.

The Metropolitan Museum of Art, New York. Rogers Fund, 1906.

> "A religious conservative, Sophocles was deeply concerned with the individual's need to find a place in the existing moral and cosmic order."

Greek drinking cup (detail) showing Oedipus pondering the riddle of the Sphinx.

Vatican Museum, Rome.

ignorance, the audience pitied them and wanted to warn them of their impending doom.

The following story is the myth the Athenians knew and the one that we must also know if we are to understand *Antigone*.

The Oedipus Myth

King Laios (lī′os) and Queen Jocasta of Thebes learned from an oracle that their newborn son would kill his father and marry his mother. Horrified by this prediction, they gave their baby to a shepherd with orders to leave the infant to die on a nearby mountainside with his ankles pinned together. But the shepherd took pity on the baby. Instead of abandoning him, he gave him to a Corinthian shepherd, who in turn gave the baby to the childless king and queen of Corinth. They named him Oedipus, which means "swollen foot" or "club foot," and raised him as their son. They never told him he was adopted.

When Oedipus was a young man, he learned of the prediction that made his true parents forsake him. Believing the king and queen of Corinth to be his real parents, he ran away from home to avoid such a terrible fate. In the course of his travels, he encountered an arrogant old man who tried to run him off the road with his chariot. Because honor was at stake, the two men fought, and Opedipus killed the stranger. Thinking no more of the incident—such occurrences were probably common on the roads in those days—Oedipus continued on his journey to the city of Thebes.

At the outskirts of the city, he encountered the Sphinx, a terrible monster with the wings of an eagle, the body of a lion, and the head of a woman. This Sphinx had been menacing Thebes by lying in ambush for travelers and then challenging them to answer a riddle. If they could answer it correctly, they could proceed on their way; if not, the Sphinx would devour them. So far, no one had been able to solve the riddle, which went like this: "What creature goes on four legs in the morning, two legs in the afternoon, and three legs in the evening?" Oedipus immediately guessed that the answer was "man": He crawls on all fours as an infant, walks on two legs as an adult, and leans on a cane in old age. Upon hearing Oedipus's answer, the defeated Sphinx leaped into the sea.

When Oedipus arrived in Thebes, the people welcomed him as their savior. Since Laios, their king, had recently been killed, they offered Oedipus their throne and the young widowed queen, Jocasta, as his bride. So Oedipus became king of Thebes, married Jocasta, and had four children with her: two sons, Polyneices (po·li·nī′səz) and Eteocles (e·tē′ə·klēz); and two daughters, Antigone (an·tig′ə·nē′) and Ismene (is·men′ē).

All went well for many years until a plague struck Thebes. Desperate to learn the cause, Oedipus sent Jocasta's brother, Creon, to consult the great oracle at Delphi. The oracle warned that the plague would not end until Thebes had punished the murderer of King Laios, who lived among them undetected. Oedipus vowed to save Thebes once again by finding this murderer. After questioning several people, including the blind prophet Teiresias (tī·rē′sē·əs), he discovered that the man he had killed on the road years before was none other than King Laios. Furthermore, he learned that he was not the son of the king and queen of Corinth, but rather the son of Laios and Jocasta. Thus Oedipus had in fact fulfilled the oracle—he had killed his father and married his mother. When Oedipus and Jocasta discovered this horrible truth, she killed herself and he gouged out his eyes to punish himself for having been blind to the truth.

After these disasters, Creon took over as regent (acting ruler) of Thebes, and after several years he decided to exile Oedipus. Accompanied only by his daughter Antigone (in some versions of the myth, also by Ismene), Oedipus wandered the countryside as a beggar until he reached the sanctuary of Colonus, where he died.

Antigone returned to Thebes, where her two brothers had agreed to rule in alternate years. Eteocles' turn came first, but when it ended, he refused to give up his throne to Polyneices. Polyneices fled to the city of Argos, where he raised an army and attacked the seven gates of Thebes. The Thebans repulsed each assault, but in the course of the battle, Eteocles and Polyneices killed each other.

Creon then became king of Thebes and gave Eteocles, his ally, a hero's burial. Creon considered Polyneices a traitor, so he decreed that his body be left unburied, to rot in the sun outside the city gates. To the Greeks, this was a terrible punishment: Their holiest laws demanded that certain burial rites be performed, or else the soul of the dead person would be condemned to eternal unrest. This is the basis of Creon's conflict with the strong-willed Antigone: As you will see, she believes that God's laws must be obeyed, whatever the consequences.

The Themes of *Antigone*

The conflict in *Antigone*—individual conscience at odds with established authority—is eternally relevant. When we know that those in power are morally wrong, do we break their laws, or do we collaborate with them by obeying? This was a crucial question for some Europeans during World War II. It was against the law, for instance, to help Jews escape the Nazis in Germany and Nazi-occupied Europe. Despite the official censorship that existed in occupied France during World War II, the French playwright Jean Anouilh (ȧ·nü′y′) presented his own version of *Antigone*. His characters wore modern military uniforms and carried guns instead of swords; Creon is portrayed as the dictator of a contemporary police state. Anouilh's play was an outcry against French collaboration with the Nazis. In writing this play, Anouilh himself could be considered a kind of Antigone figure—the voice of conscience speaking out against moral wrongs at the risk of his own life. Perhaps both Sophocles and Anouilh are asking us whether we would be so brave if put to the test.

> " **A**ntigone believes that God's laws must be obeyed, whatever the consequences."

The Temple of Athene at Delphi (4th century B.C.). Delphi, the site of the famous oracle, was thought to be the center of the earth.

> " **T**he conflict in *Antigone*— individual conscience at odds with established authority—is eternally relevant."

ANTIGONE

Sophocles, translated by **Dudley Fitts and Robert Fitzgerald**

The photographs illustrating this play are from a 1971 production starring
Philip Bosco as Creon at the Lincoln Center Repertory Theater in New York.

Characters

Antigone
Ismene } daughters of Oedipus and Jocasta
Creon, king of Thebes, uncle of Antigone and Ismene, brother of Jocasta
Haimon, Creon's son, engaged to Antigone
Eurydice, Creon's wife
Teiresias, a blind prophet
Chorus, made up of about fifteen elders of Thebes
Choragos, leader of the Chorus
A Boy, who leads Teiresias
A Sentry

Guards
Servants
A Messenger

Scene: Before the palace of Creon, King of Thebes. A central double door, and two side doors. A platform extends the length of the stage, and from this platform three steps lead down into the "orchestra," or chorus-ground.

Time: Dawn of the day after the repulse of the Argive army from the assault on Thebes.

Prologue

ANTIGONE and ISMENE *enter from the central door of the Palace.*

Antigone.

Ismene, dear sister,
You would think that we had already suffered enough
For the curse on Oedipus.
I cannot imagine any grief
5   That you and I have not gone through. And now—
Have they told you of the new decree of our King Creon?

Ismene.

I have heard nothing: I know
That two sisters lost two brothers, a double death
In a single hour; and I know that the Argive army
10   Fled in the night; but beyond this, nothing.

Antigone.

I thought so. And that is why I wanted you
To come out here with me. There is something we must do.

Ismene.

Why do you speak so strangely?

Antigone.

Listen, Ismene:
15   Creon buried our brother Eteocles
With military honors, gave him a soldier's funeral,

And it was right that he should; but Polyneices,
Who fought as bravely and died as miserably—
They say that Creon has sworn
20 No one shall bury him, no one mourn for him,
But his body must lie in the fields, a sweet treasure
For carrion birds to find as they search for food.
That is what they say, and our good Creon is coming here
To announce it publicly; and the penalty—
Stoning to death in the public square!
25   There it is,
And now you can prove what you are:
A true sister, or a traitor to your family.

Ismene.
Antigone, you are mad! What could I possibly do?

Antigone.
You must decide whether you will help me or not.

Ismene.
30 I do not understand you. Help you in what?

Antigone.
Ismene, I am going to bury him. Will you come?

Ismene.
Bury him! You have just said the new law forbids it.

Antigone.
He is my brother. And he is your brother, too.

Ismene.
But think of the danger! Think what Creon will do!

Antigone.
35 Creon is not strong enough to stand in my way.

Ismene.
Ah sister!
Oedipus died, everyone hating him
For what his own search brought to light, his eyes
Ripped out by his own hand; and Jocasta died,
40 His mother and wife at once: she twisted the cords
That strangled her life; and our two brothers died,
Each killed by the other's sword. And we are left:
But oh, Antigone,
Think how much more terrible than these
45 Our own death would be if we should go against Creon
And do what he has forbidden! We are only women,
We cannot fight with men, Antigone!
The law is strong, we must give in to the law
In this thing, and in worse. I beg the Dead
50 To forgive me, but I am helpless: I must yield
To those in authority. And I think it is dangerous business
To be always meddling.

"Ismene, I am going to bury him. Will you come?"

Antigone.   If that is what you think,
I should not want you, even if you asked to come.
You have made your choice, you can be what you want
    to be.
55 But I will bury him; and if I must die,
I say that this crime is holy: I shall lie down
With him in death, and I shall be as dear
To him as he to me.
                        It is the dead,
Not the living, who make the longest demands:
We die forever . . .
60   You may do as you like,
Since apparently the laws of the gods mean nothing to
    you.

Ismene.
They mean a great deal to me; but I have no strength
To break laws that were made for the public good.

Antigone.
That must be your excuse, I suppose. But as for me,
I will bury the brother I love.

65 **Ismene.**   Antigone,
I am so afraid for you!

Antigone.   You need not be:
You have yourself to consider, after all.

Ismene.
But no one must hear of this, you must tell no one!
I will keep it a secret, I promise!

Antigone.   Oh tell it! Tell everyone!
70 Think how they'll hate you when it all comes out
If they learn that you knew about it all the time!

Ismene.
So fiery! You should be cold with fear.

Antigone.
Perhaps. But I am doing only what I must.

Ismene.
But can you do it? I say that you cannot.

Antigone.
Very well: when my strength gives out, I shall do no
75   more.

Ismene.
Impossible things should not be tried at all.

Antigone.
Go away, Ismene:
I shall be hating you soon, and the dead will too,
For your words are hateful. Leave me my foolish plan:
80 I am not afraid of the danger; if it means death,
It will not be the worst of deaths—death without
    honor.

Ismene.

　　Go then, if you feel that you must.
　　You are unwise,
　　But a loyal friend indeed to those who love you.
　　　　[*Exit into the Palace.* ANTIGONE *goes off left.*]

[*Enter the* CHORUS.]

Parodos°

Parodos (par′ə·dəs): the first ode, or choral song, in a Greek tragedy, chanted by the Chorus as it enters the Orchestra.

Strophe° 1

Chorus.

　　Now the long blade of the sun, lying
　　Level east to west, touches with glory
　　Thebes of the Seven Gates. Open, unlidded
　　Eye of golden day! O marching light
5　Across the eddy and rush of Dirce's stream,°
　　Striking the white shields of the enemy
　　Thrown headlong backward from the blaze of morn-
　　　　ing!

Choragos.

　　Polyneices their commander
　　Roused them with windy phrases,
10　He the wild eagle screaming
　　Insults above our land,
　　His wings their shields of snow,
　　His crest their marshalled helms.

Strophe (strō′fē): the part of the ode that the Chorus chants as it moves from right to left across the stage.

5. **Dirce's stream:** a stream near Thebes. Dirce (dᵾr′sē), an early queen of Thebes, was murdered and her body thrown into the stream.

Antistrophe° 1

Chorus.

　　Against our seven gates in a yawning ring
15　The famished spears came onward in the night;
　　But before his jaws were sated with our blood,
　　Or pinefire took the garland of our towers,
　　He was thrown back; and as he turned, great Thebes—
　　No tender victim for his noisy power—
20　Rose like a dragon behind him, shouting war.

Choragos.

　　For God hates utterly
　　The bray of bragging tongues;
　　And when he beheld their smiling,
　　Their swagger of golden helms,
25　The frown of his thunder blasted
　　Their first man from our walls.°

Antistrophe (an·tis′trə·fē): chanted as the Chorus moves from left to right across the stage.

26. **For God . . . walls:** Zeus, who sided with the Thebans, struck the first Argive attacker with a thunderbolt.

Antigone, Parodos 753

Strophe 2

Chorus.
  We heard his shout of triumph high in the air
  Turn to a scream; far out in a flaming arc
  He fell with his windy torch, and the earth struck him.
30 And others storming in fury no less than his
  Found shock of death in the dusty joy of battle.

Choragos.
  Seven captains at seven gates
  Yielded their clanging arms to the god
  That bends the battle-line and breaks it.
35 These two only, brothers in blood,
  Face to face in matchless rage,
  Mirroring each the other's death,
  Clashed in long combat.

Antistrophe 2

Chorus.
  But now in the beautiful morning of victory
40 Let Thebes of the many chariots sing for joy!
  With hearts for dancing we'll take leave of war:
  Our temples shall be sweet with hymns of praise,
  And the long night shall echo with our chorus.

Responding to the Play

Analyzing the Prologue and Parodos

Identifying Facts

1. At the beginning of the play, what is Antigone's **conflict** or problem?
2. What does she ask Ismene to help her do? What is Ismene's response?
3. What arguments does Antigone use to defend her decision to break Creon's law? What arguments does Ismene use to defend her position?
4. In the Parodos, what information do we learn about the war Thebes has just fought?

Interpreting Meanings

5. From what you've seen of Antigone and Ismene in the Prologue, how would you **characterize** each sister? Does Sophocles seem to side with one sister over the other? Explain.

6. Where does Antigone use **verbal irony** to ridicule and attack Ismene? In contrast, how would you describe Ismene's **tone**, or attitude, toward her sister? Cite lines from the play to support your answers.
7. In lines 46–47 of the Prologue, Ismene says, "We are only women / We cannot fight with men, Antigone!" What do you think of this argument? Is it an argument that some people—either men or women—might use today? Explain.
8. In the Parodos, what animal does the Choragos compare Polyneices to? How does this **metaphor** make you feel about Polyneices? Explain your response.
9. At the end of the Parodos, what hopes for the future does the Chorus express? Based on what you have learned in the Prologue, do you think these hopes will be fulfilled? Why or why not?

Scene 1

Choragos.

But now at last our new King is coming:
Creon of Thebes, Menoikeus'° son.
In this auspicious dawn of his reign
What are the new complexities

5   That shifting Fate has woven for him?
What is his counsel? Why has he summoned
The old men to hear him?

[*Enter* CREON *from the palace, center. He addresses the* CHORUS *from the top step.*]

Creon. Gentlemen: I have the honor to inform you that
our Ship of State, which recent storms have threatened

10   to destroy, has come safely to harbor at last, guided
by the merciful wisdom of Heaven. I have summoned
you here this morning because I know that I can depend upon you: your devotion to King Laios was absolute; you never hesitated in your duty to our late ruler

15   Oedipus; and when Oedipus died, your loyalty was
transferred to his children. Unfortunately, as you
know, his two sons, the princes Eteocles and Polyneices, have killed each other in battle; and I, as the
next in blood, have succeeded to the full power of the

20   throne.
    I am aware, of course, that no Ruler can expect complete
loyalty from his subjects until he has been tested in
office. Nevertheless, I say to you at the very outset
that I have nothing but contempt for the kind of Gov-

25   ernor who is afraid, for whatever reason, to follow the
course that he knows is best for the State; and as for
the man who sets private friendship above the public
welfare—I have no use for him, either. I call God to
witness that if I saw my country headed for ruin, I

30   should not be afraid to speak out plainly; and I need
hardly remind you that I would never have any dealings with an enemy of the people. No one values
friendship more highly than I; but we must remember
that friends made at the risk of wrecking our Ship are

35   not real friends at all.
    These are my principles, at any rate, and that is why I
have made the following decision concerning the sons
of Oedipus: Eteocles, who died as a man should die,
fighting for his country, is to be buried with full military

40   honors, with all the ceremony that is usual when the
greatest heroes die; but his brother Polyneices, who

2. **Menoikeus** (me·noi′kē·əs): an early hero, the father of Creon and Jocasta.

broke his exile to come back with fire and sword against his native city and the shrines of his fathers' gods, whose one idea was to spill the blood of his

45 blood and sell his own people into slavery—Polyneices, I say, is to have no burial: no man is to touch him or say the least prayer for him; he shall lie on the plain, unburied; and the birds and the scavenging dogs can do with him whatever they like.

50 This is my command, and you can see the wisdom behind it. As long as I am King, no traitor is going to be honored with the loyal man. But whoever shows by word and deed that he is on the side of the State—he shall have my respect while he is living, and my re-

55 verence when he is dead.

Choragos.
If that is your will, Creon son of Menoikeus,
You have the right to enforce it: we are yours.

Creon.
That is my will. Take care that you do your part.

Choragos.
We are old men: let the younger ones carry it out.

Creon.
60 I do not mean that: the sentries have been appointed.

Choragos.
Then what is it that you would have us do?

Creon.
You will give no support to whoever breaks this law.

Choragos.
Only a crazy man is in love with death!

Creon.
And death it is; yet money talks, and the wisest
Have sometimes been known to count a few coins too
65 many.

[*Enter* SENTRY *from left.*]

Sentry. I'll not say that I'm out of breath from running,
King, because every time I stopped to think about
what I have to tell you, I felt like going back. And all
the time a voice kept saying, "You fool, don't you
70 know you're walking straight into trouble?"; and then
another voice: "Yes, but if you let somebody else get
the news to Creon first, it will be even worse than that
for you!" But good sense won out, at least I hope it
was good sense, and here I am with a story that makes
75 no sense at all; but I'll tell it anyhow, because, as they
say, what's going to happen's going to happen, and—

Creon.
Come to the point. What have you to say?

". . . the birds and the scavenging dogs can do with him whatever they like."

Sentry. I did not do it. I did not see who did it. You must
    not punish me for what someone else has done.
Creon.
80   A comprehensive defense! More effective, perhaps,
    If I knew its purpose. Come: what is it?
Sentry.
    A dreadful thing . . . I don't know how to put it—
Creon.
    Out with it!
Sentry.   Well, then;
    The dead man—
             Polyneices—

[*Pause. The* SENTRY *is overcome, fumbles for words.*
CREON *waits impassively.*]

                  out there—
                          someone—

85   New dust on the slimy flesh!

[*Pause. No sign from* CREON.]

    Someone has given it burial that way, and
    Gone . . .

[*Long pause.* CREON *finally speaks with deadly control.*]

Creon.
    And the man who dared do this?
Sentry.   I swear I
    Do not know! You must believe me!
                        Listen:
90   The ground was dry, not a sign of digging, no,
    Not a wheeltrack in the dust, no trace of anyone.
    It was when they relieved us this morning: and one of
        them,
    The corporal, pointed to it.
                There it was,
    The strangest—
           Look:
95   The body, just mounded over with light dust: you see?
    Not buried really, but as if they'd covered it
    Just enough for the ghost's peace. And no sign
    Of dogs or any wild animal that had been there.
    And then what a scene there was! Every man of us
    Accusing the other: we all proved the other man did
100   it,
    We all had proof that we could not have done it.
    We were ready to take hot iron in our hands,
    Walk through fire, swear by all the gods,
    It was not I!
105   *I do not know who it was, but it was not I!*

[CREON's *rage had been mounting steadily, but the* SEN-
TRY *is too intent upon his story to notice it.*]

And then, when this came to nothing, someone said
A thing that silenced us and made us stare
Down at the ground: you had to be told the news,
And one of us had to do it! We threw the dice,
110   And the bad luck fell to me. So here I am,
No happier to be here than you are to have me:
Nobody likes the man who brings bad news.

Choragos.
I have been wondering, King: can it be that the gods
   have done this?

Creon.
(*Furiously*) Stop!
115   Must you doddering wrecks
Go out of your heads entirely? "The gods!"
Intolerable!
The gods favor this corpse? Why? How had he served
   them?
Tried to loot their temples, burn their images,
120   Yes, and the whole State, and its laws with it!
Is it your senile opinion that the gods love to honor
   bad men?
A pious thought!
                         No, from the very beginning
There have been those who have whispered together,
Stiff-necked anarchists,° putting their heads together,
125   Scheming against me in alleys. These are the men,
And they have bribed my own guard to do this thing.
(*Sententiously*°) Money!
There's nothing in the world so demoralizing as
   money,
Down go your cities,
130   Homes gone, men gone, honest hearts corrupted,
Crookedness of all kinds, and all for money!
                              (*To* SENTRY) But you—!
I swear by God and by the throne of God,
The man who has done this thing shall pay for it!
Find that man, bring him here to me, or your death
135   Will be the least of your problems: I'll string you up
Alive, and there will be certain ways to make you
Discover your employer before you die;
And the process may teach you a lesson you seem to
   have missed:
The dearest profit is sometimes all too dear:
140   That depends on the source. Do you understand me?
A fortune won is often misfortune.

124. **anarchists** (an'ər·kists): people opposed to any kind of law or organized form
of government.

127. **sententiously** (sen·ten'shəs·lē): speaking in a trite, moralizing way.

Sentry.

King, may I speak?

Creon.   Your very voice distresses me.

Sentry.

Are you sure that it is my voice, and not your conscience?

Creon.

By God, he wants to analyze me now!

Sentry.

It is not what I say, but what has been done, that hurts
145   you.

Creon.

You talk too much.

Sentry.   Maybe; but I've done nothing.

Creon.

Sold your soul for some silver: that's all you've done.

Sentry.

How dreadful it is when the right judge judges wrong!

Creon.

Your figures of speech
May entertain you now; but unless you bring me the
150   man,
You will get little profit from them in the end.

                                    [*Exit* CREON *into the Palace.*]

Sentry.

"Bring me the man"—!
I'd like nothing better than bringing him the man!
But bring him or not, you have seen the last of me
here.
155   At any rate, I am safe!   [*Exit* SENTRY.]

Ode° 1

Ode: Each scene is followed by an ode. These odes serve both to separate one scene from the next, since there were no curtains, and to provide the Chorus's response to the preceding scene.

Strophe 1

Chorus.

Numberless are the world's wonders, but none
More wonderful than man; the storm-gray sea
Yields to his prows, the huge crests bear him high;
Earth, holy and inexhaustible, is graven
5   With shining furrows where his plows have gone
Year after year, the timeless labor of stallions.

Antistrophe 1

The lightboned birds and beasts that cling to cover,
The lithe fish lighting their reaches of dim water,
All are taken, tamed in the net of his mind;
10   The lion on the hill, the wild horse windy-maned,
Resign to him; and his blunt yoke has broken
The sultry shoulders of the mountain bull.

Strophe 2

Words also, and thought as rapid as air,
He fashions to his good use; statecraft is his,
15   And his the skill that deflects the arrows of snow,
The spears of winter rain: from every wind
He has made himself secure—from all but one:
In the late wind of death he cannot stand.

Antistrophe 2

O clear intelligence, force beyond all measure!
20   O fate of man, working both good and evil!
When the laws are kept, how proudly his city stands!
When the laws are broken, what of his city then?
Never may the anarchic man find rest at my hearth,
Never be it said that my thoughts are his thoughts.

Responding to the Play

Analyzing Scene 1 and Ode 1

Identifying Facts

1. In Scene 1, what reason does Creon give for refusing to bury Polyneices?
2. How does the Choragos react to Creon's decree?
3. In lines 83–87, what news does the Sentry announce to Creon? Why is the Sentry so reluctant to deliver his message?
4. According to Ode 1, why are human beings the most wonderful of the world's wonders? In what single respect are they limited?

Interpreting Meanings

5. In line 113, the Choragos asks Creon, "King, can it be that the gods have done this?" Why does this suggestion so enrage Creon? What does it imply?

6. At this point in the play, what **dramatic irony** do we feel—that is, what do we realize that Creon doesn't?
7. What does Creon accuse the Sentry of having done? What accusation is the Sentry making when he says, "How dreadful it is when the right judge judges wrong"?
8. Based on Scene 1, how would you **characterize** Creon? Describe what you think his strengths and weaknesses as a leader are. Do you think he is a believable character? Explain.
9. In Ode 1, what opinion does the Chorus express about the importance of law in society? Explain how this opinion is a comment on the basic **conflict** in the play so far.
10. What do you think will happen when Creon discovers the truth about Polyneices' burial? What possible **resolutions** to the conflict can you predict?

Scene 2

Reenter SENTRY *leading* ANTIGONE.

Choragos.
    What does this mean? Surely this captive woman
    Is the princess Antigone. Why should she be taken?
Sentry.
    Here is the one who did it! We caught her
    In the very act of burying him. Where is Creon?
Choragos.
    Just coming from the house.

[*Enter* CREON, *center.*]

5
Creon.   What has happened?
    Why have you come back so soon?
Sentry (*expansively*).   O King,
    A man should never be too sure of anything:
    I would have sworn
    That you'd not see me here again: your anger
    Frightened me so, and the things you threatened me
10   with;
    But how could I tell then
    That I'd be able to solve the case so soon?

    No dice-throwing this time: I was only too glad to
     come!

    Here is this woman. She is the guilty one:
15   We found her trying to bury him.
    Take her, then; question her; judge her as you will.
    I am through with the whole thing now, and glad of it.
Creon.
    But this is Antigone! Why have you brought her here?
Sentry.
    She was burying him, I tell you!
Creon (*severely*).   Is this the truth?
Sentry.
20   I saw her with my own eyes. Can I say more?
Creon.
    The details: come, tell me quickly!
Sentry.   It was like this:
    After those terrible threats of yours, King,
    We went back and brushed the dust away from the
     body.
    The flesh was soft by now, and stinking,
25   So we sat on a hill to windward and kept guard.
    No napping this time! We kept each other awake.

But nothing happened until the white round sun
Whirled in the center of the round sky over us:
Then, suddenly,

30 A storm of dust roared up from the earth, and the sky
Went out, the plain vanished with all its trees
In the stinging dark. We closed our eyes and endured
    it.
The whirlwind lasted a long time, but it passed;
And then we looked, and there was Antigone!

35 I have seen
A mother bird come back to a stripped nest, heard
Her crying bitterly a broken note or two
For the young ones stolen. Just so, when this girl
Found the bare corpse, and all her love's work wasted,

40 She wept, and cried on heaven to damn the hands
That had done this thing.
                          And then she brought more dust
And sprinkled wine three times for her brother's ghost.

We ran and took her at once. She was not afraid,
Not even when we charged her with what she had
    done.
She denied nothing.

45   And this was a comfort to me,
And some uneasiness: for it is a good thing
To escape from death, but it is no great pleasure
To bring death to a friend.
                          Yet I always say
There is nothing so comfortable as your own safe
    skin!

Creon.

50 (*Slowly, dangerously*) And you, Antigone,
You with your head hanging, do you confess this
    thing?

Antigone.

I do. I deny nothing.

Creon (*to* SENTRY).   You may go.   [*Exit* SENTRY.]
(*To* ANTIGONE) Tell me, tell me briefly:
Had you heard my proclamation touching this matter?

Antigone.

55 It was public. Could I help hearing it?

Creon.

And yet you dared defy the law.

Antigone.   I dared.
It was not God's proclamation. That final Justice
That rules the world below makes no such laws.
Your edict, King, was strong,

60 But all your strength is weakness itself against

The immortal unrecorded laws of God.
They are not merely now: they were, and shall be,
Operative forever, beyond man utterly.

65   I knew I must die, even without your decree:
I am only mortal. And if I must die
Now, before it is my time to die,
Surely this is no hardship: can anyone
Living, as I live, with evil all about me,
Think Death less than a friend? This death of mine
70   Is of no importance; but if I had left my brother
Lying in death unburied, I should have suffered.
Now I do not.
               You smile at me. Ah Creon,
Think me a fool, if you like; but it may well be
That a fool convicts me of folly.

Choragos.
Like father, like daughter: both headstrong, deaf to
75   reason!
She has never learned to yield.

Creon.   She has much to learn.
The inflexible heart breaks first, the toughest iron
Cracks first, and the wildest horses bend their necks
At the pull of the smallest curb.
                      Pride? In a slave?
80   This girl is guilty of a double insolence,
Breaking the given laws and boasting of it.
Who is the man here,
She or I, if this crime goes unpunished?
Sister's child, or more than sister's child,
85   Or closer yet in blood—she and her sister
Win bitter death for this!
         (*To* SERVANTS.) Go, some of you,
Arrest Ismene. I accuse her equally.
Bring her: you will find her sniffling in the house there.

Her mind's a traitor: crimes kept in the dark
90   Cry for light, and the guardian brain shudders;
But how much worse than this
Is brazen boasting of barefaced anarchy!

Antigone.
Creon, what more do you want than my death?

Creon.   Nothing.
That gives me everything.

Antigone.   Then I beg you: kill me.
95   This talking is a great weariness: your words
Are distasteful to me, and I am sure that mine
Seem so to you. And yet they should not seem so:
I should have praise and honor for what I have done.

All these men here would praise me
100 Were their lips not frozen shut with fear of you.
(Bitterly) Ah the good fortune of kings,
Licensed to say and do whatever they please!

Creon.
You are alone here in that opinion.

Antigone.
No, they are with me. But they keep their tongues in
leash.

Creon.
105 Maybe. But you are guilty, and they are not.

> *. . . can anyone*
> *Living, as I live, with evil all about*
> *me,*
> *Think Death less than a friend?''*

Antigone.

There is no guilt in reverence for the dead.

Creon.

But Eteocles—was he not your brother too?

Antigone.

My brother too.

Creon.   And you insult his memory?

Antigone.

(*Softly*) The dead man would not say that I insult it.

Creon.

110   He would: for you honor a traitor as much as him.

Antigone.

His own brother, traitor or not, and equal in blood.

Creon.

He made war on his country. Eteocles defended it.

Antigone.

Nevertheless, there are honors due all the dead.

Creon.

But not the same for the wicked as for the just.

Antigone.

115   Ah Creon, Creon,

Which of us can say what the gods hold wicked?

Creon.

An enemy is an enemy, even dead.

Antigone.

It is my nature to join in love, not hate.

Creon.

(*Finally losing patience*) Go join them, then; if you
    must have your love,

120   Find it in hell!

Choragos.

But see, Ismene comes:

[*Enter* ISMENE, *guarded.*]

Those tears are sisterly, the cloud
That shadows her eyes rains down gentle sorrow.

Creon.

You too, Ismene,

125   Snake in my ordered house, sucking my blood
Stealthily—and all the time I never knew
That these two sisters were aiming at my throne!

                                                  Ismene,
Do you confess your share in this crime, or deny it?
Answer me.

Ismene.

130   Yes, if she will let me say so. I am guilty.

Antigone.
   (*Coldly*) No, Ismene. You have no right to say so.
   You would not help me, and I will not have you help
      me.
Ismene.
   But now I know what you meant; and I am here
   To join you, to take my share of punishment.
Antigone.
135   The dead man and the gods who rule the dead
   Know whose act this was. Words are not friends.
Ismene.
   Do you refuse me, Antigone? I want to die with you:
   I too have a duty that I must discharge to the dead.
Antigone.
   You shall not lessen my death by sharing it.
Ismene.
140   What do I care for life when you are dead?
Antigone.
   Ask Creon. You're always hanging on his opinions.
Ismene.
   You are laughing at me. Why, Antigone?
Antigone.
   It's a joyless laughter, Ismene.
Ismene.   But can I do nothing?
Antigone.
   Yes. Save yourself, I shall not envy you.
   There are those who will praise you; I shall have
145   honor, too.
Ismene.
   But we are equally guilty!
Antigone.   No more, Ismene.
   You are alive, but I belong to Death.
Creon.
   (*To the* CHORUS) Gentlemen, I beg you to observe
      these girls:
   One has just now lost her mind; the other,
150   It seems, has never had a mind at all.
Ismene.
   Grief teaches the steadiest minds to waver, King.
Creon.
   Yours certainly did, when you assumed guilt with the
      guilty!
Ismene.
   But how could I go on living without her?
Creon.   You are.
   She is already dead.
Ismene.   But your own son's bride!

Creon.

155   There are places enough for him to push his plow.
        I want no wicked women for my sons!

Ismene.

        O dearest Haimon, how your father wrongs you!

Creon.

        I've had enough of your childish talk of marriage!

Choragos.

        Do you really intend to steal this girl from your son?

Creon.

        No; Death will do that for me.

160 **Choragos.**   Then she must die?

Creon.

        (*Ironically*) You dazzle me.

                                —But enough of this talk!

        (*To* GUARDS) You, there, take them away and guard
            them well:
        For they are but women, and even brave men run
        When they see Death coming.

                [*Exeunt* ISMENE, ANTIGONE, *and* GUARDS.]

Ode 2

Strophe 1

Chorus.

        Fortunate is the man who has never tasted God's
            vengeance!
        Where once the anger of heaven has struck, that house
            is shaken
        For ever: damnation rises behind each child
        Like a wave cresting out of the black northeast,
5   When the long darkness under sea roars up
        And bursts drumming death upon the windwhipped
            sand.

Antistrophe 1

        I have seen this gathering sorrow from time long past
        Loom upon Oedipus' children: generation from gener-
            ation
        Takes the compulsive rage of the enemy god.
10   So lately this last flower of Oedipus' line
        Drank the sunlight! but now a passionate word
        And a handful of dust have closed up all its beauty.

Strophe 2

What mortal arrogance
Transcends the wrath of Zeus?
15 Sleep cannot lull him, nor the effortless long months
Of the timeless gods: but he is young for ever,
And his house is the shining day of high Olympus.
All that is and shall be,
And all the past, is his.
20 No pride on earth is free of the curse of heaven.

Antistrophe 2

The straying dreams of men
May bring them ghosts of joy:
But as they drowse, the waking embers burn them;
Or they walk with fixed eyes, as blind men walk.
25 But the ancient wisdom speaks for our own time:
Fate works most for woe
With Folly's fairest show.
Man's little pleasure is the spring of sorrow.

Responding to the Play

Analyzing Scene 2 and Ode 2

Identifying Facts

1. How does Antigone defend her actions? Explain why she says she welcomes death.
2. In line 80, Creon says that Antigone is guilty of "a double insolence." What two faults does he accuse her of? What does he accuse Ismene of?

Interpreting Meanings

3. Since there is usually only one stage setting in a Greek drama, important actions often take place offstage. In Scene 2 the Sentry describes a crucial event that we do not witness. What does he compare Antigone to when she discovers that Polyneices' corpse has been unburied? How does this **simile** make you feel about Antigone?
4. In lines 75–76, the Choragos accuses Antigone of being "headstrong, deaf to reason," and un-yielding. Later Creon calls her behavior "bare-faced anarchy." Do you think this assessment of her **character** is valid? Does any of it also apply to Creon himself? Explain.
5. Why do you think Ismene changes her mind about her brother's burial? Do you think Antigone is justified in rejecting Ismene's support, or is she being too hard on her sister? Explain.
6. In lines 99–100, Antigone tells Creon, "All these men here would praise me / Were their lips not frozen shut with fear of you." Based on what the Choragos says to Creon in this scene, do you think Antigone's statement is correct?
7. According to Ode 2, "God's vengeance" looms over the house of Oedipus. What human fault does the Chorus say is responsible for this "curse of heaven"? So far in the play, which character or characters have shown themselves to be guilty of this fault? Explain.

Scene 3

Choragos.

But here is Haimon, King, the last of all your sons.
Is it grief for Antigone that brings him here,
And bitterness at being robbed of his bride?

[*Enter* HAIMON.]

Creon.

We shall soon see, and no need of diviners.°

—Son,

5   You have heard my final judgment on that girl:
Have you come here hating me, or have you come
With deference and with love, whatever I do?

Haimon.

I am your son, father. You are my guide.
You make things clear for me, and I obey you.
No marriage means more to me than your continuing
10   wisdom.

Creon.

Good. That is the way to behave: subordinate
Everything else, my son, to your father's will.
This is what a man prays for, that he may get
Sons attentive and dutiful in his house,
15   Each one hating his father's enemies,
Honoring his father's friends. But if his sons
Fail him, if they turn out unprofitably,
What has he fathered but trouble for himself
And amusement for the malicious?

So you are right

20   Not to lose your head over this woman.
Your pleasure with her would soon grow cold, Hai-
      mon,
And then you'd have a hellcat in bed and elsewhere.
Let her find her husband in hell!
Of all the people in this city, only she
25   Has had contempt for my law and broken it.
Do you want me to show myself weak before the
      people?
Or to break my sworn word? No, and I will not.
The woman dies.
I suppose she'll plead "family ties." Well, let her.
30   If I permit my own family to rebel,
How shall I earn the world's obedience?
Show me the man who keeps his house in hand,
He's fit for public authority.

I'll have no dealings

With law-breakers, critics of the government:

4. **diviners:** people who can foretell the future by interpreting certain omens.

35   Whoever is chosen to govern should be obeyed—
      Must be obeyed, in all things, great and small,
      Just and unjust! O Haimon,
      The man who knows how to obey, and that man only,
      Knows how to give commands when the time comes.
40   You can depend on him, no matter how fast
      The spears come: he's a good soldier, he'll stick it out.

      Anarchy, anarchy! Show me a greater evil!
      This is why cities tumble and the great houses rain
         down,
      This is what scatters armies!

45   No, no: good lives are made so by discipline.
      We keep the laws then, and the lawmakers,
      And no woman shall seduce us. If we must lose,
      Let's lose to a man, at least! Is a woman stronger than
         we?

Choragos.
      Unless time has rusted my wits,
50   What you say, King, is said with point and dignity.

Haimon.
      (*Boyishly earnest*) Father:
      Reason is God's crowning gift to man, and you are
         right
      To warn me against losing mine. I cannot say—
      I hope that I shall never want to say!—that you
55   Have reasoned badly. Yet there are other men
      Who can reason, too; and their opinions might be
         helpful.
      You are not in a position to know everything
      That people say or do, or what they feel:
      Your temper terrifies them—everyone
60   Will tell you only what you like to hear.
      But I, at any rate, can listen; and I have heard them
      Muttering and whispering in the dark about this girl.
      They say no woman has ever, so unreasonably,
      Died so shameful a death for a generous act:
65   "She covered her brother's body. Is this indecent?
      She kept him from dogs and vultures. Is this a crime?
      Death?—She should have all the honor that we can
         give her!"

      This is the way they talk out there in the city.

      You must believe me:
70   Nothing is closer to me than your happiness.
      What could be closer? Must not any son
      Value his father's fortune as his father does his?

I beg you, do not be unchangeable:
Do not believe that you alone can be right.

75   The man who thinks that,
The man who maintains that only he has the power
To reason correctly, the gift to speak, the soul—
A man like that, when you know him, turns out empty.

It is not reason never to yield to reason!

80   In flood time you can see how some trees bend,
And because they bend, even their twigs are safe,
While stubborn trees are torn up, roots and all.

"It is no City if it takes orders from one voice."

And the same thing happens in sailing:
Make your sheet fast, never slacken—and over you go,

85   Head over heels and under: and there's your voyage.
Forget you are angry! Let yourself be moved!
I know I am young; but please let me say this:
The ideal condition
Would be, I admit, that men should be right by instinct;

90   But since we are all too likely to go astray,
The reasonable thing is to learn from those who can teach.

Choragos.
You will do well to listen to him, King,
If what he says is sensible. And you, Haimon,
Must listen to your father. Both speak well.

Creon.
You consider it right for a man of my years and ex-

95   perience
To go to school to a boy?

Haimon.   It is not right
If I am wrong. But if I am young, and right,
What does my age matter?

Creon.
You think it right to stand up for an anarchist?

Haimon.
100   Not at all. I pay no respect to criminals.

Creon.
Then she is not a criminal?

Haimon.
The City would deny it, to a man.

Creon.
And the City proposes to teach me how to rule?

Haimon.
Ah. Who is it that's talking like a boy now?

Creon.
105   My voice is the one voice giving orders in this City!

Haimon.
It is no City if it takes orders from one voice.

Creon.
The State is the King!

Haimon.   Yes, if the State is a desert.

Creon.
(*Pause*) This boy, it seems, has sold out to a woman.

Haimon.
If you are a woman: my concern is only for you.

Creon.
So? Your ''concern''! In a public brawl with your
110   father!

Haimon.

How about you, in a public brawl with justice?

Creon.

With justice, when all that I do is within my rights?

Haimon.

You have no right to trample on God's right.

Creon.

(*Completely out of control*) Fool, adolescent fool!
  Taken in by a woman!

Haimon.

115   You'll never see me taken in by anything vile.

Creon.

Every word you say is for her!

Haimon (*quietly, darkly*).   And for you.
  And for me. And for the gods under the earth.

Creon.

You'll never marry her while she lives.

Haimon.

Then she must die. But her death will cause another.

Creon.

120   Another?
  Have you lost your senses? Is this an open threat?

Haimon.

There is no threat in speaking to emptiness.

Creon.

I swear you'll regret this superior tone of yours!
  You are the empty one!

Haimon.   If you were not my father,

125   I'd say you were perverse.

Creon.

You girlstruck fool, don't play at words with me!

Haimon.

I am sorry. You prefer silence.

Creon.   Now, by God—!
  I swear, by all the gods in heaven above us,
  You'll watch it, I swear you shall!
           (*To the* SERVANTS) Bring her out!

130   Bring the woman out! Let her die before his eyes!
  Here, this instant, with her bridegroom beside her!

Haimon.

Not here, no; she will not die here, King.
  And you will never see my face again.
  Go on raving as long as you've a friend to endure you.
                   [*Exit* HAIMON.]

Choragos.

135   Gone, gone.
  Creon, a young man in a rage is dangerous!

Creon.
    Let him do, or dream to do, more than a man can.
    He shall not save these girls from death.
Choragos.   These girls?
    You have sentenced them both?
Creon.   No, you are right.
140   I will not kill the one whose hands are clean.
Choragos.
    But Antigone?
Creon (*somberly*). I will carry her far away
    Out there in the wilderness, and lock her
    Living in a vault of stone. She shall have food,
145   As the custom is, to absolve the State of her death.
    And there let her pray to the gods of hell:
    They are her only gods:
    Perhaps they will show her an escape from death,
    Or she may learn,
              though late,
150   That piety shown the dead is pity in vain.

                                      [*Exit* CREON.]

Ode 3

Strophe

Chorus.
    Love, unconquerable
    Waster of rich men, keeper
    Of warm lights and all-night vigil
    In the soft face of a girl:
5   Sea-wanderer, forest-visitor!
    Even the pure Immortals cannot escape you,
    And mortal man, in his one day's dusk,
    Trembles before your glory.

Antistrophe

    Surely you swerve upon ruin
10   The just man's consenting heart,
    As here you have made bright anger
    Strike between father and son—
    And none has conquered but Love!
    A girl's glance working the will of heaven:
15   Pleasure to her alone who mocks us,
    Merciless Aphrodite.°

16. **Aphrodite** (af′rə·dīt′ē): goddess of love and beauty.

The theater at Epidaurus, Greece (c. 350 B.C.).

Responding to the Play

Analyzing Scene 3 and Ode 3

Identifying Facts

1. In Creon's first speech to Haimon, what arguments does he use to justify his decision to sentence Antigone to death?
2. What arguments does Haimon use to try to persuade his father to change his mind?
3. What does Haimon threaten to do if Antigone dies? How does Creon respond to this threat?

Interpreting Meanings

4. In line 29, Creon says that Antigone will probably plead "family ties" to avoid being punished for breaking the law. Explain how Creon has completely misread (or misrepresented) Antigone's **character.**
5. What **metaphors** does Haimon use to argue that Creon should be flexible? In lines 76–79 of Scene 2, Creon uses a similar argument against Antigone. At this point in the play, do you think that both Antigone and Creon should be more yielding, or do you believe that there are some principles that a person cannot compromise? Explain your opinion.

6. Why do you think Creon refuses to change his mind? Does he believe that he is doing what is best for Thebes, or is he afraid to appear weak? How do Creon's attitudes toward women seem to influence his decision about Antigone?
7. At the end of Scene 3, how has Creon changed his mind about Antigone's punishment? Why do you think he has done so? Do you agree that the method he proposes absolves the State of her death? Why or why not?
8. In Scene 1, Creon accuses the Sentry of having sold out for money. In Scene 3, what does he accuse Haimon of having sold out to? Do you agree with the Chorus in Ode 3 that Haimon's **motive** in defending Antigone is love? Or is Haimon motivated by something else? Explain.
9. "The State is the King!" declares Creon in line 107. "Yes," replies Haimon, "if the State is a desert." What do you think Haimon means? Do you agree with him? Why or why not?
10. At this point in the play, how do you respond to Haimon's threat in line 119? Do you take it seriously, or do you think he is just trying to pressure his father into changing his mind? Explain.

Scene 4

Choragos.

(*As* ANTIGONE *enters, guarded*) But I can no longer
  stand in awe of this
Nor, seeing what I see, keep back my tears.
Here is Antigone, passing to that chamber
Where all find sleep at last.

Strophe 1

Antigone.

5   Look upon me, friends, and pity me
    Turning back at the night's edge to say
    Goodbye to the sun that shines for me no longer;
    Now sleepy Death
    Summons me down to Acheron,° that cold shore:
10   There is no bridesong there, nor any music.

Chorus.

    Yet not unpraised, not without a kind of honor,
    You walk at last into the underworld;
    Untouched by sickness, broken by no sword.
    What woman has ever found your way to death?

Antistrophe 1

Antigone.

15   How often I have heard the story of Niobe,°
    Tantalos'° wretched daughter, how the stone
    Clung fast about her, ivy-close: and they say
    The rain falls endlessly
    And sifting soft snow; her tears are never done.
20   I feel the loneliness of her death in mine.

Chorus.

    But she was born of heaven, and you
    Are woman, woman-born. If her death is yours,
    A mortal woman's, is this not for you
    Glory in our world and in the world beyond?

Strophe 2

Antigone.

25   You laugh at me. Ah, friends, friends,
    Can you not wait until I am dead? O Thebes,
    O men many-charioted, in love with Fortune,
    Dear springs of Dirce, sacred Theban grove,
    Be witnesses for me, denied all pity,
30   Unjustly judged! and think a word of love
    For her whose path turns
    Under dark earth, where there are no more tears.

9. **Acheron** (ak′ə·rän′): one of the rivers
that dead souls were ferried across to reach
Hades, the Underworld. (Hades is also the
name of the god of the Underworld.)

15. **Niobe** (nī′ə·bē): an ancient queen of
Thebes who had seven sons and seven
daughters. Niobe boasted that she was superior to Leto because Leto only had twins,
Apollo and Artemis. Insulted, Leto complained to her children, who then slaughtered all of Niobe's children. Zeus turned
the weeping Niobe into a column of stone.
But she continued to weep, and her tears
became a stream.

16. **Tantalos** (tan′tə·ləs): a king whose punishment in the Underworld was to suffer
unending hunger and thirst. Though he
stood in a lake, the waters receded whenever he tried to drink. Though branches of
luscious fruit hung over his head, they always remained just out of his reach.

Chorus.

> You have passed beyond human daring and come at
> last
> Into a place of stone where Justice sits.
> 35   I cannot tell
> What shape of your father's guilt appears in this.

Antistrophe 2

Antigone.

> You have touched it at last: that bridal bed
> Unspeakable, horror of son and mother mingling:
> Their crime, infection of all our family!
> 40   O Oedipus, father and brother!
> Your marriage strikes from the grave to murder mine
> I have been a stranger here in my own land:
> All my life
> The blasphemy of my birth has followed me.

Chorus.

> 45   Reverence is a virtue, but strength
> Lives in established law: that must prevail.
> You have made your choice,
> Your death is the doing of your conscious hand.

Epode°

Antigone.

> Then let me go, since all your words are bitter,
> 50   And the very light of the sun is cold to me.
> Lead me to my vigil, where I must have
> Neither love nor lamentation; no song, but silence.

[CREON *interrupts impatiently.*]

Creon.

> If dirges and planned lamentations could put off death,
> Men would be singing forever.
>   (*To the* SERVANTS) Take her, go!
> 55   You know your orders: take her to the vault
> And leave her alone there. And if she lives or dies,
> That's her affair, not ours: our hands are clean.

Antigone.

> O tomb, vaulted bride-bed in eternal rock,
> Soon I shall be with my own again°
> Where Persephone welcomes the thin ghosts under-
> 60   ground.
> And I shall see my father again, and you, mother,
> And dearest Polyneices—
>   dearest indeed
> To me, since it was my hand

Epode (ep'ōd): the final stanza of the ode,
following the strophe and antistrophe.
59. **own again:** Antigone is looking forward
to a reunion with her family. The Greeks
considered the Underworld a place where
all dead souls wander as ghosts, or shades.

That washed him clean and poured the ritual wine:
65   And my reward is death before my time!

And yet, as men's hearts know, I have done no wrong,
I have not sinned before God. Or if I have,
I shall know the truth in death. But if the guilt
Lies upon Creon who judged me, then, I pray,
May his punishment equal my own.

"All my life
The blasphemy of my birth has
  followed me."

| 70 | **Choragos.** | O passionate heart, |

      Unyielding, tormented still by the same winds!

Creon.

      Her guards shall have good cause to regret their de-
        laying.

Antigone.

      Ah! That voice is like the voice of death!

Creon.

      I can give you no reason to think you are mistaken.

Antigone.

75   Thebes, and you my fathers' gods,

      And rulers of Thebes, you see me now, the last

      Unhappy daughter of a line of kings,

      Your kings, led away to death. You will remember

      What things I suffer, and at what men's hands,

80   Because I would not transgress the laws of heaven.

      (*To the* GUARDS, *simply*) Come: let us wait no longer.

            [*Exit* ANTIGONE, *left, guarded.*]

Ode 4

Strophe 1

Chorus.

      All Danae's° beauty was locked away

      In a brazen cell where the sunlight could not come;

      A small room, still as any grave, enclosed her.

      Yet she was a princess too,

5   And Zeus in a rain of gold poured love upon her.

      O child, child,

      No power in wealth or war

      Or tough sea-blackened ships

      Can prevail against untiring Destiny!

Antistrophe 1

10   And Dryas' son° also, that furious king,

      Bore the god's prisoning anger for his pride:

      Sealed up by Dionysos in deaf stone,

      His madness died among echoes.

      So at the last he learned what dreadful power

15   His tongue had mocked:

      For he had profaned the revels,

      And fired the wrath of the nine

      Implacable Sisters° that love the sound of the flute.

1. **Danae** (dan'ə·ē'): the daughter of an ancient king of Argos. The king imprisoned Danae in a bronze (brazen) tower when he learned from an oracle that she would have a son who would kill him. Zeus fell in love with Danae and visited her in her prison as a shower of gold. When Danae gave birth to Zeus's son Perseus, the frightened king put Danae and her baby in a wooden chest and tossed them into the sea. But Zeus saved them, and when Perseus grew up, he did (unknowingly) kill his grandfather, as prophesied.

10. **Dryas' son:** Lycurgos (lī·kʉr'gəs), an ancient king of Thrace who disapproved of the worship of Dionysos and drove the god and his followers into the sea. According to some accounts, Dionysos then punished Lycurgos by making him go mad and imprisoning him in a rocky cave until he regained his sanity. Later, Zeus blinded Lycurgos as further punishment.

18. **nine implacable** (im·plak'ə·b'l) **Sisters:** the Muses, goddesses of poetry, music, the arts, and the sciences. The Muses are called implacable because they cannot be appeased once they have been offended; they will no longer offer their inspiration.

Strophe 2

20
And old men tell a half-remembered tale°
Of horror done where a dark ledge splits the sea
And a double surf beats on the gray shores:
How a king's new woman, sick
With hatred for the queen he had imprisoned,
Ripped out his two sons' eyes with her bloody hands

25
While grinning Ares° watched the shuttle plunge
Four times: four blind wounds crying for revenge,

Antistrophe 2

Crying, tears and blood mingled. Piteously born,
Those sons whose mother was of heavenly birth!
Her father was the god of the North Wind

30
And she was cradled by gales,
She raced with young colts on the glittering hills
And walked untrammeled in the open light:
But in her marriage deathless Fate found means
To build a tomb like yours for all her joy.

19. **half-remembered tale:** King Phineus of Thrace imprisoned his first wife, Cleopatra, who was the daughter of Boreas, the god of the North Wind. Then the king's jealous new wife blinded Cleopatra's two sons.

25. **Ares** (er'ēz): god of war and violence, who lived in Thrace.

Responding to the Play

Analyzing Scene 4 and Ode 4

Identifying Facts

1. In lines 15–20, whose fate does Antigone compare to her own?
2. What does Antigone look forward to in death? What curse does she place on Creon?

Interpreting Meanings

3. In line 25, Antigone rebukes the Chorus for laughing at her and denying her "all pity." Is she right about the Chorus? Why or why not?
4. In line 41, what does Antigone mean when she says that her father's "marriage strikes from the grave to murder" her own? In lines 45–48, how does the Chorus argue against her?

5. Do you agree with the Chorus's opinion that Antigone is responsible for her own death? Why or why not?
6. In Antigone's last lines, what does she ask the gods to "remember"? What do these words suggest about her possible **motives**?
7. What are your feelings about Antigone in this scene? Does she seem to have changed in any way since Scene 2? If so, do you find her more sympathetic as a **character** or less? Explain your response.
8. In Ode 4, the Chorus **alludes** to three Greek myths. What fate does Antigone share with Danae, Lycurgos, and Cleopatra? Would you say that the purpose of this ode is to glorify Antigone's fate or to condemn her pride? Explain.

Scene 5

Enter blind TEIRESIAS, *led by a boy. The opening speeches of* TEIRESIAS *should be in singsong contrast to the realistic lines of* CREON.

Teiresias.
This is the way the blind man comes, Princes, Princes,
Lock-step, two heads lit by the eyes of one.

Creon.
What new thing have you to tell us, old Teiresias?

Teiresias.
I have much to tell you: listen to the prophet, Creon.

Creon.
5   I am not aware that I have ever failed to listen.

Teiresias.
Then you have done wisely, King, and ruled well.

Creon.
I admit my debt to you.° But what have you to say?

Teiresias.
This, Creon: you stand once more on the edge of fate.

Creon.
What do you mean? Your words are a kind of dread.

Teiresias.
10   Listen, Creon:
I was sitting in my chair of augury,° at the place
Where the birds gather about me. They were all a-
    chatter,
As is their habit, when suddenly I heard
A strange note in their jangling, a scream, a
15   Whirring fury; I knew that they were fighting,
Tearing each other, dying
In a whirlwind of wings clashing. And I was afraid.
I began the rites of burnt-offering at the altar,
But Hephaistos° failed me: instead of bright flame,
There was only the sputtering slime of the fat thigh-
20   flesh
Melting: the entrails dissolved in gray smoke,
The bare bone burst from the welter. And no blaze!

This was a sign from heaven. My boy described it,
Seeing for me as I see for others.

25   I tell you, Creon, you yourself have brought
This new calamity upon us. Our hearths and altars
Are stained with the corruption of dogs and carrion
    birds
That glut themselves on the corpse of Oedipus' son.

7. **my debt to you:** Teiresias is indirectly responsible for Creon's ascension to the throne; it was Teiresias who helped reveal the terrible truth to Oedipus, which resulted in his exile.

11. **augury** (ô′gyər·ē): the skill of foretelling the future from omens, such as the flight of birds or the appearance of a comet.

19. **Hephaistos** (hi·fes′təs): god of fire and the forge; the son of Zeus and Hera.

The gods are deaf when we pray to them, their fire
30 Recoils from our offering, their birds of omen
Have no cry of comfort, for they are gorged
With the thick blood of the dead.

                      O my son,
These are not trifles! Think: all men make mistakes,
But a good man yields when he knows his course is
      wrong,
35 And repairs the evil. The only crime is pride.

Give in to the dead man, then: do not fight with a
      corpse—
What glory is it to kill a man who is dead?
Think, I beg you:
It is for your own good that I speak as I do.
40 You should be able to yield for your own good.

Creon.
It seems that prophets have made me their especial
      province.
All my life long
I have been a kind of butt for the dull arrows
Of doddering fortune-tellers!

                No, Teiresias:
45 If your birds—if the great eagles of God himself
Should carry him stinking bit by bit to heaven,
I would not yield. I am not afraid of pollution:
No man can defile the gods.

               Do what you will,
Go into business, make money, speculate
50 In India gold or that synthetic gold from Sardis,°
Get rich otherwise than by my consent to bury him.
Teiresias, it is a sorry thing when a wise man
Sells his wisdom, lets out his words for hire!

Teiresias.
Ah Creon! Is there no man left in the world—

Creon.
55 To do what? Come, let's have the aphorism!°

Teiresias.
No man who knows that wisdom outweighs any
      wealth?

Creon.
As surely as bribes are baser than any baseness.

Teiresias.
You are sick, Creon! You are deathly sick!

Creon.
As you say: it is not my place to challenge a prophet.

Teiresias.
60 Yet you have said my prophecy is for sale.

50. **Sardis:** an ancient city where the first metal coins were made from a natural alloy of gold and silver.

55. **aphorism** (af'ə·riz'm): a short, wise, often clever saying.

Creon.

    The generation of prophets has always loved gold.

Teiresias.

    The generation of kings has always loved brass.

Creon.

    You forget yourself! You are speaking to your King.

Teiresias.

    I know it. You are a king because of me.

Creon.

65   You have a certain skill; but you have sold out.

Teiresias.

    King, you will drive me to words that—

Creon.   Say them, say them!

    Only remember: I will not pay you for them.

Teiresias.

    No, you will find them too costly.

Creon.   No doubt. Speak:

    Whatever you say, you will not change my will.

"The time is not far off when you
   shall pay back
Corpse for corpse, flesh of your own
   flesh."

Teiresias.

70   Then take this, and take it to heart!

    The time is not far off when you shall pay back

    Corpse for corpse, flesh of your own flesh.

    You have thrust the child of this world into living night,

    You have kept from the gods below the child that is

        theirs:

75   The one in a grave before her death, the other,

    Dead, denied the grave. This is your crime:

    And the Furies° and the dark gods of hell

    Are swift with terrible punishment for you.

    Do you want to buy me now, Creon?

                         Not many days,

    And your house will be full of men and women

80   weeping,

    And curses will be hurled at you from far

    Cities grieving for sons unburied, left to rot

    Before the walls of Thebes.

    These are my arrows, Creon: they are all for you.

85   (*To* BOY) But come, child: lead me home.

    Let him waste his fine anger upon younger men.

    Maybe he will learn at last

    To control a wiser tongue in a better head.

                     [*Exit* TEIRESIAS.]

Choragos.

    The old man has gone, King, but his words

90   Remain to plague us. I am old, too,

    But I cannot remember that he was ever false.

Creon.

    That is true. . . . It troubles me.

    Oh it is hard to give in! but it is worse

    To risk everything for stubborn pride.

Choragos.

    Creon: take my advice.

95 **Creon.**   What shall I do?

Choragos.

    Go quickly: free Antigone from her vault

    And build a tomb for the body of Polyneices.

Creon.

    You would have me do this?

Choragos.   Creon, yes!

    And it must be done at once: God moves

100   Swiftly to cancel the folly of stubborn men.

Creon.

    It is hard to deny the heart! But I

    Will do it: I will not fight with destiny.

77. **Furies:** the three goddesses of vengeance who tormented unpunished wrongdoers, especially those who had committed crimes against their own families. The Furies had snakes entwined in their hair and drove their victims mad.

Choragos.

You must go yourself, you cannot leave it to others.

Creon.

I will go.

—Bring axes, servants:

105　Come with me to the tomb. I buried her, I

Will set her free

Oh quickly!

My mind misgives—

The laws of the gods are mighty, and a man must serve
them

To the last day of his life!　　　　　　*[Exit* CREON.]

Paean°

Paean (pē′ən): a choral hymn in praise of a
god—in this case Dionysos, in whose honor
the Greeks presented their plays.

Strophe 1

Choragos.

God of many names

Chorus.　　　　　　O Iacchos°

son

of Kadmeian Semele

O born of the Thunder!°

Guardian of the West

Regent

of Eleusis' plain°

O Prince of maenad° Thebes

5　and the Dragon Field° by rippling Ismenos:°

Antistrophe 1

Choragos.

God of many names

Chorus.　　　　　　the flame of torches

flares on our hills

the nymphs of Iacchos

dance at the spring of Castalia:°

from the vine-close mountain

come ah come in ivy:

10　*Evohé*° *evohé!* sings through the streets of Thebes

Strophe 2

Choragos.

God of many names

1. **Iacchos** (ē′ə·kəs): another name for
Dionysos.
2. **Iacchos . . . Thunder:** Dionysos was the
son of Zeus, god of thunder, and the mortal
Semele (sem′ə·lē′), daughter of Kadmos.
Kadmos was the founder of Thebes (see
note, line 5).
4. **Eleusis'** (i·loo′sis) **plain:** an ancient
Greek city northwest of Athens, site of the
secret religious festivals honoring the two
great gods of the earth's bounty: Dionysos
and Demeter, the goddess of corn and the
harvest. **maenad** (mē′nad): female wor-
shiper or priestess of Dionysos. The Chorus
is describing the city of Thebes as a priestess.
5. **Dragon Field:** The oracle at Delphi had
instructed Kadmos to follow a cow marked
with a white full moon on each haunch and
to build a city on the spot where the cow
lay down from fatigue. Soon Kadmos saw a
cow that fit this description, and he followed
it until it stopped near a stream guarded by
a dragon. Kadmos killed the dragon, cut off
its head, and scattered its teeth in the field.
Warriors sprang from these teeth and fought
each other until there were only five left.
With these five warriors, Kadmos founded
the city of Thebes. **Ismenos** (is·mē′nəs): a
river near Thebes, sacred to Apollo.
8. **Castalia** (kas·tā′lē·ə): a spring sacred to
the Muses.
10. *Evohé* (ē·vō′ē): a cry of joy, like "hal-
lelujah," shouted by the worshipers at Dionysian festivals.

Chorus.   Iacchos of Thebes
    heavenly Child
         of Semele bride of the Thunderer!
    The shadow of plague is upon us:
               come
    with clement° feet
         oh come from Parnasos°
    down the long slopes
15   across the lamenting water

14. clement: mild, healing, merciful. **Parnasos** (par·nas′əs): mountain in central Greece, sacred to Apollo and Dionysos. Castalia (see note, line 8) is located at its base.

Antistrophe 2

Choragos.
    Io° Fire! Chorister° of the throbbing stars!
    O purest among the voices of the night!
    Thou son of God, blaze for us!
Chorus.
    Come with choric rapture of circling Maenads
    Who cry *Io Iacche!*°
20   *God of many names!*

16. Io (ī′ō): Hail! **Chorister:** choir leader.

20. *Iacche* (ē′ə·kē): another ritual cry of joy shouted by the worshipers of Dionysos. (The name Iacchos comes from this cry.)

Exodos°

Exodos: the final, or exit, scene.

Enter MESSENGER, *left.*

Messenger.
    Men of the line of Kadmos, you who live
    Near Amphion's° citadel:
             I cannot say
    Of any condition of human life "This is fixed,
    This is clearly good or bad." Fate raises up,
5   And Fate casts down the happy and unhappy alike:
    No man can foretell his Fate.
             Take the case of Creon:
    Creon was happy once, as I count happiness:
    Victorious in battle, sole governor of the land,
    Fortunate father of children nobly born.
10   And now it has all gone from him! Who can say
    That a man is still alive when his life's joy fails?
    He is a walking dead man. Grant him rich,
    Let him live like a king in his great house:
    If his pleasure is gone, I would not give
15   So much as the shadow of smoke for all he owns.
Choragos.
    Your words hint at sorrow: what is your news for us?

2. Amphion (am·fī′ən): an ancient king of Thebes who was a son of Zeus and the husband of Niobe (see note, Scene 4, line 15). Amphion built the wall around Thebes by playing his lyre so well that he enchanted the stones into their proper places.

Messenger.
  They are dead. The living are guilty of their death.
Choragos.
  Who is guilty? Who is dead? Speak!
Messenger.   Haimon.
  Haimon is dead; and the hand that killed him
  Is his own hand.
20 **Choragos.**   His father's? or his own?
Messenger.
  His own, driven mad by the murder his father had
      done.
Choragos.
  Teiresias, Teiresias, how clearly you saw it all!
Messenger.
  This is my news: you must draw what conclusions you
      can from it.
Choragos.
  But look: Eurydice, our Queen:
25 Has she overheard us?

[*Enter* EURYDICE *from the Palace, center.*]

Eurydice.
  I have heard something, friends:
  As I was unlocking the gate of Pallas'° shrine,
  For I needed her help today, I heard a voice
  Telling of some new sorrow. And I fainted
30 There at the temple with all my maidens about me.
  But speak again: whatever it is, I can bear it:
  Grief and I are no strangers.°
Messenger.   Dearest Lady,
  I will tell you plainly all that I have seen.
  I shall not try to comfort you: what is the use,
35 Since comfort could lie only in what is not true?
  The truth is always best.

                          I went with Creon
  To the outer plain where Polyneices was lying,
  No friend to pity him, his body shredded by dogs.
  We made our prayers in that place to Hecate°
  And Pluto,° that they would be merciful. And we
40   bathed
  The corpse with holy water, and we brought
  Fresh-broken branches to burn what was left of it,
  And upon the urn we heaped up a towering barrow
  Of the earth of his own land.

                          When we were done, we ran
45 To the vault where Antigone lay on her couch of stone.
  One of the servants had gone ahead,
  And while he was yet far off he heard a voice

27. **Pallas:** Pallas Athena, goddess of wisdom.

32. **Grief . . . strangers:** Eurydice and Creon's older son, Megareus (mə·ga′rē·əs), died during the Argive assault on Thebes.

39. **Hecate** (hek′ə·tē): goddess of sorcery and witchcraft. Offerings were left to her at crossroads, thought to be the best location for performing magic.
40. **Pluto:** another name for Hades, god of the Underworld.

Grieving within the chamber, and he came back
And told Creon. And as the King went closer,
50   The air was full of wailing, the words lost,
And he begged us to make all haste. "Am I a
        prophet?"
He said, weeping, "And must I walk this road,
The saddest of all that I have gone before?
My son's voice calls me on. Oh quickly, quickly!
55   Look through the crevice there, and tell me
If it is Haimon, or some deception of the gods!"
We obeyed; and in the cavern's farthest corner
We saw her lying:
She had made a noose of her fine linen veil
60   And hanged herself. Haimon lay beside her,
His arms about her waist, lamenting her,
His love lost under ground, crying out
That his father had stolen her away from him.
When Creon saw him the tears rushed to his eyes
And he called to him: "What have you done, child?
65   Speak to me.
What are you thinking that makes your eyes so
        strange?
O my son, my son, I come to you on my knees!"
But Haimon spat in his face. He said not a word,
Staring—
            And suddenly drew his sword
And lunged. Creon shrank back, the blade missed; and
70   the boy,
Desperate against himself, drove it half its length
Into his own side, and fell. And as he died
He gathered Antigone close in his arms again,
Choking, his blood bright red on her white cheek.
75   And now he lies dead with the dead, and she is his
At last, his bride in the houses of the dead.
                    [*Exit* EURYDICE *into the Palace.*]

Choragos.
She has left us without a word. What can this mean?
Messenger.
It troubles me, too; yet she knows what is best,
Her grief is too great for public lamentation,
80   And doubtless she has gone to her chamber to weep
For her dead son, leading her maidens in his dirge.
Choragos.
It may be so: but I fear this deep silence.
[*Pause*]
Messenger.
I will see what she is doing. I will go in.
                    [*Exit* MESSENGER *into the Palace.*]

[*Enter* CREON *with attendants, bearing* HAIMON'*s body.*]

Choragos.
  But here is the King himself: oh look at him,
85 Bearing his own damnation in his arms.
Creon.
  Nothing you say can touch me any more.
  My own blind heart has brought me
  From darkness to final darkness. Here you see
  The father murdering, the murdered son—
90 And all my civic wisdom!

  Haimon my son, so young, so young to die,
  I was the fool, not you; and you died for me.
Choragos.
  That is the truth; but you were late in learning it.
Creon.
  This truth is hard to bear. Surely a god
95 Has crushed me beneath the hugest weight of heaven,
  And driven me headlong a barbaric way
  To trample out the thing I held most dear.

  The pains that men will take to come to pain!

[*Enter* MESSENGER *from the Palace.*]

Messenger.
  The burden you carry in your hands is heavy,
100 But it is not all: you will find more in your house.
Creon.
  What burden worse than this shall I find there?
Messenger.
  The Queen is dead.
Creon.
  O port of death, deaf world,
  Is there no pity for me? And you, Angel of evil,
105 I was dead, and your words are death again.
  Is it true, boy? Can it be true?
  Is my wife dead? Has death bred death?
Messenger.
  You can see for yourself.

[*The doors are opened, and the body of* EURYDICE *is disclosed within.*]

Creon.
  Oh pity!
110 All true, all true, and more than I can bear!
  O my wife, my son!

"I look for comfort; my comfort lies here dead."

Messenger.

　　She stood before the altar, and her heart
　　Welcomed the knife her own hand guided,
　　And a great cry burst from her lips for Megareus dead,
115　And for Haimon dead, her sons; and her last breath
　　Was a curse for their father, the murderer of her sons.
　　And she fell, and the dark flowed in through her clos-
　　　　ing eyes.

Creon.

　　O God, I am sick with fear.
　　Are there no swords here? Has no one a blow for me?

Messenger.

120　Her curse is upon you for the deaths of both.

Creon.

　　It is right that it should be. I alone am guilty.
　　I know it, and I say it. Lead me in,
　　Quickly, friends.
　　I have neither life nor substance. Lead me in.

Choragos.

125　You are right, if there can be right in so much wrong.
　　The briefest way is best in a world of sorrow.

Creon.

　　Let it come,
　　Let death come quickly, and be kind to me.
　　I would not ever see the sun again.

Choragos.

130　All that will come when it will; but we, meanwhile,
　　Have much to do. Leave the future to itself.

Creon.

　　All my heart was in that prayer!

Choragos.

　　Then do not pray any more: the sky is deaf.

Creon.

　　Lead me away. I have been rash and foolish.
135　I have killed my son and wife.
　　I look for comfort; my comfort lies here dead.
　　Whatever my hands have touched has come to noth-
　　　　ing.
　　Fate has brought all my pride to a thought of dust.

[As CREON *is being led into the house, the* CHORAGOS
advances and speaks directly to the audience.]

Choragos.

　　There is no happiness where there is no wisdom;
140　No wisdom but in submission to the gods.
　　Big words are always punished,
　　And proud men in old age learn to be wise.

Responding to the Play

Analyzing Scene 5, Paean, and Exodos

Identifying Facts

1. In lines 70–76 of Scene 5, what mistakes does Teiresias say Creon has made? What does he advise Creon to do?
2. What does Creon accuse Teiresias of? After this accusation, what fate does Teiresias prophesy for Creon?
3. The violent **resolution** of the plot takes place offstage. Briefly summarize the news the Messenger brings in lines 32–76 of the Exodos and the reaction of the characters who hear this news.

Intepreting Meanings

4. Why is it **ironic** that the prophet Teiresias is blind? What added meaning does this irony give to his prophecy?
5. Why do you think Creon finally changes his mind about freeing Antigone and burying Polyneices?
6. Find two passages in this scene that comment on pride. How would you define *pride*? In your opinion, has Creon been guilty of pride, or has he been acting according to the dictates of his conscience? Explain your response.
7. The Paean is recited after Creon has changed his mind but before the plot is **resolved**. At this point in the play, why is it appropriate for the Chorus to call on the god Dionysos to "come with clement feet"? What is the Chorus asking the god to heal?
8. Reread the Messenger's speech in lines 32–76, and notice that Creon goes to bury Polyneices *before* he rushes to free Antigone. What do you think of his decision? Might he have prevented the tragedy if he had freed Antigone first?
9. At the end of the play, Eurydice blames Creon for the tragic turn of events, and Creon accepts her curse, saying, "I alone am guilty" (line 121). Do you agree that Creon is completely responsible for the play's tragic ending? Or do you think the blame should be shared—or even that Creon was merely an innocent instrument of the gods' revenge on the House of Oedipus? Explain your opinion.

The Play as a Whole

1. Describe the major **conflict** in *Antigone*. Is it a conflict between absolute good and absolute evil, or a more subtle conflict between two opposing goods? What seems to be Sophocles' stand on this conflict? Do you agree with him?
2. Do you think that Antigone is a completely admirable **character**, or is she just as proud, unyielding, and foolish as Creon? In your opinion, is Antigone an innocent martyr, or do the gods punish her for her pride, just as they punish Creon for his? Explain your opinion.
3. Did your feelings about Creon change during the course of the play? Did you pity him in the Exodos, or did you feel that he got what he deserved? Explain your response.
4. What is the role of the Chorus and Choragos in *Antigone*? To what extent do they influence the action of the play, and to what extent do they simply comment upon it or serve as a barometer of public opinion?
5. Find at least three passages in the play that seem to summarize the **theme** of *Antigone*. How would you state this theme in your own words?
6. How does the level of violence in *Antigone* contrast with what we are used to seeing today in movies and on television? In your opinion, what is the effect of having violent actions take place offstage and then described to us, rather than letting us witness them directly? Did you react as strongly to the violence and tragedy as you would have if you had seen it take place?

Writing About the Play

A Creative Response

1. **Updating the Play.** Think about how you might update *Antigone* to take place today, either in the United States or in some other part of the world. What kind of figure would Creon be: an elected politician, a dictator, a business leader, a family patriarch? What would his conflict with Antigone be about? Write a brief synopsis, or summary, of your modern version. (First reread the discussion on page 747 about the French playwright Jean Anouilh's version of the play.)

A Critical Response

2. **Identifying the Tragic Hero or Heroine.** Read the discussion under "Focusing on Background" (page 796) about the tragic hero or heroine. According to Aristotle's definition, who would you say is the tragic figure in *Antigone:* Creon, Antigone, or both? In a paragraph, state your opinion and support it with evidence from the play. Before you begin writing, you might organize your thoughts by filling out a chart like the following one.

	Antigone	Creon
Is this character neither completely virtuous nor villainous?		
Does this character's downfall come about "not by vice or depravity, but by some error or frailty"? If so, what is this error or **tragic flaw**?		
Which character suffers more?		
Whose downfall arouses more pity and fear in us? Why?		
Does this character eventually recognize his or her own weakness or error?		

3. **Responding to Two Interpretations.** Here are two different interpretations of *Antigone*:

Antigone, as a heroine of the resistance to tyrannical power, has deservedly become one of the Western world's great symbolic figures; she is clearly presented, in her famous speech, as a champion of a higher morality against the overriding claims of state necessity, which the . . . intellectuals of Sophocles' time had begun to formulate in philosophical terms. But Creon, too, is given his due; he is not a mere tyrant of melodrama but a ruler whose action stems from political and religious attitudes which were probably shared by many of the audience. Antigone and Creon clash not only as individuals, . . . but also as representatives of two irreconcilable social and religious positions. . . . The nature of Creon's assertion of state against family, refusal of burial to a corpse, is repellent, but the principle behind it was one most Athenians would have accepted as valid.

—Bernard W. M. Knox

In discussions of *Antigone* critics have tended to choose sides. Some have argued that Antigone is right and that sacred matters, the laws of the gods, always take precedence over the laws of the state. Others have argued with equal strength that Creon is right and that the good of the city must come before any "higher laws," for it is in the city that man must live. The question is complicated by the unattractive natures of Antigone and Creon; but it now seems clear that Sophocles was not writing a *thesis play* proving that man should obey the state or the gods, but rather a tragedy in which one good in human life is somehow always opposed to another good. . . . Choose one good to the exclusion of another—and it seems to be the nature of great men to do so—the play shows, and *this* will inevitably happen. *This* is the plot of the play, and the play is shaped in all its parts to reveal and define this plot.

—Alvin B. Kernan

Write a brief essay of two or three paragraphs responding to one of these interpretations. You may agree or disagree with the comment you choose to write about, and you may also use the other comment to support your argument. Cite specific passages form the play to support your opinion.

4. **Commenting on the Issue of Fate Versus Free Will.** Write a brief essay of two or three paragraphs discussing what *Antigone* reveals about Sophocles' concept of fate. Are the characters in this play free to make choices about their actions? Or are their destinies predetermined and controlled? Is Creon's fate the consequence of his own character and conduct? Is Antigone's? Or are both Creon and Antigone victims of forces they cannot control? Give specific evidence from the play to support your opinion.

Analyzing Language and Vocabulary

Extended Metaphors

An **extended metaphor** is a figure of speech that is developed and sustained over several lines or throughout an entire poem. Like any metaphor, it compares two things that are basically dissimilar but that share some quality.

Here are some extended metaphors from *Antigone*. Answer the questions following each passage.

1. **Choragos.** Polyneices their commander
   Roused them with windy phrases,
   He the wild eagle screaming
   Insults above our land,
   His wings their shields of snow,
   His crest their marshalled helms.

   —Parodos, lines 8–13

   a. Who is the wild eagle?
   b. What is compared to the eagle's call?
   c. What is compared to the eagle's wings? Its crest?

2. **Chorus.** Fortunate is the man who has never tasted God's vengeance!
   Where once the anger of heaven has struck, that house is shaken
   For ever: damnation rises behind each child
   Like a wave cresting out of the black northeast,
   When the long darkness under sea roars up
   and bursts drumming death upon the wind-whipped sand.

   —Ode 2, lines 1–6

   a. "God's vengeance" is compared to two things in this passage. The first metaphor is **implied,** rather than directly stated. What is the "anger of heaven"?
   b. What words suggest the unnamed term of this **metaphor?**
   c. What is the second comparison? What word in line 5 refers back to "vengeance"?
   d. According to these two **metaphors,** is "God's vengeance" slow or sudden?

3. **Haimon** (to Creon). In flood time you can see how some trees bend,
   And because they bend, even their twigs are safe,
   While stubborn trees are torn up, roots and all.
   And the same thing happens in sailing:
   Make your sheet fast, never slacken—and over you go,
   Head over heels and under: and there's your voyage.
   Forget you are angry! Let yourself be moved!

   —Scene 3, lines 80–86

   a. What two things is Creon compared to?
   b. What **images** does Haimon use to make these comparisons?
   c. What point is Haimon trying to make to Creon about the consequences of being inflexible?

Lines from the Play to Talk About

Like every great work of literature, *Antigone* contains a number of passages that express opinions about life or human nature.

Which of the following statements from the play seem relevant to modern life? Do any seem out of date or about issues that are unimportant today? Which statements express a view of life that you agree with? Why? Which statements seem to express Sophocles' viewpoint?

See if you can remember which characters in *Antigone* made each of these statements. Then check your answers by looking back through the play. Has any one character spoken most of these lines?

1. "Only a crazy man is in love with death!" (Scene 1, line 63)
2. "Nobody likes the man who brings bad news." (Scene 1, line 112)
3. "A fortune won is often misfortune." (Scene 1, line 141)
4. "How dreadful it is when the right judge judges wrong!" (Scene 1, line 148)
5. "Numberless are the world's wonders, but none / More wonderful than man. . . . (Ode 1, lines 1–2)
6. "There is nothing so comfortable as your own safe skin!" (Scene 2, line 49)
7. "Which of us can say what the gods hold wicked?" (Scene 2, line 116)
8. "Grief teaches the steadiest minds to waver. . . ." (Scene 2, line 151)
9. ". . . good lives are made so by discipline." (Scene 3, line 45)
10. "It is not reason never to yield to reason!" (Scene 3, line 79)
11. ". . . if I am young, and right, / What does my age matter?" (Scene 3, lines 97–98)
12. "Reverence is a virtue, but strength / Lives in established law. . . . " (Scene 4, lines 45–46)
13. ". . . The only crime is pride." (Scene 5, line 35)
14. "The pains that men will take to come to pain!" (Exodos, line 98)
15. "There is no happiness where there is no wisdom. . . ." (Exodos, line 139)
16. " . . . proud men in old age learn to be wise." (Exodos, line 142)

What other wise sayings can you find in the play? Try to find at least three more.

Focusing on Background
Aristotle's View of Tragedy and the Tragic Hero

Tragedy was first defined by the Greek philosopher Aristotle (384–322 B.C.), and critics have been arguing about it ever since. Aristotle's definition is not a rule for what tragedy *should* be; it is a description of what he believed tragedy *was*, based on his observations of Greek drama, particularly the works of Sophocles.

According to Aristotle, the function of **tragedy** is to arouse pity and fear in the audience so that we may be purged, or cleansed, of these unsettling emotions. Aristotle's term for this emotional purging is the Greek word *catharsis*, and it is one of the most analyzed of all literary expressions. Although no one is exactly sure what Aristotle meant by *catharsis*, it seems clear that he was referring to that strangely pleasurable sense of emotional release we experience after watching a great tragedy. For some reason, we usually feel exhilarated, not depressed, at the end. It is as if we feel a sense of calm after the storm.

According to Aristotle, a tragedy can only arouse these twin emotions of pity and fear if it presents a certain type of hero or heroine. This character is neither completely good nor completely bad, but rather somewhere in the middle:

". . . the change of fortune presented must not be the spectacle of a virtuous man brought from prosperity to adversity: For this moves neither pity nor fear; it merely shocks us. Nor again, that of a bad man passing from adversity to prosperity: For nothing can be more alien to the spirit of tragedy; . . . it neither satisfies the moral sense nor calls forth pity or fear. Nor, again, should the downfall of the utter villain be exhibited. A plot of this kind would, doubtless, satisfy the moral sense, but it would inspire neither pity nor fear; for pity is aroused by unmerited misfortune, fear by the misfortune of a man like ourselves. . . . There remains, then, the character between these two extremes—that of a man who is not eminently good and just, yet whose misfortune is brought about not by vice or depravity, but by some error or frailty. . . ."

—from *The Poetics*,
Aristotle,
translated by S. H. Butcher

Aristotle goes on to say that the tragic hero should be someone "who is highly renowned and prosperous," which in Aristotle's day meant a member of a royal family. Why not an ordinary working person, we might ask: simply because the hero's fall from good fortune must be from a tremendous height if it is to arouse our pity and fear.

Just as critics have argued over the meaning of Aristotle's term *catharsis*, they have disagreed sharply over what he meant by the tragic hero's "error or frailty." Is the hero's undoing a single error of judgment, as some have maintained? Or is it what other critics have termed a **tragic flaw,** a fundamental character weakness such as excessive pride, ambition, or jealousy? In both of these interpretations, the key point is that the hero is on some level responsible for his own downfall. He is not the mere plaything of the gods—the helpless victim of fate or of someone else's villainy. Furthermore, by the end of the play, the hero comes to recognize his own error and to accept its tragic consequences. He does not curse his fate or shake his fists at the gods. He is humbled—and enlightened.

Yet we, the audience, feel that the hero's punishment exceeds his crime, that he gets more than he deserves. Thus we feel pity for the hero because he is a suffering human being who is flawed like us. And we feel fear because the hero is *better* than we are (think of Oedipus, who not only was king, but whose exceptional courage and intelligence earned him his throne) and *still* he failed. What hope, then, can there be for us?

Publius Ovidius Naso (43 B.C.–A.D. 17?) lived during the most decadent period in ancient Roman history. His poetry, for the most part light and comic in theme, was directed toward an upper-class "society" audience. Yet it was also poetry of great elegance that demonstrated keen psychological insight.

Ovid's work reflects the general sense of disillusionment that pervaded Roman society in the later years of the reign of Caesar Augustus, the first Roman emperor and the grandnephew of Julius Caesar. (In another part of the empire, in Palestine, these were the years of the early life of Jesus.) During this period, the earlier values of the Roman republic were permanently replaced by those of the aristocratic and autocratic empire. Romans had once valued patriotism, religion, and idealism; now they valued pleasure, wealth, and power. Ovid was a skeptical observer of the frivolous and changeable existence of his times.

Ovid was the son of a well-to-do family from the mountains northeast of Rome. As a boy he was sent to Athens and then Rome to be educated. Ovid's parents wanted their brilliant son to become a lawyer, but in Rome he developed a taste for a good time and for writing verse. Gradually he dropped law and became a poet.

Ovid soon became a popular favorite among the Roman "fast set." But at the age of seventy, the Emperor Augustus suddenly changed his ways and announced a program of moral austerity. As a result, Ovid was charged with inciting immorality through his works and with irreverence to the state. In A.D. 8 Ovid was exiled beyond the pale of civilization to a desolate fishing village on the edge of the Black Sea. He never returned to Rome.

By the Middle Ages, Ovid was once again admired for his poetry. His simple, flowing verse—especially the *Metamorphoses*—served as a source of information about ancient mythology and wisdom.

The Metamorphoses
by Ovid

The Fall of Icarus. Engraving.

Daedalus and Icarus

The *Metamorphoses* is a verse narrative that begins with the Greek story of the creation of the universe and ends with the deification of the Emperor Augustus. Ovid collected myths from all over the Roman Empire, including Greece, Crete, and Egypt, and retold them with great subtlety. As the title suggests (a *metamorphosis* is a change of form), the theme of the work is transformation.

One of the most famous of Ovid's transformation stories is the tale of Daedalus (ded″l·əs), a skilled Athenian craftsman and sculptor, and his son Icarus (ik′ə·rəs). According to the Greek myth, the wife of King Minos of Crete gave birth to a child who had a human body and a bull's head. In order to hide this monster-child, called the Minotaur, from public view, King Minos hired Daedalus to build a labyrinth, or maze, for it. When Daedalus's task was completed, King Minos refused to let him leave Crete because he thought the clever craftsman was too valuable to lose. But Daedalus devised an ingenious plan for escape—he fashioned wings for himself and Icarus. Ovid's tale of the drowned boy is the eternal story of the youth who inevitably goes too far and too fast.

"**O**vid's tale of the drowned boy is the eternal story of the youth who inevitably goes too far and too fast."

Daedalus and Icarus

Ovid, translated by **Horace Gregory**

Weary of exile, hating Crete, his prison,
Old Daedalus grew homesick for his country
Far out of sight beyond his walls—the sea.
"Though Minos owns this island, rules the waves,
5   The skies are open: my direction's clear.
Though he commands all else on earth below
His tyranny does not control the air."
So Daedalus turned his mind to subtle craft,
An unknown art that seemed to outwit nature:
10   He placed a row of feathers in neat order,
Each longer than the one that came before it
Until the feathers traced an inclined plane
That cast a shadow like the ancient pipes
That shepherds played, each reed another step
15   Unequal to the next. With cord and wax
He fixed them smartly at one end and middle,
Then curved them till they looked like eagles' wings.
And as he worked, boy Icarus stood near him,
His brilliant face lit up by his father's skill.
20   He played at snatching feathers from the air
And sealing them with wax (nor did he know
How close to danger came his lightest touch);
And as the artist made his miracles
The artless boy was often in his way.
25   At last the wings were done and Daedalus
Slipped them across his shoulders for a test
And flapped them cautiously to keep his balance,
And for a moment glided into air.
He taught his son the trick and said, "Remember
30   To fly midway, for if you dip too low
The waves will weight your wings with thick saltwater,
And if you fly too high the flames of heaven
Will burn them from your sides. Then take your flight
Between the two. Your route is not toward Boötes
35   Nor Helice, nor where Orion° swings
His naked sword. Steer where I lead the way."
With this he gave instructions how to fly
And made a pair of wings to fit the boy.
Though his swift fingers were as deft as ever,
40   The old man's face was wet with tears; he chattered
More fatherly advice on how to fly.
He kissed his son—and, as the future showed,

35. **Boötes . . . Orion:** northern constellations of stars.

This was a last farewell—then he took off.
And as a bird who drifts down from her nest
45   Instructs her young to follow her in flight,
So Daedalus flapped wings to guide his son.
Far off, below them, some stray fisherman,
Attention startled from his bending rod,
Or a bland shepherd resting on his crook,
50   Or a dazed farmer leaning on his plough,
Glanced up to see the pair float through the sky,
And, taking them for gods, stood still in wonder.
They flew past Juno's Samos° on the left

The Fall of Icarus by Pieter
Brueghel, the Elder (c. 1555). Oil.

Musée des Beaux Arts, Brussels.

53. **Juno's Samos:** Juno (akin to the Greek
goddess Hera), the Roman queen of the
gods, was married to Jupiter (akin to the
Greek god Zeus). The island of Samos in
the Aegean Sea off the coast of western
Turkey was sacred to Juno.

And over Delos and the isle of Paros,
55 And on the right lay Lebinthus, Calymne,°
A place made famous for its wealth in honey.
By this time Icarus began to feel the joy
Of beating wings in air and steered his course
Beyond his father's lead: all the wide sky
60 Was there to tempt him as he steered toward heaven.
Meanwhile the heat of sun struck at his back
And where his wings were joined, sweet-smelling fluid
Ran hot that once was wax. His naked arms
Whirled into wind; his lips, still calling out
65 His father's name, were gulfed in the dark sea.
And the unlucky man, no longer father,
Cried, "Icarus, where are you, Icarus,
Where are you hiding, Icarus, from me?"
Then as he called again, his eyes discovered
70 The boy's torn wings washed on the climbing waves.
He damned his art, his wretched cleverness,
Rescued the body and placed it in a tomb,
And where it lies the land's called Icarus.

As Daedalus gave his ill-starred son to earth,
75 A talking partridge in a swamp near by
Glanced up at him and with a cheerful noise
The creature clapped its wings. And this moment
The partridge was a new bird come to earth—
And a reminder, Daedalus, of crime.
80 For the inventor's sister, ignorant
Of what the Fates had planned, sent him her son°—
A brilliant boy and scarcely twelve years old.
The boy studied the backbone of a fish;
This image in his mind, he made a saw
85 And was the first to bolt two arms of iron
In a loose joint: while one was held at rest,
The other traced a circle in the sand.°
Daedalus, jealous of his nephew's skill,
Murdered the child by tossing him head-first
90 Down the steep stairs that mount Minerva's temple,°
Then lied by saying the boy slipped and fell.
But Pallas,° who rewards quick-witted creatures
Restored him with the feathers of a bird,
Saved in midair. The quickness of his mind
95 Was in his wings and feet; he kept his name.
Even now the bird does not take wing too high,
Nor makes her nest in trees or up a cliff,
But claps her wings in shallow flight near earth;
Her eggs drop in thick brush, and not forgetting
100 Her ancient fall, she fears high resting regions.

55. **Delos . . . Calymne** (ka·lim'nē): various islands in the Aegean Sea. Daedalus and Icarus are headed toward Athens.

81. **her son:** Talos.

87. **traced . . . sand:** Talos is said to have invented the compass as well as the potter's wheel.

90. **Minerva's temple:** Minerva was the Roman goddess of wisdom and invention (akin to the Greek goddess Athena). Minerva's temple was the Acropolis in Athens.
92. **Pallas:** Pallas Athena, Greek goddess of wisdom.

Responding to the Poem

Analyzing the Poem

Identifying Details

1. What warning does Daedalus give his son before they take flight? Explain why Icarus ignores his father's warning.
2. In lines 1–73, Daedalus seems to be a sympathetic character. What do we learn about him in lines 74–91 that makes us see him differently?
3. What **metamorphosis**, or transformation, does Ovid describe in lines 74–100? How is the transformed creature like the original?

Interpreting Meanings

4. Icarus's death might be interpreted as a punishment arranged by the gods. What have Daedalus and Icarus done that deserves punishment? Why is each punishment appropriate?
5. According to Greek mythology, Daedalus's nephew, Talos, died long before Icarus was born. Why do you think Ovid chose to tell these stories in reverse chronological order?
6. There are several characters to feel sorry for in this story. Which character did you pity most? Explain your response.
7. The Greeks believed that human actions should embrace the principle of "the golden mean"—moderation, the prudent middle way between extremes of behavior. How does the myth of Daedalus and Icarus relate to this theme? Is there another lesson or message in this story? If so, what is it?
8. The myth of Daedalus and Icarus can be interpreted as a timeless, ever-relevant story about the character and behavior of youth. Do you think its psychological insights still hold true today? Why or why not?

Writing About the Poem

A Creative Response

1. **Describing a Character's Thoughts.** Imagine Icarus's thoughts while he is feeling "the joy of beating wings in air." Then imagine his thoughts as his wings begin to melt and he plummets to the sea. Narrate Icarus's thoughts, using the first-person pronoun *I*.

2. **Updating the Myth.** How would you update this story to take place today? Who would Daedalus and Icarus be? What would they be trying to accomplish or escape from when the tragedy occurs? Would the tragedy be a punishment for an old crime? Write a modern version of the myth, in which Icarus dies as the result of going too far, too fast, or too high—despite the warnings of his father.

A Critical Response

3. **Responding to a Critic's Comment.** Horace Gregory, the twentieth-century American poet whose translation of Ovid appears in the text, had this to say about Ovid:

> No writer of this Golden Age in Roman literature has excelled [Ovid] in the rapid unfolding of a narrative, nor has any surpassed him in the direct revelations of psychological detail. . . . However farfetched . . . his situations may seem to the twentieth-century reader, they never fail to create the illusion of life. . . .
>
> —Horace Gregory

Write a brief essay of two or three paragraphs discussing the psychological details that Ovid includes in the story of Daedalus and Icarus. Be sure to consider the following questions: What do we learn about how Daedalus feels? How are his feelings revealed? Why do we learn about Daedalus's **motivation** for murdering Talos? Does Ovid's tale indeed "create the illusion of life," as Gregory maintains, or do you find the characters and situation unbelievable?

Analyzing Language and Vocabulary

Etymologies of Names

An **etymology** traces a word's origin. The word *invent*, for example, comes from two Latin roots: *in-*, which means "in" or "on"; and *venire*, which means "to come." An inventor literally "comes upon" ideas for new tools, devices, or creations.

Names have meanings, too. According to the English poet Robert Graves, who was a scholar of

Greek mythology, Daedalus means "the artful craftsman," and Icarus comes from a Greek word meaning "dedicated to the moon-goddess Car." Poor Talos's name, some people think, means "sufferer." The name of King Minos of Crete may mean "the moon's creature," and the Minotaur's name means "Minos's bull."

Every language and culture has names that mean something, even though the meanings are no longer obvious or even pertinent. Find out the meanings of at least five "given names" (first names) and five surnames (last names) in your community. What do these names reveal about the people who originally bore them?

Focusing on Connections
The Theme of Daedalus and Icarus in Literature and Art

Here is a poem by the twentieth-century British poet W. H. Auden. Think about the poem's connections to Ovid's story of Daedalus and Icarus and to Brueghel's painting *The Fall of Icarus* on pages 798–799. Then consider the following questions: How is Auden's focus different from Ovid's? What point is Auden making about the Brueghel painting in particular and about art in general? What point is he making about suffering and its "human position"? What is it that the "Old Masters" were "never wrong" about? Is the **theme** of Auden's poem the same as the theme of Ovid's—or is his poem really about something else entirely?

Musée des Beaux Arts°

About suffering they were never wrong,
The Old Masters: how well they understood
Its human position; how it takes place
While someone else is eating or opening a window
    or just walking dully along;
How, when the aged are reverently, passionately
    waiting

Musée des Beaux Arts: the Museum of Fine Arts in Brussels, Belgium, which owns Brueghel's painting.

For the miraculous birth, there always must be
Children who did not specially want it to happen,
    skating
On a pond at the edge of the wood:
They never forgot
That even the dreadful martyrdom must run its
    course
Anyhow in a corner, some untidy spot
Where the dogs go on with their doggy life, and
    the torturer's horse
Scratches its innocent behind on a tree.

In Brueghel's *Icarus,* for instance: how every-
    thing turns away
Quite leisurely from the disaster; the ploughman
    may
Have heard the splash, the forsaken cry,
But for him it was not an important failure; the
    sun shone
As it had to on the white legs disappearing into
    the green
Water; and the expensive delicate ship that must
    have seen
Something amazing, a boy falling out of the sky,
Had somewhere to get to and sailed calmly on.
              —W. H. Auden

The Old and New Testaments are the great code of art.

—William Blake

It is impossible to imagine Western culture without the Bible. The Bible is central to the way we act, think, and communicate. Consider our basic standards of behavior. Whatever our religion or politics, most of us share certain assumptions about what is right and wrong. We agree that murder, theft, adultery, envy, lying, and dishonoring our parents are wrong—all acts that were first clearly prohibited in the Ten Commandments of the Bible.

The Biblical concept that perhaps most strongly pervades our culture is the idea that time moves in a straight line from past to future, that history can be seen as a kind of narrative with a beginning and an end—whether that end be Heaven, Hell, the arrival of a Messiah, the establishment of the Kingdom of God on earth, or another sort of millenium. The Western world view is very much geared to this linear conception of time, and in this it follows the world view of the Bible.

The Bible's Impact on Our Imaginations

The Bible has enormous importance as a sacred book and as a chronicle of history. But it is also of crucial significance as a work of literature that has influenced every aspect of our imaginative lives. What would literature be without the Bible? Writers as different from one another as John Milton and Ernest Hemingway, Walt Whitman and T. S. Eliot, Emily Dickinson and James Baldwin, William Blake and F. Scott Fitzgerald, Herman Melville and Flannery O'Connor, have been influenced not only by the Bible's text, but also by its rhythms and tones.

Literature is not the only art form indebted to the Bible. It is virtually impossible to visit an art museum without seeing a picture with a Biblical theme: Adam and Eve's expulsion from the Garden of Eden, Moses and the Ten Commandments, David's slaying of Goliath, the birth of Jesus, The Last Supper, or the Crucifixion. And how long could we listen to a classical music station without hearing music based on Biblical themes: Handel's *Messiah,* Haydn's *The Creation,* or Bach's *Easter Oratorio?*

Biblical images and stories abound in our vocabulary. We might call a person who helps others a "good Samaritan." A person who betrays a friend is a "Judas," and a particularly good or fine person is the "salt of the earth." Or we might talk about a "mass exodus" from the city on a holiday weekend or a job that requires the "patience of Job." All of these words and expressions have their source in the Bible. Many of our names are Biblical, too: Daniel, David, Jason, Samuel, Joshua, Matthew, Paul, Timothy, Peter, Mary, Sarah, Ruth, Madeline, Rachel, Deborah, Rebecca, Elizabeth, to mention only a few.

Literature and the Bible

"What would literature be without the Bible?"

David by Gianlorenzo Bernini (1623). Marble.

Borghese Gallery, Rome.

What Is the Bible?

It is important to keep in mind that the Bible is really two different books to two different religions. The Jewish, or Hebrew, Bible consists of what Jews call simply the Bible or the Holy Scriptures and what Christians call the Old Testament. The Christian Bible consists of the Hebrew Bible, or Old Testament, and the New Testament.

The Hebrew Bible is made up of many different books containing poetry, narratives, historical records, prophecies, and legal writings. The primary theme of these books is the relationship between God and His people. The first five books of the Hebrew Bible and the most sacred texts of Judaism are called the *Torah* (Hebrew for "the Law"). These books are sometimes called the Five Books of Moses, or in the Christian tradition, the Pentateuch (Greek for "five books").

Parts of the Hebrew Bible were probably handed down orally from about the thirteenth century B.C., when the ancient Hebrews returned to Canaan (later called Palestine) after their captivity in Egypt. The first fully developed written texts probably date from the tenth century B.C., about two centuries before the time of Homer. Most of the Old Testament was written in Hebrew, but a few of the later books were written in a Syrian dialect called Aramaic, the language probably spoken by Jesus.

The early Christians were Jews, and so they considered the Hebrew Bible their sacred text, but believed that it had not completed the story of God's relationship with His people. Thus the Holy Scriptures, or Old Testament, became the first part of the Christian Bible. The second part is called the New Testament. The New Testament contains four Gospels, which are accounts of the life and teachings of Jesus. The Gospels are followed by historical accounts of the early days of the Christian Church; by letters from the apostles, or early Christian missionaries; and by the Book of Revelation, a vision of the end of time. The Gospels were first written down between A.D. 50 and 150 in Koine Greek, which was the everyday "international" language spoken throughout the Middle East at that time.

Reading the Bible

Most of us read the Bible in one of its many translations, rather than in the original Hebrew or Greek. While the literary value of the Bible depends to some extent on the quality of the translations we read, even in imperfect translations the Bible has enormous power. Many of its narratives, poems, songs, epics, and parables are as basic to the world's literature as are the epics of Homer and the plays of Shakespeare.

This unit includes a very small sampling of some key selections from the Bible. These narratives and poems are presented in a variety of translations ranging from the famous seventeenth-century King James Version to the most recent contemporary editions.

Moses by Michelangelo (c. 1513–1515). Marble.

San Pietro in Vincoli, Rome.

This account of Abraham and his son Isaac occurs near the middle of the Book of Genesis, the first book of the Bible. (In Hebrew this book is called *Bereshith,* which means "in the beginning.") The poignant narrative about Abraham's near-sacrifice of Isaac is thought to have been written in the eighth century B.C., perhaps around the time of Homer.

Abraham—a name meaning "the father of many"—was the patriarch of the ancient Hebrews. He lived during one of the periods of migration in the Middle East, probably during the nineteenth century B.C. According to the Book of Genesis, God ordered Abraham to journey from his home in Mesopotamia to Canaan (later named Palestine by the Greeks). Then God made a promise to Abraham:

> I will give unto thee, and to thy seed after thee, the land wherein thou art a stranger, all the land of Canaan, for an everlasting possession; and I will be their God.

Despite this promise that the land of Canaan would belong to his descendants, Abraham and his wife, Sarah, remained childless until he was ninety-nine years old and she was ninety. But one day three angels disguised as men came to visit Abraham. When Sarah overheard one of these visitors say that she would bear a child within a year's time, she laughed to herself, believing that she and Abraham were far too old to conceive a child. But a miracle happened: Sarah did bear a child, a son God told them to name Isaac (which means "laughter"). Through this one child, Abraham's covenant, or agreement, with God would be fulfilled:

> . . . walk before me, and be thou perfect. And I will make my covenant between me and thee, and will multiply thee exceedingly . . . , and thou shalt be a father of many nations . . . , and kings shall come out of thee. And I will establish my covenant between me and thee and thy seed after thee in their generations, for an everlasting covenant. . . .

Abraham and Isaac
From the Book of Genesis

> " " **W**alk
> . . .
> **before me,
> and be thou perfect.' "
> —Genesis**

The Sacrifice of Isaac by Lucas Cranach, the Elder.

New Residence, Bamberg, Germany.

ABRAHAM AND ISAAC

Tanakh: The New Jewish Publication Society Translation

Sacrifice of Isaac by Filippo Brunelleschi (1401–1402).
Detail of gilt bronze Bapistry doors.

Bargello, Florence.

Some time afterward, God put Abraham to the test. He said to him, "Abraham," and he answered, "Here I am." And He said, "Take your son, your favored one, Isaac, whom you love, and go to the land of Moriah,[1] and offer him there as a burnt offering on one of the heights that I will point out to you." So early next morning Abraham saddled his ass and took with him two of his servants and his son Isaac. He split the wood for the burnt offering, and he set out for the place of which God had told him. On the third day Abraham looked up and saw the place from afar. Then Abraham said to his servants, "You stay here with the ass. The boy and I will go up there; we will worship and we will return to you."

Abraham took the wood for the burnt offering and put it on his son Isaac. He himself took the firestone and the knife; and the two walked off together. Then Isaac said to his father Abraham, "Father!" And he answered, "Yes, my son." And he said, "Here are the firestone and the wood; but where is the sheep for the burnt offering?" And Abraham said, "God will see to the sheep for His burnt offering, my son." And the two of them walked on together.

They arrived at the place of which God had told him. Abraham built an altar there; he laid out the wood; he bound his son Isaac; he laid him on the altar, on top of the wood. And Abraham picked up the knife to slay his son. Then an angel of the Lord called to him from heaven: "Abraham! Abraham!" And he answered, "Here I am." And he said, "Do not raise your hand against the boy, or do anything to him. For now I know that you fear God, since you have not withheld your son, your favored one, from Me."

When Abraham looked up, his eye fell upon a ram, caught in the thicket by its horns. So Abraham went and took the ram and offered it up as a burnt offering in place of his son. And Abraham named that site Adonai-yireh,[2] whence the present saying, "On the mount of the Lord there is vision."

The angel of the Lord called to Abraham a second time from heaven, and said, "By Myself I swear, the Lord declares: Because you have done this and have not withheld your son, your favored one, I will bestow My blessing upon you and make your descendants as numerous as the stars of heaven and the sands on the seashore; and your descendants shall seize the gates of their foes. All the nations of the earth shall bless themselves by your descendants, because you have obeyed My command." Abraham then returned to his servants, and they departed together for Beer-sheba; and Abraham stayed in Beer-sheba.

---

1. **the land of Moriah:** the exact location is unknown, but according to tradition it is Mount Moriah, one of the hills of Jerusalem on which Solomon built his temple.

2. **Adonai-yireh:** the Lord will see, or the Lord will provide.

Responding to the Narrative

Analyzing the Narrative

Identifying Facts

1. The account begins: "Some time afterward, God put Abraham to the test." Describe this test, and explain why God tests Abraham.
2. Does Abraham pass or fail the test? Explain.
3. What is the **climax** of this episode?
4. What does God promise Abraham after the test?

Interpreting Meanings

5. What would you say is the essential **conflict** in this brief account? Is it primarily an **external** or an **internal** conflict? Is the conflict dealt with directly in the story, or must we imagine it? Explain.
6. This narrative is remarkable for its spare style. Much is told in very few words with a minimum of detail. What details are missing from the ac-

count? (Remember that Isaac was the much-cherished son of parents who were in their nineties when he was born.) How would the narrative be different if this information had been included?

7. Clearly, Abraham made a "sacrifice" when he followed God's order to leave his homeland and move to the alien land of Canaan. But Abraham's willingness to sacrifice Isaac is of a completely different order. What does Isaac represent to Abraham? What might have been the long-term results if Abraham had sacrificed Isaac? Name two possibilities.

8. What is the message or **theme** of this famous account of a father willing to sacrifice his only child at God's command?

Writing About the Narrative

A Creative Response

Using a Different Point of View. Many artists and writers have interpreted this compelling account of Abraham and Isaac in their own works. Most of them have attempted to depict the emotions that the characters must have felt but that the narrative does not mention. (For instance, consider the paintings on pages 805 and 862.) Narrate this journey to the land of Moriah from the point of view of Isaac, using the first-person pronoun *I*. You may tell about the whole episode, beginning with the journey from home, or you may focus only on the events of the near-sacrifice itself. Include Isaac's thoughts and feelings in your retelling.

Focusing on Connections
The Theme of Abraham and Isaac in Literature

Here is a poem by the British poet Wilfred Owen, who was killed in action during World War I at the age of twenty-six, one week before the signing of the Armistice. Think about the poem's connections to the Biblical account of Abraham and Isaac. Then consider the following questions: Who are the old men in the title? Who are the young? What central **irony** does the poem contain? Why does the old man sacrifice his son—what is he unwilling to sacrifice instead? What does the last line of the poem mean? What is the poem *really* about?

The Parable of the Old Men and the Young

So Abram rose, and clave° the wood, and went,
And took the fire with him, and a knife.
And as they journeyed both of them together,

Isaac the first-born spake and said, My Father,
Behold the preparations, fire and iron,
But where the lamb for this burnt-offering?
Then Abram bound the youth with belts and
    straps,
And builded parapets and trenches there,
And stretched forth the knife to slay his son.
When lo! an angel called him out of Heaven,
Saying, Lay not thy hand upon the lad,
Neither do anything to him. Behold,
A ram, caught in a thicket by its horns;
Offer the Ram of Pride instead of him.
But the old man would not so, but slew his son—
And half the seed of Europe, one by one.

—Wilfred Owen

1. **clave:** split with an ax (archaic form of *cleaved*).

Although the Book of Ruth takes place in around 1100 B.C. (roughly the time of the Trojan War in Asia Minor), it was probably written much later, during the fifth century B.C., when the Jews had just returned to Israel after a long and painful captivity in Babylon. While they were in exile, many Jewish men had married foreign women. Fearing that these wives would introduce idolatry, Jewish leaders condemned mixed marriages and urged the expulsion of all foreign wives. Some scholars believe that the Book of Ruth may have been written as a protest against this attitude of religious intolerance.

The Book of Ruth is the story of a foreign wife from Moab, a kingdom to the east of the Dead Sea whose language was similar to Hebrew but whose pagan religion was completely different from that of Israel. The Book of Ruth seems to have been written to teach a lesson about compassion and tolerance: Its heroine is an outsider whose exceptional loyalty and devotion to her dead husband's family earns her their love and acceptance.

Originally preserved on a single wooden roller, the Book of Ruth is one of the five *Megillot* (mə·gil′lot), or scrolls, that are read aloud on certain Jewish religious festivals. The Book of Ruth is read during *Shavuot* (shə·vōō′ət), or Pentecost, the holiday celebrating the spring grain harvest. As you will see, the harvest plays an important part in the story.

There is an ancient Biblical custom that is central to the Book of Ruth. According to Hebrew law, if a husband died without leaving a son, it was the duty of his brother (or next-of-kin) to marry the widow. The first-born son of this second marriage then took the name of the dead husband and became his legal heir. This custom, called the levirate marriage law (from *levir,* the Latin word for brother-in-law), insured that the dead man's name would be perpetuated.

> " **I**ts heroine is an outsider whose exceptional loyalty and devotion to her dead husband's family earns her their love and acceptance."

Illustration of wheat fields by Jacob Steinhardt from *The Book of Ruth* (1957). Woodcut.

THE BOOK OF RUTH

King James Bible

Chapter 1

Now it came to pass in the days when the judges ruled that there was a famine in the land. And a certain man of Bethlehem-Judah[1] went to sojourn in the country of Moab, he, and his wife, and his two sons.

And the name of the man was Elimelech, and the name of his wife Naomi, and the name of his two sons Mahlon and Chilion, Ephrathites[2] of Bethlehem-Judah. And they came into the country of Moab and continued there.

And Elimelech, Naomi's husband died; and she was left, and her two sons.

And they took them wives of the women of Moab; the name of the one was Orpah, and the name of the other Ruth: and they dwelled there about ten years.

And Mahlon and Chilion died also, both of them; and the woman was left of her two sons and her husband.

Then she arose with her daughters-in-law, that she might return from the country of Moab: for she had heard in the country of Moab how that the Lord had visited his people in giving them bread.

Wherefore she went forth out of the place where she was, and her two daughters-in-law with her; and they went on the way to return unto the land of Judah.

And Naomi said unto her two daughters-in-law, "Go, return each to her mother's house: the Lord deal kindly with you, as ye have dealt with the dead and with me. The Lord grant you that ye may find rest, each of you in the house of her husband." Then she kissed them; and they lifted up their voice and wept.

And they said unto her, "Surely we will return with thee unto thy people."

And Naomi said, "Turn again, my daughters: why will ye go with me? Are there yet any more sons in my womb, that they may be your husbands?

"Turn again, my daughters, go your way; for I am too old to have a husband. If I should say I have hope, if I should have a husband also tonight and should also bear sons, would ye tarry for them till they were grown? Would ye stay for them from having husbands? Nay, my daughters; for it grieveth me much for your sakes that the hand of the Lord is gone out against me."

And they lifted up their voice and wept again: and Orpah kissed her mother-in-law, but Ruth clave[3] unto her.

And she said, "Behold, thy sister-in-law is gone back unto her people and unto her gods: Return thou after thy sister-in-law."

And Ruth said, "Entreat me not to leave thee or to return from following after thee: for whither thou goest, I will go; and where thou lodgest, I will lodge: thy people shall be my people, and thy God my God: where thou diest, will I die, and there will I be buried: the Lord do so to me, and more also, if ought but death part thee and me."

When she saw that she was steadfastly minded to go with her, then she left speaking unto her.

So they two went until they came to Bethlehem. And it came to pass, when they were come to Bethlehem, that all the city was moved about them, and they said, "Is this Naomi?"

---

1. **Bethlehem-Judah:** that is, Bethlehem in Judah. Judah was a region in southern Palestine that eventually became a kingdom rivaling Israel to the north.
2. **Ephrathites** (ef′rə·thīts): natives of Bethlehem, once known as Ephrath.

3. **clave unto:** clung to, was faithful to (archaic form of *cleaved*).

Illustration of Boaz and Ruth by Jacob Steinhardt
from *The Book of Ruth* (1957). Woodcut.

And she said unto them, "Call me not Naomi, call me Mara:[4] for the Almighty hath dealt very bitterly with me. I went out full, and the Lord hath brought me home again empty: Why then call ye me Naomi, seeing the Lord hath testified against me, and the Almighty hath afflicted me?"

So Naomi returned, and Ruth the Moabitess, her daughter-in-law, with her, which returned out of the country of Moab: and they came to Bethlehem in the beginning of barley harvest.

Chapter 2

And Naomi had a kinsman of her husband's, a mighty man of wealth, of the family of Elimelech; and his name was Boaz.

And Ruth the Moabitess said unto Naomi, "Let me now go to the field and glean ears of corn after him in whose sight I shall find grace."[5] And she said unto her, "Go, my daughter."

And she went, and came, and gleaned in the field after the reapers: and her hap[6] was to light on a part of the field belonging unto Boaz, who was of the kindred of Elimelech.

And, behold, Boaz came from Bethlehem and said unto the reapers, "The Lord be with you." And they answered him, "The Lord bless thee."

Then said Boaz unto his servant that was set over the reapers, "Whose damsel is this?"

And the servant that was set over the reapers answered and said, "It is the Moabitish damsel that came back with Naomi out of the country of Moab. And she said, 'I pray you, let me glean and gather after the reapers among the sheaves': so she came, and hath continued even from the morning until now, that she tarried a little in the house."

Then said Boaz unto Ruth, "Hearest thou not, my daughter? Go not to glean in another field, neither go from hence, but abide here fast by my maidens. Let thine eyes be on the field that they do reap, and go thou after them: Have I not charged the young men that they shall not touch thee? And when thou art athirst, go unto the vessels, and drink of that which the young men have drawn."

Then she fell on her face and bowed herself to the ground and said unto him, "Why have I found grace in thine eyes, that thou shouldest take knowledge of me, seeing I am a stranger?"

And Boaz answered and said unto her, "It hath fully been showed me all that thou hast done unto thy mother-in-law since the death of thine husband: and how thou hast left thy father and thy mother, and the land of thy nativity and art come unto a people which thou knewest not heretofore. The Lord recompense thy work, and a full reward be given thee of the Lord God of Israel, under whose wings thou art come to trust."

Then she said, "Let me find favor in thy sight, my lord; for that thou hast comforted me, and for that thou hast spoken friendly unto thine handmaid, though I be not like unto one of thine handmaidens."

And Boaz said unto her, "At mealtime come thou hither, and eat of the bread, and dip thy morsel in the vinegar." And she sat beside the reapers: and he reached her parched corn, and she did eat, and was sufficed, and left.

And when she was risen up to glean, Boaz commanded his young men, saying, "Let her glean even among the sheaves, and reproach her not. And let fall also some of the handfuls on purpose for her, and leave them, that she may glean them, and rebuke her not."

So she gleaned in the field until even, and beat out that she had gleaned: and it was about an ephah[7] of barley.

And she took it up and went into the city: and her mother-in-law saw what she had gleaned: and

---

4. **Naomi . . . Mara:** In Hebrew Naomi means "pleasantness" or "my pleasant one," and Mara means "bitterness" or "the bitter one."
5. **glean . . . grace:** According to Biblical law, the poor were entitled to glean in the fields—that is, to gather the bits of grain left or dropped by the reapers. The corners of the fields were also left for the poor to reap.
6. **hap:** luck.

---

7. **ephah** (ē′fə): a little more than a bushel.

she brought forth and gave to her what she had reserved after she was sufficed.

And her mother-in-law said unto her, "Where hast thou gleaned today? and where wroughtest thou? Blessed be he that did take knowledge of thee." And she showed her mother-in-law with whom she had wrought, and said, "The man's name with whom I wrought today is Boaz."

And Naomi said unto her daughter-in-law, "Blessed be he of the Lord, who hath not left off his kindness to the living and to the dead." And Naomi said unto her, "The man is near of kin unto us, one of our next kinsmen."

And Ruth the Moabitess said, "He said unto me also, 'Thou shalt keep fast by my young men, until they have ended all my harvest.' "

And Naomi said unto Ruth her daughter-in-law, "It is good, my daughter, that thou go out with his maidens, that they meet thee not in any other field."

So she kept fast by the maidens of Boaz to glean unto the end of barley harvest and of wheat harvest; and dwelt with her mother-in-law.

Chapter 3

Then Naomi her mother-in-law said unto her, "My daughter, shall I not seek rest for thee,[8] that it may be well with thee? And now is not Boaz of our kindred, with whose maidens thou wast? Behold, he winnoweth barley tonight in the threshingfloor. Wash thyself therefore, and anoint thee, and put thy raiment upon thee, and get thee down to the floor: but make not thyself known unto the man, until he shall have done eating and drinking. And it shall be, when he lieth down, that thou shalt mark the place where he shall lie, and thou shalt go in and uncover his feet and lay thee down; and he will tell thee what thou shalt do."

And she said unto her, "All that thou sayest unto me I will do."

And she went down unto the floor and did according to all that her mother-in-law bade her.

And when Boaz had eaten and drunk and his heart was merry, he went to lie down at the end of the heap of corn: and she came softly and uncovered his feet and laid her down.

And it came to pass at midnight, that the man was afraid and turned himself: and, behold, a woman lay at his feet.

And he said, "Who art thou?" And she answered, "I am Ruth thine handmaid: Spread therefore thy skirt over thine handmaid;[9] for thou art a near kinsman."

And he said, "Blessed be thou of the Lord, my daughter: for thou hast showed more kindness in the latter end than at the beginning, inasmuch as thou followedst not young men,[10] whether poor or rich. And now, my daughter, fear not; I will do to thee all that thou requirest: for all the city of my people doth know that thou art a virtuous woman. And now it is true that I am thy near kinsman: howbeit, there is a kinsman nearer than I. Tarry this night, and it shall be in the morning that if he will perform unto thee the part of a kinsman, well; let him do the kinsman's part: but if he will not do the part of a kinsman to thee, then will I do the part of a kinsman to thee, as the Lord liveth: lie down until the morning."

And she lay at his feet until the morning: and she rose up before one could know another. And he said, "Let it not be known that a woman came into the floor."

Also he said, "Bring the vail that thou hast upon thee, and hold it." And when she held it, he measured six measures of barley and laid it on her: and she went into the city.

And when she came to her mother-in-law, she said, 'Who art thou, my daughter?" And she told her all that the man had done to her.

And she said, "These six measures of barley gave he me; for he said to me, 'Go not empty unto thy mother-in-law.' "

Then said she, "Sit still, my daughter, until

---

8. **seek rest for thee:** that is, seek a husband. Naomi is trying to fulfill the responsibility of a parent for arranging the marriage of a child.

9. **Spread therefore thy skirt:** a formal act of betrothal.
10. **thou followest not young men:** Boaz is eighty years old. He is praising Ruth for her willingness to fulfill the levirate marriage obligation even by marrying an old man.

thou know how the matter will fall: for the man will not be in rest until he have finished the thing this day.''

Then went Boaz up to the gate and sat him down there: and, behold, the kinsman of whom Boaz spake came by; unto whom he said, ''Ho, such a one! turn aside, sit down here.'' And he turned aside and sat down.

And he took ten men of the elders of the city and said, ''Sit ye down here.'' And they sat down.

And he said unto the kinsman, ''Naomi, that is come again out of the country of Moab, selleth a parcel of land, which was our brother Elimelech's. And I thought to advertise thee, saying, Buy it before the inhabitants and before the elders of my people. If thou wilt redeem it, redeem it: but if thou wilt not redeem it, then tell me, that I may know: for there is none to redeem it beside thee; and I am after thee.'' And he said, ''I will redeem it.''

Then said Boaz, ''What day thou buyest the field of the hand of Naomi, thou must buy it also of Ruth the Moabitess, the wife of the dead, to raise up the name of the dead upon his inheritance.''

And the kinsman said, ''I cannot redeem it for myself, lest I mar mine own inheritance:[11] Redeem thou my right to thyself; for I cannot redeem it.''

Now this was the manner in former time in Israel concerning redeeming and concerning changing, for to confirm all things; a man plucked off his shoe, and gave it to his neighbor: and this was a testimony in Israel.

Therefore the kinsman said unto Boaz, ''Buy it for thee.'' So he drew off his shoe.

And Boaz said unto the elders and unto all the people, ''Ye are witnesses this day, that I have bought all that was Elimelech's, and all that was Chilion's and Mahlon's, of the hand of Naomi. Moreover, Ruth the Moabitess, the wife of Mahlon, have I purchased to be my wife, to raise up the name of the dead upon his inheritance, that the name of the dead be not cut off from among his brethren and from the gate of his place: Ye are witnesses this day.''

And all the people that were in the gate and the elders said, ''We are witnesses. The Lord make the woman that is come into thine house like Rachel and like Leah,[12] which two did build the house of Israel: and do thou worthily in Ephratah, and be famous in Bethlehem. And let thy house be like the house of Pharez, whom Tamar bare unto Judah,[13] of the seed which the Lord shall give thee of this young woman.''

So Boaz took Ruth, and she was his wife: and when he went in unto her, the Lord gave her conception, and she bare a son.

And the women said unto Naomi, ''Blessed be the Lord, which hath not left thee this day without a kinsman, that his name may be famous in Israel. And he shall be unto thee a restorer of thy life and a nourisher of thine old age: for thy daughter-in-law, which loveth thee, which is better to thee than seven sons, hath born him.''

And Naomi took the child and laid it in her bosom and became nurse unto it.

And the women her neighbors gave it a name, saying, ''There is a son born to Naomi'';[14] and they called his name Obed: He is the father of Jesse, the father of David.

Now these are the generations of Pharez: Pharez begat Hezron, and Hezron begat Ram, and Ram begat Amminadab, and Amminadab begat Nahshon, and Nahshon begat Salmon, and Salmon begat Boaz, and Boaz begat Obed, and Obed begat Jesse, and Jesse begat David.

---

11. **lest I mar mine own inheritance:** that is, by spending money on property that will go to the son legally regarded as Mahlon's, rather than his own.

12. **like Rachel and like Leah:** two sisters who were Jacob's wives. Their sons were among the twelve sons of Jacob who founded the twelve tribes of Israel.

13. **Pharez . . . Judah:** Judah was the fourth son of Jacob and Leah. After his daughter-in-law Tamar had twice been left a childless widow after two of his sons died, she tricked Judah into becoming the father of her twin sons, Pharez and Zarah.

14. **a son born to Naomi:** not literally, but rather a son in the sense of a legal heir to both her dead husband and dead sons. Some Biblical scholars suggest that the child may have been legally regarded as Naomi's.

Responding to the Story

Analyzing the Story

Identifying Facts

1. Explain why Naomi and her family travel from Bethlehem to Moab. What happens to the family during the ten years they live there?
2. How does Naomi try to dissuade her two daughters-in-law from returning with her to Bethlehem? Describe how Ruth and Orpah each respond to her arguments.
3. Why does Boaz admire Ruth? Name the ways in which he shows remarkable kindness to her.
4. Explain how Naomi "arranges" Ruth's marriage to Boaz. What are her **motives**?

Interpreting Meanings

5. How does the harvest figure in the story? On a **symbolic** level, what harvest does Ruth reap? What is her good fortune the consequence of—that is, from what "seeds" has she reaped her "harvest"?
6. What is the significance of ending the story with a reference to David, who later became the most famous king of Israel? What do you think the story is subtly trying to show?
7. In your opinion, is the Book of Ruth primarily a story about religious toleration, about devotion and loyalty, or about something else? Explain. If the Book of Ruth is meant to teach a **moral,** what would you say that moral is?
8. Ruth is sometimes called the first convert to Judaism. (Converts are often given the name Ruth when they become Jews.) What words does Ruth speak as she accepts Naomi's religion? Why do you suppose these words are also often used in marriage ceremonies today?
9. Suppose this story were the only remnant we had from ancient Hebrew literature. What would it reveal about that society's customs regarding agriculture, charity, marriage, and the role of women? What does it reveal about that society's values?
10. What do you think would happen today to an old woman whose children and husband died, leaving her without any property or family? What would our society expect that woman's widowed daughter-in-law to do to help?

Writing About the Story

A Creative Response

1. **Writing a Journal or Letter.** We do not know how Ruth felt about leaving her own parents and homeland to go with Naomi to Bethlehem. Was it difficult for her to leave the land of Moab? Did she have **motives** other than the ones stated in the story? Did she feel like a stranger or an outsider when she got to Bethlehem? Write a series of journal entries that Ruth might have written anytime after leaving Moab with Naomi. Or write a letter that Ruth might have written to her sister-in-law Orpah.

A Critical Response

2. **Analyzing the Story's Elements.** The Book of Ruth has often been called the world's first short story. Do you think it fits the generally accepted standards of the short story genre? Does it have a **conflict**? A **climax**? A **resolution**? Does it have a **protagonist** who sets the **plot** in motion? (Is this protagonist Ruth or someone else?) Is there an **antagonist**—someone who blocks the protagonist? Is there a **theme**? Write a brief essay of about three paragraphs analyzing how the Book of Ruth "works" as a short story. If you don't think it does, be sure to explain what elements you feel are missing.

Analyzing Language and Vocabulary

Hebrew Names

When she returns to Bethlehem after having lost her husband and two sons, Naomi says that her name should be changed to Mara—that is, from "pleasantness" to "bitterness." God, she feels, has dealt bitterly with her, and so her old name is no longer appropriate.

One of the beauties of ancient Hebrew names is this quality of appropriateness. They are rich in meaning, even symbolic. Sometimes a Biblical name expressed a characteristic of a person, such as Esau ("hairy"). Sometimes it described the condition of the mother, such as Benoni ("son of my pain"), the child Rachel died giving birth to. Sometimes a person's name was changed to reflect a significant event in his or her life. Thus Jacob ("the supplanter") became Israel ("the prince") after he successfully wrestled with an angel.

Here is what some of the other names in the Book of Ruth mean in Hebrew:

Ruth: "beloved"
Orpah: "turns away"
Mahlon: "sickness"
Chilion: "pining away"
Boaz: "swiftness"

Explain how each of these names is appropriate in some way.

Use a dictionary to find out what the following names from the Bible mean. If you can, explain why you think each name is appropriate.

Adam	Joseph
Eve	Noah
Cain	Joshua
Sarah	Leah
Isaac	Jonah

Focusing on Connections
Biblical Allusions

Western writers have always turned to the Bible as a source for **allusions, metaphors,** and **symbols.** For instance, the title of Bernard Malamud's story "The First Seven Years" (page 59) is an allusion to the Biblical account of Jacob, Rachel, and Leah. To fully understand the meaning of Malamud's story, you must be familiar with Chapter 29 of the Book of Genesis.

One of the most famous poems in the English language contains an allusion to the Book of Ruth:

Thou wast not born for death, immortal Bird!
No hungry generations tread thee down;
The voice I hear this passing night was heard
In ancient days by emperor and clown:
Perhaps the self-same song that found a path
Through the sad heart of Ruth, when, sick for
home,
She stood in tears amid the alien corn;
The same that oft-times hath
Charmed magic casements, opening on the
foam
Of perilous seas, in faery lands forlorn.
——from "Ode to a Nightingale,"
John Keats

Keats uses Ruth as a symbol of the outsider. He expects his readers to know that she was a foreigner in a strange land. Notice that Keats attributes certain feelings to Ruth that are never actually mentioned in the Biblical account. What are these feelings? Do you agree with the way Keats has read between the lines? How would you explain the allusion to "alien corn"?

Boaz and Ruth by Hans Holbein, the Younger. Engraving.

The Book of Psalms is an anthology of Hebrew poetry written over a span of several centuries. Traditionally, nearly half of the one hundred and fifty Psalms have been attributed to King David (c. 1040–970 B.C.). However, current scholarship suggests that most of the Psalms were actually written much later than David, and a few may have been written even earlier.

The word *psalm* derives from the Greek word *psalmos,* which means "a plucking of strings." Originally, the Psalms were chanted by a cantor (solo singer) and choir to the accompaniment of stringed instruments, cymbals, and, on High Holy Days, the flute. The Psalms might also have been chanted *antiphonally*—that is, with different voices or groups of voices addressing each other alternately. (This structural device explains the shift from one speaker to another that seems to occur in some of the Psalms.)

The Hebrew name for the Book of Psalms is *tehillah,* which means "praise-songs." While many of the Psalms sing praise and thanks to God, the collection also includes personal meditations, laments, battle songs, and even a marriage ode. Like most Hebrew poetry, the Psalms are written in unrhymed, usually unmetered verse, and the rhythm is created through the use of **parallelism** (see page 826).

The Twenty-third Psalm is one of the most famous of all the Psalms and one of the best known passages from the whole Bible. It is frequently read at funeral services. As you read the Psalm, think about what kind of consolation it might offer to mourners.

The Twenty-third Psalm

King James Bible

The Lord is my shepherd; I shall not want.
He maketh me to lie down in green pastures:
He leadeth me beside the still waters.
He restoreth my soul:
5   He leadeth me in the paths of righteousness for his name's sake.
Yea, though I walk through the valley of the shadow of death,
I will fear no evil: for thou art with me;
Thy rod and thy staff they comfort me.
Thou preparest a table before me in the presence of mine enemies:
10   Thou anointest my head with oil; my cup runneth over.
Surely goodness and mercy shall follow me all the days of my life:
And I will dwell in the house of the Lord for ever.

The Twenty-third Psalm

> " **T**he Twenty-third psalm is one of the best known passages from the whole Bible."

Bas-relief of shepherds and sheep from a portal of Chartres Cathedral (1194–1225).

Chartres, France.

Responding to the Psalm

Analyzing the Psalm

Identifying Details

1. What does the word *want* mean in line 1?
2. Identify the Psalm's two central **metaphors**. By implication, what is the speaker compared to?
3. List the words that **extend** the first metaphor throughout the first eight lines.
4. In the Middle East, it was a sign of hospitality to anoint a guest's head with oil (because his hair and beard might be dusty from traveling or working in the fields). What other **images** of hospitality does the Psalm include?

Interpreting Meanings

5. How do you interpret the speaker's two **extended metaphors**? In the first one, what do you think God is really guiding the speaker through? In the second, what do you think God is welcoming the speaker to?
6. What do the **metaphors** and **images** in this Psalm reveal about the concerns of its original audience? Does modern life offer any metaphors that would suggest care and security?

Writing About the Psalm

A Critical Response

Comparing Translations. The following chart shows the opening lines of the Twenty-third Psalm in several translations. Note the differences in the **images** and **metaphors**. Which version is the most metaphorical? Which is the most literal? Which is most beautiful? Write a brief essay of one or two paragraphs giving your response to these translations. Be sure to say which you like best, and why.

Wycliffe (1382)	The Lord gouerneth me, and no thing schal faile to me; in the place of pasture there he hath set me. He nurschide me on the watir of refreischyng; he conuertide my soule.
Coverdale (1535)	The Lord is my shepherd, I can want nothing. He feedeth me in a green pasture, and leadeth me to a fresh water. He quickeneth my soul.
Geneva (1560)	The Lord is my shepherd, I shall not want. He maketh me to rest in green pasture, and leadeth me by the still waters. He restoreth my soul.
Bishops' (1568)	God is my shepherd, therefore I can lack nothing: He will cause me to repose myself in pasture full of grass, and he will lead me unto calm waters. He will convert my soul.
King James (1611)	The Lord is my shepherd; I shall not want. He maketh me to lie down in green pastures: He leadeth me beside the still waters. He restoreth my soul.
Jerusalem Bible (1966)	Yahweh is my shepherd, I lack nothing. In meadows of green grass he lets me lie. To the waters of repose he leads me; there he revives my soul.
Living Bible (1971)	Because the Lord is my Shepherd, I have everything I need! He lets me rest in the meadow grass and leads me beside the quiet streams. He restores my failing health.
Tanakh: New Jewish Publication Society Translation (1986)	The Lord is my shepherd; I lack nothing. He makes me lie down in green pastures; He leads me to water in places of repose; He renews my life. . . .

Separation of the sheep from the goats. Front of Roman sarcophagus lid (early 4th century).

The Metropolitan Museum of Art, New York.

No one knows for certain who wrote the Song of Songs, sometimes called the Song of Solomon or Canticles (from a Latin word meaning "chant" or "song"). The phrase "song of songs" is a translation of a Hebrew idiom meaning "the best of all songs."

Traditionally, these passionate love poems have been attributed to King Solomon (c. 961–922 B.C.). The book was interpreted as the story of a peasant girl who is taken into the king's harem but is finally allowed to return to her shepherd lover. Most modern scholars, however, interpret the Song of Songs quite differently—as an anthology of love poems spanning several centuries, rather than as one long dramatic poem. It is possible that the Song of Songs developed from ancient Egyptian love poetry that had been passed down orally. Some scholars have suggested that these poems were originally sung or recited at wedding celebrations.

The Song of Songs has always been interpreted **allegorically:** Its characters and events have been seen as having symbolic meaning. In Judaism, the bride is viewed as the Jewish people and the bridegroom as God. Christians interpret these love poems as an allegory of Christ's love for the Church.

Like the Book of Ruth, the Song of Songs is one of the five *Megillot,* or scrolls, that are read aloud on certain Jewish holidays. The Song of Songs is read during Passover, which commemorates the Israelites' escape from slavery in Egypt.

For the sake of clarity, dialogue tags have been added to the text to indicate who is speaking. You may want to read the poem aloud, using two speakers.

The Song of Songs

> "It is possible that the Song of Songs developed from ancient Egyptian love poetry."

I Am the Rose of Sharon

King James Bible

Bride

I am the rose of Sharon,°
And the lily of the valleys.

Bridegroom

As the lily among thorns,
So is my love among the daughters.

Bride

5   As the apple tree among the trees of the wood,
So is my beloved among the sons.
I sat down under his shadow with great delight,
And his fruit was sweet to my taste.

1. **Sharon:** a coastal plain in north central Israel.

A Bridal Pair (detail) by an anonymous German master
(c. 1470). Tempera.

Cleveland Museum of Art. Purchase, Delia E. Holden
Fund and L. E. Holden Fund.

He brought me to the banqueting house,

10   And his banner over me was love.
Stay me with flagons,° comfort me with apples:
For I am sick of love.°
His left hand is under my head,
And his right hand doth embrace me.

15   I charge you, O ye daughters of Jerusalem,
By the roes, and by the hinds° of the field,
That ye stir not up, nor awake my love,
Till he please.°
The voice of my beloved! behold, he cometh

20   Leaping upon the mountains, skipping upon the hills.
My beloved is like a roe or a young hart:°
Behold, he standeth behind our wall,
He looketh forth at the windows,
Showing himself through the lattice.

25   My beloved spake, and said unto me,
Rise up, my love, my fair one, and come away.
For, lo, the winter is past,
The rain is over and gone;
The flowers appear on the earth;

11. **flagons** (flag′ənz): vessels for holding wine.
12. **sick of love:** lovesick.

16. **roes . . . hinds:** gazelles and female deer.

18. In some modern translations, lines 15–18 are spoken by the bridegroom. ("Do not rouse her, do not disturb my love until she is ready.")

21. **hart:** male deer.

30 The time of the singing of birds is come,
And the voice of the turtle° is heard in our land;
The fig tree putteth forth her green figs,
And the vines with the tender grape give a good smell.
Arise, my love, my fair one, and come away.
35 O my dove, that art in the clefts of the rocks,
In the secret places of the stairs,
Let me see thy countenance, let me hear thy voice;
For sweet is thy voice, and thy countenance is comely.
Take us the foxes,
40 The little foxes,° that spoil the vines:
For our vines have tender grapes.
My beloved is mine, and I am his:
He feedeth among the lilies.
Until the day break, and the shadows flee away,
45 Turn, my beloved,
And be thou like a roe or a young hart
Upon the mountains of Bether.°

31. **turtle:** turtledove.

40. **little foxes:** Some scholars believe that this is a reference to neighboring nations (such as the Philistines and the Samaritans) who wanted to destroy Israel.

47. **mountains of Bether:** possibly "hills of spices."

Responding to the Poem

Analyzing the Poem

Identifying Details

1. In the first two lines of the poem, what two **metaphors** does the bride use to describe herself?
2. In the next two lines, how does the bridegroom say his beloved compares to other women? How is his **metaphor** an extension of the bride's metaphor in line 2?
3. When the bride begins to speak again in line 5, what **images** does she use to describe her beloved? What is he like, compared to other men?
4. In lines 25–34, the bride is speaking, but she is quoting her beloved. What did he ask her to do? At the end of the poem, what is her answer to his request?

Interpreting Meanings

5. When the bridegroom appears behind the wall (line 22), what **images** tell us what season it is? Why is this season appropriate for a love poem?

6. What **images** or descriptions of love do you find particularly effective or unusual in this poem? How would you say they compare to love imagery in contemporary poetry or songs?

Writing About the Poem

A Critical Response

Comparing and Contrasting Translations. The King James Version of the Song of Songs contains some of the most famous lines from the Bible. Other, more modern versions of the Bible have translated these lines quite differently—in most cases, with greater attention to the literal meaning of the original Hebrew. The following chart shows some key lines from the Song of Songs. The lines in the left-hand column are from the King James Bible; those in the right-hand column are from the New English Bible (published in 1970). Write a brief essay comparing and contrasting the translations. State which translation you prefer, and give reasons to support your opinion.

King James Bible	New English Bible	King James Bible	New English Bible
I am the rose of Sharon	I am an asphodel in Sharon	Take us the foxes, The little foxes, that spoil the vines: For our vines have tender grapes.	Catch for us the jackals, the little jackals, that spoil our vineyards, when the vines are in flower.
As the apple tree among the trees of the wood, So is my beloved among the sons.	Like an apricot-tree among the trees of the wood, so is my beloved among boys.	My beloved is mine, and I am his: He feedeth among the lilies.	My beloved is mine and I am his; he delights in the lilies.
Stay me with flagons, comfort me with apples: For I am sick of love.	He refreshed me with raisins, he revived me with apricots; for I was faint with love.	Until the day break, and the shadows flee away, Turn my beloved, And be thou like a roe or a young hart Upon the mountains of Bether.	While the day is cool and the shadows are dispersing, turn, my beloved, and show yourself a gazelle or a young wild goat on the hills where cinnamon grows.
I charge you, O ye daughters of Jerusalem, By the roes, and by the hinds of the field	I charge you, daughters of Jerusalem, by the spirits and the goddess of the field:		
My beloved is like a roe or a young hart	My beloved is like a gazelle or a young wild goat		

Focusing on Connections
Biblical Allusions

Over the centuries, writers have often used the names of Biblical books as the titles of their own works. For example, Leon Uris wrote a novel called *Exodus,* and Toni Morrison wrote a novel called *The Song of Solomon* (another name for the Song of Songs).

Other writers have used actual lines from the Bible as their titles. Each of the following titles is a quote from the Song of Songs:

> *The Voice of the Turtle,* a play by John Van Druten
> *Comfort Me with Apples,* a novel by Peter de Vries
> *The Little Foxes,* a play by Lillian Hellman

See if you can locate these lines in the text. Based on your reading of the Song of Songs, what would you guess each of these works is about?

Here are some titles that consist of lines (or approximate lines) from other parts of the Bible. The references in parentheses will help you locate the complete quotation.

1. *Absalom! Absalom!,* a novel by William Faulkner (2 Samuel 19)

2. *East of Eden,* a novel by John Steinbeck (Genesis 2)
3. *The Sun Also Rises,* a novel by Ernest Hemingway (Ecclesiastes 1)
4. *The Power and the Glory,* a novel by Graham Greene (Matthew 6)
5. *The Lilies of the Field,* a novel by William E. Barrett (Matthew 6)
6. *Stranger in a Strange Land,* a novel by Robert A. Heinlein (Exodus 2)
7. "By the Waters of Babylon," a short story by Stephen Vincent Benét (Psalm 137)
8. *The Skin of Our Teeth,* a play by Thornton Wilder (Job 19)

Movie and song titles can also contain Biblical allusions. Can you identify the references in the following titles? Which one is an actual quote from the King James Bible?

9. *Adam's Rib,* a movie by James Cukor
10. *Through a Glass Darkly,* a movie by Ingmar Bergman
11. "Adam Raised a Cain," a song by Bruce Springsteen

The Book of Ecclesiastes (*Koheleth* in Hebrew) is a collection of poetry and wisdom. The word *ecclesiastes* is a Greek word meaning "a speaker before an assembly." *Koheleth* might mean "a debator" or "a wise man who preaches to the young," or it might just be the name of the person who wrote the book. Some scholars believe that the book is actually a collection of extracts from a sage's notebook.

For many years, people believed that King Solomon wrote Ecclesiastes in his old age (and that he wrote the Song of Songs in his youth). But now, based on the type of Hebrew used in the book, scholars think that Ecclesiastes was written in about the third century B.C., more than six hundred years after King Solomon died.

Whoever wrote the book seems to have had a somewhat skeptical view of the world. Human existence consists of one fruitless struggle after another, he seems to be saying. Life proceeds in endless cycles, and death is inevitable. The only valid intellectual stance is to say that the ways of God are unknowable. The best we can do is to live moderately and accept what comes.

Few books of the Bible have had more of an impact on modern thinking than Ecclesiastes. Its questions about the purpose of human existence have appealed to such twentieth-century writers as Jean-Paul Sartre and Albert Camus. Its style has colored the work of writers as diverse as Walt Whitman and Ernest Hemingway. The verses from Chapter 3 that follow have even found their way into popular music.

Ecclesiastes, like the Book of Ruth and the Song of Songs, is one of the five festival scrolls in the Jewish Bible. It is read during the autumn harvest festival of Succoth. Why do you think the following passage might be especially appropriate for a harvest celebration?

Ecclesiastes

"Few books of the Bible have had more of an impact on modern thinking than Ecclesiastes."

Illustration (detail) by the Limbourg Brothers for the month of July from *Les Très Riches Heures du Duc de Berry* (1413–1416). Illuminated manuscript.

Musée Condé, Chantilly, France.

Illustration (detail) by the Limbourg Brothers for the month of September from
Les Très Riches Heures du Duc de Berry (1413–1416). Illuminated manuscript.

Museé Condé.
Chantilly, France.

To Every Thing There Is a Season

King James Bible

To every thing there is a season,
And a time to every purpose under the heaven:
A time to be born, and a time to die;
A time to plant, and a time to pluck up that which is planted;
5   A time to kill, and a time to heal;
A time to break down, and a time to build up;
A time to weep, and a time to laugh;
A time to mourn, and a time to dance;
A time to cast away stones, and a time to gather stones together;
10   A time to embrace, and a time to refrain from embracing;
A time to get, and a time to lose;
A time to keep, and a time to cast away;
A time to rend, and a time to sew;
A time to keep silence, and a time to speak;
15   A time to love, and a time to hate;
A time of war, and a time of peace.

Responding to the Poem

Analyzing the Poem

Identifying Details

1. Which lines function as the "topic sentence" of the poem? How would you **paraphrase,** or state in your own words, the main idea these lines express?
2. The rest of the poem provides examples to support this topic sentence. Describe the **pattern** or **structure** that is repeated in these examples.

Interpreting Meanings

3. What do you think the phrase "a time to cast away stones" means? What does "gather stones together" mean? How might these ideas be worded using more modern **figures of speech**?
4. When do you think it might be appropriate "to lose" rather than "to get"? Can you suggest times when it might be best "to keep silence" and times when it would be better "to speak"?

5. Do you think the examples in lines 3–16 cover all aspects of human existence? Do they still apply today, even though they were written over two thousand years ago?
6. Do you agree with all of these examples? For instance, do you think that there is ever an appropriate "time to hate" or "to kill"? Explain.
7. How would you describe the **theme** of this poem? Do you think it is intended to teach a **moral** lesson? Explain.

Writing About the Poem

A Creative Response

1. **Writing Additional Examples.** Study the language and form of the poem, and add another five examples written in the same style. Each example should consist of two opposing statements. Try to cover ideas that are not already presented in the poem.

A Critical Response

2. **Analyzing Tone.** Ecclesiastes is sometimes called a cynical or pessimistic book. Do you think this excerpt is pessimistic in any way? Is it cynical, or is it wise? Write a brief essay explaining your response. Be sure to cite examples from the poem to support your opinion.

Analyzing Language and Vocabulary

Parallelism

According to the nineteenth-century English poet Matthew Arnold, ''the effect of Hebrew poetry can be preserved and transferred in a foreign language as the effect of other great poetry cannot.'' This is because Hebrew poetry rarely uses either of the two elements that make most poetry so difficult, if not impossible, to translate—**meter** and **rhyme**. Instead it relies on a poetic convention that is much more easily transferred into another language—a technique called parallelism.

Parallelism is the repetition of words, phrases, or sentences that have the same grammatical structure. In the excerpt from Ecclesiastes, the parallel structure in each line is formed by a noun phrase, *a time,* repeated and modified by two infinitive phrases with opposite or contrasting meanings (such as *to be born, to die*).

In Biblical poetry, parallelism can also involve the restatement of an entire idea in slightly different words, usually in successive lines. The following excerpt from the Ninety-first Psalm includes several examples of this second type of parallelism:

> Thou shalt not be afraid for the terror by
>   night;
> Nor for the arrow that flieth by day;
> Nor for the pestilence that walketh in
>   darkness;
> Nor for the destruction that wasteth at
>   noonday.
> 5 A thousand shall fall at thy side,
> And ten thousand at thy right hand;
> But it shall not come nigh thee.
> Only with thine eyes shalt thou behold
> And see the reward of the wicked.
> Because thou hast made the Lord, which
> 10   is my refuge,
> Even the Most High, thy habitation;
> There shall no evil befall thee,

> Neither shall any plague come nigh thy
>   dwelling.
> For he shall give his angels charge over
>   thee,
> 15 To keep thee in all thy ways.
> They shall bear thee up in their hands,
> Lest thou dash thy foot against a stone.
> Thou shalt tread upon the lion and adder:
> The young lion and the dragon shalt thou
>   trample under feet.

> —from the Ninety-first Psalm,
> King James Bible

1. Which lines restate an idea that has been expressed in a previous line?
2. What examples of structural **parallelism** can you find?

Many writers and orators throughout history have been influenced by the style and rhythm of Biblical poetry. Here is an excerpt from a famous speech that Martin Luther King, Jr., delivered at the 1963 civil rights march on Washington:

> I say to you today, my friends, that in spite of the difficulties and frustrations of the moment I still have a dream. It is a dream deeply rooted in the American dream.
> I have a dream that one day this nation will rise up and live out the true meaning of its creed: ''We hold these truths to be self-evident; that all men are created equal.''
> I have a dream that one day on the red hills of Georgia the sons of former slaves and the sons of former slaveowners will be able to sit down together at the table of brotherhood. . . .
> I have a dream that my four little children will one day live in a nation where they will not be judged by the color of their skin but by the content of their character.
> I have a dream today. . . .

> —from ''I Have a Dream,''
> Martin Luther King, Jr.

1. What examples of **parallelism** can you find in this speech?
2. Does King use only structural **parallelism,** or does he also restate the same idea in different words, as in the Ninety-first Psalm?

In the New Testament, there are four Gospels, or narrative books about the life and teachings of Jesus—the Gospels of Matthew, Mark, Luke, and John. The English word *gospel* comes from the Old English word *godspell,* which means "good news" (*god:* "good," and *spel:* "news").

Scholars believe that the Gospel of Luke was written in around A.D. 90. Luke was probably a physician who accompanied the apostle Paul on his missionary journeys. In writing his Gospel, Luke seems to have relied on the earlier Gospel of Mark, on an earlier collection of the sayings of Jesus, and on an unknown source of his own. Traditionally, Luke is also believed to be the author of the Acts of the Apostles, a New Testament book that traces Paul's missionary journeys. Many scholars believe that the Gospel of Luke and the Acts were written as a single work.

The Parable of the Prodigal Son is one of the most popular stories in the New Testament, and it appears only in Luke. A **parable** is a short, simple story that teaches a **moral** or lesson. Jesus, like many Jewish teachers of the time, frequently used such stories to make his message clear.

The word *prodigal* means "recklessly wasteful" or "extravagant." It also means "lavish" or "abundant." As you read this parable, think about how these different meanings of the word *prodigal* might be applied to both the son and the father.

The Parable of the Prodigal Son
From the Gospel of Luke

Return of the Prodigal Son by Guercino (c. 1619). Oil.

Kunsthistorisches Museum, Vienna.

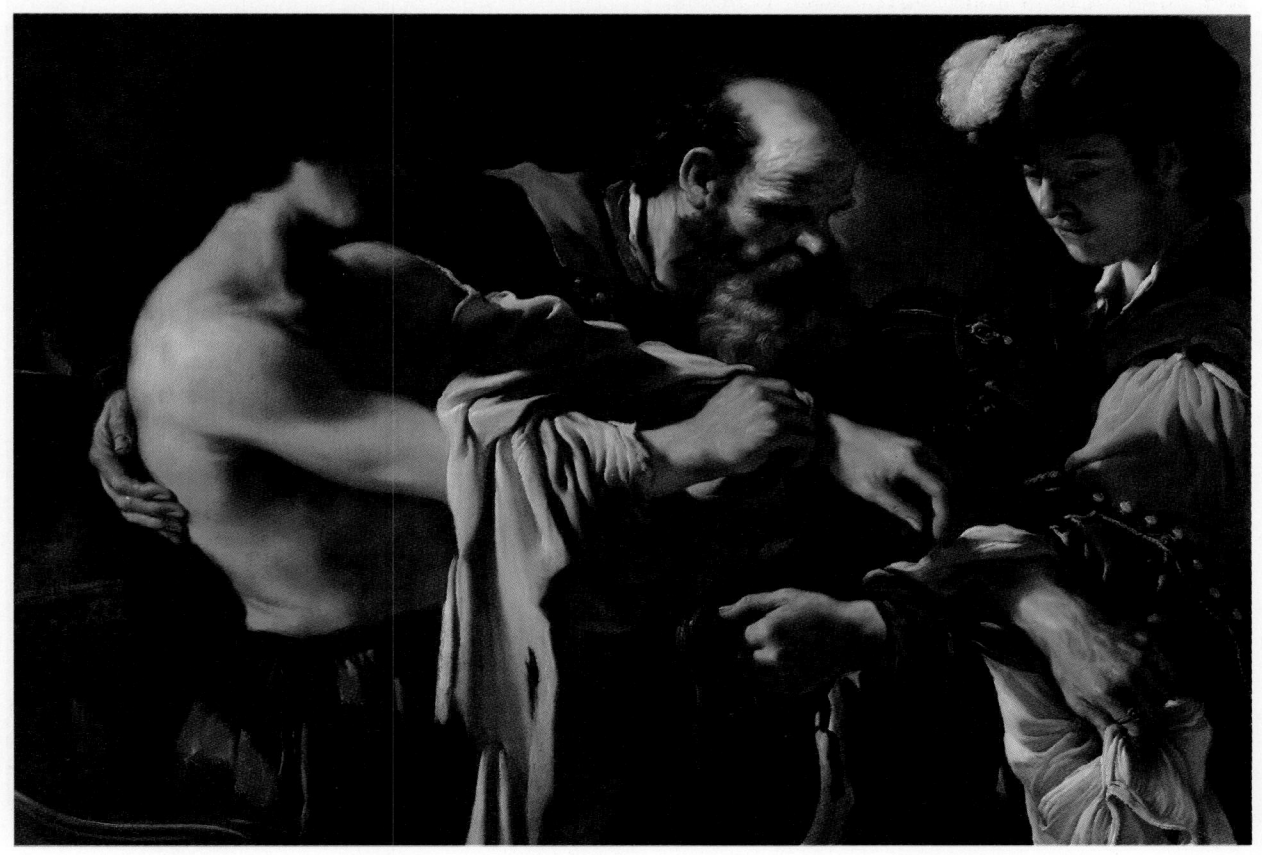

THE PARABLE OF THE PRODIGAL SON

New English Bible

The Return of the Prodigal Son by Rembrandt (c. 1665). Oil.   Hermitage Museum, Leningrad.

There was once a man who had two sons; and the younger said to his father, "Father, give me my share of the property." So he divided his estate between them.[1] A few days later the younger son turned the whole of his share into cash and left home for a distant country, where he squandered it in reckless living. He had spent it all, when a severe famine fell upon that country and he began to feel the pinch.

So he went and attached himself to one of the local landowners, who sent him on to his farm to mind the pigs.[2] He would have been glad to fill his belly with the pods that the pigs were eating; and no one gave him anything. Then he came to his senses and said, "How many of my father's paid servants have more food than they can eat, and here am I, starving to death! I will set off and go to my father, and say to him, 'Father, I have sinned, against God and against you; I am no longer fit to be called your son; treat me as one of your paid servants.'"

So he set out for his father's house. But while he was still a long way off his father saw him, and his heart went out to him. He ran to meet him, flung his arms round him, and kissed him. The son said, "Father, I have sinned, against God and against you; I am no longer fit to be called your son."

But the father said to his servants, "Quick! fetch a robe, my best one, and put it on him; put a ring on his finger and shoes on his feet. Bring the fatted calf and kill it, and let us have a feast to celebrate the day. For this son of mine was dead and has come back to life; he was lost and is found." And the festivities began.

Now the elder son was out on the farm; and on his way back, as he approached the house, he heard music and dancing. He called one of the servants and asked what it meant. The servant told him, "Your brother has come home, and your father has killed the fatted calf because he has him back safe and sound."

But he was angry and refused to go in. His father came out and pleaded with him; but he retorted, "You know how I have slaved for you all these years; I never once disobeyed your orders; and you never gave me so much as a kid, for a feast with my friends. But now that this son of yours turns up, after running through your money with his women, you kill the fatted calf for him."

"My boy," said the father, "you are always with me, and everything I have is yours. How could we help celebrating this happy day? Your brother here was dead and has come back to life, was lost and is found."

---

1. **So he divided his estate between them:** The younger son's share would be one third.
2. **mind the pigs:** For a Jew, tending pigs would be especially repugnant because pigs are considered unclean animals.

Responding to the Parable

Analyzing the Parable

Identifying Facts

1. Explain why the son decides to return to his father's home. What does he say to his father when he comes home?
2. Describe how the father receives his younger son.
3. Why is the older son angry at his father's behavior? How does the father explain his actions?

Interpreting Meanings

4. Which **character** in this story do you sympathize with most? Why? Is there a way in which each of us might, in the course of our lives, be able to identify with all three characters?
5. What would you say is the message or **moral** lesson of this parable? If you interpret the parable **allegorically,** whom do you think each of the main characters (the father, the younger son, the older son) stands for?

6. The word *prodigal* appears nowhere in the parable; it is part of a title that was added to the text in later translations. In what ways is the son prodigal? In what ways is the father prodigal with his love?

Writing About the Parable

A Creative Response

1. Writing a Parable. Write a parable of your own, or turn an event you have experienced, witnessed, or read about into a parable. Remember that a parable is a short, simple story that uses an episode from everyday life to teach a moral or ethical lesson. Its teaching is not always directly stated but can nevertheless be clearly inferred from the story.

A Critical Response

2. Comparing and Contrasting Themes. Write a brief essay comparing and contrasting the theme of the Prodigal Son with the theme of another Biblical selection in this unit. Before you begin, write a statement of theme for each selection. Then decide whether the two selections you chose share more similarities or differences.

Focusing on Connections
The Theme of the Prodigal Son in Literature

Here is a poem by the twentieth-century American poet Elizabeth Bishop. (Another of Bishop's poems appears on page 258.) Think about the poem's connections to the Parable of the Prodigal Son. Then consider the following questions: How are the focus and point of view of the poem different from that of the parable? In lines 1–3, what does the poet mean by saying that "the brown enormous odor he lived by / was too close . . . / for him to judge"? (Why do you think the poet says "lived by" instead of "lived with"?) In line 7, why does the poet mention "the sow that always ate her young"? What are the "shuddering insights" in line 26? Why do you think it took the prodigal "a long time / to finally make his mind up to go home"?

The Prodigal

The brown enormous odor he lived by
was too close, with its breathing and thick
  hair,
for him to judge. The floor was rotten; the
  sty
was plastered halfway up with glass-smooth
  dung.
Light-lashed, self-righteous, above moving
  snouts,
the pigs' eyes followed him, a cheerful
  stare—
even to the sow that always ate her young—

till, sickening, he leaned to scratch her
  head.
But sometimes mornings after drinking
  bouts
10 (he hid the pints behind a two-by-four),
the sunrise glazed the barnyard mud with
  red;
the burning puddles seemed to reassure.
And then he thought he almost might endure
his exile yet another year or more.

15 But evenings the first star came to warn.
The farmer whom he worked for came at
  dark
to shut the cows and horses in the barn
beneath their overhanging clouds of hay,
with pitchforks, faint forked lightnings,
  catching light,
20 safe and companionable as in the Ark.
The pigs stuck out their little feet and
  snored.
The lantern—like the sun, going away—
laid on the mud a pacing aureole.
Carrying a bucket along a slimy board,
25 he felt the bats' uncertain staggering flight,
his shuddering insights, beyond his control,
touching him. But it took him a long time
finally to make his mind up to go home.
                            —Elizabeth Bishop

> *. . . what is in the power of magicians to accomplish, that the heart also can accomplish by dint of love and bravery.*
>
> —from *The Romance of Tristan and Iseult*

The Literature of Romance

During the Middle Ages, a new form of literature called the romance developed in France and then spread throughout Europe. Originally, **romances** were long verse narratives about the adventures of knights and other heroes. These tales are called romances because they were originally made popular in Old French and Provençal, which are Romance languages (languages that derived from Roman, the popular form of Latin).

Most romances took as their subject matter the great Western hero cycles—legends such as those surrounding King Arthur and his Knights of the Round Table, King Charlemagne and Roland, Tristan and Iseult, and Alexander the Great. However, some medieval romances chronicled tales that had reached Europe from as far away as India and Persia.

Jugglers of Tales

Storytelling was the major form of entertainment in the early Middle Ages. Whether they were called *scops, bards, gesteurs, conteurs, jongleurs,* or *minstrels,* storytellers were essential to the life of the period. Most of these storytellers were illiterate: They collected, developed, and spread their romances orally, in the tradition of "primitive" narrative poets everywhere.

By the middle of the twelfth century, however, romances began to fall into the hands of literate poets, such as the great Chrétien de Troyes (krā·tyan′ də trwä), the most important compiler of the legends of King Arthur. Whereas the old oral romances had belonged to "the people," the new, more polished "courtly" versions were addressed to "ladies and gentlemen." It even became popular to recite romances aloud at court celebrations. By the fourteenth century, the old oral storytellers had become displaced: They were now crude entertainers for the lower classes, performing in public squares. The *jongleur* (literally, "juggler" of tales) of the tenth century became the juggler of sticks and balls of the fourteenth. The early medieval *gesteur,* who told about the old *gestes* (feats of heroes) became a jester, or a clown.

By Dint of Love and Bravery

The primary purpose of the romance was to celebrate the ideals of chivalry, the code of behavior that the medieval knight was supposed to follow: bravery, honor, loyalty, piety, the generous treatment of foes, and a readiness to help the weak and protect women.

Flemish decorated shield (15th century). Gilded wood and tempera.

The knight of the early oral romances was primarily a brave, but rather crude, warrior who fought for a king or feudal lord. By the courtly period, however, when the ideals of chivalry had developed more fully, this knight had become a much smoother character. This refinement was brought about both by the knight's Christian faith and by his idealized love for an aristocratic "lady" who was rarely his wife and whom he could probably never even hope to marry. According to the conventions of chivalry, it was for his lady's sake that a knight performed his heroic deeds. He was motivated by *corteisie* (courtesy in love and war), and he proved himself, and his devotion to his lady, by *avanture* (adventure).

The Marvelous Quest

The world of romance is a world of idealization and exaggeration, of enchantment and wish-fulfillment, a world where the forces of good always triumph over the forces of evil.

The typical plot of a romance consists of a series of marvelous adventures filled with magical or supernatural events. The hero's adventures usually assume the form of a **quest**, or long journey, in search of something desirable: the Holy Grail, a beautiful maiden, or a treasure trove. During the course of this quest, the hero comes into conflict with a host of adversaries—evil knights, witches, giants, and dragons—whom he must fight or outsmart. He is often aided in his quest by wizards or fairy queens, and by his own mysterious rapport with nature. In its purest form, the hero's quest is the struggle between good and evil. Interpreted **metaphorically,** it is a journey into the darker side of human nature and back again.

Escape To or Escape From?

Although there was always a lighter, less orthodox side to the genre, as you will see in the Middle Eastern tales of *The Thousand and One Nights*, romance through the thirteenth century was primarily an escape from the ordinary world to a vision or a more profound, even spiritual ideal. After the thirteenth century, however, the form became corrupted, but pleasantly so. The later romances provided not an escape *to* a vision but rather an escape *from* reality. Some expressed nostalgia for a past age, as you will see in Sir Thomas Malory's King Arthur tales. Others became a biting satire of the form itself, as you will find in Miguel de Cervantes' *Don Quixote*.

The romance form still exists today. Modern "romances," like their forebears, are marked by an exotic tone and a concern with exaggerated exploits of love and adventure. In today's romances, good is still pitted against evil, and the hero still triumphs "by dint of love and bravery." J. R. R. Tolkein's *The Lord of the Rings* is a classic example of a romance in which the forces of good undertake a heroic quest to battle the forces of evil. So are most Westerns. And what are *Superman, The Wizard of Oz, Star Wars, Star Trek,* and *Raiders of the Lost Ark* if not modern romances?

Combat armor made for King Charles V of Spain (16th century).

> " **T**he later romances provided not an escape *to* a vision but rather an escape *from* reality."

The story of King Arthur is an ancient one. Modern scholars believe that the legend may be based on a sixth-century Celtic warlord who lived in Wales and led his people to victory against Saxon invaders from Germany. Arthur was said to have been wounded in battle and buried at the abbey of Glastonbury in England, where a gravestone can still be seen bearing his name.

The legend of King Arthur emerged gradually, beginning perhaps with stories that were first told by Arthur's comrades and were then passed down orally. As the Celtic storytellers told and retold these popular tales about Arthur, characters and details were changed and added. By 817, long before the first printing presses, a monk named Nennius composed the first written account of the life of Arthur, working in Latin. Later writers added to the legend. Geoffrey of Monmouth, a twelfth-century historian, included Arthur in his history of the British kings and was the first to tell of the magician Merlin and Arthur's wife, Guinevere.

The cycle of Arthur stories kept growing as the legend spread to France, Spain, Germany, and Italy. A whole new cast of characters was added, among them Lancelot, Tristan, Mark, Iseult, Galahad, and Percival. In the twelfth century, the great French poet Chrétien de Troyes wrote his version of the Arthur legend, which became popular all over Europe.

Malory's *Le Morte d'Arthur*

Sir Thomas Malory (1405?–1471) completed his prose version of the Arthurian saga in late 1469 or early 1470. Working from French, English, and Latin sources, Malory gathered together for the first time the various King Arthur tales that had been circulating throughout Europe during the Middle Ages. In 1485 William Caxton, the first English printer, published Malory's text as *Le Morte d'Arthur*, making various revisions, dividing it into books and chapters, and adding a preface. However, recently discovered manuscripts indicate that Malory intended his work to be eight separate romances, rather than a single narrative. An excerpt from one of these romances, *The Tale of King Arthur* (as modernized and rewritten by the American novelist John Steinbeck) is included here.

We know only a little about Sir Thomas Malory's life. His title indicates that he was a knight, and we know he was a soldier during the Hundred Years' War and for a brief time was a member of parliament. We also know that he spent most of the last twenty years of his life in prison, accused, ironically enough, of some rather unchivalrous crimes: assault, extortion, poaching, cattle rustling, jailbreaking, plundering an abbey, and "waylaying the Duke of Buckingham." Malory pleaded innocent to all charges, and it is in fact quite likely that his imprisonment stemmed—at least in part—from his opposition to King Edward IV during the bloody Wars of the Roses. (It is also possible that Malory *was* something of a rogue.) It was during Malory's miserable years in jail that he wrote his great romance, completing it a year before he died.

The Legend of King Arthur

French tapestry of King Arthur (14th century).

The Metropolitan Museum of Art, New York. The Cloisters Collection, Munsey Fund, 1932, and Gift of John D. Rockefeller, Jr., 1947.

> "The legend of King Arthur emerged gradually, beginning perhaps with stories that were first told by Arthur's comrades."

Merlin. Illustration by T. H. White for his novel *The Once and Future King*.

Reprinted by permission of The Putnam Publishing Group from *The Once and Future King* by T. H. White. © 1939, 1940 by T. H. White. Renewed.

"John Steinbeck was nine years old when he first read what became to him a 'magic, secret book'—an abridged version of Malory's King Arthur tales."

It is important to bear in mind that the appealing twelfth-century world of chivalrous knights in shining armor was nearly as foreign to Malory in the fifteenth century as it is to us today. With the invention of gunpowder and the rise of the middle class, the old feudal order had broken down. English political and social life were in a state of turmoil that no amount of chivalry seemed likely to cure. It has been suggested that in writing *Le Morte d'Arthur*, Malory was proposing a return to the ideals of chivalry, to a simpler way of life with established codes of behavior. This seems unlikely. Rather, Malory seems to have been trying to create a nostalgic— we might perhaps say romantic—escape from the realities of a difficult age and a difficult personal life.

Le Morte d'Arthur is considered the first English prose epic, the last great medieval romance, and (with Chaucer's *Canterbury Tales*) one of the two most important English literary works of the Middle Ages. Malory's masterpiece gained immediate popularity as soon as it was published, and since then it has influenced generations of writers. The English poet Alfred, Lord Tennyson popularized Malory's tales in his *Idylls of the King*, as did Mark Twain in his comic novel *A Connecticut Yankee in King Arthur's Court* and T. H. White in his novel *The Once and Future King*. And these are only a few examples of writers who have retold Malory's tales. There have even been movie versions, such as the musical *Camelot* and the hilarious parody *Monty Python and the Holy Grail*.

John Steinbeck's Retelling

The American novelist John Steinbeck (1902–1968), author of *The Grapes of Wrath, Of Mice and Men,* and *The Pearl,* was nine years old when he first read what became to him a "magic, secret book"—an abridged version of Malory's King Arthur tales. "I think my sense of right and wrong, my feelings of noblesse oblige, and any thought I may have against the oppressor and for the oppressed came from this secret book."

Throughout his life, Steinbeck maintained a profound interest in Malory and the Arthur legends, and for a long time he thought about writing a modernized version of these tales. In 1957 Steinbeck went to England to do research for his reworking of the Arthurian legend. Rather than using Caxton's printed edition of *Le Morte d'Arthur*, Steinbeck worked from the Winchester manuscript of Malory's tales. This manuscript had been hand-written by monks during the fifteenth century, lost for almost five hundred years, and then discovered at Winchester College in 1936.

For several years Steinbeck worked enthusiastically on his retelling of the Arthur legend but then stopped for reasons we do not know. He died before completing what had become his own "quest," but he did finish seven stories. The excerpt that follows is from the first of these tales, which Steinbeck titled "Merlin." We enter the legend just after the birth of Arthur. The old king, Uther Pendragon, a Celtic war leader, has promised to give up his child to Merlin, the wizard and protector of English kings.

MERLIN: THE COMING OF ARTHUR

Sir Thomas Malory, retold by **John Steinbeck**

Merlin and the king Vortigern (in ermine) watching a pair
of fighting dragons that symbolize Arthur (red dragon) and the
Saxons (white dragon). Manuscript illumination (15th century).

Lambeth Palace Library, London.

And when Queen Igraine came to be delivered, the king commanded the knights and two ladies to wrap the child in cloth of gold and to carry him through a little postern[1] gate and give him to a poor man who would be waiting there.

Thus was the child delivered to Merlin, who carried it to Sir Ector, and his wife nursed the baby at her own breast. Then Merlin brought a holy man to christen the child, and it was named Arthur.

Within two years of the birth of Arthur, a wasting sickness fell on Uther Pendragon. Then, seeing the king helpless, his enemies raided the realm and overthrew his knights and killed many of his people. And Merlin sent to the king and said gruffly, "You do not have the right to lie here in your bed, no matter what your illness. You must go into the field to lead your men, even if you are carried there in a horse litter, for your enemies will never be defeated until you yourself are there. Only then will you win a victory."

King Uther agreed to this, and his knights carried him out and placed him on a litter between two horses, and in this way he led his army against his enemies. At St. Albans they met a great force of invaders from the north and joined battle. And on that day Sir Ulfius and Sir Brastias performed great deeds of arms, and King Uther's men took heart and attacked with fury and killed many of the enemy and put the rest to flight. When it was over, the king returned to London to celebrate his victory. But his strength was gone, and he fell into a coma, and for three days and nights he was paralyzed and could not speak. His barons were sad and apprehensive, and they asked Merlin what they should do.

Then Merlin said, "Only God has the remedy. But if all of you will come before the king tomorrow in the morning, I shall through the help of God try to make him speak." And in the morning the barons gathered, and Merlin approached the bed where the king lay and cried aloud, "Sir, is it your will that your son, Arthur, shall be king when you are dead?"

Then Uther Pendragon turned and struggled and at last he was able to say in the hearing of all his barons, "I give Arthur God's blessing and mine. I ask that he pray for my soul." Then Uther gathered his strength and he cried, "If Arthur does not rightly and honorably claim the crown of England, he will forfeit my blessing." And with that the king fell back, and very soon he died.

King Uther was interred with all the ceremony proper for a king, and his queen, the fair Igraine, and all his barons mourned for him. His court was filled with sorrow, and for a long time there was no King of England. Then danger arose everywhere, on the borders from outside enemies and within the realm from ambitious lords. The barons surrounded themselves with armed men, and many of them wished to take the crown for themselves. In this anarchy no man was safe and the laws were forgotten, so that at last Merlin went to the Archbishop of Canterbury[2] and advised him to issue a call to all the lords and all the gentlemen of arms in the kingdom to gather in London by Christmas on pain of excommunication. It was believed that since Jesus was born on Christmas Eve, He might on that holy night give some miraculous sign who should rightly be king of the realm. When the archbishop's message was sent out to the lords and knights, many of them were moved by the call and purified their lives so that their prayers might be more acceptable to God.

In the greatest church in London, perhaps St. Paul's, the lords and knights gathered to pray long before dawn. And when matins[3] and first Mass were over, there was seen in the churchyard, in a place nearest the high altar, a great block of marble, and in the marble was set a steel anvil in which a sword was driven. In letters of gold was written:

> WHOEVER PULLS THIS SWORD
> FROM THIS STONE AND ANVIL
> IS KING OF ALL ENGLAND
> BY RIGHT OF BIRTH.

The people were amazed and carried the news of the miracle to the archbishop, who said, "Go

---

1. **postern:** rear or private entrance.

2. **Archbishop of Canterbury:** head of the Church of England.
3. **matins** (mat´′nz): morning prayers.

back into the church and pray to God. And let no man touch the sword until High Mass is sung." And this they did, but when the service was over all the lords went to look at the stone and the sword, and some tried to draw out the blade, but no one could move it.

"The man is not here who will draw this sword," said the archbishop, "but do not doubt that God will make him known. Until that happens," he went on, "I suggest that ten knights, men of good fame, be appointed to guard this sword."

And it was so ordered and further proclaimed that any man who wished might try to release the sword. For New Year's Day a great tournament was planned, and this was designed by the archbishop to keep the lords and knights together, for he reckoned that God would at that time make known who should win the sword.

On New Year's Day, when holy service was over, the knights and barons rode to the field where some would joust—two armored men riding in single combat, each seeking to unhorse his opponent. Others joined the tourney, a military sport wherein chosen groups of armed and mounted men engaged in general melee. By these sports the knights and barons kept themselves hard and practiced for war and also won honor and renown for bravery and expertness with horse, with shield, with lance and sword, for all the barons and the knights were fighting men.

It happened that Sir Ector, who was the lord of lands nearby to London, rode in for the jousting, and with him came his son Sir Kay, only made a knight at Allhallows[4] of that year, and also young Arthur came, who had been reared in Sir Ector's house and who was Sir Kay's foster brother. As they rode toward the jousting field, Sir Kay discovered that he had forgotten his sword at his father's lodging, and he asked young Arthur to ride back for it.

"I will do it gladly," said Arthur, and he turned his horse and galloped back to bring his foster brother's sword to him. But when he came to the lodging he found it empty and locked up, for

---

4. **Allhallows:** All Saints' Day, November 1, a church festival honoring all of the saints.

everyone had gone out to see the jousting.

Then Arthur was angry and he said to himself, "Very well, I will ride to the churchyard and take the sword that is sticking in the stone there. I do not want my brother, Sir Kay, to be without a sword today."

When he came to the churchyard, Arthur dismounted and tied his horse to the stile and walked to the tent, and he found no guardian knights there, for they too had gone to the jousting. Then Arthur grasped the sword by its handle and easily and fiercely drew it from the anvil and the stone, and he mounted his horse and rode quickly until he overtook Sir Kay and gave him the sword.

As soon as Sir Kay saw the sword, he knew it came from the stone, and he went quickly to his father and held it out to him. "Sir, look here! I have the sword of the stone and therefore I must be King of England."

Sir Ector recognized the sword and he called Arthur and Sir Kay to him and all three returned quickly to church. And there Sir Ector made Sir Kay swear how he had got the sword.

"My brother, Arthur, brought it to me," Sir Kay answered.

Then Sir Ector turned to Arthur. "And how did you get this sword?"

Arthur said, "When I rode back for my brother's sword, I found no one at home, so I could not get it. I did not want my brother to be without a sword, and so I came here and took the sword from the stone for him."

"Were there no knights here guarding the sword?" Sir Ector asked.

"No, sir," said Arthur. "There was no one here."

Sir Ector was silent for a time and then he said, "I understand now that you must be king of this land."

"Why should that be?" said Arthur. "For what reason should I be king?"

"My lord," Sir Ector said, "God has willed that only the man who can draw this sword from this stone shall be the rightful king of this land. Now let me see whether you can put the sword back as it was and then draw it out again."

"That is not difficult," said Arthur, and he drove the blade into the anvil. Then Sir Ector tried to draw it out and he could not and he told Sir Kay to try. Sir Kay pulled at the sword with all his might and he could not move it.

"Now it is your turn," said Sir Ector to Arthur.

"I will," said Arthur. And he drew the sword out easily.

Then Sir Ector and Sir Kay kneeled down on the earth before him.

And Arthur cried, "What is this? My own dear father and my brother, why do you kneel to me?"

Sir Ector said, "My lord Arthur, I am not your father nor of your blood. I believe that you are of nobler blood than I." Then Sir Ector told Arthur how he had taken him to rear and by Uther's order. And he told him how it was Merlin's doing.

When he heard that Sir Ector was not his father, Arthur was sad and even more sad when Sir Ector said, "Sir, will you be my good and gracious lord when you are king?"

"Why should I not be?" Arthur cried. "I owe you more than anyone in the world, you and your wife, my good lady mother who nursed me and kept me as though I were her own. And if, as you say, it is God's will that I must be king—ask anything of me! I will not fail you."

"My lord," said Sir Ector, "I shall ask only one thing of you, that you will make my son Sir Kay, your foster brother, seneschal[5] and keeper of your lands."

"That shall be done and more," Arthur said. "On my honor, no other man but Sir Kay shall have that office while I live."

Then they three went to the archbishop and told him how the sword had been drawn from the stone, and by his order all of the barons gathered again to try to draw the sword, and all failed except Arthur.

Then many of the lords were jealous and angry, and they said it was an insult and a shame that the realm should be governed by a boy who was not of royal blood. The decision was put off until Candlemas,[6] when all the barons agreed to meet again. Ten knights were delegated to watch over the sword and the stone. A tent was put up to shelter it, and five knights were on guard at all times.

At Candlemas an even greater number of lords gathered to try for the sword, and no one could draw it. But Arthur, as he had done before, drew it without effort. Then the angry barons put it off until the high feast of Easter, and again only Arthur could draw the sword. Some of the great lords were opposed to Arthur as king, and they delayed the final test until the feast of Pentecost.[7] Such was their anger that Arthur's life was in danger. The Archbishop of Canterbury by Merlin's advice gathered those knights whom Uther Pendragon had loved and trusted most. Such men as Sir Bawdewyn of Bretagne, Sir Kaynes, Sir Ulfius, and Sir Brastias, all these and many more stayed near to Arthur day and night to protect him until the feast of Pentecost.

When Pentecost had come, a great gathering assembled and all manner of men struggled to pull the sword from the stone and no one succeeded. Then Arthur mounted the stone with all the lords and common people watching him, and he drew the sword easily out and held it up to them. The common people were convinced, and they cried with one great shout, "We want Arthur for our king without any more delay. We see that God wills him to be king and we will kill anyone who stands in his way."

And with that, both rich and poor kneeled down and begged Arthur's pardon for having delayed so long. Arthur forgave them, and then he took the sword in his hands and placed it on the high altar. The archbishop took the sword and touched Arthur on the shoulder and made him a knight. Then Arthur swore an oath to all the lords and commons that he would be a just and true king to them all the days of his life.

---

5. **seneschal** (sen′ə·shəl): a person in charge of the household and estate of a high-ranking person. During the Middle Ages, this was a powerful and respected position.

6. **Candlemas:** A Christian feast celebrated on February 2, commemorating the presentation of Jesus in the Temple.
7. **Pentecost:** a Christian festival celebrated on the seventh Sunday after Easter, commemorating the descent of the Holy Spirit upon the Apostles.

Responding to the Story

Analyzing the Story

Identifying Facts

1. Explain why the country is without a king for so long after Uther dies. Why doesn't Arthur come forward immediately to claim the throne?
2. Why does Merlin ask the Archbishop of Canterbury to call a meeting of lords and knights? Describe the outcome of this meeting.
3. Explain how Arthur proves himself the rightful heir of the English crown. What opposition does he encounter, and what finally establishes him as king?

Interpreting Meanings

4. Look back over the story, and notice the many references to God and religion. Discuss the part that religion seems to have played in establishing Arthur as king.
5. According to the critic Northrop Frye, "the hero of **romance** moves in a world in which the ordinary laws of nature are slightly suspended." What elements of magic appear in this tale that move it out of the realm of history and into the realm of romance?
6. This episode is only a small part of the hero cycle about Arthur and his knights, and it takes place when Arthur is only fifteen. Summarize what we learn about his **character** even in this early episode. Give details to support your statement.
7. In the typical **romance,** the hero's origins are mysterious: He is frequently raised in obscurity before taking his rightful place as leader. How do the stories of Arthur and Oedipus (pages 746–747) reflect this pattern? In what important respect are their stories different?
8. Can you think of stories about other heroes or heroines whose origins are mysterious and who are raised in obscurity? How does this mystery affect their lives?
9. In what other ways does Arthur, even at fifteen, resemble the typical **romance** hero? How does he embody some of the ideals of chivalry?
10. What would you say is the **theme** of this story? What values does it teach? Are they still pertinent today?

Writing About the Story

A Creative Response

1. **Writing a Journal Entry.** Write a journal entry for the fateful day on which Arthur pulls the sword from the stone, learns that he is not Sir Ector's son, and discovers that he is to become King of England. What might Arthur be thinking and feeling about his true parents, whose identity he still doesn't know; about his childhood in Sir Ector's home; about his new relationship to his adopted family; about his apparent destiny? Be sure to make Arthur's journal entry consistent with his **character** as revealed in the story.
2. **Resetting a Story.** Suppose that either "The Cold Equations" (page 8) or "Where Have You Gone, Charming Billy?" (page 212) were set in the world of **romance.** In a brief essay of one or two paragraphs, summarize how these stories would change if they took place in a world where people frequently had magical control over nature and even over death itself.

A Critical Response

3. **Responding to Steinbeck's Analysis of Arthur.** Read Steinbeck's remarks under "Focusing on Background" (page 840). Do you agree with his analysis that the King Arthur legend is like an American Western? In a brief essay of one or two paragraphs, give your response to Steinbeck's comparison.

Analyzing Language and Vocabulary

Changes in the English Language

Malory wrote *Le Morte d'Arthur* in the Midland dialect spoken in fifteenth-century London. By using this dialect instead of one of the several other Middle English dialects spoken at the time, Malory influenced the course of the English language: He is one of the reasons the Midland dialect became the basis for modern English.

In retelling *Le Morte d'Arthur,* Steinbeck was faced with "translating" Malory's prose into modern English. As Steinbeck notes, some words had greatly changed their meanings:

... Let us take *worship* in the Malorian sense. It is an old English word *worth-ship,* and it meant eminence gained by one's personal qualities of courage or honor. You could not inherit worshipfulness. It was solely due to your own nature and actions. Beginning in the thirteenth century, the word moved into a religious connotation which it did not have originally. And now it has lost its original meaning and has become solely a religious word. Perhaps the word *honor* has taken its place or even better, *renown.* Once *renown* meant to be renamed because of one's own personal qualities, but now it means to be celebrated but still for personal matters. You can't inherit renown. ...

—John Steinbeck

Try to translate the following passage from *Le Morte d'Arthur* into modern English. Although the Midland dialect looks quite different from the English you are used to, if you read the words aloud and do some intelligent guessing, you can understand their meaning. In this passage Sir Ector is talking about Sir Lancelot, one of the most famous of King Arthur's knights, who has just died:

"A, Launcelot!" he sayd, "thou were hede of al Crysten knyghtes! And now I dare say," sayd syr Ector, "thou sir Launcelot, there thou lyest, that thou were never matched of erthely knyghtes hande. And thou werre the curtest knyght that ever bare shelde! And thou were the truest frende to thy lover that ever bestrade hors, and thou were the trewest lover of a synful man that ever loved woman, and thou were the kyndest man that ever strake with swerde. And thou were the godelyest persone that ever cam among prees of knyghtes, and thou was the mekest man and the jentyllest that ever ete in halle among ladyes, and thou were the sternest knyght to thy mortal foo that ever put spere in the reeste."

—Sir Thomas Malory

Focusing on Background
A Letter from John Steinbeck

During the years when he was working on *The Acts of King Arthur and His Noble Knights,* Steinbeck often wrote about his project to his literary agent, Elizabeth Otis, whom he called ERO (her initials) in his letters. Here is an excerpt from one of Steinbeck's letters:

"To ERO—New York, March 1958

... My purpose will be to put [*Le Morte d'Arthur*] into a language which is understandable and acceptable to a modern-day reader. I think this is not only an important thing to do, but also a highly practical thing to do, since these stories form, with the New Testament, the basis of most modern English literature. And it can be shown and will be shown that the myth of King Arthur continues even into the present day and is an inherent part of the so-called 'Western' with which television is filled at the present time—same characters, same methods, same stories, only slightly different weapons and certainly a different topography. But if you change Indians or outlaws for Saxons and Picts and Danes, you have exactly the same story. You have the cult of the horse, the cult of the knight. The application with the present is very close, and also the present day with its uncertainties very closely parallels the uncertainties of the fifteenth century.

"It is actually a kind of nostalgic return to the good old days. I think Malory did it, and I think our writers for television are doing it—exactly the same thing, and oddly enough, finding exactly the same symbols and methods.

"Thus we find that the work I propose is not a period piece necessarily, and certainly not a specialized piece of work, but one with applications in the present day and definite roots in our living literature."

—John Steinbeck

The Thousand and One Nights (or *The Arabian Nights' Entertainment*, as it became known in Europe) is a collection of Indian, Persian, and Arab folktales spanning several centuries. It was compiled in its present form in the mid-fifteenth century, probably in Cairo, Egypt, and first published in 1548 in Arabic. Although the exact origins of these stories remain uncertain, scholars believe that the oldest tales date from the tenth century and were transmitted orally by Arab storytellers during the Middle Ages. Over the centuries, this core group of stories evolved and expanded as new tales reached the Arab world.

This ever-growing, ever-changing collection of stories gathered around one standard structural feature—a **frame story** that is probably Indian in origin but that first appeared as the prologue to a book of Persian fairy tales. Stories from a variety of cultures attached themselves to this frame story, and as they were retold and updated with each generation, they gradually assumed a Middle Eastern, and Moslem, character.

Although returning Crusaders undoubtedly brought some of these tales to Europe during the Middle Ages, the first Western translation of *The Thousand and One Nights* was a French version published in the early eighteenth century by Antoine Gallant. The most famous English translation is Sir Richard Burton's sixteen-volume edition, published between 1885 and 1888 and heavily annotated with his observations about Arab life.

The frame story that unifies *The Thousand and One Nights* is very much in the tradition of romance literature. It tells the story of how King Shahrihar of India, convinced that all women are unfaithful, acquired the unfortunate habit of marrying a new wife each day and then killing her the next morning. Just as the supply of marriageable young women was getting dangerously low, the clever Scheherazade became the king's latest bride and devised a scheme to avoid becoming his next victim. On her wedding night, she told her husband a fascinating story but left him with a "cliffhanger," refusing to reveal the ending of the story until the next night. Then she began a new tale, which she also left unfinished. By this ruse, Scheherazade bought time for a thousand and one nights—until the king no longer wished to have her killed.

Some of the best-known tales from *The Thousand and One Nights* are "Aladdin and the Magic Lamp," "Ali Baba and the Forty Thieves," and the Sindbad the Sailor tales. Sindbad is a merchant from Baghdad (in present-day Iraq) who gathers great riches during his seven exotic voyages. The strange voyage is a popular motif in the literature of romance, and Sindbad (along with Odysseus and Gulliver) is among fiction's greatest voyagers. In fact, the Sindbad stories were influenced by the Odysseus legend, which had reached the Middle Ages over the course of centuries. (See page 848 under "Focusing on Background.")

Like many of the tales in *The Thousand and One Nights*, the Sindbad stories are structured around their own frame story: Sindbad the Sailor tells his tales to a porter who is also named Sindbad. His purpose is to teach the value of hard work and perseverance to those less fortunate—and wealthy—than himself.

The Thousand and One Nights

Frontispiece by Edmund Dulac from *Sindbad the Sailor and Other Stories* (1914).

" **O**n her wedding night, Scheherazade told her husband a fascinating story but left him with a 'cliffhanger.' "

THE FOURTH VOYAGE OF SINDBAD THE SAILOR

Translated by **N. J. Dawood**

The jovial and extravagant life which I led after my return did not cause me to forget the delights and benefits of travel in distant lands; and my thirst for seeing the world, despite the perils I had encountered, continued as violent as ever. My restless soul at length yielded to the call of the sea, and after making preparations for a long voyage, I set sail with merchandise from Basrah, together with some eminent merchants of that city.

Blessed with a favoring wind, we sped upon the foamy highways of the sea, trading from port to port and from island to island. One day, however, a howling gale suddenly sprang up in mid-ocean, rolling against our ship massive waves as high as mountains. The captain at once ordered the crew to cast anchor, and we all fell on our knees in prayer and lamentation. A furious squall[1] tore the sails to ribbons and snapped the mast in two; then a giant wave came hurtling down upon us from above, shattering our vessel and tossing us all into the raging sea.

With Allah's help, I clung fast to a floating beam, and bestriding it firmly, fought the downrush of the waves with those of my companions who had managed to reach it also. Now paddling with our hands and feet, now swept by wind and current, we were at length thrown, half-dead with cold and exhaustion, on the shore of an island.

We lay down upon the sand and fell asleep. Next morning we rose and, striking inland, came after a few hours in sight of a lofty building among the trees. As we drew nearer, a number of naked and wild-looking men emerged from the door and without a word took hold of my companions and myself and led us into the building, where we saw their King seated upon a throne.

The King bade us sit down, and presently his servants set before us dishes of such meats as we had never seen before in all our lives. My famished companions ate ravenously; but my stomach revolted at the sight of this food and, in spite of my hunger, I could not eat a single mouthful. As things turned out, however, my abstinence saved my life. For as soon as they had swallowed a few morsels my comrades began to lose their intelligence and to act like gluttonous maniacs, so that after a few hours of incessant guzzling they were little better than savages.

Whilst my companions were thus feeding, the naked men brought in a vessel filled with a strange ointment, with which they anointed their victims' bodies. The change my companions suffered was astonishing; their eyes sank into their heads and their bellies grew horribly distended, so that the more they swelled, the more insatiable their appetites became.

My horror at this spectacle knew no bounds, especially when I soon discovered that our captors were cannibals who fattened their victims in this way before slaughtering them. The King feasted every day on a roasted stranger; his men preferred their diet raw.

When my transformed companions had thus been robbed entirely of all their human faculties,

---

1. **squall:** a sudden, violent wind, often accompanied by rain or snow.

Illustration by Edmund Dulac from *Sindbad the Sailor and Other Stories* (1914).

they were committed to the charge of a herdsman, who led them out every day to pasture in the meadows. I myself was reduced to a shadow by hunger and fear, and my skin shriveled upon my bones. Therefore the savages lost all interest in me and no longer cared even to watch my movements.

One day I slipped out of my captors' dwelling and made off across the island. On reaching the distant grasslands, I met the herdsman with his once-human charges. But instead of pursuing me or ordering me to return, he appeared to take pity on my helpless condition and pointing to his right, made signs to me which seemed to say: "Go this way: Have no fear."

I ran on and on across the rolling plains in the direction he indicated. When evening came, I ate a scanty meal of roots and herbs and lay down to rest upon the grass; but fear of the cannibals had robbed me of all desire to sleep, and at midnight I rose again and trudged painfully on.

Thus I journeyed for seven days and nights, and on the morning of the eighth day came at last to the opposite side of the island, where I could faintly discern human figures in the distance. Drawing nearer, I rejoiced to find that they were a party of peasants gathering pepper in a field.

They crowded round me and speaking in my own language, inquired who I was and whence I had come. In reply I recounted the story of my misfortunes, and they were all amazed at my adventure. They congratulated me on my escape and, after offering me food and water, allowed me to rest till evening. When their day's work was done, they took me with them in a boat to their capital, which was in a neighboring island.

There I was presented to their King, who received me kindly and listened in astonishment to my story. I found their city prosperous and densely populated, abounding in markets and well-stocked shops, and filled with the bustle of commercial activity. The people, both rich and poor, possessed the rarest thoroughbred horses; but I was bewildered to see them ride their steeds bare-backed.

In my next audience with the King, I ventured to express my surprise at his subjects' ignorance of the use of saddles and stirrups. "My noble master," I remarked, "why is it that no one in this island uses a saddle? It makes both for the comfort of the rider and his mastery over his horse."

"What may that be?" he asked, somewhat puzzled. "I have never seen a saddle in all my life."

"Pray allow me to make one for you," I replied, "that you may try it and find how comfortable and useful it can be."

The King was pleased at my offer. At once I sought out a skillful carpenter and instructed him to make a wooden frame for a saddle of my own design; then I taught a blacksmith to forge a bit and a pair of stirrups. I fitted out the frame with a padding of wool and leather and furnished it with a girth and tassels. When all was ready, I chose the finest of the royal horses, saddled and bridled it, and led it before the King.

The King was highly delighted with the splendor and usefulness of his horse's novel equipment and in reward bestowed on me precious gifts and a large sum of money.

When his Vizer[2] saw the saddle, he begged me to make one for him. I did so; and it was not long before every courtier and noble in the kingdom became the owner of a handsome saddle.

My skill soon made me the richest man in the island. The King conferred upon me many honors, and I became a trusted courtier. One day, as we sat conversing together in his palace, he said: "You must know, Sindbad, that we have grown to love you like a brother. Indeed, our regard for you is such that we cannot bear the thought that you might some day leave our kingdom. Therefore, we will ask you a favor, which we hope you will not refuse."

"Allah forbid," I replied, "that I should refuse you anything, your majesty."

"We wish you to marry a beautiful girl who has been brought up in our court," he said. "She is intelligent and wealthy, and will make you an excellent wife. I trust that you will settle down happily with her in this city for the rest of your days. Do not refuse me this, I pray you."

I was deeply embarrassed and did not know what to answer. "Why do you not speak, my son?" he asked.

---

2. **Vizier** (viz′yər): a Moslem minister of state.

"Your majesty," I faltered, "I am in duty bound to obey you."

The King sent at once for a cadi[3] and witnesses, and I was married that day to a rich woman of noble lineage. The King gave us a magnificent palace and assigned to us a retinue of slaves and servants.

We lived happily and contentedly together, although in my heart-of-hearts I never ceased to cherish a longing to return home—together with my wife; for I loved her dearly. But, alas, no mortal can control his destiny or trifle with the decrees of Fate.

One day death took my neighbor's wife to eternal rest, and as he was one of my closest friends, I visited him at his house to offer my condolence. Finding him overcome with grief, I tried to comfort him, saying: "Have patience, my friend. Allah in His great bounty may soon give you another wife as loving and as worthy as the one He has taken from you. May He lighten your sorrow and prolong your years!"

But he never raised his eyes from the ground.

"Alas!" he sighed. "How can you wish me a long life when I have but a few hours to live?"

"Take heart, my friend," I said. "Why do you speak of death when, thank Allah, you are in perfect health, sound in mind and body?"

"In a few hours," he replied, "I shall be consigned to the earth with the body of my wife. It is an ancient custom in this country that when a wife dies, her husband is buried with her, and if he should die first, his wife is buried with him: Both must leave this world together."

"By Allah," I cried in horror, "this is a most barbarous custom! No civilized people could ever tolerate such monstrous cruelty!"

Whilst we were talking, my neighbor's friends and kinsfolk, together with a large crowd, came into the house and began to condole with him upon his wife's and his own impending death. Presently the funeral preparations were completed; the woman's body was laid in a coffin, and a long procession of mourners, headed by the husband, formed outside the house. And we all set out toward the burial ground.

The procession halted at the foot of a steep mound overlooking the sea, where a stone was rolled away from the mouth of a deep pit, and into this pit the corpse was thrown. Next the mourners laid hold of my friend and lowered him by a long rope, together with seven loaves of bread and a pitcher of water. Then the stone was rolled back, and we all returned to the city.

I hastened with a heavy heart to the King's palace, and when I was admitted to his presence, I fell on my knees before him, crying: "My noble master, I have visited many far countries and lived amongst all manner of men, but in all my life I have never seen or heard of anything so barbarous as your custom of burying the living with the dead. Are strangers, too, subject to this law, your majesty?"

"Certainly they are," he replied. "They must be interred with their dead wives. It is a time-hallowed custom to which all must submit."

At this reply I felt as though my gallbladder would burst open. I ran in haste to my own house, dreading lest my wife should have died since I last saw her. Finding her in perfect health, I comforted myself as best I could with the thought that I might one day find means of returning to my own country, or even die before my wife.

But Allah ordained otherwise. Soon afterward my wife was stricken with an illness and in a few days surrendered her soul to the Merciful.

The King and all his courtiers came to my house to comfort me. The body of my wife was perfumed and arrayed in fine robes and rich ornaments. And when all was ready for the burial, I was led behind the bier,[4] at the head of a long procession.

When we came to the mound, the stone was lifted from the mouth of the pit and the body of my wife thrown in; then the mourners gathered round to bid me farewell, paying no heed to my protests and entreaties. They bound me with a long rope and lowered me into the pit, together with the customary loaves and pitcher of water. Then they rolled back the stone and went their way.

When I touched the bottom of the pit, I found myself in a vast cavern filled with skeletons and

---

3. **cadi** (kä′dē): a minor Moslem magistrate or judge.

4. **bier** (bir): a coffin and its surrounding platform.

reeking with the foul stench of decaying corpses. I threw myself upon the earth, crying: ''You deserve this fate, Sindbad! Here you have come to pay the last penalty for your avarice, your insatiable greed! What need had you to marry in this island? Would that you had died on the bare mountains or perished in the merciless sea!''

Tormented by the vision of a protracted death, I lay in an agony of despair for many hours. At length, feeling the effects of thirst and hunger, I unfastened the loaves and the pitcher of water and ate and drank sparingly. Then I lay in a corner which I had carefully cleared of bones.

For several days I languished in that charnel[5] cave, and at length the time came when my provisions were exhausted. As I lay down, commending myself to Allah and waiting for my approaching end, the covering of the pit was suddenly lifted, and there appeared at its mouth a crowd of mourners, who presently lowered into the cavern a dead man accompanied by his screaming wife, together with seven loaves and a pitcher of water.

As soon as the stone was rolled back I rose and, snatching up a leg-bone from one of the skeletons, sprang upon the woman and dealt her a violent blow upon the head, so that she fell down lifeless upon the instant. Then I stole her provisions, which kept me alive for several days longer. When these in turn were finished, the stone was once again rolled away from the pit and a man lowered in with his dead wife. He, too, met the same end as the unfortunate woman before him.

In this way I lived on for many weeks, killing every newcomer and eating his food. One day, as I was sleeping in my accustomed place, I was awakened by a sound of movement nearby. At once I sprang to my feet, and picking up my weapon, followed the noise until I could faintly discern the form of some animal scurrying before me. As I pressed forward in pursuit of the strange intruder, stumbling in the dark over the bones and corpses, I suddenly made out at the far side of the cavern a tremulous speck of light which grew larger and brighter as I advanced toward it. When

I had reached the end of the cave the fleeing animal leapt through the light and disappeared. To my inexpressible joy, I realized that I had come upon a tunnel which the wild beasts, attracted by the carrion in the cave, had burrowed from the other side of the mound. I scrambled into this tunnel, crawling on all fours, and soon found myself at the foot of a high cliff, beneath the open sky.

I fell upon my knees in prayer and thanked the Almighty for my salvation. The warm and wholesome air breathed new life into my veins, and I rejoiced to gaze upon the loveliness of earth and sky.

Fortified with hope and courage, I made my way back into the cave and brought out the store of food which I had laid aside during my sojourn there. I also gathered up all the jewels, pearls, and precious ornaments that I could find upon the corpses, and tying them in the shrouds and garments of the dead, carried the bundles to the seashore.

I remained there several days, surveying the horizon from morning till night. One day, as I was sitting beneath a rock praying for a speedy rescue, I saw a sail far off upon the ocean. I hoisted a winding sheet[6] on my staff and waved it frantically as I ran up and down the beach. The crew observed my signal, and a boat was promptly sent off to fetch me.

''How did you find your way to this wild region?'' asked the captain in astonishment. ''I have never seen a living man on this desolate spot in all the days of my life.''

''Sir,'' I replied, ''I was shipwrecked off this shore many days ago. These bales are the remnants of my goods which I managed to save.'' And I kept the truth from him, lest there be some on board who were citizens of that island.

Then I took out a rare pearl from one of my packages and offered it to him. ''Pray accept this,'' I said, ''as a token of my gratitude to you for saving my life.''

But the captain politely refused the gift. ''It is not our custom,'' he said, ''to accept payment for

---

5. **charnel:** (chär′n′l): a place where corpses or bones are deposited.

6. **winding sheet:** a shroud.

a good deed. We have rescued many a ship-wrecked voyager, fed him and clothed him and finally set him ashore with a little present of our own besides. Allah alone is the giver of rewards.''

I thanked him with all my heart and called down blessings upon him.

Then the ship resumed its voyage. And as we sailed from island to island and from sea to sea, I rejoiced at the prospect of seeing my native land again. At times, however, a memory of my sojourn with the dead would come back to me, and I would be beside myself with terror.

At length, by the grace of Allah, we arrived safely in Basrah. I stayed a few days in that town, and then proceeded up the river to Baghdad. Loaded with treasure, I hastened to my own house, where I was rapturously welcomed by my friends and kinsfolk. I sold for a fabulous sum the precious stones I had brought back from that barbarous city, and gave lavish alms to widows and orphans.

That is the story of my fourth voyage. Tomorrow, if Allah wills, I shall recount to you the adventures of my fifth voyage.

Responding to the Story

Analyzing the Story

Identifying Facts

1. The basic **plot** of a **romance** involves a sequence of marvelous adventures. Explain how Sindbad escapes from the cannibals. Describe what happens to his shipmates.
2. After his escape, how does Sindbad become the rich and trusted courtier of a foreign king?
3. Explain why this king wants Sindbad to marry.
4. What strange custom of this kingdom suddenly places Sindbad in grave danger once again? Briefly describe his remarkable escape.

Interpreting Meanings

5. Summarize what we learn in this story about Sindbad's **character**. In particular, what traits are responsible for his remarkable ability to escape from danger? Are there any traits that we expect to find in a **romance** hero that we do not see in Sindbad? Explain.
6. The perilous journey or **quest** is a central pattern in **romance** literature. What is the nature of Sindbad's quest—what is he going after, and what perils must he overcome to obtain his goals? Does his quest seem worthwhile, or do you prefer heroes with loftier **motives**?
7. In what ways does Sindbad resemble the heroes of modern **romances** (such as Captain Kirk or Luke Skywalker)? Is he different from them in any significant way? Explain your opinion.

Writing About the Story

A Creative Response

1. **Describing an Escape.** Write a description of an ingenious escape from a terrifying **setting** such as the burial pit Sindbad escapes from in this story. You may invent a new character or imagine Sindbad on another exotic voyage.

A Critical Response

2. **Comparing and Contrasting Stories.** The human race seems to share certain collective nightmares, and on his voyages Sindbad manages to confront some of our most fundamental ones. For instance, on his fourth voyage, Sindbad is first almost eaten by cannibals and then almost buried alive. Write two paragraphs comparing and contrasting the element of horror in the Sindbad story with the element of horror in Edgar Allan Poe's ''The Pit and the Pendulum'' (page 168). Before you begin, consider the following question: Why is the Poe tale essentially a horror story, while the Sindbad story is not?
3. **Responding to a Critic's Viewpoint.** Here is what the English novelist C. S. Forester had to say about the **character** of Sindbad the Sailor. (Forester is perhaps best known for his Captain Horatio Hornblower adventure novels.) Write a brief essay of one or two paragraphs responding to Forester's comment. Be sure to cite evidence from the story to support your opinion.

Sindbad is very much a human being, and a typical man of his time. His thoughts are tinged by the fatalism and resignation of Mohammedanism, and yet he displays the restlessness and energy which carried that religion from one end of the Old World to the other in two centuries. He is charitable, even generous, and yet desperately self-centered. He can actually note that his shipmates are honest and good-hearted—"of the kind who can live contentedly together and render aid when aid is needed"—yet he never utters a word of regret when these selfsame companions are roasted on spits, and drowned, and swallowed by snakes. He kills the new arrivals in the living tomb so that he can eat their provisions without sharing them, and when he finds a way of escape, it does not occur to him to leave behind any signpost to help those unfortunates who will come later. He accepts, almost without comment, the extraordinary charity and honesty of the various sea captains with whom he comes in contact (although in this connection we must make allowances for the strongly felt brotherhood of Islam), but he is not beyond a little sharp practice himself. He is both resolute and smug, restless and resigned, and we cannot help but like him.

—C. S. Forester

Focusing on Background
Comparing Two Sea Voyages

Scholars believe that although the author or authors of the Sindbad stories were not familiar with Homer's *Odyssey,* they were acquainted with the Odysseus legend, which Homer used as the basis of his epic. Over the course of centuries, this oral legend had reached the Middle East in the form of a romantic tale of sea adventures.

Here is an excerpt from the *Odyssey* that bears a striking resemblance to Sindbad's experiences on his fourth voyage:

"My party found a track—a wagon road
for bringing wood down from the heights to town;
and near the settlement they met a daughter
of Antiphates the Laeistrygon—a stalwart
young girl taking her pail to Artacia,
the fountain where these people go for water.
My fellows hailed her, put their questions to her:
who might the king be? ruling over whom?
She waved her hand, showing her father's lodge,
so they approached it. In its gloom they saw
a woman like a mountain crag, the queen—
and loathed the sight of her. But she, for greeting,
called from the meeting ground her lord and master,
Antiphates, who came to drink their blood.

He seized one man and tore him on the spot,
making a meal of him; the other two
leaped out of doors and ran to join the ships.
Behind, he raised the whole tribe howling, countless
Laeistrygonians—and more than men they seemed,
gigantic when they gathered on the sky line
to shoot great boulders down from slings; and hell's own
crashing rose, and crying from the ships,
as planks and men were smashed to bits—poor gobbets
the wildmen speared like fish and bore away.
But long before it ended in the anchorage—
havoc and slaughter—I had drawn my sword
and cut my own ship's cable. 'Men,' I shouted,
'man the oars and pull till your hearts break
if you would put this butchery behind!'
The oarsmen rent the sea in mortal fear
and my ship spurted out of range, far out
from that deep canyon where the rest were lost.
So we fared onward, and death fell behind,
and we took breath to grieve for our companions."

—from the *Odyssey,* Book 10,
Homer, translated by Robert Fitzgerald

Miguel de Cervantes Saavedra (1547–1616) was born into an aristocratic Spanish family that had fallen on hard times. Cervantes' father was an apothecary and surgeon who wandered about Spain looking for work and fleeing his creditors. We know little about Cervantes' youth except that he attended a Jesuit school as a child, probably studied in Madrid with a famous theologian, and showed an early talent for writing poetry.

Cervantes' life story reads like an adventure tale itself. When he was twenty-two, he fought in an illegal duel, and to avoid punishment he fled to Rome. There he entered the service of a cardinal-elect who had recently visited Spain. The following year Cervantes joined the Pope's Holy League, the Christian forces that were fighting the Ottoman Turks. In 1571, during the famous naval Battle of Lepanto, Cervantes received three gunshot wounds—two in the chest and one that permanently crippled his left hand.

After several more years of military service in Italy, Cervantes and his brother were returning to Spain when their ship was captured by pirates off the coast of Marseilles. The two brothers were taken to Algiers and held for ransom. In 1580, after four attempts at escape and five years of captivity, Cervantes was finally ransomed at a price that brought his family financial ruin.

Cervantes returned to Spain heavily burdened with debt and eager to begin a literary career, but for the rest of his life he struggled with the enormous difficulties of earning a living. His heroism during the Battle of Lepanto had been forgotten, and he had trouble simply finding a job. In 1584, at the age of thirty-seven, Cervantes married a nineteen-year-old girl, Catalina de Palacios, and the next year he published his first book, a pastoral romance called *Galatea*. It was a financial failure, and Cervantes soon took a job as a roving purchasing agent for the Spanish Armada, while his young wife remained with her family. Unfortunately, Cervantes' naive and unbusinesslike methods resulted in deficits for which he was held responsible, and he was imprisoned for bankruptcy several times. Legend has it that *Don Quixote* (dôn' kē·hô'te) was conceived and planned while Cervantes was serving time in the Seville jail.

In 1605 Cervantes achieved his first success with the publication of *Don Quixote*. The novel quickly became enormously popular both in and out of Spain: "Children handle it, youngsters read it, grown men understand it, and old people applaud it," wrote Cervantes. Yet the literary establishment ignored him for the most part, and five months after the book's appearance, Cervantes was still living in poverty. In 1615 he published Part II of *Don Quixote*, partly in response to a false sequel by another writer published the previous year.

During his life, Cervantes wrote more than thirty plays, prose and verse romances, and two other novels. But it is *Don Quixote*, his masterpiece, that earned him his stature as Spain's greatest writer. According to the English writer J. B. Priestley, "Probably only Shakespeare has captured and delighted more minds than Cervantes. And by the strangest chance, they died on the same day, the twenty-third of April, 1616."

Don Quixote
by Miguel de Cervantes

> " **C**hildren handle it, youngsters read it, grown men understand it, and old people applaud it.' "
> —Miguel de Cervantes

Don Quixote by Honoré Daumier. Oil.

Ny Carlsberg Glyptotek, Copenhagen.

> " **D**on Quixote is not only one of the profoundest literary works ever conceived: It is also one of the funniest."

A Parody of the Romance

Don Quixote is often called the first modern novel. It is written in the **picaresque** tradition, in which the hero—a *picaro,* or rogue—has a series of adventures as he wanders about with a companion. Unlike the modern novel, the plot is loosely structured, consisting of a series of separate episodes told chronologically.

Clearly, *Don Quixote* is a **satire** on the codes of chivalry and the style of the old romances, which had begun to lose popularity by Cervantes' time. But in some deeper sense, it is much more than a **parody.** It is a novel that upholds the basic human nobility that lies behind the chivalric code, the romance style, and Don Quixote's mad deeds. No doubt Cervantes found such nobility sadly lacking in his own hard life. As we read the novel, we confront the worst in human nature: violence, prejudice, greed, foolhardiness, and shallow morality. Yet our dominant reaction is almost always laughter, for *Don Quixote* is not only one of the profoundest literary works ever conceived: It is also one of the funniest.

The following excerpts are from Part I of the novel. One of them relates the most famous of Don Quixote's adventures.

TILTING AT WINDMILLS

Miguel de Cervantes, translated by **Samuel Putnam**

Chapter 1

*Which treats of the station in life
and the pursuits of the famous
gentleman, Don Quixote de la Mancha.*

In a village of La Mancha,[1] the name of which I have no desire to recall, there lived not so long ago one of those gentlemen who always have a lance in the rack, an ancient buckler, a skinny nag, and a greyhound for the chase. A stew with more beef than mutton in it,[2] chopped meat for his evening meal, scraps for a Saturday, lentils on Friday, and a young pigeon as a special delicacy for Sunday went to account for three quarters of his income. The rest of it he laid out on a broadcloth greatcoat and velvet stockings for feast days, with slippers to match, while the other days of the week he cut a figure in a suit of the finest homespun. Living with him were a housekeeper in her forties, a niece who was not yet twenty, and a lad of the field and market place who saddled his horse for him and wielded the pruning knife.

This gentleman of ours was close on to fifty, of a robust constitution but with little flesh on his bones and a face that was lean and gaunt. He was noted for his early rising, being very fond of the hunt. They will try to tell you that his surname was Quijada or Quesada[3]—there is some difference of opinion among those who have written on the subject—but according to the most likely conjectures we are to understand that it was really Quejana. But all this means very little so far as our story is concerned, providing that in the telling of it we do not depart one iota from the truth.

You may know, then, that the aforesaid gentleman, on those occasions when he was at leisure, which was most of the year around, was in the habit of reading books of chivalry with such pleasure and devotion as to lead him almost wholly to forget the life of a hunter and even the administration of his estate. So great was his curiosity and infatuation in this regard that he even sold many acres of tillable land in order to be able to buy and read the books that he loved, and he would carry home with him as many of them as he could obtain.

Of all those that he thus devoured, none pleased him so well as the ones that had been composed by the famous Feliciano de Silva,[4] whose lucid prose style and involved conceits[5] were as precious to him as pearls; especially when he came to read those tales of love and amorous challenges that are to be met with in many places, such a passage as the following, for example: "The reason of the unreason that afflicts my reason, in such a manner weakens my reason that I with reason lament me of your comeliness." And he was similarly affected when his eyes fell upon such lines as these: ". . . the high heaven of your divinity divinely fortifies you with the stars and renders you deserving of that desert your greatness doth deserve."

The poor fellow used to lie awake nights in an effort to disentangle the meaning and make sense out of passages such as these, although Aristotle himself would not have been able to understand them, even if he had been resurrected for that sole purpose. He was not at ease in his mind over those wounds that Don Belianís gave and received; for

---

1. **La Mancha:** a poor, sparsely populated province in south-central Spain.
2. **more beef than mutton in it:** Mutton was considered more desirable than beef.
3. **Quijada or Quesada:** names of distinguished Spanish families.

4. **Feliciano de Silva:** a writer of romances popular in Cervantes' day. The titles and authors that Cervantes mentions are all of popular romances.
5. **conceits:** elaborate comparisons or metaphors.

Don Quixote by Honoré Daumier. Oil.

no matter how great the surgeons who treated him, the poor fellow must have been left with his face and his entire body covered with marks and scars. Nevertheless, he was grateful to the author for closing the book with the promise of an interminable adventure to come; many a time he was tempted to take up his pen and literally finish the tale as had been promised, and he undoubtedly would have done so, and would have succeeded at it very well, if his thoughts had not been constantly occupied with other things of greater moment.

He often talked it over with the village curate, who was a learned man, a graduate of Sigüenza,[6] and they would hold long discussions as to who had been the better knight, Palmerin of England or Amadis of Gaul; but Master Nicholas, the barber of the same village, was in the habit of saying that no one could come up to the Knight of Phoebus, and that if anyone *could* compare with him it was Don Galaor, brother of Amadis of Gaul, for Galaor was ready for anything—he was none of your finical[7] knights who went around whimpering as his brother did, and in point of valor he did not lag behind him.

In short, our gentleman became so immersed in his reading that he spent whole nights from sundown to sunup and his days from dawn to dusk in poring over his books, until finally, from so little sleeping and so much reading, his brain dried up and he went completely out of his mind. He had filled his imagination with everything that he had read, with enchantments, knightly encounters, battles, challenges, wounds, with tales of love and its torments, and all sorts of impossible things, and as a result had come to believe that all these fictitious happenings were true; they were more real to him than anything else in the world. He would remark that the Cid Ruy Díaz[8] had been a very good knight, but there was no comparison between him and the Knight of the Flaming Sword, who with a single backward stroke had cut in half two fierce and monstrous giants. He preferred Bernardo del Carpio, who at Roncesvalles had slain Roland despite the charm the latter bore, availing himself of the stratagem which Hercules employed when he strangled Antaeus, the son of Earth, in his arms.

He had much good to say for Morgante, who though he belonged to the haughty, overbearing race of giants, was of an affable disposition and well brought up. But above all, he cherished an admiration for Rinaldo of Montalbán,[9] especially as he beheld him sallying forth from his castle to rob all those that crossed his path, or when he thought of him overseas stealing the image of Mohammed, which, so the story has it, was all of gold. And he would have liked very well to have had his fill of kicking that traitor Galalón,[10] a privilege for which he would have given his housekeeper with his niece thrown into the bargain.

At last, when his wits were gone beyond repair, he came to conceive the strangest idea that ever occurred to any madman in this world. It now appeared to him fitting and necessary, in order to win a greater amount of honor for himself and serve his country at the same time, to become a knight errant[11] and roam the world on horseback, in a suit of armor; he would go in quest of adventures, by way of putting into practice all that he had read in his books; he would right every manner of wrong, placing himself in situations of the greatest peril such as would redound to the eternal glory of his name. As a reward for his valor and the might of his arm, the poor fellow could already see himself crowned Emperor of Trebizond[12] at the very least; and so, carried away by the strange pleasure that he found in such thoughts as these, he at once set about putting his plan into effect.

The first thing he did was to burnish up some old pieces of armor, left him by his great-grandfather, which for ages had lain in a corner, moldering and forgotten. He polished and adjusted them as best he could, and then he noticed that

---

6. **Sigüenza:** a Spanish university that was often the subject of jokes because of the poor quality of its education.
7. **finical:** finicky; fussy; overly particular.
8. **the Cid Ruy Díaz:** The great Spanish soldier and hero Ruy (or Rodrigo) Díaz de Vivar (1040?–1099) was called the Cid, a corruption of the Arabic word for lord.

---

9. **Rinaldo of Montalbán:** one of Charlemagne's knights.
10. **Galalón:** the villain of the Charlemagne legend who betrayed the French at Roncevalles.
11. **errant:** roving or wandering in search of adventure.
12. **Trebizond:** a medieval Greek empire on the southeast coast of the Black Sea, an offshoot of the Byzantine Empire.

one very important thing was lacking: there was no closed helmet, but only a morion, or visorless headpiece, with turned-up brim of the kind foot soldiers wore. His ingenuity, however, enabled him to remedy this, and he proceeded to fashion out of cardboard a kind of half-helmet, which, when attached to the morion, gave the appearance of a whole one. True, when he went to see if it was strong enough to withstand a good slashing blow, he was somewhat disappointed; for when he drew his sword and gave it a couple of thrusts, he succeeded only in undoing a whole week's labor. The ease with which he had hewed it to bits disturbed him no little, and he decided to make it over. This time he placed a few strips of iron on the inside, and then, convinced that it was strong enough, refrained from putting it to any further test; instead, he adopted it then and there as the finest helmet ever made.

After this, he went out to have a look at his nag; and although the animal had more *cuartos,* or cracks, in its hoof than there are quarters in a real,[13] and more blemishes than Gonela's[14] steed, which *tantum pellis et ossa fuit,*[15] it nonetheless looked to its master like a far better horse than Alexander's Bucephalus[16] or the Babieca[17] of the Cid. He spent all of four days in trying to think up a name for his mount; for—so he told himself— seeing that it belonged to so famous and worthy a knight, there was no reason why it should not have a name of equal renown. The kind of name he wanted was one that would at once indicate what the nag had been before it came to belong to a knight errant and what its present status was; for it stood to reason that, when the master's worldly condition changed, his horse also ought to have a famous, high-sounding appellation, one suited to the new order of things and the new profession that it was to follow.

After he in his memory and imagination had made up, struck out, and discarded many names, now adding to and now subtracting from the list,

he finally hit upon "Rocinante,"[18] a name that impressed him as being sonorous and at the same time indicative of what the steed had been when it was but a hack, whereas now it was nothing other than the first and foremost of all the hacks in the world.

Having found a name for his horse that pleased his fancy, he then desired to do as much for himself, and this required another week, and by the end of that period he had made up his mind that he was henceforth to be known as Don Quixote,[19] which, as has been stated, has led the authors of this veracious history to assume that his real name must undoubtedly have been Quijada, and not Quesada, as others would have it. But remembering that the valiant Amadis was not content to call himself that and nothing more, but added the name of his kingdom and fatherland that he might make it famous also, and thus came to take the name Amadis of Gaul, so our good knight chose to add his place of origin and become "Don Quixote de la Mancha"; for by this means, as he saw it, he was making very plain his lineage and was conferring honor upon his country by taking its name as his own.

And so, having polished up his armor and made the morion over into a closed helmet, and having given himself and his horse a name, he naturally found but one thing lacking still: He must seek out a lady of whom he could become enamored; for a knight errant without a ladylove was like a tree without leaves or fruit, a body without a soul.

"If," he said to himself, "as a punishment for my sins or by a stroke of fortune I should come upon some giant hereabouts, a thing that very commonly happens to knights errant, and if I should slay him in a hand-to-hand encounter or perhaps cut him in two, or finally, if I should vanquish and subdue him, would it not be well to have someone to whom I may send him as a present, in order that he, if he is living, may come in, fall upon his knees in front of my sweet lady, and

---

13. **real** (rä·äl'): old Spanish silver coin.
14. **Gonela:** a fifteenth-century Italian court jester whose skinny horse was the subject of many jokes.
15. *tantum pellis et ossa fuit:* (Latin) was nothing but skin and bones.
16. **Bucephalus:** Alexander the Great's war horse.
17. **Babieca:** the Cid's war horse.

18. **Rocinante** (rō'sē·nän'tä): coined from the Spanish word *rocin,* meaning a nag or hack.
19. **Quixote:** named for a piece of armor that covers the thigh. *Don* is a Spanish title of nobility, similar to the English *Sir* or the German *von.*

say in a humble and submissive tone of voice, 'I, lady, am the giant Caraculiambro, lord of the island Malindrania, who has been overcome in single combat by that knight who never can be praised enough, Don Quixote de la Mancha, the same who sent me to present myself before your Grace that your Highness may dispose of me as you see fit'?''

Oh, how our good knight reveled in this speech, and more than ever when he came to think of the name that he should give his lady! As the story goes, there was a very good-looking farm girl who lived near by, with whom he had once been smitten, although it is generally believed that she never knew or suspected it. Her name was Aldonza Lorenzo, and it seemed to him that she was the one upon whom he should bestow the title of mistress of his thoughts. For her he wished a name that should not be incongruous with his own and that would convey the suggestion of a princess or a great lady; and accordingly, he resolved to call her ''Dulcinea[20] del Toboso,'' she being a native of that place. A musical name to his ears, out of the ordinary and significant, like the others he had chosen for himself and his appurtenances.[21]

In Chapter 7 Don Quixote convinces a peasant neighbor to serve as his squire:

. . . In the meanwhile Don Quixote was bringing his powers of persuasion to bear upon a farmer who lived nearby, a good man—if this title may be applied to one who is poor—but with very few wits in his head. The short of it is, by pleas and promises, he got the hapless rustic to agree to ride forth with him and serve him as his squire. Among other things, Don Quixote told him that he ought to be more than willing to go, because no telling what adventure might occur which would win them an island, and then he (the farmer) would be left to be the governor of it. As a result of these and other similar assurances, Sancho Panza forsook his wife and children and consented to take upon himself the duties of squire to his neighbor. . . .

From

Chapter 8

Of the good fortune which the valorous Don Quixote had in the terrifying and never-before-imagined adventure of the windmills, along with other events that deserve to be suitably recorded.

At this point [Don Quixote and Sancho Panza] caught sight of thirty or forty windmills which were standing on the plain there, and no sooner had Don Quixote laid eyes upon them than he turned to his squire and said, ''Fortune is guiding our affairs better than we could have wished; for you see there before you, friend Sancho Panza, some thirty or more lawless giants with whom I mean to do battle. I shall deprive them of their lives, and with the spoils from this encounter we shall begin to enrich ourselves; for this is righteous warfare, and it is a great service to God to remove so accursed a breed from the face of the earth.''

''What giants?'' said Sancho Panza.

''Those that you see there,'' replied his master, ''those with the long arms, some of which are as much as two leagues[22] in length.''

''But look, your Grace, those are not giants but windmills, and what appear to be arms are their wings, which when whirled in the breeze, cause the millstone to go.''

''It is plain to be seen,'' said Don Quixote, ''that you have had little experience in this matter of adventures. If you are afraid, go off to one side and say your prayers while I am engaging them in fierce, unequal combat.''

Saying this, he gave spurs to his steed Rocinante, without paying any heed to Sancho's warning that these were truly windmills and not giants that he was riding forth to attack. Nor even when he was close upon them did he perceive what they really were, but shouted at the top of his lungs, ''Do not seek to flee, cowards and vile creatures that you are, for it is but a single knight with whom you have to deal!''

---

20. **Dulcinea** (dul'sē·nā'ä): coined from the Spanish word *dulce,* meaning sweet.
21. **appurtenances:** equipment; accessories.

22. **leagues:** A league is a somewhat variable measure of distance, usually about three miles.

At that moment a little wind came up and the big wings began turning.

"Though you flourish as many arms as did the giant Briareus,"[23] said Don Quixote when he perceived this, "you still shall have to answer to me."

He thereupon commended himself with all his heart to his lady Dulcinea, beseeching her to succor him in this peril; and being well covered with his shield and with his lance at rest, he bore down upon them at a full gallop and fell upon the first mill that stood in his way, giving a thrust at the wing, which was whirling at such a speed that his lance was broken into bits and both horse and horseman went rolling over the plain, very much battered indeed. Sancho, upon his donkey, came hurrying to his master's assistance as fast as he could, but when he reached the spot, the knight was unable to move, so great was the shock with which he and Rocinante had hit the ground.

"God help us!" exclaimed Sancho, "did I not tell your Grace to look well, that those were nothing but windmills, a fact which no one could fail to see unless he had other mills of the same sort in his head?"

"Be quiet, friend Sancho," said Don Quixote. "Such are the fortunes of war, which more than any other are subject to constant change. What is more, when I come to think of it, I am sure that this must be the work of that magician Frestón, the one who robbed me of my study and my books,[24] and who has thus changed the giants into windmills in order to deprive me of the glory of overcoming them, so great is the enmity that he bears me; but in the end his evil arts shall not prevail against this trusty sword of mine."

"May God's will be done," was Sancho Panza's response. And with the aid of his squire, the knight was once more mounted on Rocinante, who stood there with one shoulder half out of joint. And so, speaking of the adventure that had just befallen them, they continued along the Puerto Lápice highway; for there, Don Quixote said, they could not fail to find many and varied adventures, this being a much-traveled thoroughfare. The only thing was, the knight was exceedingly downcast over the loss of his lance.

"I remember," he said to his squire, "having read of a Spanish knight by the name of Diego Pérez de Vargas, who, having broken his sword in battle, tore from an oak a heavy bough or branch and with it did such feats of valor that day, and pounded so many Moors, that he came to be known as Machuca,[25] and he and his descendants from that day forth have been called Vargas y Machuca. I tell you this because I, too, intend to provide myself with just such a bough as the one he wielded, and with it I propose to do such exploits that you shall deem yourself fortunate to have been found worthy to come with me and behold and witness things that are almost beyond belief."

"God's will be done," said Sancho. "I believe everything that your Grace says; but straighten yourself up in the saddle a little, for you seem to be slipping down on one side, owing, no doubt, to the shaking up that you received in your fall."

"Ah, that is the truth," replied Don Quixote, "and if I do not speak of my sufferings, it is for the reason that it is not permitted knights errant to complain of any wound whatsoever, even though their bowels may be dropping out."

"If that is the way it is," said Sancho, "I have nothing more to say; but, God knows, it would suit me better if your Grace did complain when something hurts him. I can assure you that I mean to do so, over the least little thing that ails me— that is, unless the same rule applies to squires as well."

Don Quixote laughed long and heartily over Sancho's simplicity, telling him that he might com-

---

23. **Briareus** (brī·ar′ē·əs): in Greek mythology, a giant with a hundred hands.
24. **Frestón . . . books:** In Chapter 7 Don Quixote's housekeeper burns all of his books, thinking this will cure his madness. Then his friends wall up his study and decide to tell him that an enchanter has whisked everything away. Remarkably, this strange explanation makes perfect sense to Don Quixote, who even tells them that the name of this enchanter is Frestón, and that he is a great enemy of his.

25. **Machuca** (mä·shoo′kə): literally, "the pounder"; he was the hero of a folk ballad.

plain as much as he liked and where and when he liked, whether he had good cause or not; for he had read nothing to the contrary in the ordinances of chivalry. Sancho then called his master's attention to the fact that it was time to eat. The knight replied that he himself had no need of food at the moment, but his squire might eat whenever he chose. Having been granted this permission, Sancho seated himself as best he could upon his beast, and, taking out from his saddlebags the provisions that he had stored there, he rode along leisurely behind his master, munching his victuals and taking a good, hearty swig now and then at the leather flask in a manner that might well have caused the biggest-bellied tavernkeeper of Málaga to envy him. Between draughts he gave not so much as a thought to any promise that his master might have made him, nor did he look upon it as any hardship, but rather as good sport, to go in quest of adventures however hazardous they might be.

The short of the matter is, they spent the night under some trees, from one of which Don Quixote tore off a withered bough to serve him as a lance, placing it in the lance head from which he had removed the broken one. He did not sleep all night long for thinking of his lady Dulcinea; for this was in accordance with what he had read in his books, of men of arms in the forest or desert places who kept a wakeful vigil, sustained by the memory of their ladies fair. Not so with Sancho, whose stomach was full, and not with chicory water. He fell into a dreamless slumber, and had not his master called him, he would not have been awakened either by the rays of the sun in his face or by the many birds who greeted the coming of the new day with their merry song.

Upon arising, he had another go at the flask, finding it somewhat more flaccid than it had been the night before, a circumstance which grieved his heart, for he could not see that they were on the way to remedying the deficiency within any very short space of time. Don Quixote did not wish any breakfast; for, as has been said, he was in the habit of nourishing himself on savorous memories. They then set out once more along the road to Puerto Lápice, and around three in the afternoon they came in sight of the pass that bears that name.

"There," said Don Quixote as his eyes fell upon it, "we may plunge our arms up to the elbow in what are known as adventures. But I must warn you that even though you see me in the greatest peril in the world, you are not to lay hand upon your sword to defend me, unless it be that those who attack me are rabble and men of low degree, in which case you may very well come to my aid; but if they be gentlemen, it is in no wise permitted by the laws of chivalry that you should assist me until you yourself shall have been dubbed a knight."

"Most certainly, sir," replied Sancho, "your Grace shall be very well obeyed in this; all the more so for the reason that I myself am of a peaceful disposition and not fond of meddling in the quarrels and feuds of others. However, when it comes to protecting my own person, I shall not take account of those laws of which you speak, seeing that all laws, human and divine, permit each one to defend himself whenever he is attacked."

"I am willing to grant you that," assented Don Quixote, "but in this matter of defending me against gentlemen you must restrain your natural impulses."

"I promise you I shall do so," said Sancho, "I will observe this precept as I would the Sabbath day."

Responding to the Story

Analyzing the Story

Identifying Facts

1. Explain why Don Quixote goes "completely out of his mind." What are the two reasons he gives for setting out on his adventures as a knight errant?
2. How does Don Quixote equip himself with the trappings appropriate to a knight errant?
3. In discussing Don Quixote's addiction to reading and thinking about the romances of his day, Cervantes takes a moment to poke fun at these romances. What specific aspects does he make fun of? Cite the passages.
4. Explain why Don Quixote attacks the windmills. What happens to him as a result?
5. What explanation does Don Quixote give for the fact that the giants have become windmills?
6. At the end of Chapter 8, Don Quixote tells Sancho Panza some of the rules of chivalric behavior that apply to knights errant and their squires. What are these rules?

Interpreting Meanings

7. How do you know, from the outset of the novel, that this is a **satire** and not a serious **romance** about the glorious and noble adventures of a heroic knight? In what ways is Don Quixote a **parody** of a knight in the true romances? What makes him ridiculous?
8. Part of the novel's humor comes from the stark contrast between the **romantic** ideal (as we know it from romances) and the actual reality that Don Quixote experiences. We see this contrast in Don Quixote's horse, his armor, and his ladylove. Describe these contrasts, and explain why we perceive them as comic, rather than as pathetic or tragic. How does the narrator's **tone** contribute to our perception of Don Quixote as an essentially comic character?
9. A **foil** is a person who sets off or enhances another person by contrast. (In comedy teams such as Abbott and Costello or Ralph Kramden and Ed Norton on *The Honeymooners,* one of the characters serves as a foil for the other.) Sancho Panza serves as the perfect foil for Don Quixote. In what ways are Sancho Panza and Don Quixote different from one another? Cite specific examples of their contrasting viewpoints, habits, and character traits.
10. Where did your sympathies lie in the tale of the windmills—with Sancho Panza or with Don Quixote? Are most people in the world "Sanchos" or "Quixotes"? Explain.

Writing About the Story

A Creative Response

1. **Updating the Story.** Imagine that Don Quixote and Sancho Panza are suddenly transplanted into the twentieth century. Write a short story about Don Quixote's adventure with a modern machine (such as a helicopter, a computer, a crane, a vacuum cleaner, a photocopier, a VCR, a washing machine). Be sure to include dialogue between Don Quixote and Sancho Panza. If you prefer, you may vary the model slightly by having Don Quixote's madness be the result of reading modern romances, rather than old romances about knights in shining armor. Or you may have it be the result of some other obsession, such as watching too much television.

A Critical Response

2. **Responding to a Critic's Comment.** Here is what one critic has written about *Don Quixote:*

> Generally speaking, the encounters between the ordinary world and Don Quixote are encounters between the world of reality and that of illusion, between reason and imagination, ultimately between the world in which action is prompted by material considerations and interests and a world in which action is prompted by ideal motives. . . . Don Quixote . . . sees windmills and decides they are giants; country inns become castles; flocks of sheep, armies. Though the conclusions of such episodes often have the ludicrousness of slapstick comedy, there is a powerfully imposing quality about Don Quixote's insanity: His madness always has method, a commanding persistence and coherence. And there is perhaps an inevitable sense of moral grandeur in the spec-

tacle of anyone remaining so unflinchingly faithful to his own vision. The world of "reason" may win in point of fact, but we come to wonder whether from a moral point of view Quixote is not the victor.

—P. M. Pasinetti

Write a brief essay of two or three paragraphs in which you respond to this comment, based on the excerpts you have read. Do you agree that there is a "moral grandeur" to Don Quixote's madness? Do you agree that there is a "method" to it? Be sure to cite evidence from the text to support your opinion.

Focusing on Background
The Brutal World of Don Quixote

In 1952 the Russian-born novelist Vladimir Nabokov delivered a series of lectures on *Don Quixote* at Harvard University. In these lectures, Nabokov rejected the standard interpretation of the book as a warm satire, a genteel and whimsical myth about appearance versus reality. Instead he presented *Don Quixote* as a book whose essential cruelty had been glossed over for centuries. Here is an excerpt from one of Nabokov's lectures. What is your response to his interpretation?

"Both parts of *Don Quixote* form a veritable encyclopedia of cruelty. From that viewpoint it is one of the most bitter and barbarous books ever penned. And its cruelty is artistic. The extraordinary commentators who talk through their academic caps or birettas of the humorous and humane mellowly Christian atmosphere of the book, of a happy world where 'all is sweetened by the humanities of love and good fellowship,' . . .—these gushing experts have probably been reading some other book or are looking through some rosy gauze at the brutal world of Cervantes' novel. There is a legend that one sunny morning King Philip the Third of Spain (a freak in his own right, who had succeeded in 1598 his father, the gloomy and fish-cold Philip the Second) upon looking from the balcony of his palace was struck by the singular behavior of a young student who was sitting on a bench in the shade of a cork oak . . . with a book and frantically clapping his thigh and giving vent to wild shrieks of laughter. The king remarked that the fellow was either crazy or was reading *Don Quixote*. A rapid courtier ran out to find the answer. The fellow, as you have guessed, was reading *Don Quixote*.

"What exactly provoked this outburst of wild merriment in the gloomy world of the Philips? I have listed a whole set of jollities for the merry young student to choose from. . . . So we start in Chapter 3 with the innkeeper who allows a haggard madman to stay at his inn just in order to laugh at him and have his guests laugh at him. We go on with a shriek of hilarity to the half-naked lad flogged with a belt by a hefty farmer (Chapter 4). We are convulsed with laughter again in Chapter 4 when a mule driver pounds the helpless Don Quixote like wheat in a mill. In Chapter 8 another belly laugh is given unto us by the servants of some traveling monks, who pull every hair from Sancho's beard and kick him mercilessly. What a riot, what a panic! Some carriers in Chapter 15 beat Rocinante so hard that he drops to the ground half-dead. . . .

". . . Attitudes of excruciating pain such as that of Sancho Panza in the same Chapter 15 provoke another moan of mirth. By this time Don Quixote has lost half an ear—and nothing can be funnier than losing half an ear except of course losing three-quarters of an ear—and now, please, notice the blows that he received during one day and one night: (1) wallops with packstaves, (2) a punch on the jaw at the inn, (3) sundry blows in the dark, (4) a bang on the pate with an iron lantern. And the next day is nicely started by his losing most of his teeth when stoned by some shepherds. The fun becomes positively rollicking by Chapter 17, when in the famous blanket-tossing scene, some artisans—woolcombers and needlemakers, described as 'merry fellows all of them, well intentioned, mischievous, and playful'—amuse themselves at Sancho's expense by tossing him in a blanket as men do with dogs at Shrovetide—a casual allusion to humane and humorous customs.'"

Literature & Language

Recognizing Allusions

You have seen in this unit that classical mythology, the Bible, and the masterpieces of the Romance tradition have been rich sources of **allusions** for writers throughout history. The following poems contain allusions; read them carefully and answer the questions that follow.

I.

Like W. H. Auden's poem on page 802, this poem is a twentieth-century response to the Daedalus and Icarus myth (page 798) and to Brueghel's painting *The Fall of Icarus* (pages 798–799).

Landscape with the Fall of Icarus

According to Brueghel
When Icarus fell
it was spring

a farmer was ploughing
5 his field
the whole pageantry

of the year was
awake tingling
near

10 the edge of the sea
concerned
with itself

sweating in the sun
that melted
15 the wings' wax

insignificantly
off the coast
there was

a splash quite unnoticed
20 this was
Icarus drowning

—William Carlos Williams

---

1. According to lines 11–12, who or what was "concerned with itself"?
2. What does *insignificantly* modify in line 16?
3. What point do both Auden and Williams make about the Brueghel painting?
4. What is **ironic** about the fact that it is spring when ıcarus falls?
5. Is the **theme** of Williams's poem the same as the theme of Ovid's story? Is it the same as Auden's theme? Explain.
6. What do you think Williams is using Icarus to **symbolize**?

II.

The next two poems allude to the Parable of the Prodigal Son (page 829).

The Prodigal

They made a feast in the banquet hall,
And the calf was slain for the prodigal.
And here I sit, while the last guests
    linger,
With a robe on my back, and a ring on
    my finger.

Well, home calls somehow, the whole
5   world through,
And its threshold portal is a dream come
    true,
And the glow of the home hearth is
    beautiful to see
When one has been a vagrant, in a Far
    Country.

Oh it's not much fun to be swine herd
    keeping,
And to bed with the hard earth is cold
10   enough sleeping,
And after the husks were gone, I
    fasted—
But Oh my friends—while the money
    lasted!

—Sara Henderson Hay

The Father

Well, he's come home, this younger son
   of mine.
But something in his penitence betrays
He had been guardian of fouler swine,
Before those latter days. . . .

5   For there's a furtive something sliding
   under
His speech; he sits and twists his ring
   around
And stares at it. My son was lost—I
   wonder,
Is he so truly found?

Oh I am glad I did not hesitate
10   To run and clasp him hard in my embrace.
Still, it was rather more than fortunate
He could not see *my* face.

           —Sara Henderson Hay

1. Who is speaking in the first poem?
2. What event has just taken place?
3. How does the speaker feel about his recent experience? Why has he come home?
4. Who is speaking in the second poem?
5. Who is "he" in line 1?
6. What does this speaker wonder about? What does he seem to be afraid of?
7. Why is he glad his son did not see his face?
8. Are the thoughts and feelings of these speakers like or unlike what you'd expect them to be from the original parable? What **irony** do you find in these **allusions** to the Prodigal Son?
9. What point do you think the writer is making in these two poems? How is her focus different from Elizabeth Bishop's in her poem "The Prodigal" (page 830)?

III.

To understand the allusions in the next poem, you will have to read (or reread) a legend in the King Arthur cycle called "The Fair Maid of Astolat." You probably already know who Lancelot is.

Launcelot with Bicycle

Her window looks upon the lane.
From it, anonymous and shy,
Twice daily she can see him plain,
Wheeling heroic by.
5   She droops her cheek against the pane
And gives a little sigh.

Above him maples at their bloom
Shake April pollen down like stars
While he goes whistling past her room
10   Toward unimagined wars,
A tennis visor for his plume,
Scornful of handlebars.

And, counting over in her mind
His favors, gleaned like windfall fruit
15   (A morning when he spoke her kind,
An afterschool salute,
A number that she helped him find,
Once, for his paper route),

Sadly she twists a stubby braid
20   And closer to the casement leans—
A wistful and a lily maid
In moccasins and jeans,
Despairing from the seventh grade
To match his lordly teens.

25   And so she grieves in Astolat
(Where other girls have grieved the same)
For being young and therefore not
Sufficient to his fame—
Who will by summer have forgot
30   Grief, April, and his name.

           —Phyllis McGinley

1. Cite the lines that indicate that the boy is identified with a knight of the old **romances.**
2. Does the boy imagine he is a knight, or are these the girl's thoughts? Explain.
3. Based on the favors the boy has given her (lines 14-18), what can you infer about his feelings for the girl? What **simile** indicates how she feels about these favors?

Literature & Language / cont.

4. The poet suggests that the season of year has something to do with the girl's feelings. Why would spring make the girl feel the way she does?
5. Why is the girl despairing?
6. Does the Arthurian story explain the **allusion** to a "lily maid" (line 21)?
7. What happened to the real lady of Astolat?
8. What humorous **ironic** twist does the poet give *her* story in the last lines?
9. In **alluding** to the Arthurian tales, with all their emphasis on the eternal nature of romantic love, what point do you think this poet is making about the real nature of love—at least of adolescent love? What do you think of her point of view?

Writing

1. **Writing Monologues.** Write two internal monologues that describe what you imagine the Prodigal Son and his father are thinking ten years after the son's return.
2. **Writing Monologues.** Write two internal monologues telling what Ruth and Naomi are thinking after the birth of Ruth's child.
3. **Updating a Story.** Take one of the selections in this unit that you have not already updated, and retell it as a contemporary story. You will have to decide how you will modernize the **conflict,** the **characters,** and the **setting.** Just be sure you keep to the basic **plot** of the narrative, and include some **allusions** in your story so readers will recognize the older story you are basing it on. You might try one of the following:

   a. A modern Ruth and Naomi
   b. A modern Prodigal Son (or daughter) and his father (or mother)
   c. A modern King Arthur
   d. A modern Sindbad the Sailor
   e. A modern Don Quixote and Sancho Panza

4. **Describing a Painting.** Study the following painting, *The Sacrifice of Isaac,* by the seventeenth-century Dutch artist Rembrandt. Then write a short poem or paragraph that describes what is happening in this painting and **alludes** to the Biblical account it is based on. In your verse or prose description, indicate how you feel Rembrandt has interpreted his subject matter. What is his point of view? Has he read between the lines in any way—added details or emotions that the Biblical account does not mention?

The Sacrifice of Isaac by Rembrandt. Oil.

Alte Pinakothek, Munich.

FOLKTALES FROM AROUND THE WORLD

Krishna and Radha in the Rain with Two Musicians (detail). School of Raj-putana.   New Delhi National Museum.

UNIT SEVEN   **Virginia Hamilton**

FOLKTALES FROM AROUND THE WORLD

An introduction by **Virginia Hamilton**

I got a story in me and I aim to tell it as long and as loud as I please.

—An anonymous storyteller

I am a writer who invents stories and characters that make up an entire world of *the book*. I also tell **folktales,** stories that have been told before by anonymous tellers from long ago. These stories were passed down orally for many years and eventually were written down. In my folktale collections, I tell these stories in ways that express my personal views, in my own style of writing. Many of these retold stories are ages old. By means of the story collections, I feel I have somehow made contact with the early tellers. I have touched the ancients who first invented the stories.

Household Tales

Folktales can come from close to home, from people like my own father, who was a musician, a wanderer, and a natural storyteller. My father told us fantastic stories about how, when he was a young man, he worked as a porter and waiter on the Transcontinental Canadian Railroad and saw portions of it being built; how he witnessed the last huge gatherings of the Native American tribal nations; how he played his mandolin on the radio; how he ran dance halls in the old Western mining towns, where you had to check your gun at the door. (We're talking about ninety-odd years ago.)

Some of my dad's stories sound like "tall tales" (you might even call them "lies"). For example, did he really once meet a fellow named Louis Augustus Leopold Dr. Williams John Applegate Jones, who said *his* father had named him after all his closest friends? You could say that the stories my father told his children are "household" tales. They've stayed in the family, passed from parent to children to grandchildren—and to uncles, aunts, and cousins too. That's how some folktales begin—at home, among families sharing their experiences. If you've "talked story" to your own parents, you must know household tales of your own. Stories are always being made. Sometimes they have such a profound meaning that they leave the household in search of a wider audience. They become folktales.

All Around the Mulberry Bush by Woodie Long (1990). Acrylic on canvas.

Collection of the artist. Courtesy of the Leon Loard Gallery, Montgomery, Alabama.

> "**D**id my father really once meet a fellow named Louis Augustus Leopold Dr. Williams John Applegate Jones, who said *his* father had named him after all his closest friends?"

The Birth of a Folktale

Folktales can also evolve in other ways. Here's the story of how a new folktale came into existence some forty years ago, in Australia. This folktale isn't a "household" story; it seems to have grown out of an older myth combined with a modern-day historical disaster. To understand how this story originated, you have to know something about the Aborigines, Australia's native inhabitants.

According to the Aborigines, their earliest ancestors created themselves from clay. Then they began to wander over Australia, singing out the names of everything they encountered: animals, plants, hills, rocks, streams. In this way the ancestors sang the world into being. Present-day Aborigines believe that Australia is crisscrossed with their ancestors' invisible pathways—known as "songlines." The Aborigines say they can follow the trails of the songs left along their ancestors' footprints. A song is like a map: If they know the song, they can sing-find their way across the country.

Songlines make all of Australia sacred to the Aborigines; they feel the land should remain untouched, just as it was when their ancestors sang it into existence. This belief has pitted the Aborigines against outsiders—particularly mining and railway companies, who've disturbed the songlines by "scarring" and "wounding" the land.

Now, the story I want to tell you takes place in Australia's bare scrub country, the Burt Plain. Several years ago, a railway company decided to cut through a small hill to save a few miles of track. When the Aborigines learned what the railroad intended to do, they became extremely agitated. They warned that disaster would occur if the hillside were cut: "Blackfella die! Whitefella die! All people die! End of Australia! End of world! Finish!"

It turned out that the songline along that hill told of an ancestor who had failed to perform the correct ritual for controlling the breeding cycle of the bush-fly. As a result, hordes of maggots had overrun the Burt Plain, stripping it bare of vegetation (the way it appears today). This ancestor rounded up the maggots and crammed them back under the rock, where they've been breeding underground ever since. According to the present-day Aborigines, if the railroad cut into the hillside, there would be a gigantic explosion. A cloud of flies would spew up, covering the whole earth and killing every living creature.

What does this tale mean? How did it originate? Perhaps this is the answer:

During the 1950's and early '60's, Great Britain tested a series of atomic bombs and weapons on Aboriginal tribal lands in Maralinga and Emu Field, in South Australia. The British made feeble attempts to clear the Aborigines from the test areas and then posted KEEP OUT signs—but many of the Aborigines didn't see the signs or couldn't read English. Aborigines throughout the region later reported hearing the bombs go off and feeling the ground shake. After one particular explosion, they saw a strange,

> " **T**he Aborigines say they can follow the trails of the songs left along their ancestors' footprints."

Waijara Spirit by Mandaark (1979).

Queensland Art Gallery, Brisbane, Australia.

dark cloud drifting across the sky, trickling streams of sticky dust. This cloud of radioactive fallout (which became known as the "Black Mist") drifted across the outback, and the whole area was contaminated with plutonium and other radioactive debris. Many Aborigines were stricken with terrible illnesses soon afterward. No one knows exactly how many cancers, stillbirths, and deaths resulted from the Aborigines' exposure to radioactive fallout.

Apparently, the Aborigines' tragic encounter with test bombs and "Black Mist" fit so well with their ancestor myth about hordes of maggots that the modern historical event was grafted onto the ancient story. And so a new, extraordinary folktale came into existence.

Collective Wisdom, World Saga

Each time someone tells a story in the folk tradition, it is changed at least slightly. (I've told the Aborigines' maggot/bomb tale in my own way, but I first read the story in a book called *The Songlines* by Bruce Chatwin.) Each storyteller has an individual "sound," pacing, and style. You can think of this "sound" as the storyteller's signature—there's no other signature quite like it. Try writing down your own version of the Aboriginal tale from memory. I guarantee that your telling will be different from mine, and from your classmates' versions.

Folktales are part of a group's **folklore,** the body of a people's popular, traditional knowledge that also includes their proverbs, nursery rhymes, folk songs, riddles, and even their superstitions. Folklore is woven into the fabric of every society in the world, from tribal cultures like the Aborigines of Australia to technological cultures like our own. We might even say that there's a "world saga" composed of a multitude of stories and songs describing people's fears, dreams, and values. This wealth of folklore, made by ourselves for ourselves, holds our collective wisdom and our personal vision of what the world means to us—or what we wish the world could be.

Universal Wishes and Fears

The folktales in this unit come from a variety of cultures from all over the world. As you read these Chinese, Japanese, Indian, Italian, Nigerian, Native American, and African American stories, you'll see that they share certain subjects, characters, plots, and themes. These recurring elements are called **motifs.** There are stories about the nature of wisdom, stories that explain how and why the world came to be the way it is, tales of wonder and magic, and tales of trickery and deceit. (See the list of common folktale motifs on the next page.)

In fact, remarkably similar stories, with remarkably similar char-

Illustration by Edmund Dulac for "The Story of the Fisherman" from *The Arabian Nights*.

acters, plots, and themes, can be found in every corner of the globe. (Did you realize that there are over four hundred versions of the Cinderella tale?) How can we explain these amazing similarities? Some scholars believe that most of the world's folktales originated in one place (perhaps India) and spread to other countries, carried by pilgrims, merchants, immigrants, and other travelers. Other people believe that similar stories have emerged independently in different places because they address universal wishes and fears that are bound to arise in all cultures. Probably, the answer lies in a combination of these two views.

Reading the Tales, Telling the Tales

When you've finished reading these stories, try telling one of them aloud to a friend or family member. How have you changed the tale? How is it different, simply because it's spoken rather than written? Now ask your listener to tell the same story to someone else . . .

The American storyteller Stephen Vincent Benét wrote that "folktales are as much a part of the real history of a country as proclamations and provisions and constitutional amendments." As you read these folktales, remember that they spring from the imaginations of ordinary people—people with stories to tell, people not that different from yourself. As long as there are people in this world, the urge to tell stories will exist, and the wide stream of folktales will flow on.

The Fairy Feller's Master-Stroke (detail) by Richard Dadd (1855–1864).

Tate Gallery, London.

Common Folktale Motifs

Threatened children
A false parent (wicked stepmother)
A supernatural helper (fairy godmother)
A supernatural adversary (dragon, giant, witch, demon)
Magic words, potion, or object
Magical transformations
Testing of the hero or heroine
A perilous journey
A threatened kingdom
Kindness rewarded
Evil punished
A helpful/grateful animal
A stupid ogre
A rescued princess (maiden in tower)
Deception and disguise

"As long as there are people in this world, the urge to tell stories will exist . . ."

The Wise and the Foolish

The philosopher Lieh Tzu (lyē dzu) teaches that all of us view the world based on what we think we know, which often is not the whole truth. This anecdote shows how quickly reason can be colored by emotion when our suspicions are aroused.

Here, a man finds a "scapegoat," that is, a person made to bear the blame or to suffer for someone else's crimes or misdeeds. Before you read, think about the ways "scapegoatism" is still alive today.

The Missing Axe

A Chinese Anecdote

Told by **Lieh Tzu,** *translated by* **Moss Roberts** *and* **C. N. Tay**

A man whose axe was missing suspected his neighbor's son. The boy walked like a thief, looked like a thief, and spoke like a thief. But the man found his axe while he was digging in the valley, and the next time he saw his neighbor's son, the boy walked, looked, and spoke like any other child.

Lantern Festival View by Ma Qiufang, Wangxia, China.

Courtesy China Books and Periodicals, San Francisco.

Night is followed by day, good is often followed by bad. Where there is beauty, there is also ugliness. Ease and hardship are two sides of a coin, and what we think is right may turn out to be wrong. The philosopher Liu An (lyōō än) bases this next anecdote on the philosophy called Tao (dow), or "the way." Tao is the first principle of the universe—the way of *doing nothing* (wu wei) or the way of *doing everything by doing nothing* (wei wu wei). According to Taoism, the universe is composed of opposites, of being and nonbeing. Think about your own life. Did anything good ever come out of a bad experience? Did anything bad ever result from something good?

The Lost Horse

A Chinese Anecdote

Told by **Liu An,** *translated by* **Moss Roberts** *and* **C. N. Tay**

A man who lived on the northern frontier of China was skilled in interpreting events. One day, for no reason, his horse ran away to the nomads across the border. Everyone tried to console him, but his father said, "What makes

Glazed pottery figure of a horse. Tang dynasty, China.

you so sure this isn't a blessing?" Some months later his horse returned, bringing a splendid nomad stallion. Everyone congratulated him, but his father said, "What makes you so sure this isn't a disaster?" Their household was richer by a fine horse, which the son loved to ride. One day he fell and broke his hip. Everyone tried to console him, but his father said, "What makes you so sure this isn't a blessing?"

A year later the nomads came in force across the border, and every able-bodied man took his bow and went into battle. The Chinese frontiersmen lost nine of every ten men. Only because the son was lame did father and son survive to take care of each other. Truly, blessing turns to disaster, and disaster to blessing: The changes have no end, nor can the mystery be fathomed.

The judge, or magistrate, was the lowest government official in the ancient Chinese imperial system based on the teachings of Confucius. The Taoist philosophers were critical of this system, which was often unjust and corrupt. However, this story pays tribute to a skilled judge. In order to catch a thief, this judge takes advantage of a basic principle of Confucian government—unquestioning trust in authority. Do you think it's all right for a government official to lie in order to achieve some good?

A Clever Judge

A Chinese Anecdote

Told by **Chang Shih-nan,** *translated by* **Moss Roberts** *and* **C. N. Tay**

In the days when Ch'en Shu-ku[1] was a magistrate in Chienchou,[2] there was a man who had lost an article of some value. A number of people were arrested, but no one could discover exactly who the thief was. So Shu-ku laid a trap for the suspects. "I know of a temple," he told them, "whose bell can tell a thief from an honest man. It has great spiritual powers."

The magistrate had the bell fetched and reverently enshrined in a rear chamber. Then he had the suspects brought before the bell to stand and testify to their guilt or innocence. He explained to them that if an innocent man touched the bell it would remain silent, but that if the man was guilty it would ring out.

Then the magistrate led his staff in solemn worship to the bell. The sacrifices concluded, he had the bell placed behind a curtain, while one of his assistants secretly smeared it with ink. After a time he took the suspects to the bell and had each one in turn extend his hands through the curtain and touch the bell. As each man withdrew his hands, Shu-ku examined them. Everyone's hands were stained except for those of one man, who confessed to the theft under questioning. He had not dared touch the bell for fear it would ring.

---

1. **Ch'en Shu-ku** (chen sho͞o·ko͞o).
2. **Chienchou** (jyen·jō).

The Seven Sages of the Bamboo Grove by Fu Pao-Shih (1904–1965).

Private collection.

Focusing on Connections
Confucianism and Taoism

The warring nomads that appear at the end of "The Lost Horse" were a fact of life in ancient China. When the Chou (jō) Dynasty collapsed around 800 B.C., China was plunged into chaos after three hundred years of stable rule. For the next five centuries, local princes warred among themselves. No one was safe because soldiers were paid according to the number of severed heads they presented to their commanders.

In the midst of this period of bloody turmoil, a great teacher was born: K'ung Fu-tzu (kung foo'dzu), more commonly known in the West as Confucius (551?–479 B.C.). Traveling from state to state, Confucius was determined to transform the social order of China—and he succeeded, though not during his lifetime. To this day, his ideas exert a powerful influence on Chinese life.

Confucius taught that society could be held together if individuals adhered to tradition and morality. In his writing, he stressed the importance of family, duty, obedience, respect for elders, and proper conduct in social relationships.

> Where there's nobility of spirit, there's beauty of character.
> Where there's beauty of character, there's a harmonious home.
> Where there's a harmonious home, there's an orderly nation.
> Where there's an orderly nation, there's peace in the world.
>
> —from *The Great Learning*

As Confucianism spread and transformed Chinese society, a less rigid, more mystical philosophy called Taoism rose up to challenge it. In fact, the conflict between these two great philosophies has given shape to Chinese culture. We know very little about Taoism's legendary founder, Lao Tzu (lou' dzu)—his name simply means "The Old Master." Scholars disagree on when he lived and even who he was. The traditional view is that Lao Tzu was born around 600 B.C.; no one knows when he died. Confucius supposedly met the old sage and came away bewildered by his ideas but full of respect for him. According to tradition, Lao Tzu's only written expression of his philosophy is a short, mystical book called the *Tao Te Ching* (dou de jing), or "The Way and Its Power." It is an exploration of the *Tao*—the mysterious "way" or "path" of the universe.

Though the two philosophies have much in common, Taoism differs from Confucianism on many basic points. Taoists objected to the Confucian stress on duty, social hierarchy, and materialism. They also rejected the Confucian emphasis on status and getting ahead in the world. Instead, Taoists valued humility and simplicity—"doing by not doing," freedom from desire. While Confucianism focused on relationships among people, Taoism stressed the relationship between people and nature. Most significantly, Taoists saw the world as fluid, made up of counterbalanced opposites flowing in and out of one another. This belief is embodied in the Yin and Yang symbol, the constantly spinning wheel of the universe that has come to symbolize Taoism itself. (Literally, *Yin* means the "dark side" and *Yang* means the "sunny side" of the hill.)

Another important distinction is that unlike Confucians, who made rigid distinctions between proper and improper social conduct, Taoists believed in the relativity of all values. In the Taoist tales you have just read, for example, nothing is fixed, nothing is what it seems at first glance. In "The Missing Axe," first the boy is a thief, and then he's not. In "The Lost Horse," the runaway horse is a disaster and then a blessing and then a disaster again—but ultimately it leads to salvation from those marauding nomads.

THE HAPPY MAN'S SHIRT

An Italian Tale

Told by **Italo Calvino,** *translated by* **George Martin**

We think material things will make us happy, and they certainly can. However, there are times when we have the material things we want, but we are still unhappy. Surely the son who has everything in this story should be happy. But happiness can-not be bought, and contentment needs no external sign. Before you read, write a few sentences in your journal defining what you think it means to be happy. (Say "Happiness is when _____" or "A happy person is someone who _____.")

A king had an only son that he thought the world of. But this prince was always unhappy. He would spend days on end at his window staring into space.

"What on earth do you lack?" asked the king. "What's wrong with you?"

"I don't even know myself, Father."

"Are you in love? If there's a particular girl you fancy, tell me, and I'll arrange for you to marry her, no matter whether she's the daughter of the most powerful king on earth or the poorest peasant girl alive!"

"No, Father, I'm not in love."

The king tried in every way imaginable to cheer him up, but theaters, balls, concerts, and singing were all useless, and day by day the rosy hue drained from the prince's face.

The king issued a decree, and from every corner of the earth came the most learned philosophers, doctors, and professors. The king showed them the prince and asked for their advice. The wise men withdrew to think, then returned to the king. "Majesty, we have given the matter close thought and we have studied the stars. Here's what you must do. Look for a happy man, a man who's happy through and through, and exchange your son's shirt for his."

That same day the king sent ambassadors to all parts of the world in search of the happy man.

A priest was taken to the king. "Are you happy?" asked the king.

"Yes, indeed, Majesty."

"Fine. How would you like to be my bishop?"

"Oh, Majesty, if only it were so!"

"Away with you! Get out of my sight! I'm seeking a man who's happy just as he is, not one who's trying to better his lot."

Thus the search resumed, and before long the king was told about a neighboring king, who everybody said was a truly happy man. He had a wife as good as she was beautiful and a whole slew of children. He had conquered all his enemies, and his country was at peace. Again hopeful, the king immediately sent ambassadors to him to ask for his shirt.

The neighboring king received the ambassadors and said, "Yes, indeed, I have everything anybody could possibly want. But at the same time I worry because I'll have to die one day and leave it all. I can't sleep at night for worrying about that!" The ambassadors thought it wiser to go home without this man's shirt.

At his wit's end, the king went hunting. He fired at a hare but only wounded it, and the hare scampered away on three legs. The king pursued it, leaving the hunting party far behind him. Out in the open field he heard a man singing a refrain. The king stopped in his tracks. "Whoever sings like that is bound to be happy!'' The song led him into a vineyard, where he found a young man singing and pruning the vines.

"Good day, Majesty,'' said the youth. "So early and already out in the country?''

"Bless you! Would you like me to take you to the capital? You will be my friend.''

"Much obliged, Majesty, but I wouldn't even consider it. I wouldn't even change places with the Pope.''

"Why not? Such a fine young man like you . . .''

"No, no, I tell you. I'm content with just what I have and want nothing more.''

"A happy man at last!'' thought the king. "Listen, young man. Do me a favor.''

"With all my heart, Majesty, if I can.''

"Wait just a minute,'' said the king, who, unable to contain his joy any longer, ran to get his retinue.[1] "Come with me! My son is saved! My son is saved!'' And he took them to the young man. "My dear lad,'' he began, "I'll give you whatever you want! But give me . . . give me . . .''

"What, Majesty?''

"My son is dying! Only you can save him. Come here!''

The king grabbed him and started unbuttoning the youth's jacket. All of a sudden he stopped, and his arms fell to his sides.

The happy man wore no shirt.

---

1. **retinue** (ret''n·o͞o', ret''n·yo͞o'): group of servants or followers attending an important person.

March (Gardening) from a Flemish calendar. Early sixteenth century.

By permission of The British Library, London.

Responding to the Folktales

Analyzing the Folktales

"The Missing Axe"
Interpreting Meanings
1. Describe the faulty reasoning that leads the man to conclude that his neighbor's son is a thief. How do you think the man felt about the boy *before* the axe disappeared?
2. What does this anecdote teach about the danger of distrust? Do you think the story has meaning for us today?

"The Lost Horse"
Interpreting Meanings
1. At first, the father in this tale seems to be a spoilsport—but as it turns out, he's the voice of wisdom. What does he believe is the true nature of life's blessings and disasters?
2. Based on your own experience, do you agree with the observation this tale makes about life's changing fortunes? Explain your opinion.

"A Clever Judge"
Interpreting Meanings
1. The magistrate's trick is like a modern-day "sting" operation, in which the police try to trap a criminal. In your opinion, is the magistrate justified in misleading innocent—or even guilty—citizens in order to catch the real thief? (Does the end justify the means?) Explain your reasoning.
2. Do you think this approach to justice would be dangerous in our own society today?
3. King Solomon, the Biblical ruler, is famous for his wisdom (see page 819). Once two women confronted the king, each claiming to be the mother of a baby. Read the account of how Solomon tricked the women into revealing who was telling the truth and who was lying (I Kings 3:16–28). Do you see any connections between Solomon's method of administering justice and that of the clever magistrate in this anecdote? Talk about your responses.

"The Happy Man's Shirt"
Interpreting Meanings
1. What does this tale suggest is the nature of true happiness? What do you think is the source of happiness?
2. The teller of this tale never reveals the reason for the prince's unhappiness. Do you have any theories that might explain it?

Writing About the Folktales

A Creative Response
Writing an Anecdote. An **anecdote** is a very short account of a particular incident. Teachers throughout the ages have used anecdotes to point out truths about life. "The Missing Axe," for example, is an anecdote that teaches the danger of suspicion. Try writing an anecdote of your own. Begin by jotting down some truth you want to teach. Then think of an incident that will get that idea across to your readers.

Reading About the Writers

Lieh Tzu (450–375 B.C.) was one of the three most important Taoist philosophers. Like many Chinese thinkers, Lieh Tzu used anecdotes, legends, folktales, allegories, and parables in his teachings.

Liu An (172?–122 B.C.), also known as the Prince of Huai-nan (hwī·nan), was a Taoist scholar and the grandson of the founder of the Han Dynasty (206 B.C.–221 A.D.).

Little is known about the life of **Chang Shih-nan** (jong shē·nan), other than that he lived during the Song (sōōng) Dynasty (960–1279).

Italo Calvino (1923–1985) is probably Italy's most renowned contemporary fiction writer. Though Calvino's earliest books are realistic in style, he soon turned to experiments that combine fantasy, folklore, philosophy, allegory, and science fiction. Calvino was inspired by fairy tales and fables, which he viewed as the model for all storytelling. Critics have described Calvino's tales as "legends for our time" and "fables for adults." Another story by Calvino appears on page 193.

Tales of Wonder

URASHIMA TARO

A Japanese Tale
Told by **Keigo Seki,** *translated by* **Robert J. Adams**

This ancient story may remind you of the American story of Rip Van Winkle, the man who went to sleep one day and woke up to find that twenty years had passed. In this tale from Japan, Urashima Taro makes a similar, shocking discovery.

This story is one of the most popular of all Japanese folktales. The Crane and Turtle Dances at Ise (ē·sā), mentioned at the end of the tale, are ritual dances performed at the oldest and most sacred shrine of Shinto, the chief religion of Japan.

Long ago a man named Urashima Taro lived at Kitamae Oshima. He lived with his mother, who was nearly eighty years old. He was a fisherman and was still unmarried. One day his mother said to him, "Urashima, Urashima, while I still have my health, won't you please take a bride."

"I am as yet unable to earn a living. Even if I took a bride, I could not support her; while you are still living, I shall continue fishing and go on living like this," he said.

The days and months passed, and the mother became eighty years old. Urashima was forty. It was autumn, and the north wind blew day after

Mountain View (detail). Watercolor.   By courtesy of the Board of Trustees of the Victoria and Albert Museum, London.

In the Well of the Great Wave by Katsushika Hokusai (1760–1849). Woodcut.

day so that it was impossible to go out to fish. Since he could catch no fish, he could make no money, and it began to appear that he would be unable even to get food for his mother. "Ah, if we could only have good weather tomorrow," he thought, as he lay around with nothing to do.

Suddenly the sky began to clear. Urashima Taro jumped up, climbed onto his raft, and set out to fish. He fished until it began to get light in the east, but he could not catch a single fish. He was greatly troubled, but as the sun rose higher in the sky, a large fish finally struck the hook. Quickly he hauled in the line and found that he had caught a turtle. The turtle clung to the end of the raft and made no move to go away.

"I thought maybe you were a sea bream, but you are only a turtle. Since you're here, no other fish will take the hook. Here, I'll take you off the hook; now please go away somewhere," said Urashima, throwing the turtle back into the sea.

Urashima lit his pipe and smoked as he continued fishing, but he caught nothing. He was greatly troubled, but just before noon it again felt as if a large fish had struck the hook. He hauled it in, and it was the turtle again. "No matter how much I ask him to go away, the turtle keeps coming back and the fish won't bite. I'm having very bad luck," he said and again chased the turtle away. Since he could not return home with nothing at all, he patiently kept fishing until midafternoon, when again something struck the hook. Thinking that surely this time it must be a fish, he hauled in the line and saw that it was the turtle again; so again he chased it away. It kept on like this until the sun began to set, and he had not caught a single fish. Soon the sun sank from sight, and he started home, wondering what to say to his mother.

He was paddling the raft along when he noticed a seagoing ship in the distance. For some reason or other it was coming toward him. Urashima steered his boat to starboard, and the ship did the same; he steered to port, and the seagoing ship also steered to port. Finally the ship came alongside Urashima's boat. The captain called out, "Urashima, please come on board this ship; we have come to you from the princess of Ryugu[1]."

"If I went to the dragon kingdom, my mother would be all alone, so I cannot go."

"We will see that your mother is well taken care of; please come on board our ship," urged the captain, and so Urashima, without further thought, boarded the ship.

As soon as Urashima was on board, the ship sank into the water and went to the world at the bottom of the sea. When Urashima arrived, he saw that there was a beautiful palace there; the princess came and, saying that he surely must be hungry, gave him a feast. "Please stay two or three days and enjoy yourself," she said. "Then you can return home."

Urashima saw that the princess and many other beautiful young girls were there; he was given new kimonos, and in this way days and months passed without his noticing, until three years had gone by. Urashima felt that he must return home. When he asked the princess if he might go, she gave him a three-tiered jewel box. "In case of necessity, you may open the box," she said. Then Urashima was put on board the seagoing ship, and they landed at a place similar to this one here, which looks like a mountain's nose.

Urashima went to his village and looked around, but even the face of the mountain had changed; the trees on the hills had died or disappeared. "How could all this have happened in only three years?" he thought to himself as he went to where his house was. There in a thatched house was an old man working with straw. Urashima entered the house, greeted the old man, and inquired about himself, asking, "Do you know a man by the name of Urashima?"

The old man replied, "There was a story that in my grandfather's time a man named Urashima went to the dragon kingdom at the bottom of the sea, but no matter how long his relatives waited, he never returned."

"What became of that man's mother?" asked Urashima and was told that she had died long, long ago.

Urashima went to see the remains of his own house. Only the stone wash basin and the garden steppingstones remained; other than that, there was nothing. Lost in reverie, he opened the lid of the box; in the first box there was a crane's feather. He opened the next box, and a puff of white smoke came from it; at this Urashima was turned into an old man. In the third box there was a mirror. He looked in the mirror and saw to his surprise that he had become an old man.

While he was looking in the mirror, the crane's feather from the first box attached itself to his back. He flew up into the sky and circled around his mother's grave. When he did this, the princess from the sea, who had turned herself into a turtle, came up on the beach to see him.

It is said that this is the origin of the Crane and Turtle Dance at Ise.

Steward Pouring Water to Make Tea by Harunobu (1724–1770).
Musée Guimet, Paris.

THE PEOPLE COULD FLY

An African American Tale

Told by **Virginia Hamilton**

In all of African American folklore, this tale is the most moving. It is a testament to millions of men, women, and children held in slavery—those who escaped and those who could not. There are many separate recorded fragments about flying Africans in black lore. Slaves "vanishing" under cover of darkness may be one explanation for these narratives about flight and disappearance. "Steal away home!" (an important phrase in the spiritual "Steal Away to Jesus!") could have been a code for *Escape!,* murmured from slave to slave.

There are numerous accounts of people flying in African American folklore. Angolan (Gullah) Africans, in particular, were believed by other slaves to have powerful magic and the ability to disappear at will.

As you read, think about who might have started telling this tale. Think also about those tale tellers of the early slave generations, who had only their imaginations to set them free.

They say the people could fly. Say that long ago in Africa, some of the people knew magic. And they would walk up on the air like climbin up on a gate. And they flew like blackbirds over the fields. Black, shiny wings flappin against the blue up there.

Then, many of the people were captured for Slavery. The ones that could fly shed their wings. They couldn't take their wings across the water on the slave ships. Too crowded, don't you know.

The folks were full of misery, then. Got sick with the up and down of the sea. So they forgot about flyin when they could no longer breathe the sweet scent of Africa.

Say the people who could fly kept their power, although they shed their wings. They kept their secret magic in the land of slavery. They looked the same as the other people from Africa who had been coming over, who had dark skin. Say you couldn't tell anymore one who could fly from one who couldn't.

One such who could was an old man, call him Toby. And standin tall, yet afraid, was a young woman who once had wings. Call her Sarah. Now Sarah carried a babe tied to her back. She trembled to be so hard worked and scorned.

The slaves labored in the fields from sunup to sundown. The owner of the slaves callin himself their Master. Say he was a hard lump of clay. A hard, glinty coal. A hard rock pile, wouldn't be moved. His Overseer on horseback pointed out the slaves who were slowin down. So the one called Driver cracked his whip over the slow ones to make them move faster. That whip was a slice-open cut of pain. So they did move faster. Had to.

Sarah hoed and chopped the row as the babe on her back slept.

Say the child grew hungry. That babe started up bawling too loud. Sarah couldn't stop to feed it. Couldn't stop to soothe and quiet it down. She let it cry. She didn't want to. She had no heart to croon to it.

"Keep that thing quiet," called the Overseer. He pointed his finger at the babe. The woman scrunched low. The Driver cracked his whip across the babe anyhow. The babe hollered like any hurt child, and the woman fell to the earth.

The old man that was there, Toby, came and helped her to her feet.

"I must go soon," she told him.

"Soon," he said.

Sarah couldn't stand up straight any longer. She was too weak. The sun burned her face. The babe cried and cried, "Pity me, oh, pity me," say it sounded like. Sarah was so sad and starvin, she sat down in the row.

"Get up, you black cow," called the Overseer. He pointed his hand, and the Driver's whip snarled around Sarah's legs. Her sack dress tore into rags. Her legs bled onto the earth. She couldn't get up.

Toby was there where there was no one to help her and the babe.

Into Bondage by Aaron Douglass (1936). Oil on canvas.

Evans-Tibbs Collection, Washington, D.C.

"Now, before it's too late," panted Sarah. "Now, Father!"

"Yes, Daughter, the time is come," Toby answered. "Go, as you know how to go!"

He raised his arms, holding them out to her. *"Kum . . . yali, kum buba tambe,"* and more magic words, said so quickly, they sounded like whispers and sighs.

The young woman lifted one foot on the air. Then the other. She flew clumsily at first, with the child now held tightly in her arms. Then she felt the magic, the African mystery. Say she rose just as free as a bird. As light as a feather.

The Overseer rode after her, hollerin. Sarah flew over the fences. She flew over the woods. Tall trees could not snag her. Nor could the Overseer. She flew like an eagle now, until she was gone from sight. No one dared speak about it. Couldn't believe it. But it was, because they that was there saw that it was.

Say the next day was dead hot in the fields. A young man slave fell from the heat. The Driver come and whipped him. Toby come over and spoke words to the fallen one. The words of ancient Africa once heard are never remembered completely. The young man forgot them as soon as he heard them. They went way inside him. He got up and rolled over on the air. He rode it awhile. And he flew away.

Another and another fell from the heat. Toby was there. He cried out to the fallen and reached his arms out to them. *"Kum kunka yali, kum . . . tambe!"* Whispers and sighs. And they too rose on the air. They rode the hot breezes. The ones flyin were black and shinin sticks, wheelin above the head of the Overseer. They crossed the rows, the fields, the fences, the streams, and were away.

"Seize the old man!" cried the Overseer. "I heard him say the magic *words*. Seize him!"

The one callin himself Master come runnin. The Driver got his whip ready to curl around old Toby and tie him up. The slaveowner took his hip gun from its place. He meant to kill old, black Toby.

But Toby just laughed. Say he threw back his head and said, "Hee, hee! Don't you know who I am? Don't you know some of us in this field?" He said it to their faces. "We are ones who fly!"

And he sighed the ancient words that were a dark promise. He said them all around to the others in the field under the whip, ". . . *buba yali . . . buba tambe. . . .*"

There was a great outcryin. The bent backs

Night Migration by Jean Lacy (1988).
Mixed media on museum board.

Collection of Mr. and Mrs. Richard Brettell.

straighted up. Old and young who were called slaves and could fly joined hands. Say like they would ring-sing. But they didn't shuffle in a circle. They didn't sing. They rose on the air. They flew in a flock that was black against the heavenly blue. Black crows or black shadows. It didn't matter, they went so high. Way above the plantation, way over the slavery land. Say they flew away to *Free-dom*.

And the old man, old Toby, flew behind them, takin care of them. He wasn't cryin. He wasn't laughin. He was the seer. His gaze fell on the plantation where the slaves who could not fly waited.

"Take us with you!" Their looks spoke it but they were afraid to shout it. Toby couldn't take them with him. Hadn't the time to teach them to fly. They must wait for a chance to run.

"Goodie-bye!" The old man called Toby spoke to them, poor souls! And he was flyin gone.

So they say. The Overseer told it. The one called Master said it was a lie, a trick of the light. The Driver kept his mouth shut.

The slaves who could not fly told about the people who could fly to their children. When they were free. When they sat close before the fire in the free land, they told it. They did so love firelight and *Free-dom*, and tellin.

They say that the children of the ones who could not fly told their children. And now, me, I have told it to you.

Responding to the Folktales

Analyzing the Folktales

"Urashima Taro"
Interpreting Meanings
1. Why do you suppose the princess summons Urashima to be her guest? (What connection do you see between the princess and the turtle Urashima keeps releasing from his hook?)
2. This tale contains several traditional Japanese **symbols.** For example, the crane represents long life, immortality, and faithfulness. The turtle stands for long life and good luck. The mirror is a Shinto symbol of purity and truth, and it often possesses magical properties. Think about these symbols and Urashima's transformation at the end of the story. In your opinion, is what happens to Urashima a punishment or a reward? (What is he being punished or rewarded for?) Explain your interpretation.
3. In many versions of this folktale, Urashima opens the box even though the princess has warned him not to. In these versions, the box contains only a puff of smoke, and Urashima suddenly grows old and dies. Which ending do you prefer? Why?

"The People Could Fly"
Interpreting Meanings
1. The people who could fly had forgotten their power. What do you think makes them remember it?
2. Were you surprised—or angry—that Toby didn't stay behind to help everyone escape? Do you think he made the right decision? Tell why.
3. Why do you think people have continued to tell this story? What relevance does it have to those who are suffering oppression today?

Writing About the Folktales

A Creative Response
1. **Writing a Tale of Transformation.** Transformation is a common **motif** in folklore and myth, where people are transformed into things like toads, beasts, snakes, flowers, and trees. Write a short tale about someone turning into something else—perhaps an animal or a flower or even the wind. Will the transformation be a reward or a punishment? Will it **symbolize** something—a spiritual awakening, a physical escape, or the imprisonment of the true self?

A Critical Response

2. **Comparing and Contrasting Folktales.** As tales of wonder, "Urashima Taro" and "The People Could Fly" use the same **motif**—transformation into birds—but for very different effects. Write an essay comparing and contrasting each tale's use of this motif. The following chart will help you organize your thoughts.

	"Urashima"	"People"
Reason for transformation (reward or punishment?)		
Character who causes transformation		
Result of transformation		
Symbolic meaning		

Reading About the Writers

Keigo Seki (1899–   ) (kā'gō sek'ē) is the leading folklore scholar of Japan. His three-volume collection of Japanese folktales includes two hundred and forty tales. He selected these tales from some fifteen thousand that had been collected by folklorists during the twentieth century. Seki chose versions that had been transcribed directly from oral storytellers. The only change he made was to translate the various regional dialects into standard Japanese.

Virginia Hamilton (1936–   ) is a celebrated author of children's and young adult books whose writing is flavored by her lifelong interest in folklore. The granddaughter of a man who escaped slavery, Hamilton was born in Yellow Springs, Ohio. She describes her extended family of storytellers in the introduction to this unit, which she wrote especially for this book.

In 1974 Hamilton won the prestigious Newbery Medal for her novel *M. C. Higgins, the Great.* It tells the story of a rural Ohio family threatened by the arrival of two outsiders. Her other novels include *The House of Dies Drear,* a mystery story about a boy who moves into a house that was once an Underground Railroad station; *The Planet of Junior Brown,* about a talented but troubled boy who runs away from home; and *Sweet Whispers, Brother Rush,* the story of a teen-ager whose dead uncle returns as a ghost.

Hamilton has also written several prize-winning collections of folktales (including *The People Could Fly*), plus a book of her own tales called *The All Jahdu Storybook,* about a magical character named Jahdu who was born in an oven beside two loaves of baking bread.

Focusing on Background
"I Wanted You to Understand the Horrors of Slavery"

"In doing research for my retelling of 'The People Could Fly,' I discovered that the tale is quite old. There are hundreds of reports about flying people, flying Africans. Some people say there used to be actual wing shops, where wings could be purchased to size!

"African words are used to tell 'The People Could Fly' tale. This device helped the enslaved Africans remember some of the languages of their homeland. Forbidden to speak their native languages on the New World plantations, the slaves spoke a combination of English, African jargon, and Caribbean colloquial speech called Gullah. (At one time, Gullah was a widely known black English.) The African words used in black folktales were meant to make magic and to keep the language and memories of the homeland alive.

"In my research, I also discovered that the old man who spoke the magic words and the young woman with the child were nameless, so I gave them names—Toby and Sarah. The name Toby is of African origin and means 'to make magic.'

"I wrote this tale because I wanted you to understand the horrors of slavery and to be touched by these courageous human beings, long gone, who spent their entire lives in bondage, as did their children. Because they wanted us to know and remember them, they told this tale.

"Proudly, the people who could fly have soared as high as dreams, with only their imaginations to set them free."

—Virginia Hamilton

HOW THE LEOPARD GOT HIS CLAWS

A Nigerian Tale

Told by **Chinua Achebe** *and* **John Iroaganachi**

The oral folktale is still an integral part of African life today. Those people who know the tales pass on their communal wisdom to their listeners. These listeners in turn are shaped by the stories, and then pass them on to yet another generation. This origin story is also a *por quoi* (pôr qwa′) or "how-and-why" story, one of the vast number of such tales in the classic African oral tradition.

Tales like this one explaining the origin of some feature of the world were told on all occasions—weddings, ceremonies for births, and religious rites. As you read this Nigerian tale, think about whether the story reflects any values held in our present society. Do we have an "In the beginning" account, in which everyone lives as friends in one harmonious "neighborhood"?

In the beginning . . . all the animals in the forest lived as friends. Their king was the leopard. He was strong, but gentle and wise. He ruled the animals well, and they all liked him.

At that time the animals did not fight one another. Most of them had no sharp teeth or claws. They did not need them. Even King Leopard had only small teeth. He had no claws at all.

Only the dog had big, sharp teeth. The other animals said he was ugly, and they laughed at him.

"It is foolish to carry sharp things in the mouth," said the tortoise.

"I think so too," said the goat.

The monkey jumped in and began to tease the dog.

"Don't worry, my dear friend," said the monkey. "You need your teeth to clear your farm."

The animals laughed at the monkey's joke.

When the farming season came round, King Leopard led the animals to their farmland. They

Arm jewel in the form of a leopard, probably part of a royal costume. Benin (Nigeria). Ivory and copper.

British Museum, London.

all worked hard to prepare their plots. At the end of the day, they returned home tired. They sat on log benches in the village square. As they rested they told stories and drank palm wine.

But soon it would be the rainy season, and the animals would have no shelter from the rain.

The deer took this problem to King Leopard. They talked about it for a long time. King Leopard decided to call the animals together to discuss it.

One bright morning . . . King Leopard beat his royal drum. When the animals heard the drum, they gathered at the village square. The tortoise was there. The goat was there too. The sheep, the grass-cutter, the monkey, the hedgehog, the baboon, the dog, and many others were there.

King Leopard greeted them and said, "I have called you together to plan how we can make ourselves a common shelter."

"This is a good idea," said the giraffe.

"Yes, a very good idea," said many other animals.

"But why do we need a common house?" said the dog. He had never liked King Leopard.

"The dog has asked a good question," said the duck. "Why do we need a common shelter?"

"We do need somewhere to rest when we return from our farms," replied King Leopard.

"And besides," said the goat, "we need a shelter from the rain."

"I don't mind being wet," said the duck. "In fact, I like it. I know that the goat does not like water on his body. Let him go and build a shelter."

"We need a shelter," said the monkey, jumping up and down in excitement.

"Perhaps we need one, perhaps we don't," said the lazy baboon sitting on the low fence of the square.

The dog spoke again. "We are wasting our time. Those who need a shelter should build it. I live in a cave, and it is enough for me." Then he walked away. The duck followed him out.

"Does anyone else want to leave?" asked King Leopard. No one answered or made a move to go.

"Very well," said King Leopard. "Let the rest of us build the village hall."

The animals soon scattered about to find building materials. The tortoise copied the pattern on his back and made the plan of the roof. The giant rat and mouse dug the foundation. Some animals brought sticks, some ropes, others made roof-mats.

As they built the house, they sang many happy songs. They also told many jokes. Although they worked very hard, everyone was merry.

After many weeks they finished the building.

It was a fine building. The animals were pleased with it. They agreed to open it with a very special meeting.

On the opening day the animals, their wives, and children gathered in the hall. King Leopard then made a short speech. He said: "This hall is yours to enjoy. You worked very hard together to build it. I am proud of you."

The animals clapped their hands and gave three cheers to their king.

From that day, they rested in their new hall whenever they returned from their farm.

But the dog and the duck kept away from the hall.

One morning the animals went to their farms as usual. King Leopard went to visit a chief in another village.

At first the sun was shining. Then strong winds began to blow. Dark clouds hid the sun. The first rain was coming. The songbirds stopped their singing. The humming insects became quiet. Lightning flashed across the dark clouds. Claps of thunder sounded. The rain poured and poured.

The animals in their farms saw the rain coming and began to hurry to the village hall.

The dog also saw the rain coming and returned to his cave. But it was a very, very heavy rain. Water began to enter the cave. Soon it was flooded.

The dog ran from one end of his cave to the other. But the water followed him everywhere. At last he ran out of the cave altogether and made straight for the hall of the animals.

The deer was already there. He was surprised to see the dog enter the hall.

"What do you want here?" said the deer to the dog.

"It is none of your business," replied the dog.

"It is my business," said the deer. "Please go out. This hall is for those who built it."

Then the dog attacked the deer and bit him with

his big, sharp teeth. The deer cried with pain. The dog seized him by the neck and threw him out into the rain.

The other animals came in one after the other.

The dog barked and threw each of them out. They stood together shivering and crying in the rain. The dog kept barking and showing his teeth.

Then the deer cried out:

> O Leopard our noble king,
> Where are you?
> Spotted king of the forest,
> Where are you?
> Even if you are far away
> Come, hurry home:
> The worst has happened to us
> The worst has happened to us . . . .
> The house the animals built
> The cruel dog keeps us from it,
> The common shelter we built
> The cruel dog keeps us from it,
> The worst has happened to us
> The worst has happened to us . . .

The cry of the deer rang out loud and clear. It was carried by the wind. King Leopard heard it on his way back from his journey and began to run towards the village hall.

As he got near, he saw the animals, wet and sheltering under a tree. They were all crying. As he got nearer still, he could see the dog walking up and down inside the hall.

King Leopard was very angry. "Come out of the hall at once," he said to the dog. The dog barked and rushed at him. They began to fight. The dog bit the leopard and tore his skin with his claws. King Leopard was covered with blood. The dog went back to the hall. He stood at the door barking and barking. "Who is next? Who! Who!" he barked.

King Leopard turned to the animals and said: "Let us go in together and drive out the enemy. He is strong, but he is alone. We are many. Together we can drive him out of our house."

But the goat said: "We cannot face him. Look at his strong teeth! He will only tear us to pieces!"

"The goat is right," said the animals. "He is too strong for us."

The tortoise stood up and said: "I am sure we are all sorry about what has happened to the leopard. But he was foolish to talk to the dog the way he did. It is foolish to annoy such a powerful person as the dog. Let us make peace with him. I don't know what you others think. But I think he should have been our king all along. He is strong; he is handsome. Let us go on our knees and salute him."

"Hear! Hear!" said all the animals. "Hail the dog!"

Tears began to roll down the face of the leopard. His heart was heavy. He loved the animals greatly. But they had turned their backs on him. Now he knew they were cowards. So he turned his back on them and went away. Because of his many wounds he was weak and tired. So he lay down after a while to rest under a tree, far from the village.

The animals saw him go. But they did not care. They were too busy praising their new king, the dog. The tortoise carved a new staff for him. The toad made a new song in his praise:

> The dog is great
> The dog is good
> The dog gives us our daily food.
> We love his head, we love his jaws
> We love his feet and all his claws.

The dog looked round the circle of animals and asked, "Where is the leopard?"

"We think he has gone away, O King," said the goat.

"Why? He has no right to go away," said the dog. "Nobody has a right to leave our village and its beautiful hall. We must all stay together."

"Indeed," shouted the animals, "We must stay together! The leopard must return to the village! Our wise king has spoken! It is good to have a wise king!"

The dog then called out the names of six strong animals and said to them: "Go at once and bring back the leopard. If he should refuse to follow you, you must drag him along. If we let him go, others may soon follow his wicked example until there is no one left in our village. That would be a very bad thing indeed. It is my duty as your king to make sure that we all live together. The leopard is a wicked animal. That is why he wants to go

*Kalila wa Dimna (Book of Fables)
of Bidpai: The Leopard's Court*
(detail). Mid-sixteenth century.
Opaque watercolor on paper.

The Metropolitan Museum of Art, New
York. The Nasli Heeramaneck
Collection. Gift of Alice Heeramaneck,
1981. (1981.373)

away and live by himself. It is our duty to stop him. Nobody has a right to go away from our village and our beautiful hall.''

''Nobody has a right to go away from the village,'' sang all the animals as the six messengers went to look for the leopard.

They found him resting under the tree beyond the village. Although he was wounded and weak he still looked like a king. So the six messengers stood at a little distance and spoke to him.

''Our new king, the dog, has ordered you to return to the village,'' they said.

''He says that no one has a right to leave the village,'' said the pig.

''Yes, no one has a right to leave our village and its beautiful hall,'' said the others.

The leopard looked at them with contempt. Then he got up slowly. The six animals fell back. But the leopard did not go towards them. He turned his back on them and began to go away— slowly and painfully. One of the animals picked up a stone and threw it at him. Then all the others immediately picked up stones and began to throw. As they threw they chanted: ''No one has a right to leave our village! No one has a right to leave our village!''

Although some of the stones hit the leopard and hurt him, he did not turn round even once.

He continued walking until he no longer heard the noise of the animals.

The leopard traveled seven days and seven nights. Then he came to the house of the blacksmith. The old man was sitting at his forge. The leopard said to him: "I want the strongest teeth you can make from iron. And I want the most deadly claws you can make from bronze."

The blacksmith said: "Why do you need such terrible things?" The leopard told his story. Then the blacksmith said: "I do not blame you."

The blacksmith worked a whole day on the teeth, and another full day on the claws. The leopard was pleased with them. He put them on and thanked the blacksmith. Then he left and went to the house of Thunder.

The leopard knocked at the door, and Thunder roared across the sky.

"I want some of your sound in my voice," said the leopard. "Even a little bit."

"Why do you want my sound in your voice?" asked Thunder. "And why have you got those terrible teeth and claws?"

The leopard told his story. "I do not blame you," said Thunder. He gave the sound to the leopard.

"Thank you for the gift," said the leopard. And he began his journey home.

The leopard journeyed for seven days and seven nights and returned to the village of the animals. There he found the animals dancing in a circle round the dog. He stood for a while watching them with contempt and great anger. They were too busy to notice his presence. He made a deep, terrifying roar. At the same time he sprang into the center of the circle. The animals stopped their song. The dog dropped his staff. The leopard seized him and bit and clawed him without mercy. Then he threw him out of the circle.

All the animals TREMBLED.

But they were too afraid to run. The leopard turned to them and said:

"You miserable worms. You shameless cowards. I was a kind and gentle king, but you turned against me. From today I shall rule the forest with terror. The life of our village is ended."

"What about our hall?" asked the tortoise with a trembling voice.

"Let everyone take from the hall what he put into it," said the leopard.

The animals began to weep as they had wept long ago in the rain. "Please forgive us, O Leopard," they cried.

"Let everyone take from the hall what he put into it," repeated the leopard. "And hurry up!" he thundered.

So the animals pulled their hall apart. Some carried away the wood, and some took the roofmats. Others took away doors and windows. The toad brought his talking drum and began to beat it to the leopard and to sing:

Alive or dead the leopard is king.
Beware my friend, don't twist his tail.

But the leopard roared like thunder and the toad dropped his drum and the animals scattered in the forest.

The dog had already run a long way when the leopard roared. Now he ran faster and faster. His body was covered with blood, and he was very, very weak. He wanted to stop and rest a little. But the fear of the leopard was greater than his weakness. So he staggered and fell and got up and staggered on and on and on. . . .

After many days the dog came to the house of the hunter.

"Please protect me from the leopard," he cried.

"What will you do for me in return?" asked the hunter.

"I will be your slave," said the dog. "Any day you are hungry for meat, I shall show you the way to the forest. There we can hunt together and kill my fellow animals."

"All right, come in," said the hunter.

Today the animals are no longer friends, but enemies. The strong among them attack and kill the weak. The leopard, full of anger, eats up anyone he can lay his hands on. The hunter, led by the dog, goes to the forest from time to time and shoots any animals he can find. Perhaps the animals will make peace among themselves someday and live together again. Then they can keep away the hunter, who is their common enemy.

HOW THE SNAKE GOT POISON

An African American Tale

Told by **Zora Neale Hurston**

This folktale can be found in Hurston's collection entitled *Mules and Men*. Most of the stories in this book are told on the porch of Mr. Joe Clarke's general store in Eatonville, Florida. There a group of black people are taking turns telling "big old lies" about Brer Rabbit, the Devil, Brer Fox, Sis Cat, and other "woodfolk" who walk and talk like "natural men" through the magic of "telling." The tale is recorded in one of many black folktelling vernaculars. It is a rich expression from the complex, imaginative lore of an oppressed people. I've replaced the *de*'s and *dem*'s (a popular convention of the 1930's, which many people today find offensive) with the *the*'s and *them*'s of ordinary usage. Be sure to read the story aloud.

Well, when God made the snake he put him in the bushes to ornament the ground. But things didn't suit the snake so one day he got on the ladder and went up to see God.

"Good mawnin', God."

"How do you do, Snake?"

"I ain't so many, God, you put me down there on my belly in the dust and everything trods upon me and kills off my generations. I ain't got no kind of protection at all."

God looked off toward immensity and thought about the subject for awhile. Then he said, "I didn't mean for nothin' to be stompin' you snakes like that. You got to have some kind of a protection. Here, take this poison and put it in your mouth and when they tromps on you, protect yourself."

So the snake took the poison in his mouth and went on back.

So after a while all the other varmints went up to God.

"Good evenin', God."

"How you makin' it, varmints?"

"God, please do somethin' 'bout that snake. He's layin' in the bushes there with poison in his mouth and he's strikin' everything that shakes the bush. He's killin' up our generations. We're scared to walk the earth."

So God sent for the snake and told him:

"Snake, when I give you that poison, I didn't mean for you to be hittin' and killin' everything that shakes the bush. I give you that poison and told you to protect yourself when they tromples on you. But you killin' everything that moves. I didn't mean for you to do that."

The snake say, "Lord, you know I'm down here in the dust. I ain't got no claws to fight with, and I ain't got no feet to get me out the way. All I can see is feet comin' to tromple me. I can't tell who my enemy is and who is my friend. You give me this protection in my mouth and I use it."

God thought it over for a while then he says:

"Well, Snake, I don't want your generations all stomped out and I don't want you killin' everything else that moves. Here, take this bell and tie it to your tail. When you hear feet comin' you ring your bell and if it's your friend, he'll be careful. If it's your enemy, it's you and him."

So that's how the snake got his poison and that's how come he got rattles.

Biddy, biddy, bend, my story is end.
Turn loose the rooster and hold the hen!

Responding to the Folktales

Analyzing the Folktales

"How the Leopard Got His Claws"
Interpreting Meanings
1. Do you think the animals are justified in turning their backs on the leopard? Is the leopard justified in his response to the animals' betrayal? Explain your opinions.
2. What kind of life do you suspect the animals would have led if the dog had remained king?
3. Who do you think deserves most of the blame for destroying the communal harmony the animals enjoyed "in the beginning": the dog, the leopard, the tortoise, or the rest of the animals? Why?
4. What **lessons** does this tale teach about what it takes to live together in harmony in the real world? What lessons does it teach about the nature of political power?

"How the Snake Got Poison"
Interpreting Meanings
1. What witty expressions and humorous **images** in this tale make you laugh?
2. Do you think this tale has something serious to say about how to deal with people who threaten you? Is this sound advice for individuals? For nations? Explain your opinion.

Writing About the Folktales

A Creative Response
Writing a How-and-Why Story. Write a brief imaginative tale explaining how a particular animal got the characteristics it has, or why it behaves the way it does. Here are some possibilities:

> Why birds build nests
> Why the frog has bulgy eyes
> Why the cat purrs
> How the porcupine got quills
> Why the skunk stinks

Rattlesnake #3 by William Hawkins (1988). Enamel paint and collage on masonite.

Courtesy Edward Thorp Gallery, New York.

Reading About the Writers

The Nigerian writer **Chinua Achebe** (1930–   ) is one of Africa's most acclaimed novelists. His great themes are the impact of European colonialism on traditional African society and the role of tribal values in modern urban life. Achebe says he began writing children's books because he was disturbed by what his daughter was reading at school. Though "How the Leopard Got His Claws" seems to be a simple tale for children, many readers have interpreted it as a political allegory about Nigeria.

John Iroaganachi (1940–   ) is a Nigerian writer and educator who has been actively involved in teaching and translating Ibo (also called Igbo), one of Nigeria's chief languages.

Zora Neale Hurston (1891–1960) was born and raised in Eatonville, Florida, the first self-governing black township in the United States. With $1.50 in her pocket, Hurston moved to New York City in 1925, during the height of the black cultural movement known as the Harlem Renaissance. Very soon, she began winning prizes for her writing. She also became famous for her wit, her flamboyance, and her hilarious tales of Southern life. While in New York, Hurston studied anthropology and folklore at Barnard College. Her field work recording Southern folktales and customs resulted in *Mules and Men*, the first book of black folklore by an African American.

During Hurston's lifetime, many African American writers accused her of ignoring racial oppression and of exposing black life to ridicule. In the late 1940's and '50's, Hurston slipped into obscurity and then poverty, as the new African American novels of protest made her writing seem old-fashioned. In the 1970's, however, years after Hurston had died in a welfare home in Florida, critics began reevaluating her work. Her writing is now seen as an affirmation of black culture, and she is considered one of the most distinctive voices in American literature.

Thirteen years after Hurston's death, the writer Alice Walker (see pages 129 and 429) tracked down her unmarked, overgrown grave in a cemetery in Ft. Pierce, Florida, and placed a tombstone on it. Walker had carved on the stone the words: "A genius of the South."

Focusing on Background
"Here Was This Perfect Book!"

The writer Alice Walker has been a key figure in the critical reevaluation of Zora Neale Hurston that began in the 1970's. Here is an excerpt from her foreword to a 1977 biography of Hurston by Robert E. Hemenway:

"When I read *Mules and Men* I was delighted. Here was this perfect book! The 'perfection' of it I immediately tested on my relatives, who are such typical black Americans they are useful for every sort of political, cultural, or economic survey. Very regular people from the South, rapidly forgetting their southern cultural inheritance in the suburbs and ghettos of Boston and New York, they sat around reading the book themselves, listening to me read the book, listening to each other read the book, and a kind of paradise was regained. For Zora's book gave them back all the stories they had forgotten or of which they had grown ashamed (told to us years ago by our parents and grandparents—not one of whom could *not* tell a story to make us weep, or laugh) and showed how marvelous, and, indeed, priceless, they are. *This is not exaggerated*. No matter how they read the stories Zora had collected, no matter how much distance they tried to maintain between themselves, as new sophisticates, and the lives their parents and grandparents lived, no matter how they tried to remain cool toward all Zora revealed, in the end they could not hold back the smiles, the laughter, the *joy* over who she was showing them to be: descendants of an inventive, joyous, courageous, and outrageous people: loving drama, appreciating wit, and, most of all, relishing the pleasure of each other's loquacious and *bodacious* company.

"This was my first indication of the quality I feel is most characteristic of Zora's work: racial health—a sense of black people as complete, complex, *undiminished* human beings, a sense that is lacking in so much black writing and literature. . . ."

—Alice Walker

COYOTE STEALS THE SUN AND MOON

A Zuni Tale

Told by **Alfonso Ortiz** *and* **Richard Erdoes**

Native Americans of the Zuni people tell this tale. Many Zuni live in the Southwest United States in settlements known as pueblos. They are descended from the prehistoric Anasazi peoples, who once lived in places like Mesa Verde and Canyon de Chelly. Coyote, the chief animal of the mythical age when animals were said to have talked, is a trickster who lives by his wits. He can also be at times a magician, a creator, and a culture hero.

In this story, he is portrayed as a trickster, and like a busybody, he "noses" where he shouldn't.

Among the various Pueblo tribes, men often wear masks and costumes to impersonate friendly ancestral spirits called *kachinas*. Coyote in this story is invited to watch a sacred kachina dance.

This story might remind you of the story of Pandora's box, in Greek mythology, in which the opening of a box brings misery to the world.

C oyote is a bad hunter who never kills anything. Once he watched Eagle hunting rabbits, catching one after another—more rabbits than he could eat. Coyote thought, "I'll team up with Eagle so I can have enough meat." Coyote is always up to something.

"Friend," Coyote said to Eagle, "we should hunt together. Two can catch more than one."

"Why not?" Eagle said, and so they began to hunt in partnership. Eagle caught many rabbits, but all Coyote caught was some little bugs.

At this time the world was still dark; the sun and moon had not yet been put in the sky. "Friend," Coyote said to Eagle, "no wonder I can't catch anything; I can't see. Do you know where we can get some light?"

"You're right, friend, there should be some light," Eagle said. "I think there's a little toward the west. Let's try and find it."

And so they went looking for the sun and moon.

A pipe carved in the shape of a dog. Discovered in 1915 during the excavation of Tremper Mound in Scioto County, Ohio, a prehistoric Hopewell Indian site.

They came to a big river, which Eagle flew over. Coyote swam and swallowed so much water that he almost drowned. He crawled out with his fur full of mud, and Eagle asked, "Why don't you fly like me?"

"You have wings, I just have hair," Coyote said. "I can't fly without feathers."

At last they came to a pueblo, where the Kachinas happened to be dancing. The people invited Eagle and Coyote to sit down and have something to eat while they watched the sacred dances. Seeing the power of the Kachinas, Eagle said, "I believe these are the people who have light."

Coyote, who had been looking all around, pointed out two boxes, one large and one small, that the people opened whenever they wanted light. To produce a lot of light, they opened the lid of the big box, which contained the sun. For less light, they opened the small box, which held the moon.

Coyote nudged Eagle. "Friend, did you see that? They have all the light we need in the big box. Let's steal it."

"You always want to steal and rob. I say we should just borrow it."

"They won't lend it to us."

"You may be right," said Eagle. "Let's wait till they finish dancing and then steal it."

After a while the Kachinas went home to sleep, and Eagle scooped up the large box and flew off. Coyote ran along trying to keep up, panting, his tongue hanging out. Soon he yelled up to Eagle, "Ho, friend, let me carry the box a little way."

"No, no," said Eagle, "you never do anything right."

He flew on, and Coyote ran after him. After a while Coyote shouted again: "Friend, you're my chief, and it's not right for you to carry the box; people will call me lazy. Let me have it."

"No, no, you always mess everything up." And Eagle flew on and Coyote ran along.

So it went for a stretch, and then Coyote started again. "Ho, friend, it isn't right for you to do this. What will people think of you and me?"

"I don't care what people think. I'm going to carry this box."

Again Eagle flew on and again Coyote ran after him. Finally Coyote begged for the fourth time: "Let me carry it. You're the chief, and I'm just Coyote. Let me carry it."

Eagle couldn't stand any more pestering. Also, Coyote had asked him four times, and if someone asks four times, you better give him what he wants. Eagle said, "Since you won't let up on me, go ahead and carry the box for a while. But promise not to open it."

"Oh, sure, oh yes, I promise." They went on as before, but now Coyote had the box. Soon Eagle was far ahead, and Coyote lagged behind a hill where Eagle couldn't see him. "I wonder what the light looks like, inside there," he said to himself. "Why shouldn't I take a peek? Probably there's something extra in the box, something good that Eagle wants to keep to himself."

And Coyote opened the lid. Now, not only was the sun inside, but the moon also. Eagle had put them both together, thinking that it would be easier to carry one box than two.

As soon as Coyote opened the lid, the moon escaped, flying high into the sky. At once all the plants shriveled up and turned brown. Just as quickly, all the leaves fell off the trees, and it was winter. Trying to catch the moon and put it back in the box, Coyote ran in pursuit as it skipped away from him. Meanwhile, the sun flew out and rose into the sky. It drifted far away, and the peaches, squashes, and melons shriveled up with cold.

Eagle turned and flew back to see what had delayed Coyote. "You fool! Look what you've done!" he said. "You let the sun and moon escape, and now it's cold." Indeed, it began to snow, and Coyote shivered. "Now your teeth are chattering," Eagle said, "and it's your fault that cold has come into the world."

It's true. If it weren't for Coyote's curiosity and mischief-making, we wouldn't have winter; we could enjoy summer all the time.

THE TIGER, THE BRAHMAN, AND THE JACKAL

An Indian Tale

Told by **Joseph Jacobs**

This beast fable comes from a cycle of Sanskrit tales from India called the *Panchatantra* (pan·chə·ton′trə) or the "Five Tantras" or "Books." The tales teach the art of wise ruling. They were intended as a conduct book of *artha* ("worldly wisdom") and were used to instruct the sons of royalty. The stories embody keen observations and general truths that glorify shrewd thinking.

The individual tales are told within the framework of a larger story. In this frame story, a king in southern India hires a Hindu priest to teach the king's three stupid sons how to be wise rulers.

The fable that follows uses the motif of the three questions. All of the main characters are clearly sketched. The one human character, the Brahman (brä′mən), is quite poor, although he is a member of the highest or priestly class of Hinduism. As you read, think about the kinds of real-life people that the tiger and the Brahman represent.

O nce upon a time, a tiger was caught in a trap. He tried in vain to get out through the bars, and rolled and bit with rage and grief when he failed.

By chance a poor Brahman came by.

"Let me out of this cage, oh, pious one!" cried the tiger.

"Nay, my friend," replied the Brahman mildly, "you would probably eat me if I did."

"Not at all!" swore the tiger with many oaths; "on the contrary, I should be forever grateful, and serve you as a slave!"

Now when the tiger sobbed and sighed and wept and swore, the pious Brahman's heart softened, and at last he consented to open the door of the cage. Out popped the tiger, and, seizing the

A Royal Tiger Hunt, India (detail) (1730–1734).
Opaque watercolors on paper.

Los Angeles County Museum of Art. Gift of Paul F. Walter.
M.85.297.3.

poor man, he cried, "What a fool you are! What is to prevent my eating you now, for after being cooped up so long I am just terribly hungry!"

In vain the Brahman pleaded for his life; the most he could gain was a promise to abide by the decision of the first three things he chose to question as to the justice of the tiger's action.

So the Brahman first asked a pipal tree[1] what it thought of the matter, but the pipal tree replied coldly: "What have you to complain about? Don't I give shade and shelter to everyone who passes by, and don't they in return tear down my branches to feed their cattle? Don't whimper—be a man!"

Then the Brahman, sad at heart, went farther afield till he saw a buffalo turning a well-wheel; but he fared no better from it, for it answered: "You are a fool to expect gratitude! Look at me! While I gave milk they fed me on cottonseed and oil-cake, but now I am dry they yoke me here, and give me refuse as fodder!"

The Brahman, still more sad, asked the road to give him its opinion.

"My dear sir," said the road, "how foolish you are to expect anything else! Here am I, useful to everybody, yet all, rich and poor, great and small, trample on me as they go past, giving me nothing but the ashes of their pipes and the husks of their grain!"

On this the Brahman turned back sorrowfully, and on the way he met a jackal, who called out: "Why, what's the matter, Mr. Brahman? You look as miserable as a fish out of water!"

The Brahman told him all that had occurred. "How very confusing!" said the jackal, when the recital was ended; "would you mind telling me over again, for everything has got so mixed up?"

The Brahman told it all over again, but the jackal shook his head in a distracted sort of way and still could not understand.

"It's very odd," said he, sadly, "but it all seems to go in at one ear and out at the other! I will go to the place where it all happened, and then perhaps I shall be able to give a judgment."

So they returned to the cage, by which the tiger

was waiting for the Brahman, and sharpening his teeth and claws.

"You've been away a long time!" growled the savage beast, "but now let us begin our dinner."

"*Our* dinner!" thought the wretched Brahman, as his knees knocked together with fright; "what a remarkably delicate way of putting it!"

"Give me five minutes, my lord!" he pleaded, "in order that I may explain matters to the jackal here, who is somewhat slow in his wits."

The tiger consented, and the Brahman began the whole story over again, not missing a single detail and spinning as long a yarn as possible.

"Oh, my poor brain! oh, my poor brain!" cried the jackal, wringing its paws. "Let me see! how did it all begin? You were in the cage, and the tiger came walking by——"

"Pooh!" interrupted the tiger, "what a fool you are! *I* was in the cage."

"Of course!" cried the jackal, pretending to tremble with fright; "yes! I was in the cage—no I wasn't—dear! dear! where are my wits? Let me see—the tiger was in the Brahman, and the cage came walking by—no, that's not it, either! Well, don't mind me, but begin your dinner, for I shall never understand!"

"Yes, you shall!" returned the tiger, in a rage at the jackal's stupidity; "I'll *make* you understand! Look here—I am the tiger——"

"Yes, my lord!"

"And that is the Brahman——"

"Yes, my lord!"

"And that is the cage——"

"Yes, my lord!"

"And I was in the cage—do you understand?"

"Yes—no— Please, my lord——"

"Well?" cried the tiger impatiently.

"Please, my lord!—how did you get in?"

"How!—why in the usual way, of course!"

"Oh, dear me!—my head is beginning to whirl again! Please don't be angry, my lord, but what is the usual way?"

At this the tiger lost patience and, jumping into the cage, cried: "This way! Now do you understand how it was?"

"Perfectly!" grinned the jackal, as he dexterously shut the door, "and if you will permit me to say so, I think matters will remain as they were!"

---

1. **pipal tree** (pē′pəl): an Indian fig tree.

Responding to the Folktales

Analyzing the Folktales

"Coyote Steals the Sun and Moon"
Interpreting Meanings
1. Besides day and night, what else are the sun and the moon associated with in this tale? Explain how Coyote disrupts the order of the world by opening the box.
2. Can you see any good coming from Coyote's actions in this tale—or did he really "mess everything up," as Eagle predicted he would?
3. Look up the ancient Greek myth of Pandora's Box. How is the Pandora story similar to this tale about Coyote? How is it different?

"The Tiger, the Brahman, and the Jackal"
Interpreting Meanings
1. In an animal fable, the **characters** usually represent human types. What kind of person do you think the tiger represents? The Brahman?
2. What **lesson** in worldly wisdom do you think the tiger's behavior demonstrates?
3. What political lesson would you say the jackal's behavior teaches?
4. Do you think the jackal's kind of cunning—pretended stupidity—can work in real-life situations? Explain.
5. What "tigers" have you noticed recently in world politics? What steps were taken to return them to their "cages"? In your opinion, were these steps wise or foolish?

Writing About the Folktales

A Creative Response
Writing a Trickster Tale. Try your hand at writing about a trickster. First decide on who or what your trickster will be, and then choose an adversary. (There are modern-day tricksters, such as Bugs Bunny and the diehard cartoon underdog Wile E. Coyote, Road Runner's adversary.) What does your trickster want? What threat does he or she face? Does your trickster come out ahead, or does the trick backfire? Is your trickster basically a hero or a villain? Read your tale aloud or tell it from memory during a class storytelling session. If you like to draw, you might illustrate your trickster tale.

Reading About the Writers

Alfonso Ortiz (1939–   ) was born on a Tewa pueblo in New Mexico called San Juan. Ortiz holds a doctorate in anthropology from the University of Chicago. He is the author of *The Tewa World* and *The Pueblo: Southwest*, a children's book that's part of a series on the Indians of North America.

Richard Erdoes (1912–   ) was born in Frankfurt, Germany. One of his first books was a biography of a Sioux medicine man named Lame Deer, whom Erdoes befriended while painting and photographing a Sioux reservation for *Life* magazine. "Coyote Steals the Sun and Moon" is from *American Indian Myths and Legends*, which Erdoes coedited with Ortiz.

Joseph Jacobs (1854–1916) was one of the leading folklorists and Jewish historians of his day. Born in Sydney, Australia, Jacobs lived in England for many years before immigrating to the United States in 1900. Look for his masterful retellings of English, Celtic, and Indian fairy tales.

Tender Years by Alvin Amason (1985). Oil on canvas.

Courtesy of Suzanne Brown Gallery, Phoenix, Arizona.

Literature & Language

Recognizing Storytelling Motifs

As you've seen in this unit, when people the world over tell stories, they often repeat certain subjects, themes, plots, and character types called **motifs**. The list on page 867 shows some of these recurring elements—folklorists have classified thousands of others.

The following tales contain a shared motif. "Bye-Bye" is from Haiti; "The Angel Wedding" is from Morocco.

Bye-Bye

All the birds were flying from Haiti to New York. But Turtle could not go, for he had no wings.

Pigeon felt sorry for Turtle and said, "Turtle, I'll take you with me. This is what we'll do. I'll hold in my mouth one end of a piece of wood and you hold on to the other end. But you must not let go. No matter what happens, do not let go or you'll fall into the water."

Pigeon took one end of a piece of wood and Turtle the other end. Up into the air Pigeon flew and Turtle with him, across the land and toward the sea.

As they came near the ocean, Turtle and Pigeon saw on the shore a group of animals who had gathered together to wave goodbye to the birds who were leaving. They were waving steadily until they noticed Turtle and Pigeon. Turtle? They stopped waving, and a great hubbub broke out.

"Look!" they cried to each other. "Turtle is going to New York. Even Turtle is going to New York!"

And Turtle was so pleased to hear everyone talking about him that he called out the one English word he knew:

"Bye-bye!"

Oh-oh. Turtle had opened his mouth, and in opening his mouth to speak, he let go of the piece of wood and fell into the sea.

For that reason there are many Pigeons in New York, but Turtle is still in Haiti.

—told by Diane Wolkstein

The Angel Wedding

Once the raven said to the tortoise, "Come, I'll carry you on my back and take you for a ride through the sky. Let's fly up and help the angels celebrate a wedding! We'll be back by evening."

The tortoise accepted the invitation and climbed behind the raven's wings. They set off, and when they had been flying for some time the raven asked, "Can you see paradise yet?" "No," said the tortoise. "What about the earth?" asked the raven. "The mountains look like rocks and the rivers like threads of silk," said the tortoise. "What does the earth look like now?" asked the raven after a while. "No larger than one of the round baskets that women carry on their heads to market," said the tortoise. "And now?" "Now it is like a bird's nest," answered the tortoise. The next time the raven asked the question, the tortoise said, "I see nothing except a mist like the blue smoke from a village bake oven."

When he heard this, the raven threw the tortoise off his back so that he fell and fell and fell down onto some sharp rocks. The raven swooped down after him and devoured him until nothing was left except his hard shell.

Such is what befalls him who would feast in heaven!

—told by Inea Bushnaq

Examining the Writers' Techniques

1. Explain how "Bye-Bye" is a **how-and-why story.**
2. What kind of tale is "The Angel Wedding"?
3. What would you say are the tales' **morals**?
4. What **motif** do the two tales share?
5. How do these tales connect with the myth of Daedalus and Icarus (page 798)?

Writing a Folktale

Writing a Tale. Write a **how-and-why** or **trickster tale** using one of the **motifs** on page 867. Share your tale in a storytelling session.

THE ELEMENTS OF A NOVEL

Blue Interior with Two Girls by Henri Matisse (1947).
Oil, 21½″ × 25¾″.

UNIT EIGHT   **John Leggett**

THE ELEMENTS OF A NOVEL

An introduction by **John Leggett**

A novelist is a person who lives in other people's skins.

—E. L. Doctorow

> " **T**hese episodic adventure novels all emphasize plot, just as the modern television soap opera does."

The word *novel* comes from the Latin word for "new" (*novellus*), and the novel as a literary form is still one of the newest developments among the literary genres. The novel rose in popularity several centuries ago—at the same time as the world's so-called "middle classes" were rising to social and political prominence in much of the world. Generally, these "middle classes" have favored a good story, a plain style that resembles actual speech, a moral theme, and characters with whom ordinary people can easily identify.

The first recognizable novels in the English language appeared in England in the middle of the eighteenth century. Among the most famous of these early novels are Daniel Defoe's *Robinson Crusoe;* Samuel Richardson's *Pamela, or Virtue Rewarded;* and Henry Fielding's *The History of Tom Jones.* These episodic adventure novels all emphasize plot, just as the modern television soap opera does. And they are about middle-class characters who resolve their dilemmas in accordance with accepted morality.

Considered as a worldwide phenomenon, however, the novel has much older sources that are not necessarily middle-class or moralistic in any obvious sense. Henry Fielding claims in his preface to *The Adventures of Joseph Andrews* that the novel could really be considered a descendant of Homer's *Iliad* and *Odyssey,* of Virgil's *Aeneid,* and of the other ancient epic narratives that, although written in verse rather than prose, were dominated by strong story lines. But there are two crucial differences between these epics and the novels that Fielding and his contemporaries produced. First, the eighteenth-century authors wrote about ordinary individuals, not lofty, larger-than-life gods or super-heroes: Odysseus was a king, but Robinson Crusoe was a seafarer, Pamela was a servant, and Tom Jones was an orphan boy. Second, these early novels were written in a relatively accessible, everyday language to entertain a diverse audience; the ancient epics were composed in elegant, dignified verse to sum up the history of an entire culture.

The New Novel by Winslow Homer (1877). Watercolor.

Museum of Fine Arts, Springfield, Massachusetts. The Horace P. Wright Collection.

Defining the Novel

It is not easy to define this "new" form called the novel, since it is a genre characterized by great variety and few rules. We can say with some confidence that the **novel** is a long narrative work of more than fifty thousand words written in prose. And we can suggest that its length makes it possible for **characters, plots,** and **themes** to be more fully developed than they are in short stories. Yet even this rather loose definition becomes shaky when we consider much of modern fiction. If Defoe and Fielding could be revived to read some recent novels, they might not recognize them as offspring of their own work. Just as modern painting distorts the reality we are used to, the modern novel often abandons plot and even characterization in favor of an impressionistic or stream-of-consciousness prose. At times the language itself seems to be the "subject" of the fiction. Some modern novels even come close to being "prose poems."

Early illustration from *Robinson Crusoe*.

A scene from the 1972 movie *A Separate Peace,* starring Parker Stevenson.

The Elements of a Novel

Yet we can still approach even modern novels through those elements of fiction that we have examined in short stories. In most novels the key elements are **character** and **plot.** In a sense, the interplay betweeen these two elements is somewhat like the proverbial relationship between the chicken and the egg—one develops from the other. A plot is a coherent series of related incidents, each of which results from the conflicts that come about when a character's desires are blocked in some way.

As we have seen in short fiction, **conflict** is what gives a story its energy, what propels the plot and keeps us reading. This is just as true in the novel as it is in the short story. In the simplest of novels, the conflict is likely to take place **externally** between the **protagonist** and another character or some hostile force in nature. In more complex novels, particularly modern novels, the conflict is more likely to be psychological, taking place **internally** between warring feelings within a single character's mind.

Another crucial element in a novel is its **setting.** Setting can offer clues to the social and economic backgrounds of the characters. It can also have a marked effect on the novel's mood, or **atmosphere.** In some novels, the setting even provides one side of the conflict. John Knowles's *A Separate Peace* is set at a boys' prep school in New Hampshire during World War II—a setting that might strike you as rather removed from your own experiences. Yet the novel has struck a chord with readers from all backgrounds, proving that even an elite setting can show us what is common to all humanity.

When we study a novel, we must always ask: What is this story, beneath its surface, really about? On the surface, *A Separate Peace* is about the tensions and rivalries in a friendship between two prep-school boys. Yet the real meaning of the novel—its **theme**—is what Knowles is using this relationship to say about human nature.

In our search for meaning, we will need to ask ourselves about two other elements that play important roles in prose fiction today: **point of view** and **tone.** As soon as the storyteller starts the novel, we should begin asking: From whose point of view is this narrative being told? Should I believe the narrator completely? What facets of the story might the narrator be ignorant of or biased about or unwilling to reveal? We also become aware of the tone created by the novel's point of view. Is it marked at all by **irony**? Is the story **satirical**—that is, does it ridicule human faults or social institutions? Or is the story simply an objective picture of life, devoid of any "comment" by the author?

What is so grand about the concept of the novel is that it has the possibility of capturing the essence and the truth about a particular society and a particular time in history. Every so often a novelist finds a character or a situation or a conflict that catches the imagination of us all, that tells us about our own lives, that makes us laugh and cry over our plight as human beings, and that clears up some of the mystery of our existence here on earth.

A SEPARATE PEACE

John Knowles

This story takes place many years ago in an imaginary New England prep school, a high school to which boys come from all over the country to prepare for college and for what their parents expect will be a privileged education and a privileged life.

Devon in this story is an old school with a proud tradition rooted in the hundreds of classes of boys who have gone forth over the years to assume responsibility as leaders of the nation, or so the school authorities hope. (There are no girls at Devon in 1942. As you read, you'll want to think about how a strong female character might have changed the outcome of this story.)

If a boy doesn't come to Devon with character, he may well learn it from the school itself—its very bricks and straight paths suggest the kind of men Devon intends to make of its students. The masters demand high standards in scholarship and behavior and a tough combativeness in sports.

But during these years of 1942 and 1943, there is a war on. It is a big war, World War II, and it is making people question the elite values of a school like Devon. The war is also reaching out for these teen-age boys; it is asking each one if he's yet ready to face a *real* battlefield, which, in its brutality and confusion, bears no resemblance to the games played on Devon's well-tended hockey and football fields.

Before you read the novel, write a paragraph about envy and friendship. Who is hurt more, the envied or the envier?

1

I went back to the Devon School not long ago, and found it looking oddly newer than when I was a student there fifteen years before. It seemed more sedate than I remembered it, more perpendicular and strait-laced, with narrower windows and shinier woodwork, as though a coat of varnish had been put over everything for better preservation. But, of course, fifteen years before there had been a war going on. Perhaps the school wasn't as well kept up in those days; perhaps varnish, along with everything else, had gone to war.

I didn't entirely like this glossy new surface, because it made the school look like a museum, and that's exactly what it was to me, and what I did not want it to be. In the deep, tacit way in which feeling becomes stronger than thought, I had always felt that the Devon School came into existence the day I entered it, was vibrantly real while I was a student there, and then blinked out like a candle the day I left.

Now here it was after all, preserved by some considerate hand with varnish and wax. Preserved along with it, like stale air in an unopened room, was the well-known fear which had surrounded and filled those days, so much of it that I hadn't even known it was there. Because, unfamiliar with the absence of fear and what that was like, I had not been able to identify its presence.

Looking back now across fifteen years, I could see with great clarity the fear I had lived in, which must mean that in the interval I had succeeded in a very important undertaking: I must have made my escape from it.

I felt fear's echo, and along with that I felt the unhinged, uncontrollable joy which had been its accompaniment and opposite face, joy which had broken out sometimes in those days like Northern Lights across black sky.

There were a couple of places now which I wanted to see. Both were fearful sites, and that was why I wanted to see them. So after lunch at the Devon Inn, I walked back toward the school. It was a raw, nondescript time of year, toward the end of November, the kind of wet, self-pitying November day when every speck of dirt stands out clearly. Devon luckily had very little of such weather—the icy clamp of winter, or the radiant New Hampshire summers, were more characteristic of it—but this day it blew wet, moody gusts all around me.

I walked along Gilman Street, the best street in town. The houses were as handsome and as unusual as I remembered. Clever modernizations of old Colonial manses,[1] extensions in Victorian wood, capacious Greek Revival[2] temples lined the street, as impressive and just as forbidding as ever. I had rarely seen anyone go into one of them, or anyone playing on a lawn, or even an open window. Today, with their failing ivy and stripped, moaning trees, the houses looked both more elegant and more lifeless than ever.

Like all old, good schools, Devon did not stand isolated behind walls and gates but emerged nat-

---

1. **manses:** parsonages; mansions.
2. **Greek Revival:** nineteenth-century style of architecture that imitated ancient Greek buildings.

urally from the town which had produced it. So there was no sudden moment of encounter as I approached it; the houses along Gilman Street began to look more defensive, which meant that I was near the school, and then more exhausted, which meant that I was in it.

It was early afternoon and the grounds and buildings were deserted, since everyone was at sports. There was nothing to distract me as I made my way across a wide yard, called the Far Commons, and up to a building as red brick and balanced as the other major buildings, but with a large cupola and a bell and a clock and Latin over the doorway—the First Academy Building.

In through swinging doors I reached a marble foyer, and stopped at the foot of a long white marble flight of stairs. Although they were old stairs, the worn moons in the middle of each step were not very deep. The marble must be unusually hard. That seemed very likely, only too likely, although with all my thought about these stairs, this exceptional hardness had not occurred to me. It was surprising that I had overlooked that, that crucial fact.

There was nothing else to notice; they of course were the same stairs I had walked up and down at least once every day of my Devon life. They were the same as ever. And I? Well, I naturally felt older—I began at that point the emotional examination to note how far my convalescence had gone—I was taller, bigger generally in relation to these stairs. I had more money and success and "security" than in the days when specters seemed to go up and down them with me.

I turned away and went back outside. The Far Common was still empty, and I walked alone down the wide gravel paths among those most Republican, bankerish of trees, New England elms, toward the far side of the school.

Devon is sometimes considered the most beautiful school in New England, and even on this dismal afternoon its power was asserted. It is the beauty of small areas of order—a large yard, a group of trees, three similar dormitories, a circle of old houses—living together in contentious harmony. You felt that an argument might begin again any time; in fact it had: out of the Dean's Residence, a pure and authentic Colonial house, there now sprouted an ell[3] with a big bare picture window. Someday the Dean would probably live entirely encased in a house of glass and be happy as a sandpiper. Everything at Devon slowly changed and slowly harmonized with what had gone before. So it was logical to hope that since the buildings and the Deans and the curriculum could achieve this, I could achieve, perhaps unknowingly already had achieved, this growth and harmony myself.

I would know more about that when I had seen the second place I had come to see. So I roamed on past the balanced red brick dormitories with webs of leafless ivy clinging to them, through a ramshackle salient[4] of the town which invaded the school for a hundred yards, past the solid gymnasium, full of students at this hour but silent as a monument on the outside, past the Field House, called The Cage—I remembered now what a mystery references to "The Cage" had been during my first weeks at Devon; I had thought it must be a place of severe punishment—and I reached the huge open sweep of ground known as the Playing Fields.

Devon was both scholarly and very athletic, so the playing fields were vast and, except at such a time of year, constantly in use. Now they reached soggily and emptily away from me, forlorn tennis courts on the left, enormous football and soccer and lacrosse fields in the center, woods on the right, and at the far end a small river detectable from this distance by the few bare trees along its banks. It was such a gray and misty day that I could not see the other side of the river, where there was a small stadium.

I started the long trudge across the fields and had gone some distance before I paid any attention to the soft and muddy ground, which was dooming my city shoes. I didn't stop. Near the center of the fields, there were thin lakes of muddy water which I had to make my way around, my unrecognizable shoes making obscene noises as I lifted them out of the mire. With nothing to block it, the wind flung wet gusts at me; at any other time, I would have felt like a fool slogging through mud and rain, only to look at a tree.

A little fog hung over the river so that as I neared it I felt myself becoming isolated from everything except the river and the few trees beside it. The wind was blowing more steadily here, and I was beginning to feel cold. I never wore a hat and had forgotten gloves. There were several trees bleakly reaching into the fog. Any one of them might have been the one I was looking for. Unbelievable that there were other trees which looked like it here. It had loomed in my memory as a huge lone spike dominating the riverbank, forbidding as an artillery piece, high as the beanstalk. Yet here was a scattered grove of trees, none of them of any particular grandeur.

Moving through the soaked, coarse grass, I began to examine each one closely, and finally identified the tree I was looking for by means of certain small scars rising along its trunk, and by a limb extending over the river, and another thinner limb growing near it. This was the tree, and it seemed to me standing there to resemble those men, the giants of your childhood, whom you encounter years later and find that they are not merely smaller in relation to your growth, but that they are absolutely smaller, shrunken by age. In this double demotion the old giants have become pigmies while you were looking the other way.

The tree was not only stripped by the cold season, it seemed weary from age, enfeebled, dry. I was thankful, very thankful that I had seen it. So the more things remain the same, the more they change after all—*plus c'est la même chose, plus ça change.*[5] Nothing endures, not a tree, not love, not even a death by violence.

Changed, I headed back through the mud. I was drenched; anybody could see it was time to come in out of the rain.

The tree was tremendous, an irate, steely black steeple beside the river. I was darned if I'd climb it. The heck with it. No one but Phineas could think up such a crazy idea.

---

3. **ell:** an extension to a building, usually at a right angle.
4. **salient** (sāl′yənt): here, a building that projects out from its surroundings.

5. *plus . . . change:* a reversal of the French expression "the more things change, the more they remain the same."

He, of course, saw nothing the slightest bit intimidating about it. He wouldn't, or wouldn't admit it if he did. Not Phineas.

"What I like best about this tree," he said in that voice of his, the equivalent in sound of a hypnotist's eyes, "what I like is that it's such a cinch!" He opened his green eyes wider and gave us his maniac look, and only the smirk on his wide mouth with its droll, slightly protruding upper lip reassured us that he wasn't completely goofy.

"Is that what you like best?" I said sarcastically. I said a lot of things sarcastically that summer; that was my sarcastic summer, 1942.

"Aey-uh," he said. This weird New England affirmative—maybe it is spelled "aie-huh"—always made me laugh, as Finny knew, so I had to laugh, which made me feel less sarcastic and less scared.

There were three others with us—Phineas in those days almost always moved in groups the size of a hockey team—and they stood with me looking with masked apprehension from him to the tree. Its soaring black trunk was set with rough wooden pegs leading up to a substantial limb which extended farther toward the water. Stand-ing on this limb, you could by a prodigious effort jump far enough out into the river for safety. So we had heard. At least the seventeen-year-old bunch could do it; but they had a crucial year's advantage over us. No Upper Middler, which was the name for our class in the Devon School, had ever tried. Naturally, Finny was going to be the first to try, and just as naturally, he was going to inveigle others, us, into trying it with him.

We were not even Upper Middler exactly. For this was the Summer Session, just established to keep up with the pace of the war. We were in shaky transit that summer from the groveling status of Lower Middlers to the near-respectability of Upper Middlers. The class above, seniors, draft-bait, practically soldiers, rushed ahead of us toward the war. They were caught up in accelerated courses and first-aid programs and a physical hardening regimen, which included jumping from this tree. We were still calmly, numbly reading Virgil[6] and playing tag in the river farther downstream. Until Finny thought of the tree.

---

6. **Virgil** (70–19 B.C.): Latin poet, author of the *Aeneid*.

We stood looking up at it, four looks of consternation, one of excitement. "Do you want to go first?" Finny asked us, rhetorically. We just looked quietly back at him, and so he began taking off his clothes, stripping down to his underpants. For such an extraordinary athlete—even as a Lower Middler Phineas had been the best athlete in the school—he was not spectacularly built. He was my height—five feet eight and a half inches (I had been claiming five feet nine inches before he became my roommate, but he had said in public with that simple, shocking self-acceptance of his, "No, you're the same height I am, five-eight and a half. We're on the short side"). He weighed a hundred and fifty pounds, a galling ten pounds more than I did, which flowed from his legs to torso around shoulders to arms and full strong neck in an uninterrupted, unemphatic unity of strength.

He began scrambling up the wooden pegs nailed to the side of the tree, his back muscles working like a panther's. The pegs didn't seem strong enough to hold his weight. At last he stepped onto the branch which reached a little farther toward the water. "Is this the one they jump from?" None of us knew. "If I do it, you're all going to do it, aren't you?" We didn't say anything very clearly. "Well," he cried out, "here's my contribution to the war effort!" and he sprang out, fell through the tops of some lower branches, and smashed into the water.

"Great!" he said, bobbing instantly to the surface again, his wet hair plastered in droll bangs on his forehead. "That's the most fun I've had this week. Who's next?"

I was. This tree flooded me with a sensation of alarm all the way to my tingling fingers. My head began to feel unnaturally light, and the vague rustling sounds from the nearby woods came to me as though muffled and filtered. I must have been entering a mild state of shock. Insulated by this, I took off my clothes and started to climb the pegs. I don't remember saying anything. The branch he had jumped from was slenderer than it looked from the ground and much higher. It was impossible to walk out on it far enough to be well over the river. I would have to spring far out or risk falling into the shallow water next to the bank. "Come on," drawled Finny from below, "stop standing there showing off." I recognized with automatic tenseness that the view was very impressive from here. "When they torpedo the troopship," he shouted, "you can't stand around admiring the view. Jump!"

What was I doing up here anyway? Why did I let Finny talk me into stupid things like this? Was he getting some kind of hold over me?

"Jump!"

With the sensation that I was throwing my life away, I jumped into space. Some tips of branches snapped past me and then I crashed into the water. My legs hit the soft mud of the bottom, and immediately I was on the surface being congratulated. I felt fine.

"I think that was better than Finny's," said Elwin—better known as Leper—Lepellier, who was bidding for an ally in the dispute he foresaw.

"All right, pal," Finny spoke in his cordial, penetrating voice, that reverberant instrument in his chest, "don't start awarding prizes until you've passed the course. The tree is waiting."

Leper closed his mouth as though forever. He didn't argue or refuse. He didn't back away. He became inanimate. But the other two, Chet Douglass and Bobby Zane, were vocal enough, complaining shrilly about school regulations, the danger of stomach cramps, physical disabilities they had never mentioned before.

"It's you, pal," Finny said to me at last, "just you and me." He and I started back across the fields, preceding the others like two seigneurs.[7]

We were the best of friends at that moment.

"You were very good," said Finny good-humoredly, "once I shamed you into it."

"You didn't shame anybody into anything."

"Oh yes I did. I'm good for you that way. You have a tendency to back away from things otherwise."

"I never backed away from anything in my life!" I cried, my indignation at this charge naturally stronger because it was so true. "You're goofy!"

Phineas just walked serenely on, or rather flowed on, rolling forward in his white sneakers with such unthinking unity of movement that "walk" didn't describe it.

I went along beside him across the enormous playing fields toward the gym. Underfoot, the healthy green turf was brushed with dew, and ahead of us we could see a faint green haze hanging above the grass, shot through with the twilight sun. Phineas stopped talking for once, so that now I could hear cricket noises and bird cries of dusk, a gymnasium truck gunning along an empty athletic road a quarter of a mile away, a burst of faint, isolated laughter carried to us from the back door of the gym, and then over all, cool and matriarchal, the six o'clock bell from the Academy Building cupola, the calmest, most carrying bell toll in the world, civilized, calm, invincible, and final.

The toll sailed over the expansive tops of all

---

7. **seigneurs** (sen·yəz): feudal lords.

the elms, the great slanting roofs and formidable chimneys of the dormitories, the narrow and brittle old housetops, across the open New Hampshire sky to us coming back from the river. "We'd better hurry or we'll be late for dinner," I said, breaking into what Finny called my "West Point[8] stride." Phineas didn't really dislike West Point in particular or authority in general, but just considered authority the necessary evil against which happiness was achieved by reaction, the backboard which returned all the insults he threw at it. My "West Point stride" was intolerable; his right foot flashed into the middle of my fast walk and I went pitching forward into the grass. "Get those hundred and fifty pounds off me!" I shouted, because he was sitting on my back. Finny got up, patted my head genially, and moved on across the field, not deigning to glance around for my counterattack, but relying on his extrasensory ears, his ability to feel in the air someone coming on him from behind. As I sprang at him he side-stepped easily, but I just managed to kick him as I shot past. He caught my leg and there was a brief wrestling match on the turf, which he won. "Better hurry," he said, "or they'll put you in the guardhouse." We were walking again, faster; Bobby and Leper and Chet were urging us from ahead for heaven's sake to hurry up, and then Finny trapped me again in his strongest trap; that is, I suddenly became his collaborator. As we walked rapidly along I abruptly resented the bell and my West Point stride and hurrying and conforming. Finny was right. And there was only one way to show him this. I threw my hip against his, catching him by surprise, and he was instantly down, definitely pleased. This was why he liked me so much. When I jumped on top of him, my knees on his chest, he couldn't ask for anything better. We struggled in some equality for a while, and then, when we were sure we were too late for dinner, we broke off.

He and I passed the gym and came on toward the first group of dormitories, which were dark and silent. There were only two hundred of us at Devon in the summer, not enough to fill most of the school. We passed the sprawling Headmaster's house—empty, he was doing something for the government in Washington; past the Chapel—empty again, used only for a short time in the mornings; past the First Academy Building, where there were some dim lights shining from a few of its many windows, masters at work in their classrooms there; down a short slope into the broad and well-clipped Common, on which light fell from the big surrounding Georgian[9] buildings. A dozen boys were loafing there on the grass after dinner, and a kitchen rattle from the wing of one of the buildings accompanied their talk. The sky was darkening steadily, which brought up the lights in the dormitories and the old houses; a loud phonograph a long way off played "Don't Sit Under the Apple Tree," rejected that and played "They're Either Too Young or Too Old," grew more ambitious with *The Warsaw Concerto,* mellower with *The Nutcracker Suite,* and then stopped.

Finny and I went to our room. Under the yellow study lights we read our Hardy[10] assignments; I was halfway through *Tess of the D'Urbervilles,* he carried on his baffled struggle with *Far from the Madding Crowd,* amused that there should be people named Gabriel Oak and Bathsheba Everdene. Our illegal radio, turned too low to be intelligible, was broadcasting the news. Outside there was a rustling early-summer movement of the wind; the seniors, allowed out later than we were, came fairly quietly back as the bell sounded ten stately times. Boys ambled past our door toward the bathroom, and there was a period of steadily pouring shower water. Then lights began to snap out all over the school. We undressed, and I put on some pajamas, but Phineas, who had heard they were unmilitary, didn't; there was the silence in which it was understood we were saying some prayers, and then that summer school day came to an end.

2

Our absence from dinner had been noticed. The following morning—the clean-washed shine of summer mornings in the north country—Mr. Prud'homme stopped at our door. He was broad-shouldered, grave, and he wore a gray business suit. He did not have the careless, almost British look of most of the Devon masters, because he was a substitute for the summer. He enforced such rules as he knew; missing dinner was one of them.

We had been swimming in the river, Finny explained; then there had been a wrestling match,

---

8. **West Point:** U.S. Military Academy.

9. **Georgian:** eighteenth-century style of architecture characterized by red brick and white or green wooden trim.
10. **Hardy:** Thomas Hardy (1840–1928), English novelist and poet.

then there was that sunset that anybody would want to watch, then there'd been several friends we had to see on business—he rambled on, his voice soaring and plunging in its vibrant sound box, his eyes now and then widening to fire a flash of green across the room. Standing in the shadows, with the bright window behind him, he blazed with sunburned health. As Mr. Prud'homme looked at him and listened to the scatterbrained eloquence of his explanation, he could be seen rapidly losing his grip on sternness.

"If you hadn't already missed nine meals in the last two weeks . . ." he broke in.

But Finny pressed his advantage. Not because he wanted to be forgiven for missing the meal—that didn't interest him at all, he might have rather enjoyed the punishment if it was done in some novel and unknown way. He pressed his advantage because he saw that Mr. Prud'homme was pleased, won over in spite of himself. The master was slipping from his official position momentarily, and it was just possible, if Phineas pressed hard enough, that there might be a flow of simple, unregulated friendliness between them, and such flows were one of Finny's reasons for living.

"The real reason, sir, was that we just had to jump out of that tree. You know that tree . . ." I knew, Mr. Prud'homme must have known, Finny knew, if he stopped to think, that jumping out of the tree was even more forbidden than missing a meal. "We had to do that, naturally," he went on, "because we're all getting ready for the war. What if they lower the draft age to seventeen? Gene and I are both going to be seventeen at the end of the summer, which is a very convenient time since it's the start of the academic year and there's never any doubt about which class you should be in. Leper Lepellier is already seventeen, and if I'm not mistaken he will be draftable before the end of this next academic year, and so conceivably he ought to have been in the class ahead, he ought to have been a senior now, if you see what I mean, so that he would have been graduated and been all set to be drafted. But we're all right, Gene and I are perfectly all right. There isn't any question that we are conforming in every possible way to everything that's happening and everything that's going to happen. It's all a question of birthdays, unless you want to be more specific and look at it from the sexual point of view, which I have never cared to do myself, since it's a question of my mother and my father, and I have never felt I wanted to think about their sexual lives too much." Everything he said was true and sincere; Finny always said what he happened to be thinking, and if this stunned people, then he was surprised.

Mr. Prud'homme released his breath with a sort of amazed laugh, stared at Finny for a while, and that was all there was to it.

This was the way the masters tended to treat us that summer. They seemed to be modifying their usual attitude of floating, chronic disapproval. During the winter most of them regarded anything unexpected in a student with suspicion, seeming to feel that anything we said or did was potentially illegal. Now on these clear June days in New Hampshire, they appeared to uncoil, they seemed to believe that we were with them about half the time, and only spent the other half trying to make fools of them. A streak of tolerance was detectable; Finny decided that they were beginning to show commendable signs of maturity.

It was partly his doing. The Devon faculty had never before experienced a student who combined a calm ignorance of the rules with a winning urge to be good, who seemed to love the school truly and deeply, and never more than when he was breaking the regulations, a model boy who was most comfortable in the truant's corner. The faculty threw up its hands over Phineas, and so loosened its grip on all of us.

But there was another reason. I think we reminded them of what peace was like, we boys of sixteen. We were registered with no draft board, we had taken no physical examinations. No one had ever tested us for hernia or colorblindness. Trick knees and punctured eardrums were minor complaints and not yet disabilities which would separate a few from the fate of the rest. We were careless and wild, and I suppose we could be thought of as a sign of the life the war was being fought to preserve. Anyway, they were more indulgent toward us than at any other time; they snapped at the heels of the seniors, driving and molding and arming them for the war. They noticed our games tolerantly. We reminded them of what peace was like, of lives which were not bound up with destruction.

Phineas was the essence of this careless peace. Not that he was unconcerned about the war. After Mr. Prud'homme left, he began to dress; that is, he began reaching for whatever clothes were nearest, some of them mine. Then he stopped to consider and went over to the dresser. Out of one of the drawers he lifted a finely woven broadcloth shirt, carefully cut, and very pink.

"What's *that* thing?"

"This is a tablecloth," he said out of the side of his mouth.

"No, cut it out. What is it?"

"This," he then answered with some pride, "is going to be my emblem. Ma sent it up last week. Did you ever see stuff like this, and a color like this? It doesn't even button all the way down. You have to pull it over your head, like this."

"Over your head? Pink! It makes you look like a *fairy*!"

"Does it?" He used this preoccupied tone when he was thinking of something more interesting than what you had said. But his mind always recorded what was said and played it back to him when there was time, so as he was buttoning the high collar in front of the mirror he said mildly, "I wonder what would happen if I looked like a fairy to everyone."

"You're nuts."

"Well, in case suitors begin clamoring at the door, you can tell them I'm wearing this as an emblem." He turned around to let me admire it. "I was reading in the paper that we bombed Central Europe for the first time the other day." Only someone who knew Phineas as well as I did could realize that he was not changing the subject. I waited quietly for him to make whatever fantastic connection there might be between this and his shirt. "Well, we've got to do something to *celebrate*. We haven't got a flag, we can't float Old Glory proudly out the window. So I'm going to wear this, as an emblem."

He did wear it. No one else in the school could have done so without some risk of having it torn from his back. When the sternest of the Summer Sessions masters, old Mr. Patch-Withers, came up to him after history class and asked about it, I watched his drawn but pink face become pinker with amusement as Finny politely explained the meaning of the shirt.

It was hypnotism. I was beginning to see that Phineas could get away with anything. I couldn't help envying him that a little, which was perfectly normal. There was no harm in envying even your best friend a little.

In the afternoon Mr. Patch-Withers, who was substitute Headmaster for the summer, offered the traditional term tea to the Upper Middle class. It was held in the deserted Headmaster's house, and Mr. Patch-Withers' wife trembled at every cup tinkle. We were in a kind of sun porch and conservatory combined, spacious and damp and without many plants. Those there were had large nonflowering stalks, with big barbaric leaves. The chocolate brown wicker furniture shot out menacing twigs, and three dozen of us stood tensely teetering our cups amid the wicker and leaves, trying hard not to sound as inane in our conversation with the four present masters and their wives as they sounded to us.

Phineas had soaked and brushed his hair for the occasion. This gave his head a sleek look, which was contradicted by the surprised, honest expression which he wore on his face. His ears, I had never noticed before, were fairly small and set close to his head, and combined with his plastered hair, they now gave his bold nose and cheekbones the sharp look of a prow.

He alone talked easily. He discussed the bombing of Central Europe. No one else happened to have seen the story, and since Phineas could not recall exactly what target in which country had been hit, or whether it was the American, British, or even Russian air force which had hit it, or what day he read it in which newspaper, the discussion was one-sided.

That didn't matter. It was the event which counted. But after a while Finny felt he should carry the discussion to others. "I think we ought to bomb the daylights out of them, as long as we don't hit any women or children or old people, don't you?" he was saying to Mrs. Patch-Withers, perched nervously behind her urn. "Or hospitals," he went on. "And naturally no schools. Or churches."

"We must also be careful about works of art," she put in, "if they are of permanent value."

"A lot of nonsense," Mr. Patch-Withers grumbled, with a flushed face. "How do you expect our boys to be as precise as that thousands of feet up with bombs weighing tons! Look at what the Germans did to Amsterdam! Look at what they did to Coventry!"

"The Germans aren't the Central Europeans, dear," his wife said very gently.

He didn't like being brought up short. But he seemed to be just able to bear it, from his wife. After a temperamental pause he said gruffly, "There isn't any 'permanent art' in Central Europe anyway."

Finny was enjoying this. He unbuttoned his seersucker jacket, as though he needed greater body freedom for the discussion. Mrs. Patch-Withers' glance then happened to fall on his belt. In a tentative voice she said, "Isn't that the . . . our . . ." Her husband looked; I panicked. In his haste that morning, Finny had not unexpectedly used a tie for a belt. But this morning the first tie at hand had been the Devon School tie.

This time he wasn't going to get away with it. I could feel myself becoming unexpectedly excited at that. Mr. Patch-Withers' face was reaching a brilliant shade, and his wife's head fell as though before the guillotine. Even Finny seemed to color a little, unless it was the reflection from his pink shirt. But his expression was composed, and he said in his resonant voice, "I wore this, you see, because it goes with the shirt and it all ties in together—I didn't mean that to be a pun, I don't think they're very funny, especially in polite company, do you?—it all ties in together with what we've been talking about, this bombing in Central Europe, because when you come right down to it the school is involved in everything that happens in the war, it's all the same war and the same world, and I think Devon ought to be included. I don't know whether you think the way I do on that.''

Mr. Patch-Withers' face had been shifting expressions and changing colors continuously, and now it settled into fixed surprise. ''I never heard anything so illogical as that in my life!'' He didn't sound very indignant, though. ''That's probably the strangest tribute this school has had in a hundred and sixty years.'' He seemed pleased or amused in some unknown corner of his mind. Phineas was going to get away with even this.

His eyes gave their wider, magical gleam and his voice continued on a more compelling level, ''Although I have to admit I didn't think of that when I put it on this morning.'' He smiled pleasantly after supplying this interesting additional information. Mr. Patch-Withers settled into a hearty silence at this, and so Finny added, ''I'm glad I put on *something* for a belt! I certainly would hate the embarrassment of having my pants fall down at the Headmaster's tea. Of course he isn't here. But it would be just as embarrassing in front of you and Mrs. Patch-Withers,'' and he smiled politely down at her.

Mr. Patch-Withers' laughter surprised us all, including himself. His face, whose shades we had often labeled, now achieved a new one. Phineas was very happy; sour and stern Mr. Patch-Withers had been given a good laugh for once, and he had done it! He broke into the charmed, thoughtless grin of a man fulfilled.

He had gotten away with everything. I felt a sudden stab of disappointment. That was because I just wanted to see some more excitement; that must have been it.

We left the party, both of us feeling fine. I laughed along with Finny, my best friend, and also unique, able to get away with anything at all. And not because he was a conniver either; I was sure of that. He got away with everything because of the extraordinary kind of person he was. It was quite a compliment to me, as a matter of fact, to have such a person choose me for his best friend.

Finny never left anything alone, not when it was well enough, not when it was perfect. ''Let's go jump in the river,'' he said under his breath as we went out of the sun porch. He forced compliance by leaning against me as we walked along, changing my direction; like a police car squeezing me to the side of the road, he directed me unwill-ingly toward the gym and the river. ''We need to clear our heads of that party,'' he said, ''all that talk!''

''Yes. It sure was boring. Who did most of the talking anyway?''

Finny concentrated. ''Mr. Patch-Withers was pretty gassy, and his wife, and . . .''

''Yeah. And?''

Turning a look of mock shock on me, ''You don't mean to imply that *I* talked too much!''

Returning, with interest, his gaping shock,

"You? Talk too much? How can you accuse me of accusing you of that!" As I said, this was my sarcastic summer. It was only long after that I recognized sarcasm as the protest of people who are weak.

We walked along through the shining afternoon to the river. "I don't really believe we bombed Central Europe, do you?" said Finny thoughtfully. The dormitories we passed were massive and almost anonymous behind their thick layers of ivy, big, old-looking leaves you would have thought stayed there winter and summer, permanent hanging gardens in New Hampshire. Between the buildings, elms curved so high that you ceased to remember their height until you looked above the familiar trunks and the lowest umbrellas of leaves and took in the lofty complex they held high above, branches and branches of branches, a world of branches with an infinity of leaves. They too seemed permanent and never-changing, an untouched, unreachable world high in space, like the ornamental towers and spires of a great church, too high to be enjoyed, too high for anything, great and remote and never useful. "No, I don't think I believe it either," I answered.

Far ahead of us, four boys, looking like white flags on the endless green playing fields, crossed toward the tennis courts. To the right of them, the gym meditated behind its gray walls, the high, wide, oval-topped windows shining back at the sun. Beyond the gym and the fields began the woods, our, the Devon School's woods, which in my imagination were the beginning of the great northern forests. I thought that, from the Devon Woods, trees reached in an unbroken, widening corridor so far to the north that no one had ever seen the other end, somewhere up in the far unorganized tips of Canada. We seemed to be playing on the tame fringe of the last and greatest wilderness. I never found out whether this is so and perhaps it is.

Bombs in Central Europe were completely unreal to us here, not because we couldn't imagine it—a thousand newspaper photographs and newsreels had given us a pretty accurate idea of such a sight—but because our place here was too fair for us to accept something like that. We spent that summer in complete selfishness, I'm happy to say. The people in the world who could be selfish in the summer of 1942 were a small band, and I'm glad we took advantage of it.

"The first person who says anything unpleasant will get a swift kick in the butt," said Finny reflectively as we came to the river.

"All right."

"Are you still afraid to jump out of the tree?"

"There's something unpleasant about that question, isn't there?"

"That question? No, of course not. It depends on how you answer it."

"Afraid to jump out of that tree? I expect it'll be a very pleasant jump."

After we had swum around in the water for a while Finny said, "Will you do me the pleasure of jumping out of the tree first?"

"My pleasure."

Rigid, I began climbing the rungs, slightly reassured by having Finny right behind me. "We'll jump together to cement our partnership," he said. "We'll form a suicide society, and the membership requirement is one jump out of this tree."

"A suicide society," I said stiffly. "The Suicide Society of the Summer Session."

"Good! The *Super* Suicide Society of the Summer Session! How's that?"

"That's fine, that's okay."

We were standing on a limb, I a little farther out than Finny. I turned to say something else, some stalling remark, something to delay even a few seconds more, and then I realized that in turning I had begun to lose my balance. There was a moment of total, impersonal panic, and then Finny's hand shot out and grabbed my arm, and with my balance restored, the panic immediately disappeared. I turned back toward the river, moved a few more steps along the limb, sprang far out and fell into the deep water. Finny also made a good jump, and the Super Suicide Society of the Summer Session was officially established.

It was only after dinner, when I was on my way alone to the library, that the full danger I had brushed on the limb shook me again. If Finny hadn't come up right behind me . . . if he hadn't been there . . . I could have fallen on the bank and broken my back! If I had fallen awkwardly enough I could have been killed. Finny had practically saved my life.

3

Yes, he had practically saved my life. He had also practically lost it for me. I wouldn't have been on that limb except for him. I wouldn't have turned around, and so lost my balance, if he hadn't been there. I didn't need to feel any tremendous rush of gratitude toward Phineas.

The Super Suicide Society of the Summer Session was a success from the start. That night Finny began to talk abstractly about it, as though it were a venerable, entrenched institution of the

Devon School. The half-dozen friends who were there in our room listening began to bring up small questions on details without ever quite saying that they had never heard of such a club. Schools are supposed to be catacombed with secret societies and underground brotherhoods, and, as far as they knew, here was one which had just come to the surface. They signed up as "trainees" on the spot.

We began to meet every night to initiate them. The Charter Members, he and I, had to open every meeting by jumping ourselves. This was the first of the many rules which Finny created without notice during the summer. I hated it. I never got inured to the jumping. At every meeting the limb seemed higher, thinner, the deeper water harder to reach. Every time, when I got myself into position to jump, I felt a flash of disbelief that I was doing anything so perilous. But I always jumped. Otherwise I would have lost face with Phineas, and that would have been unthinkable.

We met every night, because Finny's life was ruled by inspiration and anarchy, and so he prized a set of rules. His own, not those imposed on him by other people, such as the faculty of the Devon School. The Super Suicide Society of the Summer Session was a club; clubs by definition met regularly; we met every night. Nothing could be more regular than that. To meet once a week seemed to him much less regular, entirely too haphazard, bordering on carelessness.

I went along; I never missed a meeting. At that time it would never have occurred to me to say, "I don't feel like it tonight," which was the plain truth every night. I was subject to the dictates of my mind, which gave me the maneuverability of a strait jacket. "We're off, pal," Finny would call out, and acting against every instinct of my nature, I went without a thought of protest.

Scene from the 1972 movie *A Separate Peace*, starring Parker Stevenson.

As we drifted on through the summer, with this one inflexible appointment every day—classes could be cut, meals missed, chapel skipped—I noticed something about Finny's own mind, which was such an opposite from mine. It wasn't completely unleashed after all. I noticed that he did abide by certain rules, which he seemed to cast in the form of Commandments. "Never say you are five feet nine when you are five feet eight and a half" was the first one I encountered. Another was, "Always say some prayers at night because it might turn out that there is a God."

But the one which had the most urgent influence in his life was, "You always win at sports." This "you" was collective. Everyone always won at sports. When you played a game you won, in the same way as when you sat down to a meal you ate it. It inevitably and naturally followed. Finny never permitted himself to realize that when you won, they lost. That would have destroyed the perfect beauty which was sport. Nothing bad ever happened in sports; they were the absolute good.

He was disgusted with that summer's athletic

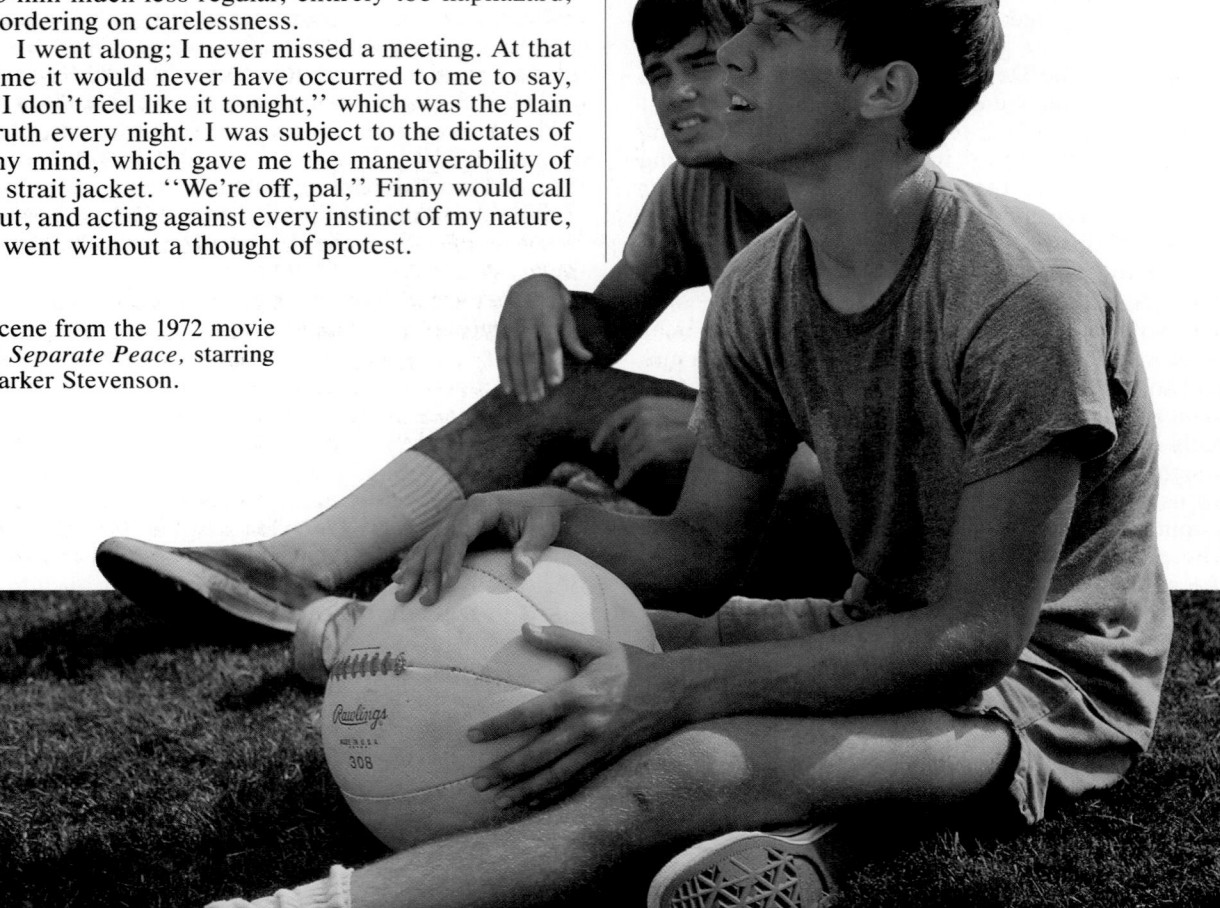

program—a little tennis, some swimming, clumsy softball games, badminton. "Badminton!" he exploded the day it entered the schedule. He said nothing else, but the shocked, outraged, despairing note of anguish in the word said all the rest. *"Badminton!"*

"At least it's not as bad as the seniors," I said, handing him the fragile racquet and the fey shuttlecock. "They're doing calisthenics."

"What are they trying to do?" He swatted the shuttlecock the length of the locker room. "Destroy us?" Humor infiltrated the outrage in his voice, which meant that he was thinking of a way out.

We went outside into the cordial afternoon sunshine. The playing fields were optimistically green and empty before us. The tennis courts were full. The softball diamond was busy. A pattern of badminton nets swayed sensually in the breeze. Finny eyed them with quiet astonishment. Far down the field toward the river there was a wooden tower about ten feet high where the instructor had stood to direct the senior calisthenics. It was empty now. The seniors had been trotted off to the improvised obstacle course in the woods, or to have their blood pressure taken again, or to undergo an insidious exercise in The Cage which consisted of stepping up on a box and down again in rapid rhythm for five minutes. They were off somewhere, shaping up for the war. All of the fields were ours.

Finny began to walk slowly in the direction of the tower. Perhaps he was thinking that we might carry it the rest of the way to the river and throw it in; perhaps he was just interested in looking at it, as he was in everything. Whatever he thought, he forgot it when we reached the tower. Beside it someone had left a large and heavy leather-covered ball, a medicine ball.[1]

He picked it up. "Now this, you see, is everything in the world you need for sports. When they discovered the circle, they created sports. As for this thing," embracing the medicine ball in his left arm, he held up the shuttlecock, contaminated, in his outstretched right, "this idiot tickler, the only thing it's good for is eeny-meeny-miney-mo." He dropped the ball and proceeded to pick the feathers out of the shuttlecock, distastefully, as though removing ticks from a dog. The remaining rubber plug he then threw out of sight down the field, with a single lunge ending in a powerful downward thrust of his wrist. Badminton was gone.

He stood balancing the medicine ball, enjoying the feel of it. "All you really need is a round ball."

Although he was rarely conscious of it, Phineas was always being watched, like the weather. Up the field, the others at badminton sensed a shift in the wind; their voices carried down to us, calling us. When we didn't come, they began gradually to come down to us.

"I think it's about time we started to get a little *exercise* around here, don't you?" he said, cocking his head at me. Then he slowly looked around at the others with the expression of dazed determination he used when the object was to carry people along with his latest idea. He blinked twice, and then said, "We can always start with this ball."

"Let's make it have something to do with the war," suggested Bobby Zane. "Like a blitzkrieg[2] or something."

"Blitzkrieg," repeated Finny doubtfully.

"We could figure out some kind of blitzkrieg baseball," I said.

"We'll call it blitzkrieg ball," said Bobby.

"Or just blitzball," reflected Finny. "Yes, blitzball." Then, with an expectant glance around, "Well, let's get started," he threw the big, heavy ball at me. I grasped it against my chest with both arms. "Well, run!" ordered Finny. "No, not *that* way! Toward the river! Run!" I headed toward the river surrounded by the others in a hesitant herd; they sensed that in all probability they were my adversaries in blitzball. "Don't hog it!" Finny yelled. "Throw it to somebody else. Otherwise, naturally," he talked steadily as he ran along beside me, "now that we've got you surrounded, one of us will knock you down."

"Do what!" I veered away from him, hanging on to the clumsy ball. "What kind of a game is that?"

"Blitzball!" Chet Douglass shouted, throwing himself around my legs, knocking me down.

"That, naturally, was completely illegal," said Finny. "You don't use your *arms* when you knock the ball carrier down."

"You don't?" mumbled Chet from on top of me.

"No. You keep your arms crossed like this on your chest, and you just butt the ball carrier. No elbowing allowed either. All right, Gene, start again."

I began quickly, "Wouldn't somebody else have possession of the ball after——"

---

1. **medicine ball:** so named because it's used for conditioning exercises.

2. **blitzkrieg** (blits′krēg): sudden, large-scale attack intended to win a quick victory; German for "lightning war."

"Not when you've been knocked down illegally. The ball carrier retains possession in a case like that. So it's perfectly okay, you still have the ball. Go ahead."

There was nothing to do but start running again, with the others trampling with stronger will around me. "Throw it!" ordered Phineas. Bobby Zane was more or less in the clear and so I threw it at him; it was so heavy that he had to scoop my throw up from the ground. "Perfectly okay," commented Finny, running forward at top speed, "perfectly okay for the ball to touch the ground when it is being passed." Bobby doubled back closer to me for protection. "Knock him down," Finny yelled at me.

"Knock him down! Are you crazy? He's on my team!"

"There aren't any teams in blitzball," he yelled somewhat irritably, "we're all enemies. Knock him down!"

I knocked him down. "All right," said Finny as he disentangled us. "Now you have possession again." He handed the leaden ball to me.

"I would have thought that possession passed—"

"Naturally you gained possession of the ball when you knocked him down. Run."

So I began running again. Leper Lepellier was loping along outside my perimeter, not noticing the game, tagging along without reason, like a porpoise escorting a passing ship. "Leper!" I threw the ball past a few heads at him.

Taken by surprise, Leper looked up in anguish, shrank away from the ball, and voiced his first thought, a typical one. "I don't want it!"

"Stop, stop!" cried Finny in a referee's tone. Everybody halted, and Finny retrieved the ball; he talked better holding it. "Now Leper has just brought out a really important fine point of the game. The receiver can *refuse* a pass if he happens to choose to. Since we're all enemies, we can and will turn on each other all the time. We call that the Lepellier Refusal." We all nodded without speaking. "Here, Gene, the ball is of course still yours."

"Still mine? Nobody else has had the ball but me, for heaven sakes!"

"They'll get their chance. Now if you are refused three times in the course of running from the tower to the river, you go all the way back to the tower and start over. Naturally."

Blitzball was the surprise of the summer. Everybody played it; I believe a form of it is still popular at Devon. But nobody can be playing it as it was played by Phineas. He had unconsciously invented a game which brought his own athletic

gifts to their highest pitch. The odds were tremendously against the ball carrier, so that Phineas was driven to exceed himself practically every day when he carried the ball. To escape the wolf pack which all the other players became, he created reverses and deceptions and acts of sheer mass hypnotism which were so extraordinary that they surprised even him; after some of these plays I would notice him chuckling quietly to himself, in a kind of happy disbelief. In such a nonstop game he also had the natural advantage of a flow of energy which I never saw interrupted. I never saw him tired, never really winded, never overcharged and never restless. At dawn, all day long, and at midnight, Phineas always had a steady and formidable flow of usable energy.

Right from the start, it was clear that no one had ever been better adapted to a sport than Finny was to blitzball. I saw that right away. Why not? He had made it up, hadn't he? It needn't be surprising that he was sensationally good at it, and that the rest of us were more or less bumblers in our different ways. I suppose it served us right for letting him do all the planning. I didn't really think about it myself. What difference did it make? It was just a game. It was good that Finny could shine at it. He could also shine at many other things, with people for instance, the others in our dormitory, the faculty; in fact, if you stopped to think about it, Finny could shine with everyone, he attracted everyone he met. I was glad of that too. Naturally. He was my roommate and my best friend.

Everyone has a moment in history which belongs particularly to him. It is the moment when his emotions achieve their most powerful sway over him, and afterward when you say to this person "the world today" or "life" or "reality" he will assume that you mean this moment, even if it is fifty years past. The world, through his unleashed emotions, imprinted itself upon him, and he carries the stamp of that passing moment forever.

For me, this moment—four years is a moment in history—was the war. The war was and is reality for me. I still instinctively live and think in its atmosphere. These are some of its characteristics: Franklin Delano Roosevelt is the President of the United States, and he always has been. The other two eternal world leaders are Winston Churchill[3] and Josef Stalin.[4] America is not, never has been,

---

3. **Winston Churchill** (1874–1965): prime minister of Great Britain during World War II.
4. **Josef Stalin** (1879–1953): Communist dictator of the Soviet Union.

and never will be what the songs and poems call it, a land of plenty. Nylon, meat, gasoline, and steel are rare. There are too many jobs and not enough workers. Money is very easy to earn but rather hard to spend, because there isn't very much to buy. Trains are always late and always crowded with "servicemen." The war will always be fought very far from America and it will never end. Nothing in America stands still for very long, including the people, who are always either leaving or on leave. People in America cry often. Sixteen is the key and crucial and natural age for a human being to be, and people of all other ages are ranged in an orderly manner ahead of and behind you as a harmonious setting for the sixteen-year-olds of this world. When you are sixteen, adults are slightly impressed and almost intimidated by you. This is a puzzle, finally solved by the realization that they foresee your military future, fighting for them. You do not foresee it. To waste anything in America is immoral. String and tinfoil are treasures. Newspapers are always crowded with strange maps and names of towns, and every few months the earth seems to lurch from its path when you see something in the newspapers, such as the time Mussolini, who had al-

most seemed one of the eternal leaders, is photographed hanging upside down on a meathook.[5] Everyone listens to news broadcasts five or six times every day. All pleasurable things, all travel and sports and entertainment and good food and fine clothes, are in the very shortest supply, always were and always will be. There are just tiny fragments of pleasure and luxury in the world, and there is something unpatriotic about enjoying them. All foreign lands are inaccessible except to servicemen; they are vague, distant, and sealed off as though behind a curtain of plastic. The prevailing color of life in America is a dull, dark green called olive drab. That color is always respectable and always important. Most other colors risk being unpatriotic.

It is this special America, a very untypical one I guess, an unfamiliar transitional blur in the memories of most people, which is the real America for me. In that short-lived and special country, we spent this summer at Devon when Finny achieved

---

5. **Mussolini . . . meathook:** Benito Mussolini (1883–1945), Italy's Fascist dictator during World War II, was executed by members of the Resistance. His body was hung upside down on public display.

certain feats as an athlete. In such a period no one notices or rewards any achievements involving the body unless the result is to kill it or save it on the battlefield, so that there were only a few of us to applaud and wonder at what he was able to do.

One day he broke the school swimming record. He and I were fooling around in the pool, near a big bronze plaque marked with events for which the school kept records—50 yards, 100 yards, 220 yards. Under each was a slot with a marker fitted into it, showing the name of the record-holder, his year, and his time. Under "100 Yards Free Style" there was "A. Hopkins Parker—1940—53.0 seconds."

"A. Hopkins Parker?" Finny squinted up at the name. "I don't remember any A. Hopkins Parker."

"He graduated before we got here."

"You mean that record has been up there the *whole time* we've been at Devon, and nobody's busted it yet?" It was an insult to the class, and Finny had tremendous loyalty to the class, as he did to any group he belonged to, beginning with him and me and radiating outward past the limits of humanity toward spirits and clouds and stars.

No one else happened to be in the pool. Around us gleamed white tile and glass brick; the green, artificial-looking water rocked gently in its shining basin, releasing vague chemical smells and a sense of many pipes and filters; even Finny's voice, trapped in this closed, high-ceilinged room, lost its special resonance and blurred into a general well of noise gathered up toward the ceiling. He said blurringly, "I have a feeling *I* can swim faster than A. Hopkins Parker."

We found a stopwatch in the office. He mounted a starting box, leaned forward from the waist as he had seen racing swimmers do but never had occasion to do himself—I noticed a preparatory looseness coming into his shoulders and arms, a controlled ease about his stance which was unexpected in anyone trying to break a record. I said, "On your mark—Go!" There was a complex moment when his body uncoiled and shot forward with sudden metallic tension. He planed up the pool, his shoulders dominating the water while his legs and feet rode so low that I couldn't distinguish them; a wake rippled hurriedly by him and then at the end of the pool his position broke, he relaxed, dived, an instant's confusion and then his suddenly and metallically tense body shot back toward the other end of the pool. Another turn and up the pool again—I noticed no particular slackening of his pace—another turn, down the pool again, his hand touched the end, and he looked up at me with a composed, interested expression. "Well, how did I do?" I looked at the watch; he had broken A. Hopkins Parker's record by .7 second.

"My gosh! So I really did it. You know what? I thought I was going to do it. It felt as though I had that stopwatch in my head and I could hear myself going just a little bit faster than A. Hopkins Parker."

"The worst thing is there weren't any witnesses. And I'm no official timekeeper. I don't think it will count."

"Well of course it won't *count*."

"You can try it again and break it again. Tomorrow. We'll get the coach in here, and all the official time-keepers and I'll call up *The Devonian* to send a reporter and a photographer——"

He climbed out of the pool. "I'm not going to do it again," he said quietly.

"Of course you are!"

"No, I just wanted to see if I could do it. Now I know. But I don't want to do it in public." Some other swimmers drifted in through the door. Finny glanced sharply at them. "By the way," he said in an even more subdued voice, "we aren't going to talk about this. It's just between you and me. Don't say anything about it, to . . . anyone."

"Not say anything about it! When you broke the school record!"

"Sh-h-h-h-h!" He shot a blazing, agitated glance at me.

I stopped and looked at him up and down. He didn't look directly back at me. "You're too good to be true," I said after a while.

He glanced at me, and then said, "Thanks a lot," in a somewhat expressionless voice.

Was he trying to impress me or something? Not tell anybody? When he had broken a school record without a day of practice? I knew he was serious about it, so I didn't tell anybody. Perhaps for that reason his accomplishment took root in my mind and grew rapidly in the darkness where I was forced to hide it. The Devon School record books contained a mistake, a lie, and nobody knew it but Finny and me. A. Hopkins Parker was living in a fool's paradise, wherever he was. His defeated name remained in bronze on the school record plaque, while Finny deliberately evaded an athletic honor. It was true that he had many already—the Winslow Galbraith Memorial Football Trophy for having brought the most Christian sportsmanship to the game during the 1941–1942 season, the Margaret Duke Bonaventura ribbon and prize for the student who conducted himself at hockey most like the way her son had done, the Devon School Contact Sport Award, Presented Each Year to That Student Who in the Opinion of the Athletic Advisors Excels His Fellows in the Sportsmanlike Performance of Any Game Involving Bodily Contact. But these were in the past, and they were prizes, not school records. The sports Finny played officially—football, hockey, baseball, lacrosse—didn't have school records. To switch to a new sport suddenly, just for a day, and immediately break a record in it— that was about as neat a trick, as dazzling a reversal as I could, to be perfectly honest, possibly imagine. There was something inebriating in the suppleness of this feat. When I thought about it my head felt a little dizzy and my stomach began to tingle. It had, in one word, glamour, absolute schoolboy glamour. When I looked down at that stopwatch and realized a split second before I permitted my face to show it or my voice to announce it that Finny had broken a school record, I had experienced a feeling that also can be described in one word—shock.

To keep silent about this amazing happening deepened the shock for me. It made Finny seem too unusual for—not friendship, but too unusual for rivalry. And there were few relationships among us at Devon not based on rivalry.

"Swimming in pools is screwy anyway," he said after a long, unusual silence as we walked toward the dormitory. "The only real swimming is in the ocean." Then in the everyday, mediocre tone he used when he was proposing something really outrageous, he added, "Let's go to the beach."

The beach was hours away by bicycle, forbidden, completely out of all bounds. Going there risked expulsion, destroyed the studying I was going to do for an important test the next morning, blasted the reasonable amount of order I wanted to maintain in my life, and it also involved the kind of long, labored bicycle ride I hated. "All right," I said.

We got our bikes and slipped away from Devon along a back road. Having invited me, Finny now felt he had to keep me entertained. He told long, wild stories about his childhood; as I pumped panting up steep hills he glided along beside me, joking steadily. He analyzed my character, and he insisted on knowing what I disliked most about him ("You're too conventional," I said). He rode backward with no hands, he rode on his own handlebars, he jumped off and back on his moving bike as he had seen trick horseback riders do in the movies. He sang. Despite the steady musical undertone in his speaking voice, Finny couldn't carry a tune, and he couldn't remember the melody or the words to any song. But he loved listening to music, any music, and he liked to sing.

We reached the beach late in the afternoon. The tide was high and the surf was heavy. I dived in and rode a couple of waves, but they had reached that stage of power in which you could feel the whole strength of the ocean in them. The second wave, as it tore toward the beach with me, spewed me a little ahead of it, encroaching rapidly; suddenly it was immeasurably bigger than I was, it rushed me from the control of gravity and took control of me itself; the wave threw me down in a primitive plunge without a bottom, then there was a bottom, grinding sand, and I skidded onto the shore. The wave hestitated, balanced there, and then hissed back toward the deep water, its tentacles not quite interested enough in me to drag me with it.

I made my way up on the beach and lay down. Finny came, ceremoniously took my pulse, and then went back into the ocean. He stayed in an hour, breaking off every few minutes to come back to me and talk. The sand was so hot from the all-day sunshine that I had to brush the top layer away in order to lie down on it, and Finny's progress across the beach became a series of high, startled leaps.

The ocean, throwing up foaming sun-sprays across some nearby rocks, was winter cold. This kind of sunshine and ocean, with the accumulating roar of the surf and the salty, adventurous, flirting wind from the sea, always intoxicated Phineas. He was everywhere, he enjoyed himself hugely, he laughed out loud at passing sea gulls. And he did everything he could think of for me.

We had dinnner at a hot dog stand, with our backs to the ocean and its now cooler wind, our faces toward the heat of the cooking range. Then we walked on toward the center of the beach, where there was a subdued New England strip of honky-tonks. The Boardwalk lights against the deepening blue sky gained an ideal, starry beauty, and the lights from the belt of honky-tonks and shooting galleries and beer gardens gleamed with a quiet purity in the clear twilight.

Finny and I went along the Boardwalk in our sneakers and white slacks, Finny in a light blue polo shirt and I in a T-shirt. I noticed that people were looking fixedly at him, so I took a look myself to see why. His skin radiated a reddish copper glow of tan, his brown hair had been a little bleached by the sun, and I noticed that the tan made his eyes shine with a cool blue-green fire.

"Everybody's staring at you," he suddenly said to me. "It's because of that movie-star tan you picked up this afternoon . . . showing off again."

Enough broken rules were enough that night. Neither of us suggested going into any of the honky-tonks or beer gardens. We did have one glass of beer each at a fairly respectable-looking bar, convincing, or seeming to convince the bartender that we were old enough by a show of forged draft cards. Then we found a good spot among some sand dunes at the lonely end of the beach, and there we settled down to sleep for the night. The last words of Finny's usual nighttime monologue were, "I hope you're having a pretty good time here. I know I kind of dragged you away at the point of a gun, but after all you can't come to the shore with just anybody, and you can't come by yourself, and at this teen-age period in life the proper person is your best pal." He hesitated and then added, "which is what you are," and there was silence on his dune.

It was a courageous thing to say. Exposing a sincere emotion nakedly like that at the Devon School was the next thing to suicide. I should have told him then that he was my best friend also and rounded off what he had said. I started to; I nearly did. But something held me back. Perhaps I was stopped by that level of feeling, deeper than thought, which contains the truth.

4

The next morning I saw dawn for the first time. It began not as the gorgeous fanfare over the ocean I had expected, but as a strange gray thing, like sunshine seen through burlap. I looked over to see if Phineas was awake. He was still asleep, although in this drained light he looked more dead than asleep. The ocean looked dead too, dead gray waves hissing mordantly along the beach, which was gray and dead-looking itself.

I turned over and tried to sleep again but couldn't, and so lay on my back looking at this gray burlap sky. Very gradually, like one instrument after another being tentatively rehearsed, beacons of color began to pierce the sky. The ocean perked up a little from the reflection of these colored slivers in the sky. Bright high lights shone on the tips of waves, and beneath its gray surface I could see lurking a deep midnight green. The beach shed its deadness and became a spectral gray-white, then more white than gray, and finally it was totally white and stainless, as pure as the shores of Eden. Phineas, still asleep on his dune, made me think of Lazarus, brought back to life by the touch of God.[1]

---

1. **Lazarus . . . God:** In the New Testament (John 11), Jesus raises Lazarus from the dead.

I didn't contemplate this transformation for long. Inside my head, for as long as I could remember, there had always been a sense of time ticking steadily. I looked at the sky and the ocean and knew that it was around six-thirty. The ride back to Devon would take three hours at least. My important test, trigonometry, was going to be held at ten o'clock.

Phineas woke up talking. "That was one of the best night's sleep I ever had."

"When did you ever have a bad one?"

"The time I broke my ankle in football. I like the way this beach looks now. Shall we have a morning swim?"

"Are you crazy? It's too late for that."

"What time is it anyway?" Finny knew I was a walking clock.

"It's going on seven o'clock."

"There's time for just a short swim," and before I could say anything he was trotting down the beach, shedding clothes as he went, and into the ocean. I waited for him where I was. He came back after a while full of chilly glow and energy and talk. I didn't have much to say. "Do you have the money?" I asked once, suddenly suspecting that he had lost our joint seventy-five cents during the night. There was a search, a hopeless one, in the sand, and so we set off on the long ride back

without any breakfast, and got to Devon just in time for my test. I flunked it; I knew I was going to as soon as I looked at the test problems. It was the first test I had ever flunked.

But Finny gave me little time to worry about that. Right after lunch there was a game of blitzball which took most of the afternoon, and right after dinner there was the meeting of the Super Suicide Society of the Summer Session.

That night in our room, even though I was worn out from all the exercise, I tried to catch up to what had been happening in trigonometry.

"You work too hard," Finney said, sitting opposite me at the table where we read. The study lamp cast a round yellow pool between us. "You know all about History and English and French and everything else. What good will Trigonometry do you?"

"I'll have to pass it to graduate, for one thing."

"Don't give me that line. Nobody at Devon has ever been surer of graduating than you are. You aren't working for *that*. You want to be head of the class, valedictorian, so you can make a speech on Graduation Day—in Latin or something boring like that probably—and be the boy wonder of the school. I know you."

"Don't be stupid. I wouldn't waste my time on anything like that."

"You never waste your time. That's why I have to do it for you."

"Anyway," I grudgingly added, "somebody's got to be the head of the class."

"You see, I knew that's what you were aiming at," he concluded quietly.

"Fooey."

What if I was. It was a pretty good goal to have, it seemed to me. After all, he should talk. He had won and been proud to win the Galbraith Football Trophy and the Contact Sport Award, and there were two or three other athletic prizes he was sure to get this year or next. If I was head of the class on Graduation Day and made a speech and won the Ne Plus Ultra Scholastic Achievement Citation, then we would both have come out on top, we would be even, that was all. We would be even. . . .

Was that it! My eyes snapped from the textbook toward him. Did he notice this sudden glance shot across the pool of light? He didn't seem to; he went on writing down his strange curlicue notes about Thomas Hardy in Phineas Shorthand. *Was that it!* With his head bent over in the lamplight, I could discern a slight mound in his brow above the eyebrows, the faint bulge which is usually believed to indicate mental power. Phineas would

be the first to disclaim any great mental power in himself. But what did go on in his mind? If I was the head of the class and won that prize, then we would be even. . . .

His head started to come up, and mine snapped down. I glared at the textbook. "Relax," he said. "Your brain'll explode if you keep this up."

"You don't need to worry about me, Finny."

"I'm not worried."

"You wouldn't——" I wasn't sure I had the control to put this question—"mind if I wound up head of the class, would you?"

"Mind?" Two clear green-blue eyes looked at me. "Fat chance you've got, anyway, with Chet Douglass around."

"But you wouldn't mind, would you?" I repeated in a lower and more distinct voice.

He gave me that half-smile of his, which had won him a thousand conflicts. "I'd kill myself out of jealous envy."

I believed him. The joking manner was a screen; I believed him. In front of my eyes the trigonometry textbook blurred into a jumble. I couldn't see. My brain exploded. He minded, despised the possibility that I might be the head of the school. There was a swift chain of explosions in my brain, one certainty after another blasted—

up like a detonation went the idea of any best friend, up went affection and partnership and sticking by someone and relying on someone absolutely in the jungle of a boys' school, up went the hope that there was anyone in this school—in this world—whom I could trust. "Chet Douglass," I said uncertainly, "is a sure thing for it."

My misery was too deep to speak any more. I scanned the page; I was having trouble breathing, as though the oxygen were leaving the room. Amid its devastation my mind flashed from thought to thought, despairingly in search of something left which it could rely on. Not rely on absolutely, that was obliterated as a possibility, just rely on a little, some solace, something surviving in the ruins.

I found it. I found a single sustaining thought. The thought was, You and Phineas are even already. You are even in enmity. You are both coldly driving ahead for yourselves alone. You did hate him for breaking that school swimming record, but so what? He hated you for getting an A in every course but one last term. You would have had an A in that one except for him. Except for him.

Then a second realization broke as clearly and bleakly as dawn at the beach. Finny had deliberately set out to wreck my studies. That explained blitzball, that explained the nightly meetings of the Super Suicide Society, that explained his insistence that I share all his diversions. The way I believed that you're-my-best-friend blabber! The shadow falling across his face if I didn't want to do something with him! His instinct for sharing everything with me? Sure, he wanted to share everything with me, especially his procession of D's in every subject. That way he, the great athlete, would be way ahead of me. It was all cold trickery, it was all calculated, it was all enmity.

I felt better. Yes, I sensed it like the sweat of relief when nausea passes away; I felt better. We were even after all, even in enmity. The deadly rivalry was on both sides after all.

I became quite a student after that. I had always been a good one, although I wasn't really interested and excited by learning itself, the way Chet Douglass was. Now I became not just good but exceptional, with Chet Douglass my only rival in sight. But I began to see that Chet was weakened by the very genuineness of his interest in learning. He got carried away by things; for example, he was so fascinated by the tilting planes of solid geometry that he did almost as badly in trigonometry as I did myself. When we read *Candide*, it opened up a new way of looking at the world to Chet, and he continued hungrily reading Voltaire, in French, while the class went on to other people.

He was vulnerable there, because to me they were all pretty much alike—Voltaire and Molière and the laws of motion and the Magna Carta and the Pathetic Fallacy and *Tess of the D'Urbervilles*—and I worked indiscriminately on all of them.

Finny had no way of knowing this, because it all happened so far ahead of him scholastically. In class he generally sat slouched in his chair, his alert face following the discussion with an expression of philosophical comprehension, and when he was forced to speak himself, the hypnotic power of his voice combined with the singularity of his mind to produce answers which were often not right but could rarely be branded as wrong. Written tests were his downfall because he could not speak them, and as a result he got grades which were barely passing. It wasn't that he never worked, because he did work, in short, intense bouts now and then. As that crucial summer wore on and I tightened the discipline on myself Phineas increased his bouts of studying.

I could see through that. I was more and more certainly becoming the best student in the school; Phineas was without question the best athlete, so in that way we were even. But while he was a very poor student, I was a pretty good athlete, and when everything was thrown into the scales they would in the end tilt definitely toward me. The new attacks of studying were his emergency measures to save himself. I redoubled my effort.

It was surprising how well we got along in these weeks. Sometimes I found it hard to remember his treachery; sometimes I discovered myself thoughtlessly slipping back into affection for him again. It was hard to remember when one summer day after another broke with a cool effulgence over us, and there was a breath of widening life in the morning air—something hard to describe—an oxygen intoxicant, a shining northern paganism, some odor, some feeling so hopelessly promising that I would fall back in my bed on guard against it. It was hard to remember in the heady and sensual clarity of these mornings; I forgot whom I hated and who hated me. I wanted to break out crying from stabs of hopeless joy, or intolerable promise, or because these mornings were too full of beauty for me, because I knew of too much hate to be contained in a world like this.

Summer lazed on. No one paid any attention to us. One day I found myself describing to Mr. Prud'homme how Phineas and I had slept on the beach, and he seemed to be quite interested in it, in all the details, so much so that he missed the point: that we had flatly broken a basic rule.

No one cared, no one exercised any real discipline over us; we were on our own.

August arrived with a deepening of all the summertime splendors of New Hampshire. Early in the month we had two days of light, steady rain which aroused a final fullness everywhere. The branches of the old trees, which had been familiar to me either half-denuded or completely gaunt during the winter terms at Devon, now seemed about to break from their storms of leaves. Little disregarded patches of ground revealed that they had been gardens all along, and nondescript underbrush around the gymnasium and the river broke into color. There was a latent freshness in the air, as though spring were returning in the middle of the summer.

But examinations were at hand. I wasn't as ready for them as I wanted to be. The Suicide Society continued to meet every evening, and I continued to attend, because I didn't want Finny to understand me as I understood him.

And also I didn't want to let him excel me in this, even though I knew that it didn't matter whether he showed me up at the tree or not. Because it was what you had in your heart that counted. And I had detected that Finny's was a den of lonely, selfish ambition. He was no better than I was, no matter who won all the contests.

A French examination was announced for one Friday late in August. Finny and I studied for it in the library Thursday afternoon; I went over vocabulary lists, and he wrote messages—je ne give a darn pas about le francais, les filles en France ne wear pas les pantelons—and passed them with great seriousness to me, as *aides-mémoire*.[2] Of course I didn't get any work done. After supper I went to our room to try again. Phineas came in a couple of minutes later.

"Arise," he began airily, "Senior Overseer Charter Member! Elwin 'Leper' Lepellier has announced his intention to make the leap this very night, to qualify, to save his face at last."

I didn't believe it for a second. Leper Lepellier would go down paralyzed with panic on any sinking troopship before making such a jump. Finny had put him up to it, to finish me for good on the exam. I turned around with elaborate resignation. "If he jumps out of that tree I'm Mahatma Gandhi."[3]

"All right," agreed Finny absently. He had a way of turning clichés inside out like that. "Come on, let's go. We've got to be there. You never know, maybe he *will* do it this time."

2. *aides-mémoire:* (French) memory aids.
3. **Mahatma Gandhi** (1869–1948): Indian political activist and spiritual leader, who was a key figure in India's struggle for independence from Great Britain.

"Oh, for heaven's sake." I slammed closed the French book.

"What's the matter?"

What a performance! His face was completely questioning and candid.

"Studying!" I snarled. "Studying! You know, books. Work. Examinations."

"Yeah . . ." He waited for me to go on, as though he didn't see what I was getting at.

"Oh for heaven's sake! You don't know what I'm talking about. No, of course not. Not you." I stood up and slammed the chair against the desk. "Okay, we go. We watch little lily-liver Lepellier not jump from the tree, and I ruin my grade."

He looked at me with an interested, surprised expression. "You want to study?"

I began to feel a little uneasy at this mildness of his, so I sighed heavily. "Never mind, forget it. I know, I joined the club, I'm going. What else can I do?"

"Don't go." He said it very simply and casually, as though he were saying, "Nice day." He shrugged, "Don't go. What the heck, it's only a game."

I had stopped halfway across the room, and now I just looked at him. "What d'you mean?" I muttered. What he meant was clear enough, but I was groping for what lay behind his words, for what his thoughts could possibly be. I might have asked, "Who are you, then?" instead. I was facing a total stranger.

"I didn't know you needed to *study*," he said simply, "I didn't think you ever did. I thought it just came to you."

It seemed that he had made some kind of parallel between my studies and his sports. He probably thought anything you were good at came without effort. He didn't know yet that he was unique.

I couldn't quite achieve a normal speaking voice. "If I need to study, then so do you."

"Me?" He smiled faintly. "Listen, I could study forever and I'd never break C. But it's different for you, you're good. You really are. If I had a brain like that, I'd—I'd have my head cut open so people could look at it."

"Now wait a second . . ."

He put his hands on the back of a chair and leaned toward me. "I know. We kid around a lot and everything, but you have to be serious sometime, about something. If you're really good at something, I mean if there's nobody, or hardly anybody, who's as good as you are, then you've got to be serious about that. Don't mess around, for heaven's sake." He frowned disapprovingly at me. "Why didn't you say you had to study before?

Don't move from that desk. It's going to be all A's for you.''

"Wait a minute," I said, without any reason.

"It's okay. I'll oversee old Leper. I know he's not going to do it." He was at the door.

"Wait a minute," I said more sharply. "Wait just a minute. I'm coming."

"No, you aren't, pal, you're going to study."

"Never mind my studying."

"You think you've done enough already?"

"Yes." I let this drop curtly to bar him from telling me what to do about my work. He let it go at that, and went out the door ahead of me, whistling off key.

We followed our gigantic shadows across the campus, and Phineas began talking in wild French, to give me a little extra practice. I said nothing, my mind exploring the new dimensions of isolation around me. Any fear I had ever had of the tree was nothing beside this. It wasn't my neck, but my understanding which was menaced. He had never been jealous of me for a second. Now I knew that there never was and never could have been any rivalry between us. I was not of the same quality as he.

I couldn't stand this. We reached the others loitering around the base of the tree, and Phineas began exuberantly to throw off his clothes, delighted by the fading glow of the day, the challenge of the tree, the competitive tension of all of us. He lived and flourished in such moments. "Let's go, you and me," he called. A new idea struck him. "We'll go together, a double jump! Neat, eh?"

None of this mattered now; I would have listlessly agreed to anything. He started up the wooden rungs and I began climbing behind, up to the limb high over the bank. Phineas ventured a little way along it, holding a thin nearby branch for support. "Come out a little way," he said, "and then we'll jump side by side." The countryside was striking from here, a deep green sweep of playing fields and bordering shrubbery, with the school stadium white and miniature-looking across the river. From behind us the last long rays of light played across the campus, accenting every slight undulation of the land, emphasizing the separateness of each bush.

Holding firmly to the trunk, I took a step toward him, and then my knees bent and I jounced the limb. Finny, his balance gone, swung his head around to look at me for an instant with extreme interest, and then he tumbled sideways, broke through the little branches below and hit the bank with a sickening, unnatural thud. It was the first clumsy physical action I had ever seen him make.

With unthinking sureness I moved out on the limb and jumped into the river, every trace of my fear of this forgotten.

Responding to the Novel

Analyzing Chapters 1–4

Identifying Facts

1. How does the Devon campus seem different to Gene, the narrator, when he sees it for the first time after fifteen years?
2. Most of the novel consists of a **flashback**. To what time and season does the story flash back? Explain how world events have affected life at the Devon School.
3. When Finny breaks a school swimming record, what does he make Gene promise? How does Gene respond?

4. In Chapter 4, what does Gene conclude about his relationship with Finny? Later, what makes Gene decide he has misjudged Finny?

Interpreting Meanings

5. On several occasions, Gene refers to Finny as "hypnotic." For example, on page 905, he describes Finny's voice as "the equivalent in sound of a hypnotist's eyes." Look back through this section of the novel, and find other words and phrases that **characterize** Finny in this way. What else do you learn about Finny's character—particularly about the rules he breaks and the rules he lives by?
6. In many respects, Gene is Finny's **foil**, or opposite. At this point in the novel, what do you think are Gene's dominant **character** traits?
7. At the end of Chapter 3, after Finny "courageously" calls Gene his "best pal," Gene is unable to return the compliment. Why does he hold back? What "truth" do you think Gene is feeling that prevents him from speaking? (Or do you think he is just less courageous, or honest, than Finny?)
8. How reliable or perceptive is Gene as a **narrator**? Does he make any statements or come to any conclusions that you're skeptical about? (Were you immediately skeptical?) How would the novel be different if Finny were the narrator, or if it were told from the **omniscient point of view**?
9. At the end of Chapter 4, Gene realizes that he has misjudged Finny—"that there never was and never could have been any rivalry" between them. Yet Gene doesn't seem at all relieved by this insight. When he says, "I couldn't stand this," what do you think he means? Do you see any **irony** in his new response to Finny?
10. Reread the last paragraph in Chapter 4. Why do you think Gene jounces the limb? Is his action deliberate, or does he simply lose his balance? Is it premeditated or impulsive? Can you think of any other interpretation?

5

None of us was allowed near the infirmary during the next days, but I heard all the rumors that came out of it. Eventually a fact emerged; it was one of his legs, which had been "shattered." I couldn't figure out exactly what this word meant, whether it meant broken in one or several places, cleanly or badly, and I didn't ask. I learned no more, although the subject was discussed endlessly. Out of my hearing people must have talked of other things, but everyone talked about Phineas to me. I suppose this was only natural. I had been right beside him when it happened, I was his roommate.

The effect of his injury on the masters seemed deeper than after other disasters I remembered there. It was as though they felt it was especially unfair that it should strike one of the sixteen-year-olds, one of the few young men who could be free and happy in the summer of 1942.

I couldn't go on hearing about it much longer. If anyone had been suspicious of me, I might have developed some strength to defend myself. But there was nothing. No one suspected. Phineas must still be too sick, or too noble, to tell them.

I spent as much time as I could alone in our room, trying to empty my mind of every thought, to forget where I was, even who I was. One evening when I was dressing for dinner in this numbed frame of mind, an idea occurred to me, the first with any energy behind it since Finny fell from the tree. I decided to put on his clothes. We wore the same size, and although he always criticized mine, he used to wear them frequently, quickly forgetting what belonged to him and what to me. I never forgot, and that evening I put on his cordovan shoes, his pants, and I looked for and finally found his pink shirt, neatly laundered in a drawer. Its high, somewhat stiff collar against my neck, the wide cuffs touching my wrists, the rich material against my skin excited a sense of strangeness and distinction; I felt like some nobleman, some Spanish grandee.

But when I looked in the mirror, it was no remote aristocrat I had become, no character out of daydreams. I was Phineas, Phineas to the life. I even had his humorous expression in my face, his sharp, optimistic awareness. I had no idea why this gave me such intense relief, but it seemed, standing there in Finny's triumphant shirt, that I would never stumble through the confusions of my own character again.

I didn't go down to dinner. The sense of transformation stayed with me throughout the evening, and even when I undressed and went to bed. That night I slept easily, and it was only on waking up that this illusion was gone, and I was confronted with myself, and what I had done to Finny.

Sooner or later it had to happen, and that morning it did. "Finny's better!" Dr. Stanpole called to me on the chapel steps over the organ recessional thundering behind us. I made my way haltingly past the members of the choir with their black robes flapping in the morning breeze, the doctor's words reverberating around me. He might denounce me there before the whole school. Instead he steered me amiably into the lane leading toward the infirmary. "He could stand a visitor or two now, after these very nasty few days."

"You don't think I'll upset him or anything?"

"You? No, why? I don't want any of these teachers flapping around him. But a pal or two, it'll do him good."

"I suppose he's still pretty sick."

"It was a messy break."

"But how does he—how is he feeling? I mean, is he cheerful at all, or——"

"Oh, you know Finny." I didn't, I was pretty sure I didn't know Finny at all. "It was a messy break," he went on, "but we'll have him out of it eventually. He'll be walking again."

"*Walking* again!"

"Yes." The doctor didn't look at me, and barely changed his tone of voice. "Sports are finished for him, after an accident like that. Of course."

"But he must be able to," I burst out, "if his leg's still there, if you aren't going to amputate it—you aren't, are you?—then if it isn't amputated and the bones are still there, then it must come back the way it was, why wouldn't it? Of course it will."

Dr. Stanpole hesitated, and, I think, glanced at me for a moment. "Sports are finished. As a friend, you ought to help him face that and accept it. The sooner he does, the better off he'll be. If I had the slightest hope that he could do more than walk, I'd be all for trying for everything. There is no such hope. I'm sorry, as of course everyone is. It's a tragedy, but there it is."

I grabbed my head, fingers digging into my skin, and the doctor, thinking to be kind, put his hand on my shoulder. At his touch I lost all hope of controlling myself. I burst out crying into my hands; I cried for Phineas and for myself and for this doctor who believed in facing things. Most of all I cried because of kindness, which I had not expected.

"Now, that's no good. You've got to be cheerful and hopeful. He needs that from you. He wanted especially to see you. You were the one person he asked for."

That stopped my tears. I brought my hands down and watched the red brick exterior of the infirmary, a cheerful building, coming closer. Of course I was the first person he wanted to see. Phineas would say nothing behind my back; he would accuse me, face to face.

We were walking up the steps of the infirmary, everything was very swift, and next I was in a corridor being nudged by Dr. Stanpole toward a door. "He's in there. I'll be with you in a minute."

The door was slightly ajar, and I pushed it back and stood transfixed on the threshold. Phineas lay among pillows and sheets, his left leg, enormous in its white bindings, suspended a little above the bed. A tube led from a glass bottle into his right arm. Some channel began to close inside me, and I knew I was about to black out.

"Come on in," I heard him say. "You look worse than I do." The fact that he could still make a light remark pulled me back a little, and I went to a chair beside his bed. He seemed to have diminished physically in the few days which had passed, and to have lost his tan. His eyes studied me as though I were the patient. They no longer had their sharp good humor, but had become clouded and visionary. After a while I realized he had been given a drug. "What are *you* looking so sick about?" he went on.

"Finny, I——" there was no controlling what I said, the words were instinctive, like the reactions of someone cornered. "What happened there at the tree? That darn tree. I'm going to cut down that tree. Who cares who can jump out of it. What happened, what happened? How did you fall, how could you fall off like that?"

"I just fell," his eyes were vaguely on my face, "something jiggled and I fell over. I remember I turned around and looked at you, it was like I had all the time in the world. I thought I could reach out and get hold of you."

I flinched violently away from him. "To drag me down too!"

He kept looking vaguely over my face. "To get hold of you, so I wouldn't fall off."

"Yes, naturally." I was fighting for air in this close room. "I tried, you remember? I reached out but you were gone, you went down through those little branches underneath, and when I reached out there was only air."

"I just remember looking at your face for a second. Awfully funny expression you had. Very shocked, like you have right now."

"Right now? Well, of course, I *am* shocked. Who wouldn't be shocked, for heaven sakes. It's terrible, everything's terrible."

"But I don't see why you should look so *per-*sonally shocked. You look like it happened to you or something."

"It's almost like it did! I was right there, right on the limb beside you."

"Yes, I know. I remember it all."

There was a hard block of silence, and then I said quietly, as though my words might detonate the room, "Do you remember what made you fall?"

His eyes continued their roaming across my face. "I don't know, I must have just lost my balance. It must have been that. I did have this idea, this feeling that when you were standing there beside me, y—— I don't know, I had a kind of feeling. But you can't say anything for sure from just feelings. And this feeling doesn't make any sense. It was a crazy idea, I must have been delirious. So I just have to forget it. I just fell," he turned away to grope for something among the pillows, "that's all." Then he glanced back at me. "I'm sorry about that feeling I had."

I couldn't say anything to this sincere, drugged apology for having suspected the truth. He was never going to accuse me. It was only a feeling he had, and at this moment he must have been formulating a new commandment in his personal decalogue:[1] Never accuse a friend of a crime if you only have a feeling he did it.

And I thought we were competitors! It was so ludicrous I wanted to cry.

If Phineas had been sitting here in this pool of guilt, how would he have felt, what would he have done?

He would have told me the truth.

I got up so suddenly that the chair overturned. I stared at him in amazement, and he stared back, his mouth breaking into a grin as the moments passed. "Well," he said at last in his friendly, knowing voice, "what are you going to do, hypnotize me?"

"Finny, I've got something to tell you. You're going to hate it, but there's something I have to tell you."

"My gosh, what energy," he said, falling back against the pillows. "You sound like General MacArthur."[2]

"I don't care who I sound like, and you won't think so when I tell you. This is the worst thing in the world, and I'm sorry and I hate to tell you but I've got to tell you."

But I didn't tell him. Dr. Stanpole came in be-

---

1. **decalogue** (dek′ə·lôg′): basic set of rules carrying binding authority; literally, the Ten Commandments.
2. **General MacArthur:** Douglas MacArthur (1880–1964), commander of all U.S. forces in the Far East during World War II, noted for his superior speaking ability.

fore I was able to, and then a nurse came in, and I was sent away. The next day the doctor decided that Finny was not yet well enough to see visitors, even old pals like me. Soon after he was taken in an ambulance to his home outside Boston.

The Summer Session closed, officially came to an end. But to me it seemed irresolutely suspended, halted strangely before its time. I went south for a month's vacation in my home town and spent it in an atmosphere of reverie and unreality, as though I had lived that month once already and had not been interested by it the first time either.

At the end of September I started back toward Devon on the jammed, erratic trains of September 1942. I reached Boston seventeen hours behind schedule; there would be prestige in that at Devon, where those of us from long distances with travel adventures to report or invent held the floor for several days after a vacation.

By luck I got a taxi at South Station, and instead of saying "North Station" to the driver, instead of just crossing Boston and catching the final train for the short last leg of the trip to Devon, instead of that I sat back in the seat and heard myself give the address of Finny's house on the outskirts.

We found it fairly easily, on a street with a nave[3] of ancient elms branching over it. The house itself was high, white, and oddly proper to be the home of Phineas. It presented a face of definite elegance to the street, although behind that wings and ells dwindled quickly in formality until the house ended in a big plain barn.

Nothing surprised Phineas. A cleaning woman answered the door, and when I came into the room where he was sitting, he looked very pleased and not at all surprised.

"So you *are* going to show up!" his voice took off in one of its flights, "and you brought me something to eat from down South, didn't you? Honeysuckle and molasses or something like that?" I tried to think of something funny. "Corn bread? You did bring something. You didn't go all the way to Dixie and then come back with nothing but your dismal face to show for it." His talk rolled on, ignoring and covering my look of shock and clumsiness. I was silenced by the sight of him propped by white hospital-looking pillows in a big armchair. Despite everything at the Devon Infirmary, he had seemed an athlete there, temporarily injured in a game; as though the trainer would come in any minute and tape him up. Propped now before a great New England fireplace, on this

quiet old street, he looked to me like an invalid, house-bound.

"I brought . . . Well, I never remember to bring anyone anything." I struggled to get my voice above this self-accusing murmur. "I'll send you something. Flowers or something."

"Flowers! What happened to you in Dixie anyway?"

"Well then," there was no light remark anywhere in my head, "I'll get you some books."

"Never mind about books. I'd rather have some talk. What happened down South?"

"As a matter of fact," I brought out all the cheerfulness I could find for this, "there was a fire. It was just a grass fire out behind our house. We . . . took some brooms and beat it. I guess what we really did was fan it because it just kept getting bigger until the Fire Department finally came. They could tell where it was because of all the flaming brooms we were waving around in the air, trying to put them out."

Finny liked that story. But it put us on the familiar friendly level, pals trading stories. How was I going to begin talking about it? It would not be just a thunderbolt. It wouldn't even seem real.

Not in this conversation, not in this room. I wished I had met him in a railroad station, or at some highway intersection. Not here. Here the small window panes shone from much polishing and the walls were hung with miniatures and old portraits. The chairs were either heavily upholstered and too comfortable to stay awake in or Early American and never used. There were several square, solid tables covered with family pictures and random books and magazines, and also three small, elegant tables not used for anything. It was a compromise of a room, with a few good "pieces" for guests to look at, and the rest of it for people to use.

But I had known Finny in an impersonal dormitory, a gym, a playing field. In the room we shared at Devon many strangers had lived before us, and many would afterward. It was there that I had done it, but it was here that I would have to tell it. I felt like a wild man who had stumbled in from the jungle to tear the place apart.

I moved back in the Early American chair. Its rigid back and high armrests immediately forced me into a righteous posture. My blood could start to pound if it wanted to; let it. I was going ahead. "I was thinking about you most of the trip up."

"Oh yeah?" He glanced briefly into my eyes.

"I was thinking about you . . . and the accident."

"There's loyalty for you. To think about me when you were on a vacation."

---

3. **nave** (nāv): a large central space.

"I was thinking about it . . . about you be-cause—I was thinking about you and the accident because I caused it."

Finny looked steadily at me, his face very hand-some and expressionless. "What do you mean, you caused it?" His voice was as steady as his eyes.

My own voice sounded quiet and foreign. "I jounced the limb. I caused it." One more sen-tence. "I deliberately jounced the limb so you would fall off."

He looked older than I had ever seen him. "Of course you didn't."

"Yes I did. I did!"

"Of course you didn't do it. You darn fool. Sit down, you darn fool."

"Of course I did!"

"I'm going to hit you if you don't sit down."

"*Hit* me!" I looked at him. "*Hit* me! You can't even get up! You can't even come near me!"

"I'll kill you if you don't shut up."

"You see! Kill me! Now you know what it is! I did it because I felt like that! Now you know yourself!"

"I don't know anything. Go away. I'm tired and you make me sick. Go away." He held his forehead wearily, an unlikely way.

It struck me then that I was injuring him again. It occurred to me that this could be an even deeper injury than what I had done before. I would have to back out of it, I would have to disown it. Could it be that he might even be right? Had I really and definitely and knowingly done it to him after all? I couldn't remember, I couldn't think. However it was, it was worse for him to know it. I had to take it back.

But not here. "You'll be back at Devon in a few weeks, won't you?" I muttered after both of us had sat in silence for a while.

"Sure, I'll be there by Thanksgiving anyway."

At Devon, where every stick of furniture didn't assert that Finny was a part of it, I could make it up to him.

Now I had to get out of there. There was only one way to do it; I would have to make every move false. "I've had an awfully long trip," I said, "I never sleep much on trains. I guess I'm not making too much sense today."

"Don't worry about it."

"I think I'd better get to the station. I'm already a day late at Devon."

"You aren't going to start living by the rules, are you?"

I grinned at him. "Oh no, I wouldn't do that," and that was the most false thing, the biggest lie of all.

6

Peace had deserted Devon. Although not in the look of the campus and village; they retained much of their dreaming summer calm. Fall had barely touched the full splendor of the trees, and during the height of the day, the sun briefly regained its summertime power. In the air there was only an edge of coolness to imply the coming winter.

But all had been caught up, like the first fallen leaves, by a new and energetic wind. The Summer Session—a few dozen boys being force-fed edu-cation, a stopgap while most of the masters were away and most of the traditions stored against sultriness—the Summer Session was over. It had been the school's first, but this was its one hun-dred and sixty-third Winter Session, and the forces reassembled for it scattered the easygoing summer spirit like so many fallen leaves.

The masters were in their places for the first chapel, seated in stalls in front of and at right angles to us, suggesting by their worn expressions and careless postures that they had never been away at all.

In an apse[1] of the church sat their wives and children, the objects during the tedious winter months of our ceaseless, ritual speculation (Why did he marry *her?* What in the world ever made her marry *him?* How could the two of them ever have produced *those* little monsters?). The masters favored seersucker on this mild first day, the wives broke out their hats. Five of the younger teachers were missing, gone into the war. Mr. Pike had come in his Naval ensign's uniform; some reflex must have survived Midshipman's School and brought him back to Devon for the day. His face was as mild and hopeless as ever; mooning above the snappy, rigid blouse, it gave him the air of an impostor.

Continuity was the keynote. The same hymns were played, the same sermon given, the same announcements made. There was one surprise; maids had disappeared "for the Duration,"[2] a new phrase then. But continuity was stressed, not be-ginning again but continuing the education of young men according to the unbroken traditions of Devon.

I knew, perhaps I alone knew, that this was false. Devon had slipped through their fingers dur-ing the warm overlooked months. The traditions had been broken, the standards let down, all rules

---

1. **apse:** semicircular projection in a building with domed or vaulted roof, such as a church.
2. **"for the Duration":** until the end of the war.

forgotten. In those bright days of truancy we had never thought of What We Owed Devon, as the sermon this opening day exhorted us to do. We had thought of ourselves, of what Devon owed us, and we had taken all of that and much more. Today's hymn was "Dear Lord and Father of Mankind Forgive Our Foolish Ways"; we had never heard that during the summer either. Ours had been a wayward gypsy music, leading us down all kinds of foolish gypsy ways, unforgiven. I was glad of it, I had almost caught the rhythm of it, the dancing, clicking jangle of it during the summer.

Still it had come to an end, in the last long rays of daylight at the tree, when Phineas fell. It was forced on me as I sat chilled through the chapel service, that this probably vindicated the rules of Devon after all, wintery Devon. If you broke the rules, then they broke you. That, I think, was the real point of the sermon on this first morning.

After the service ended we set out seven hundred strong, the regular winter throng of the Devon School, to hustle through our lists of appointments. All classrooms were crowded, swarms were on the crosswalks, the dormitories were as noisy as factories, every bulletin board was a forest of notices.

We had been an idiosyncratic, leaderless band in the summer, undirected except by the eccentric notions of Phineas. Now the official class leaders and politicians could be seen taking charge, assuming as a matter of course their control of these walks and fields which had belonged only to us. I had the same room which Finny and I had shared during the summer, but across the hall, in the large suite where Leper Lepellier had dreamed his way through July and August amid sunshine and dust motes and windows through which the ivy had reached tentatively into the room, here Brinker Hadley had established his headquarters. Emissaries were already dropping in to confer with him. Leper, luckless in his last year as in all the others, had been moved to a room lost in an old building off somewhere in the trees toward the gym.

After morning classes and lunch I went across to see Brinker, started into the room and then stopped. Suddenly I did not want to see the trays of snails which Leper had passed the summer collecting replaced by Brinker's files. Not yet. Although it was something to have this year's dominant student across the way. Ordinarily he should have been a magnet for me, the center of all the excitement and influences in the class. Ordinarily this would have been so—if the summer, the gypsy days, had not intervened. Now Brinker,

with his steady wit and ceaseless plans, Brinker had nothing to offer in place of Leper's dust motes and creeping ivy and snails.

I didn't go in. In any case, I was late for my afternoon appointment. I never used to be late. But today I was, later even than I had to be. I was supposed to report to the Crew House, down on the banks of the lower river. There are two rivers at Devon, divided by a small dam. On my way I stopped on the footbridge which crosses the top of the dam separating them and looked upstream, at the narrow little Devon River sliding toward me between its thick fringe of pine and birch.

As I had to do whenever I glimpsed this river, I thought of Phineas. Not of the tree and pain, but of one of his favorite tricks, Phineas in exaltation, balancing on one foot on the prow of a canoe like a river god, his raised arms invoking the air to support him, face transfigured, body a complex set of balances and compensations, each muscle aligned in perfection with all the others to maintain this supreme fantasy of achievement, his skin glowing from immersions, his whole body hanging between river and sky as though he had transcended gravity and might by gently pushing upward with his foot glide a little way higher and remain suspended in space, encompassing all the glory of the summer and offering it to the sky.

Then, an infinitesimal veering of the canoe, and the line of his body would break, the soaring arms collapse, up shoot an uncontrollable leg, and Phineas would tumble into the water, roaring with rage.

I stopped in the middle of this hurrying day to remember him like that, and then, feeling refreshed, I went on to the Crew House beside the tidewater river below the dam.

We had never used this lower river, the Naguamsett, during the summer. It was ugly, saline, fringed with marsh, mud and seaweed. A few miles away it was joined to the ocean, so that its movements were governed by unimaginable factors like the Gulf Stream, the Polar Ice Cap, and the moon. It was nothing like the freshwater Devon above the dam where we'd had so much fun, all the summer. The Devon's course was determined by some familiar hills a little inland; it rose among highland farms and forests which we knew, passed at the end of its course through the school grounds, and then threw itself with little spectacle over a small waterfall beside the diving dam, and into the turbid Naguamsett.

The Devon School was astride these two rivers.

At the Crew House, Quackenbush, in the midst of some milling oarsmen in the damp main room,

spotted me the instant I came in, with his dark expressionless eyes. Quackenbush was the crew manager, and there was something wrong about him. I didn't know exactly what it was. In the throng of the winter terms at Devon, we were at opposite extremities of the class, and to me there only came the disliked edge of Quackenbush's reputation. A clue to it was that his first name was never used—I didn't even know what it was—and he had no nickname, not even an unfriendly one.

"Late, Forrester," he said in his already-matured voice. He was a firmly masculine type; perhaps he was disliked only because he had matured before the rest of us.

"Yes, sorry, I got held up."

"The crew waits for no man." He didn't seem to think this was a funny thing to say. I did, and had to chuckle.

"Well, if you think it's all a joke . . ."

"I didn't say it was a joke."

"I've got to have some real help around here. This crew is going to win the New England scholastics, or my name isn't Cliff Quackenbush."

With that blank filled, I took up my duties as assistant senior crew manager. There is no such position officially, but it sometimes came into existence through necessity, and was the opposite of a sinecure.[3] It was all work and no advantages. The official assistant to the crew manager was a member of the class below, and the following year he could come into the senior managership with its rights and status. An assistant who was already a senior ranked nowhere. Since I had applied for such a nonentity of a job, Quackenbush, who had known as little about me as I had about him, knew now.

"Get some towels," he said without looking at me, pointing at a door.

"How many?"

"Who knows? Get some. As many as you can carry. *That* won't be too many."

Jobs like mine were usually taken by boys with some physical disability, since everyone had to take part in sports, and this was all disabled boys could do. As I walked toward the door I supposed that Quackenbush was studying me to see if he could detect a limp. But I knew that his flat black eyes would never detect my trouble.

Quackenbush felt mellower by the end of the afternoon as we stood on the float in front of the Crew House, gathering up towels.

---

3. **sinecure** (sī′nə·kyōor′): position that brings advantage but little or no work.

"You never rowed, did you." He opened the conversation like that, without pause or question mark. His voice sounded almost too mature, as though he were putting it on a little; he sounded as though he were speaking through a tube.

"No, I never did."

"I rowed on the lightweight crew for two years."

He had a tough bantam[4] body, easily detectable under the tight sweat shirt he wore. "I wrestle in the winter," he went on. "What are you doing in the winter?"

"I don't know, manage something else."

"You're a senior, aren't you?"

He knew that I was a senior. "Yeah."

"Starting a little late to manage teams, aren't you?"

"Am I?"

"Darn right you are!" He put indignant conviction into this, pouncing on the first sprig of assertiveness in me.

"Well, it doesn't matter."

"Yes, it matters."

"I don't think it does."

"Go to the devil, Forrester. Who the heck are you anyway."

I turned with an inward groan to look at him. Quackenbush wasn't going to let me just do the work for him like the automaton[5] I wished to be. We were going to have to be pitted against each other. It was easy enough now to see why. For Quackenbush had been systematically disliked since he first set foot in Devon, with careless, disinterested insults coming at him from the beginning, voting for and applauding the class leaders through years of attaining nothing he wanted for himself. I didn't want to add to his humiliations; I even sympathized with his trembling, goaded egotism he could no longer contain, the furious arrogance which sprang out now at the mere hint of opposition from someone he had at last found whom he could consider inferior to himself. I realized that all this explained him, and it wasn't the words he said which angered me. It was only that he was so ignorant, that he knew nothing of the gypsy summer, nothing of the loss I was fighting to endure, of skylarks and splashes and petal-bearing breezes, he had not seen Leper's snails or the Charter of the Super Suicide Society; he shared nothing, knew nothing, felt nothing as Phineas had done.

"You, Quackenbush, don't know anything about who I am." That launched me, and I had to go on and say, "or anything else."

---

4. **bantam:** small but aggressive, like a tough little bantam hen.
5. **automation:** robot; one who acts in a monotonous, routine way.

"Listen, you maimed . . ."

I hit him hard across the face. I didn't know why for an instant; it was almost as though I were maimed. Then the realization that there was someone who was flashed over me.

Quackenbush had clamped his arm in some kind of tight wrestling grip around my neck, and I was glad in this moment not to be a cripple. I reached over, grasped the back of his sweat shirt, wrenched, and it came away in my hand. I tried to throw him off, he lunged at the same time, and we catapulted into the water.

The dousing extinguished Quackenbush's rage, and he let go of me. I scrambled back onto the float, still seared by what he had said. "The next time you call anybody maimed," I bit off the words harshly so he would understand all of them, "you better make sure they are first."

"Get out of here, Forrester," he said bitterly from the water, "you're not wanted around here, Forrester. Get out of here."

I fought that battle, that first skirmish of a long campaign, for Finny. Until the back of my hand cracked against Quackenbush's face I had never pictured myself in the role of Finny's defender, and I didn't suppose that he would have thanked me for it now. He was too loyal to anything connected with himself—his roommate, his dormitory, his class, his school, outward in vastly expanded circles of loyalty until I couldn't imagine who would be excluded. But it didn't feel exactly as though I had done it for Phineas. It felt as though I had done it for myself.

If so, I had little profit to show as I straggled back toward the dormitory dripping wet, with the job I had wanted gone, temper gone, mind circling over and over through the whole soured afternoon. I knew now that it was fall all right; I could feel it pressing clammily against my wet clothes, an unfriendly, discomforting breath in the air, an edge of wintery chill, air that shriveled, soon to put out the lights on the countryside. One of my legs wouldn't stop trembling, whether from cold or anger I couldn't tell. I wished I had hit him harder.

Someone was coming toward me along the bent, broken lane which led to the dormitory, a lane out of old London, ancient houses on either side leaning as though soon to tumble into it, cobblestones heaving underfoot like a bricked-over ocean squall—a figure of great height advanced down them toward me. It could only be Mr. Ludsbury; no one else could pass over these stones with such contempt for the idea of tripping.

The houses on either side were inhabited by I didn't know who; wispy, fragile old ladies seemed most likely. I couldn't duck into one of them. There were angles and bumps and bends everywhere, but none big enough to conceal me. Mr. Ludsbury loomed on like a high-masted clipper ship in this rocking passage, and I tried to go stealthily by him on my watery, squeaking sneakers.

"Just one moment, Forrester, if you please." Mr. Ludsbury's voice was bass, British, and his Adam's apple seemed to move as much as his mouth when he spoke. "Has there been a cloudburst in your part of town?"

"No, sir. I'm sorry, sir, I fell into the river." I apologized by instinct to him for this mishap which discomforted only me.

"And could you tell me how and why you fell into the river?"

"I slipped."

"Yes." After a pause he went on. "I think you have slipped in any number of ways since last year. I understand, for example, that there was gaming in my dormitory this summer while you were living there." He was in charge of the dormitory; one of the dispensations of those days of deliverance, I realized now, had been his absence.

"Gaming? What kind of gaming, sir?"

"Cards, dice," he shook his long hand dismissingly. "I didn't inquire. It didn't matter. There won't be any more of it."

"I don't know who that would have been." Nights of blackjack and poker and unpredictable games invented by Phineas rose up in my mind; the back room of Leper's suite, a lamp hung with a blanket so that only a small blazing circle of light fell sharply amid the surrounding darkness; Phineas losing even in those games he invented, betting always for what *should* win, for what would have been the most brilliant success of all, if only the cards hadn't betrayed him. Finny finally betting his icebox and losing it, that contraption, to me.

I thought of it because Mr. Ludsbury was just then saying, "And while I'm putting the dormitory back together, I'd better tell you to get rid of that leaking icebox. Nothing like that is ever permitted in the dormitory, of course. I notice that everything went straight to seed during the summer and that none of you old boys who knew our standards so much as lifted a finger to help Mr. Prud'homme maintain order. As a substitute for the summer he couldn't have been expected to know everything there was to be known at once. You old boys simply took advantage of the situation."

I stood there shaking in my wet sneakers. If only I had truly taken advantage of the situation, seized and held and prized the multitudes of advantages the summer offered me; if only I had.

I said nothing, on my face I registered the bleak look of a defendant who knows the court will never be swayed by all the favorable evidence he has. It was a schoolboy look; Mr. Ludsbury knew it well.

"There's a long-distance call for you," he continued in the tone of the judge performing the disagreeable duty of telling the defendant his right. "I've written the operator's number on the pad beside the telephone in my study. You may go in and call."

"Thank you very much, sir."

He sailed on down the lane without further reference to me, and I wondered who was sick at home.

But when I reached his study—low-ceilinged, gloomy with books, black leather chairs, a pipe rack, frayed brown rug, a room which students rarely entered except for a reprimand—I saw on the pad not an operator's number from my home town, but one which seemed to interrupt the beating of my heart.

I called this operator, and listened in wonder while she went through her routine as though this were just any long-distance call, and then her voice left the line, and it was preempted, and charged, by the voice of Phineas. "Happy first day of the new academic year!"

"Thanks, thanks a lot, it's a—you sound—I'm glad to hear your——"

"Stop stuttering, I'm paying for this. Who're you rooming with?"

"Nobody. They didn't put anyone else in the room."

"Saving my place for me! Good old Devon. But anyway, you wouldn't have let them put anyone else in there, would you?" Friendliness, simple outgoing affection, that was all I could hear in his voice.

"No, of course not."

"I didn't think you would. Roommates are roommates. Even if they do have an occasional fight. Gosh, you were crazy when you were here."

"I guess I was. I guess I must have been."

"Completely over the falls. I wanted to be sure you'd recovered. That's why I called up. I knew that if you'd let them put anybody else in the room in my place, then you really *were* crazy. But you didn't, I knew you wouldn't. Well, I did have just a *trace* of doubt, that was because you talked so crazy here. I have to admit I had just a *second* when I wondered. I'm sorry about that, Gene. Naturally I was completely wrong. You didn't let them put anybody else in my spot."

"No, I didn't let them."

"I could shoot myself for thinking you might. I really knew you wouldn't."

"No, I wouldn't."

"And I spent my money on a long-distance call! All for nothing. Well, it's spent, on you too. So start talking, pal. And it better be good. Start with sports. What are you going out for?"

"Crew. Well, not exactly crew. Managing crew. Assistant crew manager."

"Assistant *crew* manager!"

"I don't think I've got the job——"

"Assistant crew *manager!*"

"I got in a fight this after——"

"*Assistant crew manager!*" No voice could course with dumfoundment like Finny's. "You *are* crazy!"

"Listen, Finny, I don't care about being a big man on the campus or anything."

"Whaaat?" Much more clearly than anything in Mr. Ludsbury's study I could see his face now, grimacing in wide, obsessed stupefaction. "Who said anything about whoever *they* are!"

"Well, then, what are you so worked up for?"

"What do you want to manage crew for? What do you want to *manage* for? What's that got to do with sports?"

The point was, the grace of it was, that it had nothing to do with sports. For I wanted no more of sports. They were barred from me, as though when Dr. Stanpole said, "Sports are finished," he had been speaking of me. I didn't trust myself in them, and I didn't trust anyone else. It was as though football players were really bent on crushing the life out of each other, as though boxers were in combat to the death, as though even a tennis ball might turn into a bullet. This didn't seem completely crazy imagination in 1942, when jumping out of trees stood for abandoning a torpedoed ship. Later, in the school swimming pool, we were given the second stage in that rehearsal: after you hit the water you made big splashes with your hands, to scatter the flaming oil which would be on the surface.

So to Phineas I said, "I'm too busy for sports," and he went into his incoherent groans and jumbles of words, and I thought the issue was settled until at the end he said, "Listen, pal, if *I* can't play sports, *you're* going to play them for me," and I lost part of myself to him then, and a soaring sense of freedom revealed that this must have been my purpose from the first: to become a part of Phineas.

7

Brinker Hadley came across to see me late that afternoon. I had taken a shower to wash off the sticky salt of the Naguamsett River—going into the Devon was like taking a refreshing shower itself, you never had to clean up after it, but the Naguamsett was something else entirely. I had never been in it before; it seemed appropriate that my baptism there had taken place on the first day of this winter session, and that I had been thrown into it, in the middle of a fight.

I washed the traces off me and then put on a pair of chocolate brown slacks, a pair which Phineas had been particularly critical of when he wasn't wearing them, and a blue flannel shirt. Then, with nothing to do until my French class at five o'clock, I began turning over in my mind this question of sports.

But Brinker came in. I think he made a point of visiting all the rooms near him the first day. "Well, Gene," his beaming face appeared around the door. Brinker looked the standard preparatory school article in his gray gabardine suit with square, hand-sewn-looking jacket pockets, a conservative necktie, and dark brown cordovan shoes. His face was all straight lines—eyebrows, mouth, nose, everything—and he carried his six feet of height straight as well. He looked but happened not to be athletic, being too busy with politics, arrangements, and offices. There was nothing idiosyncratic about Brinker unless you saw him from behind; I did as he turned to close the door after him. The flaps of his gabardine jacket parted slightly over his healthy rump, and it is that, without any sense of derision at all, that I recall as Brinker's salient characteristic, those healthy, determined, not over-exaggerated but definite and substantial buttocks.

"Here you are in your solitary splendor," he went on genially. "I can see you have real influence around here. This big room all to yourself. I wish I knew how to manage things like you." He grinned confidingly and sank down on my cot, leaning on his elbow in a relaxed, at-home way.

It didn't seem fitting for Brinker Hadley, the hub of the class, to be congratulating me on influence. I was going to say that, while he had a roommate, it was frightened Brownie Perkins, who would never impinge on Brinker's comfort in any way, and that they had two rooms, the front one with a fireplace. Not that I grudged him any of this. I liked Brinker in spite of his Winter Session efficiency; almost everyone liked Brinker.

But in the pause I took before replying, he started talking in his lighthearted way again. He never let a dull spot appear in conversation if he could help it.

"I'll bet you knew all the time Finny wouldn't be back this fall. That's why you picked him for a roommate, right?"

"What?" I pulled quickly around in my chair, away from the desk, and faced him. "No, of course not. How could I know a thing like that in advance?"

Brinker glanced swiftly at me. "You fixed it," he smiled widely. "You knew all the time. I'll bet it was *all* your doing."

"Don't be nutty, Brinker," I turned back toward the desk and began moving books with rapid pointlessness, "what a crazy thing to say." My voice sounded too strained even to my own blood-pounded ears.

"Ah-h-h. The truth hurts, eh?"

I looked at him as sharply as eyes can look. He had struck an accusing pose.

"Sure," I gave a short laugh, "sure." Then these words came out of me by themselves, "But the truth will out."

His hand fell leadenly on my shoulder. "Rest assured of that, my son. In our free democracy, even fighting for its life, the truth will out."

I got up. "I feel like a smoke, don't you? Let's go down to the Butt Room."

"Yes, yes. To the dungeon with you."

The Butt Room was something like a dungeon. It was in the basement, or the bowels, of the dormitory. There were about ten smokers already there. Everyone at Devon had many public faces; in class we looked, if not exactly scholarly, at least respectably alert; on the playing fields we looked like innocent extroverts; and in the Butt Room we looked, very strongly, like criminals. The school's policy, in order to discourage smoking, was to make these rooms as depressing as possible. The windows near the ceiling were small and dirty, the old leather furniture spilled its inwards, the tables were mutilated, the walls ash-colored, the floor concrete. A radio with a faulty connection played loud and rasping for a while, then suddenly quiet and insinuating.

"Here's your prisoner, gentlemen," announced Brinker, seizing my neck and pushing me into the Butt Room ahead of him, "I'm turning him over to the proper authorities."

High spirits came hard in the haze of the Butt Room. A slumped figure near the radio, which happened to be playing loud at the moment, finally roused himself to say, "What's the charge?"

"Doing away with his roommate so he could have a whole room to himself. Rankest treachery." He paused impressively. "Practically fratricide."

With a snap of the neck I shook his hand off me, my teeth set. "Brinker . . ."

He raised an arresting hand. "Not a word. Not a sound. You'll have your day in court."

"Shut up! I swear you ride a joke longer than anybody I know."

It was a mistake; the radio had suddenly gone quiet, and my voice ringing in the abrupt, releasing hush galvanized them all.

"So, you killed him, did you?" A boy uncoiled tensely from the couch.

"Well," Brinker qualified judiciously, "not actually killed. Finny's hanging between life and death at home, in the arms of his grief-stricken old mother."

I had to take part in this, or risk losing control completely. "I didn't do hardly a thing," I began as easily as it was possible for me to do, "I—all I did was drop a little bit . . . a little pinch of arsenic in his morning coffee."

"Liar!" Brinker glowered at me. "Trying to weasel out of it with a false confession, eh?"

I laughed at that, laughed uncontrollably for a moment at that.

"We know the scene of the crime," Brinker went on, "high in that . . . that *funereal* tree by the river. There wasn't any poison, nothing as subtle as that."

"Oh, you know about the tree," I tried to let my face fall guiltily, but it felt instead as though it

were being dragged downward. "Yes, huh, yes there was a small, a little *contretemps*[1] at the tree."

No one was diverted from the issue by this try at a funny French pronunciation.

"Tell us everything," a younger boy at the table said huskily. There was an unsettling current in his voice, a genuinely conspiratorial note, as though he believed literally everything that had been said. His attitude seemed to me almost obscene, the attitude of someone who discovers a sexual secret of yours and promises not to tell a soul if you will describe it in detail to him.

"Well," I replied in a stronger voice, "first I stole all his money. Then I found that he cheated on his entrance tests to Devon and I blackmailed his parents about that, then I made love to his sister in Mr. Ludsbury's study, then I . . ." it was going well, faint grins were appearing around the room, even the younger boy seemed to suspect that he was being "sincere" about a joke, a bad mistake to make at Devon, "then I . . ." I only had to add, "pushed him out of the tree" and the chain of implausibility would be complete, "then I . . ." just those few words and perhaps this dungeon nightmare would end.

But I could feel my throat closing on them; I could never say them, never.

I swung on the younger boy. "What did I do then?" I demanded. "I'll bet you've got a lot of theories. Come on, reconstruct the crime. There we were at the tree. Then what happened, Sherlock Holmes?"

His eyes swung guiltily back and forth. "Then you just pushed him off, I'll bet."

"Lousy bet," I said offhandedly, falling into a chair as though losing interest in the game. "You lose. I guess you're Dr. Watson, after all."

They laughed at him a little, and he squirmed and looked guiltier than ever. He had a very weak foothold among the Butt Room crowd, and I had pretty well pushed him off it. His glance flickered out at me from his defeat, and I saw to my surprise that I had, by making a little fun of him, brought upon myself his unmixed hatred. For my escape this was a price I was willing to pay.

"French, French," I exclaimed. "Enough of this *contretemps*. I've got to study my French." And I went out.

Going up the stairs I heard a voice from the Butt Room say, "Funny, he came all the way down here and didn't even have a smoke."

But this was a clue they soon seemed to forget. I detected no Sherlock Holmes among them, nor even a Dr. Watson. No one showed any interest in tracking me, no one pried, no one insinuated. The daily lists of appointments lengthened with the rays of the receding autumn sun until the summer, the opening day, even yesterday became by the middle of October something gotten out of the way and forgotten, because tomorrow bristled with so much to do.

In addition to classes and sports and clubs, there was the war. Brinker Hadley could compose his Shortest War Poem Ever Written:

> The War
> Is a bore

if he wanted to, but all of us had to take stronger action than that. First, there was the local apple

---

1. *contretemps* (kōn·trə·tän'): (French) awkward mishap.

crop, threatening to rot because the harvesters had all gone into the army or war factories. We spent several shining days picking them and were paid in cash for it. Brinker was inspired to write his Apple Ode:

> Our chore
> Is the core
> of the war

and the novelty and money of these days excited us. Life at Devon was revealed as still very close to the ways of peace; the war was at worst only a bore, as Brinker said, no more taxing to us than a day spent at harvesting in an apple orchard.

Not long afterward, early even for New Hampshire, snow came. It came theatrically, late one afternoon; I looked up from my desk and saw that suddenly there were big flakes twirling down into the quadrangle, settling on the carefully pruned shrubbery bordering the crosswalks, the three elms still holding many of their leaves, the still-green lawns. They gathered there thicker by the minute, like noiseless invaders conquering because they took possession so gently. I watched them whirl past my window—don't take this seriously, the playful way they fell seemed to imply, this little show, this harmless trick.

It seemed to be true. The school was thinly blanketed that night, but the next morning, a bright, almost balmy day, every flake disappeared. The following weekend, however, it snowed again, then two days later much harder, and by the end of that week the ground had been clamped under snow for the winter.

In the same way the war, beginning almost humorously with announcements about maids and days spent at apple-picking, commenced its invasion of the school. The early snow was commandeered as its advance guard.

Leper Lepellier didn't suspect this. It was not, in fact, evident to anyone at first. But Leper stands out for me as the person who was most often and most emphatically taken by surprise, by this and every other shift in our life at Devon.

The heavy snow paralyzed the railroad yards of one of the large towns south of us on the Boston and Maine line. At chapel the day following the heaviest snowfall, two hundred volunteers were solicited to spend the day shoveling them out, as part of the Emergency Usefulness policy adopted by the faculty that fall. Again we would be paid. So we all volunteered, Brinker and I and Chet Douglass and even, I noticed, Quackenbush.

But not Leper. He generally made little sketches of birds and trees in the back of his notebook during chapel, so that he had probably not heard the announcement. The train to take us south to the work did not arrive until after lunch, and on my way to the station, taking a shortcut through a meadow not far from the river, I met Leper. I had hardly seen him all fall, and I hardly recognized him now. He was standing motionless on the top of a small ridge, and he seemed from a distance to be a scarecrow left over from the growing season. As I plodded toward him through the snow, I began to differentiate items of clothing—a dull green deer-stalker's cap, brown earmuffs, a thick gray woolen scarf—then at last I recognized the face in the midst of them, Leper's, pinched and pink, his eyes peering curiously toward some distant woods through steel-rimmed glasses. As I got nearer, I noticed that below his long tan canvas coat with sagging pockets, below the red and black plaid woolen knickers and green puttees,[2] he was wearing skis. They were very long, wooden and battered, and had two decorative, old-fashioned knobs on their tips.

"You think there's a path through those woods?" he asked in his mild, tentative voice when I got near. Leper did not switch easily from one train of thought to another, and even though I was an old friend whom he had not talked to in months, I didn't mind his taking me for granted now, even at this improbable meeting in a wide, empty field of snow.

"I'm not sure, Leper, but I think there's one at the bottom of the slope."

"Oh yeah, I guess there is." We always called him Leper to his face; he wouldn't have remembered to respond to any other name.

I couldn't keep from staring at him, at the burlesque explorer look of him. "What are you," I asked at last, "um, what are you doing, anyway?"

"I'm touring."

"Touring." I examined the long bamboo ski poles he held. "How do you mean, touring?"

"Touring. It's the way you get around the countryside in the winter. Touring skiing. It's how you go overland in the snow."

"Where are you going?"

"Well, I'm not *going* anywhere." He bent down to tighten the lacings on a puttee. "I'm just touring around."

"There's that place across the river where you could ski. The place where they have the rope tow on that steep hill across from the railroad station. You could go over there."

"No, I don't think so." He surveyed the woods again, although his breath had fogged his glasses. "That's not skiing."

---

2. **puttees** (pu·tēz′): leather coverings for the lower legs.

"Why, sure that's skiing. It's a good little run, you can get going pretty fast on that hill."

"Yeah, but that's it, that's why it isn't skiing. Skiing isn't supposed to be fast. Skis are for useful locomotion." He turned his inquiring eyes on me. "You can break a leg with that downhill stuff."

"Not on that little hill."

"Well, it's the same thing. It's part of the whole wrong idea. They're ruining skiing in this country, rope tows and chair lifts and all that stuff. You get carted up, and then you whizz down. You never get to see the trees or anything. Oh you see a lot of trees shoot by, but you never get to really look at trees, at a tree. I just like to go along and see what I'm passing and enjoy myself." He had come to the end of his thought, and now he slowly took me in, noticing my layers of old clothes. "What are you doing, anyway?" he asked mildly and curiously.

"Going to work on the railroad." He kept gazing mildly and curiously at me. "Shovel out those tracks. That work they talked about in chapel this morning. You remember."

"Have a nice day at it, anyway," he said.

"I will. You too."

"I will if I find what I'm looking for—a beaver dam. It used to be up the Devon a ways, in a little stream that flows into the Devon. It's interesting to see the way beavers adapt to the winter. Have you ever seen it?"

"No, I never have seen that."

"Well, you might want to come sometime, if I find the place."

"Tell me if you find it."

With Leper it was always a fight, a hard fight to win when you were seventeen years old and lived in a keyed-up, competing school, to avoid making fun of him. But as I had gotten to know him better, this fight had been easier to win.

Shoving in his long bamboo poles, he pushed deliberately forward and slid slowly away from me down the gradual slope, standing very upright, his skis far apart to guard against any threat to his balance, his poles sticking out on either side of him, as though to ward off any interference.

I turned and trudged off to help shovel out New England for the war.

We spent an odd day, toiling in that railroad yard. By the time we arrived there, the snow had become drab and sooted, wet and heavy. We were divided into gangs, each under an old railroad man. Brinker, Chet, and I managed to be in the same group, but the playful atmosphere of the apple orchard was gone. Of the town we could only see some dull red brick mills and warehouses surrounding the yards, and we labored away among what the old man directing us called "rolling stock"—grim freight cars from many parts of the country immobilized in the snow. Brinker asked him if it shouldn't be called "unrolling stock" now, and the old man looked back at him with bleary dislike and didn't reply. Nothing was

very funny that day, the work became hard and unvarying; I began to sweat under my layers of clothes. By the middle of the afternoon, we had lost our fresh volunteer look; the grime of the railroad and the exhaustion of manual laborers were on us all; we seemed of a piece with the railroad yards and the mills and warehouses. The old man resented us, or we made him nervous, or maybe he was as sick as he looked. For whatever reason, he grumbled and spat and alternated between growling orders and rubbing his big, unhealthy belly.

Around 4:30 there was a moment of cheer. The main line had been cleared, and the first train rattled slowly through. We watched it advance toward us, the engine throwing up balls of steam to add to the heavy overcast.

All of us lined both sides of the track and got ready to cheer the engineer and passengers. The coach windows were open, and the passengers surprisingly were hanging out; they were all men, I could discern, all young, all alike. It was a troop train.

Over the clatter and banging of the wheels and couplings, we cheered and they yelled back, both sides taken by surprise. They were not much older than we were and although probably just recruits, they gave the impression of being an elite as they were carried past our drab ranks. They seemed to be having a wonderful time, their uniforms looked new and good; they were clean and energetic; they were going places.

After they had gone, we laborers looked rather emptily across the newly cleared rails at each other, at ourselves, and not even Brinker thought of the timely remark. We turned away. The old man told us to go back to other parts of the yard, but there was no more real work done that afternoon. Stranded in this mill town railroad yard while the whole world was converging elsewhere, we seemed to be nothing but children playing among heroic men.

The day ended at last. Gray from the beginning, its end was announced by a deepening gray, of sky, snow, faces, spirits. We piled back into the old, dispiritedly lit coaches waiting for us, slumped into the uncomfortable green seats, and no one said much until we were miles away.

When we did speak, it was about aviation training programs and brothers in the service and requirements for enlistment and the futility of Devon and how we would never have war stories to tell our grandchildren and how long the war might last and who ever heard of studying dead languages at a time like this.

Quackenbush took advantage of a break in this line of conversation to announce that he would certainly stay at Devon through the year, however half-cocked others might rush off. He elaborated without encouragement, citing the advantages of Devon's physical hardening program and of a high school diploma when he did in good time reach basic training. He for one would advance into the army step by step.

"You for one," echoed someone contemptuously.

"You *are* one," someone else said.

"Which army, Quackenbush? Mussolini's?"

"Naw, he's a Kraut."[3]

"He's a Kraut spy."

"How many rails did you sabotage today, Quackenbush?"

"I thought they interned all Quackenbushes the day after Pearl Harbor."[4]

To which Brinker added: "They didn't find him. He hid his light under a Quackenbush."

We were all tired at the end of that day.

Walking back to the school grounds from the railroad station in the descending darkness, we overtook a lone figure sliding along the snow-covered edge of the street.

"Will you look at Lepellier," began Brinker irritably. "Who does he think he is, the Abominable Snowman?"

"He's just been out skiing around," I said quickly. I didn't want to see today's strained tempers exploding on Leper. Then as we came up beside him, "Did you find the dam, Leper?"

He turned his head slowly, without breaking his forward movement of alternately planted poles and thrust skis, rhythmically but feebly continuous like a homemade piston engine's. "You know what? I did find it," his smile was wide and unfocused, as though not for me alone but for anyone and anything which wished to share this pleasure with him, "and it was really interesting to see. I took some pictures of it, and if they come out I'll bring them over and show you."

"What dam is that?" Brinker asked me.

"It's a . . . well a little dam up the river he knows about," I said.

"I don't know of any dam up the river."

"Well, it's not in the Devon itself, it's in one of the . . . tributaries."

"Tributaries! To the *Devon?*"

"You know, a little creek or something."

---

3. **Kraut** (krout): (contemptuous slang) German.
4. **Pearl Harbor:** The U.S. entered World War II after Japan bombed a military base at Pearl Harbor in Oahu, Hawaii, on December 7, 1941. The speaker refers to the almost immediate expulsion of those Japanese Americans living on America's west coast to "internment camps" in the middle of the country.

He knit his brows in mystification. "What kind of a dam is this, anyway?"

"Well," he couldn't be put off with half a story, "it's a beaver dam."

Brinker's shoulders fell under the weight of this news. "That's the kind of a place I'm in with a world war going on. A school for photographers of beaver dams."

"The beaver never appeared himself," Leper offered.

Brinker turned elaborately toward him. "Didn't he really?"

"No. But I guess I was pretty clumsy getting close to it, so he might have heard me and been frightened."

"Well." Brinker's expansive, dazed tone suggested that here was one of life's giant ironies. "There you are!"

"Yes," agreed Leper after a thoughtful pause, "there you are."

"Here we are," I said, pulling Brinker around the corner we had reached which led to our dormitory. "So long, Leper. Glad you found it."

"Oh," he raised his voice after us, "how was your day? How did the work go?"

"Just like a stag at eve," Brinker roared back. "It was a winter wonderland, every minute." And out of the side of his mouth, to me, "Everybody in this place is either a draft-dodging Kraut or a . . . a . . ." the scornful force of his tone turned the word into a curse, "a *nat-u-ral-ist!*" He grabbed my arm agitatedly. "I'm giving it up, I'm going to enlist. Tomorrow."

I felt a thrill when he said it. This was the logical climax of the whole misbegotten day, this whole out-of-joint term at Devon. I think I had been waiting for a long time for someone to say this so that I could entertain these decisive words myself.

To enlist. To slam the door impulsively on the past, to shed everything down to my last bit of clothing, to break the pattern of my life—that complex design I had been weaving since birth with all its dark threads, its unexplainable symbols set against a conventional background of domestic white and schoolboy blue, all those tangled strands which required the dexterity of a virtuoso to keep flowing—I yearned to take giant military shears to it, snap! bitten off in an instant, and nothing left in my hands but spools of khaki which could weave only a plain, flat, khaki design, however twisted they might be.

Not that it would be a good life. The war would be deadly, all right. But I was used to finding something deadly in things that attracted me; there was always something deadly lurking in anything I wanted, anything I loved. And if it wasn't there,

as for example with Phineas, then I put it there myself.

But in the war, there was no question about it at all; it was there.

I separated from Brinker in the quadrangle, since one of his clubs was meeting and he could not go back to the dormitory yet—"I've got to preside at a meeting of the Golden Fleece Debating Society tonight," he said in a tone of amazed contempt, "the Golden Fleece Debating Society! We're mad here, all mad," and he went off raving to himself in the dark.

It was a night made for hard thoughts. Sharp stars pierced singly through the blackness, not sweeps of them or clusters or Milky Ways as there might have been in the South, but single, chilled points of light, as unromantic as knife blades. Devon, muffled under the gentle occupation of the snow, was dominated by them; the cold Yankee stars ruled this night. They did not invoke in me thoughts of God, or sailing before the mast, or some great love, as crowded night skies at home had done; I thought instead, in the light of those cold points, of the decision facing me.

Why go through the motions of getting an education and watch the war slowly chip away at the one thing I had loved here, the peace, the measureless, careless peace of the Devon summer? Others, the Quackenbushes of this world, could calmly watch the war approach them and jump into it at the last and most advantageous instant, as though buying into the stock market. But I couldn't.

There was no one to stop me but myself. Putting aside soft reservations about What I Owed Devon and my duty to my parents and so on, I reckoned my responsibilities by the light of the unsentimental night sky and knew that I owed no one anything. I owed it to myself to meet this crisis in my life when I chose, and I chose now.

I bounced zestfully up the dormitory stairs. Perhaps because my mind still retained the image of the sharp night stars, those few fixed points of light in the darkness, perhaps because of that the warm yellow light streaming from under my own door came as such a shock. It was a simple case of a change of expectation. The light should have been off. Instead, as though alive itself, it poured in a thin yellow slab of brightness from under the door, illuminating the dust and splinters of the hall floor.

I grabbed the knob and swung open the door. He was seated in my chair at the desk, bending down to adjust the gross encumbrance of his leg, so that only the familiar ears set close against his head were visible, and his short-cut brown hair.

He looked up with a provocative grin. "Hi pal, where's the brass band?"

Everything that had happened throughout the day faded like that first false snowfall of the winter. Phineas was back.

8

"I can see I never should have left you alone," Phineas went on before I could recover from the impact of finding him there. "Where did you get *those* clothes!" His bright, indignant eyes swept from my battered gray cap, down the frayed sweater and paint-stained pants to a pair of clodhoppers. "You don't have to advertise like that, we all know you're the worst-dressed man in the class."

"I've been working, that's all. These are just work clothes."

"In the boiler room?"

"On the railroad. Shoveling snow."

He sat back in the chair. "Shoveling railroad snow. Well, that makes sense, we always did that the first term."

I pulled off the sweater, under which I was wearing a rain slicker I used to go sailing in, a kind of canvas sack. Phineas just studied it in wordless absorption. "I like the cut of it," he finally murmured. I pulled that off revealing an Army fatigue shirt my brother had given me. "Very topical," said Phineas through his teeth. After that came off there was just my undershirt, stained with sweat. He smiled at it for a while and then said as he heaved himself out of the chair, "There. You should have worn that all day, just that. That has real taste. The rest of your outfit was just gilding that lily of a sweat shirt."

"Glad to hear you like it."

"Not at all," he replied ambiguously, reaching for a pair of crutches which leaned against the desk.

I took the sight of this all right, I had seen him on crutches the year before when he broke his ankle playing football. At Devon, crutches had almost as many athletic associations as shoulder pads. And I had never seen an invalid whose skin glowed with such health, accenting the sharp clarity of his eyes, or one who used his arms and shoulders on crutches as though on parallel bars, as though he would do a somersault on them if he felt like it. Phineas vaulted across the room to his cot, yanked back the spread, and then groaned. 'It's not made up. What is all this crap about no maids?"

"No maids," I said. "After all, there's a war on. It's not much of a sacrifice, when you think of people starving and being bombed and all the other things." My unselfishness was responding properly to the influences of 1942. In these past months Phineas and I had grown apart on this; I felt a certain disapproval of him for grumbling about a lost luxury, with a war on. "After all," I repeated, "there is a war on."

"Is there?" he murmured absently. I didn't pay any attention; he was always speaking when his thoughts were somewhere else, asking rhetorical questions and echoing other people's words.

I found some sheets and made up his bed for him. He wasn't a bit sensitive about being helped, not a bit like an invalid striving to seem independent. I put this on the list of things to include when I said some prayers, the first in a long time, that night in bed. Now that Phineas was back, it seemed time to start saying prayers again.

After the lights went out, the special quality of my silence let him know that I was saying them, and he kept quiet for approximately three minutes. Then he began to talk; he never went to sleep without talking first, and he seemed to feel that prayers lasting more than three minutes were showing off. God was always unoccupied in Finny's universe, ready to lend an ear any time at all. Anyone who failed to get his message through in three minutes, as I sometimes failed to do when trying to impress him, Phineas, with my sanctity, wasn't trying.

He was still talking when I fell asleep, and the next morning, through the icy atmosphere which one window raised an inch had admitted to our room, he woke me with the overindignant shout, "What *is* all this crap about no maids!" He was sitting up in bed, as though ready to spring out of it, totally and energetically awake. I had to laugh at this indignant athlete, with the strength of five people, complaining about the service. He threw back his bedclothes and said, "Hand me my crutches, will you?"

Until now, in spite of everything, I had welcomed each new day as though it were a new life, where all past failures and problems were erased, and all future possibilities and joys open and available, to be achieved probably before night fell again. Now, in this winter of snow and crutches with Phineas, I began to know that each morning reasserted the problems of the night before, that sleep suspended all but changed nothing, that you couldn't make yourself over between dawn and dusk. Phineas, however, did not believe this. I'm sure that he looked down at his leg every morning first thing, as soon as he remembered it, to see if it had not been totally restored while he slept. When he found on this first morning back at

Devon that it happened still to be crippled and in a cast, he said in his usual self-contained way, "Hand me my crutches, will you?"

Brinker Hadley, next door, always awoke like an express train. There was a gathering rumble through the wall, as Brinker reared up in bed, coughed hoarsely, slammed his feet on the floor, pounded through the freezing air to the closet for something in the way of clothes, and thundered down the hall to the bathroom. Today, however, he veered and broke into our room instead.

"Ready to sign up?" he shouted before he was through the door. "You ready to en—Finny!"

"You ready to en—what?" pursued Finny from his bed. "Who's ready to sign and en what?"

"Finny. You're back!"

"Sure," confirmed Finny with a slight, pleased grin.

"So," Brinker curled his lip at me, "your little plot didn't work so well after all."

"What's he talking about?" said Finny as I thrust his crutches beneath his shoulders.

"Just talking," I said shortly. "What does Brinker ever talk about?"

"*You* know what I'm talking about well enough."

"No I don't."

"Oh yes you do."

"Are you telling me what I know?"

"Darn right I am."

"What's he *talking* about," said Finny.

The room was bitterly cold. I stood trembling in front of Phineas, still holding his crutches in place, unable to turn and face Brinker and this joke he had gotten into his head, this catastrophic joke.

"He wants to know if I'll sign up with him," I said, "enlist." It was the ultimate question for all seventeen-year-olds that year, and it drove Brinker's insinuations from every mind but mine.

"Yeah," said Brinker.

"Enlist!" cried Finny at the same time. His large and clear eyes turned with an odd expression on me. I had never seen such a look in them before. After looking at me closely, he said, "You're going to enlist?"

"Well, I just thought—last night after the railroad work——"

"You thought you might sign up?" he went on, looking carefully away.

Brinker drew one of his deep senatorial breaths, but he found nothing to say. We three stood shivering in the thin New Hampshire morning light, Finny and I in pajamas, Brinker in a blue flannel bathrobe and ripped moccasins. "When will you?" Finny went on.

"Oh, I don't know," I said. "It was just something Brinker happened to say last night, that's all."

"I said," Brinker began in an unusually guarded voice, glancing quickly at Phineas, "I said something about enlisting today."

Finny hobbled over to the dresser and took up his soap dish. "I'm first in the shower," he said.

"You can't get that cast wet, can you?" asked Brinker.

"No, I'll keep it outside the curtain."

"I'll help," said Brinker.

"No," said Finny without looking at him, "I can manage all right."

"How can you manage all right?" Brinker persisted aggressively.

"I can *manage* all right," Finny repeated with a set face.

I could hardly believe it, but it was too plainly printed in the closed expression of his face to mistake, too discernible beneath the even tone of his voice: Phineas was shocked at the idea of my leaving. In some way he needed me. He needed me. I was the least trustworthy person he had ever met. I knew that; he knew or should know that too. I had even told him. I had told him. But there was no mistaking the shield of remoteness in his face and voice. He wanted me around. The war then passed away from me, and dreams of enlistment and escape and a clean start lost their meaning for me.

"Sure you can manage the shower all right," I said, "but what difference does it make? Come on. Brinker's always . . . Brinker's always getting there first. Enlist! What a nutty idea. It's just Brinker wanting to get there first again. I wouldn't enlist with you if you were General MacArthur's eldest son."

Brinker reared back arrogantly. "And who do you think I am!" But Finny hadn't heard that. His face had broken into a wide and dazzled smile at what I had said, lighting up his whole face. "Enlist!" I drove on, "I wouldn't enlist with you if you were Elliott Roosevelt."[1]

"First cousin," said Brinker over his chin, "once removed."

"He wouldn't enlist with you," Finny plunged in, "if you were Madame Chiang Kai-shek."[2]

"Well," I qualified in an undertone, "he really *is* Madame Chiang Kai-shek."

"Well, fan my brow," cried Finny, giving us his

---

1. **Elliot Roosevelt:** President Roosevelt's eldest son.
2. **Madame Chiang Kai-shek:** wife of the leader of the Nationalist Chinese government.

face when he thought that on the first day of his return to Devon I was going to desert him. I didn't know why he had chosen me, why it was only to me that he could show the most humbling sides of his handicap. I didn't care. For the war was no longer eroding the peaceful summertime stillness I had prized so much at Devon, and although the playing fields were crusted under a foot of congealed snow and the river was now a hard gray-white lane of ice between gaunt trees, peace had come back to Devon for me.

So the war swept over like a wave at the seashore, gathering power and size as it bore on us, overwhelming in its rush, seemingly inescapable, and then at the last moment eluded by a word from Phineas; I had simply ducked, that was all, and the wave's concentrated power had hurtled harmlessly overhead, no doubt throwing others roughly up on the beach, but leaving me peaceably treading water as before. I did not stop to think that one wave is inevitably followed by another even larger and more powerful, when the tide is coming in.

"I *like* the winter," Finny assured me for the fourth time, as we came back from chapel that morning.

"Well, it doesn't like you." Wooden plank walks had been placed on many of the school paths for better footing, but there were icy patches everywhere on them. A crutch misplaced and he could be thrown down upon the frozen wooden planking, or into the ice-encrusted snow.

Even indoors Devon was a nest of traps for him. The school had been largely rebuilt with a massive bequest from an oil family some years before in a peculiar style of Puritan grandeur, as though Versailles had been modified for the needs of a Sunday school. This opulent sobriety betrayed the divided nature of the school, just as in a different way the two rivers that it straddled did. From the outside the buildings were reticent, severe straight lines of red brick or white clapboard, with shutters standing sentinel beside each window, and a few unassuming white cupolas placed here and there on the roofs because they were expected and not pretty, like Pilgrim bonnets.

But once you passed through the Colonial doorways, with only an occasional fan window or low relief pillar to suggest that a certain muted adornment was permissible, you entered an extravaganza of Pompadour[4] splendor. Pink marble walls

stunned look of total appalled horrified amazement, "who would have thought that! Chinese. The Yellow Peril,[3] right here at Devon."

And as far as the history of the Class of 1943 at the Devon School is concerned, this was the only part of our conservation worth preserving. Brinker Hadley had been tagged with a nickname at last, after four years of creating them for others and eluding one himself. "Yellow Peril" Hadley swept through the school with the speed of a flu epidemic, and it must be said to his credit that Brinker took it well enough except when, in its inevitable abbreviation, people sometimes called him "Yellow" instead of "Peril."

But in a week I had forgotten that, and I have never since forgotten the dazed look on Finny's

---

3. **Yellow Peril:** an offensive racist term for Asian people.

4. **Pompadour:** reference to the Marquise de Pompadour, mistress of King Louis XV of France.

and white marble floors were enclosed by arched and vaulted ceilings; an assembly room had been done in the manner of the High Italian Renaissance, another was illuminated by chandeliers flashing with crystal teardrops; there was a wall of fragile French windows overlooking an Italian garden of marble bric-à-brac; the library was Provençal[5] on the first floor, rococo[6] on the second. And everywhere, except in the dormitories, the floors and stairs were of smooth, slick marble, more treacherous even than the icy walks.

"The winter loves me," he retorted, and then, disliking the whimsical sound of that, added, "I mean as much as you can say a season can love. What I mean is, I love winter, and when you really love something, then it loves you back, in whatever way it has to love." I didn't think that this

was true, my seventeen years of experience had shown this to be much more false than true, but it was like every other thought and belief of Finny's: It should have been true. So I didn't argue.

The board walk ended, and he moved a little ahead of me as we descended a sloping path toward our first class. He picked his way with surprising care, surprising in anyone who before had used the ground mainly as a point of departure, as the given element in a suspended world of leaps in space. And now I remembered what I had never taken any special note of before: how Phineas used to walk. Around Devon we had gaits of every description; gangling shuffles from boys who had suddenly grown a foot taller, swinging cowboy lopes from those thinking of how wide their shoulders had become, ambles, waddles, light trippings, gigantic Bunyan strides. But Phineas had moved in continuous flowing balance, so that he had seemed to drift along with no effort at all, relaxation on the move. He hobbled now among the patches of ice. There was the one certainty that Dr. Stanpole had given—Phineas would walk again. But the thought was there before me that he would never walk like that again.

"Do you have a class?" he said as we reached the steps of the building.

"Yes."

"So do I. Let's not go."

"Not go? But what'll we use for an excuse?"

"We'll say I fainted from exertion on the way from chapel," he looked at me with a phantom's smile, "and you had to tend me."

"This is your first day back, Finny. You're no one to cut classes."

"I know, I know. I'm going to work. I really am going to work. You're going to pull me through mostly, but I *am* going to work as hard as I can. Only not today, not the first thing. *Not* now, not conjugating verbs when I haven't even looked at the school yet. I want to see this place; I haven't seen anything except the inside of our room, and the inside of chapel. I don't feel like seeing the inside of a classroom. Not now. Not yet."

"What do you want to see?"

He had started to turn around so that his back was to me. "Let's go to the gym," he said shortly.

The gym was at the other end of the school, a quarter of a mile away at least, separated from us by a field of ice. We set off without saying anything else.

By the time we had reached it, sweat was running like oil from Finny's face, and when he paused, involuntary tremors shook his hands and arms. The leg in its cast was like a sea anchor dragged behind. The illusion of strength I had seen

---

5. **Provençal** (prô·vän·säl´): in the Mediterranean style of Provence, a region in southeast France.
6. **rococo**: eighteenth-century French style of architecture characterized by elaborate decoration.

in our room that morning must have been the same illusion he had used at home to deceive his doctor and his family into sending him back to Devon.

We stood on the ice-coated lawn in front of the gym while he got ready to enter it, resting himself so that he could go in with a show of energy. Later this became his habit; I often caught up with him standing in front of a building, pretending to be thinking or examining the sky or taking off gloves, but it was never a convincing show. Phineas was a poor deceiver, having had no practice.

We went into the gym, along a marble hallway, and to my surprise we went on past the Trophy Room, where his name was already inscribed on one cup, one banner, and one embalmed football. I was sure that this was his goal, to mull over these lost glories. I had prepared myself for that, and even thought of several positive, uplifting aphorisms to cheer him up. But he went by it without a thought, down a stairway, steep and marble, and into the locker room. I went along mystified beside him. There was a pile of dirty towels in a corner. Finny shoved them with a crutch. "What is all this crap," he muttered with a little smile, "about no maids?"

The locker room was empty at this hour, row after row of dull green lockers separated by wide wooden benches. The ceiling was hung with pipes. It was a drab room for Devon, dull green and brown and gray, but at the far end there was a big marble archway, glisteningly white, which led to the pool.

Finny sat down on a bench, struggled out of his sheep-lined winter coat, and took a deep breath of gymnasium air. No locker room could have more pungent air than Devon's; sweat predominated, but it was richly mingled with smells of paraffin and singed rubber, of soaked wool and liniment, and for those who could interpret it, of exhaustion, lost hope and triumph, and bodies battling against each other. I thought it anything but a bad smell. It was preeminently the smell of the human body after it had been used to the limit, such a smell as has meaning and poignance for any athlete, just as it has for any lover.

Phineas looked down here and there, at the exercise bar over a sand pit next to the wall, at a set of weights on the floor, at the rolled-up wrestling mat, at a pair of spiked shoes kicked under a locker.

"Same old place, isn't it?" he said, turning to me and nodding slightly.

After a moment I answered in a quiet voice, "Not exactly."

He made no pretense of not understanding me. After a pause he said, "You're going to be the big star now," in an optimistic tone, and then added with some embarrassment, "you can fill any gaps or anything." He slapped me on the back, "Get over there and chin yourself a few dozen times. What did you finally go out for anyway?"

"I finally didn't go out."

"You aren't," his eyes burned at me from his grimacing face, "still the assistant senior crew manager!"

"No, I quit that. I've just been going to gym classes. The ones they have for guys who aren't going out for anything."

He wrenched himself around on the bench. Joking was past; his mouth widened irritably. "What did you do that for?"

"It was too late to sign up for anything else," and seeing the energy to blast this excuse rushing to his face and neck, I stumbled on, "and anyway, with the war on there won't be many trips for the teams. I don't know, sports don't seem so important with the war on."

"Have you swallowed all that war stuff?"

"No, of course I——" I was so committed to refuting him that I had half-denied the charge before I understood it; now my eyes swung back to his face. "All what war stuff?"

"All that stuff about there being a war."

"I don't think I get what you mean."

"Do you really think that the United States of America is in a state of war with Nazi Germany and Imperial Japan?"

"Do I really think . . ." My voice trailed off.

He stood up, his weight on the good leg, the other resting lightly on the floor in front of him. "Don't be a sap," he gazed with cool self-possession at me, "there isn't any war."

"I know why you're talking like this," I said, struggling to keep up with him. "Now I understand. You're still under the influence of some medicinal drug."

"No, you are. Everybody is." He pivoted so that he was facing directly at me. "That's what this whole war story is. A medicinal drug. Listen, did you ever hear of the 'Roaring Twenties'?" I nodded very slowly and cautiously. "When they all drank bathtub gin and everybody who was young did just what they wanted?"

"Yes."

"Well, what happened was that they didn't like that, the preachers and the old ladies and all the stuffed shirts. So then they tried Prohibition[7] and everybody just got drunker, so then they really

---

7. **Prohibition:** a ban on the sale and consumption of all alcoholic beverages in the U.S., lasting from 1919 to 1933.

got desperate and arranged the Depression.[8] That kept the people who were young in the thirties in their places. But they couldn't use that trick forever, so for us in the forties they've cooked up this war fake."

"Who are 'they,' anyway?"

"The fat old men who don't want us crowding them out of their jobs. They've made it all up. There isn't any real food shortage, for instance. The men have all the best steaks delivered to their clubs now. You've noticed how they've been getting fatter lately, haven't you?"

His tone took it thoroughly for granted that I had. For a moment I was almost taken in by it. Then my eyes fell on the bound and cast white mass pointing at me, and as it was always to do, it brought me down out of Finny's world of invention, down again as I had fallen after awakening that morning, down to reality, to the facts.

"Phineas, this is all pretty amusing and everything, but I hope you don't play this game too much with yourself. You might start to believe it, and then I'd have to make a reservation for you at the Funny Farm."

"In a way," deep in argument, his eyes never wavered from mine, "the whole world is on a Funny Farm now. But it's only the fat old men who get the joke."

"And you."

"Yes, and me."

"What makes you so special? Why should you get it and all the rest of us be in the dark?"

The momentum of the argument abruptly broke from his control. His face froze. "Because I've suffered," he burst out.

We drew back in amazement from this. In the silence all the flighty spirits of the morning ended between us. He sat down and turned his flushed face away from me. I sat next to him without moving for as long as my beating nerves would permit, and then I stood up and walked slowly toward anything which presented itself. It turned out to be the exercise bar. I sprang up, grabbed it, and then, in a fumbling and perhaps grotesque offering to Phineas, I chinned myself. I couldn't think of anything else, not the right words, not the right gesture. I did what I could think of.

---

8. **Depression:** the economic crisis in the U.S. and other countries, beginning with a stock market crash on October 29, 1929, and lasting through most of the 1930's.

"Do thirty of them," he mumbled in a bored voice.

I had never done ten of them. At the twelfth I discovered that he had been counting to himself, because he began to count aloud in a noncommittal, half-heard voice. At eighteen there was a certain enlargement in his tone, and at twenty-three the last edges of boredom left it; he stood up, and the urgency with which he brought out the next numbers was like an invisible boost lifting me the distance of my arms, until he sang out "thirty!" with a flare of pleasure.

The moment was past. Phineas, I know, had been even more startled than I to discover this bitterness in himself. Neither of us ever mentioned it again, and neither of us ever forgot that it was there.

He sat down and studied his clenched hands. "Did I ever tell you," he began in a husky tone, "that I used to be aiming for the Olympics?" He wouldn't have mentioned it except that after what he had said he had to say something very personal, something deeply held. To do otherwise, to begin joking, would have been a hypocritical denial of what had happened, and Phineas was not capable of that.

I was still hanging from the bar; my hands felt as though they had sunk into it. "No, you never told me that," I mumbled into my arm.

"Well, I was. And now I'm not sure, not a hundred percent sure I'll be completely, you know, in shape by 1944. So I'm going to coach you for them instead."

"But there isn't going to be any Olympics in '44. That's only a couple of years away. The war——"

"Leave your fantasy life out of this. We're grooming you for the Olympics, pal, in 1944."

And not believing him, not forgetting that troops were being shuttled toward battlefields all over the world, I went along, as I always did, with any new invention of Finny's. There was no harm in taking aim, even if the target was a dream.

But since we were so far out of the line of fire, the chief sustenance for any sense of the war was mental. We saw nothing real of it; all our impressions of the war were in the false medium of two dimensions—photographs in the papers and magazines, newsreels, posters—or artificially conveyed to us by a voice on the radio, or headlines across the top of a newspaper. I found that only through a continuous use of the imagination could I hold out against Finny's driving offensive in favor of peace.

And now, when we were served chicken livers for dinner, I couldn't help conceiving a mental picture of President Roosevelt and my father and Finny's father and numbers of other large old men sitting down to porterhouse steak in some elaborate but secluded men's secret society room. When a letter from home told me that a trip to visit relatives had been canceled because of gas rationing, it was easy to visualize my father smiling silently with knowing eyes—at least as easy as it was to imagine an American force crawling through the jungles of a place called Guadalcanal[9]—"Wherever that is," as Phineas said.

And when in chapel day after day we were exhorted to new levels of self-deprivation and hard work, with the war as their justification, it was impossible not to see that the faculty were using this excuse to drive us as they had always wanted to drive us, regardless of any war or peace.

What a joke if Finny was right after all!

But of course I didn't believe him. I was too well protected against the great fear of boys' school life, which is to be "taken in." Along with everyone else, except a few professional gulls such as Leper, I rejected anything which had the smallest possibility of doubt about it. So of course I didn't believe him. But one day after our chaplain, Mr. Carhart, had become very moved by his own sermon in chapel about God in the Foxholes, I came away thinking that if Finny's opinion of the war was unreal, Mr. Carhart's was at least as unreal. But of course I didn't believe him.

And anyway, I was too occupied to think about it all. In addition to my own work, I was dividing my time between tutoring Finny in studies and being tutored by him in sports. Since so much of learning anything depends on the atmosphere in which it is taught, Finny and I, to our joint double amazement, began to make flashing progress where we had been bumblers before.

Mornings we got up at six to run. I dressed in a gym sweat suit with a towel tucked around my throat, and Finny in pajamas, ski boots and his sheep-lined coat.

A morning shortly before Christmas vacation brought my reward. I was to run the course Finny had laid out, four times around an oval walk which circled the Headmaster's home, a large rambling, doubtfully Colonial white mansion. Next to the house there was a patriarchal elm tree, against the trunk of which Finny leaned and shouted at me as I ran a large circle around him.

This plain of snow shone a powdery white that

---

9. **Guadalcanal** (gwä′d·l·kə·nal′): largest of the Solomon Islands in the southwest Pacific, site of a major U.S. victory over Japan in November 1942.

morning; the sun blazed icily somewhere too low on the horizon to be seen directly, but its clean rays shed a blue-white glimmer all around us. The northern sunshine seemed to pick up faint particles of whiteness floating in the air and powdering the sleek blue sky. Nothing stirred. The bare, arching branches of the elm seemed laid into this motionless sky. As I ran, the sound of my footfalls was pinched off short in the vast immobile dawn, as though there was no room amid so many glittering sights for any sound to intrude. The figure of Phineas was set against the bulk of the tree; he shouted now and then, but these sounds too were quickly absorbed and dispelled.

And he needed to give no advice that morning. After making two circuits of the walk, every trace of energy was, as usual, completely used up, and as I drove myself on, all my scattered aches found their usual way to a profound seat of pain in my side. My lungs, as usual, were fed up with all this work and from now on would only go rackingly through the motions. My knees were boneless again, ready any minute to let my lower legs telescope up into the thighs. My head felt as though different sections of the cranium were grinding into each other.

Then, for no reason at all, I felt magnificent. It was as though my body until that instant had simply been lazy, as though the aches and exhaustion were all imagined, created from nothing in order to keep me from truly exerting myself. Now my body seemed at last to say, "Well, if you must have it, here!" and an accession of strength came flooding through me. Buoyed up, I forgot my usual feeling of routine self-pity when working out; I lost myself, oppressed mind along with aching body. All entanglements were shed, I broke into the clear.

After the fourth circuit, like sitting in a chair, I pulled up in front of Phineas.

"You're not even winded," he said.

"I know."

"You found your rhythm, didn't you, that third time around. Just as you came into the straight part there."

"Yes, right there."

"You've been pretty lazy all along, haven't you?"

"Yes, I guess I have been."

"You didn't even know anything about yourself."

"I don't guess I did, in a way."

"Well," he gathered the sheepskin collar around his throat, "now you know. And stop talking like a Georgia cracker—'don't guess I did'!" Despite this gibe he was rather impersonal toward me. He seemed older that morning, and leaning quietly against that great tree wrapped in his heavy coat, he seemed smaller too. Or perhaps it was only that I, inside the same body, had felt myself all at once grown bigger.

We proceeded slowly back to the dormitory. On the steps going in we met Mr. Ludsbury coming out.

"I've been watching you from my window," he said in his hooting voice with a rare trace of personal interest. "What are you up to, Forrester, training for the Commandos?" There was no rule explicitly forbidding exercise at such an hour, but it was not expected; ordinarily, therefore, Mr. Ludsbury would have disapproved. But the war had modified even his standards; all forms of physical exercise had become conventional for the Duration.

I mumbled some abashed answer, but it was Phineas who made the clear response.

"He's developing into a real athlete," he said matter-of-factly. "We're aiming for the '44 Olympics."

Mr. Ludsbury emitted a single chuckle from deep in his throat, then his face turned brick red momentarily and he assumed his customary sententiousness. "Games are all right in their place," he said, "and I won't bore you with the Eton Playing Fields observation, but all exercise today is aimed of course at the approaching Waterloo.[10] Keep that in your sights at all times, won't you."

Finny's face set in determination, with the older look I had just detected in him. "No," he said.

I don't believe any student had ever said "No" flatly to Mr. Ludsbury before. It flustered him uncontrollably. His face turned brick red again, and for a moment I thought he was going to run away. Then he said something so rapid, throaty, and clipped that neither of us understood it, turned quickly, and strode off across the quadrangle.

"He's really sincere, he thinks there's a war on," said Finny in simple wonder. "Now why wouldn't he know?" He pondered Mr. Ludsbury's exclusion from the plot of the fat old men as we watched his figure, reedy even in his winter wraps, move away from us. Then the light broke. "Oh, of course!" he cried. "Too thin. Of course."

I stood there pitying Mr. Ludsbury for his fatal thinness and reflecting that, after all, he had always had a gullible side.

---

10. **Eton Playing Fields . . . Waterloo:** allusion to the saying "The battle of Waterloo was won on the playing fields of Eton." Eton is a prestigious English boys' school. In other words, the British soldiers who defeated Napoleon at Waterloo in 1815 learned their military strategies through sports.

9

This was my first but not my last lapse into Finny's vision of peace. For hours, and sometimes for days, I fell without realizing it into the private explanation of the world. Not that I ever believed that the whole production of World War II was a trick of the eye manipulated by a bunch of calculating fat old men, appealing though this idea was. What deceived me was my own happiness; for peace is indivisible, and the surrounding world confusion found no reflection inside me. So I ceased to have any real sense of it.

This was not shaken even by the enlistment of Leper Lepellier. In fact, that made the war seem more unreal than ever. No real war could draw Leper voluntarily away from his snails and beaver dams. His enlistment seemed just another of Leper's vagaries, such as the time he slept on top of Mount Katahdin in Maine, where each morning the sun first strikes United States territory. On that morning, satisfying one of his urges to participate in nature, Leper Lepellier was the first thing the rising sun struck in the United States.

Early in January, when we had all just returned from the Christmas holidays, a recruiter from the United States ski troops showed a film to the senior class in the Renaissance Room. To Leper it revealed what all of us were seeking: a recognizable and friendly face to the war. Skiers in white shrouds winged down virgin slopes, silent as angels, and then, realistically, herringboned up again, but herringboned in cheerful, sunburned bands, with clear eyes and white teeth and chests full of vigor-laden mountain air. It was the cleanest image of war I had ever seen; even the Air Force, reputedly so high above the infantry's mud, was stained with axle grease by comparison, and the Navy was vulnerable to scurvy. Nothing tainted these white warriors of winter as they swooped down their spotless mountainsides, and this cool, clear response to war glided straight into Leper's Vermont heart.

"How do you like that!" he whispered to me in a wondering voice during these scenes. "How do you like that!"

"You know, I think these are pictures of Finnish ski troops," Phineas whispered on the other side, "and I want to know when they start shooting our allies the Bolsheviks.[1] Unless that war between them was a fake too, which I'm pretty sure it was."

After the movie ended and the lights came on to illuminate the murals of Tuscany and the painted classical galleries around us, Leper still sat amazed in his folding chair. Ordinarily he talked little, and the number of words which came from him now indicated that this was a turning point in his life.

"You know what? Now I see what racing skiing is all about. It's all right to miss seeing the trees and the countryside and all the other things when you've got to be in a hurry. And when you're in

---

1. **Bolsheviks:** that is, the Soviets. The Bolsheviks were the faction that seized power during the 1917 Russian Revolution and later formed the Communist Party. The Soviets fought with the United States and its allies in World War II.

a War you've got to be in a hurry. Don't you? So I guess maybe racing skiers weren't ruining the sport after all. They were preparing it, if you see what I mean, for the future. Everything has to evolve or else it perishes." Finny and I had stood up, and Leper looked earnestly from one to the other of us from his chair. "Take the housefly. If it hadn't developed all those split-second reflexes, it would have become extinct long ago."

"You mean it adapted itself to the fly swatter?" queried Phineas.

"That's right. And skiing had to learn to move just as fast or it would have been wiped out by this war. Yes, sir. You know what? I'm almost glad this war came along. It's like a test, isn't it, and only the things and the people who've been evolving the right way survive."

You usually listened to Leper's quiet talking with half a mind, but this theory of his brought me to close attention. How did it apply to me, and to Phineas? How, most of all, did it apply to Leper?

"I'm going to enlist in these ski troops," he went on mildly, so unemphatically that my mind went back to half-listening. Threats to enlist that winter were always declaimed like Brinker's, with a grinding of back teeth and a flashing of eyes; I had already heard plenty of them. But only Leper's was serious.

A week later he was gone. He had been within a few weeks of his eighteenth birthday, and with it all chance of enlistment, of choosing a service rather than being drafted into one, would have disappeared. The ski movie had decided him. "I always thought the war would come for me when it wanted me," he said when he came to say good-bye the last day. "I never thought I'd be going to it. I'm really glad I saw that movie in time, you bet I am." Then, as the Devon School's first recruit to World War II, he went out my doorway with his white stocking cap bobbing behind.

It probably would have been better for all of us if someone like Brinker had been the first to go. He could have been depended upon to take a loud, dramatic departure, so that the school would have reverberated for weeks afterward with Brinker's Last Words, Brinker's Military Bearing, Brinker's Sense of Duty. And all of us, influenced by the vacuum of his absence, would have felt the touch of war as a daily fact.

But the disappearing tail of Leper's cap inspired none of this. For a few days the war was more unimaginable than ever. We didn't mention it and we didn't mention Leper, until at last Brinker found a workable point of view. One day in the Butt Room he read aloud a rumor in a newspaper

about an attempt on Hitler's life. He lowered the paper, gazed in a visionary way in front of him, and then remarked, "That was Leper, of course."

This established our liaison with World War II. The Tunisian campaign[2] became "Leper's liberation"; the bombing of the Ruhr[3] was greeted by Brinker with hurt surprise: "He didn't tell us he'd left the ski troops"; the torpedoing of the *Scharnhorst*:[4] "At it again." Leper sprang up all over the world at the core of every Allied success. We talked about Leper's stand at Stalingrad,[5] Leper on the Burma Road,[6] Leper's convoy to Archangel;[7] we surmised that the crisis over the leadership of the Free French would be resolved by the appointment of neither de Gaulle[8] nor Giraud[9] but Lepellier; we knew, better than the newspapers, that it was not the Big Three[10] but the Big Four who were running the war.

In the silences between jokes about Leper's glories, we wondered whether we ourselves would measure up to the humblest minimum standard of the army. I did not know everything there was to know about myself, and knew that I did not know it; I wondered in the silences between jokes about Leper whether the still hidden parts of myself might contain the Sad Sack,[11] the outcast, or the coward. We were all at our funniest about Leper, and we all secretly hoped that Leper, that incompetent, was as heroic as we said.

Everyone contributed to this legend except Phineas. At the outset, with the attempt on Hitler's life, Finny had said, "If someone gave Leper a loaded gun and put it at Hitler's temple, he'd miss." There was a general shout of outrage, and then we recommended the building of Leper's

---

2. **Tunisian campaign:** Allied campaign in 1942 and 1943 to liberate German-occupied Tunisia, in North Africa.
3. **Ruhr:** a river valley in Germany where many coal mines and munitions factories were located.
4. *Scharnhorst:* German battleship sunk by the British navy on December 26, 1943.
5. **Stalingrad:** city in the Soviet Union, now called Volgograd. Germany's defeat at the Battle of Stalingrad, fought from August 1942 to February 1943, was a major turning point in the war.
6. **Burma Road:** Allied supply route stretching seven hundred miles through southeast Asia.
7. **Archangel:** important Arctic port in the Soviet Union.
8. **de Gaulle:** Charles de Gaulle (1890–1970), commander of the Free French Forces during World War II and later president of France.
9. **Giraud** (zhē·rō′): Henri Giraud, French general and in 1943 co-president with de Gaulle of the French Committee of National Liberation.
10. **Big Three:** the United States, Great Britain, and the Soviet Union under the leadership of Roosevelt, Churchill, and Stalin.
11. **Sad Sack:** a comic-strip character who was a hopelessly incompetent soldier; any inept person.

triumphal arch around Brinker's keystone. Phineas took no part in it, and since little else was talked about in the Butt Room, he soon stopped going there and stopped me from going as well—"How do you expect to be an athlete if you smoke like a forest fire?" He drew me increasingly away from the Butt Room crowd, away from Brinker and Chet and all other friends, into a world inhabited by just himself and me, where there was no war at all, just Phineas and me alone among all the people of the world, training for the Olympics of 1944.

Saturday afternoons are terrible in a boys' school, especially in the winter. There is no football game; it is not possible, as it is in the spring, to take bicycle trips into the surrounding country. Not even the most grinding student can feel required to lose himself in his books, since there is Sunday ahead, long, lazy, quiet Sunday, to do any homework.

And these Saturdays are worst in the late winter when the snow has lost its novelty and its shine, and the school seems to have been reduced to only a network of drains. During the brief thaw in the early afternoon, there is a dismal gurgling of dirty water seeping down pipes and along gutters, a gray seamy shifting beneath the crust of snow, which cracks to show patches of frozen mud beneath. Shrubbery loses its bright snow headgear and stands bare and frail, too undernourished to hide the drains it was intended to hide. These are the days when, going into any building, you cross a mat of dirt and cinders led in by others before you, thinning and finally trailing off in the corridors. The sky is an empty, hopeless gray and gives the impression that this is its eternal shade. Winter's occupation seems to have conquered, overrun, and destroyed everything, so that now there is no longer any resistance movement left in nature; all the juices are dead, every sprig of vitality snapped, and now winter itself, an old, corrupt, tired conqueror, loosens its grip on the desolation, recedes a little, grows careless in its watch; sick of victory and enfeebled by the absence of challenge, it begins itself to withdraw from the ruined countryside. The drains alone are active, and on these Saturdays their noises sound a dull recessional to winter.

Only Phineas failed to see what was so depressing. Just as there was no war in his philosophy, there was also no dreary weather. As I have said, all weathers delighted Phineas. "You know what we'd better do next Saturday?" he began in one of his voices, the low-pitched and evenly melodic one which for some reason always reminded me of a Rolls-Royce moving along a highway. "We'd better organize the Winter Carnival."

We were sitting in our room, on either side of the single large window framing a square of fea-

tureless gray sky. Phineas was resting his cast, which was a considerably smaller one now, on the desk and thoughtfully pressing designs into it with a pocket knife. "What Winter Carnival?" I asked.

"*The* Winter Carnival. The Devon Winter Carnival."

"There isn't any Devon Winter Carnival and never has been."

"There is now. We'll have it in that park next to the Naguamsett. The main attraction will be sports, naturally, featuring, I expect, a ski jump——"

"A ski jump! That park's as flat as a pancake."

"——and some slalom races, and I think a little track. But we've got to have some snow statues too, and a little music, and something to eat. Now, which committee do you want to head?"

I gave him a wintry smile. "The snow statues committee."

"I knew you would. You always were secretly arty, weren't you? I'll organize the sports, Brinker can handle the music and food, and then we need somebody to kind of beautify the place, a few holly wreaths and things like that. Someone good with plants and shrubbery. I know. Leper."

From looking at the star he was imprinting in his cast I looked quickly up at his face. "Leper's gone."

"Oh yeah, so he is. Leper *would* be gone. Well, somebody else then."

And because it was Finny's idea, it happened as he said, although not as easily as some of his earlier inspirations. For our dormitory was less enthusiastic about almost everything with each succeeding week. Brinker, for example, had begun a long, decisive sequence of withdrawals from school activity ever since the morning I deserted his enlistment plan. He had not resented my change of heart, and in fact had immediately undergone one himself. If he could not enlist—and for all his self-sufficiency Brinker could not do much without company—he could at least cease to be so multifariously civilian. So he resigned the presidency of the Golden Fleece Debating Society, stopped writing his school spirit column for the newspaper, dropped the chairmanship of the Underprivileged Local Children subcommittee of the Good Samaritan Confraternity, stilled his baritone in the chapel choir, and even, in his most impressive burst of irresponsibility, resigned from the Student Advisory Committee to the Headmaster's Discretionary Benevolent Fund. His well-bred clothes had disappeared; these days he wore khaki pants supported by a garrison belt, and boots which rattled when he walked.

"Who wants a Winter Carnival?" he said in the disillusioned way he had lately developed, when I brought it up. "What are we supposed to be celebrating?"

"Winter, I guess."

"Winter!" He gazed out of his window at the vacant sky and seeping ground. "Frankly, I just don't see anything to celebrate, winter or spring or anything else."

"This is the first time Finny's gotten going on anything since . . . he came back."

"He has been kind of nonfunctional, hasn't he? He isn't *brooding,* is he?"

"No, he wouldn't brood."

"No, I don't suppose he would. Well, if you think it's something Finny really wants. Still, there's never been a Winter Carnival here. I think there's probably a rule against it."

"I see," I said in a tone which made Brinker raise his eyes and lock them with mine. In that plotters' glance all his doubts vanished, for Brinker the Lawgiver had turned rebel for the Duration.

The Saturday was battleship gray. Throughout the morning, equipment for the Winter Carnival had been spirited out of the dormitory and down to the small, incomplete public park on the bank of the Naguamsett River. Brinker supervised the transfer, rattling up and down the stairwell and giving orders. He made me think of a pirate captain disposing of the booty. Several jugs of very hard cider which he had browbeaten away from some lowerclassmen were the most cautiously guarded treasure. They were buried in the snow near a clump of evergreens in the center of the park, and Brinker stationed his roommate, Brownie Perkins, to guard them with his life. He meant this literally, and Brownie knew it. So he trembled alone there in the middle of the park for hours, wondering what would happen if he had an attack of appendicitis, unnerved by the thoughts of a fainting spell, horrified by the realization that he might have to move his bowels, until at last we came. Then Brownie crept back to the dormitory, too exhausted to enjoy the carnival at all. On this day of high illegal competitiveness, no one noticed.

The buried cider was half-consciously plotted at the hub of the carnival. Around it sprang up large, sloppy statues, easily modeled because of the snow's dampness. Nearby, entirely out of place in this snowscape, like a dowager in a saloon, there was a heavy circular classroom table, carried there by superhuman exertions the night before on Finny's insistence that he had to have *something* to display the prizes on. On it rested the prizes—Finny's icebox, hidden all these months in the dormitory basement, a Webster's

Collegiate Dictionary with all the most stimulating words marked, a set of York barbells, the *Iliad* with the English translation of each sentence written above it, Brinker's file of Betty Grable[12] photographs, a lock of hair cut under duress from the head of Hazel Brewster, the professional town belle, a handwoven rope ladder with the proviso that it should be awarded to someone occupying a room on the third floor or higher, a forged draft registration card, and $4.13 from the Headmaster's Discretionary Benevolent Fund. Brinker placed this last prize on the table with such silent dignity that we all thought it was better not to ask any questions about it.

Phineas sat behind the table in a heavily carved black walnut chair; the arms ended in two lions' heads, and the legs ended in paws gripping wheels now sunk in the snow. He had made the purchase that morning. Phineas bought things only on impulse and only when he had the money, and since the two states rarely coincided, his purchases were few and strange.

Chet Douglass stood next to him, holding his trumpet. Finny had regretfully given up the plan of inviting the school band to supply music, since it would have spread news of our carnival to every corner of the campus. Chet in any case was an improvement over that cacophony. He was a slim, fair-skinned boy with a ball of curly auburn hair curving over his forehead, and he devoted himself to playing two things, tennis and the trumpet. He did both with such easy, inborn skill that after observing him, I had begun to think that I could master either one any weekend I tried. Much like the rest of us on the surface, he had an underlying obliging and considerate strain which barred him from being a really important member of the class. You had to be rude at least sometimes and edgy often to be credited with "personality," and without that accolade no one at Devon could be anyone. No one, with the exception of course of Phineas.

To the left of the Prize Table, Brinker straddled his cache of cider; behind him was the clump of evergreens, and behind them there was after all a gentle rise, where the Ski Jump Committee was pounding snow into a little take-off ramp whose lip was perhaps a foot higher than the slope of the rise. From there our line of snow statues, unrecognizable artistic attacks on the Headmaster, Mr. Ludsbury, Mr. Patch-Withers, Dr. Stanpole, the new dietitian, and Hazel Brewster curved in an enclosing half-circle to the icy, muddy, lisping edge of the tidewater Naguamsett and back to the other side of the Prize Table.

When the ski jump was ready, there was a certain amount of milling around; twenty boys, tightly reined in all winter, stood now as though with the bit firmly clamped between their teeth, ready to stampede. Phineas should have started the sports events, but he was absorbed in cataloging the prizes. All eyes swung next upon Brinker. He had been holding a pose above his cider of Gibraltar[13] invulnerability; he continued to gaze challengingly around him until he began to realize that wherever he looked, calculating eyes looked back.

"All right, all right," he said roughly, "let's get started."

The ragged circle around him moved perceptibly closer.

"Let's get going," he yelled. "Come on, Finny. What's first?"

Phineas had one of those minds which could record what is happening in the background and do nothing about it because something else was preoccupying him. He seemed to sink deeper into his list.

"Phineas!" Brinker pronounced his name with a maximum use of the teeth. "What is next?"

Still the sleek brown head bent mesmerized over the list.

"What's the big hurry, Brinker?" someone from the tightening circle asked with dangerous gentleness. "What's the big rush?"

"We can't stand here all day," he blurted. "We've got to get started if we're going to have this darn thing. What's *next*? Phineas!"

At last the recording in Finny's mind reached its climax. He looked vaguely up, studied the straddling, at-bay figure of Brinker at the core of the poised perimeter of boys, hesitated, blinked, and then in his organ voice said good-naturedly, "Next? Well, that's pretty clear. You are."

Chet released from his trumpet the opening, lifting, barbaric call of a bullfight, and the circle of boys broke wildly over Brinker. He flailed back against the evergreens, and the jugs appeared to spring out of the snow. "What the heck," he kept yelling, off balance among the branches. "*What . . . the . . . heck!*" By then his cider, which he had apparently expected to dole out according to his own governing whim, was disappearing. There was going to be no government, even by whim, even by Brinker's whim, on this Saturday at Devon.

---

12. **Betty Grable:** glamorous American film star, famous as a pin-up girl during World War II.

13. **Gibraltar:** like the Rock of Gibraltar, a small peninsula with a mass of rock at the southern tip of Spain.

From a scramble of contenders I got one of the jugs, elbowed off a counterattack, opened it, sampled it, choked, and then went through with my original plan by stopping Brinker's mouth with it. His eyes bulged, and blood vessels in his throat began to pulsate, until at length I lowered the jug.

He gave me a long, pondering look, his face closed and concentrating while behind it his mind plainly teetered between fury and hilarity; I think if I had batted an eye, he would have hit me. The carnival's breaking apart into a riot hung like a bomb between us. I kept on looking expressionlessly back at him until beneath a blackening scowl his mouth opened enough to fire out the words, "I've been violated."

I jerked the jug to my mouth and took a huge gulp of cider in relief, and the violence latent in the day drifted away; perhaps the Naguamsett carried it out on the receding tide. Brinker strode through the swirl of boys to Phineas. "I formally declare," he bellowed, "that these Games are open."

"You can't do that," Finny said rebukingly. "Who ever heard of opening the Games without the sacred fire from Olympus?"

Sensing that I must act as the Chorus, I registered on my face the universally unheard-of quality of the Games without fire. "Fire, fire," I said across the damp snow.

"We'll sacrifice one of the prizes," said Phineas, seizing the *Iliad*. He sprinkled the pages with cider to make them more inflammable, touched a match to them, and a little jet of flame curled upward. The Games, alight with Homer and cider, were open.

Chet Douglass, leaning against the side of the Prize Table, continued to blow musical figures for his own enlightenment. Forgetful of us and the athletic programming Finny now put into motion, he strolled here and there, sometimes at the start of the ski jump competition, blowing an appropriate call, more often invoking the serene order of Haydn,[14] or a high, remote, arrogant Spanish world, or the cheerful, lowdown carelessness of New Orleans.

The hard cider began to take charge of us. Or I wonder now whether it wasn't cider but our own exuberance which intoxicated us, sent restraint flying, causing Brinker to throw the football block on the statue of the Headmaster, giving me, as I put on the skis and slid down the small slope and off the miniature ski jump, a sensation of soaring flight, of hurtling high and far through space; inspiring Phineas, during one of Chet's Spanish inventions, to climb onto the Prize Table and with only one leg to create a droll dance among the prizes, springing and spinning from one bare space to another, cleanly missing Hazel Brewster's hair, never marring by a misstep the pictures of Betty Grable. Under the influence not, I know, of the hardest cider but of his own inner joy at life for a moment as it should be, as it was meant to be in his nature, Phineas recaptured that magic gift for existing primarily in space, one foot conceding briefly to gravity its rights before spinning him off again into the air. It was his wildest demonstration of himself, of himself in the kind of world he loved; it was his choreography of peace.

And when he stopped and sat down among the prizes and said, "Now we're going to have the Decathlon. Quiet everybody, our Olympic candidate, Gene Forrester, is now going to qualify," it wasn't cider which made me in this moment champion of everything he ordered, to run as though I were the abstraction of speed, to walk the half-circle of statues on my hands, to balance on my head on top of the icebox on top of the Prize Table, to jump if he had asked it across the Naguamsett and land crashing in the middle of Quackenbush's boathouse, to accept at the end of it amid a clatter of applause—for on this day even the schoolboy egotism of Devon was conjured away—a wreath made from the evergreen trees which Phineas placed on my head. It wasn't the cider which made me surpass myself, it was this liberation we had torn from the gray encroachments of 1943, the escape we had concocted, this afternoon of momentary, illusory, special and separate peace.

And it was this which caused me not to notice Brownie Perkins rejoin us from the dormitory, and not to hear what he was saying until Finny cried hilariously, "A telegram for Gene? It's the Olympic Committee. They want you! Of course they want you! Give it to me, Brownie, I'll read it aloud to this assembled host." And it was this which drained away as I watched Finny's face pass through all the gradations between uproariousness and shock.

I took the telegram from Phineas, facing in advance whatever the destruction was. That was what I learned to do that winter.

I HAVE ESCAPED AND NEED HELP. I AM AT CHRISTMAS LOCATION. YOU UNDERSTAND. NO NEED TO RISK ADDRESS HERE. MY SAFETY DEPENDS ON YOU COMING AT ONCE.
(signed) YOUR BEST FRIEND,
ELWIN LEPER LEPELLIER.

---

14. **Haydn:** Franz Joseph Haydn (1732–1809), Austrian composer.

10

That night I made for the first time the kind of journey which later became the monotonous routine of my life: traveling through an unknown countryside from one unknown settlement to another. The next year this became the dominant activity, or rather passivity, of my army career, not fighting, not marching, but this kind of nighttime ricochet; for, as it turned out, I never got to the war.

I went into uniform at the time when our enemies began to recede so fast that there had to be a hurried telescoping of military training plans. Programs scheduled to culminate in two years became outmoded in six months, and crowds of men gathered for them in one place were dispersed to twenty others. A new weapon appeared and those of us who had traveled to three or four bases mastering the old one were sent on to a fifth, sixth, and seventh to master the new. The closer victory came, the faster we were shuttled around America in pursuit of a role to play in a drama which suddenly, underpopulated from the first, now had too many actors. Or so it seemed. In reality there would have been, as always, too few, except that the last act, a mass assault against suicidally defended Japan, never took place. I and my year—not "my generation," for destiny now cut too finely for that old phrase—I and those of my year were preeminently eligible for that. Most of us, so it was estimated, would be killed. But the men a little bit older closed in on the enemy faster than predicted, and then there was the final holocaust of the Bomb. It seemed to have saved our lives.[1]

So journeys through unknown parts of America became my chief war memory, and I think of the first of them as this nighttime trip to Leper's. There was no question of where to find him; "I am at Christmas location" meant that he was at home. He lived far up in Vermont, where at this season of the year even the paved main highways are bumpy and buckling from the freezing weather, and each house executes a lonely holding action against the cold. The natural state of things is coldness, and houses are fragile havens, holdouts in a death landscape, unforgettably comfortable, simple though they are, just because of their warmth.

Leper's was one of these hearths perched by

itself on a frozen hillside. I reached it in the early morning after this night which presaged my war; a bleak, draughty train ride, a damp depot seemingly near no town whatever, a bus station in which none of the people were fully awake, or seemed clean, or looked as though they had homes anywhere; a bus which passengers entered and left at desolate stopping places in the blackness; a chilled nighttime wandering in which I tried to decipher, between lapses into stale sleep, the meaning of Leper's telegram.

I reached the town at dawn, and encouraged by the returning light, and coffee in a thick white cup, I accepted a hopeful interpretation. Leper had "escaped." You didn't "escape" from the army, so he must have escaped from something else. The most logical thing a soldier escapes from is danger, death, the enemy. Since Leper hadn't been overseas, the enemy must have been in this country. And the only enemies in this country would be spies. Leper had escaped from spies.

I seized this conclusion and didn't try to go beyond it. I suppose all our Butt Room stories about him intriguing around the world had made me half-ready to half-believe something like this. I felt a measureless relief when it occurred to me. There was some color, some hope, some life in this war after all. The first friend of mine who ever went into it tangled almost immediately with spies. I began to hope that after all this wasn't going to be such a bad war.

The Lepellier house was not far out of town, I was told. There was no taxi, I was also told, and there was no one, I did not need to be told, who would offer to drive me out there. This was Vermont. But if that meant austerity toward strangers, it also meant mornings of glory such as this one, in which the snow, white almost to blueness, lay like a soft comforter over the hills, and birches and pines indestructibly held their ground, rigid lines against the snow and sky, very thin and very strong like Vermonters.

The sun was the blessing of the morning, the one celebrating element, an aesthete with no purpose except to shed radiance. Everything else was sharp and hard, but this Grecian sun evoked joy from every angularity and blurred with brightness the stiff face of the countryside. As I walked briskly out the road the wind knifed at my face, but this sun caressed the back of my neck.

The road led out along the side of a ridge, and after a mile or so I saw the house that must be Leper's, riding the top of the slope. It was another brittle-looking Vermont house, white of course, with long and narrow windows like New England faces. Behind one of them hung a gold star which

---

1. The dropping of the atomic bombs on the Japanese cities of Hiroshima (August 6, 1945) and Nagasaki (August 9, 1945) made a prolonged, bloody ground war in Japan unnecessary.

announced that a son of the house was serving the country, and behind another stood Leper.

Although I was walking straight toward his front door, he beckoned me on several times, and he never took his eyes from me, as though it was they which held me to my course. He was still at this ground-floor window when I reached the door, and so I opened it myself and stepped into the hallway. Leper had come to the entrance of the room on the right, the dining room.

"Come in here," he said, "I spend most of my time in here."

As usual there were no preliminaries. "What do you do that for, Leper? It's not very comfortable, is it?"

"Well, it's a useful room."

"Yes, I guess it's useful, all right."

"You aren't lost for something to do in dining rooms. It's in the living room where people can't figure out what to do with themselves. People get problems in living rooms."

"Bedrooms too." It was a try toward relieving the foreboding in his manner; it only worked to deepen it.

He turned away, and I followed him into an underfurnished dining room of high-backed chairs, rugless floor, and cold fireplace. "If you want to be in a really functional room," I began with false heartiness, "you ought to spend your time in the bathroom, then."

He looked at me, and I noticed the left side of his upper lip lift once or twice as though he was about to snarl or cry. Then I realized that this had nothing to do with his mood, that it was involuntary.

He sat down at the head of the table in the only chair with arms, his father's chair, I supposed. I took off my coat and sat in a place at the middle of the table, with my back to the fireplace. There at least I could look at the sun rejoicing on the snow.

"In here you never wonder what's going to happen. You know the meals will come in three times a day for instance."

"I'll bet your mother isn't too pleased when she's trying to get one ready."

Force sprang into his expression for the first time. "What's she got to be pleased about!" He glared challengingly into my startled face. "I'm pleasing *myself!*" he cried fervently, and I saw tears trembling in his eyes.

"Well, she's probably pleased." Any words would serve, the more irrelevant and superficial the better, any words which would stop him; I didn't want to see this. "She's probably pleased to have you home again."

His face resumed its dull expression. The responsibility for continuing the conversation, since I had forced it to be superficial, was mine. "How long'll you be here?"

He shrugged, a look of disgust with my question crossing his face. The careful politeness he had always had was gone.

"Well, if you're on furlough you must know when you have to be back." I said this in what I thought of at the time as my older voice, a little businesslike and experienced. "The army doesn't give out passes and then say, "Come back when you've had enough, hear?""

"I didn't get any pass," he groaned; with the sliding despair of his face and his clenched hands, that's what it was; a groan.

"I know you said," I spoke in short, expressionless syllables, "that you 'escaped.'" I no longer wanted this to be true, I no longer wanted it to be connected with spies or desertion or anything out of the ordinary. I knew it was going to be, and I no longer wanted it to be.

"I *escaped!*" the word surging out in a voice and intensity that was not Leper's. His face was furious, but his eyes denied the fury; instead they saw it before them. They were filled with terror.

"What do you mean, you escaped?" I said sharply. "You don't escape from the army."

"That's what you say. But that's because you're talking through your hat." His eyes were furious now too, glaring blindly at me. "What do you know about it, anyway?" None of this could have been said by the Leper of the beaver dam.

"Well I—how am I supposed to answer that? I know what's normal in the army, that's all."

"Normal," he repeated bitterly. "What a stupid word that is. I suppose that's what you're thinking about, isn't it? That's what you would be thinking about, somebody like you. You're thinking I'm not normal, aren't you? I can see what you're thinking—I see a lot I never saw before"—his voice fell to a querulous whisper—"you're thinking I'm psycho."

I gathered what the word meant. I hated the sound of it at once. It opened up a world I had not known existed—"mad" or "crazy" or "a screw loose," those were the familiar words. "Psycho" had a sudden mental-ward reality about it, a systematic, diagnostic sound. It was as though Leper had learned it while in captivity, far from Devon or Vermont or any experience we had in common, as thought it were in Japanese.

Fear seized my stomach like a cramp. I didn't care what I said to him now; it was myself I was worried about. For if Leper was psycho, it was the army which had done it to him, and I and all of us were on the brink of the army. "You make me sick, you and your darn army words."

"They were going to give me," he was almost laughing, everywhere but in his eyes, which continued to oppose all he said, "they were going to give me a discharge, a Section Eight discharge."

As a last defense I had always taken refuge in a scornful superiority, based on nothing. I sank back in the chair, eyebrows up, shoulders shrugging. "I don't even know what you're talking about. You just don't make any sense at all. It's all Japanese to me."

"A Section Eight discharge is for the nuts in the service, the psychos, the Funny Farm candidates. Now do you know what I'm talking about? They give you a Section Eight discharge, like a dishonorable discharge, only worse. You can't get a job after that. Everybody wants to see your discharge, and when they see a Section Eight, they look at you kind of funny—the kind of expression you've got on your face, like you were looking at someone with their nose blown off but don't want them to know you're disgusted—they look at you that way and then they say, 'Well, there doesn't seem to be an opening here at present.' You're messed up for life, that's what a Section Eight discharge means."

"You don't have to yell at me, there's nothing wrong with my hearing."

"Then that's tough stuff for you, Buster. Then they've got you."

"Nobody's *got* me."

"Oh, they've got you all right."

"Don't tell me who's got me and who hasn't got me. Who do you think you're talking to? Stick to your snails, Lepellier."

He began to laugh again. "You always were a lord of the manor, weren't you? A swell guy, except when the chips were down. You always were a savage underneath. I always knew that, only I never admitted it. But in the last few weeks," despair broke into his face again, "I admitted a heck of a lot to myself. Not about you. Don't flatter yourself. I wasn't thinking about you. Why the heck should I think about you? Did you ever think about me? I thought about myself, and Ma, and the old man, and *pleasing* them all the time. Well, never mind about that now. It's you we happen to be talking about now. Like a savage underneath. Like," now there was the blind confusion in his eyes again, a wild slyness around his mouth, "like that time you knocked Finny out of the tree."

I sprang out of the chair. "You stupid crazy . . ."

Still laughing, "Like that time you crippled him for life."

I shoved my foot against the rung of his chair and kicked. Leper went over in his chair and collapsed against the floor. Laughing and crying he lay with his head on the floor and his knees up, ". . . always were a savage underneath."

Quick heels coming down the stairs, and his mother, large, soft, and gentle-looking, quivered at the entrance. "What on earth happened? Elwin!"

"I'm terribly—it was a mistake," I listened objectively to my own voice, "he said something crazy. I forgot myself—I forgot that he's, there's something the matter with his nerves, isn't there? He didn't know what he was saying."

"Well, good heaven, the boy is ill." We both moved swiftly to help up the chuckling Leper. "Did you come here to abuse him?"

"I'm terribly sorry," I muttered. "I'd better get going."

Mrs. Lepellier was helping Leper toward the stairs. "Don't go," he said between chuckles, "stay for lunch. You can count on it. Always three meals a day, war or peace, in this room."

And I did stay. Sometimes you are too ashamed to leave. That was true now. And sometimes you need too much to know the facts, and so humbly and stupidly you stay. That was true now, too.

It was an abundant Vermont lunch, more like a dinner, and at first it had no more reality than a meal in the theater. Leper ate almost nothing, but my own appetite deepened my disgrace. I ate everything within reach, and then had to ask, face aflame with embarrassment, for more to be passed to me. But that led to this hard-to-believe transformation: Mrs. Lepellier began to be reconciled to me because I liked her cooking. Toward the end of the meal, she became able to speak to me directly, in her high but gentle and modulated voice, and I was so clumsy and fumbling and embarrassed that my behavior throughout lunch amounted to one long and elaborate apology which, when she offered me a second dessert, I saw she had accepted. "He's a good boy underneath," she must have thought, "a terrible temper, no self-control, but he's sorry, and he is a good boy underneath." Leper was closer to the truth.

She suggested he and I take a walk after lunch. Leper now seemed all obedience, and except for the fact that he never looked at his mother, the ideal son. So he put on some odds and ends of clothing, some canvas and woolen and flannel pulled on to form a patchwork against the cutting wind, and we trailed out the back door into the splendor of the failing sunshine. I did not have

New England in my bones; I was a guest in this country, even though by now a familiar one, and I could never see a totally extinguished winter field without thinking it unnatural. I would tramp along, trying to decide whether corn had grown there in the summer, or whether it had been a pasture, or what it could have been, and in that deep layer of the mind where all is judged by the five senses and primitive expectation, I knew that nothing would ever grow there again. We roamed across one of these wastes, our feet breaking through at each step the thin surface crust of ice into a layer of soft snow underneath, and I waited for Leper, in this wintery outdoors he loved, to come to himself again. Just as I knew the field could never grow again, I knew that Leper could not be wild or bitter or psycho tramping across the hills of Vermont.

"Is there an army camp in Vermont?" I asked, so sure in my illusion that I risked making him talk, risked even making him talk about the army.

"I don't think there is."

"There ought to be. That's where they should have sent you. Then you wouldn't have gotten nervous."

"Yeah." A half chuckle. "I was what they call 'nervous in the service.'"

Exaggerated laughter from me. "Is that what they call it?"

Leper didn't bother to make a rejoinder. Before there had always been his polite capping of remarks like this: "Yes, they do, that's what they call it"—but today he glanced speculatively at me and said nothing.

We walked on, the crust cracking uneasily under us. "Nervous in the service," I said. "That sounds like one of Brinker's poems."

"That jerk!"

"You wouldn't know Brinker these days the way he's changed——"

"I'd know that jerk if he'd changed into Snow White."

"Well. He hasn't changed into Snow White."

"That's too bad," the strained laughter was back in his voice, "Snow White with Brinker's face on her. There's a picture," then he broke into sobs.

"Leper! What is it? What's the matter, Leper? Leper!"

Hoarse, cracking sobs broke from him; another ounce of grief and he would have begun tearing his country-store clothes. "Leper! Leper!" This exposure drew us violently together; I was the closest person in the world to him now, and he to me. "Leper, for heaven's sakes, Leper." I was about to cry myself. "Stop that, now just stop. Don't do that. Stop doing that, Leper."

When he became quieter, not less despairing but too exhausted to keep on, I said, "I'm sorry I brought up Brinker. I didn't know you hated him so much." Leper didn't look capable of such hates. Especially now, with his rapid plumes of breath puffing out as from a toiling steam engine, his nose and eyes gone red, and his cheeks red too, in large, irregular blotches—Leper had the kind of fragile fair skin given to high, unhealthy coloring. He was all color, painted at random, but none of it highlighted his grief. Instead of desperate and hate-filled, he looked, with his checkered outfit and blotchy face, like a half-prepared clown.

"I don't really hate Brinker, I don't really hate him, not any more than anybody else." His swimming eyes cautiously explored me. The wind lifted a sail of snow and billowed it past us. "It was only—" he drew in his breath so sharply that it made a whistling sound—"the idea of *his* face on a *woman's* body. That's what made me psycho. Ideas like that. I don't know. I guess they must be right. I guess I am psycho. I guess I must be. I must be. Did you ever have ideas like that?"

"No."

"Would they bother you if you did, if you happened to keep imagining a man's head on a woman's body, or if sometimes the arm of a chair turned into a human arm if you looked at it too long, things like that? Would they bother you?"

I didn't say anything.

"Maybe everybody imagines things like that when they're away from home, really far away, for the first time. Do you think so? The camp I went to first, they called it a 'Reception center,' got us up every morning when it was pitch black, and there was food like the kind we throw out here, and all my clothes were gone and I got this uniform that didn't even smell familiar. All day I wanted to sleep, after we got to Basic Training. I kept falling asleep, all day long, at the lectures we went to, and on the firing range, and everywhere else. But not at night. Next to me there was a man who had a cough that sounded like his stomach was going to come up, one of these times, it sounded like it would come up through his mouth and land with a splatter on the floor. He always faced my way. We did sleep head to foot, but I knew it would land near me. I never slept at night. During the day I couldn't eat this food that should have been thrown away, so I was always hungry except in the Mess Hall. The Mess Hall. The army has the perfect word for everything, did you ever think of that?"

I imperceptibly nodded and shook my head, yes-and-no.

"And the perfect word for me," he added in a distorted voice, as though his tongue had swollen, "psycho. I guess I am. I must be. Am I, though, or is the army? Because they turned everything inside out. I couldn't sleep in bed, I had to sleep everywhere else. I couldn't eat in the Mess Hall, I had to eat everywhere else. Everything began to be inside out. And the man next to me at night, coughing himself inside out. That was when things began to change. One day I couldn't make out what was happening to the corporal's face. It kept changing into faces I knew from somewhere else, and then I began to think he looked like me, and then he . . ." Leper's voice had thickened unrecognizably, "he changed into a woman, I was looking at him as close as I'm looking at you and his face turned into a woman's face and I started to yell for everybody, I began to yell so that everyone would see it too, I didn't want to be the only one to see a thing like that, I yelled louder and louder to make sure everyone within reach of my voice would hear—you can see there wasn't anything crazy in the way I was thinking, can't you, I had a good reason for everything I did, didn't I—but I couldn't yell soon enough, or loud enough, and when somebody did finally come up to me, it was this man with the cough who slept in the next cot, and he was holding a broom because we had been sweeping out the barracks, but I saw right away that it wasn't a broom, it was a man's leg which had been cut off. I remember thinking that he must have been at the hospital helping with an amputation when he heard my yell. You can see there's logic in that." The crust beneath us continued to crack and as we reached the border of the field the frigid trees also were cracking with the cold. The two sharp groups of noises sounded to my ears like rifles being fired in the distance.

I said nothing, and Leper, having said so much, went on to say more, to speak above the wind and crackings as though his story would never be finished. "Then they grabbed me and there were arms and legs and heads everywhere and I couldn't tell when any minute——"

"*Shut up!*"

Softer, more timidly, "when any minute——"

"Do you think I want to hear every gory detail! Shut up! I don't care! I don't care what happened to you, Leper. I don't give a darn! Do you understand that? This has nothing to do with me! Nothing at all! I don't care!"

I turned around and began a clumsy run across the field in a line which avoided his house and aimed toward the road leading back into the town. I left Leper telling his story into the wind. He might tell it forever, I didn't care. I didn't want to hear any more of it. I had already heard too much. What did he mean by telling me a story like that! I didn't want to hear any more of it. Not now or ever. I didn't care because it had nothing to do with me. And I didn't want to hear any more of it. Ever.

Responding to the Novel

Analyzing Chapters 5–10

Identifying Facts

1. In Chapter 5, what is Finny's reaction when Gene tells him he caused his accident? When Gene realizes he's hurting Finny by admitting the truth, what does Gene do?
2. In Chapter 6, why does Gene first decide to renounce sports, and then change his mind? At the end of the chapter, what does he realize his "purpose" must have been all along?
3. Summarize Finny's theory about the war. Why does he claim that he alone gets the joke?
4. Why does Leper "escape" from the army? How does Gene react when Leper tries to tell him what happened?

Interpreting Meanings

5. In your opinion, what are Gene's **motives** for telling Finny the truth about what happened on the tree limb? Do you see any connection between Finny's response to Gene's confession and Gene's response to Leper's story in Chapter 10? Explain.
6. Gene is aware that the 1944 Olympics would probably be canceled (as indeed they were). Yet he allows himself to fall under Finny's spell and be coached for something he knows is a "dream." Why do you think Gene is so willing to submit to Finny and live in a dream world inhabited by just the two of them?
7. Explain what the Winter Carnival represents to Gene. Why is it significant that Finny opens the Carnival by burning a copy of Homer's *Iliad*? Why is it **ironic** that the Carnival ends with the arrival of Leper's telegram announcing his "escape"?
8. On one level, Leper is Finny's **foil,** just as Gene is. Finny is a charismatic golden boy, while Leper, as his name implies, is an oddball misfit. Yet they also share certain similarities. How does each **character** respond to rules and regulations? How does each lose touch with reality? How are both Finny and Leper "broken," though in different ways?
9. In Chapter 10, Gene's visit to Leper's home parallels his visit to Finny's home in Chapter 5. But this time, rather than confessing to a crime, he is accused of one. What exactly does Leper mean when he claims that Gene always was "a savage underneath"? Do you think this is an accurate insight into Gene's **character?** Explain.
10. What is Gene unwilling to face about himself and the world when he refuses to listen to the "gory details" of Leper's story? Were you shocked by Gene's desertion of his friend? How would you react to a friend who was experiencing a crisis like Leper's?

11

I wanted to see Phineas, and Phineas only. With him there was no conflict except between athletes, something Greek-inspired and Olympian in which victory would go to whoever was the strongest in body and heart. This was the only conflict he had ever believed in.

When I got back, I found him in the middle of a snowball fight in a place called the Fields Beyond. At Devon the open ground among the buildings had been given carefully English names—the Center Common, the Far Common, the Fields, and the Fields Beyond. These last were past the gym, the tennis courts, the river, and the stadium, on the edge of the woods which, however English in name, were in my mind primevally American, reaching in unbroken forests far to the north, into the great northern wilderness. I found Finny beside the woods playing and fighting—the two were approximately the same thing to him—and I stood there wondering whether things weren't simpler and better at the northern terminus of these woods, a thousand miles due north into the wilderness, somewhere deep in the Arctic, where the peninsula of trees which began at Devon would end at last in an untouched grove of pine, austere and beautiful.

There is no such grove, I know now, but the morning of my return to Devon I imagined that it might be just over the visible horizon, or the horizon after that.

A few of the fighters paused to yell a greeting at me, but no one broke off to ask about Leper. But I knew it was a mistake for me to stay there; at any moment someone might.

This gathering had obviously been Finny's work. Who else could have inveigled twenty people to the farthest extremity of the school to throw snowballs at each other? I could just picture him, at the end of his ten o'clock class, organizing it with the easy authority which always came into his manner when he had an idea which was particularly preposterous. There they all were now, the cream of the school, the lights and leaders of the senior class, with their high I.Q.'s and expensive shoes, as Brinker had said, pasting each other with snowballs.

I hesitated on the edge of the fight and the edge of the woods, too tangled in my mind to enter either one or the other. So I glanced at my wristwatch, brought my hand dramatically to my mouth as though remembering something urgent and important, repeated the pantomime in case anybody had missed it, and with this tacit explanation started briskly back toward the center of the school. A snowball caught me on the back of the head. Finny's voice followed it. "You're on our side, even if you do have a lousy aim. We need *somebody* else. Even you." He came toward me, without his cane at the moment, his new walking cast so much smaller and lighter that an ordinary person could have managed it with hardly a limp noticeable. Finny's coordination, however, was such that any slight flaw became obvious; there was an interruption, brief as a drumbeat, in the continuous flow of his walk, as though with each step he forgot for a split-second where he was going.

"How's Leper?" he asked in an offhand way.

"Oh Leper's—how would he be? You know Leper——" The fight was moving toward us; I stalled a little more, a stray snowball caught Finny on the side of the face, he shot one back, I seized some ammunition from the ground, and we were engulfed.

Someone knocked me down; I pushed Brinker over a small slope; someone was trying to tackle me from behind. Everywhere there was the smell of vitality in clothes, the vital something in wool and flannel and corduroy which spring releases. I had forgotten that this existed, this smell which instead of the first robin, or the first bud or leaf, means to me that spring has come. I had always welcomed vitality and energy and warmth radiating from thick and sturdy winter clothes. It made me happy, but I kept wondering about next spring, about whether khaki, or suntans or whatever the uniform of the season was, had this aura of promise in it. I felt fairly sure it didn't.

The fight veered. Finny had recruited me and others as allies, so that two sides fighting it out had been taking form. Suddenly he turned his fire against me, he betrayed several of his other friends; he went over to the other, to Brinker's side for a short time, enough to ensure that his betrayal of them would heighten the disorder. Loyalties became hopelessly entangled. No one was going to win or lose after all. Somewhere in the maze, Brinker's sense of generalship disappeared . . . We ended the fight in the only way possible: all of us turned on Phineas. Slowly, with a steadily widening grin, he was driven down beneath a blizzard of snowballs.

When he had surrendered, I bent cheerfully over to help him up, seizing his wrist to stop the final treacherous snowball he had ready, and he remarked, "Well, I guess that takes care of the Hitler Youth[1] outing for one day." All of us

---

1. **Hitler Youth:** a Nazi organization formed to indoctrinate German children and teen-agers.

laughed. On the way back to the gym he said, "That was a good fight. I thought it was pretty funny, didn't you?"

Hours later it occurred to me to ask him, "Do you think you ought to get into fights like that? After all, there's your leg——"

"Stanpole said something about not falling again, but I'm very careful."

"Hey, don't break it again!"

"No, of course I won't break it again. Isn't the bone supposed to be stronger when it grows together over a place where it's been broken once?"

"Yes, I think it is."

"I think so too. In fact I think I can feel it getting stronger."

"You think you can? Can you feel it?"

"Yes, I think so."

"Thank God."

"What?"

"I said that's good."

"Yes, I guess it is. I guess that's good, all right."

After dinner that night Brinker came to our room to pay us one of his formal calls. Our room had by this time of year the exhausted look of a place where two people had lived too long without taking any interest in their surroundings. Our cots at either end of the room were sway-backed beneath their pink and brown cotton spreads. The walls, which were much farther off white than normal, expressed two forgotten interests: Finny had scotch-taped newspaper pictures of the Roosevelt-Churchill meeting above his cot ("They're the two most important of the old men," he had explained, "getting together to make up what to tell us next about the war"). Over my cot I had long ago taped pictures which together amounted to a bare-faced lie about my background—weepingly romantic views of plantation mansions, moss-hung trees by moonlight, lazy roads winding dustily past the cabins of the Negroes. When asked about them, I had acquired an accent appropriate to a town three states south of my own, and I had transmitted the impression, without actually stating it, that this was the old family place. But by now I no longer needed this vivid false identity; now I was acquiring, I felt, a sense of my own real authority and worth, I had had many new experiences, and I was growing up.

"How's Leper?" said Brinker as he came in.

"Yeah," said Phineas, "I meant to ask you before."

"Leper? Why he's—he's on leave." But my resentment against having to mislead people seemed to be growing stronger every day. "As a matter of fact, Leper is 'Absent Without Leave.' he just took off by himself."

"Leper?" both of them exclaimed together.

"Yes," I shrugged, "Leper. Leper's not the little rabbit we used to know any more."

"Nobody can change that much," said Brinker in his new tough-minded way.

Finny said, "He just didn't like the army, I bet. Why should he? What's the point of it anyway?"

"Phineas," Brinker said with dignity, "please don't give us your infantile lecture on world affairs at this time." And to me, "He was too scared to stay, wasn't he?"

I narrowed my eyes as though thinking hard about that. Finally I said, "Yes, I think you could put it that way."

"He panicked."

I didn't say anything.

"He must be out of his mind," said Brinker energetically, "to do a thing like that. I'll bet he cracked up, didn't he? That's what happened. Leper found out that the army was just too much for him. I've heard about guys like that. Some morning they don't get out of bed with everybody else. They just lie there crying. I'll bet something like that happened to Leper." He looked at me. "Didn't it?"

"Yes. It did."

Brinker had closed with such energy, almost enthusiasm, on the truth that I gave it to him without many misgivings. The moment he had it he crumbled. "Well, I'll be darned. I'll be darned. Old Leper. Quiet old Leper. Quiet old Leper from Vermont. He never could fight worth a darn. You'd think somebody would have realized that when he tried to enlist. Poor old Leper. What's he act like?"

"He cries a lot of the time."

"Oh gosh. What's the matter with our class anyway? It isn't even June yet and we've already got two men sidelined for the Duration."

"Two?"

Brinker hesitated briefly. "Well, there's Finny here."

"Yes," agreed Phineas in his deepest and most musical tone, "there's me."

"Finny isn't out of it," I said.

"Of course he is."

"Yes, I'm out of it."

"Not that there's anything to be out of!" I wondered if my face matched the heartiness of my voice. "Just this dizzy war, this fake, this thing with the old men making . . ." I couldn't help watching Finny as I spoke, and so I ran out of momentum. I waited for him to take it up, to unravel once again his tale of plotting statesmen and deluded public, his great joke, his private toehold on the world. He was sitting on his cot, elbows on knees, looking down. He brought his wide-set eyes up, his grin flashed and faded, and then he murmured, "Sure. There isn't any war."

It was one of the few ironic remarks Phineas ever made, and with it he quietly brought to a close all his special inventions which had carried us through the winter. Now the facts were re-established, and gone were all the fantasies, such as the Olympic Games for A.D. 1944, closed before they had ever been opened.

There was little left at Devon anymore which had not been recruited for the war. The few stray activities and dreamy people not caught up in it were being systematically corralled by Brinker. And every day in chapel there was some announcement about qualifying for "V-12," an officer-training program the Navy had set up in many colleges and universities. It sounded very safe, almost like peacetime, almost like just going normally on to college. It was also very popular; groups the size of LST[2] crews joined it, almost everyone who could qualify, except for a few who "wanted to fly" and so chose the Army Air Force, or something called V-5 instead. There were also a special few with energetic fathers, who were expecting appointments to Annapolis or West Point or the Coast Guard Academy or even—this alternative had been unexpectedly stumbled on—the Merchant Marine Academy. Devon was by tradition and choice the most civilian of schools, and there was a certain strained hospitality in the way both the faculty and students worked to get along with the leathery recruiting officers who kept appearing on the campus. There was no latent snobbery in us; we didn't find any in them. It was only that we could feel a deep and sincere difference between us and them, a difference which everyone struggled with awkward fortitude to bridge. It was as though Athens and Sparta were trying to establish not just a truce but an alliance—although we were not as civilized as Athens and they were not as brave as Sparta.

Neither were we. There was no rush to get into the fighting; no one seemed to feel the need to get into the infantry, and only a few were talking about the Marines. The thing to be was careful and self-preserving. It was going to be a long war. Quack-

enbush, I heard, had two possible appointments to the Military Academy, with carefully prepared positions in V-12 and dentistry school to fall back on if necessary.

I myself took no action. I didn't feel free to, and I didn't know why this was so. Brinker, in his accelerating change from absolute to relative virtue, came up with plan after plan, each more insulated from the fighting than the last. But I did nothing.

One morning, after a Naval officer had turned many heads in chapel with an address on convoy duty, Brinker put his hand on the back of my neck in the vestibule outside and steered me into a room used for piano practice near the entrance. It was soundproofed, and he swung the vaultlike door closed behind us.

"You've been putting off enlisting in something for only one reason," he said at once. "You know that, don't you?"

"No, I don't know that."

"Well, I know, and I'll tell you what it is. It's Finny. You pity him."

"Pity him!"

---

2. **LST:** abbreviation for "landing ship tank," a vessel used for landing troops and heavy equipment on beaches.

"Yes, pity him. And if you don't watch out, he's going to start pitying himself. Nobody ever mentions his leg to him except me. Keep that up and he'll be sloppy with self-pity any day now. What's everybody beating around the bush for? He's crippled and that's that. He's got to accept it, and unless we start acting perfectly natural about it, even kid him about it once in a while, he never will."

"You're so wrong I can't even—I can't even *hear* you, you're so wrong."

"Well, I'm going to do it anyway."

"No. You're not."

"The heck I'm not. I don't have to have your approval, do I?"

"I'm his roommate, and I'm his best friend——"

"And you were there when it happened. I know. And I don't give a darn. And don't forget," he looked at me sharply, "you've got a little personal stake in this. What I mean is it wouldn't do you any harm, you know, if everything about Finny's accident was cleared up and forgotten."

I felt my face grimacing in the way Finny's did when he was really irritated. "What do you mean by that?"

"I don't know," he shrugged and chuckled in his best manner, "nobody knows." Then the charm disappeared and he added, "unless you know," and his mouth closed in its straight expressionless line, and that was all that was said.

I had no idea what Brinker might say or do. Before he had always known and done whatever occurred to him because he was certain that whatever occurred to him was right. In the world of the Golden Fleece Debating Society and the Underprivileged Local Children subcommittee of the Good Samaritan Confraternity, this had created no problems. But I was afraid of that simple executive directness now.

I walked back from chapel and found Finny in our dormitory, blocking the staircase until the others who wanted to go up sang "A Mighty Fortress Is Our God" under his direction. No one who was tone deaf ever loved music so much. I think his shortcoming increased his appreciation; he loved it all indiscriminately—Beethoven, the latest love ditty, jazz, a hymn—it was all profoundly musical to Phineas.

". . . Our helper He a-mid the floods," wafted out across the Common in the tempo of a football march, "Of mortal ills prevailing!"

"Everything was all right," said Finny at the end, "phrasing, rhythm, all that. But I'm not sure about your pitch. Half a tone off, I would estimate offhand."

We went on to our room. I sat down at the translation of Caesar I was doing for him, since he had to pass Latin at last this year or fail to graduate. I thought I was doing a pretty good job of it.

"Is anything exciting happening now?"

"This part is pretty interesting," I said, "if I understand it right. About a surprise attack."

"Read me that."

"Well, let's see. It begins, 'When Caesar noticed that the enemy was remaining for several days at the camp fortified by a swamp and by the nature of the terrain, he sent a letter to Trebonius instructing him'—'instructing him' isn't actually in the text but it's understood; you know about that."

"Sure. Go on."

"'Instructing him to come as quickly as possible by long forced marches to him'—this 'him' refers to Caesar of course."

Finny looked at me with glazed interest and said, "Of course."

"'Instructing him to come as quickly as possible by long forced marches to him with three legions; he himself'—Caesar, that is—'sent cavalry to withstand any sudden attacks of the enemy. Now when the Gauls learned what was going on, they scattered a selected band of foot soldiers in ambushes; who, overtaking our horsemen after the leader Vertiscus had been killed, followed our disorderly men up to our camp.'"

"I have a feeling that's what Mr. Horn is going to call a 'muddy translation.' What's it mean?"

"Caesar isn't doing so well."

"But he won it in the end."

"Sure. If you mean the whole campaign——" I broke off. "He won it, if you really think there was a Gallic War . . ." Caesar, from the first, had been the one historical figure Phineas refused absolutely to believe in. Lost two thousand years in the past, master of a dead language and a dead empire, the bane and bore of schoolboys, Caesar he believed to be more of a tyrant at Devon than he had ever been in Rome. Phineas felt a personal and sincere grudge against Caesar, and he was outraged most by his conviction that Caesar and Rome and Latin had never been alive at all . . . "If you really think there ever was a Caesar," I said.

Finny got up from the cot, picking up his cane as an afterthought. He looked oddly at me, his face set to burst out laughing, I thought. "Naturally, I don't believe books and I don't believe teachers," he came across a few paces, "but I do believe—it's important after all for me to believe *you*. I've got to believe you, at least. I know you better than anybody.'' I waited without saying anything. ''And you told me about Leper, that he's gone crazy. That's the word, we might as well admit it. Leper's gone crazy. When I heard that about Leper, then I knew that the war was real, this war and all the wars. If a war can drive somebody crazy, then it's real, all right. Oh, I guess I always *knew,* but I didn't have to admit it.'' He perched his foot, small cast with metal bar across the bottom to walk on, next to where I was sitting on the cot. ''To tell you the truth, I wasn't too completely sure about *you,* when you told me how Leper was. Of course I believed you,'' he added hurriedly, ''but you're the nervous type, you know, and I thought maybe your imagination got a little inflamed up there in Vermont. I thought he might not be quite as mixed up as you made out.'' Finny's face tried to prepare me for what came next. ''Then I saw him myself.''

I turned incredulously. ''You saw Leper?''

''I saw him here this morning, after chapel. He was—well, there's nothing inflamed about my imagination, and I saw Leper *hiding* in the shrubbery next to the chapel. I slipped out the side door the way I always do—to miss the rush—and I saw Leper and he must have seen me. He didn't say a darn word. He looked at me like I was a gorilla or something, and then he ducked into Mr. Carhart's office.''

''He must be crazy,'' I said automatically, and then my eyes involuntarily met Finny's. We both broke into sudden laughter.

''We can't do a darn thing about it,'' he said ruefully.

''I don't want to see him,'' I muttered. Then, trying to be more responsible, ''Who else knows he's here?''

''No one, I would think.''

''There's nothing for us to do, maybe Carhart or Dr. Stanpole can do something. We won't tell anybody about it because . . . because they would just scare Leper, and he would scare them.''

''Anyway,'' said Finny, ''then I knew there was a real war on.''

''Yes, I guess it's a real war, all right. But I liked yours a lot better.''

''So did I.''

''I wish you hadn't found out. What did you have to find out for!'' We started to laugh again, with a half-guilty exchange of glances, in the way that two people who had gone on a gigantic binge when they were last together would laugh when they met again at the parson's tea. ''Well,'' he said, ''you did a beautiful job in the Olympics.''

''And you were the greatest news analyst who ever lived.''

''Do you realize you won every gold medal in every Olympic event? No one's ever done anything like that in history.''

''And you scooped every newspaper in the world on every story.'' The sun was doing antics among the million specks of dust hanging between us and casting a brilliant, unstable pool of light on the floor. ''No one's ever done anything like that before.''

Brinker and three cohorts came with much commotion into our room at 10:05 P.M. that night. ''We're taking you out,'' he said flatly.

''It's after hours,'' I said; ''Where?'' said Finny with interest at the same time.

''You'll see. Get them.'' His friends half-lifted us half-roughly, and we hustled down the stairs. I thought it must be some kind of culminating prank, the senior class leaving Devon with a flourish. Were we going to steal the clapper of the school bell, or would we tether a cow in chapel?

They steered us toward the First Building—burned down and rebuilt several times but still known as the First Building of the Devon School. It contained only classrooms and so at this hour was perfectly empty, which made us stealthier than ever. Brinker's many keys, surviving from his class-officer period, jingled softly as we reached the main door. Above us in Latin flowed the inscription, Here Boys Come to Be Made Men.

The lock turned; we went in, entering the doubtful reality of a hallway familiar only in daylight and bustle. Our footsteps fell guiltily on the marble floor. We continued across the foyer to a dreamlike bank of windows, turned left up a pale flight of marble steps, left again, through two doorways, and into the Assembly Room. From the high ceiling one of the celebrated Devon chandeliers, all glittering tears, scattered thin illumination. Row after row of black Early American benches spread emptily back through the shadows to long, vague windows. At the front of the room there was a raised platform with a balustrade in front of it. About ten members of the senior class sat on the platform; all of them were wearing their black graduation robes. This is going to be some kind of schoolboy masquerade, I thought, some masquerade with masks and candles.

''You see how Phineas limps,'' said Brinker loudly as we walked in. It was too coarse and too loud; I wanted to hit him for shocking me like that. Phineas looked perplexed. ''Sit down,'' he went on, ''take a load off your feet.'' We sat in

the front row of the benches, where eight or ten others were sitting, smirking uneasily at the students on the platform.

Whatever Brinker had in his mind to do, I thought he had chosen a terrible place for it. There was nothing funny about the Assembly Room. I could remember staring torpidly through these windows a hundred times out at the elms of the Center Common. The windows now had the closed blankness of night, a deadened look about them, a look of being blind or deaf. The great expanses of wall space were opaque with canvas, portraits in oil of deceased headmasters, a founder or two, forgotten leaders of the faculty, a beloved athletic coach none of us had ever heard of, a lady we could not identify—her fortune had largely rebuilt the school; a nameless poet who was thought when under the school's protection to be destined primarily for future generations; a young hero now anonymous who looked theatrical in the First World War uniform in which he had died.

I thought any prank was bound to fall flat here.

The Assembly Hall was used for large lectures, debates, plays, and concerts; it had the worst acoustics in the school. I couldn't make out what Brinker was saying. He stood on the polished marble floor in front of us, but facing the platform, talking to the boys behind the balustrade. I heard him say the word "inquiry" to them, and something about "the country demands. . . ."

"What is all this hot air?" I said into the blur.

"I don't know," Phineas answered shortly.

As he turned toward us Brinker was saying ". . . blame on the responsible party. We will begin with a brief prayer." He paused, surveying us with the kind of wide-eyed surmise Mr. Carhart always used at this point, and then added in Mr. Carhart's urbane murmur, "Let us pray."

We all slumped immediately and unthinkingly into the awkward crouch in which God was addressed at Devon, leaning forward with elbows on knees. Brinker had caught us, and in a moment it was too late to escape, for he had moved swiftly into the Lord's Prayer. If when Brinker had said "Let us pray," I had said "Go to heck," everything might have been saved.

At the end there was an indecisive, semiserious silence, and then Brinker said, "Phineas, if you please." Finny got up with a shrug and walked to the center of the floor, between us and the platform. Brinker got an armchair from behind the balustrade and seated Finny on it with courtly politeness. "Now, just in your own words," he said.

"What own words?" said Phineas, grimacing up at him with his best you-are-an-idiot expression.

"I know you haven't got many of your own," said Brinker with a charitable smile. "Use some of Gene's then."

"What shall I talk about? You? I've got plenty of words of my own for that."

"*I'm* all right," Brinker glanced gravely around the room for confirmation, "you're the casualty."

"Brinker," began Finny in a constricted voice I did not recognize, "are you off your head or what?"

"No," said Brinker evenly, "that's Leper, our other casualty. Tonight we're investigating you."

"What the heck are you talking about!" I cut in suddenly.

"Investigating Finny's accident!" He spoke as though this was the most natural and self-evident and inevitable thing we could be doing.

I felt the blood flooding into my head. "After all," Brinker continued, "there *is* a war on. Here's one soldier our side has already lost. We've got to find out what happened."

"Just for the record," said someone from the platform. "You agree, don't you, Gene?"

"I told Brinker this morning," I began in a voice treacherously shaking, "that I thought this was the worst——"

"And I said," Brinker's voice was full of authority and perfectly under control, "that for Finny's good," and with an additional timbre of sincerity, "and for your own good too, by the way, Gene, that we should get all this out into the open. We don't want any mysteries or any stray rumors and suspicions left in the air at the end of the year, do we?"

A collective assent to this rumbled through the blurring atmosphere of the Assembly Room.

"What are you talking about!" Finny's voice was full of contemptuous music. "What rumors and suspicions?"

"Never mind about that," said Brinker with his face responsibly grave. He's enjoying this, I thought bitterly, he's imagining himself Justice incarnate, balancing the scales. He's forgotten that Justice incarnate is not only balancing the scales but also blindfolded. "Why don't you just tell us in your words what happened?" Brinker continued. "Just humor us, if you want to think of it that way. We aren't trying to make you feel bad. Just tell us. You know we wouldn't ask you if we didn't have a good reason . . . good reasons."

"There's nothing to tell."

"Nothing to tell?" Brinker looked pointedly at the small cast around Finny's lower leg and the cane he held between his knees.

"Well, then, I fell out of a tree."

"Why?" said someone on the platform. The acoustics were so bad and the light so dim that I could rarely tell who was speaking, except for Finny and Brinker, who were isolated on the wide strip of marble floor between us in the seats and the others on the platform.

"Why?" repeated Phineas. "Because I took a wrong step."

"Did you lose your balance?" continued the voice.

"Yes," echoed Finny grimly, "I lost my balance."

"You had better balance than anyone in the school."

"Thanks a lot."

"I didn't say it for a compliment."

"Well, then, no thanks."

"Have you ever thought that you didn't just fall out of that tree?"

This touched an interesting point Phineas had been turning over in his mind for a long time. I could tell that because the obstinate, competitive look left his face as his mind became engaged for the first time. "It's very funny," he said, "but ever since then I've had a feeling that the tree did it by itself. It's an impression I've had. Almost as though the tree shook me out by itself."

The acoustics in the Assembly Room were so poor that silences there had a heavy hum of their own.

"Someone else was in the tree, isn't that so?"

"No," said Finny spontaneously, "I don't think so." He looked at the ceiling. "Or was there? Maybe there was somebody climbing up the rungs of the trunk. I kind of forget."

This time the hum of silence was prolonged to a point where I would be forced to fill it with some kind of sound if it didn't end. Then someone else on the platform spoke up. "I thought that somebody told me that Gene Forrester was——"

"Finny was there," Brinker interrupted commandingly, "he knows better than anyone."

"You were there too, weren't you, Gene?" this new voice from the platform continued.

"Yes," I said with interest, "yes, I was there too."

Finny turned toward me. "You were down at the bottom, weren't you?" he asked, not in the official courtroom tone he had used before, but in a friend's voice.

I had been studying very carefully the way my hands wrinkled when tightly clenched, but I was able to bring my head up and return his inquiring look. "Down at the bottom, yes."

Finny went on. "Did you see the tree shake or anything?" He flushed faintly at what seemed to him the absurdity of his own question. "I've always meant to ask you, just for the heck of it."

I took this under consideration. "I don't recall anything like that . . ."

"Nutty question," he muttered.

"I thought you were in the tree," the platform voice cut in.

"Well of course," Finny said with an exasperated chuckle, "of course I was in the tree—oh, you mean Gene?—he wasn't in—is that what you mean, or——" Finny floundered with muddled honesty between me and my questioner.

"I meant Gene," the voice said.

"Of course Finny was in the tree," I said. But I couldn't make the confusion last, "and I was down at the bottom, or climbing the rungs, I think . . ."

"How do you expect him to remember?" said Finny sharply. "There was a heck of a lot of confusion right then."

"A kid I used to play with was hit by a car once when I was about eleven years old," said Brinker seriously, "and I remember every single thing about it, exactly where I was standing, the color of the sky, the noise the brakes of the car made—I never will forget anything about it."

"You and I are two different people," I said.

"No one's accusing you of anything," Brinker responded in an odd tone.

"Well, of course no one's *accusing* me——"

"Don't argue so much," his voice tried for a hard compromise, full of warning and yet striving to pass unnoticed by the others.

"No, we're not accusing you," a boy on the platform said evenly, and then I stood accused.

"I think I remember now!" Finny broke in, his eyes bright and relieved. "Yes, I remember seeing you standing on the bank. You were looking up and your hair was plastered down over your forehead so that you had that dumb look you always have when you've been in the water—what was it you said? 'Stop posing up there' or one of those best-pal cracks you're always making." He was very happy. "And I think I did start to pose just to make you madder, and I said, what did I say? something about the two of us . . . yes, I said 'Let's make a double jump,' because I thought if we went together it would be something that had never been done before, holding hands in a jump——" Then it was as though someone suddenly slapped him. "No, that was on the ground when I said that to you. I said that to you on the ground, and then the two of us started to climb . . ." he broke off.

"The two of you," the boy on the platform went on harshly for him, "started to climb up the tree together, was that it? And he's just said he was on the ground!"

"Or on the rungs!" I burst out. "I said I might have been on the rungs!"

"Who else was there?" said Brinker quietly. "Leper Lepellier was there, wasn't he?"

"Yes," someone said, "Leper was there."

"Leper always was the exact type when it came to details," continued Brinker. "He could have told us where everybody was standing, what everybody was wearing, the whole conversation that day, and what the temperature was. He could have cleared the whole thing up. Too bad."

No one said anything. Phineas had been sitting motionless, leaning slightly forward, not far from the position in which we prayed at Devon. After a long time he turned and reluctantly looked at me. I did not return his look or move or speak. Then at last Finny straightened from this prayerful position slowly, as though it was painful for him. "Leper's here," he said in a voice so quiet, and with such quiet unconscious dignity, that he was suddenly terrifyingly strange to me. "I saw him go into Dr. Carhart's office this morning."

"Here! Go get him," said Brinker immediately to the two boys who had come with us. "He must be in Carhart's rooms if he hasn't gone back home."

I kept quiet. To myself, however, I made a number of swift, automatic calculations: that Leper was no threat, no one would ever believe Leper; Leper was deranged, he was not of sound mind, and if people couldn't make out their own wills when not in sound mind, certainly they couldn't testify in something like this.

The two boys left, and the atmosphere immediately cleared. Action had been taken, so the whole issue was dropped for now. Someone began making fun of "Captain Marvel," the head of the football team, saying how girlish he looked in his graduation gown. Captain Marvel minced for us in his size 12 shoes, the sides of his gown swaying drunkenly back and forth from his big hips. Someone wound himself in the folds of the red velvet curtain and peered out from it like an exotic spy. Someone made a long speech listing every infraction of the rules we were committing that night. Someone else made a speech showing how by careful planning we could break all the others before dawn.

But although the acoustics in the Assembly Hall were poor, those outside the room were admirable. All the talk and horseplay ended within a few seconds of the instant when the first person, that is myself, heard the footsteps returning along the marble stairway and corridors toward us. I knew with absolute certainty moments before they came in that there were three sets of footsteps coming.

Leper entered ahead of the other two. He looked unusually well; his face was glowing, his eyes were bright, his manner was all energy. "Yes?" he said in a clear voice, resonant even in this room, "what can I do for you?" He made this confident remark almost but not quite to Phineas, who was still sitting alone in the middle of the room. Finny muttered something which was too indecisive for Leper, who turned with a cleanly energetic gesture toward Brinker. Brinker began talking to him in the elaborately casual manner of someone being watched. Gradually the noise in the room, which had revived when the three of them came in, subsided again.

Brinker managed it. He never raised his voice, but instead he let the noise surrounding it gradually sink so that his voice emerged in the ensuing silence without any emphasis on his part—"so that you were standing next to the river bank, watching Phineas climb the tree?" he was saying, and had waited, I knew, until this silence to say.

"Sure. Right there by the trunk of the tree. I was looking up. It was almost sunset, and I remember the way the sun was shining in my eyes."

"So you couldn't . . ." I began before I could stop myself.

There was a short pause during which every ear and no eyes were directed toward me, and then Brinker went on. "And what did you see? Could you see anything with the sun in your eyes?"

"Oh, sure," said Leper in his new, confident, false voice. "I just shaded my eyes a little, like this," he demonstrated how a hand shades the eyes, "and then I could see. I could see both of them clearly enough because the sun was blazing all around them," a certain singsong sincerity was developing in his voice, as though he were trying to hold the interest of young children, "and the rays of the sun were shooting past them, millions of rays shooting past them like—like golden machine-gun fire." He paused to let us consider the profoundly revealing exactness of this phrase. "That's what it was like, if you want to know. The two of them looked as black as—as black as death standing up there with this fire burning all around them."

Everyone could hear, couldn't they? the derangement in his voice. Everyone must be able to see how false his confidence was. Any fool could see that. But whatever I said would be a self-indictment; others would have to fight for me.

"Up there where?" said Brinker brusquely. "Where were the two of them standing up there?"

"On the limb!" Leper's annoyed, this-is-obvious tone would discount what he said in their minds; they would know that he had never been like this before, that he had changed and was not responsible.

"Who was where on the limb? Was one of them ahead of the other?"

"Well, of course."

"Who was ahead?"

Leper smiled waggishly. "I couldn't see *that*. There were just two shapes, and with that fire shooting past them they looked as black as——"

"You've already told us that. You couldn't see who was ahead?"

"No, naturally I couldn't."

"But you could see how they were standing. Where were they exactly?"

"One of them was next to the trunk, holding the trunk of the tree. I'll never forget that because the tree was a huge black shape too, and his hand touching the black trunk anchored him, if you see what I mean, to something solid in the bright fire they were standing in up there. And the other one was a little farther out on the limb."

"Then what happened?"

"Then they both moved."

"How did they move?"

"They moved," now Leper was smiling, a charming and slightly arch smile, like a child who knows he is going to say something clever, "they moved like an engine."

In the baffled silence I began to uncoil slowly.

"Like an engine!" Brinker's expression was a struggle between surprise and disgust.

"I can't think of the name of the engine. But it has two pistons. What is that engine? Well anyway, in this engine first one piston sinks, and then the next one sinks. The one holding on to the trunk sank for a second, up and down like a piston, and then the other one sank and fell."

Someone on the platform exclaimed, "The one who moved first shook the other one's balance!"

"I suppose so." Leper seemed to be rapidly losing interest.

"Was the one who fell," Brinker said slowly, "was Phineas, in other words the one who moved first or second?"

Leper's face became guileful, his voice flat and impersonal. "I don't intend to implicate myself. I'm no fool, you know. I'm not going to tell you everything and then have it used against me later. You always did take me for a fool, didn't you? But I'm no fool anymore. I know when I have information that might be dangerous." He was working himself up to indignation. "Why should I tell you! Just because it happens to suit you!"

"Leper," Brinker pleaded, "Leper, this is very important——"

"So am I," he said thinly, "I'm important. You've never realized it, but I'm important too. You be the fool," he gazed shrewdly at Brinker, "you do whatever anyone wants whenever they want it. You be the fool now."

Phineas had gotten up unnoticed from his chair. "I don't care," he interrupted in an even voice, so full of richness that it overrode all the others. "I don't care."

I tore myself from the bench toward him. "Phineas——!"

He shook his head sharply, closing his eyes, and then he turned to regard me with a handsome mask of face. "I just don't care. Never mind," and he started across the marble floor toward the doors.

"Wait a minute!" cried Brinker. "We haven't heard everything yet. We haven't got all the facts!"

The words shocked Phineas into awareness. He whirled as though being attacked from behind. "You get the rest of the facts, Brinker!" he cried. "You get all your facts!" I had never seen Finny crying. "You collect every fact there is in the world!" He plunged out the doors.

The excellent exterior acoustics recorded his rushing steps and the quick rapping of his cane along the corridor and on the first steps of the marble stairway. Then these separate sounds collided into the general tumult of his body falling clumsily down the white marble stairs.

12

Everyone behaved with complete presence of mind. Brinker shouted that Phineas must not be moved; someone else, realizing that only a night nurse would be at the Infirmary, did not waste time going there but rushed to bring Dr. Stanpole from his house. Others remembered that Phil Latham, the wrestling coach, lived just across the Common and that he was an expert in first aid. It was Phil who made Finny stretch out on one of the wide shallow steps of the staircase, and kept him still until Dr. Stanpole arrived.

The foyer and the staircase of the First Building were soon as crowded as at midday. Phil Latham found the main light switch, and all the marble blazed up under full illumination. But surrounding it was the stillness of near-midnight in a country town, so that the hurrying feet and the repressed voices had a hollow reverberance. The windows, blind and black, retained their look of dull emptiness.

Once Brinker turned to me and said, "Go back to the Assembly Room, and see if there's any kind of blanket on the platform." I dashed back up the stairs, found a blanket, and gave it to Phil Latham. He carefully wrapped it around Phineas.

I would have liked very much to have done that myself; it would have meant a lot to me. But Phineas might begin to curse me with every word he knew, he might lose his head completely, he would certainly be worse off for it. So I kept out of the way.

He was entirely conscious and from the glimpses I caught of his face seemed to be fairly calm. Everyone behaved with complete presence of mind, and that included Phineas.

When Dr. Stanpole arrived, there was silence on the stairs. Wrapped tightly in his blanket, with light flooding down on him from the chandelier, Finny lay isolated at the center of a tight circle of faces. The rest of the crowd looked on from above or below on the stairs, and I stood on the lower edge. Behind me the foyer was now empty.

After a short, silent examination, Dr. Stanpole had a chair brought from the Assembly Room, and Finny was lifted cautiously into it. People aren't ordinarily carried in chairs in New Hampshire, and as they raised him up he looked very strange to me, like some tragic and exalted personage, a stricken pontiff.[1] Once again I had the desolating sense of having all along ignored what was finest in him. Perhaps it was just the incongruity of seeing him aloft and stricken, since he was by nature someone who carried others. I didn't think he knew how to act or even how to feel as the object of help. He went past with his eyes closed and his mouth tense. I knew that nor-

---

1. **pontiff:** Pope. The reference is to the old practice of carrying the Pope in a chair in solemn procession.

mally I would have been one of those carrying the chair, saying something into his ear as we went along. My aid alone had never seemed to him in the category of help. The reason for this occurred to me as the procession moved slowly across the brilliant foyer to the doors; Phineas had thought of me as an extension of himself.

Dr. Stanpole stopped near the doors, looking for the light switch. There was an interval of a few seconds when no one was near him. I came up to him and tried to phrase my question, but nothing came out, I couldn't find the word to begin. I was being torn irreconcilably between "Is he" and "What is" when Dr. Stanpole, without appearing to notice my tangle, said conversationally, "It's the leg again. Broken again. But a much cleaner break, I think, much cleaner. A simple fracture." He found the light switch and the foyer was plunged into darkness.

Outside, the doctor's car was surrounded by boys while Finny was being lifted inside it by Phil Latham. Phil and Dr. Stanpole then got into the car and drove slowly away, the headlights forming a bright parallel as they receded down the road, and then swinging into another parallel at right angles to the first as they turned into the Infirmary driveway. The crowd began to thin rapidly; the faculty had at last heard that something was amiss in the night, and several alarmed and alarming masters materialized in the darkness and ordered the students to their dormitories.

Mr. Ludsbury loomed abruptly out of a background of shrubbery. "Get along to the dormitory, Forrester," he said with a dry certainty in my obedience which suddenly struck me as funny, definitely funny. Since it was beneath his dignity to wait and see that I actually followed his order, I was, by not budging, free of him a moment later. I walked into the bank of shrubbery, circled past trees in the direction of the chapel, doubled back along a large building donated by the alumni, which no one had ever been able to put to use, recrossed the street, and walked noiselessly up the emerging grass next to the Infirmary driveway.

Dr. Stanpole's car was at the top of it, headlights on and motor running, empty. I idly considered stealing it, in the way that people idly consider many crimes it would be possible for them to commit. I took an academic interest in the thought of stealing the car, knowing all the time that it would be not so much criminal as meaningless, a lapse into nothing, an escape into nowhere. As I walked past it, the motor was throbbing with wheezy reluctance—prep school doctors don't own very desirable getaway cars, I remember thinking to myself—and then I turned the corner of the building and began to creep along behind it. There was only one window lighted, at the far end, and opposite it I found some thin shrubbery which provided enough cover for me to study the window. It was too high for me to see directly into the room, but after I made sure that the ground had softened enough so that I could jump without making much noise, I sprang

as high as I could. I had a flashing glimpse of a door at the other end of the room, opening on the corridor. I jumped again; someone's back. Again; nothing new. I jumped again and saw a head and shoulders partially turned away from me; Phil Latham's. This was the room.

The ground was too damp to sit on, so I crouched down and waited. I could hear their blurred voices droning monotonously through the window. If they do nothing worse, they're going to bore Finny to death, I said to myself. My head seemed to be full of bright remarks this evening. It was cold, crouching motionless next to the ground. I stood up and jumped several times, not so much to see into the room as to warm up. The only sounds were occasional snorts from the engine of Dr. Stanpole's car when it turned over with special reluctance, and a thin, lonely whistling the wind sometimes made high in the still-bare trees. These formed the background for the dull hum of talk in Finny's room as Phil Latham, Dr. Stanpole, and the night nurse worked over him.

What could they be talking about? The night nurse had always been the biggest windbag in the school. Miss Windbag, R.N. Phil Latham, on the other hand, hardly ever spoke. One of the few things he said was "Give it the old college try"— he thought of everything in terms of the old college try, and he had told students to attack their studies, their sports, religious waverings, sexual maladjustments, physical handicaps, and a constellation of other problems with the old college try. I listened tensely for his voice. I listened so hard that I nearly differentiated it from the others, and it seemed to be saying, "Finny, give that bone the old college try."

I was quite a card tonight myself.

Phil Latham's college was Harvard, although I had heard that he only lasted there a year. Probably he had said to someone to give something the old college try, and that had finished him; that would probably be grounds for expulsion at Harvard. There couldn't possibly be such a thing as the old Harvard try. Could there be the old Devon try? The old Devon endeavor? The decrepit Devon endeavor? That was good, the decrepit Devon endeavor. I'd use that some time in the Butt Room. That was pretty funny. I'll bet I could get a rise out of Finny with——

Dr. Stanpole was fairly gabby too. What was he always saying. Nothing. Nothing? Well there must be something he was always saying. Everybody had something, some word, some phrase that they were always saying. The trouble with Dr. Stanpole was that his vocabulary was too large. He talked in a huge circle, he probably had a million words in his vocabulary and he had to use them all before he started over again.

That's probably the way they were talking in there now. Dr. Stanpole was working his way as fast as possible around his big circle, Miss Windbag was gasping out something or other all the time, and Phil Latham was saying, "Give 'er the old college try, Finny." Phineas, of course, was answering them only in Latin.

I nearly laughed out loud at that.

Gallia est omnis divisa in partes tres[2]—Finny probably answered that whenever Phil Latham spoke. Phil Latham would look rather blank at that.

Did Finny like Phil Latham? Yes, of course he did. But wouldn't it be funny if he suddenly turned to him and said, "Phil Latham, you're a boob." That would be funny in a way. And what about if he said, "Dr. Stanpole, old pal, you're the most long-winded licensed medical man alive." And it would be even funnier if he interrupted that night nurse and said, "Miss Windbag, you're rotten, rotten to the core. I just thought I ought to tell you." It would never occur to Finny to say any of these things, but they struck me as so outrageous that I couldn't stop myself from laughing. I put my hand over my mouth; then I tried to stop my mouth with my fist; if I couldn't get control of this laughing, they would hear me in the room. I was laughing so hard it hurt my stomach, and I could feel my face getting more and more flushed; I dug my teeth into my fist to try to gain control, and then I noticed that there were tears all over my hand.

The engine of Dr. Stanpole's car roared exhaustedly. The headlights turned in an erratic arc away from me, and then I heard the engine laboriously recede into the distance, and I continued to listen until not only had it ceased, but my memory of how it sounded had also ceased. The light had gone out in the room, and there was no sound coming from it. The only noise was the peculiarly bleak whistling of the wind through the upper branches.

There was a street light behind me somewhere through the trees, and the windows of the Infirmary dimly reflected it. I came up close beneath the window of Finny's room, found a foothold on a grating beneath it, straightened up so that my shoulders were at a level with the windowsill, reached up with both hands, and since I was convinced that the window would be stuck shut I

pushed it hard. The window shot up and there was a startled rustling from the bed in the shadows. I whispered, "Finny!" sharply into the black room.

"Who is it!" he demanded, leaning out from the bed so that the light fell waveringly on his face. Then he recognized me, and I thought at first he was going to get out of bed and help me through the window. He struggled clumsily for such a length of time that even my mind, shocked and slowed as it had been, was able to formulate two realizations: that his leg was bound so that he could not move very well, and that he was struggling to unleash his hate against me.

"I came to ———"

"You want to break something else in me! Is that why you're here!" He thrashed wildly in the darkness, the bed groaning under him and the sheets hissing as he fought against them. But he was not going to be able to get to me, because his matchless coordination was gone. He could not even get up from the bed.

"I want to fix your leg up," I said crazily but in a perfectly natural tone of voice which made my words sound even crazier, even to me.

"You'll fix my . . ." and he arched out, lunging hopelessly into the space between us. He arched out and then fell, his legs still on the bed, his hands falling with a loud slap against the floor. Then after a pause all the tension drained out of him, and he let his head come slowly down between his hands. He had not hurt himself. But he brought his head slowly down between his hands and rested it against the floor, not moving, not making any sound.

"I'm sorry," I said blindly, "I'm sorry, I'm sorry."

I had just control enough to stay out of his room, to let him struggle back into the bed by himself. I slid down from the window, and I remember lying on the ground, staring up at the night sky, which was neither clear nor overcast. And I remember later walking alone down a rather aimless road which leads past the gym to an old water hole. I was trying to cope with something that might be called double vision. I saw the gym in the glow of a couple of outside lights near it, and I knew of course that it was the Devon gym which I entered every day. It was and it wasn't. There was something innately strange about it, as though there had always been an inner core to the gym which I had never perceived before, quite different from its generally accepted appearance. It seemed to alter moment by moment before my eyes, becoming for brief flashes a totally unknown building with a significance much deeper and far more real than any I had noticed before. The same

---

2. *Gallia . . . tres:* (Latin) "All Gaul is divided into three parts" (the famous first words of Julius Caesar's *Commentaries on the Gallic Wars*).

was true of the water hole, where unauthorized games of hockey were played during the winter. The ice was breaking up on it now, with just a few glazed islands of ice remaining in the center and a fringe of hard surface glinting along the banks. The old trees surrounding it all were intensely meaningful, with a message that was very pressing and entirely indecipherable. Here the road turned to the left and became dirt. It proceeded along the lower end of the playing fields, and under the pale night glow the playing fields swept away from me in slight frosty undulations which bespoke meanings upon meanings, levels of reality I had never suspected before, a kind of thronging and epic grandeur which my superficial eyes and cluttered mind had been blind to before. They unrolled away impervious to me as though I were a roaming ghost, not only tonight but always, as though I had never played on them a hundred times, as though my feet had never touched them, as though my whole life at Devon had been a dream, or rather that everything at Devon, the playing fields, the gym, the water hole, and all the other buildings and all the people there were intensely real, wildly alive, and totally meaningful, and I alone was a dream, a figment which had never really touched anything. I felt that I was not, never had been, and never would be a living part of this overpoweringly solid and deeply meaningful world around me.

I reached the bridge which arches over the little Devon River and beyond it the dirt track which curves toward the stadium. The stadium itself, two white concrete banks of seats, was as powerful and alien to me as an Aztec ruin, filled with the traces of vanished people and vanished rites, of supreme emotions and supreme tragedies. The old phrase about "If these walls could only speak" occurred to me, and I felt it more deeply than anyone has ever felt it, I felt that the stadium could not only speak, but that its words could hold me spellbound. In fact, the stadium did speak powerfully and at all times, including this moment. But I could not hear, and that was because I did not exist.

I awoke the next morning in a dry and fairly sheltered corner of the ramp underneath the stadium. My neck was stiff from sleeping in an awkward position. The sun was high and the air freshened.

I walked back to the center of the school and had breakfast and then went to my room to get a notebook, because this was Wednesday and I had a class at 9:10. But at the door of the room I found a note from Dr. Stanpole. "Please bring some of Finny's clothes and his toilet things to the Infirmary."

I took his suitcase from the corner where it had been accumulating dust and put what he would need into it. I didn't know what I was going to say at the Infirmary. I couldn't escape a confusing sense of having lived through all of this before—Phineas in the Infirmary, and myself responsible. I seemed to be less shocked by it now than I had the first time last August, when it had broken over our heads like a thunderclap in a flawless sky. There were hints of much worse things around us now like a faint odor in the air, evoked by words like "plasma" and "psycho" and "sulfa," strange words like that with endings like Latin nouns. The newsreels and magazines were choked with images of blazing artillery and bodies half sunk in the sand of a beach somewhere. We members of the Class of 1943 were moving very fast toward the war now, so fast that there were casualties even before we reached it, a mind was clouded and a leg was broken—maybe these should be thought of as minor and inevitable mishaps in the accelerating rush. The air around us was filled with much worse things.

In this way I tried to calm myself as I walked with Finny's suitcase toward the Infirmary. After all, I reflected to myself, people were shooting flames into caves and grilling other people alive, ships were being torpedoed and dropping thousands of men in the icy ocean, whole city blocks were exploding into flame in an instant. My brief burst of animosity, lasting only a second, a part of a second, something which came before I could recognize it and was gone before I knew it had possessed me, what was that in the midst of this holocaust?

I reached the Infirmary with Finny's suitcase and went inside. The air was laden with hospital smells, not unlike those of the gym except that the Infirmary lacked that sense of spent human vitality. This was becoming the new background of Finny's life, this purely medical element from which bodily health was absent.

The corridor happened to be empty, and I walked along it in the grip of a kind of fatal exhilaration. All doubt had been resolved at last. There was a wartime phrase coming into style just then— "this is it"—and although it later became a parody of itself, it had a final flat accuracy which was all that could be said at certain times. This was one of the times: this was it.

I knocked and went in. He was stripped to the waist, sitting up in bed leafing through a magazine. I carried my head low by instinct, and I had the courage for only a short glance at him before I said quietly, "I've brought your stuff."

"Put the suitcase on the bed here, will you?" The tone of his words fell dead center, without a trace of friendliness or unfriendliness, not interested and not bored, not energetic and not languid.

I put it down beside him, and he opened it and began to look through the extra underwear and shirts and socks I had packed. I stood precariously in the middle of the room, trying to find somewhere to look and something to say, wanting desperately to leave and powerless to do so. Phineas went carefully over his clothes, apparently very calm. But it wasn't like him to check with such care, not like him at all. He was taking a long time at it, and then I noticed that as he tried to slide a hairbrush out from under a flap holding it in the case his hands were shaking so badly that he couldn't get it out. Seeing that released me on the spot.

"Finny, I tried to tell you before, I tried to tell you when I came to Boston that time——"

"I know, I remember that." He couldn't, after all, always keep his voice under control. "What'd you come around here for last night?"

"I don't know." I went over to the window and placed my hands on the sill. I looked down at them with a sense of detachment, as though they were hands somebody had sculptured and put on exhibition somewhere. "I had to." Then I added, with great difficulty, "I thought I belonged here."

I felt him turning to look at me, and so I looked

up. He had a particular expression which his face assumed when he understood but didn't think he should show it, a settled, enlightened look; its appearance now was the first decent thing I had seen in a long time.

He suddenly slammed his fist against the suitcase. "I wish there wasn't any war."

I looked sharply at him. "What made you say that?"

"I don't know if I can take this with a war on. I don't know."

"If you can take——"

"What good are you in a war with a busted leg!"

"Well you—why there are lots—you can——"

He bent over the suitcase again. "I've been writing to the Army and the Navy and the Marines and the Canadians and everybody else all winter. Did you know that? No, you didn't know that. I used the Post Office in town for my return address. They all gave me the same answer after they saw the medical report on me. The answer was no soap. We can't use you. I also wrote the Coast Guard, the Merchant Marine, I wrote to General de Gaulle personally, I also wrote Chiang Kai-shek, and I was about ready to write somebody in Russia."

I made an attempt at a grin. "You wouldn't like it in Russia."

"I'll *hate* it *everywhere* if I'm not in this war! Why do you think I kept saying there wasn't any war all winter? I was going to keep on saying it until two seconds after I got a letter from Ottawa or Chungking[3] or some place saying, 'Yes, you can enlist with us.'" A look of pleased achievement flickered over his face momentarily, as though he had really gotten such a letter. "Then there would have been a war."

"Finny," my voice broke but I went on. "Phineas, you wouldn't be any good in the war, even if nothing had happened to your leg."

A look of amazement fell over him. It scared me, but I knew what I said was important and right, and my voice found that full tone voices have when they are expressing something long-felt and long-understood and released at last. "They'd get you some place at the front and there'd be a lull in the fighting, and the next thing anyone knew you'd be over with the Germans or the Japs, asking if they'd like to field a baseball team against our side. You'd be sitting in one of their command posts, teaching them English. Yes, you'd get confused and borrow one of their uniforms, and you'd lend them one of yours. Sure,

that's just what would happen. You'd get things so scrambled up nobody would know who to fight any more. You'd make a mess, a terrible mess, Finny, out of the war."

His face had been struggling to stay calm as he listened to me, but now he was crying but trying to control himself. "It was just some kind of blind impulse you had in the tree there, you didn't know what you were doing. Was that it?"

"Yes, yes, that was it. Oh, that was it, but how can you believe that? How can you believe that? I can't even make myself pretend that you could believe that."

"I do, I think I can believe that. I've gotten awfully mad sometimes and almost forgotten what I was doing. I think I believe you, I think I can believe that. Then that was it. Something just seized you. It wasn't anything you really felt against me, it wasn't some kind of hate you've felt all along. It wasn't anything personal."

"No, I don't know how to show you, how can I show you, Finny? Tell me how to show you. It was just some ignorance inside me, some crazy thing inside me, something blind, that's all it was."

He was nodding his head, his jaw tightening, and his eyes closed on the tears. "I believe you. It's okay because I understand and I believe you. You've already shown me and I believe you."

The rest of the day passed quickly. Dr. Stanpole had told me in the corridor that he was going to set the bone that afternoon. Come back around 5 o'clock, he had said, when Finny should be coming out of the anaesthesia.

I left the Infirmary and went to my 10:10 class, which was on American history. Mr. Patch-Withers gave us a five-minute written quiz on the "necessary and proper" clause of the Constitution. At 11 o'clock I left that building and crossed the Center Common, where a few students were already lounging, although it was still a little early in the season for that. I went into the First Building, walked up the stairs where Finny had fallen, and joined my 11:10 class, which was in mathematics. We were given a ten-minute trigonometry problem which appeared to solve itself on my paper.

At 12 I left the First Building, recrossed the Common and went into the Jared Potter Building for lunch. It was a breaded veal cutlet, spinach, mashed potatoes, and prune whip. At the table we discussed whether there was any saltpeter[4] in the mashed potatoes. I defended the negative.

---

3. **Ottawa . . . Chungking:** Ottawa is the capital of Canada; Chungking was the capital of China during World War II.

4. **saltpeter:** colorless compound (a nitrate). Boarding-school students used to joke that saltpeter was put in their food to lower their sexual drive.

After lunch I walked back to the dormitory with Brinker. He alluded to last night only by asking how Phineas was; I said he seemed to be in good spirits. I went on to my room and read the assigned pages of *Le bourgeois gentilhomme.*[5] At 2:30 I left my room, and walking along one side of the oval Finny had used for my track workouts during the winter, I reached the Far Common and beyond it the gym. I went past the Trophy Room, downstairs into the pungent air of the locker room, changed into gym pants, and spent an hour wrestling. I pinned my opponent once and he pinned me once. Phil Latham showed me an involved method of escape in which you executed a modified somersault over your opponent's back. He started to talk about the accident, but I concentrated on the escape method and the subject was dropped. Then I took a shower, dressed, and went back to the dormitory, reread part of *Le bourgeois gentilhomme,* and at 4:45, instead of going to a scheduled meeting of the Commencement Arrangements Committee, on which I had been persuaded to take Brinker's place, I went to the Infirmary.

Dr. Stanpole was not patrolling the corridor as he habitually did when he was not busy, so I sat down on a bench amid the medical smells and waited. After about ten minutes he came walking rapidly out of his office, his head down and his hands sunk in the pockets of his white smock. He didn't notice me until he was almost past me, and then he stopped short. His eyes met mine carefully, and I said, "Well, how is he, sir?" in a calm voice which, the moment after I had spoken, alarmed me unreasonably.

Dr. Stanpole sat down next to me and put his capable-looking hand on my leg. "This is something I think boys of your generation are going to see a lot of," he said quietly, "and I will have to tell you about it now. Your friend is dead."

He was incomprehensible. I felt an extremely cold chill along my back and neck, that was all. Dr. Stanpole went on talking incomprehensibly. "It was such a simple, clean break. Anyone could have set it. Of course, I didn't send him to Boston. Why should I?"

He seemed to expect an answer from me, so I shook my head and repeated, "Why should you?"

"In the middle of it his heart simply stopped, without warning. I can't explain it. Yes, I can. There is only one explanation. As I was moving the bone some of the marrow must have escaped into his bloodstream and gone directly to his heart and stopped it. That's the only possible explanation. The only one. There are risks, there are always risks. An operating room is a place where the risks are just more formal than in other places. An operating room and a war." And I noticed that his self-control was breaking up. "Why did it have to happen to you boys so soon, here at Devon?"

"The marrow of his bone . . ." I repeated aimlessly. This at last penetrated my mind. Phineas had died from the marrow of his bone flowing down his bloodstream to his heart.

I did not cry then or ever about Finny. I did not cry even when I stood watching him being lowered into his family's strait-laced burial ground outside of Boston. I could not escape a feeling that this was my own funeral, and you do not cry in that case.

13

The quadrangle surrounding the Far Common was never considered absolutely essential to the Devon School. The essence was elsewhere, in the older, uglier, more comfortable halls enclosing the Center Common. There the School's history had unrolled, the fabled riot scenes and Presidential visits and Civil War musterings, if not in these buildings, then in their predecessors on the same site. The upperclassmen and the faculty met there, the budget was compiled there, and there students were expelled. When you said "Devon" to an alumnus ten years after graduation, he visualized the Center Common.

The Far Common was different, a gift of the rich lady benefactress. It was Georgian like the rest of the school, and it combined scholasticism with grace in the way which made Devon architecturally interesting. But the bricks had been laid a little too skillfully, and the woodwork was not as brittle and chipped as it should have been. It was not the essence of Devon, and so it was donated, without too serious a wrench, to the war.

The Far Common could be seen from the window of my room, and early in June I stood at the window and watched the war moving in to occupy it. The advance guard which came down the street from the railroad station consisted of a number of Jeeps, being driven with a certain restraint, their gyration-prone wheels inactive on these old ways which offered nothing bumpier than a few cobblestones. I thought the Jeeps looked noticeably uncomfortable from all the power they were not

---

5. *Le bourgeois gentilhomme* (lə boor·zhwä zhôn·tē·yôm): *The Bourgeois Gentleman* (also translated as *The Would-be Gentleman*), a play by the seventeenth-century French playwright Molière.

Ghost Trail by Kerr Eby (1943). Charcoal drawing with pastel.

being allowed to use. There is no stage you comprehend better than the one you have just left, and as I watched the Jeeps almost asserting a wish to bounce up the side of Mount Washington[1] at eighty miles an hour instead of rolling along this dull street, they reminded me, in a comical and a poignant way, of adolescents.

Following them there were some heavy trucks painted olive drab, and behind them came the troops. They were not very bellicose-looking[2];

their columns were straggling, their suntan uniforms had gotten rumpled in the train, and they were singing "Roll Out the Barrel."

"What's that?" Brinker said from behind me, pointing across my shoulder at some open trucks bringing up the rear. "What's in those trucks?"

"They look like sewing machines."

"They *are* sewing machines!"

"I guess a Parachute Riggers' school has to have sewing machines."

"If only Leper had enlisted in the Army Air Force and been assigned to Parachute Riggers' school . . ."

---

1. **Mount Washington:** mountain in northern New Hampshire.
2. **bellicose-looking:** warlike-looking.

U.S. Navy Art Collection.

"I don't think it would have made any difference," I said. "Let's not talk about Leper."

"Leper'll be all right. There's nothing like a discharge. Two years after the war's over people will think a Section Eight means a berth on a Pullman car."

"Right. Now do you mind? Why talk about something you can't do anything about?"

"Right."

I had to be right in never talking about what you could not change, and I had to make many people agree that I was right. None of them ever accused me of being responsible for what had hap-pened to Phineas, either because they could not believe it or else because they could not understand it. I would have talked about that, but they would not, and I would not talk about Phineas in any other way.

The Jeeps, troops, and sewing machines were now drawn up next to the Far Common quadrangle. There was some kind of consultation or ceremony underway on the steps of one of the buildings, Veazy Hall. The Headmaster and a few of the senior members of the faculty stood in a group before the door, and a number of Army Air Force officers stood in another group within easy speaking distance of them. Then the Headmaster advanced several steps and enlarged his gestures; he was apparently addressing the troops. Then an officer took his place and spoke longer and louder; we could hear his voice fairly well but not make out the words.

Around them spread a beautiful New England day. Peace lay on Devon like a blessing, the summer's peace, the reprieve, New Hampshire's response to all the cogitation and deadness of winter. There could be no urgency in work during such summers; any parachutes rigged would be no more effective than napkins.

Or perhaps that was only true for me and a few others, our gypsy band of the summer before. Or was it rarer even than that; had Chet and Bobby sensed it then, for instance? Had Leper, despite his trays of snails? I could be certain of only two people, Phineas and myself. So now it might be true only for me.

The company fell out and began scattering through the Far Common. Dormitory windows began to fly open, and olive drab blankets were hung over the sills by the dozens to air. The sewing machines were carried with considerable exertion into Veazy Hall.

"Dad's here," said Brinker. "I told him to take his cigar down to the Butt Room. He wants to meet you."

We went downstairs and found Mr. Hadley sitting in one of the lumpy chairs, trying not to look offended by the surroundings. But he stood up and shook my hand with genuine cordiality when we came in. He was a distinguished-looking man, taller than Brinker, so that his portliness was not very noticeable. His hair was white, thick, and healthy-looking, and his face was healthily pink.

"You boys look fine, fine," he said in his full and cordial voice, "better I would say than those doughboys—G.I.'s—I saw marching in. And how about their artillery! Sewing machines!"

Brinker slid his fingers into the back pockets of his slacks. "This war's so technical they've got to use all kinds of machines, even sewing machines, don't you think so, Gene?"

"Well," Mr. Hadley went on emphatically, "I can't imagine any man in my time settling for duty on a sewing machine. I can't picture that at all." Then his temper switched tracks and he smiled cordially again. "But then times change, and wars change. But men don't change, do they? You boys are the image of me and my gang in the old days. It does me good to see you. What are you enlisting in, son," he said, meaning me, "the Marines, the Paratroops? There are doggone many exciting things to enlist in these days. There's that bunch they call the Frogmen, underwater demolition stuff. I'd give something to be a kid again with all that to choose from."

"I was going to wait and be drafted," I replied, trying to be polite and answer his question honestly, "but if I did that they might put me straight in the infantry, and that's not only the dirtiest but also the most dangerous branch of all, the worst branch of all. So I've joined the Navy, and they're sending me to Pensacola.[3] I'll probably have a lot of training, and I'll never see a foxhole.[4] I hope."

"Foxhole" was still a fairly new term and I wasn't sure Mr. Hadley knew what it meant. But I saw that he didn't care for the sound of what I said. "And then Brinker," I added, "is all set for the Coast Guard, which is good too." Mr. Hadley's scowl deepened, although his experienced face partially masked it.

"You know, Dad," Brinker broke in, "the Coast Guard does some very rough stuff, putting the men on the beaches, all that dangerous amphibious stuff."

His father nodded slightly, looking at the floor, and then said, "You have to do what you think is the right thing, but just make sure it's the right thing in the long run, and not just for the moment. Your war memories will be with you forever, you'll be asked about them thousands of times after the war is over. People will get their respect for you from that—*partly* from that, don't get me wrong—but if you can say that you were up front where there was some real shooting going on, then that will mean a whole lot to you in years to come. I know you boys want to see plenty of action, but don't go around talking too much about being comfortable, and which branch of the service has too much dirt and stuff like that. Now, I know

you—I feel I know you, Gene, as well as I know Brink here—but other people might misunderstand you. You want to serve, that's all. It's your greatest moment, greatest privilege, to serve your country. We're all proud of you, and we're all—old guys like me—we're all darn jealous of you too."

I could see that Brinker was more embarrassed by this than I was, but I felt it was his responsibility to answer it. "Well, Dad," he mumbled, "we'll do what we have to."

"That's not a very good answer, Brink," he said in a tone struggling to remain reasonable.

"After all, that's all we can do."

"You can do more! A lot more. If you want a military record you can be proud of, you'll do a heck of a lot more than just what you have to. Believe me."

Brinker sighed under his breath, his father stiffened, paused, then relaxed with an effort. "Your mother's out in the car. I'd better get back to her. You boys clean up—ah, those shoes," he added reluctantly, in spite of himself, having to, "those shoes, Brink, a little polish?—and we'll see you at the Inn at six."

"Okay, Dad."

His father left, trailing the faint, unfamiliar, prosperous aroma of his cigar.

"Dad keeps making that speech about serving the country," Brinker said apologetically, "I wish to heck he wouldn't."

"That's all right." I knew that part of friendship consisted in accepting a friend's shortcomings, which sometimes included his parents.

"I'm enlisting," he went on, "I'm going to 'serve' as he puts it, I may even get killed. But I'll be darned if I'll have that Nathan Hale[5] attitude of his about it. It's all that World War I malarkey that gets me. They're all children about that war, did you never notice?" He flopped comfortably into the chair which had been disconcerting his father. "It gives me a pain, personally. I'm not any kind of hero, and neither are you. And neither is the old man, and he never was, and I don't care what he says he almost did at Château-Thierry.[6]"

"He's just trying to keep up with the times. He probably feels left out, being too old this time."

"Left out!" Brinker's eyes lighted up. "Left out! He and his crowd are responsible for it! And *we're* going to fight it!"

---

3. **Pensacola:** seaport in Florida and site of a naval air station.
4. **foxhole:** hole dug in the ground for one or two soldiers as protection against enemy gunfire.

5. **Nathan Hale:** young hero of the American Revolutionary War, who was hanged by the British as a spy. Hale's last words were supposedly "I only regret that I have but one life to lose for my country."
6. **Château-Thierry** (shä·tō′tye·rē′): town in northern France, site of one of the final battles of World War I.

I had heard this generation-complaint from Brinker before, so often that I finally identified this as the source of his disillusionment during the winter, this generalized, faintly self-pitying resentment against millions of people he did not know. He did know his father, however, and so they were not getting along well now. In a way this was Finny's view, except that naturally he saw it comically, as a huge and intensely practical joke, played by fat and foolish old men bungling away behind the scenes.

I could never agree with either of them. It would have been comfortable, but I could not believe it. Because it seemed clear that wars were not made by generations and their special stupidities, but that wars were made instead by something ignorant in the human heart.

Brinker went upstairs to continue his packing, and I walked over to the gym to clear out my locker. As I crossed the Far Common, I saw that it was rapidly becoming unrecognizable, with huge green barrels placed at many strategic points, the ground punctuated by white markers identifying offices and areas, and also certain less tangible things: a kind of snap in the atmosphere, a professional optimism, a conscious maintenance of high morale. I myself had often been happy at Devon, but such times, it seemed to me that afternoon, were over now. Happiness had disappeared along with rubber, silk, and many other staples, to be replaced by the wartime synthetic, high morale, for the Duration.

At the gym a platoon was undressing in the locker room. The best that could be said for them physically was that they looked wiry in their startling sets of underwear, which were the color of moss.

I never talked about Phineas and neither did anyone else; he was, however, present in every moment of every day since Dr. Stanpole had told me. Finny had a vitality which could not be quenched so suddenly, even by the marrow of his bone. That was why I couldn't say anything or listen to anything about him, because he endured so forcefully that what I had to say would have seemed crazy to anyone else—I could not use the past tense, for instance—and what they had to say would be incomprehensible to me. During the time I was with him, Phineas created an atmosphere in which I continued now to live, a way of sizing up the world with erratic and entirely personal reservations, letting its rocklike facts sift through and be accepted only a little at a time, only as much as he could assimilate without a sense of chaos and loss.

No one else I have ever met could do this. All others at some point found something in themselves pitted violently against something in the world around them. With those of my year this point often came when they grasped the fact of the war. When they began to feel that there was this overwhelmingly hostile thing in the world with them, then the simplicity and unity of their characters broke and they were not the same again.

Phineas alone had escaped this. He possessed an extra vigor, a heightened confidence in himself, a serene capacity for affection which saved him. Nothing as he was growing up at home, nothing at Devon, nothing even about the war had broken his harmonious and natural unity. So at last I had.

The parachute riggers sprinted out of the hallway toward the playing fields. From my locker I collected my sneakers, jock strap, and gym pants and then turned away, leaving the door ajar for the first time, forlornly open and abandoned, the locker unlocked. This was more final than the moment when the Headmaster handed me my diploma. My schooling was over now.

I walked down the aisle past the rows of lockers, and instead of turning left toward the exit leading back to my dormitory, I turned right and followed the Army Air Force out onto the playing fields of Devon. A high wooden platform had been erected there, and on it stood a barking instructor, giving the rows of men below him calisthenics by the numbers.

This kind of regimentation would fasten itself on me in a few weeks. I no longer had any qualms about that, although I couldn't help being glad that it would not be at Devon, at anywhere like Devon, that I would have that. I had no qualms at all; in fact I could feel now the gathering, glowing sense of sureness in the face of it. I was ready for the war, now that I no longer had any hatred to contribute to it. My fury was gone, I felt it gone, dried up at the source, withered and lifeless. Phineas had absorbed it and taken it with him, and I was rid of it forever.

The P.T.[7] instructor's voice, like a frog's croak amplified a hundred times, blared out the Army's numerals, "Hut! Hew! Hee! Hore!" behind me as I started back toward the dormitory, and my feet, of course, could not help but begin to fall involuntarily into step with that coarse, compelling voice, which carried to me like an air-raid siren across the fields and commons.

They fell into step then, as they fell into step a few weeks later under the influence of an even louder voice and a stronger sun. Down there I fell

---

7. **P.T.:** abbreviation for "physical training."

into step as well as my nature, Phineas-filled, would allow.

I never killed anybody, and I never developed an intense level of hatred for the enemy. Because my war ended before I ever put on a uniform; I was on active duty all my time at school; I killed my enemy there.

Only Phineas never was afraid, only Phineas never hated anyone. Other people experienced this fearful shock somewhere, this sighting of the enemy, and so began an obsessive labor of defense, began to parry the menace they saw facing them by developing a particular frame of mind, "You see," their behavior toward everything and everyone proclaimed, "I am a humble ant, I am nothing, I am not worthy of this menace," or else, like Mr. Ludsbury, "How dare this threaten me, I am much too good for this sort of handling, I shall rise above this," or else, like Quackenbush, strike out at it always and everywhere, or else, like Brinker, develop a careless general resentment against it, or else, like Leper, emerge from a protective cloud of vagueness only to meet it, the horror, face to face, just as he had always feared, and so give up the struggle absolutely.

All of them, all except Phineas, constructed at infinite cost to themselves these Maginot Lines[8] against this enemy they thought they saw across the frontier, this enemy who never attacked that way—if he ever attacked at all; if he was indeed the enemy.

---

8. **Maginot** (mazh′ə·nō′) **Lines:** any elaborate but ineffective barriers. The reference is to the line of fortifications erected by the French along their border with Germany, before World War II. The invading German armies simply went around the barricades.

Responding to the Novel

Analyzing Chapters 11–13

Identifying Facts

1. What finally convinces Finny that the war is real?
2. Describe the inquiry Brinker conducts into Finny's accident. How does this inquiry lead to Finny's second fall?
3. When Gene calls out to Finny through the Infirmary window, what accusation does Finny make? Describe the reconciliation that takes place the next day.
4. Explain why Gene says that his war ended before he ever put on a uniform.

Interpreting Meanings

5. When Gene and Finny have their final conversation in the Infirmary, it is actually Finny who first proposes an explanation for Gene's behavior in the tree—that "it was just some kind of blind impulse," rather than "some kind of hate" or "anything personal" he'd felt all along. Gene agrees with this interpretation, adding: "it was just some ignorance inside me, some crazy thing inside me, something blind." Does this explanation make sense to you? Why or why not? (Can you think of any other kinds of behavior that could be classified as "blind impulse"?)
6. Why do you think Finny believes and forgives Gene so readily for all the suffering he has caused him? What do you think Finny means when he says that Gene has already shown him that he's telling the truth?
7. What do you think of Brinker's father's attitude toward the war? Is he right to suggest that the boys go where there's "some real shooting going on," or is his view "inside out," as Leper would say? What do you think of Brinker's attitude—that old men start the wars that young men have to fight?
8. Gene expresses a third opinion about war. Explain how his attitude relates to the self-knowledge he has gained during the course of the novel.
9. On page 982, Gene says that his nature has become "Phineas-filled." By the end of the novel, which of Finny's characteristics have become Gene's? In what ways is he still quite different from Finny?
10. Reread the last paragraph of the novel, remem-

bering Gene's assertion that he had been on "active duty" all his time at school; that he had killed his enemy there. In what way was Finny Gene's enemy, or **antagonist**? If it wasn't Finny, who or what do you think Gene's real enemy was? Explain your answer.

The Novel as a Whole

1. Gene is the novel's **protagonist**—the main character whose conflict sets the plot in motion. In most stories, people identify closely with the protagonist. Did you sympathize with Gene throughout the novel, or did you identify with him more at certain points than at others? Are there any aspects of his character that you find puzzling or unconvincing?

2. How do you feel about the **character** of Finny? Are his personality traits and actions believable? Or is he "too good to be true," as Gene suggests in Chapter 3?

3. In Chapter 11, during the first part of the inquiry into Finny's accident, Finny acts as though he is trying to cover up for Gene. Why, then, is Finny so devastated when he learns the truth about what happened?

4. One reviewer has suggested that *A Separate Peace* is a young adult classic because readers are "moved by the desire to be like Phineas and the fear of turning out like Gene." What do you think of this interpretation?

5. The action of *A Separate Peace* is set against a backdrop not only of World War II, but also of life at an elite boys' prep school. Explain how this **setting** directly affects the development of both the **plot** and the **characters**. It might help to imagine how the action would be different if the book were set, for example, in an inner-city coed school in the South during peacetime in the 1990's.

6. What do you think is the novel's central **theme**—the insight it reveals about life or human nature? Which incidents and characters from the novel support your interpretation of theme? You might even be able to find some **subthemes** in the novel. In class discussion, consider what Knowles is trying to say about these subjects: war, aggression, loyalty, friendship, rivalry, goodness, hatred, fear, and idealism. Are the novel's themes relevant to life today? Explain.

Writing About the Novel

A Creative Response

1. **Creating an Alternate Ending.** Imagine that Finny doesn't die at the end of Chapter 12. Write a synopsis, or summary, of what you think might happen after Finny is released from the Infirmary. What, for example, will happen to his relationship with Gene? What will happen to both boys after they graduate?

2. **Changing the Novel's Setting.** Pretend you're going to make a movie of *A Separate Peace,* and you've decided to have the action take place today in one of these settings:

   a. A coed inner-city school in Miami
   b. An all-girls' school in New York City
   c. Your own high school

   In three paragraphs, tell what details in the novel you'd have to change to set the story in this new time and place. In the first paragraph, describe the movie's main **characters**. In the second paragraph, describe its major **conflicts**. In the third paragraph, describe the locations where you'd set the movie's key scenes. If you think the **plot** would have to be **resolved** differently because of your changes in setting, explain why.

3. **Using a Different Point of View.** Imagine what *A Separate Peace* would be like if Finny were the narrator, rather than Gene. Pick a key scene from the novel, and retell it from Finny's point of view. Try to come up with a narrative "voice" that sounds like Finny, and that reveals his inner thoughts and feelings.

4. **Writing a Letter of Apology.** Imagine that you're Gene. It has been a year since graduation, and you're now in the Navy, stationed in Pensacola, Florida. You haven't seen or spoken to Leper since the inquiry at which he testified about Finny's fall from the tree. Since then, you've been doing a lot of hard thinking and maturing, and you now regret your behavior when you visited Leper in Vermont. Write a letter to Leper in which you apologize for your behavior that day and explain why you acted the way you did.

A Critical Response

5. **Responding to a Writer's Comment.** Read John Knowles's comment about *A Separate Peace* under "Focusing on Background" (page 986).

Then write a brief essay of two or three paragraphs in which you respond to his claim that the novel's restrictive setting and all-male cast of characters do *not* affect its appeal to a wide audience. Use specific references to the novel to support your opinion.

6. **Responding to a Critic.** Here is what one critic has written about Knowles's use of **symbolism** in *A Separate Peace:*

What happens in the novel is that Gene Forrester and Phineas, denying the existence of the Second World War as they enjoy the summer peace of Devon School, move gradually to a realization of an uglier adult world—mirrored in the winter and the Naguamsett River—whose central fact is the war. This moving from innocence to adulthood is contained within three sets of interconnected symbols. These three—summer and winter; the Devon River and the Naguamsett River; and peace and war—serve as a backdrop against which the novel is developed, the first of each pair dominating the early novel and giving way to the second only after Gene has discovered the evil of his own heart.

—James Ellis

In a brief essay of two or three paragraphs, tell whether or not you agree with Ellis's analysis of the novel's symbolism. Be sure to present details from the book that either support or refute his argument.

7. **Interpreting the Novel's Title.** What do you think the novel's title refers to? Here are some possibilities:

   a. The "measureless, careless peace of the Devon summer" that Gene prizes so much
   b. The private world inhabited by just Gene and Finny, where "there was no war at all"
   c. The feeling of liberation the boys experience at Finny's Winter Carnival
   d. The understanding Gene and Finny come to at the end of the novel
   e. The detached attitude Gene develops toward the war after Finny's death

Write a two- or three-paragraph essay in which you explore the meaning of the novel's title. Do you think this is the best title Knowles could have chosen? If not, what title would you have used instead?

8. **Comparing a Book and a Movie.** View the 1972 film version of *A Separate Peace,* and compare and contrast it with the novel. Pay particular attention to the ways in which the movie is different from the book. Do the film's **characters** and **setting** look the way you imagined them? What aspects of the novel do you find missing in the movie? (How would you have included them?) Do you prefer the book or the movie? Why?

Analyzing Language and Vocabulary

Extended Metaphors

One of the distinctive features of Knowles's writing style is his vivid use of figurative language, particularly **extended metaphors**—figures of speech that are developed and sustained over several lines of writing. Here are some extended metaphors from *A Separate Peace.* Answer the questions following each passage.

1. "To enlist. To slam the door impulsively on the past, to shed everything down to my last bit of clothing, to break the pattern of my life—that complex design I had been weaving since birth with all its dark threads, its unexplainable symbols set against a conventional background of domestic white and schoolboy blue, all those tangled strands which required the dexterity of a virtuoso to keep flowing—I yearned to take giant military shears to it, snap! bitten off in an instant, and nothing left in my hands but spools of khaki which could weave only a plain, flat, khaki design, however twisted they might be." (Chapter 7, page 939)

   a. What is Gene comparing his life to?
   b. List the different words that establish and then **extend** this comparison.
   c. Without using any **figures of speech,** how would you paraphrase this **extended metaphor** to explain why Gene wants to enlist? What does he yearn for in his life?

2. "So the war swept over like a wave at the seashore, gathering power and size as it bore on us, overwhelming in its rush, seemingly inescapable, and then at the last moment eluded by a word from Phineas; I had simply ducked, that was all, and the wave's concentrated power had hurtled harmlessly overhead, no doubt throwing

others roughly up on the beach, but leaving me peaceably treading water as before. I did not stop to think that one wave is inevitably followed by another even larger and more powerful, when the tide is coming in." (Chapter 8, page 942)

a. What two things is Gene comparing?
b. Specifically, what is Gene comparing to "a word from Phineas"?
c. Sophocles uses a similar **extended metaphor** in *Antigone* (see Ode 2, lines 1–6). Which metaphor do you prefer? Why?

3. "Winter's occupation seems to have conquered, overrun, and destroyed everything, so that now there is no longer any resistance movement left in nature; all the juices are dead, every sprig of vitality snapped, and now winter itself, an old, corrupt, tired conqueror, loosens its grip on the desolation, recedes a little, grows careless in its watch; sick of victory and enfeebled by the absence of challenge, it begins itself to withdraw from the ruined countryside." (Chapter 9, page 950)

a. What is Gene comparing winter to?
b. How do you think Gene's use of a warlike metaphor for nature reflects (1) his own outlook on life, (2) the values of Devon, and (3) world events at the time?
c. How might a different narrator, with a different set of concerns, have described the end of winter?

Reading About the Writer

John Knowles (1926–   ) was born in Fairmont, West Virginia. He based *A Separate Peace* on his experiences during World War II as a student at Phillips Exeter Academy, an exclusive preparatory school in New Hampshire. He modeled the narrator, Gene, after himself, and the other characters after his classmates—Brinker Hadley, for example, was patterned on the young Gore Vidal, who later became a renowned novelist. Even Finny's fall from the tree grew out of a less serious accident to Knowles himself.

After receiving his diploma from Exeter, Knowles served in the Air Force as an aviation cadet, and then returned to study English at Yale University. He remained in Connecticut after college as a reporter for the *Hartford Courant,* and then went to Europe, where he traveled, worked as a freelance writer, and "in general tried to live a varied life preparatory to doing my life's work: writing."

Knowles wrote *A Separate Peace* in longhand on yellow legal pads, working in the mornings before he went to his job as an associate editor for *Holiday* magazine. "No book can have been easier to get down on paper," he writes. Every major publisher in the United States initially rejected the novel, which was finally accepted by a British company and published to great acclaim.

The critical and commercial success of *A Separate Peace* enabled Knowles to become a full-time writer. He has since published several novels and works of nonfiction and has been a writer-in-residence at Princeton University and the University of North Carolina. He currently lives in New York.

Scene from *The Dead Poets Society,* a movie about a group of boys at a New England prep school, starring Robin Williams as their inspiring teacher.

© 1989 Touchstone Pictures.

Focusing on Background
"It Has Reached Out to the Readers Who Need It"

Here is an excerpt from an article John Knowles wrote for *Esquire* magazine in 1985, to mark the twenty-fifth anniversary of the publication of *A Separate Peace.* Do you agree with Knowles's assessment of the universal relevance of his novel?

"*A Separate Peace* is one long and abject confession . . . a tale of crime—if a crime had been committed—and of no punishment, or only interior punishment. It is a story of growth through tragedy. Young people, on their deepest emotional level, respond to that. It makes not the slightest difference that the story's externals may be totally foreign to them. In the novel there is not a girl in sight; that means nothing—women of all ages and every background treat it as central to their view of life.

It takes place among some privileged kids in a first-class preparatory school: that doesn't mean anything either. One of the most moving letters I ever got was from the teen-age participants in a drug treatment program in the Bedford-Stuyvesant section of Brooklyn. Another was from a group of paraplegic veterans of the Vietnam War. Co-eds in Finland, old ladies in Italy, a murderer on death row in Utah—all have communicated their depth of feeling about the book.

". . . The book has affected millions of lives, influenced them deeply, modified what they saw and felt in the world about them. The ultimate importance of *A Separate Peace* is that it has reached out to the readers who need it."

—John Knowles

DEVELOPING AND SUPPORTING A THESIS STATEMENT

Writing Assignment

Write a five-paragraph essay in which you first develop a thesis statement about *A Separate Peace* and then support that statement with evidence from the novel.

Background

In literature, a **thesis** is a position, proposition, or interpretation that a person presents and then attempts to defend. An essay about literature usually begins with a **thesis statement**—one or two sentences in the first paragraph that briefly sum up the argument or **main idea** the essay is defending.

For example, on page 984 you are asked to write an essay interpreting the title of *A Separate Peace.* Note that to write this essay, you must first come up with an interpretation of the title's meaning. You might decide that it refers to one or more of the possibilities suggested in the question. Or you might come up with your own interpretation of what Knowles means.

The next step in preparing your essay is to summarize your interpretation, or thesis, in one or two sentences. Here is a sample thesis statement:

> Clearly, the title *A Separate Peace* works on several different levels. Yet its most important meaning is the private, personal peace that Gene makes with Finny at the end of the novel.

If you used this thesis statement in the introductory paragraph of your essay, the remaining paragraphs would provide evidence to support this interpretation of the novel. Specifically, you would need to show why the final peace between Gene and Finny is central to the story's theme. You would also need to show how that peace relates to some of the title's other levels of meaning.

Prewriting

Here are some key points to keep in mind in developing a thesis statement:

1. A thesis statement presents an **opinion** that you will be attempting to defend, not a fact that you will be able to prove.
2. The opinion you set forth in your thesis statement should be **focused** enough to examine within the scope of your essay. If you are planning on writing five paragraphs, do not begin with a thesis statement that would take a two-hundred-page book to defend.
3. A thesis statement is different from a **topic.** For example, you might write an essay about the **characterization** of Finny in *A Separate Peace.* This is your topic; your thesis statement is the position you take on this topic—your interpretation of Finny's character. Here are two possible thesis statements on this topic:

> Finny in *A Separate Peace* is a magnetic, charismatic character whom people can't help liking—but he is also manipulative, immature, and self-centered. He is not nearly as innocent as he seems.

> The character of Finny represents innocence—an innocence that is destroyed when it is forced to confront the hatred and evil in the real world.

4. A good thesis statement is based on a **close reading** of the text. This means that you might

have to go back over the work to come up with an interesting idea to write about, taking notes as you reread.

5. Keep **revising** and refining your thesis statement until it expresses the precise point you want to defend in your essay. Most writers find that if they can't write a good thesis statement in one or two sentences, then they haven't clarified their thoughts enough to begin writing the essay.

6. A good thesis statement doesn't have to present an earth-shatteringly original idea. But you'll bore both your audience and yourself if you write about the most obvious aspect of the work, if you present a position that no one could possibly disagree with. In fact, one way to come up with an interesting thesis statement is to think of a seemingly obvious interpretation and then try to find a way to argue *against* it. For example, you might attempt to defend the position that the protagonist of *A Separate Peace* is really Finny, not Gene.

7. Even if you choose an interpretation that isn't quite so controversial, it is often helpful to think of arguments against your position so that you can **refute** them in your essay. (For a similar technique used in debating, see page 617.)

8. If you have trouble thinking of a good thesis to write about, try examining each of the literary **elements** you have studied. Is there one element in particular that strikes you as the most important in the work? If so, why? Is there one element that seems especially complex or open to multiple interpretations? For example, many critics who have written about *A Separate Peace* have examined the effect of the novel's first-person point of view.

Once you've developed a good thesis statement, your next step is to gather **supporting evidence**—details, quotes, and incidents from the literary work that defend your interpretation or idea. You might also wish to include quotes from book reviews, critical essays, or interviews with the writer about the work. Here is a paragraph that presents several pieces of evidence to support the writer's thesis:

It must be noted that the separate peace Finny and Gene carve out is no idyllic escape from reality. By founding the Super Suicide Society of the Summer Session, membership in which requires a dangerous leap into the Devon River, the boys admit both danger and death into their golden gypsy days. Accordingly, the game of blitzball, which Finny invents the same summer, includes the bellicosity and treachery that perhaps count as humanity's worst features: "Since we're all enemies, we can and will turn on each other all the time."

—Peter Wolfe

After you have gathered your evidence, you need to sort through it (discarding weak points if necessary) and arrange it into a strong, logical argument. Usually the most effective organization is to save your most persuasive point for last.

Writing

Use the guidelines in the Prewriting list to develop a **thesis statement** about *A Separate Peace*. Then present at least three pieces of evidence to support your thesis statement, plus any arguments you wish to refute. In your final paragraph, briefly restate your thesis and summarize your argument.

Checklist for Revision

1. Have you included a thesis statement that is focused enough to defend in your essay?
2. Have you supported your thesis statement with at least three pieces of evidence?
3. If you have quoted directly from the novel or from other sources, have you checked the quotation for accuracy, used quotation marks, and cited the page on which the quotation appears?
4. Have you checked: Spelling? Punctuation? Capitalization? Sentence structure? Paragraph organization?

WRITING ABOUT LITERATURE

Writing Answers to Essay Questions

The following strategies will help you organize and write your answers to the essay questions following each selection in this book. Step-by-step instructions in the writing process may also be found in the Exercises in Critical Thinking and Writing. A list of these exercises appears in the index on page 1052.

1. Begin by reading the essay question carefully. Make sure you understand exactly what the question is asking you to do, and note how much evidence it asks you to provide.

2. Identify the key verb in the question. It will help you pinpoint your assignment. Look for these key verbs:

● **Analyze (Examine).** To *analyze* something is to take it apart and see how it works. Usually you will be asked to analyze one element of a work and explain its effect on the other elements and on the work as a whole. For example, you might be asked to analyze the tone of Theodore Roethke's poem "The Meadow Mouse" (page 276). Begin by identifying the speaker's attitude toward his subject; come up with one or two adjectives (such as *protective* or *anguished*). As evidence, cite specific lines, images, or figures of speech that indicate the speaker's feelings. Then explain how the tone of the poem affects its total meaning.

● **Compare/Contrast.** When you *compare*, you point out similarities; when you *contrast*, you point out differences. For example, you might be asked to compare and contrast "The Road Not Taken" by Robert Frost (page 253) and "George Gray" by Edgar Lee Masters (page 256), two poems whose speakers are looking back at the decisions they have made during their lives. Make a chart listing the similarities and differences between the two poems. Consider each speaker's decision and feelings about that decision. Also examine each poem's imagery, symbolism, tone, sound effects, and rhythm if you feel there are important similarities or differences.

● **Describe.** To *describe* means to paint a picture in words. For example, if you were asked to describe Maggie in Alice Walker's "Everyday Use" (page 129), you would state what you know about her through direct and indirect characterization—how she looks, acts, speaks, feels, and affects other people.

● **Discuss.** To *discuss* means to comment about something in a general way. For example, an essay question might ask you to discuss the use of irony in Guy de Maupassant's "The Piece of String" (page 30). First identify all the examples of irony you can find in the story, and then comment on their importance to the story's overall effect. You might also state your response to the writer's use of irony. (Did you find it a powerful thematic device? Did the story's ironic ending strike you as believable?)

● **Evaluate.** To evaluate something is to judge how good or bad—or effective or ineffective—it is. For example, you might be asked to evaluate Ray Bradbury's "The Pedestrian" (page 137). Although you probably have a gut response to the story (which you should pay attention to), you need to back up your feelings with reasons and evidence. You can arrive at a well-supported judgment of the story's quality by analyzing the effectiveness of each of its different elements. (For a list of the criteria for evaluating works of literature, see pages 163, 339, and 444).

● **Illustrate.** To *illustrate* means to provide examples to support an idea or statement. For example, you might be asked to illustrate Creon's excessive pride in Sophocles' *Antigone* (page 748). Provide several examples of Creon's words and actions that demonstrate this character trait. If necessary, explain why a particular example indicates pride, rather than some other quality.

● **Interpret.** To *interpret* something means to explain its meaning and importance. For example, you might be asked to interpret the theme of Bernard Malamud's story "The First Seven Years" (page 59). Reread the story carefully and decide what you think its theme is. Then cite specific details from the story to support your interpretation.

● **Respond.** To *respond* is to give your personal reaction to something. If you are asked to explain your response to a work, you should state whether you liked or disliked it, how it made you feel, and what it made you think about. Whenever possible, you should give reasons for your response.

3. Write a thesis statement stating the main idea of your essay. Include your thesis statement in the first paragraph, along with any additional sentences that help you catch the reader's attention.

4. Gather evidence to support this thesis statement. If you can use your book, look back over the work for examples and illustrations. For a closed-book essay, make notes on all the supporting details you can remember.

5. Write one paragraph for each main point. Include a topic sentence for each paragraph, and try to express your ideas as clearly and simply as you can. Don't pad your answer with unrelated details or ideas.

6. End with a concluding paragraph. Summarize or re-state your main points, and if you wish, give your personal response to the work. Try to end your essay with a dynamic "clincher sentence."

Writing and Revising an Essay About a Literary Work

You may be asked to choose your own topic for an essay on a specific work.

Prewriting

1. Choose a limited topic that you can cover adequately. If your assignment is an essay of four paragraphs or five hundred words, you can't possibly analyze all the characters in *A Separate Peace.* But you do have room to analyze one character or the novel's setting. For ideas on the kinds of topics you can choose, review the list of key verbs on page 989.

2. Write a thesis statement. Ask yourself, "What main idea about my topic do I want to discuss?" Then write one or two sentences that state this main idea. If you have trouble expressing your idea in only one or two sentences, you should consider narrowing the topic of your essay. For help with formulating a thesis statement, see pages 987–988.

3. List two or three main ideas that develop your thesis statement. Jot down the ideas that come to mind when you think about your thesis statement, and choose the strongest two or three. Then go back over the work and do a close reading to come up with specific points you may have overlooked. Don't rely simply on your memory.

4. Gather and arrange supporting evidence. Your essay should include quotations, specific details, examples, and incidents from the literary work you are writing about—known as the **primary source.** You might also wish to refer to other works, letters, or interviews by the same writer. Finally, you can also include information from **secondary sources**—books, reviews, and critical essays about the work or the writer.

Before you begin writing, decide which evidence best supports your thesis statement. Then discard any weak or unrelated material. Once you've arranged your main

ideas and evidence in the order that seems the most logical, you'll have an informal outline to work from.

Writing

Write a draft of your essay, following your outline and notes. Be sure to include enough evidence to support your thesis statement and the main idea of each paragraph. Structure your essay according to this plan.

I. INTRODUCTORY PARAGRAPH
Catches the reader's interest.
Tells what the essay will be about.
Begins or ends with the thesis statement.

II. BODY (Paragraphs 2, 3, etc.)
Develops the thesis statement.
Includes a topic sentence and supporting evidence in each paragraph.

III. CONCLUDING PARAGRAPH
Tells the reader the essay is completed.
Restates or summarizes the thesis statement and main ideas.
Often includes a personal response.

Revising

Reread your first draft at least twice, checking once for content and once for style.

1. Content. Check to see that you've supported your thesis statement with at least two main ideas and that you've supported each main idea with sufficient evidence. If any part of your essay sounds weak or vague, go back over the work to find more convincing evidence.

2. Style. To make your essay read smoothly, you may need to combine related sentences or break up long sentences into shorter ones. Cut unnecessary or repetitive words and phrases. Make sure your ideas are clear and easy to follow, and that your wording "sounds" right.

Proofreading

The titles of poems, short stories, and essays should be enclosed in quotation marks; the titles of plays, novels, and other long works (such as epic poems) should be in italics. (However, the Bible and the individual books of the Bible are neither italicized nor placed in quotation marks.) In handwriting and typing, italics are indicated by underlining. If you are working with typewritten copy, use the following proofreader's symbols to correct errors in spelling, punctuation, and style.

Proofreader's Symbols

Symbol	Example	Meaning
≡	John knowles	Capitalize a lower-case letter.
/	"The Pit And the Pendulum"	Change a capital letter to lower case.
∧	*The* "Cold Equations"	Insert a word.
∧	Sinbad the Sailer *d, o*	Insert or change a letter.
⊙	W. H Auden	Insert a period.
⌃	Brutus Cassius, and Casca	Insert a comma.
∨	Sea Fever	Insert quotation marks.
—	A Separate Peace	Set in italics.
∿	Mark Twian	Change the order of letters.
∿	"With All Flying Flags"	Change the order of words.
⌒	A. E. Houseman	Delete and close up space.
#	#Gene Garrison is the play's protagonist.	Indent to begin a new paragraph.

A Model Essay

The following essay shows revisions that the writer made
in the first draft of a typewritten manuscript:

Humor in "The Bride comes to Yellow Sky"

Stephen short
    Crane's story "The Bride comes to Yellow Sky" is considered by many to be

a masterpiece. One writer even called it "the greatest story ever written."

One of the reasons why the story is so good is that Crane uses

some in general in particular
humor to make serious points about people and the Old West.

INTRODUCTORY PARAGRAPH

Catches reader's interest.

Presents thesis statement about the story's humor.

BODY States topic sentence.	In the first part ^of the story, Crane portrays Jack Potter and his new wife ~are~ as humorous
Adds supporting details analyzing the humor in Part I.	characters. ~They are~ Not only awkward with each other ~and~ ,but they are also completely out
	of place in the fancy railroad car that is taking them ~home~ to Yellow Sky. Crane
	makes us see them through the eyes of the condescending porter
Quotes from story.	and the other passengers, who keep giving the couple "stares of
	derisive enjoyment" (page 123). Jack's fear ~of~ about how the ~men in~
	~town~ people of Yellow Sky will react to his marriage is also comical, because ~We do not expect~ would
	~the~ a ~brave~ town marshal ~to be~ brave, not afraid of the people he is paid to
	protect.
States another topic sentence.	Part II ~gives us the comical~ presents another humorous situation ~of~ — a lone drunk ~who~ is
Adds supporting details analyzing the humor in Part II.	able to ~can~ frighten a whole town just because Jack Potter is away. This
	situation is ~even~ especially ~funnier~ funny because of ~a~ an ironic contrast that the reader
	already knows about. The man the townspeople are depending on to protect
	them is the same man ~who is~ we have just learned afraid to tell them he is married.
	Part II also includes the ~humorous~ comical character of the unsuspecting traveling sales-
	man, whose questions about Scratchy Wilson set the stage for the con- increasingly agitated
	frontation ~that~ the reader knows will occur. Crane is in fact setting us up for the
	"punchline" of his story. First we hear about the raging, fearsome
	drunk who ~is terrifying~ terrorizing the town—and then we see him.
States another topic sentence.	In Part III we get a close look at this Scratchy Wilson, whom
	we are supposedly prepared for. At first glance, he does behave like
	a typical Wild West villain. However, we soon learn details about
Adds supporting details analyzing the humor in Part III.	him that make him seem ridiculous. For one thing, he wears a shirt
	made by women in New York City and boots favored by little boys in New
	England (page 125), hardly the outfit we'd expect an authentic

western villain to wear. (In fact, these details are the reader's first hint of what will develop as Crane's major theme: that the West is no longer a terribly wild place). The lengths Scratchy goes to in order to frighten a dog also show him to be a bit ~~ridiculous~~ *ludicrous* as a bad guy. Scratchy may roar and below "terrible invitations to fight, but Crane lets us know exactly how ~~important~~ *terrifying really* he is: "The calm adobe preserved their demeanor at the passing of this small thing in the middle of the street" (page 125).

Quotes from story.

In Part IV, Crane *finally* brings his two major characters together for a ~~comical~~ showdown *is comical because it* that disappoints our expectations. Facing Scratchy down without a gun, Potter proves to be as brave as ~~the townspeople think he is~~ *we just have been led to believe*. But as a villain, Scratchy turns out to be pretty easily subdued. Presented with the news ~~that~~ *of* Potter ~~is married~~ *us marriage*, he loses all his menace and sadly walks away. Ironically, he is ~~subdued~~ *defeated* not by ~~force~~ *brute* or ~~courage~~ *sheer* but *instead* by "a foreign condition" (page 126) that he cannot understand. His world is suddenly turned upside down *by Potter's news*. Ferocious ~~drunks~~ *gun-toting* and the *courageous* ~~town marshals~~ who fight them are not supposed to have ~~married~~ *wives*. Once the bride comes to Yellow Sky, the rules of the game ~~have changed so much~~ *are so different* that Scratchy no longer knows how to play.

States another topic sentence.

Adds supporting details about the humor in Part IV.

Quotes from story.

According to one critic, Donald B. Gibson, the point of ~~the~~ *Crane's* story is that the Wild West ~~is~~ *was* dead *by the late 1800's,* even though some people living there ~~do~~ *did* not realize it (~~Gibson~~ *page*, 126). *While* Jack Potter has taken a big step toward adjusting to the changed word he lives in, Scratchy is ~~just~~ *simply* ~~confused by the changes~~ *befuddled by it*,

Cites critic's interpretation as topic sentence.

Adds supporting details.

Writing About Literature

	Gibson's interpretation makes sense to me, and I think it gets
CONCLUDING PARAGRAPH Gives personal response to critic's interpretation.	

at the heart of the humor in Crane's story. But I ~~think~~ *suspect that* Crane is

doing more than simply mocking the conventions of the ~~typical~~ *typical*

WEstern. That would make his story a funny parody, but *certainly* not a

Elaborates on thesis statement.

masterpiece. Crane is *also* showing us what happens to a society in

Quotes from story.

transition, a culture whose values are ~~changing~~ *in a state of flux*. A "simple child

of the earlier plains" (page 126), Scratchy Wilson is an anachro-

nism, a man who *finds himself* is out of place historically. Luckily, he has the

good grace—and the good sense—to realize ~~this fact~~ *his predicament* and walk away

Ends with "clincher sentence."

from what he cannot understand. But who knows—perhaps some

day he'll find himself a bride and bring her back to Yellow Sky.

Documenting Sources

Find out the method of documenting sources your teacher prefers: parenthetical citations, footnotes, or end notes.

1. Parenthetical citations give brief information in parentheses immediately after a quotation or other reference. More detailed information about each source is then given in the bibliography. Here are some examples.

Type of Quotation	Example
From a prose passage by a writer identified in the essay	In "The Mojave," Steinbeck describes the Southwest as "a great and mysterious wasteland" (page 387).
From a prose passage by a writer who is not identified in the essay	According to one critic, Scratchy "is the ridiculous victim of his own routinized mind" (Levenson, 838).
From a play	Antony claims he comes "to bury Caesar, not to praise him" (Act III, Scene 2, line 75).
From a poem	The speaker calls the meadow mouse his "thumb of a child" (line 27).

2. Footnotes are placed at the bottom of the page on which the reference appears. They are indicated by a raised number at the end of the reference, and are numbered consecutively.

[1] Richard B. Sewell, *The Life of Emily Dickinson* (New York: Farrar, Straus & Giroux, 1980).

3. End notes are identical to footnotes except that they are listed at the end of the essay on a separate page entitled "Notes." End notes are numbered consecutively.

4. Include a **bibliography** at the end of your essay. This is an alphabetical list of all the sources you consulted in researching your essay, even if you didn't use them in footnotes or end notes. Bibliography entries are listed alphabetically by the author's last name. Here is a bibliography that lists the writer's sources for the model essay on "The Bride Comes to Yellow Sky":

Bibliography

Bassan, Maurice, editor, *Stephen Crane: A Collection of Critical Essays* (Englewood Cliffs, NJ: Prentice-Hall, 1967).

Gibson, Donald B., *The Fiction of Stephen Crane* (Carbondale and Edwardsville, IL: Southern Illinois University Press, 1968).

Katz, Joseph, editor, *Stephen Crane in Transition* (DeKalb, IL: Northern Illinois University Press, 1973).

Levenson, J. C. "Stephen Crane" in *Major Writers of America, Shorter Edition,* edited by Perry Miller et al. (New York: Harcourt Brace Jovanovich, 1966).

A HANDBOOK OF LITERARY TERMS

ALLITERATION   **The repetition of consonant sounds in words that are close to one another.** Alliteration occurs most often at the beginning of words, as in "<u>s</u>weet and <u>s</u>our." However, consonants within words sometimes alliterate, as in "ga<u>gg</u>le of <u>g</u>eese." The echoes alliteration creates can increase a poem's rhythmic and musical effects and make its lines especially memorable. This line is haunting partly because of its repeated <u>w</u> sounds:

> <u>Wh</u>ere the quail is <u>wh</u>istling bet<u>w</u>ixt the <u>w</u>oods
> and the <u>wh</u>eat-lot
>
> —from "Song of Myself,"
> Walt Whitman

See pages 323, 336.
See also *Assonance, Onomatopoeia, Rhythm.*

ALLUSION   **A reference to a statement, person, place, event, or thing that is known from literature, history, religion, myth, politics, sports, science, or pop culture.** The following lines allude to Midas, the king in Greek mythology who turned everything he touched to gold. Pastan uses the allusion to suggest that the ability of poets to transform everything they "touch" in ordinary life to poetry is like Midas's golden touch.

> Someone who knows told me
> writers have fifteen years:
> then comes repetition,
> even madness.
> Like Midas, I guess
> everything we touch turns
> to a poem—
> when the spell is on.
> But think of the poet after that
> touching the trees
> he's always touched,
> but this time nothing happens.
>
> —from "Voices,"
> Linda Pastan

Can you identify the literary allusion in the following cartoon?

"Et tu, Baxter?"

Drawing by Robert Mankoff; © 1987
The New Yorker Magazine, Inc.

See pages 66, 67, 205, 245, 347, 816, 822, 860–861.

ANACHRONISM   **An event or detail in a literary work that is placed outside its proper historical time period.** For example, it would be anachronistic to describe a scene in which a nineteenth-century poet is composing lyrics on a word processor. Sometimes anachronisms are simply unintentional mistakes, but they can also be used for comic effect. For example, in Cervantes' *Don Quixote* (page 851), a seventeenth-century character assumes the outdated romantic ideals and chivalrous behavior of the twelfth century.

See page 707.

ANECDOTE   **A brief account of a particular incident.** Like **parables,** anecdotes are often used by philosophers and religious teachers to point out truths about life. Anecdotes are also a common feature of biographies and autobiographies.

See pages 422, 868, 869, 870, 874.
See also *Folktale, Parable.*

ASIDE Private words that a character in a play speaks to the audience or to another character, which are not supposed to be overheard by others onstage. Stage directions usually tell when a speech is an aside. For example, in Act II, Scene 4 (page 664) of Shakespeare's play *Julius Caesar,* Trebonius and Brutus make ominous asides that Caesar, whom they are planning to murder, cannot hear.

See pages 664, 677.

ASSONANCE The repetition of similar vowel sounds followed by different consonant sounds in words that are close together. Assonance differs from **exact rhyme** in that it does not repeat the consonant sound following the vowel. The words *sake* and *lake* rhyme, while the words *sake* and *late* are assonant. Like alliteration, assonance can create musical and rhythmic effects, as in the following lines:

> And so all the night-tide, I lie down by the side,
> Of my darling, my darling, my life and my bride
> —from ''Annabel Lee,''
> Edgar Allan Poe

See also *Alliteration, Onomatopoeia, Rhyme.*

ATMOSPHERE The mood or feeling in a work of literature. Atmosphere is usually created through descriptive details and evocative language. One of the supreme creators of atmosphere is Edgar Allan Poe. In ''The Pit and the Pendulum'' (page 168) he creates a dizzying atmosphere of horror.

See pages 146, 161–162, 900.
See also *Setting.*

AUTOBIOGRAPHY An account of a person's own life. This book contains excerpts from the autobiographies *Growing Up* by Russell Baker (page 446), *A Childhood* by Harry Crews (page 453), *Blooming* by Susan Allen Toth (page 460), and *Hunger of Memory* by Richard Rodriguez (page 470).

See page 445.
See also *Biography, Nonfiction.*

BALLAD A song or song-like poem that tells a story. Most ballads have a regular pattern of **rhythm** and **rhyme,** and they use simple language with a great deal of repetition. Ballads generally have **refrains**—lines or words that are repeated at regular intervals. They usually tell sensational adventure stories that end tragically. **Folk ballads** are composed by anonymous singers and are passed down orally from generation to generation before they are written down (often in several different versions). ''Bonny Barbara Allan'' (page 305) is an example of a folk ballad.

Literary ballads, on the other hand, are composed and written down by a known poet, usually in the style of folk ballads. Some popular country-and-western songs are written in the style of the old ballads.

See pages 305, 307.

BIOGRAPHY An account of a person's life written or told by another person. Biographies of writers, actors, sports stars, TV personalities, and historical figures are popular today. This book contains excerpts from several biographies, including *The Life of Emily Dickinson* by Richard Sewell (page 329) and *The Life of Caesar* by the Roman historian Plutarch (page 725).

See also *Autobiography, Nonfiction.*

BLANK VERSE Poetry written in unrhymed iambic pentameter. ''Blank'' means the poetry is unrhymed. ''Iambic pentameter'' means that each line contains five iambs, or metrical **feet,** each consisting of an unstressed syllable followed by a stressed syllable (⌣ ′). Blank verse is the most important metrical form used in English dramatic and epic poetry. It is the verse line used in Shakespeare's plays and Milton's *Paradise Lost.* One of the reasons blank verse has been so popular, even among modern poets, is that it combines the naturalness of unrhymed verse with the structure of metrical verse. Except for free verse, it is the poetic form that sounds the most like natural English speech. It also lends itself easily to slight variations within the basic pattern. Here are the first three lines of a blank-verse poem by Robert Frost:

> When I see birches bend to left and right
> Across the line of straighter darker trees,
> I like to think some boy's been swinging them.
> —from ''Birches,''
> Robert Frost

See page 625.
See also *Iambic Pentameter, Meter.*

CHARACTER An individual in a story or play. A character always has human traits, even if the character is an animal, as in Aesop's fables, or a god, as in the Greek and Roman myths. A character may also be a godlike human, like Superman. But most characters are ordinary human beings, like Gene Forrester in the novel *A Separate Peace* (page 901).

The process by which the writer reveals the personality of a character is called **characterization.** A writer can reveal a character in the following ways:

1. By telling us directly what the character is like: generous, deceitful, timid, and so on

2. By describing how the character looks and dresses

3. By letting us hear the character speak

4. By revealing the character's private thoughts and feelings

5. By revealing the character's effect on other people—showing how other characters feel or behave toward the character

6. By showing the character's actions

The first method of revealing a character is called **direct characterization.** When a writer uses this method, we do not have to figure out what a character's personality is like—the writer tells us directly. The other five methods of revealing a character are known as **indirect characterization.** When a writer uses these methods, we have to exercise our own judgment, putting clues together to figure out what a character is like—just as we do in real life when we are getting to know someone.

Characters can be classified as static or dynamic. A **static character** is one who does not change much in the course of a story. A **dynamic character,** on the other hand, changes in some important way as a result of the story's action. Characters can also be classified as flat or round. **Flat characters** have only one or two personality traits. They are one-dimensional—they can be summed up by a single phrase. In contrast, **round characters** have more dimensions to their personalities—they are complex and multi-faceted, like real people.

> See pages 41–45, 74–75, 76–77, 514, 900.
> See also *Protagonist.*

COMEDY   In general, a story that ends happily. The hero or heroine of a comedy is usually an ordinary character who overcomes a series of obstacles that block what he or she wants. Comedy is distinct from **tragedy,** in which a great person comes to an unhappy or disastrous end, often through some character flaw or weakness. Comedies are often, though not always, intended to make us laugh. *The Brute* by Anton Chekhov (page 601) is a comedy.

> See page 600.
> See also *Farce, Tragedy.*

CONFLICT   A struggle or clash between opposing characters, forces, or emotions. In an **external conflict,** a character struggles against some outside force: another character, society as a whole, or some natural force. *The Brute* by Anton Chekhov (page 601) centers around the external conflict between Popov and Smirnov. An **internal conflict,** on the other hand, is a struggle between opposing needs, desires, or emotions within a single character. In Amy Tan's "Two Kinds" (page 46), Jing-mei undergoes an internal conflict between her desire to please her

mother and her need to be herself. Many works, especially longer ones, contain both internal and external conflicts.

> See pages 5, 513–514, 900.

CONNOTATIONS   All the meanings, associations, or emotions that a word suggests. For example, an expensive restaurant might prefer to advertise its "delicious cuisine" rather than its "delicious cooking." *Cuisine* and *cooking* have the same literal meaning—"prepared food." But *cuisine* has connotations of elegance and sophistication, while *cooking* does not. The same restaurant would certainly not describe its food as "great grub."

Notice the difference between the following pairs of words: *unusual/odd, proud/smug, assertive/pushy, frugal/stingy.* We might describe ourselves using the first word but someone else using the second. Or consider a rather recent advertising trend—describing certain cars as *preowned* rather than *used.* (In a few years, these cars will undoubtedly become *antique* or *vintage* rather than just plain *old.*)

> See pages 73, 108, 118, 141, 162, 273, 283, 315, 382, 468, 728.
> See also *Denotation, Diction, Tone.*

COUPLET   Two consecutive lines of poetry that rhyme. The couplet has been widely used since the Middle Ages, especially to express a completed thought or to provide a sense of closure. In Shakespeare's plays, for example, an important speech or scene often ends with a couplet. Here are the final words of *Julius Caesar,* spoken by Octavius:

> So call the field to rest, and let's away,
> To part the glories of this happy day.

> See pages 286, 337.

DENOTATION   The literal, dictionary definition of a word.

> See pages 108, 315, 468.
> See also *Connotations.*

DESCRIPTION   A kind of writing that is intended to recreate a person, place, thing, event, or experience. Description uses language that appeals to the senses to inform us about how a subject looks, sounds, smells, tastes, or feels to the touch. Fiction, nonfiction, and poetry all may contain description. Here is a descriptive passage from a contemporary novel. The narrator is describing a visit home from college to the Chippewa reservation in North Dakota where she grew up. Notice how the writer selects **images** that appeal to the senses of sight, hearing, smell, and touch:

All along the highway that early summer the land was beautiful. The sky stretched bare. Tattered silver windbreaks bounded flat, plowed fields that the government had paid to lie fallow. Everything else was dull tan—the dry ditches, the dying crops, the buildings of farms and towns. Rain would come just in time that year. Driving north, I could see the earth lifting. The wind was hot and smelled of tar and the moving dust.

At the end of the big farms and the blowing fields was the reservation. I always knew it was coming a long way off. . . . The highway narrowed off and tangled, then turned to gravel with ruts, holes, and tall alfalfa bunching in the ditches. Small hills reared up. Dogs leaped from nowhere and ran themselves out fiercely. The dust hung thick.

—from *Love Medicine*,
Louise Erdrich

See pages 74–75, 383, 406.
See also *Imagery*.

DIALECT A way of speaking that is characteristic of a particular region or group of people. A dialect may have a distinct vocabulary, pronunciation system, and grammar. Generally, one dialect becomes accepted as the standard for a country or culture. In the United States today, the dialect used in formal writing and spoken by most TV and radio announcers is known as standard English. Writers often use other dialects, however, to establish character or to create local color. In his autobiographical account "The Mail-Order Catalogue" (page 453), Harry Crews captures the dialect of rural Georgia.

See pages 66, 233, 423, 459.

DICTION A writer's or speaker's choice of words. People use different types of words depending on the audience they're addressing, the subject they're discussing, and the effect they're trying to produce. For example, slang words that would be suitable in a casual conversation with a friend ("That guy really bugs me") would be unsuitable in a newspaper editorial. Similarly, the language that a marine biologist would use to describe the ocean would be different from the language used by a sailor—or a poet.

Diction is an essential element of a writer's **style**. A writer's diction can be simple or flowery (*clothing/apparel*), modern or old-fashioned (*dress/frock*), general or specific (*pants/designer jeans*). Notice that the **connotations** of words (rather than their strict, literal meanings, or **denotations**) are an important aspect of diction.

In this dialogue between a fireman and a minister, Mark Twain shows how contrasting diction can create confusion—and humor.

"Are you the duck that runs the gospel-mill next door?"

"Am I the—pardon me, I believe I do not understand?"

With another sigh and a half-sob, Scotty rejoined:

"Why you see we are in a bit of trouble, and the boys thought maybe you would give us a lift, if we'd tackle you—that is, if I've got the rights of it and you are the head clerk of the doxology-works next door."

"I am the shepherd in charge of the flock whose fold is next door."

"The which?"

"The spiritual adviser of the little company of believers whose sanctuary adjoins these premises."

Scotty scratched his head, reflected a moment, and then said: "You ruther hold over me, pard. I reckon I can't call that hand. Ante and pass the buck."

—from *Roughing It*,
Mark Twain

See pages 285, 313, 328, 468–469.
See also *Connotations, Tone*.

DRAMA A story that is written to be acted out in front of an audience. The action of a drama is driven by a character who wants something badly and who takes steps to get it. A drama usually contains these elements: a character or characters in some kind of **desperate situation** that involves a **conflict;** mounting **suspense** that leads to a **climax;** and a resulting **change** in the main character that **resolves** the story.

See pages 512–517, 613–615, 623–624, 744, 796.
See also *Comedy, Plot, Tragedy*.

EPIC A long narrative poem that relates the great deeds of a larger-than-life hero who embodies the values of a particular society. Most epics include elements of myth, legend, folklore, and history. Their tone is serious and their language grand. Most epic heroes undertake quests to achieve something of tremendous value to themselves or their society. Homer's *Odyssey* and *Iliad* (page 736) and Virgil's *Aeneid* are the best known epics in the Western tradition. An important English epic is *Beowulf*. The great epic of India is *The Mahabharata*.

See page 735.

EPITHET An adjective or descriptive phrase that is regularly used to characterize a person, place, or thing. We speak of "Honest Abe," for example, and "America the Beautiful."

Homer created so many descriptive epithets in his *Iliad* and *Odyssey* that his name has been permanently associated with a type of epithet. The **Homeric epithet** consists of a compound adjective that is regularly used to modify a particular noun. Famous examples are "the wine-dark sea," "the gray-eyed goddess Athena," and "swift-footed Achilleus."

See page 743.

ESSAY **A short piece of nonfiction prose that examines a single subject from a limited point of view.** There are two major types of essays. **Informal essays** (also called **personal essays**) generally reveal a great deal about the personalities and feelings of their authors. They tend to be conversational, sometimes even humorous in tone, and they are usually highly subjective. **Formal essays** (also called **traditional essays**) are usually serious and impersonal in tone. Because they are written to inform or persuade, they are expected to be factual, logical, and tightly organized.

See pages 410, 444.
See also *Nonfiction.*

EXPOSITION **A kind of writing that explains a subject, gives information, or clarifies an idea.** Exposition, or expository writing, is generally objective and formal in tone. A magazine article on nutrition, an instruction manual for a stereo, and the entries in this *Handbook of Literary Terms* are all examples of exposition.

Exposition is also the term for the first part of a plot. The exposition (also called the **basic situation**) presents the main characters and their conflict.

See pages 4, 383, 410, 506–509, 534, 579.
See also *Nonfiction.*

FABLE **A very brief story in prose or verse that teaches a moral, or a practical lesson about life.** The characters of

"Henry, is there a moral to our story?"

Drawing by Mischa Richter; © 1987
The New Yorker Magazine, Inc.

most fables are animals that behave and speak like human beings. Some of the most popular fables are those attributed to Aesop, who was supposed to have been a slave in ancient Greece. Other widely read fables are those in the *Panchatantra* (page 893), a collection of Indian tales about the art of wise ruling.

See pages 219, 326, 893, 895.
See also *Anecdote, Folktale, Parable.*

FARCE **A type of comedy in which ridiculous and often stereotyped characters are involved in farfetched, silly situations.** The humor in farce is based on crude physical action, slapstick, and clowning. Characters may slip on banana peels, get pies thrown in their faces, and knock one another on the head with ladders. Abbott and Costello, Laurel and Hardy, and Marx Brothers movies are examples of farces. So is the movie *Home Alone.*

The word *farce* comes from a Latin word for "stuffing," and in fact farces were originally used to fill in the waiting time between the acts of serious plays. Even in tragedies, farcical elements are often included to provide comic relief. Shakespeare, for example, frequently lets his "common" characters (such as servants) engage in farcical actions.

See pages 335, 611.
See also *Comedy.*

FICTION **Prose writing that includes invented material and that does not claim to be factually true.** The term *fiction* most often refers to prose narratives such as novels and short stories. Even though plays and poems are also works of the imagination, they are not usually classified as fiction.

See also *Nonfiction, Novel, Short Story.*

FIGURE OF SPEECH **A word or phrase that describes one thing in terms of another and is not meant to be understood on a literal level.** Figures of speech always involve some sort of imaginative comparison between seemingly unlike things. Some 250 different types of figures of speech have been identified, but the most common are the **simile** ("My heart is like a singing bird"), the **metaphor** ("Life's but a walking shadow"), and **personification** ("Death has reared himself a throne").

See pages 58, 135, 166, 186, 227, 248.
See also *Metaphor, Personification, Simile, Symbol.*

FLASHBACK **A scene in a movie, play, short story, novel, or narrative poem that interrupts the present action of the plot to "flash backward" and tell what happened at an earlier time.** The drugstore scene between George and Emily in Act Two of *Our Town* (page 539) is an example of a flashback. The act begins on George and Emily's wedding morning but then "flashes back" in time to show us the day when they discovered they loved each other.

See pages 97, 428, 924.

FOIL A character who is used as a contrast to another character. This contrast emphasizes the differences between the two characters, bringing out the distinctive qualities in each. For example, in *Julius Caesar* (page 630), Shakespeare uses the solemn, self-controlled Octavius as a foil for the excitable, impetuous Antony. In Cervantes' *Don Quixote* (page 851), the sensible, down-to-earth Sancho Panza serves as a foil for the romantic, deluded Don Quixote.

See pages 858, 924, 960.

FOLKTALE An anonymous traditional story that was originally passed down orally from generation to generation. Every culture tells folktales, and there are similar tales told throughout the world. Eventually, people began writing these stories down—sometimes retelling them in a literary way, and sometimes transcribing them directly from oral storytellers. "The Tiger, the Brahman, and the Jackal" (page 893) is an example of the first kind of tale; "Urashima Taro" (page 875) is an example of the second. Some scholars draw a sharp distinction between folktales and **myths.** Myths, unlike folktales, are seen as stories about humans and gods that are basically religious in nature. Examples of folktales include fairy tales, fables, legends, ghost stories, tall tales, anecdotes, and even jokes.

See pages 864–867.
See also Anecdote, Fable, How-and-Why Story,
Motif, Myth, Trickster Tale.

FORESHADOWING The use of clues to hint at what is going to happen later in the plot. Foreshadowing arouses the reader's curiosity and increases **suspense.** In John Knowles's *A Separate Peace* (page 901), clues in the first chapter suggest that important—and tragic—events will occur at the tree and the marble staircase.

See pages 6, 513.
See also Plot, Suspense.

FRAME STORY A story that contains another story or stories. Isaac Bashevis Singer's "The Fatalist" (page 25) and Saki's "The Storyteller" (page 206) both use this story-within-a-story structure. The frame story is also a common device for unifying a series of tales, such as those collected in *The Thousand and One Nights* (page 842) and the *Panchatantra* (page 893).

See pages 28, 209, 841, 893.

FREE VERSE Poetry that has no regular meter or rhyme scheme. Free verse usually relies instead on the natural **rhythms** of ordinary speech. Poets writing in free verse may use pauses, repetition, **alliteration, internal rhyme, onomatopoeia,** and other musical devices to achieve their effects. They may also place great emphasis on **imagery.** Here is a brief free-verse poem by Walt Whitman. Notice how much like spoken language Whitman's diction is:

Beautiful Women

Women sit or move to and fro, some old, some young,
The young are beautiful—but the old are more
    beautiful than the young.

—Walt Whitman

See pages 300, 303, 317, 318, 321, 376.
See also Rhythm.

HAIKU A Japanese verse form consisting of three lines and usually seventeen syllables (five, seven, five). Using association and suggestion, a haiku tries to create a picture of a particular moment of discovery or enlightenment. A haiku usually presents an image of daily life that relates to a particular season. Many modern American poets (such as William Carlos Williams, Amy Lowell, Ezra Pound, Richard Wright, and Gary Snyder) have attempted to capture the spirit of haiku in English, though they have not always followed the form strictly.

See page 289.

HOW-AND-WHY STORY A type of folktale that explains how and why some feature of the world came to be the way it is. Every culture tells stories that explain why animals look or act the way they do, how a natural phenomenon came into existence, or how a custom originated. A how-and-why story might explain why dogs chase cats, how the stars got into the sky, why the ocean is salty, or how misery entered the world. Some how-and-why stories are told simply to make us laugh. Others are cautionary tales told to teach a moral lesson—perhaps about the consequences of stupidity or arrogance or greed.

See pages 883, 889.
See also Folktale.

IAMBIC PENTAMETER A line of poetry made up of five iambs. An **iamb** is a metrical **foot,** or unit of measure, consisting of an unstressed syllable followed by a stressed syllable ($\smile\,\prime$). The word *dený,* for example, is made up of one iamb. *Pentameter* derives from the Greek words *penta* ("five") and *meter* ("measure"). Here are two lines of poetry written in iambic pentameter:

When forty winters shall besiege thy brow,
And dig deep trenches in thy beauty's field
—from Sonnet 2,
William Shakespeare

Iambic pentameter is by far the most common verse line in English poetry. Shakespeare's poems and plays, for example, are written primarily in this meter. Many modern poets, such as Robert Frost, have continued to use iambic pentameter. Other than free verse, it is the poetic form that sounds the most like natural speech.

See page 625.
See also *Blank Verse, Meter, Rhythm, Sonnet.*

IMAGERY **Language that appeals to the senses.** Most images are visual—that is, they appeal to the sense of sight. But imagery may also appeal to the senses of sound, smell, touch, and taste. While imagery is used in all writing, it is especially important in poetry. The following lines enable us to see, feel, hear, smell, and almost taste some winter sensations. (The "crabs" Shakespeare refers to are crab apples. A "saw" is a wise saying, and to "keel" is to cool by stirring.)

When all aloud the wind doth blow,
  And coughing drowns the parson's saw,
And birds sit brooding in the snow,
  And Marian's nose looks red and raw,
When roasted crabs hiss in the bowl,
Then nightly sings the staring owl, "Tu-whit,
Tu-who!" a merry note,
While greasy Joan doth keel the pot.

—from *Love's Labor's Lost,*
William Shakespeare

See pages 217, 267, 289, 294.

INVERSION **The reversal of the normal word order of a sentence.** The elements of a normal English sentence are subject, verb, and complement, and in most sentences this is the order in which they appear. (*He made pancakes.*) In most sentences modifiers precede the words they modify (*heavy books,* not *books heavy*). Writers use inversion for emphasis and variety. They may also use it for more technical reasons—to create a rhyme or accommodate a given meter. This line by Walt Whitman uses inversion: "With music strong I come, with my cornets and my drums." The usual word order of the first part of this line would be "I come with strong music," but Whit-

man has inverted this statement to give the line a march rhythm and an internal rhyme.

See pages 265, 280, 288, 320.

IRONY **A contrast or discrepancy between expectation and reality—between what is said and what is really meant, between what is expected and what really happens, or between what appears to be true and what really is true.**

1. **Verbal irony** occurs when a speaker says one thing but means the opposite. If you say, "Having a little snack?" to someone who is consuming an entire pizza, you are using verbal irony. In Shakespeare's *Julius Caesar,* Antony is using verbal irony during his funeral oration for Caesar when he keeps insisting that "Brutus is an honorable man" (pages 682–687). Antony actually believes that it was extremely dishonorable of Brutus to have conspired in Caesar's murder.

2. **Situational irony** occurs when what actually happens is the opposite of what is expected or appropriate. In Evan S. Connell's historical account "Amundsen and Scott" (page 474), we feel a strong sense of irony when Connell points out that, while Amundsen actually reached the South Pole before Scott and Scott died in his attempt, Scott's name is far more famous today.

3. **Dramatic irony** occurs when the reader or the audience knows something important that a character in a story or drama does not know. In "The Cold Equations" by Tom Godwin (page 7), we feel a chill of dramatic irony when Marilyn mischievously asks what her punishment for stowing away on the spaceship will be. Marilyn expects simply to be fined, but we know that her penalty will be death.

See pages 197–199, 342, 467, 534.
See also *Satire.*

LYRIC POETRY **Poetry that focuses on expressing emotions or thoughts, rather than on telling a story.** Most lyrics are short, and they usually imply rather than directly state a single strong emotion. The term *lyric* comes from the Greek. In ancient Greece, lyric poems were recited to the accompaniment of a stringed instrument called the lyre. Today poets still try to make their lyrics melodious, but they rely only on the musical effects they can create with words—such as **rhyme, rhythm, alliteration,** and **onomatopoeia.** A. E. Housman's "Loveliest of Trees" (page 272) and John Masefield's "Sea Fever" (page 305) are both lyric poems.

See also *Poetry, Sonnet.*

METAPHOR **A figure of speech that makes a comparison between two seemingly unlike things without using the connective words *like, as, than,* or *resembles.*** You are using a metaphor if you call someone a "rat" or describe a job as a "noose around your neck."

Some metaphors are **directly** stated, like Gerard Manley Hopkins's comparison "I am soft sift / In an hourglass." (If he had written, "I am *like* soft sift . . . ," he would have been using a **simile.**) Other metaphors are **implied,** or suggested, as in John Keats's lines "When I have fears that I may cease to be / Before my pen has gleaned my teeming brain." The word *gleaned* implies a comparison between a reaper gathering up the last grains of a harvest and the poet's pen extracting the last bits of verse from his brain.

An **extended metaphor** is a metaphor that is extended, or developed, over several lines of writing or even throughout an entire poem—as in Langston Hughes's "Mother to Son" (page 232), E. E. Cummings's "Spring Is Like a Perhaps Hand" (page 246), and Emily Dickinson's "I Like to See It Lap the Miles" (page 327).

A **dead metaphor** is a metaphor that has become so common that we no longer even notice that it is a figure of speech. Our everyday speech is filled with dead metaphors, such as *the neck of a bottle, an iron will,* and *the hands of a clock.*

A **mixed metaphor** is the inconsistent mixture of two or more metaphors. Mixed metaphors are usually unintentional and often conjure up ludicrous images: "If you open up that can of worms, you'll be biting off more than you can chew."

See pages 228–229, 233, 246–247, 328, 349, 405, 794, 984.
See also *Figure of Speech, Personification, Simile.*

METER A generally regular pattern of stressed and unstressed syllables in poetry. When we want to indicate the metrical pattern of a poem, we mark the stressed syllables with the symbol ʹ and the unstressed syllables with the symbol ˘ . Analyzing the metrical pattern of a poem in this way is called **scanning** the poem, or **scansion.** Here is how to scan these lines from *Julius Caesar:*

> Cowards die many times before their deaths;
> The valiant never taste of death but once.

Meter is measured in units called feet. A **foot** consists of one stressed syllable and usually one or more unstressed syllables. The standard feet used in English poetry are the **iamb** (as in *believe*), the **trochee** (as in *mercy*), the **anapest** (as in *understand*), the **dactyl** (as in *desperate*), and the **spondee** (as in *snowstorm*).

A metrical line is named both for the type and number of feet it contains. For example, a line of iambic pentameter consists of five iambs, while a line of trochaic tetrameter consists of four trochees.

See pages 300–302, 319–320, 377.
See also *Iambic Pentameter, Rhythm.*

MOTIF A particular element in a folktale or literary work that is found in many other stories. This recurring element may be a certain character type, subject matter, narrative detail, theme, or image. Folklorists have identified and indexed hundreds of motifs, such as those listed on page 867. A short folktale may consist of a single motif; a longer tale may contain many interconnected motifs.

See pages 866, 881, 882, 896.
See also *Folktale, Myth, Trickster Tale.*

MYTH An anonymous traditional story that is basically religious in nature, and that usually serves to explain a belief, ritual, or mysterious natural phenomenon. Most myths grew out of religious rituals, and almost all of them involve the exploits of gods and humans. Every culture has its own mythology, but in the Western world, for many centuries the most influential myths were those of ancient Greece and Rome.

See pages 733–734, 746, 797.
See also *Folktale, Motif.*

NARRATION A kind of writing that tells a story or relates a series of events. Narration is most often found in fiction, drama, and narrative poetry (such as epics and ballads), but narration also occurs in nonfiction works (such as biographies, essays, and newspaper stories) that "tell what happened."

See pages 36–37, 383, 410.

NONFICTION Prose writing that deals with real people, events, and places. The most common forms of nonfiction are the **biography,** the **autobiography,** and the **essay.** Other examples of nonfiction include newspaper stories, magazine articles, historical accounts, scientific reports, and even personal diaries and letters.

See pages 380–383.
See also *Autobiography, Biography, Essay, Fiction.*

NOVEL A long fictional prose narrative, usually of more than fifty thousand words. In general, the novel uses the same basic literary elements as the short story: **plot, character, setting, theme,** and **point of view.** The novel's length usually permits these elements to be more fully developed than they are in the short story. However, this is not always true of the modern novel. Some are basically character studies, with only the barest plot structures. Others reveal little about their characters and concentrate instead on setting or **tone** or even language itself.

Some famous novels include *Pride and Prejudice* by Jane Austen, *Jane Eyre* by Charlotte Brontë, *Great Expectations* by Charles Dickens, *Nectar in a Sieve* by Kamala Markandaya, *The Good Earth* by Pearl Buck, *The Color Purple* by Alice Walker, *Animal Farm* by George Orwell, and *The Yearling* by Marjorie Kinnan Rawlings.

See pages 898–900.

ONOMATOPOEIA   The use of a word whose sound imitates or suggests its meaning. Many familiar words, such as *buzz, knock, splash,* and *bark,* are examples of onomatopoeia. In poetry, onomatopoeia can reinforce meaning while creating evocative and musical sound effects. These lines use onomatopoeia to evoke noises caused by the wind:

> A thin whine of wires, a rattling and flapping of leaves,
> And the small street lamp swinging and slamming against the lamp pole.
>
> —from ''The Storm,''
> Theodore Roethke

See pages 323, 336–338.
See also *Alliteration, Assonance.*

OVERSTATEMENT   A figure of speech that uses exaggeration to express strong emotion or create a comic effect. While overstatement (also known as **hyperbole**) does not express the *literal* truth, it is often used in the service of truth to capture a sense of intensity or to emphasize the essential nature of something. For instance, if you claim that it was 250 degrees in the subway, you are using hyperbole to express the truth that it was miserably hot. Mark Twain (page 391) is a master of humorous overstatement.

See pages 396, 452.

PARABLE   A story that teaches a lesson about life. A parable is like a fable, except that its characters are human and its lesson illustrates a moral attitude or religious principle.

See page 827.
See also *Anecdote, Fable.*

PARALLELISM   The repetition of words, phrases, or sentences that have the same grammatical structure, or that restate a similar idea. Parallelism, or **parallel structure**, is used frequently in literature meant to be spoken aloud, such as poetry, drama, and speeches, because it can help make lines emotional, rhythmic, and memorable. It is also one of the most important techniques used in Biblical poetry. The parallelism in the following lines heightens their emotional effect:

> Bring me my Bow of burning gold!
> Bring me my Arrows of desire!
> Bring me my Spear! O clouds, unfold!
> Bring me my Chariot of fire!
>
> —from ''Jerusalem,''
> William Blake

See pages 318, 406–407, 509, 817, 826.

PARODY   The imitation of a work of literature, art, or music for amusement or instruction. Parodies usually use exaggeration or inappropriate subject matter to make a serious style seem ridiculous. The passage by T. Coraghessan Boyle on page 220 is a parody of the popular TV show *Lassie.*

See pages 127, 210, 220, 342–343, 375, 850.
See also *Satire.*

PERSONIFICATION   A kind of metaphor in which a nonhuman thing or quality is talked about as if it were human. In these lines, the poet describes trees as if they were people and their autumn leaves as if they were colorful clothes:

> The trees are undressing, and fling in many places—
> On the gray road, the roof, the window sill—
> Their radiant robes and ribbons and yellow laces.
>
> —from ''Last Week in October,''
> Thomas Hardy

See pages 229, 246–247.
See also *Figure of Speech, Metaphor.*

PERSUASION   A kind of writing that aims at convincing the reader or listener to think or act in a certain way. Examples of persuasion include political speeches, newspaper editorials, and advertisements, as well as many essays and longer works of literature. Persuasion may create its effect by appealing to reason, to the emotions, or to both. Persuasive writing that appeals to reason is also called **argument**.

See pages 383, 410, 428, 506–509, 723, 728–730.

PLOT   The series of related events that make up a story or drama. The plot is the underlying structure of a story. Most plots are built on these ''bare bones'': A **basic situation,** or **exposition,** that introduces the characters, setting, and, usually, the story's major **conflict.** Out of this basic situation, **complications** develop that intensify the conflict. **Suspense** mounts until a **climax**—the tensest or most exciting part of the plot—is reached, where something happens to determine the outcome of the conflict. Finally, all the problems or mysteries of the plot are unraveled in the **resolution,** or **denouement.**

In some modern fiction and drama, plot has a relatively minor function. These works may focus instead on **characterization** or **point of view.**

See pages 4–6, 513–515, 900.

POETRY **A kind of rhythmic, compressed language that uses figures of speech and imagery designed to appeal to our emotions and imaginations.** The major forms of poetry are the **lyric,** the **epic,** and the **ballad.** Though poetry is one of the oldest forms of human expression, it is extremely difficult to define. Here are three famous "definitions" of poetry:

> . . . the spontaneous overflow of powerful feelings.
> —William Wordsworth

> . . . the clear expression of mixed feelings.
> —A. E. Housman

> . . . the rhythmical creation of beauty in words.
> —Edgar Allan Poe

See page 226.
See also *Ballad, Epic, Lyric.*

POINT OF VIEW **The vantage point from which a writer tells a story.** There are three main points of view: **omniscient, first-person,** and **limited third-person.**

1. In the **omniscient** (or "all-knowing") **point of view,** the person telling the story knows everything that's going on in the story. This omniscient narrator is outside the story, a god-like observer who can tell us what all the characters are thinking and feeling, as well as what is happening anywhere in the story. For example, in Stephen Crane's "The Bride Comes to Yellow Sky" (page 120), the narrator enters the minds of Jack Potter, his bride, the characters in the Weary Gentleman Saloon, and Scratchy Wilson. The narrator also jumps effortlessly from a railroad car to the streets and barrooms of Yellow Sky, miles away.

2. In the **first-person point of view,** the narrator is a character in the story. Using the pronoun *I,* this narrator tells us his or her own experiences but cannot reveal any other character's private thoughts. When we read a story told in the first person, we hear and see only what the narrator hears and sees. We may have to interpret what this narrator says because a first-person narrator may or may not be objective, honest, or perceptive. Alice Munro's "Boys and Girls" (page 98) is told from the first-person point of view of a girl just entering adolescence.

She reveals her own turbulent thoughts and feelings, and we see the other characters in the story through her eyes.

3. In the **limited third-person point of view,** the narrator is outside the story—like an omniscient narrator—but tells the story from the vantage point of only one character. The narrator can enter the mind of this chosen character but cannot tell what any other characters are thinking except by observation. This narrator also can go only where the chosen character goes. "The Cold Equations" by Tom Godwin (page 7) is told from the point of view of the spaceship's pilot. We enter his head and share all of his thoughts and feelings, but the emotions of the stowaway, Marilyn, are revealed to us only through her words and the pilot's observations.

See pages 116–119, 467, 900.

PROTAGONIST **The main character in fiction or drama.** The protagonist is the character we focus our attention on—the person whose conflict sets the plot in motion. (The character or force that blocks the protagonist is called the **antagonist.**) Most protagonists are **rounded, dynamic characters** who change in some important way by the end of the story. Whatever the protagonist's weaknesses, we still usually identify with his or her conflict and care about how it is resolved.

See pages 43–44, 900.
See also *Character.*

PUN **A play on the multiple meanings of a word, or on two words that sound alike but have different meanings.** Many jokes and riddles are based on puns. ("When is a doctor most annoyed?" Answer: "When he runs out of patients.") Shakespeare was one of the greatest punsters of all time. Some of his puns are humorous, like the bantering of the commoners in the opening scene of *Julius Caesar* (page 632). Others are more serious and subtle word plays. For example, in Antony's speech to the conspirators after Caesar's murder in Act III (page 676), he puns on the double meaning of the expression *to let blood.* One meaning has to do with healing, the other with killing.

See pages 335, 649.

REFRAIN **A repeated word, phrase, line, or group of lines.** While refrains are most common in poetry and songs, they are sometimes used in prose, particularly speeches. Refrains are used to create rhythm, build suspense, or emphasize important words or ideas. In the ballad "Bonny Barbara Allan" (page 305), the refrain "Hardhearted Barbara Allan" echoes William's dying words, resounding like an accusing voice in the remorseful Barbara Allan's head.

See page 299.

RHYME **The repetition of accented vowel sounds and all sounds following them in words that are close together in a poem.** *Heart* and *start* rhyme, as do *plaster* and *faster*. The most common type of rhyme, **end rhyme**, occurs at the ends of lines, as in this stanza:

> When she I loved looked every day
> Fresh as a rose in June,
> I to her cottage bent my way,
> Beneath the evening moon.
>
> —from ''Strange Fits of
> Passion Have I Known,''
> William Wordsworth

Internal rhymes occur within lines. The first and third lines of this passage contain internal rhymes that add to the poem's light, playful tone:

> Pussy said to the Owl, ''You elegant fowl!
> How charmingly sweet you sing!
> O let us be married! too long have we tarried!
> But what shall we do for a ring?''
>
> —from ''The Owl and the Pussy Cat,''
> Edward Lear

When words sound similar but do not rhyme exactly, they are called **approximate rhymes** (or **half rhymes, slant rhymes,** or **imperfect rhymes**). The approximate rhymes in this stanza keep the reader deliberately off-balance and even uneasy, a mood in keeping with the poem's subject:

> Let the boy try along this bayonet blade
> How cold steel is, and keen with hunger of blood;
> Blue with all malice, like a madman's flash;
> And thinly drawn with famishing for flesh.
>
> —from ''Arms and the Boy,''
> Wilfred Owen

The pattern of rhymed lines in a poem is called its **rhyme scheme.** A rhyme scheme is indicated by giving each new rhyme a new letter of the alphabet. For example, the rhyme scheme of Wordsworth's lines is *abab*.

See pages 322, 337–338.

RHYTHM **The alternation of stressed and unstressed syllables in language.** Rhythm occurs naturally in all forms of spoken and written language. The most obvious kind of rhythm is produced by **meter,** the regular pattern of stressed and unstressed syllables found in some poetry. Writers can also create less structured rhythms by using **rhyme,** repetition, pauses, and variations in line length, and by balancing long and short words or phrases. (Poetry

without any regular meter or rhyme scheme is called **free verse.**) In this stanza, notice how the rhythm created by the alternating long and short lines seems to imitate the natural ebb-and-flow rhythm of waves. While the long lines are irregular in rhythm, like waves crashing toward the shore, each of the short lines has the same regular meter, like waves sliding smoothly back to sea.

> All day I hear the noise of waters
>   Making moan,
> Sad as the sea-bird is, when going
>   Forth alone,
> He hears the winds cry to the waters'
>   Monotone.
>
> —from ''All Day I Hear,''
> James Joyce

See pages 298–304, 319–321.
See also *Free Verse, Meter.*

ROMANCE **Historically, a medieval verse narrative chronicling the adventures of a hero who undergoes a quest for a high ideal.** The term *romance* later came to mean any story set in a world of wish fulfillment, with larger-than-life characters who often have supernatural powers. Romances usually involve a series of adventures, which end with good triumphing over evil. Fairy tales are examples of romances. Some Western movies are modern versions of romances, with the cowboy becoming the super-good questing hero.

See pages 198, 831–832.

SATIRE **A kind of writing that ridicules human weakness, vice, or folly in order to bring about social reform.** Satires often try to persuade the reader to do or believe something by showing the opposite view as absurd—or even as vicious and inhumane. Cervantes' *Don Quixote* (page 851) is a famous satire that gently ridicules the old ideals of chivalry, while more sharply pointing out the cruelty and shallowness of human nature.

See pages 199, 219, 324, 850.
See also *Irony, Parody.*

SETTING **The time and place of a story or play.** Usually the setting is established early in a story. It may be presented immediately through descriptive details, as in O. Henry's ''The Gift of the Magi'' (page 200), or it may be revealed more gradually through a combination of description and action, as in Guy de Maupassant's ''The Piece of String'' (page 30). Setting often contributes greatly to a story's **emotional effect.** The descriptions of the narrator's terrible prison in Edgar Allan Poe's ''The Pit and the Pendulum'' (page 168) help establish the story's **atmosphere** of horror. Setting may also play a role in a story's **conflict,** as the torture chamber does in this same story, and the jungle does in Tim O'Brien's "Where Have You Gone, Charming Billy?" (page 212). One of the most important functions of setting is to reveal **character.** In Alice Walker's "Everyday Use" (page 129), the narrator's home helps show us who she is, what her life is like, and what she believes in.

See pages 146–148, 900.
See also *Atmosphere.*

SHORT STORY   A short fictional prose narrative. It is impossible to say exactly when a narrative becomes too long or complex to be considered a short story and becomes a **novel** (though the novel is usually defined as being longer than fifty thousand words). Edgar Allan Poe, who is often credited with writing the first short stories, defined the short story (which he called the "prose tale") as a narrative that can be read in a single sitting and that creates a "single effect." Most short stories use these literary elements: **plot, character, setting, theme,** and **point of view.** The plot of a traditional story consists of a **basic situation** (or **exposition**) involving a **conflict, complications,** a **climax,** and a **resolution.** However, many modern short stories concentrate less on "what happens" and more on revealing a character or evoking a vivid emotional effect.

See pages 2–3.

SIMILE   A figure of speech that makes a comparison between two seemingly unlike things by using a connective word such as *like, as, than,* **or** *resembles.* Here is a simile that creates a dramatic visual image:

> The Roman Road runs straight and bare
> As the pale parting-line in hair
>
> —from "The Roman Road,"
> Thomas Hardy

A road and a part in a person's hair are different in scale and in many other ways; yet Hardy shows that they have qualities in common. Like any good figure of speech, Hardy's simile is surprising and vivid.

See pages 227–228, 246, 405.
See also *Figure of Speech, Metaphor.*

SOLILOQUY   A long speech in which a character who is alone onstage expresses private thoughts or feelings. The soliloquy is an old dramatic convention that was particularly popular in Shakespeare's day. Perhaps the most famous soliloquy is the "To be or not to be" speech in Shakespeare's play *Hamlet.* There are several soliloquies in *Julius Caesar,* such as Brutus's speech at the beginning of Act II, in which he weighs the reasons and finally decides to join the conspiracy against Caesar (page 650). Another soliloquy occurs toward the end of Act III, Scene 1, when Antony speaks in agony over Caesar's body (page 679).

See page 666.

SONNET   A fourteen-line lyric poem, usually written in iambic pentameter, that has one of several rhyme schemes. There are two major types of sonnets. The oldest sonnet form is the **Italian sonnet,** also called the **Petrarchan sonnet** (after the fourteenth-century Italian poet Francesco Petrarch, who popularized the form). The Petrarchan sonnet is divided into two parts: an eight-line **octave** with the rhyme scheme *abbaabba,* and a six-line **sestet** with the rhyme scheme *cdecde.* The octave usually presents a problem, poses a question, or expresses an idea, which the sestet then resolves, answers, or drives home. A modern variation of an Italian sonnet, by E. E. Cummings, can be found on page 338. Like many sonnets, Cummings's poem is about love.

The other major sonnet form, which was widely used by Shakespeare, is called the **Shakespearean sonnet,** or the **English sonnet.** It has three four-line units, or **quatrains,** followed by a concluding two-line unit, or **couplet.** The organization of thought in the Shakespearean sonnet usually corresponds to this structure. The three quatrains often express related ideas or examples, while the couplet sums up the poet's conclusion or message. The most common rhyme scheme for the Shakespearean sonnet is *abab cdcd efef gg.* Love sonnets by Shakespeare can be found on pages 286 and 337.

An example of a third type of sonnet, the **Spenserian sonnet,** appears on page 288. Like the Shakespearean sonnet, it is divided into three quatrains and a couplet, but it uses a rhyme scheme that links the quatrains: *abab bcbc cdcd ee.*

See pages 286, 337–338.

SPEAKER   The voice that is talking to us in a poem. Sometimes the speaker is the same as the poet, but often the poet assumes a different voice, speaking as a child, a woman, a man, a nation, an animal, or even an object. For example, the speaker in George MacBeth's "Bedtime Story" (page 369) is a giant insect-like creature.

See page 361.

STANZA   A group of consecutive lines in a poem that form a single unit. A stanza in a poem is something like a paragraph in prose: It often expresses a unit of thought. A stanza may consist of only one line, or of any number of lines beyond that. The word *stanza* is an Italian word for "stopping place" or "place to rest." A. E. Housman's poem "When I Was in Love with You" (page 361) consists of two four-line stanzas, or **quatrains,** each expressing a contrasting but related idea.

See page 299.
See also *Sonnet.*

SUSPENSE **The uncertainty or anxiety we feel about what is going to happen next in a story.** Writers often create suspense by dropping hints or clues that something—especially something bad—is going to happen. In "The Bride Comes to Yellow Sky" (page 120), we begin to feel suspense when we learn that Scratchy Wilson is on a rampage; our anxiety increases sharply when Scratchy decides to look for his enemy (and the story's likable main character), Jack Potter; and our suspense reaches a **climax** as Jack approaches his house, where Scratchy is armed and waiting.

See pages 6, 514.
See also *Foreshadowing, Plot.*

SYMBOL **A person, place, thing, or event that stands both for itself and for something beyond itself.** Many symbols have become widely recognized: A heart is a symbol of love; a snake is a symbol of evil. These established symbols are sometimes called **public symbols.** But writers often invent new, personal symbols, whose meaning is revealed in a work of poetry or prose. For example, the tiny flower in Alfred, Lord Tennyson's "Flower in the Crannied Wall" (page 367) is a symbol of the mystery of life.

See pages 165–167, 248–249, 264.
See also *Figure of Speech.*

THEME **The central idea or insight of a work of literature.** A theme is not the same as the **subject** of a work, which can usually be expressed in a word or two: old age, ambition, love. The theme is the idea the writer wishes to convey *about* that subject—the writer's view of the world or revelation about human nature. For example, one theme of John Knowles's novel *A Separate Peace* (page 901) might be stated this way: Even thoughtful, well-meaning people can be capable of great savagery and hatred.

A theme may also be different from a **moral,** which is a lesson or rule about how to live. The theme of *A Separate Peace* mentioned above, for example, would not make sense as a moral.

While some stories, poems, and plays have themes that are directly stated, most themes are implied. It is up to the reader to piece together all the clues the writer has provided about the work's total meaning. Two of the most important clues to consider are how the main character has changed and how the conflict has been resolved.

See pages 78–80, 113–115, 629, 734, 747, 802, 808, 830, 900.

TONE **The attitude a writer takes toward the reader, a subject, or a character.** Tone is conveyed through the writer's choice of words and details. For example, Saki's "The Storyteller" (page 206) is dry and ironic in tone, while A. E. Housman's poem "Loveliest of Trees" (page 272) is tender and impassioned in tone.

See pages 117–119, 341–343, 374–375, 900
See also *Connotations, Diction.*

TRAGEDY **A play, novel, or other narrative depicting serious and important events, in which the main character comes to an unhappy end.** In a tragedy, the main character is usually dignified and courageous, and often high ranking. This character's downfall may be caused by a **tragic flaw,** or character weakness. Or the downfall may result from forces beyond the hero's control. The tragic hero or heroine usually wins some self-knowledge and wisdom, even though he or she suffers defeat, possibly even death. Tragedy is distinct from **comedy,** in which an ordinary character overcomes obstacles to get what he or she wants. Shakespeare's play *Julius Caesar* (page 630) and Sophocles' play *Antigone* are both tragedies.

See pages 722, 796.
See also *Comedy.*

TRICKSTER TALE **A type of folktale featuring the exploits of a sometimes foolish, sometimes heroic character known as the trickster.** In some tales the trickster character is human, but usually he's a small animal who has to rely on his wits to survive among all the larger, stronger creatures. In some folktales the trickster is a hero—an underdog whose cleverness we admire even though we reject his morals. (Everyone seems to enjoy hearing about a good con job—particularly against a bully.) Sometimes he's even a creator, whose thefts and deceptions prove helpful to his people. In most folktales, however, the trickster is pretty much of a greedy, unscrupulous wiseguy whose antics backfire—showing us how *not* to behave.

Some of the most famous tricksters in folklore are the European Reynard the Fox, the West African spider Anansi, the Native American Coyote (see page 891), and the African American Brer Rabbit.

See pages 891, 895, 896.
See also *Folktale, Motif.*

GRAMMAR, USAGE, AND MECHANICS: A REFERENCE GUIDE

NOTE TO STUDENTS
As you write and revise formal essays and papers on topics in literature, you may want to review points of grammar, usage, capitalization, punctuation, and spelling. This reference section provides rules and examples that you will find helpful in your writing.

PARTS OF SPEECH

Nouns

1. A *noun* is a word used to name a person, place, thing, or idea.

   EXAMPLES
   man, teacher, Milton, Prof. Arne [people]
   state, country, Ohio, Brazil [places]
   car, money, Honda, ruble [things]
   strength, joy, love, liberty [ideas]

2. A *common noun* names general persons, places, and things. A *proper noun* names a particular person, place, or thing.

   EXAMPLES
Common	*Proper*
sea	Caspian Sea
building	Sears Tower

3. A *compound noun* is a single noun made up of two or more words. Compound nouns may be common or proper.

   EXAMPLES
   paperweight, sandalwood, blackboard
   left field, right of way, teen-ager, son-in-law
   Neil Armstrong, Oak Park, Sri Lanka

Pronouns

1. A *pronoun* is a word used in place of one or more than one noun. The noun that the pronoun stands for is called its *antecedent.*

   EXAMPLE
   Biff told **his** aunt **he** had bought a new computer. [The pronouns *his* and *he* refer to the antecedent *Biff.*]

2. *Personal pronouns* stand for people, places, and things. Here are the personal pronouns:

   EXAMPLES
   I, me, mine, my, myself; you, your, yours, yourself, yourselves; he, him, his, himself; she, her, hers, herself; it, its, itself; we, us, our, ours, ourselves; they, them, their, theirs, themselves

Adjectives

1. An *adjective* is a word used to modify a noun or a pronoun. Adjectives answer questions such as *What kind? Which one? How much?* or *How many?*

   EXAMPLES
   a **red** coat [What kind?] **that** jar [Which one?]
   fifty cents [How much?] **two** shoes [How many?]

2. *A, an,* and *the* are special adjectives called *articles.*

3. A *proper adjective* is an adjective that is formed from a proper noun. Proper adjectives, like proper nouns, are always capitalized.

   EXAMPLES
   Nordic winter, **French** pastry, **Edwardian** era, **A**merican food

Verbs

1. A *verb* is a word that expresses action or otherwise helps to make a sentence. An *action verb* is a word that expresses a physical or mental action.

   EXAMPLES
   stir, pour, sift, drip [physical actions]
   think, forget, consider [mental actions]

2. A *linking verb* is a word that does not express an action. A linking verb helps to make a sentence by joining the subject with a noun or adjective in the predicate.

   EXAMPLES
   Paula Abdul is an exciting **performer.** [*Is* links the subject *Paula Abdul* with the noun *performer* in the predicate.]
   She looks **vibrant** onstage. [*Looks* links the subject *she* with the adjective *vibrant* in the predicate.]

3. A one-word verb is called a *main verb.* Sometimes a main verb is accompanied by other verbs called *helping* (or *auxiliary*) *verbs.* The main verb and any helping verbs together make up a *verb phrase.*

EXAMPLES
The puppy **has found** its food. [The verb phrase is *has found.* The main verb is *found* and *has* is the helping verb.]
Tomorrow **will be** sunny. [The verb phrase is *will be.* The main verb is *be* and *will* is the helping verb.]

Adverbs

An *adverb* is a word used to modify a verb, an adjective, or another adverb. Adverbs usually answer questions such as *Where? When? How? To what extent?*

EXAMPLES
She drove **upstate.** [Where?]
I am leaving **tonight.** [When?]
Please guard this **carefully.** [How?]
The refrigerator was **almost** empty. [To what extent?]

TIPS FOR WRITERS
Use an adverb only after an action verb. Use an adjective after a linking verb to modify a noun or pronoun that is the subject of a sentence.

EXAMPLES
The peach tasted good. [*Good* is an adjective that appears after the linking verb *tasted* and modifies the subject noun *peach.*]
She spoke well. [*Well* is an adverb that modifies the action verb *spoke.*]

Prepositions

1. A *preposition* is a word used to show the relationship of a noun or a pronoun to some other word in the sentence. Below are common prepositions.

EXAMPLES

above	behind	for	on
across	below	from	over
after	beside	in	since
amid	between	into	to
among	by	like	through
around	down	near	under
at	during	of	with
before	except	off	within

2. The noun or pronoun following the preposition is called the *object of the preposition.* Words that modify the object may come between the preposition and the object. Taken together, the preposition, its object, and the modifiers of the object are called a *prepositional phrase.*

EXAMPLE
She took a walk **in the quiet garden.** [The prepositional phrase is *in the quiet garden. In* is the preposition, *garden* is the object of the preposition, and the words *the quiet* modify *garden.*]

Conjunctions

1. A *conjunction* is a word that joins words or groups of words. *Coordinating conjunctions* join two or more words, phrases, or sentence parts of equal rank. The words *and, but, or, nor, for, so,* and *yet* are coordinating conjunctions.

EXAMPLES
Light **and** sound behave like waves. [The two words *light* and *sound* are joined by *and.*]
The electrical cord on the lamp needs repair **or** the light bulb is burned out. [Two sentences are joined by *or.*]

2. *Correlative conjunctions* are always found in pairs that have other words separating them: *either . . . or, neither . . . nor, both . . . and, not only . . . but also.*

EXAMPLES
Either Fran **or** Alice will buy a new shade for the lamp.
We **not only** went to the movies **but also** saw a double feature.

3. *Subordinating conjunctions* are used to introduce subordinate clauses in complex sentences. Common subordinating conjunctions include *after, as soon as, because, if, so that, until, when,* and *while.* (See page 1011 for an exploration of complex sentences.)

Interjections

An *interjection* is a word that expresses emotion and that is not related grammatically to other words in the sentence.

EXAMPLES
Gee! That coat is very stylish.
Well, you wouldn't believe how little it cost.
Ah, that was a wonderful day.

THE SENTENCE

Elements of a Sentence

1. A *sentence* is a group of words expressing a complete thought. A group of words that does not express a complete thought is a *fragment.*

FRAGMENTS
Washed the windows. [We do not know *who* washed the windows.]
After he cleaned the stove. [We do not know *what happened* after he cleaned the stove.]
The person on the ladder. [We do not know *what* the person on the ladder did.]

SENTENCES
Bo Watson washed the windows. [The sentence expresses a complete thought.]
After he cleaned the stove, Ben sat down.
The person on the ladder began to plaster the ceiling.

2. The *subject* of a sentence is the part about which something is being said. The *simple subject* is the main word in a subject. The *complete subject* is the simple subject and all the words that go with it.

EXAMPLE
The weary commuters waited for the bus. [*The weary commuters* is the complete subject. *Commuters* is the simple subject.]

3. The *predicate* of a sentence is the part that says something about the subject. The *simple predicate,* or *verb,* is the main word in a predicate. The *complete predicate* is the simple predicate and all the words that go with it.

EXAMPLE
The weary commuters **waited for the bus.** [*Waited for the bus* is the complete predicate. *Waited* is the simple predicate.]

4. A *phrase* is a group of related words that is used as a single part of speech and does not contain a verb and its subject. Three common types of phrases include verb phrases, noun phrases, and prepositional phrases.

EXAMPLE
The two puppies were sleeping in the backseat. [*The two puppies* is a noun phrase, *were sleeping* is a verb phrase, and *in the backseat* is a prepositional phrase.]

5. A *clause* is a group of words that contains a verb and its subject and is used as part of a sentence. An *independent clause* expresses a complete thought and can stand by itself as a sentence. A *subordinate* (or *dependent*) *clause* does not express a complete thought and cannot stand alone. Subordinate clauses can be used as adjectives, nouns, or adverbs.

EXAMPLES
As the guests arrived, **we greeted them at the door.** [independent clause]
We cleaned up **after the party was over.** [subordinate clause]

Sentence Complements

1. A *complement* is a word or phrase that completes the meaning begun by the subject and verb.

2. The *direct object* receives the action expressed by the verb or names the result of the action. A direct object answers the question *What?* or *Whom?* after the action verb.

EXAMPLE
He sliced the **meat.** [*Meat* is the direct object; it receives the action of the verb *sliced.*]

3. The *indirect object* of the verb precedes the direct object and tells *to whom* (or *what*) or *for whom* (or *what*) the action of the verb is done.

EXAMPLES
Mother bought **us** a typewriter. [*Us* is the indirect object because it tells *for whom* mother bought a typewriter.]
Bill sent his **aunt** a birthday card. [*Aunt* is the indirect object because it tells *to whom* Bill sent a birthday card.]

4. A *subject complement* is a word that follows a linking verb and refers to (explains or describes) the subject.

5. If the subject complement is a noun or pronoun, it is called a *predicate nominative.*

EXAMPLES
This book is a **thesaurus.** [*Thesaurus* is a predicate nominative. It is a noun that renames the subject *book.*]
The speaker was **she.** [*She* is a predicate nominative. It is a pronoun that renames the subject *speaker.*]

6. If the subject complement is an adjective, it is called a *predicate adjective*. A predicate adjective modifies the subject of the sentence.

EXAMPLE

The painting is very **old**. [*Old* is a predicate adjective modifying the subject *painting*.]

Sentence Structure

1. A *simple sentence* has one independent clause and no subordinate (or dependent) clauses. A simple sentence may have a compound subject, a compound predicate, or both.

EXAMPLES

These plants bloom in the autumn. [simple sentence]
The asters and the pansies are planted near each other. [simple sentence with compound subject]
I watered the lawn and weeded the garden. [simple sentence with compound predicate]

2. A *compound sentence* has two or more independent clauses but no subordinate (or dependent) clauses.

EXAMPLE

Nathaniel read a book of poems by Wallace Stevens, but his brother Irwin read a different one by Edgar Lee Masters. [This sentence has two independent clauses joined by the conjunction *but*.]

3. A *complex sentence* has one independent clause and at least one subordinate (dependent) clause.

EXAMPLE

After we arrived, we took a bus tour. [*We took a bus tour* is the independent clause, and *after we arrived* is the subordinate clause.]

TIPS FOR WRITERS

Do not use a comma in a compound subject or predicate in which two elements are joined by a conjunction. If there are three or more elements, use commas to separate all the elements.

EXAMPLES

Ben and his wife are driving to Canada. [Two elements in a compound subject are not separated by a comma.]
Ben, his wife, and her sister are driving to Canada. [Three elements are separated by commas.]

4. A *compound-complex sentence* has two or more independent clauses and at least one dependent (subordinate) clause.

EXAMPLE

Everyone enjoyed the cooking class, and guys who really like to cook plan to take the next course. [*Everyone enjoyed the cooking class* and *guys plan to take the next course* are both independent clauses. *Who really like to cook* is a dependent (or subordinate) clause.]

PROBLEMS OF AGREEMENT

Agreement of Subject and Verb

1. A verb should agree with its subject in number. Singular subjects take singular verbs. Plural subjects take plural verbs.

EXAMPLES

She designs book covers. [The singular verb *designs* agrees with the singular subject *she*.]
They design book covers. [The plural verb *design* agrees with the plural subject *they*.]

Like single-word verbs, verb phrases also agree with their subjects. However, in a verb phrase, only the first auxiliary (helping) verb changes its form to agree with a singular or plural subject.

EXAMPLES

A **bird was sitting** in the nest.
Two **birds were sitting** in the nest.

2. The number of the subject is not changed by a phrase following the subject.

EXAMPLES

This **book** of essays **is** new. [*Book* is the subject, not *essays*.]
These **essays** about fishing **are** interesting. [*Essays* is the subject, not *fishing*.]

3. Compound prepositions such as *together with, in addition to, as well as,* and *along with* following the subject do not affect the number of the subject.

EXAMPLE

Lee, together with her brothers, **is visiting** friends in Maine this summer. [The subject of the sentence is singular because it names one person, *Lee*. Therefore, the predicate of the sentence uses the singular verb form *is*.]

4. The following indefinite pronouns are singular: *each, either, neither, one, everyone, everybody, no one, nobody, anyone, anybody, someone, somebody.*

EXAMPLES
Each of the actors **reads** well. [*Each one* reads.]
Neither of the actors **is** too tall. [*Neither one* is too tall.]
Someone was talking backstage during rehearsal. [*One* person was talking.]
No one is ready to begin. [*Not one* person is ready.]

5. The following pronouns are plural: *several, few, both, many.*

EXAMPLES
Several of the actors **have** been in other famous plays.
Few of the actors **are** here now.
Were both of the plays performed?
Many of the actors **study** fencing.

6. The pronouns *some, all, most, any,* and *none* may be either singular or plural. These pronouns are singular when they refer to a singular word and plural when they refer to a plural word.

EXAMPLES
Some of the action **is** suspenseful. [*Some* refers to the singular noun *action.*]
Some of the actors **are** awkward. [*Some* refers to the plural noun *actors.*]

All of the scenery **is** new.
All of the actors **seem** nervous.

Most of the action **occurs** in one room.
Most of the lines **sound** familiar by now.

TIPS FOR WRITERS

The words *any* and *none* may be singular even when they refer to a plural word if the speaker is thinking of each item individually. The words *any* and *none* are plural only if the speaker is thinking of several items as a group.

Any of these plays **is** worth seeing. [*Any one play* is worth seeing.]
None of the plays **was** bad. [*Not one play* was bad.]
Any of these plays **are** worth seeing. [*All the plays* are worth seeing.]
None of the plays **were** bad. [*No plays* were bad.]

---

7. Compound subjects joined by the word *and* are usually plural in form and therefore take a plural verb.

A **compound subject** contains two or more nouns or pronouns that are the subject of the same verb.

EXAMPLES
Sam Shepard and **David Mamet are** playwrights. [Two persons are *playwrights.*]
Plot, character, and **setting give** form to drama. [Three things *give.*]

8. A few compound subjects are thought to name a single person or thing and so take a singular verb.

EXAMPLES
My **coach and director is** Ms. Carlton. [One person is your coach and director.]
Ham and eggs is my favorite breakfast meal. [*Ham and eggs* are thought to be one dish.]

9. Singular subjects joined by the words *or* or *nor* take a singular verb.

EXAMPLE
After the performance, **Ben or Val sweeps** the stage. [*Either* Ben *or* Val sweeps the stage, not both.]

10. When a singular subject and a plural subject are joined by *or* or *nor,* the verb agrees with the subject nearer the verb.

ACCEPTABLE
Neither the coach nor the **athletes were** happy.
Neither the athletes nor the **coach was** happy.

Try to avoid awkward constructions.

BETTER
The athletes were not happy, and neither was the coach.

Other Problems in Subject–Verb Agreement

1. The contractions *don't* and *doesn't* must agree with their subjects.

With the subjects *I* and *you* and with plural subjects, use the contraction *don't* (*do not*).

EXAMPLES
I **don't** have to.   They **don't** blend.   We **don't** dare.
Men **don't** know.   You **don't** say.   These **don't** melt.

With singular subjects, use the singular *doesn't* (does not).

EXAMPLES
He **doesn't** dare to.   One **doesn't** wait.
She **doesn't** fret.   This **doesn't** leak.
It **doesn't** start.   Donna **doesn't** forget.

2. **Use a plural verb with a singular collective noun when you are referring to the individual parts or members of the group acting separately. Use a singular verb when you refer to the group acting together as a unit.** *Collective nouns* **are singular in form, but they name a group of persons or things.**

EXAMPLES
army	club	fleet	jury
assembly	committee	flock	panel
audience	faculty	group	swarm
class	family	herd	team

EXAMPLES
The audience **are** all in their seats. [*Audience* is thought of as individuals.]
The audience **is** showing its approval. [*Audience* is thought of as a unit.]

Be sure that any pronoun referring to the collective noun has the same number as the noun (*their* in the first example above, *its* in the second).

TIPS FOR WRITERS
When the subject follows the verb, find the subject and make sure that the verb agrees with it. The most common uses of the subject-following-verb form are in sentences beginning with *here* and *there* and in questions.

Here **is** a **book** of recipes.   Here **are books** of recipes.
There **is** my **package**.   There **are** my **packages**.
Where **is Dan**?   Where **are Dan and Miko**?

---

3. **A verb agrees with its subject, not with its predicate nominative.**

STANDARD
         S   V   PN
American **rivers are** our project.

      S   V   PN
Our **project is** American rivers.

4. **Contractions such as** *here's, where's, how's,* **and** *what's* **include the verb** *is.* **Do not use one of these contractions unless a singular subject follows it.**

NONSTANDARD
There's some entries for that topic in the index.

STANDARD
There **are** some **entries** for that topic in the index.
In the index, there**'s** an **entry** for that topic.

5. **A word or a phrase stating a weight, a measurement, or an amount of money or time is usually considered one item and takes a singular verb.**

EXAMPLE
Ten dollars is too much for that scarf.

Sometimes, however, the amount is thought of as individual pieces or parts. If so, a plural verb is used.

EXAMPLES
Five of the films **were** given awards.
Three fourths of the films **are** on videotape.

6. **The title of a work of art, literature, or music, even when plural in form, takes a singular verb.**

EXAMPLE
Porgy and Bess **is** a musical by George Gershwin. [one musical]

7. *Every* **or** *many a* **before a subject calls for a singular verb.**

EXAMPLES
Every teacher and parent **was** concerned.
Many a problem **was** solved at the meeting.

8. *The number of* **takes a singular verb;** *a number of* **takes a plural verb.**

EXAMPLES
The number of contestants **was** large.
A number of them are sophomores.

Agreement of Pronoun and Antecedent
1. **A pronoun should agree with its antecedent in number and gender.**

A pronoun usually refers to a noun or another pronoun that comes before it. The word that a pronoun refers to is called its **antecedent.**

A few singular personal pronouns have forms that indicate the gender of the antecedent. *He, him,* and *his* are masculine; *she, her,* and *hers* are feminine; *it* and *its* are neuter.

EXAMPLES
Vicki takes **her** first test today.
Max has **his** last exam tomorrow.
The **team** has **its** own clubhouse.

2. **When the antecedent of a personal pronoun is another kind of pronoun, look in a phrase following the antecedent to determine gender.**

EXAMPLES
Each of the **women** rents **her** own studio.
One of the **boys** took **his** project home.

3. **When the antecedent may be either masculine or feminine, use both the masculine and the feminine forms.**

EXAMPLES
Everyone of the students wrote reports of **his or her** experiment.
A **student** should always have **his or her** notebook handy.

4. **Use a singular pronoun to refer to *each, either, neither, one, everyone, everybody, no one, nobody, anyone, anybody, someone,* or *somebody.***

EXAMPLES
Somebody forgot to return **his or her** new tennis racket.
One of the cats has a thorn in **its** paw.
No one has made **his or her** report yet.

When the meaning of *everyone* and *everybody* is clearly plural, use the plural pronoun.

TIPS FOR WRITERS
In many cases you can avoid the awkward *his or her* construction by rephrasing the sentence and using the plural form of the pronoun.

AWKWARD
Everyone of the candidates expressed his or her views.

REVISED
All of the candidates expressed **their** views.

CONFUSING
Everyone complained when **he or she** learned that the train would be late.

CLEAR
Everyone complained when **they** learned that the train would be late.

5. **Two or more singular antecedents joined by *or* or *nor* should be referred to by a singular pronoun.**

EXAMPLES
Neither **Alan nor Guido** hurt **himself** while playing.
Dena or Ilia will show **her** film today.

6. **Two or more antecedents joined by *and* should be referred to by a plural pronoun.**

EXAMPLES
Kira and Floyd ran quickly because **they** didn't want to be late.
Viola and Flora took **their** time.

7. **The number of a relative pronoun is determined by the number of its antecedent.**

EXAMPLES
Anyone who wants a ride should call Susan. [*Who* refers to the singular pronoun *anyone* and thus takes the singular verb form *wants.*]
All who need rides should call Susan. [*Who* refers to the plural pronoun *all* and thus takes the plural verb form *need.*]

TIPS FOR WRITERS
Sentences with two or more singular antecedents joined by *or* or *nor* can sound awkward if the antecedents are of different genders. If a sentence sounds awkward, revise it to avoid the problem.

AWKWARD
Ned or **Clara** will tell **his** or **her** story.

REVISED
Ned will tell **his** story, or **Clara** will tell **hers**.

USING VERBS CORRECTLY

The Principal Parts of Verbs
1. **The four principal parts of a verb are the *infinitive*, the *present participle*, the *past*, and the *past participle*.**

The principal parts of the verb *run,* for example, are *run* (infinitive), *running* (present participle), *ran* (past), and *run* (past participle). These principal parts are used to form all of the verb tenses.

EXAMPLES
Alta **runs** every day.
Alta is **running** in the race.
Alta **ran** two miles.
Alta has **run** the race well.

Regular Verbs

2. **A regular verb forms its past and past participle by adding -*d* or -*ed* to the infinitive.**

INFINITIVE	PRESENT PARTICIPLE	PAST	PAST PARTICIPLE
ask	asking	asked	(have) asked
fill	filling	filled	(have) filled
print	printing	printed	(have) printed
vote	voting	voted	(have) voted
face	facing	faced	(have) faced
taste	tasting	tasted	(have) tasted

The present participle of most regular verbs ending in *-e* drops the *-e* before adding *-ing.*

One common error in the use of the past and the past participle forms is to leave off the *-d* or *-ed* ending.

NONSTANDARD
She use to enjoy cooking.

STANDARD
She **used** to enjoy cooking.

NONSTANDARD
Alexandra was suppose to go to the mountains with them.

STANDARD
Alexandra was **supposed** to go to the mountains with them.

A few regular verbs have an alternate past form ending in *-t.* For example, the past form of *dream* may be written *dreamed* or *dreamt* and the past form of *burn* may be *burned* or *burnt.*

Irregular Verbs

3. **An *irregular verb* forms its past and past participle in some other way than by adding -*d* or -*ed.***

Irregular verbs form their past and past participle in one or more of these ways: changing a vowel, changing consonants, adding *-en,* making no change at all.

INFINITIVE	PAST	PAST PARTICIPLE
ring	rang	(have) rung
think	thought	(have) thought
drive	drove	(have) driven
burst	burst	(have) burst
freeze	froze	(have) frozen

If you are not sure about the parts of a verb, look in a dictionary, which lists the principal parts of irregular verbs. In the next column, you will find a list of frequently misused irregular verbs.

Irregular Verbs Frequently Misused

INFINITIVE	PRESENT PARTICIPLE	PAST	PAST PARTICIPLE
arise	arising	arose	(have) arisen
begin	beginning	began	(have) begun
bet	betting	bet	(have) bet
bleed	bleeding	bled	(have) bled
blow	blowing	blew	(have) blown
break	breaking	broke	(have) broken
bring	bringing	brought	(have) brought
burst	bursting	burst	(have) burst
choose	choosing	chose	(have) chosen
come	coming	came	(have) come
dig	digging	dug	(have) dug
do	doing	did	(have) done
drink	drinking	drank	(have) drunk
drive	driving	drove	(have) driven
eat	eating	ate	(have) eaten
fall	falling	fell	(have) fallen
fly	flying	flew	(have) flown
freeze	freezing	froze	(have) frozen
give	giving	gave	(have) given
go	going	went	(have) gone
grow	growing	grew	(have) grown
know	knowing	knew	(have) known
leave	leaving	left	(have) left
lend	lending	lent	(have) lent
put	putting	put	(have) put
ride	riding	rode	(have) ridden
ring	ringing	rang	(have) rung
run	running	ran	(have) run
see	seeing	saw	(have) seen
seek	seeking	sought	(have) sought
shake	shaking	shook	(have) shaken
shrink	shrinking	shrank	(have) shrunk

sink	sinking	sank	(have) sunk
speak	speaking	spoke	(have) spoken
steal	stealing	stole	(have) stolen
sting	stinging	stung	(have) stung
strike	striking	struck	(have) struck
swear	swearing	swore	(have) sworn
swim	swimming	swam	(have) swum
take	taking	took	(have) taken
tear	tearing	tore	(have) torn
throw	throwing	threw	(have) thrown
wear	wearing	wore	(have) worn
win	winning	won	(have) won
write	writing	wrote	(have) written

4. **The time expressed by a verb is called the *tense* of the verb. Every verb in English has six tenses: present, past, future, present perfect, past perfect, future perfect.**

The following list shows six tense forms of *go*. Giving all the forms of a verb in this way is called **conjugating** the verb.

Conjugation of *Go*

Present Tense

Singular	*Plural*
I go	we go
you go	you go
he, she, *or* it goes	they go

Past Tense

Singular	*Plural*
I went	we went
you went	you went
he, she, *or* it went	they went

Future Tense

Singular	*Plural*
I will (shall) go	we will (shall) go
you will go	you will go
he, she, *or* it will go	they will go

Present Perfect Tense

Singular	*Plural*
I have gone	we have gone
you have gone	you have gone
he, she, *or* it has gone	they have gone

Past Perfect Tense

Singular	*Plural*
I had gone	we had gone
you had gone	you had gone
he, she, *or* it had gone	they had gone

Future Perfect Tense

Singular	*Plural*
I will (shall) have gone	we will (shall) have gone
you will have gone	you will have gone
he, she, *or* it will have gone	they will have gone

Each of the six tenses has an additional form called the **progressive form**, which expresses continuing action. It consists of a form of the verb *be* plus the present participle of the verb. The progressive is not a separate tense but an additional form of each of the six tenses in the conjugation.

Progressive Forms

Present Progressive: am, are, is going

Past Progressive: was, were going

Future Progressive: will (shall) be going

Present Perfect Progressive: has, have been going

Past Perfect Progressive: had been going

Future Perfect Progressive: will (shall) have been going

Consistency of Tenses

5. **Do not change needlessly from one tense to another.**

NONSTANDARD
Myron made the sauce and boils the noodles. [*Made* is past tense; *boils* is present tense.]

STANDARD
Myron **made** the sauce and **boiled** the noodles. [*Made* and *boiled* are past tense.]

The perfect tenses are used to express completed action.

NONSTANDARD
She told us that she moved to Iowa City two years ago. [Since the action of moving was completed before the action of telling, the verb should be *had moved,* not *moved.*]

STANDARD
She told us that she **had moved** to Iowa City last year.

Active and Passive Voices

6. A verb in the active voice expresses an action done *by* its subject. A verb in the passive voice expresses an action done *to* its subject.

ACTIVE VOICE

The mechanic **repaired** the brakes and the transmission. [The subject, *mechanic,* performs the action of repairing.]

PASSIVE VOICE

The brakes and the transmission **were repaired** by the mechanic. [The subject, *brakes* and *transmission*, receives the action.]

ACTIVE VOICE

My mother **baked** the birthday cake. [The subject, *mother*, performs the act of baking.]

PASSIVE VOICE

The birthday cake **was baked** by my mother. [The subject, *cake*, receives the action.]

Special Problems with Verbs

Using *Lie* and *Lay* Correctly

1. The verb *lie* means "to rest or recline," "to remain lying in a position." *Lie* never takes an object. The verb *lay* means "to put or place" (something). *Lay* usually takes an object. Problems result from the fact that the past tense of *lie* is *lay.* Be sure you know whether you mean "to rest" or "to put."

INFINITIVE	PRESENT PARTICIPLE	PAST	PAST PARTICIPLE
lie	lying	lay	(have) lain
lay	laying	laid	(have) laid

EXAMPLES

At night I like to **lie** on my back and look at the stars.
The books **are lying** on the sofa.
She **has** just **lain** down to take a nap before she must return again to work.
Yesterday the tomatoes **lay** in the sun for three hours.
How long **has** that package **lain** there?

Lay the curtains down.
I **am laying** your mail on this chair.
Pat **laid** bricks in a row.
Have you **laid** the pen on the desk?
Please **lay** your test booklet down.

Using *Sit* and *Set* Correctly

2. The verb *sit* means "to rest in an upright, seated position." *Sit* almost never takes an object. The verb *set* means "to put or place" (something). *Set* usually takes an object. Notice that *set* does not change form in the past or past participle.

INFINITIVE	PRESENT PARTICIPLE	PAST	PAST PARTICIPLE
sit	sitting	sat	(have) sat
set	setting	set	(have) set

EXAMPLES

Please **sit** in this chair.
They **are sitting** in the library.
How long **have** they **been sitting** there?
She **has** just **sat** down to dinner.
Yesterday the cat **sat** on the windowsill all day.
They **had sat** in the docter's waiting room for three hours.

Set the books down on the table.
I **am setting** your lunch on the table.
Pat **set** the clock for the next morning.
Have you **set** aside some time for working on the computer?
They **have set** the bricks in the backyard.

Using *Rise* and *Raise* Correctly

3. The verb *rise* means "to go in an upward direction." *Rise* never has an object. The verb *raise* means "to move something in an upward direction." *Raise* usually takes an object.

INFINITIVE	PRESENT PARTICIPLE	PAST	PAST PARTICIPLE
rise	rising	rose	(have) risen
raise	raising	raised	(have) raised

EXAMPLES

Look, the moon **is rising** over the hills.
Please **rise** and say the Pledge of Allegiance.
After a long career he **has risen** to the rank of a four-star general.
Yesterday my sister **rose** at four in the morning to go skiing.

Raise your hand if you need help.
They **raised** some interesting questions about the new law.
The city **is raising** its sales tax.
Have you **raised** chickens before?
I **am raising** money for our club.

USING PRONOUNS CORRECTLY

Nominative and Objective Uses

Case

1. *Case* **is the form of a noun or pronoun that shows its use in a sentence. In English, there are three cases: *nominative*, *objective*, and *possessive*.**

Choosing the correct case form for a noun is no problem, because the form remains the same in the nominative and objective cases.

EXAMPLE
My former **dentist** has sent my X-rays to my new **dentist.**

Only in the possessive case does a noun change its form, usually by adding an apostrophe and *s.*

EXAMPLE
My **dentist's** office is well equipped.

Personal pronouns, however, have various case forms. In the following example, the boldfaced pronouns all refer to the same person. They have three different forms because of their different uses.

EXAMPLE
He [nominative] forgot to bring **his** [possessive] ticket with **him** [objective].

The Case Forms of Personal Pronouns

2. **Here are the case forms of personal pronouns. Notice that all personal pronouns, except *you* and *it*, have different nominative and objective forms.**

PERSONAL PRONOUNS

SINGULAR

Nominative Case	Objective Case	Possessive Case
I	me	my, mine
you	you	your, yours
he, she, it	him, her, it	his, her, hers, its

PLURAL

Nominative Case	Objective Case	Possessive Case
we	us	our, ours
you	you	your, yours
they	them	their, theirs

The Nominative Case

1. **The subject of a verb is in the nominative case.**

EXAMPLE
She was relieved that **they** were safe. [*She* is the subject of *was*; *they* is the subject of *were.*]

Sometimes you may be unsure about which pronoun to use when both parts of a compound subject are pronouns. To help you choose the correct form, try each pronoun separately with the verb.

EXAMPLE
(She, Her) or (they, them) will buy rolls.

"*She* will buy rolls." "*They* will buy rolls." "*Her* will buy rolls" and "*them* will buy rolls" sound strange. "*She or they will buy rolls*" is correct.

TIPS FOR WRITERS

Sometimes the pronouns *we* and *they* sound awkward when used as parts of a compound subject. In such cases, it is a good idea to revise the sentence.

AWKWARD
We and they plan to go together to the fair.

BETTER
We plan to go with **them** to the fair.

2. **A *predicate nominative* is in the nominative case.**

A **predicate nominative** is a noun or pronoun that follows a linking verb and explains or identifies the subject of the sentence.

A pronoun used as a predicate nominative always follows a form of the verb *be* or a verb phrase ending in *be* or *been.*

EXAMPLES
Where **is he?**
It might **be she.**
It could **have been they.**

TIPS FOR WRITERS

Widespread usage has made such expressions as *It's me, That's him,* or *Could it have been her?* acceptable in speaking. If possible, you should avoid such expressions in your written work unless you are writing conversational English in a dialogue.

The Objective Case

3. The *direct object* of a verb is in the objective case.

A *direct object* is a noun or pronoun that receives the action of the verb or shows the result of the action.

EXAMPLES
Nan told **us** about the article. [*Nan* is the subject of the verb *told*. Nan told *whom?* The answer is *us*.]

He thanked **us**. [*He* is the subject of the verb *thanked*. He thanked *whom?* He thanked *us*.]

When the object is compound, try each pronoun separately. All parts of the compound must be correct for the sentence to be correct.

NONSTANDARD
Nan's story amused him and I. [*Nan's story amused him* is correct. *Nan's story amused I* is incorrect. Therefore, *Nan's story amused him and I* is incorrect. The second pronoun should be *me*.]

STANDARD
Nan's story amused him and **me**.

TIPS FOR WRITERS

Some mistakes in usage are more common than others. In speech, for example, people often incorrectly use the pronoun *me* for *I* in a compound subject.

INCORRECT
Aretha and me prepared all the food.

CORRECT
Aretha and **I** prepared all the food.

4. The *indirect object* of the verb is in the objective case.

An *indirect object* is a noun or pronoun that tells to whom or for whom something is done. Pronouns used as indirect objects are in the objective case: *me, him, her, us, them.*

EXAMPLE
The receptionist gave **her** an appointment.

5. The *object of a preposition* is in the objective case.

A prepositional phrase begins with a preposition and ends with a noun or pronoun, which is the *object of the preposition*. A pronoun used as an object of a preposition must be in the objective case.

EXAMPLES
Peg was seated next to **us**.
Rhea sat behind **him** and **me**.

Many people use the incorrect pronoun forms with the preposition *between*. You have probably heard phrases such as *between you and I* and *between you and he*. These phrases are incorrect. The pronouns are objects of a preposition and should be in the objective case. The correct phrases are *between you and me* and *between you and him.*

Special Pronoun Problems

Using *Who* and *Whom* Correctly

1. *Who* is used as subject or predicate nominative, and *whom* is used as an object.

NOMINATIVE	OBJECTIVE
who	whom
whoever	whomever

In spoken English, the use of *whom* is becoming less common. In fact, when you are speaking, you may correctly begin any question with *who,* regardless of the grammar of the sentence. In written English, however, you should make a distinction between *who* and *whom*.

2. The use of *who* or *whom* in a subordinate clause depends on how the pronoun functions in the clause.

When you are choosing between *who* and *whom* in a subordinate clause, follow these steps to make the correct choice:

STEP 1: Find the subordinate clause.
STEP 2: Decide how the pronoun is used in the clause—as subject, predicate nominative, object of the verb, or object of a preposition.
STEP 3: Determine the case of the pronoun according to the rules of standard English.
STEP 4: Select the correct form of the pronoun.

EXAMPLE
Alexander Graham Bell, (*who, whom*) I reported on, invented the telephone.

STEP 1: The subordinate clause is (*who, whom*) *I reported on.*

STEP 2: In this clause, the subject is *I,* and the verb is *reported.* The pronoun is the object of the preposition *on: I reported on* (*who, whom*).

STEP 3: The object of a preposition is in the objective case.

STEP 4: The objective form is *whom.*

ANSWER: Alexander Graham Bell, **whom** I reported on, invented the telephone.

3. **Pronouns used as *appositives* are in the same case as the word to which they refer.**

An *appositive* is a noun or pronoun that follows another noun or pronoun to identify or explain it.

EXAMPLES
The winners, **he, she,** and **I,** received awards. [Since *winners* is the subject of the sentence, the pronouns in apposition with it (*he, she, I*) must be in the nominative case.]

The editor thanked the authors, Jill and **me.** [Since *authors* is the direct object of *thanked,* the pronoun *me,* which is in apposition to *authors,* must be in the objective case.]

TIPS FOR WRITERS
To figure out the correct form for a pronoun used with an appositive or as an appositive, read the sentence with only the pronoun.

EXAMPLES
Ms. Sato asked two students, Polly and (*he, him*), to help. [Omit the direct object, *students:* Ms. Sato asked Polly and him to help.]
(*We, us*) classmates offered to help. [Omit the appositive, *classmates:* We offered to help.]

The Pronoun in an Incomplete Construction

After *than* and *as* introducing an incomplete construction, use the form of the pronoun that you would use if the construction were completed.

Notice how pronouns change the meaning of sentences with incomplete constructions.

EXAMPLES
Li Hua knows Amy better than **I.**
Li Hua knows Amy better than **me.**

In the first sentence, the nominative case pronoun *I* is the subject of an understood verb: *Li Hua knows Amy better than I* [*know Amy*]. In the second sentence, the objective case pronoun *me* is the object of the understood verb: *Li Hua knows Amy better than* [*Li Hua knows*] *me.*

EXAMPLES
I pitch to you more often than **he** [pitches to you].
I pitch to you more often than [I pitch] to **him.**

USING MODIFIERS CORRECTLY

1. **Adjectives and adverbs are modifiers, that is, they state qualities of other parts of speech. Adjectives modify nouns and pronouns. Adverbs modify verbs, adjectives, and other adverbs.**

EXAMPLES
soft gloves   [adjective]
woolen scarf   [adjective]
speak **quietly**   [adverb]
do **better**   [adverb]

2. **Use adjectives to compare one noun with another noun that has the same quality.**

EXAMPLES
This lawn is **greener** than that one.
That chair is **wider** than this one.

3. **Use adverbs to make comparisons between verbs.**

EXAMPLE
I learned the dance easily, but Tom learned it even **more easily.**

4. **There are three degrees of comparison: *positive, comparative,* and *superlative.***

POSITIVE	COMPARATIVE	SUPERLATIVE
high	higher	highest
late	later	latest
fluffy	fluffier	fluffiest
strong	stronger	strongest
careful	more careful	most careful
lightly	more lightly	most lightly
deeply	more deeply	most deeply
curious	more curious	most curious

5. **A one-syllable modifier regularly forms its comparative and superlative degrees by adding -er and -est.**

POSITIVE	COMPARATIVE	SUPERLATIVE
thick	thicker	thickest
hot	hotter	hottest
short	shorter	shortest

6. **Some two-syllable modifiers form their comparative and superlative degrees by adding -er and -est. Other two-syllable modifiers form their comparative and superlative degrees with *more* and *most*.**

POSITIVE	COMPARATIVE	SUPERLATIVE
humble	humbler	humblest
lovely	lovelier	loveliest
hopeful	more hopeful	most hopeful
comic	more comic	most comic
tautly	more tautly	most tautly

Some two-syllable modifiers may take either *-er, -est* or *more, most: happy, happier, happiest* or *happy, more happy, most happy.*

If you are unsure of how a two-syllable modifier is compared, look in an unabridged dictionary.

7. **Modifiers that have more than two syllables form their comparative and superlative degrees with *more* and *most*.**

POSITIVE	COMPARATIVE	SUPERLATIVE
honorable	more honorable	most honorable
bountiful	more bountiful	most bountiful
accurately	more accurately	most accurately

8. **Modifiers that indicate less of a quality use the word *less* or *least* before the modifier.**

POSITIVE	COMPARATIVE	SUPERLATIVE
likely	less likely	least likely
rapidly	less rapidly	least rapidly
useful	less useful	least useful

Irregular Comparison

9. **Here are some commonly used modifiers which do not follow the regular methods of forming their comparative and superlative degrees.**

POSITIVE	COMPARATIVE	SUPERLATIVE
bad	worse	worst
good	better	best
well	better	best
many	more	most
much	more	most

Do not add the *-er, -est* or *more, most* forms to irregularly compared forms: *worse*, not *worser* or *more worse.*

Use of Comparative and Superlative Forms

10. **Use the comparative degree when comparing two things. Use the superlative degree when comparing more than two.**

COMPARATIVE
Playing basketball can be **more exhausting** than playing tennis.
Paul thinks that baseball is a **better** game than football.

SUPERLATIVE
Gone with the Wind is the **longest** movie I have ever seen.
Memorizing two speeches from *Macbeth* is the **most challenging** assignment I've had so far.

In everyday conversation, people sometimes use the superlative degree in comparing two things: *Put your best foot forward.*

11. **Include the word *other* or *else* when comparing one thing with others that belong in the same group.**

NONSTANDARD
Vanna is taller than any member of her family. [Vanna is a member of her own family, and she cannot be taller than herself. The word *other* should be added.]

STANDARD
Vanna is taller than any **other** member of her family.

12. **Avoid double comparisons.**

A **double comparison** is incorrect because it contains both *-er* and *more* or *-est* and *most.*

NONSTANDARD
She is more neater than I.
This is the most smallest size I could find.

STANDARD
She is **neater** than I.
This is the **smallest** size I could find.

13. Be sure your comparisons are clear.

UNCLEAR
The coastline of Maine is rockier than Georgia. [This sentence incorrectly compares a coastline to a state.]

CLEAR
The coastline of Maine is rockier than the coastline of Georgia.

Both parts of an incomplete comparison should be stated if there is any chance of misunderstanding.

UNCLEAR
I like her better than Jim.

CLEAR
I like her better than I like Jim.
I like her better than Jim likes her.

Dangling Modifiers
1. **A modifying phrase or clause that does not clearly and sensibly modify a word in a sentence is a *dangling modifier*.**

When a modifying phrase containing a verbal comes at the beginning of a sentence, the phrase is followed by a comma. Immediately after that comma should come the word that the phrase modifies.

UNCLEAR
Cleaning the windows, the glass broke.

CLEAR
Cleaning the windows, he broke the glass.

Correcting Dangling Modifiers
2. **To correct a dangling modifier, rearrange the words in the sentence or add words to make the meaning logical and clear.**

DANGLING
Lying on the shelf, Giorgio found the book.

CORRECTED
Giorgio found the **book** that was lying on the shelf.

Misplaced Modifiers
3. **A *modifying phrase* is a phrase or clause that sounds awkward because it modifies the wrong word(s). Modifying phrases should be placed as near as possible to the words they modify.**

MISPLACED
We talked about the blizzard on the bus.

CORRECTED
On the bus, we talked about the blizzard.

Misplaced Clause Modifiers
4. **Place an adjective or adverb clause as near as possible to the word it modifies.**

MISPLACED
I found a painting in an attic that was worth a lot of money.
He is making a sculpture for his cousin that is twelve feet tall.

CORRECTED
In an attic, I found a painting that was worth a lot of money.
He is making a sculpture that is twelve feet tall for his cousin.

COMMON USAGE PROBLEMS

a, an
These *indefinite articles* refer to one of a general group. Use *a* before words beginning with a consonant sound; use *an* before words beginning with a vowel sound.

EXAMPLES
We have **a** stamp and **an** envelope.
A hatful of coins was collected in less than **an** hour.

A is used before *hatful* because the *h* in *hatful* is pronounced. *An* is used before *hour* because the *h* in *hour* is not pronounced.

accept, except
Accept is a verb that means "to receive." *Except* may be either a verb or a preposition. As a verb, it means "to leave out" or "to omit." As a preposition, *except* means "excluding."

EXAMPLES
I shall **accept** her invitation, of course.
The ruling **excepts** those who have not registered.
Everyone **except** Rose heard the news.

affect, effect
Affect is a verb meaning "to influence." *Effect* used as a verb means "to accomplish." Used as a noun, *effect* means "the result of some action."

EXAMPLES

The drought **affects** the water level at the reservoir.

The last rainfall had not **affected** the water level enough to make a difference in the emergency.

The scientists know that only the correct medication will **effect** a cure for the disease.

The talk had a good **effect** on the student's grades.

between, among

Use *between* when you are referring to two people or things.

EXAMPLES

The price will be **between** forty and fifty dollars.

We could not decide which of the two toasters to buy because there was not much difference in price **between** them.

The referee tossed the ball **between** the two players.

Use *among* when more than two things or persons are involved.

EXAMPLES

We divided the six coins **among** the three of us.

The club members discussed the problems **among** themselves.

bring, take

Bring means "to come carrying something." *Take* means "to go carrying something." Think of *bring* as related to *come, take* as related to *go.*

EXAMPLES

Bring your compass with you.

Take your mother to the dentist.

bust, busted

Avoid using these words as verbs. Use a form of either *burst* or *break.*

EXAMPLES

The gas main **burst** [not *busted*].

The pipe **burst** [not *busted*] from the cold weather.

I **broke** [not *busted*] three plates.

He **broke** [not *busted*] his sister's doll.

could of

Do not write *of* with the helping verb *could.* Write *could have.* Also avoid *ought to of, should of, would of, might of,* and *must of.*

EXAMPLE

Luisa could **have** [not *of*] called me.

don't, doesn't

Don't is the contraction of *do not. Doesn't* is the contraction of *does not.* Use *doesn't,* not *don't,* with *he, she, it, this,* and singular nouns.

EXAMPLES

It **doesn't** [not *don't*] matter.

The bus **doesn't** [not *don't*] stop here anymore.

fewer, less

Fewer refers to number; *less* refers to quantity. *Fewer* tells "how many"; *less* tells "how much."

EXAMPLES

There were **fewer** bushels of corn harvested this year than last.

The result is **less** grain for the markets.

good, well

Good is always an adjective. Never use *good* to modify a verb; use *well,* which is an adverb.

NONSTANDARD
Mica ran good in the race.

STANDARD
Mica ran **well** in the race.

Well is used as an adjective to mean "healthy."

EXAMPLE
You look **well.**

Feel good and *feel well* mean different things. *Feel good* means "to feel happy or pleased." *Feel well* simply means "to feel healthy."

EXAMPLES
The hat made him look **good.**

I didn't feel **well,** so I went to bed.

The use of *good* as an adverb is increasing in conversational English, but it should not be used that way in writing.

had ought, hadn't ought

Unlike other verbs, *ought* is not used with *had.*

NONSTANDARD
Vera had ought to be more careful; she hadn't ought to leave her tools lying around.

STANDARD
Vera **ought** to be more careful; she **ought not** to leave her tools lying around.

haven't but, haven't only

In these expressions *but* and *only* convey a negative idea. Avoid using them with *not* in formal writing.

INFORMAL
I haven't but one essay left to type.

FORMAL
I **have but** one essay left to type.
I **have only** one essay left to type.

learn, teach

Learn means "to acquire knowledge." *Teach* means "to instruct" or "to show how."

EXAMPLE
My uncle **taught** me to drive a car; I **am learning** to drive a tractor now.

like, as

Like is a preposition. In informal English, *like* is often used as a conjunction meaning "as." In formal English, always use *as*.

EXAMPLES
It is just **like** her to send me a get-well card. [The preposition *like* introduces the pronoun *her*.]
You should do **as** your dentist recommends and floss your teeth. [*Your dentist recommends* is a clause and needs the subordinating conjunction *as* to introduce it.]

like, as if

In formal written English, *like* should not be used for the compound conjunctions *as if* or *as though*.

EXAMPLE
The wallet looks **as though** [not *like*] it had been dropped in a mud puddle.

no, none, nothing

Do not use the words *no, none,* and *nothing* with another negative.

NONSTANDARD
That kettle doesn't have no lid.

STANDARD
That kettle has **no** lid.
That kettle **doesn't have any** lid.

NONSTANDARD
She doesn't do nothing but complain.

STANDARD
She **doesn't do anything** but complain.
She **does nothing** but complain.

NONSTANDARD
I looked for twine, but I couldn't find none.

STANDARD
I looked for twine, but I **couldn't find any.**
I looked for twine, but I **could find none.**

same

Same is used as an adjective (the *same* day, the *same* person) and as a pronoun (more of the *same*). In the latter use, *same* should always be used with *the*.

NONSTANDARD
We found the exhibit and enjoyed same.

STANDARD
We found the exhibit and enjoyed it.

shall, will

Some people prefer to use *shall* with first person pronouns and *will* with second and third person pronouns in the future and future perfect tenses. Nowadays, most Americans do not make this distinction. *Will* is acceptable in the first person as well as in the other two.

than, then

Do not confuse these words. *Than* is a conjunction; it is used to make comparisons. *Then* is an adverb; it tells about time.

EXAMPLES
Your hair is longer **than** mine.
We planted radishes. **Then** we planted peas.

which, that, who

The relative pronoun *who* refers to people only; *which* refers to things only; *that* refers to either people or things and is used to begin a restrictive clause, that is, one that is essential to the meaning of the sentence.

EXAMPLES
Here is the clerk **who** will fill your order. [person]
I need this tool, **which** I use in my work. [thing]
These brackets are ones **that** will hold shelves. [thing, introducing an essential clause]
The dealer is a person **that** enjoys the hardware business. [person, introducing an essential clause]

THE RULES FOR CAPITALIZATION

First Words
1. **Capitalize the first word in every sentence.**

   EXAMPLES
   Many sights along the road were delightful. **O**ne night we saw two fawns feeding by the highway.

   Traditionally, the first word of a line of poetry is capitalized.

   EXAMPLE
   I wandered lonely as a cloud
   That floats on high o'er vales and hills,
   When all at once I saw a crowd,
   A host, of golden daffodils.

   —from "I Wandered Lonely as a Cloud,"
   William Wordsworth

   Some writers do not follow these practices. When you are quoting, use capital letters exactly as they are used in the source of the quotation.

Pronoun *I*
2. **Capitalize the pronoun *I*.**

   EXAMPLE
   Bill and **I** went to Maine.

Proper Nouns and Proper Adjectives
3. **Capitalize proper nouns and proper adjectives.**

   Common nouns name people, places, and things. **Proper nouns** name a particular person, place, or thing. Proper adjectives are formed from proper nouns.

   Common nouns are not capitalized unless they begin a sentence or a direct quotation or are included in a title (see pages 1027, 1032). Proper nouns are always capitalized.

   COMMON NOUNS
   a **c**omposer, a **l**anguage, a **k**ing, a **s**ea

   PROPER NOUNS
   Wagner, **L**atin, **E**dward VIII, **A**tlantic

   PROPER ADJECTIVES
   Wagnerian soprano, **L**atin poetry, **E**dwardian design

   Some proper names consist of more than one word. In these names, short prepositions (generally, fewer than five letters) and articles are not capitalized.

   EXAMPLES
   Museum **o**f Modern Art
   Alexander **t**he Great

   Proper nouns and adjectives sometimes lose their capitals through frequent usage.

   ampere, **v**enetian blinds

   To find out whether a noun should be capitalized, check in a dictionary. The dictionary will tell you if a word should always be capitalized or if it should be capitalized only in certain uses.

Names of People
4. **Capitalize the names of people.**

   EXAMPLES
   Marta **S**amoza, **J**ohn **D**river

Geographical Names
5. **Capitalize geographical names.**

   TOWNS, CITIES, COUNTIES, TOWNSHIPS
   Denver, **S**eattle, **Z**urich, **R**ichmond, **D**unbar, **O**range **C**ounty, **O**ld **B**ridge Township

   STATES, PROVINCES, COUNTRIES
   Maryland, **G**eorgia, **O**ntario, **F**rance, **S**witzerland

   REGIONS
   the **W**est, the **S**outh, the **N**ortheast, **N**ew **E**ngland

   Words such as *north, west,* and *southeast* are not capitalized when they indicate direction.

   EXAMPLES
   She lives somewhere **n**orth of here.
   We spent Saturday afternoon driving **w**est.

   However, these words are capitalized when they name a particular place.

   EXAMPLES
   She is living somewhere in the **N**ortheast.
   I spent my vacation traveling in the **S**outhwest.

   CONTINENTS
   South **A**merica, **A**ntarctica, **A**sia, **A**ustralia, **A**frica

   ISLANDS, MOUNTAINS, BODIES OF WATER
   Long **I**sland, the **G**reater **A**ntilles, **M**ont **B**lanc, the **C**atskills, **P**acific **O**cean, **R**appahannock **R**iver

PARKS
Queen Elizabeth Park, Devil's Lake State Park

ROADS, HIGHWAYS, STREETS
Route 211, Interstate 81, Garden State Parkway, Atlantic Avenue, Corey Street

In a hyphenated number, the second word begins with a small letter.

EXAMPLES
Thirty-third Street, Twenty-first Avenue

Organizations

6. **Capitalize names of organizations, businesses, institutions, and government bodies.**

The word *party* is usually written without a capital letter when it follows a proper adjective.

EXAMPLES
Republican party, Democratic party

BUSINESSES
International Business Machines, Exxon Corporation, Ford Motor Company

INSTITUTIONS, ORGANIZATIONS
United States Naval Academy, Yale University, World Bank, Federal Communications Commission

Do not capitalize words like *hotel, theater, college, high school,* and *post office* unless they are part of a proper name.

EXAMPLES
Lee High School   a high school
Joyce Theater   a theater

GOVERNMENT BODIES
Congress, Senate, Department of State

Historical Events

7. **Capitalize the names of historical events and periods, special events, and calendar items.**

HISTORICAL EVENTS AND PERIODS
Taiping Rebellion, World War II, Stone Age

SPECIAL EVENTS
Olympic Games, Super Bowl, World Series

CALENDAR ITEMS
Monday, December, Labor Day, Valentine's Day

Nationalities and Races

8. **Capitalize the names of nationalities, races, and peoples.**

EXAMPLES
American, German, Irish, Mayan, Slavic, Sioux

Brand Names

9. **Capitalize the brand names of business products. Do not capitalize the noun that often follows the brand name.**

EXAMPLES
Xerox copiers, Chrysler automobile, Pyrex pie plate

Particular Places, Things, Events

10. **Capitalize the names of ships, planets, monuments, awards, and any other particular places, things, or events.**

SHIPS, TRAINS, AIRCRAFT, SPACECRAFT
the *Titanic,* the *U.S.S. Missouri,* the *Metroliner, Saturn V,* the *Atlantis*

PLANETS, STARS
Saturn, Rigel, the Big Dipper

Sun, moon and *earth* are not capitalized unless they are listed with other heavenly bodies.

MONUMENTS, MEMORIALS, BUILDINGS
Lincoln Memorial, Washington Monument, Empire State Building, Sears Tower, St. Paul's Cathedral, Wrigley Building

AWARDS
Nobel Prize, Emmy Award, Pulitzer Prize

Specific Courses, Languages

11. **Do *not* capitalize names of school subjects, except for languages or course names followed by a number.**

EXAMPLE
I am taking English literature, world history, Typing I, Latin II, and American history.

Do *not* capitalize the name of a class (*freshman, sophomore, junior, senior*) unless it is used as part of a proper noun.

EXAMPLE
All juniors should meet after the assembly to discuss the Junior-Senior Prom.

Titles of People

12. Capitalize the title of a person when it comes before a name.

EXAMPLES

President Grant, **K**ing Faisal, **M**s. Johnson

Do not capitalize a title used alone or following a person's name, especially if the title is preceded by *a* or *the*.

EXAMPLE

We discussed the problem with the **k**ing of England.

13. Capitalize words showing family relationship when used with a person's name but *not* when preceded by a possessive.

EXAMPLES

Could I speak with **A**unt Doris or with **C**ousin Bill?
My **c**ousin Dana went skiing.

Titles of Literary and Other Creative Works

14. Capitalize the first and last words and all important words in titles of books, periodicals, poems, stories, historical documents, movies, television programs, works of art, and musical compositions.

Unimportant words in a title are
articles: *a, an, the*
short prepositions (fewer than five letters): *of, to, for, from*
coordinating conjunctions: *and, but, so, nor, or, yet, for*

BOOKS
Anna Karenina, The Mayor of Casterbridge

PERIODICALS
Harper's, Reader's Digest, Newsweek, TV Guide

POEMS
"The **R**aven," "**O**de **o**n **a** **G**recian **U**rn"

STORIES
"The **M**ost **D**angerous **G**ame," "The **L**ady, **o**r the **T**iger?"

HISTORICAL DOCUMENTS
Constitution, **M**agna **C**arta, **B**ill **o**f **R**ights

TELEVISION PROGRAMS
MacNeil-Lehrer Report, The Simpsons, L.A. Law

WORKS OF ART, MUSICAL COMPOSITIONS
The Wood Gatherers, Portrait of a Youth, New World Symphony, "**A**merica the **B**eautiful"

The words *a, an,* and *the* written before a title are capitalized only when they are the first word of a title.

EXAMPLES
A Bell for Adano, The Hobbit, The Oregon Trail

Before the names of magazines and newspapers, *a, an,* and *the* are usually not capitalized.

EXAMPLE
Did you buy a copy of the *Atlantic* today?

Religions

15. Capitalize names of religions and their followers, holy celebrations, holy writings, and specific deities.

RELIGIONS AND FOLLOWERS, SPECIFIC DEITIES
Judaism, **I**slam, **M**ormon, **G**od, **B**rahma

HOLY DAYS AND SEASONS, HOLY WRITINGS
Hanukkah, **R**amadan, **G**ood **F**riday, **Y**om **K**ippur, the **B**ible, **K**oran, **U**panishads, the **N**ew **T**estament

The word *god* is not capitalized when it refers to the several gods of ancient mythology.

EXAMPLE
She loved to read stories about the Greek **g**ods.

PUNCTUATION

End Marks

End marks—*periods, question marks,* and *exclamation points*—are used to indicate the purpose of a sentence.

1. **Use a period to end a statement (*or* declarative sentence).**

   EXAMPLES
   I bought three cucumbers.
   Ron asked me what I wanted.
   A kitten appeared at our farmhouse door last week.

   Notice in the second example that a declarative sentence containing an indirect question is followed by a period.

2. **Use a question mark to end a question (*or* an interrogative sentence).**

   EXAMPLES
   Is this bridge closed?
   Has there been a flood?
   Whose car is that?

   A direct question may have the same word order as a declarative sentence. Since it is a question, however, it is followed by a question mark.

   EXAMPLES
   You are going anyway?
   It is raining?

TIPS FOR WRITERS

Be sure to distinguish between a declarative sentence that contains an indirect question and an interrogative sentence, which asks a direct question.

INDIRECT QUESTION
Miranda asked me what my name was. [declarative]

DIRECT QUESTION
Miranda Quigley asked Tony, "What is your last name?" [interrogative]

---

3. **Use an exclamation point to end an exclamation—that is, a statement that shows strong feeling. Use an exclamation point after an interjection—that is, a word that shows strong feeling.**

EXAMPLES
The team just won!
Aren't you amazed!

EXAMPLES
Wow! What a meal!
Whee!

4. **Use a period or exclamation point to end an imperative sentence.**

When an imperative sentence makes a request, it is generally followed by a period. Imperative sentences, particularly commands, may also show strong feeling. In such cases, an exclamation point should be used.

EXAMPLES
Please don't go.
Don't go!

Sometimes, a command or request is stated in the form of a question. Because of the purpose, however, the sentence is really an imperative sentence and is followed by a period or an exclamation point.

EXAMPLES
May I give you some advice.
Will you tell me!

5. **Use a period after an abbreviation.**

Personal Names: T. S. Eliot, O. Henry
Titles Used with Names: Mr., Ms., Mrs., Dr., Prof.
States: Ala., Mo., Fla., Minn., N.C.
Time of Day: A.M., P.M.
Years: B.C., A.D.
Addresses: Ave., St., Rd., Blvd., Pkwy.
Organizations and Companies: Assn., Co., Inc.
Units of Measure: lb., oz., in., ft., yd., mi.

Abbreviations for government agencies and international organizations and some other frequently used abbreviations are written without periods. Abbreviations in the metric system are often written without periods, especially in science books.

EXAMPLES
TV, IQ, FM, IRS, UN, rpm, dm, cm, mm, kg

The two-letter state abbreviations without periods are used only when the ZIP code number is included.

EXAMPLE
New York, NY 10128

If you are unsure about whether to use periods with an abbreviation, look in a dictionary.

Commas

1. **Use commas to separate items in a series.**

   Notice in the following examples that the number of commas in a series is one less than the number of items in the series.

   EXAMPLES
   The pencils, pens, and pads were missing. [words]
   The sunlight played on the walls, on the lawn, and in the treetops. [phrases]
   You who have decorated the halls, who have written invitations, and who have planned the entertainment deserve praise for your efforts. [clauses]

   When the last two items in a series are joined by *and,* you may omit the comma before the *and* if the comma is not needed to clarify the meaning.

   CLEAR WITH COMMA OMITTED
   The train stops at Chatham, Morristown and Dover.

   NOT CLEAR WITH COMMA OMITTED
   Our yearbook staff has editors for music, theater, sports, academic and social events. [How many editors are there, four or five? Does one person handle academic and social events together, or is there an editor for each one?]

   CLEAR WITH COMMA INCLUDED
   Our yearbook staff has editors for music, theater, sports, academic, and social events. [five editors]

   Some words—such as *bread and butter, table and chairs*—are often used in pairs and usually are considered one item when they appear in a series.

EXAMPLE
My favorite drinks are cream soda, coffee, and **tea and honey.**

2. **If all items in a series are joined by *and* or *or,* do not use commas to separate them.**

   EXAMPLES
   I bought **tea and coffee and milk.**
   Frank or Kate or Luisa will provide the donation.

3. **Independent clauses in a series are usually separated by semicolons. Short independent clauses, however, may be separated by commas.**

   EXAMPLES
   As the show continued, armies of tap-dancers flooded the stage; complex rhythms were heard; arms and legs moved in unison.
   Tap-dancers flooded the stage, complex rhythms were heard, and arms and legs moved in unison.

4. **Use commas to separate two or more adjectives preceding a noun.**

   EXAMPLE
   Have you finished reading that **new, exciting** novel?

   When the last adjective in a series is thought of as part of the noun, the comma before the adjective is omitted.

   EXAMPLES
   We just built a **new recreation room.**
   I had **hot, nourishing vegetable soup** for lunch last Friday.

   You can use two tests to determine whether an adjective and a noun form a unit.

   TEST 1:
   Insert the word *and* between the adjectives. If *and* fits sensibly between the adjectives, use a comma. In the first example sentence, *and* cannot be logically inserted: *new and recreation room.* In the second sentence, *and* sounds logical between the first two adjectives (*hot and nourishing*) but not between the second and third adjectives (*nourishing and vegetable*).

   TEST 2:
   Change the order of the adjectives. If the order of the adjectives can be reversed sensibly, use a comma. *Nourishing, hot vegetable soup* makes

sense, but *vegetable, hot, nourishing soup* and *recreation new room* do not.

5. Use commas before *and, but, or, nor, for, so,* and *yet* when they join independent clauses.

Do not be misled by compound verbs, which often make a sentence look as though it contains two independent clauses.

COMPOUND SENTENCE
Mother made lentil soup, and **Father made fresh biscuits.** [two independent clauses]

SIMPLE SENTENCE
Father **mixed** the dough and then **greased** the pan. [one subject with a compound verb]

In the following correctly punctuated compound sentences, notice that independent clauses appear on both sides of the coordinating conjunctions.

EXAMPLES
He turned the ignition on, and **the car started.**
It is only 3 o'clock, yet **the sky is dark.**

TIPS FOR WRITERS
A comma is always used before *for, so,* and *yet* joining two independent clauses. The comma may be omitted, however, before *and, but, or,* or *nor* when the independent clauses are very short and when there is no chance of confusion.

EXAMPLES
The train was late, so we missed our bus.
I read the book and I saw the movie too.

---

6. Use commas to set off nonessential clauses and nonessential participial phrases.

A *nonessential* (or *nonrestrictive*) clause or participial phrase adds information that is not necessary to the main idea in the sentence. Omitting such a clause or phrase will not change the meaning of the sentence.

NONESSENTIAL CLAUSES
Dr. Frank Miller, **who is my dentist,** plays viola in our city orchestra.
This magazine, **to which I subscribe,** always has several good short stories.

NONESSENTIAL PHRASES
The dog, **hunting for its bone,** dug holes in the yard.
Our house, **built in the eighteenth century,** is very old.

When a clause or phrase is necessary to the meaning of a sentence—that is, when it tells *which ones*—the clause or phrase is *essential* (or *restrictive*), and commas are *not* used.

Notice how the meaning of each sentence below changes when the essential clause or phrase is omitted.

ESSENTIAL CLAUSES
All students **who need bus passes** must go to the principal's office.
The cereal **that we eat** has no sugar in it.

An adjective clause beginning with *that* is always essential.

ESSENTIAL PHRASES
Seniors **that hope to graduate** must get passing grades on all their tests.
The novels **that were written by Dickens** are all shelved on the second floor.

7. Use a comma after introductory words such as *well, yes, no,* and *why* when they begin a sentence.

EXAMPLES
No, we've never been to Montana.
Ah, the mountain stream is so cold!

8. Use a comma after an introductory participial phrase.

EXAMPLES
Hoping for a victory, the coach changed pitchers three times.
Excited by their win, the team could not stop talking about it.

9. Use a comma after a series of introductory prepositional phrases.

EXAMPLES
At the end of the dry, hot summer, the reservoir was far from full.
By the end of the dry winter, the water shortage was a problem.

A short introductory prepositional phrase does not require a comma unless the comma is necessary to make the meaning clear.

EXAMPLES

In winter we have more snow than rain. [No comma is needed since the meaning is clear.]
In winter, snow is common. [The comma is necessary to avoid reading *winter snow*.]

10. **Use a comma after an introductory adverb clause.**

EXAMPLE

Because there was no oil in the lamp, I could not light the wick.

11. **Use commas to set off elements that interrupt the sentence.**

EXAMPLES

There is, **in fact,** no right answer.
Nevertheless, the trip is necessary.
I offered to go with him, **of course.**

12. **Use commas to set off appositives and appositive phrases.**

EXAMPLE

Mr. Evans, **her track coach,** expected her to win.

When an appositive has no modifiers and is closely related to the word preceding it, it should not be set off by commas.

EXAMPLE

My friend **Eartha** is a potter.

13. **Use commas to set off words used in direct address.**

EXAMPLES

Kuri, I'd like to introduce you to Lisa.
I will memorize that sonata for next week, **Ms. Samson.**
Your grades, **Dena,** have improved.

14. **Use a comma to separate items in dates and addresses.**

EXAMPLES

My sister moved to **San Francisco, California,** on **Thursday, September 26, 1991.**
On **September 26, 1991,** my sister's address became **1592 Union Street, San Francisco, CA 94123.**

Notice that no comma separates the month and day (September 26) or the house number and street name (1592 Union Street) because each is considered one item. Also, the ZIP code is not separated from the name of the state by a comma: San Francisco, CA 94123.

15. **Use a comma after the salutation of a friendly letter and after the closing of any letter.**

EXAMPLES

Dear Ms. Acevedo,   My dear Luna,
Sincerely yours,   Very truly yours,

16. **Use a comma after a name followed by an abbreviation such as *Jr., Sr.,* and *M.D.***

EXAMPLES

Lloyd Elmore, **Jr.**   Lt. Marc Stein, **U.S.M.C.**

Semicolons

1. **Use a semicolon between independent clauses in a sentence if they are not joined by *and, but, or, nor, for, so,* or *yet.***

Notice in the following example that the semicolon replaces the comma and the conjunction joining the independent clauses.

EXAMPLE

First I washed the lettuce, **and** then I peeled the potatoes and carrots.
First I washed the lettuce; then I peeled the potatoes and carrots.

A semicolon can be used between two closely related independent clauses.

EXAMPLE

Leon organized his note cards. Then he began to make an outline.
Leon organized his note cards; then he began to make an outline.

2. **Use a semicolon between independent clauses joined by conjunctive adverbs or transitional expressions.**

EXAMPLES

Melinda was late; **however,** the train was also not on time.
The house is quite large; **as a result,** cleaning it takes a long time.

3. **Use a semicolon (rather than a comma) to separate independent clauses joined by a coordinating conjunction when there are commas within the clauses.**

EXAMPLE

Opening the cookbook and thumbing through the pages in search of a good recipe, Jason read each one carefully, checking the lists of ingredients; but, unfortunately, Jason didn't understand the instructions.

4. Use a semicolon between items in a series if the items contain commas.

EXAMPLE

Performances are scheduled for **Tuesday, August 20; Thursday, August 22; Saturday, August 24; and Sunday, August 25.**

Colons

1. Use a colon before a list of items, especially after expressions like *the following* and *as follows*.

EXAMPLES

You will take **the following courses:** Acting I, basic scene design, makeup, and fencing.
The menu will be **as follows:** fruit cup, tossed salad, roast chicken, peas, baked potato, and rolls.

2. Use a colon between the hour and the minute.

EXAMPLES

9:15 P.M.   10:45 A.M.

3. Use a colon between chapter and verse in referring to passages from the Bible.

EXAMPLES

Luke 2:7   Psalms 91:1-7

4. Use a colon after the salutation of a business letter.

EXAMPLES

Dear Ms. Mercado: To Whom It May Concern:

Italics

When writing or typing, indicate italics by underlining. If your composition were to be printed, the underlined words would be set in italics. For example, if you type

Stephen Sondheim wrote <u>Into the Woods</u>.

the sentence would be printed like this:

Stephen Sondheim wrote *Into the Woods*.

If you use a personal computer, you can probably set words in italics yourself.

1. Use italics (underlining) for titles of books, plays, films, periodicals, works of art, long musical compositions, long poems, television programs, ships, aircraft, and so on.

BOOK: *Two Years Before the Mast*
PLAY: *Macbeth*
FILMS: *The Band Wagon, Singin' in the Rain*
PERIODICALS: *Life, Newsweek*
WORKS OF ART: *Musical Forms, The City*
LONG MUSICAL COMPOSITIONS: Mahler's *Third Symphony, Appalachian Spring*
TELEVISION SERIES: *Frontline, Golden Girls*
LONG POEM: *Hiawatha*
SHIPS: *Pequod, USS Intrepid*
AIRCRAFT, SPACECRAFT: *Skylab, Soyuz 19*

The words *a, an,* and *the* written before a title are italicized only when they are part of the title. Before the names of newspapers and magazines, however, they are not italicized, even if they are capitalized on the front page of the newspaper or on the cover of the magazine.

EXAMPLE

Do you read the *New Republic?*
In Chicago I saw the original of Picasso's *The Old Guitarist.*
I subscribe to the *Chicago Tribune.*

2. Use italics (underlining) for words, letters, and figures referred to as such and for foreign words.

EXAMPLES

The word ***algebra*** comes from Arabic.
The word ***Hawaii*** has two *a*'s and two *i*'s.
The *7* on my application looks like a *1.*

Quotation Marks

1. Use quotation marks to enclose a direct quotation—a person's exact words.

EXAMPLES

Jamie said, "Honesty is the best policy."
"I think so too," agreed his brother.

2. Begin a direct quotation with a capital letter.

EXAMPLES

After the game, the coach said, "**M**y team has never played better."
Father said, "**T**here on the table, no doubt."
[Although this quotation is not a sentence, it is Father's complete remark.]

If the quotation is a fragment of the original quotation, it may begin with a small letter.

EXAMPLE
Is beauty, as Emerson wrote, "in the eye of the beholder"? [The quotation is obviously only a phrase from Emerson's poem.]

3. **When a quoted sentence is divided into two parts by an interrupting expression, begin the second part with a small letter.**

EXAMPLE
"I hear," she said, "that you are playing the leading role."

If the second part of a quotation is a new sentence, a period (not a comma) follows the interrupting expression; and the second part begins with a capital letter.

EXAMPLE
"We rode on the merry-go-round," Ralph said. "The parachute jump was not working."

4. **Set off a direct quotation from the rest of the sentence by commas or by a question mark or an exclamation point.**

EXAMPLES
The dentist said, "Brush your teeth at least twice a day," as he gave me a toothbrush.
Alan shouted, "Have a happy holiday!"

5. **Place commas and periods inside closing quotation marks.**

EXAMPLES
"I haven't seen the movie yet," said Felicia, "but I understand many people liked it."
We took turns reading lines from "The Death of the Hired Man," by Robert Frost.
I think it was Plato who wrote, "The life that is unexamined is not worth living."

6. **Place semicolons and colons outside closing quotation marks.**

EXAMPLES
John Keats wrote, "A thing of beauty is a joy forever"; I wonder in which poem that line appears.
The following students were nominated for "associate membership": Douglas Green, Felix Castillo, and Katrina Hansen.

7. **If the quotation is a question or an exclamation, place question marks and exclamation points inside the closing quotation marks. Otherwise, place them outside.**

EXAMPLES
"Did you win the contest?" Niko asked as I walked into the room.
"Yes, I won first place!" I exclaimed.
What does it mean to "toe the mark"?

8. **When you write dialogue (a conversation), begin a new paragraph every time the speaker changes.**

EXAMPLE
"Who are you?" the boy said. "What are you doing here?"
"Trying to get warm," the young man said, the voice hoarse, the speech American.
—Kay Boyle

9. **When a quoted passage consists of more than one paragraph, put quotation marks at the beginning of each paragraph and at the end of the entire passage. Do not put quotation marks after any paragraph but the last.**

EXAMPLE
"Last Saturday," the letter began, "I arrived for my annual summer visit at my grandparents' farm. The farm, as you know, is a large one in Illinois. Imagine me taking care of horses, pigs, and chickens!
"To tell you the truth, I love it, and I am thinking of going to school here, so that I can help my grandparents all year long."

10. **Use single quotation marks to enclose a quotation within a quotation.**

EXAMPLE
Franco, our exchange student, asked me, "What does the phrase 'in one ear and out the other' mean?"

11. **Use quotation marks to enclose titles of articles, short stories, essays, poems, songs, individual episodes of TV shows, chapters, and other parts of books or periodicals.**

EXAMPLES
Please read the essay entitled "The Dog That Bit People" by James Thurber.
The poem "Mending Wall" is one I know well.

Apostrophes

With the Possessive Case

1. **Add an apostrophe and an** *s* **to form the possessive case of a singular noun. The** *possessive* **of a noun or pronoun shows ownership or relationship.**

   EXAMPLES
   the **lawyer's** briefcase   the **team's** mascot
   the **principal's** office   **Earl's** bicycle
   one **hour's** time   the **coin's** value

2. **Add only an apostrophe to a proper name if the name has two or more syllables or if the addition of** *'s* **would make the name awkward to pronounce.**

   EXAMPLES
   Mrs. Divilbiss' daughter-in-law
   Massachusetts' capital

3. **Add only an apostrophe to form the possessive case of a plural noun ending in** *s.*

   EXAMPLES
   states' governors   **passengers'** comfort

   Although most plural nouns end in *s*, some are irregular. To form the possessive case of a plural noun that does not end in *s*, add an apostrophe and an *s*.

   EXAMPLES
   mice's tails   **children's** clothing
   women's rights   **men's** neckties

4. **Add an apostrophe and an** *s* **to form the possessive case of an indefinite pronoun.**

   EXAMPLES
   nobody**'s** fault   someone**'s** glove
   another**'s** wish   neither**'s** response

TIPS FOR WRITERS

Do not use an apostrophe to form the *plural* of a noun. Remember that the apostrophe shows ownership or relationship.

INCORRECT
The two runners' ran the race in identical times.

CORRECT
The two **runners** ran the race in identical times.
The two **runners'** times for the race were identical.

---

5. **For possessives of compound words, names of organizations and businesses, and words showing joint possession, make only the last word possessive in form.**

   COMPOUND WORDS
   city council's decision   **brother-in-law's** car

   ORGANIZATIONS
   Department of Agriculture's pamphlet list
   National Kidney Foundation's home office
   ASPCA's charitable work

   BUSINESSES
   Lever Brothers' products   **Kraft's** cheeses

   JOINT POSSESSION
   Lou and Pat**'s** record collection [The collection belongs to both Lou and Pat.]

   When one of the words showing joint possession is a pronoun, both words should be possessive in form.

   EXAMPLES
   Don's and **your** travel plans [not *Don and your travel plans*] got fouled up.
   Bob's and **my** batting averages are higher this year than last.

6. **When two or more persons possess something individually, make each of their names possessive in form.**

   EXAMPLES
   Alejandro's and **Marcelo's** poems were long. [the poems of two different people]
   Dana's and **Rob's** projects earned them each a good grade. [individual, not joint, possession]

With Contractions

7. **Use an apostrophe to show where letters or numbers have been omitted in a contraction.**

   A *contraction* is a shortened form of a word, a figure, or a group of words. The apostrophes in contractions indicate where letters or numerals have been left out.

   EXAMPLES
   who is . . . who's   we are . . . we're
   He is . . . he's   were not . . . weren't
   1991 . . . '91   is not . . . isn't

EXCEPTIONS
will not . . . won't
shall not . . . shan't

8. **Use an apostrophe and an _s_ to form the plurals of lowercase letters, some uppercase letters, numerals, and some words referred to as words.**

EXAMPLES
Good writers dot their _i_'s and cross their _t_'s.
Her writing always has too many _so_'s.

Hyphens

1. **Use a hyphen in some compound nouns.**

EXAMPLES
two-step, great-uncle, daughter-in-law

2. **Use a hyphen to divide a word at the end of a line.**

EXAMPLE
So far as I know, French is her **na-tive** language.

Divide an already hyphenated word only at a hyphen.

INCORRECT
My brother has started a toy-re-pair business.

CORRECT
My brother has started a **toy-repair** business.

INCORRECT
Janet has old-fash-ioned ideas sometimes.

CORRECT
Janet has **old-fashioned** ideas sometimes.

Do not divide a word so that one letter stands alone.

INCORRECT
We return to the a-forementioned point.

CORRECT
We return to the **afore-mentioned** point.

3. **Use a hyphen with compound numbers from _twenty-one_ to _ninety-nine_ and with fractions used as adjectives.**

EXAMPLES
thirty-two pennies
two-thirds cup [but _two thirds_ of the liquid]

4. **Use a hyphen with the prefixes _ex-, self-, all-,_ and with the suffix _-elect,_ and with all prefixes before a proper noun or proper adjective.**

EXAMPLES
ex-member   **pro-**British
mid-February   president-**elect**

Dashes
Use a dash to indicate an abrupt break in thought or speech or an unfinished statement or question.

Many words and phrases are used parenthetically: that is, they break into the main thought of a sentence. Most parenthetical elements are set off by commas.

EXAMPLES
You will, **nonetheless,** be invited to speak.
The topic, **she realized,** did not interest her.

Sometimes, however, these elements demand a stronger emphasis. In such cases, a dash is used.

EXAMPLES
Every time I hear that melody—but we have more important things to discuss.
A touch of spring—could it be spring?—was in the air that day.

Parentheses
Use parentheses to enclose material that is added to a sentence but is not of major importance.

EXAMPLES
Our net profit **(gross profits less expenses)** has grown each year.
The Italian Renaissance painter Botticelli **(1444–1510)** was not a popular artist in his own time.

Punctuation marks are used within parentheses when they belong with the parenthetical matter. However, a punctuation mark is not placed within parentheses if the mark belongs to the sentence as a whole.

EXAMPLES
Print your name legibly. (Do not use pencil.)
This new frying pan has a special coating (it is manufactured in Germany).

SPELLING

Words with *ie* and *ei*

1. **Write *ie* when the sound is long *e*, except after *c*.**

EXAMPLES

achieve	shield	ceiling	receive	conceit
chief	thief	liege	lien	wield
grief	belief	niece	deceive	yield

2. **Write *ei* when the sound is not long *e*.**

EXAMPLES

neighbor	weigh	surfeit
reign	eight	height
vein	foreign	sleigh

EXCEPTIONS
friend, mischief, financier, kerchief

Words with *-cede, -ceed,* and *-sede*

3. **Only one English word ends in *-sede*: *supersede*; only three words end in *-ceed*: *exceed, proceed,* and *succeed*; all other words with this sound end in *-cede*.**

EXAMPLES

precede	recede	secede
intercede	concede	accede

Adding Prefixes

4. **When a prefix is added to a word, the spelling of the original word itself remains the same.**

EXAMPLES
pre + digest = **pre**digest
il + logical = **il**logical
mis + lay = **mis**lay
im + measurable = **im**measurable

Adding Suffixes

5. **When the suffix *-ness* or *-ly* is added to a word, the spelling of the original word remains the same.**

EXAMPLES
quick + ly = quick**ly**   fair + ness = fair**ness**

EXCEPTIONS
Words ending in *y* usually change the *y* to *i* before *-ness* and *-ly*:

*hearty—heart**i**ness; ready—read**i**ly*

But most one-syllable adjectives ending in *y* follow rule 5: *sly—slyness; dry—dryly*
True, due, and *whole* drop the final *e* before *-ly*: truly, duly, wholly

6. **Drop the final silent *e* before adding a suffix that begins with a vowel.**

EXAMPLES
note + ing = noting   debate + able = debatable
idle + ed = idled   desire + ous = desirous

EXCEPTIONS
1. Keep the final silent *e* in words ending in *ce* or *ge* before a suffix that begins with *a* or *o*: *salvageable, peaceable*
2. To avoid confusion with other words, keep the final silent *e* in some words: *dyeing* and *dying, singeing* and *singing.*

7. **Keep the final silent *e* before adding a suffix that begins with a consonant.**

EXAMPLES
nine + ty = nin**e**ty   fine + ly = fin**e**ly
fate + ful = fat**e**ful   case + ment = cas**e**ment

EXCEPTIONS
nine + th = ninth   argue + ment = argument

8. **When a word ends in *y* preceded by a consonant, change the *y* to *i* before any suffix except one beginning with *i*.**

EXAMPLES
sixty + eth = sixt**i**eth   defy + ed = def**i**ed
fury + ous = fur**i**ous   ferry + ing = ferr**y**ing

EXCEPTIONS
1. Some one-syllable words:
shy + ness = shyness
sky + ward = skyward
2. *lady* and *baby* with suffixes:
ladylike   ladyship   babyhood

9. **When a word ends in _y_ preceded by a vowel, simply add the suffix.**

EXAMPLES
pay + able = payable   boy + hood = boyhood
replay + ed = replayed   pray + ing = praying

EXCEPTIONS
day + ly = daily   pay + ed = paid
say + ed = said

Doubling Final Consonants

10. **When a word ends in a consonant, double the final consonant before a suffix that begins with a vowel only if the word: (1) has only one syllable or is accented on the last syllable, and (2) ends in a single consonant preceded by a single vowel.**

EXAMPLES
mop + ing = mo**pp**ing   occur + ed = occu**rr**ed
propel + ant = prope**ll**ant   sit + er = si**tt**er

Otherwise, simply add the suffix.

EXAMPLES
dump + ed = dump**ed**
burrow + ing = burrow**ing**
refer + ence = refer**ence**

Plurals of Nouns

11. **To form the plurals of most English nouns, add _s_.**

joke / joke**s**   package / package**s**
hedge / hedge**s**   theater / theater**s**

12. **To form the plurals of other nouns, follow these rules.**

If the noun ends in _s, x, z, ch,_ or _sh,_ add _es_.

pass / pass**es**   waltz / waltz**es**   thatch / thatch**es**
wax / wax**es**   rash / rash**es**

If the noun ends in _y_ preceded by a consonant, change the _y_ to _i_ and add _es_.

cry / cr**ies**   gantry / gantr**ies**   worry / worr**ies**

EXCEPTION
The plurals of proper nouns: the _Bradys,_ the _Kerrys_

If the noun ends in _y_ preceded by a vowel add _s_.

turkey / turkey**s**   tray / tray**s**   key / key**s**

For some nouns ending in _f_ or _fe,_ change the _f_ to _v_ and add _s_ or _es_.

Noticing how the plural is pronounced will help you remember whether to change the _f_ to _v_.

bluff / bluff**s**   wolf / wol**ves**   half / hal**ves**

If the noun ends in _o_ preceded by a consonant, add _es_.

echo / echo**es**   potato / potato**es**

If the noun ends in _o_ preceded by a vowel, add _s_.

patio / patio**s**   radio / radio**s**   video / video**s**

Nouns for musical terms that end in _o_ preceded by a consonant form the plural by adding only _s_.

soprano / soprano**s**   cello / cello**s**   piano / piano**s**

A number of nouns that end in _o_ preceded by a consonant have two plural forms.

cargo   cargo**s** _or_ cargo**es**
halo   halo**s** _or_ halo**es**
zero   zero**s** _or_ zero**es**

The best way to handle plurals of words ending in _o_ preceded by a consonant is to check their spelling in a dictionary.

The plurals of some nouns are formed in irregular ways.

foot / feet   man / men   mouse / mice
child / children   tooth / teeth   ox / oxen

Some nouns have the same form in both the singular and the plural.

SINGULAR AND PLURAL
deer   moose   Burmese   Polish   sheep   Welsh

Plurals of Compound Nouns

13. **If a compound noun is written as one word, form the plural by adding _s_ or _es_.**

cupful / cupful**s**   eyelash / eyelash**es**

If a compound noun containing a noun plus a modifier is hyphenated or written as two words, make the noun plural.

brother-in-law / brother**s**-in-law
passer-by / passer**s**-by

The plurals of a few hyphenated compound nouns are irregular.

lean-to / lean-to**s**   ten-year-old / ten-year-old**s**
lead-in / lead-in**s**

Plurals of Latin and Greek Loan Words

14. **Some nouns borrowed from Latin and Greek form their plurals as in the original language.**

emphasis / emphas**es**   diagnosis / diagnos**es**
alumnus / alumn**i**

A few Latin and Greek loan words have two plural forms.

index / ind**exes** *or* ind**ices**
curriculum / curricul**a** *or* curriculum**s**

Check a dictionary to find the preferred spelling of such plurals.

Plurals of Numbers, Letters, Symbols, and Words Used as Words

15. **To form the plurals of numerals, most capital letters, symbols, and words used as words, add an** *s.*

EXAMPLES
Put the **100s** and the **Ls** in separate columns.
Do not change any **&s** to **ands.**

To prevent confusion, use an apostrophe and an *s* to form the plurals of lowercase letters, certain capital letters, and some words used as words.

EXAMPLES
Your **a's** look like **o's.**
Felix got all **A's** in mathematics.
The speaker's constant **you know's** irritated the audience.

The plurals of decades and centuries may be formed by adding an *s* or an apostrophe and an *s.*

EXAMPLES
My grandparents were in the armed services during the **'40s.**
Shakespeare wrote during the late **1500's** and early **1600's** (or **1500s** and **1600s**).

Spelling Numbers

16. **Always spell out a number that begins a sentence.**

EXAMPLE
One thousand four hundred stamps were used to send out the invitations.

17. **Within a sentence, spell out numbers that can be written in one word or two words; use numerals for other numbers.**

EXAMPLES
I have only **two** tests in the next **three** weeks.
We invited **twenty-seven** guests to the party.
Noah has recordings of **115** different compositions.

18. **Spell out numbers used to indicate order.**

EXAMPLE
My sister placed **fourth** [not 4th] in the contest.

EXCEPTION
Use numerals for dates when you include the name of the month.

EXAMPLE
School begins on September **3.** [not 3rd] [Writing *the third of September* is also correct.]

Always use numerals for years.

EXAMPLE
The Civil War ended in **1865.**

Words Often Confused

You can prevent many spelling errors by learning the difference between the words grouped together in this section. Some of them are confusing because they are *homonyms*—that is, they're pronounced alike. Others are confusing because they're spelled the same or nearly the same.

affect	[verb] *to influence* The lack of rain will surely *affect* the grain harvest.
effect	[verb] *to accomplish*; [noun] *consequence or result* The antibiotic *effected* a cure. Closing down a factory may have a major *effect* on unemployment.
all ready	[pronoun plus adjective] *everyone ready* By noon we were *all ready* to eat.

already	[adverb] *beforehand* I have *already* paid the bill.
all right	[This is the only acceptable spelling. Although the spelling *alright* appears in some dictionaries, it has not become standard usage.]
all together	*everyone in the same place* *All together* now, repeat these verbs.
altogether	*entirely* You are *altogether* right in your judgment.
complement	[noun] *something that completes or makes perfect*; [verb] *to complete or make perfect* What is the *complement* of this acute angle? That dark shade of green *complements* your eyes.
compliment	[noun] *a remark that expresses approval, praise, or admiration*; [verb] *to pay a compliment* Her *compliment* was sincere and much appreciated. Let me *compliment* you on that delightful meal.
consul	*the representative of a foreign country* The Peruvian *consul* will speak at our meeting.
council	*a group called together to accomplish a job* The advisory *council* has delegates from each district.
councilor	*a member of a council* District *councilors* voted for the hiring freeze.
counsel	[noun] *advice*; [verb] *to give advice* I came to seek your *counsel* about the dilemma. Did you *counsel* her to see another pediatrician?
counselor	*one who gives advice* My consultation with the career *counselor* was far from helpful.
des´ert	[noun] *a dry region* Wind storms in the *desert* made travel nearly impossible.
desert´	[verb] *to leave, abandon* I hope you won't *desert* us if we have a blizzard.
dessert	[noun] *the final course of a meal* *Dessert* was served on the patio.
miner	*a worker in a mine* The *miners* have just won an increase in wages.
minor	*under legal age*; also, *smaller or less important* (as opposed to *major*) *Minors* may not purchase cigarettes in any state. Only a few *minor* adjustments remain to be made.
moral	[adjective] *having to do with good or right*; [noun] *a lesson in conduct* *Moral* issues were not on the syllabus. What is the *moral* of that fable?
morale	[noun] *mental condition, spirit* The team's *morale* was lifted by the victory.
personal	*individual; private* My *personal* responsibilities are increasing.
personnel	*a group of people employed in the same work or service; a staff* Our *personnel* all have extensive experience with teen-agers and their problems.
principal	[noun] *head of a school*; [adjective] *main, most important* The *principal* greeted the counselor. The *principal* concern was her high blood pressure.
principle	[noun] *a rule of conduct*; also *a law or a main fact* My father was guided by his *principles*. The *principles* of logic fascinate me.
stationary	*in a fixed position* Are the posts *stationary*?
stationery	*writing paper* The *stationery* was old and torn.
who's	[contraction of *who is, who has*] I don't know *who's* been invited. [*who has*] *Who's* going to the mall? [*who is*]
whose	[possessive of who] I don't know *whose* blue raincoat this is.

GLOSSARY

The glossary below is an alphabetical list of words found in the selections in this book. Use this glossary just as you use a dictionary—to find out the meanings of unfamiliar words. (A few technical, foreign, or more obscure words in this book are not listed here, but instead are defined for you in the footnotes that accompany each selection.)

Many words in the English language have more than one meaning. This glossary gives the meanings that apply to the words as they are used in the selections in this book. Words closely related in form and meaning are usually listed together in one entry (*acute* and *acutely*), and the definition is given for the first form.

The following abbreviations are used:

adj., adjective	**n.,** noun	**v.,** verb
adv., adverb	**pl.,** plural form	

Unless a word is very simple to pronounce, its pronunciation is given in parentheses. A guide to the pronunciation symbols appears at the bottom of each right-hand glossary page.

For more information about the words in this glossary, or about words not listed here, consult a dictionary.

abash (ə·bash′) *v.* To make ashamed and ill at ease.

abound *v.* To be plentiful; exist in large amounts or numbers.

abridge (ə·brij′) *v.* To shorten.

absolve (əb·zälv′) *v.* To free from guilt or blame.

abstain (əb·stān′) *v.* To hold oneself back; do without.

abstinence (ab′stə·nəns) *n.* The act of doing without some food, drink, or other pleasures.

abyss (ə·bis′) *n.* A deep or bottomless hole.

adage (ad′ij) *n.* An old saying.

adhere (əd·hir′) *v.* **1.** To stick; stay attached. **2.** To stay firm in supporting or approving.

adroit (ə·droit′) *adj.* Skillful.

affable (af′ə·b'l) *adj.* Pleasant, friendly, and easy to talk to. —**affability** *n.*

affluent (af′loo·wənt) *adj.* Wealthy.

aghast (ə·gast′) *adj.* Horrified.

akimbo (ə·kim′bō) *adv., adj.* With hands on hips and elbows bent outward.

alacrity (ə·lak′rə·tē) *n.* Eager willingness.

alienate (āl′yən·āt′) *v.* To make unfriendly.

allege (ə·lej′) *v.* To assert without proof.

alleviate (ə·lē′vē·āt′) *v.* To make less hard to bear.

allocate (al′ə·kāt′) *v.* To distribute or give out.

alluring (ə·loor′iŋ) *adj.* highly attractive; charming; tempting.

alluvial (ə·loo′vē·əl) *adj.* Of, found in, or made up of, sand and clay gradually deposited by moving water, as along a river bed.

aloof *adj.* Distant; reserved.

anemic (ə·nē′mik) *adj.* **1.** Deficient in red blood corpuscles. **2.** Weak and sickly.

animosity (an′ə·mäs′ə·tē) *n.* Strong dislike or hatred.

annihilate (ə·nī′ə·lāt′) *v.* To destroy completely. —**annihilation** *n.*

aperture (ap′ər·chər) *n.* An opening.

apex (ā′peks) *n.* **1.** The highest point. **2.** The pointed end; tip.

apparition (ap′ə·rish′ən) *n.* An unexpected or extraordinary sight, especially a strange, ghostly figure that appears suddenly. —**apparitional** *adj.*

appease *v.* To quiet, especially by giving in to the demands of.

appertain (ap′ər·tān′) *v.* To belong or be a part.

appraise *v.* To estimate the value of. —**appraisal** *n.*

appurtenances (ə·purt′n·əns·əz) *n. pl.* Equipment; accessories.

aptitude (ap′tə·tood′) *n.* A natural ability or talent.

arduous (är′joo·wəs) *adj.* Difficult; laborious.

array *v.* To place in order.

arroyo (ə·roi′ō) *n.* A dry gully or channel.

artless *adj.* **1.** Lacking skill; clumsy. **2.** Without artificiality or deceit; natural.

ascribe *v.* To regard as coming from someone.

assail (ə·sāl′) *v.* To attack.

attire (ə·tīr′) *n.* Clothes.

attribute (a′trə·byoot′) *n.* A characteristic.

audacity (ô·das′ə·tē) *n.* Shameless boldness.

augment (ôg·ment') *v.* To increase or make greater.

august (ô·gust') *adj.* Worthy of respect because of age, dignity, or high position.

autocratic (ôt'ə·krat'ik) *adj.* Ruling with absolute power; dictatorial.

avarice (av'ər·is) *n.* Greed for wealth.

baleful *adj.* Threatening harm or evil.

balm *n.* **1.** An aromatic healing ointment. **2.** Anything that heals or soothes the mind or spirit.

banal (bā'n'l, bə·nal') *adj.* Dull or trite; commonplace.

barbaric (bär·ber'ik) *adj.* Uncivilized; crude.

bard *n.* A poet.

bastion (bas'chən) *n.* Any place fortified against attack.

batholith (bath'ə·lith') *n.* A large natural rock mass.

belligerent (bə·lij'ər·ənt) *adj.* Ready or eager to fight.

bemuse (bi·myōōz') *v.* **1.** To confuse. **2.** To plunge into thought.

benediction (ben'ə·dik'shən) *n.* A blessing.

benefactor (ben'ə·fak'tər) *n.* A person who has given help.

benevolent (bə·nev'ə·lənt) *adj.* Kindly. —**benevolently** *adv.* —**benevolence** *n.*

berate (bi·rāt') *v.* To scold severely.

bereaved (bi·rēvd') *adj.* Suffering the recent death of a loved one. —**the bereaved** *n.* The survivors of a person who has recently died.

blasphemy (blas'fə·mē) *n.* Speech, writing, or action that is disrespectful of God or of anything held as divine.

blight *v.* To ruin or destroy.

bludgeon (bluj''n) *v.* **1.** To strike with, or as with, a bludgeon or club. **2.** To bully.

brigand (brig'ənd) *v.* A bandit or robber.

brisk *adj.* **1.** Quick; energetic. **2.** Sharp in manner.

bulwark (bul'wərk) *n.* A person or thing that is a strong protection.

cadaverous (kə·dav'ər·əs) *adj.* Like a cadaver or corpse; gaunt and pale.

cajole (kə·jōl') *v.* To coax with flattery.

calamity (kə·lam'ə·tē) *n.* A disaster. —**calamitous** *adj.*

callous (kal'əs) *adj.* Unfeeling; insensitive. —**callousness** *n.*

calumny (kal'əm·nē) *n.* A false statement meant to hurt someone else's reputation.

candid *adj.* Honest; frank. —**candidly** *adv.*

capital *n.* Money or property owned or used in business.

cascade *n.* A waterfall.

cataclysm (kat'ə·kliz'm) *n.* A great, violent disaster or upheaval.

cessation (se·sā'shən) *n.* A complete stop; ending.

chagrin (shə·grin') *n.* A feeling of distress caused by embarrassment, disappointment, or failure.

chasm (kaz''m) *n.* A deep crack in the earth's surface.

chastise (chas'tīz) *n.* To punish or scold. —**chastisement** *n.*

chide *v.* To scold.

citadel (sit'ə·del') *n.* A fortress for defense of a city.

clad *adj.* Dressed.

cognizance (käg'nə·zəns) *n.* Knowledge gained through observation.

commensurate (kə·men'shər·it) *adj.* Corresponding in extent; proportionate. —**commensurately** *adj.*

composure (kəm·pō'zhər) *n.* Calmness.

compulsion (kəm·pul'shən) *n.* A driving force; irresistible impulse to do something.

concord (kän'kôrd) *n.* Agreement or peace.

condolence (kən·dō'ləns) *n.* Expression of sympathy.

conjecture (kən·jek'chər) *n.* Guessing or a guess.

connive (kə·nīv') *v.* To scheme secretly. —**connivance** *n.*

consign (kən·sīn') *v.* To hand over or deliver.

contemptuous (kən·temp'choo·wəs) *adj.* Scornful. —**contemptuously** *adv.*

convulsive (kən·vul'siv) *adj.* Marked by violent spasms or shaking. —**convulsively** *adj.*

coquetry kō'ket·rē) *n.* Flirtatiousness.

corporal (kôr'pər·əl) *adj.* Of the body; bodily.

corroborate (kə·räb'ə·rāt') *v.* To confirm or support.

countenance (koun'tə·nəns) *n.* The face.

covert (kuv'ərt; kō'vərt) *adj.* Secret or hidden.

cow *v.* To fill with fear; intimidate.

coy *adj.* Pretending shyness or innocence.

credence (krēd''ns) *n.* Belief.

credulity (krə·dōō'lə·tē) *n.* A tendency to believe too readily.

crematorium (krē'mə·tôr'ē·əm) *n., pl.* **crematoria.** A building where bodies are burned.

crestfallen *adj.* Dejected; depressed.

crevice (krev'is) *n.* A narrow opening or crack.

cumulative (kyōōm'yə·lə·tiv) *adj.* Increasing by addition; accumulated.

debris (də·brē') *n.* Broken bits and pieces.

deference (def'ər·əns) *n.* A yielding in opinion, judgment, or wishes.

defile *v.* To make unclean.

deflect *v.* To turn or make go to one side; swerve.

delusion *n.* A false belief.

demeanor (di·mēn'ər) *n.* Outward behavior, especially proper behavior.

---

fat, āpe, cär; ten, ēven; is, bīte; gō, hôrn, tōōl, look; oil, out; up, fʉr; get; joy; yet; chin; she; thin, then; zh, leisure; ŋ, ring; ə for *a* in *ago*, *e* in *agent*, *i* in *sanity*, *o* in *comply*, *u* in *focus*; ' as in *able* (ā'b'l).

demoralize (di·môr'ə·līz') *adj.* **1.** To lower the morale of; weaken the spirit or courage of. **2.** To corrupt the morals of. —**demoralizing** *adj.*

denounce *v.* To inform against.

denunciation (di·nun'sē·ā'shən) *n.* The act of informing against.

deplorable (di·plôr'ə·b'l) *adj.* Very bad. —**deplorably** *adv.*

deploy (dē·ploi') *v.* To spread out or place.

deposition (dep'ə·zish'ən) *n.* The testimony of a witness.

depraved (di·prāvd') *adj.* Morally bad; corrupt.

deranged (di·rānjd') *adj.* Insane.

derisive (di·rī'siv) *adj.* Showing contempt or ridicule.

desolate (des'ə·lit) *adj.* Deserted or uninhabitable.

devoid *adj.* Completely without.

diffuse (di·fyōōs') *adj.* Spread out in every direction.

diligence (dil'ə·jəns) *n.* Constant, careful effort. —**diligent** *adj.*

dirge (dʉrj) *n.* A funeral hymn.

dirigible (dir'i·jə·b'l) *n.* A blimp or airship.

discern *v.* To perceive or recognize.

disconsolate (dis·kän'sə·lit) *adj.* So unhappy that nothing will comfort.

discretion (dis·kresh'ən) *n.* The quality of being discreet, or careful about what one does or says.

disparage (dis·par'ij) *v.* To speak slightingly of; show disrespect for. —**disparagement** *n.*

disquiet *v.* To make anxious, uneasy, or restless.

dissemble (di·sem'b'l) *v.* To conceal the truth, or one's true feelings, by pretense.

dissension (di·sen'shən) *n.* Disagreement or quarreling.

dissipate (dis'ə·pāt') *v.* To break up and scatter; vanish. —**dissipation** *n.*

dividend (div'ə·dend') *n.* A profit divided among the shareholders of a company.

doctrine (däk'trən) *n.* The beliefs taught as the principles of a religion, political system, or philosophy.

dowager (dou'ə·jər) *n.* An elderly woman of wealth and dignity.

dowry (dou'rē) *n.* Property or money that a woman brings to her husband at marriage.

ebullient (i·bool'yənt) *adj.* Overflowing with enthusiasm.

ecstatic (ek·stat'ik) *adj.* Joyful. —**ecstatically** *adv.*

edict (ē'dikt) *n.* An official public order; decree.

effrontery (e·frun'tər·ē) *n.* Shameless and disrespectful boldness.

elegy (el'ə·jē) *n.* A poem or song mourning or praising the dead.

elongated (i·lôŋ'gāt·əd) *adj.* Lengthened; stretched out.

eloquent (el'ə·kwənt) *adj.* Graceful and persuasive in speech or writing.

emaciated (i·mā'shē·āt'əd) *adj.* Abnormally thin.

emanate (em'ə·nāt) *v.* To come forth.

emancipation (i·man'sə·pā'shən) *n.* Release from slavery or servitude; freeing.

eminent *adj.* Standing high by comparison with others; distinguished.

enamor (in·am'ər) *v.* To fill with love.

encompass (in·kum'pəs) *v.* To contain.

endeavor (in·dev'ər) *v.* To try.

enjoin *v.* To order to do something.

ennui (än·wē') *n.* Boredom.

entreat *v.* To beg.

enunciate (i·nun'sē·āt') *v.* To pronounce or speak clearly and distinctly.

epithet (ep'ə·thet') *n.* A word or phrase, often a scornful one, used to describe some person or thing.

equanimity (ek'wə·nim'ə·tē) *n.* Calmness.

estuary (es'choo·wer'ē) *n.* An arm of the sea; inlet.

evangelist (i·van'jə·list) *n.* A person who tries to convert others to Christianity.

evict (i·vikt') *v.* To remove or throw out.

evince (i·vins') *v.* To show plainly.

exalt (ig·zôlt') *v.* To glorify.

exaltation (eg'zôl·tā'shən) *n.* **1.** Glorification. **2.** Great joy or pride.

exasperate (ig·zas'pə·rāt') *n.* To irritate or annoy very much. —**exasperation** *n.*

excommunicate (eks'kə·myōō'nə·kāt') *v.* To exclude from the sacraments, rights, and privileges of a religion. —**excommunication** *n.*

exemplary (ig·zem'plə·rē) *adj.* Serving as an example or warning.

exhort (ig·zôrt') *v.* To urge strongly.

exonerate (ig·zän'ə·rāt) *v.* To free from a charge; prove blameless.

exorcize (ek'sôr·sīz') *v.* To drive out or away by prayers or rituals.

expatiate (ik·spa'shē·āt') *v.* To speak or write in great detail.

expedite (ek'spə·dīt') *v.* To speed up or make easier.

expenditure (ik·spen'də·chər) *n.* The act of spending or using up.

extremity (ik·strem'ə·tē) *n.* **1.** The outermost part; end. **2.** The end of life. **3.** An extreme measure; severe or strong action.

exuberant (ig·zōō'bər·ənt) *adj.* **1.** Growing abundantly. **2.** Full of health and high spirits.

exultation (eg'zəl·tā'shən) *n.* Rejoicing; triumph.

fabrication (fab'rə·kā'shən) *n.* Making up or invention.

famished (fam'isht) *adj.* Very hungry.

fastidious (fas·tid'ē·əs) *adj.* Extremely careful or critical. —**fastidiously** *adv.*

fatalist (fāt''l·ist) *n.* A person who believes that all events are determined by fate and are therefore inevitable.

fathom *v.* To get to the bottom of; understand.
fatigue (fə·tēg′) *n.* Exhaustion; tiredness.
fatuous (fach′oo·wəs) *adj.* Stupid; foolish. —**fatuously** *adv.*
fawn *v.* To try to win favor by flattering and acting extremely humble.
feign (fān) *v.* To pretend.
feint (fānt) *v.* To deliver a pretended blow or attack.
filial (fil′ē·əl) *adj.* Of or befitting a son or daughter.
fissure (fish′ər) *n.* A deep crack.
flaccid (flas′id) *adj.* Hanging in loose folds; limp.
forestall (fôr·stôl′) *v.* To prevent or restrain by taking prior action.
forfeit (fôr′fit) *v.* To lose or give up because of some fault of crime.
formidable (fôr′mə·də·b'l) *adj.* Awe-inspiring.
frigid (frij′id) *adj.* Extremely cold.
frond *n.* A leaf.
frowzy (frou′zē) *adj.* Dirty and untidy.
frugal (froo′g'l) *adj.* **1.** Thrifty. **2.** Inexpensive or meager.
fugitive (fyoo′jə·tiv) *adj.* Fleeing from something.
fume *n.* To show anger.
furtive (fur′tiv) *adj.* Secret; sneaky.
fusillade (fyoo′sə·läd′) *v.* To fire many shots at.

gall¹ *n.* Rude boldness.
gall² *v.* To annoy.
gambol (gam′b'l) *v.* To jump and skip about in play.
garb *v.* To dress.
garrison (gar′ə·s'n) *n.* Troops stationed in a fort.
gingerly *adv.* In a very cautious way.
glean *v.* To collect or find out gradually, or bit by bit.
grisly (griz′lē) *adj.* Horrible; terrifying.
grovel (gruv′'l) *v.* To lie face down or crawl in a face-down position.
gullible (gul′ə·b'l) *adj.* Easily cheated and tricked.

hamlet *n.* A very small village.
haphazard (hap′haz′ərd) *adj.* Not planned; random. —**haphazardly** *adv.*
hapless *adj.* Unfortunate; unlucky.
hearken (här′kən) *v.* [Archaic] To hear or pay attention to.
heinous (hā′nəs) *adj.* Very evil or wicked.
hereditary (hə·red′ə·ter′ē) *adj.* Passed genetically from generation to generation.
homage (häm′ij) *n.* Anything done to show honor or respect.
hover (huv′ər) *v.* **1.** To stay suspended in the air. **2.** To wait close by, especially in an overprotective or anxious way.
hulking *adj.* Large and heavy.
humanitarian *adj.* Helping people, especially through the elimination of pain and suffering.

idolatry (ī·däl′ə·trē) *n.* The worship of idols.
idyllic (ī·dil′ik) *adj.* Pleasant and peaceful.
illustrious (i·lus′trē·əs) *adj.* Famous because of dignity or achievements.
immaculate (i·mak′yə·lit) *adj.* Perfectly clean.
imminent (im′ə·nənt) *adj.* Likely to happen soon. —**imminence** *n.*
impecunious (im′pi·kyoo′nē·əs) *adj.* Poor.
impede *v.* To obstruct or block.
impediment (im·ped′ə·mənt) *n.* An obstruction; block.
impending (im·pend′iŋ) *adj.* About to happen.
imperative (im·per′ə·tiv) *adj.* Absolutely necessary; urgent.
impetuous (im·pech′oo·wəs) *adj.* Moving with great force or violence; impulsive.
impostor (im·päs′tər) *n.* A person who pretends to be something he or she is not.
imprecation (im′prə·kā′shən) *n.* A curse.
impregnable (im·preg′nə·b'l) *adj.* Unconquerable; unyielding.
improbable (im·präb′ə·b'l) *adj.* Not likely to happen or be true. —**improbably** *adv.*
impudence (im′pyoo·dəns) *n.* Shamelessly bold or disrespectful behavior.
imputation (im′pyoo·tā′shən) *n.* Accusation; charge.
incandescence (in′kən·des′əns) *n.* Great brightness; brilliant shine.
incessant (in·ses′'nt) *adj.* Never stopping; constant. —**incessantly** *adv.*
incompetence (in·käm′pə·təns) *n.* Lack of skill or ability.
incongruous (in·käŋ′groo·wəs) *adj.* Out of place; inappropriate.
increment (in′krə·mənt) *n.* Amount of increase.
incubator (iŋ′kyə·bāt′ər) *n.* An artificially heated container for hatching eggs.
incursion (in·kur′zhən) *n.* An invasion or undesired entrance.
indecorous (in·dek′ər·əs) *adj.* Not suitable or proper.
indefatigable (in′di·fat′i·gə·b'l) *adj.* Never tiring.
indelible (in·del′ə·b'l) *adj.* That cannot be erased; lasting.
indifferent (in·dif′ər·ənt) *adj.* Having no preference; neutral.
indigent (in′di·jənt) *adj.* Poor.

fat, āpe, cär; ten, ēven; is, bīte; gō, hôrn, tool, look; oil, out; up, fur; get; joy; yet; chin; she; thin, then; zh, leisure; ŋ, ring; ə for a in ago, e in agent, i in sanity, o in comply, u in focus; ' as in able (ā′b'l).

induce *v.* To persuade.

indulgent (in·dul′jənt) *adj.* Lenient; overly generous.

ineffable (in·ef′ə·b'l) *adj.* Too overwhelming to be expressed in words. —**ineffably** *adv.*

inert (in·urt′) *adj.* Not moving or active.

infamous (in′fə·məs) *adj.* Having a very bad reputation.

infidel (in′fə·d'l) *n.* A person who does not believe in Christianity, or a person who does not believe in the prevailing religion.

infirmity (in·fur′mə·tē) *n.* A weakness or defect.

injunction (in·juŋk′shən) *n.* A command or order.

inquisitorial (in·kwiz′ə·tôr′ē·əl) *adj.* Questioning, especially in a hostile or overly curious manner.

insatiable (in·sā′shə·b'l) *adj.* Constantly wanting more; incapable of being satisfied.

inscrutable (in·skrōōt′ə·b'l) *adj.* Hard to understand; mysterious.

insensible (in·sen′sə·b'l) *adj.* Without feeling.

insinuate (in·sin′yoo·wāt′) *v.* **1.** To work into gradually, indirectly, and artfully. **2.** To hint; imply.

insolence (in′sə·ləns) *n.* Bold disrespect.

instigate (in′stə·gāt′) *v.* To urge on; cause.

insuperable (in·sōō′pər·ə·b'l) *adj.* Unconquerable.

insurrection (in′sə·rek′shən) *n.* A rebellion.

integral (in′tə·grəl) *adj.* Necessary for completeness; essential.

integrity (in·teg′rə·tē) *n.* **1.** Unbroken condition; wholeness. **2.** Honesty and sincerity.

inter (in·tur′) *v.* To put into a grave or tomb; to bury.

interim (in′tər·im) *n.* The period of time between; meantime.

intervene (in′tər·vēn′) *v.* To come between as an influencing force, as in order to settle some argument.

intractable (in·trak′tə·b'l) *adj.* Hard or impossible to treat or manage.

inventory (in′vən·tôr′ē) *n.* A list of goods or property.

involuntary (in·väl′ən·ter′ē) *adj.* Not done on purpose; unintentional.

irrevocable (i·rev′ə·kə·b'l) *adj.* That cannot be undone; unalterable.

jettison *v.* To throw overboard.

jilt *v.* To reject (a previously accepted lover or fiancé).

jocular (jäk′yə·lər) *adj.* Joking; full of fun.

jovial *adj.* Full of good humor; merry.

judicious jōō·dish′əs) *adj.* Wise and careful.

juxtaposition (juk′stə·pə·zi′shən) *n.* Placement close together.

kindred (kin′drid) *adj.* Similar in nature; related.

labyrinth (lab′ə·rinth′) *n.* A maze.

lamentation (lam′ən·tā′shən) *n.* The art of lamenting, or expressing grief; wailing.

languid (laŋ′gwid) *adj.* Without energy or spirit.

lenient (lē′ni·ənt) *n.* Mild in punishing or judging. —**leniency** *n.*

leonine (lē′ə·nīn′) *adj.* Of or like a lion.

libertine (lib′ər·tēn′) *n.* A person who leads an immoral life.

loath *adj.* Reluctant.

locution (lō·kyōō′shən) *n.* A word, phrase, or expression.

logistics (lō·jis′tiks) *n. pl.* The handling of the details of an undertaking.

loquacity (lō·kwas′ə·tē) *n.* Talkativeness.

lugubrious (loo·gōō′brē·əs) *adj.* Very sad or mournful, especially in an exaggerated way. —**lugubriousness** *n.*

luminous (lōō′mə·nəs) *adj.* Shining; glowing.

magnanimous (mag·nan′ə·məs) *adj.* Generous in overlooking injury or insult.

maim *v.* To cripple or mutilate.

malefaction (mal′ə·fak′shən) *n.* Wrongdoing; crime.

malice (mal′is) *n.* Ill will or evil intent.

manacles (man′ə·k'lz) *n. pl.* Handcuffs.

manifest (man′ə·fest′) *v.* To appear.

manifesto (man′ə·fes′tō) *n.* A public declaration of motives and intentions by a government or public person or group.

martial (mär′shəl) *adj.* Of or suitable for war.

massive (mas′iv) *adj.* Extremely large.

maxim *n.* A briefly worded rule of behavior or statement of a general truth.

mean *adj.* In the middle of two extremes; average.

melancholy (mel′ən·käl′ē) *adj.* Sad and gloomy.

melodramatic (mel′ə·drə·mat′ik) *adj.* Exaggeratedly emotional —**melodramatically** *adv.*

mentor *n.* A teacher or wise advisor.

meticulous (mə·tik′yoo·ləs) *adj.* Extremely careful about details.

minion (min′yən) *n.* A servant or follower.

miscreant (mis′krē·ənt) *n.* An evil person; criminal.

modish (mōd′ish) *adj.* Fashionable. —**modishness** *n.*

mode *n.* A manner or method.

mollify (mäl′ə·fī′) *v.* To soothe the temper of; calm.

monosyllabic (män′ə·si·lab′ik) *adj.* Having only one syllable or using words of only one syllable.

monotonous (mə·nät′'n·əs) *adj.* Continuing without varying; tediously unvarying. —**monotonous** *adv.*

mope *v.* To be gloomy; to give oneself up to brooding.

morbid *adj.* Tending to dwell on gruesome or gloomy matters.

morose (mə·rōs′) *adj.* Gloomy. —**morosely** *adv.*

mortal *adj.* That must eventually die.

musingly (myōō′ziŋ·lē) *adv.* Thoughtfully; in a meditative way.

myopic (mī·äp′ik) *adj.* Nearsighted.

myriad (mir′ē·əd) *adj.* **1.** Countless. **2.** Highly varied.

naiveté (nä·ēv·tā′) *n.* Innocent or foolish simplicity.

negligent (neg′li·jənt) *adj.* Careless. **—negligently** *adv.*

neuter (nōōt′ər) *adj.* Neither masculine nor feminine.

nonchalant (nän′shə·länt′) *adj.* Showing cool lack of concern; casually indifferent.

nondescript (nän′di·skript′) *adj.* Lacking in recognizable qualities; hard to classify or describe.

nonentity (nän·en′tə·tē) *n.* A person of little or no importance.

obscure *v.* To make dim or hide from view.

obsequious (əb·sē′kwē·əs) *adj.* Much too willing to serve or obey.

obsolete (äb′sə·lēt′) *adj.* No longer in use; outdated.

obstinacy (äb′stə·nə·sē) *n.* Stubbornness or resistance.

ominous (äm′ə·nəs) *adj.* Sinister; threatening.

opportune (äp′ər·tōōn′) *adj.* Right for the purpose or circumstances; well-timed.

opportunist (äp′ər·tōōn′ist) *n.* A person who acts primarily to further his or her own interests.

optimum (äp′tə·məm) *adj.* Most favorable; best.

oration *n.* A public speech.

oscillation (äs′ə·lā′shən) *n.* The act of swinging back and forth.

palisade (pal′ə·sād′) *n.* A fence used for a defense.

pander *v.* To gratify others' desires. To pander *to.*)

parasite (par′ə·sīt′) *n.* **1.** A person who lives at the expense of others without making a useful or adequate return. **2.** An organism that lives in or on another organism of a different species, deriving food or protection from the host, which it usually harms. **—parasitic** *adj.*

parley *n.* A conference with an enemy.

parsimony (pär′sə·mō′nē) *n.* Stinginess.

patronage (pā′trən·ij) *n.* Support given by a patron.

pauper (pô′pər) *n.* An extremely poor person.

peremptory (pə·remp′tər·ē) *adj.* Commanding in an overbearing way; imperious.

perfunctory (pər·fuŋk′tər·ē) *adj.* Done without care or effort, merely as a form or routine.

perplexity (pər·plek′sə·tē) *n.* Confusion; bewilderment.

pertinacity (purt′ə·nas′ə·tē) *n.* Stubborn firmness; persistence.

peruse (pə·rōōz′) *v.* To read carefully **—perusal** *n.*

perverse (pər·vurs′) *adj.* Stubbornly contrary or unreasonable. **—perversity** *adj.*

petty *adj.* Showing a tendency to make much of small matters; small-minded.

petulant (pech′oo·lənt) *adj.* Irritable; complaining.

picturesque (pik′chə·resk′) *adj.* Charming visually; quaint. **—picturesquely** *adv.*

pillage (pil′ij) *v.* To take money or property by violence.

pique (pēk) *v.* To ruffle the pride of; offend.

pittance (pit′′ns) *n.* A small amount of money.

placid (plas′id) *adj.* Calm.

plague (plāg) *n.* A contagious disease epidemic or other disaster.

plateau (pla·tō′) *n.* A raised area of level land.

plausible (plô′zə·b′l) *adj.* Seemingly true or acceptable.

ponderous (pän′dər·əs) *adj.* Heavy or bulky.

populace (päp′yə·lis) *n.* All the people in an area.

portage (pôr′tij) *n.* The carrying of boats and supplies overland between waterways.

posterity (päs·ter′ə·tē) *n.* Future generations.

potent (pōt′′nt) *adj.* Powerful.

poultice (pōl′tis) *n.* A hot, soft, moist mass applied to a sore or inflamed part of the body.

precipice (pres′ə·pis) *n.* A steep cliff.

precipitate (pri·sip′ə·tət′) *adj.* Very sudden or unexpected.

precipitation (pri·sip′ə·tā′shən) *n.* Rain, snow, sleet, or hail.

predilection (pred′′l·ek′shən) *n.* A preference.

predominate (pri·däm′ə·nāt′) *v.* To be greatest in number or amount.

preeminent (prē·em′ə·nənt) *adj.* Excelling over others in some way; prominent.

preoccupied (prē·äk′yə·pīd′) *adj.* Wholly absorbed in one's thoughts; engrossed.

preordain (prē′ôr·dān′) *v.* To order or determine beforehand.

preside (pri·zīd′) *v.* To be in the position of authority in an assembled group.

pretext (prē′tekst) *n.* A false reason; excuse.

prevail (pri·vāl′) *v.* To gain the upper hand; triumph.

privation (prī·vā′shən) *n.* Lack of the ordinary necessities of life.

profane (prə·fān′) *v.* To treat (sacred things) with disrespect.

profess (prə·fes′) *v.* To claim; make an open declaration.

proliferate (prō·lif′ə·rāt′) *v.* To increase greatly.

prophetic (prə·fet′ik) *adj.* Predicting the future, or having the powers to predict the future.

prostrate (präs′trāt) *adj.* Lying face downward.

prototype (prōt′ə·tīp′) *n.* A typical example; a perfect example of a particular type.

protracted (prō·trakt′əd) *adj.* Lengthened in time; prolonged.

---

fat, āpe, cär; ten, ēven; is, bīte; gō, hôrn, tōōl, look; oil, out; up, fʉr; get; joy; yet; **ch**in; **sh**e; **th**in, *th*en; **zh,** leisure; **ŋ,** ring; ə for *a* in *ago,* e in *agent,* i in *sanity, o* in *comply, u* in *focus; ʼ* as in *able* (ā′b′l).

provincial (prə·vin'shəl) *adj.* Of the country; unsophisticated.

provocation (präv'ə·kā'shən) *n.* An act or cause of provoking or irritating.

proximity (präk·sim'ə·tē) *n.* Nearness.

prudent (prōōd''nt) *adj.* Cautious or discreet in conduct.

raiment (rā'mənt) *n.* Clothing.

rake *n.* A person who overindulges in pleasures such as drinking or gambling. —**rakish** *adj.*

rancid (ran'sid) *adj.* Spoiled.

rancor (raŋ'kər) *n.* Deep hate or ill will. —**rancorous** *adj.*

rankle *v.* To cause lasting anger or resentment.

ravage (rav'ij) *n.* Severe damage; ruin.

ravine (rə·vēn') *n.* A long, deep hollow in the earth's surface.

recoil *v.* To draw back.

reconcile (rek'ən·sīl') *v.* To make friendly again or win over to a friendly attitude.

recriminate (ri·krim'ə·nāt') *v.* To answer an accuser by accusing him or her in return. —**recrimination** *n.*

redress (ri·dres') *v.* To set right; make amends for.

reflex (rē'fleks) *n.* A quick, automatic response.

refute (ri·fyōōt') *v.* To prove to be false; disprove.

regressive (ri·gres'iv) *adj.* Tending to move backward or toward an earlier state.

reminiscence (rem'ə·nis''ns) *n.* **1.** The act of remembering. **2.** A memory or recollection.

rendezvous (rän'dā·vōō') *n.* A place chosen for meeting.

renowned (ri·nound') *adj.* Famous.

repugnant (ri·pug'nənt) *adj.* Distasteful; disagreeable.

repulsion (ri·pul'shən) *n.* A strong dislike.

resolute (rez'ə·lōōt') *adj.* Determined; unwavering.

retinue (ret''n·ōō') *n.* A group of followers or servants.

reverberation (ri·vur'bə·rā'shən) *n.* A repeated sound or echo.

reverential (rev'ə·ren'shəl) *adj.* Showing deep respect and awe.

reverie (rev'ər·ē) *n.* A daydream.

revile (ri·vīl') *v.* To call bad names.

rift *n.* A break or estrangement in a friendship.

robust (rō·bust') *adj.* Strong and healthy.

rogue (rōg) *n.* A mischievous rascal. —**roguish** *adj.*

ruminate (rōō'mə·nāt') *v.* **1.** To chew the cud, as a cow does. **2.** To turn something over in the mind.

rustic *n.* A country person.

sacrament (sak'rə·mənt) *n.* In Christianity, one of several ceremonies regarded as sacred, including baptism, confirmation, and marriage.

sagacity (sə·gas'ə·tē) *n.* Wisdom and sound judgment.

sage *adj.* Wise.

sally *n.* A sudden rushing forth to attack.

salutary (sal'yoo·ter'ē) *adj.* Healthful or favorable.

sanctified (saŋk'tə·fīd') *adj.* Holy.

sardonic (sär·dän'ik) *adj.* Bitterly sneering or sarcastic.

saturated (sach'ə·rāt'id) *adj.* Filled to the point where no more can be absorbed.

scruple (skrōō'p'l) *n.* A feeling of uneasiness about doing something one believes is wrong; qualm. —*v.* To have scruples (about).

scrupulous (skrōō'pyə·ləs) *adj.* Showing careful attention to what is right, proper, or exact. —**scrupulously** *adv.*

scrutiny (skrōōt''n·ē) *n.* A close examination.

sear *v.* To scorch or burn the surface of.

seditious (si·dish'əs) *adj.* Stirring up rebellion.

seizure (sē'zhər) *n.* A sudden attack, as of disease.

semblance (sem'bləns) *n.* A false appearance.

senescence (sə·nes''ns) *n.* Old age.

senile (sē'nīl) *adj.* Showing mental impairment and memory loss resulting from old age. —**senility** *n.*

sepia (sē'pē·ə) *adj.* Printed in sepia, a brown ink.

servile *adj.* Like a servant; humble and submissive. —**servility** *n.*

sheepish *adj.* Embarrassed because of a fault or failure. —**sheepishly** *adv.*

shroud *n.* A cloth used to wrap a body for burial.

siesta (sē·es'tə) *n.* A brief nap taken after the noon meal, especially in Spain or Latin American countries.

simper *v.* To speak with a silly or affected smile.

skeptical (skep'ti·k'l) *adj.* Not easily convinced; doubting.

slander *n.* A spoken statement that damages another person's character or reputation. —*v.* To utter slander about.

slovenly (sluv'ən·lē) *adj.* Careless and untidy.

sobriety (sə·brī'ə·tē) *n.* **1.** Moderation, especially in the use of alcohol. **2.** Seriousness; sedateness.

solarium (sō·ler'ē·əm) *n.* A glassed-in room or porch.

solicitude (sə·lis'ə·tōōd') *n.* Concern; care.

sonorous (sə·nôr'əs, sä'nôr·əs) *adj.* Having a full, rich sound.

spectral *adj.* Ghostly.

squander *v.* To spend wastefully.

stature (stach'ər) *n.* Position considered worthy of esteem.

stilted *adj.* Artificially formal.

stint *v.* To limit to a small amount.

stoic (stō'ik) *adj.* Calm under suffering. —**stoicism** *n.*

stolid (stäl'id) *adj.* Showing little or no emotion or sensitivity.

strangulation (strang'gyə·lā'shən) *n.* The cutting off of a flow or circulation.

strenuous (stren'yoo·wəs) *adj.* Requiring great effort.

subject (sub'jikt) *adj.* Under the control of another. —**subjection** *n.*

subjugate (sub′jə·gāt′) *v.* To bring under control; conquer.

subservient (səb·sur′vē·ənt) *adj.* Condition of being an inferior or servant; subordinant.

subside *v.* To sink to a lower level.

superfluity (sōō′pər·flōō′ə·tē) *n.* An amount beyond what is needed; excess.

superlative (sə·pur′lə·tiv) *adj.* Superior to all others.

suppliant (sup′lē·ənt) *adj.* Requesting humbly.

supplicate (sup′lə·kāt) *v.* To request humbly.

supposition (sup′ə·zish′ən) *n.* A guess or assumption.

suppression (sə·presh′ən) *n.* A putting down or crushing by force.

surly *adj.* Sullenly rude; bad-tempered.

surreptitious (sur′əp·tish′əs) *adj.* Secret and stealthy. —**surreptitiously** *adv.*

susceptible (sə·sep′tə·b'l) *adj.* Easily affected or influenced.

swarthy *adj.* Having a dark complexion.

swathe (swā*th*) *n.* A long strip or row.

tarry *v.* To wait or stay.

temerity (tə·mer′ə·tē) *n.* Rash boldness; recklessness.

temper *v.* To moderate or lessen by mixing with something else.

temperamental (tem′prə·men′t'l) *adj.* Changing in mood or behavior.

temperance (tem′pər·əns) *n.* Moderation in, or abstinence from, drinking alcoholic beverages.

terrestrial (tə·res′trē·əl) *adj.* Of the earth.

timorous (tim′ər·əs) *adj.* Fearful; timid. —**timorously** *adv.*

tolerate (täl′ə·rāt′) *v.* To bear; put up with.

tolerable (täl′ər·ə·b'l) *adj.* Bearable.

transcendent (tran·sen′dənt) *adj.* Excelling; extraordinary; exceeding usual limits or lying beyond the limits of ordinary experience.

transgress *v.* To overstep or break (a law or commandment).

traverse (tra·vurs′) *v.* To cross.

trepidation (trep′ə·dā′shən) *n.* Fearful anxiety.

tribunal (trī·byōō′n'l) *n.* A court of justice.

truant (trōō′ənt) *adj.* Away from school without permission.

tumult (tōō′mult) *n.* A commotion or confusion; uproar. —**tumultuous** *adj.*

tutelage (tōōt′lij) *n.* Teaching.

ultimatum (ul′tə·māt′əm) *n.* A final offer, demand, or order.

ungainly *adj.* **1.** Awkward; clumsy. **2.** Coarse and unattractive.

uninitiated (un′i·nish′ē·ā·təd) *adj.* Not having learned the basics of some subject.

unscrupulous (un·skrōōp′yə·ləs) *adj.* Not restrained by ideas of right and wrong; unprincipled.

untenable (un·ten′ə·b'l) *adj.* Impossible to hold, occupy, or defend.

untoward *adj.* Not favorable.

unwonted (un·wôn′tid) *adj.* Not common or usual.

vacuum *n.* A completely empty space; void.

valise (və·lēs′) *n.* A suitcase.

vaunt *v.* To boast about.

velocity (və·läs′ə·tē) *n.* Speed.

vertebra (vur′tə·brə) *n., pl.* **vertebrae** (vur′tə·brē′) Any bone of the spinal column.

vestige (ves′tij) *n.* A trace; last remaining bit.

vicarious (vī·ker′ē·əs) *adj.* Experienced by imagined participation in another's experience. —**vicariously** *adv.*

vicissitudes (vi·sis′ə·tōōdz) *n. pl.* Unpredictable changes that keep occurring.

victuals (vit′'lz) *n. pl.* Food.

vigil *n.* A watch kept during the usual hours of sleep.

vile *adj.* **1.** Wicked; sinful. **2.** Highly disagreeable; very bad.

vindictive (vin·dik′tiv) *adj.* Inclined to seek revenge. —**vindictiveness** *n.*

visage (viz′ij) *n.* The face.

voracity (vô·ras′ə·tē) *n.* Great hunger; greed.

wane *v.* To grow less in amount or importance.

wince *v.* To draw back slightly, as in pain or embarrassment.

zeal (zēl) *n.* Intense enthusiasm. —**zealously** (zel′əs·lē) *adv.*

---

fat, āpe, cär; ten, ēven; is, bīte; gō, hôrn, tōōl, look; oil, out; up, fur; get; joy; yet; **chin**; **she**; **thin**, *th*en; **zh,** leisure; **ŋ,** ring; ə for *a* in *ago*, *e* in *agent*, *i* in *sanity*, *o* in *comply*, *u* in *focus*; ' as in *able* (ā′b'l).

INDEX OF SKILLS AND FEATURES

LITERATURE AND LANGUAGE SKILLS

The following is a selective index of literary and related language terms. Some language terms not included below can be found in the **Language and Vocabulary Exercises** index on page 1049 or the **Literature and Language Exercises** index on page 1052.

Allegory 819, 829
Alliteration 323, 336, 995
Allusion 67, 205, 347, 816, 822, 860, 995
Anachronism 707, 994, 995
Anapest 302, 319, 1002
Anecdote 422, 423, 868, 869, 870, 874, 995
Antagonist 43, 148, 155, 983
Apostrophe 364
Approximate rhyme (Half rhyme, Slant rhyme) 322, 338, 378, 1004
Archaic words 626
Argument 509
Aside 664, 677, 996
Atmosphere 146, 161, 466, 900, 996
Audience 444, 517, 624, 745
Autobiography 445, 452, 467, 996
Ballad 299, 305, 307, 996
"Bare bones" 4, 513, 515, 597, 1003
Basic situation (See **Exposition**)
Blank verse 625, 996
Cadence 304, 311, 407, 441
Cause and effect 37
Character (Characterization) 41, 74, 76, 163, 514, 900, 996
Chronological order 37
Circular reasoning 196
Cliché 163, 164, 452, 469
Climax 4, 27, 185, 413, 514, 807, 1003
Comedy 600, 997
Complications 4, 1003
Conflict 5, 513, 900, 997
Connotations 73, 108, 118, 141, 161, 273, 283, 315, 376, 382, 468, 485, 728, 997
Contraction 280
Couplet 286, 326, 337, 377, 997
Dactyl 302, 1002
Denotation 108, 315, 468, 997

Denouement (See **Resolution**)
Description 74, 383, 395, 406, 507, 509, 997
Desperate situation 513
Dialect 66, 128, 164, 233, 423, 459, 998
Dialogue 219, 556, 557, 613
Diction 164, 285, 313, 328, 363, 444, 468, 998
Direct characterization 41, 75, 996
Direct metaphor 238, 1001
Drama 512, 518, 559, 600, 613, 623, 628, 744, 796, 998
Dramatic irony 198, 534, 1001
Dynamic character 44, 163, 996
Elegy 299
Elizabethan English 626, 667
Emotional appeal 428, 509, 728
Emotional effect 75, 147, 164, 178, 285, 307, 357, 1005
End rhyme 322, 326, 378, 1004
End-stopped line 321, 338, 625
English sonnet (See **Shakespearean sonnet**)
Epic 735, 998
Epithet 743, 998
Essay 410, 444, 999
Exact rhyme 322, 338
Exaggeration (See **Overstatement**)
Exposition (plot) 4, 534, 579, 1003
Exposition (writing) 383, 410, 506, 999
Extended metaphor 233, 247, 328, 794, 818, 984, 1001
External conflict 6, 513, 900, 997
Fable 219, 324, 326, 893, 895, 999
Fact 381, 444, 445, 473, 507, 510
Fairy tale (Tale of wonder) 210, 344, 347, 841, 867, 875
Farce 335, 611, 999
Faulty reasoning 196, 509, 874
Figure of speech (Figurative language) 58, 135, 166, 186, 227, 238, 245, 248, 339, 999
First-person point of view 116, 988, 1004
Flashback 37, 97, 428, 924, 999
Flat character 44, 163, 996
Foil 858, 924, 960, 999
Folklore 192, 866
Folktale 841, 864, 999
Foot 301, 625, 1002
Foreshadowing 6, 513, 1000
Form 298, 376

Formal essay (Traditional essay) 410, 999
Frame story 28, 209, 841, 893, 1000
Free verse 300, 303, 317, 318, 321, 376, 1000
Generalization 80, 113, 196, 452
Haiku 289, 1000
Half rhyme (see **Approximate rhyme**)
History 473, 507, 510
How-and-why story 866, 883, 889, 896, 1000
Humor 335, 395, 452, 889
Hyperbole (See **Overstatement**)
Iamb 302, 319, 320, 377, 625, 1000, 1002
Iambic pentameter 625, 1000
Idiom 66, 231, 242
Imagery (Image) 75, 162, 217, 267, 289, 294, 339, 1000
Implied meaning (See **Inference**)
Implied metaphor 228, 238, 795, 1001
Indirect characterization 42, 75, 76, 996
Inference (Implied meaning) 210, 310, 428, 470
Informal essay (Personal essay) 410, 999
Internal conflict 6, 513, 900, 997
Internal rhyme 322, 326, 337, 338, 366, 1004
Inversion (Inverted word order) 265, 280, 288, 320, 328, 1001
Irony 197, 342, 467, 534, 900, 989, 1001
Italian sonnet (see **Petrarchan sonnet**)
Jargon 242, 310, 497, 505
Journal 280, 281, 384, 405, 408
Legend 833
Limited third-person point of view 117, 143, 1004
Loaded words 196, 485, 510, 728
Magic realism 187, 192
Main idea 108, 404, 467, 470, 507, 987, 989
Metamorphosis (See **Transformation**)
Metaphor 186, 228, 233, 246, 328, 349, 405, 794, 984, 1001
Meter 300, 319, 377, 1002
Mixed metaphor 247, 1001
Monologue 232, 862
Mood 75, 161, 164, 278, 285, 497
Moral (Lesson) 79, 210, 219, 326, 827, 830, 896

Motif 866, 881, 882, 893, 896, 1002
Motivation 45, 163
Myth 192, 733, 746, 797, 865, 1002
Narration 36, 383, 395, 410, 467, 497, 507, 509, 1002
Narrator 116, 135, 140, 559, 924, 1004
Nonfiction 380, 384, 408, 410, 444, 445, 470, 473, 507, 510, 950, 1002
Novel 850, 898, 1002
Objective writing 382, 408, 469, 507
Octave 338, 1006
Omniscient point of view 116, 143, 1004
Onomatopoeia 323, 336, 1002
Opinion 163, 444, 473, 507, 509, 510, 987
Overstatement (Hyperbole) 396, 452, 1003
Parable 808, 827, 830, 1003
Paradox 433, 438, 600
Parallelism (Parallel structure) 318, 406, 441, 509, 817, 826, 1003
Paraphrasing 265, 352, 691, 727, 825
Parody 127, 210, 220, 342, 375, 850, 858, 1003
Personal Essay (See **Informal essay**)
Personification 229, 246, 1003
Persuasion 383, 410, 414, 428, 506, 723, 728, 1003
Petrarchan sonnet (Italian sonnet) 338, 1006
Picaresque 850
Plot 4, 38, 163, 513, 900, 1003
Poetry 226, 246, 248, 264, 265, 267, 294, 296, 298, 319, 322, 336, 339, 341, 374, 376, 625, 826, 1004
Point of view 116, 163, 467, 900, 1004
Prose 227, 300, 307
Protagonist 43, 79, 690, 900, 983, 988, 1004
Psalm 817, 826
Pun 335, 649, 1004
Purpose (Aim) 114, 383, 444, 506
Quatrain 286, 337, 338, 377, 1006
Quest 217, 832, 847
Refrain 299, 305, 307, 312, 321, 346, 1004
Repetition 178, 299, 322, 323, 357, 610, 728, 826
Resolution (Denouement) 4, 22, 66, 1003

Rhyme 322, 337, 377, 1004
Rhyme scheme 286, 335, 337, 338, 1004, 1006
Rhythm 298, 319, 1005
Romance 198, 831, 1005
Round character 44, 163, 204, 996
Run-on line 308, 309, 321, 337, 338, 369, 625
Sarcasm 197, 510
Satire 199, 219, 324, 428, 850, 900, 1005
Scanning 301, 319, 320, 1002
Second-person point of view 140, 144
Sentence fragment 613
Sestet 338, 1006
Setting 146, 163, 900, 983, 1005
Shakespearean sonnet (English sonnet) 286, 337, 338, 1006
Short story 2, 4, 38, 41, 76, 78, 113, 116, 145, 146, 163, 165, 197, 222, 815, 1006
Simile 186, 227, 246, 405, 1006
Situational irony 197, 204, 1001
Slang 335, 468, 505
Slant rhyme (See **Approximate rhyme**)
Soliloquy 666, 1006
Sonnet 286, 337, 338, 1006
Speaker 361, 371, 1006
Spondee 302, 312, 1002
Stage directions 598
Stanza 286, 299, 1006
Static character 44, 163, 996
Stereotype 196
Stock character 44, 163
Stress (Accent) 300, 1002
Style 112, 144, 162, 164, 178, 195, 205, 378, 407, 443, 468, 469, 505, 615, 984, 990
Subject (of literary work) 79, 217, 339, 376
Subjective writing 382, 408, 469
Subordinate clause 193, 1010, 1011
Subtheme 983
Suspense 6, 514, 728, 745, 1007
Symbol (Symbolism) 165, 195, 248, 264, 984, 1007
Theme 78, 113, 163, 167, 518, 629, 734, 747, 802, 808, 830, 900, 983, 1007
Thesis statement 987, 989
Title 79, 114, 315, 984, 987
Tone (Attitude) 117, 163, 341, 371, 374, 375, 389, 469, 826, 900, 1007
Traditional essay (See **Formal essay**)
Tragedy 722, 796, 1007
Tragic flaw 794, 796
Tragic hero/heroine 722, 794, 796

Transformation (Metamorphosis) 797, 801, 867, 881, 882
Translation 235, 742, 818, 821
Travel literature 384, 408
Trickster tale 891, 895, 896, 1007
Trochee 302, 377, 1002
Turning point 691
Understatement 360
Verbal irony 197, 395, 649, 728, 1001
Verisimilitude 146
Vignette 58

LANGUAGE AND VOCABULARY EXERCISES

The following is an index of topics discussed in the Analyzing Language and Vocabulary exercises. Additional page references for some terms, as well as other language terms not included here, can also be found in the **Literature and Language Skills** index on page 1048 and the **Literature and Language Exercises** index on page 1052.

Allusions 205, 347
Americanisms 128, 160
Anachronisms 707
Appositives 23
Ballad formulas 307
Brand names 363
Changes in the English language 839
Clichés 452
Connotations 73, 108, 141, 273, 283, 315
Context clues 22, 277, 389, 505
Contractions 233, 280
Denotations 108, 315
Dialect (See also **Specialized vocabulary**) 66, 233, 423, 459
Diction 285, 313
Elizabethan English 667
Epithets 743
Etymologies 235, 260, 354, 371, 389, 438, 557, 801, 815
Etymologies of names 801, 815
Exact meanings 557
Extended metaphors 794, 984
Figures of speech 58, 135, 186, 242, 349, 405, 794, 984
Food as metaphor 349
Grammar (See also **Syntax**) 423, 459
Greek names 801
Greek roots and word origins 260, 396, 438
Hebrew names 815
Homophones 649

Idioms 66, 231, 242
Imagery 217
Implied meanings 210
Inferences 210
Inverted sentences 66, 280, 288
Irony 467
Jargon (See also **Specialized vocabulary**) 242, 310, 497, 505
Latin roots and word origins 235, 260, 354, 371, 389, 438, 801
Loaded words 485
Metaphors 186, 349, 405, 794, 984
Monitoring your reading 366
Multiple meanings 263, 275
Names 257, 363, 801, 815
Oral reading 326, 331, 441, 459
Overstatement 396
Parallelism 826
Paraphrasing 353, 691
Persuasion 428
Poetic words 280
Point of view 267
Prefixes 23, 438
Pronunciation 66, 326, 423, 459
Proper nouns 363
Punctuation 291, 505
Puns 335, 649
Reading aloud (See **Oral reading**)
Related words 235, 263, 354, 371, 389, 396, 438, 557
Root words 235, 354, 371, 389, 396, 438, 557, 801
Similes 186, 405
Slang 505
Spanish words 235
Specialized vocabulary (See also **Dialect, Jargon**) 155, 438, 497
Stage directions 598
Standard English 67, 233, 459
Strong verbs 88, 414
Style 178, 505, 984
Suffixes 28, 438
Synonyms 313, 328
Syntax 66, 291, 333, 423, 459
Verbal irony 649
Word analysis 23, 438
Word histories (See also **Etymologies**) 260
Words often confused 255

COMPOSITION SKILLS

Writing: A Creative Response
  Answering the poet 288
  Assuming a character's point of view 192
  Changing a poem's tone 375
  Changing the novel's setting 983

Changing the resolution 22, 108, 155, 983
Changing the speaker in the poem 361
Choosing visual images 371
Continuing the story 66, 112, 140
Contrasting two characters 72
Creating a character from a photograph 441
Creating an extended metaphor 328
Creating metaphors 257
Creating sound images 274
Describing a ceremony 160
Describing a character 88
Describing a character's thoughts 801
Describing a fear 414
Describing a modern-dress production 723
Describing an escape 847
Describing an ideal place 407
Describing an imaginary place 210
Describing an object 135, 283
Describing a painting 862
Describing a person 469
Describing sights and sounds 338
Describing the United States from an outsider's point of view 405
Evoking a mood 162
Expressing a different attitude 231
Expressing an opinion 28
Expressing a wish 332
Extending a metaphor 247
Extending the poem 233, 242, 252, 368, 371
Extending the story 66, 112, 140, 723
Filling in the gaps 314, 357
Imagining a character's reaction 485
Imitating the poem 235, 238, 273, 277, 291, 331, 349, 360, 373, 375
Imitating the writer's technique 58, 210, 217, 271, 389, 423, 459
Making a poem out of a journal entry 280
Narrating an event 467
Narrating an experience 395
Narrating a scene 37
Questioning the poet 293
Reacting to a scientific discovery 443
Resetting a story 839, 983
Reworking Uriah Heep 75
Rewriting the passage as a poem 407
Telling a story 357, 459
Translating a poem 235

Updating the characters 723
Updating the farewell scene 742
Updating the myth 801
Updating the play 793
Updating the poem 352
Updating the story 35, 177, 185, 204, 858, 862
Updating the story for a movie 35
Using a different point of view 135, 141, 144, 310, 318, 366, 371, 505, 808, 983
Using figures of speech 245
Using imagery to express emotion 295
Using images 285
Using magic realism 192
Using symbols 264
Using the descriptive mode to create a character 75
Writing about an historical event 509
Writing about the future 22
Writing a character sketch 433
Writing additional examples 825
Writing a dialogue 221, 556, 615
Writing a fable 326
Writing a free-verse poem 321
Writing a how-and-why story 889
Writing a journal entry 28, 271, 815, 839
Writing a letter 97, 485, 815, 983
Writing an anecdote 874
Writing an animal tale 896
Writing a narrative in the form of a log 497
Writing an autobiographical essay 452
Writing an essay 438
Writing a new stage manager's speech 556
Writing a new version of an old story 347
Writing an eyewitness report 497
Writing an opinion column 509
Writing an original scene 597
Writing a parable 830
Writing a parody 127
Writing a persuasive essay 414, 723
Writing a plan for a movie version 127
Writing a poem 260, 263, 311, 313, 376
Writing a resolution for the story 66, 112, 140
Writing a tale of transformation 881
Writing a trickster tale 895
Writing haiku 289
Writing monologues 862

Writing realistic dialogue 615
Writing the next act 556, 611

Writing: A Critical Response
Analyzing advertisements 428
Analyzing a character 76, 97, 405, 452, 485, 597, 724
Analyzing a poem 254, 363
Analyzing a story 222
Analyzing persuasion 728
Analyzing relationships 459
Analyzing symbolism 195
Analyzing the essay 441
Analyzing the essay's beginning 423
Analyzing the essay's purpose 414
Analyzing the humor 395
Analyzing the play as a farce 611
Analyzing the poem's effect 242
Analyzing the poem's humor 335
Analyzing the poem's message 315
Analyzing the story's elements 222, 815
Analyzing the writer's attitude 371, 389
Analyzing the writer's techniques 438
Analyzing tone 826
Analyzing "what happened" in the poem 260
Answering the poet 366
Commenting on the issue of fate versus free will 794
Comparing a book and a movie 984
Comparing a journal entry and a poem 280
Comparing and contrasting autobiographies 467
Comparing and contrasting characters 505, 724
Comparing and contrasting poems 252, 273, 283, 285, 288, 291, 296, 354, 366, 368
Comparing and contrasting stories 141, 145, 155, 847
Comparing and contrasting themes 830
Comparing and contrasting translations 742, 818, 821
Comparing an essay and a short story 433
Comparing a poem to the story 135
Comparing plays 612
Comparing poetry to prose 307, 407
Comparing the passage with a poem 727
Comparing the play with its source 724

Connecting ideas 254
Describing the main character 73
Developing a thesis statement 987
Distinguishing between subjective and objective details 407
Evaluating a character 66, 88, 204
Evaluating an essay 444
Evaluating a poem 311, 339
Evaluating a story 128, 163, 428
Evaluating history 510
Evaluating persuasion 510, 728
Evaluating poetic diction 328
Evaluating the frame story 28
Evaluating the metaphor 233
Evaluating the plot 22, 177
Evaluating the story's point of view 185
Evaluating the title 315
Explaining an opinion 598
Explaining a theme 556
Explaining the actions in a ballad 307
Explaining the poet's comment 254
Expressing an opinion 108
Identifying the tragic hero or heroine 794
Inferring an explanation 310
Inferring the main idea 470
Interpreting a poem 265
Interpreting the novel's title 984
Interpreting the poem's message 293
Making generalizations 113
Paraphrasing a poem 265
Predicting outcomes 38
Recognizing faulty reasoning 196
Relating a passage to contemporary life 727
Responding to a critic 556, 742, 794, 801, 847, 858, 984
Responding to an attitude 485
Responding to a story 160, 222
Responding to a writer's comment 983
Responding to figures of speech 238
Responding to Steinbeck's analysis of Arthur 839
Responding to the account 505
Responding to the characters 53
Responding to the journal 405
Responding to the play 557
Responding to the poem 360
Responding to the poem's message 347
Responding to the story 35
Responding to the story's subject 217
Responding to the story's theme 113, 141

Responding to the writer's style 205
Responding to two interpretations 794
Stating a theme 113, 598
Supporting an opinion 22
Supporting a thesis statement 987
Supporting a topic sentence 108
Writing a factual summary 497
Writing a letter to the editor 196

SPEAKING AND LISTENING SKILLS

Acting out a dialogue 615
Comparing speeches read aloud 690
Conducting a debate 616
Hearing different voices 353
Hearing the effect of inversion 281
Listening to approximate rhymes 328
Listening to poetry read aloud 304
Preparing a choral reading 326
Preparing different oral readings 331
Reading a folktale aloud 867, 888, 895, 896
Reading aloud to hear cadence 407, 441
Reading aloud to hear parallelism 318, 407, 441
Reading a narrative aloud 37
Reading a story aloud to hear its rhythm 110
Reading dialect aloud 459
Reading dialogue aloud 615
Reading free verse aloud to hear its rhythm 311, 317, 331
Reading poetry aloud 291, 300, 304, 308, 311, 314, 317, 321, 324, 326, 331, 332, 347, 364, 369, 407, 819
  to hear alliteration 332
  to hear humorous sound effects 324
  to hear rhyme 326
  to hear rhythm and meter 300, 301, 307, 311, 312, 314, 317, 331
  using different speakers 326, 819
  with correct pronunciation 326
Reading run-on lines aloud 308, 321, 369
Recognizing how poetic form affects oral reading 291, 331
Recognizing how tone of voice affects meaning 117, 277, 331, 341, 347
Recognizing the difference between oral and written folktales 867
Telling a folktale from memory 895

LITERATURE AND LANGUAGE EXERCISES

The following is a list of skills covered in the Literature and Language exercises, presented in the order in which they appear in the book. Additional page references for some skills can also be found in the **Literature and Language Skills** index on page 1048 and the **Language and Vocabulary Exercises** index on page 1049.

Using the Narrative Mode 36
Using the Descriptive Mode in Characterization 74
Combining Sentences 110
Using Pronouns Correctly 143
Using Words to Create Atmosphere 161
Using Subordinate Clauses 193
Punctuating Dialogue 219
Using Similes, Metaphor, and Personification 246
Using Symbols 264
Using Imagery 294
Creating Rhythm and Meter 319
Creating Sound Effects 336
Creating a Tone 374
Using Parallel Structure 406
Using Vivid Adjectives 442
Using Effective Diction 468
Using the Expository and Persuasive Aims 506
Recognizing Sentence Fragments in Dialogue 613
Famous Passages from the Play 727
Recognizing Allusions 860
Recognizing Storytelling Motifs 896

CRITICAL THINKING AND WRITING EXERCISES

The following is a list of skills covered in the Exercises in Critical Thinking and Writing, presented in the order in which they appear in the book. Additional exercises calling for critical thinking skills, including synthesis, can be found in the **Composition Skills** index on page 1050.

Predicting Outcomes 38
Analyzing a Character 76
Making Generalizations and Stating a Theme 113

Comparing and Contrasting Stories 145
Evaluating a Short Story 163
Recognizing Faulty Reasoning 196
Analyzing and Responding to a Story 222
Paraphrasing and Interpreting a Poem 265
Comparing and Contrasting Poems 296
Evaluating a Poem 339
Distinguishing Between Subjective and Objective Details 408
Evaluating an Essay 444
Inferring the Main Idea 470
Evaluating History 510
Debating: Developing a Logical Argument 616
Analyzing and Evaluating Persuasion 728
Developing and Supporting a Thesis Statement 987

INDEX OF FEATURES

Focusing on Background
  Another View of Sisters ("Everyday Use") 136
  Aristotle's View of Tragedy and the Tragic Hero (Antigone) 796
  Autobiography of a Poet, The ("Theme for English B") 360
  Biblical Allusion, A ("The First Seven Years") 67
  Brutal World of Don Quixote, The ("Tilting at Windmills") 859
  Comments from the Poet
    Brooks, Gwendolyn ("The Bean Eaters") 316
    Nye, Naomi Shihab ("The Flying Cat") 318
    Stone, John ("Double Header") 243
  Comments from the Writer
    Bradbury, Ray ("The Pedestrian") 142
    Crews, Harry ("The Mail-Order Catalogue") 459
    Munro, Alice ("Boys and Girls") 109
    Twain, Mark ("The Genuine Mexican Plug") 396
    Tyler, Anne ("With All Flags Flying") 89
  Comparing Two Sea Voyages ("The Fourth Voyage of Sindbad the Sailor") 848
  Emily Dickinson and the Train ("I Like to See It Lap the Miles") 329
  Episode from Real Life, An ("Where Have You Gone, Charming Billy?") 218
  From the Preface to Our Town 558
  Getting a Play Produced (I Never Sang for My Father) 599
  "Here Was This Perfect Book!" ("How the Snake Got Poison") 890
  "It Has Reached Out to the Readers Who Need It" (A Separate Peace) 986
  "I Wanted You to Understand the Horrors of Slavery" ("The People Could Fly") 882
  Letter from John Steinbeck, A ("Merlin: The Coming of Arthur") 840
  Shakespeare's Source: Plutarch (Julius Caesar) 725
  Singer on Yiddish, Ghosts, and Stories for Children ("The Fatalist") 29
  Sister's View of Saki, A ("The Storyteller") 211
  Tricky Poem, A ("The Road Not Taken") 255
  Where Did the Poem Come From? ("I Wandered Lonely as a Cloud") 281
  Where Did the Story Come From? ("The Pit and the Pendulum") 179

Focusing on Connections
  Biblical Allusions (The Book of Ruth) 816
  Biblical Allusions (The Song of Songs) 822
  Confucianism and Taoism (Chinese anecdotes) 871
  Theme of Abraham and Isaac in Literature, The 808
  Theme of Daedalus and Icarus in Literature and Art, The 802
  Theme of the Prodigal Son in Literature, The 830

A Critical Comment
  Brute, The 610
  I Never Sang for My Father 595
  Our Town 554
  Two Interpretations of the Play (Julius Caesar) 721

PICTURE CREDITS

INDEX OF AUTHORS AND TITLES

Page numbers in italics refer to the pages on which author biographies appear.

Abandoned Farmhouse 270
Aboard at a Ship's Helm 249
Abraham and Isaac 806
Achebe, Chinua 883, *890*
Adams, Robert J. 875
Aldington, Richard 294
All Day I Hear, from 1005
Allen, William *424*, 424
All Watched Over by Machines of Loving Grace 372
Alvarez, Julia 348, *349*
Alvarez, Lynne 336
Amundsen and Scott 474
Anderson, Robert 561, *598*, 599
Angel Wedding, The 896
Annabel Lee, from 996
Antigone 748
Apartment in Moscow, An 397
Aristotle 796
Arms and the Boy, from 1005
Artist, The 290
At Barstow, from 377
Atlas, James 557
Auden, W. H. 375, 802
Avenue Bearing the Initial of Christ into the New World, The from 336

Baker, Russell *446*, 446
Baldwin, Hanson W. *486*, 486
Barefoot in the Park, from 613
Bashō, Matsuo *289*, 289
Bean Eaters, The 314
Bears 324
Beautiful Women 1000
Bedtime Story 369
Bentley, Eric 601
Berry, Wendell 297
Bet, The 90
Bible, The, selections from 67, 805, 806, 810, 817, 819, 825, 826, 828
Big Sea, The, from 360
Billington, Rachel 408
Bishop, Elizabeth 258, *260*, 830
Birches, from 997
Blake, William 264, 1003
Bonny Barbara Allan 305
Bownas, Geoffrey 289
Boyle, T. Coraghessan 220

Boys and Girls 98
Bradbury, Ray 137, *141*, 142
Brautigan, Richard 372, *373*
Bread Loaf to Omaha, Twenty-eight Hours 362
Bride Comes to Yellow Sky, The 120
Brooks, Gwendolyn 314, *316*, 316
Brown, John Mason 724
Brute, The 601
Bushnaq, Inea 896
Buson, Yosa *289*, 289
Buzzati, Dino 110
Bye-Bye 896
Byron, Lord 246

Calvino, Italo 193, 872, *874*
Carroll, Lewis 322
Cervantes, Miguel de *849*, 851
Chang Shih-nan 870, *874*
Charge of the Light Brigade, The, from 320
Chekhov, Anton 90, 601, *612*
Children and Sir Nameless, The 351
Choice of Weapons, A 337
Cinderella 344
Cisneros, Sandra 54, *58*
Cleghorn, Sarah N. 342
Clever Judge, A 870
Clifton, Lucille 230, *231*
Cold Equations, The 7
Coleridge, Samuel Taylor 301
Colet, Roger 30
Colwin, Laurie 68, *73*
Concord Hymn, The, from 298
Confucius 871
Connell, Evan S. 474, *475*
Courage 237
Courage That My Mother Had, The 265
Coyote Steals the Sun and Moon 891
Crane, Hart 247
Crane, Stephen 120, *128*
Crews, Harry *453*, 453, 459
Cullen, Countee 247
Cummings, E. E. 246, 330, *331*, 338

Daedalus and Icarus 798
David Copperfield, from 74
Davies, W. H. 339
Dawood, N. J. 842
Day in the Life of the Jemaa el Fna, A, from 408
Day Is Done, The, from 246

Dickens, Charles 74
Dickinson, Emily 229, 269, 296, 320, 322, 327, *329*
Discovering the Land of Light, from 406
Doll's House, The 180
Don Quixote, from 849
Double Header 239

Ecclesiastes, The Book of, from 825
Elk, The 274
Ellis, James 984
Emerson, Ralph Waldo 298
Epitaph on a Tyrant 375
Erdoes, Richard 891, *895*
Erdrich, Louise 284, *285*, 998
Everyday Use 129
Ex-Basketball Player 308
Excelsior, from 342

Fatalist, The 24
Father, The 861
Father William, from 322
Fear 247
Figure a Poem Makes, The, from 254
First Fig 375
First Seven Years, The 59
Fish, The 258
Fitts, Dudley 748
Fitzgerald, Robert 748, 848
.05 311
Flower in the Crannied Wall 367
Flying Cat, The 317
Foggy Street 244
Forester, C. S. 848
For My Grandmother 247
For My Sister Molly Who in the Fifties, from 136
Forster, E. M. 724
For the Union Dead, from 229
Fourth Voyage of Sindbad the Sailor, The 842
Frame, Janet *411*, 411
Frost: A Literary Life Reconsidered, from 255
Frost, Robert 251, *252*, 253, 254, 337, 997

García Márquez, Gabriel 161, 187, *192*
Garnett, Constance 90
Garrow, David J. 506
Genesis, The Book of, from 67, 805
Genuine Mexican Plug, The 391
George Gray 256

Gift of the Magi, The 200
Ginsberg, Allen 282, 283
Godwin, Tom 7, 23
Golf Links, The 342
Gray, Patrick Worth 362, 363
Great Learning, The, from 871
Gregory, Horace 798, 801
Guiterman, Arthur 324, 326

Haiku 289
Haines, John 267
Hamilton, Virginia 878, 882, 882
Happy Man's Shirt, The 872
Hardy, Thomas 351, 352, 1003, 1006
Hayden, Robert 292, 293
Hay, Sara Henderson 860, 861
Heart of a Champion, from 220
Hektor's Farewell to Andromache 736
Henry, O. 200, 205
Her Heart Belongs to "Father," from 595
High School Band, The 321
Hoffenstein, Samuel 375
Homer 735, 736, 848
House on Mango Street, The 54
Housman, A. E. 272, 273, 343, 361, 1004
How the Leopard Got His Spots 883
How the Snake Got Poison 888
Hughes, Langston 232, 233, 264, 358, 360
Hunger of Memory, from 470
Hurston, Zora Neale 888, 890

I Am the Rose of Sharon 819
I Burned My Candle at Both Ends 375
If I Die in a Combat Zone, Box Me Up and Ship Me Home, from 218
Ignatow, David 332, 333
I Have a Dream, from 826
Iliad, The, from 735
I Like to See It Lap the Miles 327
Images 294
I May, I Might, I Must 337
In Back of the Real 282
I Never Sang for My Father 561
in Just- 330
In Search of Our Mothers' Gardens, from 429
Iroaganachi, John 883, 890
Issa, Kobayashi 289, 289
I Wandered Lonely as a Cloud 278

Jacobs, Joseph 893, 895
Jerusalem, from 1003
Joyce, James 1005

Julius Caesar, from 998, 1002
Just Lather, That's All, from 38

Keats, John 320, 374, 816
Keene, Donald 289
Kernan, Alvin B. 794
Kerr, Walter 616
King, Martin Luther, Jr. 506, 826
Kinnell, Galway 336
Knowles, John 901, 985, 986
Knox, Bernard W. M. 794
Kooser, Ted 270, 271, 374

L'Amour, Louis 149, 155
Landscape with the Fall of Icarus 860
Last Week in October, from 1003
Lattimore, Richmond 736, 742
Launcelot with Bicycle 861
Lear, Edward 1005
Lectures on Don Quixote, from 859
Lee, Andrea 397, 397
Leisure 339
Letter from Birmingham City Jail, from 507
Lieh Tzu 868, 874
Life of Caesar, The, from 725
Life of Emily Dickinson, The, from 329
Limits of the Envelope, The 499
Lines Supposed to Have Been Written to Fanny Brawne 374
Liu An 869, 874
Lloréns Torres, Luis 234, 235
Longfellow, Henry Wadsworth 246, 247, 342
Lost Horse, The 869
Loveliest of Trees 272
Love Medicine, from 998
Love's Labors Lost, from 1001
Love Without Love 234
Lowell, Amy, 294, 374, 377
Lowell, Robert 229
Luke, The Gospel of, from 827

MacBeth, George 369, 371
Mackenzie, Lewis 289
McGinley, Phyllis 337, 861
McNamar, Hugh 274
Mail-Order Catalogue, The 453
Make Something of Yourself 446
Malamud, Bernard 59, 67
Malory, Sir Thomas 833, 835, 840
Mannes, Marya 595
Mansfield, Katherine 180, 186
Man to Send Rain Clouds, The 156
Martin, George 872
Marzán, Julio 234
Masefield, John 312, 313

Masters, Edgar Lee 256, 257
Maupassant, Guy de 30, 35
Meadow Mouse, The 276
Meeting-House Hill, from 377
Merlin: The Coming of Arthur 835
Merwin, W. S., 356
Metamorphoses, The, from 797
Millay, Edna St. Vincent 247, 265, 375
Missing Axe, The 868
Miss Rosie 230
Mojave, The 385
Momaday, N. Scott 406
Monologue of Isabel Watching It Rain in Macondo, from 161
Moons, 267
Moon was but a Chin of Gold, The 269
Moore, Marianne 337
Moore, Richard 364, 366
Morte d'Arthur, Le, from 833, 840
Mother to Son 232
Mountain sat upon the Plain, The 229
Mr. Parker 68
Munro, Alice 98, 109, 109
Munro, Ethel M. 211
Musée des Beaux Arts 802
Mushrooms in the City 193
My Friend Moe 415

Nabokov, Vladimir 859
Narrow Fellow in the Grass, A 296, 320
Neruda, Pablo 356, 357
Night of Spring 252
Ninety-first Psalm, The, from 826
No News from Auschwitz 439
Nothing Happened 460
Nye, Naomi Shihab 317, 318, 318

Oates, Joyce Carol 143
O'Brien, Tim 212, 218, 218
Ode to a Nightingale, from 816
Odyssey, The, from 848
Oh, God of dust and rainbows, help us see 264
Oh, When I Was in Love with You 361
One day I wrote her name upon the strand 288
O'Neill, Jaime M. 347
One Writer's Beginnings, from 468
On the Grasshopper and Cricket 320
On Warts 434
Ortiz, Alfonso 891, 895
Our Town 519
Ovid 797, 798
Owen, Wilfred 808, 1005

Owl and the Pussy Cat, The, from 1005
Ozymandias 353

Parable of the Old Men and the Young, The 808
Parable of the Prodigal Son, The 828
Pasinetti, P. M. 858
Pastan, Linda 378, 995
Pedestrian, The 137
People Could Fly, The 878
Piece of String, The 30
Pit and the Pendulum, The 168
Plutarch 725
Pocket Poem 374
Poe, Edgar Allan 168, *178,* 996, 1004
Poet 378
Poetics, The, from 796
Pop Smash, Out of Echo Chamber 334
Portis, Charles 36
Pritchard, William H. 255
Prodigal, The (Bishop) 830
Prodigal, The (Hay) 860
Psalms, The Book of, from 817, 826
Putnam, Samuel 851

Rabassa, Gregory 161, 187
Raizan, Konishi 289, *289*
Rawlings, Marjorie Kinnan *415,* 415
Recital, from *378*
Red Wheelbarrow, The 294
Reed, Ishmael *311,* 311
Rime of the Ancient Mariner, The, from 301
R.M.S. Titanic 486
Road Not Taken, The 253
Roberts, Moss 868, 869, 870
Rodriguez, Richard 470
Roethke, Theodore 276, *277*
Roman Road, The 1005
Rosenthal, A. M. *439,* 439
Roughing It, from 391, 998
Ruth, The Book of 810

Saki 206, *211*
Sea Fever 312
Seki, Keigo 875, *882*
Separate Peace, A 901
Sewell, Richard 329
Sexton, Anne 237, *238,* 344
Shades of Night, The, from 343
Shakespeare, William 286, 337, *621,* 630, 998, 1000, 1001
Shall I Compare Thee to a Summer's Day? 286
Shelley, Percy Bysshe 353, *354*

She Walks in Beauty, from 246
Sick Rose, The 264
Silko, Leslie Marmon 156, *160*
Simon, Neil 613
Simultaneously 332
Singer, Isaac Bashevis 24, *28,* 29
Singer, Joseph 24
Slumber Did My Spirit Seal, A, from 320
Snake, The 297
Snowstorm, from 336
Song of Myself, from 995
Song of Songs, The, from 819
Sonnet 2, from 1000
Sonnet 29 337
Sophocles *745,* 748
Span of Life, The 337
Spatial Remarks, from 442
Spenser, Edmund 288
Spring is like a perhaps hand 246
Steinbeck, John *385,* 385, *834,* 835, 840
Still Just Writing, from 89
Stone, John 239, *242,* 243
Stopping by Woods on a Snowy Evening 251
Storm, The, from 1002
Storyteller, The 206
Strange Fits of Passion Have I Known, from 1004

Tan, Amy 46, *53*
Taxi, The 374
Tay, C. N. 868, 869, 870
Téllez, Hernando 38
Tennyson, Alfred, Lord 320, 367, 368
Theme for English B 358
This Is Just to Say 304
This is the land the Sunset washes 322
Thomas, Lewis *434,* 434
Thoreau, Henry David 254
Thousand and One Nights, The, from 841
Thwaite, Anthony 289
Thurber, James 219
Tichborne, Chidiock 299
Tichborne's Elegy 299
Tiger, the Brahman, and the Jackal, The 893
Tilting at Windmills 851
To Every Thing There Is a Season 825
Tomlinson, Charles 377
Tonight I Can Write 356
Toth, Susan Allen *460,* 460
Tragedy of Julius Caesar, The 630
Trap of Gold 149

True Grit, from 36
Tumbleweed 261
Twain, Mark *390, 391, 396,* 998
Twenty-third Psalm, The 817
Two Kinds 46
Tyler, Anne 81, *89,* 89

Updike, John 308, *310,* 334, 378, 442
Urashima Taro 875

Van Doren, Mark 724
Venuti, Lawrence 110
Very Old Man with Enormous Wings, A 187
Voices, from 995
Voznesensky, Andrei 244, *245*

Wagoner, David 261, *263*
Walden, from 254
Walker, Alice 129, *136,* 136, 429, 890
Walking in the Breakdown Lane 284
Walls of Anagoor, The 110
Weaver, William 193
Welty, Eudora 468
Westwood, Thomas 252
What Could It Be? 348
What Happened to Charles 219
when my love comes to see me it's 338
Where Are You Going, Where Have You Been? from 143
Where Have You Gone, Charming Billy? 212
Whipping, The 292
Whitman, Walt 247, 249, 995, 1000
Whittemore, Reed 321
Whole Society of Loners and Dreamers, A 424
Wilbur, Richard 244
Wilder, Thornton 519, *558,* 558
Williams, William Carlos 290, *291,* 294, 304, 860
Willy 364
Wind and Silver, 294
With All Flags Flying, 81
Wolfe, Peter 988
Wolfe, Tom *498,* 499
Wolkstein, Diane 896
Wordsworth, Dorothy 281
Wordsworth, William 278, *281,* 320, 1004

You Are Now Entering the Human Heart 411